Harper's Dictionary of HINDUISM

Margaret and James Stutley are private scholars who retired over twenty years ago to North Wales to devote themselves to this work. Previous to that James Stutley had been an Oriental bookseller and lecturer on Chinese art. Both he and Margaret Stutley, who is a Fellow of the Royal Asiatic Society, became interested in Hinduism in their teenage years and have since formed a massive library of Indological works, including the important works of modern scholarship upon which *Harper's Dictionary of Hinduism* is based.

Harper's Dictionary of
HINDUISM

Its Mythology, Folklore, Philosophy, Literature, and History

Margaret and James Stutley

1817

Harper & Row, Publishers
New York, Hagerstown, San Francisco, London

 For information address Harper & Row, Publishers, Inc., 10 East 53rd Street, New York, N.Y. 10022.

FIRST UNITED STATES EDITION

ISBN: 0-06-067763-5

Library of Congress Catalog Number: 76-9999

HARPER'S DICTIONARY OF HINDUISM is published in Great Britain under the title A DICTIONARY OF HINDUISM.

Contents

Preface

The need for a new Dictionary of Hinduism that would meet the requirements of the modern student and general reader has long been recognized. The attempt to meet this need has been for us an exacting but interesting task during the past twenty years.

Now that it is over we wish to thank those who have directly contributed to its completion, and those who have indirectly done so through the media of their translations and commentaries, from which we have quoted, such quotations being acknowledged in footnotes. But to those who, during the early stages of our task gave much practical help, we tender special thanks. They include Miss I.B. Horner, Professor P.S. Jaini, Colonel E.F.J. Payne, and Mr. A.H. Prior.

We wish to thank also the Hon. Editor of *Folklore* for permission to use part of the entry entitled 'Aśvamedha', contributed to *Folklore*, vol. 80, Winter 1969.

Margaret and James Stutley

General Abbreviations and Symbols

App.	Appendix
AS.	Anglo-Saxon
c.	circa, approximate date
Cal.	Calcutta
cf.	compare
ch.	chapter
col.	column
comp.	compound
ed.	edition, or edited
e.g.	exempli gratia, for example
E. or Eng.	English
et al.	and others
etc.	et cetera, and others similar to
f.	feminine gender
fasc.	fascicule
F. or Fr.	French
G.	German
Goth.	Gothic
Gr.	Greek
H.	Hebrew
Hind.	Hindi
ibid.	ibidem, 'in the same place or book'
IE.	Indo-European
i.e.	id est, 'that is'
Intro.	Introduction
L.	Latin
lit.	literally
Lith.	Lithuanian
m.	masculine gender
MS. or MSS.	manuscript(s)
n.	neuter gender
N.E.	north-east
nom.	nominative case
N.W.	north-west
OE.	Old English
OFries.	Old Friesian
OG.	Old German
OHG.	Old High German
OP.	Old Persian
OSl.	Old Slavonic
pa.	parvan
Pā.	Pāli
priv.	privative
q.v.	quod vide, 'which see'
rev.	revised edition or version
s. or sing.	singular
Sem.	Semitic
seq. or et seq.	sequens, 'following'
Skt.	Sanskrit
Sl. or Slav.	Slavonic
S.W.	south-west
tr.	translation or translated
v.	vide, 'see'
viz.	videlicet, 'namely'
W.	Welsh

Symbols

=	'equivalent to', 'equal'
( )	parentheses enclosing remarks, descriptions and explanatory statements
[ ]	brackets enclosing words introduced to link portions of a quoted passage
$\sqrt{\quad}$	denotes an etymological root

Abbreviated Titles of Works referred to

The names of Sanskrit and Pāli compositions, and of other works quoted from, or cited or referred to; full details of these works are given in the Bibliography.

ABORI — Annals of the Bhāndārkar Oriental Research Institute
AGP. — *Agni Purāṇa*, tr. by Manmatha Nath Dutt Shastri, 2 vols
AHI. — *An Advanced History of India*, 2nd edn., R.C. Majumdar, *et al.*
AIA — *The Art of Indian Asia*, H. Zimmer
Ait. Br. — *Aitareya Brāhmaṇa*, tr. by A.B. Keith
Ancestor Worship. — *Origin and Development of the Rituals of Ancestor Worship*, Dakshina Ranjan Shastri
AOS. — American Oriental Society, New Haven
Aspects. — *Aspects of Early Viṣṇuism*, J. Gonda
AV. — *Atharva-Veda Saṁhitā*, tr. by W. Dwight Whitney, 2 vols
AVB. — *Hymns of the Atharva-Veda*, tr. by M. Bloomfield
BG. — *Bhagavadgītā*, various translations
BH. — *Brahmanism and Hinduism*, M. Monier-Williams
Bhāg. P. — *Bhāgavata Purāṇa*
BIP. — *The Beginnings of Indian Philosophy*, F. Edgerton
Br. — *Brāhmaṇa*
Brah. P. — *Brahmāṇḍa Purāṇa*, tr. G.C. Bosch
Bṛhad-Ār. Up. — *Bṛhad-Āraṇyaka Upaniṣad*
Bṛhadd. — *Bṛhad-Devatā*, tr. by A.A. Macdonell
BSOAS. — *Bulletin of the School of Oriental and African Studies*, London
CC. — *Change and Continuity in Indian Religion*, J. Gonda
CD. — *Century Dictionary*, ed. by W.D. Whitney
CG. — *Cosmography and Geography in Early Indian Literature*, D.C. Sircar
Chān. Up. — *Chāndogya Upaniṣad*
C. Herit. I. — *The Cultural Heritage of India*, Sri Ramakrishna Centenary Memorial, 3 vols
CHI. — *The Cambridge History of India*, ed. by E.J. Rapson, 6 vols, 1922–
CHS. — *Principles of Composition in Hindu Sculpture*, Alice Boner
CI., or *Cyclo I.* — *The Cyclopaedia of India*, 3 vols, E. Balfour
CII. — *Corpus Inscriptionum Indicarum*, 3 vols, 1888–1929
Cults. — *The Cults of the Greek States*, Lewis Richard Farnell
DHA. — *A Dictionary of Hindu Architecture*, Prasanna Kumar Acharya
DHI. — *The Development of Hindu Iconography*, J.N. Banerjea
EB. — *Encyclopaedia of Buddhism*, ed. by G.P. Malalasekera, fasc. 1–
EBS. — *The Early Brahmanical System of Gotra and Pravara*, John Brough
EHI. — *Elements of Hindu Iconography*, T.A.G. Rao, 2 vols
EM. — *Epic Mythology*, E.W. Hopkins
ERE. — *Encyclopaedia of Religion and Ethics*, ed. by James Hastings, 13 vols
ES. — *Encyclopaedia of Superstitions*, E. and M.A. Radford.
EW. — *History of Philosophy: Eastern and Western*, S. Radhakrishnan, 2 vols
Facets. — *Facets of Indian Thought*, Betty Heimann
GG. — *The Golden Germ*, F.D.K. Bosch
Hariv. — *Harivaṁśa*
HCD. or *HD.* — *A Classical Dictionary of Hindu Mythology and Religion*, John Dowson
HCIP. — *The History and Culture of the Indian People*, ed. by R.C. Majumdar, *et al.*, vols 1–5
HIIA. — *A History of Indian and Indonesian Art*, A.K. Coomaraswamy
HIL. — *A History of Indian Literature*, M. Winternitz
HIP. — *A History of Indian Philosophy*, S. Dasgupta
HOS. — Harvard Oriental Series
HP. — *Hindu Polytheism*. A. Daniélou
HW. — *Hindu World*, 2 vols, Benjamin Walker.

Abbreviated Titles

IA. or *Ind. Ant.*	*The Indian Antiquary*
IAL.	*A Comparative Dictionary of the Indo-Āryan Languages*, R.L. Turner
IHQ.	*Indian Historical Quarterly*
Images.	*Images and Symbols*, Mircea Eliade
India.	*India and World Civilization*, D.P. Singhal
IRA.	*India in the Rāmāyaṇa Age*, S.N. Vyas
IT.	*The Indian Theogony*, Sukumari Bhattacharji
IW.	*Indian Wisdom*, M. Monier-Williams
IWP.	*Indian and Western Philosophy*, Betty Heimann
JA.	*Journal Asiatique*
JAOS.	*Journal of the American Oriental Society*
JRAS.	*Journal of the Royal Asiatic Society*, London
JRASB.	*Journal of the Royal Asiatic Society of Bengal*
Kauś.	*Kauśika Sūtra*
Kauṣ	*Kauṣītaki Upaniṣad*
Kauṣ. Br.	*Kauṣītaki Brāhmaṇa*, tr. by A.B. Keith
Legends.	*Legends in the Mahābhārata*, S.A. Dange
Loka.	*Loka. World and Heaven in the Veda*, J. Gonda
Māṇḍ. Up.	*Māṇḍukya Upaniṣad*
Manu	*The Laws of Manu*, tr. by G. Bühler
Mārk. P.	*Mārkaṇḍeya Purāṇa*, tr. by F.E. Pargiter
Matsya Pur.	*Matsya Purāṇa*—A Study, V.S. Agrawala
MBh.	*Mahābhārata*, sponsored by Pratap Chandra Roy, 2nd ed., 12 vols
MBh. Crit. Edn.	The Critical Edition of the Mahābhārata, ed. by V.S. Sukthankar, F. Edgerton, S.K. De, *et al.*
MBh., EM.	This refers to E.W. Hopkins' references to the *Mahābhārata* in his *Epic Mythology*
MCB.	*Mélanges chinois et bouddhiques*, Brussels
Muṇḍ Up.	*Muṇḍaka Upaniṣad*
Myths.	*Myths and Symbols in Indian Art and Civilization*, H. Zimmer, ed. by J. Campbell
Nir.	*The Nighaṇṭu and the Nirukta*, tr. by Lakshman Sarup
Notes.	*Notes on Names and the Name of God in Ancient India*, J. Gonda
OHI.	*The Oxford History of India*, V.A. Smith, rev. by Sir Mortimer Wheeler *et al.*
OM.	*The Masks of God*, vol. II, *Oriental Mythology*, J. Campbell
ORC.	*Obscure Religious Cults*, Shashibhusan Dasgupta
OST.	*Original Sanskrit Texts*, 5 vols, J. Muir
P. or *Pur.*	*Purāṇa*
Patterns.	*Patterns in Comparative Religion*, Mircea Eliade
PI.	*The Purāṇa Index*, 3 vols, V.R. Ramachandra Dikshitar
PSPT.	*The Significance of Prefixes in Sanskrit Philosophical Terminology*, Betty Heimann
PTR.	*Paurānic and Tantric Religion*, J.N. Banerjea
PTS.	The Pāli Text Society's *Pāli-English Dictionary*, ed. by T.W. Rhys Davids and William Stede
RAA.	*Religion in Art and Archaeology*, J.N. Banerjea
Rām.	*The Rāmāyaṇa*. tr. by Hari Prasad Shastri, 3 vols
RV.	*The Hymns of the Ṛgveda*, various translations
SBE.	*Sacred Books of the East*, ed. by F. Max Müller
ŚBr.	*Śatapatha Brāhmaṇa*, tr. by Julius Eggeling, 5 vols, *SBE.*
SED.	*Sanskrit-English Dictionary*, M. Monier-Williams
Seers.	*The Seers of the Ṛgveda*, V.G. Rahurkar
Shamanism.	*Shamanism, Archaic Techniques of Ecstasy*, Mircea Eliade
SS.	*Śūnyasaṁpādane*, 3 vols, tr. by S.C. Nandimath, *et al.*
Suś. Saṁ.	*Sushruta Saṁhitā*, tr. and ed. by Kaviraj Kunjalal Bhishagratna, 3 vols
SV.	*Sāma Veda*, tr. by R.T. Griffith
Śvet. Up.	*Śvetāśvatara Upaniṣad*
Tait. Br.	*Taittirīya Brāhmaṇa*
Tait. Saṁ.	*The Veda of the Black Yajus School entitled Taittirīya Saṁhitā*, tr. by A.B. Keith

TPU.	*Thirteen Principal Upaniṣads*, R.E. Hume
TT.	*The Tantric Tradition*, Agehananda Bharati
Up.	*Upaniṣad*
Vāj. Saṁ.	*Vājasaneyi-saṁhitā*
VF.	*Sparks from the Vedic Fire*, Vasudeva S. Agrawala
VI.	*Vedic Index of Names and Subjects*, A.A. Macdonell and A.B. Keith, 2 vols
VM.	*Vedic Mythology*, A.A. Macdonell
VP.	*Viṣṇu Purāṇa*, tr. by H.H. Wilson
VS.	*Viṣṇuism and Śaivism. A Comparison*, J. Gonda
VSM.	*Vaiṣṇavism and Śaivism and Minor Religious Systems*, R.G. Bhandarkar
WI.	*The Wonder that was India*, A.L. Basham
Yakṣas.	*Yakṣas*, A.K. Coomaraswamy, 2 vols
Yoga	*Yoga: Immortality and Freedom*, Mircea Eliade
YV.	*Yajur-Veda*

List of romanized Sanskrit characters in English alphabetical order, and their pronunciation

The transliteration follows that of Monier-Williams's *Sanskrit-English Dictionary*, with a few exceptions. The letter *ṛ* replaces his *ṛi*, and *ṣ* his *sh*; the nasal symbol, called the *anusvāra*, represented by his *ṃ* or *ṇ* is here rendered *ṁ* or *ṅ* as in *Sāṁkhya* or *Sāṅkhya*. The *SED*. states that 'the *visarga*, as a substitute for final *s*, is a distinctly audible aspirate, so that the *ḥ* at the end of such a word as *devaḥ* must be clearly heard'.

a	Like u as in cut; never as in bat
ā	father
ai	aisle
au	loud
b	bag
bh	abhor
c	church (but in compounds, expressed or implied, like vac, ṛc, etc., changes to k).
ch	church-hill
d	dice
ḍ	drum
dh	adhere
ḍh	red-haired
e	prey
g	gun
gh	log-hut
h	hit
i	lip
ī	police
j	jet
jh	hedge-hog
k	kit
kh	ink-horn
l	lull
ḷ	label
m	man
n	nut
ṇ	none
ñ	singe
o	so
p	pat
ph	up-hill
r	rat
ṛ	rich
ṛī	marine
s	sit
ś	hiss
ṣ = sh	sure
t	dot
ṭ	true
th	nut-hook
ṭh	boat-hook
u	full
ū	rude
v	ivy (but pronounced as w after some consonants)
y	yet

Diacritical Marks

These denote family, tribal or national relationship, gender, etc., and determine pronunciation; but consonants with diacritical dots, such as *ṭ*, *ṭh*, *ḍ*, *ḍh*, *ṇ*, do not differ greatly in pronunciation from their unmarked counterparts.

Mutations

These occur when a particular terminal vowel of one word coalesces with the initial vowel of the following word. Thus *a* + *a* merge and become *ā*; *a* + *ā* become *ā* as in Śaṅkara and ācārya, which become Śaṅkarācārya. A terminal *u* before an initial *a* changes to *v*, as in Manu + antara (Manvantara). A terminal *a* followed by an initial *u* coalesce and become *o* as in Kaṭha Upaniṣad (Kaṭhopaniṣad).

Introduction

'Hinduism' is now generally used as a term to summarize the aspirations—both unsophisticated and intellectual—of the majority of the Indian people. But any simple definition of it is difficult, perhaps impossible. This is partly owing to the nuances of the Sanskrit language, in which many texts are written, and partly to the too literal interpretation of Hindu imagery and mythology that often veils its real significance. This has often led to the epithets 'heathen' and 'polytheistic' being applied to Hinduism.

Such misunderstanding is now gradually being dispelled, as is the view that Religion is a congeries of disparate and even antipathetic systems, instead of the modern view that they are aspects of a single concept. The latter view is particularly noticeable since Hinduism has been studied in historical perspective, which shows that an early form of Hinduism existed in proto-historical India. It began, like the early forms of religion in the Middle East, with man's attempt to come to terms with his physical environment, and subsequently with the mysterious world beyond it. The process of cultural advance in India was inevitably influenced by conditions peculiar to it, but its development gradually generated its own momentum and created its own expanding horizon. It recognized energy, as does modern science, to be the ultimate source of manifestation, and as Hinduism developed, to be also the fount of all human aspirations.

Now it is possible to survey the long vista of Indian history which, despite the disparity and fluctuations of its cultural levels, reveals a continuity and a genius for analysis and synthesis that has never been surpassed.

Note on arrangement

If the names or terms which occur in entries call for detailed exposition, they will be found under individual headings, thus avoiding unnecessary repetition. Most entries are supplemented by relevant cross-references placed at the foot of an entry immediately below the notes.

Map of Ancient India

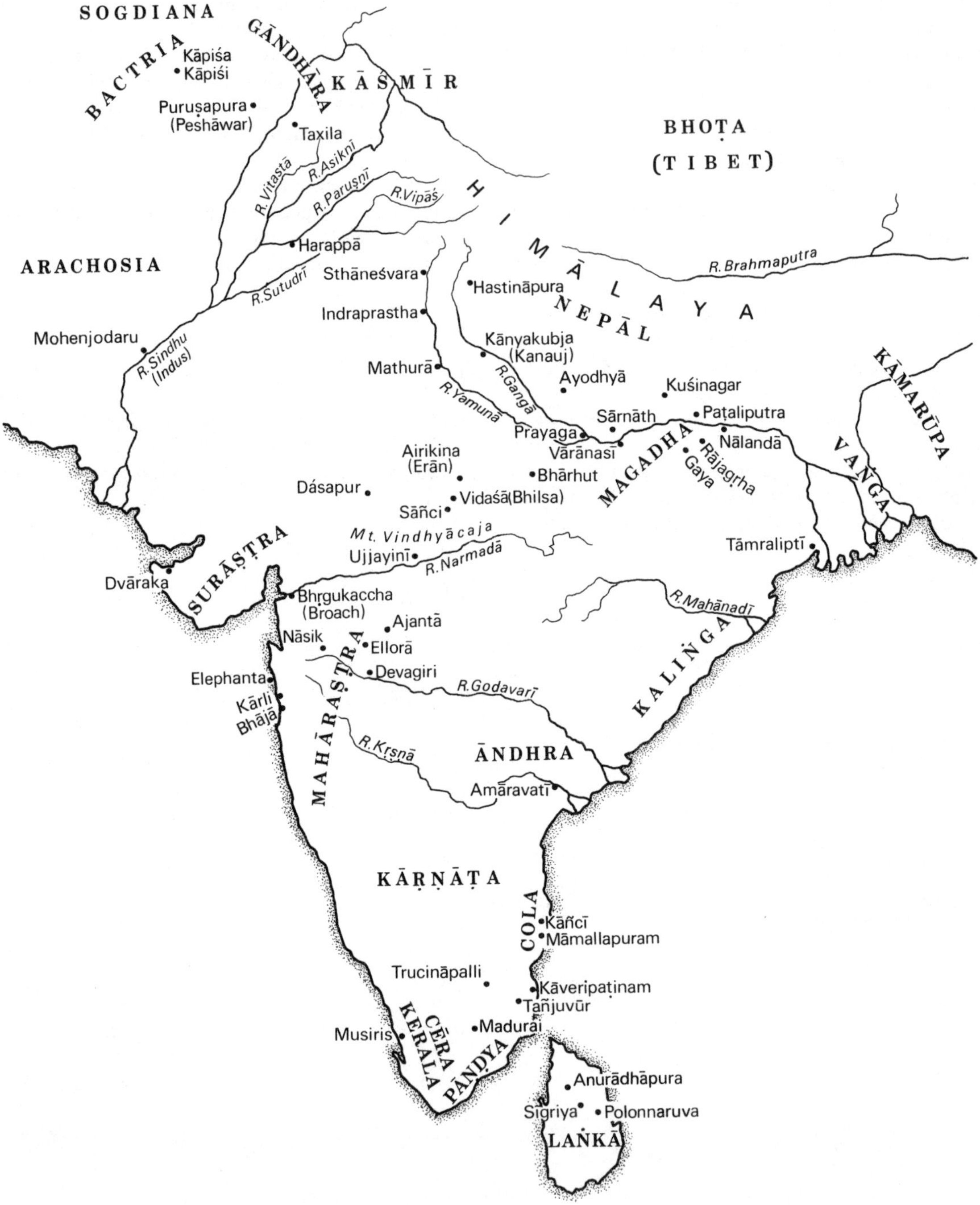

Veil after veil will lift
But there must be veil after veil behind.

Edwin Arnold

From the unreal lead me to the real!
From darkness lead me to light!

Bṛhad-Āraṇyaka Upaniṣad, I.3,28

A

A The first letter of the Sanskrit 'alphabet', regarded as the perfect letter, imperishable, the first sound and hence the beginning of all knowledge. It is the essence of the Veda and is equated with *brahman*.
v. Akṣara; Śabda-brahman.

Ābhāsvaras The 'Shining Ones'. A category of sixty-four minor deities who inhabit an ethereal world and preside over spiritual enlightenment. They are attendant on Śiva.

Abhaya-hasta The *abhaya* or fear-dispelling gesture, expressed by raising the right hand (*hasta*) with the palm and fingers extended.[1] The Buddha and many Indian gods are often thus depicted. In the *Bhāgavata Pur.* fearlessness is personified as a child of Dharma (Law, Justice, Duty, etc.).
[1] Cf. the assuring gesture which accompanies the benediction pronounced by the Pope or other dignitaries of the Christian Church.
v. Mudrā.

Abhicāra 'Magic.' The employment of incantations, spells or rites designed to achieve maleficent ends.[1] A girdle (*mekhalā*) giving protection and power to the wearer is worn during these rites, and when tied impedes the progress of the enemy (*AV.*, VI.133). These rites are performed from right to left, which is opposite to those designed to achieve beneficent ends. The latter are performed in the direction that the life-giving sun appears to move. To go against the sun[2] was believed to strengthen the power of darkness and to cause many calamities.
[1] For magic in the Brāhmaṇas v. Lévi, *La Doctrine du sacrifice*, p. 139. In the description of the powers inherent in the *vaṣat* ritual call, information is given concerning the way in which the priest may injure the sacrificer by pronouncing the call in a certain manner (*Ait. Br.*, III.7). Cf. the rite of cursing in medieval Christianity, which drew upon particular Psalms, the Psalter being regarded as 'a powerful defence against demons . . . For a "Slaying prayer" . . . Psalm 108 "Deus laudem" was most used' (von Dobschütz, *ERE.*, III. p. 425).
[2] Cf. the European 'widdershins'.
v. Abhicārikamūrti; Pradakṣiṇā; Dakṣiṇāgni; Dhūmāvatī; Chinnamastā; Bharaṇī; Kṛtyā; Śānti II.

Abhicārikamūrti A form (*mūrti*) of Viṣṇu worshipped for the purpose of inflicting injury and death on enemies. An image of this aspect of Viṣṇu should be placed only in forests and other lonely places.[1]
[1] *EHI.*, I. pt. i, pp. 20f.
v. Abhicāra.

Abhijñānaśakuntalā *'The Recognition of Śakuntalā.'* The name of a play by Kālidāsa, regarded as the best of all his works.

Abhimānī 'Proud.' An epithet of Agni, the eldest son of Brahmā. Abhimānī had three sons by Svāhā, viz., Pāvaka, Pavamāna and Śuci who represent the fires of lightning, fire produced by friction, and the solar fire which 'drinks up' water (*VP.*, I.10). According to the *Bhāg. P.* these fires are the various 'appellations of fire employed in the invocations with which different oblations to fire are offered in the ritual of the Vedas' (*VP.*, p. 71, n.9).

Abhimantraṇa Consecration by means of special *mantras*.

Abhimanyu A son of Arjuna and Subhadrā. He married Uttarā who gave birth to a still-born premature child. The child had been burnt by Aśvatthāman's magic weapon *brahmāstra*, and so was deprived of strength and energy, but Vāsudeva (Kṛṣṇa) revived the infant and endowed him with great strength. He was called Parikṣit and later succeeded Yudhiṣṭhira to the throne of Hastināpura (*MBh.*, Ādi pa., 95).
v. Pāṇḍava(s).

Abhinavagupta (7th century.) A Śākta notable for his great learning and spiritual attainments. Forty-one of his works are known including commentaries on the sixty-four monistic Śaivāgamas.

Abhiṣeka A consecration rite, primarily by anointing or sprinkling, usually with water, followed by a series of subsidiary rites over a period of about a year. Its purpose was to define or confirm the divine status of the king,[1] but originally it appears to have been to ensure continuity of life and even immortality.[2] It was an important part of a more extensive ceremonial, the *rājasūya* or consecration of a king, and of the *aśvamedha* (horse sacrifice) by which imperial status was confirmed. But the king, though he regarded himself as divinely appointed, represented only the secular members of the community, comprising the *kṣatra* and *rājanya*, or nobility and royalty, and the *vaiśyas*. The *brāhmaṇas* also regarded themselves as divinely appointed, but later when class was defined, claimed their descendants both lay and priestly to be the superior class. Thus the stability and welfare of the community were dependent on the goodwill of both priest and king, the duty of the priest being to ensure that the gods continued to inseminate the land, that of the king to ensure its uninterrupted fertility.[3]

The entire *abhiṣeka* ceremony is described in the *ŚBr.*,[4] and begins with the preparation of offerings of cakes made of various cereals, after which the king is anointed. He then dons a silk under-garment (*tārpya*), the symbol of 'inner' knighthood (*kṣatra*). This is followed by the donning of a cloak of undyed wool, the outer or visible sign of knighthood. Over this is placed a mantle, representing the womb or source of knighthood. Finally a band of linen or similar material is drawn round the king's head, the ends being tucked into the front of the mantle. This symbolizes the 'navel' or central point of sovereignty. The successive donning of these garments, and of the *uṣṇīsa* symbolizes the several stages of development of the embryo, the final stage indicating the re-birth of the newly consecrated king (*ŚBr.*, V.3. 5,23–4).[5]

[1]The first mention of which appears to have been in the *Ait. Br.*, I.14.

[2]*CC.*, p.454.

[3]J. M. Allegro, *The Sacred Mushroom and the Cross*, p. 58.

[4]Eggeling's translation, pt. III. pp. 68–126.

[5]The waters represent seed and thus the consecrated became 'possessed of seed' (*Ait. Br.*, I.3).

v. Abhimantraṇa.

Abhiṣṭadevatā or **Iṣṭadevatā** The 'chosen' deity of a worshipper.

Abhragaṅgā v. Gaṅgā.

Abhramātaṅga v. Airāvata.

Abhramu A cow-elephant, the mate of Indra's elephant Airāvata.

Abhranāga(s) v. Airāvata; Lokapāla(s); Gaja.

Ācārya I. A spiritual guide or teacher.

v. Guru.

II. A class of Tamil Vaiṣṇava teachers who regarded the Āḷvārs as worthy of worship, and also considered them to be the incarnations of Viṣṇu's weapons. The first *ācārya* Nāthamuni (c. 9th century A.D.) arranged the Āḷvār hymns into a compendium called the *Nālāyira-prabandham* (Collection of Four Thousand Songs) which was regarded as the Tamil Veda.

v. Āyudhapuruṣa.

Acyuta 'Never-falling.' One of the twenty-four *avatāras* of Viṣṇu. The utterance of the name Acyuta, as well as those of Ananta and Govinda (all names of Viṣṇu), will destroy every disease (*AGP.*, I. p. 125).

Ādāra The plant sometimes used as a substitute for *soma*. It is said to have sprung from the sap of the personified Sacrifice, i.e., Viṣṇu (*ŚBr.*, IV.5.10,4). When placed on a fire this plant burns fiercely and gives off fragrance (XIX.1.2,12).

Adhāraṇi v. Araṇi(s); Aśvattha; Śamī.

Adharma The personification of injustice, unrighteousness and vice; and hence Himsā (violence or injury) is personified as his wife and their children as Anṛta (falsehood) and Nikṛtī (immorality) (*VP.*, I.7). But according to the *Bhāg. P.* Adharma's wife is called Mṛṣā (falsehood), and their children are Dambha (hypocrisy) and Māyā (deceit), who were adopted by the goddess of misery Nirṛti. Different texts give various names to their descendants, but in every case they are always twins (*VP.*, p. 49, n.14).

Heimann defines *adharma* as 'unnatural laws of statics and non-motion ... [which being] against the law of dynamics, stands for "evil"'.[1]

[1]*Facets*, p. 176.

Adhideha v. Adhiśarīra.

Adhiratha The name of Karṇa's foster-father.

Adhiśarīra or **adhideha** An 'intermediate body' believed to clothe and support the departed spirit in the *pitṛloka* (spirit world).

v. Pitṛ(s); Yama; Ekoddiṣṭa.

Adhvara A sacrifice, especially the *soma* sacrifice.

v. Adhvaryu.

Adhvaryu A priest whose duties were to supervise the offerings and to build the altar, prepare the sacrificial vessels, light the fire, bring and immolate the sacrificial animal, and repeat the hymns of the *Yajurveda*. Haug maintains that the *raspi* priest in the Irānian *haoma* ritual corresponds to the *adhvaryu* priest in the *soma* ritual. An *adhvaryu* or *Yajurveda* priest has the power to destroy offspring.[1]

Five *adhvaryus* and seven holy singers guard Agni, here likened to a bird (*RV.*, III.7,7), but Hillebrandt considers these refer not to five priests but to 'the five planets which move about in the heavens like the *adhvaryu* priests on the sacrificial ground'.[2] According to the *ŚBr.* (XII.8.2,22) the Aśvins are the *adhvaryus* of the gods. The sacrificial 'gift' for the *adhvaryu* is a chariot (*Manu*, VIII.209).

[1]v. *OST.*, III. p. 54.

[2]*Vedische Mythologie*, 3, 423, cited by Macdonell and Keith, VI., vol. I. p. 21.

v. Agnicayana; Ṛtvij; Dakṣiṇā.

Āḍi A son of the *asura* Andhaka. To avenge his father's death at the hands of Śiva, he assumed the form of a snake and entered Śiva's abode, where he transformed himself into the beautiful Umā, but Śiva was not deceived and killed him with his *vajra* (*Matsya P.*, 156.12–37, *PI.*).

Ādimātā v. Manasā.

Ādimūrti v. Viṣṇu.

Ādinātha or **Ṛṣabhanātha** The first of the twenty-four *tīrthaṅkaras* of the Jains.

Aditi The Vedic goddess of space, i.e., *a* 'not', and *diti* 'limited'. But she is also associated or identified in the *RV.* with other phenomena, such as Earth, Nature, etc. Müller[1] considers that Aditi, in her cosmic character, is the 'Beyond, the unbounded realm beyond the earth, sky, and heaven ... [and] though in more general language she may be identified with heaven and earth in their unlimited character', the original significance of her name is retained in these other contexts. Gonda[2] considers her name to signify 'Freedom', and her nature to be manifested 'in any expansion of phenomenal life'. Thus one passage refers to her as a fertility goddess, the Cosmic Cow;[3] another declares her 'to be all that has been, and is yet to be', in whom all the gods are comprised (*RV.*, I. 89,10). Other passages state that Aditi was born of Dakṣa and that Dakṣa was born of Aditi,[4] and that existence from non-existence sprang. These enigmatic statements suggest the attempts of the Vedic *ṛṣis* to define the abstract nature of existence, as in X.129, when 'there was neither ought nor nought'.

[1] *Vedic Hymns*, *SBE.*, vol. XXXII, pp. 248f.

[2] *VS.*, p. 7.

[3] Cf. the ancient Egyptian sky-goddess Nut who appears as a great cow with stars on her body; her legs form the four cardinal points (James, *Tree of Life*, p. 177); also the goddess Hathor, 'one of the oldest Egyptian deities, worshipped from Gerzean times under the fertility emblem of a cow with a variety of names' (ibid., p. 267).

[4] *OST.*, IV. p. 13.

v. Āditya(s).

Āditya(s) The sons of Aditi, who personify particular aspects of nature. They represent a cosmogonic tradition like that of the divine Asuras who, though a dominant feature of Avestan cosmogonic theory, appear in that sense only occasionally in the *RV.*

Unlike Aditi, who represents cosmic energy or force, the Ādityas collectively represent the whole range of phenomenal manifestation, each individual aspect of it being generally assigned to a particular Āditya. But there is consistency neither in the ascription of individual qualities and functions, nor of the enumeration of the Ādityas, which in the *RV.* varies from five to eight, and in the Brāhmaṇas reaches twelve. In *RV.*, IX.114,3 the Ādityas are said to be seven, but X.72–8 gives eight, which includes Mārtāṇḍa whom Aditi cast away. According to Sāyaṇa, the eight are: Mitra, Varuṇa, Dhātar, Aryaman, Aṁśa, Bhaga, Vivasvat and Āditya (Sūrya).[1]

The *Śatapatha Brāhmaṇa* presents a bewildering portrayal of the functions of the Ādityas, who are said to number twelve (XI.6.3,8), representing the twelve months of the solar year. Their names are variously given in different works,[2] but many are names of the sun, such as Savitṛ, the solar Viṣṇu, etc. As all Ādityas are fundamentally aspects of light, they are collectively regarded as one, called the Āditya, i.e., the Sun. The latter, like the gods of Fire and Wind, is regarded as one of the regents of the three worlds (*Chān. Up.*, 2.21,1). The Sun is also Death, therefore those creatures living on the earth-side of him die, but the gods living on his heavenly side are immortal (*ŚBr.*, II. 3.3,7). All the worlds are attached to the Āditya by threads, like beads on a necklace (VII.3.2,13). The sun is one of the six doors to the impersonal *brahman* (XI.4.4,1).[3] At the dissolution of the world the Ādityas will appear as twelve suns; hence the sun is said to be 'twelve-souled' (*MBh.*, 3.3,26, *EM.*).

In Buddhism Āditya is the name of a Buddha, and also the *gotra* name of the historic Buddha; hence his epithet, 'Kinsman of the sun' (Ādiccabandhu).[4]

[1] *RV.*, II. p. 487, n.8.

[2] The *VP.* (I. 15) enumerates them as Viṣṇu, Śakra, Aryaman, Dhūti, Tvaṣṭṛ, Pūṣan, Vivasvat, Savitṛ, Mitra, Varuṇa, Aṁśa and Bhaga.

[3] The others are: Fire, Wind, the Waters, the moon and lightning.

[4] *EB.*, p. 226.

v. Ajita(s); Ṛta.

Ādivarāha The 'first boar'. An epithet of Viṣṇu, referring to his boar (*varāha*) *avatāra*.

Adri or **Grāvan**[1] 'Rock', 'stone'. In the *RV.* (X.175) *adri* denotes the pressing-stones used ritually to extract the sacred *soma* juice. They were deified and likened to horses or bulls, and invoked to drive away calamity and demons and to give fertility and prosperity. They are said to be immortal and mightier than heaven, which was regarded as an inverted stone bowl.

[1] The *Nir.* (9.8) derives *grāvāṇaḥ* (stones) from the root *han* (to kill), or from *gṛ* (to praise), or from *grah* (to seize).

Adrijā 'Mountain-born.' An epithet of the goddess Pārvatī, whose father was Himavat, the personification of the Himālaya.

Adrikā The name of a nymph (*apsaras*). By a *brāhmaṇa*'s curse she was transformed into a fish and lived in the Yamunā river, where she picked up a leaf dropped by a hawk or eagle (Śyena), on which the sperm of King Uparicara had fallen. The fish ate the sperm and was later caught by fishermen who cut it open, when to their amazement a girl and boy emerged. The fishermen took the twins to the king who adopted the boy, who later became the virtuous King Matsya. The girl, who had a strong fishy smell, was given to the fishermen and called Satyavatī. After the 'birth' of the twins Adrikā was released from the curse and ascended to the heavens on the path trodden by the *siddhas*, *ṛṣis*, etc. (*MBh.*, Ādi pa., 63).

v. Parāśara.

Aduḥkhanavamī v. Devī.

Advaita Vedānta v. Darśana; Vedānta; Brahman (neuter).

Āgama(s) 'That which has come down', i.e., traditional religious teaching, contained in non-Vedic texts and thus distinguished from Vedic texts of the brahmanic schools. The texts of the early Śaiva sects were called Āgamas, and unlike the Vedas were accessible to women and to the menials of the household. Āgama was also used by the Jainas as a description of their sacred texts.

Some early Śaivāgamas were composed in Sanskrit but in southern India were re-written in Tamil[1] or another of the South Indian languages.

The traditional Śaiva texts comprise twenty-eight Āgamas and 108 Upāgamas (minor texts); those of the Śāktas, seventy-seven Śāktāgamas or Tantras.

[1] *WI.*, pp. 333f.; *EW.*, Vol. I, p. 36.

Agastya or **Agasti** A Vedic seer who is traditionally credited with the authorship of *RV.*, I.166–91. His birth from an urn or jar (*kumbha*)[1] along with Vasiṣṭha is attributed to Mitra-Varuṇa, whose procreative activity was stimulated by the sight of the beautiful goddess of the dawn (Urvaśī). A sociological interpretation of the birth of the two seers suggests that Urvaśī was a non-Āryan goddess,[2] which may account for the colonizing activities attributed to Agastya and his descendants.

The Vedic Agastya was not included in 'the charmed circles of Bhṛgus, Āṅgirasas, and the Seven'[3] great *ṛṣis*. Nonetheless, he is credited with the reconciliation of Indra and the Maruts after their quarrel (*RV.*, I.165; 170), Indra's right to separate or preferential worship being established, without depriving the Maruts of their rights. But beyond referring to Agastya's marriage relationship as strained owing to his coldness and neglect of his wife Lopāmudrā (*RV.*, 179), the *saṁhitā* gives little more information about him.

The Vedic account of Agastya is expanded and embellished in the Purāṇas, the Mahābhārata and Rāmāyaṇa, one legend giving the reason for his marriage as his discovery of his 'dead' forebears. He found them suspended by their heels over a pit, a single thread holding them to the world of the living. They informed him that only when he had begotten a son would their release be effected, and hence his marriage.[4]

Another *MBh.* legend relates that when Agastya arranged to hold a twelve-year sacrifice Indra threatened to withhold all rain. The *ṛṣis*, assembled for the sacrifice, fearing that Indra intended to maintain a twelve-year drought, besought Agastya to cancel the sacrifice. But Agastya was not intimidated and threatened to supplant Indra unless he produced rain.[5] Indra, knowing that the power Agastya had derived through sacrifices (*yajña*) and austerities (*tapas*) was greater than his own, released the rain.

The chief claim to fame of Agastya's family is based on the missionary and colonizing efforts of a later Agastya, whose name is syncretized with that of the Vedic seer, known also as Māna (the Measurer). Agastya's journey through the Vindhya mountains, dividing northern India from the Deccan, was difficult owing to the terrain, and hazardous because of hostile tribes, but he finally succeeded in crossing the mountains.

To ensure that the mountain passes would not again be quickly overgrown as is usual in tropical forests, Agastya persuaded them to stop growing, promising that on his return they should have complete freedom to grow, but he never returned and the way from the north remained open. By his tact he gained the confidence of some tribes but failed with the Kāleyas who, from the security of their lake and river retreat, menaced the northern travellers. Agastya resolved the difficulty by 'drinking the ocean dry', a description probably denoting that he drained the area, thus leading to the subjugation of the Kāleyas.

His exploits aroused the fears of two wealthy native rulers, the brothers Vātāpi and Ilvala, whose extortionate demands on the people had not been unnoticed by Agastya, against whom the brothers concocted an ingenious and macabre plot, but they were outwitted and forced to give up their ill-gotten wealth.

When Rāma was on his way to Laṅkā to rescue Sītā, he met Agastya, who gave him magic[6] weapons to enable him to pass safely through the demon-infested forests. Agastya, having decided to remain in the Deccan, built himself a hermitage, which became a great place of pilgrimage (*Rām.*, III.11,94). Of him it was said that by his great merit he 'has restrained death . . . and who through his benevolence to mankind has rendered the southern regions secure' (*Rām.*, III.11,79). Agastya's influence spread to Java, Cambodia and Borneo where in the hierarchy of gods, the highest rank is accorded him.[7]

Agastya's name was later added to the list of the Seven Great Seers, which forms the original basis of '*gotra*' genealogy. Agastya, like other great *ṛṣis* was accorded stellar status and identified with Canopus, the brightest star in the sky of southern India. When reflected in water, it cleanses the most turbid lake or river. His fame is such that many Tamil Hindus believe that he still lives, and that though invisible, he dwells on the sacred mountain called Agastya Malai (Agastya's hill).

[1]Hence the epithet Kumbhayoni, applied to Agastya, and Kuṇḍina to Vasiṣṭha.

[2]Rahurkar, *Seers*, p. 203 (citing D. D. Kosambi, 'Urvaśī and Purūravas').

[3]*EM.*, p. 185.

[4]A reference to the *ekoddiṣṭa* rite which, being unknown in Vedic times, confirms the existence of the Agastya family in post-Vedic times. Cf. the legend of Jaratkāru.

[5]*Seers*, pp. 205f. Cf. the Nepalese legend of Gorakhnāth, who tied up the clouds in a bundle on which he sat in deep meditation for twelve years (Briggs, *Gorakhnāth and the Kanphaṭa Yogīs*, p. 196).

[6]Agastya was reputed to be an adept in sorcery and witchcraft.

[7]*Seers*, p. 207.

v. Kumbhamātā; Māna II.

Aghamarṣaṇa A Vedic *ṛṣi* and reputed author of hymn X.190 of the *RV*. 'He may be credited with having formulated the views which came to be known in later ages as "doctrine of time" (*kāla-vāda*).'[1] The hymn was probably composed a little earlier than the famous 'Creation Hymn' (X.129), ascribed to Parameṣṭhin, but shares with it the theory that creation of the visible world arose from the effects of warmth or 'creative fervour' (*tapas*) on the primeval substance water.

Aghamarṣaṇa's exposition of creation differs from that of Parameṣṭhin in regarding time as the principal feature of creation. He refers to time as 'the Year', in which the succession of the seasons represents 'order' (*ṛtu*), without which the empirical world would disintegrate, and the maintenance and continuity of the universe be impossible.

[1]Barua, *A History of Pre-Buddhistic Indian Philosophy*, p. 8. *RV.*, X.190 is the 'sin-destroying' hymn (*AGP.*, I. p. 595; II. p. 774) and is said to be more efficacious than the performance of a horse sacrifice (*aśvamedha*) (*Manu*, XI.260–1).

Aghāsura A demonic Asura who assumed the form of an enormous boa-constrictor to devour Kṛṣṇa, his companions and their cattle. Thinking that the demon's huge mouth was the entrance to a cavern the cowherds entered it, but Kṛṣṇa knowing what had happened, entered and choked the Asura to death (*Bhāg. P.*, X.12, 31–8, *PI.*).

Aghāśva 'Having vicious horses.' An epithet of the royal *ṛṣi* Pedu (*RV.*, I.116, 6; cf. *AV.*, X.4, 10).

v. Paidva; Aśvin(s).

Aghora 'Non-terrifying.'[1] A term euphemistically applied to Śiva for the purpose of propitiating him. It is also applied to the personification of Śiva's southern face which represents eternal law (*dharma*), or the principle of intellect (*buddhi tattva*).[2]

[1]*TT.*, p. 162. Aghora 'denotes the absence of, and restraint in, awful, terrific and violent action and attitude and, hence friendliness' (*VS.*, pp. 43f., and his *Four Studies in the Language of the Veda*, pp. 95ff.).

[2]*HP.*, p. 212.

Agni 'Fire'; the 'god of fire'. Fire and its relation to the sacrifice was the dominating feature of the fire-cult in Vedic times. The sacrifice was a rite of sympathetic magic, in which an offering was made to the gods, the celestial controllers of the mysterious and potent forces of nature, to ensure the continuance of conditions favourable to mankind. To be effective it was essential that the oblation should reach these all-powerful beings. None was more suitable to act as messenger than Agni,[1] whose flames on the altar tended always to rise, as did the aroma of the 'burnt offerings', symbolizing the ascent of the oblation itself.

Almost as important as fire itself was the means of producing it, and the method common to the Indo-Āryans was by the friction of two fire-sticks (*araṇis*).

Owing to their nature, gods like Agni and Vāyu (Wind) generally lend themselves to metaphor rather than to anthropomorphic description. Thus Agni is described as butter-backed, butter-faced, seven-tongued, as having flaming hair (*RV.*, I.45, 6), golden-toothed, thousand-eyed, etc., but these are epithets referring to qualities rather than to inconographic representation.[2]

In addition important functions are attributed to Agni. He is inherent in every god; he is the priest of the gods, as well as the god of the priests; the honoured guest in every home, who by his magical power drives away the demons of darkness (*RV.*, III.20, 3). Because he is born anew with every kindling, he is forever young and is thus the bestower of life and of children (I.39, 1; X.88, 10), and places seed in women (*Ait. Br.*, VI. 3). Being immortal he is able to confer immortality on his devotees (*RV.*, I.31,7). His chariot is drawn by red horses, who leave behind them a blackened trail. He clears a way through the impenetrable jungle and consumes the unwanted forest, so providing 'space' for his followers.

Many of the references to Agni in the *RV.* may be regarded as metaphorical, such as his association with the waters, in which he sometimes hides, an allusion to the storm-clouds from which the lightning appears to originate (II.9, 2 and 4).

Although basically one, Agni has a number of aspects. The *ŚBr.* (II.1,1, etc.) gives to the three-fold nature of Agni a distinctively ritualistic interpretation, and defines it as the three sacrificial fires, the *gārhapatya*, *āhavanīya* and *dakṣiṇa*. Elsewhere he is said to have been originally four-fold, but three of the forms passed away (I.2.3,2). In the same work he is said to have eight forms named Rudra, Śarva, Paśupati, Ugra, Aśani, Bhava, Mahāndevaḥ, Īśāna, and in his *trivṛt* state (of being three times three), he has a ninth name, Kumāra (VI.I.3,10–18).

The Purāṇas present Agni anthropomorphically rather than as a Vedic concept. His attributes are more personal and he is given a new parentage. He is sometimes called Abhimānī (proud), the eldest son of the Creator Brahmā; or is said to have sprung from the mouth of Cosmic-Man (*virāṭ-puruṣa*). On the terrestrial plane Agni was born as the ritual fire from Vasubhāryā (the daughter of light) and Dharma (Eternal Law; Duty).[3] By his wife Svāhā Agni had three sons, Pāvaka, Pāvamāna and Śuci, who begot forty-five sons, the three generations totalling forty-nine, who are identified with the 'Forty-nine Fires'. The *Harivaṁśa* describes Agni as one of the eight regents of space, as clothed in black, with smoke as his banner and headpiece, and armed with a fiery javelin. He is four-handed; the seven winds are the wheels of his chariot; and he is accompanied by a goat (*aja*).

Agni's ultimate destructive aspect is the subterranean fire (*vaḍabāgni*)[4] which will finally emerge from the cavity called Vaḍabāmukha (mare's mouth), and destroy the world. The fire of the funeral pyre is the altar of the dead, the last oblation to Agni.

As a wise god Agni is called Kavi, Jātavedas, Pracetas; as lord he is Dhātṛ, Kastṛ, Bhūtādi, Sureśa; as the child of water, Apāṁgarbha; as maker of gold, Hiraṇyakṛt, Hiraṇyaretas, Vasuretas; as universal, Vaiśvānara and Pāñcajanya; as springing from the fire-stick, Śamīgarbha and Araṇīsuta. Agni 'has as many forms as there are sacrifices, with parents and sons in each form',[5] and thus belongs not to a single category but represents every aspect of divinity.

[1] *RV.*, I.12, 1.

[2] This question is discussed by Yāska (c. 500 B.C.) in the *Nirukta*. He refers to those who consider that some gods are described anthropomorphically (*puruṣavidhāḥ*), and to others who consider that particular gods like Agni have no human form (*apuruṣavidhāḥ*).

[3] *HP.*, p. 88.

[4] *SED.* 'The image of fire in water is the ultimate resolution of oppositions; held in suspended union, each retains its full power and nothing is lost in compromises, but there is complete balance. In ritual fire and water combine to burn away sinful elements and then to wash them away' (W. D. O'Flaherty, 'The Submarine Mare in the Mythology of Śiva', *JRAS.*, no. 1, 1971, p. 8).

[5] *EM.*, p. 104.

v. Anala I; Angiras; Agnicayana; Agnīdh; Āpaḥ; Apāṁ-Napāt; Adharāraṇi; Atharvan; Bhṛgu I and II; Garuḍa; Mātariśvan; Yūpa; Śamī; Havyavāhana; Siṁha; Dakṣiṇāgni; Trita Āptya(s).

Agnicayana The preparing of the sacrifical fireplace or altar (*vedi*). Eggeling considers that this complex and important rite was a priestly compromise, added to the *soma* ritual.[1]

According to the Vedic conception of the universe, it had originated as the Cosmic Man (Puruṣa), from whose dismembered body all the forms of the universe came into being. The bricks of the fire-altar represent the material elements of the Puruṣa, and are laid according to the cardinal points, thereby denoting the expansion of the universe in all directions and man's integration into the cosmic order. The bricks[2] also represent the Year, and the endless round of birth, life and death. The heart of the altar is Agni's tongue of flame, and with this ascending flame individual man identifies himself with Cosmic Man. P. Mus in his work on *Barabuḍur* proves that the Vedic fire-altar was the prototype of the *stūpa*, and not of the tumulus as was formerly thought.

With each new building of the altar, the *brāhmaṇas* re-enact the sacrificial dismemberment and re-integration, so ensuring the continuation of the Puruṣa's creative acts by which the cosmic processes are maintained.[3] For this reason all sacrificial rites are said to be included in the *agnicayana* (*ŚBr.*, IX.5.1,42).

[1] *ŚBr.*, pt. iii. Pref. xxvi–xxvii, *SBE.*, XLI.

[2] The biggest altar was in the shape of a large bird with outstretched wings, consisting of 10,800 bricks individually named.

[3] *CC.*, p. 18.

v. Vedi; Adhvaryu; Puruṣamedha; Yajña; Kūrma; Dhiṣṇya II; Agnihotra.

Agnīdh 'Kindler', i.e., the priest who lights the sacrificial fire, having first sprinkled the altar (*vedi*) three times with water to appease Agni. When the fire is burning well Agni is invited to drink the sacred *soma* from the Agnīdh's bowl (*RV.*, II.36,4).

v. Ṛtvij.

Agnihotra 'Fire-offering.' The name of an important

Vedic rite consisting of a daily oblation to the domestic and sacrificial fires (*gārhapatya* and *āhavanīya* respectively) performed by householders. It consists chiefly of milk, oil and sour gruel. According to the *Ait. Br.* (V.26) it is connected with the All-gods (Viśvedevatās) and finds 'support in cattle'.[1]

If three unclean animals, viz., a boar, ram or dog, should come near the sacrificial fires during the rite, an expiatory ceremony must be performed, which consists of pouring water in front of and between the *gārhapatya* and *āhavanīya* fires, with the words: 'Here Viṣṇu strode' (*ŚBr.*, XI.4.1, 5).

The *agnihotra* is personified as the son of Pṛśni.

[1]For expiations connected with the *agnihotra* cow, v. *Ait. Br.*, V. 27. For the use of the heated cauldron (identified with the sun) in the *agnihotra*, v. *Kauṣ. Br.* (II.1f.).

Agni Purāṇa v. Purāṇa(s).

Agniveśa A *ṛṣi*, said to be the author of an early work on medicine.

v. Āyurveda.

Agrasaṁdhānī v. Citragupta; Yama I.

Ahalyā Also called Maitreyī. The wife of the *ṛṣi* Gautama[1] whom Indra seduced while her husband was performing his early morning devotions (*ŚBr.*, III.3.4, 18). When the *ṛṣi* learned of his wife's infidelity he drove her from the hermitage and cursed her to become invisible. He revenged himself on Indra by inflicting him with a skin complaint which consisted of a thousand marks resembling the female pudenda.[2]

This myth was extended in the *Rām.*, and became the basis of variant accounts, in one of which Rāma restored Ahalyā to her normal form and reconciled her with Gautama. Indra was punished by the gods who allowed Rāvaṇa to defeat him.

The *Mārk. P.* (V.1–19) makes use of the myth to denigrate Indra and to glorify Viṣṇu.

[1]Ahalyā was the first woman created by Brahmā who gave her to Gautama (*VP.*, IV.19).

[2]In a later myth these marks were changed to eyes, and Indra became known as Sahasrākṣa (Thousand-eyed). Another myth states that on learning of the seduction, Gautama deprived Indra of his genitals (*vṛṣaṇa*) and substituted those of a goat (*Rām.*, I.48, 16f., *EM.*).

Āhavanīya The eastern fire, one of the three sacrificial fires. It is the first to be lit and to receive the offering. Should this fire go out and atonement not be made, it would result in the death of the eldest son of the institutor of the sacrifice (*ŚBr.*, XI.5.3,8).[1] The *āhavanīya* is called the womb (i.e., seat) of the god (XII.9.3,10), and at death one who reverences it 'falls away from this world' and ascends to the celestial world (*Tait. Saṁ.*, I.5,8; 1.6,7).

[1]For various expiations connected with the fires v. *Ait. Br.*, VII.12.

v. Agni; Gārhapatya; Dakṣiṇāgni; Dhiṣṇya II.

Ahi I. The 'hissing' serpent. The Vedic Ahi is probably another designation of the serpent Vṛtra, the demon of drought and darkness, who envelops mankind in its coils, and absorbs the atmospheric waters. He is called the Enchanter (*RV.*, II.11, 5). It has been suggested that Ahi is the personification of winter whose death releases the frozen streams, but it seems more probable that he is associated with the struggle between the powers of good and evil, which precedes each creation. To the delight of the gods Indra slew Ahi with his keen-edged thunderbolt (*vajra*) and also made the channels for the released waters (*RV.*, I.32; 103, 7; 130, 4; VI.18, 14).

The name Ahi[1] is sometimes applied to Agni; the Maruts also bear the epithet 'Shining like Ahi' (*ahibhānavaḥ*), or 'Shining like serpents' (*ahibhānu*). Ahi is described as brilliant and armed with lightning and hail. When used in the plural this term refers to a certain class of demons of whom Ahi is the first-born.[2] The *Mārk. P.* (xlviii. 21ff.) states that the Ahis were snakes formed of Brahmā's hair when it lost its erectibility.

[1]The name Ahi has cognate Greek forms, *ophis* or *echis* 'serpent' (*IT.*, p. 255).

[2]Cf. the Avestan Azhi, and the ancient Egyptian snake-god Apep, lord of the powers of darkness, who every morning menaces the rising sun.

v. Ahirbudhnya I.

II. An epithet of Rāhu, the demon who causes eclipses.

Ahiṁsā 'Not to injure or harm'; from *a* 'not', and *hiṁsā*, 'harmful or injurious'. *Ahiṁsā* is one of the cardinal virtues of most Hindu cults. It may have originated as a protest against blood sacrifice, and was later directed against capital punishment, and by Buddhists and Jains against war. But the need of the Āryan settlers for more territory and the subsequent ambitions of rulers precluded the general acceptance of the practice of *ahiṁsā*. The savagery of Vedic warfare and the absence of a moral code governing its conduct is evident in the use of poisoned arrows, even in late Vedic times,[1] and also by the harsh treatment of prisoners. This is referred to in the *AV.* (VIII. 8, 10) which states they are to be bound and put to death. For the women-folk of the defeated enemy there was only slavery or concubinage. Doubtless there was little to choose between the conduct of the Āryans and the indigenes (*dasyus*, *asuras*, *daityas*, etc.), the latter also being frequently referred to as *a-mitra*, those 'who do not recognize the sacredness of contracts or treaties' (*RV.*, X.89, 9). But any obvious evidence of moral consciousness is not apparent until the composition of the Upaniṣads which, in the *Chān. Up.* (3.17, 4), associates *ahiṁsā* with austerity, charity and truthfulness, and declares that non-injury and truth are inseparable. Whilst the credit for the doctrine belongs to the Upaniṣads, its dissemination and practical application belong to the Jains[2] and Buddhists, and to the influence of the Emperor Aśoka.

Although the *MBh.* frequently condemns war and emphasizes the virtues of peace, it offers only an impracticable code of conduct in the event of its occurrence, and failed to prevent the reprehensible breaches of the generally accepted rules of warfare by Arjuna and others in the Pāṇḍava-Kaurava war. By contrast the record of Aśoka after the Kaliṅga campaign is an outstanding application of the doctrine of *ahiṁsā*.

Ahiṁsā is said to be one of the means by which the faculty of remembering former existences may be attained (*Manu*, IV.148; VI.39). In the *Vāmana P.*, *ahiṁsā* is personified as the wife of Dharma, whose offspring Nara and Nārāyaṇa taught the way to spiritual enlightenment.

[1] *Majjhima Nikāya*, II. 216; 256.

[2] According to the Jaina *Ācārāṅga Sūtra* (I.2,3,1–4), 'A wise man ... should know and consider the happiness of all things ... For nothing is inaccessible to death, and all beings are fond of themselves ... they shun destruction and cling to life ... To all things life is dear' (cited in *WI.*, p. 293). This is in line with modern scientific views, such as that of the biologist H. J. Campbell who states that all animals are pleasure-seekers (*The Pleasure Areas*, Prelude 11). Cf. also the Orphics and the vegetarian Pythagoreans who abstained from killing animals (Nilsson, *A History of Greek Religion*, p. 220).

Ahirbudhnya I. The great serpent of the deep, probably an atmospheric deity (*Nir.*, 10, 44) who sometimes assumes a maleficent aspect. He lives in the atmospheric 'ocean' and presides over the firmament (*RV.*, I.186, 5). Heesterman[1] suggests that he may represent the vertical rotation of the cosmic forces of fertility 'from sky to earth and back again to the sky, recalling the well-known cycle in which the two fundamental elements fire and water alternate with each other in upward and downward movement'. Banerjea considers he may be the beneficent aspect of Ahi Vṛtra.[2]

In post-Vedic literature Ahirbudhnya is an epithet of a Rudra; of Śiva; and of one of the eleven Maruts.

[1] *Ancient Indian Royal Consecration*, pp. 120, 121, n. 37. Ahirbudhnya unites in his nature fire and water (*RV.*, VII.34, 16).

[2] *DHI.*, p. 345.

v. Ahi I.

II. Name of an early Pāñcarātra *saṁhitā*.

Ahiśuva A drought-demon and a son of Ūrṇavābha. After drinking *soma*, Indra in a state of 'wild delight' killed Ahiśuva and released the waters (*RV.*, VIII.32, 1, 26).

Aiṅginī Gaṇeśa's *śakti*, also called Gaṇeśānī.

Airaṁmadīya 'Giving refreshment and ecstasy.' The name of the lake in Brahmā's world where the *soma*-yielding fig-tree *Somasavana* grows (*Chān. Up.*, VIII.5, 3).

Airāvata or **Airāvaṇa** The white, four-tusked elephant which emerged from the Churning of the Ocean (*samudramathana*) and was appropriated by Indra as his mount (*vāhana*). No cosmological myths associated with Airāvata appear in the *RV.* or other early texts.[1] When elephants are mentioned they are called *nāga*, *vāraṇa* or *śukladant*.

Airāvata is said to be the prototype of all elephants and was made king of elephants by Pṛthu (*VP.*, I.22). Brahmā held in his hands two halves of an egg-shell over which he intoned seven holy songs. From the right half eight elephants (*abhranāgas*) including Airāvata emerged, and from the left half eight cow-elephants. These sixteen animals (in pairs) support the earth at the four cardinal and the four intermediate points. All world-elephants have four tusks and are large and white. Elephants originally had wings but when one descended heavily on to a tree under which a *ṛṣi* was teaching, the branches broke, whereupon the *ṛṣi* laid a curse on all elephants that they should lose their wings, but they are still believed to be capable of producing clouds; hence Indra when seated on Airāvata sends rain (*MBh.*, 6.95, 34), the water being first drawn up from the underworld by Airāvata (5.99, 7, *EM.*).

The cult of the white elephant practised by the Thai kings and by the late dynasty of Upper Burma may have originated in the worship of Airāvata.

[1] Indra's elephant is not a Vedic conception, nor is it 'likely that a purely Āryan deity should originally have been associated with a distinctively Indian animal symbol. In all probability the elephant, like the horse, was an ancient symbolic element in the water cosmology' (Coomaraswamy, *Yakṣas*, pt. ii. p. 32).

v. Gaja; Mārtāṇḍa; Lokapāla(s).

Aitareya Brāhmaṇa v. Brāhmaṇa(s).

Aitareya Upaniṣad v. Upaniṣad(s).

Aiyanār A Tamil tutelary deity adopted into the Hindu pantheon and said to be a son of Viṣṇu or Śiva. Horses in South India are today dedicated to Aiyanār as the son of Śiva, and are worshipped together with the *liṅga*.[1]

[1]Kramrisch, *Unknown India*, p. 56. There are variant spellings of the name.

Aja 'Goat.' The he-goat, sacred to Pūṣan (*RV*., I.138,4) and associated with the sacrificial horse (I.162, 2–4) in the horse sacrifice, where it was believed to precede and guide the horse to the next world.

In Vedic funerary rites the corpse was laid on the skin of a sacrificed goat, and its kidneys put into the hands of the dead man as a sop to the hounds of Yama (*AV*., XVIII.2,11–13).[1]

In astronomy *aja* is equated with the sign Aries. The plural form occurs once in the *RV*. (I.18,19) as the name of a tribe, probably non-Āryan.

[1]Cf. the Gr. 'sop to Cerberus'.

v. Aśvamedha; Ajavīthī; Chāga.

Ajagava I. The southern path of the sun, moon and planets.

v. Ajavīthī.

II. The name of Śiva's bow which came down from heaven at the birth of Pṛthu (*VP*., I.13). It is also called Pināka and resembles the rainbow.

Ajanani 'Non-birth', 'cessation of existence'. A term often used in cursing, such as 'may he cease to exist!'

Ajaśṛṅgī 'Having a goat's horn.' The shrub (Odina wodier) whose fruit resembles a goat's horn. In a hymn (*AV*., IV.37,1–3) dedicated to this plant it is addressed as follows: 'By thee of old the Atharvans slew the demons, O herb; by thee also did Kaśyapa, Kaṇva, Agastya slay. By thee do we expel *apsarasas* and *gandharvas*; O goat-horned one, drive away the demon; make all disappear by [thy] smell ... Let the *apsarasas* ... Guggulū, Pīlā, Naladī, Aukṣagandhi, Pramandanī ... go away ... ye have been recognized.'[1]

[1]Spirits, when called by name become powerless. Cf. Jung's technique for dealing with the unconscious, which was to personify and talk to one's inner powers, so removing 'their dangerous autonomy' and bringing them 'into a proper relationship with consciousness' (Brome, *Freud and His Early Circle*, p. 78).

Ajavīthī 'Goat's road.' One of the three paths in which the sun, moon and planets move.

Ajita(s) A class of deified beings belonging to the first *manvantara*. Brahmā created twelve deities called Jayas to be his assistants at the beginning of the first *kalpa*, but they neglected his commands, whereupon he cursed them to be reborn in each succeeding *manvantara* up to the seventh, in each of which they would bear a different name—Tuṣitas, Satyas, Haris, Vaikuṇṭhas, Sādhyas and Ādityas.[1]

v. Wilson, *VP*., p. 102, n. 20.

Ājivika Name of the Order of monks established by Gośāla, a former friend and associate of Vardhamāna, the Jaina *tīrthaṅkara*, Mahāvīra. Initially the Ājivikas had much in common with the Digambara Jains, and like them went about naked. Though generally living in communities and practising extreme austerity (*tapas*), they were accused by Buddhists and Jains of immorality and ritual laxity. But they gained much popular support during the Buddha's lifetime and were an important factor in the religious life of India during the reign of Aśoka, who dedicated caves in the hills near Gayā to them and mentioned them as one of the chief sects in the seventh Pillar Edict.

The only traces of the Ājivikas to survive are in South India. These consist of numerous inscriptions from Madras, Mysore and Andhra, which show that the cult survived in these regions until the fourteenth century.[1] They are also mentioned in Tamil works. Their basic tenet was rigidly deterministic, and held that the entire cosmic process was governed by an inflexible principle called *niyati* or destiny.

[1]Basham, '*Ājivikas*' (*EB*., p. 332). They practised an extremely painful form of initiation, which often resulted in deformities. It is probable that many extreme Tantric techniques derived from them.

Ājya v. *Ghṛta* (ghee).

Ākāśa I. 'All-pervading; space; vacuity.' The chief and most subtle of the five elements, with which Brahmā is equated (*Chān. Up*., 7.12,1–2).

II. A god to be worshipped when building a house (*Matsya P*., 253.24; 265.39, *PI*.).

Ākāśagaṅgā The name of the celestial *gaṅgā* (Ganges).

Ākhurāja The name of the king of moles. At certain times of the year the village agriculturists must offer a sacrifice to Ākhurāja at mole-heaps.

Akrūra A Yādava prince and uncle of Kṛṣṇa. He was a son of Śvaphalka and Gāndinī. Satadhanvan gave him the *syamantaka* jewel (*VP*., IV.13).

Akṣa A die. Originally dice consisted of small nuts called *vibhītaka* or *vibhīdaka*, later oblong dice with four scoring sides, were used.

v. Kali I.

Akṣara 'Imperishable, indestructible'; a term applied to the syllable *OM* and equated with *brahman*, and hence with the whole world (*Māṇḍūkya Up*., 1).

v. Om; Akṣara-Brahmā; Akṣarā; Vāc.

Akṣarā A personification of Speech (when expressed as praise or prayer), who is invoked not to neglect her followers (*RV*., VII. 15,9; 36,7).

v. Akṣara; Vāc.

Akṣayā 'Undecaying.' A name of the Earth-goddess, also called Pṛthivī.

Akṣaya Vaṭa The so-called 'undying banyan'. A sacred tree at Allāhābād, reputed to be the place where

Rāma, Sītā and Lakṣmaṇa took refuge. Hsüan-tsang, the seventh-century Chinese pilgrim, describes it as a huge tree in which dwelt a man-eating demon. Pilgrims used to fling themselves into the water nearby, and later their bones were collected and placed at the foot of the tree. The successor of this banyan 'is still worshipped in an underground temple near the fort of Allāhābād'.[1]

[1]Crooke, *Things Indian*, p. 48.

v. Vṛkṣa.

Akūpāra The tortoise or turtle on which the earth was thought to rest.

v. Kūrma.

Ākūti 'Will, intention', personified as the daughter of Svāyambhuva Manu. She became the wife of Ruci, the Lord of Progeny, by whom she had the twins Yajña and Dakṣiṇā who afterwards became husband and wife (*VP.*, I 7). This myth is designed to show the inseparability of sacrifices (*yajña*) and the 'gift' (*dakṣiṇā*) to the *brāhmaṇas* for their services at the sacrifice.

Alakā Also called *Vasudhārā*, *vasusthalī* and *prabhā*. The name of the dwelling-place of the *gandharvas*, and also the name of Kubera's capital (*MBh.*, Ādi pa., 85) situated on Mount Kailāsa.

Alakanandā 'Light and joy.' One of the four branches of the river Ganges (*gaṅgā*), believed by Vaiṣṇavas to be the celestial river which Śiva bore on his head for more than a hundred years. By means of this river Sagara's sixty thousand sons were purified and raised to heaven (*VP.*,II.8).

Alakṣmī 'Misfortune', personified as the sister of Lakṣmī (goddess of good fortune). Alakṣmī is also called Jyeṣṭhā (elder sister), with whom the seventh *mahāvidyā* Dhūmāvatī is identified.

Alarka I. A fabulous animal with eight legs.

II. A rabid dog. The name of a *yakṣa* said to be the lord of all dogs, and hence he is invoked to remove the poison from a person bitten by a mad dog (*Suś. Saṁ.*, II. p. 736).

Allāhābād The Islamic name of one of the seven sacred cities of the Hindus, situated at the confluence of the Ganges, Jumna and the mythical subterranean Sarasvatī. Hence it is called *triveṇī* ('triple-braid'). Its ancient name was Prayāga, 'the place of sacrifice', where Brahmā is reputed to have performed *aśvamedhas*.

Āḷvār(s) A group of Tamil Vaiṣṇava 'saints' (7th-9th cent. A.D.),[1] who were especially concerned with the personal experience of the Supreme Being and of his compassion and love. They chanted Vedic hymns and sang ecstatic songs praising Nārāyaṇa, Rāma, Kṛṣṇa and the *gopīs*.

The greatest of the twelve famous Āḷvārs was the *śūdra* Nammāḷvār (c. A.D. 800), who is reputed to have remained in trance for the first sixteen years of his life, and then composed four hymns believed to contain the essence of the four Vedas.

The other important Āḷvārs are Poygai, Pūdam, Pey, Tirumaḷiśai, Kulaśekhara a king of Malabār, Āṇḍal (or Godā) the only woman, Tiruppāṇ a 'pariah', and the last Āḷvār Tirumaṅgai a military chief. A collection of devotional poetry called *nālāyiram* is attributed to the twelve Āḷvārs.

[1]v. J. S. M. Hooper, *Hymns of the Āḷvārs*; *EW.*, vol. I. p. 36.

v. Ācārya II.

Amarakoṣa or **Nāmaliṅgānuśāsana**[1] A dictionary (*koṣa*) of Sanskrit synonyms and homonyms written in verse by Amara, an eminent lexicographer of the Gupta period, of whom, despite his fame, little is known except that he was acquainted with Mahāyāna Buddhism and the works of Kālidāsa and other contemporary writers. He owes his fame to the compilation of his *koṣa* which like Pāṇini's *Aṣṭādhyāyī* superseded all its predecessors. He is mentioned as one of the 'nine jewels' of the Court of an unidentified Gupta king. Thus his date can only be conjectured, but is generally assigned to a period between A.D. 400 and 600.

The *Koṣa* is arranged in three parts, each divided into chapters, and subdivided into sections according to the subjects dealt with. The most informative part is perhaps the second, which deals with words relating to agriculture, trade, medicine, textiles, dress, jewellery, and incidentally with the importance of women in social and educational life.

[1]v. S. K. Nanayakkara, 'Amarakoṣa', in *EB.*, pp. 405f.

Amarāvatī I. 'Abode of the immortals.' The capital of Indra's Paradise (*Svarga*), situated on the eastern side of Mount Meru. It is also called Devapura, 'City of the gods', and Pūṣabhāsā, 'Sun-splendour'. It has one thousand gates and a hundred palaces (*MBh.*, 3.43,7, *EM.*). Fragrant flowers and sacred trees abound, as well as a large number of celestial chariots which can move anywhere at will. *Siddhas*, *apsarasas*, *gandharvas*, the Aśvins, Rudras, *brahmarṣis*, etc., dwell there, but only those who have undergone extreme asceticism (*tapas*), and offered libations of ghee (*ghṛta*) to the sacred fire, and who have been brave in battle, are able to see this region. The road to it is the 'path of the stars'. The dead remain in Amarāvatī until the time for their rebirth on earth; hence 'to enter Amarāvatī' is a euphemism for dying.

II. Once a great city, now only a village, situated on the south bank of the Kistna (Kṛṣṇā) river, about twenty miles from Guntur. It was formerly known as Dhanakaṭaka, the capital of Mahā Andhra—one of the greatest centres of Buddhism towards the end of Aśoka's reign and for some centuries later.

The city was noted for its *mahā caitya* or great *stūpa*, one of the finest architectural monuments and most elaborate examples of sculpture in India.[1]

[1]Some of the sculptures were saved and are now in the British Museum v. Douglas Barrett, *Sculptures from Amarāvatī in the British Museum*.

Amāvāsyā 'The night of the new moon (when the sun and moon "dwell together"), the first day of the first quarter on which the moon is invisible. From *vas* "to dwell" and *amā* "together".'[1]

[1]*SED*., p. 81, col. 2. v. also *AV*., VII.79.

Ambā I. 'Mother.' A name of Durgā; of one of the seven Kṛttikās.

II. The name of the King of Kāśī's eldest daughter. She and her sisters were carried off by Bhīṣma to be the wives of his brother Vicitravīrya. Ambā had previously been betrothed to the Rāja of Śalva to whom Bhīṣma sent her, but the Rāja rejected her because she had been in another man's house. Ambā then retired to the forest to gain power by extreme asceticism (*tapas*) and thus avenge herself. Śiva promised her vengeance, but in another life, whereupon she committed suttee (*satī*) and was reborn as Śikhaṇḍin, the slayer of Bhīṣma.

III. In southern Indian languages *ambā* becomes *ammā* and is frequently affixed to the names of goddesses and females in general.[1]

[1]Cf. German *Amme*, 'nurse'; OG. *amma*.

Ambikā 'Mother.' A nature-goddess around whom many earlier myths gathered.[1]

Ambikā was formed from the energies of all the gods to destroy the buffalo-demon and his army who were attacking the gods. She overcame the demons, but later the gods were again attacked and conquered by the demons Śumbha and Niśumbha. Śumbha greatly desired Ambikā but she rejected him, and in revenge he sent a great army against her under Caṇḍa, but Kālī defeated this army and received from Ambikā the name Cāmuṇḍā.

The Jaina *tīrthaṅkara* Nemi has as his messenger the old mother-goddess Ambikā, who 'often figures as the tutelary genius or *sampradāya-devī* of the Jaina religion'.[2]

According to Sāyaṇa, Ambikā assumed the form of autumn and so destroys beings through fever and other autumnal diseases, and hence she is propitiated at the height of the harvest season.[3] She is also worshipped before the digging of water-tanks (*Matsya P*., 58, 26, *PI*.). The *Kālikā P*. (c. 14th cent.) gives directions for human and animal sacrifices to be offered to Caṇḍikā (Ambikā).

[1]Gaurī, Kālī and Umā are called Ambikās.

[2]R. Williams, 'Before Mahāvīra', *JRAS*., pts 1 and 2, p. 4, 1966).

[3]Ambikā is also a name applied to the harvest as the most productive season.

v. Durgā; Hemāmbikā; Mahiṣa II; Pārvatī.

Ambudeśvara 'Lord of rain.' An epithet of Indra, referring to his rain-making powers.

v. Airāvata.

Ambuvācī The four days in *āṣāḍha* (the 10th–13th of the dark half of the month, i.e., June–July), when the earth is believed to be unclean and agriculture is prohibited.

Amṛta 'Immortal', from *a*, privative, and *mṛta*, 'dead', from the root *mar*, 'to die'. It is the beverage of immortality in Vedic and Hindu mythology; the etymological source of the Greek *am(b)rotos*, the am(b) rosia (food or drink) of the gods,[1] who alone may partake of it and by whom immortality is bestowed.

Some confusion has arisen about the distinction of *amṛta* and *soma*, the former being—etymologically—a celestial elixir, and *soma*, by ritualistic definition, a sacrificial libation offered to the gods, though drunk by the officiating priests. Although these distinctions are not always made, *amṛta* is usually described in mythical terms, whereas the *soma* juice is almost invariably referred to as derived from a plant. In *RV*. (I.23,19–20) '*amṛta* is in the waters,[2] wherein is healing balm. Within the waters—Soma thus hath told me—dwell all balms that heal.' But in other hymns *amṛta* is likened to milk or to rain, such as VII.57,6: 'May the Maruts (the storm-gods) give us *amṛta* for the sake of offspring'; or IX.74,4: '. . . from animated cloud . . . is *amṛta* produced'; or X.139,6: 'The cow-pen flowed with *amṛta*'. The connexion of *amṛta* with rain is also evident in *AV*., 1.4,4; IV.15,10 and 35,6.

In late Vedic texts Soma (the moon-god) is regarded as the receptacle of *soma* juice (the sacrificial oblation), or alternatively of *amṛta*. a belief which was the basis of many Paurāṇic legends, among them being that attributing the waxing of the moon to the replenishment of its store of *amṛta* by sunbeams.

Concerning the origin of *amṛta* the *AV*. (IV.35,6) says it is produced during the cooking of the sacrificial rice-mess, and possesses a potency that overpowers death. So precious was *amṛta* that the gods protected it with all manner of defences, but despite these, Garuḍa succeeded in stealing it, a feat described in the *MBh*. (Ādi pa., 32 and 33). Another myth states that Dhanvantari, the physician of the gods, emerged from the Churning of the Ocean holding a chalice of *amṛta*.

[1]Cf. Latin *im-mor-talis*, and the Teutonic Immurt'hal (Vale of Immortality) at Neufchatel. Coomaraswamy (*Yakṣas*, pt. ii, p. 19) points out that the Semitic view of immortality is that it lasts forever, whereas in Indian

sacrifices (*RV.*, I.83,4). By *tapas* (asceticism) they produced cows (X.169,2). The healing herbs which grow on plains and mountains are said to belong to them (*AV.*, VIII.7,17).

[1] Āṅgiras is an epithet of Agni in the *RV.*, and from it the Āṅgirasas probably derived their name (*EBS.*, p. 18). The *Nir.*, 11.17 states that the Āṅgirasas were 'born of Agni'.

Anila I. The 'immortal air', to which at death mortal breath returns, as the body burns to ashes (*Īśā Up.*, 17). 'The idea that at death the several parts of microcosmic man revert to the corresponding elements of the macrocosm is expressed several times in Sanskrit literature.'[1]

[1] *TPU.*, p. 365, n. 1.

v. Prāṇa.

II. 'Wind.' Name of one of the eight Vasus (*VP.*, I.15).

Animiṣa I. 'Unblinking.' A characteristic or mark (*lakṣaṇa*) of the gods. Various allusions to this characteristic occur in the *MBh.* At the wedding of Nala and Damayantī the gods Agni, Varuṇa and Indra assumed the form of Nala, but the bride was able to identify the real Nala by the blinking of his eyes. The twin Aśvins attempted the same trick upon Cyavana's wife, hoping to seduce her, but she also recognized her husband by the absence of this divine 'mark'.[1]

[1] Heliodorus refers to this characteristic: 'The gods may be known by the eyes looking with a fixed regard and never closing the eyelids', and he cites Homer as proof of his observation. The Nāga guardians of the *soma* were also 'winkless' (*MBh.*, Ādi pa., 33).

II. The name of a demon who must be propitiated with offerings of a mixture of mustard seeds and rice-chaff.[1]

[1] *DHI.*, p. 70, n.1.

Aniruddha I. 'Unobstructed', 'unopposed'. The son of Pradyumna (Kṛṣṇa's son), around whom a minor cult grew up. The *daitya* princess Uṣā, the daughter of Bāṇa, fell in love with Aniruddha who was magically conveyed by Citralekhā to her apartments. When Bāṇa learnt that Aniruddha was in the palace precincts, he ordered his guards to seize him, but Aniruddha defended himself with an iron club and defeated his assailants. Then Bāṇa by magical means captured him, but Kṛṣṇa, Balarāma and Pradyumna went to his rescue and Bāṇa was defeated (*VP.*, V.33). Uṣā and Aniruddha married, and had a son called Vajra.

In the Pāñcarātra system Saṅkarṣaṇa (Balarāma), Pradyumna and Aniruddha are 'gods in their own right, as they were with the early Bhāgavatas'.[1]

[1] *WI.*, p. 329.

v. Subhadrā.

II. One of the four forms of Hari, said to be the source of all sounds (*śabda-yoni*) (*Bhāg. P.*, I.5,37; III.1,34, *PI.*).

Añjanā Name of the wife of a Vānara chief, who was seduced by the wind-god Vāyu. She gave birth to Hanumat.

Āñjana An eye-ointment from the Himālaya or from the region of the Yamunā river, which gives protection against demons and spells, as well as curing jaundice and other diseases (*AV.*, IV.9).

Anna 'Food'; 'sustenance in a mystical sense'.[1] It is the lowest form in which the Supreme Essence is manifested. Metaphorically it is called honey (*madhu*) (*Bṛhad-Ār. Up.*, 2.5,1ff.), and he who recognizes it as the *ātman* figuratively partakes of it and is called the honey-eater (*madhvad*) (*Kaṭha Up.*, 4.5).

Food is especially significant because it is 'continuously transformed substance and energy, a theory in agreement with modern Western science as exemplified by Mayer's Law of the Conservation of Energy'.[2]

[1] The ancient Egyptians also had 'a spiritual view of food; the same word, *ka*, which denotes man's impalpable vital force also means, in the plural, his sustenance' (Frankfort, *Ancient Egyptian Religion*, p. 91).

[2] *IWP.*, p. 120. Food is the primary cause of the origin, continuance and dissolution of all beings (*Suś. Saṁ.*, I, p. 469).

v. Annapatnī; Annapūrṇā.

Annapatnī A goddess presiding over food.

Annapūrṇā[1] 'Giver (or possessor) of food.' A household goddess who is a beneficent form of Durgā. Her worship ensures that the household and the world shall never lack food.[2]

[1] Annapūrṇā is one of Śiva's female aspects (*Facets*, p. 47).

[2] Cf. the Babylonian Anna, the prototype of the Roman Anna Perenna whose festival was held during the Ides of March. Annapūrṇā's festival is held between mid-March and mid-April during the waxing of the moon. v. also E. J. Thompson and A. M. Spencer, *Bengali Religious Lyrics*, pp. 41f., 1923).

v. Anna.

Antarīkṣa The firmament, the sphere of the winds where dwell the *gandharvas*, *apsarsas* and *yakṣas*.

Anugrahamūrti(s) The beneficent forms of Śiva.

v. Saṁhāramūrti(s).

Anumati 'Divine favour', approbation', personified as a goddess who is invoked to give her worshippers wealth, inspiration, insight, offspring and longevity (*Tait. Saṁ.*, III.11). She is also identified with the earth (*ŚBr.*, V.2.3,4), and personifies the earlier day of full-moon (*Nir.*, 11.29), when the gods and *pitṛs* are said to receive the oblations with special favour (*VP.*, II.8). With Prajāpati and Sinīvālī she is invoked to form the embryo in the womb and to make it male (*AV.*, VI.11,3).

Oblations are made to Rākā, Sinīvālī, Kuhū and Anumati, who are 'deliberately brought into conjunction with the moon, which forms part of the Agni Soma ritual' (*Tait. Saṁ.*, III.4,8 and n. 4).

v. Rākā.

Anustaraṇī The cow sacrificed at the funeral ceremony which ensured that the dead had a 'supply of the essence of beef for their journey'.[1]

[1] *BH.*, p. 282; v. also *Ancestor Worship*, p. 39.

Anvāhāryapacana v. Gārhapatya.

Anyataḥplakṣā The beautiful lotus-lake in Kurukṣetra where nymphs dwell in the shape of aquatic birds. Urvaśī lived on this lake when she left her mortal lover Purūravas (*ŚBr.*, XI.5.1,4).

Āpadeva The god of the waters, i.e., Varuṇa.

Āpaḥ The 'waters.'[1] The personification of the celestial and terrestrial waters as maidens (*RV.*, II.35,4), or as goddesses (*Ait. Br.*, II.20) who give boons and attend the sacrifice. As mothers they produce all things, and represent all the deities (*Ait. Br.*, II.16; *Kauṣ. Br.*, XI.4). They also cure, purify, free from 'sin' and from evil dreams, etc. (*AV.*, X.5.24); give immortality (*Kauṣ. Br.*, XII.1), and accompany Agni to the *soma* sacrifice.

From the cosmic point of view the all-pervading waters symbolize the undifferentiated state of the cosmos before creation, as can be seen in the myth of the golden embryo Hiraṇyagarbha. According to *Chān. Up.* (7.10, 1–2), all things, animate and inanimate, are but water solidified, and hence it should always be reverenced. Coomaraswamy points out that saliva is used in the *Tait. Ār.*, I.23,1, as synonymous with *āpaḥ*.[2] So powerful was magically prepared water that handfuls—the so-called water-thunderbolts—were sometimes hurled at enemies.[3]

[1] Cf. the Sumerian *apsu*, the eternal and un-created primeval abyss of sweet water, personified as the goddess Nammu who created heaven and earth. In the Babylonian myth the waters were personified as Apsu, the primeval male, who mingled with the salt waters of the ocean, personified as Tiamat, his consort (E.O. James, *Tree of Life*, p. 11).

[2] *Yakṣas*, pt. ii. p. 24, n.l.

[3] Caland, *Altindischer Zauberritual*, pp. 171ff.

v. Apāṁ Napāt; Varuṇa.

Apālā I. A woman who suffered from a severe skin disease and hence was repudiated by her husband. Indra is said to have cleansed her thrice by drawing her successively through the hole of the chariot, of the wagon and of the yoke (*RV.*, VIII.80,7; *AV.*, XIV.1,41).[1] According to Sāyaṇa she cast off one skin when drawn through each hole, these skins became a hedgehog, alligator and chameleon respectively.

[1] Cf. the curative properties attributed to holed stones such as the Crick and Mēn-an-Tol in Cornwall; the Shargar stone in the Orkneys, and others in the Hebrides, Eire, etc.

II. A daughter or relation of the seer Atri, and a composer of some *RV.* hymns[1]

[1] v. Rahurkar, *Seers*, p. 303.

Apāmārga The plant (Achyranthes aspera) which is found all over India. It has long spikes of retroflected leaves. Death by starvation or thirst, lack of children or cattle, can be 'wiped away' by the *apāmārga* (*AV.*, IV.17,6). It is called the 'reverted one' (*punaḥsara*), which may mean that it averts spells from a victim and causes them to revert, with all their evil intentions, to their originator.

By means of this plant the gods destroyed the *rākṣasas*, and hence the Sacrificer uses it to repel fiends who might attack the sacrifice (*ŚBr.*, V.2.4,14). It is also used in the rite for cleansing or purifying[1] those having attended a burial, which includes the invocation: 'O *apāmārga*, drive away from us sin, guilt, witchery, infirmity and evil dreams' (XIII.8.4,4). In necromancy the oblations should consist of twigs of the *apāmārga* or *vaṭa* tree (*AGP.*, II. p. 955).

[1] In ancient times purification was not physical cleansing, but a magical riddance of evil spirits and their influence. Cf. Aeschines who 'purified the initiated and wiped them clean with mud and pitch' (Harrison, *Prolegomena to the Study of Greek Religion*, p. 492). Impurity 'was conceived of as infection, as a material substance which could be washed away with water or the blood of sacrificial victims, rubbed off or else burned away with fire, or smoked out with sulphur' (Nilsson, *History of Greek Religion*, p. 85). For cleansing by blood of birds v. Leviticus, 14,4ff. Aesculapius was said to have 'wiped away' disease (Nilsson, op. cit., p. 86).

Apāṁ-napāt 'Son of the waters'; probably an aspect of the celestial fire (Agni) who is born as lightning from the waters of the aerial ocean, i.e., the firmament. Apāṁ-napāt became a separate deity[1] by whom all things were engendered (*RV.*, II.35). In another version Mātariśvan, the Indian Prometheus, brings Agni down from the heavens in the form of Apāṁ-napāt.[2]

[1] *HCIP.*, I. p. 373.

[2] Cf. the Avestan Apām-napāṭ, the spirit of the water, who like Agni lives in the depths and is surrounded by nymphs. Napāṭ means 'offspring of' and 'navel of'. Cf. Zend *nāfyo*, 'offspring', from *nāfa*, 'navel'.

Aparājita 'Invincible.' An epithet of Viṣṇu and Śiva; of the eleven Rudras (*VP.*, I.15); of a mythical sword; and of a class of Jaina divinities.

Aparājitā I. 'Invincible.' A name of Durgā.

II. The name of Brahmā's citadel (*Chān. Up.*, VIII.5,3).

Aparṇā Originally a non-Āryan goddess who was worshipped by the Śabaras, Barbaras, Pulindas, and other tribes. She is said to be the eldest daughter of Himavat and Menā. Aparṇā and her sisters Ekaparṇā and Ekapāṭalā practised such extreme austerities (*tapas*) and abstinence that two of them were able to exist on one leaf (*parṇa*) each, but Aparṇā denied herself even this meagre portion, and hence her name Aparṇā (without a leaf). Such extremes of self-denial caused her despairing mother to cry out, 'Umā! Umā!' (lit. 'Desist, desist'), but her pleas were unavailing and Aparṇā, as the great female ascetic, became the *śakti* of the great male ascetic Śiva and became known as Umā. The goddess Durgā is sometimes described as *aparṇā* ('not having even a leaf for a garment').[1]

[1] *DHI.*, p. 492.

Apasmāra The demon-dwarf, who personifies the evils of ignorance and forgetfulness; but according to the *Suś. Saṁ.*, (I. p. 302) he is the personification of epilepsy.

Śiva as Naṭarāja is depicted dancing or stamping on the dwarf. Coomaraswamy states that the *yakṣa* vehicle (*vāhana*) of Naṭarāja 'has come to be regarded as a demon, symbol of spiritual darkness (*apasmāra puruṣa*).[1]

[1] *Yakṣas*, pt. i. p. 8.

Āpastamba v. Yajurveda.

Āprī(s) Propitiatory invocations or offering prayers (*yājyās*) at the 'fore-offerings' of the animal sacrifice, which vary according to different families.[1] The *Tait. Saṁ.* (III.1,3) states that the *āprīs* are uttered over the head of the sacrificial animal. Some *RV.* hymns are devoted to the *āprīs* (I.142; 188; II.3; IV.4; VIII.2, etc.). The *āpri* verses are said to be brilliant and splendid, and thus they cause the sacrificer to prosper (*Ait. Br.*, II.4).

In the school of Kaṇva twelve *āprīs* are said to propitiate twelve deities, the *āprīs* being the personified objects associated with the fire-cult, such as the fuel; the *yūpa*; the sacred grass on which the gods sit; the enclosure, etc.[2] The twelve *āprīs* are also identified with the twelve months of the year, and hence with Agni who represents the Year (*ŚBr.*, VI.2.1,28; 2.2,5; XII. 8.2,19).

[1] Eggeling, *ŚBr.*, pt. ii. p. 185, n.1. The *āprī* hymns appear to stem from Indo-Irānian times, as the Pārsīs have 'Afrigan *mantras* corresponding to the Āprīgaṇas' (*C. Herit. I.*, vol. I. p. 161).

[2] Cf. the Sumerian Tablet IX which consists of a 'collection of conjurations ... addressed to the objects, used in the ritual ceremony and intended to enhance their purifying properties' (E. Reiner, *Śurpu*, Intro., p. 2).

v. Yajña; Barhis.

Apsarasas 'Essence of the waters'; 'moving in the waters or between the waters', viz., the clouds (*RV.*, X.123,5). The name of the seductive celestial nymphs (the mistresses of the *gandharvas*) who dwell in *svarga*, Indra's paradise. They are the dancers of the gods (*Manu*, I.37), who may have symbolized clouds or the mists drawn up by the sun.[1] The chief *apsaras* was Urvaśī who became the lover of King Purūravas. The hymn *RV.*, X.95, consists of a dialogue between them which contains the germ of a very entertaining story related in the *ŚBr.*, *MBh.* and *Purāṇas*, which forms the plot of Kālidāsa's well-known drama Vikramorvaśī, 'The Hero and the Nymph'.

The *apsarasas* can assume any form at will, and often appear as aquatic birds (*ŚBr.*, XI.5.1,4). Warriors who die in battle are taken by the *apsarasas* in brilliantly coloured chariots to Indra's paradise (*MBh.*, 8.4,9, etc., *EM.*), a role similar to that of the Teutonic Valkyries.

The parentage of these nymphs is variously given; they and the *gandharvas* sprang from Prajāpati's dismembered body (*ŚBr.*, IX.4.1,2); or they rose from the Churning of the Ocean after the emergence of the wish-fulfilling *pārijāta*, their favourite tree (*VP.*, I.9); or they sprang from Bhāsī, the 'mother of birds'; or from Vāc.

The gods often sent *apsarasas* to seduce *ṛṣis* and ascetics,[2] and were thus accused of causing madness (*Tait. Saṁ.*, III.4,8). Their other characteristics were promiscuity, lack of maternal feelings, and the discarding of their earthly offspring when they wished to return to their celestial abode.

The *AV.* (IV.37) includes a spell to be used against supernatural foes, particularly against *apsarasas* whose names represent certain odours. Among these nymphs are Guggulū (bdellium), Naladī (nard), Pramandanī (a pungent-smelling plant), and Aukṣagandhī (having an ox-smell).[3] But the scent of the Earth-mother, which *apsarasas* and *gandharvas* shared, was regarded with favour (*AV.*, XII.1,23). In the same work they are told to go away to the trees, because they have been recognized, recognition of supernatural creatures being said to take away much of their power.[4]

Both the *gandharvas* and the *apsarasas* are said to 'stand' on forest trees, or to dwell in them, especially in the *nyagrodha*, *aśvattha* and *udumbara* (*Tait. Saṁ.*, III.4,8; *AV.*, IV.37,4) from which the sounds of their cymbals and lutes may be heard. They are besought to bestow their favours on wedding processions and to bring luck at games of dice (*AV.*, IV.38,3; XIV.2,9).

The *Skanda P.* gives the number of the *apsarasas* as thirty-five millions, of whom one thousand and sixty are important; but according to the *MBh.* (7.61,7, *EM.*) they number 'seven times six thousand . . . [who] dance on the point of Dilīpa's sacrificial post to the music of Viśvāvasu'.

Popular Buddhism adopted the nymphs, and the *Mahāvastu* states that they wore garlands of flowers and many jewels; they are also described in several of the *Jātaka* tales as 'dove-footed' (*kakuṭa-pādiniyo*) and attendant on Sakka (Pā.), i.e., Indra.

[1]*EM.*, p. 158. The *ŚBr.* (XIII.4.3,7–8) states that Varuṇa's attendants are *gandharvas*, and Soma's *apsarasas*. The latter are closely associated with the waters and fertility and were originally of more significance in early than in late literature (Coomaraswamy, *Yakṣas*, pt. ii. p. 33).

[2]Cf. the temptation of St. Anthony.

[3]Whitney, *AV.*, I. p. 211, n.

[4]v. *Ajaśṛṅgī*, n.l.

v. Rambhā I; Ghṛtācī; Antarikṣa; Tilottamā; Aṣṭāvakra; Brahmaloka; Urvaśī.

Apvā Possibly the personification of a kind of colic to which warriors in the field were subject (*RV.*, X.103, 12; *AV.*, IX.8,9; *Nir.*, 9.33). According to Sāyaṇa, Apvā is a goddess presiding over fear.

v. Śakaṁbhara.

Ara I. The name of one of the two seas in Brahmā's sphere, the other being called Ṇya. They can only be found by one who has lived the chaste life of a student (*Chān. Up.*, VIII.5,3–4).

v. Brahmaloka; Brahmacārin.

II. A spoke of a wheel-shaped altar (*vedi*); and a spoke of the Jaina time-wheel.

Aramati 'Devotion', 'piety'. Name of a goddess personifying these virtues (*RV.*, VII.34,21; 36,8, etc.). She is also the protectress of the worshippers of the gods and of good works in general. According to Sāyaṇa she personifies the earth, and there are some similarities between her and the Avestan Ārmaiti, genius of Wisdom and the Earth, who also symbolizes modesty and piety.

Araṇi The fire-drill, consisting of two pieces of wood used to produce fire. This is achieved by friction; the lower piece, *adharāraṇi*, is laid flat; the upper piece, *uttarāraṇi*, is held upright, so that it rests on an indentation in the lower. When rapidly twirled to and fro, sufficient heat is generated to ignite the kindling.

This process is poetically likened to that of procreation, the lower stick being regarded as the mother, the upper the father, and the fire (Agni) as the offspring. During the *soma* sacrifice the *araṇis* are addressed as the two lovers, Purūravas and Urvaśī (*ŚBr.*, III.4.1,22). Taking up the lower *araṇi*, the priest says: 'Thou art the birth-place of Agni.' He then lays two blades of sacred grass upon it saying: 'You are the testicles.' Then he lays the lower *araṇi* down, declaring: 'Thou art Urvaśī.' He then touches the sacrificial cooking vessel, with the words: 'Thou art Āyus.' Placing the upper stick in the lower, he concludes this part of the ritual by declaring: 'And thou art Purūravas.' Then he twists the stick to and fro, uttering the formula: 'I twirl thee with the *gāyatrī* metre, the *triṣṭubh* metre and the *jagatī* metre.'[1] The two *araṇis* are also called 'a chariot of the gods' which conveys the sacrifice to the celestial world (*Kauṣ. Br.*, II.6).

The *RV.* states that the upper *araṇi* was made from the wood of the *śamī*, a hardwood tree (Acacia suma), the lower and softer from that of the *aśvattha* (Ficus religiosa).[2] But according to the *ŚBr.* (XI.5.1,4; 12–17) both *araṇis* were fashioned by Purūravas from *aśvattha* wood. The *araṇis* symbolize Agni, i.e., energy transformed into matter.[3]

[1]*HIL.*, I. pt. i. pp. 156f.; v. also *OST.*, II. pp. 46f. and n. 52.

[2]Wilson, cited by Griffith, *RV.*, II. p. 426, n. 10.

[3]*VF.*, p. 101.

v. Mātariśvan; Tanūnapāt; Yajña.

Āraṇyaka(s) 'Forest texts.' These are essentially sacred esoteric writings which form the core of the Upaniṣads. They were considered to be 'of a secret uncanny character, and spelt danger to the uninitiated',[1] being intended only for those *brāhmaṇas* and *kṣatriyas* who had renounced the world and retired to forest solitudes.

[1]*HIL.*, I. pt. i. p. 203; *EW.*, I. p. 57.

Araṇyānī Name of the goddess who personifies woods and forests (*RV.*, X.146, 1–6).[1]

[1]Cf. *Nir.*, 9,29.

Araru The name of a four-footed demon (*RV.*, X.99,10).

Arāṭakī Perhaps the name of a herb, which is used against evil spirits (*AV.*, IV.37,6).

Arāti 'Non-liberality; envy; malignity.' The personification of meanness, envy, etc.

Arāyī 'Mean.' Name of one of a particular class of demonesses consisting of one-eyed limping hags who destroy embryos (*RV.*, X.155, 1–4).

Arbuda The serpent adversary of Indra, who appears to be cognate with Vṛtra (=Ahi). Indra drove out Arbuda's cows, and knocked him down by striking him with ice (or frost) (*RV.*, VIII.32,26; X.67,12).

Arbuda Kādraveya Name of a mythical seer mentioned in the *Ait. Br.* (VI.I) and the *Kauṣ. Br.* (XXIX.1) as a maker of spells (*mantras*).

Arbudi A serpent-like demon, perhaps the same as

Arbuda. By his creative powers (*māyā*) he projects apparitions of terrifying phantom armies and is thus often invoked to destroy enemies. He is also associated with Nyarbudi who is invoked to send forth seven spectres to terrify the enemy (*AV.*, XI.9).

Arcā An image or icon. When sanctified by special rites the deity represented by it is said to take up his abode in it, and thus it becomes a proper object of worship.

Ardhagaṅgā v. Kāverī.

Ardhalakṣmīhari 'Part Lakṣmī and part Hari.' A form of Viṣṇu.

Ardhanārī The androgynous form of Śiva in which the left side of the body is depicted as female and the right as male, representing the culmination of all male and female forms. From the union of the male and female energies lust arises, and hence this form of Śiva symbolizes lust (*kāma*). Ardhanārī carries out the creative process and begets Skanda or Kumāra.[1] The feminine half is considered more violent, impulsive and creative than the male half, and only when the distinction and limitation of male and female is overstepped and the impersonal *brahman* realized can liberation occur. Thus Ardhanārī conducts 'the mind beyond the objective experience in a symbolic realm where duality is left behind'.[2]

Śiva is said to have become this form by worshipping *śakti* (*Brah. P.*, II.27,98; IV.5,30; 44,48, *PI.*).[3] Banerjea suggests that it emphasizes 'the union of the principal cult deities of Śaivism and Śāktism'.[4]

It is suggested that the distinction of sex evolved from a primordial hermaphroditism (*Suś. Saṁ.*, I. Intro., xxxii).

[1] *VF.*, p. 129, and v. *RV.*, I.164,16.

[2] Campbell, *The Hero with a Thousand Faces*, p. 152.

[3] Cf. the androgynous forms of the ancient Egyptian god of the Nile Hapi, and of Nu, the god of the primeval waters from which the world was created; or Adam before the separation of Eve. The Venus Barbata of Cyprus was regarded as both male and female (Farnell, *Cults*, vol. II, p. 628); the Navajo Indian god Ahsonnutli was also bi-sexual. In Tantrism the Supreme Being is believed to include male and female elements within himself.

[4] *DHI.*, p. 552.

v. Bhṛṅgi; Harihara.

Ari 'Enemy', 'hostile'. One of the four kinds of *mantras*. The *ari mantras* 'destroy those who utter them' (*Mantra Mahodadhi* 24.23, cited by Daniélou, *HP.*, p. 337).[1]

[1] Cf. *AV.*, VII. 88.

Ariṣṭa I. A *daitya*, the son of Bali, who assumed the form of a savage bull and attacked the herdsmen and *gopīs* (*VP.*, V.14). He was slain by Kṛṣṇa (*AGP.*, I. p. 54).

II. The personification of Mount Ariṣṭa, described as waking at dawn, opening eyes of metal, stretching, etc. (*Rām.*, 5.56,10f., *EM.*).

III. Any form of mental disturbance, hallucination, delirium, etc. Also certain signs observed in a patient on the threshold of death (*Suś. Saṁ.*, I. pp. 284f.).

Ariṣṭanemi I. A Prajāpati who married four of Dakṣa's daughters.

II. The name of the twenty-second *tīrthaṅkara* of the Jainas.

III. The name of the *yakṣa* who resides in the sun's chariot during the month of *pauṣa*.

Arjuna I. One of the five Pāṇḍava princes (son of King Pāṇḍu and Pṛthā), whose paternity is mythically ascribed to Indra. The diverse accounts of Arjuna's life, especially those of his several marriages and some of his exploits, related in the *MBh.*, suggest that he is either a composite figure, representing several legendary heroes, possibly of two ethnic groups, or that these accounts are regional and relate to a single figure.[1] Either conclusion would account both for their fictional character and their characteristic disregard of chronology and historical probability.

His first great exploit was his feat of archery at the tournament (*svayaṁbara*) held in honour of his cousin Draupadī (known also as Kṛṣṇā), which gained him both the championship of the contest and the hand of Draupadī. Another legend states that she, in accordance with the custom of some Himālayan non-Āryan tribes, became the common wife of all five Pāṇḍavas; yet another tradition declares that she became the wife of Arjuna's eldest brother Yudhiṣṭhira.

Arjuna is said to have married Kṛṣṇa's sister Subhadrā, by whom he begot Abhimanyu; later he married Ulūpī, a Nāga princess, who bore him another son Irāvat; later still he married a daughter of the king of Maṇipura, who bore him a third son Babhru-vāhana (*Bhāg. P.*, IX.22,29–33, *PI.*).

Some of the late Arjuna legends suggest the transition from Vedic theogony to Hinduism, and reflect also the rivalry of the early Śaiva and Vaiṣṇava sects. One story recounts that Arjuna possessed a magical arrow with which he dispersed a rain-storm precipitated by Indra. A Śaiva legend relates that Arjuna fought unsuccessfully with Kirāta, a mountaineer whose form Śiva had assumed. When Arjuna discovered the identity of his all-powerful opponent he knelt down and worshipped him.

But the most important events of the legendary Arjuna are his exploits in the Pāṇḍava-Kaurava war, in which heroism and tragedy are vividly presented and to the present day remain a source of never-failing interest. But above all they present the most highly prized legacy of ancient times, the *Bhagavadgītā* which Kṛṣṇa is said to have imparted to Arjuna on the eve of the great eighteen-day battle.

[1]According to the *ŚBr.*, V.4.3,7, Arjuna is a mystical name of Indra, who is said in the Epic to be the progenitor of the Pāṇḍava Arjuna.

v. Mahābhārata; Kapiketana.

II. The son of Kṛtavīrya, a ruler of the Haihaya branch of the Yādavas. Under the leadership of Arjuna the Haihaya kingdom became the paramount power in Upper India after the decline of the Kingdom of Ayodhyā. Arjuna's attempt to gain control of the sea-trade of Western India and his demands on the Bhṛgus were the reasons for Paraśurāma's revolt against the Haihayas, which resulted in the death of Arjuna.[1]

His namesake, the Pāṇḍava Arjuna, was a direct descendant of Kṛtavīrya, the Pāṇḍu prince's mother Pṛthā being the daughter of Sūra, third son of the Haihaya Arjuna, the son of Kṛtavīrya.

[1]*HCIP.*, vol. I, pp. 282f.

Arka I. 'Light-bringer', 'shining'. An epithet of the sun (*RV.*, X.107,4).[1]

[1]Arka is identified with *ātman* in the *Maitrī Up.*, 6.8.

II. A plant (Calotropis gigantea) closely associated with Rudra and therefore regarded as inauspicious, although an amulet of *arka* wood is said to give virility (*AV.*, VI.72), and its leaves, if worn on a Prince's body, ensure the success of his mission (*AGP.*, vol. I, p. 496). Sacrificial oblations to Rudra are offered on its leaves which are then burnt separately so that no one should tread on them and thereby suffer injury (*ŚBr.*, IX.1.1,4; 9 and 42).

Arthaśāstra A treatise on political science traditionally ascribed to Kauṭilya, styled Cānakya, the minister of Candragupta Maurya. It is the earliest extant work of its class, and though the constitutional laws it enumerates agree with those recorded centuries later by Megasthenes, he does not mention Kauṭilya. Also, 'the rules of government laid down by the *Arthaśāstra* pertain to a small state and not a vast empire as that of Candragupta'.[1] Moreover, the *Artha* makes no mention of Candragupta or his capital Pāṭaliputra; and its metre, style and arrangement belong to a later period, but this may be the result of subsequent recensions.[2] Thus the view that the *Artha* was mainly compiled about A.D. 300 instead of 500 B.C., is confirmed by the modern statistical analysis of its vocabulary.[3] Nonetheless, the existence of a treatise by Kauṭilya is indicated in later recensions by such passages as: 'This is the view of Kauṭilya (*iti kauṭilyaḥ*) or is not (*niti kauṭilyaḥ*).'

The fifteen *adhikaraṇas* comprising the *Artha* survey the whole field of government: the routine duties of the ruler, the training of princes, the qualifications of ministers of state, the Home and Foreign Office, Civil Service, Defence, the Judiciary, civil and criminal law, corporation and guilds.

The purpose of the *Artha* is evident. It sought to establish a social relationship both social and economic between the various groups comprising the State, and between the State and its neighbours; an ideal often initially achieved peaceably, but the ambitions of princes and the demands of the economy, especially those depending on overseas trade, led to wars to protect trade routes, and the acquisition of territory to provide new sources of food and raw materials. Thus the ideal of Candragupta and his grandson Aśoka was of an Indian empire, a world complete in itself.[4]

[1]*HCIP.*, vol. II, p. 275. v. also *EW.*, vol. I, ch. V.

[2]The language is mainly correct Sanskrit, but a few non-Pāṇinian forms occur.

[3]The method used by T. R. Trautmann, *Kauṭilya and the Arthaśāstra.*

[4]Cf. the similar ambitions of the rulers of Persia, Greece, Rome, and of Charlemagne, Napoleon, Hitler, etc.

v. Cakravartin.

Aruṇa I. The 'Reddish One', the god of the morning, a late personification, the equivalent of the Vedic Uṣas, the goddess of the dawn. The male conception probably goes 'back to some pre-Āryan stratum'.[1]

Vinitā, the daughter of Dakṣa and one of the wives of Kaśyapa, bore two sons, Aruṇa and Garuḍa, both associated with some aspect of the sun (*VP.*, I.21). They were born in the form of eggs of which initially there were three, but in her impatience to hatch them Vinitā broke one from which streaked forth a lightning flash. She broke another which revealed a youth, radiant as the dawn, but with unformed feet. Though able to stand he could not walk.[2]

[1]*AIA.*, I. p. 53.

[2]According to one of the Hindu theories of embryology an embryo develops from the head downwards.

II. The name of a skin disease, perhaps a form of leprosy, of which the symptoms are red spots; the remedy for it is a particular spell given in *AV.*, V.22.

Arundhatī I. 'Fidelity.' A daughter of Dakṣa and wife of Dharma. From her were 'born' the divisions of the earth (*VP.*, I.15).

II. The star Alcor, belonging to the Great Bear, and personified as the wife of Vasiṣṭha, one of its chief stars, or the common wife of the seven stars called the seven ṛṣis. Alcor is invoked in marriage ceremonies and represents conjugal perfection.[1]

Arundhatī became jealous of the illustrious Vasiṣṭha, and as a result she became a tiny star like fire mixed with smoke, which appears intermittently among the seven bright stars (*MBh.*, Ādi pa., 235).

To be unable to see the Pole Star, the Milky Way and Arundhatī indicates that one is 'already with death' (*Suś. Saṁ.*, I. p. 287), and to see Arundhatī and the Pole Star intermittently presages death within a year (*MBh.*, 12.318,9, *EM.*, p. 182).

[1]Diehl, *Instrument and Purpose*, p. 188.

III. The name of a plant used to heal serious wounds (*AV.*, IV.12). According to Sāyaṇa it was used to stop the flow of blood from sword-cuts. It is said to 'arise', from the *aśvattha*, *khadira*, *nyagrodha* and *parṇa* trees, etc. (*AV.*, V.5,5), and hence it may be some kind of fungus or parasitic plant, but in the ninth verse of the same hymn, it is said to have 'fallen from the horse's mouth', and may refer to saliva possessing soothing and curative properties.[1] Arundhatī also protects cattle from Rudra's 'hurled missile' (lightning?) (*AV.*, VI.59,3).

[1]Radford, *Encyclopaedia of Superstitions*, p. 54; or it may refer to knowledge (*jñāna*) which is symbolized by the horse.

v. Hayagrīva.

Aruṇodā A lake (*VP.*, II.2) or river of celestial mango juice flowing from Mount Mandara, in which *yakṣiṇīs*, the attendants of Pārvatī, bathe (*Bhāg. P.*, V.16,17–18, *PI.*).

Arvan I. 'Running', 'quick'. Name of one of the horses of the moon.

II. A mythical animal on which the *asuras* ride (*Tait. Saṁ.*, VII.5,25).

Ārya Name—assumed or applied—of fair-skinned nomadic horse and cattle breeders who occupied the plains north of the Caucasus between the Caspian and the Black Sea. About the beginning of the second millennium B.C. they began to migrate, probably owing to over-population. Some went north and then north-west and spread into northern Europe, becoming the ancestors of the Āryo-European peoples. Others, after journeying northwards, turned south-east around the Caspian and finally reached India and Irān via the Indus Valley. Some groups, like the Kassites and Mitanni, appear to have moved westward from Irān and settled in parts of the Middle East.

Attempts to formulate a proto-Āryan language have failed, owing to dialectal variants, a diversity that has persisted in the Āryo-European and Indo-Āryan languages to the present day. Finally the Indian grammarian Pāṇini (c. 300 B.C.) succeeded in producing from the Indo-Āryan dialects a classical spoken and written language (called Sanskrit, meaning 'orderly or arranged'). It was as basic to Indo-Āryan languages as were its European counterparts, classical Greek and Latin, to the languages of Europe.

The origin of the term Āryan has generally been regarded as uncertain, but it appears initially to have been connected with land and later with agriculture.[1] Its early significance is retained in the Welsh '*ar-glwydd*' (lord or overlord), *ar* meaning 'before' 'above', implying precedence; *glwydd* meaning 'lord', especially of land and implicitly of cattle, a significance apparent in the Welsh translation of the Old Testament,[2] and in the hereditary title of the Welsh nobility.[3]

The Āryan 'lords of the land' were the prototypes of the Vedic kings and nobles (*rājanya*) and knightly warriors (*kṣatra*), whose distinction from the Indian indigenes was emphasized by Āryan ethnic characteristics, and hence the pleas to the gods to preserve their blond hair and fair skins (*ārya-varṇa*) from contamination through intermarriage with the dark-skinned (*dasyu-varṇa*) indigenes.[4] Despite their prayers, fusion of Āryans and some of the indigenes occurred and with it the disappearance of the ethnic significance of Ārya'. But it retained some of its prestige as a synonym of 'noble', 'valid', 'trustworthy', etc.[5]

The Āryans were also distinguished by the patriarchal character of their society, and the worship of male deities, Indra, Agni and Mitra, in contradistinction to the mother-goddess concept common to Indian communities. But the fusion of the races resulted in a pantheon of gods and goddesses and a complex ritual, devised by increasingly influential priestly families. The process by which this assimilation was achieved has been lost in the periodic redaction of ancient texts, but particular passages of the *RV.* and *AV.* suggest that Indian rather than Āryan influence predominated in the assimilation and became the basis of modern Hinduism. But however opinions may vary about the degree of Āryan or Indian influence, there is unanimity about the Āryan contribution, not only to many of the languages of India, but also to the Āryo-European languages of the world.[6]

[1]Cf. E. *arable*; Lat. *arvum*, an arable field; W. *aradr*, plough.

[2]Cf. the Welsh translation of Psalm 50, 10, where the Lord (Arglwydd) claims that 'Every beast of the forest is mine, and the cattle on a thousand hills'.

[3]Such as Lord (Arglwydd) So-and-So.

[4]Even today in India marriage advertisements stress the desirability of light-skinned brides and bridegrooms.

[5]Cf. the Four Noble (*ariya*) Truths of Theravāda Buddhism.

[6]A great number of words occurring in European languages, hitherto generally considered to be derived directly from Greek and Latin, may now be traced to a proto-Āryan source, and confirmed by their Indo-Āryan equivalents.

Āryabhaṭa A famous Indian mathematician and astronomer (c. 5th cent. A.D.) to whom is attributed the introduction of the decimal place-value system. Although there are divergent views about this claim,[1] the earliest use of the system occurs in his work, the *Āryabhaṭīya*.

[1]For these views, v. Datta and Singh, *History of Indian Mathematics*; and *EW*., vol. I, p. 446.

v. Jyotiṣa.

Aryaman The Avestan Airyaman. In Vedic mythology Aryaman is an Āditya, one of the sons of Aditi. He is frequently invoked with Mitra and Varuṇa to ensure that the sun's path, which lies above the region of Bṛhaspati, is clear (*ŚBr*., V.3.1,2). Aryaman is a wise ruler, who forgives 'sins' and guides his worshippers along safe and easy paths (*RV*., VII.36,4; 38,4; 63,6; 93,7).[1] He also presides over twilight and the *nakṣatra* Uttaraphalgunī, and regulates the external performance of rituals (*Tait. Saṁ*., II.1,11), whilst Dakṣa attends to the technical and magical efficacy of rites. He also controls marriage contracts and finds husbands for unmarried girls (*AV*., VI.60,1; XIV.1,17).

[1]Hopkins suggests that he was originally a clan-god (*EM*., p. 81).

v. Āditya(s).

Āryāvarta A portion of northern India dominated by the Āryans in the second millennium B.C., which later was extended, according to *Manu* (II.21–2), from the western to the eastern oceans.

v. Ārya.

Āṣāḍha v. Ambuvācī.

Āśāgaja One of the four (or eight) mythical elephants supporting the world.

Asamañja v. Sagara.

Āsana 'Seat or throne'; 'position or posture'. The term usually refers to any yogic posture assumed as a means of attaining 'one-pointed' meditation. It is essential that the extremities of the limbs be pressed together to ensure an uninterrupted flow of the life-circle, so that the radiations of the yogin's 'nerve-centres in toes and fingers are concentrated in a kind of closed circuit and their forces are not wastingly diffused'.[1]

Particular poses are depicted in representations of the Vedic and Paurāṇic divinities, and of the Buddhist *bodhisattvas* and of the Buddha himself. Eighty-four postures are enumerated in various works, but traditionally the *āsanas* are believed to number 8,400,000, of which only eighty-four are known to man. Śiva is said to have created each of them by assuming their characteristic *sthāna* (stance). Some *āsanas* have passed into the dance; others have been taken over from the stances of warriors in battle. The positions of the various limbs of the body are collectively known as *āsana-mūrti*, i.e., the entire form, the sum of its symbolic parts. The *siṁhāsana* (lion-throne) is associated with royal power.[2]

[1]*Facets*, p. 75.

[2]Auboyer, *Le Trône et son symbolisme dans l'Inde ancienne*, ch. 3. The ancient Egyptian goddess Isis was the deified throne (James, *Tree of Life*, p. 168).

v. Āsanamantra; Mudrā.

Āsanamantra A *mantra* which is to be uttered when taking a seat (*āsana*). Diehl states that the *āsanas* may be mentally visualized by the *ācārya*, and the postures themselves worshipped.[1]

[1]*Instrument and Purpose*, pp. 105 and 116, n.l. Cf. the Canaanite myth which states that when Baal's palace was built, he supplied the seat-gods and the throne-goddesses with wine (G. R. Driver, *Canaanite Myths*, p. 101, n.1). v also *āsana* n.2.

Aśani I. 'Thunderbolt', i.e., 'meteorite'; 'lightning'. Agni is invoked to pierce through the Yātudhana's skin and to let the fiery dart destroy him (*RV*., X.37, 4–5).

II. The name of one of the eight forms of Agni (*ŚBr*., VI. 1.3,14).

III. One of the eight elemental forms of Śiva (also called Ugra, 'fearful'), which denotes the power of destruction exercised through the elements.

Asiknī v. Vīriṇī; Dakṣa.

Asipattra One of the twenty-eight hells. It consists of a forest, the leaves of whose trees are sharp swords (*asi*) (*VP*., II.6). Those who stray from the Vedic path, such as hunters and slaughterers of camels, go to this hell (*Bhāg. P*., V.26,7 and 15; *Brah. P*., II.28,84, etc., *PI*.). Those who wantonly cut down trees also suffer the same fate.

Āśis 'Hope', personified as the daughter of Bhaga.

Asita I. The name of the Lord of darkness and of magic.

II. A sage and also the name of the hill on which he dwells.

III. A *siddha* who acted as *purohita* at Kṛṣṇa's sacrifice in Kurukṣetra.

Aśiva 'Inauspicious', 'dangerous' (*RV*., I.116,24). The name of a demon causing disease (*Hariv*., 9560, *SED*.).

Aśmaka The name of Madayantī's child. After bearing the child in her womb for seven years, she performed a 'Caesarean' operation with a sharp stone (*aśman*), and hence the name of her child (*VP*., IV.4; cf. *MBh*., Ādi pa., 179).

Aśman I. 'Rock', 'stone', i.e., Indra's *vajra.*
II. The firmament, which was regarded as an inverted stone bowl (*RV.*, V.56,4, etc.).[1]
[1]Cf. Zend *asman*; Persian *aṣmān*; Lith. *akmu.*
Aśna 'Voracious.' An epithet applied to one of the many demons overthrown by Indra (*RV.*, II.20,5).
Aśoka I. A tree (Saraca indica) sacred to Śiva.

When Damayantī was seeking Nala she circumambulated an aśoka tree thrice, and begged it to free her from grief (*MBh.*, Vana pa., 64).

The *Rāmāyaṇa* describes an *aśoka* grove in which Sītā was illtreated before being compelled to yield to Rāvaṇa. Hindu women accordingly associated the *aśoka* tree with constancy and chastity, and at certain times worshipped it and ate its buds. An *aśoka* is said to bloom when touched by a beautiful girl's leg (*AGP.*, II. p. 892).
II. Name of the famous Mauryan Emperor.
v. Buddhism; Maurya(s).
Āśrama I. A popular term for the hermitage of a *ṛṣi* or holy man.
II. Name of the four stages into which the life of the individual Hindu was divided. The *āśramas* are 1. *brahmacārin*; 2. *gṛhasthya*; 3. *vānaprastha*; 4. *sannyāsin.*
Aśrī 'Bad luck', personified as a goddess.
Aṣṭādhyayī 'Eight chapters.' The name of Pāṇini's great Sanskrit grammar. The language developed little after Pāṇini, except in its vocabulary. His 'grammar is one of the greatest intellectual achievements of any ancient civilization, and the most detailed and scientific grammar composed before the nineteenth century'.[1]
[1] *WI.*, p. 388.
Aṣṭākṣara 'Containing eight syllables'. The *mantra* of Viṣṇu: '*Aum nama Nārāyaṇāya*' is repeated thrice daily to attain liberation.
Aṣṭamaṅgala Eight auspicious objects necessary for a great occasion such as a coronation, etc., viz., a lion, bull, elephant, water-jar, fan, flag, trumpet, lamp; or alternatively a *brahmin*, cow, fire, gold, ghee, sun, water and a king.
Aṣṭamūrti The 'eight forms' of Śiva, viz., the five elements, and the sun, moon and sacrificer. 'Śiva fulfils all functions which belong to these eight realities or constituents. The world is a product of his eight forms . . . and can only exist and fulfil its task because these forms co-operate.'[1]
[1] *VS.*, p. 41.
Aṣṭāpada 'Having eight legs.' The fabulous animal Śarabha.
Aṣṭāvakra A *muni* noted for his extreme asceticism. Owing to the pre-natal curse of his father Kahoḍa, he was born with eight (*aṣṭa*) parts of his body deformed (*vakra*), and hence his name.

Whilst engaged in austerity (*tapas*), which consisted of standing up to his neck in water, some nymphs (*apsarasas*) on their way to Mount Meru saw his head projecting from the water. Realizing that he must be a great *muni* they paid homage to him. This gratified Aṣṭāvakra and he offered them a boon, but two of the nymphs replied that to know he was so well-disposed towards them was enough. The others replied, 'If, exalted sir, you are indeed pleased with us, then grant us a husband, the best of men.' 'So be it,' replied Aṣṭāvakra, emerging from the water, and presenting himself as a suitor. But when they saw how ugly he was they laughed at him. 'Very well', he said, 'you shall have the husband you desire, but afterwards you shall fall into the hands of thieves.'

This story (*VP.*, V.38) was related by Vyāsa to Arjuna to console him for the loss of the women he had loved, and to remind him of the vanity of all earthly things. 'Death', said Vyāsa, 'is the doom of everyone. Union inevitably terminates in separation; growth tends but to decay. Do you, therefore, along with your brothers, relinquish everything, and repair to the holy forest.'

The Pāṇḍu princes followed Vyāsa's advice, placed Parikṣit on the throne and ended their days as sannyāsins.
Asthimālin 'Having a necklace of bones', i.e., skulls. An epithet of Śiva.
Asthisambhava 'Consisting of bones', i.e., the *vajra.*
v. Dadhyac.
Āstika 'Orthodox.' The acceptance of the Veda as divinely inspired and authoritative. To the Vedic fundamentalists even the sounds of its words were divine. Thus its opposite *nāstika* 'unorthodox' was the rejection of the divine origin of the Veda. But the term does not imply that *nāstika* schools or systems, such as the Buddhists and Jainas, entirely rejected the Veda, though most of its dogmas were regarded with scepticism by the materialist Cārvāka School.
v. Darśana(s); Pūrva-Mīmāṁsā.
Āstīka v. Jaratkāru; Janamejaya.
Astramantra A *mantra* used to charm weapons (*Raghuvaṁśa*, V.59), and as a protection against malevolent forces. Water consecrated by this *mantra* also removes the impurities of child-birth (*AGP.*, I. p. 275).
Asunīta 'World of spirits'; 'Lord of spirits', i.e., Yama (*AV.*, XVIII.2,56).
v. Asunīti.
Asunīti 'Spirit-life'; 'world of spirits', personified as a goddess who is invoked to prolong life and give strength and nourishment (*RV.*, X.59,5,6). Muir[1] considers she

may be a deity presiding over funerals; or perhaps it is an epithet of Yama.

[1]*OST.*, V, p. 297.

Asura 'Lord'; it also means 'demon', but only the latter is in use from the later Vedic period onwards.[1] Various derivations have been suggested for this word, some of which are rejected by modern Sanskritists. Its earliest use supports the view that it is derived from *as*, to be, to exist, or from *aśu*, breath, life. Because of the association of *asura* with light, the derivation from *svar*, to shine, has also been suggested. The word appears to be of Indo-Āryan-Irānian origin and to signify the personification of the imperfectly understood forces of nature, especially of those favourably associated with fertility. But other natural phenomena, like drought, eclipses, disease, etc., were regarded as demons, always in conflict with personified beneficent phenomena, and thus called Asuras.

These two categories are distinguished in the Irānian Avesta as Ahura (Vedic Asura) a god, and Daeva, signifying one of the demons or anti-gods. But in the *RV.*, possibly following another tradition, Asura and Deva are sometimes used synonymously, both signifying divine beings possessed of creative vitality. This tradition is acknowledged in a myth in the *ŚBr.* (IX.5.1,12ff.), which purports to explain their subsequent distinction as gods and anti-gods. It relates that the Devas (gods) and Asuras, both of them sprung from the Creator Prajāpati, inherited speech—both true and false, but that finally the gods rejected untruth, whilst the Asuras spurned truth which led to their downfall. Another tradition states that though the gods and Asuras were equally powerful, their power was divided, the gods exercising it by day and the Asuras by night (*Ait. Br.*, IV.5.). Later the term *asura* denoted the hostile native rulers and tribes opposed to Āryan religious and political expansion.

The synonymous significance of Deva and Asura in the *RV.* is apparent in the invocation to Varuṇa as the great Asura, the Lord God, the great king (I.24,14); in the identification of Savitar with the gold-handed Asura (I.35,9); or Rudra as the Asura of mighty heaven (II.1,6). Similar references apply to Dyaus (I.131,1), Indra (I.174,1, etc.), Agni (V.12,1, etc.), Pūṣan (V.51,11), and Soma (IX.72,1). On the other hand, in a solitary passage of the *RV.* (V.40,5–9), Svarbhānu,[2] one of the demons of eclipse, is referred to as a descendant of Asuras.[3]

The advanced style and contents of the final *maṇḍala* of the *RV.* indicate that it is a 'supplement' to the earlier *maṇḍalas.*[4] In it the superficial duality of natural forces is recognized, as is the distinction of two categories of celestial Asuras, beneficent and maleficent, the latter being regarded as 'evil spirits in perpetual hostility to the gods' (X.53,4).

This distinction, which was accompanied by the general use of *deva* when referring to the gods, reflects also the recognition of their relative importance. This more critical attitude also marks the beginning of the end for most of the ancient animistic concepts. Even the traditional status of the 'great Asuras', Agni, Varuṇa and Soma, was questioned by Indra when he declared: 'These Asuras have lost their powers of magic.' His subsequent appointment of Varuṇa as the Lord and Ruler, who discerns 'truth and right from falsehood' (X.124,5), suggests a new concept of divinity which may be said to be one of the great steps in 'the evolution of the idea of God' in Vedic speculative thought, as great perhaps as the transition from the Hebraic notion of Elohim to that of Jehovah.

According to the *ŚBr.* (VIII.8.1,5), people 'who are godly make their burial places four-cornered, whilst those who are of the Asura nature, the Easterners and others, make them round, and the gods drove them from the regions'. There is also the so-called Asura form of marriage in which the bride is sold (*AGP.*, I. p. 594).

[1]Heimann, *Facets*, p. 159. Filliozat suggests that the Asuras were lesser gods 'charged with expounding the teachings of the gods themselves' (in *Ancient and Medieval Science*, p. 141). The *Ait. Br.* (VI.4) states that the gods' sacrifice was thrown into confusion by the Asuras.

[2]He is identified with Rāhu in post-Vedic works.

[3]Cf. the Old Testament myth of Lucifer.

[4]*HCIP.*, Vol. I, pp. 229, 238, n. 17, *et al.*, considers that the *RV.* originally consisted only of the first eight *maṇḍalas.*

v. Daitya(s); Dānava(s); Durgā; Kālanemi I; Hiraṇyapura; Aghāsura; Andhaka I; Arbuda; Asuravidyā; Aśvagrīva; Madhu II; Marka I; Rudra; Āsurī I and II; Anārya; Namuci.

Asuravidyā 'Science of the Asuras', i.e., magic.

Āsurī I. A 'demoness' who was the first to produce a remedy for leprosy (*AV.*, I.24). The Asuras are said to dig for the remedy (II.3,3).

II. Name of a plant (Sinapsis ramosa). The demoness Āsurī may be a personification of this plant.

Aśva, also **Haya**[1] 'Horse.' The symbol of luminous deities, especially the sun. In *Ait. Br.* (VI.35), the sun is said to have taken the form of a white horse. Seven golden horses, symbolizing the seven days of the week, pull the sun's chariot. 'The horse is a natural symbol of power . . . an aspect which was surely strengthened by the fact that the horse-drawn chariot gave the Indo-

Āryans the decisive advantage in their invasion of the Indian sub-continent; for the Vedic Indians, the horse was the emblem of war.'[2] Cavalry was later used but it never reached the standard of that of Alexander. In *RV.*, I.64,6, the horse is identified with the rain-cloud; the Aśvins are horsemen; Indra has bay horses;[3] and the Maruts' chariot is drawn by red horses and mares (V.56,6–7).

The horse was produced from water and hence is particularly 'Varuṇa's own', because Varuṇa is the god of the waters (*ŚBr.*, V.1.4,5; 3.1,5; VIII.4.3,13; cf. IV.3.4,31).[4] The various forms of Agni are invoked to become horses and carry the sacrificer to heaven where men dwell joyously with the gods (*AV.*, XVIII. 4,10; v. also *Ait. Br.*, III.49), and those institutors of sacrifices who give horses as their 'gift' (*dakṣiṇā*) to the officiating priests will dwell forever with the sun (*RV.*, X.107,2). Eating horse-flesh was abhorrent to the Vedic Indians (*Tait. Saṁ.*, VII.2,10).[5]

, The head of the horse is particularly sacred and potent. Among other things, it represents knowledge (*jñāna*). The mythical celestial musicians called *aśvamukhas* had human bodies and horse-heads. Some mare-headed female *yakṣīs* are depicted on an erotic frieze at Aihole, and are familiar Indian 'night-mares' who carry men off for sexual purposes.[6]

Crooke states that many Indians when buying a horse do not look for its points but for lucky or unlucky marks and colours, the most highly prized animals being those having the five auspicious markings, viz., four white stockings and a white blaze on the forehead. In the Deccan a piebald horse and a cream wall-eyed mare are equally valued, but a mare of any other colour or with one wall-eye is most unlucky.[7]

[1] *Haya* appears in early Indian dialects as *hi*, *hya* and *hyvor*; hence the Gothic, *hyrsa*, Teutonic, *hors*, and Saxon, *horse*.

[2] O'Flaherty, 'The Submarine Mare', *JRAS.*, no. 1, 1971, p. 17. A document from Mitanni, the Kikkuli Text (c. 1360 B.C.), gives detailed instructions for the training of chariot horses, and it contains 'several technical expressions ... reminiscent of Sanskrit expressions' (Zeuner, *A History of Domesticated Animals*, p. 319; v. also Hrozný, 'L'entraînement des chevaux chez les anciens Indo-européens d'après un texte mîtannien-hittite provenant du 14 siècle av. J. C.' (*Archiv. orientálni*, Praha, 3e, 431–61).

[3] Perhaps similar to the ancient Przevalsky horse (v. Bökönyi, *The Przevalsky Horse*, illus. fig. 33).

[4] The Greek Poseidon created the horse by a blow on a rock with his trident (Nilsson, *A History of Greek Religion*, p. 71). He is also the god of horses, and in Arcadia he took the form of a horse (ibid., p. 121).

[5] v. Oldenberg, *Religion des Veda*, p. 356, n.3.

[6] P. Rawson, *Erotic Art of the East*, Pl. 42.

[7] *Things Indian*, p. 256. *AGP.* (Ch. 289) lists the unlucky markings of a horse.

v. Aśvamedha; Arvan I; Tārkṣya; Uccaiḥśravas; Dadhikrā; Vājin; Hayagrīva; Saraṇyū; Vaḍabāgni; Kalkin.

Aśvagrīva 'Horse-neck.' Name of an Asura.

Āśvalāyana A famous author of Śrauta and Gṛhya Sūtras and other works on ritual. He was a pupil of Śaunaka.

Aśvamedha The horse-sacrifice. The Indo-Āryan horse sacrifice appears initially to have assimilated an ancient Indian fertility rite in which some native animal, probably a bull, was replaced by the Asian horse introduced by the Āryans. This is indicated by the fact that the horse was not indigenous to India, and that, owing to the Indian climate, the breeding of horses there—without constant renewal—was seldom successful.[1]

The development of the ritual of the *aśvamedha* during the three phases of Indo-Āryan expansion in Upper India is clearly apparent, though not always chronologically definable. The earliest source of information about it is in two hymns (I.162 and 163) of the *RV.*, but beyond extolling the horse, asserting its divine origin and identifying it with the sun,[2] they give only meagre details of the rite itself.[3] The principal function of the horse was to draw the chariots used by members of the aristocratic warrior-class in sport and war; only once is it mentioned as being ridden (V.61,2).

As a fertility rite the horse sacrifice was associated with the Spring community festival, and was probably originally offered to Varuṇa,[4] king of heaven and earth and of the waters, who was also the representative of law and order; alternatively, it may have been offered first to Dyaus, the Indo-Irānian sky-god.[5] The celestial association of the horse is indicated in *RV.*, I.163, which states that Trita (in this context the personification of the rising sun) puts the bridle on the horse for Indra (the chief of the gods) to mount. According to hymn 162 a dappled goat[6] precedes the horse to announce the sacrifice to the gods. On the arrival of the horse it joins Indra's bay horses, the two dappled mares of the Maruts (the storm-gods), and the ass which draws the Aśvins' chariot. The rite ensures wealth and benefits for the sacrificer, provides good horses, fine sons and continued lordship; and fills the rivers. In the *Tait. Saṁ.* (V.7,25) and the *Bṛhad-Ār. Up.* (I.1) the *aśvamedha* has a cosmic significance, its performance being regarded as taking place at the centre of the earth, and as representing in miniature a re-creation of the world. In the later phases the fertility aspect remains, but is largely obscured by changing conditions, and hence it became a festival of great pomp and included the distribution of largesse on a grand scale, especially to the officiating priests. Its secular character thus distinguished it from the exclusively priestly sacrifices.[7] The rite, in its fully developed form, consisted of two parts, one preparatory, the other culminatory, the former including a military challenge, the latter the celebration of its success.

The preparatory rite began with the selection of a stallion which was then purified by the magic properties of a rope of *darbha* grass and dedicated to Agni, the god of fire, without whom no sacrifice is complete. This was followed by the dedication to the god Soma (the deification of the sacrificial libation offered to the gods); to the Waters; to Savitṛ (an aspect of the sun); and to Vāyu (the Wind-god). Finally it was dedicated to Viṣṇu (a Vedic solar divinity, not the post-Vedic Supreme Being of the Vaiṣṇavas); to Indra (the Āryan warrior-god); to Bṛhaspati (the preceptor of the gods); and to Mitra and Varuṇa.

The horse was then released in a north-easterly direction, the way that leads to the gods,[8] where lay also the territory as yet unconquered. The animal was allowed to wander at will for a year, and was escorted by a hundred princes 'born in wedlock', a hundred sons of chiefs and heralds, and a hundred sons of attendants and charioteers, all armed according to their rank. Thus the horse was a challenge to the neighbouring native rulers. If the escort was attacked and defeated and the animal captured, the challenger was unable to perform the sacrifice and became an object of ridicule. The *Tait. Br.* (III.8.9,4) declares that a weakling who aspires to the performance of the *aśvamedha* shall be destroyed. This reflects the early beliefs of many peoples that a king must be strong and healthy, etc.

To ensure success the escort had not only to guard against attack but also against unpredictable risks that might nullify the rite. Special rites were laid down if the horse should couple with a mare during its wanderings, or become diseased. If it should die or be stolen, another must be consecrated by sprinkling water on it.

As part of the preparatory rite, and to sustain the animal during its wanderings, daily offerings were made to Savitṛ, the horse being associated or identified with the sun and the solar year; and the lute-players sang of the ruler's exploits and valour. Only those of the escort who remained to the end of the expedition were eligible to share the royal power that derived from the performance of an *aśvamedha*.

The sacrifice took place in Spring or Summer, preferably the former. The return of the horse marked the beginning of the king's consecration which included the pressing of juice from the *soma* plant. After the horse had been bathed in a pool or stream[9] in the sacrificial area, a 'four-eyed' dog[10] was killed by a blow from a club of *sidhraka* wood, and the body floated off under the belly of the horse in a southerly direction. The slaying of the dog may initially have been intended to drive away evil spirits from the horse, or alternatively to represent Indra's conquest of the drought-demon Vṛtra. Another interpretation is that it was an offering to the *pitṛs* (ancestors) who dwelt in the South, where lies the realm of Yama (the ruler of the dead), whose two hounds were 'four-eyed'; or the dog may have been a kind of scape-goat who bore away the 'sins' of those taking part in the ceremony, the dog often being regarded as the embodiment of evil and misfortune.

The horse is bound to the central stake, fifteen other animals being roped to various parts of the horse. These animals are identified with the magical thunderbolt (*vajra*), which in turn is equated with vigour and the power to repel evil. A number of other sacrificial animals are bound to various stakes. During this rite the horse is believed to assume the form of a great bird who takes the sacrificer to heaven (*ŚBr.*, pt. v. p. 315n.).

The slaughtering knife for the horse is of gold, for gold represents royalty; a copper knife is used for the 'body-encircling' animals, who represent the chiefs, heralds and minor aristocracy; and an iron knife for the remaining animals who represent the commonalty.

Only the horse knows which is the heavenly world, and hence the gods hold on to its tail for guidance.[11] When the horse sees the mares penned up in the sacrificial area he utters (i.e. neighs) 'hiṇ'.[12] In so doing he is supposed to be reciting the *udgītha*, the principal part of the *sāman* or chanted verse (usually the duty of the *udgātṛ* priest).

The sacrificial horse and three others, all richly caparisoned, are harnessed to a chariot and driven around the sacrificial area and then unharnessed. The Queen Consort anoints the fore-part of the sacrificial horse; the king's favourite wife the middle; and a discarded or neglected, or possibly a barren wife, the hindquarters.

A gold cloth is spread on the ground and the horse killed. Four of the king's wives, and a girl who takes the part of a fifth wife, together with four hundred female attendants, are led up to the dead animal. The Queen Consort lies down with the horse and a cloth is thrown over them and the officiant says: 'In heaven ye envelop yourselves—for that indeed is heaven where they immolate the victim!' The Queen adds (for the completeness of the union): 'May the vigorous male, the layer of seed, lay seed!' The priests and the assembled women then take part in an erotic dialogue. Meyer draws attention to the parallel rite in the *hieros gamos* (the so-called sacred marriage) of the Queen of Athens with Dionysos, which was celebrated in the 'Cattle Stall', when Dionysos probably assumed the form of a bull, just as Varuṇa is identified with the stallion in the erotic scene with the queen.[13] The belief that mimic copulation confers fertility is common to many cultures, and the horse in folklore is closely associated with the sun, fertility, and with water, hence Varuṇa is the presiding deity of the horse (*vājin*), the latter being especially associated with the notion of generative strength (*vāja*).

Propitiatory oblations of blood are offered to the fearsome god Rudra and to Death. The first oblation is offered 'in the throat' of the *gomṛga* (an unidentifiable animal), to shield the cattle from Rudra, and a second and third is offered on a horse-hoof and in an iron bowl, to protect one-hoofed animals and people respectively from him. As Death is in all the worlds, a sacrificer who failed to make an oblation to Death would die.

After the Queen had risen from under the robe, the horse was then dissected. The portions were roasted and some offered to Prajāpati; the remainder being divided amongst those present. The ceremony closes with a purificatory bath and the offering of gifts or an honorarium (*dakṣiṇā*) to the officiating priests. The *dakṣiṇā* often consisted of booty captured during the horse's wanderings.

For several centuries the performance of the *aśvamedha* lapsed. In the *MBh.* (Aśvamedha pa.) the *aśvamedha* is described as a rite performed by Yudhiṣṭhira, to atone for the slaughter by the Pāṇḍavas of their kinsmen the Kauravas, an intention probably in accordance with the views of late post-Vedic times, but far from its earlier significance. The efforts of the Emperor Aśoka (273–231 B.C.) and of the Jainas and Buddhists to prevent blood sacrifices, may have contributed to the brahmanic reaction which led to its revival on a grand scale during the subsequent Śuṅga dynasty founded by Puṣyamitra (187–151 B.C.), a general of the last Mauryan King Bṛhadratha. To celebrate his son's and grandsons' defeat of the Greek successors of Alexander, Puṣyamitra ordered the performance of two *aśvamedhas*, not to proclaim new suzerainty but to signalize their victories. It again fell into abeyance during the Kuṣāṇa dynasty, but was revived in the fifth century A.D. during the Gupta dynasty,[14] and again in the seventh century by Ādityasena Gupta of the later Gupta dynasty. One of the rare records of the performance of the *aśvamedha* in southern India is that of Śivaskandavarman of the Pallava dynasty, who is mentioned in the early *prakṛt* records of the family as a 'righteous king of kings'. Another instance is that of Pulaskeśin of the Cālukya dynasty (6th cent. A.D.). Basham[15] states that the last recorded performance of an *aśvamedha* was in Orissa in the ninth century A.D.

[1]Thus the assertion of Coomaraswamy (*Yakṣas*, pt. ii, p. 30) that the *aśvamedha* was certainly pre-Vedic lacks probability.

[2]The Cretans, as did the Greeks, sacrificed horses to Poseidon Hippios (Farnell, *Cults*, IV, p. 20). The Rhodians annually dedicated to the sun-god a quadriga which was driven into the sea in which the sun nightly disappeared. Among other communities a horse-sun cult also existed. At one time the kings of Judah dedicated horses and chariots to the sun (II. Kings xxiii, 11). But the suggestion that the horses were bronze models kept in the temple lacks validity, as in xi, 16 reference is made to the road by which the horses travelled to the temple, though if for sacrifice is not explicitly stated. That this was the intention is suggested by the identification by the Hebrews of the Canaanite (probably Hittite) sun-god Shamash with the Hebrew sky-god Yahweh. The horse-sacrifice, probably introduced by the Scythians, was also performed in China (J. Needham, *Science and Civilization in China*, I, p. 90; v. also Warde Fowler, *Roman Festivals*, p. 330; Frazer, *Pausanias*, IV, p. 198).

[3]The basis of the *aśvamedha* was a simple rite of sympathetic magic which became greatly elaborated and inclusive of 'everything which could make an appeal to the warrior Indian king and induce him to distribute abundant largesse on the celebrators' (*CHI.*, vol. I, p.142).

[4]Dumont, *L'Aśvamedha*, p. xii. The *Ait. Br.*, VIII.21, mentions a number of 'world-conquerors' who performed *aśvamedhas.*

[5]*Patterns*, p. 96.

[6]The goat and horse are the only animals mentioned in the *RV.* accounts of the *aśvamedha*, but according to Eggeling (*ŚBr.*, pt. v, p. 311, n.1), this Brāhmaṇa appears to have incorporated several versions of the rite, and lists as victims 349 domestic animals and 260 wild ones, though some, if not all, of the latter were probably released.

[7]K. Geldner, *ERE.*, II, p. 160.

[8]Cf. *RV.*, X.2,3 'To the gods' pathway have we travelled ready to execute what work we may accomplish.' This journey, traditionally in a clock-wise direction, is also compared to that of the sun and hence 'was a solemn confirmation of the king in his role as Regent

of the Year, and was also an exaltation for the valour of the warrior-caste' (Broderick, *Animals in Archaeology*, p. 128).

[9]This may indicate the expulsion of Death or Winter. At Tabor (Bohemia) it was said that 'Death floats down the stream' (Grimm, *Teutonic Mythology*, p. 771, v. also p. 767). v. also Micah, 7, 19: 'all our sins will be cast into the depths of the sea'. Southward running water was believed to possess magical properties (K. Thomas, *Religion and the Decline of Magic*, p. 624); v. also *Folklore*, VI (1888), p. 211.

[10]Dogs that have a yellow spot on each side of the eyelids are called 'four-eyed'. They are believed to be able to see evil spirits (Crooke, *Things Indian*, p. 147). The 'four-eyed' dog may represent the evil in the four quarters of the world which menaces the sacrifice and which must be eliminated (Dumont, *L'Aśvamedha*, p. 27), and by killing the dog the danger is rendered harmless (*ŚBr.*, XIII.1.2,9). Many demons are said to have four eyes (*AV.*, V.19,7; VIII.6,22), physical malformations are said to endow one with magical powers, divination, etc. (v. H. Webster, *Magic*, pp. 144ff.).

[11]It was the custom of some Hindus to give a black cow to the priest so that at death they might grasp its tail and be guided across the river of death (Vaitaraṇī). There is also a North European parallel which states that he who gives a cow to the poor will find another to guide him safely over the bridge of death (Tylor, *Primitive Culture*, I, p. 427).

[12]Cf. Lat. *hinnire*, to neigh; Fr. *hennir*; E. *hinny* and *whinny*.

[13]*Trilogie altindischer Mächte und Feste der Vegetation*, pt. iii, 248, cited by Campbell, *Masks of God*, II, p. 196. The sacred marriage was an 'economic' measure designed 'to galvanize the vitality of the topocosm' (Gaster, *Thespis*, p. 79).

[14]The members of the Gupta dynasty claimed descent from the Maurya ruler Samudra (A.D. 333–75).

[15]*Journ. of the Andhra Hist. Research Soc.*, X, p. 14.

Zeuner in his *History of Domesticated Animals* (illus. p. 332) includes a photograph of a sacrificial horse from northern Gujarāt made of burnt clay—the legs, tail and mouth form flues. The figure is stuffed with hay which is lit and the smoke emerges from the holes. This is probably a relic of the horse sacrifice when a real horse was burnt.

v. Daśaratha; Rājasūya.

Aśvattha A tree (Ficus religiosa), sacred to Hindus as the eternal tree of life whose roots are in heaven, i.e. in the divine essence, the impersonal *brahman* (*Kaṭha Up.*, VI.1; *Maitri Up.*, VI.4). It is also especially sacred to Buddhists as the *bodhi* tree under which the Buddha gained Enlightenment.[1]

The antiquity of tree worship in India is indicated by a third millennium B.C. clay tablet from Mohenjo-daro depicting an *aśvattha* and its worshippers;[2] and by the use of its wood for making the fire-sticks (*araṇi*) and particular sacrificial vessels. The *aśvattha* was adored as the abode of a deity or was itself worshipped. Parts of it were used in rites to drive away or overcome enemies (*AV.*, III.6). The gods sit under a celestial *aśvattha* (*AV.*, V.4,3); on earth the holy man who sits in its shade is endowed with oracular powers and the ability to remember former births, as well as to understand the language of animals. The eating of its fruit is forbidden to all except ascetics, for it represents the male element in fire.[3]

The *aśvattha* is said to have issued from Indra's skin and his honour, after his limbs fell asunder when Tvaṣṭṛ exorcized him (*ŚBr.*, XII.7.1, 1–9). So magically powerful is this tree that graves should never be placed near it (XIII.8.1,16).

[1]Kṛṣṇa, on the eve of his ascension to heaven, is said to have meditated on the *aśvattha* (*Bhāg. P.*, III.4.3 and 8; *Brah. P.*, III.11,35 and 109, etc., *PI.*). In the *Gītā* Kṛṣṇa is made to say 'amongst all trees I am the *aśvattha*'. (Cf. Christ's words: 'I am the true vine'.)

[2]*GG.*, pp. 67f.

[3]*EM.*, p. 6. According to the *Suś. Saṁ.*, II, p. 513, the fruits, bark, roots, etc., of the *aśvattha*, when sweetened and boiled in milk, are said to be a powerful aphrodisiac.

v. Purūravas.

Aśvatthāman 'Horse-voiced.' A son of Droṇa and Kṛpī, so-called because his first cry when he was born was likened to the neighing of the celestial steed Uccaiḥśravas (*MBh.*, Ādi pa., 131).

Aśvatthāman fought with the Kauravas against the Pāṇḍavas at Kurukṣetra. On the last day of the battle the only surviving Kaurava leaders (apart from the dying king, Duryodhana) were Aśvatthāman, Kṛpa and Kṛtavarman. In a last desperate attempt to avenge themselves all three entered the Pāṇḍava camp during the night.[1] Finding Dhṛṣṭadyumna asleep, Aśvatthāman trampled him to death. He then killed Śikhaṇḍin, King Drupada's son, and the five young sons of the Pāṇḍu princes whose heads he took to Duryodhana. Finally, with his magical weapon *brahmāstra*, he killed the unborn child (Parikṣit) while in the womb of Uttarā, Abhimanyu's widow.[2] For this final act Kṛṣṇa laid upon Aśvatthāman a curse that caused him to flee. But he was overtaken by Arjuna and Kṛṣṇa, who spared his life but compelled him to give up the magical jewel which he wore as an amulet on his head-dress. They presented it to Draupadī who gave it to her husband Yudhiṣṭhira, now the undisputed ruler of the Bhāratas.

[1]Contrary to military tradition.

[2]Kṛṣṇa restored Parikṣit to life.

v. Mahābhārata; Daśarājña.

Aśvinī 'Mare.' The wife of the Aśvins, later considered to be their mother.

v. Vaḍabā; Aśvinīkumāra.

Aśvinīkumāra The 'mare's boys'. An epithet of the Aśvins, their mother Aśvinī having assumed the form of a mare.[1]

[1]Cf. Poseidon, who in the form of a stallion, pursued Demeter in the form of a mare.

Aśvin(s) 'Possessed of horses.' The name of two divinities who appear in the sky before the dawn in a golden carriage drawn by horses or birds. They are sometimes said to be twin stars and identified with the Greek Dioscuri and the Latin Gemini, a constellation represented as two youths, Castor and Pollux, sitting side by side, whose heads are two bright stars which bear their names. But this identification appears to be relatively late, and as a zodiacal sign has no connexion with the Vedic notion of the twin Aśvins, especially as the sun is in Gemini in only one month of the year, between 20 May and 21 June. It is possible that the Aśvins are connected with the Canaanite twin stars Shachar (dawn) and Shalim (dusk).[1]

In early Vedic[2] and Mazdean mythologies the Aśvins were also called Nāsatyas (Inseparables), and Dasras (Wonder-workers).[3] Their numerous attributes and functions probably reflect ancient non-Indian traditions as well as those originating in India. This diversity is also apparent in the several interpretations of their name in the *Nirukta* (XII.1f.), which states that they are so-called 'because they two pervade ($\sqrt{}$*aś*) everything, one with moisture, the other with light'; or because they have horses (*aśva*). The *Nirukta* adds that 'some regard them as heaven and earth; others as day and night, or take them to be the sun and moon; while historians regard them as two virtuous kings'.

Despite etymological variations, the principal characteristic of the Aśvins is clear. This associates them primarily with light and the sun Sūrya—represented as a horse, and portrays them as horse-headed charioteers; they are secondarily associated with agriculture, cattle and horses. He-goats, as symbols of fertility, are similarly regarded as sacred to the Aśvins (*ŚBr.*, XII.7.2,7).

Subsequently, because of their connexion with plants, especially with those having medicinal properties, the Aśvins were credited with healing powers. In addition, being forever young, they could restore youth to the aged, and even avert death. They were regarded as the physicians of mankind—especially of warriors wounded in battle—and also of the gods.

Maṇḍala I of the *RV.* briefly refers to their many functions, attributes and magical exploits, which possibly reflect ancient popular myths rather than priestly invention. Thus in hymn I.15,11 they are said to drink *soma* with *ṛtu* (the personified seasons), and in hymn 22, 1–3 they sprinkle the sacrifice with their honey-whip (*madhukaśā*), a rite elaborated in *AV.*, IX.I. In *RV.*, I.34,5–8 the Aśvins are the source of heavenly medicaments, and guard the vault of heaven by day and night. In 46, 2–6 they are referred to as sons of the sea, i.e., of the atmosphere, regarded as an ocean of air whose ultimate shores are heaven and earth; thus they are the mariners' guides. They also reveal the riches of the earth and lighten darkness. At the sacrifice they are offered *soma* by the Kaṇvas. Their bounty is generous, as is evident by the supplies of food given to the army of King Sudās during the war of the Ten Kings (Daśarājña). In hymn 112, 3–21 they cure the blind and the lame, restore fertility to the barren cow and cause the rain to fall in times of drought. They gave speed to the horse entered in a race by Kṛṣānu,[4] one of the guardians of the celestial *soma.* In hymn 116, 6–24 they are said to have presented a white horse to the royal seer Pedu, one of their most ardent followers; rescued Atri when he was a captive of the *asuras*; rejuvenated the aged *ṛṣi* Cyavana; to have given a son to Vadhrimatī, the wife of an impotent man; replaced a leg lost in battle by a woman named Viśpalā, by a metal one (the first reference to surgery in Vedic times); restored Ṛjrāśva's sight; rescued the *ṛṣi* Rebha who, after being wounded in a battle with the *asuras*, was bound and flung into a well. They are invoked to drive away the *asuras* and *dasyus* by the blasts of their trumpets (*bakura*); and to preserve the germ of life in all female creatures. From the hoofs of their horses pour wine, i.e., rain.[5]

The *Puruṣa-sūkta* (*RV.*, X.90) contains the first reference to social distinction, which is repeated in the allegorical account of the dismemberment of Prajāpati (*ŚBr.*, VIII.2.1,11–14). In this myth the Aśvins, like their earthly counterparts, the surgeons and physicians, are regarded as of minor importance and relegated to the third social class, i.e., the celestial equivalent of the *viś* or commonalty.[6]

The Prajāpati allegory appears to be the basis of the Paurāṇic myths relating to the exclusion of the Aśvins from the sacrifice, no evidence of which is to be found in the *RV.* The stigma attaching to surgeons and physicians was a post-Vedic development, coinciding with the dogma which condemned the mutilation of the body, whether of a corpse or of a warrior wounded in battle. Surgery, especially if it involved the removal of any portion of the body, was looked upon with horror by orthodox Hindus, because it was considered to prevent the spirit from entirely purging itself in the funeral fire and thus barring its access to a higher spiritual life.[7]

Among the epithets of the Aśvins are: Abhijan (Ocean-born) and Vāḍabeyau (Sons of the submarine fire). They are also said to have been born from the 'tears of Agni' (*MBh.*, 13,85,109, *EM.*). Przyluski[8] considers that the Aśvins were originally horse-gods who later became identified with horsemen, and thus like many Vedic astral gods may have been the apotheoses of historic figures whose deeds are enshrined in legend. One of these ascribes their parentage to the sun-god Dharma-Vivasvat and his wife Saṁjñā, the daughter of Tvaṣṭṛ who, finding her husband's brilliant splendour overwhelming, left him, leaving behind only her shadow (*chāyā*). She then assumed the form of a mare and began a life of extreme austerity (*tapas*). Her husband finally found her and assumed the form of a stallion. From this reunion the Aśvins were begotten, and hence their epithet, Aśvinīkumāra (the mare's boys).[9] This story is probably the origin of the practice of invoking the Aśvins at marriage ceremonies.

In the early hymns of the *RV.* the description of the Aśvins puts them in a special category, in which they perhaps surpass all other Vedic personifications of nature.[10] They are the focus of the supreme belief in divine goodwill towards mankind, and of a simple, uncritical faith, shared by both priests and people in early Vedic India and lacking the complex dogma and ritual that was later to supersede it.

[1]G.R. Driver, *Canaanite Myths*, p. 23. The Aśvins' Avestan counterparts were the Aspinas. The divine pair of sons of the Supreme God El, born of mortal women, constitute in some respects 'a Canaanite counterpart of the Classical Dioscuri ... who are likewise frequently identified—as are also the analogous Vedic Aśvins—with the morning and evening star Phosphoros and Hesperos, and who are likewise known as "Princes"' (Th. Gaster, *Thespis*, p. 411). It has also been suggested that the Aśvins 'were a tribe of horsemen ... who were also skilled in healing and who later became identified with the dual kings who ruled over them' (*HW.*, I, p. 93).

[2]*RV.*, I.3,3.

[3]*RV.*, I.116,10. The Heavenly Twins identified with the constellation Gemini are frequently mentioned in Babylonian texts. 'They appear also, under the Indic name of Nāsatya, in the Hittite treaty of Suppiluliuma with Mattiwaza of Mitanni' (Gaster, *Thespis*, p. 412; v. also *CHI.*, p. 110; and Thième, 'Āryan gods of the Mitanni Treaties', *JAOS.*, vol. 80 (December 1960), pp. 301f.).

[4]The Kereṣāni of the Avesta.

[5]Cf. the Greek myth of Pegasus and the Hippocrene fountain.

[6]When Prajāpati was dismembered the Aśvins and other gods appropriated the limbs of his body. The Aśvins are said to have taken the part above the feet and below the waist, the portions above this being taken by the major gods, who correspond to the *brāhmaṇa* and *rājanya* classes.

[7]*Suś. Saṁ.*, I. Intro., pp. xxiiif., n.2. v. Ekoddiṣta.

[8]*HCIP.*, vol. III, p. 617.

[9]The Dioscuri were called 'boys', and regarded as heroic young men (Nilsson, *A History of Greek Religion*, p. 34).

[10]In the *MBh.*, I.66,40, the Aśvins, plants and animals are all called *guhyakas*—their chief is Kubera which points to the Aśvins being *yakṣas* (Coomaraswamy, *Yakṣas*, pt. ii, p. 22).

v. Atri; Paidva; Ṛjrāśva; Saptavadhri; Saraṇyū: Dadhyac; Mainda; Pṛthā.

Atala 'Bottomless.' The name of one of the three lower worlds, and an epithet of Śiva.

Atharvan The name of the priest who was the first to generate fire, to institute its worship, and to offer *soma* (*RV.*, I.83,5; v. *Tait. Saṁ.*, IV.1,3); hence he was called the 'father of agni' (fire).

He is the reputed author of the *Atharvaveda*, and is classed as a Prajāpati. He is also represented as the eldest son of Brahmā, who imparted to him the essence of all knowledge (*brahmavidyā*) (*Muṇḍ. Up.*, I.1,1). His descendants (Atharvāṇas) were often associated with the Āṅgirasas, but the 'expressions, *atharvan* and *aṅgiras*, denote white and black magic respectively'.[1]

Atharvan as a form of fire appears 'in the demoniac ceremony to raise an apparition from fire in secret rites ... performed by means of the *mantras* of Bṛhaspati and Uśanas as declared in the *Atharvaveda*'.[2] He and his descendants also excelled in the expulsion of demons, especially with the plant Odina wodier, called 'goat-horned' (*ajaśṛṅgī*) (*AV.*, IV.37,1).

[1]*HIL.*, vol. I, pt.i. p. 105.

[2]*EM.*, p. 102.

v. Dadhyac.

Atharvaveda The 'Veda of the Atharvan' or 'knowledge of magic formulas'. Another tradition calls it the *Bhṛgvaṅgirasaveda*, both Bhṛgu and Aṅgiras as well as Atharvan being ancient fire-priests and regarded as founders of the Atharvanic popular cult.

To what extent the *AV.* may have drawn upon ancient Indus Valley and Dravidian magico-religious cults can at present only be conjectured, but that they greatly influenced early Āryan culture seems certain. It is likely that sacrificial fire and its ritual also antedated the Āryan occupation of north-western India. This may account for Bhṛgu having been credited with its origination as a religious rite, and for the 'special relationship' that existed between his descendants, the Bhārgavas, and the non-Āryan peoples, termed *asuras*.[1] The antiquity of the sponsors of the Atharvanic formulas seems certain from the fact that in early Vedic times their names and their historical origin had long since been forgotten.

The *Atharvaveda* (listed as the fourth Veda), by the nature of its contents, is distinguished from the three earlier Vedas, which were originally regarded as the definitive corpus of Vedic religious knowledge. It is distinguished from the other Vedas by the nature of its accompanying *Brāhmaṇa*, the *Gopatha*, appended probably to conform to the custom of providing each Veda with one or more Brāhmaṇas. But as the *Gopatha* is really a Vedāṅga, it is irrelevant as an appendage to the *AV.* Its three attached Upaniṣads are also relatively late compositions, the *Muṇḍaka* and *Praśna* being of the middle Upaniṣad period (post-Vedic, but pre-Buddhist), the *Māṇḍūkya* being slightly earlier.

Comparison of existing recensions[2] suggests that the *AV.* originally consisted of eighteen books. Subsequently two more were added, Book XIX being similar to the main body of the work; Book XX generally consisting of excerpts from *maṇḍala* X of the *RV.*, or of passages drawn from a source common to both Vedas. This is apparent in the creation hymn (*RV.*, X.129), repeated in the *AV.* with some variation in the order of the verses, but comparatively little in the readings.

The eighteen books comprise three divisions. The first (Books I-VII) consists mainly of charms and imprecations of a popular character in verse form. Since the books of the first division are the most representative of the entire collection, and as Books I-VI may well have been its nucleus, their initial position is not inappropriate. The second division (Books VIII-XII) consists of both verse and prose, the latter resembling a Brāhmaṇa in style and content. This is indicated in passages relating to the sacrifice for which a goat and five rice dishes comprise the offering (IX.5); the praise of the virāj, symbolizing the universe (VIII.9), and the *ucchiṣṭa* or sacrificial remnant (XI.7). Other portions consist of mystic hymns (VIII.9; IX.9–10, etc.), or comprise *brahmodyas* or priestly riddles (X.2 and 20–5). Some passages condemn witchcraft and those who practise it; praise the marvels of human anatomy; extol the virtues of a special amulet; and give a list of remedies for snake-venom. Each of the books of the third division (XIII–XVIII) is devoted to a particular subject, Book XIV relating to the wedding ceremony; XVIII to funeral rites.

The *AV.* depicts a world reflecting popular animistic beliefs, ignored for the most part by the priestly composers of the earlier Vedas, but later becoming too widespread to be suppressed. That world consisted mainly of malevolent demons and spirits, seeking continually to injure those unprotected by magical rites, spells, incantations, *mantras* and exorcism.[3] Nor did the threat come only from demons and spirits; a person against whom another bore a grudge might be injured by a curse or spell. On the other hand protective weapons and amulets could be made more efficacious by means of particular rites. Doubtless there was a role for the priest in averting these threats, and an opportunity to assert 'the inviolability of the *brahmins* and their possessions',[4] and to emphasize the importance of the *dakṣiṇā* or 'gift' to the priests.

Many of the magical instructions given in some Tantras are similar to those of the *AV.* Winternitz also points out the remarkable agreement between Indian and German magic incantations. Fifty-five, seventy-seven or ninety-nine diseases are mentioned in the *AV.*, so in German incantations the same numbers of diseases are often referred to. One German spell declares that: '"This water and the blood of Christ is good for the seventy-seven kinds of fever"'.[5] Another belief, common to the Vedic Indians and other peoples, is that many diseases are caused by worms.[6]

[1] v. Devayānī.

[2] Only two of the nine redactions of this work are extant, viz., the Paippalāda and Śaunaka recensions. v. E. tr. by Whitney, with Intro. and notes by C.R. Lanman.

[3] Therapeutic charms or conjurations recited in the presence of the patient are common to most forms of so-called primitive culture (H.E. Sigerist, *A History of Medicine*, vol. I, pp. 191–216). For the therapeutic charms of the Assyrians and Babylonians, v. Contenau, *La Médicine en Assyrie et en Babylonie*, pp. 146ff.).

[4] *HIL.*, I. pt. i, p. 129.

[5] Ibid., p. 115.

[6] Many of the Marsh Arabs of southern Iraq believe that toothache is caused by worms in the teeth (M. al Hamdani and M. Wenzel, 'The Worm in the Tooth', *Folklore*, vol. 77, 1966, pp. 60–4).

v. Āyurveda.

Atithigva v. Divodāsa I.

Ātivāhika v. Ekoddiṣṭa.

Ātmabhava 'Mind-born.' An epithet of Kāma, the god of love.

Ātman The 'essence or principle of life'. This term is variously derived from *an*, to breathe; *at*, to move; *va*, to blow.[1] Later the term was used in a metaphysical sense to denote the individuated notion of reality, and thus to distinguish it from the empirical self (*jīva*), which was regarded merely as the sum of the sense faculties. Therefore, while the equation of 'soul' and the empirical self may be justified, it is incorrect to define *ātman* as 'soul'.

The early use of the term *ātman* lacks any mystical or esoteric significance, as is indicated in the following: 'The Sun, the essence (*ātman*) of all—the inanimate as well as the animate—who has filled the air and earth and heaven' (*RV.*, I.115,1). From this simple notion of cosmic unity were derived various symbolically presented theories of the nature of the universe,[2] evolved not in logical sequence, but 'like radiations from a common nucleus'.[3] From this notion was developed the idea of immanence and transcendence, the two aspects of a single entity. This is indicated in the *ŚBr.* (X.5.3,2–3) which paraphrases the opening lines of the Creation hymn (*RV.*, X.129): 'Then, there was neither Aught nor Nought ... that One, a void in chaos wrapt', from which Mind arose, and from it Speech, whence Breath, and finally self. The idea was not further developed until the composers of the Āraṇyakas and Upaniṣads attempted to define the nature of this 'self'.

In the process new expressions were used and analogies improvised, which often tended to obscure rather than clarify. Often, too, the notion of cosmic unity is presented in terms having an apparent—though not actual—dual significance, such as the use of two terms, *ātman* and *brahman*, to express a single identity. There is an implicit dualism also in the gender of '*brahman*', which is neuter, lit. *ne* 'not', and *uter* 'either', signifying 'neither one nor the other'.[4] Similarly, the phrase '*tat tvam asi*' (that thou art) synthesizes two notions, man's real self (*ātman*) and the Cosmic Self (*brahman* or *paramātman*). To explain these anomalies use was made of the word *iva*, meaning 'as it were' or 'as if there were', which was prefixed to phrases having an apparent dualistic significance. There is no such ambiguity in the *Bṛhad-Ār. Up.* (I.3,22) which declares that the vital force (*ātman*) is not only operative in Man, but also in every form of life, a truth amply demonstrated by the experiments of modern science. Thus, as Heimann points out, 'the concept of the *Ātman* ... cannot be isolated and separated from the cosmic *Brahman*-principle'.[5] Apprehension of the abstract is limited by the nature of the subject and by the subjective processes of the mind, which can only think of the transcendent *brahman*-principle as it relates to the individuated *ātman*-principle, i.e., from the universal to the particular, or vice versa. The two aspects may be likened to the individual waves of the ocean; the senses perceive their distinction, the mind their identity.

[1] *SED*. Edgerton suggests that 'breath' is probably its oldest meaning (*BIP.*, p. 141, n.3).

[2] Such as the Puruṣa, Hiraṇyagarbha, the Sāṁkhya theory, etc.

[3] *Facets*, p. 65.

[4] *CD*.

[5] *Facets*, p. 60.

v. Vedānta; Bhakti; Bhagavadgītā; Buddhism; Nirvāṇa.

Ātreya I. v. Āyurveda.

II. v. Atri(s).

Atri An ancient *ṛṣi* and sacrificer, and author of a number of Vedic hymns and of a code of law, who is often associated with the Āṅgirasas and others as progenitors of mankind, and hence is included among the Prajāpatis. He is also said to have been the *purohita* of the Five Tribes, the earliest of the Āryan settlers in India.

One of the roles of Atri and his descendants appears to have been to protect the sun against the eclipse demon Svarbhānu (the Rāhu of post-Vedic mythology). This is referred to in the *AV.* (XIII.2,12) as the maintenance of the sun in the sky, and in *RV.* (V.40,8) as the establishment in the heavens of the eye of Sūrya (the Sun), which became obscured during an eclipse. To defeat Svarbhānu and deliver the sun from the darkness, Atri composed a 'fourth prayer'[1] which enabled him to find the sun again.

The names of the Seven Seers, including Atri's, were originally epithets of fire,[2] which may explain the magical potency of his name, as even the gods have 'no alternative but to make effective such prayers as are either associated with Atri's name or are composed according to the pattern evolved by Atri'.[3]

It was probably during the early period of Āryan expansion, when Atri was the *purohita* of the Five Tribes, that he was captured by hostile indigenes and thrown into a 'fiery pit'. He was succoured by the Aśvins (*RV.*, I.112,7) and finally freed by them (I.117,3). Inevitably, owing to the lack of reliable knowledge of the early Vedic *ṛṣis*, legend and other fictional devices were used to account for their origin. Thus the *ŚBr.* (I.5.5,13) describes Atri as an emanation of Vāc; the *MBh.* (13,65,1, *EM.*) as one of the nine mind-born sons of Brahmā, who were all—as the result of a curse laid upon them by Śiva—forced to immolate themselves on the sacrificial fire, Brahmā himself being compelled to perform the ceremony. From this fire Atri was reborn and united with his wife Anasūyā, a daughter of Dakṣa.

Astral myths refer to Atri as one of the stars in the constellation of the Great Bear. According to Paurāṇic myth he produced the moon from a glance of his eyes during *tapas*.

[1]It has been suggested by Ludwig that this was in addition to the usual liturgy of three prayers against an eclipse (v. Griffith, *RV.*, I. p. 502, n.6).

[2]*EM.*, p. 184.

[3]*Seers*, p. 62.

v. Dattātreya.

Atri(s) A son or descendant of Atri (Ātreya). Some of Atri's family are traditionally regarded as the composers of several *RV.* hymns. There were two female seers of this family, Apālā and Viśvavārā, also said to have composed hymns. Other descendants include Dattātreya, Durvāsas, the Bhāratas, Pāṇḍavas, Kauravas, etc.

Aum v. OM.

Aurṇavābha The son of Urṇavābha. A *dānava* who was killed by Indra (*RV.*, II.11,18). Sāyaṇa identifies him with the drought-demon Vṛtra.

Aurva Name of a *ṛṣi*, the descendant of Ūrva.[1] In the *RV.* (VIII.91,4) the name Aurva appears jointly with that of Bhṛgu. Post-Vedic mythology builds on the scanty *RV.* references a precise genealogy of Aurva as the son of Cyavana and grandson of Bhṛgu, or attributes to him a miraculous birth from the thigh (*uru*)[2] of an unnamed Bhārgava mother.

Aurva underwent intense austerities (*tapas*) to the consternation of the gods who greatly feared his powers, but finally the *pitṛs* persuaded him to expel his fiery energy (which had assumed the form of the horse-headed Hayaśiras) into the sub-marine Vaḍabā.[3]

[1]*SED.*

[2]O'Flaherty suggests that the primary meaning of Ūrva was perhaps 'derived from *uru*, "broad", or *vṛ*, "to enclose" ('The Submarine Mare in the Mythology of Śiva', *JRAS.*, no. 1, 1971, p. 21). Cf. the mythical accounts of the birth of the Buddha and Indra from their mothers' sides.

[3]Ibid.

v. Sagara; Vaḍabāgni

Aurvaśīya v. Agastya.

Avakā A plant with sharp sword-like leaves which grows in marsh-land and hence represents water or moisture. Its leaves are put under and on top of the tortoise (representing heaven and earth) which is placed on the altar. The *avakā* is also spread over the burial mound (*ŚBr.*, VII.5.1,11; XIII.8,3,13). According to the *AV.* (IV.37, 8–9), it is the food of the *gandharvas*, but in verse 10 it is invoked to overpower both *gandharvas* and *piśācas*. According to the *Āśvalāyana Gṛhya Sūtra* (II.814) the central post of a building should be placed in a pit filled with the *avakā* plant, which will prevent fire.

Avara(s) v. *Ṛṣi*(s).

Avatāra According to Pāṇini (III.3,120) the word means 'descent', especially of a god from heaven to earth. Gonda states that an *avatāra* is an 'appearance' (*Erscheinung*) of the deity.[1]

In the Purāṇas and Epic an *avatāra* is an incarnation, and is distinguished from a divine emanation (*vyūha*), both of which are associated with Viṣṇu and Śiva, but particularly with the former. The *avatāra* concept is probably a development of the ancient myth that, by the creative power of his *māyā*, a god can assume any form at will, as did Indra (*RV.*, III.53,8; VI.47,18).[2] It has been suggested by some scholars that the animal forms (fish, tortoise, boar, etc.) assumed by Viṣṇu may have originally been the objects of individual cults. The incarnatory act is not simply an expression of the will or whim of a god, but is a response to necessity, such as that referred to in the *Bhagavadgītā* (IV.7–8),[3] which declares that 'whenever there is decay of righteousness ... and there is exaltation of unrighteousness, then I Viṣṇu will come forth ... for the protection of the good, for the destruction of evil-doers, for the sake of firmly establishing righteousness. For this purpose I am born from age to age.'

The Viṣṇu *avatāra* concept represents 'the syncretism of three god-concepts, Vīra or the hero-god Vāsudeva-Kṛṣṇa; the Vedic solar Viṣṇu; and the cosmic god Nārāyaṇa of the Brāhmaṇas'.[4] Though given variant interpretative emphasis, this threefold concept is generally considered by Vaiṣṇavas to represent the five fundamental aspects of Viṣṇu, viz., Para, the Supreme Being; Vyūha, the emanatory; Vibhava or Avatāra, the incarnatory; Antaryāmin, the divine presence in all beings; and the Vigrahas, the visible and veritable bodies of the god.

The variant lists of the *avatāras* of Viṣṇu suggest regional or sectarian preferences, which would account for the existence of different Vaiṣṇava schools by whom these lists were compiled. Among these schools are the Ekāntika, Vyūhavāda, Avatāravāda and Pāñcarātra. But the *avatāra* concept is further complicated by its extension which may not only relate to a composite Viṣṇu, but also to his Vyūhas, sub-Vyūhas and Pāriṣadas (companions), or even to his attributes or emblems,[5] and may possibly account for his thousand epithets. But these distinctions are a late development, apparent only when belief in the cosmic Vāsudeva-Viṣṇu-Nārāyaṇa triad as the Supreme Being became the cornerstone of Vaiṣṇavism.[6]

The list of *avatāras* of the Pāñcarātra school later became stereotyped as the 'ten' (*daśāvatāras*).[7] The enumeration in the several schools of Northern India differs slightly, as do the lists of those of the South. The *MBh.* (XII.389,104, *EM.*) lists them as Haṁsa, Kūrma, Matsya, Varāha, Narasiṁha, Vāmana, Rāma (Bhārgava), Rāma (Dāśarathi), Sātvata (i.e., Vāsudeva or Baladeva), and Kalkin. Apparently the Buddha had not yet been recognized as an *avatāra*; nor is the included in the *Vāyu Pur.* list which enumerates them as Yajña, Narasiṁha, Vāmana, Dattātreya, (a fifth, unnamed), Jāmadagnya Rāma, Dāśarathi Rāma, Vedavyāsa, Vāsudeva-Kṛṣṇa, and Kalkin, the future incarnation.[8] The *Bhāg. P.* contains three lists of *avatāras*. In I.3,6–22, twenty-two names are given; in II.7,1ff., twenty-three; and in XI.4,3ff., sixteen. All three lists include the Buddha, and Ṛṣabha the first Jaina *tīrthaṇkara*, and the usual ten of the stereotyped list, but the compiler declares emphatically that '"the divine descents are innumerable" (*avatārāḥ hyasaṁkheyāḥ*).'[9]

An early Pāñcarātra Saṁhitā enumerates thirty-nine incarnatory forms, in which are included the conventional list of ten, and also Vāgīśvara (no. 13) and Lokanātha (no. 24), both Mahāyāna Buddhist divinities, and under the name of Śāntātman (no. 25) the Buddha himself. The mythical metamorphoses of Śiva[10] were probably devised to counter-balance those of Viṣṇu. Today any 'distinguished person could be called an Avatar . . . though this diminishes the original theological purpose of the term'.[11]

The notion of successive Buddhas and Jainas may have had some influence on the *avatāra* doctrine, but an important difference is that the Buddha and the Jaina *tīrthaṇkaras* are not regarded as incarnations of a divine being, as are the Hindu *avatāras*.

[1] *Die Religionen Indiens*, I, p. 269.

[2] Cf. the ancient Egyptian god Horus as the avatar of Osiris (Gaster, *Thespis*, p. 400).

[3] Adapted from the translation by Annie Besant and Bhagavan Das.

[4] *DHI.*, p. 386. Parrinder suggests that Viṣṇu's *avatāras* 'may incorporate Indus Valley or forest divinities' (*Avatar and Incarnation*, p. 16).

[5] *DHI.*, p. 389.

[6] But to the masses of India, *avatāras*, like the saints of the medieval Christian Church, are besought to confer boons on the worshipper. v. also *Aspects*, p. 243.

[7] *DHI.*, p. 390. These divinities and heroes 'were adopted by Vaiṣṇavism at different times, but all were incorporated by the eleventh century' (*WI.*, p. 302).

[8] *DHI.*, p. 390.

[9] Ibid., p. 391.

[10] In the *Liṅga Pur.* Śiva is the Lord of all Being, the Divine Cause, who expresses himself through his *vibhavas* and *vyūhas* (*VP.*, Pref., p. xlii). All *ṛṣis*, *munis* and kings should be deemed *avatāras* of Viṣṇu (*AGP.*, CCLXXVI,22–5).

[11] Parrinder, op. cit., p. 20.

v. Avatāramantra; Hayagrīva; Āveśāvatāra(s).

Avatāra Mantra The formula by which the 'descent' of a deity is effected.

v. Mantra; Avatāra.

Āveśāvatāra(s) The designation of *ṛṣis*, *munis* and those dedicated to religious practices. They are said to be 'possessed' (*āveśa*) of god-given power, but unlike *avatāras* are to be venerated but not worshipped.

v. Avatāra.

Avidyā 'Ignorance, lack of true knowledge (*vidyā* or *jñāna*).' As a general term it lacks any ambiguity, but when applied by the composers of the Upaniṣads and by the quasi-philosophical schools (*darśanas*), and later still by the metaphysical theologians of the sectaries, the term acquired a significance of bewildering complexity. The result was an attempt to define true knowledge and its sources; to distinguish the real from the often inconsistent empirical real; to determine the nature of the essence (*ātman*) of existence; and to reconcile the apparent gap between its cosmic and individual aspects.

The complexity of the problem was increased by the necessity of relating knowledge *per se* to the 'dogma' of *saṁsāra* or concept of the individual's evolution through a series of re-births or new lives; to enable him to shed his *avidyā* and thus realize his unity with the Ultimate Essence of Existence (*brahman-ātman*). As the attainment of such knowledge was recognized as intellectually impossible, meditation of the most profound kind was advocated. Subsequently, faith (*śraddhā*) and devotion (*bhakti*) were presented as 'aids' to meditation. Radhakrishnan considers that *avidyā* is not intellectual ignorance but spiritual blindness.[1]

[1] The *Brahma-Sūtra*, p. 21. In the Advaita Vedānta school *avidyā* is said to be beginningless (*anādi*), and may be either negative, i.e., 'ignorance' of the unity underlying the diversity of things, or positive in the sense that it gives rise to misapprehension (*EW.*, vol. I, p. 280). In Yoga *avidyā* is primal ignorance, an entity which manifests itself in perverted cognitions (ibid., p. 256).

Avimukta The name of a sacred place (*tīrtha*) near

Banāras. Here the devotee will see the god of gods (Śiva), and thus will be immediately cleansed of every 'sin' including that of brahminicide (*MBh.*, II. Vana pa., 84).

Avis A sheep. According to the *ŚBr.* (VI.1.2,34), it is identified with the earth and is sacred to Varuṇa (VII.5.2,35).

Prajāpati, being alone at the beginning of creation, desired to create food and reproduce himself. He produced a number of different animals from his body, including a sheep from his ear (VII.5.2,6); but in 5.2,25 the sheep is said to have been fashioned by Tvaṣṭṛ.

Ayana The sun's path north and south of the equator. The southern *ayana* is a night of the gods, and the northern a day (*VP.*, I.3).

Ayas A term used in the *RV.* for metal, later used to denote iron.

Ayodhyā 'Invincible.' An ancient city on the banks of the Gogrā river, said to have been founded by Ikṣvāku, the first king of the Solar dynasty; or by Manu, first of the traditional kings of India. It is notable as Rāma's capital, and is one of the seven Hindu sacred cities. To die in any of them ensures eternal bliss. Ayodhyā was also sacred to Jainas and Buddhists.

Ayonijā v. Sītā.

Āyudha Weapons in general, but Indra's bow in particular.

Āyudhapuruṣa A weapon of a deity represented anthropomorphically. An early parallel exists in the Canaanite myth of Baal's two weapons called Aymur and Yagrush which were invoked to drive away enemies.[1]

A twelfth-century stone image of the four-armed Viṣṇu, now in the Indian Museum (no. 2,592), depicts the following personified objects, the mace (*gadādevī*), the *cakra* called Sudarśana, the conch-shell trumpet and a lotus. The conch and lotus here replace Viṣṇu's consorts, Śrī and Puṣṭi.[2]

The sex of the *āyudhapuruṣas* is usually determined by the gender of the word denoting them.[3] Thus *gadā* (fem.) is represented by a female figure, but *cakra* and *padma* being neuter should therefore be shown as eunuchs, though in late Gupta and medieval art they are depicted as male. The *Viṣṇudharmottara* describes *cakrapuruṣa* as a round-eyed fat male figure with drooping belly, whose eyes gaze intently on Viṣṇu. In the Śaiva temple at Dhokeśvara (sixty miles south of Aurangabad) Śiva's trident (*triśūla*) is personified as a thin figure with a 'three-pronged projection on his head'.[4] The *āyudhapuruṣas* can usually be identified by the weapons they represent being shown behind them, or in their hands, or on their heads as at Dhokeśvara.

Visnu's *cakra*, Sudarśana, has its own *mantra* (as have his other weapons) which has the power of neutralizing poison, and exorcizing the influence of malignant demons and planets.

[1] But it is not altogether clear from the text whether or not they were fully anthropomorphized (Driver, *Canaanite Myths*, pp. 79–81). The naming of weapons and emblems was also common in Europe, with Thor's hammer Miölnir; the iron glove Iarn Greiper; the magic belt Megingiörd; Arthur's sword Excalibur; and the famous Irish sword Caladbolg of Fergus, etc. The Celts worshipped their personified weapons, as well as ascribing magic powers to those of gods and heroes.

[2] *DHI.*, pp. 403–4.

[3] The *āyudhapuruṣas* have a place in ritual and also in 'ceremonies for protection' (*VS.*, p. 178, n.91).

[4] G. Tarr, 'The Śiva Cave-Temple of Dhokeśvara', *Oriental Art*, Winter 1969, p. 275 and illus., p. 276.

v. Dhanus; Kṛśāśva; Śaṅkhapuruṣa; Śastradevatā(s); Ācārya II.

Āyurveda The Veda (science or knowledge) of *āyus* 'life, vitality, health, longevity'. It is sometimes regarded as an *Upaveda*, closely associated with the *AV.* Āyurveda is a traditional and naturalistic system, which in its early stages largely depended on the use of water, herbs, minerals and the formic acid of ant-hills for the cure of disease. Some of these remedies had a therapeutic value, but others relied mainly on sympathetic magic.

The origin of the Āyurveda was ascribed to the gods, and its methodology to the *AV.* which, despite its limitations, is generally recognized as the basis of Hindu medicine. Thus in the *AV.* (II.33) reference is made to particular parts of the body, though the distinction of veins and arteries from ducts is confused (I.17,3; VII.35,2). The diagnosis of disease is similarly limited, cause and cure being regarded as supernatural, the former ascribed to demons, the latter to the gods. Thus the distinction between disease and demonic possession was of the slightest (II.4), though occasionally even disease is regarded as of divine origin, and to be the penalty for evil-doing, like that of dropsy (*jalodara*).[1] inflicted by Varuṇa on those guilty of falsehood (I.10, 1–4). But the commonest and most dreaded disease was 'fever', probably malarial, and known as *takman* (I.25; V.22, etc.).[2]

There is no clear evidence in the *RV.* that those associated with the cure of disease were of inferior status. This assertion came later when the conflict of theological and secular judgments came to a head.[3]

It was not until about the sixth century B.C. that the study of Hindu medicine was divested of some of its mythical elements and was studied rationally. This development was accelerated as the result of Persian and Greek influences in north-western India.

Indian medicine, like that of medieval Europe, was based on the diagnosis of the bodily 'humours' (*doṣa*). According to most Indian authorities 'health was maintained through the even balance of the three vital fluids of the body—wind, gall and mucus, to which some added blood as a fourth humour. The three primary humours were connected with the scheme of the three *guṇas* . . . and associated with virtue, passion and dullness respectively.'[4]

The Buddhist Canonical writings (*Vinaya*, I., p. 274) refer to the physician and surgeon Jīvaka Komārabhacca (Pā.), Jīvaka Kaumārabhṛtya (Skt), who is said to have been the Buddha's physician and to have cured several people, including King Bimbisāra. The Pāli and Sanskrit Vinayas also mention medical prescriptions allowed by the Buddha for diseases affecting the monks, but the data of the Pāli *Tipitaka* on the whole differs little from that of the classical Āyurveda, the practice of which was already fixed. On the other hand, it is to the Buddhists, with their unrivalled genius for organization, that credit is due for the establishment of free hospitals for both animals and humans, and to the Emperor Aśoka for their extension throughout India. Notable also was the subsequent establishment of monastic centres of learning, like that at Nālandā in Bihār, capable of accommodating up to ten thousand students. Its reputation was such that it attracted students and scholars from all parts of India and abroad, and led to an increasing interest in philosophy, medicine and other sciences.

The most important Āyurvedic texts of this period are the *Caraka*[5] and *Suśruta*[6] *Saṁhitās*, which represent the first successful attempt to distinguish 'between magico-religious treatments and rational therapeutics based upon yukti, i.e., rational connection of observed facts . . . [which give the] same general representation of the nature and functions of the human body and of the nature and causes of ailments'.[7] Caraka was possibly a court physician of the Kuṣāṇa emperor Kaniṣka (c. A.D. 70–110), traditionally regarded as a Buddhist. Caraka's original treatise has been lost, but a redaction of it, with additions, is extant and is attributed to Dṛḍhabala (ninth century).[8] Both systems were regarded as of divine origin, but they differ about their historical introduction. According to Caraka, Indra revealed the Āyurveda to Bharadvāja who taught it to his disciples, among whom was Ātreya Punarvasu from whom it passed to Agniveśa, whose teaching Caraka mainly followed, hence his *saṁhitā* is called the *Agniveśatantra*. According to the *Suśruta*, Indra revealed the Āyurveda to Dhanvantari in his incarnate form of Divodāsa, king of Kāśī; his system is the basis of the *Suśruta saṁhitā*, the date of which is uncertain, but probably about a century later than Caraka's. Nāgārjuna, the great Buddhist teacher, is said to have edited the *Suśruta* text.

The so-called Bower MS. found at Kaṣgar in 1890, and named after its discoverer, consists of medical tracts and is assigned to the fourth century A.D. This and other fragments from Central Asia exceed the range of topics discussed in the *Caraka* and *Suśruta Saṁhitās*. Such treatises were succeeded during the following centuries by an important Buddhist medical treatise called *Rgyud-bzi*, which originated in the border regions of China and Tibet. This treatise is divided into four parts, and is considered to have been translated from a lost Sanskrit original in eight parts, entitled the *Amṛtahṛdayāṣṭāṅgaguhyo-padeśatantra*. It accords generally with the classical Āyurveda of Caraka and Suśruta, but includes matters like the investigation of the pulse which do not exist in the old texts and appear only in later Āyurveda literature.[9]

Other texts, purporting to be the Chinese and Tibetan translations of lost Sanskrit texts, appeared from the tenth to twelfth centuries. But the only important contributor to Āyurveda during this period was Vāgbhaṭa, who ranks next to Caraka and Suśruta. There were probably two writers of this name, both Buddhists, the authors of two famous works—the *Aṣṭāṅga-saṁgraha* (c. 7th cent.), and the *Aṣṭāṅga-hṛdayasaṁhitā* (c. 8th cent.). The former, like the *Suśruta*, is in prose mixed with verse, and is cited as the work of Vṛddha Vāgbhaṭa.[10] The other is entirely in verse and its author referred to simply as Vāgbhaṭa, whose treatise clearly reveals the influence of his namesake.

The only other notable Āyurvedic teacher of the period was Mādhava (c. 1370), brother of the famous commentator Sāyaṇa. Mādhava is regarded as the foremost early authority of medical diagnosis (*nidaṇa*), and ranks next in importance to Vāgbhaṭa. From Mādhava onwards medical knowledge came increasingly under the influence of tantrism and alchemy, which became the subjects of innumerable treatises, mostly of little value.[11] In the eighteenth century Western medical practice was introduced into India and was combined with the best of the traditional Hindu Āyurveda.

[1]Correctly diagnosed as being connected with heart disease.

[2]*ERE.*, IV, p. 764. *Takman* was later known as *jvara.*

[3]The polluting effect of contact with corpses was probably the chief reason for the inferior status accorded to surgeons. v. Aśvin(s).

[4] *WI.*, p. 499. The Āyurveda contributed to the development of chemistry by 'propounding a theory of chemical combination and division and classification of substances. The "*pañcabhūtas*" (*kṣiti, ap, tejas, marut* and *vyoman*) were responsible for the formation of chemical compounds, and depending on the number of *bhūtas* [elements] involved, they were named, *mono-*, *bi-*, *tri-*, *tetra-* and *penta-valent* (somewhat like the the binary, tertiary, and quaternary compounds of Dalton)' (*EW.*, vol. I, p. 463).

[5] Translated by A. Kaviratna.

[6] Translated by K. L. Bhishagratna.

[7] J. Filliozat ('Āyurveda', *EB.*, p. 477).

Indian medicine, being based 'on nature, generally ignored all supernatural diseases, or else discussed them outside the more rational texts. Thus all references to demons, and all prognoses based on omens and oneiromancy, are confined to special chapters whose resemblance to an Akkadian treatise used by the Persians suggests that they were imported into India by the Parthians' (Filliozat in *Ancient and Medieval Science*, p. 156).

[8] *HCIP.*, vol. II, p. 277.

[9] v. Filliozat, *EB.*, p. 479.

[10] *HCIP.*, vol. III, p. 320.

[11] Nonetheless, in Hindu medicine notice was taken not only of 'the effects of the drugs and foods on the physical organism, but also on the nervous centres and, through them, on the subtle body, character, mental faculties, etc.' (Daniélou, *Yoga: the Method of Re-Integration*, p. 11).

Āyu I. Life, vitality'. A divine personification presiding over life (*RV.*, X.17,4).

II. A name of the king of the frogs.

Āyus Name of the oldest son of Purūravas and the nymph Urvaśī.

v. Araṇi.

B

Babhru A Vedic *ṛṣi* who mixed *soma* for Indra who rewarded him with cattle (*RV.*, V.30,11).

Babhru-vāhana A son of Arjuna who was adopted by his maternal grandfather the king of Maṇipura. On his grandfather's death he succeeded to the throne.

When Arjuna went to Maṇipura with the sacrificial horse selected for the *aśvamedha*, he quarrelled violently with his son who killed him with an arrow. Suffering great remorse, Babhru-vāhana decided to kill himself, but his step-mother, the Nāga princess Ulūpī, gave him a magic gem which restored Arjuna to life.

Baḍabāgni v. Vaḍabāgni.

Baḍabāmukha v. Vaḍabāmukha.

Bādarāyaṇa[1] The first teacher to formulate the system (*darśana*) called Vedānta, or cosmotheistic doctrine of *brahman*, the All-One. This he presented in the *Brahma-sūtra* variously known as *Vedānta-sūtra*, *Śārīraka-sūtra*, etc., upon which Śaṅkarācārya based the doctrine of Advaita-vedānta.

[1]His date is uncertain but according to Jacobi (*JAOS.*, xxxi, 1911, 1 ff.), it was between A.D. 200 and 450.

Badarī I. The jujube tree (Zizyphus jujuba Lam.), the dwelling place of the goddess Durgā.

II. The present Badarīnātha,[1] situated in the Himālaya, and sacred to Viṣṇu in his dual form of Nara-Nārāyaṇa.

[1]Also a title of Viṣṇu as Lord of Badarī.

Baḍavā v. Vaḍabā.

Bagalā 'Deceitful.' The designation of cranes, regarded as the most deceitful of birds, and hence the name of the crane-headed goddess (the eighth *mahāvidyā*), who represents the power of cruelty, black magic, poison, and all destructive desires. She was originally a village-goddess (*grāmadevatā*), but is now identified with Durgā.

v. Vaka I.

Bāhu A king of the Solar dynasty and father of Sagara.

Bāhuja 'Arm-born.' A *kṣatriya* said to have issued from Brahmā's arm. According to *Manu* (I.31) the *kṣatra* (the warrior class) was produced from the arm of the creator.

v. Puruṣa.

Baja A herb, said to be the white mustard (*śvetasarṣapa*). An amulet made of *baja* will expel the demons from between the thighs of pregnant women (*AV.*, VIII.6,3).

Baka v. Vaka.

Bakula or **Vakula** A name of Śiva, and of the tree (Mimusops elengi) with which he is identified (*MBh.*, 13.17,110, *EM.*). It puts forth blossoms when sprinkled with nectar from the mouths of lovely women.

v. Candramukha.

Bakura A horn, trumpet or other wind instrument used to rally troops in battle, but Yāska considers it to be a lightning flash or thunderbolt, metaphorically called a horn, trumpet, etc. The *bakura* was used by the twin Aśvins to frighten away the Dasyus during the advance of the Āryan settlers (*RV.*, I.117,21). The drum (*dundubhi*) and the '*bakura* provided the music of war'.[1]

[1]S. D. Singh, *Ancient Indian Warfare*, p. 10. The very sound of a trumpet caused the enemy to die (*AGP.*, 269,35–7).

v. Dundubhi I.

Bala v. Vala.

Bālā The mother of Bālin and Sugrīva, said to have been formed by Prajāpati from dust that had fallen into his eyes.

Baladeva v. Balarāma.

Bālagraha 'Seizer of children'. A malevolent spirit which causes nine kinds of demoniac possession.

v. Grāhi(s).

Balāhaka I. One of Kṛṣṇa's four horses, the others being Meghapuṣpa, Śaibya and Sugrīva.

II. The name of one of the seven clouds which will appear at the dissolution of the world.

Bālāmbikā 'Girl-mother.' A goddess whose shrine is held in high esteem by South Indian Tantrists. She is identical with Kanyā Kumārī, the divinity of Cape Comorin.[1]

[1]*TT.*, p. 99, n.11.

v. Hemāmbikā; Mukhāmbikā.

Balarāma 'Rāma the strong', also called Bala, Baladeva, Balabhadra, Halāyudha, Lāṅgalin, Musalī, etc. Like his younger brother Kṛṣṇa, Balarāma appears to have been a historical figure who became identified with an agricultural deity. He appears as a culture-hero in the *VP.* (V.25) where he is associated with irrigation and viticulture, as well as with agriculture, but factual and mythical elements are so intermingled that it is often impossible to distinguish them.

Tradition states that Balarāma was the seventh child of Devakī. Owing to a prediction that one of her children would later kill Kaṁsa the tyrannical King of

Mathurā and usurp his throne, an edict was issued stating that each child born to Devakī was to be destroyed. Six of her children were thus disposed of, but during her seventh pregnancy a celestial voice directed her to transfer the unborn child to the womb of the second queen, Rohiṇī, who later gave birth to Balarāma. Another legend states that Balarāma and Kṛṣṇa were formed from a white and a black hair respectively from Viṣṇu's head (*VP.*, V.1).

Balarāma had many adventures. He slew the ape Dvivida who had stolen his weapons, and also the *asura* Dhenuka who had assumed the form of an ass, and whose dead body he threw into a tree. He forced Duryodhana and the Kauravas to give up Kṛṣṇa's son, by throwing his ploughshare under the ramparts of their city and pulling down the walls.

According to legend, when Varuṇa asked his wife Vāruṇī (goddess of wine) to get some wine for Balarāma, she took up her abode in a Kaḍamba tree (Ipomoea aquatica)[1] and collected the juice of the flowers. As Balarāma drew near he was attracted by the fragrance of the exuding drops, which he drank. So potent was the wine that he became intoxicated and shouted to the river-goddess Yamunā to come to him as he wished to bathe, but the river continued on its course. Balarāma thereupon threw his ploughshare into it and dragged it behind him during his wanderings until the river-goddess cried for mercy. Only when the country was well-watered[2] did he release her.

Balarāma married Revatī, the daughter of King Raivata, by whom he had two sons, Niśaṭha and Ulmuka. His death occurred under a banyan tree on the outskirts of Dvārakā. As he lay dying the great serpent Ananta issued from his mouth and glided towards the ocean from which the Ocean-god arose with offerings to meet him (*VP.*, V.37), and hence the myth that Balarāma was an incarnation (*avatāra*) of the world-snake Ananta or Śeṣa, which led to the production of images of Balarāma as a snake-man (Nāga). Although temples dedicated to Balarāma existed at one time, his importance waned in the Middle Ages, when the Kṛṣṇa cult became paramount.

[1]A spiritous liquor is distilled from the flowers of the Kaḍamba.

[2]The *Bhāg. P.* and the *Hariv.* repeat the story, which probably alludes to the construction of canals from the Jumna (*VP.*, pp. 452–3 n.).

v. Raivata I; Dhenuka I; Rāma; Avatāra.

Balbaja A species of coarse grass (Eleusine indica), said to be produced from the urine of cows (*Tait. Saṁ.*, II. 2.8,1). The *Kāṭhaka Saṁ.* states that it is used for the sacrificial litter or seat (*barhis*) of the gods, and for fuel,[1] but according to *RV.*, I.3,3 the grass used was *kuśa*.

[1] *VI.*, vol. II, p. 63.

v. Kuśa II.

Bali I. A technical term for an offering of grain or rice to certain gods, household divinities, spirits (*bhūtas*), birds, animals and inanimate objects. It is part of the daily ritual carried out by a householder.[1] In the morning rite the *bali* offerings are thrown in the direction of the four cardinal points, or into the fire. Some of the offerings should be placed near the main door accompanied by praise of the Maruts; the next portion, placed in water, is similarly addressed to the waters; that put in the pestle and mortar, to trees. At the head of the bed an offering is made to Śrī; at the foot to Bhadrākālī; at the centre of the house conjointly to Brahmā and to Vāstoṣpati, the lord of the dwelling. In the evening a *bali* must be offered to the spirits who roam about at night, and an offering placed on the upper floor of the house to Sarvātmabhūti. The remainder of the food forms the offering to the *pitṛs*, and is thrown towards the south, the abode of the dead (*Manu*, III.87–93; *VP.*, III.11).

Bali offerings of all kinds, whether Buddhist or Brahmanical, are so similar that they must have been derived from a common source of ancient rites.

[1]This ensures that at death, the householder will immediately attain *brahman*. The '*bali*-offering implies a cult midway between that of the Vedic sacrifice and the sectarian sacrifice not countenanced by the orthodox' (*CHI.*, vol. I, p. 230).

v. Bhūtabali.

II. The name of the good but proud Daitya king, the son of Virocana. He assisted Brahmā in designating the various castes (*Hariv.*, 1688, *EM.*).

Hopkins points out that as Kṛṣṇa represents both right and wrong, he can become the demon Bali, even 'as Śiva becomes the eclipse demon' (*EM.*, p. 217; v. also *VP.*, V.26).

v. Bāṇa III; Vāmana; Puṇḍra I; Avatāra.

Bāli or **Bālin** 'Tailed.' A monkey, the elder brother of the monkey-king Sugrīva. Bāli, the son of Indra, was born from his mother's hair (*bāla*); hence his name. His wife was Tārā (or Śudeṣṇā), and his sons, Aṅgada and Tāra. During Sugrīva's absence from his kingdom Bāli usurped the throne, but on Sugrīva's return he fled.

v. Rāmacandra; Vānara(s).

Bambhāri The name of one of the seven tutelary deities of the sacred *soma* plant (*Tait. Saṁ.*, I.2,7).

Bāṇa or **Vāṇa** I. 'Arrow.' In the *RV.* (IV.3,7) *bāṇa* refers to lightning, called the 'lofty arrow', and in (VIII.66,7 and n.7) it refers to Indra's thousand-feathered and hundred-barbed arrow. The Aśvins are implored to turn away the arrow of disease and death (VII.71,1).[1]

In the *MBh.* and *Rām.* arrows are likened to serpents gliding noiselessly through the air; and real serpents are said to have become Śiva's bow and arrows, as also those of Rāvaṇa (*Rām.*, 6.103, 18, *EM.*).

Arrows also have phallic significance and are used in a rite to ensure male offspring, when an arrow is broken above the mother's head accompanied by the words: 'Unto thy womb let a foetus come, a male one, as an arrow to a quiver' (*AV.*, III.23,2).[2] The bow and arrow also symbolize power and strength (*ŚBr.*, VI.5.2–10). Indrāṇī, Indra's wife, is said to be the goddess of arrows (*Tait. Saṁ.*, II.2,8).

[1]The deer-horn or iron tips of arrows used in Vedic warfare were sometimes smeared with poison (*RV.*, VI.75,5). Metal arrows were called *nārāca*; the aboriginals used an arrow or dart (*kāṇḍa*) blown from a blowpipe (*nālīka*).

[2]Śiva's arrow and *liṅgam* are the vehicles of his energy; the two are the same (Zimmer, *Myths*, p. 187).

v. Iṣu; Dhanus; Bāṇagaṅgā; Bāṇaliṅga; Puṁsavana.

II. Name of the number five, a reference to the five arrows of Kāma, the god of love.

III. The thousand-armed eldest son of Bali (*VP.*, I.21). Bāṇa was a devotee of Śambhu (Śiva) to whom he appealed to cause a war as his many arms were useless in peace time. Śiva replied that when Bāṇa's peacock banner was broken strife would ensue.

v. Aniruddha I; Ūṣā.

IV. Author of the 'Deeds of Harṣa' (*Harṣacarita*) written in the seventh century, which purports to tell of the events leading to Harṣa's rise to power. But the work appears to be unfinished. His other unfinished work was called *Kādambarī*, a romance, which was completed by his son.

Bāṇa spent his youth wandering from town to town, mixing with philosophers, actors, doctors, ascetics of various cults, and people of low caste, which shows 'how lightly the rules of caste weighed on the educated man'.[1]

[1]*WI.*, p. 447.

Bāṇagaṅgā The name of a river produced by Rāvaṇa whose arrow cut through a mountain, so making a channel for it.

Bāṇaliṅga A white stone found in the Narmadā river and worshipped as the *liṅga* of Śiva.

Bāṇaparṇī The name of a poisonous plant used in sorcery against a woman rival (*AV.*, VII.113).

Banāras v. Kāśī.

Barhis The grassy bank or couch[1] on which the gods sit when attending the sacrifice (*Nir.*, 8.8–9). This grass is also strewn over the sacrificial area and on the altar to serve as a sacred surface on which to present the oblations. It is also one of the deified objects (*āprī*) of the sacrifice (*RV.*, V.5,4).

The *barhis* symbolize all plants, and the altar (*vedi*) the earth; thus the Sacrificer ensures the continuance of plant life (*ŚBr.*, I.3.3–9f.; 8.2,11; but cf. XII. 8.2,36).

An Emperor's throne is also covered with this grass, said to have emerged from the vital sap of the personified Sacrifice (XIV.1.3,11).[2]

[1]Cf. the setting up of seats for the divine guests in some Canaanite ceremonies which 'reflects the *lectisternium* . . . characteristic of many seasonal festivals among the Greeks and Romans, and a feature especially of the Attis mysteries. The rite is well attested, at a late date, at Palmyra and in the Hauran' (Gaster, *Thespis*, p. 408).

[2]For its connexion with funeral rites v. *AV.*, XVIII.4,51,52.

v. Kuśa I.

Barhiṣads The sons of Atri and ancestors of the *daityas*, *dānavas*, *yakṣas*, *gandharvas*, etc. (*Manu*, III. 196). According to the *Matsya* and *Padma Purs.* and the *Hariv.*, the Barhiṣads are the sons of Pulastya.

Basanti v. Śītalā.

Basava (12th cent.) The minister of a Jaina king who was instrumental in developing the Vīra-Śaiva system. He organized a religious house called Śivānubhava-mantapa, intended to make man realize his place in the universe; to give women equality of status; to abolish caste distinctions; to encourage manual labour and simple living. The *Vacana-śāstra* is a collection of the sayings of Basava and of his colleagues.

Baṭuka 'Boy', 'youth'. A form of Śiva (Bhairava)[1] represented in Śākta rites by boys.

[1]Baṭuka is worshipped in northern India. He is depicted as a hideous youth, usually accompanied by a dog.

Bauddha v. Buddhism.

Bhadra 'Auspicious', 'fortunate'. An epithet of Śiva; Mount Meru, etc.

Bhadrā I. 'Auspicious', 'fortunate'. A name of Durgā; of Vaiśravaṇa's wife; of a daughter of Soma and wife of Utathya; and of one of Kṛṣṇa's queens.

II. The name of one of the four branches of the celestial Ganges (*gaṅgā*) which flows from Mount Meru through the land of the Uttarakurus to the northern ocean. The other three branches are the Sītā, Alakanandā and the Cakṣu (*VP.*, II.2).

III. Name of a daughter of Rohiṇī and mother of goats and sheep (*Brah. P.*, III. 3.74–5, *PI.*).

IV. The wife of the fabulous bird Garuḍa (*Vāyu P.*, 69.328, *PI.*).

Bhadraghaṭa v. Kalaśa.

Bhadrākālī I. A form of Durgā who sprang from Devī's (Umā's) wrath when her husband Śiva was insulted by Dakṣa (*VP.*, I.8). She was probably a nature-goddess adopted by Śaivas. She bestows boons on children when propitiated by human sacrifice, but became enraged when she discovered that the virtuous *brāhmaṇa* Bharata was to be the victim (*Bhāg. P.*, V.9.12–18, *PI.*). Bhadrākālī fought on the side of Śumbha and Niśumbha in the war of the gods and the *asuras*.

II. Name of one of the Mātṛs attendant on Skanda.

Bhadrakumbha v. Kalaśa.

Bhadranidhi v. Kalaśa.

Bhaga An Āditya, a son of the cosmic mother-goddess Aditi; or name of the sun in the month *puṣya*; or one of the divisions (*muhūrta*) of a day and night. The *Purāṇa Index* (vol. II, p. 525) derives Bhaga from *bha*, cherisher or supporter, and *ga*, leader, whence Bhagavat, lord.[1] Though late, the Paurāṇic definitions of Bhaga generally accord with its Vedic significance, i.e. 'sharer or dispenser', an epithet applied to a tribal lord or chieftain who, according to ancient Āryan custom, annually divided the spoils of war and the products of communal activity among the adult members of the tribe. In the *RV.* (I.24,5; VII.38,1) the epithet was applied to one of the Ādityas, who as Bhaga became the celestial dispenser of wealth and other boons.[2]

Bhaga is sometimes associated with the lunar asterism Uttara-Phalgunī, a constellation astrologically considered to be favourable to marriage.

Bhaga's wife is called Siddhi (Realization). His sons are Vibhu (Power), Prabhu (Sovereignty) and Mahimān (Greatness), and his daughter is Āśis, the personification of Hope.

[1]Cf. Zend *bagha*; Gr. *Bagaios*; Slav. *Bogŭ*.

[2]Bhaga is the god who gives human beings their share of happiness (Gonda, *Loka*, p. 142). Edgerton states that Bhaga is Fortune personified (*BIP.*, p. 115). Wallis (*Cosmology of the RV.*, p, 11) considers him to be a survival from an ancient sun-cult; and Yāska states that he is the sun which presides over the forenoon.

v. Aṁśa I; Hara; Vīrabhadra I.

Bhagavadgītā[1] The 'Lord's Song', i.e., the Song of Kṛṣṇa. It forms part of the sixth (*parvan*) of the *MBh.* and presents the views of Kṛṣṇa Devakīputra, whom the *Chān. Up.* represents as the disciple of a solar priest who declared that righteous conduct is more efficacious than gifts made to a priestly sacrificer.[2] The theme of the *Gītā* goes much further and declares that the ancient faith in sacrifice as the sole means of liberation is no longer valid. Only deeds springing from altruistic motives (*niṣkāma karma*), and devotion (*bhakti*) to Īśvara[3] and faith in his grace (*prasāda*) can lead to the realization of *brahman*.

The *Gītā* confirms the definition of *avatāra* as an incarnation of the Supreme Being, which occurs from age to age in response to a particular need or crisis.

Opinions vary about the date of the original composition of the *Gītā*, some placing it in or about the fourth century B.C., others in the third or second centuries. Whichever of these is correct, the work in its present form indicates considerable revision.

[1]Of the thirty-four MSS. used to compile the critical edition of the *MBh.*, two omit the *Bhagavadgītā* entirely (*BIP.*, p. 197). On sound text-critical grounds 'all stanzas above 700 are, in all MSS. unquestionably secondary insertions' (ibid., p. 197, n.1.).

For an E. translation with Sanskrit text, notes, etc. v. Nataraja Guru, *The Bhagavad Gītā*. There are said to be over fifty translations of this work (v. Bibliography).

[2]*AHI.*, p. 83. The *MBh.* was originally a secular work in which a number of sacred works were interpolated.

[3]'Bhandarkar has rightly pointed out that the *Bhagavadgītā* is the earliest exposition of the Bhakti system of Ekāntika Dharma' (*PTR.*, p. 31). v. also *VS.*, pp. 22–4; cf. *CHI.*, vol. I, p. 273.

v. Kurukṣetra; Bhakti.

Bhagavat A term generally used as an honorific, as a form of address, expressing veneration or great respect.[1] As such it is applied to the Vedic gods, godlings and *ṛṣis*; to Kṛṣṇa, Viṣṇu, Śiva, etc; and to the Buddha and *bodhisattvas*. According to the *Bhāg. P.*, Kapila is regarded as one of the *avatāras* of Bhagavat (*EW.*, vol. I, p. 124).

[1]In the Purs. it is applied to one possessing *bhaga* (spiritual power) (*AGP.*, I, p. 2, n.); or dignity, majesty, excellence, etc. (*VS.*, p. 35).

Bhāgavata Relating to or coming from Bhagavat, i.e., Viṣṇu or Kṛṣṇa. The name of a theistic cult which stressed the importance of worship rather than sacrifice. The devotees of Kṛṣṇa became known as Bhāgavatas, who later merged with the Pāñcarātra, a Vaiṣṇava sect.[1]

[1]*PTR.*, p. 20.

v. Bhakti.

Bhāgavata Purāṇa v. Purāṇa (s).

Bhagīratha A son of Dilīpa and a great-great grandson of Sagara, a legendary king of Ayodhyā, who with his 60,000 'sons' are the chief figures in a myth which, among other things, relates the miraculous origin of the Ganges and the part played by Bhagīratha in guiding it during its long journey to the sea, and hence Bhāgīrathī, the name by which Gaṅgā is also known (*VP.*, IV.4).

Bhāgīrathī A name of the Ganges (*gaṅgā*).
v. Bhagīratha.

Bhairava I. 'Frightful', 'terrible'. A name of one of the eight *ugra* or *ghora* forms of Rudra, especially worshipped by outcaste groups. Bhairava is also a name of the southern face of the five-faced Śiva.

Śiva, inconsolable after the death of his wife Śatī at Dakṣa's sacrifice, wandered aimlessly over the earth carrying her corpse on his shoulders. To cure him of his obsession Viṣṇu cut up Śatī's body with his *cakra* and had her limbs scattered. The places where they fell became sacred and known as *śaktipīṭhas*, each being guarded by Śiva in the form of a Bhairava.[1]

Bhairava is often depicted accompanied by a dog[2] or riding on one; hence his epithet Śvāśva, 'Whose horse is a dog'. He often serves as the doorkeeper of Śaiva temples, and has been identified with the village-godling Bhairon, worshipped as a black dog or a red stone. Bhairava is invoked in rites designed to destroy enemies (*AGP*., Vol. I, p. 509).

[1]*DHI*., p. 495, n.l.

[2]The association of the dog with the worship of the Bhairavas by outcastes probably stems from Manu's rule that only those who are caste-less should be allowed to keep dogs and asses.

v. Kṣetrapāla; Baṭuka; Śvan.

II. Name of a chief of Śiva's host (*gaṇa*).

Bhairavā I. A class of *apsarasas*.
II. Epithet of the goddess of misery, Nirṛti.

Bhairavī 'Terror', or 'the power to cause terror'. The name of a goddess who is the sixth *mahāvidyā* and one of the ten personifications of Śiva's energy. Bhairavī represents the power of death, which continues throughout life. In carrying out this silent process of perpetual decay and destruction (*nitya pralaya*), Bhairavī is often popularly regarded as a demoness. Her image appears in many temples, but is never placed in the principal shrine.[1]

[1]*PI*., vol. II, p. 584.

v. Bhairava I; Mahāvidyā(s).

Bhairon A village godling, the personification of a field-spirit, often confused with the *bhūmiya* form of the earth-god. Bhairon on the other hand was elevated to the Hindu theogony. He began as a peasant godling, by stages became an attendant of a brahmanic god, and was then regarded as a form of the god, culminating in the only form of the god (Śiva) recognized by particular peasant communities, chiefly in northern India.[1]

[1]*ERE*., II, p. 539.

Bhakti 'Devotion', 'worship'. From *bhaj*, meaning in a religious context adoration or loving devotion. From the same root are derived Bhagavat (Adorable One), and Bhāgavata, a worshipper of Bhagavat, both words being closely associated with *bhakti* or *bhakti-mārga* (the devotional path), the doctrine of liberation by faith, as opposed to the Vedic doctrine of liberation by works (*karma-mārga*), or by knowledge (*jñāna-mārga*).[1]

But Heimann[2] considers that *bhakti* does not only mean devotion offered to a single divinity, 'but reciprocal participation', its verbal root *bhaj*, meaning 'to share, to partake, to enjoy'. *Bhakti* thus appears to be a later expression of the magical partnership of the sacrificer and the chosen deity (*iṣṭadevatā*) to whom the oblation is made. The male *bhakta* regards himself as feminine in relation to the deity and believes that love given attracts counter-love, even as the Ṛgvedic sacrifice 'brought about' the desired result.

For the notion of *karman* as an inexorable process of cause and effect, *bhakti* substitutes the belief that by the exercise of divine grace (*prasāda*) the karmic process may be modified.

It has been suggested that the earliest allusion to *bhakti* is to be found in two *RV*. hymns (V. 85, 7–8; VII.87,7) addressed to Varuṇa, in which he is implored to forgive the trespasses of his devotees.[3] But it seems strange that of the 1,017 hymns comprising the *RV*. these two hymns alone express such sentiments, and that they should have had so little impact on Vedic ethics, which are generally materialistic and whose altruism is limited to the family or the tribe. The gods are invoked mainly to grant wealth, and increased fertility of cattle and crops, etc.

But if the notion of *bhakti* exists in the *RV*., then the solar Viṣṇu, often addressed as Bhagavat, and also identified with Bhaga, may well have been its source, and finally have become 'the germ of the "god" of the Bhāgavatas'[4] and an important link in the early Viṣṇu cult. Thus the distinction between Varuṇa as the forgiver of 'sins' and the altruistic (*niṣkāma*) and mystical adoration (*bhakti*) of the Supreme Being is as great perhaps as that between the original definition of Yoga, i.e., 'concentration of thought' and its later significance of 'devotion to God'. The stress on *bhakti* in the *BG*.[5] marks the beginning of the final development of the *bhakti* ideal, which now permeates every Vaiṣṇava and Śaiva cult.

[1]'Works' in this context refer to those prescribed by the Vedic sacerdotalists; by 'knowledge' is meant knowledge of the Veda.

[2]*IWP*., pp. 73f.

[3]*AHI*., p. 38; and v. *VS*., p. 22. Although the *bhakti* cults came into prominence in the centuries immediately preceding the beginning of the Christian era, they were not an isolated sectarian development, but a

general tendency which can be seen in early Buddhism and in Śaivism. Bhagavat 'Worshipful' was applied to Viṣṇu (Vāsudeva); the Four Great Kings; Kubera; and the Buddha himself, as well as to the Nāga Dadhikarṇa (Coomaraswamy, *Yakṣas*, pt. i, pp. 27 and n. 3; 28).

[4]*C. Herit. I.*, vol. II, p. 66.

[5](XI. 43–6) appears to be more a state of humble reverence towards a mighty potentate, rather than adoration, but according to the *Nārada Bhakti Sūtras*, *bhakti* is said to have three modes, viz., the servant, refugee, and friendly attitude towards the object of worship (v. Nataraja Guru, *The Bhagavad Gītā*, p. 503).

Bhaṅgā Also called *vijayā*. Hemp (Cannabis sativa),[1] a narcotic drug commonly called '*bhang*'. The dried leaves and capsules of the plant contain a powerful narcotic resin and a volatile oil. It is used for smoking, and is also made up with flour, sugar, etc., into a kind of sweetmeat called *majūn*. The pounded leaves when infused in cold water make an intoxicating drink, and it is employed medically for its anodyne, hypnotic and anti-spasmodic qualities.

According to the *AV.* (XI.6,15) *bhaṅgā* is one of the 'five kingdoms of plants' ruled by Soma, all of which are invoked to 'free us from disease'. Diehl, citing Sandegren, states that in South Indian divinatory ceremonies hemp is sometimes smoked as an 'aid' to achieving an ecstatic state.[2] The Order or Sect of the Assassins (lit. 'hashish-eaters') used hemp before committing the murders for which they had been selected by their chief.[3] Some Śāktas and members of similar cults still use opium and hashish.[4]

[1]As prepared by the Arabs it is called hashish. The British in India set up a Hemp Drug Commission in 1893–4 (7 vols and Supplementary vol. Repr. 1970).

[2]*Instrument and Purpose*, p. 222, n.l.

[3]But it has recently been suggested that hashish was given as a reward *after* the murder had been committed.

[4]Lindquist, *Die Methoden des Yoga*, pp. 194ff.

v. Vijayā II.

Bharadvāja A member of an ancient Āryan pastoralist tribal group of that name,[1] and also the name of one of its members who became a *ṛṣi*. Some of his descendants (Bhāradvājas) also became notable *ṛṣis* and *brāhmaṇas*. The early tribal Bhāradvājas worshipped Pūṣan, a local god and the protector of pastoralists, who was apparently not initially recognized by the major Āryan tribes. But later hymns of the *RV.* include Pūṣan in the Vedic 'pantheon' by making him Indra's brother (VI.55,5), or helper (VI.56,2), and also by associating him with the god Soma (II.40, 1–6). Probably because of Pūṣan's enhanced status, the Bhāradvājas became the sacrificial officiants of the pastoralist tribes, and their hymns were given a place in the *RV.*[2] One of these (VI.28) relates solely to praise of the cow, and is the earliest reference to its sacred character and its special association with Bhaga, Indra, and Soma.

The *ŚBr.* has one reference to a Bhāradvāja, a teacher; only in the Purs. and *MBh.* is the name again given prominence, but the legends in which it occurs, even when related to a specific event, are often inconsistent to the point of absurdity. One such legend, variously recounted, refers to the adoption by a Bhārata prince of a son of the *ṛṣi* Bṛhaspati, who was given the name of Bharadvāja,[3] the meaning of which the *VP.* (IV.19) gives as '*bhara dvā-jam*' (born of two fathers). This refers to the double pregnancy of Mamātā, a condition attributed to her husband Utathya and Bṛhaspati. The point of this legend is given in the *Bhāg. P.* which states that from Bharadvāja, a *brahmin* by birth, and king by adoption, descended *brahmins* and *kṣatriyas*, the children of two fathers.

The *Brahma P.* and the *Hariv.* appear to have modified this legend, perhaps to reconcile the account of Bharadvāja as a sage, who was brought by the Maruts[4] to perform a sacrifice, by which Bharata might obtain a son, and the other account which states that Bharadvāja was brought by the Maruts, not as a sage, but as a child, of whom Bharata said, 'this Bharadvāja shall be Vitatha', signifying that the king regarded him as a compensation for the unprofitable (*vitatha*) birth of his nine sons murdered by their mothers. But the *MBh.* (Ādi pa., 3,710) gives a simpler account. Bharata, because of the loss of his children, obtained from Bharadvāja by great sacrifices, a son Bhūmanyu; or as suggested in another passage (verse 3,785) he was the son of Bharata and his wife Sunandā, the daughter of Sarvasena, King of Kāśī, born apparently without the aid either of the Maruts or of Bharadvāja, or of any sacrificial rites.[5]

Other references to the Bhāradvājas who were sages or *brāhmaṇas* occur in the *MBh.* and the Purs. One Bhāradvāja by the performance of a sacrifice enabled Pratardana, a son of King Divodāsa, to be born fully adult. Another begot the heroic Droṇa, by the nymph Ghṛtācī (*MBh.*, I.166, 1f., *EM.*). A Vaiṣṇava myth refers to a Bhāradvāja *ṛṣi* who sprinkled Viṣṇu's chest with water which transformed itself into the *śrīvatsa* mark.

[1]*Brah. P.*, II.16.50; *Matsya P.*, 114, 43, *PI.*

[2]With a few exceptions all the hymns of *RV.* VI are attributed to the *ṛṣi* Bharadvāja or to members of his family (*RV.*, I. p. 555, n.).

[3]Griffith's reference to Bharadvāja as the son of Bṛhaspati appears to be based on this legend (*RV.*, I. p. 147, n.13).

[4]The introduction of the mythological Maruts 'seems to have grown out of a confusion of the names, Marut and Marutta'; the latter being the ruler of the kingdom of Vaiśālī, of whose people the Maruttas, Bṛhaspati was priest (*Seers*, p. 98).

[5]*VP.*, p. 359n.

Bharaṇī Name of the seventh *nakṣatra*, consisting of three stars and figured by the *pudendum muliebre*. Hostile rites (*abhicāra*) should be performed under this *nakṣatra* (*AGP.*, I, p. 512).

Bharata Primarily the name of an Āryan tribal group, prominent in early Vedic times; or that of its post-Vedic descendants, the Bhāratas; or it may signify the land of the Bharatas which, because of its great extent, made Bhārata one of the alternative names for India—or at least of its northern regions.

The word *bharata* is derived from *bhṛ*, to carry off, and hence to rob, plunder or raid, the significance given to it in the *RV.* (III.53,24; V.54,14; VII.8,4, etc.). As an epithet it may have been applicable to many of the Āryan pastoralist tribes and later have become the name of the most successful, or of a combination of them.

In Vedic times the Āryan tribes warred not only against their indigenous neighbours but also against their compatriots, especially the Kuru tribes, which finally led to a confederation of them, determined to destroy the power of the Tṛtsu king Sudās. Uncertain of the ability of Viśvāmitra his *purohita*, Sudās dismissed him and appointed Vasiṣṭha as his priestly adviser and protector. In the campaign that followed, known as the Daśarājña or Battle of the Ten Kings, Sudās was successful, his supremacy subsequently leading to the founding of the Bhārata kingdom. This formerly consisted of the lands between the rivers Sarasvatī and Yamunā, now extended eastwards, being bounded on the north by the Himālaya and on the south by the Vindhya mountains.[1]

Bharata, the most notable of its rulers, was the son of Śakuntalā and Duṣyanta, probably a Puru ruler, whose kingdom now formed part of the Bhārata empire. The importance of the Lunar Dynasty, of which the Bhārata kings represented the direct line, is indicated by the number of legends invented to support what were often dubious genealogical records, such as those of the birth of an heir to Bharata,[2] and of his descendants Śāntanu, Kṛṣṇa Dvaipāyana, Dhṛtarāṣṭra and Pāṇḍu, and finally the Kauravas and Pāṇḍavas, whose quarrel led to the tragic war of the Mahābhārata. Through their descent from Bharata, these two princely families, especially the Pāṇḍavas, are often referred to as Bhāratas. The later Bhāratas became noted for the 'superiority of their cult and ritual practices'.[3] But by the sixth century B.C., they cease to be mentioned in the geographical lists, either of the *Ait. Br.* (VIII.14) or the *Mānava Dharma Śāstra*; nor is there any reference to them in the Buddhist texts. But in the *MBh.* they are romantically referred to, and their land, Bhāratavarṣa, is given an emotionally evocative significance, like that given in modern times to La Patrie by the French or 'Hen Wlad fy nhadau' to Wales by the Welsh.

[1]'The origin of the name Bhāratavarṣa (Land of the Bhāratas) offers another instance of the diversity of traditions. According to many of the Purs., the name was derived from Bharata, son of Ṛṣabha and grandson of Nābhi who was a descendant of Vaivasvata Manu, while certain other Paurāṇic passages represent Bharata as the second name of Manu himself' (*CG.*, p. 37).

[2]One passage in the *MBh.* (Ādi pa., verse 3,785), in contrast to these fanciful legends, simply states that the son Bhūmanyu, was born to Bharata and his queen Sunantā, a daughter of Sarvasena, King of Kāśī, probably one of the vassal kings of the Bhārata empire (Wilson, *VP.*, p. 359, n.15).

[3]*HCIP.*, I, p. 245.

v. Bharadvāja; Bhāratī; Menā II.

Bhāratī A goddess who is included among the *āprī* deities (*RV.*, I.188,8; II.1,11). She is often associated with the goddesses Sarasvatī and Ilā (= Iḍā), who also represent various forms of worship, and who protect the sacred grass on which the gods sit when attending the sacrifice (II.3,8). Probably because of her connexion with Sarasvatī she became the tutelary deity of the Bhāratas, a people who dwelt in the valley of the Sarasvatī River.[1]

[1]*CG.*, p. 22.

v. Mahī; Barhis.

Bhārgava A descendant of Bhṛgu, such as Cyavana, Jamadagni, Paraśurāma, etc. Bhārgava appears as the name of some authors of hymns, and also of mythical as well as of historical persons.

That Bhārgava is also the name of a special class of priests, having no connexion with either the original Bhṛgu or the fire-cult, is indicated by the legend of the Bhārgava priest Śukra, the preceptor, not of *dasyus*, but of *daityas*, the name applied to the mixed racial groups belonging to the small independent states which later became part of the kingdom of Magadha. These mixed ethnic groups, of predominantly Turanian and Āryan origin,[1] included the Bhargas of Sumsumāra Hill, the Śākyas of Kapilavastu and the Mauryas of Pipphalivana, and several others, all warrior tribes.[2]

Thus the appointment of Bhārgava priests, who were probably of similar ethnic origin to the people whose preceptors they became, represents a tactical move to further the brahmanization of these warrior tribes. The failure to complete their conversion to brahmanic orthodoxy appears to be indicated by the emergence from their midst of the founders of Jainism and Buddhism.

[1]v. *OHI.*, p. 8.

[2]*AHI.*, p. 57.

v. Yayāti; Devayānī.

Bhartṛhari (7th cent.) A famous poet and grammarian who wrote a number of fine short poems, on love, worldly wisdom, etc., and the grammatical work called *vākyapadīya*.

Bhāsa A dramatist and author of several notable plays including the *Svapnavāsavadatta* (The Vision of Vāsavadatta), and *Pratijñāyaugandharāyaṇa* (Yaugandharāyaṇa's Vows). He also wrote some short dramas based on epic stories. His date is unknown, but some scholars consider him to be earlier than Kālidāsa.

Bhāsī A daughter of Tāmrā and Kaśyapa. Bhāsī became the mother of kites (*VP.*, I.21). The *Vāyu* and *Brahmāṇḍa* Purs. make her the mother of crows, doves sparrows, owls, partridges, etc.

Bhasman Sacred ash, said to be the *semen virile* (*vīrya*) of Śiva. Burning was believed to reduce substances to their pure primal state, thus ashes were considered to be the sign of a pure substance. Cf. the ash-altar of Ge at Olympia, which was believed to be 'charged with the presence of the divinity'.[1]

[1]Farnell, *Cults*, IV, p. 221, n. c.

v. Vibhūti II.

Bhaṭṭa An honorific affixed or prefixed to the names of learned brahmins.

Bhaṭṭa Kallaṭa A pupil of Vasugupta, who publicized his teacher's work.

Bhaṭṭārikā 'Noble lady.' An epithet of the goddess Durgā.

Bhauma I. The personification of the planet Mars whose octagonal chariot is drawn by eight red horses (*V.P.*, II.12) who sprang from fire.

II. A magical weapon with which Arjuna created land (*MBh.*, Ādi pa., 137).

Bhaumī 'Produced from the earth.' An epithet of Sītā.

v. Sītā I; Bhūmi.

Bhava I. 'Existence', 'becoming'. One of the eight elemental forms of Rudra representing the forces of nature; the other forms being Śarva, Rudra, Paśupati, Ugra, Mahān (Mahādeva), Bhīma and Iśāna (*ŚBr.*, VI.1.3,10–18; *Kauṣ. Br.*, VI. 1–9).

Bhava is lord of cattle and men; the possessor of heaven, earth, and the atmosphere; the protector of his worshippers against jackals (the mere sight of which is a bad omen),[1] and against other evil influences. Those who do not sacrifice he kills and also those who mock the gods. He is often associated with Śarva and both are invoked to destroy with lightning (i.e., the missile of the gods) all evil-doers and sorcerers (*AV.*, X.1,23; XI.2).

The notions of destruction and renewal, or perpetual becoming, the chief characteristic of Rudra, are developed in the Purs. devoted to Śiva, with whom Rudra became identified.

It is evident that as early as the period of the Brāhmaṇas the dualistic theory of nature was being developed, the eight forms of Rudra being divided into two groups of four, one of them *ghora* (terrific), the other, in which Bhava is included, being *saumya* (peaceful).[2] This interpretation of the nature of Bhava pervades the Purs. He is the essence of life, the reservoir of the seven worlds and their protector (*Liṅga P.*, 2,13,5–6).

In Buddhism *bhava* is a technical term meaning 'becoming, (a form of) rebirth, existence'.[3]

[1]Cf. the Egyptian jackal-headed god of death, Anubis.

[2]*DHI.*, p. 448.

[3]*PTS.*

v. Bhāvanī.

II. A form and name of Agni who is identified with Parjanya, the rain-god (*ŚBr.*, VI.1.3,15).

Bhavabhūti A famous playwright (8th cent.) who lived at Kānya-kubja. His surviving plays include the *Mahāvīracarita* (The Deeds of the Great Hero), and the *Uttararāmacarita* (The Later Deeds of Rāma).

Bhāvaja 'Heart-born.' An epithet of Kāma, the god of love.

Bhavānī 'Giver of existence.' The female counterpart of Bhava and the popular name of Devī in the Śākta cult.

v. Ṭhag(s).

Bhāvinī(s) I. A class of women who, in certain regions of India, are dedicated to the service of the temple. In one town near Madras members of the weaver caste used to devote the eldest daughter of every family to the temple. The dedication consisted of a marriage ceremony in which the girl was wedded to a dagger (a well-known phallic symbol), or to a mask of the god.

v. Deva-dāsī.

II. A name of one of the *matṛs* attendant on Skanda.

Bhaviṣya Purāṇa v. Purāṇas.

Bhaya 'Fear', personified[1] as a grand-son of Adharma (Vice) and Hiṁsa (Violence). Bhaya's son was Mṛtyu (Death) (*VP.*, I.7).

[1]Cf. the Gr. personification of Fear (Phobos) to whom Alexander offered mystic rites at night whilst his army slept (Farnell, *Cults*, V, p. 445, n. c.).

v. Yātanā.

Bheda A man who incurred the wrath of the gods by his refusal to give a cow to the priests. The gods 'talked about' Bheda and so destroyed him (*AV.*, XII.4,49).

Bheḍī 'Ewe.' A name of one of the *matṛs* attendant on Skanda.

Bheruṇḍā A name of the goddess Kālī and of a *yakṣiṇī*.

Bhikṣāṭana Śiva in the form of a naked mendicant accompanied by a dwarf who carries a *pātra* (alms-bowl).

Having cut off one of Brahmā's heads, Śiva was guilty of brahminicide (*brahmahatyā*), and the skull stuck fast to his palm. For a long time he wandered about the country as a naked beggar until he reached Banāras, where he expiated his crime and the skull dropped from his hand (*Matsya P.*, 182,15; 183, 101, *PI.*).

Bhīma I. 'Tremendous', 'Fearful', 'Terrible'. One of the eight elemental forms of Rudra (*VP.*, I.8), the presiding deity of *ākāśa* (space).

II. The second of the five sons of Pāṇḍu.[1] His adventures and exploits both before and during the war between the Pāṇḍavas and Kauravas are recounted in the *MBh.* One story refers to Bhīma's struggles against native tribes (*asuras*) and his killing of Hiḍimba, one of their chiefs, whose sister Hiḍimbā he married. Bhīma is also called Bhīmasena and Vṛkodara (Wolf's belly), and according to de Gubernatis[2] he represents 'the solar hero enclosed in the nocturnal or winter darkness'.

Bhīma was huge, coarse and belligerent. His cousin Duryodhana, jealous of his great strength, poisoned him and threw the body into the Ganges, where it sank to the realms of the Nāgas who immediately bit him, but the vegetable poison in his blood neutralized their venom and he recovered. The Nāgas then presented him with eight jars of nectar to drink which gave him the strength of thousands of elephants (*MBh.* Ādi pa., 128).

During the exile of the five Pāṇḍu princes Duryodhana instigated a plot to burn them in their house, but he was frustrated by Bhīma. In the thirteenth year of their exile the princes entered the service of the Rāja of Virāṭa, where Bhīma acted as cook. Once he was matched against the famous wrestler Jīmūta whom he killed.

In the Mahābhārata war Bhīma finally fought Duryodhana. The two were well matched, but when Bhīma was losing he struck an unfair blow with his mace, thus disregarding an ancient rule that a blow should never be dealt below the navel. This blow broke his adversary's thigh, and hence his epithet Jihmayodhin, the 'unfair fighter'.

He is said to have made an iron image of one of his greatest enemies and then beaten it (*MBh.*, 9.33.4; 11.12.15, *EM.*)[3].

[1]According to mythology his father was the wind-god Vāyu.

[2]*Zoological Mythology*, II, p. 144.

[3]Cf. the image-magic recorded in European witch trials.

v. Ghaṭotkaca; Durvāsas; Pṛthā.

Bhīmā A form of Durgā.

Bhīmanāda The name of one of the seven clouds which will appear at the destruction of the world.

Bhīmarathī The 'night of fear'. The seventh night of the seventh month of the seventy-seventh year of life, after which a man is regarded as in his dotage, and hence exempt from religious duties.

Bhīṣanā A terror-inspiring goddess.

Bhīṣma The eighth and last of the sons (the Vasus) of Gaṅgā, the goddess of the river Ganges, and King Śāntanu (*VP.*, IV.20), all of whom, except Bhīṣma, were drowned at birth by their mother.

Bhīṣma is one of the prominent figures of the *MBh.*, especially in the legends relating to the war between the Pāṇḍavas and Kauravas. He commanded the forces of the latter and was fatally wounded. Legend ascribes his survival for fifty-eight days to his possession of the power of prolonging life.[1]

Bhīṣma is portrayed as a man of honour, chivalrous and loyal, whose memory is greatly venerated. Among his epithets are: Gāṅgeya and Nadīja (River-born); Tālaketu (Palm-banner).

[1]The Siddhas in general maintain that death may be postponed indefinitely. The historical Buddha is said to have possessed this yogic power. Although this belief cuts across the *karman* theory, in which the duration of any individual existence is determined by its *karman*, it appears that two kinds of life-duration are envisaged, 'the original one generated by the *karman* and the other by yogic powers.' P. S. Jaini, 'Buddha's Prolongation of Life', *BSOAS.*, XXI. pt. 3 (1958), p. 548.

v. Vasu(s) III.

Bhīṣmaka A King of Vidarbha and father of Rukmiṇī.

Bhogavatī I. The magnificent subterranean capital of the Nāgas, which is also called Pūtkārī.

v. Pātāla.

II. The name of a serpent-nymph.

III. One of the *mātṛs* attendant on Skanda.

IV. The name of the sacred river of the serpent-demons, and of their king Vāsuki.

Bhṛgu(s) I. 'Roasters.' From *bhṛj* or *bhrāj*, 'to burn or roast.' Thus Bhṛgu became the name of the fire-priest by whose magical power the altar fire was kindled. The belief that the Bhṛgus (Bhṛgavaḥ) and the Āṅgirasas and Atharvans alone possessed this gift is possibly the basis of the myth that it was of celestial origin, i.e., lightning, brought to the Bhṛgus by the mysterious, semi-divine Mātariśvan, who taught them the use of the fire-sticks (*araṇi*). This priestly prerogative suggests that the ceremony was initially conducted in secret and that the process was not yet common knowledge. The artificial production of fire (*agni*) was regarded by the people as magical and hence the veneration accorded to its personification, the god Agni, to whom a great number of the *RV.* hymns are addressed. Similarly, the fire-priests were invested with a semi-divine aura and regarded as 'akin to the gods'.

In the Vedic fire-cult the altar was regarded as the centre of the world (*RV.*, I.143,4), but it had also a mundane significance 'as a treasure, established among mankind, for mankind' (*RV.*, I.58,6). Thus when the process of ignition became generally understood, the family hearth became the family altar, and the head of the household the conductor of its simple rites. But the gradual elaboration of ritual necessitated the creation of special classes of priests like the Adhvaryu, Potṛ and Hotṛ, to whom specific duties were assigned, a development that deprived the fire-priest of his unique position.

Nonetheless the Bhṛgus continued to be the central figures of numerous legends, and the first Bhṛgu was given a divine origin. He is described as a son of Varuṇa (*ŚBr.*, XI.6.1,1); or of Indra; or of Prajāpati (*Ait. Br.*, 3,34). Later texts state that he was created by the first Manu (*Manu*, I.34–5); or that he was one of Brahmā's mind-born sons (*VP.*, I.7). In the sectarian legends of the Purāṇas, *MBh.* and *Rām.*, Bhṛgu becomes the focus of Vaiṣṇava and Śaiva rivalry. One of these legends relates that when the *ṛṣis* were undecided whether to worship Brahmā, Viṣṇu or Śiva, Bhṛgu was sent to interview them. On finding Śiva obsessed with his *śakti*, Pārvatī, Bhṛgu condemned him to take the form of a *liṅgam* and be deprived of all future oblations. Bhṛgu found Brahmā completely wrapped up in himself and so considered him unworthy of worship. When he visited Viṣṇu, the god was asleep, and Bhṛgu kicked him, but Viṣṇu, instead of rebuking him, said that he was honoured to be awakened by so great a *ṛṣi*. On his return to the other *ṛṣis* Bhṛgu announced that Viṣṇu alone was worthy of worship.

v. Bhārgava; Śukra I; Vedi.

II. The term applied to the subtle inner fire of the body which 'burns up' water or semen; hence Śiva's title Bhṛgupati, 'Lord of continence'.

Bhṛṅga 'Bee.' This insect was included among the victims offered at an *aśvamedha* (horse sacrifice).

Bhṛṅgi I. A *ṛṣi* who was completely devoted to the worship of Śiva. When the *devas* and *ṛṣis* were circumambulating Śiva and Pārvatī in Kailāsa, Bhṛṅgi refused to worship Pārvatī. To punish him she weakened him so much that he was unable to stand, but Śiva took pity on him and provided him with a third leg. But to save Pārvatī's honour and to pacify her[1] Śiva assumed the Ardhanārī form (by uniting his body with hers), thereby forcing Bhṛṅgi to venerate them both, but the *ṛṣi* assumed the form of a beetle and bored through the composite body and so continued to circumambulate Śiva alone.[2]

[1]Śiva and Pārvatī are essentially one.

[2]*EHI.*, II, pp. 322f. This naïve story no doubt emphasizes the disagreements of some devotees when the principal cult-deities of Śaivism and Śāktaism were amalgamated.

II. The name of Śiva's bull, also called Nandin. By extreme asceticism it gained Śiva's favour and became his vehicle (*vāhana*) and emblem.[1] The bull personifies justice and virtue.

[1]*HP.*, p. 316.

v. Kāmadhenu; Tapas.

Bhūḥ v. Vyāhṛti(s).

Bhūmi 'Existing', i.e., the earth as one of the three worlds or spheres of existence, viz., the celestial, atmospheric and the terrestrial. Later Bhūmi became a synonym of Pṛthivī or Bhūdevī, the goddess personifying the earth.

v. Varāha I; Hiraṇyākṣa; Emūṣa; Vyāhṛti(s); Bhaumī.

Bhūmiya A godling connected with the earth[1] and particularly with its cultivation, who may be either masculine or feminine—according to local tradition. Bhūmiya is sometimes one of the consorts of the earth-goddess, and a shrine dedicated to him is erected on the site of a new village. He is believed to be a *brāhmaṇa* 'missionary' who introduced new agricultural methods and was subsequently deified.

Among his epithets are: Kṣetrapāla or Khera (Guardian of the mound on which the village stands); Śyāma (Black One); and Zamīndār (Landholder).[2]

[1]Cf. Pā. *bhummā*, the 'earthly ones', viz., the gods inhabiting the earth, especially tree-gods (*yakṣas* (Skt.), *yakkhas*, Pā.).

[2]Crooke, *Religion and Folklore of Northern India*, p. 93.

Bhūrrloka The earth and the lower regions. From the earth to the sun is the *bhuvar-loka* (atmospheric sphere) and from the sun to Dhruva (the Pole Star) is the *svar-loka* (the celestial region) (*VP.*, II. 7).

Bhūtabālagrahonmāda A form of madness which attacks children, said to be produced by *bhūtas*.

Bhūtabali Offerings to propitiate *bhūtas*, demons and other maleficent spirits. When an image of Viṣṇu is to be made, the *homa* ceremony is performed, and after the final oblation the *guru* or officiating priest offers the *bhūtabali* with these words: 'We have come here for the purpose of making an image of the god Viṣṇu, and we have undertaken the journey at the instance of the god Keśava. Anything done to please the god Viṣṇu, is also pleasant to you.[1] Therefore quietly and quickly depart ye spirits, quitting this place, being pleased with the sacrifice we have offered' (*AGP*., I.43.18–21).

[1]Viṣṇu/Kṛṣṇa may be equated with demons, etc., because Viṣṇu is immanent in all things; therefore no acts of any kind can affect him (*VP*., V. 26).

v. Bhūtavidyā; Bali I.

Bhūtamālā 'Garland of the elements' (*bhūta*). A name of Viṣṇu's garland, consisting of five rows of fragrant flowers or five rows of jewels, viz., pearl, ruby, emerald, sapphire, and diamond, representing the five elements (*VP*., I.22).

v. Bhūta(s) II.

Bhūtamātṛ 'Mother of Spirits.' Her festival was held during May–June when the crops were ripening, and was of the nature of an orgy. The women dressed as men and vice versa. Erotic songs were sung and much promiscuity took place.[1]

[1]Auboyer, *Daily Life in Ancient India*, p. 146.

v. Bhūta(s), I.

Bhūtanātha v. Bhūta(s) I.

Bhūtapati v. Rudra; Paśupati I.

Bhūtapūrṇimā The day of the full moon of the month *āśvina* when the *bhūtas* are worshipped.

Bhūta(s) I. Malignant spirits, goblins. One of the earliest references to *bhūtas* appears in the *ŚBr*. (VIII.4.2, 12), where the word means 'living beings' created by Prajāpati. But in post-Brāhmaṇa works (*Maitrī Up*., I.4) *bhūtas* are represented as 'ghosts, spirit-bands, goblins, serpent-spirits, vampires and the like'—not to be confused with *asuras* (demons), *yakṣas*[1] (sprites) and *rākṣasas* (ogres). According to the *VP*. (I.5), *bhūtas* are malignant fiends and eaters of flesh, created by Brahmā from himself.[2] *Manu* (III.90) refers to them as spirits that roam about by day and night and to which a *bali* offering should be made in the morning and evening as a propitiation.

Later the malevolent qualities of the *bhūtas* became assimilated with those of particular *pretas*, such as those who have met with violent deaths, or who have died without the performance of the correct funerary rites. The *bhūtas* then become increasingly malignant and incessantly plague those who omit to perform them. Like the so-called vampires and witches of medieval Europe the *bhūtas* were blamed for every domestic calamity, including acts of revenge by neighbours with a grudge, as well as events arising from unknown causes, such as contaminated wells, blighted crops, diseased live-stock, and the death of children through sickness. In the *Suś. Saṁ*. (II, p. 526) cutaneous diseases, chronic fever, epilepsy and insanity are said to be caused by them. Such diseases may prove fatal, and medicines and *mantras* are often of no avail (ibid., pp. 41 and 292).

Because the *bhūtas* cast no shadow, their presence is not always evident, so that it is necessary to burn turmeric frequently—a deterrent greatly feared by these malignant spirits. They haunt forests and desolate houses, and to avoid them it is necessary to lie prone on the ground, since *bhūtas* never rest on it, but hover above it at a height related to their status.[3] In early Buddhism a *bhūta* (Pā. *bhūtā*) is the guardian spirit of a city, but the word was also applied to ghosts, demons and *yakṣas*. In modern India they represent the spirits of the dead.[4]

Bhūtanātha (Lord of *bhūtas*) is the title given to the Buddhist Tantric deity, Vajrasattva or Hevajra, and it is also applied to Śiva in the Hindu Tantras.[5]

[1]Although according to Coomaraswamy these are often called *bhūtas*, he suggests that the name *bhūta* may mean 'those who have become *yakṣas*' (*Yakṣas*, pt. i, p. 5, n.2). For a full discussion of this word v. E. Arbman, *Rudra*, pp. 165ff.

[2]According to the *Padma P*. their mother was Krodhā.

[3]'On Demonology in Southern India', p. 99 (*Journal of the Anthropological Soc. of Bombay*, 1887).

[4]*Ancestor Worship*, p. 333.

[5]*ORC*., p. 195; *AGP*., I, p. 404.

v. Bhūtapūrṇimā; Bhūtavidyā; Bhūteśvara; Bhūtavināyas; Bhūtonmāda; Śrāddha; Bhūtabali.

II. An element.

v. Bhūtamālā.

Bhūtavidyā 'Knowledge of spirits', i.e., demonology. One of the eight branches of medicine dealing with maladies caused by demoniac possession.

v. Bhūta(s) I.

Bhūtavināyas Leaders of *bhūtas* and attendants of Rudra (*Bhāg. P*., VI.6,18, *PI*.).

Bhūteśvara 'Lord of *bhūtas*.' An epithet of Śiva, Viṣṇu, Brahmā, Kubera and Kṛṣṇa.

Śiva as Bhūteśvara haunts cremation grounds and is attended by troops of imps and *bhūtas*.

Bhūti I. 'Well-being', 'prosperity', 'good fortune'. A name of the goddess Lakṣmī personifying prosperity, etc. The gods, wishing to attain prosperity, were the first to render homage to Bhūti (*ŚBr*., VII.2.1,17). II. Superhuman powers attained by the practice of austerity (*tapas*) and thaumaturgy.

Bhūtonmāda Insanity produced by the influence of evil spirits.
v. Bhūta(s) I.

Bhuvaḥ v. Vyāhṛti(s).

Bhuvaneśvara 'Lord of the world.' A title of Śiva.

Bhuvaneśvarī 'Mistress of the world.' An epithet of many goddesses including the goddess ruling over creation. As ruler of the universe she is called Rājarājeśvarī (Queen of Queens), and she embodies the totality of the transcendent knowledge that sustains the world, 'fragments of which are revealed in the Vedas'.[1] Bhuvaneśvarī is the tutelary deity of Orissa.[2]

[1] Karapātrī, 'Śrī Bhagavatī tattva', *HP.*, p. 280.
[2] *TT.*, p. 334.
v. Mahāvidyā(s).

Bhuvarloka The region above the earth corresponding to the atmosphere, where dwell Munis, Siddhas, numerous spirits of the dead and superhuman beings.[1] It reaches upwards from the earth to the planetary sphere (*svarloka*) (*VP.*, II.7).

[1] *BH.*, p. 234.

Biḍāli The name of a particular disease and of the demoniacal spirit presiding over it.

Bilhaṇa (11th–12th cent.). The author of the *Caurapañcāśikā*, 'Fifty Stanzas of the Thief', describing the secret love of a burglar and a princess.

Bīja v. Mantra.

Bilva A tree (Aegle marmelos), commonly called Bel. It is sacred to Śiva and represents his vegetal form,[1] and thus is associated also with Śākta cults. Amulets are made from it, and also medicine from its unripe fruit. Its wood is never used for fuel from fear of arousing Śiva's wrath.[2]

The 'pledge of the Bel' is one of the most sacred oaths a Hindu can take.

[1] *AIA.*, I. p. 165.
[2] *VS.*, p. 112, and v. p. 203, n. 11.

Bodha 'Understanding', 'knowledge', personified as a son of Buddhi (Intellect), one of Dakṣa's daughters (*VP.*, I.7).

Brahmā The masculine form of '*brahman*' (neuter). Brahmā is represented as the Creator in late Vedic and subsequent works, but in the context of monistic speculation Brahmā appears to have been a theological intrusion, incompatible with the notion of an eternal, impersonal Universal Principle (brahman). This intrusion served a necessary purpose during the transition from the early Vedic personification of natural forces and phenomena to the concept of a personal, monotheistic ideal.

The Upaniṣad presentation of Brahmā as a mental image of the abstract *brahman* temporarily solved one problem of the monotheistic theory, but raised another, represented by the cults of Viṣṇu and Śiva, which necessitated further theological adjustment. This was accomplished by the introduction of a triad (*trimūrti*) in which Brahmā, Viṣṇu and Śiva constituted in one form the three aspects of *brahman*. But this too conflicted with the notion of an eternal universe of which continuity, not creativity, was the dominant characteristic, and thus Brahmā had to be given a new role. He became the equilibrium (*rajas*) between two opposing principles (the centripetal and centrifugal), represented by Viṣṇu and Śiva respectively,[1] the former representing preservation and renewal, the latter elimination or destruction.

The *paurāṇic* revival of ancient myths and legends, designed to reinterpret allegorically the early Vedic cosmogonic views, made use of one or another of the Creator-concepts, but they seldom succeed in advancing the philosophical notion of cosmic unity. This is indicated by the reference to ancient quasi-historical figures, or by interpreting ancient myths in the light of current post-Vedic ideas, but which, because of their inadequacy, were later modified.

In one of these myths Brahmā assumes an androgynous form, from which man and woman were created.[2] In another, Brahmā is called Nārāyaṇa because he arose from the primeval waters (*nārāḥ*) to set in motion the creative process. Other myths of a similar kind are related, in which the attributes of the earlier Creators, Puruṣa, Prajāpati and Hiraṇyagarbha are ascribed to Brahmā who is now conceived as the creative instrument of eternal *brahman*.

Many of the *paurāṇic* and Epic myths are undisguisedly sectarian. In one of these, of Vaiṣṇava origin, Bhṛgu is deputed to visit the three 'gods' of the *trimūrti* to ascertain which one of them was most worthy of worship. He found Brahmā 'too wrapped up in himself', and Śiva too engrossed with his wife Pārvatī. Viṣṇu alone proved to be worthy. The story of Dakṣa's sacrifice is the subject of another myth of Śaiva origin, obviously intended to indicate the struggle between the worshippers of Śiva and Viṣṇu, in which at first the latter, but finally the former, acquired the ascendancy.[3] But the theory of periodic creation or re-creation and the subsequent recognition of Śiva and Viṣṇu as the media for the mystical realization of *brahman*, made Brahmā philosophically irrelevant, and by the nineteenth century his cult had virtually ceased to exist, so that of all the temples of India, there remained only two dedicated solely to Brahmā.

[1] *HP.*, pp. 23f.
[2] Brahmā converted himself into two persons, the first male, Manu Svāyambhuva, and the first female,

Śatarūpā (*VP.*, I.7. n. 5). Cf. the Ardhanārī form of Śiva, and the androgynous Adam, from one of whose ribs Eve was formed (*Genesis*, II.21–2).

[3] *VP.*, p. 53, n.l.

v. Kalpa I; Brahmāṇī; Brahmapralaya; Brahmāstra; Brahmaśiras; Kratu I; Bhikṣāṭana; Brahmarandhra; Citragupta; Haṁsa; Jagannātha; Ahalyā; Ākāśa I; Brahmavidyā; Brahmāṇḍa I; Aṅgiras I; Nārada; Rākṣasa(s) I; Ṛbhu; Rudra; Sanatkumāra; Sandhyā; Vāstoṣpati I; Veda; Vedhasa; Kumāra(s); Brahmaloka; Brahmarekha I; Brahmacakra; Brahmadaṇḍa; Svayambhū I; Madhu II.

Brahmacakra 'Brahmā's wheel', i.e., the universe; the name of a particular magic circle.

Brahmacārin A religious student or pupil, whose education began after a ceremony (*upanayana*), regarded as an initiation into a new spiritual life, entailing a rigorous discipline for a prescribed period, during which he was required to live as a student in the house of his teacher (*guru*). His daily routine included begging for alms, tending the sacrificial fires, household duties, and practising austerities in addition to his studies. Chastity was a most solemn obligation.

This 'religious living' is one of four *aśramas* or stages of the life of a Hindu, the others being *gṛhasthya*, the stage of the married householder, including procreation, performance of prescribed daily sacrifices, and the responsibility of living in a community; *vānaprasthya*, the stage when the householder gives up his duties and retires to the forest to practise meditation, *tapas*, etc., preparatory to the complete renunciation of all worldly goods; and *saṁnyāsa* 'renunciation', when all possessions are given up except for a loin-cloth, water-pot and begging bowl. He must subsist on the food given him on his begging-round, and he is free from all worldly duties, obligations and observances, and by deep meditation he acquires a calm tranquil spirit.

Though some form of studentship must have existed in priestly families from early Vedic times, systematic education of the *brahmacārin* seems not to have been given prominence until the period of the Upaniṣads.[1] Their liberal attitude towards education, like their rejection of priestly fundamentalism, is indicated in several Upaniṣads which clearly show that education should not be regarded as a priestly prerogative, but be available to all.

[1] In an obscure hymn of the *AV.*, XI.5.1, great powers are ascribed to the *brahmacārin*.

v. Vidyā; Gṛhya-sūtras; Vedāṅga(s); Lokāyata(s); Janaka II.

Brahmadaṇḍa I. 'Brahmā's staff', his mythical weapon. II. The curse of a *brāhmaṇa*.

Brahmagāyatrī A magical *mantra* modelled on the *gāyatrī*.

Brahmagupta (7th cent.) A mathematician and astronomer of Ujjain. He was able 'to solve indeterminate equations of the second degree, and initiated a period of constant progress in mathematics which culminated in the work of the ninth-century Jaina master, Mahāvīra of Mysore, the *Gaṇitasāraṇagraha* ('Brief Explanation of the Compendium of Calculation').'[1]

Brahmagupta estimated the size of the circumference of the earth as 5,000 yojanas. Assuming his 'yojana to be the short league of about four and a half miles, this figure is not far out, and is as accurate as any given by ancient astronomers'.[2] Furthermore, he correctly defined zero.

[1] Filliozat, in *Ancient and Medieval Science*, p. 152.

[2] *WI.*, App. I., p. 488.

Brahmaloka or **Satyaloka** The eternal Brahmā-world or world of Truth (*satya*), consisting of infinite wisdom. It is the highest of the worlds. No distinctions exist in it and it is always light (*Chān. Up.*, 8.4.2; *Bṛhad-Ār. Up.*, 4.3.33).

Those persons possessing true knowledge metaphorically cross the river Vijarā (Ageless), and are cleansed of their good and bad deeds, illnesses and other defects, and never return to the world, because they are beyond rebirth (*Bṛhad-Ār. Up.*, 6.2,15).

Brahman (neuter) 'All-pervading, self-existent power'. From *bṛh*, lit. 'growth or development'. Though the masculine form 'Brahman', denoting a priest, occurs in the *RV.* neither the neuter form nor the masculine 'Brahmā' appear.[1] In later literature *brahman* is equated with cosmic unity, a notion rooted in the age-old problem of man's relation to his immediate, and subsequently to his supramundane environment.

The notion of cosmic unity was developed during two fairly distinct periods, the first mainly represented by the interpretation of '*brahman*' in the Upaniṣads, the second by the formulation of the notion by the Vedāntins. The first period begins with early Vedic symbolic representation, in which the imperfectly understood forces of nature are personified, and whose immense powers can only be influenced by an equally powerful magic.[2] When this power was exercised by the officiating priest the propitious powers of the *devas*[3] were strengthened and the unpropitious weakened or destroyed. But occasionally a Vedic seer, like Dīrghatamas, penetrates the veil of materialistic aspirations and sees the collective powers of nature as a single sovereign power. 'To what is One, sages give many a title' (*RV.*, I.164,46); or according to another seer: 'that One wherein abide all things existing' (X.82,6).

Brahman

Generally the early Vedic seers were concerned only with a pantheistic notion of the phenomenal world, regarding it as the work of a specific Creator or of 'secondary' Creators. The notion of *brahman* as a cosmic principle is a later development. It is traceable in the Brāhmaṇas, and to particular passages of the *Atharvaveda.*[4] 'But various passages in different Brāhmaṇas contain so many assertions about *brahman* of a somewhat conflicting nature that it is very difficult to form a definite idea about it'.[5] In the earlier Upaniṣads the expression *ekamevādvitīyam* is introduced to denote an impersonal, eternal, self-existent unifying principle. This notion is supported by such comprehensive 'expressions as *sarvaṁ khalvidaṁ brahma* (all this really is *brahman*), *tajjalan* ("in it everything is born, everything exists, and everything is absorbed")'.[6] *Brahman* 'is invisible, ungraspable, eternal, without qualities; it is the imperishable source of all things' (*Muṇḍ. Up.*, I.1,6–7). It is the 'falling-together' and hence unification of all opposites. But in many passages of the Upaniṣads the notion of *brahman* is obscured by the traditional views of Creation and Creator. The re-naming of the creative instrument as Brahmā, so as to associate it with *brahman*, left the problem of cosmic unity no nearer to a solution than when the Creator was called Puruṣa or Prajāpati. Some passages reflect other traditional views, such as those declaring that 'One should worship It as magical formula (*brahman*)', or that 'by It one becomes possessed of magic formula' (*Tait. Up.*, III.10,4–5). The *Chān. Up.* (I.7,1, etc.) declares that *brahman* denotes prayer which sometimes also implies a form of magical power. R. E. Hume[7] suggests that, despite their insight, the *aupaniṣadic* visionaries failed to grasp fully the stupendous notion of *brahman* as all-pervading power; and that because of their persistence in figurative thinking, they still clung to old cosmologies which the *brahman* theory itself was intended to transcend.

In the second phase the idea of cosmic unity is subject to theological influences, represented by the variant views of the Vaiṣṇava, Śaiva and Śākta sects, as well as by *Paurāṇic* and Epic re-interpretation of ancient Vedic myths, which were represented in the form of allegory, fable and pseudo-historical legend. Despite these influences, the notion of *brahman* became firmly established among the Vedāntins and began profoundly to affect popular religious beliefs. Nonetheless, despite the incompatibility of the theory of a creative Brahmā and that of the uncreated and eternal *brahman*, the traditional belief in a creative instrument persisted. The problem was temporarily solved by the doctrine of the *trimūrti* (the Three-in-One), which presents Brahmā, Viṣṇu and Śiva as three aspects of *brahman*. But this theological expedient represents only the monotheistic manifestation of *brahman*, little different from that of Prajāpati and other Creators. The problem is philosophical rather than theological, and was only solved by the recognition of Viṣṇu and Śiva as the instruments of renewal and destruction, the two chief characteristics of cosmic continuity.

As the notion of unity gradually permeated Hindu religious life, so with the theory of *ātman-paramātman* the notion of *brahman* became less of an abstraction. Viṣṇu and Śiva also lose their theistic differentiation in the title Īśvara, the Lord of all Being. A further contribution to the monistic theory was the notion of zero, introduced by Indian mathematicians in the fourth century A.D., which was 'conceived as a symbol of *brahman* and *nirvāṇam* ... [as] the unifying point of indifference and the matrix of the All and the None'.[8] The ancient realistic view of life was no longer regarded as valid. Zero represented the reconciliation of opposites, of plus and minus, of light and darkness, of opposite moral values, of all dualistic concepts, a notion which by means of yogic techniques was of great therapeutic value in resolving psychological problems. Zero also confirmed the use of the expression 'as if', or 'as it were' (*iva*) in the *Bṛhad-Ār. Up.* (II.4,14), which declares that it is only 'as if' there were any duality (*dvaitam iva*). Deussen considers that 'the unknown is only "as it were" (*iva*) unknown ... only "as it were" ... a plurality'.[9]

This view is summed up in the closing passage of *Manu* (XII.123,125), in the statement: 'Some call him Agni, others Manu, others the Vital Breath, and again others eternal *brahman* ... He who thus recognizes the Self (*ātman*) in all created beings, [shares the harmonious relationship of all Being], and enters the highest state, *brahman*'.

[1] But Sāyaṇa interprets some *RV.* passages as allusions to Brahmā.

[2] Most early religious cults indicate a belief in magical power, a belief originating in the use of intoxicants and hallucinogenic drugs, in the practice of extreme asceticism (*tapas*), or in the utterance of *mantras* and the performance of sacrificial rites. On the other hand, yogic techniques have often proved to be a source of extra-sensory perception and of increased mental powers.

[3] Both Devas and Asuras were originally regarded as being sometimes beneficent and sometimes maleficent.

[4] The *AV.* references to *brahman* sometimes imply the possession of magical power.

[5] *PTR.*, p.6.

[6] Ibid.

[7] *TPU.*, p. 15.

[8]*Facets*, p. 24.
[9]*Religion and Philosophy of India*, p. 158.
Cf. Vaihinger, *The Philosophy of 'As If'*; and the Jaina doctrine of *syādvāda*, i.e., that ordinary judgment is valid only of a particular aspect of an object, and hence is relative.
v. Skambha; Om; Ātman; Nirvāṇa.

Brahman[1] or **Brāhman**[2] (masc.) 'A man belonging to the first of the three twice-born classes and of the four original divisions of the Hindu body (generally a priest, but often . . . a layman engaged in non-priestly occupations, although the name is strictly applicable to one who knows and repeats the Veda.'[3] An alternative designation (*brahman*)[4] generally denotes a descendant of a priestly family or of a member of the superior class.

But as Vedic sacrificial ritual expanded it became necessary to have an organized body of priestly officiants consisting of sixteen members, called the *ṛtvij*, each of whom was designated and individually responsible for a particular sacrificial role, the superviser being called the *Brāhman* or *Brahman*.

With the rise of the Vaiṣṇava and Śaiva cults, Vedic ritual and the need for the *ṛtvij* became an anachronism, and thus the precise role of priestly officiants a merely academic question, especially after the passing of the Indian Act of Independence.

[1]The transliteration of Macdonell and Keith, *VI.*, vol. I, pp. 112ff.
[2]*SED.*, p. 741.
[3]Ibid.
[4]Ibid.
v. Brāhmaṇa I; Varṇa; Yajñopavīta.

Brāhmaṇa I. In the *RV.* it is the collective designation of priests, though one passage (I.15,5)[1] appears to denote an individual priest, irrespective of his function in the performance of the sacrifice, i.e., as Brahman, Hotṛ and Adhvaryu (X.88,19). In subsequent texts, *brāhmaṇa* denotes a member or descendant of a priestly family. In the *RV.* there is no evidence of a claim to superiority by the *brāhmaṇa*. This is indicated by the fact that in early Vedic times any member of the Āryan tribes, if competent, could become a priest, or be eligible for election as chief of the clan or tribe.

On the other hand, the later Saṁhitās, and the Brāhmaṇas and Sūtras all reflect social, political and economic changes, and indicate the establishment of a class system, in which the priests were dominant. They claimed also to be the repository of sacred knowledge, and alone privileged to perform sacrifices, a prerogative formerly shared with the *kṣatra* (the noble and warrior class). The *ŚBr.* describes in great detail the status of the priestly class and its relation to secular authority (*rājanya*), and to the commonalty (*viś*). Whilst acknowledging the rights of the ruler *brāhmaṇas* claimed exemption from particular statutes of Civil Law. This claim was based on the assertion that the *brāhmaṇas* were the earthly counterparts of the gods, and when descended from a *ṛṣi* they claimed to represent all the deities (XII.4.4,6). Their prerogatives are enumerated (XI.5.7,1 *et seq.*), particularly those referring to the honour (*arcā*) and gifts (*dakṣiṇā*) due to them. They should not be subject to oppression (*ajyeyatā*) or to the death penalty (*avadhyatā*), even when guilty of a capital crime.[2] In addition to these privileges, only the priests may partake of the sacrificial *soma*, and eat the remains (*ucchiṣṭa*) of the sacrifice, no one else being regarded as sufficiently holy to consume food of which the gods have partaken.[3] The priest's wife and cow were also sacred. The priest's sacerdotal status gave him the opportunity of becoming a *purohita* or adviser to a chieftain or king, originally a modest preferment, but in later times a position of great influence, combining the posts of Chancellor or Prime Minister and chief adviser to the ruler.[4]

In a hymn extolling the *brāhmaṇa*, he is said to be the essence (*tattva*) of the sacrifice (*AV.*, XIX.42,2), and his anger to be more dangerous than a venomous serpent, or a weapon (*Matsya P.*, 30, 23–5, 30, *PI.*).

Although the *brāhmaṇas* had privileges they also had obligations. Without them the tedious task of orally transmitting the Saṁhitās and other texts could not have been undertaken; nor without their erudition would it have been possible for them to Sanskritize Vedic dialects and provide the medium for the secular and religious literature of the post-Vedic era.

The *brāhmana* was thus required to be proficient in sacred knowledge, which implied that he must be of priestly descent (*brāhmaṇya*); that his deportment should at all times befit his vocation; that he should be diligent in his task of teaching and improving the people; he should always be kind and gentle and an example to all; be ever ready to officiate at the sacrifice, though not without expectation of the customary gift (*dakṣiṇā*) (*ŚBr.*, XIII.1.5,6). Though entitled to the best of food and entertainment, such attention applied only to the true *brāhmaṇa* and not to the unworthy.[5]

With the establishment of large kingdoms and a more complex economy, many of the descendants of the Vedic priestly families were unable or unwilling to become priests, and instead took up secular occupations. In modern times these descendants form a class generally referred to as *brahmins*, thus distinguishing them from priests. Owing to the many cultural changes, social and political, as well as religious that have occurred in the life of the Indian people, the power and influence of the priests have gradually declined, so that they have become merely the custodians of the temple and the officiants of domestic ceremonies.

[1]Priestesses were unknown in Vedic ritual; in certain circumstances a wife might be deputed to perform a sacrifice for her husband, but in one text the gods are said to 'despise the offering of a woman' (Hillebrandt, *Ritualliteratur*, p. 70).

[2]Cf. the quarrel of Henry II and Thomas à Becket over the non-liability of his monks to punishment under Civil Law for the many murders committed by them during the king's reign. The worst penalty that could be imposed on *brāhmaṇas* was 'the humiliation of losing their topknot, followed by confiscation of property and banishment' (*WI.*, p. 120).

[3]*VI.*, vol. II. p. 83. It is said that nothing can injure the stomachs of *brāhmaṇas* (*Ancestor Worship*, p. 194).

[4]Kauṭilya, Purohita to the Mauryan Emperor Candragupta, was not only an eminent statesman, but also the reputed author of a classic work on statecraft.

[5]Cf. *Manu*, XII.71, which states that a *brāhmaṇa* who fails in his sacred duty shall be reborn an Ulkāmukha (demonic spirit) whose only food is vomit.

Originally *brāhmaṇa* meant '"one possessed of *brahman*", a mysterious magical force of the type widely known to modern anthropologists by the Polynesian word *mana*' (*WI.*, p. 139).

v. Brāhmaṇa II; Agastya; Ṛtvij.

II. The name of priestly compositions severally appended over a long period to each of the four Vedas.[1] Initially they consisted of manuals of simple rites, which subsequently became elaborated. This elaboration demanded 'the intellectual activity of a sacerdotal caste which ... succeeded in transforming a primitive worship of the powers of nature into a highly artificial system of sacrificial ceremonies ... [by a priestly class which simultaneously deepened and extended] its hold on the minds of the people, by surrounding its own vocation with the halo of sanctity and divine inspiration'.[2]

The quality of the Brāhmaṇas varies, as does their relevance to the particular Veda to which they are appended. Thus the *Gopatha Br.*, attached to the *AV.*, is really a Vedāṅga, and was only added when the *Atharvaveda* received canonical acceptance, probably to conform to the current convention that each Veda should have at least one Brāhmaṅa.

In contrast to the *Gopatha* is the massive *Śatapatha Br.*, attached to the White Yajus (*Vājasaneyi-Saṁ.*) of the *YV.* Besides a great deal of interesting but extraneous information, it presents systematically the ritual of the general sacrifice, as distinct from that of the earlier *soma*. The ritual of the Black Yajus, which is almost identical with that of the White Yajus, is preserved in the *Taittirīya Saṁ.*, their only difference being in the method of presentation. *Taittirīya* and *Śatapatha Brāhmaṇas* present the views of a number of priestly schools, and together with the *Aitareya Br.*, attached to the *RV.*, and the three principal Brāhmaṇas of the *Sāmaveda*, form a corpus of ritual and dogma from which was derived a degree of priestly authority and influence hitherto unparalleled in the religious life of India.

Some passages in the Brāhmaṇas are full of genuine thought and feeling, and are the chief source of information of one of the most important periods of social and intellectual development of India. But these works—'for wearisome prolixity of exposition, characterised by dogmatic assertion and a flimsy symbolism rather than by serious reasoning ... are perhaps not equalled anywhere.'[3] Nonetheless, the ultra-conservative tradition gave a stimulus to the esoteric coteries and the appearance of the Āraṇyakas and Upaniṣads, and provided the basis of modern Hinduism.

[1]*CHI.*, I, p. 149 suggests 800–600 B.C. as a reasonable date for the Brāhmaṇa period.

[2]Eggeling, *ŚBr.*, I, Intro., p. ix.

[3]Ibid.

v. Ṛtvij.

Brahmaṇaspati The deity of prayer (or possibly of the text of the Veda). But Wilson considers that this definition, though etymologically acceptable, does not justify the assumption that Brahmaṇaspati 'is to be considered as a distinct personification, or as a modified form of one of those already recognized'.[1] Neither Brahmaṇaspati nor Bṛhaspati differ functionally from Indra, Soma and other gods, with whom they are collectively invoked to give protection and to grant prosperity (*RV.*, I.18,5, etc.). When Brahmaṇaspati[2] is especially invoked, it is perhaps because his priestly suppliants believed that their prayers would be more efficacious, and divine bounties more abundant, if addressed to the 'lord of prayer' (I.18,2–3), especially as he is said to have become 'omnipotent through prayer' (II.24,15). According to (X.72,2)[3] he produced the gods 'with blast and smelting, like a smith'.

In the Brāhmaṇas Brahmaṇaspati's role as the lord of prayer is confirmed, and in the elaborate building of the fire-altar he is described as the creator of the priestly order (*brāhmaṇa*), and as Prajāpati (*ŚBr.*, VIII.4.3,3–4).

In the Upaniṣads his name is etymologically defined and given a mystical significance. 'Speech is also Brahmaṇaspati. Prayer (*brahman*) verily is speech. He is her lord (*pati*), and is therefore Brahmaṇaspati' (*Bṛhad-Ār. Up.*, I.3.21).

Brahmaṇaspati, like Bṛhaspati, is identified with sacrifice and priestly invocation, and is regarded as the special intermediary—not of the gods and the people—but of the gods and the priests.

[1]Cited by Griffith, *RV.*, I, p. 21n. The *Nir.* (10.12) states that Brahmaṇaspati is the protector or supporter of Brahmā.

[2]Banerjea, following Sāyaṇa, states that the Vedic Gaṇapati 'denoted Brahmaṇaspati; in this context he was the leader of the groups of the Devas and similar other beings belonging to his own order' (*DHI.*, App., A. p. 575; v. also *RV.*, II.23,1).

[3]Cf. *Śvet. Up.*, 3.3.

Brahmāṇḍa I. 'Brahmā's egg', i.e., the universe believed to be divided into twenty-one regions of which the earth was seventh from the top. There were six heavens above the earth, and seven stages of Pātāla under the earth. Below Pātāla lay Naraka, a kind of purgatory also divided into seven zones of increasing severity. The whole universe was thought to hang in space isolated from other universes.

II. The name of a Purāṇa and an Upapurāṇa.

Brahmāṇī or **Brāhmī** A non-Vedic goddess[1] and the *śakti* of Brahmā. She is also called Śatarūpā and Sāvitrī. According to the *Matsya* and *Śiva Purs.* she is Brahmā's daughter, and from their incestuous union the first Manu (Svāyambhuva) was born. Brahmāṇī is regarded as one of the eight divine mothers (*mātṛkās*).

[1]*CC.*, p. 446.

Brahmapāśa 'Brahmā's noose.' A mythical weapon.

Brahmapralaya Brahmā's periodic act of destruction. This universal destruction (*pralaya*) occurs at the end of every hundred years of Brahmā's life, in which he too is engulfed.

v. Yuga.

Brahma-Purāṇa v. Purāṇa(s).

Brahmarākṣasa A demoniac spirit. A *brāhmaṇa* who has associated with outcastes, seduced other men's wives, or stolen the property of other *brāhmaṇas* will at death become a Brahmarākṣasa (*Manu*, XII.60).

According to the *Bhāg.* and *Brah. Purs.* it is the name of a class of demons,[1] who usually dwell in *śleṣmātaka* trees.

[1]Or they may have been *rākṣasas*, i.e., non-Āryan tribes who had adopted Brahmanism (*IRA.*, p. 43).

v. Ulkāmukha.

Brahmarandhra 'Brahmā's crevice.' An aperture in the crown of the head[1] through which the spirit escapes at death. Only the spirits of the good leave the body in this way, those of evil men take a downward course and are expelled 'in the same manner as the excreta'.[2] But according to another myth, if the spirit escapes through the feet it goes to Viṣṇu; if from the crown of the head, to Brahmā, and if through the eyes, to Agni (*MBh.*, 12.302,20f.; 314, 1f.; 318, 1f., *EM.*).

[1]Or behind the forehead (*HP.*, p. 255). Cf. the Tibetan Buddhist death-rites connected with this aperture.

[2]*BH.*, p. 291.

Brahmarekha 'Brahmā's line.' Brahmā is said to write a child's destiny on its forehead on the sixth day after birth. To do this he uses the *brahmatandram* (an oval bead-rimmed disc).

Brahmarṣi(s) v. *Ṛṣi*(s).

Brahmasaras 'Brahmā's lake.' The name of a bathing place (*tīrtha*) sacred to the *pitṛs*. By passing one night here, one attains to the region of Brahmā. Brahmā placed a sacrificial pillar in this lake and a believer who circumambulates it achieves the merit accruing to the performance of the *Vājapeya* sacrifice (*MBh.*, II. Vana pa., 84). This lake is the source of all rivers, and in ancient times Brahmā himself dwelt on its banks. Mahādeva (Śiva) is ever-present there (ibid., 95).

Brahmaśiras Another name for Śiva's favourite weapon, the spear *pāśupata*, with which he killed the *daityas* and with which he will destroy the universe at the end of the age.[1]

[1]*HP.*, p. 217.

Brahmāstra 'Brahmā's missile.' A magical weapon that never fails to destroy the enemy, and which returns to the hand of the thrower. Crooke suggests that it was some kind of boomerang similar to the weapons used today by the Maravar and Kallar tribes.[1]

[1]*Things Indian*, p. 26. It may not refer to a real weapon, as all kinds of weapons (of a magical nature) are said to return to the thrower when the correct *mantras* are uttered. Arjuna had to learn the correct *mantras* as well as the rites of expiation and revival when he received the *brahmaśiras* (*MBh.*, Vana pa., 91).

Brahma-Sūtra Also called *Vedānta-Sūtra.* It comprises the collected sūtras of Bādarāyaṇa, and as it refers to almost all the other Indian systems (*darśanas*), its date cannot be early,[1] but may be, as Jacobi suggests, between A.D. 200 and A.D. 450.[2]

The *Brahma-Sūtra*, while expressing Bādarāyaṇa's own views, is specifically a summary of attempts by earlier expositors of the teaching of the Upaniṣads. Bādarāyaṇa thus presents *dvaita* Vedānta rather than the purely monistic (*advaita*) doctrine of the early Upaniṣads.

The *Brahma-Sūtra* comprises four chapters (*adhyāyas*), each divided into four parts (*pādas*), subdivided into sections (*adhikaraṇas*) made up of *sūtras* or aphoristic statements, each subject being fully discussed, the accompanying commentary presenting a reasoned statement of objections and the answers to them.

[1]Radhakrishnan, *Brahma-Sūtra*, p. 22, dates it about the second century B.C.

[2]*JAOS.*, XXXI, p. 29.

v. Śaṅkara: Vedānta; Brahman (neuter).

Brahmavaivarta Purāṇa v. Purāṇa(s).

Brahmavarta The land between the two divine rivers Sarasvatī and Dṛṣadvatī (*Manu*, II.17).

Brahmavidyā I. The basic or essential knowledge (*vidyā*) which Brahmā gave to his eldest son Atharvan, who taught it to Aṅgir. It was then passed down successively to Bhāradvāja Satyavāha and Aṅgiras (*Muṇḍ. Up.*, 1.1,2). It should only be imparted to a son or worthy pupil (*Chān. Up.*, 3.11,5); by means of it one is liberated from rebirth (*Śvet. Up.*, I.7). Brahmavidyā is personified as the goddess Umā who helped to dispel Indra's ignorance (*Kena Up.*, 3.25).

v. Atharvan.

II. Name of *mantras* presided over by Brahmā (*AGP.*, II. p. 1210).

Brāhmī I. v. Brahmāṇī.

II. v. Sanskrit.

Brahmodya Theological questions or riddles. In part of the *aśvamedha* (horse sacrifice) rites some of the priests 'propound to each other ... riddles on cosmogonic, cosmologic, metaphysical and ritualistic subjects, a well-known device to penetrate the mysteries of the unknown ... and liberate power and to get a hold on the potencies which are the subject of the riddles'.[1]

[1]*VS.*, p. 32.

Bṛhad-Āraṇyaka Upaniṣad v. Upaniṣad(s).

Bṛhad-devatā An index of the Vedic gods, more extensive than any of the other Anukramaṇīs. It is divided into eight *adhyāyas* corresponding to the early arrangement of the *RV.* It related each verse to a particular deity, illustrated by reference to a large number of stories and myths, which furnished the composers of the Epics and Purāṇas with material for further embellishment.

'Though *ślokas* have undoubtedly been added here and there and some modifications of diction have probably crept in, the authenticity of the text as a whole is better guaranteed than that of perhaps any other ancillary Vedic work.'[1] Tradition attributes it to Śaunaka, the author of some short Anukramaṇīs, but from references in the work itself (VII.38), the author was not Śaunaka himself, 'but a near contemporary teacher of his school'.[2] From internal and other evidence the date of the work can be fixed at between 500 and 400 B.C., which would place it between the composition of Yāska's *Nirukta* and that of the *Sarvānukramaṇī*, attributed to one of the several authors called Kātyāyana.

[1]Macdonell, *Bṛhad-devatā*, vol. I, Intro., p. xxiii.

[2]Ibid., p. xxiv.

Bṛhaspati 'Lord of Prayer.' From *bṛh*, prayer, and *pati*, lord. A Vedic god, also called Brahmaṇaspati, the celestial priest or *purohita* of the gods.[1] Unlike most Vedic deities, who personify only the forces and phenomena of nature Bṛhaspati represents moral ideas, or is regarded as the divine *brāhmaṇa* who sanctifies the sacrificial rites of his earthly counterpart. He gains and holds for the gods 'the magical powers obtained by the sacrifice',[2] and ensures the benefits which are expected by the officiants of the sacrifice. In this connexion Bṛhaspati is traditionally associated with the Āṅgirasas, one of the principal Vedic priestly families. This may account for the reference to Bṛhaspati as the son of Aṅgiras (*RV.*, VI.73,1), the ancient fire-priest, which suggests that Bṛhaspati was a deified mythical *ṛṣi*. The link with Aṅgiras may also account for the close association of Bṛhaspati and Brahmaṇaspati with Agni, the god of fire and lord of prayer (*RV.*, I.38,13). Thus the similarity of their role as mediators and as *purohitas* of the gods, lends plausibility to Müller's suggestion that these two minor *devas* are 'varieties of Agni'.[3] Edgerton stresses that both Bṛhaspati and Brahmaṇaspati are purely ritualistic deities in the older *RV.* hymns. Later they function as demiurges or epithets of them.[4]

But the activities and functions of Bṛhaspati are not limited to those referred to above. He, like other Vedic gods, was subject to the henotheistic shifts of status and function, possibly representing the different views of priestly families or coteries, or reflecting changes in popular religious beliefs. Eggeling points out that shadowy conceptions of celestial priests like Bṛhaspati could evoke no feelings of sympathy in the hearts of the people generally whereas Agni, the genial guest of every household, is indeed Vaiśvānara, the friend of all.[5]

Some of the hymns addressed to Bṛhaspati are pleas for help in the recovery of stolen cattle (*RV.*, X.68,7); for the rescue of persons in distress, like Trita who was immured in a well (*RV.*, I.105,17); or to grant increase of herds and an abundance of food, etc. Others have a moral significance. Thus in II.23, Bṛhaspati is besought to drive away all evil-minded, arrogant and rapacious persons, who without cause threaten the god's devotees. He is the protector who loves them; the averter of 'sin'; who burns up demons with his fierce-flaming brand; and is the upholder of mighty Law. But in one hymn, VI.73,3, Bṛhaspati is described as striving to win the waters (rain) and light, and with lightning to smite the foe (the drought-demon), such activities being generally associated with Indra.

In the Brāhmaṇas Bṛhaspati remains connected with Vedic sacrificial ritual, but gradually its significance and that of the gods associated with it was changed by *aupaniṣadic* views, so that the name of Bṛhaspati as the lord of prayer, seldom appears in subsequent compositions. But in the *VP.* (IV.6) Bṛhaspati is introduced for the purpose of explaining the origin of the planet Mercury and the birth of Budha, later adopted as one of the mythical progenitors of the Lunar dynasty (Candravaṁśa).

The attribution of *RV.*, X.71 to Bṛhaspati, and the following hymn to him and Aditi, are considered by Rahurkar to be a fictitious tradition.[6] Similarly the reference to Bṛhaspati as the father of Bharadvāja, a celebrated *ṛṣi*, is a synchronism of two widely separated periods in which the name occurs.

Among Bṛhaspati's many epithets are: Sadasaspati (Lord of Assemblies); Jyeṣṭharāja (King of Elders); Gaṇapati (Lord of Hosts—this is also an epithet of Gaṇeśa); Vajrin (Wielder of the Thunderbolt); Dhiṣaṇa (the Intelligent).

[1] *Ait. Br.*, III. 17. With Bṛhaspati as *purohita* the gods conquered heaven and the world, as does the sacrificer who has Bṛhaspati as *purohita* (ibid).

[2] *EM.*, p. 65.

[3] Cited by Griffith, *RV.*, I, p. 55, n. 14.

[4] *BIP.*, p. 20, n.l.

[5] *ŚBr.*, I, Intro., p. xvi n.

[6] *Seers*, p. 256.

v. Śukra I; Kaca; Bṛhatī III; Utathya; Tārā I.

Bṛhaspatisava A festival celebrating the accession of a *brāhmaṇa* to high office, particularly that of *purohita*. The festival follows a preliminary ceremony, the *Vājapeya*, performed by a priest seeking promotion (or by a king seeking greater power).

The *bṛhaspatisava* is the priestly counterpart of the *rājasūya*, or consecration of a king, though the *ŚBr.* (V. 15,2–3), as a defender of priestly superiority, regards the *rājasūya* as of less importance. During the *bṛhaspatisava* ceremony the priest mounts a cart-wheel (representing the sun) set up on a post acting as an axle. The wheel is revolved thrice in a sunwise motion (*Tait. Saṁ.*, I.7.3), while the priest chants a *sāman* to Savitṛ.

Bṛhatī I. The name of a particular metre of thirty-six syllables, and later applied to any metre containing this number of syllables. By means of the *bṛhatī* the gods gained heaven (*ŚBr.*, XII.2.3,1).

v. Virāj II; Gāyatrī.

II. The name of one of the seven horses of the sun's chariot which, like the names of the others, is equated with a particular metre of the Vedas (*VP.*, II.8).

III. The name of Bṛhaspati's wife who is also called Dhenā and Vāṇī (*Gopatha Br.*, 2.9; *HP.*, p. 325).

Bṛhat-kathā 'Great Story.' A large series of popular stories in various recensions. It consists of an interconnected sequence of stories, a common literary device. A well-known version in the West is the *Kathā-sarit-sāgara*.

Bṛhat-Saṁhitā v. Varāhamihira.

Buddha 'Enlightened', 'awakened'. It is not, as often transliterated, a proper name, but a title or honorific applied to 'a wise or learned man, a sage . . . a fully enlightened man who has achieved perfect knowledge of the truth'.[1] It was thus applied to the sage of the Śākyas (Śākyamuni), who became the Buddha when he attained enlightenment.

[1] *SED.*

v. Buddhism; Avatāra(s).

Buddhism Bauddha is the Sanskrit term, from *buddhi*, 'relating to intellect or understanding', and hence 'relating or belonging to the Buddha or to Buddhism.' A 'school' of Indian speculative thought founded by Siddhārtha (6th cent. B.C.) which developed into a monastic order (*saṅgha*). Siddhārtha (also called Gotama) was the son of Śuddhodana, a member of the Gotama clan and a chieftain of the Śākya tribe, whose lands were part of the Gorakhpur district, and extended from the lower Nepalese mountains to the river Raptī in Oudh. Siddhārtha was born 'at Kapilavastu (now Bhūila)—a town situated about half-way between Bastī and Ajūdhyā (Ayodhyā) in the territory of Kosala (the modern Oudh), about sixty miles from its capital city Śrāvasti'[1] (a favourite abode of Gotama).

Buddhism is one of the three heterodox (*nāstika*) *darśanas*, but shares with the 'orthodox' (*āstika*) Sāṁkhya school the distinction of being the most philosophically developed of the early Indian *darśanas*. Like the Sāṁkhya (and Jainism), Buddhism originated in a region where social, religious and political conditions had been only slightly influenced by Vedic traditions. Thus Buddhism, while rejecting brahmanic fundamentalism, later formed part of Indian religious development. In this sense Buddhism is merely a convenient name for the conclusions reached by its founder under the famous *bodhi* tree, the culmination of his experience among Sāṁkhya and other itinerant ascetics. The substance of his conclusions is contained in his first discourse, which he expounded in detail during the next forty years. Subsequently, his conclusions were variously interpreted and expounded by separate Buddhist groups, ambiguously designated Hīnayāna and Mahāyāna, which finally split into a number of distinct schools. But initially the Order consisted of small, scattered communities of monks, subject to simple disciplinary rules. Though their influence initially may have been slight, it grew rapidly and under the patronage of the Emperor Aśoka (273–232 B.C.), spread throughout India and beyond. In the course of its development additional splinter groups emerged from the original body of elders (*theras*), one of which was later called Theravāda. These splinter groups also became subdivided, each holding views varying in degree from their particular parent body. The principal groups initially were the Sarvāstivādins who were granted lands in Kāṣmir and in Gandhāra and in other parts of the north-west frontier region of India; the Mahāsaṅghikas in Āndhra; the Theravādins, led by Mahendra, Aśoka's son, in Ceylon. That the Buddhist Order flourished is attested by the great *stūpas* (relic and cult monuments) at Sāñcī, Amarāvatī and by other architectural remains in India, and at Anurādhapūra and elsewhere in Ceylon, as well as in Further India.

Another contributing factor to the success of early Buddhism was its use of local dialects (*prakṛts*), especially by the Theravādins in the *suttas* (*sūtras*) of the Pāli Canon. By the end of the first millennium B.C., Mahāsaṅghika views led to the gradual formation of the Mahāyāna (Great Vehicle), so-called to distinguish it from the Theravāda or Hīnayāna (Little Vehicle), now more appropriately designated the Northern and Southern schools.

Buddhist tradition divides its development into three phases called the 'three Turnings of the Wheel of the Law', a metaphor probably based on the ancient myth of the sun's chariot that regularly wheels across the heavens. The three phases are defined as: 1. The Pluralist-Realist view of the early Buddhist Schools. 2. The Critical-Sceptic-Monist view of the Mādhyamika. 3. The Idealistic-Monistic view of the Yogācāra-Vijñanavāda.

The system of logic of the first phase was of the conventional type, common to all Indian schools of the period. The second phase is dominated by the Mādhyamika School, whose leader Nāgārjuna introduced a dialectic by which the validity of all propositions was to be tested, which made it essentially a 'Critique of Pure Reason'. The principle of Interdependent Origination (*pratītya-samutpāda*), a prominent doctrine of early Buddhism, was now given a wider interpretation. Elements (*dharmas*) formerly regarded as real or ultimate bases of existence because interdependent, were now considered to be unreal (*śūnya*) because of their contingent nature, i.e., their relativity (*śūnyatā*). Thus only the whole was conceived to be real, and the concept of causality, especially of a *First* Cause, an illusion. This was not a denial of empirical reality, but of its ultimate nature. These two aspects of reality are the Two Truths of the Mahāyāna, which supersede the Four Truths of the Hīnayāna.

During the third phase Buddhism acquired a theistic character. The earthly Buddha gradually came to be regarded as an incarnation of the eternal, cosmical Buddha who, like the *brahman* of the Vedānta, is beyond illusion and causation. Like the Vedāntins, the Buddhists, having rejected the empirical as the ultimate source of knowledge, turned to intuition which was developed as 'psycho-experimental-speculation'.

Despite the changing views during the development of Buddhism its central philosophy continued to be based on what it considered to be a self-evident truth, that of the impermanence of all compounded entities and their preclusion from any inherent, individual permanence. This conclusion, called *anātmya* by Mahāyānists, and *anattā* (Pā.) by the early Buddhists, is often misunderstood in the West, owing to *ātman* being equated with 'soul'. Some confusion has also arisen among medieval Indian commentators owing to the Buddhist practice of adapting Hindu terminology to express particular aspects of its own philosophy.

That Buddhism greatly contributed to modern Hinduism is generally acknowledged, just as the Advaita doctrine of Hinduism influenced Buddhism during the third and final phase of its existence in India. The gap between the two systems had for some centuries been gradually closing, until it became obvious that they could not continue to function separately. History presents no evidence of a formal amalgamation, but records only the decline and virtual disappearance of organized Buddhism in India. Various reasons for this have been advanced, all having some validity, but Radhakrishnan's explanation presents the Hindu point of view and possibly the view of the historian: 'The Buddha utilized the Hindu inheritance to correct some of its expressions . . . While the teaching of the Buddha assumed distinctive forms in the other countries of the world . . . here, in the home of the Buddha, it has entered into and become an integral part of our culture . . . In a sense the Buddha is a maker of modern Hinduism.'[2]

[1] Monier-Williams, *Buddhism*, p. 21.

[2] Bapat (gen. ed.), *2,500 Years of Buddhism*, pp. xvf.

v. Avatāra; Maurya.

Budha The personification of the planet Mercury. He is said to be a son of Soma (the Moon), who seduced Tārā (*AGP*., II. p. 1007).

v. Bṛhaspati; Navagraha(s); Iḷā; Candravaṁśa.

C

Caitanya The founder of one of four principal Vaiṣṇava sects, born in Nadiya in Bengal in 1485. His father, Jagannāth Miśra, was an orthodox *brahman*, his mother the daughter of Nīlāmbar Cakravartī. Caitanya is held to have been an incarnation of Kṛṣṇa, and hence received much devotion (*bhakti*) from his followers.

In cult-images he is depicted as fair and not dark-skinned like Kṛṣṇa. This is because he is believed to incarnate Kṛṣṇa and also Rādhā who was fair.[1]

[1] *BH.*, p. 142. Sometimes he dressed as a woman and believed himself to be Rādhā, Kṛṣṇa's beloved (Kennedy, *The Caitanya Movement*, pp. 17ff.).

Caitraratha The grove of Kubera situated on Mount Meru and planted by the *gandharva* Citraratha.

Caitya Initially a mound or tree, and later a shrine or building constructed in memory of a notable hero, muni, or teacher, in which their ashes or relics were placed. Such memorials were not a chronological development, but represent contemporary customs, traditions and cultural stages over a long period. Thus the early types of *caitya* such as trees with a revetment round the stem are portrayed in pre-Vedic remains[1] and also mentioned as customary in the *Rāmāyaṇa*.

Caitya trees (*caitya-vṛkṣa*) were held in such veneration that not even a single leaf should be destroyed, for these trees 'are the resort of *devas*, *yakṣas*, *nāgas*, *apsaras*, *bhūtas*, etc.'[2] Mounds and tree *caityas* were thus contemporary with some of the most elaborate memorials, like the *caityas* or *stūpas* of the Jains and Buddhists.

The plan of the *caitya* hall is similar to the early Christian basilicas, being divided into a nave and two side aisles, which were continued round the apse.[3]

[1] Some early sealings from Harappā depict a tree enclosed within a low wall or railing.

[2] Coomaraswamy, *HIIA.*, p. 47; *Yakṣas*, pt. i, p. 23.

[3] P. K. Acharya, *A Dictionary of Hindu Architecture*, pp. 199ff.

Cakra I. The wheel of a chariot or wagon, frequently mentioned in the *RV.* as a symbol of the sun.

v. Cakra II.

II. 'Discus.' The favourite weapon of Viṣṇu-Kṛṣṇa. It was a steel disc with a hole in the centre and the outside edge sharpened, used in Indian warfare.[1] It was twirled rapidly round the forefinger and then hurled at the adversary; or the thrower faced his objective squarely, holding the *cakra* low down on his left side, between the first finger and thumb of his right hand. Then bringing his right arm and shoulder forward he flung it underhand, with the full force of his body behind it.[2] The Bhuiyas, an Orissan tribe, use a similar weapon and are said to be able to sever a two-inch sapling at forty yards.[3]

In some *RV.* hymns (I,155,6, etc.) the sun is likened to a wheel denoting 'the principle of Time, in whose revolution all creation has its being and sees its end'.[4] The year is called the revolving wheel of the gods which contains everything including immortality. On it the gods move through all the worlds (*Kauṣ. Br.*, XX.1). Brahmā holds all things together as does the hub, the spokes and felly of a wheel (*Bṛhad-Ār. Up.*, 2.5,15; *Praśna Up.*, 6.6; *Śvet Up.*, 6.1). The priests are said to know the two wheels of the sun, but the third which is invisible is revealed only to those 'who are skilled in highest truths' (*RV.*, X.85,16). The first two wheels possibly represent heaven and earth; the third the transcendental world, the source of all manifestation.

Śiva is associated with the inexorable movement of the 'Wheel of Time' (*kālacakra*) in which the endless round of births and death occur. His *śakti* Durgā has the *cakra* as one of her twelve weapons which is thus invoked: 'Om to the *cakra*, thou pervadest all nature, thou art Viṣṇu, thou art also Devī, O beautiful-shaped discus, thee I adore, O Lord!'[5]

The weapons and emblems of the gods are often personified, the *cakra* being depicted as a heavily ornamented male figure with large pendulous belly and round, wide-open eyes.[6] The personified *cakra par excellence* is Viṣṇu's wheel Sudarśana, which is 'partly endowed with the character of Viṣṇu'.[7]

Coomaraswamy considers that the *cakra* originally represented the sun,[8] which traverses the world like the triumphant chariot of a *cakravartin*. Hence it also represents celestial and cosmic order or balance (*ṛta*). The Buddhist *cakra* symbolizes the Wheel of the Law (*Dharmacakra*). The *cakra* is now depicted on the national flag of India.

[1] Some *cakras* may be seen in the Pitt Rivers Museum, Oxford, and in Lord Langford's collection of armour and weapons at Bodrhyddan Hall, Clwyd, N. Wales.

[2] Stone, *Glossary of the Construction, Decoration and Use of Arms and Armor*, p. 171.

[3] Crooke, *Things Indian*, p. 26.

[4]*VF.*, p. 127.
[5]Birdwood, *Indian Arts*, I, p. 63.
[6]*EHI.*, I, pt. i, p. 243.
[7]*DHI.*, p. 539.
[8]*HIIA.*, p. 41. Combaz considers the *cakra* has an affinity with the *triśūla* (*L'Évolution du stūpa en Asie*, II, pp. 163–305).

v. Mura; Ṛtam I; Cakravartin; Āyudhapuruṣa.

III. A mystical circle or diagram.

IV. The six circles or depressions of the body serving mystical and thaumaturgical purposes. They are: *mūlādhāra*, the part above the pubis; *svādhiṣṭhāna*, umbilical region; *maṇipūra*, pit of the stomach; *anāhata*, root of the nose; *viśuddha*, hollow between the frontal sinuses; *ājñākhya*, the union of the coronal and sagittal sutures. Various faculties and divinities are believed to dwell in these hollows.[1]

[1]F. Mann states that the Indian *cakras* correspond to the acupuncture points of ancient Chinese medicine (*Acupuncture. Cure of Many Diseases*, p. 11).

V. The stellar *cakra*, composed of *nakṣatras* and planets, regarded as rotating like a potter's wheel. 'The imagery of the wheel implies a fixed centre which is Dhruva . . . to which the whole system of moving stars is secured by certain pulls, spoken of as winds (*Vāta*) in physical form but actually invisible forces exercised by Dhruva or the Centre.'[1]

[1]Agrawala, *Matsya*, p. 209.

Cakrapūjā v. Śākta.

Cakravāka A species of aquatic bird. The Aśvins are likened to it (*RV.*, II.39,3). It is included in the list of victims of the *aśvamedha* (horse sacrifice) where it is offered to the four quarters (*Tait. Saṁ.*, V.5.13). It symbolizes conjugal fidelity and love.

Cakravāla The nine mythical mountain ranges encircling the earth with Mount Meru as the central mountain.

v. Lokāloka.

Cakravarti-kṣetra The sphere of influence of an Indian *cakravartin* which was often referred to as 'the whole earth'.[1]

[1]*CG.*, p. 19. 'There was a modified conception of the *Cakravarti-kṣetra*, which regarded South India as the sphere of influence of the South Indian rulers and North India as that of the North Indian kings. The earliest reference to South India as a *cakravarti-kṣetra* is found in the Nasik *praśasti* of Gautamīputra Śātakarṇi (c. A.D. 106–30) of the Śātavāhana dynasty' (ibid., p. 163).

Cakravartin A 'universal ruler'. The word does not occur in the Vedas; '*cakra*' in the *RV.* denotes a wheel, particularly a chariot wheel; '*vartin*' as an affix to *cakra* is post-Vedic and means 'moving or turning', or 'abiding in, or ruling over a territory called a *cakra*'.[1] The metaphorical use of the wheel is apparent in the *MBh.* (Ādi pa., 13), where '*cakra*' signifies the wheel of a monarch's chariot rolling over his dominions, and '*vartin*' its unimpeded movement. The *cakravartin*'s dominions are often referred to as 'the whole earth', i.e., stretching from sea to sea,[2] like those of the Emperor Aśoka.

Generally the Hindu concept of the *cakravartin* is one of temporal kingship, but to Buddhists and Jainas it had also an ethical significance,[3] which is confirmed in the Edicts of Aśoka and by the Buddhist *Lalitavistara*. The latter describes the inauguration of the sovereign who, after the ceremony, addresses his vassal chieftains: 'Virtuously rule these provinces, destroy not life . . . Act not fraudulently through temptation; nor utter what is false. It is sinful to conquer him who sues for mercy, or to approve of the vicious.'[4]

According to the *Matsya P.* the birth of a *cakravartin* heralds a new age, in which he embodies the attributes of the Dharma (Law, Justice, Duty, etc.).[5]

The *cakravartin* is said to possess 'Seven Treasures' (*sapta ratna*), the enumeration of which varies. The *Matsya Pur.* lists them as: *cakra*, chariot, jewel, queen, wealth, horse and elephant. According to the *VP.* (I.13), a *cakravartin* is born with the mark of Viṣṇu's *cakra* on the palm of his hand; and bears also the thirty-two major, and innumerable secondary, marks on his body.

Cakra, in its original sense of circle, has a political significance in the *Nītiśāstra* or science of politics. It refers to the position of a 'valiant king' (*vijigīṣu*) in relation to his kingly neighbours who form an alliance, usually comprising twelve members, regarded as a circle or *maṇḍala*,[6] in which the *vijigīṣu* is paramount or seeks to maintain that position.[7]

Though such notions of sovereignty were not explicitly stated in the Vedas, several late hymns of the *RV.*, notably X.90 and 129, indicate the idea of social and cosmic unity, and of law and order, of a 'fundamental unity, far more profound than that produced either by geographical isolation or by political suzerainty. That unity transcends the innumerable diversities of blood, colour, language, dress, manners, and sect.'[8]

[1]*VP.*, I.13, n.5.
[2]*Kathāsaritsāgara*, cvii, 133.
[3]The Buddhists and Jainas, whilst recognizing that the *cakravartin* represents the highest temporal power, regarded their sages as its spiritual counterpart.
[4]Cited by Jacobi, *ERE.*, III. p. 337.
[5]Similarly the ancient Egyptian Pharaohs represent Justice (*maat*) (H. Frankfort, *Ancient Egyptian Religion*, p. 43).

[6]Cf. King Arthur and the knights of the round table.
[7]Cf. *Manu*, VII.156ff.
[8]*OHI.*, p. 7.
v. Sudarśana; Ikṣvāku; Sagara; Arthaśāstra.

Cakreśvara 'Lord of the discus'. An epithet of Viṣṇu.
v. Sudarśana; Cakra II.

Cakṣu 'Eye.' The sun-god Sūrya sees beyond the sky, earth and waters, and is the eye of all that exists (*AV.*, XIII.1,45). He gives sight to all creatures (VIII.2,3); and the eyes of the dead go to him (*RV.*, X.16,3).

Indra is said to have transformed Vṛtra's eye into Mount Trikakud, from which a healing eye-ointment is obtained (*ŚBr.*, III.1.3,12).[1] But according to the *Tait. Saṁ.* (VI.1.1,5) Vṛtra's eye became collyrium.

Belief in the evil influence of the human eye (*dṛṣtidoṣa*) is common to India and to many countries. It causes death, illness, injury, poverty (children and animals being especially vulnerable); hence the use of amulets, counter-charms and certain protective gestures. Many plants are also believed to give protection against it, including the *jaṅgiḍa* in India (*AV.*, XIX.35,3), shamrock in Ireland, garlic in Greece, etc. According to the *Tait Saṁ.*, III.5.5. Agni is invoked to give protection against its baleful influence; in *RV.* (I.79,12) he drives away evil with his thousand eyes (cf. *AV.*, VI.37,1).

[1]This apparently refers to sympathetic magic, as the ointment (=Vṛtra's eye) is put on the eye of the patient.
v. Cakṣur-mantra; Cakṣurdāna.

Cakṣurdāna 'Gift of sight.' The ceremony of anointing the eyes of an image at the time of its consecration, to give it the 'gift of sight'.
v. Prāṇapratiṣthā.

Cakṣur-mantra 'Bewitching with the eye.' In a hymn directed against cursers and curses, the invoker requests that the unfriendly possessor of the Evil Eye should have his ribs crushed (*AV.*, II.7,5). An ointment made from the *jaṅgiḍa* plant was said to be a protection against bewitchment (XIX.35,3; and v. 45, 1). During the wedding ceremony a wife is implored not to have the Evil Eye, i.e., not to 'overlook' her husband (*RV.*, X.85, 44; *Pāraskara Gṛhya Sūtra* 1.4).
v. Cakṣu.

Cāmuṇḍā or **Cāmuṇḍī** A goddess of non-Āryan origin. She is one of the terrible (*ugra*) forms of Durgā and one of the seven mothers (*sapta mātṛkā*). As the goddess Kālī she sprang from the forehead of Ambikā and was created expressly to destroy the mighty *asuras* Caṇḍa and Muṇḍa. After destroying them she was given the name of Cāmuṇḍā (*Mārk. P.*, 87,24–5), and is depicted as an emaciated, terrifying old woman, robed in an elephant's hide and wearing a dreadful garland (*mālā*) of corpses. When depicted as Pretāsana she is shown seated on a corpse. This 'is really a yogic *āsana*, in which the whole body lies rigid and motionless like a corpse'.[1] Cāmuṇḍā is said to reveal herself in the form of Kaumārī (*AGP.*, I, pp. 571–2).

[1]*DHI.*, p. 274.
v. Raktavīja; Navapatrikā.

Cañcalā or **Lolā** 'Fickle One.' An epithet of Lakṣmī.

Caṇda I. 'Wrathful.' The name of a mythical being whose daughters (Caṇḍasya naptyas) constitute a class of demonesses who have to be exorcized from the household (*AV.*, II.14,1–6).
v. Cāmuṇḍā.

II. Name of one of the sixty-four Bhairavas of the Āgamic texts.[1]

[1]*DHI.*, p. 466.

III. The name of one of the seven clouds which will envelop the earth at the end of the age.

Caṇḍā v. Caṇḍī.

Caṇḍāla An outcaste, a person of the lowest of the mixed tribes; particularly one born of a *śūdra* father and a *brahmin* mother. Persons guilty of bad conduct will be reborn in the womb of a dog, swine or *caṇḍāla* (*Chān. Up.*, 5.10,7). *Caṇḍālas* are prohibited even from seeing the food offered at a *śrāddha* (*VP.*, III.16). They are required to live outside towns or villages, their function being limited to the collection of the clothes of the dead from cremation grounds (*AGP.*, I, p. 588). A necklace (*mālā*) made of the teeth of a dead *caṇḍāla* was used in incantations to cause the death of an enemy (*AGP.*, II, p. 1217). Some *caṇḍālas* are called Kaulas, viz., worshippers of *śakti* according to the so-called 'left-hand' ritual.
v. Sītalā; Mataṅga.

Caṇḍarudrikā Mystical knowledge acquired by worshipping the eight Nāyikās, i.e., various forms of Durgā.

Caṇḍi, Caṇḍikā, or **Caṇḍā**[1] 'Wrathful.' A fierce form assumed by Durgā, a *śakti* of Śiva, to destroy the *asura* Mahiṣa. This mythical event is celebrated annually in Bengal at the Durgāpūjā.

In Mysore Caṇḍī is worshipped as Cāmuṇḍī, and is 'a tutelary deity of the ruling house of the Wadiyar, worshipped by the ruler himself. Caṇḍī is also popular in Bengal.'[2]

[1]Caṇḍī is identical with Kālī as well as with the Buddhist Vajrayāna 'goddesses, and the non-Āryan autochthonous goddesses in general' (*TT.*, p. 94).
[2]*TT.*, Bibliog. Sec., p. 312.
v. Mahiṣa II; Tejas.

Candra The Moon and its personification as a deity. The name is derived from *ścandra*, 'shining', 'radiant'. Because of its radiance it was likened to gold; a glowing spark in the heavens; a bowl overflowing with *amṛta*, milk,[1] rain, etc. When the *soma* sacrifice had long since ceased to be performed, Candra became identified with some of its qualities and associated with *amṛta*, the mythical elixir of the gods. Ultimately Candra became King Soma and was given a place in stellar mythology, as the founder of the Lunar dynasty.

The mysterious waxing and waning of the moon inevitably led to their association with life and death. Sacrificial offerings were therefore made to the dead at the time of the new moon to replenish the sap drunk by the *pitṛs*.[2] The eclipse of the moon, attributed to the demon Rāhu (*AV*., XIX.9,10) was greatly feared lest the moon should not survive his onslaught.

The origin of the moon is variously given in different works. It was engendered from the mind of the Cosmic Puruṣa (*RV*., X.90,13); or it was the egg produced as the result of the union of Prajāpati with the Sky. Prajāpati touched the egg saying, 'Bear thou seed', and the Moon was created, for that also is seed (*ŚBr*., IX.1.2,39); or it arose during the Churning of the Ocean (*VP*., I.9). Candra's own world is above the seven worlds of wind[3] from whence he restores the evaporated moisture to the plants.

In India, as in many other countries, it is generally believed that certain phases of the moon are propitious and others harmful. The full moon destroys darkness and so is beneficent.[4] The hare-marked moon (*candra-śaśāṅka*) is said to destroy evil and to rise like a horned bull, but to see the full moon with broken light to its right portends death (*MBh*., 12.318, *EM*.).

[1]Originally Candra was male, but later, when regarded as a source of milk it was then called *gaus* (f.) which means both cow and moon.

[2]Hence the light of the new moon is feared because it is a sign that the dead need nourishment. Old shepherds in Oxfordshire never dock lambs' tails when the moon is 'southing' (i.e., waning), because the animals would die (Radford, *ES*.). Some Europeans believe that it is unlucky to see the new moon through trees or glass.

[3]*EM*., p. 92.

[4]Greeks, Romans and Jews shared the same belief. 'The sun shall not smite thee by day, nor the moon by night' (*Psalm*. 121,6).

v. Candravaṁśa; Kaumudī; Kuhū; Candrakānta; Candrakalā; Anumati II; Arvan I; Atri; Rākā; Rohiṇī II.

Candrakalā One-sixteenth of the moon's disc, each segment being personified as a goddess.

Candrakānta 'Moon-loved', i.e., the moon-stone, the gem supposed to be formed by the moon's rays, which also dissolves under the influence of its own light.

Candramukha The name of a *yakṣa* said to dwell in the *bakula* tree (Mimusops elengi).[1]

[1]*DHI*., p. 341 and Pl. XIII. fig. 2.

Candravaṁśa The Lunar dynasty or line of kings,[1] the counterpart of the Solar dynasty (Sūryavaṁśa).

Paurāṇic mythology ascribes the founding of the Lunar Dynasty to Candra (the moon), but traditional history ascribes it to Yayāti's two sons Puru and Yadu.

[1]For the genealogical table of the Lunar dynasty according to the *VP*., v. *HCD*., p. 69.

v. Candra; Devayānī.

Cāṇūra An *asura* and famous wrestler who attempted to kill Kṛṣṇa, but he was seized by the latter and whirled round and round a hundred times and then dashed to the ground, whereupon a hundred pools of gory mire formed (*VP*., V.20).

Caraka General name for a wandering religious student. It is also the name of the author of a medical work, the *Carakagrantha* (1st–2nd cent.),[1] which paurāṇic legend assigned to the serpent-king Śeṣa, the recipient of the *Āyur-veda*. To alleviate sickness and disease Śeṣa incarnated himself as the son of a *muni*, and was called Caraka, because he came to spy (*cara*), i.e., to carry out medical investigation and diagnosis.

Caraka, with Suśruta and Vāgbhaṭa are known as 'the triad of the ancients' (*vṛddha-trayī*), and are three of the most important figures in the practice of Indian medicine. Caraka was Court physician to King Kaniṣka.

[1]His original writings are lost and this treatise is a redaction of his work with additions by another author. For a translation, v. *The Caraka Saṁhitā*, by A. Kaviratna, Cal., 1899; and v. A.K. Majumdar, *Caraka and His Successors in Hindu Medicine*, 1901.

Carakī A demoness propitiated with offerings of meat and ghee (*ghṛta*) (*AGP*., I, p. 370).

v. Pūtanā.

Caraṇa One of a number of Vedic priestly schools, each having its own Vedic text (*śākhā*) interpreted according to its own views.

v. Śākta; Prātiśākhya; Darśana.

Cāraṇa Probably wandering minstrels,[1] who were later employed at the courts of kings. But *Manu* (XII.44) classes them with the *suparṇas* (bird-deities); *rākṣasas* and *piśācas*, all of whom were 'produced by Darkness'.

[1]Cāraṇa may denote a caste, perhaps of singers, rope-dancers, etc.

Carmaṇvatī v. Rantideva.

Cārvāka The name of a Materialist school, one of the three 'heterodox' Indian *darśanas*; its origin is attributed to *Cārvāka*, of whom little is known. The main work representing its views, the *Bārhaspati Sūtra* (c. 600 B.C.), is lost, but it is possible to reconstruct its doctrines from contemporary Jaina and Buddhist texts and also from Hindu sources of the eighth century A.D.[1] The Cārvāka views are probably the result of a growing scepticism towards Vedic dogma, apparent also in Jaina and Buddhist doctrines. Even the *RV.* (X.129) with its question: 'Who knows, who ever told, from whence this vast creation rose?'[2] is not without a sceptical element.

The Cārvāka, like Buddhism, regards the universe as an interdependent entity, subject to continual change. Like Buddhism also, the Cārvāka regards 'soul', ego or personality as nothing more than the sum of the activity of the 'conscious living body (*caityanya-viśiṣṭa deha eva ātmā*)',[3] and supports this view by quoting the *Bṛhadāraṇyaka Up.*, (II.4,12) where the self is likened to a lump of salt which, when dissolved in water, permeates it, but which they believed could not be recovered.

According to their theory of knowledge perception was the only means of knowing the truth—beyond perception everything is doubtful. But inference was admitted as a means of knowledge as long as it was applied to phenomena only. The universe 'sprang from the fortuitous combination of elementary particles of matter. This theory is called *yadṛcchāvāda* (the theory of accidental causation)'.[4]

The Cārvākas believe man's chief aim to be the 'pursuit of happiness' and the avoidance of suffering—to be achieved pragmatically—in the Kantian sense. 'Rather a pigeon today, than a peacock tomorrow' is their view. Cārvāka ethics may be summed up in the dictum that a good action conduces to happiness, a bad one to unhappiness. No charge appears to have been made that the Cārvākas were amoral, anti-social or lacking in practical humanitarianism.

The influence of Cārvāka scepticism in the development and rationalization of Hinduism has perhaps failed to gain full recognition, but it undoubtedly aroused Indian philosophy from complacent dogmatism, as Hume's scepticism aroused Kant from his 'dogmatic slumber'.

[1]Such as the *Sarvadarśanasaṁgraha* of Mādhavācārya. In addition there is the *Tattvopaplavasiṁha* of Jayarāśi Bhaṭṭa, a Cārvāka writer of the same period.

[2]Tr. by Muir.

[3]Chatterjee and Datta, *Introduction to Indian Philosophy*, p. 62.

[4]*EW.*, I. p. 135.

v. Ātman.

Cārvī 'Splendour.' An epithet of Kubera's wife Bhadrā.

Cāṣa The blue jay, one of the many sacrificial victims offered at the horse sacrifice (*aśvamedha*).

The spirit of Disease is implored to 'depart with the blue jay and the kingfisher'. This refers to the ancient belief that diseases can be transferred to, and carried away by, certain birds and animals.

v. Haritāla; Haridrā.

Cātaka The bird (Cucculus melanoleucus) which is said to live on rain-drops.

Cātanāni 'Expellers.' Hymns or verses of hymns used for exorcism such as *AV.*, I.7 in which Agni is invoked to discover the whereabouts of sorcerers.

Cāturmāsyani The seasonal or four-monthly sacrifices performed at the commencement of the three seasons (spring, rainy season and autumn). A fourth seasonal ceremony, called the *śunā-śīrīya* is usually performed at the close of the seasonal offerings.

Chāga Goat. Various fanciful origins of the goat include the following: it was derived from the moisture adhering to the shell of the cosmic egg (*ŚBr.*, VI.1.1,11); or produced from the heat of Makha's head (XIV.1.2,13); or it emerged from Indra's eyes when he was exorcized by Tvaṣṭṛ for having slain his (Tvaṣṭṛ's) son Viśvarūpa (XII.7.1,2).

Goats pull Pūṣan's chariot (*RV.*, I.138,4, etc.), and are also connected with Agni[1] in funeral rites,[2] in which their dismembered limbs (representing Agni's portion) are laid on the corpse when it is placed on the funeral pyre (*RV.*, X.16,4; *ŚBr.*, VI.2.1,5). It also represents all cattle (*ŚBr.*, VI.5.1,4). The goat is also Agni's vehicle (*vāhana*) and symbolizes his generative power.[3]

[1]Cf. the *makara*-bodied goat or 'goat-fish', the Indian and Persian zodiacal sign. This combination suggests Agni—who has goat forms and is born of the waters (Coomaraswamy, *Yakṣas*, pt. ii, p. 51). Cf. also the Sumerian goat-fish, symbol of Ea, god of the waters (v. Ward, *Seal Cylinders*, pp. 384f; 399).

[2]Goat's flesh is especially pleasing to the *pitṛs* (*Matsya P.*, 148.83; 17.32, *PI.*). 'The very look of a black goat sanctifies all things' (*Ancestor Worship*, p. 158).

[3]Hence it is equated with Prajāpati, the Lord of generation and of all creatures (*ŚBr.*, V.2.1,24).

v. Aja; Aśvamedha; Chāgavaktra; Ahalyā.

Chāgavaktra 'Goat-faced.' A companion of Skanda-Kārttikeya, or an aspect of the deity himself.[1]

[1]*DHI.*, pp. 146 and 363.

v. Naigameya; Chāga.

Chandas 'Metre.' The name of one of the six Vedāṅgas, which lays down rules intended to ensure the correct performance of sacrificial procedure, and especially of the use of the appropriate metre in the chants. In Indian prosody *chandas* denotes a succession of poetical feet (*pādas*)[1] arranged in regular order, according to certain types recognized as standards, in verses of a particular length. A metre may consist of long or short syllables, ranging from a minimum of four to a maximum of twelve.[2]

Next to language, metre is significant in determining the age of the Vedic hymns, their metres indicating the gap that exists between them and those of classical Sanskrit poetry, the latter retaining little trace of the numerous metres of the Veda. On the other hand, classical Sanskrit poetry has metres having no prototype in the Veda.

In the oldest Indian metre only the number of syllables is fixed, their quantity or measure being only partially determined,[3] the last syllable of each line being a *syllaba anceps*, i.e., either a short or long syllable regardless of the metre of the syllables preceding it. Vedic verses are generally composed of lines of eight, eleven or twelve syllables, but only the last four (or five) have a fixed rhythm. Originally the most popular metre was the *gāyatrī*, after which the *gāyatrī mantra* (*RV.*, III.62,10) is named, which is repeated by every devout Hindu at his morning and evening devotions. Its regular form consists of three lines each of eight syllables. Contemporary with it was the *anuṣṭubh* (from which derived the *śloka*), consisting of four lines, also of eight syllables each, subsequently the most popular metre for Epic poetry.

The eleven-syllabled line has a caesura or pause after the fourth or fifth syllable. The *triṣṭubh* metre consists of four such lines. The twelve-syllabled line is called *jagatī*, and except for its additional syllable follows the same pattern as the *triṣṭubh*. Another metre, the *dvipadā-virāj*, only occasionally used, consists of four or eight five-syllabled lines. A distinctive feature of Vedic verse is that two or more metres may occur in a single hymn, as in *RV.*, VII.54, where the metre of the first verse is *gāyatrī*, that of verses 2–4 *upariṣṭābṛhati*, and that of verses 5–8 *anuṣṭubh*.

Metre has always been regarded by Hindus as of the utmost importance. This is indicated 'by the excessive cultivation and elaboration bestowed upon their whole metrical system',[4] some of the most sacred metres vere personified. Nonetheless, it was not until the second century B.C. that a treatise (Vedāṅga) dealing with both Prakrit and Sanskrit metres appeared, or at least it is the earliest to have survived. This Vedāṅga called the *Chandaḥ-śāstra*, is ascribed to Piṅgala (or Piṅgalanāga).

Though metre is an important aid in repeating passages from the Veda it is not the only one. In his introduction to the first hymn of the *RV.* Sāyaṇa states that not only should anyone repeating a Vedic hymn know the name of the *ṛṣi*[5] to whom it was revealed, and the name of the god to whom it was addressed, but also be aware both of the proper accents to be used and of the correct interpretation of the *mantras*. Anyone not knowing these things and attempting to repeat a portion of the Veda is called a *mantra*-thorn (*mantra-kaṇṭaka*) whose ignorance will assuredly cancel or obstruct the efficacy of its recital.

Injuries can be caused by a particular use of the metres (*Kauṣ. Br.*, XI.5). Also certain metres are connected with the attainment of power, splendour, etc. (XVII.2). Even the gods used the metres to reach the heavenly world and thus by the metres the sacrificer too is enabled to reach heaven (*Ait. Br.*, I.9).

[1] *Pāda* also means 'fourth part' or 'quarter', and hence sometimes denotes the four *pādas* of the metre called *virāj*, which consists of eight five-syllabled lines, or sometimes of four lines of ten syllables.

[2] *CD.*, p. 3739.

[3] *HIL.*, vol. I. pt. i, p. 53.

[4] *IW.*, p. 163.

[5] The names of the seers to whom the hymns were revealed are generally those of families of singers, the songs being handed down from 'mythical ancestors' (*pitṛs*), *HIL.*, pt. i, p. 50.

v. Ṛtvij; Ṛgveda; Sāmaveda; Yajurveda; Śikṣā; Prātiśākhya; Vāc.

Chattra I. Parasol, umbrella. The seven worlds are said to be arranged one above the other like a number of parasols.

II. The white parasol symbolizes royal or delegated power. The *mantras* with which it is consecrated are given in the *AGP.* (II, pp. 991f.), and they ensure victory.

Chāyā v. Saṁjñā.

Chinnamastā The 'Beheaded' or 'she with the split skulls'. A Tantric form of Durgā who is depicted as headless.

Chinnamastā is the fifth *mahāvidyā* and represents the end of life, when the sacrificial victim is beheaded.[1] The Buddhist Tantric goddess Vajrayoginī is iconographically similar to Chinnamastā. The former is described in one *sādhana* as headless, and it seems that she has been incorporated by the Hindus into their 'Pantheon', but owing to religious fear they retained her Buddhist *mantra*.[2] Chinnamastā, Dhūmāvatī and other 'sinister' goddesses, were worshipped in *abhicāra* rites for the purpose of injuring enemies.[3]

[1] In Vedic ritual the sacrificial victim was always beheaded.

[2] Bhattacharyya, *Buddhist Iconography*, p. 155 and n. In Tantric Buddhism, the philosophical form of Vajrayoginī is Prajñāpāramitā, the goddess of wisdom (*HP.*, p. 281).

[3] C. Chakravati, 'Śakti Worship and the Śākta Saints of Bengal' (*C. Herit. I.*, vol. II, pp. 296f.). Chinnamastā is

also called Vidyā and Tārā (*TT.*, p. 73).
v. Kabandha; Mahāvidyā(s).

Citrabhavana The city ruled by Vicitra, the younger brother of Yama. It is one of the sixteen cities through which the dead have to pass.[1]

[1]*Ancestor Worship*, pp. 326, 328.

Citragupta The scribe of the gods, born from the body of Brahmā whilst the latter was engaged in deep meditation. Brahmā revealed to Citragupta all subtle and hidden things, and allowed him to share in the oblations offered at the fire sacrifices. Citragupta later became Yama's scribe[1] and records men's good and bad deeds in the Agrasamdhānī (Main Records). His caste is that of scribes (*kāyastha*), and his nine sons: Bhaṭṭa, Nāgara, Senaka, Gauḍa, Śrivāstavya, Māthura, Ahiṣṭhana, Śakasena and Ambaṣṭha, are regarded as the ancestors of particular castes of scribes.[2]

[1]*AGP.*, II, p. 1287. Citragupta is sometimes regarded as a form of Yama.

[2]*HP.*, p. 135.

Citraketu A king of Śūrasenas who had many wives, but no children. The sage Aṅgiras, aware of his disappointment, performed a sacrifice to obtain progeny for the king. The remnant (*ucchiṣṭa*) of the sacrifice was then given to the chief wife who was delivered of a son.

Citraketu once laughed when he saw Pārvatī sitting on Śiva's lap. The indignant goddess cursed him to be reborn as an *asura*, whereupon he begged for forgiveness, but Pārvatī was adamant until Śiva informed her that Citraketu was a devotee of Hari and of himself.

Citralekhā v. Ūṣā; Aniruddha I.

Citrāṅgadā v. Babhru-vāhana.

Citrapakṣa 'Speckled wing.' An epithet of a demon causing headaches.

Citraratha The name of the King of the *apsarasas* and *gandharvas* who made Indra's grove called Caitraratha situated in the country of the Northern Kurus (*Rām.*, 2.91,19, *EM.*). He promised Arjuna a hundred horses of the *gandharva* breed. These magical horses can take any shape, fulfil wishes and travel anywhere.

Citrasena 'Having a bright spear.' A *gandharva* who instructed Arjuna in celestial music and dancing, when the latter resided for five years in Indra's heaven (*MBh.*, Vana pa., 44).

Cuḍel A demoness. A woman who dies unpurified within fifteen days of childbirth becomes a demoness.[1]

[1]*BH.*, p. 229.

Cumuri Probably the name of a leader of a native tribe who with Dhuni was conquered by the *ṛṣi* Dabhīti aided by Indra. The latter destroyed 30,000 of their men by his magic power and weapons. Their cattle, horses and 'golden treasure' were given by Indra to Dabhīti (*RV.*, II.13,9; 15.4,9; IV.30,21).

Cyavāna or **Cyavana** I. Name of an ancient *ṛṣi*. The first form of the name occurs only in the *RV*; the latter in other Vedic and post-Vedic texts. The *RV.* mentions only the restoration of Cyavāna's youth and vigour by the Aśvins. Other references are of the briefest and give no indication of his history. Even the *Nirukta* (IV.19) says only that he was a *ṛṣi*. But the *Śatapatha Brāhmaṇa* contains several Cyavāna legends, one of which (IV.1.5,1f.) states that when the Bhārgavas (Bhṛgus) attained the heavenly world, Cyavāna, although a Bhārgava, was left behind, decrepit and ghostlike. Some youths of a branch of the Mānava tribe, the Śaryātas, on catching sight of the strange old man, pelted him with clods. Cyavāna thereupon 'sowed discord among the Śaryātas, so that father fought with son, and brother with brother'. Śaryāta, their chieftain, at first blamed himself for this calamity, but after making enquiries discovered what the youths had done. Taking his daughter Sukanyā with him he set out to placate Cyavana, saying: 'Reverence be to you, O *ṛṣi*. Because I knew thee not, therefore have I offended you. Here is Sukanyā, with her I make atonement to you: let my tribe live together in peace!'

Later when Sukanyā was settled in Cyavāna's hermitage, the Aśvins, who were performing cures in the neighbourhood, came upon Sukanyā and said to her: 'How come you to waste your charms on a decrepit old man. Come with us and enjoy yourself!' Sukanyā replied: 'To whom my father has given me, him will I not abandon, as long as he lives.' When Sukanyā told her husband what the Aśvins had said, he told her to tell them not to deride him, because they also were imperfect. 'If they enquire in what way, ask them to make me young again and then they will learn the reason.'

When the Aśvins appeared again, Sukanyā repeated her husband's words, and they told her to take Cyavāna to a pool nearby from which he would emerge rejuvenated. This was done, and Cyavāna then directed the Aśvins to go to Kurukṣetra where the *devas*, having chanted the *bahiṣpavamāna*[1] were performing a sacrifice. But the *devas* refused to let them share in the sacrifice because of their having 'wandered and mixed much among men, performing cures'.[2] But the Aśvins pointed out that they (the *devas*) were worshipping with a 'headless' sacrifice. The gods demanded an explanation, which the Aśvins agreed to give if they were invited to share in the sacrifice. The gods agreed, and the Aśvins, taking the part of the Adhvaryu priests, restored the 'head' of the sacrifice;[3] thus establishing their right to share in its performance.

There are variants of this legend in the Purāṇas and

the Epic, one of which recounts that the Aśvins, hoping to deceive Sukanyā, also entered the pool with Cyavāna, but when they emerged, she easily recognized her husband by the blinking of his eyes (*animiṣa*), an unblinking stare being one of the distinguishing 'marks' or 'signs' of a *deva*.

[1]Name of a *stoma* or *stotra* (generally consisting of three *tricas* and sung outside the *vedi* (altar) during the morning libation.

[2]The practice of medicine was regarded as an occupation of *śūdras*, which even minor divinities should not follow.

[3]This was accomplished by the assimilation of the *āśvina* libation with that already offered before their arrival, and by the chanting of the *divākīrtya* consisting of eleven verses not in the *Sāma-Veda*, the first of which is called the head (*śiras*), the second the neck (*grīvāḥ*), etc. (*ŚBr.*, II, p. 276, n.1). Thus this reference to the 'headless sacrifice' has nothing to do with the Vedic practice of beheading the sacrificial victim.

v. Aurva; Mada.

II. Name of a demon who causes diseases.

D

Dabhīti v. Cumuri.

Dadhi Thick sour milk, regarded as a cure for certain ailments. It is said to belong to Indra (*ŚBr.*, VII.4.1,42), and to be a form of the earth-world (VII.5.1,3).

Dadhīca v. Dadhyac.

Dadhikrā, Dadhikrās, or **Dadhikrāvan** The last is a lengthened, interchangeable form of Dadhikrās,[1] a mythical being, and the subject of several *RV.* hymns (IV.39,7, etc.). He is described as a celestial horse[2] whose prototype may have been a distinguished chariot-horse of the same name. Like Tārkṣya, he represents the morning sun, and was created by Heaven and Earth or by Mitra-Varuṇa (the latter being the tutelary deity of horses). C.K. Raja points out that the horse symbolizes *jñāna* (knowledge), and in a hymn to Dadhikrāvan he is invoked to make our mouths fragrant. This refers to the *madhuvidyā* (the sweet doctrine, i.e., the highest knowledge).[3] He is allied with Sūrya, with Morning, the Ādityas, the Āṅgirasas and Vasus, and directs the solar deities 'along the Path of Order', i.e., their ordered diurnal journey across the heavens (*RV.*, VII.44,4–5). In similar fashion Dadhikrā guides mortals along the paths of life.

[1] *RV.*, IV.39, 1 and 4, in which the last two forms occur. There are passages in the Vedas where the word is used both in the sense of a horse and a deity (*Nir.*, 2.27).

[2] Crooke suggests he may have been a divine hero; Bhattacharji, states that Dadhikrāvan 'is the sun in the shape of a horse' (*IT.*, p. 231).

[3] *C. Herit. I.*, vol. I, p. 32.

v. Dadhyac; Vājin.

Dadhyac or **Dadhyañc** (Later form Dadhīca.) 'Possessing (or sprinkling) sour milk (*dadhi*).' Name of a *ṛṣi*, the son of the fire-priest Atharvan (*RV.*, I.80,16), who kindled Agni and is mentioned with Aṅgiras and other early sacrificers.

Indra taught him the *pravargyavidyā* and *madhuvidyā* (the highest knowledge), warning him that if he divulged it he would lose his head.[1] Despite the threat, he was persuaded by the Aśvins to teach them the prohibited knowledge. To protect him from Indra's threat, the Aśvins removed the *ṛṣi*'s head, replacing it with that of a horse.[2] When Indra struck it off, they replaced it with Dadhyac's own head (*ŚBr.*, XIV.1.1,18–25).

The *Bṛhadd.* (III.21–4) gives a different version. The Aśvins persuaded Dadhyac to 'make us two receive the mead by means of a horse's head', and because he agreed Indra cut off his equine head; 'but his own head they (the Aśvins) put on (again)'. The severed head fell into a lake on Mount Śaryaṇāvat, from which it rises to bestow boons on men, and where it will remain until the close of the age (*yuga*).

Dadhyac is the subject of many legends, one of which states that he possessed a mysterious power which kept the *asuras* in check,[3] until he ascended to heaven when they spread over the earth. Another myth states that with a *vajra* made from Dadhyac's bones, Indra slew the ninety-nine Vṛtras (*RV.*, I.84,13). Thus, according to the *MBh.* (Vana pa., 100) Dadhyac died voluntarily for the 'good of the three worlds', and even his bones served to benefit mankind, and hence his presentation as the embodiment of altruistic service. This myth may be intended to stress 'the merits of meditation; for Dadhīca's meditations or their merits clung to his bones and made the bolt ... such an irresistible weapon'.[4]

[1] His head was believed to possess oracular powers (*RV.*, I.119,9). The *Bṛhadd.* III,18 states that Indra gave him the Brahmā spell which revealed to him the abode of *soma*.

[2] The horse represents knowledge (*jñāna*), and from Dadhyac's equine head issued the highest knowledge. The twin Aśvins who are also closely connected with horses, are also said to possess the highest knowledge. v. also O'Flaherty, 'The Submarine Mare in the Mythology of Śiva', *JRAS.*, no. 1, 1971, p. 19; Bosch, 'The God with the horse's head' in *Selected Studies in Indonesian Archaeology*, pp. 144f.

[3] Cf. the European belief in the auspicious and protective powers of wooden horse-heads carved on house gables (v. Professor Wolfram's letter to the Editor of *Folklore*, Spring, 1969, p. 60). Horse bones (for protection) are sometimes found embedded in the walls of old houses in England and Wales.

[4] *IT.*, p. 261.

Daitya(s) Giants or Titans, the descendants of Diti. The Daityas figure only in post-Vedic literature, where they are represented as demons, generally opposed to the *devas* (gods); or they denote native tribes opposed to Āryan expansion, both religious and political. These tribes are known also as Dānavas, Asuras, etc. To the priests, the enemies of the gods were also their enemies, and the eradication of some indigenous cults was as important to the Vedic priests as was political conquest to the Āryan rulers.

The political struggle, like the religious, ended in compromise, the former by intermarriage of Āryan and non-Āryan ruling families,[1] the latter by the assimilation of some native cults with Vedic ones.

The Daityas (or Asuras) in the legend of the Churning of the Ocean (*samudramathana*) are described as anti-gods who seized the cup of *amṛta* (ambrosia) from Dhanvantari, the physician of the gods. It was restored to the gods only by the intervention of Viṣṇu in the form of the enchantress Mohinī, whose charms diverted the Daityas (*VP.*, I.9). But in another passage (V.1) Daityas, Yakṣas, Rākṣasas, Nāgas, etc., are collectively called 'forms of the Great Spirit, Viṣṇu'.

[1]This is indicated by the marriage of Arjuna to King Vāsuki's sister, and of Bhīma's to Hiḍimbā, etc. Some native tribes also sided with the Kurus during the Pāṇḍava-Kaurava war.

v. Danu II.

Ḍāka The male counterpart of *ḍākinī*.

Ḍākinī(s) Demoniac and quasi-divine beings in Hindu tantrism and folklore. The *AGP.* (I., p. 538) calls them 'malignant spirits'. They eat raw flesh and are attendant on Kālī. The *ḍākinī* Pūtanā attempted to poison the child Kṛṣṇa.

Ḍākinīs also occur in Buddhist tantrism, such as the goddess Vajravārāhī. In one of her forms she 'is invoked in the rite of bewitching men or women and is very popular nowadays in Nepal and other Buddhist countries'.[1]

[1]Bhattacharyya, *Buddhist Iconography*, p. 104. Coomaraswamy suggests that the *ḍākinīs* must have been originally *yakṣiṇīs* (*Yakṣas*, pt. i, p. 9).

v. Ḍāka; Śākinī(s); Abhicāra.

Dakṣa A son of Brahmā and one of the six Ādityas.[1] From very early times the notion of cosmic unity is suggested, though in language often paradoxical and obscure. Thus *RV.*, X.72,2–4 reads: 'Existence . . . from non-existence sprang . . . Dakṣa was born of Aditi, and Aditi was Dakṣa's child.' The *Nir.* (11.23) suggests that this contradiction is part of the nature of the gods, who may derive their characteristics from, or be born from, each other, or have a common origin. The notion of cosmic unity is expressed also in *RV.*, X.90,1: 'Then there was neither Aught nor Nought'. The original significance of Dakṣa seems to be that of universal creative energy, which in the Brāhmaṇas is represented as the inherent power of the sacrifice. Thus Dakṣa came to be associated with priestly skill, ensuring the efficacy of the sacrifice and the maintenance of contact with the gods, without which cosmic stability and continuity would be jeopardized. In this context Dakṣa is recognized as one of the sovereign principles of the Universe. In the Purāṇas and the Epic Dakṣa is presented in various guises, but principally as a 'secondary' creator, or as a *ṛṣi* who is present in each age (*manvantara*) of re-creation (*VP.*, I.15). In the first *manvantara*[2] he is said to be a Prajāpati produced by Brahmā. Another tradition states that Dakṣa willed into existence *devas* and *ṛṣis*, and finally sons (Haryaśvas and Śabalāśvas) to people the earth.[3] But they rejected this role and devoted themselves to an ascetic life.

Convinced of the futility of mind-born progeny, Dakṣa decided to establish sexual intercourse as the alternative. This decision provides the excuse for a discourse on the virtues of marriage and the importance of begetting sons, and for the declaration that 'even *ṛṣis* cannot create creatures without women' (*MBh.*, Ādi pa., 74). To achieve his purpose Dakṣa married Asiknī, the daughter of the patriarch Viraṇa (whence her patronymic Vīraṇī or Vīriṇī, by which she is often known), and begot by her fifty daughters (*putrikās*) (*Manu*, IX.127), whose male issue he could adopt as his sons[4] and thus fulfil the final rites required by Brahmanic law. The fifty daughters were divided among three husbands: To Dharma, he gave ten; to Soma (the Moon) twenty-seven, who became lunar asterisms associated with the fortnightly waxing and waning of the moon and the division of the lunar calendar; to Kaśyapa the remaining thirteen, the eldest of whom bore him famous sons, the youngest, Manu, being the progenitor of the human race, thus fulfilling Dakṣa's great ambition.

Other accounts of Dakṣa reflect the rivalry of the Śaiva and Vaiṣṇava sects. One of these legends relates to a sacrifice initiated by Dakṣa, to which Śiva had not been invited. Rebuked by Dadhīca for the omission, Dakṣa declared that it was deliberate, as the sacrifice was dedicated to Viṣṇu who alone was the Supreme Lord.[5] The sequel was the immediate appearance of the fearful Vīrabhadra, the personification of Śiva's wrath, at the sight of whom all the sacrificial officiants except Dakṣa fled. The latter begged for mercy, and was told to take refuge in Rudra (Śiva). 'Better his anger than the blessings of other gods!'

[1]*RV.* (II.27,1) gives six; as also do most of the Brāhmaṇas; but *ŚBr.* (XI.6,3 and 8) gives twelve, and links them with the solar months as the 'cycle of destiny' whose unit is the year (v. *HP.*, p. 112).

[2]To overcome the many conflicting accounts of Dakṣa's life, the compilers of the Purāṇas tried to explain the inconsistencies by stating that in every *manvantara* the

ṛṣis reappear, but with different origins.

[3]In some versions of this legend the sons number 5,000; in others 1,000, who being childless were succeeded by a second 1,000, also childless. Both groups 'dispersed themselves through the regions ... and as rivers that lose themselves in the ocean came back no more' (*VP.*, I.15).

[4]Whence *putrikā-putra*, a daughter's son, who by agreement or adoption become the 'son' of her father. The number of Dakṣa's daughters varies: the *MBh.* gives fifty, which is probably the original enumeration. The *Bhāg.*, *Kūrma*, *Padma*, *Liṅga* and *Vāyu Purs.* give sixty (v. *VP.*, p. 99, n.11).

[5]This sectarian rivalry is reflected in the *Kūrma Pur.*, which states that neither prayers nor any portion of the sacrificial oblation should be reserved or allotted to Śiva or to his *śakti* Umā.

v. Vīrabhadra I; Satī; Bhairava I.

Dakṣiṇā The honorarium or 'gift' given by the institutor of a sacrifice to its priestly officiants. The term is derived from *da*,[1] 'give', or from *dakṣ*, 'causing the imperfect to be accomplished' (*Nir.*, I.7). It is not a fee,[2] as there is no fixed scale of charges for the services rendered; nor is a gift demanded, though one is expected. But for those who evade their obligation or are niggardly retribution inevitably follows. This is confirmed in the *Ait. Br.* (VI.35) which states that a sacrifice without a *dakṣiṇā* will come to harm.

Originally the usual offering was a cow.[3] The gift of horses ensures that the donor will dwell with the sun forever; gold gives eternal life, and robes longevity. The liberal are certain to attain wealth, a beautiful bride, as well as the assistance of the gods in battle (*RV.*, X.107). According to the *ŚBr.* (XII.7.1,14) *dakṣiṇās* are 'healing medicine'.

In some passages of the *RV.*, *AV.* and other texts the term *iṣṭapūrta*[4] is used. It signifies that the *dakṣiṇā* should not be limited to the occasion of the sacrifice but given at any time. In this sense *dakṣiṇā* is equivalent to *dāna*, the word used in the Upaniṣads and post-Vedic texts to denote charitable gifts.

Just as the secular power relied on the levying of taxes for its maintenance, so the *brāhmaṇa* depended on *dakṣiṇās* for the maintenance of sacrificial performance, which in turn sustained the gods and ensured the continuity of the universe.

The *dakṣiṇā* was personified as a goddess who is invoked to save man from harm (*RV.*, I.18,5). She represents the female power of the Sacrifice (*yajña*) by which its fruition is ensured, and hence the goddess Dakṣiṇā is identified with the Cosmic Cow (Mother Nature), the giver of all life.[5]

The *Bṛhad-Ār. Up.* (5.2,3) links gifts (*dānena*) with the practice of self-control, compassion and altruism, a point of view prominent in Jainism and Buddhism, which increasingly influenced the social ideology of Hinduism.

[1]Cf. Skt. *dāna*, gift; Lat. *donum*, *donare*; Fr. *donner*; E. *donate*, etc.

[2]But more a 'present'. It is also a life-giving and a binding device (*CC.*, p. 77, n. 30 and p. 234), as well as a recognition of the claim to divine status of the priests themselves, a claim made in numerous texts (*AV.*, V.11,11; *Tait. Saṁ.*, 1.7.3,1, etc.). The quantity and quality of a *dakṣiṇā* is related to the purpose of the sacrifice. Thus lame cattle are prescribed for a magic rite intended to injure an enemy (Heesterman, *Ancient Indian Royal Consecration*, p. 164).

[3]*SED.* Cf. *RV.*, X.107,7. Later other animals were offered, viz., horses, asses, camels, dogs and sheep (*CC.*, p. 226). At Daśaratha's *aśvamedha* his four queens were given as *dakṣiṇā*, but they could be redeemed by a gift of money (*IRA.*, p. 124).

[4]From *iṣṭa* (personal piety), and *pūrta* (altruistic piety). The *iṣṭapūrtin* is one who has 'stored up' merit in heaven by instituting sacrifices during his lifetime, for his own and others' benefit.

[5]Agrawala, *Matsya Purāṇa—A Study*, p. 130.

Dakṣiṇācāra 'Right-hand' Tantric ritual, so-called to distinguish it from the 'Left-hand' (*vāmācāra*) form. The former is also called *pratinidhi*, 'worship through substitutes'.

v. Śākta; Tantra.

Dakṣiṇāgni The 'southern fire', also called *anvāhāryapacana*. Dakṣiṇāgni is one of the three fires in which offerings are made. It receives the monthly offerings to the *pitṛs* (the ancestors, who dwell in the South), and it is also the fire in which the dead are cremated; hence it is called the 'flesh-eating' fire (*RV.*, X.16,9).

The warlike Naḍa, King of Niṣāda, is identified with the *dakṣiṇāgni* (*ŚBr.*, II.3.2,2), probably because of the deaths caused by his predatory expeditions.

Dangerous powers are inherent in the southern fire which is dedicated to the demons who dwell in the south, 'the sphere of death and destruction'.[1] In the *pitṛ yajña* rite (a form of ancestor worship), the sacrifice must be performed on the afternoon of the day of the new moon, and take place in the *dakṣiṇāgni*. The offerings are first made in the north and finally in the south. After the name of each *pitṛ* has been uttered, the officiant touches water and looks towards the south. A pit is dug south or west of the southern fire to drive away the *rākṣasas* and *asuras*, and a brand from that fire is used as an additional mode of causing fear. A sacrifice for the working of spells (*abhicāra-yajña*) is also performed in this fire. If it is allowed to go out, the sacrificer's cattle will die unless expiation is made (*ŚBr.*, XI.5.3,10).

[1]*AIA.*, I, p. 38. Originally this fire was probably intended to drive away evil spirits who constantly threatened the sacrifice, and hence the household fire (*gārhapatya*) was regarded as beneficent, the *dakṣiṇāgni* as maleficent (*ŚBr.*, II.3.2,6).

v. Āhavanīya; Dakṣiṇāmūrti; Abhicāra.

Dakṣiṇākālikā A tantric form of Durgā.

Dakṣiṇāmūrti The 'southern image'. *Dakṣiṇā*, 'south', *mūrti*, 'form; an auspicious form of Śiva as the Supreme Yogin and teacher of knowledge, music and the Veda, who represents the altruistic asceticism that leads to union with *brahman*. He is also called Paśupati, the Lord of Animals, of hunters, and of lonely places. Both these forms are linked, as Zimmer[1] has pointed out, for both are destructive. The southern form embodies that knowledge and yogic power which destroys the bonds binding the 'individual' *ātman* to the world, and Śiva as Paśupati represents the destruction of life by time, wars, disease, hunting, etc.

Rao[2] considers that the southern form is so-called because Śiva faces the south when teaching the *ṛṣis*. Daniélou states that as all knowledge exists *in potentia* in the solar sphere (*sūrya-maṇḍala*), knowledge flows from the sun, i.e., from the north to the south, from above to below, and so towards disintegration and death. Therefore Dakṣiṇāmūrti is regarded as the presiding deity of death.[3] Boner[4] states that Dakṣiṇāmūrti is regarded as 'seated in the North, upon the Pole [= Meru] around which all the worlds revolve . . . In the esoteric sense [it means] . . . one who looks from above downwards, and, who looks from within outwards.' The *ŚBr.* identifies the sun with Death, because those creatures on the earth-side of the sun die, whilst those (the gods) on the other side are immortal. By the rays of the sun all creatures are attached to *prāṇa* (the vital breath or life-force) (II.3.3,7; VII.3.2,13).

[1]*AIA.*, I, p. 14. The south is also the place of the dead and of the *pitṛs*.

[2]*EHI.*, II, p. 273.

[3]*HP.*, p. 208.

[4]*CHS.*, p. 203, citing Coomaraswamy, *A New Approach to the Vedas*, pp. 12f.

v. Dakṣiṇāgni; Yama; Dakṣiṇāpati.

Dakṣiṇāpati 'Lord of the South.' An epithet of Yama, ruler of the dead.

Damanaka The tree Artemisa vulgaris, regarded as a vegetal form of Śiva, and hence those who worship it gain great merit, and attain the heavenly world (*AGP.*, I, ch. 80).

Ḍamaru[1] A drum, shaped like an hour-glass. It denotes primordial causal sound (*nāda*);[2] the drum is also one of Śiva's emblems when he is represented as the Cosmic Dancer, Naṭarāja. In this form Śiva generally has four arms (or occasionally eight), the drum being held in the hand of the upper right arm. The drum-beats symbolize the rhythmic pulsing of the creative forces as the universe unfolds. The upward and downward pointing triangles of the *ḍamaru* represent the two aspects of creative force, the *liṅgam* and *yoni* respectively. The meeting point of the triangles is the point 'from which creation begins'.[3] When separated, the dissolution of the world occurs.

[1]This name is of non-Indian origin (Przyluski, 'Un ancien peuple du Punjab; les Udumbara', *JA.*, 1926, pp. 34ff.).

[2]According to the Tantras creation begins with sound (*C. Herit. I.*, vol. II, pp. 198f.). A Tamil text states that 'creation arises from the drum'. Śiva has the epithets Ḍa 'Sound' and Nāḍatanu 'Consisting of sound'.

[3]*HP.*, p. 219.

v. Dundubhi I.

Damayantī v. Nala.

Dambha I. 'Deceit, hypocrisy, fraud', personified as a son of Adharma and Mṛṣā.

II. A name of Indra's thunderbolt (*vajra*), also called *dambholi*.

Dambholi v. Dambha II.

Dāmodara An epithet of Kṛṣṇa which refers to the attempts of his foster-mother to tie him up with a rope (*dāma*) round his belly (*udara*).

Daṁśa An *asura* cursed by a *ṛṣi* to be reborn as a 'blood-drinking octopod'. After being released from the curse he appeared as a red *rākṣasa* riding on a cloud.

Dānava (s) Sons of Danu, one of the daughters of Diti.[1] Like the Daityas, the Dānavas figure mostly in post-Vedic texts, and are represented sometimes as celestial powers opposed to the *devas*, but generally as native tribes (*daityas*, etc.) opposed to political and religious Indo-Āryan expansion.

[1]According to the *VP.* (I.21), Danu is the wife of Kaśyapa, to whom she bore numerous renowned *dānavas*. Some other Purs. refer to Diti as his wife.

v. Samudramathana; Asura(s); Daitya(s); Madhu; Kaiṭabha.

Daṇḍa I. Staff, rod, sceptre. The *daṇḍa* symbolizes power and sovereignty, and when in the hands of the goddess Kālī, the personification of the inexorable power of Time, it denotes both power and destruction. It is also a protection against evil spirits.

II. Daṇḍa, represents punishment, and is personified as the son of Dharma and Kriyā (*Manu*, VII.14; *VP.*, I.7). In some contexts *daṇḍa* is 'the embodiment of the principle of universal law and order, the descendant of the Vedic *ṛta*'.[1]

Punishments were often regarded as religious penances; by undergoing punishment in this life the guilty escaped the consequences of crime in the next.

[1] *EW.*, I, p. 112. Viṣṇu transformed himself into Daṇḍa (*MBh.*, 12.122,24, cited by Gonda, *Aspects*, p. 124).

v. Daṇḍadhara; Daṇḍin II.

Daṇḍadhara 'Rod-bearer.' A title of Yama, the ruler of the dead.

Daṇḍaka A vast forest in the Deccan, the scene of many of Rāma's and Sītā's adventures.

Daṇḍin I. The name of one of Sūrya's two door-keepers. Yama's staff is personified as Daṇḍin or Daṇḍa, who is a form of Yama himself. It inspires 'fear of the other world, which alone makes men virtuous' (*MBh.*, 12.15,5f.; cf. 3.56,10, *EM.*).

II. A writer of ornate prose narratives (*kāvyas*). His best known work is the *Daśakumāracarita* (Tales of the Ten Princes), consisting of a number 'of exciting and ingenious stories, held together by a framing narrative and all interwoven with great skill . . . Few works of Indian literature tell us so much about low life.'[1]

[1] *WI.*, p. 442. The *Daśakumāracarita* has been tr. into E. by A. W. Ryder, *The Ten Princes*.

Danu I. A son of Śrī. Also called Dānava. He was very handsome but was transformed into the monster Kabandha when he offended Indra; or according to another myth Indra left him as a headless trunk (*Rām.*, III.71,10. *SED.*).

II. A daughter of Dakṣa and the wife of Kaśyapa. She became the mother of 'demons' (*ŚBr.*, I.6.3,9; *VP.*, I.15).

v. Dānava(s); Kuṇāru.

Darbha v. Kuśa.

Daridrā 'Poor, deprived.' A form of Dhūmāvatī (the seventh *mahāvidyā*) as the goddess of poverty, frustration and despair.

Darpa 'Pride, insolence.' An epithet of Kāma, the god of love, who is the personification of pride. Darpa led many gods and *asuras* to destruction.

Darśana or **Dṛṣṭi** From *dṛś*, lit. 'looking at', 'viewing',[1] its meaning in Vedic texts. In the post-Vedic period it is used as a technical term and signifies the respective views of the six 'orthodox' (*āstika*) Hindu priestly 'schools'. These comprise the Vaiśeṣika, founded by Kaṇāda; the Akṣapāda or Nyāya, by Gautama; the Sāṁkhya, by Kapila; the Yoga, by Patañjali; the Pūrva-Mīmāṁsā, by Jaimini; and the Uttara Mīmāṁsā or Vedānta, presented by Bādarāyaṇa in the *Brahmasūtra*. In addition to these are three 'heterodox' (*nāstika*) *darśanas*: the Cārvāka, Jaina and Buddhist.

Except for the Pūrva-Mīmāṁsā the *darśanas* represent in their respective ways the transition from a dogmatic view of the sources of knowledge to an examination of knowledge itself. Though the foundation of these 'schools' (except the Cārvāka) is attributed to various seers, their views are the crystallization of centuries of speculative thought rather than the work of particular *ṛṣis*. Nor should the traditional labels 'orthodox' and 'heterodox' be interpreted as 'conservative' and 'radical' respectively, though the latter may apply to the 'heterodox'. A radical trend is evident in some of the hymns of *maṇḍala* X of the *RV.*, which gradually gained momentum, and in the Āraṇyakas and Upaniṣads reached the first definite stage of its development.

But this reformation of ideas does not represent a break with traditional views, but rather a modification and adaptation of them. Even the extreme 'heterodox' schools do not reject all traditional views, only those which critical examination regarded as doubtful or fallacious. Thus, though the authority of the Veda as an infallible source of knowledge was challenged, the validity of much of its teaching was recognized. Similarly, some views of the priestly schools were generally accepted, but the claims of the priests to divine authority and social superiority were rejected. Though the uncomprising materialism of the Cārvākas was rejected by the other schools, all views were openly debated or discussed, often with severally beneficial results. Sometimes schools might combine to dispute views of a particular school, as happened when the Idealist Vedāntins and Mahāyāna Buddhists opposed the more extreme Realist views of the Vaiśeṣikas. Yet despite the apparent irreconcilability of some 'orthodox' and 'heterodox' views, the contribution of the latter to Indian philosophical and religious thought has helped to preserve its continuity rather than to destroy it.

Thus Vedic cosmologico-ritual, *aupaniṣadic* mysticism, and the philosophical views of the *darśanas* are merely stages in the development of modern Hinduism, which has absorbed the best elements of each.

[1] Cf. the Gr. *derkomai*, to look, contemplate, to be receptive. Each *darśana* is described under its respective name.

Dāruka Name of Kṛṣṇa's charioteer.

Dāsa or **Dasyu** Two of the epithets applied in the *RV.* by the early Āryans to the indigenes of north-western India, whose hostility was expressed by 'hit and run' and 'scorched-earth'[1] tactics, regarded by the Āryan warriors as contrary to the rules of warfare. These epithets had also religious overtones, when applied by Vedic priests, and were expressions of contempt for people who were riteless (*a-karman*) and followers of strange ordinances (*anyavrata*) (*RV.*, X.22,8), and revilers of the gods (*deva-pīyu*) (*AV.*, XII.1,37).[2] In addition there were aesthetic objections to the *dasyus* because of their dark skins (*dāsa-varṇa*) and often ugly features (*a-nās* or *an-ās*),[3] as well as to their 'barbarous' speech. But the views expressed in the *RV.* and *AV.* represent chiefly those of particular Āryan seers. From the evidence now available it is apparent that the civilization of north-western India, at the time of the Āryan immigration, had reached a high level, and that all *dasyus* were not regarded as ignorant barbarians is tacitly admitted in other passages of the *RV.* and *AV.*, which refer to their wealth and social organization (*viśaḥ*).[4] Evidence of their cultural activities, broadened by contact with adjoining countries to the west, is also indicated by the archaeological and other remains in the cities of the Indus Valley. Furthermore, as Thibaut[5] points out, the so-called *dasyus* had a long series of names for high numerals, whereas the highest unit of Āryan enumeration did not go beyond 1,000, i.e., it had no single word for million, billion, etc.

The equation of *dasyu* with slave[6] in Vedic times, had not always the stigma of social inferiority that it subsequently acquired. During the early struggles of the *dasyus* to retain their independence the lot of many of those captured was generally slavery, just as that of the wives of those slain in battle was concubinage. On the other hand there was no similar equation made during later centuries regarding the indigenes of north-eastern India. Neither were they stigmatized by the epithet *dasyu*, nor ethnically distinguished by skin-colour. Such prejudices had long since ceased to be relevant, as is indicated—among other things—by the emergence from this area of such illustrious figures as the Buddha, Mahāvīra, and such notable dynasties as those founded by the Mauryas and the Guptas.

[1] If *dāsa* and *dasyu* are derived from *das*, in the sense of 'lay waste' as Whitney suggests, the original meaning would have been 'devastator', 'ravager', and thus also equated with 'enemy' (VI., vol. I, p. 357, n. 19). Moslem gypsies of the Balkans call Christian gypsies *das* (v. Singhal, *India*, vol. I, p. 239).

[2] *HCIP.*, vol. I, p. 249. Such strange ordinances doubtless included phallic worship which are referred to with disapproval in the *RV.*

[3] Perhaps identical with those whom Piggott designates 'the South Baluchistan or Proto-Australoid type' (*Prehistoric India*, p. 148).

[4] The term *dāsa* appears to denote individual indigenous tribes such as the Paṇis, Kirātas, Kīkaṭas, Cāṇḍalās, etc., whereas *dasyu* is used in the collective sense.

[5] *Astronomie, Astrologie und Mathematick*, p. 70, cited in *VI.*, vol. I, p. 343; v. also S.V. Visvanātha, *Racial Synthesis in Hindu Culture*, p. 38.

[6] Greek writers were positive that no slavery existed in India in Mauryan times, but 'a form of slavery of the *dāsas*, or servants prevailed, but they had some rights' (*EW.*, I, p. 111; v. also *WI.*, p. 153).

v. Anārya; Asura; Daitya; Varṇa; Nāga; Namuci; Śambara; Varcin; Pipru.

Daśakumāracarita v. Daṇḍin II.

Daśarājña Lit. 'Ten Kings'. The name of the war fought by ten tribes against Sudās, King of Bhārata (*RV.*, VII.18).[1]

Sudās[2] and his *purohita* Viśvāmitra, having conquered two minor native kingdoms, began to plan the subjugation of the entire land west of the Paruṣṇī (Rāvī). To ensure success he replaced Viśvāmitra by Vasiṣṭha, whom he considered more competent. This resulted in a feud between the two *purohitas* which was maintained for centuries by their respective descendants, and also led to Viśvāmitra transferring his allegiance to ten of the neighbouring rulers whom he knew were to be the next victims of Bhārata ambition. He persuaded them to form a confederate army, instead of waiting to be attacked individually.

There is some doubt about the ethnic composition of this army, but from the names mentioned (*RV.*, VII.18),[3] viz., the Pakthas, Bhalānas, Alinas, Śivas, Vaṣānins and others, it appears to have been mainly, if not entirely, composed of non-Āryans. It took up a position on the right or further bank of the Paruṣṇī, to the west of the Bhārata army. The confederate command planned to divert the river, thus enabling its army to cross and effect a surprise attack on the Bhāratas. Whether through faulty construction of the revetments or their undermining by the enemy is not known, but the river suddenly resumed its course while the confederate army was crossing it, drowning not only many of its men but also two of its royal commanders. Utter defeat by the Bhāratas swiftly followed, and with the subjugation of the rest of the country Sudās became the paramount ruler of the Land of the Five Rivers.

[1] This hymn gives an account of the battle but as it does not contain the word *daśarājña*, 'the passages in which it is found may reasonably be considered late' (*VI.*, vol. 1, pp. 356f.).

[2] Sudās and other kings mentioned in the *RV.*, 'although they may be accepted as real persons, cannot be invested with much interest from the historian's point of view' *OHI.*, 3rd ed., p. 53.

[3] The names vary in the *RV.* and later Vedic literature. Some (probably the Āryan tribes), are referred to as the 'five peoples' (*pañcajanāḥ*) but are not named.

v. Purohita; Bharata; Tṛtsu(s); Divodāsa I.

Daśaratha A prince and a descendant of Ikṣvāku, Daśaratha had three wives who were childless. To remedy this he performed the *aśvamedha* (horse sacrifice—a fertility rite), as a result of which the three wives became pregnant. To Kauśalyā was born Rāma; to Kaikeyī, Bharata; to Sumitrā, Lakṣmaṇa and Śatrughna. All four sons are manifestations of part of Viṣṇu, Rāma representing half, Bharata, a quarter, Lakṣmaṇa and Śatrughna the remaining quarter. The purpose of these manifestations is stated to be the destruction of the demon Rāvaṇa. Another version states that Daśaratha's wives shared a vessel of fertility-inducing nectar given by Viṣṇu, half being given to Kauśalyā, and a quarter each to Kaikeyī and Sumitrā, the share of the divine nature accorded to the four sons being the same as that in the former version.

Dasyu v. Dāsa.

Dattātreya Son of Atri and Anasūyā. The name of a post-Vedic sage who, by the syncretic process commonly employed in the Purāṇas and the Epic, is linked with the Vedic *ṛṣi* Atri, said to be his father.

Dattātreya is a partial *avatāra* of Viṣṇu, and his three sons Soma, Datta and Durvāsas also received a portion of the divine essence.[1]

According to the *Bhāg. Pur.* Dattātreya was a preceptor of the non-Āryan tribes; hence the allegation that he associated with people of low birth, which made him ritually impure. But it was also said of him, 'No stain can soil the heart purified by the ablution of learning and into which the light of knowledge has entered' (*Mārk. P.*, 18, 29).[2]

Dattātreya is also a mythological combination of three gods—Brahmā, Śiva and Viṣṇu, which indicates 'definite efforts towards a rapprochement between the different sects'.[3] His cult is one of the many facets of Advaita Vedānta, 'Dattātreya being worshipped by a large number of people to this day'.[4]

Iconographically Dattātreya is represented either as Brahmā, Śiva and Viṣṇu side by side, or by a four-armed Viṣṇu with the vehicles (*vāhanas*) of Brahmā and Śiva.[5] Dattātreya is accompanied by four dogs.

[1]For another version v. *HW.*, I, p. 97. The *Vāyu P.* (ch. 98, vs. 71ff.) states that Dattātreya is one of the human incarnations of Viṣṇu (cited by Banerjea, *DHI.*, p. 390).

[2]*HP.*, p. 183.

[3]*DHI.*, p. 233; also The Mahārāja of Mysore, *Dattātreya*, pp. 23 and 75; *HW.*, I, p. 98. Dattātreya is the tutelary deity of the royal house of Mysore.

[4]*VSM.*, p. 42.

[5]*EHI.*, I, p. 251.

Dayā 'Sympathy', 'compassion', personified as a daughter of Dakṣa, and the wife of Dharma.

Deva A celestial power; the deification or personification of natural forces and phenomena, etc., each distinguished by name and by particular attributes. They are generally regarded as auspicious, or potentially so if propitiated. *Deva* is the Vedic form, *daeva* the Zend, which were used in India and Irān respectively by Āryan migrants from the Caucasus.

The term *deva*[1] is etymologically connected with *dyaus*,[2] the bright sky, and is regarded as the source of divine powers like Sūrya the sun; Agni, the god of fire; the Maruts, the storm-gods, etc. But there is a constant tendency to assimilation and interchange of attributes; the same qualities are ascribed to different deities, and the same actions performed by them, so that they tend to become indistinguishable in character.[3] The number and classification of the gods are thus subject to variation. In *RV.*, I.139,11 and 45,2 they number thirty-three, equally divided among the three spheres, the heavens, earth and waters;[4] in the *ŚBr.*, IV.5.7,2, they comprise eight Vasus, eleven Rudras, twelve Ādityas, Heaven and Earth (to which the Creator Prajāpati is added as the thirty-fourth).

The early Vedic divinities all appear to have been male, but the inclusion later of goddesses probably reflects the influence of indigenous mother-goddess cults. Among these *devīs* are Ūrmyā (Night) and her sister Uṣas (Dawn); Iḷā, goddess of sacred speech and action; Sarasvatī, the river-goddess, who is also connected with music; and Mahī, the Great, variously described (*RV.*, I.13,7–9); Nirṛti, goddess of death and destruction (V.41,17); and Sūryā, daughter of Sūrya, the Sun (VI.63,5).

As the representatives of the gods, the priests also claimed to share divinity with them. Notable heroes like Kṛṣṇa and the three Rāmas achieved divine status as *avatāras* of Viṣṇu, and like Śiva have the supreme title, Mahādeva.

The early Vedic seers,[5] like their Greek counterparts, ascribe the origin of the *devas* to Heaven and Earth, but later cosmogonic theory, ascribed the origin of both *devas* and anti-gods to Prajāpati. Initially only Agni was immortal (I.13,5, etc.), but subsequently immortality was conferred on all major Vedic divinities (*ŚBr.*, II.2.2, 8–14); etc. *RV.* VIII.48,3, records that by drinking the sacred *soma* juice men became immortal and 'discovered' the gods.[6]

According to the mythology of the *MBh.* the *devas*, when appearing to mortals, neither sweat, nor blink their eyes, nor do their feet touch the ground; they are shadowless (as are the *bhūtas*), and they wear never-fading flowery ornaments.[7] But in other passages it is stated that their flower-garlands fade when they are frightened, and that Rāma saw the shadows of *devas*, *gandharvas* and *rākṣasas* at a place called Subhūmika.

[1]According to the *Chān. Up.*, 6,3, *deva* refers to any abstract or cosmic potency.

[2]From *div*, to shine, be bright; nom. *dyaus*.

[3]*ERE.*, VI, p. 283. In Greece, as in India, new and separate personages were created out of the 'epithets of a divinity detached from the proper name and then misunderstood' (Farnell, *Cults*, I, p. 182).

[4]But *RV.*, X.52,6, declares that 3,339 gods served and honoured Agni. Allegro writing of the Near and Middle East considers that there was not a multiplicity of gods in the ancient world, but 'many aspects of the one deity of fertility . . . The god was the seed, his name and functions finding verbal expression in the one Sumerian phoneme U' (*The Sacred Mushroom and the Cross*, p. 29). In India any individual shape, either of a person, personal god or of a single universe is 'considered purely accidental and transitory' (*IWP.*, p. 38).

[5]The ancient *ṛṣis* are said to have 'seen' the gods in visions. C. Kunhan Raja considers that the gods are 'only the objects of an inner experience of a few specially gifted *ṛṣis*' (*C. Herit. I.*, vol. I, p. 28). By means of *mantras* the ordinary man can gain 'some knowledge' of the *devas*. A *deva* 'is believed to be present in any power centre or manifestation of power' (Gonda, *Loka*, p. 107).

[6]This may indicate that *soma* was a hallucinogenic drug (rather than an intoxicant), perhaps similar in its effects to the modern 'mind-expanding' drug LSD.

[7]The gods are said to detest the smell of human beings (*Ait. Br.*, III.30).

v. Vīra I; Ṛtam I; Iṣṭadevatā.

Deva-dāsī(s) A class of women dedicated to the service of the temple, who were held to be married to the god associated with it,[1] and hence their designation *deva-dāsī*, 'slaves of the god', the latter usually referring to Śiva, the lord of the dance. At one time their morals 'were generally patterns of piety and propriety',[2] but later they appear to have been intended mainly for the gratification of the *brāhmaṇas*, or in some parts of India for any who solicited them.[3] Every temple, according to its size, had eight or more dancers.

There are few references to the *deva-dāsīs* before the Middle Ages. Most temple-prostitution was 'in the South, where it survived until recent times. The wild fertility cults of the early Tamils involved orgiastic dancing, and their earliest literature shows that prostitution was common among them' (*WI.*, p. 185).

Girls destined to be *deva-dāsīs* were drawn from any caste and preparation for their future role began in infancy. They were taught to read and write, as well as to sing and dance, and also to play one or more musical instruments, and often performed at public ceremonies. The income from this source and the gifts of admirers enabled some *deva-dāsīs* to devote large sums to worthy causes. Their liberality and association with the temple gave them a certain status, so that they were allowed to sit at public ceremonies with male officials whose wives and daughters were denied this privilege.

Under Moslem rule in India many *deva-dāsīs* in northern temples were seized and put in the harems of the new rulers, but in parts of the Deccan, less subject to Moslem power and influence, the *deva-dāsīs* were unmolested.

From the middle of the nineteenth century the status of Indian women has gradually been raised, so that not only are the universities of India and elsewhere open to them, but the highest political office is occupied by one of them. No longer is the role of dancer and singer associated with the temple *deva-dāsīs*, but is now regarded, like any of the arts, as a cultural activity of a modern civilized society.[4]

[1]*BH.*, p. 451.

[2]Ibid.

[3]*Cyclo. I.*, I, p. 923.

[4]Much of this can be attributed to Shanta Rao, the great Indian danseuse who, despite parental disapproval, dedicated herself to her art and deprived it of its former stigma.

v. Bhāvinī; Nāṭya Veda.

Devadatta I. 'God-given.' Name of Arjuna's conch-shell which came from a lake north of Kailāsa. It had originally belonged to Varuṇa, the god of the waters (*MBh.*, Sabda pa., 3).

II. The white horse of Pārāśraya.

v. Kalkin.

Devakī[1] A daughter of Devaka, a descendant of the Kukura branch of the Yādava royal line. She was thus the cousin of Kaṁsa, king of Mathurā, her father's eldest brother. Devakī married Vasudeva, the Minister of Kaṁsa. The King, after deposing his father Ugrasena and usurping the throne, was threatened by a prediction that he would one day be slain by one of Devakī's sons. To avert this calamity he had her first six sons destroyed at birth, but owing to a subterfuge failed to kill the seventh and eighth, Balarāma and Kṛṣṇa. Later the prediction was fulfilled by Kṛṣṇa who restored Ugrasena to the throne, an event that vitally affected Kṛṣṇa's future and that of much of northern India.

Whatever the actual means used to conceal the birth of Balarāma and Kṛṣṇa, they were not recorded, but myth presents Balarāma's escape as an obstetrical miracle, performed by the transplanting of his embryo from the womb of Devakī to that of Rohiṇī, Vasudeva's second wife. Another myth (*VP.*, V.1) states that Viṣṇu plucked from his head one white and one black hair, the former becoming the embryo of Balarāma, the latter that of Kṛṣṇa. At birth both children were secretly taken to the country.

[1]The *AGP.* (II, p. 1013) embellishes history by making Devakī an incarnation of Aditi, and her husband Vasudeva an incarnation of Kaśyapa.

Devālā v. Rāga.

Devaloka The world or sphere of a divinity, i.e., Paradise; a term also applied to any one of the three, seven or twenty-one superior worlds.

The *devaloka* is said to be the best of the three worlds, to be reached only through knowledge (*Bṛhad-Ār. Up.*, I.5,16). If the oblation offered by the Adhvaryu priest flames upwards, this indicates that the sacrificer will attain the sphere of the gods (3.1,8). Those who have lived a pure life in the forest solitudes will at death pass into the flame of the cremation fire; from the flame into the day; from day into the half-month of the waxing moon; then into the six months when the sun moves north-ward; then to the *devaloka*; from there to the sun and finally into the fire of lightning (6.2,15).

Devanāgarī 'The divine script' developed from an early style (Brāhmī) to the highly ornamented form 'in which Sanskrit, Prākrit, Hindī and Marāthī are written at the present day'.[1] The *devanāgarī* script indicates the high standard of literacy attained in centres of learning and in cities, and the extension of the vocabulary and grammar required to meet the needs of sophisticated communities.

[1] *WI.*, p. 398.

Devapatha I. The 'path of the gods' which is the way they take from any direction to the sky. The path itself becomes visible to anyone who touches water and then sings a *gātha* to Rudra (*MBh.*, 3.114, 6–10, *EM.*, p. 59).
II. The *devapathas* of a city may refer to royal roads or ways leading to temples.

v. Devayāna.

Devarṣi A *ṛṣi* of the divine class, among which were Nārada, Parvata, Nara and Nārāyaṇa, the Vālakhilyas, etc.

v. Ṛṣis.

Devatā(s) Household and 'sylvan deities who do not share the characteristics of the supernal *devas* (also called *devatās*)',[1] but seem to belong to earth. Diehl[2] points out that the 'experience of "possession" dominates the relationship between man and god, obliterating not only the distinction between god and demon but making for but a slight variation of the divine appearance indicated by different names'. Thus a word like *tēvatai* (Tamil), *devatā* (Skt.), can mean both 'deity' and 'demon'. '*Devatā*' is also applied to the whole body of minor gods.

[1] *EM.*, p. 57. Coomaraswamy mentions references in the *MBh.* to *devatās*, *yakṣīs*, etc., dwelling in the *kaḍamba* tree (*HIIA.*, p. 64, n.2). In the Upaniṣads '*devatā*' is applied to any abstract or cosmic 'potency' (v. *Chān. Up.*, 6.3).

[2] *Instrument and Purpose*, pp. 279f. and n. 3. Cf. 'possession' in Haitian Voodoo (Maya Deren, *Divine Horsemen*, pp. 16f.; 247ff., etc.).

v. Grāmadevatā.

Devatīrtha That part of the hands sacred to the *devas*, viz., the tips of the fingers.

Devayajana v. Vināyaka I.

Devayāna 'The Path of the gods.' The way followed after death by ascetics and those who have attained knowledge and faith, which leads to complete absorption in *brahman* (*Chān. Up.*, IV.15, 5–6; *Bṛhad-Ār. Up.*, VI.2,15).

Belief in this mystical path, or of a bridge or river to be crossed, is common to 'most ancient mythologies'.[1] The *ŚBr.* (XII.7.3,7) states that the world of the gods is in the North, beyond Mount Kailāsa, whence stretches a narrow, terrifying path barely wide enough for one person.

The *Kauṣ. Up.* (1.3–6) description of the path is presented in the style of an early Vedic poet. On the way to *nirvāṇa* the pilgrim comes successively to the worlds of Agni, Vāyu, Varuṇa, Indra and Prajāpati, and finally to the world of Brahmā in which is situated the lake Āra and the river Vijarā in which the pilgrim s good and evil deeds are washed away. Here the goddesses Mānasī and Cākṣuṣī gather flowers with which they weave the worlds.

[1]Cf. the Cinvat bridge of Irānian mythology, and the part played by bridge-symbolism 'in Christian and Islamic apocalypses as well as in the initiatory traditions of the western Middle Ages' (Eliade, *Shamanism*, p. 484).

v. Devapatha I.

Devayānī The ambitious only daughter of the Bhārgava priest Śukra, the *purohita* of Yayāti, paramount ruler of several native and as yet not fully brahmanized kingdoms, one of whose vassals was King Vṛṣaparvan, father of a very attractive daughter Śarmiṣṭhā. These five—and Kaca, Śukra's pupil—comprise the *dramatis personae* of a closely woven succession of stories (*MBh.*, Ādi pa., 76–83), which include myth, folklore, magic, social customs, feminine psychology, and genealogy.

The first story concerns the mythical origin of fire (*agni*) brought to earth by the ancient fire-priest Bhṛgu, who passed on the magical element to his descendants, the Bhārgavas. Agni, alone of the gods to possess immortality, thus aroused their envy, so they deputed Kaca, Bṛhaspati's son, to become a pupil of the Bhārgava Śukra and by devious means obtain the secret of immortality.

Kaca made several attempts, each of which might have cost him his life but for Devayānī, whose motive in rescuing him was her determination that he should marry her. This was an unforeseen complication, which was aggravated by his refusal and his explanation, that as her father's pupil his relationship to her was that of a brother, and that therefore their marriage would be incestuous. That problem was resolved by Kaca's discovery of Śukra's secret and his return to the delighted gods.

The next episode is concerned with the peculiarly feminine quarrel of Devayānī and Śarmiṣṭhā, which culminated in Śarmiṣṭhā being thrown into a disused well, where she might have perished but for her discovery by Yayāti, when out hunting. Thwarted again, Devayānī repeated to her father some of Śarmiṣṭhā's taunts, undeniably true and therefore the more unforgivable —and insisted that Śarmiṣṭhā and her attendants should become her servants; a demand her father Vṛṣaparvan was powerless to refuse.

With her potential rival removed, Devayānī took the first opportunity of letting Yayāti know that she would not prove an unwilling bride. The king reminded her that she was the daughter of a priest, and he of a lower social order, saying, 'Even your father cannot bestow you on a king, however great.'[1] But finally he agreed, provided she obtained her father's consent. Despite the sin of contracting a *pratiloma* marriage and creating a mixed caste Śukra consented, provided that the king remained faithful to Devayānī. At her insistence Śukra added that Śarmiṣṭhā should be given a separate establishment and thus not be a possible rival. During the ensuing years Devayānī bore two sons, Yadu and Turvaśu, and Yayāti added to his dominions. But Śarmiṣṭhā, tired of her banishment, and realizing that her youth was slipping away, arranged a secret meeting with Yayāti, and made it clear that she wished to become his second wife.[2] She said that she had been unjustly made the slave of Devayānī and that as he was Devayānī's lord and master, therefore he must be hers also. Unable to resist her appeal, Yayāti consented.

When Śarmiṣṭhā subsequently bore a son, Devayānī, though at first suspicious, was given an explanation that allayed her doubts of her husband's fidelity. Śarmiṣṭhā was more circumspect about the births of her second and third sons, but Devayānī finally learned of them and implored her father to avenge her, adding what rankled most with her: 'O father, here is Śarmiṣṭhā with three sons, while I have only two!'

Yayāti, pressed for an explanation by Śukra, replied, 'O *brāhmaṇa*, what I did was from no selfish motive. When solicited by a woman in certain circumstances, a man may not lawfully reject her.' Śukra's reply was to curse Yayāti that he should immediately become old and decrepit. Aware of the irrevocability of a *brāhmaṇa*'s curse, Yayāti nonetheless pleaded for its mitigation. Finally Śukra declared that his youth would be restored only if one of his sons accepted the curse. The youngest, Śarmiṣṭhā's son Puru, alone agreed to do so. The intention in the subsequent account of his life appears to be merely to link it with the genealogy of the Pāṇḍavas and Kauravas.

[1]Such a marriage between two classes was forbidden.

[2]i.e., after three monthly periods have passed, a maiden (who is free to marry) may 'unite herself, of her own will, to a blameless man' (*Gautama Dharmaśāstra*, XVIII.20).

v. Puru; Uśanas Kāvya.

Devayoni I. The origin or birthplace of a god.

II. The sacred wood used for kindling fire.

v. Araṇi.

Devī The general term for a goddess; the feminine form of *deva*, a god or celestial power. The *RV.* frequently refers to the *devīs* as wives of the gods, or to parts of religious worship personified as goddesses, such as Hotrā, Bharatī and Iḷā (II.1,11, etc.).

Dawn (Uṣas) and Night (Rātrī) are similarly personified (VIII.10,2; etc.), as also are sacred rivers, including Gaṅgā, Yamunā, Śutudrī, Vipās, Paruṣṇī and Sarasvatī (III.33,1; X.75,5; etc.).

But it is not until the post-Vedic period that the term *devī* becomes Devī, *the* Goddess, or Mahādevī, Supreme Goddess, and is identified with Cosmic Energy (*śakti*), the dynamic aspect of Śiva. Such a significant notion represents a long period of philosophical speculation and the absorption of many local goddesses into the Śaiva pantheon, though many still retain a pseudo-individuality in popular festivals.[1] They comprise a great number, and include such familiar names as Pārvatī, Durgā, Kālī, Umā, Gaurī, Jagan-mātā. But such distinctions are apparent rather than real; each is Devī and Devī is each of them and the sum of all that they represent.[2]

Historically the notion of *devī* is the culmination of a long process that began with the worship of the fertility or mother-goddess, and local nature-goddesses, a common feature of most early mythologies. Thus it is not 'unreasonable to conclude that the early Indus Valley ringstones and female figurines along with the circular discs and tiny nude female figures of the historic period collectively establish the long continued existence of the worship of the female principle in aniconic and iconic forms'.[3]

Ultimately Devī became associated with the *trimūrti*, and homage paid to her is counted as homage to the three deities comprising it, since they are believed to have been born from her qualities.[4] Thus when the joint power of Brahmā, Viṣṇu and Śiva is combined in the form of Īśvara 'it becomes the Supreme-Goddess (Bhagavatī), the Resplendent-One (Devī)'.[5] Devī is all things, as is indicated by her numerous epithets. Thus she is Ambikā (the Mother), Kanyā (the Virgin), Satī (Virtuous), Kāmākṣī (Wanton-eyed), etc. On *aduḥkhanavami*, the ninth day of the first fortnight of bhādrapada, women worship Devī to avert evil during the coming year.

[1]Such as 'the present-day *navapatrikā-praveśa* ceremony in the autumnal worship of Durgā in Bengal which is based on much earlier authority' (*PTR*., p. 126).

[2]Cf. the Sumerian goddess Innina (Ishtar) who gradually absorbs 'into herself the attributes of most of the other female divinities, and is known as the goddess *par excellence*' (Hooke, *Babylonian and Assyrian Religion*, p. 30).

[3]*PTR*., p. 111.

[4]'Appropriation of Śiva's attributes by Devī', *BSOAS*., 1955, xvii/3, p. 523.

[5]*HP*., p. 253.

v. Śākta; Pārvatī.

Dhananjaya I. The name of a many-headed serpent of great power, and one of Kadrū's thousand serpent progeny (*VP*., I.21).

II. An arranger of the Vedas in the sixteenth *dvāpara* age (*VP*., III.3).

III. A title of Arjuna.

Dhanurveda The science of archery.[1] It is attributed to Viśvāmitra or Bhṛgu, and is an *upaveda* (auxiliary science) connected with the *Yajurveda*. Every king was expected to be proficient in archery.

[1]Part of the *AGP*. (II, pp. 894ff.) is devoted to the training of the archer.

v. Dhanus; Bāṇa I.

Dhanus 'Bow', derived from *dhanv* 'to go' or 'to kill' (*Nir*., 9.16). The bow, arrows and corselet were the traditional equipment of the warrior (*kṣatriya*).The bow is praised in a hymn to war-weapons as the winner of cattle and of battle, the disperser of enemies (*RV*., VI.75), and in the *ŚBr*. is said to be 'the nobleman's strength' (V.3.5,30).

A bow was placed in the right hand of a dead warrior, its removal being the final act of the funerary rites (*RV*., X.18,9). The bow is sometimes personified and depicted as an accessory, as on the Śeṣaśayana relief at Deogarh.[1]

Some deities possess bows, all of which are named. Viṣṇu possessed two called *śārṅga* and *cāpa*, the latter being successively passed down to Rāma and other heroes; Śiva's bow was called *ājagava*; Soma's *gāṇḍīva*.

In Mauryan times the usual Indian bows were powerful weapons five or six feet long and often made of bamboo. Subsequently bows became smaller and were made of horn (*śārṅga*).

[1]*DHI*., p. 538.

v. Āyudhapuruṣa; Bāṇa I; Iṣu; Dhanurveda.

Dhanvantari The physician of the gods. A *ṛṣi*[1] referred to in the *Garuḍa P*. (139, 8–11) as the first propounder of medical science (*āyurveda*). This is confirmed in the *VP*. (IV.8) which states that Dhanvantari in a former incarnation was told by Nārāyaṇa that he should be reborn in the royal family of Kāśī-rāja, and would compose the eightfold medical system. A variant of this legend claims the distinction for the king of Kāśī, styled Divodāsa or Devadāsa Kāśī-rāja, but the variation is probably the result of a confusion of names, his grandson (son of Dīrghatamas) being also called Divodāsa, the preceptor of Suśruta, to whom the authorship of the medical treatise, the *Suśruta Saṁhitā*, is traditionally attributed. As Kāśī (the modern Banāras) has from early times been a centre of learning, especially of medical science, the traditional connexion of Dhanvantari[2] is not without foundation.

To add further lustre to his reputation, he is said to have emerged from the Churning of the Ocean (*samudra-mathana*) bearing in his hands a cup of *amṛta*—the elixir of immortality. Because of his contribution to medicine Dhanvantari became entitled to share the offerings made to the gods (*VP*., IV.8; *Manu*, III.85).

[1]Daniélou (*HP*., pp. 184f.) *et al*. consider that Dhanvantari was a Vedic deity to whom offerings were made at twilight in the north-eastern quarter.

[2]Dhanvantari may have been a name or 'title' given to those who excelled in medical knowledge.

v. Caraka.

Dhāraṇā A form of one-pointed meditation or contemplation of an image, or a mental visualization of a deity; from *dhṛ*, 'to hold' (*VP*., 513, n. 17). A man who dies whilst in *dhāraṇā*, assists the 'souls' of his relations and finally enters Paradise himself (*AGP*., II, pp. 1310–11).

Dharaṇī A name of the Earth-goddess.

Dhāraṇī Lit. 'that by which something is sustained or kept up';[1] a mnemonic formula containing *mantras*. In the popular sense *dhāraṇīs* are spells which protect against demons, diseases, and other malign influences.

[1]Dasgupta, *ORC.*, p. 20.

v. Mantra.

Dharaṇīdhara Lit. 'Earth-supporter'. An epithet applied to the mythical serpent Śeṣa, to the tortoise (*kūrma*), and to the eight elephants (*abhranāgas*) upon which the earth rests. The epithet is also applied to Viṣṇu, Kṛṣṇa and Śiva.

v. Gaja; Dharaṇī.

Dharma or **Dharman** I. Moral and religious duty; law; custom. From *dhar*, 'to hold'; that which forms a foundation and upholds, or constitutes law and custom. *Dharma* implies movement, change, dynamic qualities, the chief characteristics of natural law. Thus its opposite *a-dharma*, signifies the law of statics and non-motion, and hence by comparison 'un-natural'. Initially it was applied to cosmological theory and to sacerdotal and social rules by which the community, the gods and the universe were held together. Except in a very limited sense, the notion of *dharma* as a principle or an ethical concept is lacking in the *RV*. In some passages it refers entirely to sacrificial procedure, such as the kindling of the fire in accordance with ancient custom (III.17,1); in others to ensure that the worship of the gods shall be carried out 'as the laws of men ordain' (III.60,6).

In the Brāhmaṇas *dharma* generally means 'duty', specifically that relating to the sacrifice, but the Dharmasūtras and Dharmaśāstras, like the Hebraic Decalogue, regard *dharma* as a code of rules designed to ensure the cohesion of the community. Later the extension of Brahmanic influence and the establishment of kingdoms necessitated further regulations. These were codified under three headings: Śrauta, dealing with the major sacrifices; Gṛhya, with purificatory and household rites; Dharma, with temporal duties, customs, etc.; the three constituting the 'Whole Duty of Man'.

The rights of ownership, and any other rights endorsed by *dharma* were protected by the provision of penalties or sanctions (*daṇḍa*). Thus without *daṇḍa* there was no security, social, political or religious for the three superior classes. But different laws and customs, or variant interpretations of them, were subject to regional traditions or to the respective views of rulers and of priestly schools.[1] Thus many anomalies existed in both *dharma* and *daṇḍa*, the chief of which relate to the *śūdra* or menial caste, for whom *daṇḍa* often meant death, where for the same crime, committed by one of the superior castes, the penalty was minimal.

The classical Upaniṣads are chiefly concerned with the mystical realization of the Universal Principle (*brahman*) rather than with the question of *dharma* as an ethical principle. The Purāṇas also, though for different reasons, generally lack any appreciation of the ethical aspect of *dharma*. They are chiefly concerned, as the *VP.* (III.6) declares, with 'the creation of the world and its successive reproductions, the genealogies of the patriarchs and kings, the periods of the Manus, and the transactions of the royal dynasties'. Particular Purāṇas, such as the *Viṣṇu* and *Śiva*, are of a sectarian character, and tend to be laudatory and devotional, and like the *VP.* (III.6), to regard *dharma* simply as one of the fourteen (or eighteen) principal branches of knowledge. The *MBh.* and *Rām.* suggest a growing awareness of the ethical nature of *dharma*,[2] which is indicated in some of their homilies and stories.

The earliest exposition of *dharma* as an ethical philosophy may be attributed to Buddhism, and was possibly its greatest contribution to Hinduism. The Buddhist definition, while rejecting sacerdotalism and caste, adopted the best of the current social rules. It rationalized cosmological theory and epistemology; defined ideal kingship, later exemplified by the Emperor Aśoka; and like Jainism advocated the doctrine of non-injury (*ahiṁsā*).

[1]Anomalies in the Dharmaśāstras are often due to portions having been extracted from one work and incorporated in another, or are the result of additions and alterations.

[2]It 'means an intellectual tenet and/or psychological, social and religious attitudes, all in one' (Heimann, *Facets*, pp. 158f). Potter points out that the 'attitude of *dharma* is . . . concern for others as a fundamental extension of oneself' (*Presuppositions of India's Philosophies*, p. 8). Cf. Basham, *WI.*, p. 137.

v. Ṛtam I and II.

II. A mythical *ṛṣi*, sometimes classed as a Prajāpati and mind-born son of Brahmā. His wives were thirteen (or ten) of Dakṣa's daughters by whom he had numerous children who personify virtues and religious rites and represent allegorically the moral and religious duties indicated by the word *dharma*.

v. Nandi; Yudhiṣṭhira; Dharmarāja; Dharmaputra.

Dharmapāśa The noose used by Varuṇa to control and bind demons (*RV.*, VI.74,4). Although the noose or lasso was used as a weapon of war in prehistoric times, Varuṇa's noose appears to be a magical weapon by which he effortlessly captures his enemies.[1]

[1]Eliade, *Images and Symbols*, p. 101.

v. Pāśa.

Dharmaputra 'Son of Dharma.' An epithet applied to Yudhiṣṭhira, the eldest of the Pāṇḍu princes, as a token of his virtuous qualities. Similarly Arjuna, because of his skill in arms, is referred to as Indraputra (Son of Indra).

v. Kunti; Pṛthivī.

Dharmarāja 'King of Justice.' An epithet of Yama, as the embodiment of *dharma* (law).

Dharmaśāstra The general name for a law-book or code of laws.[1] The most important are the codes of Manu and Yājñavalkya, but those of Āpastamba, Gautama, Vāsiṣṭha and Baudhāyana are frequently cited.

[1]v. P.V. Kane, *History of Dharmaśāstra*, vols I–V.

v. Dharma I; Manu-smṛti.

Dhātar (Vedic) **Dhātṛ** (Skt.) 'Establisher', 'arranger', 'founder', 'creator', 'supporter'. As one of the Ādityas, Dhātar has a cosmogonic role as Creator[1] of 'the sun and moon, heaven and earth, and the regions of air and light' (*RV*., X.190,3). Dhātar is associated with conception (*RV*., X.184,1–2; *AV*., VII.17 and 20).[2] Dhātar is also invoked to give wealth, longevity, immortality and rain, the last being contained in a huge skin-bag in the skies which Dhātar unties (*AV*., VII.18).

[1]'Dhātṛ interchanges with Vidhātṛ and both with Brahmā as creator' (*EM*., p. 81). He is also identified with the Year (*Tait. Saṁ*., I.5,1) and with *ātman* (*Maitri Up*., 6.8). In bearing a son a wife regenerates her husband and she is called a *dhātrī* (*IRA*., p. 113).

[2]This passage is incorporated in *AV*., V.25, and included in the *garbhādhāna* ceremony to ensure conception.

Dhenu A milch cow,[1] metaphorically the earth. The nectar-yielding cow was fashioned by the Ṛbhus (*Bṛhadd*., III.85) and is said to be a form of Vāc (II.78).

[1]The *Nir*. (11.42) derives *dhenu* from *dhe* (to suck); or from *dhi* (to nourish).

Dhenuka I. A fierce demon who dwelt in a grove of palm-trees. Some cowherds on seeing the ripe fruit asked Rāma and Kṛṣṇa to shake it down for them. When Dhenuka heard the noise of fruit falling he assumed the form of an ass and began furiously to kick Rāma who, seizing his hind legs, whirled him round and round till he was dead, and then tossed him up on to a tree. The other asses who came to Dhenuka's aid were similarly treated (*VP*., V.8).[1]

This legend, like some of those of Kṛṣṇa's boyhood, was probably brought to India by the Ābhīras, a cattle-breeding people,[2] but Banerjea suggests that the killing of Dhenuka, like the slaying of the bull-demon Ariṣṭa and the horse-demon Keśin, may be figurative references 'to the subjugation of some of the lower cults by the higher one'.[3]

[1]Cf. the eastern Nigerian custom of breaking the legs of live horses and then hanging the bodies on trees, described by Elizabeth Huxley in *Four Guineas*.

[2]*VSM*., pp. 37f. Wilson suggests that they are the Abhirs or Ahirs of Gujarat, the Abiria of Ptolemy (*Notes on the Sabda Parva of the Mahābhārata*, p. 5).

[3]*DHI*., p. 102. Dhenuka is also the name of a tribal group.

II. The name of a sacred bathing-place (*tīrtha*) where, by staying one night and giving away sesame and kine, the giver is cleansed of all sin and attains the region of the moon-god (Soma) (*MBh*., Vana pa., 84).

Dhiṣaṇa Name of a demon (*AV*., II.14,1).

Dhiṣaṇā A goddess of abundance and a wife of the gods (*RV*., I.26,10); a 'mother' closely associated with the preparation of the *soma* juice (IV.34,1), and with the *soma*-bowl itself, which she sometimes personifies. In the plural the *dhiṣaṇās* are divine guardians. Like Aṅgiras they kindled the sacred fire; are identified with the goddess Vāc;[1] with days and nights, with metres, the stars (*ŚBr*., VI.5.4,5–8), and with the sciences (*Tait. Saṁ*., V.1,7). They are invoked to give their worshippers strength, and not to harm them (*Tait. Saṁ*., I.4,1).

[1]According to Sāyaṇa and the *Nir*., 8.3; but Hillebrandt identifies them with the Earth.

Dhiṣṇya I. 'Mindful, attentive, liberal.' An epithet of the Aśvins (*RV*., I.3,2).

II. A side-altar, generally consisting of a mound of earth covered with sand, on which the sacrificial fire was laid. Eight *dhiṣṇyas* were used in the *soma* sacrifice, each representing a particular aspect of Agni (*ŚBr*., X.4.3,21). Special trenches were dug to provide the earth for these side-altars and in the trenches resided the demons who haunted the sacrificial ground.

v. Vedi; Agnicayana.

Dhṛṣṭa A magic formula uttered over weapons.

Dhṛṣṭadyumna A son of Drupada,[1] and commander of the Pāṇḍava army in the war against the Kauravas. He slew Droṇa who had beheaded his father, and was in turn trampled to death as he lay asleep by Droṇa's son, Aśvatthāman.

[1]He is also called a son of Agni, having been born from the sacrificial fire (*agni*), kindled for the express purpose of injuring an enemy, the strength of the foe being poured on to the fire (*EM*., p. 100).

Dhṛtarāṣṭra I. The blind eldest son of Vyāsa and Ambikā, and ruler of the Kuru kingdom. He married Gāndhārī by whom he had a hundred sons, the eldest being Duryodhana (*VP*., IV.20). Dhṛtarāṣṭra renounced the throne and Duryodhana became king and led the Kauravas in the war against the Pāṇḍavas.

v. Pāṇḍu; Mahābhārata; Arjuna.

II. The name of a huge many-headed serpent, who was

one of the thousand sons of Kadrū.[1]

[1]Cf. *AV.*, VIII,10,29.

Dhṛti 'Steadfast', resolute'. These qualities were personified as a daughter of Dakṣa and one of Dharma's wives (*VP.*, I.7).

Dhruva 'Firm, fixed, constant.' In the sūtras[1] Dhruva denotes the Pole Star which, because of its 'fixed' position in the heavens, has long been used by mariners. In the Hindu marriage ceremony it symbolizes the constancy expected of the bride.

A Vaiṣṇava legend ascribes Dhruva's position in the heavens to Viṣṇu (*VP.*, I.15). Dhruva is thus called the Pivot of the Planets (*grahādhāra*), a designation similar to those applied to the Pole Star in other countries.[2] According to the *VP.*, II.9, all the celestial luminaries are bound to the Pole Star by aerial cords.

[1]*Āśvalāyana Gṛhya*, I.7,22; *Sāṁkhyāyana Gṛhya*, I.17,2, etc.

[2]The Greeks regarded Mount Olympus as a pillar, situated at the 'navel of the earth', and reaching to the Pole Star; the Lapps know the Pole Star as *tjuöld* (the Stake); the Turks, as *deymirqazig* (the Iron Peg); and the Chinese, as the Pivot (Smythe-Palmer, cited by Gaster, *Thespis*, p. 183, n.).

Dhruvā The sacrificial ladle.

v. Juhū.

Dhūmavarṇa 'Smoke-coloured.' A king of the serpents. According to the *Harivaṁśa*, Yadu, one of King Yayāti's five sons, was captured by the Nāga King Dhūmavarṇa whose five daughters he married. The myth apparently refers to the origin of races of mixed blood, Āryan, Dravidian and Turanian.

Dhūmāvatī 'The Smoky One.' The seventh *mahāvidyā*, who represents or personifies the final stage of the destruction of the universe by fire, when only the smoke from its ashes remains. In this state she is called Daridrā, the personification of poverty, or Vidhavā, the widow (of a dead world), and is identified with the goddesses Alakṣmī (misfortune) and Nirṛti (misery). Dhūmāvatī is generally portrayed as a hideous crone, with a long nose, cruel eyes, and carrying a winnowing basket.

Because of her colour she is associated with the rainy season when the dark clouds created by the malevolent water-spirit obscure the sun. The latter's reappearance marks the end of the monsoon, which was celebrated by the festival of lamps (the modern Divālī). Thus deities like Dhūmāvatī and Chinnamastā are invoked in *abhicāra* rites to injure enemies.[1]

[1]*C. Herit. I.*, vol. II, pp. 296f.

Dhūmorṇā 'Shroud of smoke', i.e., the smoke of the funeral pyre, personified as one of the wives of Yama, the ruler of the dead.

Dhundhu Probably from *dhu*, 'shaking, trembling'. The name of a demon, the son of Madhu, who causes earthquakes and volcanic eruptions. He is said to have hidden under a sea of sand when attacked by Kuvalayāśva and his 21,000 sons (viz., subjects) at the instigation of the *ṛṣi* Uttaṅka whose devotions Dhundhu had disturbed. Though they succeeded in destroying the demon, only three of his attackers, including the king, survived his fiery breath. Thenceforth Kuvalayāśva was known as Dhundhumāra or 'Slayer of Dhundhu' (*VP.*, IV.2).[1]

[1]v. also O'Flaherty, 'The Submarine Mare in the Mythology of Śiva', *JRAS.*, no. 1, 1971, pp. 20f.

Dhuni 'Roaring.' A demon who with another called Cumuri were overcome with sleep by Indra and so conquered (*RV.*, II.15,9).

Dhvaja-stambha A flag-staff placed in front of the central shrine (*garbha-gṛha*) of Śaiva temples. It represents the fiery *liṅga* form assumed by Śiva to indicate to Brahmā and Viṣṇu his capacity for endless expansion. The flag or banner is sometimes represented by a narrow vertical wooden frame on the roof of the temple. If placed inside it must penetrate the roof so as to indicate infinite height.[1] Vaiṣṇavas believe that whoever hoists a flag on the top of a temple will dwell in Viṣṇu's realm for thousands of years, a temple being another form of the divine image of Viṣṇu (*AGP.*, I, p. 222).

A mast (*dhvaja*) representing Indra, used to be erected annually at the Indramahotsava festival. It was addressed by his various names, such as Śakra, Śatakratu, Vajrapaṇi, etc.[2]

[1]Diehl, *Instrument and Purpose*, p. 164; Gonda, *Aspects*, pp. 255ff.

[2]*GG.*, pp. 152f. Cf. the ancient Hittite custom of presenting a sacred pole *inter alia* to the god Telipinu at the annual festival of Puruli (Gaster, *Thespis*, p. 99).

v. Hari; Yūpa.

Digambara I. 'Sky-clad', i.e., naked. The name of one of the two main Jaina sects, distinguished from the Śvetāmbara 'white-robed' by more extreme and rigorous ascetism. They believed that Mahāvīra, the last *tīrthaṅkara*, was not only born miraculously, but that by means of the influx of material particles,[1] he was able to live without food or drink.

[1]W. Schubring, *Doctrine of the Jainas* (tr. by W. Beurlen), p. 61.

II. An epithet applied to Śiva as the Lord of Yoga.

Dikpāla(s) The guardians of the four quarters and of the four intermediate quarters.

v. Lokapāla(s).

Dīkṣā 'Initiation', 'consecration', 'dedication'. The early Vedic consecration of the institutor (*yajamāna*) of a sacrifice was all important, for without *dīkṣā*[1] no benefits could be derived from the sacrifice, which initially related to the *soma* ceremony, but later was associated with other sacrifices.[2]

Dīkṣā is associated with the idea of rebirth, because the initiant becomes an embryo again by means of the sacrifice (*Ait. Br.*, I.3,1), even as did Prajāpati (*ŚBr.*, III.2.1,11). *Dīkṣā* not only sanctifies the body and purifies from 'sin' in this life, but also after death (*Manu*, II.26).

In the late Vedic period, when the speculative movement was gaining momentum, the student (*brahmacārin*) had to undergo a form of *dīkṣā* called *upanayana* before being accepted as a pupil by a teacher (*ācārya*) and taught the 'secret doctrine' (*upa-niṣad*). For the consecrated there were fewer obstacles on the transmigratory journey (*saṁsāra*) to the 'imperishable source of *dīkṣā*' which is eternal *brahman* (*Muṇḍ Up.*, II.1,6).

In the Purāṇas *dīkṣā* is personified as the wife of Soma, or of Ugra (*VP.*, I.8), or of Vāmadeva.

[1]Bharati points out that the essential part of *dīkṣā* 'must be *a mantra* of some sort' (*TT.*, p. 185, and v. ch. 7). There are many kinds of *dīkṣā* including *śāmbhavī dīkṣā*, when the pupil attains knowledge instantly by the mere look, word or touch of his guru; and *mānasi dīkṣā* when the pupil is initiated in secret by his *guru*. The initiant faces the north for the *dīkṣā* giving deliverance, and the east for the *dīkṣā* giving enjoyment only. It is interesting to note that Plutarch affirmed that 'death and initiation clearly closely correspond' (James, *Tree of Life*, p. 89).

[2]*Dīkṣā* can be used for good or evil purposes. The *AGP.*, I. ch. 27, describes a *dīkṣā* that 'grants all objects of desire'. In the religions of the most unsophisticated to the most advanced, all include 'some kind of initiation-ritual and some kind of religious dramatic show' (Farnell, *Cults*, III, p. 129).

v. Nayana-dīkṣā; Yajñopavīta.

Dikśūla 'Sky-spear.' The name of any inauspicious planetary conjunction, and of days when travel is restricted to certain directions.

Dilīpa Also called Khaṭvāṅga. A King of the Ikṣvāku or Solar dynasty and father of Raghu, the great-grandfather of Rāmacandra.[1] Traditional history records little of him except that he was a great warrior intent on territorial aggrandisement. This is confirmed in Kālidāsa's poem *Raghuvaṁśa*, which allegorically refers to his extensive kingdom as Surabhi, the Cow of Plenty,[2] and Nandinī its calf as the people of the newly conquered territories.

Legend recounts that Dilīpa, lacking an heir, sought the advice of the *ṛṣi* Vasiṣṭha, who informed him that owing to his ambitions he had offended Surabhi, and that before he and his queen could hope for a son they must by way of penance tend Nandinī until they had gained its affection. They succeeded in doing so and in due course Raghu was born.

[1]According to the genealogical list in *HCIP.*, I, App. II. But the *VP.*, p. 306, n. 13 and some other works differ from this, owing to the confusion of Dilīpa, father of Raghu, with an earlier Dilīpa.

[2]Mythologically synonymous with Āryāvarta or Madhyadeśa. The capture of Surabhi was thus the cause of most of the wars in Northern India in ancient times and of the feud between Vasiṣṭha and Viśvāmitra which began with the War of the Ten Kings (*daśarājña*).

v. Khaṭvāṅga II.

Dīpāvalī Lit. a 'row of lamps'. A festival during which all the lamps of the household are lit to celebrate the reappearance of the sun which had been 'hidden' during the rainy season by the malevolent water-spirit. The festival is now known as Divālī and is held on the day of the new moon in the month of *āśvina* or *kārttika* (mid-October to mid-November). When propitiated with gifts at this time, gods and spirits will assume human form to visit the earth (*AGP.*, I, p. 245).

Dīrghatamas The name of a blind *ṛṣi* (*RV.*, I.147,3) referred to by his metronymic Māmateya (son of Mamatā), and in *RV.* (I.158,1) by his patronymic Aucathya (son of Ucathya). His name Dīrghatamas, meaning 'prolonged darkness' is an allusion to his affliction. He is traditionally regarded as the composer of *RV.* hymns I. 140 to 164.[1]

From the account given in *RV.* (I.158,4–5) Dīrghatamas appears to have been threatened several times by death, on one occasion by fire, on another when he was bound and thrown into a river by the *dāsas*; finally by a man called Traitana, an attack from which he would not have escaped had not the attacker, by an unskilful stroke, wounded himself.

The slight references to Dīrghatamas in the *RV.* are expanded in the *Bṛhadd.* (IV. 11–15), which states that his blindness resulted from a curse laid upon him while still in his mother's womb by his uncle Bṛhaspati, whose amorous advances had been rejected by Mamatā. But the gods, distressed by the child's blindness, restored his sight. In the same work (IV.21 and 24–5) the Ṛgvedic *ṛṣi* is syncretized with an ascetic of the same name, but of a later period, as is indicated in the reference to the kingdom of Aṅga, a country unknown to the Vedic Indo-Āryans. The purpose of this legend was probably to give credibility to a genealogical table of doubtful authenticity linking Dīrghatamas and his descendants with Yayāti (*VP.*, IV.18).

[1]Hymn 164 is one of the most philosophical in the *RV.*, and indicates the attempts being made to reconcile the beliefs of the non-Āryan Indians with those of the Āryans.

v. Uśij.

Diti A goddess. In the *RV. diti* signifies 'limited', 'bounded', in contradistinction to *aditi*. This distinction is clearly indicated in V.62,8, where Mitra and Varuṇa, when traversing the heavens in their gold-hued car, beheld both Aditi, the goddess of boundless space, and Diti, the goddess of earthly phenomena. This antithesis may be only a play on words, but it is more likely to have been a dualistic interpretation of the universe, represented as heaven and earth.

In Vedic cosmology Diti[1] is a fleeting shadowy figure seldom mentioned in the *RV.* Unlike Aditi and the Ādityas, she is neither lauded nor invoked. According to the *VP.* (I.15) Diti was one of Dakṣa's daughters who became the wife of the *ṛṣi* Kaśyapa. She bore him two sons, Hiraṇyakaśipu and the invincible Hiraṇyākṣa, the progenitors of the *daityas*. She begged her husband to give her a son capable of destroying Indra. He agreed, but only on condition that she remained both mentally and physically chaste and carried the child in her womb for a hundred years. She fulfilled these conditions for nearly a century, but one night retired without performing the necessary ablution of washing her feet. Indra immediately noticed the omission, and with his thunderbolt (*vajra*) divided the embryo into seven parts.[2] The mutilated child cried piteously and Indra, angered by the noise, again divided each of the seven portions into seven, and so formed the Maruts (the storm-gods) (*VP.*, I.21).[3]

[1]She may represent the mortality of the individual, whilst Aditi the mother of the Devas, symbolizes radiance and immortality.

[2]Another version is that when Indra found her sleeping in an indelicate position he entered her womb, cut the embryo into seven and then into forty-nine pieces, but at Diti's request gave them the status of gods, known as the Maruts (*Bhāg. P.*, VI.18, 23–77; *Brah. P.*, I.1,112, *PI.*; Cf. *AGP.*, I, p. 87).

[3]Probably a satirical parody of the naïve attempts at etymology by some grammarians.

Divodāsa I. Also called Atithigva (the hospitable one).[1] He was one of the most notable kings of the Vedic Tṛtsus, and the ancestor of Sudās whose exploits in the war of the ten kings (*daśarājña*) enabled him to establish the great kingdom of Bhārata.

The opinion that Divodāsa and Atithigva are different people cannot be supported in view of the complete parallelism of the incidents associated with them.[2]

[1]As Atithigva (*RV.*, VII.19,8); as Divodāsa (IX.61,2).

[2]*VI.*, vol. I, p. 364.

II. v. Bharadvāja; Āyurveda; Dhanvantari.

Draupadī Also known as Kṛṣṇā. A daughter of Drupada, King of Pañcāla. She is one of the principal figures in the traditional history of the Pāṇḍava and Kaurava families.[1]

[1]According to the *MBh.* (Ādi pa., 63), she was born from the sacrificial fire and was regarded as an incarnation of the goddess Śrī (ibid., 199).

v. *Mahābhārata*; Arjuna.

Drāviḍa Name of a people, or of the language they spoke, which after a series of phonetic changes became identified with the adjective Tamil, and thus a title strictly applicable only to a single branch, the Tamils, but extended to the whole family. Ancient Tamil tradition speaks of five Dravidian regions, viz., Andhra or Telugu and the Kanarese countries, the Mahārāṣṭra or Marāthā provinces, and Gujarāt.

At least a millennium prior to the entry of the Āryans the north-west of India was occupied mainly by a brown-skinned long-headed ethnic group having a culture from which are derived the tongues now known as Dravidian, many words of which are to be found in Vedic and Sanskrit vocabularies, and which independently entered those of some early Āryo-European languages.

The Dravidians appear to have entered India from the north and north-west, probably through Baluchistan—into the plain of the Indus, and thence ultimately to the regions south of the Vindhya.

The proto-Dravidians appear to be the originators of the Indus Valley civilization, and to have had an advanced social and political system. The Dravidian kingdoms traded with Western Asia, Egypt and later with the Greek and Roman Empires. Among their exports were ivory, apes and peacocks (v. I. Kings, X.22; II. Chronicles, IX.21), and later pepper, rice, spices, gems, muslin, etc.[1] Their religion reflects a variety of sources, which subsequently profoundly influenced Hindu culture, perhaps more profoundly than did that of the Āryans.

[1]Kennedy, 'The Early Commerce of India with Babylon', *JRAS.*, 1898, pp. 241ff. For the affiliation of the Dravidian languages with the Finno-Ugrian group, v. Caldwell, *Comparative Grammar of the Dravidian Languages*, pp. 64ff.; Burrow, 'Dravidian Studies IV', *BSOAS.*, XI. pp. 328f.

Droṇa I. The military preceptor of the Kuru and Pāṇḍu princes. He is said to have been generated by the *ṛṣi* Bharadvāja whose seed fell into a pot (droṇa) when he gazed upon the beautiful nymph Ghṛtācī (*MBh.*, Ādi pa., 168).

v. Drupada.

II. A trough-shaped altar.

Dṛṣṭidoṣa The 'Evil Eye'. Belief in the evil influence of the human eye is widespread. Diehl[1] states that in southern India a pot painted with spots was believed to avert the baleful influence of the 'evil eye'. The glance of snakes is believed to be very dangerous, hence the epithet *dṛṣṭiviṣa* 'in whose glance is poison' is applied to them.[2] Similarly the eyes of strangers are believed to carry various kinds of evil. Even chimpanzees interpret a prolonged stare as a threat.[3]

According to the *Tait. Saṁ.* (III.2,10), objects of value should be guarded from hostile or envious looks; but the 'eye' of the sun harms nothing. The man who pronounces *Tait. Saṁ.* (VI.1.7,3) temporarily identifies his own visual faculty with that of the sun and thus is able to achieve within the ritual context objects normally only reached or realized by the sun.[4]

[1] *Instrument and Purpose*, p. 324, n.6.
[2] Gonda, *Eye and Gaze in the Veda*, p. 26.
[3] J. van Lawick-Goodall, *In the Shadow of Man*, p. 63.
[4] Gonda, op. cit., p. 40. There appears to be a reference to the 'evil eye' in *Kauṣ Br.*, XXIX.1.

v. Cakṣu; Cakṣur-mantra; Netraviṣa.

Druh 'Hostile.' A male or female member of a group of demons[1] or sprites opposed to Indra (*RV.*, IV.23,7). They were probably associated with drought (X.48,10).

[1] Cf. Zend *druj*.

Druhyu A son of Yayāti and Śarmiṣṭhā (*VP.*, IV.10).

v. Devayānī.

Drupada Also called Yajñasena. King of Pañcāla and the father of Kṛṣṇā, usually referred to by her patronymic, Draupadī. Drupada in his youth was a great friend of Droṇa, but they later quarrelled and fought on opposite sides in the war of the Pāṇḍu and Kuru princes, during which Drupada was killed by Droṇa who on the following day was slain by Dhṛṣṭadyumna, Drupada's son.

v. Aśvatthāman; Mahābhārata.

Dundubha A species of non-poisonous snakes, one of which figures in a story in the *MBh.* (Ādi pa., 8–11). It begins with the betrothal of Ruru (the son of Pramati, and grandson of the *ṛṣi* Cyavana) to a daughter of the *apsaras*, Menakā. But shortly before the marriage the bride was bitten by a snake and died. Ruru's grief was so intense that the gods sent a messenger telling him that if he surrendered half of his remaining span of life, it would be transferred to his bride and she would be restored to him.

Ruru vowed that henceforth he would kill every snake he came across. One day in the forest he saw an old snake, and was about to attack it when it called out, 'I have done you no harm, why should you want to kill me?' Ruru explained, whereupon the snake gave him an account of his present plight. As a joke he had once fashioned a snake from blades of grass, and placed it near a *ṛṣi* called Khagama when he was about to perform a sacrifice. When Khagama saw it he fainted, and later cursed the practical joker to become a serpent until such time as Ruru should find him. The story concludes with a homily on the subject of *ahiṁsā* (non-injury).

Dundubhi I. A war-drum glorified in a *RV.* hymn (VI.47,28–31). Its sound strikes terror into enemies and conquers them; drives away misfortune; and endows Indra's followers with vigour (*AV.*, V.20; VI.126; *Nir.*, 9.13).

v. Ānaka.

II. The sounds[1] of a 'medicated' drum are said to cure snakebite, and a potion of herbs and cow urine when smeared on drums, banners, and the gateways of houses, will eliminate poison from the sufferer. It is also efficacious in cases of stones in the bladder, colic, coughs and asthma, etc. (*Suś. Saṁ.*, II. pp. 737f.).

[1] Great power is believed to be inherent in the rhythm of sound. Cf. the rhythmic drumming by which the Shaman is conveyed to heaven (Eliade, *Images*, pp. 46–7, and *Shamanism*, pp. 171f.).

v. Ḍamaru; Mahāvrata.

III. A buffalo-shaped demon said to resemble a cloud from which the 'roaring' sound of a drum can be heard; hence iconographically thunder is represented by a drum.

Śiva and the gods attacked the demon with tridents but were unable to kill him but finally they succeeded 'by means of incantations',[1] thereby showing that the power of sound is greater than that of weapons.

[1] *DHI.*, p. 166, quoting Mackay.

Dundubhī The name of a *gandharvī* and also the name of a particular throw of the dice in gambling. All the *gandharvīs* are associated with dice playing (*AV.*, II.2,5).

Dundubhisvana 'Drum-sound.' A *mantra* used as a protection against malevolent spirits who are supposed to possess weapons.

Durgā A composite goddess embodying a number of local divinities and demonesses associated with mountains, vegetation and fire. This assimilation began about the end of the Vedic period[1] and culminated in the Śākta cult. Many factors, now unknown, must have contributed to the development of these cults, but there is little doubt that early Indian folk-religion exerted 'a great influence in moulding the notion of the "motherly divinities".'[2] Thus there is some justification for assuming a connexion between these 'mother-goddesses', like Umā, Durgā, Pārvatī, Lakṣmī, etc., and the old fertility goddesses like Sarasvatī, Puraṁdhi, Aditi, etc.,[3] although 'maternal' is not the most fitting description either of the *śaktis* or of some village mother-goddesses of South India, whose cults[4] have persisted with only minor modifications to the present day.

Durgā is portrayed in the Purāṇas and the Epic as a notable female warrior, the bloodthirsty destroyer of giant *asuras*. This has probably a historical basis, recalling the warfare between the Indo-Āryans and native tribes. The warrior Durgā assumes ten forms: 1. As Durgā she received the messengers of the giant Śumbha; 2. As Daśabhujā she destroyed Śumbha's army commanded by Dhūmalocana; 3. As Siṁhavāhinī she rides a lion, the latter symbolizing her warlike nature and invincibility; 4. As Mahiṣāsuramardinī (the slayer of Mahiṣa) she slew Śumbha in his buffalo form; 5. As Jagaddhātrī (mother of the world) she destroyed another army of giants; 6. As Kālī or Kālī Mā, she fought the army of the giant Raktavīja who, realizing that his men were no match for her, attacked the goddess in person. Kālī wounded him repeatedly, but from every drop of blood that flowed from his wounds a thousand giants arose. She retaliated by materializing Caṇḍī,[5] another of her forms. While Caṇḍī continued the fight Kālī drank the giants' blood until only Raktavīja was left, whereupon Caṇḍī slew him with a single blow; 7. As Muktakeśī she destroyed more of the giant's troops; 8. As Tārā she slew Śumbha; 9. As Chinnamastā she slew Niśumbha; 10. As Jagadgaurī (the Yellow Woman) she is praised by gods and men for delivering them from demons.

In her fierce aspect she may represent fire and its cathartic properties. Her epithets Kālī and Karālī are also the names of two of Agni's tongues (i.e., flames) (*Muṇḍ. Up.*, I.2,4); another of her names is Jātavedasī (the feminine form of one of Agni's epithets). Durgā's connexion with vegetation is shown by the *navapatrikā* or ceremony of the Nine Plants, and her identification with Śākambharī, the nourisher of herbs; as Vindhyavāsinī she is associated with the Vindhyas where she dwells, and as Pārvatī she is the goddess of the Himālaya. Her beneficent aspect is also indicated in Yudhiṣṭhira's hymn to her: 'Thou art called Durgā by all because thou savest men from difficulty ... Thou art the sole refuge of men.'[6] Her primitive side can be seen in the human and animal sacrifices offered to her, the use of intoxicants, and her epithet Chinnamastā (the Headless).[7] In Durgā's principal temple in Calcutta, seven to eight hundred goats are slaughtered during the Durgā *pūjā* in the autumn, their heads being placed in piles before her image. Pigs, fowls, sheep and water-buffaloes are also immolated. Until 1835 when the British Government, with the help of some enlightened Indians, suppressed human sacrifice, a boy was beheaded every Friday before the altar. In 1830 a Rāja sacrificed twenty-five men to Durgā.[8]

As the *śakti* of Śiva the great ascetic[9] (also a composite god embodying several local *devas*) Durgā became the goddess of yogins; but to the masses she remains the great Mother-goddess. Banerjea considers that some concepts of Durgā stem from prehistoric times,[10] and Campbell suggests affinities with the village cults of Melanesia and New Guinea as well as with 'Near Eastern matrices of civilization'.[11]

[1]Her name appears in the *Bṛhadd.* (II.77), but Macdonell considers it an interpolation, although an early one.

[2]S. Kumar Das, *Śakti or Divine Power*, p. 41.

[3]Ibid., p. 42.

[4]The rites connected with these cults are described by H. Whitehead, *Village Gods of South India*, pp. 71ff.

[5]In this myth the disparate elements in Durgā can be seen, as both Kālī and Caṇḍī emanate from her, and do the actual killing of demons.

[6]Arthur Avalon, *Hymns to the Goddess*, pp. 70f.

[7]The *Kālikā Pur.* gives minute details of the correct method of offering a human victim to Kālī. Human blood is said to satisfy her for a thousand years (Wilson, *Selected Works*, II, p. 268). Since the Middle Ages, animals are 'decapitated before the sacred icon, in such a way that some of the blood fell on it. The ritual slaughter of animals was justified by the doctrine that the soul of the victim went straight to heaven ... its survival in Bengal and elsewhere is a matter of shame to most modern Hindus' (*WI.*, p. 336).

[8]E.A. Gait, 'Human Sacrifice (Indian)', *ERE.*

[9]Śiva's vegetal form is that of the *bilva* tree (Aegle marmelos) (*AIA.*, I, p. 165).

[10]*DHI.*, pp. 173, 490. E.A. Payne considers the name Durgā to be aboriginal (*The Śāktas.*, p. 6.).

[11]Oriental Mythology, *Masks of God*, II, p. 171.

v. Devī; Śākta: Vāmācāra.

Durga I. Name of a giant *asura*, son of Ruru. By means of extreme austerities Durga had obtained the favour of Brahmā and conquered the three worlds. He abolished all religious ceremonies so that the *brāhmaṇas* were too terrified to read the Vedas, and even rivers changed their courses. The gods appealed to Śiva, who asked the goddess Durgā to destroy the giant. She agreed and during a fearful battle the monster successively assumed the forms of an enormous elephant, a buffalo and a thousand-armed giant, but she finally killed him.

II. Name of a Commentator on the *Nirukta*.

Dūrvā A species of grass (Cynodon dactylon) common to marshland (*RV.*, X.16,13). During the dry season

when much of the vegetation is destroyed, Agni is invoked to let the 'flowery dūrvā grass spring up (X.142, 8). Later this grass became one of the substitutes for the *soma* plant (*ŚBr.*, IV.5.10, 5), and regarded as sacred to Gaṇeśa. A particular plant (thought to be a species of *dūrvā*) is said to be efficacious against curses (*AV.*, II,7).
v. Dūrvāṣṭamī.

Durvāsas A pious but irascible sage,[1] son of Atri by Anasūyā, and said to be a partial incarnation of Śiva.

One day he beheld a beautiful *vidyādharī* (nymph) holding a garland of divine flowers. Immediately he was filled with religious ecstasy and demanded the garland. The nymph gave it to him and he presented it to Indra, who nonchalantly placed it on his elephant's head, but the animal shook it off. The enraged sage then cursed Indra to lose his dominion over the three worlds. In vain did the humbled god beg for forgiveness, and so gradually the whole universe became weakened; all the vegetation and inhabitants perished, and the gods were almost overwhelmed by their enemies. In desperation the gods begged Brahmā to help them; he advised them to apply to the supreme Hari (Viṣṇu), to whom they prayed: 'O Viṣṇu, be manifest unto us . . . thou art Brahmā, thou and Śiva, Indra, fire, air, god of the waters, the sun, the lord of death, the Vasus, the Maruts, the Sādhyas and Viśvadevas.'[2] Viṣṇu then directed them to churn the ocean to obtain the *amṛta* and other precious objects (*VP.*, I.9), when the universe would be restored and their enemies destroyed.

Another legend recounts Durvāsas's quarrel with Kṛṣṇa when the latter failed to show him the respect he considered due to him. The angry sage predicted when and how Kṛṣṇa would die; hence the myth that Kṛṣṇa's death was the result of 'the imprecation of Durvāsas'. Yet another legend relates that when Durvāsas was staying with Kuntībhoga, he was so much impressed by his host's adopted daughter Kuntī that he gave her a *mantra* by which in time of need she could summon any of the gods by whose grace she might obtain children (*MBh.*, Ādi pa., 67).

[1]He 'observed the *vrata*, or vow of insanity, equivalent to the ecstasies of some religious fanatics' (*VP.*, p. 61, n.3).

[2]This myth reflects Śaiva and Vaiṣṇava rivalry and is also one of the most explicit accounts of the transition from Vedism to Hinduism.

v. Pṛthā; Karṇa; Samudramathana.

Dūrvāṣṭamī A festival held on the eighth day of the light half of the month *bhādra*, when *dūrvā* grass is deified and worshipped.

Duryodhana The name of King Dhṛtarāṣṭra's eldest son who became the leader of the Kauravas in the war against the Pāṇḍavas.
v. Mahābhārata.

Duṣyanta v. Śakuntalā; Bharata; Menā II.

Dvaipāyana v. Vyāsa; Parāśara.

Dvāpara I. v. Yuga.
II. In the games of dice the names *kṛta*, *tretā*, *dvāpara* and *kali* are given to different sides of the die, marked respectively four, three, two and one (*ŚBr.*, pt. iii, p. 107n.).

Dvāra A door or portal, which from early Vedic times had a highly symbolic significance, whether as the entrance to the sacrificial enclosure, the temple, the palace or the ordinary house. In a ritual context doors are referred to in the *RV.* as 'sovran, wide, good, many and manifold' (I.188,5); as divine, and an unfailing help in the performance of sacrificial rites (I.13,6; 142,6); and regarded as goddesses (II.3,5).[1] The gods enter the sacrificial enclosures by these divine 'doors' like the morning light which passes through the portals of the eastern sky (X.110,5; *AV.*, V.12,5). Offering verses are recited for the doors during the *soma* sacrifice. They represent 'rain bestowed on the sacrificer' (*Ait. Br.*, II.4).

In the Gṛhya Sūtras the position of doors is said to affect adversely or beneficially the fortunes of the householder. Thus a house with an eastern entrance ensures fame and vigour; a northern, offspring and cattle; a southern, the fulfilment of all desires; but one with a western or back door brings misfortune.[2] The instructions were further elaborated in the Śilpa Śāstras. If the main door was too near a tree, corner, road or temple, misfortune would overtake the householder and his sons.[3] A plain door was said to be unlucky; it should therefore be decorated with auspicious symbols such as the pitcher of abundance, fruit, foliage, birds, etc.[4] The lowest part (an eighth) of the door is regarded as inauspicious (*AGP.*, I, p. 159). In the same work (ch. 104) it is said that the doors of a temple should face the four cardinal points, and that the door-jambs should never be plain, but comprise two, three, five, seven or nine parallel perpendicular pillars, each variously carved. The lower portions (usually a quarter of the jamb) are reserved for the images of the doorkeepers (*dvārapāla*), which differ according to the deity to which the temple is dedicated.[5]

[1]Cf. the Egyptian temple which in historical times was not only regarded as a living entity, but after the performance of particular ceremonies its reliefs and statues were also thought to be imbued with latent life. v. E.A.E. Reymond, *The Mythical Origin of the Egyptian Temple*, pp. 294f.

[2]*Gobhila Sūtra*, IV.7,15–19 cited by Bhattacharyya,

Canons of Indian Art, pp. 31f.; v. also Harle, *Temple Gateways in South India*; and Barua, *A Cultural History of Assam*, I, pp. 171f.

[3]Bhattacharyya, op. cit., p. 235.

[4]Ibid., p. 237. In ancient Greece Hecate and Hermes were depicted on doors for protective purposes (Farnell, *Cults*, II, pp. 509, 516).

[5]v. also Bhattacharyya, op. cit., p. 239. *Yakṣas* were often guardians of gates (Coomaraswamy, *Yakṣas*, pt.ii, p.8).

Dvārakā 'Many-gated.' The name of the capital of Kṛṣṇa's kingdom. Kṛṣṇa built the city on a cliff overlooking the sea as a defence against attack by the Yavana king, Kālayavana. After Kṛṣṇa's death, the ocean rose and submerged the whole city except the temple (*VP*., V.23; 38), but according to the *MBh.* account both were destroyed.

v. Dvāra; Raivata; Yādava.

Dvīpa Lit. 'island', but in a geographical sense, a continent, one of the seven insular land masses which, according to the Purāṇas, comprised the known world. The *VP*. (II.2) describes these *dvīpas* as Jambu, Plakṣa, Śālmali, Kuśa, Krauñca, Śāka, and Puṣkara, which are surrounded severally by seven great seas, viz., the sea of salt water (*lāvaṇa*), of sugar-cane juice (*ikṣu*), of wine (*surā*), of clarified butter (*sarpi*), of curds (*dadhi*), of milk (*dugdha*), and of fresh water (*jala*). These seas all symbolize fertility.

Jambu-dvīpa (India) occupies the centre and most important position, as did China (the Middle Kingdom) in Chinese geography. To the Paurāṇics not only was Jambu-dvīpa the geographical centre of the world, but also its spiritual centre, symbolized by Mount Meru, the Indian Olympus, the dwelling-place of the gods. On its summit is the vast city of Brahmā and on its spurs the eight cities of the Lokapālas or heavenly regents, Indra, Yama, Varuṇa, Kubera, Vivasvat, Soma, Agni and Vāyu.

Iyer[1] considers that the so-called geography of the Purāṇas is really a way of teaching Yoga. The seven islands and seas represent the seven *prakṛtis*, viz., the five elements and individuation (*ahaṁkāra*), and the determinative faculty (*buddhi*). 'Such terminology corresponds to the yogic terminology of *cakras* or *padmas* (lotuses) in the human frame'.

[1]*Permanent History of Bhāratvarṣa*, cited by D. Bahadur K. S. Ramaswami Sastri in 'The Purāṇas and their Contribution to Indian Thought' (*C. Herit. I.*, vol. I, p. 175).

Dvita 'Second' in the numerical sense. A vague mythological figure, said by some to be a son of Atri. With Ekata and Trita[1] 'the guilt of the gods in sacrifice is transferred through them [these three] to a variety of evildoers' (*Tait. Saṁ.*, I. p. 8, n. 3; *RV*., V.18,2). Dvita is also invoked to take away bad dreams (*RV*., VII.47,16).

[1]Dvita, Ekata and Trita are called the three brothers of Agni. They represent the three principles of matter, life and mind which 'must combine for the manifestation of organic beings' (*VF*., p. 6).

Dvivida I. A huge monkey or ape who hated the gods because Kṛṣṇa had killed his friend, the *asura* Naraka. Dvivida interfered with sacrifices and religious rites, showered rocks on towns and hamlets, caused tidal waves, and assuming any shape he pleased trampled on corn-fields, causing much misery and hardship to the people. When he stole Baladeva's ploughshare and ridiculed him Baladeva seized his club, whereupon Dvivida hurled a huge rock. But Baladeva threw his club breaking the rock into a thousand fragments. Again the monkey attacked, but Baladeva felled and killed him with one blow (*VP*., V.36).

v. Mainda.

II. The name of the monkey-ally of Rāma.

Dvyāśrayakāvya v. Rāmacarita.

Dyaus The sky. From *div*, to shine. As *div* is also the root of *deva* (lit. luminous), a celestial being or god, the Vedic Dyaus was probably regarded as a celestial aspect of nature, awe-inspiring, and only vaguely associated with atmospheric phenomena. Like similar traditional nature concepts, such as Aditi and Varuṇa, the notion of Dyaus is developed in the hymns of the *RV*. in accordance with the views of priestly families. Thus from being simply a name given to the broad and luminous sky, Dyaus is given various appellations, such as 'the father of light' (*Dyu-pitar*), corresponding in this sense to the Greek Zeus or the Roman Jupiter. In the *RV*. Dyaus (Heaven) and Pṛthivī (Earth) 'are often described as parents (*janitrī*, *RV*., X.110,9; *pitarā*, III.3,11; *mātarā*, I.155,3). Or Heaven alone is called father (*pitā*) and Earth, mother (*mātā*).'[1]

Of the various Vedic cosmological views, the earliest appears to have been that the universe consisted only of earth and sky, which are likened to two bowls or hemispheres, joined together at the horizon (*RV*., III.55,20); or they are likened to the wheels at each end of an axle (X.89,4). As neither existed independently, they are almost invariably invoked as one (*dyāvāpṛthivī*). But the dual division of the universe was soon superseded by a threefold division, comprising sky, atmosphere and earth, which were subject to further metaphorical description and sub-division, according to phenomena, such as the sun, lightning, storm-clouds, fire, etc., associated with one or another of the three regions. In this context the sun, having traversed the heavens from east to west, returns from west to east—not under the earth as believed by the ancient Egyptians and others—but by the way it had come, 'turning its light side up to the sky and leaving the earth in darkness.'

Though Dyaus is called 'Infinite', and 'Incomparable Heaven' (*RV*., X.63,3 and 10), and he and Dyāvāpṛthivī are described as the parents of both gods and mankind, other cosmological views presented the heavens and the earth as the creation of Indra, of Viśvakarman, or of Tvaṣṭṛ.

[1]*BH*., p. 182.

Dyāvāpṛthivī 'Heaven (Dyaus) and Earth (Pṛthivī).' The parents of the gods, who are invoked to give their worshippers wealth, success, abundant rains, food and heroic strength.

v. Dyaus.

E

Edhas 'Fuel.' The sacred wood used for the sacrificial fire, invoked to ensure prosperity. The association of fire, and prosperity appear to be a punning of the roots *idh*, 'burn', and *edh*, 'prosper' (*AV.*, VII.89, 4 and n.).

Egāttalā The tutelary goddess of Madras. Some of her rites are performed by pariahs and not by *brāhmaṇas*, which indicates her non-Āryan origin.[1]

[1]Eliade, *Yoga*, p. 386.

Ekacakra 'One wheel'. A reference to the sun's chariot which has only one wheel (*RV.*, I.164,2). It is drawn by one horse with seven names, or by seven horses.[1] The sun was believed to move across the sky as a revolving wheel. The *ekacakra* is eternal, and the lives of all creatures are dependent on its diurnal journey across the sky.

[1]The horses symbolize the seven days of the week or the seven *chandas* (metres).

v. Cakra; Sūrya.

Ekadanta 'Having one tusk.' An epithet of Gaṇeśa.

Ekākṣara From *eka*, 'one'; *akṣara*, 'imperishable.' The one imperishable *bīja-mantra OM*, which overcomes all difficulties (*AV.*, V.28,8).

v. Mantra.

Ekalavya The brother of Śatrughna. He was abandoned in infancy, but was found and reared by members of the Niṣāda tribe,[1] and later became their king.

When unable to get certain information from his *guru*, he made a clay image of him and worshipped it and thus obtained the desired knowledge.

Ekalavya was involved in a night attack on Dvārakā, Kṛṣṇa's capital, but was finally killed by a rock flung by Kṛṣṇa.

[1]Either a non-Āryan tribe, or one composed of members of a degraded mixed caste.

Ekamevādvitīyam The 'one eternally existing entity having no second of its own'[1] i.e., *brahman*.

[1]*PTR.*, p. 6.

v. Vedānta.

Ekānaṁśā 'The single portionless one.' Epithet of *kuhū*, the new moon, personified as Durgā.[1]

[1]*DHI.*, p. 133.

Ekāntika v. Bhakti.

Ekapāda 'One-footed.' Epithet both of Śiva and of one of the eleven Rudras, 'evidently based on the Vedic Aja Ekapāda'.[1]

[1]*DHI.*, p. 232.

Ekaparṇā v. Aparṇā.

Ekapāṭalā v. Aparṇā.

Ekaśṛṅgin 'Unicorn.' Epithet of Viṣṇu. Hopkins suggests that a horn (or horns) may be the remains of Viṣṇu's animal forms,[1] especially as his *varāha* (boar) form is said to be 'one-horned'.

[1]*EM.*, p. 206; v. also *HCIP.*, I, p. 188.

Ekāṣṭakā The eighth day after the full moon.[1] It is personified as the goddess Śacī, Indra's wife.[2] She is invoked to give children who will be healthy and long-lived.

The *Tait. Saṁ.* (VII.4,8) refers to Ekāṣṭakā as the wife of the (personified) Year. The latter dwells with her on the eighth day of the full moon.

[1]*SED.* Sāyaṇa states it is the eighth day of the dark half of the month *māgha* (January–February).

[2]But according to *AV.*, III.10,12–13 and *Tait. Saṁ.*, IV.3,11, Ekāṣṭakā generated Indra by extreme austerities (*tapas*).

Ekata v. Trita; Dvita.

Ekoddiṣṭa(s) Post-Vedic funerary rites performed after the cremation of a deceased man to ensure union with his ancestors (*pitṛs*).[1]

Contary to the Vedic practice of burying the dead,[2] the post-Vedic custom was cremation which involved a complex ritual. When no body was available, owing to death by drowning or other circumstances, special rites were performed, and an image made of *kuśa* grass resembling a human figure was burnt.[3] Subsequently, in the Gṛhya period, the Vedic belief that at death the deceased immediately joined the *pitṛs* was superseded by the belief that he first became a *preta* (an ethereal form), and only after enduring this painful state for a year, was able to join the *pitṛs*. This belief was changed in the Paurāṇic period when after cremation the 'self' of the dead man was believed to assume an *ātivāhika śarīra* form, i.e., one consumed by fire (*śarīra* is derived from *śṛ*, to burn).[4] This body is less 'subtle' than that of the *preta*, and subject to an even more painful transitional period. To facilitate release from this state, a *pūraka* offering, consisting of a cake or ball of rice, is made to the starving *ātivāhika*, who is then able to assume a *preta* form. To ensure the progress of the *preta*, *ekoddiṣṭa* rites are performed at monthly intervals for six months or a year, culminating in the *sapiṇḍī karaṇa* rite. On the conclusion of the latter, the *preta* becomes a *pitṛ* and is entitled to 'take part in the *pārvaṇa* rite which is the model of all kinds of ancestor-worship popularly known as *śrāddha*'.[5]

The account of the *ekoddiṣṭa* rite in the *VP.* (III.13) generally agrees with the above description, but does not mention the intermediate 'forms' assumed by the deceased; it merely states that the dead man, 'wherever he may be', is addressed by name and offered a libation.

Post-Paurāṇic interpretation of the rite varies, but whether performed as a duty or as a reverential act by the male next-of-kin, it is generally regarded as obligatory, and is a reminder of the relation of the present to the past.

[1]*Āśvalāyana Gṛhya Sūtra*, IV.7,1; *Manu*, IV.110.

[2]The Āryan burial places were 'four-cornered' and thus distinguished from those of the indigenes which were round (*ŚBr.*, XIII.8.1,5).

[3]A knot of consecrated *kuśa* grass should be made for each spirit to be invoked (*AGP.*, I, p. 468).

[4]*Nir.*, III.5. But according to *AGP.*, II, p. 615, one who dies without any rites being performed on his behalf, attains liberation if he dies with his mind absorbed in Hari (Viṣṇu).

[5]*Ancestor Worship*, p. 2.

v. Go; Vaitaraṇī; Piṇḍa; Śrāddha.

Elāpattra A Nāga king who is depicted in both reptile and human form on the railings of the Bharhut *stūpa.*[1] The *VP.* (I.2) describes him as a son of Kadrū.

[1]*DHI.*, p.100.

Emūṣa The name of the boar (*varāha*) who raised up the earth from below the waters, when it was only one span in breadth (*ŚBr.*, XIV.1.2,11; *VP.*, 1.4).

v. Avatāra; Pṛthivī.

Eta The steed or steeds (*etāḥ*) of the Maruts; perhaps a kind of spotted deer, the skins of which the Maruts wore over their shoulders (*RV.*, I.166,10).

Etaśa I. A 'dappled horse', one of the horses which draw the chariot of the sun (Sūrya).

v. Dyaus.

II. The name of a sage, said to have cursed his children because they disturbed him when he was performing a rite. That his intolerance was not considered to have been justified is indicated by the disfavour with which his descendants were regarded. They were declared to be the worst of Bhṛgus.[1] The same story appears in the *Ait. Br.* (VI.33), where the sage is called Aitaśa, and his descendants described as the worst of the Aurvas, which similarly reflected on the character of the Bhṛgus, as Aurva was a grandson of Bhṛgu.

[1]*Kauṣ. Br.*, XXX.5.

G

Gada The name of a demon killed by Hari (Viṣṇu). Viśvakarman made a club (*gadā*) from the demon's bones and presented it to Viṣṇu (*AGP.*, I, p. 447).

Gadā A mace or club of wood or iron; a favourite weapon in ancient Indian warfare, which only the very strong, like the mighty Bhīma, were able to wield. His *gadā* was huge and gold-plated as befitted his status. Favourite maces, as well as other weapons, were often personified and called by such names as Modakī, Śikharī, etc.[1]

The mace also symbolizes the power that ensures conformity with universal law (*AGP.*, I, p. 174). It was invoked along with other weapons of the gods to protect its devotees (II. p. 786).

[1] S. D. Singh, *Ancient Indian Warfare*, pp. 111f.

v. Gada; Gadādevī; Āyudhapuruṣa; Kaumodakī; Cakra.

Gadādevī Viṣṇu's mace (*gadā*) personified as a beautiful woman. When personified, weapons are generally depicted either as male or female, according to the gender of the word denoting the particular weapon; hence *gadā*, being feminine is depicted as a woman.

v. Āyudhapuruṣa.

Gadāgada 'Gada and Agada', i.e., the two Aśvins, the physicians of the gods.

Gādhi Name of the son of Kuśāmba, referred to in the *Rāmāyaṇa* as the founder of Kauśāmbī (the modern Kosam on the Yamunā). According to the *Viṣṇu Pur.* (IV.7) Kuśāmba, desiring a son who would be the equal of Indra, engaged in extreme austerities (*tapas*). Indra, alarmed at the prospect of such a rival, decided to incarnate himself as Gādhi, Kuśāmba's son. Gādhi became the father of Jamadagni and grandfather of Paraśurāma.

v. Satyavatī II; Viśvāmitra.

Gaja The common name in Epic and later literature of the elephant (Elephas indica). The *RV.* refers to the elephant as *hastinmṛga* (the animal with a hand), an allusion to its trunk. But such references are rare, as are those in the *AV.*, which call the elephant simply *hastin* (with a hand). It is also referred to as *mātaṅga* (roaming at will). To the first Āryan settlers it was an awesome and often terrifying animal, but to the indigenes of northern India, it had been tamed and was a familiar sight. This is indicated by the seals, depicting the elephant, excavated at Mohenjo-daro and Harappā, and by the words *gaja* and *mātaṅga* which have been traced to pre-Indo-Āryan Austric speaking tribes.[1]

Although there is no explicit indication in the Vedas of the use of elephants by the indigenes in warfare, this may be inferred from the references to the capture of ten thousand elephants and a similar number of women, subsequently presented to the *brāhmaṇas*,[2] as a *dakṣiṇā* at the *aśvamedha* performed by a victorious prince. The chariot, drawn by horses, which was the Āryan equivalent of cavalry, appears to have proved more effective than the elephant, though Megasthenes (4th cent. B.C.) records that the use of war-elephants was customary in India in his time.

The mythical origin of the elephant is described in the *ŚBr.* (III.1.3,3–4). When the seven sons of Aditi were shaping her deformed eighth son, Mārtāṇḍa,[3] in the form of a man, they threw away the surplus flesh which became an elephant. Hence it is said that the elephant 'partakes of the nature of man'. Subsequently, in the post-Vedic period, elephants were trained and put to various uses, and their ownership was regarded as a sign of power, sovereignty and wealth. The king himself consecrated the State elephant by 'a ritual baptism'. A special 'staff was allocated to the white elephant which took part in every festival and in royal pilgrimages'.[4]

Elephants figure prominently in Paurāṇic mythology, and are associated with rain and likened to grey rain-clouds, the Sanskrit word *nāga* signifying both cloud and elephant.[5] Elephants both support and guard the regions of the world; they initially numbered four but were later increased to eight. In a rite designed to benumb the faculties of one's enemies, a figure of an elephant was made of earth taken from an ant-hill. This rite should be performed in a remote place, such as the top of a mountain, or in a field with only one tree, or at a place that has been struck by lightning (*AGP.*, I, p. 508). The *MBh.* (3.173,50, *EM.*) recalls the fierceness of the struggles of the indigenes, indicated by the epithet given them, *dānavas* or demons, and that of their war-elephants, *dānavanāgas*.

[1] *HCIP.*, I, p. 150. Elephants may have been sacred to the Indus Valley people (ibid., p. 185).

[2] *Ait. Br.*, VIII.22.

[3] From *mṛtāṇḍa*, lit. 'dead or addled egg'.

[4] Brodrick, *Animals in Archaeology*, p. 135.

[5] The Mayan rain-god Chac is elephant-headed and

associated with serpents. In the *Codex Troano*, Chac is depicted treading on a serpent's head and pouring out the rain from a bowl ('Representation of Deities of the Maya Manuscripts', *Papers of the Peabody Museum*, vol. IV (1904), cited by G. E. Smith, *The Evolution of the Dragon*, p. 84, and v. figs. 11 and 12).

v. Abhranāga; Airāvata; Gajendra; Gajamuktā; Gaṇeśa; Lokapāla.

Gajakūrmāśin 'Devourer of an elephant and a tortoise.' An epithet applied to Garuḍa when he seized an elephant and a tortoise in his talons. The elephant and tortoise were really two brothers who had cursed each other to assume animal form. They lived in a great lake and continually fought each other.[1] Garuḍa carried them to a large banyan tree, but as he alighted on a branch it began to crack. Seeing the Vālakhilya *ṛṣis* below hanging head downwards engaged in ascetic practices, he rose in the air with the branch in his beak, still holding the elephant and the tortoise. After this feat the *ṛṣis* named him Garuḍa (bearer of heavy weight) (*MBh.*, Ādi pa., 30).

[1]Dange, *Legends*, p. 51, suggests that the tortoise and elephant represent two Nāga tribes fighting for supremacy.

Gajamuktā The pearl or jewel believed to be set within the heads of elephants, serpents and *makaras*.

Gajendra King of elephants. When playing with his wives he was seized by an aquatic monster from whose clutches he could not free himself, whereupon he prayed fervently to Viṣṇu who appeared in his *kari-varada* aspect and rescued him.[1]

In a previous existence Gajendra had been a Pāṇḍyan king called Indrayumna. He had been a devotee of Hari (Viṣṇu), but Agastya had cursed him to be born as an elephant.

[1]*Bhāg. P.*, Bk. VIII, Chs 2–4; *DHI.*, p. 426.

Gaṇa I. 'Troop', 'multitude', especially troops of demigods, the attendants of Śiva and Devī.[1] The *gaṇas* are generally grouped in classes, viz., Ādityas, Viśvas, Vasus, Tuṣitas, Ābhāsvaras, Anilas, Mahārājikas, Sādhyas and Rudras. Twelve groups of seven *gaṇas* live with the sun during various parts of the year (*Vāyu P.*, 52, 24–35, *PI.*).

[1]Banerjea draws attention to the similarity between the hybrid figures of the *pramanthas* and *gaṇas* attendant on Śiva and some of the composite figures on seals from Mohenjo-daro and Harappā (*PTR.*, p. 65). According to *AGP.* (II, p. 1,114) the *gaṇas* are invoked to protect children.

v. Gaṇeśa.

II. A group of asterisms classed under three heads—gods, men and *rākṣasas*.

Gaṇaparvata The abode of the *gaṇas* on Mount Kailāsa, also called Rajatādri or Silver Mountain.

Gaṇapati 'Leader of the *gaṇas*.' An epithet of Brahmaṇaspati, the Lord of Prayer, as 'Lord and Leader of the heavenly hosts (*gaṇas*)' (*RV.*, II.23,1), probably a reference to those who figuratively carry out his purpose and answer the prayers of his suppliants. But the Vedic Gaṇapati has no connexion with his paurāṇic namesake, which is an epithet of Gaṇeśa, the principal object of worship of the Gāṇapatya cult.

Coomaraswamy considers that Gaṇapati is a type of *yakṣa*, and draws attention to an elephant-headed *yakṣa* depicted on an Amarāvatī coping.[1]

[1]*Yakṣas*, pt. i, p. 7. The *pāriṣadas* (*gaṇas*) described in the *MBh.* as attendant on Skanda, also have crow, owl, dog, boar, elephant and lion faces, etc. (*DHI.*, p. 356).

v. Gaṇa I; Vināyaka; Gaṇapatihṛdayā.

Gaṇapatihṛdayā A Buddhist Tantric elephant-headed goddess, probably Gaṇeśa's *śakti*. She personifies the Buddhist *mantra* of the same name, said to have been disclosed to Ānanda by the Buddha at Rājagṛha.[1]

[1]Bhattacharyya, *Buddhist Iconography*, pp. 157–8 and Pl.xlii, fig. d; Mitra, *Nepalese Buddhist Literature*, p. 89; Getty, *Gaṇeśa*, p. 37.

Gāṇapatya The cult of Gaṇapati (Gaṇeśa), lord of the *gaṇas* or minor gods and spirits.[1] This cult's doctrines are included in the *Gaṇeśa Purāṇa* and in a poem called the *Gaṇeśa-gītā* which, except for the substitution of 'Gaṇeśa' for 'Kṛṣṇa', is identical in substance with the *Bhagavadgītā*.[2]

The early Gāṇapatyas worshipped six forms of Gaṇapati, named respectively, Mahā, Haridrā, Ucchiṣṭa (also called Heramba), Navanīta, Svarṇa and Santāna-Gaṇapati.[3] Banerjea suggests that some folk-deities 'served as the central figures of such cults as that of the Gāṇapatyas, probably a later merger of the earlier cults of the Yakṣas and Nāgas'.[4]

During the development of the Gāṇapatya cult it is possible to discern 'the first stage of Gaṇeśa's embryonic existence when he was still the ungainly, but already sacred, image of a genius-elephant . . . which . . . ended in the ultimate type of a genius with the head of an elephant'.[5] This iconographical representation was accompanied by an imperfectly applied 'theological' veneer through which an ancient animism is visible.

[1]Bhandarkar, *VSM.*, p. 148. The Gāṇapatya cults may have arisen because of the close association of Śiva and his son, Gaṇeśa; the latter's worship in this cult finally superseded that of Śiva.

[2]*SED.*, *IW.*, p. 139, n. 1.

[3]*BH.*, p. 218.

[4]*PTR.*, p. 16.
[5]Getty, *Gaṇeśa*, Intro. by A. Foucher, p. xxi.
v. Hairamba(s); Vināyaka.

Gandhamādana I. 'Intoxicating fragrance'. The name of one of the four mountains enclosing the central region of the world. It forms the division between Ilāvṛta and Bhadāśva, east of Meru[1] and is renowned for its fragrant forests. Here dwell Indra, Kubera and his *yakṣas*. Gandhamādana is the home of healing herbs, and its groves are said to lead to heaven.

[1]The *VP.* places it to the south of Meru.

II. A monkey-general of Rāma's allies who was killed by Indrajit, but later resurrected by Hanumat with herbs gathered on Mount Kailāsa.

Gāndhārī The daughter of Subala, King of Gandhāra, and wife of the blind Dhṛtarāṣṭra. In sympathy with her husband she always blindfolded her eyes (*MBh.*, Ādi pa., 110).

Gāndhārī had once hospitably entertained the *ṛṣi* Dvaipāyana who in return offered her a boon. She asked for one hundred sons. Later she became pregnant but at the end of two years no child had been born. Then she struck her womb violently and was delivered of a hard lump of flesh, which Dvaipāyana sprinkled with water and divided into one hundred pieces each about the size of a thumb. He placed one piece in each of a hundred jars of ghee (*ghṛta*). After a further two years the lids of the jars were removed and Duryodhana appeared, and later ninety-nine other sons, but Gāndhārī also wished for a daughter. Then Dvaipāyana called for another jar of ghee in which he placed a small excess portion of flesh, and in due course a beautiful daughter, Duḥśalā, was born (*MBh.*, Ādi pa., 115 and 116).

Gandharvaloka The 'world or sphere of the *gandharvas*', in which *śūdras* dwell after death (*VP.*, I.6).

Gandharva-nagara 'City of the *gandharvas*.' Post-Vedic works equate this illusory city with 'mirage'.

Gandharva(s) A deity dwelling in the atmosphere, designated the heavenly Gandharva (*divya gandharva*)[1] in the *RV.* IX.86,36, and called Viśvāvasu (X.85,21–2).[2] He is the guardian of the celestial *soma*, i.e., rain, or may represent the rain-cloud itself as in (VIII.66,5), when 'Indra in . . . realms of space pierces the Gandharva through'. In IX.85,12 he is described as lighting the two worlds, heaven and earth, which are called his parents. The *gandharva* may have been a tutelary Āryan tribal godling or have a still more ancient origin, a supposition that might account for the revival in Paurāṇic times of nature myths of *gandharvas*, *rākṣasas*, and other goblins and spirits.[3]

The *AV.* describes the *gandharvas* as shaggy, half-animal beings, having a strong earthy odour and associated with water. Sometimes they are depicted with the upper half of the body human with wings attached to the shoulders, and the lower half bird-like; at other times as handsome, rather effeminate men.[4]

When the *soma* is being conveyed to the sacrificial hut, the following *mantra* is used to protect it: 'Move forward, O lord of the world, to all thy stations. Let no opponent find thee; let not robbers find thee nor the Gandharva, Viśvāvasu, injure thee' (*Tait. Saṁ.*, I.2,9). In one *AV.* hymn (II.2) the Gandharva is to be propitiated and banned 'with incantation'; amulets should also be worn as a protection against him. The *gandharvas* and the *apsarasas* may also cause madness; propitiatory offerings should therefore be made to them. The kindling material of the sacrificial fire should be of *nyagrodha*, *udumbara*, *aśvattha* or *plakṣa* wood, for these trees are the abode of *gandharvas* and *apsarasas* (*Tait. Saṁ.*, III.4,8). At the *vājapeya* sacrifice the Gandharva is a divine being 'who purifieth thoughts' (ibid., I.7,7). In another passage (ibid., I.4,7) Agni is called the Gandharva, as also are Candramas (the moon),[5] Prajāpati and Vāyu. Death, the overlord, is also called the Gandharva.

Traditional history refers to *gandharvas*, as well as to *rākṣasas*, *asuras*, *nāgas*, *yakṣas*, etc., as native tribal groups, who were at one time or another allies or adversaries of the Āryans. Thus the *nāgas*, who had been oppressed by the *gandharvas*, called Mauneyas or sons of the *muni* Kaśyapa,[6] allied themselves with Purukutsa, a renowned Solar Dynasty king, enabling him to cross the Narmadā river and defeat the *gandharvas*. In the *Viṣṇu Pur.* (IV.3) this event is transformed into a sectarian legend designed to glorify Viṣṇu, to whom the *nāgas* had appealed for help. Viṣṇu declared that he would incarnate himself in Purukutsa, whom the river-goddess Narmadā would then conduct to the secret dwellings of the *gandharvas*, take them by surprise and destroy them. In acknowledgment of Narmadā's services, a *mantra* was addressed to her. Whosoever repeats it morning and night will never be bitten by a snake or suffer from food poisoning.

In the *MBh.* (Ādi pa., 172) the *gandharvas* are said to be musicians,[7] the *apsarasas* the dancers, of the gods. They are collectively regarded as radiant beings who sing sweetly on the mountains, but may be dangerous, especially at twilight, when—together with *yakṣas* and *rākṣasas*—they roam about and haunt forest pools. But great healing powers are attributed to them as well as the capacity to cause insanity. When Varuṇa their overlord became impotent they restored his virility with an aphrodisiac.

In a section of the *Agni Pur.* (II, p. 1062), dealing with the management of horses, the horse in a previous incarnation is said to be the son of a *gandharva*[8] chieftain.

In Buddhist folklore the *gandharvas* are attendant on the *devas* who dwell in the *cāturmahārājika* realm, and in both Buddhism and Hinduism, they are connected with marriage, or rather with conception as a being seeking to be reborn.[9]

The Hindu association of the *gandharvas* with marriage and with the protection of virgins may have originated from the Vedic Gandharva's protection of Sūryā when she was about to become the bride of the sun (*RV.*, X.85,22). They are said to love women and to be thinking always of them (*Kauṣ. Br.*, XII.3) Among the various types of marriage to which Manu refers (III.21,32; *AGP.*, I, p. 594) is the 'Gandharva marriage', which is not dependent on parental consent, but on mutual agreement and affection.

[1]In the *RV.* the designation occurs generally in the singular. It is only in much later times that the *gandharvas* were regarded as a class. They are the equivalent of the Avestan *gandarewas*.

[2]Meaning 'beneficial to all'.

[3]Iconographically represented in hybrid forms, part-human, part-bird, which may have owed 'their origin and evolution to the dim memories of the remote past' (*DHI.*, p. 163). The same author also draws attention to the animal-faced forms on sealings discovered at Harappā.

[4]Such as the eleventh-century sandstone figure from Orissa, now in the Victoria and Albert Museum (274–1951).

[5]Hence the *gandharvas* are said to regulate the course of the twenty-seven lunar asterisms (*nakṣatras*). Edgerton considers they were originally male sexual demons who troubled women (*BIP.*, p. 79, n.3).

[6]But the origin of the *gandharvas* is variously described. According to *Manu* (I.37) they were created by the seven Great Manus; or by Brahmā (*VP.*, I.5); or emerged from Prajāpati's dismembered body (*ŚBr.*, IX.4.1,2), etc.

[7]Their connexion with music is indicated by the term *gandharvavidyā*, the knowledge of music. It is also the general designation of music and the name of a particular musical note.

[8]*Gandharvas* are subject to Varuṇa, the presiding deity of horses, and are thus often associated with them; especially with the horses that draw the sun's chariot whose course the *gandharvas* direct.

[9]Malalasekera, *Dictionary of Pāli Proper Names*: v. also *PTS*.

v. Gandharvī; Gandharvaloka; Gandharva-veda; Viśvāvasu; Citraratha II; Vāc; Gandharvavivāha; Kabandha; Śūrpa; Tumburu; Purūravas; Vāyu.

Gandharvaveda 'Gandharva science or knowledge.' The dramatic arts and music, dancing, etc. (*VP.*, III.6).

Gandharvavidyā v. Gandharva (s), n.7.

Gandharvavivāha A form of marriage by mutual consent.

v. Vivāha; Gandharva (s).

Gandharvī The daughter of Surabhi. In *RV.* (X.11) she appears as a seductive water-nymph haunting the banks of rivers. In later works a number of *gandharvīs* are mentioned, the chief being 'the abstract Gandharvī or ancestress of all horses, which marks the centaur character of these spirits'.[1]

Mantharā, the sister of Bali, was formerly a *gandharvī* called Dundubhī (the drum). At Brahmā's behest she was incarnated as the fomentor of hate.[2]

[1]*EM.*, p. 153.

[2]Ibid., p. 156.

v. Harī; Kinnara (s).

Gandhavatī 'Sweetly scented.'

v. Satyavatī I.

Gāndinī The daughter of Kāśīrāja who, after being in her mother's womb for twelve years without any signs of parturition, advised her father to present a cow each day to the *brāhmaṇas* to ensure that at the end of a further three years she would be born. The father acted accordingly and Gāndinī was born as she had foretold. Later she married Śvaphalka and continued the daily presentation of a cow to the end of her life (*VP.*, IV.13), and hence her name, which means a 'cow daily'.

v. Akrūra.

Gāṇḍīva The magical bow which possessed the power of a thousand bows and had two inexhaustible quivers. No other weapon could damage it, and the *gandharvas* and all other celestial beings worshipped it (*MBh.*, Ādi pa., 227). It was presented to Arjuna, but after Kṛṣṇa's departure to heaven the bow lost its power.

Gaṇeśa or **Gaṇapati** The elephant-headed god of wisdom described in the *Smṛti* of Yājñavalkya (I.270, 279, 293) as a demon who possesses men and women and hinders them, but when propitiated and praised assists them. Gaṇeśa's name does not appear in the earliest recension of the *MBh.*, or in any version of the *Rāmāyaṇa*; nor has any representation of him been discovered anterior to the fifth century.[1]

However enhanced the status of Gaṇeśa became in medieval India and Indonesia, etc., his metamorphosis fails to conceal his animistic origin. 'Thus, when dealing with a theri-anthropomorphic figure of Gaṇeśa's type, we can easily trace it back to the animal prototype from which it came; and here we plunge into the oldest layer of superstition . . .'[2] Nor is it difficult to see why Gaṇeśa, because of his probable association with an ancient elephant cult, should have been selected from the host of ancient Indian nature godlings, and to have survived so long in the popular imagination.

Owing to lack of textual references, it is impossible to trace in detail the earliest development of Gaṇeśa's metamorphosis. Bhandarkar[3] suggests his origins may have been the four malignant spirits called *vināyakas*, whose individual names were Sālakaṭaṅkata, Kūṣmāṇḍarājaputra, Usmita and Devayajana. Finally these four became incorporated in Gaṇapati-Vināyaka, whose mother was Ambikā. Crooke[4] sees in Gaṇeśa a Dravidian sun-god, an opinion confirmed by de Gubernatis[5] who suggests also that the rat (Gaṇeśa's *vāhana*) symbolizes night or darkness which the sun destroys. Sometimes Gaṇeśa (without his *vāhana*) is depicted as a scribe to whom Vyāsa is dictating the *Mahābhārata*.[6]

As rodents generally succeed in gnawing their way through every obstruction, the rat is said to symbolize Gaṇeśa's ability to destroy every obstacle. Risley's observation that the rat is a 'totem' of at least one Dravidian tribe (the Oraons) points to its early symbolism.[7] Coomaraswamy regards Gaṇeśa as a folk-godling having affinities with *yakṣas* and *nāgas*,[8] while Monier-Williams places Gaṇeśa and Skanda at the head of the tutelary village-divinities (*grāma-devatās*) who, as the controllers of good and evil actions, guard the household.

Despite his originally malignant nature, his worshippers succeeded in breaking through the barriers of brahmanic conservatism and securing his recognition as a god, if only a minor one. It may seem strange that such a cult should have emerged when speculation about the nature of the self and the universe had passed from the mythical to the philosophical, when theriomorphism had come to be generally regarded as part of ancient folklore, but these two levels are, as they have always been, characteristic of Indian religious belief.

The accounts of his parentage vary.[9] In one of these he is the son of Śiva and Pārvatī; or was formed from the unguents with which she anointed herself (*Matsya P.*, 23,38 and 84, etc., *PI.*). Another myth states that on one occasion after Pārvatī had bathed, the water was thrown into the Ganges and drunk by the elephant-headed goddess Mālinī who gave birth to a body with four arms and five elephant heads. The river-goddess Gaṅgā claimed him, but Śiva declared him to be Pārvatī's son, reduced his five heads to one and enthroned him as the 'Remover of obstacles'.[10] Perhaps the most fantastic of the myths is that giving the reason for Gaṇeśa's epithet, Gajānana or elephant-face. It states that Pārvatī, wishing to be protected, especially when bathing, from her uxorious husband Śiva, created Gaṇeśa from her sweat and appointed him to be the guardian of her apartments. When Śiva sought admission Gaṇeśa, unaware of his identity, refused him, whereupon the enraged husband summoned one of his attendants (*gaṇas*) who decapitated Gaṇeśa. Finally Śiva was induced to appeal to 'the gods of the north' to make good Gaṇeśa's loss with the head of the first animal they encountered. This happened to be an elephant, and hence Gaṇeśa's elephant head. As an explanation of Gaṇeśa's solitary tusk[11] (*ekadanta*), it is related that on one occasion, the moon and the twenty-seven asterisms (*nakṣatras*) laughed at him when his belly had burst open and released a large number of cakes which he had eaten. In his rage he broke off one of his tusks and threw it at the moon which gradually became dark.

In modern times Gaṇeśa is regarded as the personification of those qualities which overcome difficulties. He is the typical embodiment of success in life, and its accompaniments of good-living, prosperity and peace, and hence his images and shrines are seen throughout India. In all ceremonies (except funeral rites) and undertakings Gaṇeśa is first invoked.[12] Nonetheless, few, if any, temples are solely dedicated to him, and the once flourishing cult of the Gāṇapatyas has failed to maintain a place in the sophisticated philosophy of modern Hinduism, yet Gaṇeśa is still revered by most Hindus whether Vaiṣṇava or Śaiva.

[1] The earliest so far discovered is in a temple at Bhumāra, Central India (v. Getty, *Gaṇeśa*, Pl. 3b).

[2] Ibid., Intro. by A. Foucher, p. xvi. Many dwarf *yakṣas* are depicted with elephant ears which suggests a connexion with Gaṇeśa (Coomaraswamy, *Yakṣas*, pt. ii, p. 32).

[3] *VSM.*, pp. 147f. Foucher also considers Gaṇeśa was originally a kind of demon who became lord of the *gaṇas* (the hordes of spirits who follow Śiva) (Getty, *Gaṇeśa*, Intro., p. xx.).

[4] *Religion and Folklore of Northern India*, p. 98.

[5] *Zoological Mythology*, II. p. 68.

[6] Getty, op. cit., Pl.1.

[7] *Tribes and Castes of Bengal*, II, p. 113.

[8] *Yakṣas*, I, p. 7. His pot-belly (*tundila*) is a characteristic he shares with some *yakṣas*. It resembles a pitcher (*kumbha*) 'containing all prosperity' (*Kathāsaritsāgara*, 22, 162), and in the same work (22,55) an image of Gaṇeśa is mentioned which fulfils all desires (cited by Bosch, *GG.*, p. 114, n.9). Although Gaṇeśa is not named in any of the lists of *yakṣas*, he may be 'actually equivalent to Kubera or Māṇibhadra' (*Yakṣas*, pt. i,

p. 7). For illustrations of an elephant-headed *yakṣa* depicted on the Amarāvatī coping, v. Pl. 23, fig. 1.
[9]v. *EHI.*, for myths concerning Gaṇeśa's parentage.
[10]According to the *Haracarita* (18th canto) by Jayadratha, a thirteenth-century composition, claimed to be based on earlier texts.
[11]Meditation on this tusk will alleviate fever (*AGP.*, II, p. 1119).
[12]Cf. the ancient Egyptian scribe who, at the beginning of his day's work, would pour out a libation to Thoth, god of writing (Cottrell, *Land of Shinar*, p. 155).
v. Gaṇeśagītā; Gaṇeśānī; Brahmaṇaspati, n. 2; Siddhi II; Vināyikā; Gaṇeśvara; Gaṇapati-hṛdayā.

Gaṇeśagītā A work of the Gāṇapatyas giving a popular interpretation of the *BG.*, in which Gaṇeśa's name is substituted for Kṛṣṇa's. Gaṇeśa is identified with the Supreme Deity and regarded as superior even to the *trimūrti.*[1]
[1]E. tr. K. Yoroi, *Gaṇeśagītā*, The Hague, 1968.

Gaṇeśānī The *śakti* of Gaṇeśa.
v. Vināyikā.

Gaṇeśa Purāṇa A Purāṇa embodying the doctrines of the Gāṇaptyas whose supreme deity is Gaṇeśa.[1]
[1]*IW.*, p. 139, n.1. For an analysis of this Pur. v. Stevenson, *JRAS.*, 1845, VIII, p. 319.
v. Gaṇeśagītā.

Gaṇeśvara 'Lord of the *gaṇas*.' Epithet of Gaṇeśa, Viṣṇu and Śiva.

Gaṅgā 'Swift-goer.'[1] Name of the river Ganges and its personification as a goddess. The river rises from an ice-bed, 13,800 feet above sea-level, beyond Gaṅgotrī (probably Gaṅgā-avatārapuri), 'the sacred manifestation of the Gaṅges'.[2]

The Indus, Jumnā, Narmadā and other rivers have similarly become local objects of worship. But to the early Āryan intruders, temporarily halted in the Panjāb, the Indus and Sarasvatī were the only great Indian rivers known to them. Thus Gaṅgā is mentioned in two passages only of the *RV.* and is invoked in hymns to rivers (X.75,5), simply as one of a number of river-goddesses.

With the Āryan occupation of the Gangetic basin Gaṅgā gradually became the chief river-goddess of a vast area, the subject of numerous legends, and endowed with fabulous virtues. Along the banks temples were erected, each the centre of pilgrimage at which priests could officiate and expect a multiplicity of sacrificial and other 'gifts'. Legend was piled on legend, some of them obviously priestly fictions, invented to sustain the role of the priests as intermediaries between the goddess and her devotees. A celestial Gaṅgā[3] called Abhragaṅgā or Ākāśagaṅgā was invented, who bore the epithet Devabhūtī (flowing from heaven). It was also called Mandākinī (the Milky Way),[4] which issued from Viṣṇu's left foot; hence Gaṅgā's epithet Viṣṇupadī. Gaṅgā flows on to the head of Dhruva who sustains her day and night (*VP.*, II.8).

The royal *ṛṣi* Bhagīratha, descendant of Sagara, performed extreme austerities (*tapas*) for many years to effect Gaṅgā's descent from heaven[5] for the purpose of purifying the ashes of Sagara's 60,000 sons who had been destroyed by the *ṛṣi* Kapila, and enable them to attain Paradise. Bhagīratha then propitiated Śiva and Gaṅgā, and the latter swept down in three great torrents which would have flooded the earth had not Śiva caught the waters in his matted hair and broken their fall; hence his epithet Gaṅgādhara (Supporter of the Ganges). Being again propitiated by Bhagīratha, Śiva allowed Gaṅgā to flow to the sea and to the nether regions (Pātāla) and so purify Sagara's sons (*MBh.*, Vana pa., 108), and hence her epithet Bhagīrathī.

Gaṅgā initially was probably a river-spirit[6] who was finally anthropomorphized and with whom other local river-goddesses became identified, such as the river-goddess of the Tipāras (East Bengal) called Tuimā. Gaṅgā is often identified with Pārvatī, or with one of the other forms of the Mother-goddess like Annapūrṇā, goddess of food and plenty at Banāras. Gaṅgā's form varies according to local tradition. Thus in South India she is represented as a mermaid, swimming in water with folded hands, wearing a crown, and bearing on her forehead the Śaiva mark in sacred ashes. In Bengal she is depicted as a woman, coloured white (denoting her cleansing and purifying qualities), crowned and seated on her *vāhana*, a *makara.* In her right hand she holds a lotus, in her left a lute.

Not only will those who bathe in the Gaṅgā obtain Svarga ('heaven'), but also those whose bones, hair, etc., are left on the banks (*VP.*, IV.4). All the country through which the Ganges flows should be regarded as hallowed ground. Seeing, touching, or drinking the water, or addressing the goddess as 'O mother Ganges', will remove all 'sin' (*AGP.*, ch. 110).

Gaṅgā encloses Brahmā's great city situated on Mount Meru and then divides into four mighty rivers flowing in the four directions (*VP.*, II.2).[7]

King Śāntanu fell deeply in love with Gaṅgā who agreed to marry him on condition that he neither criticized nor spoke unkindly to her. If he broke either condition she would immediately disappear.[8] For many years they lived happily and had seven sons (the Vasus), but Gaṅgā threw each child at birth into the river, saying, 'This is for your good'. When the eighth child was born and she was about to drown it, Śāntanu remonstrated and called her a murderess. She then revealed that she was the goddess Gaṅgā who at the instigation of the gods had been chosen as the mother of the eight Vasus. The latter, owing to the curse of the *ṛṣi* Vasiṣṭha (here called Āpava), were condemned to be born in human form. Before leaving the king forever she requested that their last child should be called Gaṅgādatta (*MBh.*, Ādi pa., 98). This story is probably based on that of Aditi who took her seven sons to meet the gods, leaving behind the eighth, Mārtāṇḍa (*RV.*, X.72,8).

[1]From *gam* 'going' (*Nir.*, 9.26).

[2]*ERE.*, VI, p. 180. Gaṅgotrī itself is now regarded as the source.

[3]The Nile was also personified and had both a celestial and an underworld counterpart (James, *The Tree of Life*, pp. 66 and 134).

[4]*ERE.*, II, p. 809.

[5]Another reason given for bringing Gaṅgā to earth was to fill up the sea which had been consumed by Agastya (*MBh.*, Vana pa., 109).

[6]The differentiated forms of the river goddesses in northern India 'are directly derived from that of the *yakṣī-dryad*, and this implies that the latter, despite the vegetal and apparently terrestrial habitat, was still primarily a spirit of the waters' (Coomaraswamy, *Yakṣas*, pt. ii, p. 55).

[7]Cf. the river which flowed out of Eden and then divided into four rivers (Genesis, II.10).

[8]Cf. the conditions laid down by the nymph Urvaśī for Purūravas.

v. Gaṅgākṣetra; Gaṅgājala; Kārttikeya; Bhīṣma; Meru I; Anasūyā; Haridvāra; Ākāśagaṅgā.

Gaṅgādatta v. Gaṅgā.

Gaṅgādhara 'Bearer (or receiver) of the Ganges' (Gaṅgā), an epithet of Śiva and of the personified Ocean.

Gaṅgājala The water of the sacred Ganges (Gaṅgā), used when administering oaths.

Gaṅgākṣetra The land (*kṣetra*), regarded as sacred, through which the Ganges flows as well as a specified area on either bank. Those who die within these limits go immediately to the heavenly world, irrespective of their misdeeds.

Gaṅgāputra 'Son of Gaṅgā.' An epithet of Bhīṣma.

Garbhādhāna A purificatory rite performed after menstruation to ensure both conception and the perfect development of the embryo (*AGP.*, Ch. 24; v. also vol. I, p. 101, n. and p. 274). For successful conception the following prayer is recited: 'May Viṣṇu form and mould the womb; may Tvaṣṭar duly shape the forms; Prajāpati infuse the stream, and Dhātar lay the germ for thee' (*RV.*, X.184,1; *AV.*, V.25,5). To ensure that the offspring shall be male, the *garbhādhāna* is followed three months later by the *puṁsavana* rite. In South India the 'womb-fire' is worshipped and the generative process symbolically represented in these ceremonies.[1]

[1]Diehl, *Instrument and Purpose*, p. 125.

Garbha-gṛha The centre or inner sanctuary of an Indian temple enshrining its main deity, regarded as 'the container of the seed (of universal manifestation)'.[1]

[1]*CHS.*, p. 24. Cf. the Holy of Holies in the ancient Egyptian temple which 'was a small dark room in the central axis of the temple towards the back . . . Since all that exists had gone forth from this spot, it was a centre of immeasurable potency well suited for the manifestation of a divinity' (H. Frankfort, *Ancient Egyptian Religion*, p. 153).

Garga Name of an astronomer who, with the Nāga architect Śeṣa, introduced Nāgara architecture.[1] Bhattacharyya's contention that this school of architecture and painting arose after Garga had been instructed by the architect Śeṣa is corroborated by a tradition recorded by Tarānātha, the Tibetan historian, that there was a Nāga school of art in the time of Nāgārjuna.[2]

[1]Bhattacharyya, *Canons of Indian Art*, p. 315.

[2]Ibid., p. 384. Tarānātha mentions three early styles of Indian art, viz., Deva, Yakṣa and Nāga (ibid., pp. 385f.).

Gārgī Saṁhitā An astronomical work (c. A.D. 230) of great historical value. It contains a chapter called the Yuga Purāṇa, believed to date from c. A.D. 50 which gives an account of Greek influence in Pāṭaliputra. Other interesting references enhance its value as a source book of Indo-Greek history.[1]

[1]A.K. Narain, *The Indo-Greeks*, p. 174.

Gārgī Vācaknavī A daughter of Vacaknu. Her learning is representative of the high intellectual standard of the women of the upper classes in the late Vedic period.[1] Gifted women thus often took part in the philosophical and literary debates held under royal auspices.

At one of these debates held under the patronage of the learned Janaka, King of Videha, the leading contestant, Yājñavalkhya, was challenged by Gārgī, one of the questioners. Her questions and Yājñavalkhya's answers appear in the *Bṛhad-Ār. Up.*, (III.8,1–12). The first question was: 'What is the warp and woof that links all that is above the sky, beneath the earth, and between them both, or that links what people call past, present and future?' 'Space', replied Yājñavalkhya. Gārgī then asked him to elaborate. Yājñavalkhya replied with a proliferation of detail, characteristic of the earlier Upaniṣads, that the warp and woof uniting space and time and all existence in an indissoluble whole is the Self-existent, Imperishable, Impersonal *brahman*, the unheard Hearer, the unseen Seer, the uncomprehended Comprehender of all that ever was, or is, or ever shall be.

[1]A status that stands 'in sad contrast to the later age when even the study of Vedic literature was forbidden to women under the most severe penalty' (*HCIP.*, I, p. 513).

v. Vedānta.

Gārhapatya The name of the domestic fire, one of the three sacred fires. It is also the family sacrificial fire which a son received from his father and transmitted to his descendants, thus linking each generation, not only with the ancient progenitors of the family (*pitṛs*) (to whom the *dakṣiṇāgni* is dedicated), but also with the gods (associated with the *āhavanīyāgni*) (*Tait. Saṁ.*, I.5,8; 6,7; VI.1,8). The constant maintenance of the *gārhapatya* was the sacred duty of every householder, for without it there could be no performance of the rites connected with birth, marriage, death, or for averting disease and other calamities, or for the performance of exorcisms and spells.

The *gārhapatya* appears to be the prototype of all sacrificial fires, and particularly of the threefold division of fire (*tretāgni*), introduced by Purūravas (*VP.*, IV.6), which became one of the bases of the brahmanic sacrificial system. In the *tretāgni* ceremonial it was important that none of the fires should go out, but if this happened to the *gārhapatya* it was relighted from the *āhavanīya* and immediate atonement made, failing which the head of the house would die (*ŚBr.*, XI.5.3,9).

In Vedic sacrifices there were three altars, one for each of the three fires (*RV.*, II.36,4), to which great mystical significance was attached. They represent the regions of earth, atmosphere and sky, and the power inherent in them.[1]

The ancient significance of the *gārhapatya* is indicated by its etymology; it signifies 'lord of the household', i.e., Agni, the honoured guest in every home, without whom no sacrifice was effectual, for Agni sanctifies and witnesses every rite. The grass which is spread over the altar must be burnt at the end of the rite because it becomes imbued with a superhuman character' and so could injure anyone who touched it.[2]

[1]*Maitri Up.*, 6,33.

[2]*HCIP.*, I, p. 501.

v. Kuśa; Nirṛti.

Garuḍa I. Also called Tārkṣya. A mythical figure having the beak and talons of a predatory bird and the body of a man, the subject of numerous stories in the *MBh.* and Purāṇas. Like the Vedic sun-god (Savitar or Viṣṇu), Garutmat[1] (possibly, but not certainly, Garuḍa's prototype) was associated with the sun, but not apparently as Viṣṇu's *vāhana.*[2] Garuḍa is identified with the all-consuming sun's rays, and is also the devourer or destroyer of serpents, and hence his epithets Nāgāntaka and Sarpārāti. Popular belief also credits him with the power to cure those suffering from snake-bite,[3] or threatened by disease, and hence his *mantra*:[4] 'Oṁ Tārkṣya (Garuḍa), cast down my enemies, trample the diseases and venom that might invade me' (*AGP.*, I, p. 530). The emerald, traditionally regarded as the foe of poison, is also associated with Garuḍa.

The etymological significance of Garuḍa's name is further illustrated by another of his epithets, Vināyaka,[5] an epithet he shares with Gaṇeśa, both being the removers or destroyers of obstacles, and thus probably of hindrances to the attainment of knowledge. As such Garuḍa appears in the Sātvata list of the thirty-nine *avatāras* of Viṣṇu as Vihaṅgama (the ninth) and as Amṛtaharaṇa (the eighteenth).[6] In the *AGP.* (II. p. 1101) Rudra is said to be manifest in the shape of the mighty celestial bird Garuḍa.

Many of the Garuḍa stories and fables appear to be drawn from ancient non-Āryan sources, the original significance of which has been forgotten. They have thus become little more than nursery tales like their counterparts in other countries. Garuḍa is said to have stolen the sacred *amṛta*[7] from heaven, demanded by Kadrū as a ransom for the release of his mother. This was a task that was dangerous and well-nigh impossible as Kadrū well knew, but Garuḍa succeeded in defeating most of the guardians of the *amṛta*, and having got through the revolving wheel with its razor-like spokes he was finally confronted by two great serpents whose glance alone was sufficient to reduce anyone to ashes. Without a moment's hesitation Garuḍa flung dust in their eyes and destroyed them. Then picking up the *amṛta* he flew off with it, and delivered it to Kadrū and thus obtained his mother's release.

In Buddhism Garuḍa (Garuḷa, Pā.) is regarded as a kind of harpy.

[1]Banerjea considers that Garuḍa (as Garutmat) was the theriomorphic form of the Vedic Āditya Viṣṇu (*PTR.*, p. 26). Dange states that Garuḍa was the name of a sub-division of the Nāga tribe (*Legends*, Pref., p. x).

[2]Hopkins suggests that the name Viṣṇu may mean bird (*EM.*, p. 203 and n. 1).

[3]A graceful winged human figure forms the capital (all that remains) of a Garuḍa temple pillar, which if embraced cures anyone suffering from snake-bite (*DHI.*, Pl. xxvi, fig. 3). He is similarly represented in Amarāvatī sculptures (C. Sivaramamūrti, *Amarāvatī Sculptures*, p. 75). Dange suggests that Garuḍa is derived 'from *gara* and the causal of *uḍ* + the root *ḍī* meaning "one who takes of or removes the poison", or "makes the poison vanish"— (*garam ud* + *ḍayayati*)' (*Legends*, p. 100).

[4]The Garuḍa *mantra* is said to be one of the most efficacious for the expiation of 'sin' (*AGP.*, II, p. 968). According to the *Suś Saṁ.* II, p. 716, 'the *mantras*, full of occult energy of perfect truth and divine communion, disclosed by the *devarṣis* and *brahmarṣis* of yore, never fail to eliminate poison from the system', more speedily than by the use of drugs. A blow from a fist charged with the Garuḍa *mantra* is an antidote to all snake-poison (*AGP.*, II, p. 1095); it also cures all other diseases, as well as persons suffering from possession by an evil spirit (I, p. 530).

[5]Vināyikā is the name of the female counterpart of Garuḍa and of Gaṇeśa.

[6]*DHI.*, p. 529. Garuḍa personifies valour (*IRA.*, p. 312).

[7]A 'strong-pinioned' bird is said to have fetched the 'bubbling beverage' (i.e., the *soma*) from afar (*RV.*, X.144, 1–4). Cf. III.48,4 where Indra conquers Tvaṣṭṛ and carries off the *soma*, probably the basis of the Garuḍa *amṛta* myth. This exploit has some parallels with that of the Sumerian storm-bird Zu, the stealer of the 'tablets of destiny', which gave him the power over the 'destiny' of everything. He too is depicted as half-man and half-bird on cylinder seals.

Grünwedel suggests that the parrot and the West Asian griffin were the bases on which the modern iconography of Garuḍa was developed (*Buddhist Art*, p. 51). The Egyptian sun-god was also represented as an eagle, and the Mayan sun-god was borne across the sky by a giant condor.

v. Garuḍa(s); Garuḍī I, II; Gajakūrmāśin; Tāmra; Vāyu; Jāṭayu I; Suparṇa, II; Viṣavidyā; Mayūra.

II. Name of a weapon, fire-altar, and of an army-formation (*Manu*, VII, 197).

Garuḍa(s) Demonic forms which appear in battle, sometimes as great birds of prey.

Gāruḍī I. 'Relating to (or coming from) Garuḍa.' A *mantra* against poison.

II. A caste of snake-charmers in Mahārāṣṭra.

Garutmat An eagle which protects one against poison and poisoned arrows (*AV.*, IV.6,3).

v. Garuḍa I.

Gaumukha v. Gaṅgā.

Gaura A name of Śiva, and of a mountain of gold situated north of Mount Kailāsa. Lake Bindusaras lies at its foot, where Bhagīratha performed great austerities.

Gaurī 'Yellow', 'Brilliant'. Name of a goddess, the spouse of Śiva or of Varuṇa. The oceans (i.e., the fertilizing rain) flow down from her (*Nir.*, 11.40,41); she is the source of the world, the Cosmic Cow. Agrawala agrees that she symbolizes the waters (*apaḥ*), denoting the undifferentiated form of matter before creation.[1] Payne suggests she was a goddess of the harvest and ripened corn, or perhaps named after the yellow Gaura buffalo.[2] The former suggestion is borne out by the festival held on the third clear day of *caitra* (March–April) when women and girls competed to see who could swing the highest, as the higher they went the higher and better would be the plant growth.[3]

Gaurī is also the name of a class of goddesses called Gaurīs which includes Umā, Pārvatī, Rambhā, Totalā and Tripurā.[4]

[1]*VF.*, p. 50.

[2]*The Śāktas*, p. 7. The *AGP.*, I, p. 407 states that Gaurī is a symbol of universal force; Sāyaṇa equates her with Vāc.

[3]Auboyer, *Daily Life in Vedic India*, p. 145.

[4]*DHI.*, p. 502. The goddess Śrī is regarded as one of the six varieties of Gaurī, or sometimes as Gaurī herself.

v. Gaura; Godhikā.

Gautama I. A name of the *ṛṣi* Śaradvat, the husband of Ahalyā. Indra assumed the form of Gautama and seduced Ahalyā, whereupon he lost his handsome form (*Mārk. P.*, V.13).

v. Kṛpī.

II. The founder of the Nyāya school.

v. Darśana.

III. A name of Śākyamuni, the historical Buddha.

v. Buddhism.

Gaya v. Gayā; Gayāsura.

Gayā Name of a town and also of the district in which it is situated. It is one of the seven sacred Hindu centres and hence an important place of pilgrimage, notable also as the spot where the *asura* Gaya (Gayāsura) offered himself as a sacrifice 'for the good of all mankind'. It is the place where the sacred *akṣayavaṭa* tree grows to which offerings are made. As these offerings directly benefit the *pitṛs* Gayā is called Pitṛtīrtha (sacred place of the *pitṛs*).[1]

One of the villages near Gayā is called Bodh Gayā, traditionally regarded as the place where the Buddha attained Enlightenment under the *aśvattha* tree (Ficus religiosa).

[1]*Ancestor Worship*, p. 269. Grierson suggests that Gayā was originally a Hindu shrine with a sacred tree which granted offspring; then it became Buddhist, and again Hindu between the fifth and seventh centuries A.D. (*ERE.*, VI, p. 183).

Gayāsura The name of a giant demon, associated with the town of Gayā and its vicinity. Although an *asura*, Gaya was a devout Vaiṣṇava who for a thousand years had been practising rigorous austerities (*tapas*) on the Kolāhala hill. As the power engendered by such practices was believed to threaten the status of the gods themselves, they appealed in turn to Brahmā and Śiva for help. But as neither felt capable of averting the danger the gods called upon Viṣṇu who advised them to grant Gayāsura whatever boon he wished on condition that he ceased from all ascetic practices. He agreed provided that his body should be made so pure that its purity would be beyond that ever known or to be known. The gods accepted the condition, but the granting of this boon had unforeseen results. People flocked to see and touch the body of the holy *asura* whereupon they immediately ascended to the immortal world of Brahmā (Brahmaloka). As a result the worship of Indra and the other gods almost ceased and no one entered the domain of Yama, the judge of the dead. No longer able to perform their duties the gods again appealed to Viṣṇu who advised them to ask Gaya to offer his body as a sacrifice, and thus enable the rhythm of life, death and immortality to be restored. Again Gaya agreed, and on reaching the summit of Kolāhala hill he fell to the ground. When a slight movement of the body was observed Brahmā ordered Yama to fetch the *dharmaśilā* (stone of virtue) from the nether world and to place it on the giant's head. To add to its weight Brahmā and the other gods present sat on it, but the body still showed signs of life. Finally Viṣṇu struck the stone with his mace (*gadā*), whereupon the body ceased to move, but Gaya, still alive, remonstrated with Viṣṇu for his unkind act, and then prayed that the place where he lay should be named after him and that those offering oblations of water and funerary cakes there should gain great merit for themselves, as well as enabling their ancestors to reach Brahmā's world.[1] Thus Gayā became a renowned place of pilgrimage for all devout Hindus and later also for Buddhists.

[1]This is a brief account of the Gayāsura myth in the *Gayā-māhātmya* sections of the *Vāyu P.* cited by D. Shastri, *Ancestor Worship*, pp. 256f. A similar version is included in *AGP.*, I, pp. 445f.

Gāyatrī The name of a metre, consisting of twenty-four syllables (variously arranged, but generally as a triplet of eight syllables each).[1] Numerous *RV.* hymns were composed in this metre, the most sacred being the verse (also known as *gāyatrī* or *sāvitrī*) addressed to the Sun (Savitar) as the supreme generative force. It consists of a short prayer or *mantra* (*RV.*, III.62,10), translated by Wilson as: 'We meditate on that excellent light of the divine Sun; may he illuminate our minds',[2] repeated by every 'twice-born' man at his morning and evening devotions. Its repetition is forbidden to menials and to women.

From being a simple Vedic invocation of the sun to be benign to his worshippers and to bless their undertakings, it was given a gradually expanding significance.[3] One who desires to attain heaven should recite a thousand *gāyatrīs*; an unlimited number gives the fulfilment of all desires (*Ait. Br.*, II.17). By means of the *gāyatrī* a *guru* obtains for his pupil a 'second birth', which is real and exempt from old age and death (*Manu*, II. 148); and a 'twice-born' man who daily repeats the *gāyatrī* 3,000 times outside his village will be freed after a month from guilt however great (II.79).

The *gāyatrī* is personified as a goddess, the wife of Brahmā and mother of the four Vedas, and of the first three classes in their capacity of 'twice-born'. Diehl states that in southern India the *gāyatrī* is attached to Śiva and other gods 'both as *mantra* and as goddess', and that in Śaiva ritual 'there is a *gāyatrī* for each god'.[4]

The presiding deity of the *mantra* is naturally the sun-god. The *gāyatrī* should be repeated when casting libations of ghee (*ghṛta*) into the sacrificial fire, and on occasion to appease the anger of the gods; or for the propitiation of hostile planets. Each letter of the *mantra* has its own deity who 'wipes away' all 'sin' from the person who repeats it (*AGP.*, 215, 16–24). The same work mentions a demonic *gāyatrī* consisting of fifteen syllables.

[1]But sometimes consisting of 'one line of sixteen syllables and a second line of eight. There are eleven varieties of this metre, and the number of syllables in the stanza varies accordingly from nineteen to thirty-three' (Griffith, *RV.*, I. pp. 652f.). The *gāyatrī* is equated with the earth, 'for on it everything here that has come to be is established' (*Chān. Up.*, III, 12, 1–2). By means of it the sacrifice is carried to the gods (*ŚBr.*, I.3.4,6), and hence it is said to be Agni's metre (V.2.1,6).

[2]The *Nir.* (7.12) derives *gāyatrī* from *gai* 'to praise'; or from *gam* with *tri* by metathesis, i.e., 'three-coursed'.

[3]*Bṛhad-Ār. Up.*, 5.14. 1–8.

[4]*Instrument and Purpose*, p. 81, and p. 7 n.2.

v. Virāj II.

Ghaṇṭā 'Bell.' One of the numerous sacrificial objects used in Hindu ritual, and a specific attribute of Śiva. The sound of Śiva's bell or his drum (*ḍamaru*) symbolizes creation and indicates his *mantra-svarūpa* or mystic sound-form.[1] Śiva's spouse Durgā (also called Ghaṇṭī), has the bell as one of her twelve 'weapons'. It is invoked in the following way: 'Om! to the *ghaṇṭā*, by thy world-wide sound strike terror into our enemies, drive out from us all our iniquities, defend us and bless us'. The sounds of all musical instruments are said to be contained in the peals of a bell, and a man's possessions are increased by the tolling of a bell (*AGP.*, II. p. 1218).

The practice of wearing or ringing bells as a protection from evil spirits and from bodily harm is world-wide. Tibetan priests ring bells on mountains to avert hail-storms, and Church bells were rung for many centuries in Europe to avert thunderstorms. The bells often bore such inscriptions as 'Fulgura frango, dissipo ventos' (Lightning and thunder, I break asunder).[2]

[1] *EHI.*, I, pt. i, p. 294.

[2] In the Pontifical of Egbert, Archbishop of York (A.D. 732–66), *Surtees Society*, XXVII, the protective aspect of bells is prominent. 'Wherever this bell sounds let the power of enemies retire, so also the shadow of phantoms, the assault of whirlwinds, the stroke of lightnings, the harm of thunders, the injuries of tempests, and every spirit of the storm-winds'.

Ghaṇṭākarṇa 'Bell-eared.' Name of an attendant of Skanda and of Śiva. Ghaṇṭākarṇa presides over cutaneous diseases and is propitiated to give protection against them.

Ghaṇṭī v. Ghaṇṭā.

Gharma A kind of four-legged kettle or cauldron (likened to an ox),[1] used especially for boiling milk for sacrificial purposes associated with the Aśvins (*RV.*, IV.55,6 and n. 6; VIII.76,2). The boiled milk[2] was also called gharma and was used also as a battle-charm (*AV.*, VIII.8,17). The celestial gharma was brought down to earth by the *ṛṣis* (*RV.*, X. 181,3).

[1] Aufrecht suggests that this was because of its shape.

[2] In South India a ceremony called Pongal (from Tamil *pongu*, to boil) is performed, in which the manner of the heating and boiling of the milk 'is the heart of the festival ... It further prognosticates the fortunes of the family during the coming year, and is thus of crucial importance' (F. R. Allchin, *Neolithic Cattle-Keepers of South India*, p. 134).

Ghaṭodara 'Pot-bellied.' Epithet of Gaṇeśa and of a *rākṣasa*, etc.

Ghaṭotkaca 'Pot-headed.' A son of Bhīma by the demoness (*rākṣasī*) Hiḍimbā. According to another myth he was created by Indra and the other gods, who gave him a share of their own energy to enable him to be a fit antagonist of Karṇa (*MBh.*, Ādi pa., 157). He is described as bald with a head like a water-pot (*ghaṭa*), with terrifying eyes, large mouth, arrowshaped ears, sharp teeth and copper-coloured lips. Within an hour of his birth he had grown into a powerful youth, proficient in the use of all weapons.

Ghoṣiṇī(s)[1] Female attendants of Rudra (*AV.*, XI.2,31).

[1] Lit. 'Noisy ones', from *ghoṣi* 'sounding aloud'.

Ghṛta[1] Clarified butter (the modern *ghi* (Hindi), or ghee, the Anglicized form). *Ghṛta* is produced by boiling butter, and then repeatedly skimming it until all water and curds have been removed. The remainder is thus reduced to a clear oil, which is poured into a vessel to cool, and if properly processed will keep almost indefinitely. Because of its fatty nature it became a symbol of prosperity and fertility and was likened to the moisture drawn up by the sun which returns to the earth as 'fatness', i.e., fertilizing rain (*RV.*, I.164,47; III.1,7; *AV.*, VI.22,1).[2] It is said to have sprung from the ocean as a wave of sweetness, and is equated with *amṛta* (*RV.*, IV. 58,1ff.). In the Vedic ritual the ceaseless flowing of the *ghṛta* libations symbolizes 'the creative process of cosmic and individuated life',[3] and in the latter sense is offered in a rite performed after the successful birth of a son (*Bṛhad-Ār. Up.*, VI.4,24).[4] The *AGP.* (I, p. 357) promises that those who bathe images of the gods with *ghṛta* will be freed from 'sin' during subsequent rebirths; and that whoever bathes the images with 'two maunds of *ghṛta*' will himself become divine.

Ghṛta is much used medicinally and is said to be efficacious in cases of insanity, epilepsy, colic, fever, etc. It also improves sight, ensures longevity, appeases adverse fate, eliminates poisons from the body, as well as warding off monsters and demons. Various kinds of *ghṛta* are used for specific purposes, such as matured ghee which prevents mental aberrations and hysteria. *Kumbha-ghṛtam* (pitcher ghee), matured in a vessel for eleven to a hundred years, becomes possessed of the mystic potency of warding off monsters. *Mahā-ghṛtam* (great ghee), matured for more than a hundred years, improves the intellect and acts as a powerful 'prophylactic against the malignant influences of evil spirits and baneful planets (*graha*)' (*Suś. Saṁ.*, I, pp. 441 and 443). Ghee which has been cooked a hundred times in succession with a quantity of *vacā* (an aromatic root), and taken every day, extends one's life to five centuries and is also beneficial in cases of scrofula, goitre, etc. (ibid., II, p. 527); *amṛta-ghṛtam* is capable of bringing the dead back to life (ibid., II, p. 739).

The gods are said to have once put a pot of ghee on the sacrificial fire and from it emerged a boar (*ŚBr.*, V.4.3,19); hence this animal is full of fat because it was produced from *ghṛta*.[5]

[1] *Nir.* (7.24) derives *ghṛta* from *ghṛ*, 'besprinkle'.

[2] Cf. *ghṛtapruṣ*, 'sprinkling ghee or fat', i.e., bedewing with welfare and gifts (*SED*); v. also *Ait. Br.* I.3.

[3] *VF.*, p. 11.

[4] Sanctified *ghṛta* was poured on the sacrificial fire to ensure offspring to Drupada's queen (*MBh.*, Ādi pa., 169). This association of *ghṛta* with offspring probably stems from a passage in the *ŚBr.* (VI.3.3,19 and the *Kauṣ. Br.*, XVI.5) where it is equated with seed.

[5] According to Agrawala, *Matsya—A Study*, p. 325, the Sun (Sūrya) is the fat-dripping animal. From its melting 'fat the cosmos is being created'.

v. Ghṛtācī.

Ghṛtācī 'Abounding in ghee (*ghṛta*).' Name of an *apsaras* (nymph), mother of a hundred daughters by Kuśanābha. Vāyu, the god of the wind, fell in love with the girls and wanted them to accompany him to his abode in the sky but they refused. He then cursed them to become deformed, but they later regained their beauty and became the wives of Brahmadatta, King of Kāmpila.[1]

Ghṛtācī had many love affairs with great *ṛṣis* and other men. Her offspring from her alliance with the *ṛṣi* Viśvakarman are said to be the origin of the mixed castes. Bharadvāja was overcome with delight when he accidentally saw her and thus Śrutāvatī was born; on another occasion she met Bharadvāja, and Droṇa was subsequently born.

[1]*HCD*., p. 112.

Girijā 'Mountain-born.' An epithet of Pārvatī as the daughter of Himavat the personified Himālaya.

Girīśa 'Mountain lord', an epithet of Śiva.

Gītāgovinda 'Song of the Cowherd.' An erotic poem by the Court poet Jayadeva (12th cent.), written in Bengal, which recounts the early life and loves of Kṛṣṇa and the *gopīs*. It consists of a series of dramatic lyrics intended to be sung and resembles in some ways the poetry of the European troubadours.

Gñā(s) A class of goddesses, referred to in several passages of the *RV*. (III.1,9; VI.49,7, etc.). S. K. Das[1] suggests that the *gñās* belong 'to the prehistoric stage of thought when male "nature powers" were beginning to be associated with female "energies".' Some translators regard them as 'consorts of the gods', but it may be that they originally belonged to the vegetal and fertility cults of non-Āryan India. In the *Tait. Saṁ*. (VI.6,6) they are associated with Tvaṣṭar, the 'moulder (or vivifier) of forms', and also with Agni (representing generative power) who implants seed in wives. In the *aśvamedha* (horse-sacrifice), the *gñās* call forth generative power, especially 'in the sense of the restoration of the power of vegetative fertility'.[2]

The importance of these goddesses is recognized in the *AV*. (VII.49), where they are referred to as wives of the gods and separately designated as Indrāṇī, Agnāyī, Aśvinī, Rodasī and Varuṇānī. Other texts add to this list the names of Dhiṣaṇā, Sarasvatī, Bhāratī, Vāc, etc., whose roles become of ever-increasing importance. The Brāhmaṇas tended to synthesize the *gñās* with the goddess Vāc and to identify her with the Vedic metres which, as creative forces of enormous potency, reveal the secret power of the sacrifice and thus convey the sacrificer to the heavenly world (*ŚBr*., VI.5.4,7, etc.).

[1]*Śakti or Divine Power*, p. 15.

[2]Ibid., p. 19. According to the *Nir*. (12, 45) the *gñās* give protection, offspring and booty. Their sphere is the earth and they are easy to invoke.

v. Śacī; Kālī I.

Go A cow, bull, bullock, ox.[1] Cattle were the most important of the animals known to the Āryan pastoralist and agriculturist; the chief source of food and of various useful by-products; and the principal form of currency. They were highly valued but initially were not regarded as sacred. Cows and bullocks were used to draw the plough.

The *RV*. frequently eulogizes the cow and attributes to it a heavenly origin (I.73,6), yet despite its great sanctity and veneration there was never a cow-goddess in India. It was regarded as miraculous that a black or red cow should yield white milk.[2] Thus terrestrial cows came to be the counterpart of Indra's celestial cows, whose 'secret' was guarded by Agni in 'Viṣṇu's highest heaven' (V.3,3). When the cow became identified with the life-giving and life-sustaining mother-goddess, its paramount importance was established. Aditi, the goddess of nature, is called the 'perfect cow', the bountiful giver (VIII.90,15); similarly the goddess Vāc is called the divine milchcow who gladdens mankind with reinvigorating food (VIII.89,11). The importance of the cow is also indicated by the extensive vocabulary connected with it, such as *gaviṣṭi* (search or desire for cows), a euphemism for cattle-raiding, and synonymous with 'fight',[3] often the climax of a raid.

One of the earliest indications of an association of the cow with the *brāhmaṇa*, and indirectly with sacrificial rites, appears in the *AV*. (V.18 and 19) which refer to the inviolability of the *brāhmaṇa*'s cow—usually the 'present' (*dakṣiṇā*) given him for services rendered at the sacrifice. The *AV*. (XII.5) also prescribes the penalties and misfortunes incurred by those guilty of injuring or stealing a *brāhmaṇa*'s cow. When or why cattle became one of the sacrificial offerings is uncertain. Whether it was an innovation or the assimilation of ancient non-Āryan bull-cults[4] is equally uncertain; nor do the pre-Harappā (Kot Diji and Amri)[5] and Harappā cultures provide a satisfactory answer, despite the bull-motifs of their pottery wares and seals. Thus the gradual emergence of the cow-cult, and later the veneration of the bull Nandi in Śaivism, suggest a possibly early folk-origin. A traditional period is indicated in passages declaring that the sacrificial cow should not be slaughtered outside the sacred enclosure.[6] Later the sacrificial cow was replaced by birds, goats, etc., and finally by rice and similar offerings. Only in the unique *aśvamedha* did the horse continue to be the principal sacrificial victim, until through the influence of '*ahiṁsā*' this also ceased. But 'from the time of the *Ṛg Veda* down to the age of the *śrauta* rituals'[7] the sacrifice of a cow was customary in funeral rites, a male corpse being covered with cow-hide, which was invoked not to let the fire consume it, because of the belief that it possessed protective as well as revivifying powers. The cow presented to the officiating priest during a funerary rite, was believed to carry the dead man over the river of blood and filth (Vaitaraṇī) which separates the earth from the abode of the dead.[8] A cow was also sacrificed on other occasions, such as when a house was built[9] and for the sustenance of guests. The offer of the cow was a formal piece of etiquette. Any of the worthiest guests, such as a teacher, priest, father-in-law, king, friend, etc., could demand the cow's death, but probably it was seldom requested.[10] An offering of beef is said to sustain the *pitṛs* for a year; buffalo meat even longer, and rhinoceros meat longer still.[11]

When finally the sacrificial slaughter of the cow ceased, the sacred animal became one of the chief figures in Paurāṇic myth. As Surabhi it became the Cow of Plenty, one of Dakṣa's daughters, her role being based on early Vedic fertility symbolism which likened cows to rain-giving clouds. She was also called Kāmadhenu, the wish-fulfilling cow.[12] In the *VP.* (I.9), Surabhi was the first of the treasures to emerge from the Churning of the Ocean (*samudramathana*). In other myths Surabhi symbolizes India, which the warring forces, led respectively by Vasiṣṭha and Viśvāmitra sought to possess.

The five products of the cow: milk, curds, ghee, urine and dung are all used in purificatory ceremonies, and cow-dung is 'worshipped as an emblem of the discus of Viṣṇu, as is the yellow pigment from the cow'.[13] Everything that falls from the horns of a cow is said to bring good luck,[14] and even a drop of water from her horns will expiate all 'sins' (*AGP.*, II, p. 1,075); but when horns *inter alia* which have been 'charmed' are thrown into a house, discord will inevitably follow (II, p. 1,178). The effect of curses may be counteracted by the ritual bathing of a number of cows (*Varāha P.*, 147, 1–27).

[1]Among the oldest Egyptian amulets are those having the head of a cow with a woman's face (Hathor?) (Budge, *Amulets and Talismans*, p. 134).

[2]Cf. the G. nursery rhyme: 'O sage mir, wie geht es zu, gibt weisse Milch die röte Ku.' The *ŚBr.* (II.2.4,15) explains the whiteness of milk by stating that Agni copulated with a cow, the milk being his semen.

[3]V. M. Apte, *HCIP.*, I, p. 395; W. Hayes, *The Book of the Cow.*

[4]That both cow and bull cults were common to ancient Egyptian, Mediterranean and Mesopotamian cultures is well-documented, but to what extent they may have spread to prehistoric India is still conjectural. From his study of the Deccan ashmounds of burnt cow-dung, F. R. Allchin considers they were originally 'the pens in which the Neolithic cattle were herded' (*Neolithic Cattle-Keepers of South India*, p. 162).

[5]'The following Radio-Carbon dates, calculated on a half life of 5568 by the Pennsylvania University, more or less confirm . . . dating arrived at by conventional method', which date the respective excavated layers as ranging from B.C. 1975 ± 134 to B.C. 2471 ± 141 (F. A. Khan, *Indus Valley and Early Iran*, p. 55).

[6]The word *aghnyā* 'not to be killed' applied to cows, also suggests that they were not to be slaughtered except sacrificially. But according to the *Ait. Br.* (I.15) a cow that miscarries may be slaughtered for a king or other important personage.

[7]*Ancestor Worship*, p. 39.

[8]*AV.*, XII.4,36. Cf. the Egyptian cow-headed goddess Hathor who leads the dead to the next world, and the bull that carries the dead man on his back to the underworld (v. Ions, *Egyptian Mythology*, illus. p. 116); also the old North-European belief that whosoever gives a cow to the poor will after death be guided by it along the path to heaven. In Lancashire the Milky Way was called the 'cows' lane'—the way the dead entered heaven.

[9]Bhattacharyya, *Canons of Indian Art*, p. 32.

[10]*CHI.*, I. p. 232.

[11]*Ancestor Worship*, p. 162.

[12]Cf. the wish-fulfilling cow of other mythologies such as the Shilluk white cow which emerged from the Nile at the Creation; the Scandinavian cow Auðhumla, which emerged from the ice blocks and gave life-giving streams of milk (Ellis-Davidson, *Gods and Myths of Northern Europe*, p. 198): the Welsh elfin cow Fuwch Gyfeilioru; and the Irish cow Glasgavlen.

[13]*EM.*, p. 17. In English rural districts cow-dung poultices were common.

[14]Cf. the Swiss custom of decorating the horns and heads of cows at certain times to bring good luck and prosperity.

v. Goloka; Goloman; Gopāla I; Bharadvāja; Gaurī; Gokarīṣam.

Godāvarī 'Granting water or kine.' The name of a river in the Deccan. Great merit is acquired by bathing in it, and ultimately the attainment of Vāsuki's realm (*MBh.*, Vana pa., 85).

Godha 'Lizard.' This reptile was often used for divinatory purposes.

Godhikā An iguana. Emblem of the goddess Gaurī.

Gogrāsa An expiatory rite in which a mouthful of grass is presented to a cow. This rite may have some connexion with the practice of certain menial castes 'of a guilty man putting a piece of dry grass crosswise in his mouth when he goes to the head of his village to ask his pardon'. Where grass is not available the first finger of the right hand is placed crosswise in the mouth. Animals are also sacrificed before the village goddesses (*grāma-devatās*) by the villagers, in the belief that their sins will be forgiven. To avert the consequences of wrong-doing, the animal's right leg is placed crosswise in its mouth.[1]

[1]Mahārāja Sir V. S. Ranga Rao Bahadur, *Asiatic Review*, January 1919, cited by Whitehead, *The Village Gods of South India*, p. 51, n.1.

Gokarīṣam 'Dried cow-dung.' This is placed on the heads of children possessed by evil spirits. When the demoness Pūtanā tried to poison the young Kṛṣṇa, Yaśodā waved a cow-tail over him to guard him from harm, whilst Nanda placed dried powdered cow-dung on his head, and for further protection gave him an amulet,[1] calling also on Hari to protect him (*VP*., V.5).

[1]Called the *rakṣa* amulet, 'the preserver'. It consists of a piece of thread, silk or some more costly material which is bound round the wrist or arm, accompanied by a prayer for protection.

Gokarṇa 'Cow-eared.' A place of pilgrimage sacred to Śiva. Here Yama practised austerities and became a Lokapāla and lord of the *pitṛs* (*Matsya P.*, 11. 18–20 *Pl.*).

Gokula The pastoral district on the river Yamunā where Kṛṣṇa passed his boyhood with Nanda and the *gopīs*.

Gokulāṣṭamī v. Kṛṣṇāṣṭamī.

Goloka 'Cow-world.' Kṛṣṇa's Paradise situated on Mount Meru, where dwells also the wish-fulfilling cow Surabhi.

Gomeda The name of particular gems brought from the Himālaya and the Indus, used to purify water (*Suś. Saṁ.*, I, p. 424).

Gopāla or **Govinda** I. 'Cow-herd.'[1] An epithet applied to Kṛṣṇa when he lived among the herdsmen and women in Vṛndāvana.

[1]In early times the Gr. Apollo was worshipped as a goat-herd (Farnell, *Cults*, IV, p. 255).

v. Gopī(s).

II. Name of a demon causing fever.

Gopatha Brāhmaṇa Name of the Brāhmaṇa attached to the *AV*.

Gopīcandana v. Tilaka.

Gopī(s) Herdswomen among whom the youthful Kṛṣṇa lived. Many of them left their homes, children and husbands to dally with him on the banks of the Yamunā river. They often danced a circular dance[1] in which each *gopī* imagined she held Kṛṣṇa's hand (*VP*., V.13), but according to the *Bhāg. Pur*. Kṛṣṇa multiplied himself many times and danced between each pair of *gopīs*.[2] This idyllic picture of the divine Kṛṣṇa with the *gopīs* symbolizes the abstract relation of the deity to his devotees. It is 'a drama perpetually enacted in the heart of every *bhakta* or votary'.[3]

[1]Probably to promote fertility in cattle and plant growth. Some aborigines had a number of circular dances, one of which was probably adopted into Hinduism and traditionally associated with the *gopīs* and Kṛṣṇa; later it became an important part of his worship, and is performed in Rājputāna and other centres of his cult. The figure in the centre, around whom the dancers revolve, impersonates the deity (Crooke, *Things Indian*, p. 123). The early Church Father, St. Basil (4th cent.) asked whether there could be 'anything more blessed than to imitate on earth the ring-dance of the angels ... to glorify the rising Creator' (cited by Wosien, *Sacred Dance*, p. 29). The Sudanese Dinka women sometimes perform a cow-dance (Zeuner, *A History of Domesticated Animals*, p. 226).

[2]In a later account Kṛṣṇa, like the Greek Narcissus, is said to have become enamoured of his own beauty (v. *HP*., p. 313).

[3]Coomaraswamy, *Catalogue of Indian Collections*, Boston, p. 23.

v. Rādhā; Līlā.

Gopīta The name of one of the four water-wagtails, regarded as birds of augury.

Gorakhnāth or **Gorakṣa** A yogin of the Nātha cult, who lived between the 9th and 12th centuries A.D. In one of the traditional lists of Nātha leaders quoted by S. Dasgupta,[1] Śiva is Ādi-nātha, the Supreme Siddha, the Divine Source of Perfection, of whom all Siddhas (the perfected ones, or those approaching that state) are incarnations.[2] Gorakhnāth appears as a 'descendant' of Ādi-nātha, and an exponent of 'Nāthism', the general religious nature of which 'is characterized by a wide-spread belief in occult power attained through the practice of yoga.'[3] This cult embraces many Śaiva and Tantric beliefs and to a lesser extent some of those of Buddhism. The cult includes also magical and alchemical practices, and became very popular after the twelfth century.

Gorakhnāth is also credited with the 'founding' of Haṭha Yoga and the Order of Kānphaṭa Yogīs,[4] also called Gorakhnāthis. The Tibetan historian Tāranātha, states that Gorakhnāth was originally a

Buddhist, as was the Siddha Matsyendranāth, the first incarnate teacher of the Nāthas, who was identified with the Mahāyāna Buddhist *bodhisattva* Avalokiteś-vara, the tutelary deity of Nepal.[5]

A number of miraculous deeds and yogic powers were attributed to Gorakhnāth, including withholding rain; power to revive the dead; indefinite prolongation of his own life,[6] and making a banyan tree grow from a seed to maturity in a few hours. Eliade points out that the mythology and folklore associated with the Gorakh-nāthis, although containing many archaic elements, expresses 'the real spiritual longings of the superficially Hinduized masses'.[7]

[1]*ORC.*, p. 208.

[2]Cf. the Mahāyāna Buddhist *bodhisattvas.*

[3]*ORC.*, p. 211.

[4]From *kān*, 'ear' and *phaṭa* 'split'. Members of this cult wear huge earrings, one of their distinctive 'marks'. Cf. the Inca initiation ceremony in which the initiand's ears were pierced.

[5]Matsyendranāth may have brought the teachings of the Siddhas and Nāths to Nepal.

[6]This power was attributed to the Buddha, to Bhīṣma, and other great yogīs. v. P.S. Jaini. 'Buddha's Prolongation of Life', *BSOAS.*, XXI, pt. 3, 1958, pp. 546f.

[7]*Yoga*, p. 302. For the culture and tradition of the Siddhas v. *C. Herit I.*, vol. II, pp. 303ff.

v. Pāśupata.

Gotama I. A Vedic *ṛṣi*, son of Rahūgaṇa. The composition of *RV.* (I.92) is attributed to him and considered to be one of the 'finest specimens of Ṛgvedic lyric poetry'.[1]

[1]Rahurkar, *Seers*, p. 190.

II. Name of the *gotra* to which the Buddha belonged.

III. The founder of the Nyāya school of philosophy.

Gotra Indian lexicographers associate *gotra* with *santati* or *anvavāya* (lineage), *janana* (race), *kula* or *santāna* (family), and with *abhijana* (descent).[1] According to Brough, brahmanical *gotra* 'may be defined as an exogamous patrilineal sibship, whose members trace their descent back to a common ancestor'.[2] A man should marry only within his caste (*jāti*), but not within the prohibited degrees of relationship as defined by his *pravara*,[3] nor would he marry a woman of the same *gotra*.

In the fourth century B.C., the theory of *gotra* was systematized, doubtless to meet changing social conditions, when the laws of inheritance as well as marriage required clarification.[4] As the number of progenitors increased they were enumerated in stereotyped lists (*pravaras*) covering a limited period,[5] each family having its own *pravara*, which was recited during the performance of specific rites. Though *gotra* and *pravara* overlap, *pravara* is generally the criterion of ancestry, except in the case of marriage, when both have to be considered.

The theory of *gotra* appears to have been evolved to support the claim of *brāhmaṇas* to superior status, for it denied the right of the *kṣatriya*, *vaiśya* or *śūdra* to claim descent from a particular *gotra* in the proper sense of the term.[6] According to Paurāṇic tradition the *brāhmaṇas* initially derived their descent from the ancient fire-priests Atharvan, Aṅgiras and Bhṛgu, or from the *ṛṣis* Gautama, Bharadvāja and Jamadagni.[7] But later the list was extended to include Viśvāmitra, Vasiṣṭha, Kaśyapa and Atri, who comprised the 'seven great *ṛṣis*' (*Mārk. P.*, 79,9), the name of Agastya being added later. The number of these patriarchal progenitors was periodically added to and variously listed according to particular brahmanical family traditions. This proliferation of *gotrakārins* is evident in the *Āśvalāyana Śrauta Sūtra* (XII.10,6ff.) and other texts, where they number from eighteen to forty-nine.

That the early brahmanical theory of *gotra* was subject to modification is evident also in its adoption by Jainism and Buddhism, whose respective founders were both of the *kṣatra* class. Thus 'in the Pāli books, the word *gotta* is not infrequently used in the expected sense, as, for example, Bhagavā Gotomo gottena, Kakusandho Kassapo gottena, i.e., a Gautama, or a Kaśyapa by *gotra*'.[8]

Today there seems to be no certainty what constitutes the *gotras*. 'Apparently there are eight primitive *gotras* descended from the seven *ṛṣis* . . . The remaining *gotras* are possibly subdivisions of these eight, but are not all identifiable with them.'[9]

[1]*ERE.*, VI, p. 353n. The original meaning of *gotra* is 'cowshed' or 'a herd of cows' (*WI.*, p. 153).

[2]*EBS.*, p. 2.

[3]i.e., those whose common ancestry entitles them to share in the *śrāddha* offering called *piṇḍa*. Thus all members of past and present generations associated with the *piṇḍa* offering are called *sapiṇḍas* (Auboyer, *Daily Life in Ancient India*, p. 160). 'In the earliest Vedic period the *gotra* had solemn festivals of union, and of communication with the dead' (*VI.*, II, p. 257, n. 83)

[4]Thus *gotra* may be of two kinds, *vaidika* for *brahmins*, *laukika*, 'worldly', for those of other classes. The *vaidika* denotes persons distinguished by the same family name, or known to be descended from the same ancestor. Subsequently *laukika gotras* were formed from subdivisions of the original Vedic *gotras*.

[5]Thus a Hindu may not marry a female descendant as far

back as the seventh degree from his father or from one of his *sapiṇḍas*, i.e., his father's six ancestors in the male line; nor marry a female descendant as far back as the seventh degree of his father's *bandhus*, his ancestors in the female line. It does not include the mother's mother, etc., as a line of female ancestors is not regarded as a line in Hindu law (v. E.J. Trevelyan, *Hindu Family Law*, pp. 34f.). But there are exceptions to these rules.

[6]Bhattacharya, *Laws of the Joint Family*, p. 111, cited by Trevelyan, op. cit., p. 34.

[7]*Matsya Pur*., 190,8ff.

[8]*EBS*., p. 5.

[9]Trevelyan, op. cit., p. 34.

Govardhana Name of a mountain in Bṛndāvana, the scene of Kṛṣṇa's triumph over Indra. The incident described in the *VP*. (V.10–11) indicates the decline of Vedic traditions and their transition to new cults, in this instance to that of Viṣṇu-Kṛṣṇa. In this myth Indra, the focus of Vedic theism, is threatened with the loss of his sovereignty over the Govardhana mountain and the deprivation of sacrificial offerings by the people of the area, and the transfer of their allegiance to Kṛṣṇa. To retain his sovereignty Indra called upon the storm clouds to flood the countryside and destroy both the people and their herds, but Kṛṣṇa lifted the mountain and held it up[1] for seven days and so provided a shelter for both people and cattle. Realizing that he was no match for Kṛṣṇa, Indra commanded the clouds to disperse. The incident ended with Kṛṣṇa and Indra mutually embracing, and Indra mounting his elephant Airāvata and returning to heaven.

[1]Hence his epithet Govardhanadhara, 'upholder of Govardhana'.

Graha 'Seizer.' From *grah*, 'to seize or overpower'. Name of a particular class of demons who 'seize or possess' their victims and inflict upon them all manner of illnesses, especially insanity.[1] Monier-Williams defines *graha* as 'any state which proceeds from magical influences and takes possession of the whole man'. The *RV*. (X.161,1) refers to a 'grasping demoness' (*grahī*) who causes wasting diseases. According to the *AGP*. (II, p. 1115), the *grahas* cause nymphomania.

The *grahas* are of different types and may be propitiated by offerings made at a particular place and time. Those to the *devagrahas* should be made in the temple; those of *asura-grahas* at the close of day in the yard of the house; those (consisting of wine and soup) to the *gandharvagrahas* in the midst of a gathering of people; those (of cooked and raw flesh) to the *piśācagrahas* and left in an empty (?) room. Should a physician take preventive measures against any of these *grahas* (with the exception of the *piśācas*), both he and the patient may suddenly die (*Suś. Saṁ*., III, p. 380).

Later myths identify or associate *grahas* with planets[2] which 'seize' or influence men's lives, a belief on which the complex pseudo-science of astrology is based. But such myths vary regionally and reflect numerous inconsistencies. Thus *grahas* may sometimes exert favourable influences,[3] but at other times may be malevolent forces to be propitiated. They are also especially dangerous to travellers and to those living in lonely places, or by lakes, streams, on the brow of hills, or deserted moorland, on which nothing grows but a solitary haunted tree. To stay in a deserted house is equally dangerous (*AGP*., II, p. 1114).

The nine planets (*navagrahas*) comprise the sun (Sūrya), moon (Soma), Mercury (Budha), Jupiter (Bṛhaspati), Venus (Śukra), Mars (Maṅgala), Saturn (Śani), Rāhu and Ketu (a comet).[4] Rāhu 'seizes' the sun or the moon, and is thus regarded as malevolent as is also Ketu, because comets are believed to portend calamity and disaster.[5] Whole towns can be destroyed by astral influences (*Suś. Saṁ*., I, p. 52).

At the beginning of each eon 'the planets were believed to commence their revolutions in line, and to return to the same position at the end of it. The apparently irregular course of the planets was explained on the hypothesis of epicycles, as in classical and medieval astronomy'.[6]

The planets also influence vegetation and plants, so that care must be exercised in selecting 'food on certain days of the lunar month' (*Suś Saṁ*., I, p. lxvi).[7]

[1]Cf. *grahāgama*, demonical possession. The Akkadian devils 'seized', 'struck down', or 'touched' all who crossed their path. They were generally blamed for causing persistent migraine, general paralysis, etc. (R. Labat, 'Mesopotamia' in *Ancient and Medieval Science*, p. 88).

[2]In an attempt to avoid Rudra's anger the gods disguised themselves as planets (*AGP*., II, p. 1114).

[3]In a hymn for appeasement and welfare addressed to various divinities, the planets are invoked to protect their worshippers from 'land-plagues' (*AV*., XIX, 9,7,9,10).

[4]Both Rāhu and Ketu are fictitious planets, regarded as the ascending and descending nodes of the lunar orbit (Diehl, *Instrument and Purpose*, p. 201).

[5]In this context the sun is regarded as a malevolent *graha* (or *mahāgraha*) because it 'seizes' the light of the moon.

[6]Basham, *WI*., App. II, p. 491.

[7]Cf. Rudolph Steiner's theory of the planting of vegetables, etc., according to certain phases of the moon.

v. Grahabali; Grahahoma; Grahāpasmāra; Grahākuṇḍalikā; Śani; Skanda.

Grahabali Also known as *graha śānti* and *graha yajña*. A rite designed to propitiate the planets. It protects one against bows and arrows, as well as ensuring the attainment of wealth, longevity, prosperity and the removal of all troubles.

v. Grahahoma; Navagraha.

Grahāgama v. Graha.

Grahahoma The name of the burnt offering to the nine planets (*navagrahas*) which should be arranged as follows: the Sun in the centre (its presiding deity being Śiva) accompanied by a food offering of rice cooked with sugar; the Moon in the south-east (presiding deity Pārvatī), and an offering of white rice, ghee and sugar; Mars in the south (deity Skanda), and a grain offering; Mercury in the north-east (deity Hari), and an offering of milk and rice; Jupiter in the north (deity Brahmā), and an offering of yellow rice and curds; Venus in the east (deity Indra), and an offering of coarse sugar and rice; Saturn in the west (deity Yama), and rice, sesamum and pulses cooked in milk; Rāhu in the south-west (deity Kāla), and an offering of mutton; Ketu in the north-west (deity Citragupta), and an offering of coloured rice (*Matsya P.*, 93, 5–20 *PI.*).

Grahakuṇḍalikā The mutual relation of planets from which a particular prediction may be derived.

v. Graha.

Grahāpasmāra 'Hysteria', believed to be caused by the baleful effects of malignant stars and planets.

v. Graha.

Grahapati 'Lord of the planets.' A title of the Āditya (the Sun), and of Soma (the Moon).

v. Graha.

Grāhi(s) 'Seizers.' Malevolent female spirits who enter infants and cause them to die.[1] When a child is so 'possessed' propitiatory offerings of fish, meat, wine, flowers, etc., should be made to the *grāhis* (*AGP.*, II, p. 1105).

According to the *Suś. Saṁ.* (III, p. 161) the *grāhis* issue from the *rājasa* essence of the goddesses Gaṅgā, Umā and Kṛttikā who guard the new-born Guha (Skanda).

[1]They also 'seize' and kill men (*RV.*, X.161,1).

v. Graha.

Grāmadevatā(s) Minor powers or tutelary goddesses (*devatās*) of villages (*grāmas*). The *grāmadevatās* can certainly be assigned to an archaic period, even pre-Dravidian, according to Eliade.[1] Their association with the water-jar or pot (a symbol of the womb) indicates a close association with the ubiquitous fertility cult.[2] Thus they are often represented by a jar or pot.[3]

Among the rural communities of southern India religion revolves round the *grāmadevatās*, whose shrines, like those of *yakṣas*, are often situated near trees,[4] a further confirmation of their vegetal connexion. They are sometimes represented by a platform under a tree, or by a stone slab on which is carved a crude figure of a woman, who may have two, four, six or eight arms, or none at all. But their usual icons are 'simple stone images of the female organ of generation (*yoni*)'.[5]

Among the animals sacrificed[6] to these goddesses are sheep, goats and buffaloes, their blood being sprinkled on the worshippers, on lintels and door-posts of houses, cowsheds and boundary stones, or mixed with rice and scattered in the streets or around the village boundary.

Whitehead stresses that the *grāmadevatās* '*symbolize only the facts of village life*. They are related, not to great world forces, but to such simple facts as cholera, small-pox, and cattle-disease'.[7] Some of them are said actually to 'possess' their devotees.

These goddesses are also worshipped by fishermen[8] and those whose livelihood is connected with lakes and rivers. The great goddess Mahādevī or Mahā-grāmadevatā, is said to have been born 'in the waters, within the sea', thus possibly connecting her with maritime communities. With very few exceptions the village deities are feminine. The outstanding exception is Iyenar, the name is said to be a corruption of Hari-Hara (Viṣṇu-Śiva). Iyenar is concerned with the guardianship of the fields, crops and herds and is the nightwatchman of the village, and large and small clay figures of horses are offered to him. On these horses he is supposed to ride round the village at night driving off demons.

[1] *Yoga*, p. 349.

[2]Whitehead considers they were predominantly rural mother-goddesses, but Dumont does not agree (v. 'Définition structurale d'un dieu populaire tamoul,' *JA.*, ccxli, p. 259, Fas. 2, 1953).

[3]A dance called the 'pot dance' was performed by girls to ensure fertility. The great *ṛṣis* Agastya and Vasiṣṭha were born in a water-jar. Cf. the present-day Voudoun rite of reclaiming the soul of the deceased from the watery abyss. The soul is placed in a clay jar (*govi*), the latter being the substitute for the body which once housed the soul (Maya Deren, *Divine Horsemen*, p. 28).

[4]Coomaraswamy, *Yakṣas*, I, p. 17.

[5]Eliade, *Yoga*, p. 349.

[6]Animals are never sacrificed to the village god Iyenar.

[7] *Village Gods of South India*, p. 17.

[8]The village deity Mīnācī (also called Mīnākṣī) is especially worshipped by fishermen. In the great temple of Madurā she is worshipped as the *śakti* of Śiva. The *grāmadevatās* appear to be various manifesta-

tions (under different names) of the great goddess Devī. v. Gogrāsa; Kumbhamātā; Grāmadruma.

Grāmadruma A particular village tree regarded as sacred and worshipped by the villagers.

Grāmakālī(s) Protective deities of villages and forests, regarded as of the same class as Nāgas.[1]

[1] *HP.*, p. 307.

Grāmaṇī(s) A class of celestial beings, who in pairs attend the Sun-god in each of the six seasons (*Vāyu P.*, 52,1, *PI.*).

Grāvan v. Adri.

Gṛdhravaṭa The banyan tree, sacred to Śiva, which grows on the Gṛdhrakūṭa hill.

Gṛhadevī 'Goddess of the household.' A folk-deity of ancient and medieval India known as Jarā, a *rākṣasī* who has the power to assume any form and who is venerated by the people generally.
v. Jarāsandha.

Gṛhalakṣmī The guardian *devī* (goddess) of a new house who is worshipped and invoked to give happiness, comfort, wealth, children, health and longevity to its inmates.[1]

[1] *Mānasāra*, Ch. xxxvii, *DHA.*, p. 169.

Gṛhasthya v. Brahmarcārin.

Gṛhya-Sūtra(s) Collections or manuals of social and domestic rules. When the Hindu ceremonies are compared with those of other Āryan-speaking peoples it seems probable that 'the Indian ritual has preserved elements reaching far back into prehistoric times'.[1]

[1] *CHI.*, I. p. 233.

Gṛtsamada A Vedic *ṛṣi*. Traditionally said to be the son of Śunahotra of the Āṅgirasa family, but after his capture by hostile tribes (*asuras*) and release by Indra, he was adopted by Śunaka of the Bhṛgu family, and hence the tradition of his belonging to two *gotras*. Though the name Gṛtsamada does not occur in the singular in the text of *maṇḍala* II of the *RV.*, the plural form clearly points to the Gṛtsamada authorship of most of its hymns and the family's descent from Śunahotra Āṅgirasa.[1]

The Gṛtsamada hymns are of great literary interest. They consist mostly of ballads, the major portion of each being recited, while the refrain—a characteristic of these poems—being sung in chorus. The subject of each describes the heroic exploits of Indra, the refrain ending with an emphatic: 'He, O men, is Indra.'

Several stories illustrate the association of the Gṛtsamadas with the worship of Indra. One relates that Gṛtsamada through great austerities became as huge and powerful as Indra so that his body was visible in the three spheres. Mistaking it for Indra, the *daityas* Dhuni and Cumuri were about to attack it, when Gṛtsamada by his yogic powers realized their murderous intention. To protect himself he proclaimed the mighty deeds of Indra as embodied in *RV.*, II.12,[2] so effectively that the two demons were paralysed by fear and quickly slain by Indra (*Bṛhadd.*, IV.65–9). Indra then promised Gṛtsamada that he would never forsake him and that he and his family should always be secure, wealthy, and have many heroic sons (IV.70–3).

Gṛtsmada is linked with Śiva in a story which recounts that after Vasiṣṭha had cursed him to become a wild beast because of a mistake in the recitation of part of the sacrificial ritual, Śiva restored him to his usual form and made him 'immortal' and 'free from sorrow' (*MBh.*, 13.18, 20, *EM.*).

[1] Rahurkar, *Seers*, pp. 1–6.

[2] Cf. the protective powers thought to reside in Bible texts. In the *Ait Br.* (V.2) Gṛtsamada by his hymn went to the abode of Indra, the ultimate world.

Guggulu Bdellium, an aromatic gum-resin found near rivers and used in perfumes, medicines and as a disinfectant, as well as a protection against certain diseases and curses (*AV.*, XIX.38, 1–2).

Newly gathered *guggulu* is said to be an aphrodisiac and tonic; and when stored will reduce corpulency (*Suś. Saṁ.*, II, p. 314).

Guha 'Secret one.' Epithet of Skanda (Subrahmaṇya) in mantric rites. The epithet is also applied to Śiva, and Viṣṇu.

Guhyakādhipati 'Lord of the *guhyakas*.' A title of Kubera.

Guhyaka(s) 'Concealed, hidden, secret.' A class of godlings or spirits who exercise their powers from caves and other secret places (Cf. *guhā*, a hiding-place, cavern). Like the *yakṣas*, the *guhyakas* dwell on Mount Kailāsa and are attendant on Kubera,[1] the god of wealth.

The *guhyakas* are described as half-horse or half-bird beings who carry Kubera's palace from place to place. They appear as luminous bodies in the heavens and assume demonic forms in battle (*MBh.*, 3.42,36; 173,50, *EM.*). To the realm of *guhyakas* go all those who die bravely in battle.

When selecting a stone, which should be flawless, to make an image of Viṣṇu, it should first be worshipped, after which the *guhyakas* and *yakṣas* who may be concealed in or near it, should be propitiated and requested to move on to another place of concealment.[2]

[1] Kubera himself is a god of 'hiding' (*AV.*, VIII.10,28), and at his behest a *guhyaka* presented Rāma with sanctified water which makes the invisible visible (*MBh.*, Vana pa., 287). According to the *Mārk. P.* (108, 21f.) Revanta, son of the Sun (Sūrya), was made

Lord of the *guhyakas*; thus mortals who call on him when in lonely places, or in great conflagrations, or when confronted by robbers and enemies, will be saved.

[2]*DHI.*, p. 218. Hopkins suggests that *guhyaka* was probably a 'general name for all the spirits of concealment, though sometimes made a special class' (*EM.*, p. 144). The twin Aśvins, plants and animals are classed as *guhyakas* (Coomaraswamy, *Yakṣas*, pt. ii, p. 22).

Guṇa A cord or string used to bind things together, a word which the *PTS.* considers may be of non-Āryan origin, a suggestion supported by S.K. Chatterji[1] who says that 'weaving of cotton cloth was also an Austric or Proto-Australoid invention'. But the word is used in a technical sense in the Sāṁkhya system, in which 'the three *guṇas*' (*sattva*, *rajas* and *tamas*)[2] are part of its theory of creation and evolution, and in the Vaiśeṣika system are one of the categories of substance.

[1]*HCIP.*, I, p. 150.

[2]J. Przyluski, *La Théorie des Guṇas*, cited by Eliade, *Yoga*, p. 374, sees traces of Semitic elements in the idea of the three *guṇas*. There are also some similarities to Plato's *epithumia*, *thumos* and *logistikon* (Singhal, *India*, vol. I, p. 35).

v. Darsána(s); Pāñcarātra.

Guṇakeśī v. Mātali.

Gungū A lunar goddess (*RV.*, II,32,8).

v. Kuhū.

Gupta(s) Name of the dynasty in northern India in the third century A.D. It was founded as the result of the dissolution of the Kuṣāṇa empire and the political disruption that ensued. Though nothing is known of the origin of the Gupta family or clan, the names of its first two rulers are recorded, but they appear to have been little more than feudatory chieftains. Nor has the location and extent of their kingdom been established. Tradition suggests that it was Magadha, but this is based on a statement by the Chinese pilgrim I-tsing 250 years later.

Historical references to the Guptas do not appear until the reign of Candragupta I, the third ruler (crowned in A.D. 320), who assumed the imperial title of Mahārājadhirāja instead of the less grandiloquent Mahārāja of his predecessors. Candragupta's ambition to establish his kingdom firmly before embarking on its extension is indicated by his marriage to Kumāradevi, a princess of the neighbouring Licchavi kingdom. Though its people, despite their ancient lineage and eminence, were called degraded (*vratya*) *kṣatriyas* in the *Manusaṁhitā*, this referred to their brahmanical non-conformity rather than to their social character and military capability.

Candragupta formally abdicated in favour of his son Samudra, who though not the eldest was, like Aśoka six centuries before, chosen because of his outstanding ability, the choice inevitably leading to family disputes, and delaying the coronation for several years. Following this event Samudra-gupta, again like Aśoka, began a series of military campaigns, resulting in the conquest of large areas of northern, north-eastern and southern India. But the objective was not to enlarge his empire, but to unite the country and end the constant fighting among petty chieftains. In addition he established friendly relations with border kingdoms by acknowledging their autonomy and agreeing upon an alliance for mutual defence. But Samudra-gupta is renowned not only as a general and statesman, but also as a distinguished poet and musician, and a patron of learning. He was instrumental in effecting the transition of traditional Brahmanism to Hinduism, the former having declined, owing partly to the ascendancy of Buddhism during the reigns of its royal patrons, Aśoka and Kaniṣka, but more particularly to the influence of the early Upaniṣads and emergence of the nascent Vaiṣṇava and Śaiva cults. In the secular world there was also a development of the arts and sciences, the appearance of great writers, like Kālidāsa, and the stimulus engendered by contacts with other civilizations, both western and eastern, and by the adoption of classical Sanskrit as the literary and official language, instead 'of the more popular literary dialects, which had enjoyed the patronage of the Andhra kings'.[1]

Samudra-gupta was succeeded by his son Candragupta II, probably in A.D. 376, who reigned for thirty-three years. During that time he subdued the satrapies of north-western India, assumed the title Vikramāditya, a distinction adopted to commemorate a ruler's exceptional military exploits. During his reign Fa-hsien, a Chinese pilgrim, remarked on the absence of serious crime and unrest.

Candragupta II was followed by his son Kumāragupta, who reigned from A.D. 415–55, a period noted for the development of the administration and stability of the empire. But towards the end of this period peace was threatened by an enemy whose identity has not been established, and whose defeat was only accomplished after a long campaign by the Crown Prince Skandagupta. Another threat of war followed. This was from Central Asia and the Far East by tribes collectively known as Hūṇas, some of whom were also successfully invading Europe. Skanda-gupta's military skill again prevailed, but the tax on the resources of the empire led to the deterioration of its administration, a decline in its overseas trade, and thus of its power and prestige, as is indicated in the debasement of the coinage. Some outlying provinces seized the opportunity of declaring their independence under self-styled Mahārājas.

The death of Kumāra-gupta marks the end of the empire's greatness, and though the dynasty continued, it lacked the power and wealth to maintain it on the former scale. Nonetheless, the later Gupta period is noted for the development of the sciences, and of architecture and sculpture of superlative quality. But the achievement of the early Gupta period at the height of its prosperity carried on the great humanitarian traditions of the Mauryan emperor Aśoka in the third century B.C. Fa-hsien records[2] the existence of numerous charitable institutions and excellent free hospitals endowed by benevolent citizens, to which came all poor or helpless patients suffering from all kinds of infirmities. They were well cared for, food and medicine being supplied according to their wants.

[1]V.A. Smith, *The Early History of India*, 4th ed., p. 320.

'A paper by Jack Goody and Ian Watt on "The Consequences of Literacy" . . . shows how among non-literate people there can be no sense of a continuous past . . . [or] the making of any distinction between history and myth' (cited by H.R. Ellis Davidson, 'Folklore and History', *Folklore*, vol. 85 (Summer 1974), pp. 74f.).

[2]*Travels*, Ch. xxvii.

Guru[1] A religious guide or teacher, especially one who gives initiation (*dīkṣā*) to a pupil.

The very close relationship between the *guru* (regarded as a spiritual parent) and his pupil can be seen in the prohibition that a pupil may not marry his *guru*'s daughter, as she stands in the relation of a sister to him.

In modern times the *guru* acts as adviser to all who seek spiritual guidance. He is thus distinguished from the family priest, whose function is almost solely devoted to presiding over or performing specific rites.

[1]According to the *Advaya tāraka Up.*, 14–18, the syllable '*gu*' means 'darkness', '*ru*' means 'dispeller' (cited by Daniélou, *Yoga: the Method of Re-integration*, pp. 113–14). But Heimann (*Facets*, p. 118) considers that the *guru*'s 'spiritual quality is expressed in measure of quantity'—the literal meaning of *guru* being 'the Weighty One'.

A *guru*'s great spirituality should be projected by him 'into the innermost being of his disciple' (*AGP.*, I, p. 313). v. also Gonda, *CC.*, p. 233; *TT.*, pp. 186f.; *C. Herit. I.*, vol. II, p. 182.

v. Yajñopavīta.

H

Haihaya(s) A collateral branch of the Yādavas, descendants of Yadu, eldest son of Yayāti.
v. Jamadagni; Kartavīrya; Paraśurāma; Kāśī; Kosala.

Hairamba(s) Members of the esoteric section of the Ucchiṣṭa-Gaṇapatis who regard the goddess Devī as the *śakti* of Gaṇeśa rather than of Śiva. They have no caste or marriage distinctions, and regard promiscuous intercourse as the highest act of worship. The male worshipper identifies himself with Heramba (Gaṇeśa), the female with Gaṇeśa's *śakti* Gaṇeśānī.[1]

[1] *ERE.*, VI, p. 176.

Haladhara 'Plough-holder.' An epithet of Balarāma.

Halāhala A deadly poison prepared from the roots of an unknown plant. It emerged from the Churning of the Ocean (*samudramathana*). Śiva drank it and held it in his throat, thus saving all living beings from death.
v. Nīlakaṇṭha.

Hālāhala Name of the buffalo-demon killed by Śiva's attendants (*gaṇas*), assisted by the gods in the Rudrakṣetra near Avantī.[1]

[1] *DHI.*, p. 166, n.1.

Haṁsa I. 'Goose', often erroneously translated 'swan', especially by English scholars because of the epithet 'goose' used to denote foolishness and irresponsibility. But this is not characteristic of the wild goose which is noted for its discipline and beauty. The *haṁsa* is the Bar-headed goose (Anser indicus) which breeds on the lakes of Central Asia; in winter it migrates to almost every part of India.[1] In ancient times India, and North and Central Asia, had bird-cults generally associated with local mother-goddesses and fertility. Naturally, the choice of a particular bird, whether real or imaginary, was dictated by local conditions and beliefs. These birds were often accorded divine or semi-divine status and generally regarded as beneficent. The exception was the owl, which to this day is almost universally considered to be a bird of ill-omen.[2]

In Vedic India the *haṁsa* was closely associated with the sun (*RV.*, IV.40,5; *ŚBr.*, VI.7.3,11; *Maitri Up.*, VI.34),[3] and represented as the male principle of fertility. Because of the *haṁsa*'s beauty and grace in flight, and its pure whiteness it was frequently employed as a simile or metaphor by Vedic poets, so that its enhanced significance in the Upaniṣads is not unexpected. Thus in the *Bṛhad-Ār.* (4.3,11–12) the *haṁsa* is symbolically represented as 'the One Spirit; in the *Śvet.* (6,15) as 'the one soul in the midst of the world'; and in the *Maitri* (6,8) it is identified with the *ātman*.

The *haṁsa* symbolizes knowledge[4] and the life-force or cosmic breath (*prāṇa*), '*ham*' being its exhalation, and '*sa*' its inhalation which is regarded as the return of the individual life-force to *brahman*, its cosmic source. The lofty flight of the *haṁsa* is therefore likened to the spiritual efforts of the devout Hindu to attain *brahman*.

[1] A.T. Hatto, 'The Swan Maiden', p. 339, *BSOAS.*, XXIV, pt. 2,1961.

[2] In Sumerian mythology (c. 2300–2000 B.C.) Lilith, a goddess of the underworld, is depicted on a clay plaque as a winged nude figure, with claw-feet, having an owl on either side of her. She is the 'night monster' of Isaiah XXXIV, 14.

[3] The ancient Egyptian sun-god Amon-Re was believed 'to have flown in the form of a goose over the waters, his honking the first sound ever made' (H. Frankfort, *Ancient Egyptian Religion*, p. 154). In the Shamanistic cults of northern Asia the goose is associated with the sun.

[4] For this reason the goose became the *vāhana* of Brahmā and is also associated with his consort Sarasvatī, and hence her epithet Haṁsādhirūḍhā (mounted on a goose). The goose symbolizes purity (*Ait. Br.*, IV.20).

II. One of the *avatāras* of Viṣṇu (*DHI.*, p. 390).

Haṁsādhirūḍhā v. Haṁsa I, n.4.

Haṁsa Mantra The *mantra* of the goose (*haṁsa*) (which represents knowledge) consists of the two sounds produced in breathing. As inhalation and exhalation is normally an unconscious act (occurring 21,600 times every twenty-four hours), it becomes an efficacious *mantra* only when breathing is a conscious act (*AGP.*, II. pp. 767f.).
v. Yoga.

Hanumat (Hanuman only in compounds). 'Heavy-jawed.' A 'monkey-chief' and the mythical leader of a large troop of ape-like creatures. His exploits are related in great detail in the *Rāmāyaṇa*, but scantily in the *Mahābhārata* and *Agni Purāṇa*, his chief role being as the ally of Rāma in his war against Rāvaṇa, the demon-king of Laṅkā.[1]

Animals able to talk, and who possess magical powers, are common to the folk tales of all countries, especially those of early Greece, but they are nowhere as numerous or fantastic as those of Indian mythology.[2] Hanumat is one of these, and is described as having a short thick neck, a round red face, sharp white fangs, a mane like *aśoka* flowers, a tail like Indra's banner, and able to expand until he was as large as a mountain. His parents were Vāyu (the wind) and Añjanā, an *apsaras*, formerly the wife of the ape Kesarin.

When Rāma, the mortal hero (later to become an *avatāra* of Viṣṇu), fell exhausted on the battlefield, Hanumat flew to the Himālaya and uprooted an entire mountain on which grew healing herbs and carried it back to his master and so restored him. Rāma rewarded him with the gift of perpetual life, but this does not appear to mean eternal life, as Varuṇa promised him only that he should not die for a million years, which Brahmā ensured by making him invulnerable. His image is depicted on Arjuna's banner.

Many other myths surround this popular folk-divinity, among which are the following: he was swallowed by a sea-monster and vomited out again, or emerged from the monster's ear; he killed Kālanemi and thousands of *gandharvas* who assailed him; and finally jumped from India to Ceylon (Laṅkā) in one bound. Indrajit, Rāvaṇa's son, once captured him and set his tail on fire and forced him to march through the streets of Laṅkā, but Sītā invoked Agni who allowed the fire to play about the monkey's tail without burning it.[3] Later Hanumat avenged himself by setting fire to the city.[4]

Hanumat retains his popularity today. In northern India he presides over every settlement, the setting up of his image being a sign of its establishment. Popularly regarded as the patron of wandering acrobats and wrestlers, Hanumat is also noted for his great asceticism, learning and as 'the ninth author of grammar'.[5] In southern India his image often forms part of bells or lamps. In one temple a sacred tank is dedicated to him where sacrifices are performed by those wishing to have a son.[6]

[1]Crooke (*Things Indian*, p. 329) considers that Hanumat may represent 'the prognathous hero of one of the forest tribes who assisted the Āryans in their movement southwards'. Cf. M.N. Dutt Shastri, *Agni Purāṇa*, I, p. 41n.

[2]Animals were venerated and the more powerful were also feared. In India as in early Greece there were combinations of man and animal such as Gaṇeśa and Narasiṁha, or man and bird like Garuḍa. The more beneficent deities 'assumed the shape of a bull, a cow or monkey; in the main, symbols of wealth and fertility' (Heimann, *IWP.*, pp. 31f.).

[3]Monkeys are said to be able to heal scalded or burned horses (de Gubernatis, *Zoological Mythology*, II, p. 105).

[4]Crooke, op. cit., p. 330.

[5]*OST.*, IV, p. 490.

[6]Diehl, *Instrument and Purpose*, p. 244.

v. Vānara(s).

Hara 'Destroyer', 'seizer'. One of the eleven Rudras (*VP.*, I.15),[1] and one of the thousand and eight names or epithets of Śiva. Hopkins[2] suggests that in the early use of epithets like Hara, Hari, etc., 'no great difference was felt between gods and demons. When good, a god; when destructive, a demon.'

Hara represents death, the inexorable process of disintegration of the individual and of the universe, and is popularly regarded as the 'embodiment' of sleep, the remover of pain.[3]

[1]The list of these Rudras varies; some Purāṇas omit Hara.

[2]*EM.*, p. 52.

[3]*Liṅga P.*, Uṇādi Sūtra I, 153, *HP.*, p. 197. Meditation on Hara also dispels all ignorance (Bhandarkar, *VSM.*, p. 107).

Hari I. 'Pale or reddish-yellow.' In Vedic usage '*hari*' is applied to fire (Agni), the sun (Viṣṇu), lightning (Indra), etc. It is probably because of its association with the solar Viṣṇu and with light that the Purāṇic writers borrowed the epithet '*hari*' and applied it to the post-Vedic Viṣṇu.

Hari is said to be incarnate in countless gods, *ṛṣis*, lawgivers, etc.[1] Two of his *śaktis* are said to be manifested in the banner (*dhvaja*) flown above temples (*AGP.*, I, p. 225).

When a village festival has been performed in honour of inauspicious (*krūra*) deities, another festival must be held in honour of Hari, thereby ensuring universal prosperity.[2]

According to the *VP.*, I.22, 'This Hari, who is the most immediate of all the energies of *brahman*, is composed entirely of his essence; and from him, and in him, is the universe; and he, the supreme lord of all, comprises all that is perishable and imperishable.'

[1]*HP.*, p. 164.

[2]Gonda, *Aspects*, p. 254, n. 108.

v. Hara; Hari-Hara.

II. 'Tawny or bay', especially applied to Indra's horses, and hence his frequent epithets Harivān and Haryaśva, 'having bay horses', in the *RV*.

Harī One of the nine wrathful daughters of Krodhā. Harī became the mother of all monkeys, horses and of the animals called 'cow-tailed' (*MBh.*, Ādi pa., 66).

Haricandana The sandal-tree, one of the five trees of 'Paradise'.

Haridrā Turmeric (Curcuma longa). An aromatic plant of the ginger family, used as an ingredient in curry powder and as a medicine for internal and cutaneous diseases, especially leprosy (*AV.*, I. 23). Gaṇeśa as Haridrāgaṇapati has offerings of turmeric made to him. According to folk belief *haridrā* is much disliked by demons.

Diseases such as jaundice are invoked to go to the yellow porridge made from *haridrā*, on the principle that yellow diseases belong by right to 'yellow objects', such as yellow birds, plants, etc.[1]

[1]Similar beliefs and practices were common to ancient Greece and Rome and later to Germany, etc.

v. Hāridrava; Hrūḍu; Cāṣa; Lakṣmī(s).

Haridrāgaṇapati v. Haridrā.

Hāridrava The yellow wagtail. In a charm to remove jaundice it is invoked to leave the patient and go to the sun, to parrots, or to the *hāridrava* (*AV.*, I.22,4).

Haridru An inauspicious tree (Cedrus deodara) which should not be planted near graves (*ŚBr.*, XIII.8.1,6).

Haridvāra 'Hari's (Viṣṇu's) Gate.' The modern Hardwār, a famous town and sacred bathing-place (*tīrtha*) where the Ganges leaves the mountains and flows through the plains. It is said to lead to Vaikuṇṭha, Viṣṇu's Paradise or 'sphere'.

Hari-hara Viṣṇu (Hari) and Śiva (Hara) conjoined as a single deity. In images the left side represents Viṣṇu and the right Śiva.[1] This form denotes the union of the two divine personalities, and the synthesization of the two major cults of Vaiṣṇavism and Śaivism.

During the Churning of the Ocean (*samudramathana*) Viṣṇu assumed the form of the enchantress Mohinī with whom Śiva fell in love. He embraced Mohinī sexually and from their union was born the child Hari-hara, named after the two deities.

[1]The Vijayanagara kings in the Deccan patronized the Hari-Hara temples where the god is still worshipped (*WI.*, p. 311).

Hariṇa 'Gazelle.' The horns were used in a remedial rite against the unidentifiable disease called *kṣetriyā*[1] (*AV.*, III.7.1,2).

[1]Bloomfield (*AVB.*) translates *kṣetriyā* as 'hereditary disease'.

Hariśara 'Having Viṣṇu for an arrow.' This refers to the legend of Śiva's burning of the three cities (Tripura) when Viṣṇu was said to be the shaft of his arrow.

Hariścandra A royal *ṛṣi* and virtuous king of the Solar dynasty in the Treta age, and a son of Triśaṅku. According to the *Padma* and *Mārk. Purs.*, Hariścandra gave up his country, wife, son, and finally himself to satisfy the excessive demands of Viśvāmitra for *dakṣiṇā* (sacrificial gifts). After terrible sufferings the gods took pity on him and raised him and his subjects to the heavenly sphere. But the *ṛṣi* Nārada encouraged him to boast of his great merits, so causing him and his people to fall headlong to earth, but the king's immediate repentance arrested their fall in mid-air where they remain to this day. Their aerial city is said to be occasionally visible.

v. Śaibya I; Śunaḥśepa.

Haritāla A tree, according to Sāyaṇa, but none is known today by this name. Monier-Williams suggests that *haritāla* is a kind of yellowish-green pigeon.

An early example of the transference of illness to animals or birds occurs in *RV.*, I.50,12: 'Let my yellowness (jaundice) pass to starlings or to Haritāla trees.'[1]

[1]A charm against plague in ancient Greece was: 'Go to the crows.' According to Pliny, jaundice could be cured by looking at a starling, when the bird's death would follow instead of the patient's (Entralgo, *The Therapy of the Word*, p. 61).

v. Hāridrava; Haridrā; Hrūḍu.

Harivaṁśa 'The genealogy of Hari.' A work, written in Paurāṇic style, which forms an appendix (*khila*) to the *Mahābhārata* and consists of three parts (*parvans*). The first begins with an account of creation, followed by a genealogical list of the Yādavas accompanied by mythological narratives. The second, narrates the feats and love-affairs of Kṛṣṇa and the *gopīs*. The third, like some Purāṇas, contains prophecies about the *kali* age and other matters which bear no relation to the general title.

Like the *Mahābhārata* itself, the Harivaṁśa has been subjected to periodic revision, interpolation and ill-assorted additions by successive redactors, often of dubious competence. As an agglomeration of legends and myths brought together for the glorification of Viṣṇu, its contents can scarcely be considered worthy of its purpose.

Harṣa A ruler of the later Gupta dynasty who ascended the throne at the age of sixteen in A.D. 606. He reigned forty-one years and restored some of the former glory of the Guptas. He was greatly admired by the Chinese pilgrim Hsüan-tsang whom Harṣa made a member of his Court.

Three plays are attributed to King Harṣa, the Ratnāvalī, Priyadarśikā and Nāgānanda.

Haryaśva(s) The collective name of the 5,000 mind-born sons of Dakṣa who refused to people the earth, but chose instead to lead a celibate and ascetic life. v. Nārada; Vīriṇī.

Hasta I. 'Hand.' Hands, signifying power and protection, have played an important part in early beliefs as is indicated by the 'hand-impressions of Palaeolithic cavern walls . . . [which] connoted not merely power over the prey nor even the consecration of the instrument of hunter and artist, but a testimony of their presence in a sacred place'.[1] In India also the hand has protective powers, as when the sacrificer lays his hand down with the palm upwards and prays: 'Shield me from all evil spirits' (*ŚBr.*, XIV.1.3,24).[2]

[1]G. R. Levy, *Gate of Horn*, p. 49.

[2]In parts of Europe the open hand with the fingers widely extended is a charm against the Evil Eye; the raised hand conveys a blessing, like that of the Christian benediction.

v. Mudrā.

II. Name of a constellation, and of the Star of Doom which portended death to Rāvaṇa.[1]

[1]*IRA.*, p. 184.

Hastakamala 'Lotus in hand.' An epithet of Lakṣmī, goddess of good fortune, who emerged from the Churning of the Ocean (*samudramathana*) holding a lotus (symbolizing good fortune).

Hastināpura A city about fifty-seven miles north-east of Delhi, founded by Hastin, the first Bhārata King of the Lunar dynasty. Most of the city has been washed away by the Ganges.

Balarāma dragged the ramparts of the city towards him with his ploughshare when the Kauravas refused to give up their prisoner Śāmba (Kṛṣṇa's son) to him (*VP.*, IV. 35).

Havirbhū 'Oblation-born.' The personification of the place of sacrifice as the daughter of Kardama and wife of Pulastya.

Havis An oblation such as *ghṛta*, *soma*, etc., and associated with fire.

v. Havyavāhana.

Havyavāhana 'Oblation bearer (or vehicle).' Fire (*agni*) as the conveyor of oblations (*havis*) to the gods.

Haya v. Aśva; Indra.

Hayagrīva 'Horse-necked', or Hayaśiras, 'horse-headed'.[1] Hayagrīva is post-Vedic, and is first presented in the *MBh.* and the Purāṇas but lacks consistent portrayal, possibly, as van Gulik[2] suggests, because of the existence of two Hayagrīva traditions. One refers to him as a demon (*dānava* or *daitya*) who, having stolen the Vedas from Brahmā, was slain by Viṣṇu in his fish-form (*matsya avatāra*).[3] But this is contradicted by a tradition which states that Hayagrīva was divine, and had not only retrieved the lost Vedas but was also their promulgator and protector.[4] The demonic tradition was further eroded when Hayagrīva became the eighteenth *avatāra* of Viṣṇu,[5] and the Vedic and post-Vedic Viṣṇu were synthesized, and the synonymous attributes of sun and horse identified with those of Viṣṇu, the lord of all. This equation of symbol and the object symbolized is indicated in the equation of knowledge with the sun and light, and of knowledge with Dadhikrā the celestial horse, itself a form of the sun,[6] and thus finally with the Supreme Viṣṇu.

According to the *MBh.*, the future *avatāra* will appear as a *brāhmaṇa* (or a warrior) called Kalkin, riding a white horse.[7]

[1]The commonest word for horse in Vedic literature is *aśva*, but *haya* is used when referring to 'the speeding horse'.

[2]*Hayagrīva. The Mantrayanic Aspect of Horse Cult in China and Japan*, p. 19; v. also F. D. K. Bosch, 'The God with the Horse's Head', in *Selected Studies in Indonesian Archaeology*.

[3]*Bhāg. P.*, 8.24, cited by Daniélou, *HP.*, p. 167.

[4]The belief in the protective powers of the horse, or of the head alone, is indicated by the numerous carved horses' heads on the gables of houses in Central, Northern and Eastern Europe (Letter from Prof. R. Wolfram, *Folklore*, vol. 80, pp. 60f., 1969). The ancient Germans according to Tacitus regarded the horse as a prophetic animal, specially familiar with the divine world; the Persians divined the future from the neighing of horses (Farnell, *Cults*, III, p. 59).

[5]According to the *Bhaktamālā* (a late work), v. Grierson, 'Gleanings from the Bhaktamālā', *JRAS.*, 1909.

[6]Cf. *ŚBr.*, VI.31,29; 'for this horse is indeed yonder sun'; and *MBh.* (5.99,5, *EM.*), 'when the horse-headed Viṣṇu (the sun) emerged from the sea he filled the world'.

[7]Or Viṣṇu himself will appear as a white horse (Gonda, *Aspects*, p. 149). Poseidon, Athena, Aphrodite and Cronus had horse aspects. The Celtic goddess Epona sometimes assumed the form of a mare (A. Dent and D. M. Goodall, *The Foals of Epona*, p. 10); the Black Demeter was represented in the Phigalian cave (in Arcadia) as a woman with the head of a mare. While she remained in the cave, nothing grew on earth. This 'indicates that the horse was one of the animal forms assumed in ancient Greece, as in modern Europe, by the corn-spirit' (Frazer, *The Golden Bough*, Abr. ed., p. 471); v. also Farnell, *Cults*, I, 29; II,450,641.

Hayaśiras v. Hayagrīva.

Hemāmbikā 'Golden mother.' A tantric form of *śakti* as 'mother' to whom a shrine is dedicated in Palghat, South Malabar. She is represented—not as a figure—but by a pair of hands protruding from a miniature well.[1] Though there is no evidence that she was ever presented as a complete figure, legend suggests it, and attributes her present form to the 'lewd attentions' of the priestly ministrant[2] responsible for ritually bathing her.

[1]Bharati (*TT*., p. 99) considers this icon to be unique in India, and observes that neither her shrine (*pīṭha*) nor those of the two Ambikā goddesses associated with her are included in D. C. Sircar's list of Śākta *pīṭhas*.

[2]These priests are rarely *brahmins*, but are usually drawn from the *śūdra* class.

v. Mukhāmbikā; Bālāmbikā.

Hemamṛga 'Golden deer.' The *rākṣasa* Mārīca assumed the form of a golden deer and so fascinated Rāma and Sītā that the former left his home to pursue the wonderful animal. During his absence, Rāvaṇa, disguised as a mendicant, abducted Sītā.

Hiḍimba The name of the giant red-haired cannibal *rākṣasa* who dwelt in a Śāla tree. He sent his sister Hiḍimbā to decoy the Pāṇḍavas when they were living in the forest after the burning of their house. Hiḍimbā could transform herself into any shape, could fly, and also possessed knowledge of the past and the future. As soon as she saw Bhīma she fell in love with him, revealed her brother's plan and offered to protect him, but Bhīma refused. Hiḍimba then appeared and after a fierce struggle Bhīma killed him, and hence his epithet Hiḍimbajit (Conqueror of Hiḍimba). Hiḍimbā fled after the death of her brother, but later returned to Bhīma. She lived with him only by day as at nightfall she had to return him to the Pāṇḍavas. Their child, Ghaṭotkaca, was conceived and born on the same day, as is usual with the offspring of *rākṣasīs* (*MBh*., Ādi pa., 154 and 157).

Hiḍimbā I. The sister of Hiḍimba.

II. Name of the wife of Hanumat.

Himā 'Snow.' The name of a celestial damsel who dwells in mountains.

v. Urvarā.

Himālaya 'Abode of snow.' A mountainous region running in a south-easterly curve along the northern border of India. It consists of parallel ranges about 1,500 miles long and from 150–200 miles in breadth, divided by deep valleys above which tower some 114 peaks of over 20,000 feet, seventy-five of them exceeding 24,000 feet, all perpetually snow-clad and shrouded in mist. Their stupendous height and mass have always been a source of wonderment, and because of their inaccessibility in ancient times were regarded as a mysterious region. They were also subject to fierce winds and avalanches of snow, ice and rocks, and were thus forbidding and dangerous.

Mountain peaks, where earth and sky meet, being the nearest earthly things to the celestial sphere, are generally regarded as dwelling-places of the gods,[1] the Himālaya especially being so regarded. The mythical Mount Meru was said to be situated in the Himālaya, and to constitute the axis of the universe, the source of the earth's energy. Shrines and places of worship might be built on the lower peaks of the Himālaya,[2] but no one should dwell there because it was 'a region impregnated with the sacred, a spot where one can pass from one cosmic zone to another'.[3]

The Himālaya is personified as Himavat (snow-clad), whose daughters are the beautiful Pārvatī[4] and Gaṅgā.

[1]According to the *MBh*., the gods of old sacrificed on the summits of the Himālaya.

[2]*HP*., p. 264.

[3]Eliade, *Patterns*, p. 100.

[4]Pārvatī is the f. of *parvata*, a 'mountain range'; a 'hill'.

v. Menā; Maināka; Kailāsa.

Himavat v. Himālaya.

Hiṁsā 'Injury', 'harm', 'violence', the opposite of *ahiṁsā*. Hiṁsā is personified as the wife of Adharma (Injustice).[1]

[1]*VP*., p. 49. n.14; *Mārk. P*., 50, 29–32.

v. Hiṁsākarman.

Hiṁsākarman An injurious act, especially the use of magical spells designed to injure an enemy.

Hiṅgu An annual plant (asafoetida), from the roots of which is prepared a drug having a powerful alliaceous odour and bitter taste.[1] It has medicinal properties, but in India and Irān is used as a condiment by Smārta *brahmins* in South India, as a substitute for onions, the latter being regarded by them as having aphrodisiacal properties.[2]

[1]It is still widely used in North Wales as a household remedy, where it is known as 'Devil's dung' (Letter from D. F. Lewis, Secretary and Registrar of the Pharmaceutical Society of G. B., to the Editor, *Country Quest* (December 1969), pp. 53f.).

[2]But Balfour considers that asafoetida produces a sensation of heat, increased secretion in the alimentary canal, 'and the urinary and genital organs seem to be sometimes materially excited' (*CI*., vol. I. p. 179).

Hiraṇyagarbha 'Golden-womb', or Hiraṇyāṇḍa, 'Golden-egg'. The name of the creator, the source of all life, human and celestial (*RV*., X.121,1).[1] The name metaphorically associates creation with the sun or with the light of the sun, and by implication with the primordial waters from which the sun appears to rise. It is a late *RV*. theory, and contrasts with the earlier *maṇḍalas* which lack a clear notion of the origin of the world and of any primary act of creation. Aditi is described as the goddess of nature, and the Ādityas as her offspring. Natural forces are also personified, but they represent only the process by which the continuity of phenomena is maintained. Thus the introduction of Hiraṇyagarbha appears as the earliest attempt to clarify the ambiguities of earlier Indian cosmogonic myths, though the use of the egg-metaphor shows little advance on its Egyptian[2] and Greek[3] parallels.

In the Upaniṣads cosmogonic theory is further developed, but not pressed to a logical conclusion. Thus the idea of primordial chaos, when 'there was neither Aught nor Nought' (*RV.*, X. 129), is interpreted in the *Chān. Up.* (3, 19) as existence or non-being (*brahman*), which became 'being' in the form of an egg. This split into two, one part being silver, the other gold. The silver became the earth, the gold heaven, whilst the residue became clouds, oceans and rivers. Variations of this account occur in the *ŚBr.* (II.1.6,1f.; *Manu*, I.5ff.). The *MBh.* (12,312, 1–7, *EM.*) represents Brahmā also as having been born from a golden egg.

It is possible that the ancient association of birds, like the *haṁsa*, and Garutman (later Garuḍa) with the sun, and the association of birds with eggs may have led to some confusion when symbolism became over-elaborated. This is indicated when the light of the sun becomes the light shed by knowledge, and the latter's subsequent attribution to the *haṁsa*. Many similar arbitrary and obscure association of ideas occur, especially in the *MBh.* and *Rām.*, whose meaning is further obscured by the ornate poetical language in which they are expressed.

Finally, Hiraṇyagarbha, Prajāpati and Brahmā were superseded in common Hindu theology by the theory of *śakti* as the creative principle[4] and by *brahman* as the 'supreme essence' or life-force.

[1]In the last stanza Hiraṇyagarbha is equated with Prajāpati. This stanza may have been added when Prajāpati was established as the supreme creator, before being equated with and finally replaced by Brahmā.

[2]Ra (the sun) was 'the egg of the great cackler', Seb (the earth), by a play on words, being equated with goose. W. M. Flinders Petrie, *ERE.*, IV, p. 145; v. also Reymond, *Mythical Origin of the Egyptian Temple*, p. 70; James, *Tree of Life*, p. 131.

[3]Among the later Orphic cosmogonies was the theory of an 'Egg of light', the offspring of Chronos and Ether, or of Ether and Chaos. From the egg issued the first god Phanes, creator of the world (*ERE.*, IV, p. 147; Nilsson, *A History of Greek Religion*, pp. 73, 216).

[4]*HP.*, p. 254.

Hiraṇyahasta 'Golden-handed.' The name of the child 'given' by the Aśvins to Vadhrimatī, whose husband was impotent (*RV.*, I. 116,13; 117,24, etc.).

Hiraṇyakaśipu 'Golden-robed.' A mythical Daitya ruler, whose wealth and power were matched only by the costliness of his apparel.

Unfortunately for Hiraṇyakaśipu, his son Prahlāda was an extremely zealous Vaiṣṇava (*VP.*, I.15), who regarded with disfavour the materialistic ambitions of his father who, having been assured by Brahmā that no man, animal, or created being was able to kill him, took every opportunity to enrich himself and increase his power. Thus he declared himself lord of the three worlds (earth, atmosphere and the heavens), appropriated the offerings made to the gods, and finally claimed the throne of Indra. It seems probable that Hiraṇyakaśipu was a Śaiva.[1]

The conflict of views of father and son resulted in the latter's persecution, described by him with all the pride of a martyr in his power of endurance, made possible by Viṣṇu's help, specially given to him. He declared proudly that although weapons had been hurled against him, that poisonous snakes had bitten him, and that he had been thrown into a fiery furnace, his faith in Viṣṇu had never wavered. He ended his declaration by requesting Viṣṇu to pardon his father's iniquities (*VP.*, I.20). Finally his father did repent and was united with his son. But the *Bhāg. P.* account states that the father summoned his son to Court and demanded that if Viṣṇu was everywhere, why was he not in the pillars of the palace. Immediately he had spoken the pillar nearest to him burst asunder and from it sprang Narasiṁha[2] the man-(*nara*) lion (*siṁha*) *avatāra* of Viṣṇu, who tore Hiraṇyakaśipu to pieces.[3]

[1]The *MBh.* states that Śiva gave him the sovereignty of the three worlds for a million years (*HM.*, p. 122).

[2]As Narasiṁha was neither wholly man nor animal, nor a 'created being', the validity of Brahmā's promise was considered by the narrator to have remained intact.

[3]The *Śiva P.* version, as might be expected, differs considerably.

v. Hiraṇyākṣa; Śiśupāla; Śarabha.

Hiraṇyākṣa 'Golden-eyed.' A *daitya* and brother of Hiraṇyakaśipu (*AGP.*, I, p. 22). He threw the earth into the sea (*VP.*, I.15), for which deed Viṣṇu, in the form of Varāha (the boar *avatāra*), killed him.

v. Diti.

Hiraṇyapura 'Golden City.' Name of a city of the *asuras* built by the great magician Maya (or by Brahmā or Viśvakarman). It floats in the air and is situated beyond the ocean. All desirable objects are contained in it, and grief or disease never occur (*MBh.*, Vana pa., 172).

Hiraṇyavakṣas 'Golden-breasted.' Name of the goddess Vasudhārā,[1] said to conceal 'within her womb the treasures of the world'.[2]

[1]Vasudhārā is also the name of a Mahāyāna Buddhist goddess, associated with the Dhyānī-Buddha system, but she 'has a greater antiquity than the Dhyānī Buddhas themselves' (Bhattacharyya, *Buddhist Iconography*, p. 89).

[2]*Ancestor Worship*, p. 245.

Hitopadeśa 'Friendly advice, salutary instruction.' From *hita* 'of good intent', and *deśa* 'place'. A collection of fables and stories of an ideal society of pious animals, who seek to show how varied talents, however small, can give a sense of security to the weak, inspire mutual confidence, and ensure help for those menaced by stronger members of society.

Though many translations of the *Hitopadeśa* have been adapted to the religious and social ideas of different peoples, the stories are substantially the same. Thus the 'pious animal' in one may appear as a devout jackal, in another a very virtuous lion, or as either a very pious cat or one using religion as a cloak for its predatory activities. In the Sanskrit version the cat is a Hindu, Jain or Buddhist ascetic, and therefore eats no flesh. In the Persian (ante-Islamic) translation the animal is a Magian; in the Arabic the fox is an orthodox Moslem, who regularly performs his religious duties, reads the Koran, and makes at least one pilgrimage to Mecca; in the Greek the animal is a monk or hermit who talks in the Homeric hexameters of the Iliad.[1]

Twenty-five of the stories of the *Hitopadeśa* are derived from an older work entitled *Pañcatantra*, but seventeen appear to be stories composed in Bengal between the tenth and thirteenth centuries. Some of the stories of the first group appeared in an Arabic translation, called *Kalilah and Dimna* (names of the two jackals in the first story), or as the *Fables of Bilpaī*, which appeared in an English translation in 1570 as the *Fables of Pilpay*, and was apparently the source of a story called *The Dervise and the Thief*,[2] by Beaumont and Fletcher.

The version called *Fables of Bilpay* was first translated from Sanskrit into Persian in the sixth century by Barzūyeh, an eminent physician at the court of the Persian king Nuṣiravān. Other translations appeared, including Arabic (8th cent.), Greek (11th cent.), Hebrew (12th cent.), followed by others into Syriac, Turkish, Afghan, Malay, Mongolian and Latin. Modern European translations began with the German (1483), followed by the Spanish (1498), English (1570), Danish (1618), Dutch (1623) and Swedish (1743). The complete Sanskrit recension discovered by Sir Charles Wilkins and Sir William Jones was published at Serampore in 1804. In 1884 Francis Johnson, a former Professor of Oriental Languages of the East India Company's college at Haileybury, published a complete Sanskrit text, collated with the Serampore and Bonn editions and the MS. copy in the Bodleian Library at Oxford.

[1]Abridged and adapted from an essay by Prof. Tayler Lewis, contributed to an American magazine (unnamed) and quoted in the Intro. to *The Fables of Pilpay* published by Fr. Warne & Co., London.

[2]Massinger used the story in the '*Guardian*', and La Fontaine acknowledged his indebtedness to eighteen of the fables of Pilpay. The Welsh story of the killing of Llewelyn's faithful hound Gellert, reflects several transformatory stages of the Sanskrit original (v. Edgerton, *Pañcatantra*, pp. 17ff.).

Holākā[1] Commonly called Holī. A spring festival dedicated to Kṛṣṇa and the *gopīs*. It took the place of an earlier kind of Saturnalia, 'the survival of a primitive fertility ritual, combining erotic games, "comic operas" and folk-dancing'.[2] Some of the earlier elements remain, such as the singing of suggestive songs, the throwing of coloured water, and jumping over bonfires, the ashes of which were believed to possess magical powers.

[1]Perhaps derived from a cry, shout or sound in singing (*SED.*).

[2]Auboyer, *Daily Life in Ancient India*, p. 144. For further details of *holākā* v. Meyer, *Trilogie*, pt. i, Kāma, pp. 1–238.

Holī v. Holākā.

Homa The act of making an oblation or burnt offering to the gods by throwing ghee (*ghṛta*) into the sacrificial fire.

Hotṛ or **Hotar** v. Ṛtvij.

Hotrā 'Call, invocation', used in ritual and personified as the wife of Agni (*RV.*, I.22,10; II.62,3).

Hrūḍu[1] Name of the god of fever '*takman*' (*AV.*, I.25,1ff.), who is invoked to leave the patient and enter the body of a frog (VII.116,1f.).

[1]Henry suggests that this 'word may be connected with the Assyrian *ḥuraçu* and the Hebrew *ḥarūc*, and so go back to a proto-Semitic* *harūḍu*, "gold"' (*JA.*, 9.X.513, cited by Whitney, *AV.*, I. p. 26n.).

v. Haritāla.

I

Iḍā Sacrificial food or a libation,[1] especially that offered between the *prayāja* (preliminary) and *anuyāja* (final) sacrificial rites (*RV.*, I. 40,4; *ŚBr.*, I.8.1,9). A meat-offering was an important part of the *iḍā* rite.[2]

The *ŚBr.* (I.8.1, 1–6) briefly describes the Deluge, of which Manu was the sole survivor. Because he retrieved from the waters the clarified butter, sour milk, whey and curds, collectively called *iḍā*,[3] they were personified as Iḍā who claimed to be his daughter (*ŚBr.*, I.8.1, 7ff.; *VP.*, IV.1). She besought Manu to make use of her at the sacrifice, promising to be its benediction, and that whatever blessing he should invoke through her should be granted.

[1]Personified as a cow symbolizing food, nourishment and abundance, or as a goddess of abundance (*RV.*, I.13,9; 40,4; *Tait. Saṁ.*, I.7,2; VI.3,11).

[2]Iḍā is one of the *āprī* divinities (*AVB.*, p. 512).

[3]As these are all products of milk, Iḍā is called the Agnihotra cow, Manu's daughter (*ŚBr.*, XI.,5.3,5). By Iḍā the gods and sacrificers obtained food (XI.1.6, 28), the latter being the primary cause of the origin, continuance and dissolution of all beings including Brahmā (*Suś. Saṁ.*, I. p. 469). Iḍā is sometimes equated with the earth (*AV.*, XVIII.4,30).

v. Iḍā-pātra; Iḷā; Urvaśī.

Iḍā-pātra The vessel used for the *iḍā* oblation. It is placed on the head of the corpse when the deceased's sacrificial implements and body are cremated. The *iḍā-pātra* is sacred to the gods and the *pitṛs*, and in it the *soma* always purifies itself (*AV.*, XVIII.3,53–4).

Iḍaspati or **Iḷaspati** 'Lord of the libation.' A title of Pūṣan (*RV.*, VI.58,4); of Viṣṇu (*Bhāg. P.*, IX.2,35, *PI.*) and of Parjanya, god of rain (*RV.*, V.42,14).

v. Iḍā.

Iḍāviḍā or **Iḷāvilā** The name of a daughter of the royal *ṛṣi* Tṛṇabindu. She became the wife of Viśravas and mother of Kubera, the god of wealth (*Bhāg. P.*, IV.1,37; 12.9, *PI.*).

Idhmavāha 'Carrier of sacrificial fuel.' Name of one of Agastya's sons by Lopāmudrā, and of the adopted son of Kratu. Idhmavāha remained in the womb for seven years (*MBh.*, Vana pa., 99).

Īhāmṛga(s) 'Antelope',[1] or 'wolf';[2] also the name of a mythical animal made up of parts of beasts, birds and reptiles according to the sculptor's or painter's fancy.

[1]*IRA.*, p. 193, n.1.

[2]*SED.*

Ikṣvāku I. The name of a king, and of a people[1] who settled in eastern India between the rivers Son and Ganges. Opinions about their ethnic origin vary, Pargiter holding that the Aṅgas and Magadhas were non-Āryans; Oldenberg that they were early Āryan immigrants; Vincent Smith that the Magadhas and other neighbouring tribes were of mixed Turanian stock; whilst Paurāṇic tradition speaks of the Ikṣvākus and Videhas as inhabitants of the country since Ṛgvedic times, though this tradition throws no light on their origin. Politically, socially, and in their interpretation of Vedic tradition, all the people of the area, especially the Mauryas, Vajjians, and other warrior tribes collectively called Kosalans, are characterized by outstanding initiative and independence. This is apparent in the non-brahmanic Jains and Buddhists, who called themselves Kosalans.

[1]Probably the Ikṣvākus were the first planters and derived their family name from the *ikṣu* or sugarcane 'whose quality they had come to control through experiments', J. C. Ray, 'Food and Drink in Ancient India' (*Man in India*, vol. XIII, p. 225, cited by S. N. Vyas, *IRA.*, p. 239).

II. The son of Manu Vaivasvat, who was the son of Vivasvat, the sun. Ikṣvāku founded the Solar dynasty, and reigned at Ayodhyā. He had a hundred sons, one of whom called Nimi founded the Mithilā dynasty.

Iḷa v. Iḷā.

Iḷā In the *RV.* (I.13,9) Iḷā, Sarasvatī and Mahī[1] are mentioned as three goddesses 'who bring delight'. Iḷā is 'made a teacher of the sons of men' (I.31,11); and in her holy place the priest sits (I.128,1). But in another hymn (V.41,19) she is called 'mother of the herds of cattle',[2] i.e., of food intended for the sacrifice, which would seem to associate or identify her with Iḍā. Iḷā's place is the centre of the earth (III.29,4), or the northern altar (*uttaravedi*), the place of libation, prayer and worship, etc. (cf. *ŚBr.*, I.1.2,23).

In the Purs. Iḷā is the subject of various stories, apparently representing separate traditions, all of which bear little resemblance to the Vedic Iḷā. The *VP.* (IV.1) states that to obtain sons Manu offered a sacrifice[3] to Mitra-Varuṇa, but owing to a ritual error, only a daughter, Iḷā, was born. By favour of Mitra-Varuṇa her sex was changed. This legend differs in other Purs and the *MBh.* The latter states that Manu's sacrifice resulted in the birth of ten sons of whom Iḷā was one. According to the *Matsya P.* he was the eldest son who in the course of his duties entered the forest of Śambhu (Śiva), which unknown to him was Pārvatī's sacred grove. Having previously had her privacy disturbed by some sages, Pārvatī demanded of Śiva that henceforth any man who ventured into the forest should be changed into a woman. When Iḷā's brothers found him so transformed they applied to Vasiṣṭha, their father's priest, who directed them to worship Śiva and Pārvatī. Iḷā again became male and renamed Sudyumna, but was again transformed into a woman near the hermitage of Budha (Mercury), the son of the Moon (Soma). Budha married her and had by her a son, Purūravas. This legend, begun as Śaiva propaganda, is given a Vaiṣṇava sequel. After the birth of Purūravas, 'illustrious *ṛṣis*' determined that Iḷā should again have her sex changed, and prayed to Viṣṇu, by whose favour Iḷā again became Sudyumna and subsequently father of three sons. This curious story is part of a complex legend of Manu and his ten sons, which is intended to serve not only sectarian interests but also to show that the different castes originated from a common ancestor. This is illustrated by the story of one of Manu's sons, who was degraded to the *śūdra* caste as the penalty for having killed a cow.

[1]Some passages include Bhāratī (*RV.*, I.162,9) or omit Mahī (I.188,8).

[2]The *Nir.* (11.49) also calls her 'mother of the herd', i.e., of everything.

[3]According to the *Bhāg. P.* (IX.1.16,22, *Pl.*), she was ritually born from his *aśvamedha* (horse sacrifice).

v. Iḍā.

Iḷāvilā Name of Kubera's mother.

Ilībiśa A demon whose strong castles were broken down by Indra (*RV.*, I.33,12). Sāyaṇa identifies the demon with Vṛtra.

Ilvala v. Vātāpi.

Indha A corruption of *indhana* 'fuel', from the root *indh.* It is applied to Indra as god of lightning. In the *Nirukta*, the oldest extant commentary on the *Veda saṃhitā*, the gods are said to dislike being addressed by their actual names.[1]

[1]The 'name' of a god is properly his manifestation. Cf. the Hebrew prohibition against uttering Yahweh's name.

Indirā A name of Lakṣmī, the wife of Viṣṇu.

Indirālaya 'Abode of Indirā' (Lakṣmī), i.e., the blue lotus from which the goddess Indirā emerged at the creation.

Indra The tutelary god of Indo-Āryans, initially regarded as the chief of the gods, to whom many *RV.* hymns are addressed. But such a description fails to indicate the multiform activities attributed to him in the *RV.*, *AV.*, Brāhmaṇas and other texts. As Heimann observes, 'The main gods, like Indra and Agni, are called *puru-rūpavat*, "having many forms", all of equal importance.'[1]

There are many descriptions of Indra,[2] both etymological and traditional, but they are too variant to provide a single satisfactory definition, especially that of the *ŚBr.* (VI.1.1,2), where Indra is described as the 'Kindler' (Indha). 'Here some etymologies are at work which are philologically wrong but psychologically correct. Indra is Indha, the stimulating force which "kindles" thoughts and deeds.'[3] Perhaps the primary meaning of Indra is that given in the *RV.* which defines his chief characteristic as 'power' or 'strength'.[4] This is represented by his *vajra* (the thunderbolt or lightning) which destroys the demons of drought or eclipse, or metaphorically strikes the enemies of Āryans,[5] and hence his epithets, Vajrapāṇi (wielder of the *vajra*), and Vṛtrahan (destroyer of Vṛtra, the drought-demon).[6] His generative power is likened to the vigour of the stallion (*vājin*) and thus associated with his bay horses,[7] or likened to that of the bull, with whose archaic cult Indra was assimilated. In a general sense his power is indicated by the faith of his invokers in his ability to bestow cattle and other material benefits. But the functions of Indra and the other main gods are limited by contemporary cosmogonic views. Thus gods must be sustained by copious *soma* libations (*RV.*, I.5,6; III.40,2, etc.), and by oblations of various kinds by which Indra's power and vigour are increased so that he in turn can increase the material welfare of mankind.[8] Occasionally the monotonous repetition of pleas to Indra for rain and cattle is interrupted by priestly demands that he should punish those who fail to make adequate 'gifts' (*dakṣiṇā*) to the priests who constantly chant the praises of their divine benefactor (*RV.*, VI.44 and 45). Alternating with this plea is that beseeching him to smite the dark-skinned *dasyus* and thus preserve Āryan racial purity (III. 34,9).

A change of attitude towards Indra is apparent in the tenth *maṇḍala* of the *RV.*, whose supplementary character is evident in some of the Indra hymns, many of which are inferior copies of earlier hymns, while others (nos. 166–91) are literary fragments, each consisting only of three, four, five or six stanzas which differ also in character and style from the early Indra hymns. But parts of this *maṇḍala* reflect social and economic change and the desire of the people to live in freedom and peace. There is also a suggestion of nostalgia in the recollection of the power formerly exercised by Indra on their behalf. On the other hand, the question is asked whether the *ṛṣis* of old ever really understood Indra's true nature, and the suggestion is made that perhaps it has yet to be revealed (X.54 and 55). Indra's foes are no longer said to be the atmospheric demons or the *dasyus*, but those who lead evil lives, who break covenants or follow not the ordinances of Varuṇa, Aryaman and Mitra (X.89,8).

One hymn (X.161), which seems more appropriate to the *AV*. than the *RV*., is a plea to Indra and Agni to cure those suffering from *rājayakṣma* (King's disease) which the *Suś. Saṁ.* (III.41,2) defines as a wasting disease. But the great hymns of this *maṇḍala*, notably nos. 90 and 129, put those to Indra into perspective and herald the more realistic efforts to define the nature of both man and his environment, and to question the functions of the gods themselves. The final hymn, no. 191, is addressed to Agni, and may be termed an epilogue, not only to the tenth *maṇḍala* but to the entire *RV*. It appeals to the gods to 'assemble and to let their minds be all of one accord', to act in accordance with ancient custom, and to have a common purpose.

This notion of collective divinity is indicated in the *ŚBr.* (III.4.2,2) where Indra is chief of the gods (*devapati*), or that Indra is simply the title of the god temporarily regarded as their chief.[9] But it becomes obvious in later literature that the trend towards divine unity was the penultimate step to a monotheistic ideal, and a farewell to the Vedic notion of the personification of natural forces, etc. This notion of divine unity seems to have led also to that of political unity, of which the *cakravartin* or ideal universal ruler was the embodiment. Thus Indra, as the traditional war-leader, became the symbol of the power of the *kṣatra* or ruling class,[10] and his *vāhana*, the elephant Airāvata, the most powerful of animals, became the prototype of the royal elephant (symbolizing royal power) upon which the ruler rode when State ceremonial required his attendance.

The *RV*. contains only allusions to his mother, a shadowy figure whom later literature declares to be Aditi. But in the *RV*. (X.90,13) Indra and Agni are said to have been born from the mouth of the Cosmic Puruṣa. The *AV*. (III.10,12) and *Tait. Saṁ.* (IV.3,11) state that Indra's mother was Ekāṣṭakā, a daughter of Prajāpati. Other accounts ascribe his origin to those inexhaustibly fertile parents, Kaśyapa and Aditi. The *Avyakta Up*. states that he was fashioned from all the gods and is therefore the greatest of them. Other legends, often invented for a sectarian purpose, provide him with a succession of wives and offspring. One of these wives was Indrāṇī, by whom he had three sons, Jayanta (Victorious), Ṛṣabha (the Bull), and Mīḍhuṣa (Liberality) (*Bhāg. P*., 6.18,7). To Indra is also ascribed the paternity of the monkey-king Bāli, slain by Rāma.

The process of denigration of some of the Vedic gods was perhaps accentuated by brahmanic recognition of deities of Indian but non-Āryan origin, like Garuḍa. This is suggested in a *MBh.* passage cited by Dange,[11] in which Garuḍa, hitherto ignored, requests that he may carry the sacrifice, enter the Vedas, and finally be meditated on by the *brāhmaṇas*.

The establishment and gradual spread of the sectarian cults and the formulation of Vedānta philosophy appear to have led also to the exclusion of Indra from post-aupaniṣadic theism, references to him being of a clearly mythical nature. Thus in the *Mārk. P.* (V.1–19) Indra undergoes a series of transformations which originated from his alleged seduction of the wife of the *ṛṣi* Gautama, and his slaying of Tvaṣṭṛ's son.[12] As a result of this crime of brahminicide, his moral attributes and splendour were taken from him and given to Dharma; and after breaking his peace treaty with Vṛtra, his magical power was transferred to Vāyu; and following his seduction of Ahalyā his beauty passed to the Aśvins. But the *Mārk. P.* (V.20–6) provides a sequel to this legend, which says that his power and beauty were finally restored to him, apparently for the sole purpose of removing from Draupadī the stigma of having made a polyandrous marriage with the five Pāṇḍu princes, three of them the sons of Kuntī (Pṛthā), and two, the twin sons of Madrī, both she and Kuntī being the wives of Pāṇḍu. To effect this Indra's wife became incarnate as Kuntī, thus making Indra a part incarnation of her three sons. Indra also assumed the form of Yama and thus became the father of Madrī's two sons. This made all five princes indivisibly one, the collective incarnation of Indra.

The decline in Indra's prestige is indicated also by the attitude of *ṛṣis* like Durvāsas and Agastya, who contemptuously threatened to usurp his throne and exercise the powers he no longer appeared to possess. But later Indra's power was given an esoteric and erotic significance in Tantrism. His *vajra* became identified with the penis, and his generative energy regarded as the manifestation of elemental energy. In this context he is called Śakta (Potent One), and represents universal energy (*vidyutśakti*).[13]

[1] *Facets*, p. 90. Gonda states that multiformity is 'characteristic of gods concerned with the process of fertilization' (*Aspects*, p. 124). Indra was able to effect magic changes in his body (*RV*., III.53,8).

P. Thième ('The Aryan Gods of the Mitanni Treaties', *JAOS*., no. 4, 1960) points out that Indra is the culture-hero of the Vedic Āryans as well as a cosmic creator—these traits make him 'a most complex personality . . . to whom mankind owes the fundamental necessities of life'.

[2]v. also *Nir.* (10,8); Müller, *Lectures on Language*, II, p. 430n.; *HP.*, p. 108.

[3]*Facets*, p. 91. The *ŚBr.* definition is repeated in the *Bṛhad-Ār. Up.*, 4.2,2.

[4]Thus Indra is called Śatakratu, 'lord of a hundred powers' (*RV.*, VIII.32,11); Putrāḥ śavasaḥ, 'son of strength' (*RV.*, IV.24,1), an illusion to his mother Aditi, called the 'Mighty One' (*śavasī*). His wife Śacī is 'goddess of strength'. The *Chān. Up.*, 2.22, 3 and 5 identifies him with the vowels of the sung chant, which should be pronounced strongly with the thought: 'To Indra let me give strength.' T.R.V. Murti considers that Indra 'is the super-natural personality or essence activating things from within. It is an unseen presence (*parokṣa*), not overtly perceived, but felt to be the guiding and controlling spirit within' (*The Central Philosophy of Buddhism*, p. 15).

[5]Among his victories was that over the Vṛcīvans (*RV.*, VI.27,5) at Hari-yūpīyā. Wheeler suggests that the latter may be another name for Harappā (*Civilization of the Indus Valley and Beyond*, p. 78).

[6]Piggott suggests that the Vṛtra myth may refer to the destruction of the river-dams of the Indus people by the invading Āryans (*Prehistoric India*, p. 262). Cf. Heesterman, *Ancient Indian Royal Consecration*, p. 28.

[7]In *RV.* I.82,6 his power is said to be linked with his horses. The latter are usually described as bays, perhaps because such horses were favoured by the Āryans. According to Ridgeway, the Vedic horses were of Mongolian stock. The so-called tangum horses from the Tangustan Mountains of Bhotan had white legs and were marked with such large areas of bay that two or three often spread over the whole body, head and neck (*Origin and Influence of the Thoroughbred Horse*, pp. 153–4).

[8]In later literature each *manvantara* or periodic re-creation is said to have its respective Indra (*VP.*, III.2).

[9]This theistic order of precedence, which Müller calls 'henotheistic', and which is implicit in the *RV.* term 'Viśvedevas', or collective divinity, is indicated in the functional association of Indra, Agni, Mitra and Varuṇa, or in joint names such as Indra-Agni (Indrāgni) (*RV.*, I.108 and 109), Indra-Vāyu (*RV.*, I.135), or as Mitra-Varuṇa, etc.

[10]Thus in *AV.*, III.4,6 a king is addressed as a 'human Indra'. Indra makes the king victorious (IV.22,5f.); and is the maintainer of royalty (VI.87,2). v. also *ŚBr.*, V.3.1,3; X.4.1,5.

[11]*Legends in the Mahābhārata*, p. 122.

[12]According to the *Ait. Br.* (VII.28), he also conquered Vṛtra, gave the Yatis to the hyenas, contended with Bṛhaspati, etc., and for these reasons was excluded from the *soma* sacrifice by the gods.

[13]*HP.*, p. 110.

v. Śrī II; Vṛṣa; Dadhyac; Uccaiḥśravas; Indrajāla I; Indracāpa; Indradhanus; Indra-khīla; Indragopa; Indramaha; Indravrata; Indra-Varuṇa; Kapiñjala; Kutsa; Arbuda; Manyu; Sakra; Sītā I; Indra(s); Viśākha II; Airāvata.

Indracāpa Indra's bow (the rainbow).

Indradhanus Indra's bow, also called Vijaya 'victory'.

Indradyumna A pious Pāṇḍyan king devoted to Hari (Viṣṇu). Once he failed to welcome the *ṛṣi* Agastya who then cursed him to become an elephant. Subsequently he became the lord of elephants with the power to remember his past life (*Bhāg. P.*, VIII.4,7–12, *PI.*).

Indrāgni Indra and Agni conjoined. This dual form is regarded as twin brothers, handsome and wise, the sons of Dyaus and Aditi. They represent the *kṣatra* (ruling caste) and embody the Āryan ideal of heroism in battle and the 'auspicious bonds of friendship' (*RV.*, I.108,5). The fire-altar is said to belong to Indrāgni (*ŚBr.*, IX.5.2,10).

Indragopa 'Protected by Indra.' The cochineal insect which emerges from the ground after rain,[1] and hence its association with Indra as the rain-giver.

[1]*PTS.* These insects and frogs are said to be born of decomposed vegetable matter (*Suś. Saṁ.*, I, p. 12).

Indrajāla I. The 'snare' (or net) of Indra', i.e., the art of magic.[1] To frighten away an enemy army, illusions of great armies should be 'called up', or a mirage-like picture of their future defeats, as well as the appearance of immense storm clouds (*AGP.*, II, p. 870).

[1]*HP.*, p. 315. Cf. *Maitri Up.*, 4.2.

II. A weapon used by Arjuna. In Vedic warfare nets were used to entangle the enemy (*AV.*, VIII.8.5,7; 8.18).

Indrajit 'Conqueror of Indra.' An epithet applied to Meghanāda, son of Rāvaṇa king of Laṅkā. He captured Indra and refused to release him until the gods granted him (Indrajit) the gift of immortality. By the power of his *māyā* Indrajit was able to make himself invisible in battle (*MBh.*, Vana pa., 286).

v. Hanumat.

Indra-khīla 'Indra's post.' A pillar or column dedicated to Indra and placed at or before the city gate; also the name of a large slab of stone placed at the entrance of a house.[1]

[1]*PTS.*

Indraloka Indra's domain, sphere or world, to which after death go all heroic *kṣatriyas* (*VP.*, I.6), Indra

being the representative of the warrior class.
v. Loka.

Indramaha or **Indramahotsava** The raising of Indra's 'standard' (*indradhvaja*). An ancient ceremony conducted by the *purohita* for the king and celebrated as a festival (*utsava*) in parts of India, especially Orissa.

The 'standard' was a tree[1] selected from the nearby forest. After being cut down and the branches removed, it was set up in the main square seven days before the full moon of the month of *āśvina* (September–October). The base was placed in a socle braced by four clamps, and held by eight cords from the top of the standard, each cord being pegged in the earth at one of the eight points of the compass. It was lavishly decorated with white banners, mirrors, bells, garlands, fruit, etc.,[2] and formed the focal point of the festivities, being regarded as Indra himself[3] for the period of the ceremony, and addressed as Śatakratu, Vajrapāṇi, and other epithets. On the seventh or full moon day it was dismantled and taken to the river where the current carried it away.[4]

[1]According to the *Bhāratanāṭyaśāstra* it was a bamboo.

[2]Cf. the Hittite custom of erecting an evergreen with the fleece of a sheep hung on it before the god Telipinu to celebrate the return of fertility to the land. A Babylonian magical text specifies the erection of such a standard, coupled with the display of a fleece, as part of a ritual for expelling disease' (B. Meissner, *Babylonien und Assyrien*, II, p. 209 (Heidelberg 1920–5), cited by Gaster, *Thespis*, p. 313n.).

[3]Cf. Śiva's epithet Sthāṇu, 'wooden post', 'pillar'.

[4]Auboyer, *Daily Life in Ancient India*, p. 147 and n. 6; *GG*., p. 153.

v. Śakra-kumārī(s).

Indrāṇī I. Wife of Indra. She is also called Śacī (which Pischel considers was her real name in Vedic times),[1] and also Paulomī (her father being the demon Puloman). Indra chose her for his bride because of her great beauty and voluptuousness (*Tait. Br*., II.4.2.7).

[1]v. *Vedische Studien*, II, p. 52.

II. Name of the pupil of the left eye, that of the right being called *indra*.

Indraprastha 'Indra's place.' The ancient capital of the Pāṇḍavas, believed to have been situated near Old Delhi,[1] or on its site.

[1]*IRA*., App. p. 326.

Indra-Pūṣan The dual form of Indra and Pūṣan, invoked to give assistance in battle (*RV*., VII.35,1).

Indra(s) In late mythology there are many Indras, each of whom rules over the various *manvantaras*. According to the *MBh*. (Ādi pa., 199) there were five Indras of old who, when reborn on earth as men, had as their common wife the goddess Śrī. They are the five Pāṇḍu princes, and Śrī is Draupadī.

Indra-Soma The dual form of Indra and Soma whose function is to perform heroic deeds for man, invest him with great strength, and to destroy blasphemers, etc.

Indra-Soma discovered the sun and light, supported the heavens with a pillar and spread out the earth, filled the seas with water, and gave milk to cattle (*RV*., VI.72). In another hymn consisting mostly of imprecations against demons and other enemies, Indra-Soma is invoked to smite them all (VII.104).

Indrasuta 'Son of Indra.' An epithet of the monkey-king Bāli, and of Arjuna and Jayanta.

Indra-Varuṇa The dual form of Indra and Varuṇa representing heroic and kingly power. From Indra-Varuṇa comes protection, prosperity, fame, wealth and many horses (*RV*., IV.41; 42; VI.68,6).

Indra-Viṣṇu The dual form of Indra and the Vedic solar Viṣṇu, invoked to give shelter, to accept the sacrifice and give riches and unmolested pathways.

Indravrata 'Indra's rule of conduct.' One of the duties of a king, who should shower benefits on his kingdom, even as Indra showers plentiful rain (*Manu*, IX.304).
v. Kṣatra.

Indrāyudha 'Rainbow', usually a sign of good fortune, but when appearing in a cloudless sky or in the evening it is a bad omen for the State (*Matsya P*., 233.7,*PI*.).

Indrayumna v. Gajendra.

Indu[1] 'Drop' (especially of *soma*); 'spark'; and later a name for the moon.

In the *RV*. Indu is a name of Vāstoṣpati, the tutelary deity of the home (VII.54,2). In another hymn the word refers to *soma*, whose glorious drops give immortality and freedom from disease (VIII.48,3,5).

[1]The grammarian Vopadeva derives *indu* from the same root as Indra, i.e., *ind*, meaning 'to be powerful' or 'giving great power'; the *SED*. suggests the root *und*, 'to drop'. In the Brāhmaṇas *indu* is applied only to the moon but the connexion between the meaning '*soma* juice' and 'moon' in the word *indu* has led to the same two ideas being transferred in classical Sanskrit to the word *soma*, although the latter has properly only the sense of *soma* juice.

Iṅgiḍa A plant (or substance) used in magical rites to ensure the destruction of enemies. In witchcraft rites it is a substitute for ghee (*ghṛta*) (*AV*., II, p. 503; *AVB*., p. 334, n.2).

Irā I. Any drinkable fluid, especially milk. It is closely allied to *iḍā*.

II. Name of an *apsaras*, a daughter of Dakṣa and wife of Kaśyapa. Her three daughters were called Latā (creeper), Vallī (creeping plant) and Vīrudhā (a plant which grows again after having been cut). These children became the mothers of trees, plants and shrubs (*Brah. P.*, III.7,459–63, 468; *Matsya P.*, 6.2 and 46, etc., *PI.*).

Irāvatī I. A name of Durgā as wife of Rudra.

II. A Himālayan river (the Rāvī) sacred to the *pitṛs*.

III. Name of a daughter of Krodhavaśā and wife of Pulaha. She became the mother of the four royal (or divine) elephants viz., Airāvaṇa (Airāvata), Kumuda, Añjana and Vāmana.

Īśā The name of the shortest of the thirteen principal Upaniṣads, 'so-called from its first word; or sometimes "Īśāvāsyam" from its first two words'.[1]

[1]Hume, *TPU.*, p. 362.

Īśāna I. 'Ruler,' 'Master', 'Lord', from the root *īś*, 'to have power; an epithet of one of the eight forms of Agni,[1] associating his sovereign quality with that of the Sun, the ruler of all. Thus it is said of Agni that henceforth he can have no greater name than Īśāna (*ŚBr.*, VI.1.3,17). Īśāna represents the total potentiality of all knowledge and presides over all forms (*Śvet. Up.*, IV.11; V.2).

[1]Also an epithet of Śiva 'who presides over the north-eastern region [and who] is often concerned with various aspects of fecundation' (Gonda, *Aspects*, p. 250, n.76).

v. Īśvara.

II. Name of the fifth face of the five-faced Śiva 'which is beyond the comprehension of even the *yogis*'.[1]

[1]*DHI.*, pp. 460, 573.

v. Īśvara.

Īśānā An epithet of Durgā.

v. Īśāna.

Iṣṭadevatā The main deity of a temple, family or cult; or the deity 'chosen' by the individual worshipper,[1] and thus is never regarded as unique. After the abstruse speculations of the Upaniṣads the masses felt the need for a personal god, and hence arose the notion of the *iṣṭadevatās* as 'aids' or 'guides' to assist the worshipper to attain his final goal, the impersonal *brahman*. As the devotees are in different stages of spiritual growth so their worship will vary from an elementary to an advanced stage.[2]

[1]Cf. the ancient Egyptian word *netjer* which may mean 'a god, the god, or the Supreme God', hence the 'exact meaning is "the god with whom you have to reckon in the circumstances" ... the relation of the Egyptian [worshipper] to the god ... at a given moment, was, temporarily, almost exclusive of all others' (Frankfort, *Ancient Egyptian Religion*, pp. 67, 76).

[2]Eliade suggests that the 'need for a mystical devotion to personal or local divinities' is an aboriginal trait (*Yoga*, p. 361).

Iṣṭāpūrta 'Stored-up sacrificial rites'. The accumulated merit of the sacrifices offered during one's lifetime, believed to accrue to the dead.

v. Dakṣiṇā, n.2.

Iṣu The commonest word for arrow (*RV.*, II.24,8, etc.), and regarded as synonymous with *śarya*, *śārī* and *bāṇa*. The bow-string (*jyā*) consisted of a thong of cow-hide, which was drawn back to the ear when discharging the arrow. It measured five spans (three feet) according to the *ŚBr.* (VI.5.2,10). In *RV.* times a single quiver (*iṣudhi*) was worn slung on the back, but later two quivers were customary.

The arrow-head was made of deer-horn or metal and sometimes smeared with poison (*RV.*, VI.75,15; *AV.*, IV.6, etc.), though this practice was later condemned in the *Manusmṛti*. That the bow (*dhanus*) was the most highly regarded of the warrior's possessions is indicated in many early texts, and the arrow was often invoked for protection.[1] Even in death, the bow which was placed in the right hand of the dead warrior was removed only as the final act of the funeral rite (*RV.*, X.18,9).

[1]The commentator Durga states that 'certain arrows possess the power of pursuing even an invisible enemy and of discrimination in attack' (*Nir.*, p. 145, n.4). v. also Singh, *Ancient Indian Warfare*, p. 94.

v. Bāṇa I.

Īśvara 'Lord.' From the root *īś*, 'to have power'.[1] In the earliest Vedic literature *īśvara* denotes the power of a ruler, lord or master. In the *AV.* (VII.102,1) the word denotes divine power, and in XIX.6,4 it is a title of the Cosmic Puruṣa as lord (Īśvara) of immortality. Subsequently—after the final recension of the *Manusmṛti* and *Bhagavadgītā*—Īśvara was 'used almost exclusively in the sense of Parameśvara'.[2] In some late sectarian texts Īśvara and Īśāna are applied synonymously to Śiva.[3] Though Patañjali,[4] in his presentation of the Sāṁkhya and Yoga systems as a single philosophy, used the title Īśvara it lacked the comprehensive significance of the Hindu non-sectarian term Īśvara, signifying 'God'.[5]

[1]Īśāna is from the same root. v. also Gonda, *VS.*, pp. 19f. and p. 40 for the cult of Īśāna.

[2]M.D. Shastri. 'History of the Word Īśvara and its Idea', (*All India Oriental Conference*, VII. Baroda, pp. 492ff.).

[3]*PTR.*, p. 68.

[4]The significance of Patañjali's concept of Īśvara is fully discussed by Eliade, *Yoga*, pp. 74ff.

[5]Specifically the 'God' of yogins cannot be invoked by rituals, incantations or devotion, for he is the Absolute. Thus Īśvara is 'an archetype of the yogin ... [and] probably a patron of certain yogic sects' (Eliade, op. cit., p. 75). Later Īśvara represents ultimate reality

which *māyā* obscures.

Īśvaragītā The 'Song of the Lord'. The name of the first eleven chapters of the second part of the *Kūrma P.*, which are devoted to Śiva. The *Īśvaragītā* is directly inspired by the *BG*. It extols Viṣṇu but regards Śiva as the supreme deity.

Itarajana 'Other folk', a euphemism for secret or hidden spirits or *yakṣas* (*AV.*, VIII.10,28).

Itihāsa (= *iti-ha-āsa*, 'so indeed it was'.) A class of 'literature' of a popular character, associated with another class called '*purāṇa*' (not to be confused with the post-Vedic Purāṇas). Both *itihāsas* and proto-*purāṇas* were current in the early Vedic period, but were apparently not of sufficient importance to be generally included in the *RV.*, though it appears to allude to some of them, and even to include a complete story, i.e., the gambler's lament (*RV.*, X.34). The earliest references to *itihāsa* and proto-*purāṇa* occur in the *AV.* (XV.6,4, *et seq.*) and to *itihāsa* alone in the *Bṛhad-Ār. Up.* (II.4,10, etc.). The *Chān. Up.* (III.4,1,2, etc.) declares that *itihāsas* and proto-*purāṇas* constitute a fifth Veda, while the *Śāṅkhāyana Śrauta sūtra* (XVI.2.21,27) regards them as two distinct Vedas, as does the *ŚBr.* (XIII.4.3, 12–13). The *Tait. Br.* (II.9) also regards them as two classes of literature.[1]

[1] *VI.*, vol. I, pp. 76f.

J

Jabālā Mother of a natural son, Satyakāma Jābāla, who despite his lowly caste was accepted as a pupil by the *ṛṣi* Hāridrumata Gautama (*Chān. Up.*, 4.4,1–5).
v. Varṇa.

Jābāli The name of the priest of Rāma's father Daśaratha, King of Ayodhyā. After the king's death Jābāli tried unsuccessfully to induce Rāma to assert his right to the throne, using arguments common to the Lokāyatikas or Materialists. Jābāli contended that now Rāma's father was dead, traditional sacrifices like the *ekoddiṣṭha śrāddha* were mere artifices, invented to dupe people into making gifts to the priestly officiants. But Rāma denounced these views as being inconsistent with tradition and established institutions, which was undoubtedly true, but was not perhaps an adequate answer to Jābāli's assertions. Instead, Rāma's reply is made the excuse for a homily concerning 'eternal and universal truths of abiding ethical interest'.[1]

[1]*IRA.*, p. 182.

Jaḍa I. 'Insentient.' The highest stage of yogic concentration, in which the yogin becomes 'insentient' i.e., completely detached from the false discrimination between things, especially of 'fictional' opposites, such as pain and pleasure, success and failure, existence and non-existence, etc. *Jaḍa* may be equated with '*vidyā*, true knowledge, the synoptic vision of the whole; it is genuine "con-ception", "gathering-together", "consciousness" in its literal sense of "knowing-together" all things however apparently different and divergent. *Avidyā* then, like *māyā*, is the fiction of separation'.[1]

Yogins, while recognizing the apparent duality of the empirical, and the polarity of all concepts arising from intellectual processes, strive to reach the non-dual state of *jaḍa*.

[1]Heimann, *IWP.*, pp. 94f.

II. A quality of matter.

Jagad-dhātrī 'Sustainer of the world.' An epithet of Pārvatī and Sarasvatī, etc.

Jagad-Gaurī 'The fairest in the world.' An epithet of Pārvatī.

Jaganmātṛ 'World-mother.' An epithet of Durgā and Lakṣmī.

Jagannātha 'Lord of the World.'[1] A form of Kṛṣṇa. The chief centre of Jagannātha's worship is the great temple complex at Purī, Orissa. Three wooden statues of Jagannātha, his brother Balarāma and his sister Subhadrā are enshrined in the main sanctum. Every twelve years the statues are renewed 'and the old ones are buried underground in an unfrequented part of the extensive temple compound'.[2]

The temple was originally Buddhist and probably dedicated to a Buddhist tooth relic[3] or perhaps to the bone relics of a great Arhat. Its origin may account for the freedom from caste restrictions for all who come to worship there. Its Buddhist origin is also confirmed by the adaptation of the 'Three Jewels of Buddhism', viz., the Buddha, Dharma and Saṅgha, to conform with Hindu ideas. Thus the Buddha became Upaya (the male principle); the Dharma, Prajñā (the female principle); and Saṅgha the phenomenal world, the product of the male and female principles.

Although Kṛṣṇa is usually depicted as a very handsome youth, as Jagannātha his image is repulsively ugly. Various myths have grown up to explain this, including the following: a fowler called Bāsu found Jagannātha in the form of a blue-stone image at the foot of a banyan tree.[4] Another myth states that Kṛṣṇa was killed by a hunter and his body left to rot under a tree. Some people found his remains and placed the bones in a box. Then Viṣṇu directed King Indradyumna to make an image of Jagannātha and to put the bones in it.[5] Viśvakarman, the architect of the gods, undertook to make the image on condition that he was undisturbed until it was finished, but after fifteen days the King could contain his curiosity no longer, so Viśvakarman left the image in an unfinished state without arms or legs. In response to the King's plea to make the statue famous, Brahmā gave it eyes and a 'soul' and also acted as high priest at its consecration. The image at Purī perpetuates this tradition by representing Jagannātha as a crudely-carved block of wood, though in some temples arms and legs have been added by the priests.

At the Lion's Gate of the Jagannātha temple a man of the sweeper caste strikes the pilgrims with his broom to purify them of their 'sins'. He also makes them promise never to disclose the secrets of the shrine.[6]

The great Ratha-yātra festival takes place in the month *āṣāḍha* (June–July) when the three images are brought out on the Juggernaut and pulled through the streets by devotees. People are sometimes killed in the dense crowds trying to touch or get near the Juggernaut, and occasionally those with suicidal tendencies, or in great pain and misery have chosen death under its wheels, but this is completely opposed to the spirit of Vaiṣṇavism.

[1]A title also applied to Dattātreya and to Rāma as *avatāras* of Viṣṇu.

[2]*DHI.*, pp. 211f.

[3]*BH.*, p. 59, n.1.

[4]W.W. Hunter, *Orissa*, I, pp. 89f.

[5]This is against usual Vaiṣṇava practice as any part of a corpse is considered unclean.

[6]Hunter, op. cit., I, p. 142, cited by Crooke, *Religion and Folklore of Northern India*, p. 137.

Jagatī Name of a metre of 4 × 12 syllables. According to the commentator Durga, it 'spreads like the waves of water'.[1] It is said to have emerged from Brahmā's western mouth (*VP.*, I.5). Jagatī is associated with consecration and with sacrificial animals (*Tait. Saṁ.*, VI.1.6,1).

[1]The *Nir.*, 7.13 states it has 'the gait of an aquatic animal'. It is said to have entered all the gods together (*RV.*, X.130,5).

v. Gāyatrī; Bṛhati; Triṣṭubh; Virāj II.

Jāhnavī v. Jahnu.

Jahnu A *maharṣi* and the ancestor of the Kuśikas. He and his family were especially favoured by the Aśvins (*RV.*, I.116,19; III.58,6).

A prince of the same name once drank up the waters of the Ganges because they had flooded his sacrificial ground. The gods and *ṛṣis* then propitiated him and re-obtained the personified Ganges (Gaṅgā) from him as his daughter (whence she is called Jāhnavī).

Jaimini The name of a famous sage and of various authors. The *Mīmāṁsā Sūtras* are attributed to a Jaimini, as is a part of the *Sāmaveda*, but as they are of widely divergent dates, they cannot possibly be by the same hand. Again there is a *Gṛhya Sūtra* attributed to a Jaimini, which is relatively late, and also an astrological treatise of quite recent date.[1] Another Jaimini was a noted Kanarese author whose translation of the Aśvamedha pa. of the *MBh.* is regarded as the finest extant specimen of Kanarese poetry.

[1]*CI.*, vol. II. p. 402.

v. Darśana; Pūrva-Mīmāṁsā: Vedānta.

Jaina 'Relating to the Jinas', $\sqrt{ji}$ 'victorious'. Jainism is one of the three 'heterodox' Indian *darśanas* which rejected the Veda as an infallible source of knowledge. Jainism was 'founded' about the time of the closing of the three-Veda corpus and the composition of the earliest Āraṇyakas and Upaniṣads, when speculation in India and elsewhere was turning away from mythical to rational explanations of man's own nature and that of his environment. But Jainism, like Buddhism, owes its origin more to historical and geographical conditions (referred to below) than to brahmanic speculation.

Jainism soon became a celibate Order of itinerant monks, noted for extreme asceticism, but which split into two sections, one being known as Digambara (Sky-clad), whose self-denying ordinances excluded even the wearing of clothes. The other section, the Śvetāmbara (White-robed), was less extreme in its interpretation of self-denial. As the dispute was one of discipline and convention rather than of doctrine the Digambaras later adopted clothing and the two sections were re-united.

It is generally conceded that some Jaina views have influenced Vaiṣṇavism in particular, and perhaps Hinduism in general, but a clear-cut indication of such influence is difficult owing to the lack of a uniform terminology. Thus the Vedāntins use '*ātman*' in a very special sense, the Buddhists in another, while the Jainas avoid it altogether, using instead the term '*jīva*' to denote 'soul'. These terminological differences were initially aggravated by those of language, the Jainas using Ardha-māgadhī, the Buddhists Pāli. The orthodox *darśanas* used Sanskrit. But this situation was later remedied when the use of Sanskrit became general, though technical terms like *ātman*, *jīva*, *guṇa*, etc., remained unco-ordinated.

Besides the above differences between 'orthodox' and 'heterodox' schools there were others of an ethnic and political nature. Whereas the 'orthodox' schools expressed priestly views, those of the Jainas (and Buddhists) mainly represented the views of *kṣatriya* leaders. The former were developed in north-western India, in an environment very different from that of the north-east, which at the time of the founding of Jainism (and Buddhism) was less 'brahmanized' than the north-west. These differences, initially slight, resulted in the establishment of Jainism and Buddhism as two well-organized monastic institutions, each with its own educational centres catering for thousands of students from all parts of India, Further India and China.

Of the twenty-four Jaina teachers (*tīrthaṅkaras*) only two are generally regarded as historical. These are Pārśvanātha (c. 8th cent. B.C.) and Vardhamāna, styled Mahāvīra (great hero) a contemporary of the Buddha (6th cent. B.C.). Vardhamāna was born near Vaiśālī and belonged to the Nāya clan, called Nāta in Pā. or Jñātṛ in Skt. His parents were Siddhārtha, a wealthy nobleman, and Triśalā, sister of Ceṭaka, an eminent prince of Vaiśālī. Jainism takes its name from the epithet Jina (conqueror) which was applied to all *tīrthaṅkaras*, who were considered to have conquered all passions (*rāga* and *dveṣa*), and attained liberation (*kaivalya* or *nirvāṇa*). Mahāvīra claimed to be no more than the successor and co-ordinator of the teaching of Pārśva and his predecessors.

In common with the other *darśanas*, Jaina philosophy begins with an examination of the sources of knowledge (*pramāṇas*), viz., perception, inference, and the authoritative testimony of its Canonical literature. The Jaina criterion of epistemological validity is whether or not knowledge and its product comprised a harmonious equation. Thus knowledge is subject to critical appraisal, and every aspect of an object considered before a judgment (*naya*) is made. Owing to the complex nature of objects and the impossibility of absolute cognition, many judgments must of necessity be relative. Jainism therefore maintains that every judgment should be prefixed by '*syāt*', meaning 'somehow', 'in some respect', an assertion not unlike the aupaniṣadic use of 'as if, 'as it were' (*iva*).[1] *Syādvāda* insists that because human judgment has often to rely on incomplete knowledge, such judgment may be valid only of a particular aspect of an object.

Jaina philosophy, like that of the Sāṁkhya, though superficially pluralistic, is basically dualistic. The universe is divided into two eternal, uncreated, co-existent categories—the 'soul' (*jīva*) and the 'non-soul' (*ajīva*)'.[2] Though independent, the 'soul' and the 'non-soul' when conjoined are a psycho-somatic whole. This dualistic theory is applied to ethics, where *karman*, representing the residuum of all activity of a positive or negative nature, is the link between 'soul' and body. The negative is thus considered to retard the destruction of the ethically bad, the positive to expedite the conquest of the 'soul' over the desires of the body, and finally lead to the attainment of *nirvāṇa*.

Jaina dualistic theory classifies substance (*dravya*), the indefinable stuff of which the universe consists,[3] as organic (*jīva*) and inorganic (*ajīva*), a distinction common to the other Realistic schools. The inorganic is itself incapable of extension or diminution, except by external means. On the other hand, all living organisms (*jīva*) are capable of self-extension, of evolution, and are individually distinguished by the degree of their respective sense-faculties, which may vary from two (with worms) to five (with humans). Thus, because *jīva* is common to all living organisms, whether their consciousness is rudimentary or highly evolved, life is a unity, a belief that Jainism shares with Buddhism and Hinduism, but which as expressed in the doctrine of *ahiṁsā* (non-injury) is perhaps more closely adhered to by the Jainas.

Jaina cosmological theory is based on the concept of universal unity. Though substance is by its nature regarded as eternal and unchanging, it is also the medium of circumstantial, changing modes (*paryāyas*). Without these modes or mutations substance would be only an abstraction; without them the process of origination, decay, and further origination would cease.

In Jainism as in all the *darśanas*, except perhaps the Cārvāka, philosophy demands perfect faith (*samyag-darśana*) which is of value only as a means to the attainment of right knowledge (*samyag-jñāna*), which in turn is of value only if it leads to right conduct (*samyak-cāritra*), and frees the 'soul' from its sensuous fetters and finally leads to the attainment of perfection. The consummation of these three ideals; faith, right knowledge, and right conduct, are called the three gems (*triratna*) of Jaina ethics, the essence of its philosophy.

Jainism probably represents 'in its fundamental tenets one of the oldest modes of thought known to us, the idea that all nature, even that which seems to be most inanimate, possesses life and the capability of reanimation; and this doctrine the Jains have, with inflexible conservatism, kept until modern times'.[4]

[1] *Bṛhad-Ār. Up.*, 2.4,14.
[2] J. Jaini, *Principles of Jainism*, p. xxii. For yoga and Jainism, v. R. Williams, *Jaina Yoga*.
[3] Cf. the Sāṁkhya '*prakṛti*'.
[4] *CHI.*, I. p. 161.

Jaitraratha 'Car of Victory.' The name of Indra's chariot, which as lightning or as a meteor descends to earth with a thunderous noise. It is decorated with gold and drawn by golden or peacock-hued steeds; contains all weapons, and above it on a yellow staff flies Indra's dark-blue standard, symbolizing victory (*MBh.*, 3.42, 8 and 30, *EM.*).

Jaladhijā 'Ocean-born.' An epithet of Lakṣmī.

Jālapāda Finger and toe membranes, included among the distinguishing 'marks' or 'signs' of divine beings.[1]
[1] Cf. the thirty-two divine marks of the Buddha.
v. Lakṣaṇa

Jalaśāyin 'Reposing on the waters.' An allusion to Viṣṇu who sleeps upon his serpent-couch on the waters during the devolution of the world.
v. Śeṣa.

Jala-turaga v. Jalebha.

Jalebha or **Jala-hastin** The mythical water-elephant, often depicted with the water-horse (*jala-turaga*), as the vehicles (*vāhanas*) of *yakṣas* and *yakṣīs*. The *jalebha*, *makara*, *yakṣa*, or mouth or navel, or brimming vase all symbolize the waters as the source of life.[1]
[1] Coomaraswamy, *Yakṣas*, pt. ii, p. 50. Cf. the horse-headed aquatic monsters of Celtic mythology called Goborchinn. Belief in a water-spirit in the form of a horse still persists in Scotland and in Ireland (Lady

Gregory, *Visions and Beliefs in the West of Ireland*, pp. 21ff.).

Jamadagni[1] A Vedic sage, possibly one of Viśvāmitra's friends (*RV*., III.62,18; X.167,4, etc.).[2] Apart from these brief references little is known of him. He may have been a member of the priestly family of that name, mentioned in the sole *RV*. reference to them (III.53, 15–16). The *Ait. Br.* (VII. 27 and 34) and the *ŚBr*., (XIII.5.4,1) refer to a person called Jamadagni, better known as Pārikṣita 'descendant of Parikṣit'. Except for the name there is no evidence of any connexion between the two families.

Nonetheless, this slender information provided the basis for a series of Paurāṇic legends. Thus in the *VP*. (III.1) Jamadagni is designated one of the seven great *ṛṣis* of the present *manvantara*. But according to another legend he was a Bhārgava, the son of Ṛcīka (a descendant of Bhṛgu) and Satyavatī, daughter of Gādhi, King of Kānyakubja. This Jamadagni married Reṇukā (daughter of Prasenajit) who uncomplainingly shared his ascetic life, though this did not preclude her from bearing her husband five sons, of whom only Paraśurāma the youngest achieved fame.

During the absence of the sons at work in the fields, Reṇukā went to a stream nearby to bathe, but while seeking a secluded spot she caught sight of a neighbouring prince and his wife disporting themselves in the stream, and was envious of their uninhibited pleasure. The narrator of the incident states that she was 'defiled by unworthy thoughts', and though she bathed according to the customary rites, the water failed to purify her. On her return to the hermitage her husband observed her agitation, and on learning the cause of it was 'exceedingly wroth', regarding her as 'fallen from perfection, and shorn of the lustre of her sanctity'. Four of their sons returned shortly after and were each successively commanded by their father to put their mother to death. They were horrified by the command, whereupon their father cursed them to be idiots for the rest of their lives. When Paraśurāma returned the 'mighty and holy' Jamadagni commanded him to kill his mother because she had sinned. Paraśurāma accordingly struck off his mother's head with his axe (*paraśu*) and thus assuaged his father's wrath. His father commended him for his obedience and promised him any boon he desired. Paraśurāma thereupon asked that his mother's life might be restored; that she should not only be freed from the stigma of defilement, but also that no reference should ever be made to it; that his brothers should be given back their normal senses; and finally for himself the granting of longevity and invincibility in single combat (*MBh*., Vana pa., 106).

Other stories are related dealing with the theft of Jamadagni's sacred calf (the offspring of Surabhi, the Cow of Plenty); the murder of the sage by the sons of Kārtavīrya; and Paraśurāma's revenge.

[1]The *HCIP*. (I, p. 280) considers Jamadagni to be a historical figure, but as tradition is neither consistent with itself nor with the various legends, no clear portrait of the sage emerges from either source.

[2]The *Tait. Saṁ*. (III.1.7,3) states that Jamadagni and Viśvāmitra quarrelled with Vasiṣṭha.

Jāmbavat The King of the Bears (an aboriginal tribe) who assisted Rāma in his invasion of Laṅkā. According to the Rāmāyaṇa he travelled over the earth twenty-one times at the request of the gods to gather the herbs from which ambrosia (*amṛta*) was made.

Prasena who was guarding the sun-jewel syamantaka for his brother Satrājit, was killed by a lion who carried it off in his mouth. It was later stolen by a second lion which was in turn killed by Jāmbavat who took the jewel for himself. As it was known that Kṛṣṇa had always coveted the gem he was therefore suspected of having killed Prasena, but Kṛṣṇa discovered what had happened and attacked Jāmbavat in his cave. A fearful fight ensued, lasting for twenty-one days, until Jāmbavat finally admitted Kṛṣṇa's superiority, gave up the jewel and presented his daughter Jāmbavatī to Kṛṣṇa in marriage (*VP*., IV.12). The *AGP*. (275, 40–4) has a different version.

Jāmbavatī v. Jāmbavat.

Jambha 'Crusher.' The name of several demons, sometimes identified with *daityas* or *dānavas* in the *VP*. (IV.6). The *MBh*. describes them as 'disturbers of sacrifices'.

Jambhalā A *rākṣasī* who induces pregnancy if meditated upon by women.

Jambudvīpa The name of one of the seven great insular continents, each of which is surrounded by one of the seven seas of salt water (*lāvaṇa*), sugar-cane juice (*ikṣu*), wine (*surā*), clarified butter (*sarpi* or *ghṛta*), curds (*dadhi*), milk (*dugdha*), and fresh water (*jala*), all of which represent fertility and abundance. Jambudvīpa[1] is the central continent, i.e., India, and in its centre is situated the golden mountain Meru (*VP*., II.2). An enormous *jambu* tree (the rose-apple tree, Eugenia jambolana) is said to be visible on Mount Meru.

[1]Vedic writers called India Pṛthivī (Earth), but later it was called Jambudvīpa. Bharati (*TT*., p. 60) states that Jambudvīpa is merely the generic name for the regions adjacent to India in the north, north-east, east, and south-east, with India at the centre.

Jambuvṛkṣa The *jambu* tree (Eugenia jambolana). It is a wish-granting tree (*kalpavṛkṣa*), whose branches

reach the sky; it is a favourite resort of *ṛṣis*.
v. Pārijāta; Jambudvīpa.

Jāmi A goddess of femininity or maternity.

Janaka I. A Solar Dynasty king of Mithilā, who was produced by attrition from the body of his predecessor Nimi. This act was carried out by a number of *ṛṣis* who gave him this name, signifying that he was born without a progenitor.

II. King of Videha and the father of Sītā. His daughter sprang fully formed from the furrow (*sītā*) which the king had ritually ploughed when preparing a sacrifice to obtain offspring, and hence his epithet, Śīradhvaja (He of the plough-banner). He is notable not only as a just ruler and a man of great piety but also as a supporter of the claim that a pious *kṣatriya* is as fully qualified to perform sacrifices as a member of the priestly class (*Bṛhad-Ār. Up.*, III.1,1). This view was apparently shared by his priestly adviser Yājñavalkya, for both are traditionally regarded as archetypes of the liberalism current in Videha and the adjoining kingdoms, reflected centuries later by the response of their descendants to the views of the Jaina Mahāvīra and the Buddha Śākyamuni.
v. Gārgī.

Janaloka Name of one of the upper 'worlds' (*lokas*) where dwell good men and Brahmā's mind-born sons (*VP.*, II.7).

Janamejaya The name of a king, a descendant of Parikṣit. He is mentioned in the *ŚBr.* (XI.5.5,13) as the owner of horses, and in (XIII.5.4,1–3) as a performer of an *aśvamedha.*[1] According to one tradition he was the son of Puru, the youngest son of Yayāti and Śarmiṣṭhā, and ruler of the kingdom of Pratiṣṭhana.[2]

The Purāṇas and the *MBh.* refer to two Janamejaya Pārikṣitas, one a grandson of Kuru and ancestor of the Pāṇḍavas; the other a grandson of Arjuna and therefore a descendant of the Pāṇḍavas. Owing to the similarity of the names of the brothers[3] of both Janamejayas, the two traditions have apparently been syncretized, so that little reliance can be placed on either. Moreover, any historical value they might have is further bedevilled by the confusion of Nāga, the name of the hostile tribes by whom Parakṣit was killed, and *nāga*, a name for snake. Thus legend declares that to avenge Parakṣit's death Janamejaya 'sacrificed' (i.e., killed) every Nāga tribesman or snake (*nāga* or *sarpa*) he came across, and hence his epithet Sarpasattrin, 'Serpent sacrificer'. Only the intervention of the *ṛṣi* Āstīka prevented their extermination.[4]

One legend of Janamejaya is not without a sly hint of humour. It relates how the king, having committed brahminicide, a crime far more heinous than that of regicide, was condemned to listen to a recital by Vaiśampāyana of the entire *Mahābhārata*!

[1] *VI.*, vol. I, p. 273.
[2] *HCIP.*, vol. I, p. 274.
[3] This similarity, repeated by other authorities, 'appears to be an error', as the sons referred to are those of the later Parikṣit' (Wilson, *VP.*, p. 365, n.1).
[4] Cf. the legend of St. Patrick's extermination of snakes in Ireland.

Janārdana 'Giver of rewards.' One of the twenty-four *avatāras* of Viṣṇu. Janārdana takes the form of the planets[1] and gives the 'fruits' (i.e., consequences of their actions) to living beings. As the 'one god' he takes the names of Brahmā, Viṣṇu or Śiva according to whether he creates, preserves or destroys (*VP.*, I.2).

[1] As the planets must necessarily precede the beings who live on them, they determine the background of the world in which the individual develops. From the point of view of mankind they are divinities and connected with the *avatāras* of Viṣṇu. Those 'beings in whom the spiritual element is predominant are the celestial wanderers, the planets, while those in whom the life element predominates are the living beings' (*Bṛhat Parāśara Horā*, 1.26,31, cited by Daniélou, *HP.*, p. 166). The planets are believed to be conscious and to possess the power to act, each having a presiding deity whom they obey (Karapātrī, 'Śrī Viṣṇu tattva', cited by Daniélou, op. cit.).

Jaṅgiḍa A tree (Terminalia benghalensis) whose wood is regarded as a powerful amulet, capable of protecting animals as well as men, and of destroying the power of witches (*AV.*, II.4; etc.). It also has curative properties and prolongs life.

In the beginning the gods made a most excellent remedy from the *jaṅgiḍa* which the *ṛṣis*, whilst uttering Indra's[1] name, bestowed upon men (*AV.*, XIX.35,1).

[1] Indra gave the *jaṅgiḍa* its protective and curative powers (*AV.*, XIX.34.9).

Japa The repetition of a *mantra* or prayer, either verbally or mentally, accompanied by meditation on one's 'chosen deity' (*iṣṭadevatā*), or by a *maṇḍala* or *yantra*.

Jara 'Becoming old'[1] Kṛṣṇa, after the Bhārata war, retired to the solitude of the forest where he finally died, or as metaphorically expressed in legend he was killed by an arrow from the bow of a hunter called Jara, who mistook him for a deer (*VP.*, V.37).

[1] Personified as a daughter of Death (Mṛtyu).

Jarā A flesh-eating *rākṣasī*, capable of changing her form at will. She was generally propitiated and called Gṛhadevī (goddess of the household). Banerjea considers that there is a resemblance between Jarā and the Buddhist *yakṣiṇī* Hārītī.[1]

Pictures of Jarā as a young woman surrounded by children are painted or carved on a wall of the house to ensure the prosperity of the household, and to protect it from every calamity. But her duties as protectress of the household did not preclude her from carrying out at night her macabre habit of eating the remains of corpses left at cross-roads.

An obscure myth refers to her having found a still-born child, born in two parts, or according to another myth to two children, each lacking an ear, eye, leg or arm, who were left at a cross-roads. As she put them together, preparatory to taking them to her den, the parts of the two dead children became a single lusty child whom Jarā presented to the childless king of Magadha who named the child Jarāsandha 'joined by Jarā'.

[1] *DHI.*, p. 380.

Jarāsandha Lit. 'united by Jarā', a reference to an obscure myth relating to a *rākṣasī* called Jarā. But there appear to have been several notable men called Jarāsandha.

Traditional history refers to Jarāsandha as king of Magadha, one of the most powerful monarchs of his time. He twice waged war against the Yādavas, led by Kṛṣṇa, who after the second attack was forced to retire with his forces to Dvārakā.[1]

Soon afterwards Jarāsandha's power was challenged by the equally powerful Yudhiṣṭhira, the eldest of the five Pāṇḍu princes, who announced his intention of performing the *rājasūya* sacrifice, denoting his assumption of imperial status. Yudhiṣṭhira's envoys informed Jarāsandha of the forthcoming ceremony, at the same time demanding release of the kings he held captive. Jarāsandha refused and was challenged to a duel by one of the envoys, Yudhiṣṭhira's brother Bhīma, who after a long and bloody fight finally killed his opponent with his bare hands. The subsequent dismemberment of Jarāsandha's empire and the additions of parts of it to the Pāṇḍava domains aroused the jealousy of the Kauravas, and finally resulted in the great Bhārata war.

[1] According to legend, Jarāsandha flung a mace ninety-nine leagues, from Girivraja to Gadāvasāna, a metaphorical allusion, indicating that Śaivism 'flourished in the North (Kashmir) and East (Benāras, Magadha), as opposed to Kṛṣṇaism (Mathurā to Surat)' (*EM.*, p. 226).

v. Vipracitti.

Jaratkāru A *ṛṣi* and great ascetic. A *MBh.* story describes his austerities as being so great that when on a journey round the world he lived on air only and never slept. Whilst on this journey he came upon a pit or well, from the top of which some men were suspended head down, supported only by a rope of *vīraṇa* fibre, which was gradually being gnawed through by a rat. On enquiring who they were he was astounded to learn that they were his own forebears, for whose plight he was responsible, owing to his having no son to perform the *ekoddiṣṭha* rites and thus ensure the continuity of the family. The single rope represented the son he lacked, so that if he remained childless his ancestors would fall into the pit, never to attain the realm of the *pitṛs*.

Reluctant to forsake his ascetic life, and yet unwilling to leave his ancestors to their fate, Jaratkāru agreed to marry, but on two conditions: the first that his bride should have the same name as himself, the second that her father should not require a bride-price. These unusual conditions were fulfilled when Vāsuki, a Nāga king, offered his youngest sister, Jaratkāru as a gift to the *ṛṣi*, who married her and subsequently had a son by her called Āstīka.

v. Gotra; Pravara.

Jaṭā The state of the hair when left in a matted condition as a sign of mourning. It is also a characteristic of ascetics and especially of Śiva as the great yogin. Śiva's *jaṭā* represents also Vāyu (the wind-god), who in turn represents the subtle form of *soma*; its manifested form being the celestial Ganges which flows down upon Śiva's head.[1]

[1] *HP.*, p. 215.

Jaṭādhara 'Wearing the *jaṭā*.' An epithet of Śiva.

Jaṭāsura A *rākṣasa* who in the guise of a *brāhmaṇa* carried off Yudhiṣṭhira, Sahadeva, Nakula and Draupadī, because he wished to obtain the weapons of the Pāṇḍavas. He was killed by Bhīma (*MBh.*, Vana pa., 156).

Jātavedas A common Vedic epithet of Agni. In the *Bhāg. P.* (V.20,16–17) the word refers specifically to Agni's birth from the fire-sticks (*araṇis*). He is later called the son of Purūravas, who is said to have made fire threefold (*VP.*, IV.6).[1] The meaning of the word *jātavedas* varies but generally has the sense of 'all-knowing', 'possessing wisdom', etc.[2] The functions of Jātavedas vary considerably. In the *AV.* (VII.35,1) he is invoked to prevent an enemy's wife from having children; in the *MBh.* (3.134,27, *EM.*) to spare the houses of the good from being destroyed by fire; and in other texts to act beneficently or protect his worshippers from maleficent activities.

The *Kena Up.* (3–4) contains an allegory in which the Vedic gods are called upon to testify to their knowledge of *brahman*, but Agni (Jātavedas) and Vāyu failed to give satisfactory answers. Indra alone succeeded.

[1] Purūravas was probably the promulgator of some important ritual innovations.

[2]According to the *Nir.*, 7.19 (v. also *Bṛhadd.*, I.91–3) Jātavedas knows all created beings, or is known to all beings, or he pervades all beings. The same work mentions a Brāhmaṇa passage (as yet untraced) which states that as soon as he was born he 'found the cattle' and hence in all seasons the cattle move towards him. Also in the *Nir.* (7,20) he is said to be the overcomer of all obstacles confronting his worshippers.

v. Gārhapatya.

Jaṭāyu or **Jaṭāyus** A chief of the Gṛdha (Vulture) tribe.[1] Jaṭāyu and another chief called Sampāti attempted to intercept Rāvaṇa on his journey back to Laṅkā with Rāma's wife Sītā whom he had abducted. But Rāvaṇa wounded Jaṭāyu and left him to die in the forest, where Rāma and Lakṣmaṇa found him. He told them of his encounter with Rāvaṇa, assuring them that Sītā was still alive, and indicating the direction taken by her abductor (*MBh.*, Vana pa., 277). Rāma and Lakṣmaṇa performed the last rites for the heroic Jaṭāyu, who from the ashes of the funeral pyre ascended to the heavens in a fiery chariot.

[1]Some of the ancient Indian nomadic tribes were named after birds on account of their migratory habits (A.C. Das, *Ṛgvedic India*, p. 148).

v. Ratnaśikhaṇḍa.

Jāti Birth or social status based on lineage. *Jāti* is one of the conditions which determines the position of the individual or family in the caste system. In theory *jāti* is inflexible, but in practice exceptions were made; thus it was possible by performing great austerities (*tapas*) for a *kṣatriya* to become a *brāhmaṇa*; even a *śūdra*, like the 'illegitimate' Satyakāma Jābāla, was accepted as a pupil (*brahmacārin*) by the *ṛṣi* Hāridrumata Gautama (*Chān. Up.*, IV.4,1–5).

v. Varṇa; Kula; Gotra.

Jaṭilā Also called Śabarī. A woman greatly skilled in Vedic knowledge. She voluntarily burnt herself to death in the hope of being re-united with her teachers in the other world (*Rām.*, III.73–4).

Jaya One of the two gatekeepers of Viṣṇu's palace, the other being Vijaya.

Jayadeva The literary pseudonym of the twelfth-century unknown author of a pastoral poem, the *Gītā-govinda*. Though chiefly remembered as a poet, he was a great reformer, especially of the early Kṛṣṇa cult, and greatly influenced many other Vaiṣṇava cults. He was also one of the earliest Hindu writers to denounce the caste system.

Jayadeva(s) v. Ajita(s).

Jayadratha 'Possessor of victorious chariots.' A king of Sindhu and an ally of the Kauravas. He married Duḥśalā, daughter of Dhṛtarāṣṭra, the blind Kaurava king. During the exile of the Pāṇḍavas Jayadratha abducted Draupadī, the common wife of the Pāṇḍu princes, but was pursued and captured by them, though his life was spared. Despite their clemency he subsequently joined the Kauravas in their war against the Pāṇḍavas, and was killed by Arjuna on the fourteenth day of the battle.

v. Mahābhārata.

Jayanta I. 'Victorious.' An epithet of Śiva; of the Āditya (the Sun); of Skanda; of a Rudra; and of a son of Indra.

II. A son of Arjuna and Subhadrā, later called Abhimanyu because of his fearlessness. He possessed the power of remaining invisible in battle and thus was able to kill all his opponents.

Jayantī A daughter of Indra, also called Jayanī, Devasenā and Tāviṣī.

Jaya(s) v. Ajita(s).

Jayayajña The 'victory-sacrifice', i.e., the *aśvamedha* (horse-sacrifice), often performed to celebrate the successful conclusion of a war and the assumption by a ruler of imperial status.

Jīmūta The name of the famous wrestler killed by Bhīma.

Jīmūtavāhana 'Whose vehicle is the clouds.' An epithet of Indra.

Jina 'Conqueror.' An epithet of the Jaina *tīrthaṅkaras* and of Gotama the Buddha, to denote their having freed themselves from every psycho-somatic impediment.

Jiṣṇu 'Victorious', 'triumphant'. An epithet of Indra; of Pāṇḍu's son Arjuna; and of Viṣṇu.

Jīva 'Existing', 'living';[1] hence *jīva-ja*, 'born alive', or born from the womb, as distinct from *āṇḍa-ja*, 'egg-born' (*Chān. Up.*, VI.3,1). Generally in Jainism and Buddhism *jīva* signifies the empirical 'soul' or biological essence,[2] but this notion is subject to qualification by individual Jainas and Buddhists. Hinduism on the other hand uses the term *ātman* to denote the Cosmic Essence, which permeates both the individual as well as the universe.

Jīva is essentially a state of consciousness, which distinguishes it from *ajīva*, the inorganic and unconscious. *Jīva* is thus temporary and individual, and subject to the vicissitudes of the empirical world,[3] while *ātman* is unchanging and eternal.

[1]Cf. Gr. *bios*; Lat. *vivus*; E. *quick*; Lith. *gývas*.

[2]Thus in the Buddhist *Dīgha Nikāya* (I.157 and 188) the question is asked: 'Is the body the "soul", or is the body one thing and the "soul" another?'

[3]The term *jīvātman* occurs in the *Bhāg. P.* and denotes the personal or individual 'soul' (as distinct from the

paramātman, the eternal principle) (*SED.*).
v. Karman; Prāṇa.

Jñāna 'Knowing'; 'the apprehension of knowledge'. Initially *jñāna* appears to have meant the knowledge required by the warrior, herdsman, agriculturalist, craftsman, etc., in the performance of their respective duties. Later it meant also the mystical or magical knowledge required by the tribal priest to enable him to deal with the mysterious powers of nature, personified as Devas and Asuras. But the concept of the power inherent in knowledge implied that the apprehension of knowledge ensured the sharing of this power. Thus at a very early stage in Indian social and religious evolution the two spheres of knowledge became one, and priestly magical skills were applied to ensure victory to the warrior, abundance to the herdsman and agriculturalist, fecundity to women, etc. That priestly knowledge implied supernormal power became an axiom and gave an unprecedented authority to the proliferation of priestly formulas and *mantras*, and ensured that only he 'who knowing thus' shall benefit. Thus the exercise of knowledge and power became increasingly the prerogative of the priestly adept, who alone was capable of communicating with the gods through the medium of the sacrifice.

In the Purs. *jñāna* is variously defined to conform with sectarian views, though without conflicting with the monistic idea. *Manu* (XII.81.90) discusses the best means of gaining fundamental knowledge (*jñānapūrvam*), which is summed up in the closing passage (XII.125): 'He who recognises the Self through the Self in all created beings becomes equal (minded) towards all, and enters the highest state, *brahman*.'[1]

[1]Thus 'the root *jñā*, in its Vedāntic sense, does not connote cognition, but the irrefutable intuition of a single, all-including entity, other than which nothing persists' (*TT.*, p. 16).

Jñāna Dakṣiṇāmūrti The form of Śiva as the embodiment of knowledge (*jñāna*). He is thus represented as the universal *guru* (*mahāyogin*) who symbolizes transcendent consciousness.
v. Dakṣiṇāmūrti.

Jñānavāpī 'Pool of knowledge.' A sacred well in Banāras, the water of which confers knowledge.

Jñāna Yoga v. Yoga.

Juhū I. One of the two principal sacrificial offering-spoons, the other being called *upabhṛt*. The *juhū* is a tongue-shaped wooden spoon used to pour the sacred ghee on the fire. According to the *AV.* (XVIII.4,5) the *juhū* sustains the sky; the *upabhṛt* the atmosphere; the ladle (*dhruvā*) the earth. The *juhū* and *upabhṛt* are called yoke-fellows, as they represent 'the two horses that are supposed to convey the sacrifice (and consequently the sacrificer himself) to the world of the gods' (*ŚBr.*, I, p. 68, n.1; I.8,3,26f.).

If a sacrificer should inadvertently take up the *juhū* in the right hand and the *upabhṛt* in the left, this would enable an enemy to become his equal. The *juhū* should be taken up in both hands and then laid down on the *upabhṛt*, which will ensure the possession of cattle and long life. The two spoons should not be allowed to clink together, as this makes the sacrificer's property insecure (*ŚBr.*, XI.4.2,1–2).

II. Name of one of Agni's seven tongues, i.e., flames (*RV.*, I. 58,7).

Jūrṇi 'Firebrand.' A weapon frequently used by native guerrillas (often called demons) in their resistance to Āryan expansion (*RV.*, I.129,8).[1]

[1]Singh, *Ancient Indian Warfare*, pp. 106, 115.

Jvālājihva 'Flame-tongued.' A demon causing diseases, probably fever (*jvara*).

Jvālāmukhī 'Mouth of fire.' A volcano, or any place from which subterranean fire issues. It is often worshipped as a form of Durgā.

Jvara The personification of fever, called the 'king of diseases' which affects the whole organism simultaneously. According to the *MBh.* Jvara was produced from Śiva's wrath when he was excluded from Dakṣa's sacrifice.[1] In revenge he destroyed the personified Sacrifice which itself took the form of a deer and fled heavenwards. In the heat of the chase that followed a drop of sweat fell from Śiva's forehead and became fire from which the terrifying Jvara emerged. The sacrifice was burnt up and the gods put to flight. To appease Śiva, Brahmā promised that henceforth he should never be excluded from the sacrifice, and that Jvara would be allowed to range over the whole earth.

The *VP.* (V.33) describes Jvara as having three feet and three heads, and emanating from Maheśvara (Śiva). Jvara once defended Bāṇa against Kṛṣṇa, but the later generated a great heat (fever) which expelled Śiva's fever which had entered his (Kṛṣṇa's) body. As the personified Fever departed it addressed Kṛṣṇa saying: 'Those men who call to memory the combat between us shall be ever exempt from febrile disease.'

[1]The fever emanating from the wrath-fire of Śambhu (Śiva) is the most dangerous. It is always present at the death of every creature; hence it is called the destroyer of created beings (*Suś. Saṁ.*, III, p. 211).

Jyeṣṭhā A local goddess once popular in Southern India. Today she is known as Śītalā, the goddess of smallpox.[1] She is worshipped also in parts of Bengal, Orissa, Gujarāt, etc.[2]

'Some of the various names given to Jyeṣṭhā in the old Tamil Nigaṇṭus are Mugaḍi, Tauvai, Kālāḍi and

Mudevī, the crow-bannered, the ass-rider, etc., and her weapon is said to be the sweeping broom.'[3] But in the *Bodhāyana Gṛhyasūtra*[4] Jyeṣṭhā is called Kapila-patnī, Kumbhī, Jyāyā, Hastimukhā, Vighapārṣadā, and Nirṛti whose chariot is drawn by lions, accompanied by tigers.

Some iconographical texts portray Jyeṣṭhā as a kind of ogre, like Jarā the personification of old age, long-nosed, with sagging lips, long and pendulous breasts and belly, but despite her terrifying aspect she bestows gifts on her worshippers and destroys their enemies. She sometimes accompanies Yama, the ruler of the dead.[5] The *Liṅga P.* states that she came out of the ocean when it was churned (*samudramathana*) for the second time. She married a sage but he soon discovered her anti-social tendencies when she refused to perform a good deed or encourage others to do so. Neither Viṣṇu nor Śiva were of interest to her.

At this point the myth reveals its sectarian intention. The unhappy sage was advised to humour his wife and encourage her selfish and irreligious attitude. He therefore took her to shrines of local divinities and to Buddhist sanctuaries, where 'evil and inauspicious' non-Vedic rites were performed. There he left her, suggesting that she should sustain herself until his return (which he had no intention of doing) by accepting the oblations offered her by the women worshippers. Finally when she realized that her husband had deserted her, she reluctantly turned to Viṣṇu who counselled her to mix only with those who were his exclusive worshippers, and not with the followers of Śiva or other gods. But Viṣṇu nonetheless took the precaution of repeating the Rudra *mantra* to protect himself from her baneful influence!

[1]Śītalā has many affinities with the Buddhist goddess Hārītī.

[2]*DHI.*, p. 383.

[3]Ibid. Śītalā also rides a donkey and has a broom as one of her emblems. In India the crow is the bird of death and called *yama* in some Lexicons (*SED.*).

[4]Cited by Banerjea, *DHI.*, p. 382.

[5]*EHI.*, vol. I, p. 364.

Jyotir-liṅgam The unbounded *liṅgam* of light, the form assumed by Śiva which compelled both Brahmā and Viṣṇu to acknowledge his supremacy.

v. Liṅgodbhavamūrti.

Jyotiṣa One of six Vedāṅgas. In a general sense it denotes the science of astronomy, but in sacrificial ritual it refers to the Vedic calendar by which the most auspicious day for the performance of a particular sacrifice is fixed. Subsequently such calendrial decisions became a feature of astrology, so that no important undertakings such as marriage, building a house, etc., were made without reference to calendrial omens.

Though there is no Vedic text on the subject, there is ample evidence in the Vedas of a knowledge of the stars. The *RV.* lists a number of them and divides the year of 360 days (*sāvana*) into twelve months. The 'moon of later birth' (*RV.*, I.25,8) is probably an allusion to an intercalary thirteenth or supplementary month of the luni-solar year,[1] but other passages lack any precise astronomical knowledge. A notable effort to remedy this deficiency is apparent in particular passages of the Āraṇyakas and Upaniṣads, which attempt to interpret the world objectively, and to establish the relations of similarity, identity and interdependence, for which the word '*iva*' (as if, or as it were) is used. Although these attempts were an advance on earlier cosmological views, they were mainly speculative. It was not until the appearance of the *Jyotiṣavedāṅga* (Treatise on astronomy), compiled between 300 and 200 B.C., that the subject made use of the mathematics gradually being evolved. Though failing to produce a sophisticated stellar theory, the *Jyotiṣavedāṅga* provided a basis for the subsequent five astronomical treatises called Siddhāntas, of which the only surviving one is the *Sūrya Siddhānta* (Explanation or Solution of the Sun). But its scope was limited by attempts to reconcile the temporal aspect of recurring cosmic cycles with the mythical unit of time called 'a day of Brahmā', equivalent to a calendar year. The latter was divided into 10,800 'moments', the number of metrical divisions in the *RV.*, each of which consists of forty syllables, the whole totalling 432,000 syllables.[2]

At the end of the Great Cosmic Cycle, all the stars, having completed revolutions over a period of 4,320,000 years, were thought to return to their original positions. To support the authenticity of this grand total, it was subjected to the following analysis. This begins with the number 108, i.e., the product of the four phases of the moon and twenty-seven *nakṣatras* (lunar asterisms); the second, the product of the sixteen theoretical parts of the lunar disc, and twenty-seven lunar phases, totalling 432; and finally the product of the lunar years, which is 12,000 divine years, equivalent to 360 calendar years, each of 360 days, making a grand total of 4,320,000. The assumption that these figures solved all astronomical problems led to greater attention being devoted to astrology. But some amends were made later when the *Sūrya Siddhānta* was re-written and established as the basic handbook of Indian astronomy. About this time (A.D. 499) the astronomer Āryabhaṭa produced his great work the *Āryabhaṭiya* which mentions the rotation of the earth and develops the theory of epicycles. The end of the sixth century marks the birth of the astronomer Al-Bīrunī, considered to be the most accomplished of Indian astronomers despite his refusal to accept Āryabhaṭa's theory of the rotation of the earth.

Before the introduction of the signs of the zodiac, solar months were called by the names corresponding to lunar months, and subsequently by the zodiacal sign in which the sun appeared. Owing to differences in the length of lunar months and days and variations in the precession of the equinoxes it became necessary to make adjustments to reconcile them with the months and signs of the zodiac. This reconciliation was achieved in the Siddhānta period when the week of seven days was introduced, each named after a planet. The months followed the Greek zodiacal order but with Indian designations. This arrangement involved changing the three Vedic seasons to six, each consisting of two months, viz:[3]

Vasanta (Spring)	caitra (March-April)
	vaiśākha (April-May)
Grīṣma (Hot season)	jyaiṣṭha (May-June)
	āṣādha (June-July)
Varṣa (Rainy season)	śrāvaṇa (July-August)
	bhādrapada (August-September)
Śarad (Autumn)	aśvinā (September-October)
	kārttika (October-November)
Hemanta (Winter)	mārgaśīrṣa (November-December)
	pauṣa (December-January)
Śiśira (Frosty season)	māgha (January-February)
	phālguna (February-March)

Astrology has always been closely associated with astronomy in India as is indicated in the works of astronomers referred to above. In addition Varāhamihira (sixth cent. A.D.), author of several astronomical treatises, who also wrote on astrology and divination, the most important being the *Bṛhat-saṁhitā* (Great Compendium), which describes the motions and conjunctions of celestial bodies and their divinatory significance. He also wrote two books on purely horoscopic astrology, in which he introduced many Greek astrological terms, including *hora*, the hour of birth.

The subsequent Moslem invasions and contacts with Arab science influenced Indian astronomy in the medieval period, Bhāskara (twelfth century) being one of its most noted exponents.

[1]Griffith, *RV.*, I, p. 33, n.8; v. also Basham, *WI.*, App. III, pp. 492f.

[2]'The numbers 10,800 and 432,000 were also the bases of the cosmic cycles of later Indian and even foreign astronomers' (Filliozat in *Ancient and Medieval Science*, p. 138). In the list of ten Babylonian kings, composed in Greek by one of their priests called Berossos (c. 280 B.C.), the period of their reigns totals 432,000 years. Also the Icelandic Poetic Edda states that in Odin's heavenly warrior hall there were 540 doors through each of which 800 fighters will pass when they wend their way to fight with the Wolf. As 540 × 800 totals 432,000, Indian astronomical influence appears to have travelled far afield (v. Campbell, *The Masks of God*, II, p. 116).

[3]Filliozat, op. cit., p. 147.

v. Yuga; Kalpa; Manvantara; Māsa.

Jyotiṣa vedāṅga v. Jyotiṣa.

Jyotsnā 'Moonlight.' The beloved of the Moon (Soma).

K

Ka The Sanskrit interrogative pronoun 'who', frequently used as an allusion to the nameless source of universal power,[1] later called Hiraṇyagarbha, 'the golden germ', 'the source of golden light', 'the only Lord of all created beings' (*RV.*, X.121,1). Each stanza of this hymn (except the tenth and last) concludes with the refrain: 'What god (*kāsmai devāya*) shall we adore with our oblation', i.e., 'To whom (*ka*) shall we address our hymn?'[2] The last stanza identifies Ka with Prajāpati,[3] who alone comprehends all created things. But in *RV.*, I.164,6 the composer asks: 'What was that One who in the Unborn's image has established and fixed firm these worlds' six regions?' Another seer, in *RV.*, X.129,7, also alludes to a nameless being as 'He, the first origin of this creation, whether he formed it or formed it not'.

[1]The ancient Egyptian Edfu creation myth seems to be 'based on beliefs from the time when the Egyptians adored only nameless forces' (Reymond, *The Mythical Origin of the Egyptian Temple*, p. 74).

[2]St. Paul (Acts, 17,23) refers to an altar in Athens inscribed 'To an unknown god'.

[3]Oblations are offered silently to Ka (Prajāpati) because 'everything not "named" or defined belongs to Him' (*VF.*, p. 2).

Kabandha A fabulous giant, the leader of a southern Indian aboriginal tribe[1] whose grotesque masks and painted or tattooed bodies[2] resemble those of primitive tribes in many countries. The purpose of these practices varies, but each tribe has a strictly observed ritual according to the occasion. These practices may explain the descriptions in the *Rāmāyaṇa* of Kabandha and other so-called demonic beings called *rākṣasas*.[3] One of the most outstanding of these is described as a huge being, headless, devoid of neck, having the face where the belly should be, and with a single enormous eye protruding from the centre of the chest (*Rām.*, III.69,27). This hideous pot-bellied (*udaremūkha*) motif is repeated in numerous iconographic details of the architectural remains at Amarāvatī, Ghaṇṭaśālā, Ajantā, etc.[4]

The *udaremūkha* form resembles the *kabandha*, a large, round-bellied water-pot, and hence the name of the pot-bellied *rākṣasa*. To account for his deformity legend states that he was originally a *gandharva* whom Indra had struck with his thunderbolt, so driving his head into his body. He remained in this state until Rāma and Lakṣmaṇa found him and cut off his arms (*Rām.*, III.69,26ff.). Rāma granted his dying wish that he should be cremated, and as the flames rose Kabandha emerged in his *gandharva* form, free of all deformity.

The 'headless' motif appears in numerous legends, and is applied to the headless corpse called *ruṇḍa*, 'a late equivalent of the Epic Kabandha, a torso which dances on the battlefield'.[5] The same motif is also evident in the form of Śiva which presides over the Cosmic Sacrifice,[6] and in the forms of Rāhu and other eclipse demons.

[1]The Kabandhas were a class of beings whose eponymous hero was known also as Danu (*DHI.*, p. 368).

[2]Whilst this practice may owe its origin to tribal totemism, vestiges of which are apparent in the body ornamentation of Australian aborigines and of some North American Indians, no trace of totemism is evident in southern India at the time of the *Rāmāyaṇa*.

[3]Three of these tribes are described by G. Ramdas, 'Aboriginal Tribes in the Rāmāyaṇa' (*Man in India*, V, pp. 28ff.). Kabandha was the leader of the Dānavas, Virādha of the Virādhas, and Rāvaṇa of the Laṅkā Rākṣasas, the most powerful group.

[4]Illustrated in *IRA.*, p. 313.

[5]*EM.*, p. 20.

[6]*HP.*, p. 280.

v. Ketu; Chinnamastā; Danu II.

Kaca A son of Bṛhaspati, deputed by the gods to become the pupil of Śukra and to obtain from him the secret of immortality (*saṁjīvinī vidyā*)[1] so that they might share what had hitherto been the prerogative of Agni. Immortality is one of the principal themes in the *MBh.*,[2] which is illustrated in the account of the dangers undergone by Garuḍa in stealing the *amṛta* from *svarga*; and the fearsome experiences of Kaca before Śukra finally imparted to him the *saṁjīvinī vidyā*. On another occasion when Kaca went to the woods to gather flowers for Devayānī the *asuras* ground him to pieces, and then mixed them with Śukra's wine (*surā*). Devayānī insisted that Kaca's life be again restored, but by then Śukra realized that to do so would result in his own death,[3] but he resolved the problem by imparting the secret knowledge to Kaca on condition that he in turn would resuscitate his preceptor.

Being now in possession of the secret *mantra*, Kaca was about to leave Śukra's hermitage, but was confronted by Devayānī who told him plainly that she expected him to marry her, reminding him that, owing to her intercession, his life had been restored. Kaca expressed his gratitude, acknowledged her beauty and virtues, but informed her that as a preceptor's daughter and a pupil were considered to be brother and sister, their marriage would be incestuous. Devayānī, who should have been aware of this, nonetheless cursed Kaca, declaring that her father's secret would avail him nothing. 'I do not deserve your curse,' Kaca replied. 'You have acted under the influence of passion. Therefore your desire shall not be fulfilled; no *ṛṣi*'s son shall ever accept your hand in marriage!'[4]

Kaca then returned to the gods who praised him for having fulfilled his mission, adding, 'Your fame shall never die. Henceforth you shall share with us the sacrificial offerings.'[5]

[1]A term for which there is no simple English equivalent. Freely translated it can mean 'an antidote against death', or 'knowledge which will ensure immortality'. It was perhaps initially a medical term referring to the process of revivification, or restoration of life.

[2]v. Dange, *Legends*, Ch. IV. for the legend of Kaca.

[3]According to Dange, op. cit., p. 236, the swallowing of Kaca by Śukra represents 'the main features of sacrificial consecration and initiation'.

[4]*MBh.*, Ādi pa., 76 to 78.

[5]An exception to the Vedic tradition which limits offerings to the thirty-three principal gods (*HP.*, p. 84 n.).

v. Upanayana.

Kadalī I. The name of a river sacred to the *pitṛs*. Rāma at one time dwelt on its banks.

II. The plantain (Musa sapientum) which represents vegetative power.

v. Navapatrikā(s).

Kaḍamba A tree (Ipomoea acquatica Forsk.), sacred to Kṛṣṇa. The goddess Kālī is said to become 'excited' by drinking *kaḍamba*—flower wine.[1]

[1]Rawson, *The Art of Tantra*, p. 131.

v. Balarāma; Devatā.

Kadrū A daughter of Dakṣa and wife of Kaśyapa (*VP.*, I.15). The various legends of Kadrū are so interwoven that it is almost impossible to distinguish them, but the *VP.* version possibly presents the most coherent account of her activities.

That there may have been several women called Kadrū is probable, but they all have in common the serpent (*nāga*) motif,[1] representing either the reptile species or the indigenous non-Āryan tribes called Nāgas. The theme of the principal Kadrū legends represents perhaps the antagonism between the non-Āryan and Āryan cultures, symbolized by the attempts of the indigenes to get possession of the elixir of immortality (*amṛta*). One of these legends relates that the *ṛṣi* Kaśyapa, before retiring to the forest, promised his two wives Kadrū and Vinatā as many children as they desired. Kadrū asked for a thousand, Vinatā for two only, but stipulated that they must be superior to Kadrū's. At the expected time the offspring were born as eggs. From Kadrū's emerged a thousand tiny serpents, among which were Śeṣa (representing an ancient cosmogonic myth) and Vāsuki (the legendary king of serpents). Owing to Vinatā's eggs having failed to hatch, she opened one of them which revealed—not the wonderful child she expected—but a pitiful deformed creature, later called Aruṇa (Reddish One).[2] From the other egg emerged a beautiful youth, but with unformed feet, who is identified in some legends with Garuḍa, and like his brother Aruṇa, is also associated with the solar Viṣṇu (*VP.*, I.21).

By a subterfuge Kadrū succeeded in enslaving Vinatā, subjecting her to every conceivable indignity. Garuḍa, having tried by every available means to secure his mother's release, was finally informed by Kadrū that he could obtain this by procuring a portion of the *amṛta* from Indra's heaven (*svarga*). The precious elixir of immortality was so carefully guarded that the task was well-nigh impossible, but Garuḍa succeeded and obtained his mother's freedom. Then he slew Kadrū's thousand children and thereafter became the enemy of all snakes (*nāgas*).

[1]There is a *grahī* (Seizer) called Kadrū who assumes a subtle form and enters the womb of a pregnant woman and changes the embryo into a snake (*MBh.*, 3.230,37, *EM.*, p. 28).

[2]He became the Sun's charioteer and the male counterpart of the Vedic goddess of the Dawn (Uṣas), the male form probably representing an ancient non-Āryan tradition.

v. Daitya; Dānava.

Kaikeya A patronymic, denoting descent from the Kekaya, a Vedic Āryan warrior-tribe of NW. India. Kaikeya and his five sons were allies of the Pāṇḍavas in the Bhārata war.

Kaikeyī A Kaikeya princess who with Kausalyā and Sumitrā were the three principal wives of Daśaratha, King of Kosala. His three queens bore him four sons, viz., Rāma to Kausalyā, Bharata to Kaikeyī, and Lakṣmaṇa and Śatrughna to Sumitrā. According to the *AGP.*, (I.6) Daśaratha on his marriage to Kaikeyī had promised her two boons which she had never claimed. When Rāma the eldest son was about to be installed as heir-apparent, Kaikeyī—at the instigation of Mantharā, her personal attendant—demanded that Bharata should be proclaimed heir and that Rāma and his wife Sītā should be banished for fourteen years to the Daṇḍaka forest.[1] Daśaratha reluctantly honoured his promise, from which ensued the succession of events recounted by Vālmīki in his famous epic poem, the *Rāmāyaṇa*.

[1]But the *Rāmāyaṇa* states that Rāma left Ayodhyā to fight Rāvaṇa and his Rākṣasa tribesmen who were oppressing *ṛṣis* like Agastya engaged in the brahminization of the Deccan.

v. Rāmacandra.

Kailāsa A range of mountains, forming part of the Himālaya. The name means crystalline or icy, and is derived from *kelas* (crystal), a compound of '*ke*', water, and '*las*' to shine.

In Hindu mythology Kailāsa is the name of a single peak (situated south of Mount Meru), and is regarded as the paradise of the gods, especially of Śiva and Kubera. The latter was consecrated here as 'giver of wealth'. On its summit is a great *jujube* tree from whose roots the Ganges rises (*MBh.*, 3,142,4f., *EM.*).

Kaiṭabha A demon, variously referred to as an *asura*, *daitya* or *dānava* who with another demon, Madhu, figure in an obscure cosmogonic allegory which states that they issued from the root of Viṣṇu's ear whilst he was sleeping at the end of an age, their intention being to kill Brahmā who was seated on the lotus springing from Viṣṇu's navel. Brahmā saw them and invoked Mahāmāyā (the goddess personifying Viṣṇu's cosmic sleep), for help but before she could act Viṣṇu awoke and destroyed them, and hence his epithets, Kaiṭabhajit and Madhusūdana (*Mārk. P.*, canto lxxxi, 41–53).[1] According to the *Harivaṁśa*, the bodies of the two *asuras* produced so much fat or marrow (*medas*), that Viṣṇu in the form of Nārāyaṇa formed the earth from it, and hence its appellation Medinī.

Another *MBh.* legend states that Hayaśīrṣa, the horse-headed *avatāra* of Viṣṇu, killed the two *asuras* after they had stolen the Vedas and hidden them at the bottom of the ocean.

[1]According to the *Suś. Saṁ.*, II, p. 699, Kaiṭabha obstructed Brahmā when he was creating the world, but the enraged god reduced him to ashes. As Brahmā's wrath continued to build up he placed it in the mobile and immobile parts of the creation. The *Brah. P.* (II.37,2, *PI.*) attributes the killing to Durgā.

Kākākṣi 'Crow's eye.' According to Indian folklore the crow has only one eye which moves from one eye-socket to the other as occasion requires.

Kakṣīvat According to Weber[1] Kakṣīvat was a member of the Pajra, a *kṣatriya* tribe. He later became a *ṛṣi* and author of some *RV.* hymns. His mother was Uśij, his father Dīrghatamas, reputed to have been one of the earliest 'missionaries' to the kingdoms of Aṅga and Kaliṅga.[2]

Kakṣīvat married the ten daughters of Rāja Svanaya, and he received an enormous marriage settlement of bulls, cows, horses and eleven quadrigas, etc.

[1]*Episches im Vedischen Ritual*, pp. 22–5. Kakṣīvat appears to have been associated with the worship of the Aśvins, and to have lived a 'hundred autumns' (*RV.*, IX.74,8). The Aśvins rejuvenated him (X.143,1).

[2]Dīrghatamas is sometimes syncretized with an earlier *ṛṣi* of that name, to whom Aṅga and Kaliṅga could not have been known.

Kakubh I. 'Peak, summit', later 'region', 'quarter of the heavens'. Kakubh is personified as a daughter of Dakṣa and the wife of Dharma.

II. The name of a metre of three *pādas*, consisting of eight, twelve and eight syllables respectively. Bulls are said to have been produced in its form (*ŚBr.*, VIII.2.4,7). In another part of the same work it is equated with *prāṇa* (5.2,4).

Kakudmin v. Raivata I.

Kāla I. The generic expression for 'time' but it occurs only once in the *RV.*, and that in a late portion (X.42,9). To the early Vedic agriculturists and herdsmen time meant the season (*ṛtu*) of the year, a term which in the *AV.* and Brāhmaṇas was gradually superseded by '*kāla*', a word derived from '*kal*', meaning 'to calculate or enumerate'. As the sun is an important factor in seasonal change it was inevitably associated with time, as in the *RV.* (I.155,6), or in the *AV.* (XIX.53,1–10) with past, present and future. Thus time is said to have existed before creation, to be the source of the primordial waters, and the progenitor of the creator (Prajāpati).[1]

Considering the interest in the abstract shown in the Upaniṣads, it seems strange that so little attention was given to the theory of time. Except for a bare mention in the *Śvet.* (1,2) and several passages in the *Maitri* (6,14–16) which refer to the year as being composed of moments and other divisions of time, they contain nothing else of importance regarding time except the reference to the two forms of Brahmā as Time and the Timeless, an idea that is not, however, really developed.

It is perhaps not possible to distinguish the sequence of ideas about Time which were current in India and among its Western neighbours from the sixth century B.C., but in India attention appears to have been diverted from ritualistic and mystical interpretations of the universe to theories having some sort of mathematical foundation. This new approach culminated in astronomical treatises (Jyotiṣavedāṅgas), c. 300–200 B.C., and in the formulation of solar and lunar calendrial cycles. Subsequently more sophisticated Siddhānta treatises appeared, though these did not immediately supersede the ingenious but mythical theories which divided time into immense periods called *yugas*, *kalpas* and *manvantaras*.

With the postulation of 'zero' in India about the fourth century A.D., and the advent of the Indian astronomer Āryabhaṭa (A.D. 499), science was separated from traditional quasi-scientific views. About this time also the Sarvāstivādin Buddhist school[2] was critically examining the 'supposed' stability of the universe and advancing the theory that 'there is no other ultimate reality than separate, instantaneous bits of existence',[3] and that time is not an independent entity but is composed of an unending succession of moments. Thus 'past' and 'future' were considered to be fictions, only the present being real; consciousness of the past was the product of recollection (not always accurate, even when recorded), and any sense of the future the product of imagination.

Both Viṣṇu and Śiva are regarded as forms of Cosmic Time, Śiva being represented by his *śakti* Kālī. Viṣṇu, on the other hand, is considered to consist of four elements: primary matter (*pradhāna*), an activating principle (*puruṣa*), visible substance (*vyakta*) and time (*kāla*). Though the various Indian schools appear to recognize the close connexion of space and time, separate terms distinguishing them continued to be used.[4] Nonetheless, all Indian schools regard time and space as part of a fourfold whole, of which its three co-ordinates are the cycles of creation, preservation and destruction.[5]

The ancient notion of time as an ever-rolling wheel, like its position in Western classical mechanics, was superseded by new ideas. The *Aṣṭasāhasrikā Prajñāpāramitā* (a Mādhyamika Buddhist work) also robs Time of its independence by declaring that: 'There is no setting in motion of anything, nor any stopping of the motion of anything. Knowing just that is the perfection of wisdom (*prajñāpāramitā*).'[6]

[1]Time is likened to a steed with seven reins (rays?) which draws a chariot having seven wheels (the seven worlds), with immortality as their axle (*AVB.*, p. 224).

[2]And also the Mādhyamika Buddhist school.

[3]Th. Stcherbatsky, *Buddhist Logic*, I, p. 80.

[4]Lecompte du Noüy, *Biological Time*, p. 129, distinguishes time and space by pointing out that while it is possible to travel in every direction in three-dimensional space, either rapidly or slowly, or to retrace one's footsteps, or even to stand motionless, none of these things is physically possible in time. Nonetheless, as neither time nor space exists independently, the connexion between them gives at least the impression of a single identity.

[5]Cf. the four-dimensional continuum of Einstein's theory of relativity, which includes time and thus robs it of its independence (*Relativity*, by Albert Einstein, p. 56).

[6]Zimmer, *Philosophies of India*, p. 484.

v. Kāla Bhairava; Kālabhakṣa.

II. 'Dark', 'black'. Kāla sometimes refers to the skin colouration of indigenous Indian tribes.

v. Dānavas; Kālamukha.

Kāla Bhairava The divinity of death represented by the southern aspect of Śiva called Dakṣiṇāmūrti.

v. Kāla I; Kālabhakṣa; Kālanātha.

Kālabhakṣa 'The devourer of time.' An epithet of Śiva.

Kālāci The name of Yama's judgment hall. From its throne (*vicārabhū*) he announces the fate of the dead who appear before him.

Kāladaṇḍa 'The staff of death.' One of Yama's emblems. It is also the personification of Death who is called the 'measurer of eternal time'.[1]

[1]*AGP.*, 318,20.

Kāladūta 'Messenger of death.' Any omen or sign of approaching death such as illness, old age, etc., or the sight of a dove or pigeon (*kapota*) which presages death.

v. Yama; Mṛtyu.

Kālāgni The conflagration that will destroy the world at the end of the age (*yuga*).

v. Pralaya.

Kālaharamūrti A form (*mūrti*) of Śiva as the conqueror of death.

It had been decreed that the boy Mārkaṇḍeya should die in his sixteenth year. He was unafraid, being devoted to the worship of Śiva, but when the time of his death arrived the dread figure of Yama (the ruler of the dead) suddenly appeared, and Mārkaṇḍeya panicked. In his terror he clutched a *liṅga* with both hands, from which Śiva himself burst forth and vanquished Yama.

Kālahasti One of the five principal *Liṅga* temples in which each of the five elements is symbolized. That of Kālahasti is dedicated to the *liṅga* of the atmosphere; Kāśī to water; Kāñcī (Conjeeveram) to the earth; Cidambaram to space, and Tiruvannamalai to fire.[1]

[1]*HP.*, p. 221.

Kālāmra A divine mango tree, a league high, which grows east of Meru. Its juice endows women with perpetual youth (*Brah. P.*, II.15, 58 and 61, *PI.*).

Kālamukha 'Black-faced.' An epithet applied to the progeny of Āryan men and Rākṣasa women.

Kālāmukha v. Kāpālika.

Kālanātha 'Lord of time.' A form of Śiva representing time which brings all beings to disintegration and death (*mṛtyu*).

Kālanemi I. The name of *dānava* who was incarnated as Kaṁsa and slain by Kṛṣṇa. He personifies the Wheel of Time as a form of fate.[1]

[1]*EM.*, p. 76.

II. A member of the Rākṣasa tribe and an uncle of Rāvaṇa. The latter had promised him half his kingdom if he killed Hanumat the chief of the 'monkey tribe', an ally of Rāma. The attempt occurred when Kālanemi, disguised as a recluse, invited Hanumat to his hermitage for a meal. Hanumat declined and went off to bathe in a pool nearby, but as soon as he stepped into the water his foot was seized by a crocodile. He succeeded in killing it, but from its body appeared a beautiful nymph (*apsaras*) who had been cursed by Dakṣa to take the form of a crocodile until released by Hanumat. The grateful nymph then warned him of Kālanemi's murderous intentions. The monkey then returned to the hermitage, seized Kālanemi and flung him into the air with such force that he landed in Laṅkā (Ceylon) before the throne of Rāvaṇa.[1]

[1]*HCD.*, p. 141.

Kālapāśa The noose (*pāśa*) with which Yama the ruler of the dead ensnares his victims, when the time (*kāla*) for them to die arrives.

Kālarātrī The name of a goddess personifying Time which destroys the world at the end of each age.[1]

The great primary goddess Mahālakṣmī at the end of the age assumes the form of Mahākālī and is known also as Mahāmāyā, Yoganidrā, Kālarātrī, etc.

Kālarātrī is usually depicted carrying a noose with which she ensnares her victims; or she is described as a black, half-clad, blood-bespattered woman called Kuṭumbinī.[2]

[1]She is the presiding deity of the night following the dissolution of the universe (*AGP.*, 136,1).

[2]*EM.*, p. 76.

v. Kālarudra; Kālāgni; Pralaya; Kālī.

Kalaśa[1] The Indian water-pot, pitcher, ewer. These vessels varied in quality and were designated according to the intended use, and were the subject of much symbolism. Thus the *bhadrakumbha* (auspicious jar) was made of gold and used only at the consecration (*abhiṣeka*) of kings. The *bhadranidhi* (treasure of fortune) was a costly vessel offered to Viṣṇu; the *bhadraghaṭa* (vase of fortune)[2] was dedicated to Lakṣmī. From it grows the fortune-bestowing lotus.

In ancient India the *kalaśa* symbolized the universe, and in later times, when the theory of the *maṇḍala* was established, 'the vase remained as an integral part of maṇḍalic liturgy, in the same way as it still forms an indispensable element of certain *pūjā* of Hinduism . . . [hence the] vase is the first *maṇḍala* into which the deities descend and arrange themselves'.[3] Thus Brahmā holds the 'Wisdom vase', which symbolizes the earth and is the container and the sustainer of all things.

The notion of fecundity, prosperity and wealth was symbolized by the *kumbha*,[4] i.e., 'the generative pot', and was carried over to certain *devas* such as Kubera, god of wealth, and Gaṇeśa, the giver of prosperity and ensurer of success in every enterprise, both of whom were depicted as pot-bellied. Their attendants, the *yakṣas* and *gaṇas* were depicted in the same way.

[1]Also called *amṛta-kalaśa*, *kalaśa-ghaṭa*, *varṣamāna*, etc. v. also Coomaraswamy, *Artibus Asiae*, 1928–9, pp. 122f.; and *Nir.* (11.12).

[2]Cf. the Greek and Roman cornucopia.

[3]Tucci, *Tibetan Painted Scrolls*, I, p. 327, n.33.

[4]*Kumbha* is usually a large vessel of clay or costly metal, whilst the *kalaśa* is a small pitcher with unburnt base.

v. Agastya; Kalāvatī I.

Kalāvatī I. A mystical ceremony, the initiation of a Tantrika student, at which the goddess Durgā is believed to be transferred from a water jar to the body of the novice.

v. Kalaśa.

II. The name of the lute of the *gandharva* Tumburu.

Kālayavana 'Black or dark Yavana.' Yavana often denotes the Greeks, who had cultural contacts with the Indo-Āryans of north-western India from the end of the sixth century B.C., but Yavana is also synonymous with stranger, alien and barbarian, usually regarded as an enemy.

The Kālayavanas may have been of Greco-Bactrian or Scythian origin[1] who collectively constituted a threat to the Yādava kingdom of Kṛṣṇa, which was also threatened by the ruler of Magadha. To avoid war on two fronts, Kṛṣṇa transferred the inhabitants of Mathurā to Dvārakā, a western coastal town, which needed only to be fortified on the landward side. Then he returned with his army to Mathurā to meet the Kālayavanas whom he lured into the mountains where they were ambushed and defeated.[2]

[1]*VP.*, p. 449, n.2.

[2]The account of this defeat is told in the *Hariv.* and *VP.* (V.23) which state that Kṛṣṇa lured the Kālayavana king to a cavern where he was slain 'by a glance of the eyes' of its occupier, the mighty Mucukunda.

Kāleja(s) 'Demons of Time.'[1] Probably an Indian aboriginal tribe.

[1]*HP.*, p. 143.

Kalhaṇa (12th century.) A Kaṣmīrī poet, author of the Rājataraṅgiṇī (River of Kings), a history of Kaṣmīr in verse.

Kali I. The name of one of the pieces used in games of dice. It is marked with a single dot, and known as the *kali* die.[1] Various names are given to the dice (*akṣa*) but they are generally described as *kṛta, tretā, dvāpara* and *kali*, representing respectively 4,3,2,1. Some lists add *akṣarāja*, others *abhibhū*, but parallel lists in the *Tait.* and *Vāj. Saṁhitās* suggest that these two are identical. The *ŚBr.* (V.4.4,6) names only the *kali* die and states that it 'dominates the other dice'. The methods of play are not known, but it is evident that they were not uniform, some games being played with four, others with five pieces.[2] Dice were made from various materials, but generally from the hard nuts of the *vibhītaka* tree (Terminalis bellerica), and were about the size of a nutmeg, nearly round, with five slightly flattened sides. Later at ceremonial games gold dice in the form of cowries or *vibhītaka* nuts were used.[3]

Evidently dice playing involved gambling, often for high stakes, sometimes resulting in ruin for the loser, as indicated in the 'Gambler's Lament' (*RV.*, X.34), and in the loss of his kingdom by King Yudhiṣṭhira. In the *AV.* (VII.109,1) the *kali* is implored to be auspicious to his devotee and to strike, as does lightning a tree, the opponent at the gaming table.

[1]This is the formidable losing die (*AV.*, VII.109,1), later personified as the destroying spirit of time, which drives and coerces, as indicated by the root *kal*, 'to oppress'. Thus an evil and oppressive king is called a *kali* (*EM.*, p. 76).

[2]Various methods are referred to in the *VI.*, vol. I, p. 4. v. also K. de Vreese, 'The Game of Dice in Ancient India', in *Orientalia Neerlandica*, pp. 349ff., Leiden, 1948. For the ritual dice game in the *rājasūya*, v. Keith, *JRAS.*, 1908, pp. 823ff.

[3]Eggeling, *ŚBr.*, III, pp. 106f., n.l. In the later Vedic period the gambling hall of the king's palace 'had some magical or religious significance, though its import is not wholly clear' (*WI.*, p. 207).

v. Ṛṇam.

II. One of the four mythical periods (*yugas*) which together constitute a particular measure of the world's duration, preceded and succeeded respectively by two transitional periods of dawn and twilight, each comprising 100 'divine' years. The total, 1,200 'divine' years, is equivalent to one-tenth of that of the four *yugas* (12,000 'divine' years or 4,320,000 calendar years, i.e., 12,000 × 360), of which the *kaliyuga* comprises 432,000.

v. Kalpa; Kālarātrī; Manvantara.

Kālī I. The name of one of the seven tongues or flames of Agni, alluded to as the 'Seven Red Sisters' (*RV.*, X.5,5; *Muṇḍ. Up.*, 1.2,4).

II. A goddess, the *śakti* of Śiva. She is called by many names including Satī, Pārvatī, Durgā,[1] Umā, Bhavānī. From the mystical point of view she represents the supreme realization of truth, the state beyond manifestation, the *paramātman* of Hinduism and the *para-nirvāṇam* of Buddhism.

Kālī also symbolizes eternal time and hence she both gives life and destroys it. Her appearance is described as a hideous four-armed emaciated woman with fang-like teeth, who devours all beings.[2] She holds a *pāśa* (noose), *khaṭvāṅga* (skull-topped staff), *khaḍga* (sword) and a severed head. The weapons denote her powers of destruction; the severed head, that there is no escape from time, and that individual lives and deaths are merely minute episodes in the time continuum. This is also the significance of her association with crematoria and burial grounds. Her nakedness indicates that she has stripped off all the veils of existence and the illusion (*māyā*) arising from them. Her only garment is Space. Thus she is also described as black, the colour in which all distinctions are dissolved; or she is eternal night, in the midst of which she stands upon 'non-existence', the static but potentially dynamic state that precedes manifestation. The Unmanifest is represented by the corpse (*śava*) of Śiva on which she stands. Her hands show the fear-removing (*abhaya*) and boon-granting (*vara*) *mudrās*. The former indicates that she is able to allay the terrors of those who invoke her, because she understands their fears; the latter *mudrā* indicates the bestowal, not of transient gifts, but of true perception leading to liberation (*mokṣa*).

Kālī's most sacred temple, the Kālīghaṭ, is situated in a suburb south of Calcutta.[3] Its importance stems from the myth of Satī's death, when her distraught husband Mahādeva (Śiva) wandered about the world carrying his wife's body, and threatening to destroy the world, but Viṣṇu intervened and with his *cakra* (discus) cut up Satī's body into fifty-one pieces which fell to earth in various places, each place becoming sacred because imbued with Satī's divine spirit.

[1]In her non-Brahmanical form Kālī is the tutelary deity of Bengal—'Durgā being her high-caste counterpart' (*TT.*, p. 331).

[2]Cf. the goddess whose image the pre-Columbian peoples of North and Central America 'had borne with them out of Asia [and who] kept only her voracious form, and in the great sculptures of the first Mayan civilisation, she is seen as Night or Death, and the sacrificial Altar' (Levy, *The Gate of Horn*, p. 183); cf. also the Canaanite goddess Anat who slaughters Baal's rivals and ties their heads around her bosom; their limbs dangle from her girdle, and she wades up

to her knees in their blood (Gaster, *Thespis*, p. 237). At the Pontypridd Eisteddfod of 1878, in addition to the usual Gorsedd ceremony, prayers were offered 'to that sinister Hindu deity, Kālī' (Piggott, *The Druids*, p. 179).

[3]The original temple stood in what is now the city of Calcutta. At first it was known as Kālīkṣetra (the place of Kālī), and subsequently as Calcutta.

v. Devī; Kālikā Purāṇa; Mātṛkās; Cāmuṇḍā; Raktavīja; Navapatrikā.

Kālidāsa A great dramatist and lyric poet of northern India who appears to have been a member of the court of Candra-Gupta II (fourth century A.D.), but despite Kālidāsa's fame there is a great divergence among scholars regarding his date.[1] His name gives no indication of his parentage or origin; indeed, it serves only as a peg on which to hang numerous stories, none having any biographical value.

The only trustworthy information is contained in Kālidāsa's own works. These indicate that he was a *brahmin*, gentle and sympathetic, well-educated, and acquainted with the greater part of India. Though apparently a devotee of Śiva, he did not neglect to extol Viṣṇu. He appears to have conformed to all the traditions associated with his class and with the high cultural standards of the Gupta period; his views also on religion and the social and political order of his time betray no signs of extreme partisanship.

The works ascribed to him include the *Raghuvaṁśa*, *Śakuntalā*, *Kumāra-sambhava;* and *Vikramorvaśī*.

[1]*HIL.*, vol. III, Fasc. 1, p. 16.

v. Purūravas.

Kālikā A name of Durgā, the primordial *śakti* from whom Brahmā, Viṣṇu, Maheśvara and other gods were born. Kālikā is eternal and at the time of the dissolution of the world the gods will again disappear into her.[1]

[1]Nirvāṇa Tantra, cited by Rawson, *The Art of Tantra*, p. 184.

Kālikā Purāṇa (c. 10th cent. A.D.) One of the eighteen Upapurāṇas. It is dedicated to the *śakti* of Śiva in her many forms as Mahāmāyā, Bhadrā, Kālī, Durgā, etc.

Kāliya A son of Kadrū and chief of the Krodhavaśa Nāga tribe whose occupation was fishing in the Yamunā river, and charcoal burning. Legend, making a pun of the word *nāga* (snake), describes Kāliya as a five-headed serpent-king who from his dwelling in a deep pool in the Yamunā ravaged the countryside.

On one occasion the child Kṛṣṇa jumped in the pool and was quickly surrounded by snakes, but Balarāma who was near called to him to use his divine powers. In a moment Kṛṣṇa vanquished the snakes and danced upon the middle head of Kāliya until he begged for mercy and admitted the supremacy of Kṛṣṇa. The latter then directed Kāliya and his followers to leave the river and live by the sea (*VP.*, V.7).

According to the *Bhāg. P.* (16.63; 17, 1–11, *PI.*) Garuḍa[1] also attacked Kāliya when the latter failed to make the agreed fortnightly *bali* offering, but Kāliya fled to the Kālindī river where Garuḍa was unable to follow because of the curse laid upon him by the *ṛṣi* Saubhari for having taken a king-fish from the river.

[1]A form assumed by Kṛṣṇa (*VP.*, V.7).

Kali Yuga v. Yuga.

Kalkin The future incarnation (*avatāra*) of Viṣṇu,[1] variously described in the *MBh.* and Purs. as a hero mounted on a white horse, bearing a blazing sword, or as a giant with a white horse's head, or simply as a white horse. The *VP.* (IV.24) describes Kalkin's advent less poetically. He will be the son of a *brāhmaṇa* called Viṣṇuyaśas; the *Bhāg. P.* that he will be a Universal Ruler (*cakravartin*) called Pārāśraya, mounted on a white horse[2] called Devadatta. His mission, like that of Maitreya, the future Buddha, will be to restore *dharma*, the law of right and justice.

Such a hope was particularly evident among both Hindus and Buddhists during the successive Moslem invasions from the eighth century,[3] a hope not unlike that of the Jews during their deportation to Babylonia (586 B.C.) and their gradual dispersion (*diaspora*) during the successive conquests of the Persians and Romans. But neither Jew nor Hindu was alone in suffering such afflictions. 'The hope of a semi-divine Deliverer ... was common in the ancient world, especially in Egypt and Babylonia.'[4] The Greek *Sibylline Oracles*, iii.49 (168–165 B.C.) speak of 'a holy prince' who is to reign over the whole earth forever, and in another passage, iii. 652, of a king who will appear at sunrise and bring peace to all mankind.

[1]The sun is also likened to a horse and hence all solar divinities, including Viṣṇu, are associated with it (v. Dadhikrā).

[2]Cf. the Revelation of St. John, xix, 11: 'And I saw the heaven opened; and behold, a white horse, and he that sat thereon, called Faithful and True; and in righteousness he doth judge ...'

[3]Lassen suggests that the idea of the horse-*avatāra* of Viṣṇu was conceived as the result of the defeat of the Indian armies by the cavalry of Mahmoud of Ghazni (cited by Jouveau-Dubreuil, *Iconography of Southern India*, p. 99, n.1).

[4]*ERE.*, VIII, pp. 574f.

Kalmāṣa-pāda A Solar dynasty king, the son of Sudāsa. When out hunting he mortally wounded one of a pair of tigers which, as it lay dying, changed into a *rākṣasa*, while its mate fled vowing vengeance.

When Kalmāṣa instituted a sacrifice, with the *ṛṣi* Vasiṣṭha as officiant, the *rākṣasa* assumed the form of a cook and prepared human flesh for the *ṛṣi*. When the latter discovered what had happened he blamed the king and laid a curse upon him that henceforth he should desire only human flesh, but on learning the truth reduced the period of the curse to twelve years. The king, regarding this as still too severe, prepared water according to special rites so that he might call down a curse on Vasiṣṭha, but was dissuaded by his wife Madayantī. Not knowing what to do with the now magically efficacious water,[1] he poured it away, but some fell on his feet, turning one black and the other white (*VP.*, IV.4).

[1]Cf. the efforts made during the Christian baptismal service to prevent the drips of water from the infant's head returning to the hallowed water of the font (F. Bond, *Fonts and Font Covers*, pp. 60f.).

Kalmāṣī The mythical speckled cow of Jamadagni which grants all desires.

Kalpa I. 'A fabulous period of time, a day of Brahmā, or 1,000 *yugas*, a period of four thousand, three hundred and twenty millions of years of mortals, measuring the duration of the world.'[1]

Another Paurāṇic system divides a *kalpa* into fourteen periods called *manvantaras*, each containing seventy-one *mahāyugas* and totalling 994 (14 × 71) *mahāyugas*. The remaining six, required to make up the number of 1,000 *mahāyugas*, are distributed amongst the *manvantaras* as follows: one *kṛtayuga*, 0·4 of a *mahāyuga*, precedes the first *manvantara* as a dawn or introductory period. This *manvantara* and each of the remaining thirteen are followed by another *kṛtayuga* or twilight period. Thus the one 'dawn' and fourteen 'twilights' = 15 × 0·4 = 6 *mahāyugas*, which with the 994 referred to above total 1,000 *mahāyugas* or one *kalpa*. But some Purāṇas refer to a 'night of Brahmā' and others to a 'night and day of Brahmā', to denote immense periods of time. Thus a hundred 'days and nights of Brahmā' are considered to constitute the entire span of his existence. This is the longest period in the Hindu time-scale, and is called a *para*, half of which, a *parādha*, had elapsed when the present *kalpa* began. But in theory *kalpas* succeed one another *ad infinitum*.[2]

[1]*SED.*

[2]*VP.*, p. 23, n.8, p. 24, n.9; v. also Filliozat in *Ancient and Medieval Science*, pp. 143f., and Basham, *WI.*, p. 321. Owing to the development of two separate time-systems, attempts to co-ordinate them has led to some confusion over the division and duration of the successive periods of the world's existence.

v. Jyotiṣa; Pralaya.

II. The name of one of the six Vedāṅgas which prescribes the ritual and rules for sacrificial performance.[1]

[1]*SED.*, p. 262.

Kalpadruma One of the five trees (*pañca-vṛkṣa*) of *svarga* (Indra's paradise or sphere), which will fulfil all desires and bestow innumerable gifts.[1]

[1]Cf. the gifts hung on Christmas trees in Europe.

Kāma The god of love (from *kam*, 'wish', 'desire', 'longing for'). In the *RV.* (V.36,1) it is likened to 'the desire of the thirsty steer for water', and in IX.113,11 the longing for happiness and the fulfilment of desires. In the *AV.* (XIX.52,1) *kāma* denotes 'the primal germ of mind, which first arose within that One'.[1] Thus in the early use of the word there is always the suggestion of dualism, of a connexion between the subjective and objective, between will or intention and fulfilment or manifestation,[2] between premise and conclusion.

The significance of *kāma* gradually developed, as is indicated in the many shades of meaning given it in the Brāhmaṇas, Upaniṣads, Purāṇas, etc. In the latter *kāma* is personified and given an erotic role in many stories. One of which states that when Śiva was engaged in meditation, Kāma discharged an arrow at him, to divert his attention to his wife Pārvatī, but Śiva reduced him to ashes with a glance from his third eye. In response to the plea of Kāma's widow Rati (the personification of affection and sensual delight), Śiva restored her husband, but only as a mental image, representing true love and affection, not just carnal desire, and hence his epithet, Anaṅga (bodiless).

Kāma's origin is variously given. In some Brāhmaṇas and other texts he is said to be self-born (ātma-bhū) or un-born (aja); the *Tait. Br.* refers to Dharma as his father and his mother as Śraddhā.[3] His wife, Rati or Revā, is the embodiment of wifely love; their daughter Tṛṣṇā (or Tṛṣā) represents 'thirst' as a form of desire.

Kāma and Rati, attended by Vasanta (Spring), denote love's season, and the spontaneous renewal of all vegetal life. In medieval texts Kāma's constant epithet is *makara-dhvaja* (*Viṣṇudharmottara*, III.73, 20ff.), and this is also the name of an aphrodisiac advertised at the present day. It should not be forgotten that Kāma is a *yakṣa* 'and identical with the Buddhist Māra . . . Kāma is also a form of Agni, and Agni is born of the waters',[4] the source of life. Kāma is also linked with the solar Viṣṇu, the source, literally of warmth, and hence figuratively of love and union.

[1]*OST.*, V, p. 402. A variant of this stanza appears in the *RV.* (X.129,4). The Greek god of love, Eros is also associated with creation.

[2]Cf. E. F. J. Payne's translation of Schopenhauer's *Die*

Welt als Wille und Vorstellung (*The World as Will and Representation*).
[3]Lakṣmī in the *Hariv*.
[4]Coomaraswamy, *Yakṣas*, pt. ii, p. 54. In two Gandhāra reliefs Kāma's daughters bear a *makara* standard (*dhvaja*) (Foucher, *L'Art gréco-bouddhique du Gandhāra*, II, p. 196, figs. 400, 401).

In Indian symbolism heat 'has two forms, mutually opposed: *kāma*, the heat of sexual desire, and *tapas*, the heat generated by ascetic practices, particularly by chastity' (W. D. O'Flaherty, 'The Submarine Mare in the Mythology of Śiva', *JRAS*., no. 1, 1971, p. 9).
v. Kāmaloka; Kāmāṅkuśa; Kāmaśāstra; Mṛtyu; Yaśas; Pradyumna; Aniruddha; Makara I; Bāṇa II.

Kāmadhenu The mythical wish-fulfilling Cow of Plenty which emerged from the Churning of the Ocean (*samudramathana*)[1] and fulfils every desire. She is also called Surabhi,[2] Śavalā, Aditi, etc.

Kāmadhenu symbolizes the abundance and proliferation of Nature, and hence she stands for both motherhood and generation.
[1]Cf. the sacred white cow which, according to the Shilluk creation legend, emerged from the river Nile; also the cow Auðhumla of Northern mythology, which emerged from the melting ice-blocks and from whose udders life-giving streams of milk flowed. The Welsh elfin cow Fuwch Gyfeilioru was also pure white and produced endless streams of milk. She possessed the power to heal, to make fools wise, and to make everyone in the world happy (W. Sikes, *British Goblins*, p. 38).
[2]According to the *Kālikā Pur*. (adhyāya, 91) Kāmadhenu's mother was Surabhi and her (Kāmadhenu's) son was Bhṛṅgi (the Wanderer), Śiva's bull.
v. Kārtavīrya; Satyavrata II; Viśvāmitra; Vetāla II; Paraśurāma.

Kāmākhyā or **Kāmākṣī** 'Wanton-eyed.' A form of Durgā. Her chief temple is in Asssam where cruel rites were practised. Human sacrifice,[1] which was voluntary, took place in the temple up to 1832. The victims, when accepted for sacrifice, were then regarded as sacred and given whatever they desired until the time of the annual festival of the goddess, when they were sacrificed. One chapter of the *Kālikā Pur*. deals with the decapitation, etc., of the victim.
[1]Animals are now sacrificed v. E.A. Gait, *A History of Assam*, p. 58.

Kāmākṣī v. Kāmākhyā.

Kamalā I. 'Lotus.' A name of Lakṣmī, and of a number of women.
II. Name of the tenth *mahāvidyā*, the lotus girl who 'appears as pure consciousness of self, bathed by the calm water of fulfilment . . . She is enjoyer and enjoyed, the state of reconstituted unity.'[1] She rules over the auspicious sign Taurus (Rohiṇī).
[1]Rawson, *The Art of Tantra*, p. 133.

Kāmaloka The sphere or paradise of Kāma the god of love.

Kāmāṅkuśa The pointed hook or goad with which Kāma excites lovers.

Kāmāri 'Love's adversary.' Epithet of Śiva, denoting that he is beyond the sway of the emotions, being the yogin *par excellence*.
v. Dakṣiṇāmūrti.

Kāmaśāstra A manual of the art of love, attributed to Kalyāṇamalla, but its references to earlier authors and its variant style, suggest that it is a compilation. Far from treating the subject with levity as Ovid, Boccaccio and other Western authors have done, 'the Indian author has taken the opposite view, and it is impossible not to admire the delicacy with which he has handled an indelicate theme'.[1] As he assures his readers, his object is not to encourage mere sensual indulgence but to prevent disharmony between husband and wife.
[1]Pisanus Fraxi, *Bibliography of Prohibited Works*, I, p. 283.

Kambala An upper garment. This is of special significance at marriage ceremonies. Should contact with the bridal car, and any other kind of pollution occur, it is 'wiped' off on the *kambala* of the bridegroom, and thus purifies all present at the ceremony (*AV*., XIV.2.66,67).

Kambu The term for the three lines or creases of the neck regarded as a lucky sign. They appear in stylized form on the images of deities and of the Buddha.

Kaṁsa The tyrannical king of Mathurā and son of Ugrasena. He is sometimes regarded as a *dānava* and identified with Kālanemi.
v. Kṛṣṇa I.

Kaṇāda The founder of the Vaiśeṣika system (*darśana*). He is also known as Kaṇabhuj, Kaṇabhakṣa, and Kaṇabhakṣana, names meaning 'atom-eater' or 'atom-enjoyer', and referring to the atomic theory of the school. Kaṇāda's *Vaiśeṣika-sūtra* is the first systematic work of the Vaiśeṣika system.

Kāñcīpura (Conjeeveram.) One of the seven holy cities of India, situated some forty-five miles from Madras. Almost every religious movement that has affected southern India has been connected with Kāñcī.

The Chinese pilgrim Hsüan-tsang mentions a number of Buddhist *stūpas*[1] erected there by the Emperor Aśoka. At the time of Hsüan-tsang's visit (A.D. 640) it was still a stronghold of Buddhism, but also contained over eighty temples dedicated to Viṣṇu as Varadarāja, 'royal giver of boons'.
[1]All the Buddhist buildings have disappeared, most of

their stone having provided materials for the later Śaiva and Vaiṣṇava temples.

Kaṇḍu An eminent *ṛṣi* and ascetic who dwelt on the banks of the Gomatī river. His great spiritual achievements so alarmed the gods that they sent the *apsaras* (nymph) Pramlocā to distract him. She quickly succeeded in her mission and Kaṇḍu's mind became entirely immersed in pleasure and enjoyment so that he failed to observe the passing of time, although the nymph occasionally returned to the gods. At last she told him that they had been together for 907 years, six months and three days, but to the *ṛṣi* it seemed that only one day had passed. Then he realized that all his past asceticism and merit had been wiped out by his love for the nymph, and he angrily told her to leave him. She reluctantly did so, trembling and agitated, with sweat dripping from every pore, which as she passed through the air fell on the trees. The winds collected it, and the moon's rays matured it, and thus was born the *ṛṣis*'s child, the beautiful girl called Māriṣā.

Kaniṣka I. Name of a class of deities of the fourteenth *manvantara*.

II. A celebrated ruler of the Kuṣāṇa dynasty.

Kaṅkālamūrti A fierce form (*mūrti*) of Śiva, figures of which are mostly to be found in South India.

Legend states that when Viṣvaksena (Viṣṇu's doorkeeper) refused to admit Śiva to Viṣṇu's presence, Śiva killed him; hence he is often depicted with Viṣvaksena's corpse on his trident (*triśūla*).[1]

[1]The *Āditya Pur.* states that Kaṅkāla wears a necklace of skeletons (*kaṅkāla*) which comprises all the skeletons of Viṣṇu's various incarnations (*avatāras*).

Kaṅkaparvan 'Scorpion.'[1] A charm against the bite of scorpions, snakes and insects is given in *AVB.*, VII.56.

[1]Or 'a kind of serpent' (*SED.*).

Kānphaṭa Yogī(s) or **Gorakhnāthī(s)** v. Gorakhnātha.

Kaṇva I. The name of an ancient *ṛṣi*, frequently referred to in the *RV.* (I.36,8; 39,7; 47,5, etc.) and other Vedic texts. His sons and descendants are also often mentioned in *maṇḍala* VIII of the *RV.*, as well as in that part of *maṇḍala* I attributed to the family of Kaṇvas.

II. A disease-demon (or demons) who devours embryos. A plant with a spotted leaf[1] is used for protection against them. (*AV.*, II.25).

[1]This may be the *pṛśniparṇī* (Hemionitis cordifolia). The *Suś. Saṁ.* states that this plant, when mixed with milk, prevents miscarriage (*garbhasrāve*).

Kāṇva Name of one of the two known texts of the Śatapatha Brāhmaṇa.

Kāpālika A South Indian medieval tantric cult, organized in small monastic communities and temples. It was subsequently associated with the Kālāmukha and both are regarded as offshoots of the Śaiva Pāśupata cult.

Apart from fragmentary epigraphical evidence and the apparently prejudiced accounts of Rāmānuja, Mādhavācārya and others no Kāpālika or Kālāmukha texts have survived. The main objection of the Vaiṣṇava leaders to the Kāpālikas was the 'permissive' attitude towards caste distinction, implied in their initiatory vow, which 'for orthodox Hindu writers such as Rāmānuja ... was an attack on the whole divinely ordained social order (*varṇā-śrama-dharma*)'.[1]

[1]D.N. Lorenzen, *The Kāpālikas and Kālāmukhas*, p. 7. But Banerjea (*DHI.*, pp. 451f.) considers that their anti-social practices probably stem from the worship of the fierce form of Rudra-Śiva.

v. Lakulīśa.

Kapālin 'Adorned with skulls.' A name of Śiva who, at the destruction of the universe (*pralaya*), will be alone among the ashes of the destroyed worlds, wearing a garland of skulls symbolizing the endless evolution and devolution of universes, and indicating the inseparability of life and death.

Kapālinī A name of Durgā as the wife of Śiva-Kapālin.

Kaparda A small shell or cowry,[1] whence the hair-style in which the hair is braided or knotted in the shape of a cowry. Śiva's hair is dressed in this way and hence his epithet Kapardin 'wearing the *kaparda*', an epithet which Rudra and Pūṣan also share (*RV.*, I.114,1; VI.55,2).

[1]Cowry is the popular name of Cyproea moneta, a small glossy yellowish-white shell used as money by various peoples. In Egypt it is believed to be a protection against the evil eye.

Kapardin v. Kaparda.

Kapi 'Monkey or ape.' Also known as Vṛṣākapi, the 'tawny beast' of the obscure *RV.* hymn (X.86). Here Kapi appears to be Indra's friend, although he had previously attacked Indrāṇī (Indra's wife) when on her way to attend a sacrifice.

Kapi is also an epithet applied to the solar Viṣṇu.[1] Gonda suggests that this indicates the belief that the god's essence was 'present in those animals ... connected with the same phenomena as he was himself. He could then be represented by them.'[2]

[1]Cf. another of Viṣṇu's epithets Kapīndra, 'lord of monkeys'.

[2]*Aspects*, p. 106. Wild apes in many parts of India are propitiated to prevent them from damaging crops.

v. Kapiketana.

Kapiketana 'Having a monkey as symbol.' An epithet of Arjuna, the Pāṇḍu prince, whose banner-emblem was a monkey (*kapi*).

Kapila I. According to tradition the name of the founder of the Sāṁkhya system,[1] but Hindu accounts of him are so full of legends and contradictions that little historical value can be attributed to them.[2] The Buddhist references to Kapila deserve more serious consideration, since they connect his name with the city of Kapilavastu, the birthplace of the Buddha, and ascribe to him and his followers, some of whom are named, a sphere of activity which agrees well with the close relationship that existed between Buddhist and Sāṁkhya philosophy.[3]

[1]His date is unknown, but he probably lived during the seventh century B.C. (Radhakrishnan and Moore, *Sourcebook in Indian Philosophy*, p. 425).

[2]Kapila is sometimes said to be a son of Brahmā; or an incarnation of Viṣṇu (*DHI.*, p. 391); or of Agni.

[3]*ERE.*, VII, p. 659.

v. Darśana(s).

II. A *ṛṣi* who burnt up Sagara's 60,000 sons by his fiery glance (*VP.*, IV.4).

v. Aṁśumat; Bhagīratha.

Kapilavastu v. Buddhism; Kapila I.

Kapiñjala The Francoline partridge. Indra is said to have assumed the form of a *kapiñjala*. It is regarded as a bird of good omen, especially when its cry is heard coming from the south, the region of the *pitṛs*. It also protects one from thieves and evil-doers.

Kapiśā Name of one of Pulaha's wives and mother of *piśācas*.

Kapitthaka (Feronia elephantum.) A herb, probably that used by the Gandharva to cure Varuṇa of impotence (*AV.*, IV.4,1).

Kapota A dove or speckle-necked pigeon, regarded as a bird of ill-omen in the Vedas and later works, and also as a messenger of Death if it perches near the fire, when it must be driven away by 'holy verses' (*RV.*, X.165,5).

The *kapota* is associated with the owl (*ulūka*) another bird of ill-omen (*RV.*, X.165, 1–5).

v. Yama I.

Karālī Name of one of Agni's seven[1] tongues of fire. The names of the others are: Kālī, Manojavā, Sulohitā, Sudhūmravarṇa, Sphuliṅginī, and Viśvarūpī.

[1]Agni is called 'seven-rayed' in *RV.*, I.146,1; v. *Muṇḍ. Up.*, I.2,4.

Karambha 'Gruel.' A kind of porridge made of parched grain, barley or sesame. It was said to be a special sacrificial food prepared for Pūṣan whose teeth had been knocked out by Śiva; but the origin of the offering is more likely to have been connected with Pūṣan's association with agriculture.

Kardama 'Mud.'[1] The name of one of the lords of progeny (Prajāpatis), born from the shadow of Brahmā. He is said to have practised great austerities (*tapas*) for 10,000 years on the banks of the Sarasvatī river, after which Hari (Viṣṇu) appeared before him and praised him.

[1]Mythologically Kardama and Ciklīta (slime) are regarded as the sons of Śrī (Lakṣmī) the goddess of good fortune who is also called Karīṣiṇī 'abounding in dung'. In rites connected with vegetation and its growth, clay or mud are of the greatest importance (Gonda, *Aspects*, pp. 218, 262). Cf. the Greek Demeter as the goddess of the cultivated earth, the tilth, and as Karpophoros 'she who bears fruits'.

Karimuktā A pearl or precious jewel said to be found in an elephant's head, also believed to exist in the heads of serpents and *makaras*.

Kārīrīṣṭi A rain-spell which is given in the *Tait. Saṁ.* (II.4.7–10). The Aśvins, Soma, Mitra-Varuṇa, Parjanya, etc. are implored to give rain, and the Maruts begged to loosen the 'water-bag' and so permit the rain to fall.

On the principle of identification which runs through all Indian ritual, the sacrificer successively dons a dark garment with a black fringe, representing the colour of rain-clouds; he summons the east wind and drives away the west wind, for the wind rules the rain; he makes eight offerings to the four quarters and the four intermediate quarters to make the rain move from these areas; he then mixes *karīra* groats[1] with honey on a black antelope skin and ties the ends together; and also practises divination from the movements of a black horse.[2]

[1]The *SED.* considers *karīra* to be the plant and fruit of Cappararis aphylla which grows in deserts. The *Maitrāyaṇī Saṁ.* (I.10,12) states that the use of the fruit is to obtain rain and food.

[2]v. Hillebrandt, *Ritualliteratur*, p. 120.

Karīṣiṇī v. Kardama, n.l.

Karman An act or its performance, irrespective of purpose, and hence expressions like *karma-śīla*, 'assiduous in work'; *karma-kāla*, 'the proper time for action', etc. Thus action itself is regarded as essentially neutral, subject only to causal law.

In Brahmanical literature *karman* means 'the practice of religious duties' (*karmānuṣṭhāyin*), particularly those relating to the sacrifice, and performed solely to ensure divine favours. Later such action was designated *karma-mārga*, and defined as intentionally good or bad, and identified with *dharma* (law) as an expression of the kinetic process to which all phenomena are subject. It then became an ethical doctrine (*jñāna-mārga*) and associated with the idea of the consequences or 'fruits' of actions (*karmaphala*), and ultimately conceived as a mystical or metaphysical dogma, and one of the main features of the theory of metempsychosis[1] or 'bonds of action' (*karma-bandha*). But while the results of some actions might not be apparent during an individual life-time, their consequences, for better or worse, were inevitable in the ensuing life and its successors until at last liberation is achieved.

This notion was accepted (and still is by some sections of the Indian people) as part of a rigid biological process, accountable only to itself, and incapable of modification except in accordance with its own law.[2] This dogma was generally maintained until the introduction of *bhakti-mārga* or liberation through the practice of altruism and 'devotion (*bhakti*) to *brahman*, the divine essence', and the exercise of its divine grace (*prāsada*).

[1]Metempsychosis should be 'regarded from the biological angle as a quasi-mechanical urge for attaining the least impeded form for the development of the innate main tendency by means of future manifestations' (Heimann, *Facets*, p. 52).

[2]The *Bṛhad-Ār. Up.* (4.8) implies that *karman* is worked out in some 'supernatural world' and not in the empirical world.

v. Saṁsāra.

Karma Yoga v. Yoga.

Karṇa One of the principal figures in the war of the Pāṇḍavas and Kauravas, and the chief rival of the Pāṇḍu prince, Arjuna. Karṇa was ostensibly of lowly origin, having been brought up by a poor childless couple who had found him on the banks of the Yamunā river (*MBh.*, Ādi pa., 67). Actually Karṇa was the natural son of Kuntī[1] (later the wife of King Puru). Kuntī had abandoned Karṇa soon after birth to avoid the social stigma had her pre-marital lapse been discovered.

Karṇa became a highly skilled bowman and charioteer, but because of his lack of noble lineage was refused permission to compete at the tournament (*svayaṁbara*) of the princess Draupadī, whom custom decreed should become the bride of the champion. Upon Arjuna being declared the winner, Karṇa directed his ambition elsewhere and joined the Kauravas and was made King of Aṅga by Duryodhana, the Kuru prince-regent, who thus secured a valuable ally in the impending conflict with the Pāṇḍavas.

Kuntī's secretiveness about the identity of Karṇa's father is paralleled by that of the chroniclers of the *MBh.*, who make up for their reluctance to disclose it, or their ignorance of it, by endowing Karṇa with a mythological origin[2] and the patronage of Indra. The latter's gift of an irresistible javelin to Karṇa in exchange for his magically protective cuirass was an unfortunate exchange and later resulted in Karṇa's death. This occurred on the last day of the epic battle when Karṇa's chariot became stuck in the soft earth, so that his javelin, effective only in close fighting, was useless, and his lack of a cuirass left him at the mercy of Arjuna's bow. Karṇa pleaded for time to release his chariot, but Kṛṣṇa who was acting as Arjuna's charioteer reminded him that Karṇa had shown no mercy to his foes in similar circumstances, whereupon Arjuna shot an arrow and killed Karṇa.

Pṛthā was overcome with grief, not only at the loss of her eldest son, but also that, because of her secrecy, he should have been slain by his half-brother. But her remorse did not stop her from disclosing her secret to Arjuna and the rest of the family, for whom victory now became more bitter than defeat.

[1]Her patronymic by adoption, her proper name being Pṛthā. She was also the mother of Arjuna and of two of his brothers.

[2]Paurāṇic mythology—possibly to avoid any embarrassing speculation—ascribes Karṇa's birth to Sūrya, who was invoked by a *mantra* given to Kuntī by the sage Durvāsas, who had been her adopted father's guest. Karṇa was born with radiant armour and earrings (*EM.*, p. 87).

v. Adhiratha; Mahābhārata.

Karṇavedha From *karṇa*, 'ear' and *vedha*, 'boring'. A rite in which the ear of a woman is pierced to avert her death when the birth of a third son is imminent.

Karṇikā The tendril[1] of the world lotus. The great *ṛṣis* Atri, Bhṛgu, etc., each described it differently because each had only partial knowledge. Brahmā alone knows the totality of the universe (*Vāyu P.*, 34, 58–69, *PI.*).

[1]According to the *MBh.*, the pericarp (*SED*).

Kārṣmarya A tree, the wood of which was used in sacrificial rites because it was believed to possess the power to kill *rākṣasas*, who were a constant threat to the performance of religious rites (*ŚBr.*, VII.4.1,37).

Kārtavīrya The patronymic of Arjuna, a son of Kṛtavīrya, King of the Haihayas. Dattātreya endowed him with a thousand arms, and a golden chariot that would take him anywhere he wished, as well as giving him the desire to rule wisely. He was also given the assurance that he would not meet with death except at the hand of one renowned in the three regions of the world (*VP.*, IV.11).

The quarrel of the Haihayas and Jamadagni began as a relatively small affair, but developed into war when political and priestly interests clashed, resulting in the death of Jamadagni and Kārtavīrya.

v. Paraśurāma; Arjuna II.

Kārttika The name of a month,[1] mid-October to mid-November, when the full moon is near the Kṛttikās (Pleiades), the latter being the mythical foster-mothers of Kārttikeya, god of war.

[1]Considered the most suitable for making war.

Kārttikeya 'Associated with Kṛttikās, the Pleiades.' Kārttikeya is also known as Skanda, Kumāra, Subrahmaṇya, Mahāsena, Guha, etc.[1] As the god of war Kārttikeya is naturally associated with *kārttika* the month best suited to warfare. He is depicted on some ancient Indian tribal coins as well as on those of the Kuṣāṇa emperor Huviṣka. He was worshipped by Kumāragupta I and the Yaudheyas, an ancient military tribe.[2]

Some myths emphasize the connexion of Kārttikeya with his six foster-mothers, the Pleiades,[3] and are popular throughout India. In the Deccan these myths have apparently merged with one relating to the appeal of the gods for help in repelling the attacks of the *asuras*, to which Śiva responded by assuming six faces, each with a central eye from which six sparks darted forth. The sparks fell into a lake said to be situated some fifty miles north-west of Madras, and they became six infants, nursed by the six mothers who comprise the Pleiades. Pārvatī, Śiva's wife, took the infants in her arms, and squeezed them so affectionately that they became a single body, but with six heads. Other myths ascribe Kārttikeya's parentage to Agni and Gaṅgā when Śiva's semen was cast into the fire (*agni*) and thence into the Ganges. Other accounts simply state that he was the son of Śiva and Pārvatī.[4]

The peacock called Paravāṇi is his vehicle (*vāhana*); his wife is Kaumārī or Senā (the personification of the army).

[1] An analysis of the myths associated with these names indicates an amalgamation of various regional god-concepts and folk-elements on which the deity who became Skanda-Kārttikeya was built up. He is usually known as Subrahmaṇya in southern India.

[2] *DHI.*, p. 140.

[3] *VP.* (I.15) states that the Pleiades were his mothers.

[4] The *Chān. Up.* (7.26,2) identifies him with Sanat-Kumāra, one of the mind-born sons of Brahmā—'the blessed Kumāra shows the further shore of darkness. People call him Skanda.'

v. Kārttika; Kṛttikā; Krauñca II.

Kasarṇīla The name of a snake (*AV.*, X.4,5) slain by Paidva, the white snake-killing horse, which the Aśvins gave to Pedu (*RV.*, I.117,9; IX.88,4).

Kāśī One of the seven sacred cities of India, and the earliest name of the city of Vārāṇasī (Banāras).

It was originally the name of the kingdom of the Kāśīs, a people closely associated with Kosala and Videha in the late Vedic age. Kāśī seems to have been either the name of its first chieftain or simply that by which the tribe was known; but legend derives it from Kāśa, a type of grass (Saccharum spontaneum) which carpeted the site chosen by its first ruler.

The city, notable from the sixth century B.C., was a focal point in the history of north-eastern India and one of its great centres of learning. Its proximity to the holy Ganges has also served to enhance its religious importance and made it at various times a Brahminical, Buddhist, Jaina, Vaiṣṇava, Śaiva and Śākta place of pilgrimage. It was at Banāras that the Buddha first expounded his doctrine, and where stands the great *stūpa* commemorating the event. The views of the Kāśī religious authorities have always carried immense weight in the Hindu world.[1] To Śaivas it is pre-eminently the city of Śiva, the Lord of Kāśī (Kāśīnātha).

[1] Kāśī is likened to the top of the skull, considered to be the centre of knowledge which abides in the 'lotus of a thousand petals'.

v. Kuṇḍalinī; Triśūla.

Kāśikā Vṛtti The 'Banāras Commentary'. A commentary on Pāṇini's grammer (the *Aṣṭādhyayī*) by Jayāditya and Vāmana (7th century A.D.).[1]

[1] *WI.*, p. 388.

Kāśīrāja v. Kāśī; Gāndinī.

Kāṣṭhā Name of one of Kaśyapa's wives, said to be the mother of cloven-hoofed quadrupeds.

Kaśyapa I. A mythical figure whose solitary reference in the *RV.* (IX.114,2) suggests a remote folk origin. The *SV.* references are equally obscure, and their interpretation by both Indian and Western commentators, generally irreconcilable. This is indicated in Part I, IV.2.3,2: 'Those whom they call the attendant pair of Kaśyapa who knows the light', which may allude to heaven and earth, or according to Sāyaṇa, to Indra's horses. Other *SV.* passages speak of the 'sage', possibly an allusion to Kaśyapa, based on similar obscure references in *RV.*, IX.[1] But in the *AV.* as Bloomfield[2] observes, 'Kaśyapa is a name to conjure with; . . . amulets and charms handled by him are peculiarly powerful (I.14,4; IV.37,1) . . . He rises to the dignity of the supreme self-existing being (Svayambhū) in XIX.53,10 . . . He is also intimately related with forms of the sun, Sūrya and Savitar . . . In fact Kaśyapa is the sun, as a tortoise, that creeps its slow course across the sky . . . Only we must not forget that these writings neglect no opportunity of being guided in their constructions by puns, even of the most atrocious sort . . . In the *ŚBr.* (VII.5.1,5) Kaśyapa (referred to as Prajāpati) is punned with Kaśyapa (tortoise).[3] In some passages a second pun is perpetrated. Prajāpati, having assumed the form of a tortoise (*kūrma*), created living beings. What he created, he made (*kar*), and hence he is called '*kūrma*', i.e., '*kaśyapa*' (tortoise); therefore all creatures are said to be descended from Kaśyapa.[4]

In the *MBh.* and the Purs. Kaśyapa was provided with thirteen of Dakṣa's daughters (representing the thirteen months of the lunar year) as wives, including Aditi, by whom he begot the twelve Ādityas (representing the solar year). By other wives he begot demons, reptiles, birds and other living creatures, and by Diti and Danu the numerous aboriginal tribes generally designated Daityas and Dānavas—irrespective of their differences of language, customs and ethnic origin. It may thus be inferred that the recognition of non-Āryan tribal groups as part of the Kaśyapa myth occurred when the fusion of the Indo-Āryan peoples of India—north of the Narmadā—was relatively complete, and when derogatory terms like *dāsa* and *dasyu* had become obsolete. This is indicated by numerous legends, especially that of King Hiraṇyakaśipu, who claimed descent not only from Kaśyapa, but also from Diti, according to his metronymic Daitya. The identification of Kaśyapa with Prajāpati and the latter with Brahmā ended Kaśyapa's rôle as a secondary creator.

[1]Probably the ancient seer who became one of the seven great *ṛṣis* (*Bṛhad-Ār. Up.*, II.2,4). v. Gotra.

[2]*AVB.*, pp. 403f. The *AV.* (XIII.1,23) mentions a class of semi-divine beings called Kaśyapas who are connected with the sun.

[3]According to the *Mahābhāṣya*, Kaśyapa is an inverted form of *paśyaka* (seer) (*HP.*, p. 95, n.6).

[4]The post-Vedic Kaśyapa legends agree neither with each other, nor with those of the Vedas, the result perhaps of the syncretism of the mythical Kaśyapa (one of the *sapta-ṛṣis*) and the actual *ṛṣi* (son of Marīci) called Kaśyapa as were his descendants, to whom also various *RV. sūktas* are traditionally attributed.

v. Kūrma; Gotra.

II. One of the teachers of the Vājasaneya school. A priest called Kaśyapa is associated with Paraśurāma and Rāmacandra, and another with Janamejaya (*Ait. Br.*, VII.27).

Kāśyapī v. Pṛthivī.

Kaṭapūtana A ghostly form (*preta*) assumed at death by a kṣatriya who has neglected his religious duties (*Manu*, XII.71).

Kathā-sarit-sāgara The 'Ocean of the Streams of Story'. A large collection of stories, written by Somadeva Bhaṭṭa (11th century).

Katha Upaniṣad Name of an Upaniṣad generally said to belong to the *AV.*, but sometimes assigned to the Black Yajur Veda.

v. Bṛhatkathā.

Kātyāyana (c. 3rd century B.C.) Name of the author of works on ritual, grammar, etc., including the *vārttikas* or critical notes to Pāṇini's aphorisms; to the Śrauta-sūtras; and to the *Sarvānukramaṇī*, a work in *sūtra* form giving the first words of every *RV.* hymn, the number of verses and of metres, etc.

Kauberī The wife of Kubera and daughter of the *dānava* Mura. She is also called Yakṣī or Cārvī.

Kaumārī v. Cāmuṇḍā.

Kaumodakī The name of Viṣṇu-Kṛṣṇa's magical mace or club presented by Varuṇa. It symbolizes the invincible power of knowledge, and of Time the destroyer, and hence is associated with the goddess representing the power of time, Kālī.[1] It is also a symbol of sovereignty.

[1]Cf. the magical maces, both of which were named, and made by the divine craftsmen Kathir-and-Khasis for Baal (G. R. Driver, *Canaanite Myths*, p. 13).

v. Gadā.

Kaumudī or **Jyotsnā** Moonlight personified as the wife of Candra (the moon) and identified with the daughter (or bride) of Sūrya, the sun.

Kaurava(s) v. Mahābhārata; Pāṇḍavas; Duryodhana; Karṇa; Pṛthā.

Kauśika Sūtra One of the two sūtras attached to the *AV.*, the other being the Vaitāna.[1] The *Kauśika* contains directions for carrying out the magical rites mentioned in the *AV.*

[1]Bloomfield, *The Atharvaveda*, p. 16.

Kauśikī I. A river sacred to the *pitṛs*, and identified with Satyavatī, the wife of Ṛcīka.[1]

[1]According to the *Rām.*, Satyavatī became the river only after her death.

v. Paraśurāma.

II. Name of the goddess who issued from Pārvatī's body (*Mārk. P.*, 85, 40).

Kaustubha A magical jewel which emerged from the Churning of the Ocean (*samudramathana*). Viṣṇu-Kṛṣṇa wears it on his breast.

Kauṭilya v. Arthaśāstra.

Kavaca 'Cuirass.' There is no evidence that the *kavaca* of Vedic times was made of metal, though that is possible. Originally it may have consisted of a linen 'corselet-strap' (*kavaca-pāśa*)[1] like those known to Herodotus. But Bloomfield (*AVB.*, p. 129) translates *kavaca* as coat-of-mail.

[1]Or the *kavaca-pāśa* was used to keep the breastplate in place (S.D. Singh, *Ancient Indian Warfare*, p. 97).

Kavacam A mystical syllable (*bīja*) forming part of a *mantra*. Amulets and *mantras* give protection against danger as does the *kavaca* 'cuirass' (*AGP.*, 142, 6–17).

Kāvya 'Descendant of Kavi.'[1] A patronymic of Uśanas, generally referred to as Uśanas Kāvya, the 'messenger' of the *asuras* (*Tait. Saṁ.*, II.5,8). From certain passages in the *RV.* (IV.16, 2; I.51,10–11) he appears to have been a special friend and worshipper of

Indra and also his companion in some battles. Kāvya also made the bolt (*vajra*) with which Indra slew Vṛtra (I.121,12).

[1]Said to have been a Bhārgava (Rahurkar, *Seers*, p. 213).

v. Śukra.

Kāvya(s) A class of ornate poems, with which are included those of an erotic or dramatic character, the subject-matter of most being closely connected with the two great epics, the *Rāmāyaṇa* and *Mahābhārata*.

Kedāranātha A famous Śiva-*liṅga* in the form of a natural conical mass of ice, worshipped in the Himālaya.[1]

[1]Cf. the 'rude aniconic pillar [or stone] of immemorial sanctity' which was the earliest form or embodiment of the Greek Zeus (A.B. Cook, *Zeus*, I, p. 34).

v. Liṅga.

Kena The name of one of the thirteen principal Upaniṣads.

Keśava 'Long-haired.' A name of Viṣṇu-Kṛṣṇa. According to the *Matsya P.* (243,13, *PI.*) Keśava should be worshipped to counteract bad omens.

Various interpretations have been given of this name including the following: it was given to Kṛṣṇa after he had killed Keśin; or it refers to the myth of his origin from a black hair;[1] or it means 'the rayed' or 'radiant one', as Kṛṣṇa is associated with light (*keśa*) (*Nir.*, 12,25).

[1]Hair is considered to be one of the places where the 'soul-substance' may be localized. 'It is a form of the "external soul" and the "procreative life substance"' (Heesterman, *Ancient Indian Royal Consecration*, p. 215).

v. Balarāma.

Keśin In the *VP.* (V.16) Keśin is described as a *daitya* who assumed the form of a horse[1] to attack Kṛṣṇa, but the latter thrust his arm into its jaws and rent it in two. For this deed Kṛṣṇa was given the epithet Keśava.

RV., X.136 is dedicated to the Keśins. Bloomfield suggests that Keśin is the sun metaphorically alluded to as a solitary hermit (*muni*). This appears to be borne out by *Nir.*, 12.25–7. But Heesterman tentatively suggests that the Keśin may have been a human ecstatic who 'strives to conform to the model of a primordial cosmic man, whose long-hairedness may be taken to refer to his being a store of procreative life substance'.[2]

[1]Or he possessed 'dark horses' (*AV.*, XI.2,18). In the same work he is described as a hairy, embryo-destroying demon (VIII.6,23).

[2]*Ancient Indian Royal Consecration*, p. 218.

Keśinī A name of Durgā; of the mother of Rāvaṇa and Kumbhakarṇa; and of an *apsaras*.

Ketakī A flower which should never be offered to Śiva. It figures in a dispute between Brahmā and Viṣṇu, who each claimed to be the superior. Śiva, on being called upon to adjudicate, stated that whichever of them could discern either the top or the bottom of the cosmic fiery *liṅga*,[1] the axis of the universe, would be deemed the greater. Brahmā assumed the form of a goose (*haṁsa*) and soared upwards, whilst Viṣṇu, in the form of a boar (*varāha*) dug deeply into the earth. Ages passed without either reaching his goal. Then Brahmā saw a *ketakī* flower drifting down, which aeons before had fallen from Śiva's hair. Assuming that the flower had seen the top of the *liṅga*, Brahmā cited this as proof of his success, but Śiva refused to accept it as such, and cursed Brahmā that he should no longer be worshipped in temples.[2] Śiva also cut off one of Brahmā's heads, the one which had lied. Furthermore, he banned the offering of *ketakī* flowers to himself.

[1]This form or aspect of Śiva is called Liṅgobhavamūrti.

[2]Today there are very few temples dedicated to Brahmā.

Ketu Any unusual phenomenon such as a comet, meteor, etc.; it is also the personification of the descending node of the moon, whose chariot is drawn by eight green horses (*Brah. P.*, 23,90, etc., *PI.*). Ketu is also included as one of the nine Grahas (Navagrahas) who are propitiated at all times of danger and trouble, because all misfortunes are attributed to their anger.

v. Rāhu; Śani.

Ketumāla One of the nine great divisions of the known world. Here Viṣṇu revealed himself to Lakṣmī when she praised him (*Bhāg. P.*, V.16, 10; 17.7 etc., *PI.*). According to the *VP.* (II.2) Viṣṇu resides here in his boar (*varāha*) *avatāra*.

Khaḍga 'Sword'; 'large sacrificial knife'. The *khaḍga* was among the nine self-created weapons discovered by the gods in the depths of the ocean, and is one of the emblems of the *kṣatra* class.

When the *khaḍga* is held by Śiva (as the embodiment of knowledge) it represents his valour and the power of knowledge to destroy ignorance. But other swords, according to their size and markings, are deemed auspicious or inauspicious (*AGP.*, 245, 22–7). Those shaped like bamboo leaves were highly valued (*Bṛhat Saṁ.*, XLIX, 7).

v. Āyudhapuruṣa; Kṣatriya.

Khadira A tree whose wood was used for making sacrificial posts (*Ait. Br.*, II.1ff.) and ladles; its heart-wood for amulets, and the points of ploughshares.[1] So important was the plough in agriculture that the *khadira* was said to be god-given and 'born of the ploughshare'. Thus amulets of *khadira* wood were made in the shape of miniature ploughshares (*AVB.*, VIII.8,3).

During part of the *rājasūya* ceremony, the king sits on a *khadira*-wood throne, which is perforated and bound with thongs like that of the Bhārata kings (*ŚBr.*, V.4.4,1).

[1]It is considered more durable than teak and thus was used to make pestles, sword handles, the axle-pins of Vedic chariots, and is used in the construction of houses, etc. Furthermore, from the *khadira* is made an astringent, and ointment for burns, syphilis, etc. (*CI.*, vol. I, pp. 12f.).

v. Kṛṣi.

Khāṇḍava Indra's forest in Kurukṣetra which was burnt by Agni with the help of Kṛṣṇa and Arjuna.

Kharoṣṭhī A Sanskrit dialect employing an ancient Aramaic alphabet, modified to accord with the Indian. It was greatly superior to the original Aramaic, which lacked a precise vowel notation. It was written from right to left, and introduced into the Panjāb during the Persian domination in the fifth and fourth centuries B.C. Two recensions of the Fourteen Rock Edicts of Aśoka were inscribed in this script on rocks at places near the north-west frontier of India.

Khaṭvāṅga I. Also called Pānśula. A club or short staff with a skull-shaped top. It is one of Śiva's weapons and hence is carried by Śaiva ascetics and yogins.

II. A *cakravartin* of the Ikṣvāku (Solar) dynasty, also known as Dilīpa, son of Raghu, the grandfather of Rāmacandra.

Kīkaṭa A non-Āryan tribe, whose lack of success as cattlemen was attributed to their failure to acknowledge Indra and the gods (*RV.*, III.53,1–14; *Nir.*, 6.32).

Kīlāla A sweet drink, and a divine beverage similar to *amṛta*.

Kilāsī A kind of spotted deer, which drew the chariot of the Maruts.

Kilāta v. Kirāta.

Kimīdin(s) A species of beings also 'called *yātudhāna*, a term which oscillates between meaning "human sorcerer" and "hostile demon"';[1] tradition generally favours the latter definition. Thus many passages of the *AV.*, notably I.7,1–7; 8.1–4; 16.1–4, etc., are directed against sorcerers and demons, including *kimīdins*, *piśācas*, *rākṣasas* and a number of demonesses.[2]

Kimīdins are especially dangerous to pregnant women; not only can they devour embryos, but also possess the power to change a male embryo into a female (VIII.6.25).

[1]*AVB.*, pp. 237f.

[2]But *AV.*, II.24,5 suggests that these so-called demons may be only *dasyus* (aboriginals), especially as they are said to hate *brahmins* (VIII.4,2). Nonetheless, whichever they may be, the gods and especially Agni are implored to drive them away. Other Kimīdins are named in II.24, including Śevṛdhaka, Mroka, Sarpa, Jūrṇī, Arjunī, etc.

Kiṁpuruṣa(s) An ambiguous term which may refer to junglefolk[1] or to jungle sprites.[2] According to the *ŚBr.* (VII.5.2,32), 'Kiṁpuruṣas seems to have had some kind of ritual significance in rites directed against enemies.'

The Kiṁpuruṣas dwell on the Gandhamādana mountain where they go about in pairs, male and female, bearing swords and clad in fine raiment.[3]

[1]The *Ait. Br.* (II.8) and *ŚBr.* (I.2.3,9), etc., refer to them as apes, meaning probably ape-like men.

[2]Mythologically they are said to be a class of divinities born from Brahmā's shadow as were the Kinnaras. In Jaina canonical literature they and the Kinnaras are included among the *vyantara devatās* (*DHI.*, p. 336).

[3]*EM.*, pp. 158f.

Kinnara(s) Mythical beings with human bodies and the heads of horses (*VP.*, I.5), or with the bodies of horses and human heads. They may have been primitive folk-gods, who after the rise in importance of the post-Vedic cult-deities, were relegated to the position of inferior spirits, although appreciably influencing the forms of the principal deities of some major brahmanical cults.[1] Kinnaras are also mentioned in some Buddhist texts.

According to other myths Kinnaras were descended from Pulastya, having Śiva as their lord. With the *gandharvas* they form a celestial choir in Kubera's Paradise. Daniélou[2] considers that 'the Indian *kinnara* and Greek *kentauros* (centaur) are words of the same origin'.

It is possible that the horse-heads of the Kinnaras refer to masks worn by an aboriginal tribe of that name, a common practice to deceive and terrify their enemies.

[1]*DHI.*, pp. 335f.

[2]*HP.*, p. 307, n.7.

Kirāta A name initially applied to an aboriginal people of north-eastern India, living in mountain caves, and referred to in *Vāj. Saṁ.* (XXX.16).[1] The *AV.* (X.4,14) mentions a Kirātī girl who collects medicinal roots or herbs on the ridges of mountains. The name Kirāta (or Kilāta), later applied to a people located in eastern Nepal, seems to have been applied subsequently to any hill-folk, many of whom were hunters and foresters and probably warlike.[2]

Śiva assumed the form of a Kirāta when he fought with Arjuna over a boar, which each claimed to have killed. When Arjuna's weapons proved to be useless against the Kirāta he realized the identity of his adversary and worshipped him, whereupon Śiva gave him the invincible weapon, *pāśupata*.[3]

[1]In *VP.*, II.3 they are said to be a barbarous people living to the east of Bhārata. The *MBh.* refers to north-eastern mountaineers who are born of Agni (*EM.*, p. 104).

[2]According to *Manu* (X.44) they were originally *kṣatriyas*, who had neglected their duties and sunk to the condition of *śūdras.*

[3]*HCD.*, p. 22.

Kirātārjunīya 'Arjuna and the Kirāta.' A poem by Bhāravi, describing Arjuna's fight with a Kirāta.

Kirātī A girl or woman of the wild hill-tribe of Kirātas. It is also an epithet of Durgā and Gaṅgā.

Kīrtimukha A magical device in the form of a demon-mask[1] placed above the doorways of Śaiva temples to guard the threshold. It is also depicted above the aureole (*prabhā-maṇḍala*) at the back of the images of Śaiva deities. Its terrifying aspect drives away the impious, but assures the devotees of Śiva's protective powers.

The 'demon-mask' in Indian temples is represented by a *makara*-head, called a *kīrtimukha* (glory head), or by a *siṁhamukha* (lion's head). The *kīrtimukha* probably had no original connexion with the *makara*, but became connected with it after the Gupta period.

The *Skanda Pur.* relates that the Titan King Jalandhara was so carried away by his own power and conquests that he sent Rāhu[2] (the eclipse demon) to Śiva commanding him to give up his bride-to-be, the beautiful Pārvatī, as he desired her. This demand caused Śiva's rage to burst from his central eye in the form of a terrifying lion-headed demon, with emaciated body and flying mane. Rāhu, overcome by fear, took refuge in Śiva, so leaving the demon without a victim, whereupon he begged Śiva to provide him with food. Śiva suggested that he should eat his hands and feet and this he did, but his hunger was so great that he continued eating until only his head remained.[3] The head represents the cosmic fire which periodically annihilates the world[4] leaving only Śiva. The latter was much gratified with the all-consuming power shown by his creature that he vowed that henceforth he should be known as Kīrtimukha and that he should dwell forever by his door. Furthermore, those who entered and failed to worship him would never attain his (Śiva's) grace.

[1]Cf. the Gorgon Medusa whose face had the power to turn men to stone, showing that her potency resided only in her head, The Gorgoneion-mask is similar to the *kīrtimukha*, both having glaring eyes, protruding tusks and pendent tongue. Cf. also the Greek goddess of vengeance Praxidike whose images consisted of a head only (Harrison, *Prolegomena to the Study of Greek Religion*, p. 188; v. also Farnell, *Cults*, I, p. 264). The head 'is the ultimate terror of the underworld' (Halliday, *Indo-European Folk-Tales*, p. 138).

[2]Kramrisch suggests that *kīrtimukha* really stands for Rāhu.

[3]Cf. the rare, sex-linked genetic disease called the Lesch syndrome of self-mutilation, where children 'eat their own limbs, and even if tied up, nibble away their lips' (Anthony Michaelis, 'Screening Clue to Mongol Births', in the *Daily Telegraph*, London).

[4]Or it represents the Sun and Death, i.e., that which generates and destroys everything.

Kokāmukhā The wolf-faced form of Durgā who glories in battles (*SED.*).

Kokkara A primitive musical instrument consisting of an iron tube which when scraped rhythmically has a hypnotic effect similar to that of African *vodun* drums and some forms of 'beat' music. It is used as an accompaniment to the recitation of divine names.

Kolāhala I. The hill where the *asura* Gaya laid down his life.

v. Gayāsura.

II. A demon personifying noise or uproar, who was killed by Hari (*AGP.*, 276, 22–5).

Kosala One of the non-Āryan kingdoms of eastern India[1] which, like its immediate neighbours Kāśī and Videha, became prominent towards the end of the Vedic age. Adjoining them were other small states, either republican or having an elected king or chieftain, which played a significant part in the post-Vedic period.

The whole of this area, which was economically dependent on the Ganges and its tributaries, appears to have reached a cultural stage similar to that of the Indus Valley civilization. But whereas the latter failed to survive the impact of Āryan influence, the Gangetic States maintained a high degree of intellectual independence and political unity. Possibly the reason for this was that Kosala and other eastern states were ruled by an aristocracy, whose power was based on a warrior class upon which brahmanic influence had had little effect. This is also indicated by the radical religious and social movements which originated in that area, and in the personal character of two of their leaders, the Jaina Mahāvīra and the Buddha. Important rulers, like the Mauryas and the Guptas, also came from this area.

Although Kosala, Videha and Kāśī later became part of Magadha, and were finally absorbed by the great Mauryan empire, this in no way diminishes their former fame or the importance of their contribution to modern Hinduism.

[1]Rāma's kingdom on the banks of the Sarayū was called Kosala. The *VP.* (IV.24) mentions seven Kosalas, one

of which some Purs. locate in the Vindhya range.
v. Janaka.

Koṭavī A powerful demoness of southern India, later identified with Durgā. Koṭavī was the mother of Bāṇa, the tutelary deity of the *daityas*, and the embodiment of their sacred lore. She is said to be composed of incantations (*mantras*) and an eighth part of Rudrāṇī.[1]

When Kṛṣṇa was about to kill Bāṇa with his discus Sudarśana, Koṭavī appeared naked[2] before him in an attempt to divert him from his purpose, but he threw the discus and cut off Bāṇa's arms (*VP.*, V.33).

[1]Wilson, *VP.*, p. 68, n.4.

[2]Koṭavī means 'a naked woman'.

Kratu I. A personification of offerings and worship.
II. A personification of Intelligence as a mind-born son of Brahmā, and one of the seven or ten *Brahmarṣis* (*Manu*, I.35).[1]

[1]Their number varies considerably in different works, but the original number was probably seven.

v. Vālakhilya II.

Krauñca I. Perhaps a kind of curlew.[1] Curlews and also geese (*haṁsa*) were believed to have the capacity to separate mixed milk and water.

[1]The *SED.* suggests a curlew, but it may have been a species of heron (*Rāmāyaṇa*, vol. III, Glossary, tr. by H.P. Shastri).

II. Name of a mountain in the eastern part of the Himālaya said to have been split by Kārttikeya's lance.

When Indra and Kārttikeya failed to agree which was the more powerful, they decided that the first to circumambulate the mountain would be the winner, but even when they had done so they failed to agree and appealed to the mountain itself. The latter, being biased in favour of Indra, declared him the winner. To avenge this injustice Kārttikeya hurled his lance or spear (*śakti*) at the mountain and pierced it. Other accounts state that Paraśurāma and Vāyu pierced it with their arrows, thus creating a mountain pass.

III. Name of one of the seven *dvīpas* of the world which is surrounded by a sea of milk (or ghee), symbolizing abundance. Hari (Viṣṇu) is worshipped in Krauñca in the form of the waters (*Bhāg. P.*, V.1.32; 20.18–23, *PI.*).

Krauñcā A daughter of Tāmrā. Krauñcā is the mythical ancestress of curlews.
v. Krauñca I.

Kṛmi 'Worm.' In Vedic India worms were thought to infest the ribs, eyes, nose and teeth (*AV.*, V.23), and to be the general cause of disease in men and cattle.[1] Many spells and *mantras* in the *AV.* were therefore devoted to the destruction of worms. Agastya's incantation or *mantra* in the *RV.* (I.191) was believed to crush worms, and it was also used as an antidote to all kinds of poisons (*AV.*, II.32,3). The sun is said to be the great killer of worms (II.32,1; V.23,6).

[1]The Marsh Arabs of Iraq believe that toothache is caused by worms (Hamdani and Wenzel, 'The Worm in the Tooth', *Folklore*, vol. 77, pp. 60ff., Spring 1966). Such folk-notions concerning disease may have become crystallized in prehistoric times and become part of Indo-European folk-lore (*AVB.*, p. 314).

Krodha I. 'Anger', 'wrath', personified as a child of Lobha and Nikṛti, or of Death (Mṛtyu), etc.
II. Name of the mystic syllable *huṁ* or *hrūṁ* (*SED.*).

Krodhā A daughter of Dakṣa and wife of Kaśyapa. She became the mother of *bhūtas*.

Krodhavaśa (s) Native tribesmen of northern India, some of whom were slain by Bhīma. They are sometimes referred to as *rākṣasas*, or as *yakṣas*.[1]

[1]According to the *MBh.* they were spirits who take away all merit from those who keep dogs (*EM.*, p. 45).

Kṛpa I. A prince who was assisted by Indra (*RV.*, VIII.3,12; 4,2).
II. A 'son' of the *ṛsi* Śaradvat by the nymph Urvaśī, and the brother of Kṛpī. Kṛpa was also called Gautama and Śāradvata. Kṛpa was adopted by king Śāntanu.

Kṛpī Tradition ascribes her paternity to the *ṛsi* Śaradvat, also called Gautama, whence her patronymic Gautamī. But the *Vāyu P.* (99, 204, *PI.*) states that Kṛpī and her brother Kṛpa were born in a bed of *kuśa* grass, after the unsuccessful attempt of a nymph sent by Indra to seduce Śaradvat. The two children were found by King Śāntanu who adopted them out of compassion (*kṛpa*), whence their names. Kṛpī later became the wife of Droṇa and mother of Aśvatthāman.

Kṛśana 'Pearl' or 'mother-of-pearl'. Pearls adorned Savitṛ's golden chariot (*RV.*, I.35,4). In an *AV.* hymn (IV.10), directed against various kinds of evil, a pearl-shell is said to be an efficacious amulet. In the same hymn pearls are called the bones of the gods.

Kṛśānu I. 'Archer.' A semi-divine being or *gandharva* sometimes identified with Rudra, and guardian of the celestial *soma* (*RV.*, I.155,2; IV.27,3, etc.). Kṛśānu is the counterpart of the Avestan Gandarewa Keresani who is connected with *haoma*.
II. Name of a man whom the Aśvins helped to win a horse-race (*RV.*, I. 112,21).

Kṛśāśva A sage and husband of two of Dakṣa's daughters whom the *Rām.* calls Jayā and Vijayā. The deified weapons (*śastradevatās*) are regarded as his progeny (*AGP.*, 19,4; *VP.*, I.15).
v. Āyudhapuruṣa.

Kṛṣi 'Ploughing'. From $\sqrt{kṛṣ}$ 'to plough' (*RV.*, I.23,15; 176,2). Though the cultivation of the soil appears to have been known to the Āryans before their separation in Irān, it seems strange that expressions for ploughing should occur mainly in *maṇḍalas* I and X of the *RV.*, and only rarely in II to VIII.

Pṛthi (or Pṛthu)[1] is credited with the introduction of ploughing and the cultivation of grain (*AV.*, VIII.10,24), but this is also ascribed to the Aśvins (*RV.*, I.117,21). The later Saṁhitās and Brāhmaṇas frequently refer to ploughing, the use of the plough being regarded as one of the characteristics of Āryan or brahminic civilization, distinguishing it from that of the non-Āryan Indian tribes.

As much of the land was unsuitable for agriculture, specific names, such as *urvarā* or *kṣetra*, were given to suitable areas. Irrigation and the use of manure were introduced, and ploughs of various sizes, drawn by oxen in teams of six, eight, twelve, or even twenty-four were used.

Apart from enemy raiders, the agriculturalist had to contend with moles, birds, and other animals and reptiles which destroyed the seed or injured the young shoots. In addition there was the hazard of drought or excessive rain, and hence the numerous spells to avert these calamities (*AV.*, VI.91,1; VII.11).

[1] Pṛthu is said to be the first anointed king. For a survey of royal ploughing ceremonies in India and Greater India, v. H.G. Quarich Wales, *Siamese State Ceremonies*, pp. 256ff.

v. Khadira; Veṇa; Yava.

Kṛṣṇa I. Son of the Vedic Devakī, subsequently identified with the Kṛṣṇa of the *MBh.*, and finally with the Viṣṇu of the Pūraṇas. This syncretism is based on a combination of fragments of traditional history and diverse myths and legends.

The Kṛṣṇa cult is based on two traditions: one identifying him with a Yādava prince, the son of the Paurāṇic Devakī and her husband Vasudeva, whence Kṛṣṇa's patronymic, Vāsudeva. The other tradition identifies him with one of Ghora Āṅgirasa's pupils (the mother of whom was also called Devakī), to whom there is a single reference in the Upaniṣads, the *Chān.* (III.17,6).

Many of the Kṛṣṇa legends in the Purāṇas, follow the Yādava tradition which is supported by a legend relating to his uncle, Kaṁsa, the tyrannical ruler of Mathurā, whose assassination by one of the sons of Devakī (Kaṁsa's cousin) had been predicted by the *ṛṣi* Nārada. To avert this Kaṁsa had her first six sons killed at birth, but the seventh (Balarāma, also called Baladeva or Balabhadra), was transferred to the womb of Rohiṇī, Vasudeva's second wife, and the eighth (Kṛṣṇa) was smuggled out of the palace and placed in the care of foster-parents, a cow-herdswoman Yaśodā and her husband Nanda, who lived on the banks of the Yamunā (Jumna).

Kaṁsa, who had earlier deposed his father Ugrasena and usurped his throne, was later killed by Kṛṣṇa. To avoid war with Kaṁsa's powerful father-in-law, Jarāsandha, King of Magadha, the Yādavas withdrew with Kṛṣṇa and established themselves at Dvārakā on the West coast, well out of reach of Jarāsandha. The latter's death at the hands of Bhīma, one of the five Pāṇḍu princes, ensured Kṛṣṇa's alliance with the Pāṇḍavas.

But in one respect this traditional account is difficult to accept without many reservations, owing to discrepancies in the description of the geographical background of the Āryan conquest of India.[1] If the traditional date of the Mahābhārata war (c. 1400 B.C.) is accepted, it precludes any knowledge of Magadha and the other kingdoms of eastern India by either Pāṇḍavas or Kauravas, for Indo-Āryan penetration of eastern India did not occur until some centuries later. Thus Kṛṣṇa-Vāsudeva, the Yādava prince, must have belonged to the later period. Also, it is by no means certain, as is usually assumed, that Kṛṣṇa, the Pāṇḍavas, the Kauravas and Jarāsandha were Āryans, for evidence is gradually accumulating that a fairly developed culture and powerful non-Āryan kingdoms flourished in that part of India before the entry of the Āryans.[2]

The tradition of the semi-divine Kṛṣṇa[3] was not at first specifically associated with the pupil of Ghora Āṅgirasa, but it becomes apparent in the *MBh.* that the reputation of Kṛṣṇa, the *kṣatriya*, ill-accorded with that of the saintly post-Vedic Kṛṣṇa,[4] and hence the subsequent emphasis on the latter aspect of his character. This had undoubtedly become established about the fourth century B.C., as is indicated by Pāṇini (IV.3,98), and confirmed by Patañjali who states that Vāsudeva 'is the name of the "worshipful", i.e., of one who is pre-eminently worshipful'.[5] Epigraphic remains of the second century B.C. also associate Vāsudeva with the Bhāgavata cult in north-western India, as is indicated by an inscription found at Ghosundi in Rājputāna which mentions the hall of worship of Saṁkarṣaṇa (Balarāma) and Vāsudeva.[6]

The development of the Bhāgavata cult by *kṣatriyas* in western India is paralleled by that in the east where the Jaina and Buddhist cults were also founded or developed by *kṣatriyas*. All these cults not only rejected the ancient belief in the efficacy of blood-sacrifice as a means of attaining 'liberation', but were also unanimous in replacing it by a doctrine of *ahiṁsā* (non-injury, and especially non-killing). These post-Vedic cults also represent the general desire for a more personal religious relationship which philosophical speculation failed to provide. Vaiṣṇavism thus had its *avatāras* and *vyūhas*, Śaivism its *śaktis*, Jainism its *tīrthaṅkaras*, and Buddhism its *arhats* and *bodhisattvas*. This development in the apotheosis of Kṛṣṇa is indicated in the association of his name with Hari, and both with Nara and Nārāyaṇa as the four sons of Dharma, subsequently regarded as the four *vyūhas*[7] of Viṣṇu.

In the *MBh*. Vāsudeva is called Sātvata[8] and at the end of ch. 66 of the Bhīṣma *parvan*, Bhīṣma says: '"This eternal god, mysterious, beneficent and loving should be known as Vāsudeva, and *brāhmaṇas*, *kṣatriyas*, *vaiśyas* and *śūdras* should worship him by their devoted actions".'[9] But by whatever name the 'Source of all being' is called, whether Puruṣa, Virāj, Hiraṇyagarbha, Prajāpati, Brahmā, Hari, or Nārāyaṇa, all speculative ideas about the nature of man and the universe become crystallized in the notion of an impersonal cosmic essence, believed by devout Vaiṣṇavas to be manifested in Viṣṇu, the Supreme Lord (Maheśvara). Thus the validity of Kṛṣṇa's apotheosis does not depend on genealogy, or on theological assumptions (often of a dubious character),[10] still less on the accounts of his boyhood adventures among the *gopīs*, but on faith (*śraddhā*), not unlike that of the Christian belief in the divinity of Christ.

[1]*HCIP*., I, p. 311.

[2]Ibid., p. 313. In a Vedic hymn 50,000 Kṛṣṇas are said to have been slain. This probably refers to a non-Āryan tribe who fought against the Āryans.

[3]Heimann suggests that Kṛṣṇa was probably an ancient god of cattle (*IWP*., p. 36).

[4]Particularly his advice to Arjuna to ignore Karṇa's appeal for time when his chariot was stuck in the mud during the Pāṇḍava-Kaurava war.

Many of Kṛṣṇa's exploits resemble those of Indra's. The latter killed many demons including Vṛtra, protected cows and fought Vala. Kṛṣṇa killed the demons Kāliya and Śambara and many others, and also protected cows and herdsmen.

[5]Bhandarkar, *VSM*, p. 3.

[6]Both are also listed as cult names in an early Buddhist text, the *Niddesa*, which forms part of the *Khuddaka Nikāya*.

[7]These four *vyūhas* or personified forms, appear to have been introduced subsequent to the composition of the *Bhagavadgītā*, as it makes no reference to them.

[8]A genealogical allusion to the descendants of the Vṛṣṇis (a branch of the Yādavas).

[9]Bhandarkar, *VSM*, p. 8.

[10]These appear to be late inventions as, except for one allusion, the *MBh*. does not mention them. Another late myth expressed as a pun, attributes the conception of Kṛṣṇa (black) to one of Viṣṇu's black hairs (v. Balarāma). The true explanation is probably that given in the *Bhagavadgītā*, in which Kṛṣṇa refers to himself as Time (*kāla*), also meaning 'black', which leads every mortal into the sombre realm of death. Or it may indicate that he was a member of the dark-skinned aboriginals.

The Greek Zeus is described as having 'a darkling brow', i.e. '"blue here implies "black" . . . a confusion characteristic of early thought and as such well-known to anthropologists' (A. B. Cook, *Zeus*, I, p. 2, n.2). The *Nir*. (2.20) derives *kṛṣṇam* from the root *kṛṣ* (to drag away). v. also R. V. Joshi, *Le Rituel de la dévotion Kṛṣṇaite*, for ceremonies associated with the cult of Kṛṣṇa's image.

v. Avatāra; Pūtanā; Pradyumna; Satyabhāmā; Pārijāta; Tulasī; Tulasīvivāha; Kaumodakī; Jara; Govardhana; Gopāla; Ariṣta I; Aniruddha I; Balāhaka I; Cāṇūra; Kucaila; Keśin; Viṣṇu; Syamantaka; Nandaka; Rukmiṇī; Tṛṇāvarta; Śrīvatsa; Satrājita.

II. 'Black.' In some passages of Vedic literature the word denotes a dark-coloured animal or bird, but in the *Tait. Saṁ*. (V.2.6,5) and the *ŚBr*. (I.1.4,1) it refers to an antelope. A few other passages indicate a bird of prey, but all references indicate black or dark colouration. This epithet is never used to denote skin colour, i.e., of non-Āryan Indians, the term for which is *dāsa-varṇa*.

III. The name of a seer[1] (*RV*., VIII.85.3,4). This hymn ascribes to him or to Viśvaka, son of Kṛṣṇa (Kārṣṇi), the authorship of the next hymn (VIII.86). In two other hymns of the *RV*. the Aśvins are said to have restored Viṣṇāpū to Viśvaka Kṛṣṇiya (which as a patronymic would be an isolated form of Kārṣṇya), thus making Kṛṣṇa the grandfather of Viṣṇāpū, and possibly identical with Kṛṣṇa Āṅgirasa mentioned in the *Kauṣītaki Br*. (XXX.9).[2]

[1]Whatever the origin of the name, its meaning, 'black or dark-coloured', like the contrasting name of the Pāṇḍu prince Arjuna (white), or that of the famous Buddhist teacher Nāgārjuna (lit. White Nāga) has no racial significance. Cf. the English surname Black, or the German Schwartz, or the use of 'black' as an allusion to the armour of a warrior, like that of the Black Prince (of Wales), or the Black Knight of the Morte D'Arthur (v. Kṛṣṇa I. n.10).

[2]*VI*., vol. I. p. 184.

IV. The name of a hell to which go those who cause impotence in others, trespass on land, are impure, or who gain their livelihoods by fraud (*VP*., II.6).

Kṛṣṇa-dvaipayana The twenty-eighth Veda-vyāsa, the legendary compiler or arranger (*vyāsa*) of the *Mahā-*

bhārata. He was the natural son of the *ṛṣi* Parāśara and Satyavatī and was born on an island (*dvīpa*) in the Yamunā (Jumna) river, and hence his appellation Dvaipāyana.

Kṛṣṇāṣṭamī or **Gokulāṣṭamī** A fertility festival associated with the Viṣṇu cult in which the participants throw milk, coconuts and other fruits at each other.[1]

[1]Gonda, *Aspects*, p. 233.

v. Nanda ¶.

Kṛta I. The name of the side of a die marked with four dots and regarded as the lucky or winning die. It is also the collective name of the four dice in opposition to the fifth die called *kali*.

II. Name of the first of the four ages of the world; also called *satya-yuga*. In this age all people belonged to one caste called the *haṁsa*, and all worshipped the same deity and had a single *veda*. It was a 'golden age'.

v. Yuga; Kalpa; Jyotiṣa.

Kṛtaka A son by adoption who having no *gotra* of his own assumes that of his adopted father. He has the same rights as a legitimate son.

Kṛtānta I. 'Fate or destiny.' Rāma declared that 'our life and death, joy and pain ... are surely the work of fate' (*Rām*., II.22, 22f., *IRA*.).

II. An epithet of Yama, the ruler of the dead (*AGP*., 318,20).

Kṛtavīrya v. Kārtavīrya.

Kṛttikā(s) The name of the constellation, Pleiades,[1] originally the first, but later the third lunar mansion, having Agni[2] as its regent. This constellation was originally believed to contain six stars and is sometimes represented as a flame or sword. Agni's association with it indicates that he was at one time a war-god.[3]

In mythology the six *kṛttikās* are the nymphs who became the nurses of the god of war Kārttikeya.

[1]This constellation is an open star cluster in the constellation of Taurus. Six stars only are visible to the naked eye, but several hundred can be seen with a telescope. All these stars are associated and move in the same direction and speed in space.

[2]According to the *Tait. Saṁ*. (V.3,9) the gods, by means of fire, went to the celestial world and became the *kṛttikās*.

[3]*EM*., p. 106.

Kṛtyā 'Spell', 'enchantment', 'witchcraft', personified as a divinity of witchcraft (*abhicāradevatā*). Sacrifices are offered to Kṛtyā for destruction and for magical purposes.[1] She is described as blue and red and clings closely to her victim (*RV*., X.85,28–30). An *AV*. hymn (X.1) represents Kṛtyā 'as an elaborate effigy (bogey) with head, nose and ears; the ritual is well acquainted with similar artful devices'.[2] According to Utpala, Kṛtyā denotes a woman raised from the fire by means of *abhicāra* rites for the destruction of enemies; but Manu (III.58) regards her as a 'female relation' who by her curse can destroy whole families. The commentator Keśava states that the magical operator looks at the *kṛtya* whilst muttering the *mantra AV*., V.14,9, and then shoots at it with a special bow and arrow. The effect of a destructive act in the ritual sphere is enhanced when it is accompanied by a look directed towards the object which must be struck (*ŚBr*., VI.3.3,12).

When Kṛṣṇa killed the King of Kāśī, the latter's son propitiated Śaṅkara (Śiva) and implored him to destroy Kṛṣṇa. Śaṅkara agreed and from out of the southern fire (*dakṣiṇāgni*) sprang a huge terrifying female (*Kṛtyā*) blazing with light and with a fiery radiance playing about her hair. She called loudly to Kṛṣṇa and then departed to Dvārakā. Kṛṣṇa, realizing that she was a magical creation of Śaṅkara's, sent his invincible discus (*cakra*) Sudarśana against her. Kṛtyā, terrorstruck at its power, fled to Kāśī. The army of Kāśī and the hosts of demigods attendant on Śiva attacked the discus, but were powerless against it and the whole city was totally destroyed (*VP*., V.34). This legend points to rivalry between Śaivas and Vaiṣṇavas at Kāśī, which has been and still is a Śaiva centre.

[1]Cf. the Akkadian ... rite designed to counteract black magic. Wax or wooden figurines are made of the sorcerer who bewitched the supplicant, and are melted or burnt in the fire (Reiner, *Šurpu*, Intro., p.2). Information is given in the *Ait. Br*. (III.19) for those wishing to practise witchcraft. Whitney (*AV*., vol. I. p. 180n.) suggests that *kṛtyā* may be an object into which an evil influence is conveyed by sorcery, and when buried becomes a source of harm to those against whom it is directed. In Voodoo, *wanga* (an evil charm) is conveyed to one or more objects by means of a magic procedure. These objects then become injurious to those people against whom the *wanga* is directed. Today the most powerful of these charms are those in which the Roman Catholic Host is incorporated (A. Metraux, *Voodoo*, p. 285 and n.). In Haiti the power of a *wanga* is often personified (ibid.). Gonda (*Eye and Gaze in the Veda*, p. 18) suggests that *kṛtyā* is a doll or image prepared for destructive purposes. The hideous doll-like creatures suspended from Nāyar houses in Malabar attract the eye of the passer-by and so prevent him from 'overlooking' the inmates of the house (F. Fawcett, *Madras Museum Bulletin*, 1901, iii, no. 3,309).

[2]Bloomfield, *The Atharvaveda*, p. 66. 'All India is pervaded by sorcery from the *RV*. ... through the *Yajus*-literature, and curiously enough, also the Upaniṣads ... to the Tantras of the worshippers of

Śakti' (ibid.).

v. Abhicāra.

Kṣamā 'Patience', personified as a daughter of Dakṣa and wife of the *ṛṣi* Pulaha (*VP*., I.7); also an epithet of the personified Earth and of Durgā.

Kṣatra 'Supremacy', 'power', 'dominion'. The term occurs in the *RV*. (I.24,11; IV.17,1; V.62,5–6, etc.), and denotes the power of the gods, particularly of Indra and of Mitra-Varuṇa, but never that of the secular ruler. In one passage of the *AV*. (III.5,2) *kṣatra* denotes the superhuman potency secreted by the gods in the *parṇā* tree from which amulets were made. In other *AV*. passages temporal power is referred to as *rājanya*, not *kṣatra*. This is apparent in two hymns (III.3 and 4) which mention the rites to ensure the restoration of a ruler who has been driven from his dominions by a rival (*parārājena*).[1]

The first mention of *rājanya* is in *RV*., X.90, where it denotes the ruling and warrior class (later known also as *kṣatriya*), which is defined as protector of the tribe (*gopā janasya*). In addition to the *rājanya* the hymn also distinguishes the priestly class (*brāhmaṇa*); the commonalty (*viś* or *vaiśya*), which includes herdsmen, agriculturists, merchants, craftsmen etc., and lastly the menial class (*śūdra*).

References to '*rājan*', '*rājanya*', '*kṣatra*', '*kṣatra-pati*' and '*kṣatriya*' all relate to social classes having common interests, though the significance of these designations varied with changes in the social and political structure.[2] Thus it is possible, as is suggested in the *VI*. (vol. I, p. 202), that *kṣatra* became the collective term for *kṣatriyas*. Similarly *rājan* and *kṣatra-pati* were later used synonymously, and *rājanya* used as a collective term, denoting both the ruler and the aristocracy.[3] Also the *ŚBr*. (I.3.2, 14–15), whilst distinguishing the king (*rājan*) from the warrior (*kṣatriya*), makes it clear that they have equal rights in the appropriation of the *vaiśya*'s goods. It is also apparent that for a considerable period these distinctions were not as rigid as when the caste system became established. Nonetheless, learning ceased to be the prerogative of the priestly class, just as many of the traditional occupations of the commonalty were also shared by members of the brahmanical and *kṣatra* classes. Polygamy was practised mainly by the latter to provide descendants and thus preserve the *gotra* and the continuance of the *śrāddha* rites. Precedence was given to the first wife or to the one of the highest caste.[4]

[1] *AVB*., p. 327.

[2] Thus a distinction between '*rājanya*' and '*kṣatriya*' is occasionally made, as in the *Ait. Br*. (VII.20) where a *rājanya* asks a *kṣatriya* for a place to sacrifice.

[3] As in other Indo-European communities, it is probable 'that in the period of the *Ṛgveda* the priesthood and the nobility were hereditary' (*CHI*., vol. I, p. 125).

[4] Auboyer, *Daily Life in Ancient India*, p. 188.

v. Varṇa; Rājasūya; Aśvamedha.

Kṣatriya In the narrowest sense it denotes the warrior, but in the widest sense, the class collectively known as *kṣatra*. 'That it covered the royal house and the various branches of the royal family may be regarded as certain. It, no doubt, also included the nobles and their families',[1] and as the Āryan settlements became established the retainers of each noble family became trained men-at-arms, whose weapons were the bow and spear, the chariot being generally reserved for their masters. It is unlikely that the fighting forces of the Āryans were composed only of a warrior class; no doubt they included all tribesmen capable of bearing arms when threatened by hostile Indian indigenes (*dasyus*, etc.).

The connexion of *brāhmaṇa* and *kṣatra* was generally close, each class being dependent on the other, their relationship maintained by the king's domestic priest (*purohita*), who ensured that the commonalty was not—as sometimes occurred—subjected to the rapacity of the *kṣatriyas*. But the legendary accounts of sanguinary struggles between the *brāhmaṇa* and *kṣatra* classes leading to 'the final overthrow, and even annihilation, of the *kṣatriyas* can hardly deserve much credence'.[2]

According to the *Dharma Sūtra* of Vasiṣṭha (II.15–17) 'the lawful occupations of a *kṣatriya* are three: studying, sacrificing ... and bestowing gifts; and his peculiar duty being to protect the people with his weapons; let him gain his livelihood thereby.'

The *Vasiṣṭha Dharma Sūtra* (I.28–9) lists six types of marriage, including the *kṣatra*, or right to a bride captured during a military campaign. The same work (I.24) allows a *kṣatriya* two wives, but the *Baudhayana Dharma Sūtra* (I.8.16,2) permits three.[3]

With the establishment of kingdoms and secular law, the traditional view that the *brāhmaṇas* alone possessed the right to perform all sacrificial ceremonies, or that learning also was their sole prerogative ceased to be accepted by the *kṣatra* class. Thus at the ceremonial anointing of a king (*rājasūya*) the priest sat below the *kṣatriyas*.

[1] *VI*., vol. I, p. 203.

[2] *ŚBr*., I, Intro., xiv; and v. Paraśurāma.

[3] *Brāhmaṇas* were allowed four wives, and *kṣatriyas* two or three who could be of the *kṣatriya*, *vaiśya* or *śūdra* class (v. Hari Prasad Shastri's translation of the *Rāmāyaṇa*, vol. I, p. 36, n.3).

v. Indravrata; Indra; Vivāha; Varṇa.

Kṣetrapāla A tutelary deity[1] and guardian of South

Indian Śaiva temples and of the area surrounding them. Kṣetrapāla should be worshipped before each rite or its efficacy would be destroyed. He is sometimes addressed as Mahābhairava and is thus identified with Bhairava, a form of Śiva.

[1]There are said to be forty-nine Kṣetrapālas.

Kṣetrasya pati 'Lord of the soil (or field).'[1] A tutelary deity invoked to gain cattle, horses, and to fill heaven and earth with sweetness. According to the Gṛhya Sūtras special worship and sacrifices are offered to this god when the fields are ploughed.

[1]Cf. the Hattic divinity Wurunkatte 'King of the Land' (E. Laroche, *Recherches sur les noms des dieux hittites*, pp. 37f., Paris, 1947; Laroche, *Journal of Cuneiform Studies*, I, 1947, pp. 196, 215; and the Greek Erichthonios who may have been originally 'a spirit of the fertility of the fields, although mythology has converted him into a legendary ancestral king of Athens' (Nilsson, *A History of Greek Religion*, p. 32).

v. Kṣetrasya patnī.

Kṣetrasya patnī 'Queen of the soil (or field).' A tutelary deity (*AV.*, II.12,1).

Kṣetriya Some kind of incurable (or hereditary?) disease (*AV.*, II.8), which according to Pāṇini is curable only in a future life (*SED.*); but the *AV.* (III.7) states that the antidote is the horn of a gazelle (*hariṇa*). Heesterman suggests that it may refer to the membranes adhering to the newly born child, which may have been 'considered the physical form in which a hereditary illness might attach itself to the child' (*Ancient Indian Royal Consecration*, p. 18).

Kṣudhā A 'secondary' goddess. At the dissolution of the world at the end of an age, the great primary goddess Mahālakṣmī (in whom the three *guṇas* are manifested) assumes the form of Mahākālī, known also as Tṛṣā, Nidrā, Kālarātrī, Kṣudhā, etc.[1]

[1]*DHI.*, p. 496.

Kubera or **Kuvera** An earth-spirit of ancient Indian folklore mentioned in the *AV.* (VIII.10,28), who gradually became one of the principal figures in an ever-increasing corpus of Indo-Āryan myth and legend.[1]

In what are probably the oldest Kubera myths, he is described as the leader of those mysterious genii, the *yakṣas*, *guhyakas* and *rākṣasas*,[2] the guardians of his nine divine treasures (*nidhis*). The *yakṣas* also guard the minerals and precious stones hidden in the earth which, according to ancient Indian belief, wander about freely, but are occasionally revealed to man by Kubera. Hence he came to be regarded as the lord of riches (Dhanapati)[3] who dwells in the womb of jewels (*ratnagarbha*).

The main source of the Kubera legends is the *Rāmāyaṇa* and Purāṇas, where he is said to be the son of the non-Āryan seer Pulastya and of Iḍaviḍā, a daughter of the *ṛṣi* Bharadvāja, or that his father was Viśravas, the son of Bharadvāja, and hence his patronymic Vaiśravas. But according to the *MBh.* his mother was a non-Āryan woman called Bhadrā, a daughter of Mura.

The dominions of Kubera and his half-brother Rāvaṇa comprised a great deal of southern India and the whole of Laṅkā, the conquest of which is described in the *Rāmāyaṇa*. Rāvaṇa was chief of the Rākṣasa tribe. He defeated Kubera, usurped his throne, and subsequently abducted Sītā the wife of Rāma during their exile in southern India. Kubera became an ally of Rāma and hence is included in the mythology of some Vaiṣṇava sects, but he is also regarded as a companion of Śiva and hence some Śaiva sects accord him recognition.

Kubera is one of the eight guardians of the world (Lokapālas). Kings are said to be formed from the eight eternal particles of the Lokapālas (*Manu*, V.96; VII.4–5).

Images of Kubera were often of gold and adorned with numerous multi-coloured emblems. He is depicted as a pot-bellied dwarf with three legs,[4] eight teeth and one eye; his vehicle (vāhana) is a man (nara).[5] He dwells on Mount Kailāsa in a palace set in beautiful gardens. Like Śiva he is associated with generative power and is invoked at weddings.[6]

[1]Kubera attends the nineteenth Jaina *tīrthaṅkara* of the present *avasarpiṇī*.

[2]The demonic *guhyakas* and *rākṣasas*, like those connected with Paśupati and Kumāra, are attracted by the smell of putrefying matter and hence to patients suffering from ulcers (*Suś. Saṁ.*, I. p. 180).

[3]According to *Manu* (VII.42) he attained this position by means of his great humility.

[4]The Greek Priapos was also three-legged (*EM.*, p. 148).

[5]But according to Coomaraswamy *nara* in this context does not refer to man but to 'mythological beings variously described, sometimes as bird-horses, which may possibly explain the occasional representation of winged Atlantes' (*Yakṣas*, pt. i, p. 8).

[6]In his role as a marriage divinity he bears the epithet Kāmeśvara (Lord of love); hence he is closely associated with the amorous *gandharvas* (*EM.*, p. 148). For the Kubera cult in Java v. Krom, *Archaeological Description of Bārābudur*, pp. 17f.

v. Alakā; Puṣpaka; Śukra II; Caitaratha; Sūryabhānu.

Kubjikā The tutelary goddess of potters. Pottery was regarded as a menial occupation.

Kucaila The name of a poor *brāhmaṇa* who had been one of Kṛṣṇa's fellow-pupils. His wife urged him to visit Kṛṣṇa at Dvārakā, which he finally but reluctantly agreed to do. Kṛṣṇa welcomed and entertained him, but sent him away empty-handed. Kucaila wondered why the customary gift to the parting guest had not been made, but then thought no more of it. To his amazement, on nearing the end of his journey he saw—not his own poor dwelling—but a great mansion, and coming to meet him his wife and a host of servants. Kucaila henceforth became a devoted worshipper of Kṛṣṇa (*Bhāg. P.*, X.80, 6–45; 81, *PI.*).

Kūdī A plant. Small bundles of its twigs are tied to the foot of a corpse so that on its way to the realm of the dead its footsteps will be obliterated, thus preventing its return to the land of the living (*RV.*, X.18,2; *AV.*, V.19,12).[1]

[1]It was customary in parts of Lincolnshire 'to tie the feet of the dead man to prevent him walking' (K. Thomas, *Religion and the Decline of Magic*, p. 595).

v. Mṛtyu; Yama.

Kuhū The name of one of the four daughters of Aṅgiras and Śraddhā, who according to *Manu* (III.86) personifies the first day of the waxing moon, which though invisible actually rises. On the following day, when it becomes visible it is personified as Sinīvalī. But the name of the goddesses representing these lunar phases vary in different works. Thus the *VP.* (II.8) states that the day when the moon rises is called Amāvāsyā; the day when first seen, Sinīvalī; and the first day of its disappearance, Kuhū.

Kuhū is associated with particular sacrifices and invocations and is invoked to give a great hero abundance of wealth (*AV.*, VII.47). She is also implored to give her worshippers the glory and fame of their ancestors (*Nir.*, 11.33). Sāyaṇa identifies her with the *RV.* lunar goddess Gungū.

v. Candra; Sāya.

Kujambha An *asura* who commanded the army of Bṛhaspati's wife Tārā (or Tārakā).

Kujambha's chariot was drawn by mules whose heads were covered with masks of demonic appearance (*Matsya P.*, 147. 28; 148. 42–50; 150. 76–121, etc., *PI.*), intended to terrify the enemy, a common practice of many aboriginal tribes.

v. Budha.

Kukkuṭa I. 'Cock.' The emblem on the banner presented to Skanda by the wind-god Vāyu.

II. According to the *Matsya P.* (237,5) a cock crowing in the evening is an ill omen.

Kula 'Family'; 'lineage'. It denotes the 'home' or 'family domicile', and by metonymy the family itself.

Kula, like *jati* (birth) and *gotra* (theoretically denoting the original bearer of the family name, borne by his descendants or assumed by adoption), have all to be considered in defining a particular person's position in the social structure, i.e., his caste.

v. Gotra; Pravara; Kula devatās; Varṇa.

Kula devatā(s) The household gods chosen by the members of a family (*kula*) for worship on special occasions. These *devatās* are usually associated with the house and its neighbourhood rather than with the family itself. Thus if a family moves to another area, its members either return periodically to their former village to worship their chosen *devatās*, or they devote a sacred jar or pot (*kumbha*) in the new home to represent them.[1]

[1]Diehl, *Instrument and Purpose*, p. 174.

v. Kumbhamātā; Kumbha.

Kuliśa A synonym of the thunderbolt (*vajra*), the shatterer of river banks (*Nir.*, 6.17). It is also the term for an axe or hatchet.

Kumāra 'Boy', 'adolescent', 'youth'.[1] A name of Skanda, the god of war. Kumāra is identified with the ninth form of Agni (*ŚBr.*, VI.1.3,18), or is regarded as the son of Agni (*VP.*, I.15). Kumāra married Indra's daughter Devasenā, the personification of the army. Kumāra was given a cock and a peacock by Hari (Viṣṇu), and by Sarasvatī and Brahmī, a lute and goat, and by Śiva a ram (*Brah. P.*, III.3,24; 10. 35–48, *PI.*).

[1]The old Tamil god Murugan on whom Skanda's attributes were grafted is said in an early poem to appear in 'the form of a young man, fragrant and beautiful', and hence the epithet *kumāra* may have been transferred to Skanda. Cf. Apollo, called the 'boy-god' by the Laconians (Farnell, *Cults*, IV, p. 127).

Kumāra(s) The four (or five) mind-born sons of Brahmā who refused to create progeny. Their names are Sanatkumāra, Sananda, Sanaka, Sanātana; a fifth, Ṛbhu is sometimes included.

Kumārasambhava 'The Birth of the War-god Skanda.' The title of a long poem by Kālidāsa, describing *inter alia* the courtship and marriage of Śiva and Pārvatī and the birth of their son Kumāra (also called Skanda).

Kumārī Name of one of the seven holy rivers that wash away 'sin' (*VP.*, II.4).

Kumbha 'Pot, pitcher, or jar.' These water-vessels are identified with mother-goddesses, and thus represent the womb, the 'generative pot'.[1] Extensive use was made of water-vessels in Vedic ritual, a practice that has survived to the present day.[2]

[1]Cf. the *vodun* ceremony for the reclamation of the soul after death, when it is placed in a clay jar (*govi*), a substitute for the vessel of flesh which once housed the soul (Maya Deren, *The Divine Horsemen*, p. 28).

[2]Coomaraswamy, *Yakṣas*, pt. ii, p. 26.

v. Kalaśa; Kumbhamātā; Vasiṣṭha; Grāmadevatā(s); Kula devatā(s).

Kumbhaghṛta v. Ghṛta.

Kumbhakarṇa 'Pot-eared.' A *rākṣasa*, son of Viśravas and Keśinī and brother of Rāvaṇa. Kumbhakarṇa had been cursed by Brahmā[1] to sleep for six months at a time and to awake for only a single day, as a punishment for harassing gods and men.

Rāvaṇa, needing help to fight Rāma, sent messengers to arouse him, which was only achieved with difficulty. Kumbhakarṇa then joined his brother and captured the monkey (or monkey-masked) chieftain Sugrīva, and carried him to Laṅkā. But on his return to the battle he was defeated by Rāma who cut off his head.[2]

[1]According to another version Brahmā had given him the boon of six monthly periods of sleep.

[2]According to the *AGP.* (I.10), Sugrīva chopped off Kumbhakarṇa's ears and nose and Rāma his legs and head.

Kumbhamātā The Pot-goddess, the tutelary divinity of a village (*grāmadevatā*), who is often represented by or identified with a pot or vessel. This ancient belief is accepted by many Hindus, and today forms a part of their marriage ritual. It consists 'of a pile of pots in which the deities who promote fertility abide . . . By means of magic the goddess is invited to enter a jar which becomes the central object of worship.'[1] The usual method of worship of the goddess of snakes (Manasā) is with plain or decorated pots known as *manasār-bāri*. Before being fired these vessels 'are often placed one upon the other and fixed together, making columns of pots, sometimes having as many as seven tiers'.[2]

[1]Crooke, *Religion and Folklore*, etc., pp. 88–9. In parts of Bengal a pot marked with vermilion represents the snake-godling (ibid., p. 384); v. also Coomaraswamy, *Yakṣas*, pt. ii, p. 61.

[2]B. Ghose, *Paścimbaṅger Saṁskṛiti*, p. 679, cited by P.K. Maity, *Historical Studies in the Cult of the Goddess Manasā*, p. 262.

Theriomorphic and anthropomorphic vessels were also used ritually in many ancient cultures including Egypt. (v. Glanville, 'Egyptian Theriomorphic Vases in the British Museum', *Journal of Egyptian Archaeology*, vol. XII, pts i and ii, pp. 52–69, April, 1926). A double terracotta theriomorphic vessel, dating from the age of the Old Assyrian Trading Colonies (19th–18th cent. B.C.), was exhibited at the Hittite Exhibition at the Royal Academy, 1964.

v. Kumbha; Kula devatā(s); Lakṣmī n.4.

Kuṇāru The name of the 'handless' demon whom Indra crushed to death (*RV.*, III.30,8).

Kuṇḍalinī Latent energy, or the name of the goddess personifying it. Kuṇḍalinī represents the latent energy which lies at the base of the spinal column (*mūlādhāra cakra*) like a coiled serpent,[1] ready to spring. The awakening of the *kuṇḍalinī* mystically represents 'liberation' (*mokṣa*), the re-integration of the individual into the Universal Self (*ātman*).[2]

The *kuṇḍalinī* is awakened only after the exercise of difficult yogic techniques and is made to rise through the seven *cakras* (planes) to the *sahasrāra-cakra* in the head or brain.[3] This highest *cakra* is represented as a thousand-petalled lotus in the centre of which the final union of Śiva and Śakti occurs.[4] This seventh *cakra* is usually regarded as the transcendent plane where the yogin emerges from the limitations of time and hence from *saṁsāra*. Elaborate spiritual preparations are necessary before the *kuṇḍalinī* can be aroused. The yogin takes up a particular position (*āsana*); the breath is held by curling up the tongue until the tip touches the back of the throat, and the sexual energy is transmuted. When the *kuṇḍalinī* moves, great heat is engendered which courses up through each *cakra* to the seventh, provided the yogin is sufficiently advanced. As this heat passes upwards, the lower *cakras* become cold. In an attempt to hasten the process some Tantric schools combined particular *āsanas* with sexual practices to achieve the necessary 'simultaneous "immobility" of breath, thought and semen'.[5]

In mythology *śakti* (i.e., *kuṇḍalinī*) was formed from the combined energies of the gods which darted from their mouths in the form of flames and merged, finally taking the shape of the fierce eighteen-armed goddess who destroyed the buffalo demon Mahiṣa.

[1]The *kuṇḍalinī* is likened to a female serpent lying coiled eight times. This concentrated energy remains dormant in ordinary people 'after having propagated their world around them by many active coilings. She is said, by using the fifty Sanskrit letters as the strings of her instrument, to "sing her song" out of which are woven all the forms of the worlds' (Rawson, *The Art of Tantra*, p. 165).

[2]'Re-integrated into the Self, he who perceives the common essence in all things, beholds the Self in all things and all things in the Self' (*Bhagavadgītā*, 6.29, tr. by Daniélou, *Yoga, The Method of Re-integration*, p. 108).

[3]According to the tantric texts this can seldom be achieved, but when it is the mind is freed from all illusion (*māyā*). Macrocosmically the activation of *kuṇḍalinī* creates the universe (*HP.*, p. 287). According to modern medicine, the nervous system consists of a number of nerve centres, the largest and most important being the brain and the spinal cord, which together constitute the cerebro-spinal axis.

[4]*Kuṇḍalinī* represents the supreme *śakti* (*paraśakti*),

the original source of everything. Thus without *śakti* nature remains inert or 'like a corpse' (v. Eliade, *Yoga*, p. 270; Avalon, *Serpent Power*, p. 242; *HP*., p. 254).

[5]Eliade, op. cit., p. 248.

v. Yoga; Mahiṣāsuramardinī.

Kuntī v. Pṛthā.

Kuntibhoja v. Pṛthā.

Kūrkura A dog-demon who attacks children, and is perhaps the personification of a cough or similar disease.[1]

[1]*SED*.

v. Sīsara.

Kūrma I. 'Tortoise.' In the *ŚBr*. (VI.1.1,12) the tortoise figures in one of the early cosmogonic theories, which likens the cosmos to an egg which the creator Prajāpati broke open. He squeezed the shell and the juice which flowed from it became the tortoise—its lower shell represents the earth, the curved upper shell the sky, and its body, the atmosphere (VII.5,1ff.); hence the tortoise denotes the three worlds of earth, atmosphere and sky. It is also identified with the 'life-sap', the vital element in the creative process, and hence the reptile form is associated with the creator Prajāpati (VII.6.1,5).[1]

The *kūrma avatāra*, and those of the *matsya* (fish) and *varāha* (boar), are creation myths of the Brāhmaṇas, and represent an intermediate stage in the development of *avatāravāda*. The list of *avatāras* of the Pāñcarātra school later became stereotyped as the 'ten' (*daśāvatāras*), including the three Prajāpati forms, and though the list was supplemented in some Purāṇas, and slightly varied, all are recognized as *avatāras*, *vibhavas* or *vyūhas* of Viṣṇu.

The tortoise[2] was used to support[3] Mount Mandara (which was the churning-stick) when the gods and *asuras* churned the ocean (*samudramathana*). During the construction of the northern altar (*uttara vedi*) representing the universe, a live tortoise was placed in the first layer of bricks (*ŚBr*., VII.5.1,1).[4]

Later the tortoise came to symbolize the ideal man, restrained, calm and self-collected.

[1]This is probably based on the myth of the secondary creator Kaśyapa, whose name also means 'tortoise'.

[2]The figure of a tortoise is often 'in the central place of the temple' (Dange, *Legends*, p. 263). In the *Mārk. P*. (58.1ff.) Bhārata (India) is represented as resting on the back of a giant tortoise facing eastwards. The constellations and countries are arranged around it in nine divisions. The geographical positions are incorrect and are merely an attempt to make the shape of India conform to that of a tortoise lying spread out and facing east. Cf. Gonda, *Aspects*, p. 127.

[3]Cf. *kūrmaśila*, the stone base or support of an image.

[4]The tortoise placed in the base of the altar represents the source of all things. The *Mārk P*. (58.74) identifies the tortoise with Nārāyaṇa 'in whom everything is established'.

II. The name of one of the Purāṇas.

Kuru The name of a people and the country occupied by them (*kurukṣetra*). It is seldom mentioned alone but is usually coupled with that of the neighbouring Pañcālas, the two peoples being intimately associated and often referred to as Kuru-Pañcālas. They greatly influenced the development of Indian literature, as it was in their country that Sanskrit achieved its classical form and where the principal Brāhmaṇas were composed. Their mode of sacrifice was everywhere highly esteemed, as was the performance by their kings of the *rājasūya* or royal consecration, an esteem amply confirmed in the *Bṛhad-Ār. Up*. (III.1.1–20) and elsewhere.

Before their union with the Pañcālas the Kurus appear to have been connected with the Sṛñjayas, as at one time, according to the *ŚBr*. (II.4.4,5), both peoples were served by the same domestic priest (*purohita*). Among other references to the Kurus is one of a curse that they would be forced to leave Kurukṣetra, an event that may have been syncretized with the Epic tradition of the expulsion of the Kauravas by the Pāṇḍavas. But as traditional history often contains the garbled remnants of ancient tales and legends, it is necessary to rely on the evidence of the *RV*., though this is not always clear, owing to the various names by which the Kurus appear to have been known.[1]

[1]Thus Kuruśravaṇa, whose name appears to connect him with the Kurus, is called in the *RV*. Trāsadasyava 'descendant of Trasadasyu' (scourge of the *dasyus*), who was a king of the Purus (*RV*., IV.42,8–9).

Kurukṣetra 'Land of the Kurus', an extensive plain of the Madhyadeśa, mentioned in the *ŚBr*. (XIV.1.1,1–2) as a place sacred to Agni, Indra, Soma, Makha and other *devas*, who assembled there for the performance of a sacrifice from which the Aśvins were initially excluded.

Kurukṣetra and its capital Hastināpura figure in the *MBh*. as the scene of the great Bhārata war between the Pāṇḍavas and Kauravas. The men of this area are notable for their courage (*Manu*, VII.193), and at death do not go to Yama's realm, but go directly to the celestial world (*MBh*., 9.53,20, *EM*.). Five of Kṛṣṇa's wives were burnt on a funeral pyre in Kurukṣetra.[1] Kurukṣetra symbolizes the struggle to maintain right against the forces of evil.

[1]For twelve years Kṛṣṇa performed sacrifices there.

Kuśa I. A species of grass (Desmostachya bipinnata),

commonly called *darbha*, regarded by Hindus as the most sacred of Indian grasses. After the removal of the roots, the remainder was spread out on the altar (*vedi*), also on the seat reserved for the gods, and over the whole of the sacrificial area.[1] Because of its divine nature, the three goddesses, Sarasvatī, Iḷā and Bhāratī were implored to protect the 'holy grass, the flawless refuge of the gods' (*RV.*, II.3,8). Later, because of its dangerous supernatural properties, it was burnt at the close of the sacrifice lest harm should befall those who came in contact with it.

The productive 'power' of the sacrifice is indicated by the *kuśa*, which was passed from priest to priest and then given to the sacrificer and his wife.[2] But as the body of a woman below the navel is considered to be impure, it was necessary at the sacrifice that a woman should wrap a covering of *kuṣa* grass over her clothes to render her ritually pure (*ŚBr.*, V.2.1,8), because the grass was regarded as 'god-born', and the first plant to be created (*AV.*, XIX.32,7–10).

When the *soma* plant became unprocurable, yellow *kuśa* was substituted. It was believed to remove anger (*AV.*, VI.43), or as an amulet to 'burn away the heart of the hater', or to 'burst asunder the heads of enemies' (*AV.*, XIX. 28–9). But it is in the Purāṇas that most of the folk tales and mythology relating to the *kuśa* occur. When the drops of *amṛta* spilt by Garuḍa on a patch of *kuśa* were licked up by some snakes, the sharp-edged grass split their tongues, since when all snakes have this characteristic. According to the *VP.* (I.13) Veṇa, King of the Niṣādas, claimed to be 'the lord of the sacrifice, and alone entitled to the oblations'. For this irreverence the Vaiṣṇava *munis* 'beat him with consecrated blades of the holy grass and slew him'.[3] Kuśa grass was also used as a weapon when Dadhīca threw a fistful of it at the gods (*Śiva P.*, Rudrasaṁhitā II.39,23f.).

In South Indian temples five to twenty-one blades of *darbha* grass are twisted together and knotted at the top to represent the deities and *pitṛs* during worship.[4]

[1]The stalk is sacrificially pure and the top sacred to the gods (*ŚBr.*, VII.3.2,4).

[2]Cf. the ritual use of a blade or bunch of grass in Sumeria (Reiner, *Šurpu*, p. 5); and the Parsee symbolism of twigs, cited by Haugh, *The Origin of Brāhmaṇism*, p. 9.

[3]In the *Mārk P.* (51.16) the *kuśa* grass is struck against the side of the body to avert evil influences.

[4]Diehl, *Instrument and Purpose*, p. 108, n.2.

v. Barhis; Yūpa.

II. Kuśa and Lava were the twin sons of Rāma and Sītā.

v. Kuśāmba.

III. One of the seven mythical insular continents (*dvīpas*) of the world (*VP.*, II.2).

Kuśāmba A son of Kuśa and a descendant of Purūravas.

v. Gādhi.

Kuṣāṇa(s) The name of one of the tribal groups forming the Turanian and Scythian ethnic conglomerate which spread out over parts of northern and north-western Asia. Because of their skill and fighting prowess as horsemen, the Kuṣāṇas were called Yüeh-chi (lit. 'hard pads') by the Chinese whose north-western provinces they had conquered, but from which they were dislodged by a neighbouring tribe, the Hiung-nu.

Some Kuṣāṇas became separated from the other Yüeh-chi tribes and went westwards, and after defeating the Śakas dwelling on the banks of the Jaxartes,[1] they settled there until compelled to move to the valley of the Oxus (Amu Darya), only to meet again their former enemies the Śakas whom they again defeated. The Kuṣāṇas then pressed on to the south and occupied part of the former Greek satrapies in the region of Kabul, where they established a kingdom. About the beginning of the first century A.D., under their ruler Kadphises II, they entered India proper where they found more Śakas, this time not alone but with allies, the Pahlavas (Parthians). Both were soon subjugated and the greater part of the Panjāb and Sind regions occupied, whence the Kuṣāṇas spread to eastern India during the reign of their ruler Kaniṣka.

The Kuṣāṇa dynasty marks the second great era of Indian political, social and religious development. Kaniṣka I,[2] like the emperor Aśoka, was claimed by the Buddhists as a royal devotee, but whilst both rulers expressed their personal interest in Buddhism, as indicated by Aśoka's Edict Pillars and the great *stūpa* erected by Kaniṣka at Puruṣapura (Peshāwar), the reverse of the Kuṣāṇa coins depicts Greek, Elamite, Persian, as well as Indian deities, reflecting the existence of various forms of religion in the different parts of the empire.[3]

By the end of the second century Kuṣāṇa power was declining and the Śaka satraps appointed by Kaniṣka I began to rule large parts of Western and Central India as independent monarchs. Nonetheless, the achievements of the Kuṣāṇa era provided a firm foundation for those of the golden age of the Guptas, and also profoundly influenced Indian religious, social and political development.

[1]This region, often referred to as Scythia, but never specifically defined, was the land from which the Śakas originated and which the Kuṣāṇas temporarily occupied. As a result North-western India, as the final home of both Śakas and Kuṣāṇas, incorrectly 'came to be

styled Scythia by Greek mariners and geographers in the first and second centuries A.D.' (*AHI.*, p. 118).
[2]As numismatic evidence points to the existence of at least one other king of this name, this has sometimes made their identification uncertain.
[3]This included those areas of Central Asia occupied by other branches of the Yüeh-chi.

Kuśasthalī or **Kuśavatī** I. A city built by Kuśa, Rāma's son, on the brow of the Vindhya mountains.
II. A city perhaps identical with Dvārakā, built by King Raivata.

Kuṣmāṇḍa(s) The name of a class of demi-gods (attendant on Śiva) who can assume any form. When the *ṛṣi* Dhruva was engaged in deep meditation, one of them, in the form of Dhruva's mother, unsuccessfully sought to distract him (*VP.*, I.12).

Kuṣṭha An aromatic plant (Costus speciosus or arabicus),[1] said to grow alongside the *soma* plant on the mountains. Like *soma* it also grew in the third heaven under the great *aśvattha* tree where the gods forgather, and hence it is called the 'flower of immortality', i.e., the visible manifestation of *amṛta* (*AV.*, V.4,3). It possessed great curative powers and was worn as a protective amulet against sorceresses and the fever called *takman*, etc. The *kuṣṭha* also provided protection against injury and death, and hence its epithets *naghāmāra* and *naghāriṣa* (XIX.39,2).
[1]*Kuṣṭha* 'was, like cinnamon and cardamon, processed in Syria' and exported to Rome to perfume wine and as an ingredient for sauce (Auboyer, *Daily Life in Ancient India*, p. 84; Rawlinson, *Intercourse between India and the Western World*, p. 124).

Kutsa The name of an ancient mythical hero referred to in the *RV.* (IV.26.1, etc.), associated with Indra in the defeat of Śuṣṇa (the eclipse demon) and the rescue of the sun. Once when Kutsa was hard-pressed by his enemies, Indra tore off one of the wheels of the sun and so prevented darkness falling. Kutsa so closely resembled Indra that the latter's wife did not know which was her husband! At other times he is described as having been vanquished by Indra (*RV.*, I.53,10, etc.).

According to *Manu* (XI.250), if Kutsa's hymn *RV.* (I.97) is muttered it purifies those who drink intoxicants (*surā*).

Kuvalaya The miraculous horse with which Kuvalayāśva destroyed the *daitya* Pātālaketu when he attempted to disturb the *ṛṣi* Gālava during his meditations (*Mārk. P.*, XX.42ff.).
v. Pratardana.

Kuvalayāpīḍa Kaṁsa's huge state elephant[1] which was placed at the entrance to the wrestlers' arena to attack Kṛṣṇa, but the latter seized it by its tail and whirling it round killed both it and its keeper.
[1]Or it was a *daitya* who assumed the form of an elephant.

Kuvalayāśva A prince of the Solar dynasty and the father of 21,000 sons. For seven days he attacked the *asura* Dhundhu and finally slew him, and hence Kuvalayāśva was known as Dhundhumāra 'Slayer of Dhundhu'.

Kuvera v. Kubera.

L

Laghujātaka 'Short Horoscopy.' A work dealing with horoscopic astrology by Varāhamihira in which a number of Greek astrological terms are used.[1]

[1]Filliozat in *Ancient and Medieval Science*, p. 146.

Lāja Parched or puffed rice used as a household food, and also as a ritual offering.

Lajjā 'Modesty', personified as one of Dakṣa's daughters, who became a wife of Dharma and mother of Vinaya (the personification of good behaviour) (*VP.*, I.7).

Lākṣā A medicinal climbing plant, used to heal flesh-wounds (*AV.*, V.5,4–5).

Lakṣaṇa 'Marks, signs or characteristics.' The *AV.* (1.18) contains a charm to remove undesirable marks from a woman's body. These marks are regarded as demons and named. Another charm (VII. 115) is designed to remove unlucky marks from one's own body. Man is said to be born with a hundred marks, some of which are inauspicious. Marks which appear on a man's right side and on a woman's left are considered to be auspicious.

The ears of cattle were marked to indicate ownership. 'With a red (copper?) knife make thou a pair (*mithuna*)[1] on their two ears; the Aśvins have made the mark...' (VI.141,2).

[1]The Commentary states that the ears of cattle were marked with signs resembling the genitals (Whitney, AV., vol. I, p. 140, n.1).

Lakṣmaṇa A son of King Daśaratha and Sumitrā and half-brother of Rāma. Lakṣmaṇa is regarded as the embodiment of loyalty, and also as a partial (one-eighth) incarnation of Viṣṇu.

v. Śūrpaṇakhā; Tārakā; Rāmacandra.

Lakṣmaṇā Name of one of Kṛṣṇa's wives (*VP.*, V.28).

Lakṣmī A mark, sign or token (*RV.*, X.71.2), which in Vedic times had no qualitative significance—this being generally denoted by the addition of '*pāpī*' (bad) or '*puṇyā*' (good). A 'bad' sign indicated impending misfortune, ill-luck, etc.,[1] a 'good' sign prosperity, success, happiness and good fortune, both kinds being mentioned in the *AV.* (VII.115,1). But in the *MBh.* and other late literature Lakṣmī is personified as the goddess of fortune, and also as the embodiment of loveliness, grace and charm. The *Rām.* (I.45,40–3) states that she arose from the Ocean[2] when the waters were churned (*samudramathana*); hence her epithet Kṣīrābdhitanayā (daughter of the ocean of milk). In similar legends she appears either holding a lotus, or standing on the expanded petals of a lotus flower,[3] whence her name Padmā. According to some Purāṇas she is the daughter of Bhṛgu and Khyāti; or of Dakṣa and Prasūtī. The *Matsya* and *Padma Purs.* state that she is one of Dharma's wives, and the *VP.* that she is Indra's and Viṣṇu's consort. When the latter she is said to be co-existent with him and to accompany him in each of his incarnations (*avatāras*). Thus in his incarnation as Rāmacandra she is identified with Sītā, in that of Paraśurāma with Dharaṇī (Earth). As both Sītā and Dharaṇī she is associated with fertility, prosperity and abudance. In a myth (*Mārk P.*, XVIII,49f.) which refers to the seven lucky 'stations' or positions of the body from which her gifts are bestowed, it is stated that when she is 'stationed' on the feet, her gift is a house; on the thigh, wealth; in the genitals, a wife; in the bosom, offspring; in the heart, the fulfilment of desires; around the neck, contact with loved ones; in the face, beauty and poetic fire. But if Lakṣmī should be on or above the head of a man it is a sign of misfortune. Thus when the *daityas*, having defeated the gods, abducted Lakṣmī from Dattātreya's hermitage and carried her in an improvised litter above their heads, they were rendered powerless, and were utterly destroyed when the gods renewed the battle.

The assimilation of Lakṣmī with both Vaiṣṇava and Śaiva mythology, and her representation on the early coins of Indian and neighbouring non-Indian kingdoms, suggest that she was predominantly a goddess of good fortune.[4] Thus she is associated with the god of wealth Kubera. She is also the presiding deity of the magical lore called *padminī*.

Lakṣmī's figure is often depicted on the doors and lintels of houses to bring good luck and to avert evil influences (*Mārk. P.*, L. 80–2).[5]

[1]Gonda suggests that a *lakṣmī* may be an object or being whose mere presence has a good or bad effect (*Aspects*, p. 215, and v. n.19). Later the bad *lakṣmīs* were personified as Alakṣmī, Lakṣmī's sister.

[2]Cf. the deity of the Hittite monarchy, the sun-goddess of Arinna who rose from the ocean and bestowed fertility on the land (James, *The Tree of Life*, p. 115).

[3]But the lotus pedestal on which the figure of Lakṣmī stands is also common to other goddesses, so that the

identification of Lakṣmī requires other 'marks' for its confirmation.

[4]v. *DHI.*, pp. 110ff. Lakṣmī never had a cult of her own, but was worshipped as a subsidiary deity.

[5]In East Bengal Lakṣmī is often depicted on round earthenware vessels 'and worshipped on the Kojāgarī Purṇimā night (just after the Durgā pūjā) and preserved in the house for one year, to be replaced in the next year' (Bhattacharyya, *Canons of Indian Art*, p. 383). Other goddesses are also worshipped similarly (v. Kumbhamātā). Lakṣmī is also 'represented by a corn-basket filled with unhusked rice', or she manifests 'herself in the shape of seedlings grown in the winnowing basket' (Gonda, *VS.*, p. 112).

v. Nirṛti; Lakṣmīputra; Śrī.

Lakṣmī-Nārāyaṇa Lakṣmī and Nārāyaṇa (Viṣṇu) conjoined. This dual form denotes that in his supreme state Viṣṇu is one with his *śakti* (Lakṣmī). They constitute the 'one Paramātman, the Supreme Brahman without distinction'.[1]

[1]Gonda, *VS.*, p. 59.

Lakṣmīputra 'Son of Lakṣmī', i.e., Kāma, the god of love.

Lakulīśa The founder or systematizer of the Pāśupata, an extreme Śaiva cult.[1] He lived in ancient Kāyārohaṇa (modern Karvan in the Kathiawar Peninsula).[2] A late tenth- or early eleventh-century inscription in the temple of Nātha, situated 'fourteen miles to the north of Udaipur, Rājputāna ... [states] that Śiva became incarnate as a man with a club (lakula) in his hand in the country of Bhṛgukaccha'.[3] Some Purāṇas describe him as the twenty-eighth and last incarnation of Śiva.[4]

Lakulīśa's four immediate disciples were Kuśika, Mitra, Garga and Kauruṣya, reputed to be the founders of four subsects of the Pāśupata.

[1]Lakulīśa is often represented in eastern India (especially Orissa) as the Buddha, accompanied by a deer on each side of the *dharma-cakra*. This indicates that Buddhism and its art motifs were in the process of being absorbed by a rival cult (*DHI.*, p. 6).

[2]Ibid., p. 450.

[3]*VSM.*, p. 116.

[4]The Śaiva *avatāra* doctrine was a pale reflection of the Vaiṣṇava doctrine of *avatāras*.

Lalitā A goddess also called Mahādevī. According to the *Tantrarāja Tantra* 'the entrancing person of the incarnate god Kṛṣṇa ... was in fact a form assumed by the highest female Nityā [*mahāvidyā*] in the supreme *maṇḍala* of Tantric female deities, who is called Lalitā; the Great goddess herself, embracing all women and entrancing the world' (Rawson, *The Art of Tantra*, p. 99).

v. Līlā.

Lambodarī The pot-bellied goddess, wife of Gaṇeśa (*AGP.*, 144, 13ff.).

Laṅkā[1] The name is frequently used in the *Rāmāyaṇa* to denote the island of Ceylon, or its capital city. The latter was well-fortified and protected by high walls, with four massive gates. Drawbridges spanned the moat encircling the city. As an additional protection it was built on a hill, surrounded by dense forests, making mass movement of troops virtually impossible. Laṅkā was a well-planned city and possessed numerous fine houses, some of seven or eight storeys.[2]

Whether real or imaginary, and much of the *Rāmāyaṇa* belongs to the latter category, its account of Laṅkā generally agrees with the Buddhist records which indicate that the cultural standards in parts of southern India and Ceylon were as high as those in northern India, a fact for long obscured by the derogatory term '*rākṣasa*', applied in the Rām. to some of the southern tribes.

[1]Referred to in Indian literature also as Nāgadvīpa (Island of the Nāgas), or as Siṁhala-dvīpa; or by the Arabs as Serendib; or by the Portuguese as Ceilão or Zeylan, whence the later Ceylon.

[2]*IRA.*, p. 261.

v. Nikumbhilā; Laṅkinī; Hanumat; Vānara; Viśvakarman.

Laṅkinī The tutelary goddess of Laṅkā, who challenged Hanumat when he landed there, but he easily knocked her down with a blow from his left fist, the use of the left indicating contempt.

v. Nikumbhilā.

Lava A son of Rāma and brother of Kuśa to whom Vālmīki is traditionally said to have imparted the *Rāmāyaṇa*. The two brothers travelled round the country singing excerpts from it and so helped to popularize it.

Lavaṇa I. One of the seven oceans which surround the *dvīpas* in concentric belts.

II. Name of a hell to which go those who mock the Vedas, or who associate with women within the prohibited degrees (*VP.*, II.6).

III. A Rākṣasa chieftain who had inherited the invincible trident (*triśūla*) that had been given to his father by Śiva. Nonetheless he was defeated by Śatrughna and dispossessed of his capital Mathurā (*VP.*, IV.4).

Laya Yoga v. Yoga.

Lepa 'Smearing', 'anointing', 'daubing'. A reference to dirt or to other substances adhering to vessels, especially any wiped from the hand after offering oblations to the three ancestors, viz., father, grandfather, and great-grandfather. This residue is regarded as an oblation to the paternal ancestors.[1]

[1]*SED.*

Līlā 'Play' or 'display' (of ever-moving forces and energies). Līlā is often translated as 'sport' or 'whim' and applied to the spontaneous, unpremeditated act of creation or destruction.[1] This power is personified as the goddess Lalitā, whose form is the universe. She is also called Mahādevī. Thus *līlā* primarily means free motion or movement, whether regular or irregular, like the 'play' of water in a fountain.[2] From the philosophical aspect *līlā* is the manifestation of the Cosmic Principle (*brahman*) expressed in every aspect of the empirical world.[3] According to Nimbārka and other Vedāntins *līlā* is carried out through the abundance of the Supreme Being's bliss, and hence the world is said to originate from bliss (*ānanda*), is sustained in bliss and is dissolved in bliss. *Līlāvāda* is an attempt to explain the motive for creation. The adverse effects and the sufferings of the created are explained away by associating this cosmic *līlā* with justice, i.e. *karman*.

[1]Heimann, *PSPT.*, p. 75. Radhakrishnan regards *līlā* as 'the joyous exercise of spontaneity involved in the art of creation' (*Hindu View of Life*, p. 69; v. also *EW.*, vol. I, p. 125).

[2]Whitney, *CD.*, p. 4545, col. 3.

[3]Boner, *CHS.*, p. 168.

Liṅga A 'sign', 'mark', 'symbol', or the characteristic of a thing. It may also be a focal point from which something may be inferred; or which indicates a boundary or distinction between two or more objects; or as the *liṅga-vyāpta* (a term in logic) which represents the invariable mark denoting the connexion between two phenomena, like fire and smoke, the latter being the sign (*liṅga*) of the presence of fire. *Liṅga* is also a 'sign' of gender or sex, of generative power,[1] like the phallus and *yoni*, and thus often erroneously designated 'phallic worship'.[2] Though ring-stones and clay figures, displaying male and female sex organs have been found among the urban remains of the Indus Valley, similar to those of other early civilizations, it is doubtful, as Wall states, whether there was ever a real worship of the generative organs; rather they were recognized as symbols of ideas which were embodied in nature worship.[3]

Nonetheless, these ancient generative symbols, particularly the phallus, appear to be the prototypes of the *liṅga* and are 'the most numerous sacred objects by far in the whole range of contemporary religion',[4] being estimated to number 30 millions.[5] The eleventh-century temple at Tanjore is said to contain a thousand stone pillars in a room called the 'Hall of a Thousand Liṅgas'.[6] When the *liṅga* represents Svayambhū the 'self-originated' it is depicted as 'rounded at top and bottom to show that it does not "stand" or "arise from" anywhere in our space or time. It may thus look egg-shaped, and recall the Cosmic Egg'.[7] The size of a *liṅga* is generally determined by the size of the temple housing it.

Inevitably generative symbols became formalized and used as amulets by some women as an insurance against infertility. Such amulets were generally the gift of a husband to his bride on their wedding day.[8] In South India a formalized miniature *liṅga*, attached to a necklace and concealed under the clothing, is also worn by male devotees of Śiva.

In the Liṅgāyat *dīkṣā* (initiation) ceremony, corresponding to the *upanayana* ritual, the *liṅga* necklace replaces the traditional *yajñopavīta* or sacred thread bestowed on the initiate.

Sex symbolism has long been associated with husbandry and the implements connected with it. The Sanskrit for plough is '*lāṅgula*', derived from '*lak*', denoting both a digging implement and a phallus.[9] The female pudenda (*yoni*) is similarly associated with ploughing and identified with the furrow (*sītā*), and personified as the daughter of King Janaka (meaning progenitor). She emerged from the furrow whilst the King was engaged in ritual ploughing.

The fertility aspect of the *liṅga* belongs to the period of the Epics and Purāṇas, and evident during the development of Śaivism.[10] Thus the *liṅga*, as the symbol of transcendental power, is the central conception of Śaiva philosophy. Śiva is represented in beautifully sculptured forms as well as by the symbolic *liṅga*, which may be a stone pillar, a natural white stone (*bāṇa-liṅga*), a mountain (like Tiruvanamalai) or any similar aniconic form (*niṣkala*).[11] As the latter it is identified with *brahman*, the Universal Principle (*Śiva Purāṇa*, Vidyeśvara Saṁ., V.8–11).

In Śaiva temples the *liṅga* usually stands on a pedestal representing the *yoni*, their union being the supreme expression of creative energy.

[1]Cf. the ancient Persian horse-bit, whose cheek-pieces had one end fashioned as a phallus and the other as a horse's hoof, probably to indicate the generative strength of the horse (Trench, *A History of Horsemanship*, p. 20). In parts of ancient Greece during the festival of Demeter and Persephone, women devotees walked in procession carrying phalli modelled in dough and live snakes—symbols of generation and regeneration (Brodrick, *Animals in Archaeology*, p. 111).

[2]It has been suggested that '*śiśnadeva*' (*RV.*, VII.21,5; X.99,3), a word of uncertain meaning, refers to aboriginal 'phallic worshippers', but Yāska defines the word as 'non-observers of Vedic ritual'. Its significance is fully discussed by Banerjea, *DHI.*, pp. 63ff. M.R. Anand (*The Hindu View of Art*, p. 11) states that the Dravidians

had phallic and nature-spirit cults.

[3]O.A. Wall, *Sex and Sex Worship*, p. viii. In the Zhob Valley where small farming groups existed before 3000 B.C., a carved stone *liṅga* was found and nearby at the Periano-Ghundai mound, a vulva is depicted (A. Stein, *Memoirs of the Archaeological Survey of India*, no. 37, p. 60, 1925).

[4]Campbell, *Masks of God*, II. p. 170. Bharati emphasizes that 'the ithyphallic condition is not priapic, but represents precisely what the tantric aims to master, i.e., seminal retention in the laboratory setting of tantric ritualistic copulation' (*TT.*, p. 296). In the Javanese and Cambodian Devarāja cult the 'fiery *liṅgam*' represents the 'fiery essence of Kingship, a radiant earthly emanation of royal wisdom and dominion' (Coomaraswamy, *Yakṣas*, pt. ii. p. 45. n. 1).

[5]This number includes those erected to mark the burial places of ascetics and yogins who, because they are considered to have attained the form of Śiva-*liṅga*, i.e., liberation, have no need to be cremated (Coomaraswamy, 'Indian Architectural Terms', *JAOS.*, 1928, pp. 250ff.).

[6]For illus. v. A. Volwahsen, *Living Architecture: Indian*, p. 79. The Greek Eros was represented as a simple phallic pillar (R. Graves, *Greek Myths*, I, p. 58, n.1); and the symbol of Hermes was a cross with an erect phallus depicted about halfway up the shaft. It was 'known throughout the classical world and standing at crossroads was welcomed as a source of comfort and inspiration by the traveller' (J.M. Allegro, *The Sacred Mushroom and the Cross*, p. 106). The erect phallus was also the emblem of the Roman deity Fascinus (ibid., p. 81); and according to Adam of Bremen the statue of Freyr in the temple at Uppsala was phallic (Davidson, *Gods and Myths of Northern Europe*, p. 96).

[7]Rawson, *The Art of Tantra*, p. 193. The phallus has cultic importance in many religions and 'was set up as a symbol on graves in Asia Minor . . . [which] reveals a knowledge of the fertility of death which brings about transformation' (Herzog, *Psyche and Death*, p. 206).

[8]When visiting Pondicherry the Pope's Apostolic Legate admonished the Jesuit missionaries for having permitted this custom and its continuance by the female converts. Their refusal to obey led to a compromise whereby a cross was also engraved on the pendant, thus coupling 'the symbol of Christian salvation with that of the male and female pudenda' (*Index Librorum Prohibitorum*, I, p. 289).

[9]v. J. Przyluski, 'Non-Aryan loans in Indo-Aryan', in P.C. Bagchi, *Pre-Aryan and Pre-Dravidian in India*, pp. 10ff.; v. also *Tait. Saṁ.* (IV.2,5) where seed is sown in the field-womb. *Liṅga* is said to be derived from two roots '*li*' (to dissolve) and '*gam*' (to go out), meaning 'the ultimate Reality into whom the creatures of the world dissolve and out of whom they all evolve again . . . the conception of *liṅga* in Vīra-Śaivism (Liṅgāyata) represents spiritual dynamic fullness' (Radhakrishnan, *EW.*, vol. I. p. 399).

[10]Nonetheless, Śiva unequivocably 'stands for the complete control of the senses, and for supreme carnal renunciation. His phallic representation would seem to be an inane paradox unless we take into account the tantric ideological background of this symbolism, which is truly profound' (*TT.*, p. 296).

[11]The most auspicious *liṅgas* are natural forms such as the *bāṇaliṅgas*. *Mukhaliṅgas* combine both iconic and aniconic forms, and consist of a *liṅga* with Śiva's head (or sometimes his whole figure) depicted on one side (cf. the Hermes cross in n. 6).

v. Liṅga Purāṇa; Mārkaṇḍa; Nandi; Śivarātri; Svayambhū; Kalaharamūrti; Kedāranātha; Mahādeva.

Liṅga Purāṇa One of the eighteen classical Purāṇas, which is devoted to a description of Śiva, his incarnations, and ritual.

v. Liṅga; Purāṇa(s).

Liṅgaśarīra The subtle body which, after cremation, accompanies the transmigrating spirit. The *liṅgaśarīra* is an essential link in the continuity of life because it is not destroyed by the death of the individual but continues to activate it throughout *saṁsāra* until it is merged with the universal *ātman*.[1]

[1]The ancient Egyptian '*ka*', the *alter ego* or active aspect of the personality, similarly maintains consciousness after death and precedes the deceased, and thus prepares the way to the next phase.

v. Ekoddiṣṭa.

Liṅgāyat The name of a Śaiva sect often associated or identified with the Vīraśaiva, a sect which became prominent in the twelfth century A.D. at Kalyāṇa in the Karṇāṭak region of South India. But the recent publication of part of the *Śūnyasaṁpādane*,[1] the Vīraśaiva scriptural corpus, indicates that former views concerning the Liṅgāyats may have to be revised, especially as they are neither mentioned in the work itself, nor by its editors. 'Liṅgāyat' may thus have been an epithet applied to the Vīraśaiva by other Śaiva cults.

According to the *Śūnyasaṁpādane*, the Vīraśaiva movement was a reaction against superstitious practices. It was supported (or founded) by Basava, a minister of the usurper King Vijjala (or Vijjaṇa) who reigned at Kalyāṇī. It soon became a well-organized and influential cult, attracting representatives of other Śaiva sects from various parts of India. Basava denounced obscurantism, rejected caste distinction, and even condoned the marriage of an Untouchable with the daughter of a *brahmin*. He opposed cremation, sacrifices, pilgrimages and image-worship, stating that the only sacred symbol was the *liṅga*. He rejected also the Vedas and the authority of the *brāhmaṇas* whom he considered should be replaced by a new order of priests called *jaṅgamas*. Such radical views quickly aroused the anger of the Smārta *brahmins*. The situation became so acute that the king dismissed Basava and expelled him and the Vīraśaivas from Kalyāṇī. Brahminic anger was also directed against the Jain community which was regarded as having encouraged the Vīraśaivas. The subsequent persecution of the Jains may account for their rather jaundiced view of Basava and the use he made of his high position to carry out the religious reforms advocated by one sect, irrespective of the traditions of others. Thus the Jain records, which have been one of the main sources of information about the Liṅgāyat cults, are now being questioned.[2]

The *Śūnyasaṁpādane*, written in simple rhythmical prose, addressed to the common man[3] represents the quintessence of the teaching of Prabhu, one of the early Vīraśaiva *śaraṇas* (saints or holy men), and supplies much information about the development of its mystical creed, but little about its discipline and organization. It does however maintain that mystical experience is more easily gained by constant contact with a mystically oriented community and the observance of *śaraṇa* discipline, than by ascetic practices.[4]

The Vīraśaivas thus maintain a community relationship but have no temples, except those erected as memorials, nor do their priests conform to the traditional type. Priestly duties are performed by practising *jaṅgamas*, who conduct marriage and other domestic ceremonies and who also act as *gurus*.[5] Strict Liṅgāyats are not initiated with the brahmanic sacred thread (*yajñopavīta*) but with the *liṅga* emblem.[6]

The philosophic views of the Vīraśaivas are summed up in the terminology of their sacred writings: i.e., *śūnya* 'void', signifying 'void of all distinctions', the Absolute or the Real; and *saṁpādane*, 'attainment or realization'. But their traditional cosmogonic and metaphysical views can only be fully appreciated by the mystic. The Vīraśaivas accept the monism of the Vedānta and its theory of illusion (*māyā*), but their presentation of these theories is distinctly sectarian. Śiva is the Eternal Principle; the Self-existent, the Unsupported (*nirālaṁba*); the cosmic *liṅga*; the *paramātman*, devoid of all attributes (*sarva-śūnya*).

[1]Edited and tr. by S.C. Nandimath and others, Karṇāṭak Univ. Dharwar, 5 vols.

[2]'Modern historians, particularly Fleet, Bhandarkar and Dasgupta, who have based their accounts on such material, have naturally gone completely wrong' (*Śūnyasampādane*, vol. II, p. 2).

[3]Ibid., vol. I, Pref. p. x.

[4]Ibid., vol. III, p. 427, n.102.

[5]When receiving a child into the Vīraśaiva community the initiating *guru* looks intently into his eyes. 'In doing so he resorts to yoga, in the course of which he places his hand on the head of his pupil. Through this act he is believed to extract the spiritual principle from the child's body and to place it in the *liṅga* which has already been consecrated by him. Thereupon the initiate is supplied with this *liṅga* and seven other emblems . . . This important rite is considered to be a spiritual birth' (Gonda, *Eye and Gaze in the Veda*, pp. 54ff.; v. also S.C. Nandimath, *A Handbook of Vīraśaivism*, pp. 71f.).

[6]In the Bacchic '*phallophoria*' a wooden or leather phallus was carried round during the service. It was also regarded as an averter of the evil eye. In the hymn sung by Dikaiopolis the phallus 'was regarded as possessed with the "*mana*" or influence of the god of life and also as evoking it' (Farnell, *Cults*, V. p. 210). To the Vīraśaivas the *liṅga* represents the unifying principle of Śiva and Śakti (*EW*., vol. I, p. 395).

v. Marula.

Loka[1] A world; a division of the universe; the sphere of a divinity. In general the three worlds (*tri-loka*) are heaven, earth and the nether regions, but there are a number of different classifications. *Loka* appears to have originally denoted a clearing in the forest needed as space for cultivation, the clearance giving access to sunlight and rain without which the land was useless. *Loka* thus became semantically connected with sunlight, and metaphorically with divine or heavenly light,[2] but its primary significance of locality has always been its principal characteristic. In the *RV*. Indra is constantly besought to drive out the indigenes and thus provide room (*loka*) for the Āryans; or where forests needed clearing Agni is called upon to burn them with his fiery breath (*RV*., I.58,4). *Loka* also denoted the enclosed area used for the performance of the sacrifice, or when qualified by a prefix might be applied to any place or area.

In the *RV*. (X.14,2) Yamaloka denotes the world of the dead; other supraterrestrial spheres or worlds are Svarloka (Indra's paradise) and Brahmaloka (abode of Brahmā). Mention is made in the *ŚBr*. (XIII.1.7,3; etc.) and the *AV*. (X.6,31; etc.) of the 'three worlds', viz., heaven or the sky, the atmosphere or intermediate region, and the earth.

The cosmogonic world is referred to as two halves

(*RV.*, I.59,4), or as two bowls (I.3,20), one being inverted[3] and placed over the lower so that the rims meet and thus form the horizon.

The relationship between gods and men in early Vedic times was collective rather than individual. A sacrifice offered to Indra or to Agni was essentially an offering to all the gods, for it was only by their concerted efforts that the world was sustained. Similarly the sum of individual sacrifices strengthened and sustained the gods. Supplications were thus made for the tribe or people and not primarily for the individual. 'Give us', not 'give me' was the usual form of the supplication. At that stage of cultural development the ancestors (*pitṛs*), rather than the deceased individual father, were the objects of reverence. The notion of individual immortality and of a particular place (*loka*) in the celestial world were a later priestly device, a further incentive for the performance of individual sacrifice. This is indicated in such passages as *ŚBr.*, VI.2.2,27 and *Tait. Saṁ.*, III.3.5.4, which assure the devotee that by the proper performance of the appropriate sacrifice he will obtain a place (*loka*) of his own in the celestial world.[4] The *Bṛhad-Ār. Up.* (I.5,16) mentions the three worlds, viz., of men, *pitṛs* and gods, that of the latter being the best. The world of men can be obtained only by means of a son; the *pitṛloka* by sacrifice, and the world of the gods by knowledge. The same work also mentions the Gandharva, Prajāpati, and Brahmā worlds, etc., and gives the degrees of bliss experienced in each (IV.3.33). The *sāman* chants are said to lead one to Brahmā's world (*Praśna Up.*, V.5).

With the development of the notion of *karman*, the attainment of the individual *loka* was seen to depend, not on the performance of the sacrifice, but on individual moral responsibility. Thus, however complex the system of *lokas* may appear to be in Indian cosmology, or whether mythically presented for the edification of the masses, or philosophically analysed for the sophisticated, the conclusion reached seems to be that man makes his own *loka*—either a heaven or a hell.

[1]v. J. Gonda's comprehensive study entitled *Loka; World and Heaven in the Veda.*

[2]*Loka* sometimes has the meaning of a 'heaven' but not always, as can be seen in *AV.*, XVIII.2.47, 'they, going up to heaven (*div*), have found a place (*loka*), shining upon the back of the firmament'.

[3]'The inverted bowl we call the sky', as the Rubaiyat describes it.

[4]The above *Tait. Saṁ.* reference also indicates that man may participate in more than one world. He is said to conquer the 'worlds of the gods'. v. also *Chān. Up.*, II.23,1.

v. Manvantara; Śeṣa I; Pātāla; Lokapālas.

Lokāloka or **Cakravāla** A mythical mountain range encircling the outermost of the seven seas, dividing the visible world from the region of darkness.[1] The sun rises and sets within this circular barrier. Beyond it is the region of perpetual darkness which is encompassed by the shell of the mundane egg (*VP.*, II.4). But the outer darkness is no obstacle to the spirits of the dead if they have lived righteous lives (*Manu*, IV.241–3).

[1]Similar to the Cimmeria of ancient Greek legend, and regarded as a region of perpetual darkness.

Lokanātha 'Lord of worlds.' An epithet of the Sun, Brahmā, Viṣṇu, Śiva, and of the gods in general. It is also applied to the Buddha; to *bodhisattvas* and to rulers.

Lokapāla(s) or **Dikpāla(s)**[1] Guardians (*pālas*) of the regions and of the four cardinal and four intermediate points of the compass. The Hindu conception of world-guardians is old, but it was not until Paurāṇic times that their mythology was fully developed. The *AV.* (III.27) mentions six *lokapālas*,[2] each having its own overlord, Agni being ruler of the East, and its defender the black serpent; Indra of the South, its defender the 'cross-lined' serpent; Varuṇa of the West, its defender the adder (*pṛdāku*); Soma of the North, its defender the boa-constrictor (*svaja*); The 'fixed quarter' is ruled by the solar Viṣṇu and defended by the serpent with black-spotted neck (*kalmāṣa*); the 'upward quarter' ruled by Bṛhaspati, its defender the white serpent (*śvitra*).

Another version is given in the *Bṛhad-Ār. Up.* (III.9.19) which refers to the Sun as regent of the East; Yama (S); Varuṇa (W); Soma (N); Agni, the zenith. But in *Manu*, the *MBh.* and the Purs. the *lokapālas* number eight, viz., Kubera (N); Varuṇa (W); Indra (E); Yama (S); Vāyu or the Maruts (NW); Soma or Īśāna (NE); Nirṛti or Sūrya (SW); Agni (SE). According to *Manu* (V.96 and 97) a king is said to be an incarnation of the eight *lokapālas*.

The *MBh.* (VI.12,36; VII.94,47) states that each of the guardian deities is mounted on a bull-elephant also called a *lokapāla*. The winds are produced from their trunks. Each elephant is accompanied by its mate (whose name is here bracketed). Indra's elephant is Airāvata or Abhramātanga (Abharmu); Agni's, Puṇḍarīka (Kapilā); Yama's, Vāmana (Pingalā); Sūrya's, Kumuda (Anupamā); Varuṇa's, Añjana (Añjanavatī); Vāyu's, Puṣpadanta (Śubhadantī); Kubera's, Sārvabhauma (mate uncertain); Soma's, Supratīka (mate uncertain). In the *Rām.* Indra's elephant is called Virūpākṣa; Varuṇa's, Saumanasa; Yama's, Mahāpadma; Kubera's, Himapāṇḍara.

The *lokapālas* play an important part in the design of temples and cities, much of Indian architecture being based on the square—'a final and unequivocal form' which indicates the Absolute, and which is fixed by the cardinal points.[3]

[1]*Dik* (in compounds) for *diś*, to point out, and thus to indicate the direction or the relative position of a place or thing.

[2]The *Tait. Saṁ.* (V.5,10) also mentions six *lokapālas*, but omits Viṣṇu and varies the regional arrangement of the gods. In Buddhist mythology there are four divine beings (*caturmahārājas*) associated with the four principal quarters.

[3]A. Volwahsen, *Living Architecture: Indian*, p. 44.

Lokāyata 'Materialism.' A term denoting the belief that 'matter is the only substance, and that matter and its motions constitute the universe'.[1] The Sanskrit term *loka* (world), and perhaps *ayata* (unrestricted) initially denoted the study of nature and the laws governing it, independent of stereotyped brahmanical religious views. A Lokāyata, in this sense, whether priest or layman, may be regarded as one whose education was not confined to a study of the Veda, but included nature-lore, cosmogonic theory and any subject covered by the learned treatises called Vedāṅgas. 'To be a master of such lore was then considered by no means unbecoming to a learned brahmin, though it ranked below his other studies.'[2]

Thus the term *lokāyata* was specifically applied to the materialistic Cārvāka school (*darśana*), and perhaps because of this *lokāyata* became by the eighth century a term of abuse by extreme 'orthodox' sects as a peg on which to 'hang the views that they impute to their adversaries, and give them, in doing so, an odious name.'[3]

[1]Whitney, *CD.*, p. 3658.

[2]Rhys-Davids, *Dialogues of the Buddha*, pt. 1, *SBB.*, vol. II, p. 171; v. also *Aṅguttara Nikāya*, vol. I, p. 163.

[3]Rhys-Davids, op. cit., vol. I, p. 172. The stigma thus attaching to the term is not unlike that denoted in modern times by such epithets as infidel, heathen, unbeliever, etc.

Lolā or **Cañcalā** The 'Fickle One'. An epithet of Lakṣmī, the goddess of fortune.

Lopāmudrā Wife of the aged *ṛṣi* Agastya (*RV.*, I.179). In post-Vedic mythology Agastya is said to have formed Lopāmudrā from the most beautiful parts of various animals, and then secretly introduced her into the palace of the King of Vidarbha who adopted her. Upon reaching marriageable age, she married Agastya. The *MBh.* describes her as the embodiment of wifely devotion.[1]

[1]*EM.*, p. 185.

M

Mada 'Intoxication; mental disturbance; uncontrollable emotion.' But *mada* may also denote another type of mental state, expressing rapture, exhilaration, inspiration, or religious fervour. In mythology Mada is the personified rage of the *ṛṣi* Cyavana who created this demonic form to force Indra to allow the Aśvins to share in the *soma* sacrifice (*MBh.*, Vana pa., 124 and 125).

Madana 'Seducer of the mind.' An epithet of Kāma, the god of love.

Mādhava I. A son or descendant of the Yādava Madhu. Kṛṣṇa, at one time a Yādava ruler, and later an incarnation (*avatāra*) of Viṣṇu, is often regarded as a Mādhava, as was also Paraśurāma.

II. Also known as Vidyāraṇya. The brother of the fourteenth-century Scholiast Sāyaṇa. Mādhava was the foremost authority on medical diagnosis and ranks in importance just below his predecessor Vāgbhaṭa.

v. Āyurveda.

Madhavā A celestial nymph (*apsaras*) whom Indra sent to distract Viṣṇu and thus interrupt the flow of cosmic force which only the exercise of complete concentration and asceticism (*tapas*) can ensure. This myth (*Matsya P.*, 61,22, *PI.*) points to that transitional period when the Vedic gods, and Indra in particular, were being superseded by Viṣṇu and Śiva.

Mādhavī Devī The Earth-goddess. When Sītā's chastity was questioned after her return from captivity in Laṅkā, she appealed to the goddess to confirm that she had successfully resisted all attempts of Rāvaṇa, her captor, to ravish her, and that her husband Rāma was the father of the twin sons she had subsequently borne.

Despite the defence on her behalf made by the *brāhmaṇa* Vālmīki, who declared that her innocence had been divinely revealed to him, Sītā's accusers remained unconvinced. Then Sītā, attired in a yellow robe, with joined palms, her head bowed, her eyes lowered, called thrice upon the earth-goddess and declared: 'I have never let my thoughts dwell on any but Rāma. If this be true let me rejoin the earth from which I sprang.'[1] As she spoke there appeared a marvellous throne beside which stood the goddess Mādhavī, who took Sītā in her arms and placed her on the throne. Before the assembly could recover from their astonishment Sītā descended into the earth (*Rām.*, Uttarakhaṇḍa, ch. 97).

[1]Literally, 'Let the earth swallow me up.' The appeal to the earth was a form of oath in common use. When the Buddha's great spiritual attainments were questioned by Māra, he touched the earth which vouched for him.

Madhu I.[1] 'Honey'; 'sweetness'; 'exhilarating';[2] 'intoxicating'. As one of the principal means of sustenance of prehistoric man, honey must have been one of the earliest words in his limited vocabulary, and of the languages of areas where wild honey was found.[3]

In Indian works it is described as the favourite drink of warriors; as a remedy for various diseases; as the source of mental and physical powers; and as the means of attaining longevity. Hence the custom of putting a little honey into the mouth of a new-born infant. To the Vedic physician *madhu* was regarded as the essence of all plant life, and to possess fertilizing properties, and hence it was customary to sprinkle the newly ploughed furrows with *madhu* and ghee (*AV.*, III.117,9).

Madhu is also associated with the mystical doctrine called *madhuvidyā* (*Bṛhad-Ār. Up.*, II, 5, 16–18) which is equated with the esoteric doctrine imparted to the two Aśvins by Dadhyac Ātharvaṇa. The *ŚBr.* (XIV. 1.1,18) describes it as 'this pure essence, this sacrifice'. But the student (*brahmacārin*) is generally forbidden to eat honey (*ŚBr.*, XI.5.4,18) doubtless because of its supposed aphrodisiac properties (*Suś. Saṁ.*, I, p. 449).[4] But in the above *ŚBr.* passage, one student clearly states he has no intention of abstaining from honey. The offering of a drink or food, of which honey is the chief ingredient, was generally regarded as essential in social life.

[1]Allowing for dialectal changes, the Skt. *madhu* (honey) is common to all Indo-European languages, as is indicated by OS1. *medu*; OP. *meddo*; OFries. *mede*; W. *mel*; and E. *mead*, the drink made from honey. *Madhu* (sweetness), perhaps its secondary meaning, is represented in H. by *māthōq*, in Sem. by the tri-consonantal root *mtq*, and in Ugarit by *mṭq*, etc. These are all ultimately represented in Gr. by *meli*, L. *mel* (honey), which by extension signify sweetness. The intoxicating quality later attributed to *madhu* is represented by Gr. *methu*, and accounts for the English name of the semi-precious stone amethyst (Gr. amethustos = *a*, 'not' + *methustos*, 'drunk or intoxicated'), originally thought to prevent intoxication.

[2]According to the *Nir.*, 4.8 *madhu*, from the root *mad* (to exhilarate), is equated with *soma*.

[3]Numerous passages in Hebrew and other Near Eastern

literature attest the importance of honey. In Greek and Roman death-cults it was the food of the dead, and in India honey 'cakes' (*piṇḍa*) were offered to the *pitṛs* (*Vāyu P.*, 30,151; 56, 12, etc., *PI.*).

[4]But he may eat it if given to him by his teacher (*ācārya*). Honey is said to be the husk (*palāva*) of the Veda.

v. Aśvins; Madhukaśā.

II. A primordial cosmic power. In Paurāṇic mythology Madhu and Brahmā antedate creation and thus are regarded as the first-born (*pūrvaja*) powers to emerge from primordial chaos. Brahmā is represented as Light, Madhu as Darkness, who seeks continually to destroy his rival. This cosmogonic contest is only ended when the Vedic *devas* were superseded by the sectarian gods. Thus Madhu, who had for so long defied Brahmā, was then destroyed by Kṛṣṇa/Viṣṇu, and the ancient Creator (Brahmā) relegated to an insignificant niche in the post-Vedic triad (*trimūrti*).

III. The *VP.* (IV.11) mentions two Madhus; the first as one of the hundred sons of Kārtavīrya, the Haihaya king slain by Paraśurāma; the other as the son of Vṛṣa (one of Kārtavīrya's grandsons), who also had a hundred sons, the chief of whom was Vṛṣṇi, whose descendants, the Vṛṣṇis, were also called Mādhavas after their forbear Madhu.

v. Yayāti; Yadu.

Madhukaśā Lit. 'honey-whip'. The whip with which the Aśvins are said to have scattered the dew[1] and mixed honey with the *soma* juice[2] (*RV.*, I.157,4; *AV.*, IX.1; etc.), honey being regarded as a potent fertilizing fluid. But neither the mystic nor realistic background of the honey-whip is clear in the various references to it. It is personified and called 'the formidable daughter of the Maruts' (*AV.*, IX.1,3 and 10).[3]

Like other ritual entities *madhukaśā* was made into a sort of cosmogonic power which could bestow immortality (*AV.*, IX.1).[4]

[1]In the ancient Middle East dew was regarded as 'the most powerful conceptual fluid of nature' (J.M. Allegro, *The Sacred Mushroom and the Cross*, p. 111). Coomaraswamy (*Yakṣas*, pt. ii, p. 22) suggests that the *madhukaśā* represents lightning which brings the rains; it is also personified as a goddess of abundance. v. also Bloomfield. *The Atharvaveda*, p. 90. In the folklore of many countries lightning is regarded as a whip or lash (J. Rendell Harris, *Picus Who is also Zeus*, pp. 57ff.), and the bringer of rain.

[2]The Petersburg Lexicon suggests that honey was beaten at the sacrifice. Cf. the E. culinary term to whip, meaning to beat into a froth.

[3]Cf. the Canaanite goddess Pughat who knew the courses of the stars; carried the waters on her shoulder and sprinkled dew on the barley (G. R. Driver, *Canaanite Myths*, p. 61).

[4]*BIP.*, p. 94, n.4; also *AV.*, X.7.19.

v. Madhu I.

Madhusūdana 'Destroyer of Madhu.' One of the thirty-nine *avatāras* of Viṣṇu who destroyed the demon Madhu.

Madhuvidyā 'Delectable or sweet knowledge', a play on the word *madhu* (honey or sweetness), which became the basis of a sweet mystical doctrine (*Bṛhad-Ār. Up.*, II.5,16–18).

v. Madhu I.

Madhvācārya (12th–13th century.) The author of the *Sarvadarśanasaṁgraha* and founder of a Vaiṣṇava *dvaita* sect whose members are called Mādhvas. They confuted the doctrine of *māyā* advanced by Śaṅkarācārya in the ninth century, and also rejected his doctrine of *advaita* (the non-dual constitution of the universe). Instead they adopted the *dvaita* (dual) doctrine introduced by Rāmānuja in the eleventh century. This sought to show that the Supreme Being is the material as well as the efficient cause of the animate and inanimate world. Although Madhva accepted Rāmānuja's general theory, he objected to anything that tended to qualify the uniqueness of the Supreme Being.

The trend away from the Realistic theory of the early Buddhist and Hindu schools began about the second century A.D. Mahāyāna Buddhists finally rejected it for a highly sophisticated form of Idealism, which was later adapted and incorporated by Śaṅkara in his theory of *advaita*.[1]

The Mādhvas follow the Vaiśeṣika system and divide all existing things into categories of substance. Thus the Supreme Being is considered to be a substance, though mystically combining cosmic essence (*ātman*) and the functional activity of Brahmā. These functions are eight, expressed in creation, preservation, dissolution, the regulation of evolutionary law, the bestowal of knowledge, the manifestation of the divine essence, the maintenance of a correct balance between mankind and *saṁsāra*, and finally control of the process of liberation (*mokṣa*).[2]

Directions necessary for the knowledge that leads to *mokṣa* are given under eighteen headings which include altruism, worship, meditation, unqualified devotion to the Supreme Being; and sympathy for one's social inferiors and love for one's equals.

[1]Hence the charge by his opponents that he was 'a Buddhist in disguise'.

[2]*VSM.*, p. 59. A full account of the Mādhva system is given in the *Madhvasiddhāntasāra* by Padmanābhasūri, Bombay, 1883. For the Mādhva temple cult v. Gonda,

VS., p. 81.

Mythologically Madhva is said to be an *avatāra* of Vāyu, the god of the wind, in this context having an ethereal spiritual significance. Vāyu 'is his agent in the world, and has some of the features of the Holy Ghost of Christian theology. The resemblances ... to Christianity are so striking that influence, perhaps through the Syrian Christians of Malabar, is almost certain' (*WI.*, p. 333).

v. Vedānta; Brahman (neuter).

Madhyadeśa 'Middle country.' This originally seems to have consisted of that area of Central India occupied by the Āryan migrants, sometimes referred to as Āryāvarta, the land of the Āryans. But the term Madhyadeśa subsequently had perhaps a wider geographical significance and comprises the area between the Vindhya and Himālaya (*Manu*, II.21), which, though largely dominated by the Āryans, included native kingdoms or republics of differing ethnic origins.

Madhyarekhā The central or first meridian, conceived by the Hindus to pass through Laṅkā, Ujjayīnī, Kurukṣetra, etc., to Mount Meru.

Madirā The goddess of wine and wife of Varuṇa, and thus she is also called Vāruṇī. Madirā is also a name of Durgā.[1]

[1]*DHI.*, pp. 86–7 and n. 2.

v. Madyam; Surā.

Mādrī The second wife of King Pāṇḍu, and mother of twin sons, Nakula and Sahadeva, whose paternity is mythically ascribed to the Aśvins.

Madugha A species of plant yielding a honey-like substance, used in the making of love-spells (*AV.*, I.34) and in nuptial ceremonies. It was also chewed by debators to ensure their success.

Madyam Intoxicating liquor. It was generally forbidden to *brāhmaṇas*, but was used in the worship of the *śaktis*.

v. Surā; Madirā.

Magadha v. Pāṭaliputra; Kāśī; Maurya(s).

Māgha I. v. Jyotiṣa.

II. The author (7th century) of a long poem called *Śiśupālavadha* (Slaying of Śiśupāla), describing Kṛṣṇa's defeat of Śiśupāla.

Mahābhārata A vast miscellany, partly narrative, partly didactic, of myths, folk tales, legends of Vedic gods and Hindu sectarian divinities which gradually accumulated round an epic poem describing the struggle between two families for the possession of Upper India (Madhyadeśa), which in the Epic is called Bhārata, whence the title of the whole work.

Nineteenth-century translators and commentators tended to regard its references to pseudo-historical events as valid and to overlook the syncretism of Vedic and post-Vedic names and places. Though the *Mahābhārata* is one of the most important Indian compositions, it is, like the *Rāmāyaṇa*, largely a work of fiction, in which historical names and events are adapted by successive redactors. In its present form it consists of eighteen books (*parvans*), divided into chapters or sections. Its nucleus is traditionally ascribed to Kṛṣṇa Dvaipāyana, called Vyāsa, 'the arranger'. Though the date of its composition, like the names of its author, is uncertain, a version of it appears to have been known to the compilers of the Buddhist Pāli Canon. A version resembling its present form may have been compiled between 200 B.C. and A.D. 200.[1] But Winternitz[2] considers it cannot be earlier than the fourth century B.C. or later than the fourth century A.D.

The *Mahābhārata* opens with the Ādi parvan which recounts the divine origin and childhood of its heroes, the genealogy of the two main families, the rivalry between them, and Draupadi's svayaṁbara. The second *parvan* is called Sabhā, where the drama begins with the assembly of the rival princes at the city of Hastinapura. Then follows the Vana pa., which narrates the exile of the Pāṇḍavas in the Kāmyaka forest after Yudhiṣṭhira's defeat at dice. This section also includes the story of Nala and an outline of the *Rāmāyaṇa*. The fourth, the Virāṭa, is named after the king with whom the Pāṇḍavas took refuge after their twelve years' exile; the fifth, Udyoga, deals with their preparation for war against the Kauravas. The following four books are named after the Kaurava war-leaders, Bhīṣma, Droṇa, Karṇa and Śalya, whose deaths are successively recorded. The tenth, Sauptika, describes the 'night-attack' by the three surviving Kauravas on the Pāṇḍava camp and the slaughter of all but the Pāṇḍu princes. It is followed by a short book called Strī, which tells of Queen Gāndhārī's and the other women's grief for the dead. In the following two books, Śānti and Anuśāsana, Bhīṣma is miraculously resurrected, apparently for the purpose of delivering long discourses on ethics and philosophy. Yudhiṣṭhira is crowned emperor, and in the fourteenth book, the Āśvamedhika, he performs the *aśvamedha* (horse sacrifice). In this book is inserted the *Anugītā*, a poem in the style of the *Bhagavadgītā*. The fifteenth, Āśramavāsika, describes the hermitage (*āśrama*) to which Dhṛtarāṣṭra, Gāndhārī, and Pṛthā (the mother of the Pāṇḍus) retired, and refers to their death in a forest fire. The sixteenth, Mausala, recounts the death of Kṛṣṇa and his brother Balarāma, and the engulfing of their city Dvārakā by the sea; the seventeenth, Mahāprasthānika, narrates the story of the Pāṇḍus' renunciation of their kingdom and their journey with

Draupadī to the northern mountains on their way to Mount Meru, the place of Indra's heaven (*svarga*). This is achieved in the last book, Svargārohaṇa.

The *Bhagavadgītā* is included in most of the manuscripts of the *MBh.*, but two out of the thirty-four used for the Critical Edition omit it entirely.

To the eighteen books was added, at a much later date, the *Harivaṁśa*, consisting of a long account in three parts of the genealogy, birth and life of Kṛṣṇa as the *avatāra* of Viṣṇu, written in the style of a Purāṇa.

It is generally accepted that much of the first parvan is an addition, as is most of the eighteenth. The same might also be said of the remainder of the books that follow the eleventh, except for a portion of the fifteenth when the curtain falls on the final scene of the tragedy. All else is anticlimax.

The *Mahābhārata*, like the *Rāmāyaṇa*, was composed in honour of Viṣṇu, who then was not as clearly defined as in later sectarian compositions. Śiva's appearance in the *Mahābhārata* may reasonably be regarded as an early attempt to counterbalance the attention given to Viṣṇu, though the advocacy of either cult in the *MBh.* is never as pronounced as in the Purāṇas.

The *MBh.*,[3] or at least a great deal of it, was evidently intended to be sung or recited, as its dramatic form and content indicate, which has made it an unfailing source of entertainment to the present day.

The extant recensions of the *MBh.* are the Northern and the Southern, which may 'be further sub-divided into versions according to the scripts in which the text is written. The Northern recension is thus made up of the Śaradā or Kāśmīri, and the Nepālī, Maithilī, the Bengali and the Devanāgarī versions. The Southern recension comprises the Telugu, the Grantha and the Malayālam versions.'[4] There are innumerable discrepancies in the two recensions, the Southern being the longer. Of the complete versions of the work, the most important are the Calcutta, Bombay and the Kumbhakonam.[5]

[1]E. W. Hopkins, *ERE.*, VIII, p. 325, but in his *Epic Mythology*, p. 1, he suggests 300 B.C. to 100 B.C. as the most probable date.

The Mahābhārata war is paralleled 'in the legend of the Trojan War ... Each became the great central point to which the nations of the Middle Ages referred their history. To have shared ancestrally in the fame of Kurukṣetra or of Troy was for nations the patent of nobility and ancient descent' (*CHI.*, vol. I, p. 307).

[2]*HIL.*, vol. I, p.465.

[3]A large number of works have been written on different aspects of the *MBh.* and it has been translated into E. under the auspices of P. C. Roy, 12 vols, and reprinted recently by the Oriental Publishing Co., Calcutta. An important Critical Edition, edited by V. S. Sukthankar, F. Edgerton, S. K. De, *et al.* is being published by the Bhandarkar Oriental Research Institute, and will for the first time collate all important versions.

[4]*HCIP.*, vol. II, p. 250.

[5]Ibid. v. also n. 3 above.

v. Ṛṇam; Karṇa.

Mahābhāṣya 'Great Commentary.' The name of Patañjali's Commentary on Pāṇini's Sūtras and the Vārttikas of Kātyāyana.

Mahābhaya 'Terror', personified as one of the sons of Adharma (wrong) and Nirṛti (misery).

Mahādeva The 'Great God', a title often applied to Śiva and sometimes to Viṣṇu. Mahādeva is also 'taken as a substitute for the impersonal Brahman Itself'.[1]

According to the *Liṅga P.* Mahādeva's *śakti* is Rohiṇī and his son is Budha, the personification of the planet Mercury.

[1]Heimann, *Facets*, p. 66.

v. Śaivism; Mahādevī.

Mahādevī 'Great Goddess.' A title of Śiva's *śakti* who represents all aspects of his cosmic energy. She is known by many names: Pārvatī, Durgā, Kālī, Umā, etc.[1]

The *Varāha P.* describes Mahādevī as a virgin of celestial loveliness, distinguished by three colours from which at the request of the gods she created the *śaktis* of the three divinities comprising the triad (*trimūrti*). The white became Sarasvatī, the *śakti* of Brahmā; the red, Lakṣmī, the *śakti*, of Viṣṇu; and the black, Pārvatī, the *śakti* of Śiva.

[1]This title is also applied to Lakṣmī, Sarasvatī and other goddesses.

v. Mahādeva.

Mahājvāla The name of the hell destined for those who have committed incest with a daughter or daughter-in-law (*VP.*, II.6).

Mahākāla I. Śiva as Lord of Time, and hence of Death. He assumes the form of Mahākāla when leading all things to final dissolution. Mahākāla is Śiva's *alter ego.*[1]

[1]*CHS.*, p. 170.

II. In Hindu astronomy Mahākāla represents the conjunction of the sun and moon.

Mahākālī The destructive form of the great mother-goddess Kālī (representing the dynamic aspect of Śiva, or the expression of his wrath) (*Vāyu P.*, 101, 298, *PI.*). Because of her character she is popularly associated with Mahāmārī, the personification of cholera (*Mārk. Pur.*, 92, 33–7).[1]

[1]Mahālakṣmī assumes the form of Mahākālī at the dissolution of the universe (*DHI.*, p. 496).

Mahālakṣmī 'Great Lakṣmī', the *śakti* of Nārāyaṇa (Viṣṇu).[1] She is the primary goddess who embodies the three *guṇas* (*sattva*, *rajas*, *tamas*). At the dissolution of the universe she assumes the form of Mahākālī in whom the *tamas guṇa* (*tamoguṇa*) predominates. A number of other goddesses emanated from Mahālakṣmī such as Mahāmāyā, also known as Mahāmārī (the personification of cholera), Kṣudhā, Yoganidrā, Kālarātrī, etc. The goddess Mahāsarasvatī (in whom the *sattva guṇa* predominates) also emanates from Mahālakṣmī. The former was also known as Mahāvidyā, Vāc, Vedagarbhā, etc. 'From these three forms of *śakti* ... were evolved in turn Brahmā and Śrī, Rudra and Trayī or Vedavidyā, and Viṣṇu and Gaurī'.[2]

[1]Mahālakṣmī is sometimes identified with, or 'manifests her nature', in Sarasvatī, Kālī, etc. (*VS.*, p. 60).

[2]*DHI.*, pp. 496f.

Mahāmārī v. Mahālakṣmī; Mahākālī.

Mahāmāyā I. The transcendent power of illusion (*māyā*), personified as the goddess Mahāmāyā[1] who is also identified with Durgā. By the divine power of *māyā* she makes the universe appear as if really existing and thus cognizable by the senses. Though immanent in the world, she only becomes manifest when carrying out divine purposes.

[1]She also personifies Viṣṇu's fecund sleep at the end of each age (*Mārk. P.*, 81, 40–53).

v. Mahālakṣmī; Yoganidrā.

II. A *vidyā* (magical spell or type of knowledge) capable of dispelling all forms of *māyā* (*Bhāg. P.*, X.55,16,22, *PI.*). By means of this spell Pradyumna was able to vanquish Śambara.

Mahāpadma I. One of the eight 'treasures' (*nidhis*) connected with the magical art called *padminī*, which brings wealth and good fortune, extending to seven generations (*Mārk. P.*, 68, 13–16).

II. Name of one of the eight cold hells.

III. Name of the elephant supporting the southern region of the earth.

v. Abhranāga(s).

Mahāpralaya The 'dissolution of the universe' which occurs at the end of the age. The goddess Mahākālī is the ruling deity of *mahāpralaya*.

v. Pralaya; Maharloka.

Mahārātrī The 'long night', when the world is destroyed. Śiva, as the Eternal, is regarded as 'the substratum from which all the secondary cycles of time and the energies which rule them are formed.'[1]

[1]*HP.*, p. 268.

v. Kāla; Mahākāla II; Pralaya.

Maharloka or **Gandharvaloka** One of the seven worlds, the region of celestial spirits (*gandharvas* and *apsarasas*). The spiritually advanced remain in this sphere (*loka*) for a *kalpa*, i.e., a day of Brahmā. Maharloka is situated ten million leagues above the Pole Star (*VP.*, II.7).

The world is destroyed (*pralaya*) by fire at the end of the age, and the heat engendered is so great that all who dwell in Maharloka move to a higher sphere, the Janaloka (*Mārk P.*, 46, 39–40; *VP.*, VI.3).

Maharṣi(s) 'Great Seers', the collective designation of the 'Seven Great *Ṛṣis*', frequently referred to in the *RV.* though not individually named. They were held in high esteem as 'beings who speak with seven holy voices' (Vālakhilya hymn 11,3), and as 'seven god-like *ṛṣis*' (*RV.*, X.130,7). Another hymn (I.164,15), referring to six two-monthly seasons[1] and a single intercalary season, suggests their connexion with an early form of lunar reckoning.[2] It is evident that, unlike the *Śrutarṣis*, they were not singers and poets, or authors of sacred songs. The *ŚBr.* (VI.1.1,1) distinguishes them as the 'seven vital airs', i.e., the 'Sevenfold Vital Breath', thus giving them a cosmogonic significance.

In the *MBh.* and the Purāṇas the Maharṣis are variously enumerated regionally. Thus in the North the most famous group consists of Vasiṣṭha, Kaśyapa, Atri, Viśvāmitra, Gautama, Jamadagni, Bharadvāja;[3] in the East, Kauśika, Yavakrīta, Gārgya, Gālava, Kaṇva the son of Medhātithi; in the South, Svastyatreya, Namuci, Pramuci, Agastya, Atri, Sumukha, Vimukha; in the West, Nṛṣadgu, Kavaṣa, Dhaumya, Raudreya or Kauṣeya.[4]

The Maharṣis are further distinguished from Brahmaṛṣis (priestly seers); Devarṣis (priests of the gods); Rājarṣis (those of royal lineage), and other ṛṣis, variously classified. In the *VP.* (IV. 24) the seven *ṛṣis* are given astrological significance as stars in the constellation Ursa Major, in which Agastya was subsequently included.

[1]Cf. 'He thus establishes the seven *ṛṣis* in the seasons' (*ŚBr.*, IX.3.1,21).

[2]v. Nakṣatras.

[3]*Mārk. P.*, lxxix, 9.

[4]*EM.*, p. 177.

v. Ṛṣi(s).

Mahāśānti An expiatory observance for averting evil.

v. Śānti II; Ṣaṭkarman.

Mahāsiddha(s) Tantric 'saints' who have attained perfection. Traditionally there are said to be eighty-four of them. Many were probably famous teachers some of whom became the subject of myth and legend. These *siddhas* are depicted as possessing 'quasi-demonic energy in their strong, well-cared for bodies and violent eyes. They probably embody folk memories of the magical dances performed by Shamans possessed by spirits.'[1]

[1]Rawson, *Art of Tantra*, p. 136.

Mahāśveta 'Dazzling white.' An earth-goddess and one of the numerous consorts of the sun-god Sūrya.[1] It is also an epithet of Durgā and Sarasvatī.

[1]*DHI.*, p. 439.

Mahāvidyā The goddess personifying that kind of knowledge (*vidyā*) which transcends intellectual cognition (*jñāna*) and wisdom (*prajñā*). Though *mahāvidyā* is a post-Vedic notion, it probably owes something to the prehistoric cult of the mother-goddess, and particularly to that of the Vedic A-diti (lit. without limit, i.e., beyond all human apprehension). The notion of *mahāvidyā* appears to be even more closely connected with Vāc, the Vedic goddess of speech, 'the Word',[1] without whom the hymns of the Veda could not have been composed, or knowledge acquired and transmitted.

Mahāvidyā is not concerned with knowledge for its own sake, but with the apprehension of that particular knowledge which will eradicate *avidyā* (false knowledge or ignorance) and dispel the mists of illusion (*māyā*), and lead to the attainment of liberation (*mokṣa*).

[1]Cf. the Greek Logos.

Mahāvidyā(s) The ten Hindu tantric goddess-transformations. Seven of them belong to the creative manifestation-stages of the universe, and three to the withdrawal. They represent the ten forms of transcendent knowledge and magical powers collectively known as *mahāvidyā*.[1]

The usual list of the ten Mahāvidyās represents them as the source of preternatural power,[2] some of them being depicted with macabre symbolism, and each described in a Tantra bearing her name. The Mahāvidyās are: the Black Kālī (or Lalitā), the goddess of Time. When in the process of creation she sees herself as the origin of multiplicity, she assumes the aspect of the second *mahāvidyā* who 'stands on the funeral pyre in which the "world" is reduced to ashes, but is herself pregnant with the potential of re-creation; for she . . . divides the one into the many'.[3] As Tārā is an emanation of Kālī, they jointly suggest the identity of time and space, and are also regarded as the two principal goddesses of the group. Soḍaśī is portrayed as a girl of sixteen, the embodiment of the sixteen modifications of desire. As the number sixteen also represents totality, completeness, the cosmic whole, Soḍaśī symbolizes perfection. Bhuvaneśvarī, represents the forces of the material world; Bhairavī, the infinity of forms and desires which attract and distract mankind, and also the inevitability of death which begins with conception and continues throughout life. She thus represents the perpetual process of creation, dissolution and re-creation. Chinnamastā, also called Vīrarātrī, represents eternal night. She is depicted as a naked goddess holding in one hand a blood-stained knife and in the other her own severed head, the mouth of which drinks the blood gushing from her headless body. Two more streams of blood gush from her headless body into the mouths of two nude girls, which symbolizes the distribution of her life-energy into the universe; or it may refer to a particular aspect of the ritual sacrifice 'called the "joining of the head" (*śirosandhāna*), in which the head is symbolically re-attached to the body of the victim'.[4] This denotes the consummation of the process of life, death and new life, and the maintenance of cosmic continuity. Dhūmāvatī, personifies the destruction (*pralaya*) of the universe by fire, when only the smoke (*dhūma*) from its ashes remains. She is then called Daridrā, the personification of destitution, or Vidhavā, the widow of a dead world. (As numbers three to seven have a similar theme, they are classified as '*vidyās*', the minor sources of magical power). Bagalā, the crane-headed goddess, represents the hidden forces underlying jealousy, hate, cruelty, etc. Mātaṅgī is the personification of domination. Kamalā, the lotus-girl, represents pure consciousness of self; she rules over the auspicious zodiacal sign *rohiṇī*. Kamalā grants boons and allays fear and so is identified with Lakṣmī, the goddess of good fortune. The eighth to tenth are classified as *siddha-vidyās*, a term which appears to signify the attainment of supreme knowledge, the overcoming of *avidyā* (ignorance) and *māyā* (illusion). Each of these goddesses 'represents a limitation of the total *persona* of Kālī herself, but is an inevitable part of that whole. Without the drastic experience of integration, no search for integration means anything. Kālī must be known in the full gamut of her transformations'.[5]

[1]*BH.*, p. 187. The Mahāvidyā cult was prominent in medieval Bengal (*HCIP.*, vol. IV, p. 286).

[2]*BH.*, ibid. gives a description of them, drawn from the Tantras. A modern exposition is given by Daniélou, *HP.*, pp. 268ff. who transposes numbers five and six.

[3]Rawson, *The Art of Tantra*, p. 132.

[4]*HP.*, p. 281. In Vedic blood sacrifice the victim was beheaded.

[5]Rawson, op. cit., pp. 133f.

v. Nakṣatra(s); Śiva; Śakti.

Mahāvīra I. 'Great hero.' An epithet of Vardhamāna, the twenty-fourth (and last) *tīrthaṅkara* of the Jainas. Vardhamāna was born near Vaiśālī and 'belonged to the Nāya clan called Nāta (or Ñāta) in Pāli and Jñātṛ in Sanskrit. His parents were Siddhārtha, a wealthy nobleman, and Triśalā, sister of Ceṭaka, an eminent Licchavi prince of Vaiśālī'.[1]

At the age of thirty Mahāvīra became an ascetic and practised *tapas* for twelve years during which time he wandered from place to place. For some years another ascetic, Gośāla Maskarīputra shared his hardships until they quarrelled and the latter left to found the Ājīvika cult. After thirteen years Mahāvīra attained enlightenment and became a Jina (Conqueror). He gained many followers, and taught for thirty years in the Gangetic kingdoms. He died of self-starvation at the age of seventy-two (c. 468 B.C.) at Pāvā, near Rājagṛha.[2]

Unlike his contemporary, the Buddha, who founded the Buddhist Order, Mahāvīra was not an originator, but the co-ordinator of an organization that had already been systematized by Pārśvanātha, the twenty-third *tīrthaṅkara*, two centuries before.

[1]*HCIP.*, II, p. 413; *CHI.*, I, pp. 154ff. The epithet Mahāvīra is also applied to Viṣṇu, Rāma, Hanumat, Garuḍa, the *vajra*, etc.

[2]Basham, *WI.*, pp. 287ff.; v. also Parrinder, *Avatar and Incarnation*, ch. 13.

v. Jainism; Darśana(s).

II. The term for the heated metal vessel also called *gharma*, in which fresh milk is poured during the *pravargya*, a ceremony preceding the *soma* sacrifice (*RV.*, V.30,15; VIII.61,10).

Mahāvrata I. An ancient popular village fertility festival, held at the winter solstice[1] to drive away demonic influences which might impede the return of the sun and thus retard plant growth.[2] The *brāhmaṇas* took advantage of the popularity of the occasion and turned it into a religious festival, but a number of folk-elements remained, such as the use of swings, in the belief that the higher one swung the higher the crops would grow. Races were run[3] to increase the fertility of the soil, accompanied by the beating of the earth-drum.[4] Ritual abuse was exchanged between a courtesan and a *brahmacārin*; a *brahman* and a *śūdra* fought for a white round skin (a symbol of the sun); young girls danced holding water pitchers (*kumbha*), singing 'this is honey' (*madhu*), which is said to endow the sacrificers with might. Sacral coition was also carried out under a covering.[5] All this was 'amalgamated with the artificial litany and *sāman* engendered by the Agnicayana rite'.[6]

[1]The ceremonial kindling of fire is elsewhere associated with solstitial festivals in ancient Egypt and 'as far back as the third millennium B.C., the Sumerians of Nippur called the pertinent month by a name ... which means properly (Month of) the Festival of Lighting Braziers' (Gaster, *Thespis*, pp. 274f. For European examples v. p. 274).

[2]v. *Ait. Br.*, IV.14. The *mahāvrata* festival marks 'both the end and the beginning of two successive solar periods' (*ŚBr.*, V, p. 167, n.1). The *Tait. Saṁ.* (VII.2.2, etc.) declares that the rite is to 'win food'.

[3]Races were also run at the *vājapeya* ceremony.

[4]The earth-drum was made by digging a hole and covering it with hide. The power in the eerie sounds made by it enabled the sacrificers 'to conquer the earth'.

[5]A. Hillebrandt, *Rituallliteratur*, p. 157. A sacral coition also took place during the *aśvamedha*.

[6]Keith's translation of the *Tait. Sam.*, pt. i, p. cxxxi; VII.5,9–10.

II. Name of the vow taken by the Śaiva Kāpalikās; hence their epithet Mahāvratins.[1]

[1]*RAA.*, p. 56.

v. Vrātya(s).

Mahāvyahṛti A mystical formula consisting of '*bhūr, bhuvaḥ, svaḥ*', which are the names of the first three of the seven worlds. The *mahāvyahṛti* should be uttered after the sacred syllable *OM* by every *brahmin* at the commencement of his daily prayers.

The three *mahāvyahṛtis* are personified as the daughters of Savitṛ and Pṛśni.

v. Vyahṛti(s).

Mahāyuga(s) v. Kalpa.

Mahendra I. 'Great Indra.' An epithet applied to Indra, Viṣṇu and Śiva. According to the *ŚBr.* (I.6.4,21), Indra became Mahendra after he had slain Vṛtra.

An offering to Mahendra obtains for the offerer superiority, greatness and victory (*Tait. Saṁ.*, I.6. 2 and 4). In the same work it is stressed that the poor should not sacrifice to Mahendra for he is the deity of learned *brahmins*, village headmen, and warriors. Should a poor man sacrifice to him he would lose his own deity and his condition would be worsened (2.5,4).

II. Name of a mountain range sacred to Indra and Hari (Viṣṇu). Here Paraśurāma underwent a long period of austerity (*tapas*).

A *bilva* tree grows on the mountain to which offerings are made by those desiring good sight.

III. A son or brother of the Mauryan Emperor Aśoka and leader of the Buddhist monks who introduced Buddhism into Ceylon.

IV. Name of the regent of the north-east quarter.

v. Lokapāla.

Maheśvara 'Great Lord'; 'the possessor of great power',[1] an epithet generally applied to Śiva, and sometimes to Viṣṇu.

Maheśvara is the guardian of the household (*AGP.*, 40,21).

[1]*Īśvara*, like *īśāna*, is from the Vedic root *īś*, 'to have power'. In Maheśvara are co-ordinated the three energies from which knowledge arises, viz., under-

standing (*jñāna*), will (*icchā*), and action (*kriyā*). In the Śaivism of Kashmir the notion of Maheśvara 'holds that the world mind, as Will, is within the process of Nature. The world is not a finished result that is ascribed to God, an external designer; but the very march of nature is the working of the universal mind' (*EW.*, vol. I, p. 388).

Maheśvara Sūtra A Śaiva work dealing with the four sciences leading to supreme knowledge. They are symbolically attributed to Śiva and are defined as: Yoga; the monistic theory of the Vedānta; language, i.e., the relation of verbal sounds and symbols to ideas; and music, i.e., the melodic arrangement of sounds in accordance with the rules of rhythm in all its forms, whether vocal or instrumental. One of the principal early instruments was the drum (*ḍamaru*).[1] The metres of the *RV.* songs, as well as their arrangement and the form of the *mantras* in subsequent Vedic texts indicate the influence of sound and rhythm.

[1]The knowledge of the four sciences is said to have emerged from the sounds of Śiva's drum during his cosmic dance. The *Maheśvara Sūtra* 'represents one of the esoteric word-formulae in which the ancient Śaiva wisdom was condensed and which are believed to constitute the earliest revelation' (*HP.*, p. 200).

v. Tāṇḍava; Naṭarāja.

Maheśvarī The 'Supreme goddess', i.e., the *śakti* of Maheśvara (the supreme lord Śiva). Maheśvarī is variously called Durgā, Pārvatī, etc.

Mahī 'Great.' A goddess of the Earth who with the goddesses Ilā and Sarasvatī attend the sacrifice (*RV.*, I.13,9, etc.).[1] Mahī is called the universal *soma* cow, from whom flows all prosperity and abundance (*Tait. Saṁ.*, VII.1,6).

[1]The epithet Mahī is frequently applied to divine beings and powers.

v. Pṛthivī.

Mahiṣa I. 'Buffalo', the emblem of Yama and of a Jaina *tīrthaṅkara.*

II. A demon who had become so powerful that he defeated the gods and established himself in heaven. The gods wandered forlornly about the world until they were advised by Viṣṇu and Śiva to concentrate their powers which appeared as jets of fire, and from these emerged the terrifying form of the goddess Durgā.[1] Riding on a lion and armed with weapons given her by the gods, she attacked Mahiṣa who continually changed his shape, but when he finally assumed the form of a buffalo she slew him. Mahiṣa then sought to escape from the carcase, but the goddess cut off his head with her divine sword (whence her epithet Mahiṣāsuramardinī—'crusher of Mahiṣa'), and restored heaven to the gods. Mahiṣa's decapitated head blocked the entrance to the country of the Northern Kurus (*MBh.*, Vana pa., 230).[2]

[1]She has many names including Ambikā, Caṇḍikā, Caṇḍī, etc.

[2]The slaying of Mahiṣa is also related in the *Mārk. P.* (Cantos 82–4).

III. One of the Sādhyas, the 'perfected' or 'successful' militant gods.

IV. Name of a Vindhya tribe.

Mahiṣāsuramardinī v. Mahiṣa II.

Mahiṣī The chief wife of a king (*ŚBr.*, VI.5.3,1). During part of the *aśvamedha* (horse sacrifice) it was the King's chief queen who performed sacral coition (under a rich robe) with the sacrificial horse (XIII.5.2,2).

Maināka A mountain[1] situated to the north of Mount Kailāsa and personified as the son of Himavat and Menā or Menakā (*Mārk. P.*, 52,13). To prevent the mountains from moving Indra clipped the wings of all except those of Maināka because of his apparent stability, but according to the *MBh.* (Vana pa., 135) he subsided into the interior of the earth.

[1]Every mountain is a potential divinity and the abode of divine beings.

Mainda An *asura* in the form of an ape. He and his brother Dvivida are the sons of the Aśvins, but according to the *Rām.* the Aśvins were reborn as the two apes.[1]

[1]*EM.*, pp. 103, 168.

Maithuna v. Mithuna.

Maitreya I. 'Friendly.' A pupil to whom Parāśara related the *Viṣṇu Purāṇa.*[1]

[1]Wilson, *VP.*, p. 3, n.10.

II. The name of the future Buddha.

Maitri One of the eighteen principal Upaniṣads.

Makara I. A mythical aquatic animal[1] which in early art appears to have been inspired by the crocodile. In Indian sculpture it originally had four and later two or four leonine or dog-like legs; a scaly body and crocodile tail. The later medieval forms have elaborate floriated tails as in Gupta art. A full-faced *makara* is depicted on a small metal ornament from Taxila, and as part of a head-dress at Amarāvatī.[2] Like other creatures associated with water (representing the unmanifested state of the cosmos), the *makara* has a metaphysical significance which identifies it with 'absolute reality concentrated in water'.[3] The *makara* is often depicted on the architraves of early *toraṇas*; on throne-backs; as a head-dress ornament; as earrings, etc., and also as a gargoyle carrying away the offerings in water from a *liṅgam.*[4]

The *makara* figures in many legends and myths and is endowed with occult and magical powers, especially those relating to the fertility of rivers, lakes, and the sea, the last being called *makarāvāsa* (*makara*'s abode). Thus it is the vehicle (*vāhana*) of Varuṇa, god of the celestial and terrestrial waters, and of Gaṅgā, goddess of the Ganges. As the producer of fertility, it appears on the banner of Kāma,[5] the god of love. It is also depicted as an auspicious sign on the hand of Śrī. The '*makara* and *kirttimukha* forms appear on the majority of French and Spanish Churches built in the 12th century'.[6]

[1]It represents the sign of Capricorn in the Hindu zodiac (Werner, *Dictionary of Chinese Mythology*, p. 305).

[2]Coomaraswamy, *Yakṣas*, pt. ii, p. 48. Lindsay considers the *makara* motif to be of south Indian origin ('Makara in the Early Chinese Buddhist Sculpture', *JRAS*., 1951, pp. 134ff.; v. also Vogel, 'Le Makara dans la sculpture de l'Inde', *Revue des Arts Asiatiques*, 1930, pp. 133ff.).

[3]Eliade, *Patterns*, p. 193.

[4]Coomaraswamy, op. cit., pt. ii, p. 47. In some myths *makaras* are connected with pearls. (Cf. the *makara nidhi* of Kubera.) To take a pearl from a *makara*'s jaws was the proverbial example of courage (ibid., p. 50).

[5]And on the banner of Pradyumna, the incarnation of Kāma, born as the son of Kṛṣṇa and Rukmiṇī. In ancient Egypt the crocodile represented virility. Today in the Sudan, crocodile genitals are eaten as an aphrodisiac (Brodrick, *Animals in Archaeology*, p. 73).

[6]B. Rogers, 'An Archaeological Pilgrimage to Santiago de Compostela' in *Science*, vol. 131, 1180, cited by Singhal, *India*, vol. II, p. 60. The *makara* is also depicted on the fifteenth-century chancel screen in Llanrwst Parish Church in the Conway Valley (*Folklore*, vol. 77, Spring 1966, pp. 66f.).

v. Makaravyūha.

II. The name of one of the personified 'treasures' (*nidhis*) of Kubera. A man on whom the *makara* looks is born ignorant, though with a good disposition. He gains the friendship of kings; but his greatest pleasure is the buying and selling of weapons (*Mārk. P.*, 68.4,17–20).

v. Padminī-vidyā.

Makārā A goddess. Bharati suggests that she may be a Buddhist Tantric goddess who was adopted by the Hindu Tantrists, and may personify the 'five Ms' (*pañcamakāra*),[1] of the 'left-handed' tantric ritual, viz., *mada* (wine), *matsya* (fish), *māṁsa* (meat), *mudrā* (parched grain or kidney beans regarded as aphrodisiacs), and *maithuna* (ritualistic copulation).

[1]*TT*., pp. 24, 70.

Makaravyūha An army formation (*vyūha*), used for attacking on a narrow front, i.e., as a column, and hence its being likened to a *makara* or a crocodile. Jarāsandha deployed his troops in this fashion against the Yādavas, but Kṛṣṇa blocked their advance by felling trees and then ambushed them.

Makha A mysterious being whom Agni, Rudra and Indra slew (*Tait. Saṁ.*, III.2,4), hence their epithet Makhahan 'killer of Makha'.

The name, which appears once in the *RV*. (IX.101,13), may refer to a person to whom the Bhṛgus were opposed. The description in the *ŚBr*. (VI.5.2,1–2) seems to indicate that it had ritual significance. It reads: 'The priest then takes a lump of clay . . . saying, "Thou are the head of Makha!" The priest then says, apparently to himself, "Makha, doubtless, is the sacrifice,[1] and this is its head," and proceeds with the building of the *āhavaniya* fire-altar repeating, "Thou art the head of Makha!"'

A possible explanation of this obscure passage is contained in an earlier part of the *ŚBr*. (I.2.5,1–7), which recounts the quarrel of the *devas* and *asuras* over the division of the world. Placing Viṣṇu (representing the sacrifice), at their head, the *devas* confronted the *asuras* and demanded their share. The *asuras* grudgingly agreed to grant them the amount of ground which could be covered by the prostrate body of Viṣṇu, here described as a dwarf (*vāmana*).[2]

Another myth concerns a contest in which the gods were required to perform a sacrifice. The first to complete it was to be regarded as supreme. Viṣṇu won easily and so gained all the power and glory of the sacrifice for himself, thereby causing great envy among the other gods. Finally they decided to bribe the ants with the promise of a continuous supply of food if they would gnaw through Viṣṇu's bowstring. The ants agreed and Viṣṇu's head was cut off as the ends of the huge bow sprang apart. The delighted gods rushed upon Viṣṇu to take his power, but Indra arrived first and gained it for himself; hence his epithet Makhavat (*ŚBr*., XIV.1.1, 1–14; 1.2,10).[3]

[1]And hence is identified with Viṣṇu who is the personified Sacrifice.

[2]The germ of numerous stories associated with the Vāmana *avatāra*.

[3]v. also *Vāj. Saṁ.*, 37,3; *OST*., IV, p. 126, n. 125.

v. Cyavana; Yajña.

Mālā A necklace, wreath, or garland. Necklaces are generally made of berries, or of beads carved from the wood of sacred trees, to which magical properties are attributed. Perforations in the beads were believed to afford dwelling-places for spirits. Wreaths and garlands are made of auspicious flowers, and worn at festivals and weddings, or presented to guests.

Garlands also symbolize victory, as does Viṣṇu's garland. Dwarf and normal sized *yakṣas* are often depicted carrying or wearing garlands. Coomaraswamy points out that garlands are provided with nodes at regular intervals as are the lotus (*padma*) rhizomes.[1]

Rudrakṣa berries are used for Śaiva *mālās*, the *tulasī* for those of Vaiṣṇavas, and dead men's teeth or similar relics for those of Śāktas. *Mālās* are believed to possess protective powers, and snake-charmers hang them on their pipes when playing before snakes.

[1] *Yakṣas*, pt. ii, p. 59. Cf. the garland motif borne by Erotes which may have been taken over from India; also the figure of the Greek Victory (Nike) who holds in her right hand a figure of Zeus Olympios to which she presents a garland (Farnell, *Cults*, I, pp. 128f.).

v. Mālāmantra; Vaijayantī-mālā; Vanamālā; Mālinī.

Mālāmantra A sacred text or spell written in the form of a wreath or garland (*mālā*).

Mālinī Name of an *apsaras*, the daughter of Varuṇa's son Puṣkara.

A garland (*mālā*)[1] is always presented to a bride at her wedding, and thus Durgā as the spouse (*śakti*) of Śiva is often referred to as Mālinī, 'she with the garland'.[2]

Mālinī, who married the *muni* Ruci, bore him a son called Manu Raucya, destined to be the ruler of a *manvantara* (*Mārk. P.*, 98, 1f.).

[1] The name Mālinī is derived from *mālā* 'garland'.

[2] Cf. C. Autran, *L'Épopée Indoue*, p. 19. 'Mālinī—l'un des noms d'invocation de Durgā—parèdre de Śiva, le dieu au taureau, comme [Europa], parèdre du dieu au taureau de Crète, doivent leur appellatif commun de "Celle à la (belle) guirlande".'

Mallanāga v. Vātsyāyana.

Mamatā The sister-in-law of Bṛhaspati. He attempted to have intercourse with her when she was pregnant, but the foetus obstructed him, whereupon he cursed the unborn child. Fearing that her husband would desert her she decided to abandon the child, but the gods commanded her to rear the child born of two fathers (*bhara dvājam*); hence his name Bharadvāja.

v. Dīrghatamas.

Māṁsa 'Flesh.' The term generally refers to the flesh of animals, but it also signifies the pulp or fleshy parts of certain fruits.

In post-Vedic times *māṁsa* refers particularly to the flesh of the cow, an animal which, for several reasons, had come to be regarded as especially sacred and whose slaughter was forbidden. Such a view must have developed gradually, as there is no evidence of its having been held by the non-Āryan races of India; nor by the early Vedic Indians. Flesh was offered to the gods, and was subsequently consumed by the officiating priests. Agni, the god of fire, was called 'eater of the ox or cow' (*RV.*, VIII.43,11). Oxen and goats were also slaughtered to provide food for guests in the home (*RV.*, X.68,3), and for those attending wedding feasts. In the cremation ceremony the hide of a cow was used to envelop the corpse (X.16,7). That such practices were common is evident by the terms *māṁsapacana*, the vessel used for cooking meat (I.162,13), and *māṁsopajīvin*, a dealer in meat. But later a radical change took place among certain Hindu sects which forbade the eating of the flesh of the cow or any other animal.[1] Although a number of factors may have induced this change, it seems that revulsion against blood sacrifice, the concept of the unity of all life, and the influence of the Jaina and Buddhist teaching of *ahiṁsā* were among the contributing factors to what is now a fundamental tenet of many Hindu sects.

[1] But some Tantrists make use of the so-called 'Five M's' (pañcatattva or pañcamakāra), viz., *mada* (wine), *matsya* (fish), *māṁsa* (meat), *mudrā* (parched grain) and *maithuna* (coition).

Māna I. The name of a *RV.* poet and singer.

v. Māna(s).

II. 'Measurer.' An epithet of the ancient *ṛṣi* Agastya (*RV.*, VII.33,13), whom some later writers considered to be one of the founders of Vāstuvidyā (the science of architecture). The *Mānasāra* may represent a summary of his architectural treatises.[1] This traditional claim has been repeated by some modern commentators, but it lacks any textual confirmation. That there may have been a post-Vedic architect called Māna, or one given that epithet is possible, but to identify him with Māna Agastya is a Paurāṇic syncretism.

[1] Bhattacharyya, *Canons of Indian Art*, p. 13, and n. 1.

Māna(s) Descendants of Māna who invoked Indra and the Maruts for gifts of cattle and for 'universal gifts' (*RV.*, I.169,8); and the Aśvins for abundant food (I.182,8; 184,4–6).

v. Māna I.

Manas 'Mind' (in its widest sense as applied to all the mental powers), intellect, intelligence, understanding, perception, will, etc.[1] In philosophy, *manas* is the internal organ of perception and cognition.[2]

There is scant evidence in early Vedic times of interest in psychosomatic analysis or in the functioning of the sensory organs, still less an appreciation of their relation to what they called *manas*, the individual spirit. Nonetheless, some of the early Vedic seers, in their concept of *vāc* as the magical vehicle of thought and speech, unconsciously provided a basis for the later recognition of the relation of thought, speech and mind to the human spirit. The *ŚBr.* (III.2.4,11) declares: 'For indeed this speech (*vāc*) of ours is upheld by the mind (*manas*), because Mind precedes Speech (and prompts her) . . . Were it not for Mind, Speech would be incoherent'.

The Upaniṣads attempt to define mind, but not very successfully, largely owing to over-elaboration and to an association of ideas which, though related, need separate consideration. This and the use of dubious analogy and metaphor have led to some confusion, as is evident in the *Bṛhad-Ār. Up.* (I.5,3–7) which, having recognized hearing and seeing as functions of the mind, then links speech, mind and breath together as a threefold entity. They are successively declared to be the three worlds, the three Vedas, etc. In the later Upaniṣads a clearer picture of mind is drawn, as in the *Kaṭha* (6.6–7) where the senses (*indriya*) are considered to rank below the mind, just as true being (*sattva*) is ranked above it. The *Maitri* (6.30) also connects the senses with mind but identifies them with individuality, which it contrasts with the individual or subjective notion of *ātman*. Thus it strongly condemns as a snare and delusion the belief: 'This is I' and 'That is mine', and declares that only by the apprehension of the fictitious nature of such illusions will liberation (*mokṣa*) be attained.

In the subsequent Hindu quasi-philosophical systems (*darśanas*) mind is regarded as a special sense-organ, distinct from the five ordinary senses, and constituting 'a sort of inlet of thought to the soul',[3] but distinct from it. Above all mind is a means of facilitating the release of the individual from the bonds of *avidyā* and *māyā*.

[1] *SED*. Cf. OL *mānis*, 'good', which has L. pl. *mānēs*, used as noun, the 'good' (gods), a euphemism of *dī inferi*, later denoting a family's ancestral spirits worshipped as gods (Partridge, *Origins*, p. 387).

[2] v. Whitney, *CD*., and *IW*., p. 53.

[3] *IW*., pp. 64f.

Manasā A goddess of snakes, whose cult, probably derived from an archaic form of snake-worship, is mainly confined to Bengal and parts of Bihar, Orissa and Assam, and like the snake (*nāga*) cults of South India was initially limited to the unbrahmanized hill and jungle tribes who lacked political, social and cultural unity and a common language. Snake-worship was once general in those parts of India where venomous snakes abounded. Ancient man, awed by their mysterious gliding motion, the sloughing of their skins, and fearing their poisonous fangs, sought to propitiate them by the laying of offerings near their lairs.[1] In early snake-cults the snakes themselves were the objects of worship, whereas in the Manasā cult, it was the goddess herself, as their leader and controller, who was worshipped and invoked for protection against them. Thus in India there is 'no single instance of a snake-goddess who is herself not a snake, except that of Manasā in Bengal'.[2] Nonetheless, it is probable that her cult represents the merging of various snake-cults.

Literary evidence of the Manasā cult appears in the narrative poems in praise of the gods, the earliest having been composed about A.D. 1300. Some of them attempt to synthesize the mythical Śiva of the Purāṇas and the folklore of Manasā in a form intelligible to village folk, who quickly transformed Śiva into a simple peasant like themselves, whose emblem was the plough rather than the trident of the Śiva of the Hindu triad (*trimūrti*).

Manasā is closely connected with the earth and nether world, and as a fertility goddess, with marriage rites, the snake being a phallic symbol. Manasā myths, like those of some other minor divinities, were adopted to serve Śaiva interests, just as the serpent Śeṣa served those of the Vaiṣṇavas. Thus to the myth of Śiva's partial swallowing of the poison which emerged from the Churning of the Ocean (*samudramathana*) is added a sequel in which Manasā extracts the poison from his throat. Having fulfilled the role of 'remover of poison' (Viṣāharī), she distributed it among various snakes and insects, so accounting for the origin of the poisonous varieties,[3] and hence her supplementary epithet Viṣādharī, 'controller of poison'.[4] In the final canto of the *Manasā-vijaya*[5] she is referred to as Ādimātā (primal mother). Manasā can assume any form at will and can perform other miracles, such as milking a barren cow, using a wicker basket as a milk pail, and drinking the milk whilst standing on her head.[6]

A story from Bengal indicates the rivalry that once existed between the cults of Manasā and Śiva. A certain merchant, a devout Śaiva, who had steadfastly refused to worship Manasā, was persuaded to change his mind by his daughter-in-law Behulā after his son had died from snake-bite and had been restored to life by Manasā. Nonetheless, he insisted that his flower offerings should be offered with the left hand.[7]

Manasā is sometimes described as the daughter of Kaśyapa and sister of the serpent Ananta; or born from Śiva's semen which had fallen into a lotus flower, and which, when it reached the roots deep down in Pātāla, Vāsuki's mother fashioned into a beautiful girl.

The Manasā cult also exists among some Bengali Moslem communities[8] and is identified with the goddess Jāṅgulī by some Mahāyāna Buddhists. Padmāvatī, the female messenger (*śāsanadevatā*) of the twenty-third Jaina *tīrthaṅkara*, Pārśvanātha, is probably the counterpart of Manasā who is also called Padmāvatī.[9]

[1] Clay figurines of the Indus Valley depict a seated figure with an attendant on either side, and backed by an erect cobra, suggesting that at least as early as 3000 B.C. a snake-cult existed in that area.

[2] T.W. Clark, 'Evolution of Hinduism in Medieval

Bengali Literature' (*BSOAS.*, p. 507, xvii/3). But the author qualifies this statement by a reference to an eighteenth-century poem which provides an exception, but as it is at variance with the general Manasā tradition, it appears to lack authenticity.

[3]Cf. the myth of Kadrū and the origin of serpents' forked tongues.

[4]For Manasā's other epithets, v. P.S. Rawson, 'The Iconography of the Goddess Manasā', *Oriental Art*, New Series, vol. I, n. 4, 1955.

[5]Vipardās's Manasā-Vijaya, edited by Sukumar Sen, 1953, *Asiatic Society of Bengal.*

[6]T.W. Clark, op. cit., p. 507.

[7]Dange, *Legends*, pp. 354f., App. C. Offerings to the gods are always made with the right hand.

[8]Maity, *Historical Studies in the Cult of the Goddess Manasā*, p. 182.

[9]*DHI.*, p. 563.

v. Nāga III; Nāgadru.

Mānasāra The name of the standard treatise on architecture and sculpture (c. A.D. 600).[1] It comprises seventy chapters, totalling 10,000 lines.[2]

[1]There are many similarities between it and the canon of Vitruvius (15 B.C.).

[2]*DHA.*, p. 782.

Manas-pāpman 'Evil', regarded as an entity capable of entering another entity. The evil in a person is invoked to leave him and transfer itself to trees (*AV.*, VI.45).

Mānava-Dharma Śāstra The name of the Code of Laws attributed to Manu.

v. Manu-Smṛti.

Māṇḍakarṇi An aged *ṛṣi* whose extreme asceticism (*tapas*) culminated in his decision to live only on air for ten thousand years. The gods, fearing that he would thereby become more powerful than they, sent five of the most attractive *apsarasas* to distract him. He became so entranced with them that he decided to keep them all. The divine nymphs rejuvenated him and they all lived happily together. The sweet sounds of their instruments can be heard in the tinkling murmurs of streams.

v. Tapas.

Mandākinī The Milky Way. A name of the celestial river Gaṅgā, sacred to the *pitṛs*, which flowed across the sky and then fell to earth from the tangled hair of Śiva.

v. Mandodaka.

Maṇḍala I. A circle separating a particular area from its surroundings, which when consecrated becomes purified for ritual and liturgical purposes. The circle also gives protection from malevolent forces.[1]

Maṇḍalas are circular diagrams of complex design, capable of innumerable variation. Basically they consist of a circular border enclosing a square divided into four triangles. In the centre of each triangle, as well as in the circle at the centre of the *maṇḍala*, a deity or its emblem is depicted. *Maṇḍalas* may be drawn or painted on wood, paper, stone, or traced on the ground.[2] Some resemble labyrinths, palaces, or exotic gardens, etc. They are used as a 'support', either simultaneously or successively, 'of a concrete ritual or an act of spiritual concentration, or . . . of a technique of mystical physiology'.[3] As all creation is thought to flow from a centre, the Vedic fire-altar was regarded as situated at the centre of the world,[4] which thus reproduced microcosmically the creation of the world.

The Hindu temple when viewed from above represents a *maṇḍala* in stone. The most famous architectonic *maṇḍala* is that of Borobudur in Java, which the devotee circumambulates in a sunwise direction (*pradakṣiṇā*), and ascends the successive terraces (representing various psychic levels).

The adept penetrates the *maṇḍala* by certain yogic techniques which re-activate the *cakras* (circles or planes), regarded as points of intersection of the cosmic and the mental life.[5]

[1]Similarly the enclosure wall of the early Egyptian temples of the Sun-god protected 'the sacred area from the evil coming from outside' (Reymond, *The Mythical Origin of the Egyptian Temple*, p. 239).

[2]Eliade, *Myth of the Eternal Return*, p. 83, draws attention to the similarity of appearance and intent of the 'sand-paintings' of the North American Navajo Indians.

[3]Eliade, *Images*, p. 54.

[4]Cf. the Greek Omphalos, and the Christian belief that Jerusalem (as shown on early maps) was situated at the centre of the world.

[5]v. Tucci, *Theory and Practice of the Maṇḍala*; Eliade, *Yoga*, pp. 219ff.; G. Combaz, *L'Évolution du stūpa en Asie*, pp. 124ff.

v. Yantra; Kuṇḍalinī; Vedi; Agnicayana.

II. A section or division of a book, such as the ten *maṇḍalas* of the *RV.*

III. The concept of 'circles' (*maṇḍalas*) governed the relations of one king to another. The centre of the *maṇḍala* is the territory of the *vijigīṣu*, i.e., a king who desires conquest. The next circle represents the adjoining kingdom, whose king is 'the enemy' (*ari*); beyond this *maṇḍala* is the territory of the 'friend' or 'ally' of the *vijigīṣu*, and so on.

Mandara I. The mythical white mountain, supported by Viṣṇu in his tortoise (*kūrma*) incarnation (*avatāra*), and used as a pestle by the *Devas* and *Asuras* (the joint powers of nature) to churn the ocean (*samudramathana*) to gain the essential objects necessary for the survival of gods and mankind. The ocean represents the unmanifested cosmos which contains *in potentia* everything necessary to form a new world.

Kubera, the god of riches, the *yakṣa* Maṇibhadra and other divinities reside on Mount Mandara (*MBh*., Vana pa., 139). At its foot the celestial Ganges (*gaṅgā*), which fell to earth from the moon, divides into four great streams (*Mārk. P*., 56, 1f.).

II. The coral tree (Erythrina indica), one of the five trees of Indra's Paradise (*svarga*). The *Hariv*. identifies it with the *pārijāta*, whose flowers are offered to the Sun by the Vidyādharas.[1] This tree has brilliant scarlet flowers which appear before the leaves. The leaf is composed of three leaflets, which symbolize the *trimūrti*, the largest representing Viṣṇu, the one on the right Brahmā, and that on the left, Śiva.[2]

[1] *EM*., p. 7.

[2] E. Blatter and W. S. Millard, *Some Beautiful Indian Trees*, p. 68.

Mandeha(s) Demons (*rākṣasas*) of the night, who during twilight try to devour the Sun. At night they hang upon rocks and at dawn attack it, but are inevitably defeated. With the onset of darkness they revive and renew the battle the next day.[1]

The victory of the divine Sun is attributed by the *brāhmaṇas* to their performance of particular rites, which consist of the sprinkling of water, purified and consecrated by the mystical syllable *OM* and the repetition of the *gāyatrī*, the most sacred verse of the Vedas, possessing a power capable of dispelling every demonic force (*Brah. P*., II.21,110; *Vāyu P*., 50,163, *PI*.).

[1] This ancient myth appears in the *VP*. (II.8), but various versions occur in other Purāṇas.

Cf. the Teutonic myth of the dead warriors who spend their days fighting and at evening gather in Odin's great hall, Valhalla, for a feast prepared from the body of the magic boar Saehrimnir whose life is also successively renewed.

Māndhātṛ or **Māndhāta** A royal *ṛṣi* (*rājarṣi*) of Solar dynastic lineage and son of Yuvanāśva. For many years the latter had no children which grieved him deeply. Finally several sages undertook a lengthy rite to enable him to have a son. Part of the rite was the placing of a vessel of consecrated water on the altar, but during the night Yuvanāśva, feeling thirsty, drank it, unaware of its magical potency until a child emerged from his right side,[1] though without harming him. While the sages were wondering who would nurse the child, Indra appeared and gave his finger to the child to suck and said 'He shall suck me' (*mām ayam dhāsyati*). From the contraction of these words the boy was named Māndhātṛ.

Māndhātṛ ruled his extensive dominions wisely and well. He married Vindumatī by whom he had fifty daughters and three sons.

Saubhari, an aged and emaciated *ṛṣi* who had practised austerities (*tapas*) by standing in water for twelve years, finally decided to marry one of Māndhātṛ's daughters. The *rāja* was unwilling, but fearing the *ṛṣi*'s displeasure, promised to agree if one of his daughters agreed. A eunuch then conducted Saubhari to the inner apartments. As the *ṛṣi* entered he transformed himself into a handsome young man, with whom the fifty girls immediately fell in love. To avoid embarrassment he married them all (*VP*., IV.2).

[1] The *Hariv*. and some Purs. state he was born naturally from the goddess Gaurī. Cf. the mythological account of the Buddha's birth from his mother's side.

Mandodaka The mythical lake with curd-like water, situated on Mount Kailāsa, said to be the source of the terrestrial Ganges (*gaṅgā*), the counterpart of the celestial river Mandākinī (*Matsya P*., 121, 4–5).

Maṇḍodarī 'Narrow-waisted.' The beautiful daughter of Maya the architect of the *asuras* (non-Āryan tribes). She became Rāvaṇa's favourite wife, to whom she bore Indrajit (Conqueror of Indra).

Maṇḍūka 'Frog.' Because of their association with water, frogs were also associated with rain-spells. One such spell occurs in the *Nir*. (9.6–7). When Vasiṣṭha desired rain he praised the clouds, and the frogs applauded him. Being much gratified he praised them in turn and said, 'O frog, join me, O swimmer, invoke rain. Float in the middle of the pond, having spread your four feet.' Frogs also possessed cooling properties[1] and for this reason were placed on the funerary fire after it had been extinguished by water (*RV*., X.16,14). The last drops of water to drip from the fire-altar became frogs (*ŚBr*. IX.1.2,20f.).

During the elaborate rites connected with the building of the fire-altar, a frog, lotus flower and a bamboo-shoot were drawn across the centre of the altar as a gesture of appeasement.[2]

[1] The consecrated marrow of a frog when rubbed on the body enables one to walk unscathed through fire (*AGP*., 306, 18).

[2] This gesture is 'plainly intended as remedial and expiatory for the cruelty of Agni in burning a corpse; the fire is not only to be extinguished, but to be followed by its antithesis, the growth of water-plants and the appearance of their attendant frogs' (Whitney, *AV*., vol. II, p. 850n.).

v. Narasiṁha; Vedi; Pākadūrva; Takman; Agnicayana.

Māṇḍūkya The name of one of the thirteen principal

Upaniṣads, which consists of an exposition of *OM*, the most sacred syllable, a sound representing the Cosmic Principle, *brahman*.

Maṅgala I. The planet Mars, with which Kārttikeya (the god of war), is identified.

v. Navagraha(s).

II. Anything, or any event regarded as auspicious, such as an amulet, good omen, or ceremony, etc. A bride is said to be *sumaṅgala*, i.e., auspicious, because she not only brings luck to all who look at her, but is herself immune from the Evil Eye.[1]

[1]Gonda, *Eye and Gaze in the Veda*, p. 51.

Maṇi A magic pearl or jewel used as an amulet (*AV.*, I.29, 1–6), which both protects and fulfils all the wishes of the wearer.

v. Maṇidvīpa II; Kaustubha; Syamantaka.

Maṇibhadra A *yakṣa* and brother of Kubera, and tutelary deity of travellers and merchants.

v. Yamalārjuna.

Maṇidvīpa I. 'Jewel-Island.' An epithet applied to the hood of the serpent Ananta.

II. In Śaiva mythology *maṇidvīpa* is the jewel-island situated in the ocean of nectar (*amṛta*). A magnificent palace is situated on the island, which contained the wish-fulfilling gem (*cintāmaṇi*).

Maṇigrīva 'Bejewelled neck.' A son of Kubera. He and his brother Nala-Kubera were cursed by the *ṛṣi* Nārada to be transformed into two *arjuna* trees, a state in which they remained until Kṛṣṇa released them by uprooting the trees (*AGP.*, I, Ch. 12, 16–17).

v. Yamalārjuna.

Maṇikarṇikā I. A jewelled earring.

II. Name of one of the five principal *tīrthas* at Banāras, said to have appeared when Śiva's earring fell to the ground. Anyone who dies here will have all his wishes fulfilled (*Matsya P.*, 182,24; 185,69, *PI.*).

Maṇimaṇḍapa 'Jewel-palace.' The abode of Śeṣa, and of Nairṛta the ruler of the south-western quarter.

Manmatha A name of the god of love, Kāma.

Manoja 'Mind-born.' An epithet of Kāma, the god of love.

Mantharā I. A deformed slave (a servant of Queen Kaikeyī) who turned the queen against Rāmacandra.

II. A *gandharvī*, also called Dundubhī, and a sister of Bali. Indra killed her when she tried to destroy the earth.

Mantra Though generally defined as 'a formula, comprising words and sounds which possess magical or divine power', no single definition adequately expresses its significance.[1] It is a verbal instrument believed to possess power. 'A word or formula ... [which] represents a mental presence or energy; by it something is produced, crystallized, in the mind. The term *mantra-śakti* is employed to denote this magic power possessed by words when they are brought together in a formula.'[2]

In the *RV.* the gods were invoked by means of *mantras* to ensure success in impending battles (I.100), to avert drought (V.68), to grant long life (I.89,9), and in the *AV.* to ensure escape from all danger and difficulty (XIX.7), and to grant the fulfilment of all needs. The *AV. mantras* also served to expel the demons of fever and other diseases (V.22; III.31), to bewitch and destroy enemies (IV.18), and to stimulate love in unresponsive lovers (VI.130).

The sounds of *mantras* constituted a secret, initiatory language, to be uttered according to particular rules if their esoteric meaning and power were to be assimilated and the initiate fully 'awakened'.

A *mantra* may consist of a syllable (*bīja*), or a word or group of words, drawn from the three Saṁhitās, the *ṛc*, *yajus* and *sāman*, the original constituents of the Veda. Thus *mantras* correctly uttered or sung became part of the liturgy of the sacrifice which gave them an additional authority,[3] as well as ensuring communication with the chosen deity.[4] The *mantras* of the *RV.* were recited by the *hotar* (*hotṛ*), and chosen to suit the nature of each sacrificial rite; those of the *SV.* were sung by the *udgatar* (*udgatṛ*) at the *Soma* sacrifice; those of the *YV.* belong to the more formalized ritual of the Brāhmaṇas and were recited by a class of priests called *adhvaryu*. The *mantras* of the *RV.* 'are composed in an artificial style, full of archaisms and poetic constructions, and complicated, well-defined metrical forms, ... and under the influence of a fully developed literary convention'.[5]

The efficacy of a *mantra* in post-Vedic times was not dependent on its meaning, but rather on the subjective effect of the exacting mental discipline involved in its correct utterance, and the accompanying mode of breathing. Of the seventy million *mantras*, many consisted of 'bizarre and unintelligible phonemes: *hrīṁ*, *hrāṁ*, *hrūṁ*, *phaṭ*, etc.'[6] The first three of these—like *OM*, the most sacred syllable of all—belong to a special class of sounds, such as 'ṁ' or 'ṅ' which unlike most consonants can be sustained as long-drawn-out humming sounds.

In the *Agni Pur.* rite after rite is described, each requiring the constant repetition of *bīja-mantras*, often for the attainment of trivial ends. Particular attention is also devoted to the rule that the *mantra* imparted by the *guru* to his pupil must never be divulged 'even if Śiva himself should demand it' (312, 18–21). This Pur. also points out that a *mantra* softly uttered is more efficacious than if repeated loudly, and that when its utterance can only be discerned by the movement of the lips, it is a hundredfold more potent, and when mentally repeated its power increases a thousandfold (293,28). One class of *mantras* consists of a single letter, which is equated with the deity it symbolizes (348,13). *Mantras* are sometimes classified according to gender, the masculine being used as charms, or as spells to confound enemies; the feminine for trivial matters; the function of the neuter is unnoticed (293,4). Another classification is based on the vowels and particular consonants of the Sanskrit 'alphabet', which represent different phases of the moon. The short sounds denote its waxing, the long its waning.

The time in which a *mantra* becomes effective depends on the time taken to pronounce it, i.e., on the number of letters comprising it. In particular circumstances a *bīja-mantra* is repeated a hundred or even a thousand times (*Manu*, II,79); or inscribed in the centre of a *maṇḍala* as a focal point in meditation. But *mantras* are of infinite diversity and are thus all things to all men. As a type of prayer they are linked with *śraddhā* (faith) and *bhakti* (devotion), and together constitute the means by which the devout Hindu achieves *mokṣa* (liberation) and union with *brahman*.

[1]Bharati (*TT*., p. 111) defines the *mantra* as 'a quasi-morpheme, or a series of quasi-morphemes, or a series of mixed genuine and quasi-morphemes arranged in conventional patterns, based on codified esoteric traditions, and passed on from one preceptor to one disciple in the course of a prescribed initiation ritual'. Bharati (p. 103) also considers that '*mantra*' 'combines the old Vedic (and Indo-European) root "*man*" "to think" with the element—*tra*, i.e., the *kṛt*-suffix indicating instrumentality'. Both *mantra* and *sandhābhāṣā* are cryptic, esoteric utterances, unintelligible to the uninitiated. *Mantra* language is not senseless mumbo-jumbo merely because it is not intelligible to some. Thus *mantra* should not be identified with *kavaca* (protective formula), or with *yāmala* (a *mantra* based on a text); nor with *dhāraṇī* (a mnemonic formula containing *mantras* (pp. 101f.). But such distinctions are not always appreciated by devout Hindus.

Śaivas (and others) are 'convinced that the *mantra* is a form or representative of God himself, the phenomenal world being the materialization of the *mantras*, without which no cult is possible' (Gonda, *VS*., p. 65).

[2]Zimmer, *Myths*, p. 141n.; v. also Rawson, *The Art of Tantra*, pp. 195f.

According to ritual logic 'there exists a correlation between the ritual act and the results to be expected' (Gonda, *Loka*, p. 145, n.5). The ceremonies which accompanied the Babylonian 'Prayers of the Lifting of the Hand' were believed to be 'potent in themselves, and, as the efficacy of an incantation depended on its correct recital, so their power resulted from a scrupulous performance of each detail' (King, *Babylonian Magic and Sorcery*, p. xxx).

[3]'There is no doubt that suggestions of external origin gain added force when they ally themselves with auto-suggestions, and conversely an auto-suggestion will be stronger' (C. K. Ogden, *A. B. C. of Psychology*, 4th ed., p. 121).

[4]Similarly without the correct incantation (and drum-beat) in *vodun* rites, the god invoked makes no response.

[5]P. T. Srinivas Iyengar, *Life in Ancient India in the Age of the Mantras*, p. 3.

[6]Eliade, *Yoga*, p. 213. The Judaic 'Whisperers' also repeated passages of Scripture or uttered unintelligible sounds to effect cures and as a protection against snakes and scorpions (R. Patai, *Man and Temple*, p. 184). According to Josephus, Solomon also possessed the 'knowledge of the art used against demons ... [and] composed incantations for the relief of illnesses and exorcisms capable of expelling demons from the possessed' (J. M. Allegro, *The Sacred Mushroom and the Cross*, p. 31).

v. Vāc; Kavacam; Mantravidyā.

Mantravidyā The science of mantras.

Mantrodaka Water consecrated by *mantras*.

Manu I. 'Man',[1] applied in an archetypal sense in the *RV*., X.63,7, which refers to Manu as the first to offer an oblation to the gods; and in IX.92,5 to Āryan man as distinct from, and superior to, the non-Āryan *dasyu*. In X.86,23, the reference to the score of children born to Manu's daughter Parśu may be the basis of the later myth naming Manu as the first man, whose lack of a wife led him, like the Hebrew Adam, to ensure propagation by means of one of his ribs (*parśu*). The Manu myth gradually expanded, and was represented by variant accounts, which culminated in his appearance as Vaivasvata, the seventh Manu of the *manvantara* cosmic evolutionary theory. This theory was elaborated in several Purāṇas including the *VP*., and postulated a succession of worlds, or a single world divided into fourteen immense periods of time called *manvantaras*, each introduced by a 'secondary creator' regarded as a Manu, or First Man.

The Manus are usually listed as: Svāyambhuva, the son of Svayambhū, the Self-Existent. Svārociṣa, son of Svāyambhuva's daughter Ākūti. Auttami, Tāmasa, Raivata and Cākṣuṣa represent the six periods of prehistory. Vaivasvata, also called Satyavrata, the Manu of the present age, the son of Vivasvat, the Sun;

the patronymic is also that of the Vedic Svāyambhuva, the intention being apparently to add lustre to the Paurāṇic Manu, who is regarded as the progenitor of a new race,[2] the old having perished in the Deluge. Vaivasvata's rescue by Viṣṇu in the form of a fish (*Matsya avatāra*) is the theme of the *Matsya Purāṇa*.

Sāvarṇa, brother of Vaivasvata, Dakṣa-Sāvarṇa, Brahma-Sāvarṇa, Dharma-Sāvarṇa, Rudra-Sāvarṇa, Raucya, son of a *ṛṣi* named Ruci and the *apsaras* Mālinī, and Bhautya, son of the *muni* Bhūti comprise the remainder.

[1]OSl. and OHG. *man*; OFries. and G. *mann*. The *Nir.* (12,33) derives Manu from the $\sqrt{man}$, 'to think'.

[2]Cf. the Hebrew account of the Deluge and the survival of Noah (Genesis, chapters 7 and 8).

v. Matsya-avatāra.

II. The mythical author or compiler of the *Manu-smṛti* (Institutes or Code of Manu).

Manu-smṛti or **Mānava Dharma-śāstra** The Code or Institutes of Manu. A collection of laws based on custom and precedent and the teaching of the Vedas. It is traditionally attributed to the mythical first Manu, Svāyambhuva, but it is obviously the work of many hands. Bühler suggests that it was probably based on 'manuals written by the teachers of the Vedic schools for the guidance of their pupils ... [and only later] acknowledged as sources of sacred law applicable to all Āryas'.[1] Thus they represent 'the sum of the conditions of social co-existence with regard to the activity of the community and of the individual'[2] in India during almost the whole of the first millennium B.C. The *śāstra* makes no attempt to present Law as a form of political sovereignty, though it recognizes the existence of quasi-political authority, exercised jointly by the *brāhmaṇa* and *rājanya* classes—predominantly by the former.

The *Manu-smṛti* points out *inter alia* that the ultimate aim of mankind is not to achieve individual immortality, such as that of the ancestral *pitṛs*, but to attain complete undifferentiated union with *brahman*. The main part of the *śāstra* thus serves as a kind of preparation for that ideal, though not initially envisaged as such. Divine revelation (*śruti*) and empirical knowledge (*smṛti*) are drawn upon to define the Law of Conduct and to apply it, though not always impartially, to all classes of the community.

A number of myths are included in the Code, designed to endow it with greater authority and antiquity, but it has no need of this mythological material as its merits are self-evident. Manu is said to have learnt the 'Institutes' from the Creator[3] himself, and in turn transmitted them to the first ten sages; finally entrusting Bhṛgu with its exposition.

[1]*Laws of Manu*, *SBE.*, pp. xif.; v. also *CHI.*, I, p. 278.

[2]R. Pal, *History of Indian Law*, p. 2.

[3]This is paralleled by the claims made for the Mosaic Law.

v. Dharma-śāstra(s).

Manuṣyaprakṛtideva(s) Lit. a *deva* of human (*manuṣya*) origin. Renowned heroes, *ṛṣis* and others who, because of their great virtues and qualities (often enhanced by legends), have been elevated to the status of minor divinities, or in the case of Kṛṣṇa regarded as the Supreme Being.

Manvantara The life or period of a Manu (from *manv*, used in compounds for *manu*, and *antara*, period of a Manu). Each *manvantara* consists of 4,320,000 solar years, equivalent to 12,000 divine years, i.e., one-fourteenth of a day and night of Brahmā. Fourteen such periods constitute an age (*kalpa*), but according to *Manu* (I.80) the *manvantaras* and the evolutions and devolutions of the world are numberless. Each *manvantara* has its own Manu, its own Indra and *ṛṣis*, etc.

v. Yuga; Manu I; Pralaya.

Manyu[1] 'Wrath' and its personification. Wrath is regarded as an independent power and identified with Indra, the heroic Vedic god of war. Various hymns (*AV.*, IV.31 and 32; *RV.*, X.84 and 83) are addressed to Manyu as the victorious spirit of battle. He is invoked to lead the army, slay foes, share out the booty, and by force, remove scorners. Two others hymns (*AV.*, VI.42 and 43) are intended to appease wrath; in the latter hymn *darbha* (*kuśa*) grass is called the 'appeaser of wrath' (*manyuśamana*).

A myth in the *ŚBr.* (IX.1.1,6) describes how all the deities except Manyu deserted Prajāpati. The latter wept and his tears fell upon Manyu who was transformed by them into the hundred-headed Rudra. Prajāpati continued to weep and his tears spread through the worlds in the forms of terrifying Rudras (roarers).

[1]The *Nir.* 10,29, derives *manyu* from '*man*', meaning to shine, or to be angry, or to slay.

Māra 'Death', from *mṛi*, to die,[1] and hence *a-mṛta*, not mortal. Māra is associated with pestilence and fatal disease, and also with killing or destroying.

In Buddhist mythology Māra is portrayed as the Destroyer, the Evil One, who attempted to dissuade the Buddha from his mission by the vision of temporal power.

[1]Zend. *mar*; Gr. *mrotos*; L. *mors*; G. *mord*; F. *mort*, etc.

v. Mārī; Kaiṭabha.

Māraṇa I. 'Killing'; 'death'; 'destruction'. The power to kill or maim by means of a *mantra*.

v. Ṣaṭkarman.

II. The name of a magical weapon.

Mārga 'Way or path.' From *mṛga*, seeking, searching, tracking (as in hunting), looking for, or following a way or path. By extension *mārga* later acquired moral significance, denoting the right or proper path, as in the Buddhist Eightfold Way.
v. Mārgavatī; Pathyā.

Mārgavatī A goddess of paths and roads, and hence the protectress of travellers.
v. Pūṣan.

Mārī A goddess personifying pestilence and death (*māra*), and identified with the goddess Durgā.

Mārīca A Rākṣasa,[1] a son of Tārakā; who attempted to spoil Viśvāmitra's sacrifice, but was prevented by Rāma.

Mārīca became the minister of Rāvaṇa, King of Laṅkā. To enable the latter to abduct Sītā (Rāma's wife), Mārīca assumed the form of a beautiful golden deer to lure Rāma from his hermitage. The latter finally killed the deer, but as the animal lay dying, Mārīca arose from its body and resumed his Rākṣasa form.[2]

[1]The *ṛṣi* Agastya turned Mārīca and his mother into Rākṣasas (*EM.*, p. 185).

[2]Mārīca was adept at casting spells (*IRA.*, p. 40).
v. Māyābala.

Marīci The Vedic term for a particle of light, a mote or a ray of light (of the sun or moon). In post-Vedic literature it is the name of a Prajāpati, regarded as a son of Svayambhū (Brahmā);[1] as one of the seven great *ṛṣis*; as the first of the ten Prajāpatis or secondary creators; and as the father of Kaśyapa.

[1]Brahmā created the Sword (*asi*) as a divine being (v. Āyudhapuruṣa) to protect men, and then gave it to Rudra who in turn passed it on to Viṣṇu. The latter presented it to Marīci (*EM.*, p. 176).

Māriṣā v. Kaṇḍu.

Marka I. A son of Śukra (according to Sāyaṇa), who with Śaṇḍa were *purohitas* of the *asuras* (*Tait. Saṁ.*, VI.4,10).

Marka and Śaṇḍa taught the *daitya* Hiraṇyakaśipu the science of politics.[1]

[1]*HP.*, p. 326.
v. Bṛhaspati.

II. A disease-demon presiding over childhood illnesses.

III. The vital breath (*prāṇa*) that pervades the body (*SED*).

Mārkaṇḍeya Name of a *brāhmaṇa* who on seeing the whole earth engulfed by water became terrified and begged Viṣṇu to save him. Viṣṇu replied: 'Look at me who in the form of a child am lying on a *vaṭa*-tree leaf. I am Kāla (Death); enter my mouth and shelter therein.' Mārkaṇḍeya obeyed and found not only an assembly of gods, *gandharvas*, *ṛṣis*, but also the whole world. When he emerged he saw that Viṣṇu was still in the form of a child.

This *MBh.* story is an initiation myth in which the swallowing denotes the attainment of the highest knowledge by allowing the individual by 'death' or the relinquishing of the limits and constrictions of individuality, to become one with the deity; the regurgitation representing a kind of immortality to be attained through knowledge.[1]

[1]Dange, *Legends*, p. 207.

Mārkaṇḍeya Purāṇa One of the eighteen Purāṇas which is attributed to the ancient *ṛṣi* Mārkaṇḍeya, the son of Mṛkaṇḍa.

The general character of this Pur. has been summed up by Wilson,[1] who considers the manner of the narration superior to that of all other Purāṇas except the *Bhāgavata.* Pargiter[2] and others consider that Cantos 45–81 and 93–136 constitute its original form.

[1]*VP.*, Pref., xxxiv–xxxv.

[2]The *Mārkaṇḍeya Purāṇa*, Bibliotheca Indica, Intro., p. iv.

Mārtāṇḍa or **Mārtaṇḍa** (The later form.) 'Sprung from an (apparently) lifeless egg' (mṛtāṇḍa).[1] The name Mārtāṇḍa occurs in one hymn only of the *RV.* (X.72,8–9) as one of the eight sons (the Ādityas) of Aditi who was cast away to die, then brought back,[2] only to be again abandoned. In the *ŚBr.* (XI.6.3,8) the Ādityas number twelve, and represent the months of the year, but they are not named.

The *Mārk. P.* (105, 1ff.) includes a myth purporting to explain the name Mārtaṇḍa. The Sun (Sūrya) revealed himself to Aditi and promised her a boon. She requested him to allow a portion of himself to enter into the Ādityas and so assist them to destroy their enemies, the *dānavas* and *daityas.* The Sun agreed to her request and announced that in due time one of his rays would become incarnate in her womb. Aditi continued performing arduous austerities (*tapas*), including that of *cāndrāyaṇa* in which the amount of food is diminished daily during the bright half of the month, but increased in the dark half; alternatively barley gruel is eaten once on the last day of each fortnight (*Manu*, VI.20). Her husband Kaśyapa angrily condemned her for fasting and thus destroying the egg in her womb, but when the child was born a voice from the celestial region was heard: 'Whereas thou, O muni, hast spoken of this egg as destroyed, thy son shall therefore be called Mārtaṇḍa, and as Lord shall exercise the sun's sway on the earth.'

[1]From *mṛta*, without life, and *aṇḍa*, an egg.

[2]This indicates alternating death and regeneration (*RV.*, X.72,8–9). The eighth Āditya is 'the only one by whom continuity of the cosmic process is secured; at

the same time he is the remainder, which can be dangerous . . . and is thrown away to be reproduced, that is, to become the principle of continuity' (Heesterman, *Ancient Indian Royal Consecration*, p. 36, n.26).
v. Ucchiṣta.

Marula One of the five ascetics traditionally regarded as the founders of the Vīra-Śaiva sect, the others being Ekorāma, Paṇḍitārādhya, Revaṇa and Viśvārādhya. They are said to have sprung from the five heads of Śiva, and to become incarnate in each age.[1]

[1]J.N. Farquhar, *Outline of the Religious Literature of India*, p. 260.

Marutgaṇa v. Marut(s).

Marut(s) Storm-gods, the friends and allies of the Vedic god Indra. In a battle-charm, Indra is invoked to confuse enemies, and the Maruts to slay them (*AVB.*, III.1,6); in the same work the Maruts are asked to cause darkness and so prevent the enemy from seeing each other (III.2,6).

The Maruts are closely associated with Agni, the fire-god, and with Vāyu, the wind-god. They are said to roar like lions, to have teeth of iron, and like the Hittite storm-gods, to be armed with golden weapons (lightning and thunderbolts).[1] They hold apart the spheres of heaven and earth and thus control the rain (*AV.*, IV.27,5). Their offspring are the mysterious Ūrdhvanabhas (*Tait. Saṁ.*, I.3,9). The Maruts partake of the sacred *soma*, and are overlords of the northern region (*ŚBr.*, VIII.6.1,8). Indra is the divine prototype of a king, as the Maruts are of the 'common people' (*viś*).[2]

Inevitably their origin and description varies from period to period. They are the sons of Rudra and Pṛśnī, or the children of the celestial ocean or they were born of the laughter of lightning fashioned by Agni, or engendered by Vāyu, the wind-god, in the womb of heaven, or they are sons of Marutvatī, one of the wives of Dharma (*VP.*, 1.15); whilst other myths refer to them as 'self-born'.[3]

In the *RV.* (VIII.85,8, etc.) the Maruts are said to number 'three times sixty'; in the *Tait. Saṁ.*, thirty-three; in the *Ait.* and *ŚBr.* eleven; in the *MBh.* seven or eleven; in the *Viṣṇu* and *Brahmāṇḍa Purs.*, seven groups of seven, whose dwelling is the seven spheres viz., the earth, sun, moon, stars, planets, the Pole Star and the constellation Ursa Major.

[1]The *Nir.*, 11,13, states that the Maruts were the first atmospheric deities, and derives their name from *ma-rutaḥ*, 'of measured sound', from the root *mi* plus the root *ru*; or of 'measured brilliancy' from the root *mi* plus the root *ruc*; or they 'move about a great deal' (*mahad* plus *dru*).

[2]*BIP.*, p. 118, n.3; *AVB.*, p. 663.

[3]According to the *Matsya* (ch. 7) and *Viṣṇu Purs.* (I.21), they are the offspring of Diti and Kaśyapa. After Indra had cut Diti's embryo into forty-nine pieces (which became the forty-nine Maruts) she requested him to make them into a troop (*gaṇa*) of gods. He agreed and hence they are known as Marutgaṇa. They are worshipped by those requiring lasting strength and vigour (*ojas*) (*Bhāg. P.*, II.3,8, *PI.*).

Māsa The general word for 'month' in the *RV.* and later, which appears to refer solely to a lunar measure of time rather than to the solar time-scale in the Brāhmaṇas.

Subsequently the lunar year was divided into twenty-one phases (*nakṣatras*) of the moon, but in early Vedic times only the two characteristic phases were celebrated. These were the night of the new moon, Amā-vāsyā (home-staying night), and the night of the full moon, Paurṇa-māsī (*AV.*, VII. 79, 80).[1] But in the *Tait. Saṁ.* (VII.4.8,1) and elsewhere the eighth day after the full moon of *māgha*[2] was regarded as of special importance, because it marked the end of the old year or the beginning of the new.

In northern India and much of the Deccan the month began and ended with the full moon, but in Tamil areas it usually began with the new moon.

[1]*VI.*, vol. II, p. 156.

[2]For the names of the months v. Jyotiṣa.

Māṣa A kind of bean, one of the seventeen kinds of useful grain (*VP.*, I.6).[1] According to the *Tait. Saṁ.* (V.1,8) beans are said to be impure, perhaps because they are regarded as aphrodisiacs (*Suś. Saṁ.*, I. p. 475). Beans were used in Indian love-charms and represented the testicles.

[1]According to the *Mārk. P.*, 15, 8–9, a man who steals paddy, barley, sesamum, māṣa, etc., will be reborn as a large-mouthed rat.

Mātā I. 'Mother'; or 'moon'. The mother's womb determines (or measures out) the potential of each created being, and hence the mother represents the mortal, the finite, the Earth, whilst the father denotes the infinite, unmanifested source. The moon (*mātā*) is also the 'measurer' of time.[1]

[1]Gonda, *Four Studies in the Language of the Veda*, p. 168.

II. The mother of Grahas.

Mātali The name of Indra's charioteer who by his brilliant driving baffled the enemy. He took Arjuna to heaven and back in Indra's chariot; and he also advised Rāma concerning battle tactics.

Mātali's wife is Sudharmā, his son Gomukha, and his daughter Guṇakeśī.

Mataṅga A man who was the son of a *caṇḍāla*,[1] but

who was brought up as a *brāhmaṇa*. One day when he was cruelly goading a young ass its mother said that such conduct was only to be expected from one of his low birth. Mataṅga angrily demanded an explanation. The ass informed him that his mother had been a drunkard and his father only a barber. Then Mataṅga determined to become a 'real' *brāhmaṇa*, and to that end practised extreme austerities (*tapas*), but Indra still refused to recognize him as a *brāhmaṇa*. For hundreds of years he continued *tapas* until Indra relented and gave him the power to move like a bird, to change his shape at will and to become famous.

Sītā and Rāma visited Mataṅga in his hermitage near the Ṛṣyamūka mountain, where the trees are said to have grown from the sweat of his pupils.

[1]Or he had been a *caṇḍāla* in a former existence (*MBh.*, Anuśāsana pa.).

Mātaṅgī I. Name of the mythical mother of elephants. II. Name of a *mahāvidyā* who represents royal dominion (the elephant being the mount of kings and hence a symbol of sovereignty).

Mātariśvan The name of a divine being to whom fire (*agni*) was first disclosed (*RV.*, I.31,3); or who first brought forth fire from the fire-sticks (*araṇis*),[1] and gave it to the Bhṛgus who in turn communicated it to man.

According to the *AV.* (VIII.1.5) Mātariśvan is the wind which possesses cleansing properties (XI.4.15); in the *ŚBr.* (I.7.1,11) a cauldron (*gharma*) of Mātariśvan is mentioned.

[1]Monier-Williams (*SED.*) suggests that Mātariśvan may be derived from *mātari* (growing in the *mātari*, the wood of the fire-sticks). According to the *Mārk. P.*, 17.25 Mātariśvan dwells in the abodes of *caṇḍālas*.

Mathurā An ancient city situated on the Yamunā river, and the birthplace of Kṛṣṇa. It is one of the seven sacred cities of India.

The plains of Mathurā are famous as the scene of Kṛṣṇa's life with the *gopīs*, and also (*VP.*, I.12) of that of the fight between the demon Madhu and Śatrughna (Rāma's brother), who celebrated his victory by making it the site of Mathurā.[1]

[1]Cf. *VP.* IV.4.

Maṭmaṭa(s) Pot-testicled demons, having feet with toes and heels reversed. They are born from dung-smoke or from the dust of the threshing floor, and are said to be specially dangerous to pregnant women (*AV.*, VIII.6,15).

Mātṛ(s) and **Mātṛkā(s)** In the singular, both forms signify 'mother', particularly a 'divine mother', and hence figuratively 'source' or 'origin'. Both designations also refer to a class of goddesses, whose traditions link them with the Vedic Gnās (spouses of the gods) and with the still more ancient mother-goddesses, incarnations of the reproductive forces in nature.[1] This belief in a divine mother has persisted in communities long regarded as patriarchal, like the Vedic Āryans, and in a modified form in Judaism, which still regards descent from the mother as its racial criterion.[2]

In early Vedic times the *mātṛs* were generally connected with the waters and the earth, both representing latent fecundity[3] and thus associated with the sun-god (Sūrya) as the male activating element. Though not named in *RV.* (I.34,8) the *mātṛs* are called the Seven Mother Streams, probably a reference to the seven major rivers of north-western India.[4] The term *mātṛ* has also a wider significance in the concept of Aditi, the Cosmic Mother, and in that of Vāc, the goddess of speech. The seven *mātṛkās* (saptamātṛkās) are identified with the seven vowels (five pure, two mixed, e.o), and as the basis of all language they represent power.

The recognition of power as an independent entity is indicated by the growing use of the term '*śacī*' when referring to Indra's might '*śacīpatiḥ*' (*RV.*, VIII.15, 13, etc.). 'It is, perhaps, in this notion of *śacī*, though crude and simple, that we find ... the divine Śakti-principle in the earliest stage of formation'.[5] Thus the *mātṛs* became equated with the energies (*śaktis*) of the gods (*devas*). The *mātṛs* are often depicted with children on their lap or at their side, and therefore are regarded as guardians of children, a function later taken over by the goddess Ṣaṣaṭhī.[6] In some ways they are similar to the Celtic Mother-goddess Matrŏna[7] and the Gallic 'Matres, who were frequently represented holding an infant or its swaddling clothes in their laps'.[8]

Several traditions seem to have existed simultaneously concerning the mothers, and hence the disparity in their numbers as given in various works. The most usual number is seven[9] or eight. In later ritual literature sixteen *mātṛkās*[10] are mentioned, beginning with Gaurī, Padmā, Śacī, Medhā, Sāvitrī, Vijayā, Jayā, Deva-senā, Svadhā, Svāhā, Śānti, Puṣṭi, Dhṛti, Tuṣṭi, Ātma-devatā and Kula-devatā. From time to time lesser *śaktis* were added to these, making sixty-four or more.[11]

In an inscription of the early Cālukya kings, they describe themselves 'as the descendants of Hāritī [the Buddhist goddess of small-pox], and nurtured by the seven mothers'.[12]

Monier-Williams suggests that the *mātṛs* have some similarities with the village-goddesses (*grāmadevatās*), whilst other authorities consider that the term 'mothers' may be a euphemism applied to a fierce class of *yoginīs* or similar beings. The latter view is borne out by the fifth-century inscription found in the village of Gangdhar (Jhalwar, Madhya Bharat) which mentions the erection of the terrible abode of the Divine Mothers, 'filled full of

Ḍakinīs . . . who stir up the very oceans with the mighty wind rising from the Tantric rites of their religion'.[13] Furthermore, a stone inscription dating from the time of Kumāra-gupta I, mentions the construction of temples dedicated to the Divine Mothers and describes them as terrifying abodes (*veśāmatyugram*).[14]

Caṇḍikā, in her great struggle with the *asura* Śumbha and his followers, was assisted by the Seven Mothers, each personifying the power or energy of their respective *deva*. Each of the *mātṛs* have the same appearance, ornaments, emblems, etc. as their respective *devas*. The furious *mātṛs* quickly routed the enemies of the gods, whereupon the latter experienced 'unparalleled joy', and the Mothers, intoxicated by blood, broke into a wild dance of victory (*Mārk. P.*, 88.11ff.).

The Śāktas maintain that the *mātṛkās* preside over impurities (*malas*), and over the sounds of the letters of the language. The supreme *mātṛkā* is Ambikā who has three aspects, Jyeṣṭhā, Raudrī and Vāmā, each having a specific function.[15]

[1]In Babylonia the mother-goddess was known as Mylitta; the Canaanite Kathirat, the 'wise women', were associated with fertility and marriage (G.R. Driver, *Canaanite Myths*, p. 6); and the Hittite Great Goddess (MAH) also presides 'over procreation and childbirth and determines destinies' (Gaster, *Thespis*, p. 271).

In Europe, Roman dedicatory inscriptions to 'the mothers' are common. Bede (*De Temporum Ratione* 13) states that in early Anglo-Saxon times Christmas Eve was called Modraniht (Night of the Mothers) (H.R. Ellis Davidson, *Gods and Myths of Northern Europe*, pp. 112f.).

[2]The *Vasiṣṭha Dharmasūtra* (II.2–3) states that the initial birth of the 'twice-born' Hindu is from his mother's womb, the second when he is invested with the sacred thread.

[3]The Pot-goddess (Kumbhamātā), the tutelary divinity of a village, is also associated with water and is represented by or identified with a water-jar (the 'generative pot') regarded as a symbol of fertility. These jars thus figure in all village marriage ceremonies.

[4]Müller considers these to be the Indus, the five rivers of the Panjāb (Vitastā, Asiknī, Paruṣṇī, Vipāśā, Śutudrī), and the Sarasvatī.

[5]S.K. Das, *Śakti or Divine Power*, p. 10.

[6]*HCIP.*, vol. IV, p. 341.

[7]Known in northern Germany as Holda or Holle and in southern Germany as Berchte or Perahta (J. Grimm, *Teutonic Mythology*, I, pp. 267, 272).

[8]R. Loomis, 'Morgain la Fée and the Celtic Goddesses', *Speculum*, 20, 1945, p. 201.

[9]Six or seven mothers were assigned to Skanda and later many more. Cf. the seven Hathors of Egypt; the Roman Parcae; the Teutonic Norns; the Hittite Gulses, etc. (v. Gaster, *Thespis*, pp. 287n., 298).

[10]The sixteen *mātṛkās* were identified with the fourteen vowels plus the *anusvāra* and *visarga* (*SED.*).

[11]*HCIP.*, vol. IV, p. 341.

[12]*DHI.*, p. 503.

[13]Ibid., p. 494.

[14]*HCIP.*, vol. IV, p. 347.

[15]Radhakrishnan, *EW.*, vol. I, p. 420. In tantric literature *mātṛkā* is an ambiguous word; perhaps 'its equivocality is intentional. It means a little mother, a little (or minimal) measure of any kind . . . from the first meaning derives the purely tantric use as a goddess, usually auxiliary to some central deity male or female (as the *ḍākinīs* . . .); the second meaning yields the notion of the cosmic matrix symbolized by the "garland of letters" which is thought to verbalize the cosmic process in tantric *sādhanā*' (*TT.*, p. 273, n.54).

v. Mantra; Āpaḥ; Andhaka.

Matsya avatāra The fish[1] incarnation (*avatāra*) of Viṣṇu, whose function was to save the best of mankind and other precious things from the Flood.[2]

Manu Satyavrata (generally known by his patronymic Vaivasvata) corresponds to the Hebrew Noah both in status and character. One day whilst bathing Manu found a tiny fish in his hands which begged him to remove it from the sea where no small fish was ever safe. Manu accordingly placed it in a bowl of water, but it quickly outgrew the bowl and various larger vessels until finally he replaced it in the sea. It then warned him of the impending Deluge and directed him to put a pair of all living creatures as well as the seeds of every plant into a boat.[3] He was then to go on board, and when a great fish (*jhaṣa*) appeared, he should use the body of the serpent Vāsuki as a rope and attach it to the horn of the fish, which would then tow the boat to safety. On hearing this Manu realized that the miraculous fish was none other than Viṣṇu.

Later when a great storm arose the fish duly appeared, towed the ship to a mountain, and then showed Manu how to let the vessel slide down as the waters subsided. Thus the world was re-peopled by the virtuous descendants of Manu and his companions.

[1]The fish denotes growth and rapid reproduction. Cf. the Messiah who, in the Talmud is called Dag (Fish); whence the later fish symbolism associated with Jesus.

[2]Both the Hebrew and Indian versions regard the Flood as the result of man's decadence, and both stem from the Sumerian Deluge story recorded on a tablet dated c. 1750 B.C. Cf. the ancient Egyptian Atmu or Atum

who flooded the earth, saving only those who were on his boat; the Zoroastrian Yima who released a dove when the waters began to subside; and the many Deluge stories of the North American Indians.

[3]In the simpler story included in the *MBh.* Manu collects the seeds of all things, but in the highly embellished account in the *Matsya P.* he brings everything together by his yogic power.

v. Śaṅkha II.

Matsya Purāṇa One of the eighteen Purāṇas (*VP.* III.6). It includes the myth of the *matsya avatāra*; the special duties of householders; the destruction of Tripurāsura; the wars of the gods with the *daityas*; the birth of Kārttikeya and Umā; the burning of Kāma, etc. Viṣṇu in his fish *avatāra* (*matsya avatāra*) is said to have narrated this Purāṇa to Manu.

Matsyendranātha The quasi-mythical founder of the Nāth order of yogins, and one of the eighty-four great *siddhas*. He became the tutelary divinity of Nepal. Matsyendranātha's pupil and successor was the *siddha* Gorakhnātha who, having been greatly offended by his master's two sons, ritually killed them, washed their entrails and hung their skins on trees. This suggests a very ancient rite, before the use of fire for sacrificial purposes, when offerings were 'spread out on the place of sacrifice itself, or hung on trees, to which the god *must come himself and partake of them*'.[1] At Matsyendranātha's request Gorakhnātha restored the youths to life, thus indicating 'an initiatory death and resurrection' rite as well as Shamanistic elements.[2] Both Matsyendranātha and Gorakhnātha were associated with the Kānphaṭā Yogins, also called Gorakhnāthīs. According to the traditions of this cult, Matsyendranātha's two sons were the founders of Jainism. 'This anachronism probably conceals certain obscure relations between the Jain ascetics and the secret doctrine of Matsyendranāth and Gorakhnāth.'[3]

[1]O. Schrader, 'Āryan Religion', *ERE.*, II,.p. 41.

[2]Eliade, *Yoga*, p. 310.

[3]Ibid. Tucci states that the name Matsyendranātha was given to those *Siddhas* who had reached a certain stage of spiritual perfection ('Animadversiones Indicae', *JRASB.*, n.s. xxvi, 125–60, 1930).

Maurya(s) The name of one of the ancient tribes of north-eastern India, whose capital was Pipphalivana, about fifty miles to the west of Kuśīnagara.[1] The tribes of this region, having been little influenced by Āryan religion and polity, generally maintained an individual independence and a liberal measure of social freedom, and were ruled by a military (*kṣatra*)[2] or aristocratic government.

The history of the Mauryas represents the culminating stage in the development of the Magadhan empire. The first stage began in the seventh century B.C. with rulers of a dynasty known as the Great Nāga by some authorities, and by others as members of the Haryaṅka-kula (family), whose most prominent members were Bimbisāra and Ajātaśatru. Mauryan consolidation of India owes much to the conquest of the republican states, and the kingdoms of Kāśī and Kosala. But the inability to maintain political and social unity which had bedevilled the Vedic period, continued to characterize the development of the Magadhan empire. In addition the corruption of some of its rulers provided the opportunity for the Mauryas to assume power.

The early career of Candragupta, the founder of the Maurya dynasty, is obscured by conflicting traditions, some of which, after being subjected to literary dramatization, have little historical probability. One tradition attempts to denigrate Candragupta by deriving his clan-name Maurya from his mother Murā, a member of the menial (*śūdra*) class. This charge is not only etymologically incorrect, as the derivative from Murā is Maureya—not Maurya, but it is also contradicted by the more reliable Buddhist tradition which represents him as a great *kṣatriya* which his history amply proves.

Though the invasion of Gandhāra and the Sind Valley by Alexander did not directly affect Magadha, it did facilitate the consolidation of north-eastern India by Candragupta and the establishment of Pāṭaliputra as the new capital. This union of the whole of North India brought the eastern and western regions into direct contact and led to a fusion of ideas which gave an impetus to speculative thought concerning the nature of man and his world. These changed conditions, to which the diverse ethnic groups of Magadha greatly contributed, may account for the rapidity with which the so-called 'heterodox' views of Jainism and Buddhism were accepted.

During the reign of Aśoka (273–231 B.C.), the grandson of Candragupta, the ideal of Indian unity seemed to have been attained with the subjugation of Kaliṅga, the tragic cost of which changed the course of Aśoka's life and made him declare that 'the chiefest conquest is that made by the Law of Piety, therefore an end must be put to the notion that the duty of kings is armed conquest'.[3] To reinforce his views he had them inscribed on rocks and Edict Pillars in various parts of the country. A charter of rights entitled every subject to have access to the emperor, and an official was appointed to ensure it and to encourage tolerance and good-will among religious cults. The 'Civil Service' was reformed and hospitals built for animals as well as humans.

Although the extent of Aśoka's interest in Buddhism

may have been exaggerated it appears to have been sincere. On the other hand, his reference in the Pillar inscriptions to sentiments which Buddhists claim reflect those in the Pāli Suttas, might be regarded by certain Hindu sects as also expressing their views.

Aśoka's administrative genius is shown by the use he made of the organizing ability of the Buddhists to ensure the kind of peace that neither civil law nor military presence could enforce. This was effected by sending his son (or brother) Mahendra to Ceylon at the head of a Buddhist mission; by granting lands to the powerful Buddhist Sarvāstivāda sect in Gandhāra and Kashmir, and to the Mahāsaṅghika, lands in Andhra. In addition, Aśoka's responsibility for the great advance in Indian architecture stands high; whereas Candragupta used wood, Aśoka chose stone. The massive Edict Pillars, each weighing about fifty tons, are among the earliest known examples of the Indian stonecarvers' craft, as is also the magnificent palace at Pāṭaliputra, and the *stūpas* at Sārnāth and Sāñcī.

Aśoka's great qualities were not shared by his descendants, and the administration of the empire gradually ceased to be effective. It is evident also that the growing power of the 'unorthodox' Jain and Buddhist cults contributed to a brahmanic reaction against much of Aśoka's liberalism. Thus when the north-western borders of the empire were threatened with invasion by the satraps appointed by Alexander, Aśoka's dissolute and irresolute heirs proved incapable of dealing with the situation. In desperation, Puṣyamitra, the army generalissimo, usurped the throne and with the aid of his son and grandson defeated the invaders. Puṣyamitra's accession marks the beginning of the Śuṅga Dynasty and the end of the Maurya.

[1] Law, *Tribes in Ancient India*, p. 288.

[2] Because they did not perform the expected brahmanic rites they were derided as 'decadent *kṣatriyas*' by orthodox *brahmins*.

[3] Rock Edict XIII.

Maya An architect of non-Āryan stock, and hence the designation *asura* or *dānava* applied to him. He built the magnificent court of the Pāṇḍu princes at Hastināpura (*MBh.*, Sabhā pa., I and III), and is regarded as the counterpart of Viśvakarman, the architect of the gods, and as one of the great preceptors of Vāstuvidyā (science of architecture) in South India.[1] In addition he, or a man of the same name, is described as an authority on astronomy and military science.[2]

[1] Bhattacharyya, *Canons of Indian Art*, p. 37.

[2] *SED*. Mythologically Maya is said to have received the science of architecture and the treasure of Uśanas (Śukra) from Brahmā (Tarapada Bhattacharya, *A Study on Vāstuvidyā*, p. 36).

v. Tripura.

Māyā 'Illusion', personified as a goddess. A word, originally of limited significance in the *RV.*, gradually became an important Hindu and Buddhist metaphysical term. *Māyā* occurs in the *RV.* (V.85,5, etc.) in several grammatical forms,[1] all derived from the root *mā*, the source of several derivatives, each having its own distinctive significance, such as 'to measure', 'to show', 'to build', etc.[2] In the *RV. māyā* generally means supernatural power or wonderful skill; in the *AV.* magic, illusion. Von Glasenapp describes it as 'an activity at variance with the norm, as the miraculous power (of a god)'. But he also points out that it denotes cunning and crafty deception.[3] In the *RV. māyā* is particularly associated with Indra and Agni, and refers to their magical powers, as later it was to denote those of Śiva and Viṣṇu.

The composers of the Upaniṣads succeeded in rationalizing the ancient belief in personified natural forces as the explanation of all transitory forms (*meyas*) and in providing a basis for Vedānta philosophy. One conclusion of the latter, reached only after acute analysis and comparison (*prapañca*), was that phenomena and their differentiation by name and form had no real existence (*avastu*); the other conclusion was that the perception of phenomena is merely the reaction of the senses to the spontaneous and continuous projection of the indefinable Real (*brahman*). Thus 'in worshipping the illusion, or its manifestations, one worships the reality behind it, the unknowable Immensity on which it rests'.[4] The simile of the master-magician (*māyāvin*), once used to describe Indra's powers, is used in the Vedānta to denote the power of *brahman*. Similarly in the *Bhagavadgītā*, Kṛṣṇa is called Māyāvin when he reproduces the world-emanation in all its forms.

Radhakrishnan defines *māyā* as 'the principle which accounts for the apparent conditioning of the unconditioned Absolute'.[5]

[1] Thus the verb '*mame*' or noun '*mānam*', or '*māyām*' (magic deed or design), or the plural (*meyas*), are all associated with *māyā*. Furthermore, *māyā* indicates the power of gods and demons to take many measurable, visible transitory forms (*meyas*), the manifoldness of which 'are a reflection or manifestation of the Ultimate, but never the Ultimate itself. This lies before, and after, all its emanations' (Heimann, *Facets*, p. 90). But when the concept of *māyā* is 'confronted with the postulate of absolute permanency and constancy, it gains the meaning of transitoriness and thus, in its last consequence, that of illusionary reality only' (ibid.,

p. 125).

[2]P.D. Shastri, *The Doctrine of Māyā*, pp. 30f.

[3]*Entwicklungsstufen des indischen Denkens*, pt. ii, section C.3. An unpublished translation into English by E.F.J. Payne.

[4]Karapatri, 'Śrī Bhagavatī tattva', *Siddhānta*, V, (1944–5), 246, cited by Daniélou, *HP.*, p. 29.

[5]*EW.*, vol. I, p. 66; v. also Gonda *CC.*, ch. VI.

v. Mahāmāyā; Nārada; Māyābala; Varuṇa; Māyādevī.

Māyābala Military tactics intended to deceive the enemy, and also commonly employed by the Indian tribes in their attacks on the Āryans. The *Rāmāyaṇa* frequently condemns the Rākṣasa tribesmen for resorting to the use of fire, poison and magic in battle.[1]

[1]*IRA.*, p. 40.

v. Mārīca.

Māyādevī or **Māyāvatī** The goddess (*devī*) personifying illusion (*māyā*).

A legend related in the *VP.* (V.27), appears to be based on the rivalry and intrigues of Jarāsandha, king of Magadha, and Kṛṣṇa, leader of the Yādavas. War being imminent between them, both rulers sought an alliance with neighbouring kingdoms. One of them was Vidarbha (Berar), whose ruler Bhīṣmaka had a daughter Rukmiṇī whom Kṛṣṇa wished to marry, but his suit was rejected by her family, especially by her brother Rukmin. At the suggestion of Jarāsandha a marriage was arranged between Rukmiṇī and Śiśupāla. But on the eve of the wedding, Kṛṣṇa contrived to abduct the bride, leaving his brother Balarāma and the Yādavas to hold off the pursuit of her family. This they succeeded in doing, but Rukmin, vowing that he would never return to Vidarbha until he had slain Kṛṣṇa, raised an army, which was utterly destroyed, except for Rukmin, whose life was spared by the intercession of Rukmiṇī. Kṛṣṇa then married her, according to the Rākṣasa rite,[1] and by her had a son Pradyumna.

On this fragment of traditional history is superimposed the story of Pradyumna which amply illustrates the power of illusion. When Pradyumna was only six days old, he was carried off by the demon Śambara who had been warned that if the child lived it would one day destroy him. He therefore threw it into the sea where it was swallowed by a large fish,[2] which was subsequently caught by fishermen and sold to Śambara's wife Māyādevī. When the fish was cut open it was found to contain a beautiful child. Māyādevī immediately summoned the *ṛṣi* Nārada, who told her what her husband had done, and said that she must make amends by caring for the child as if he were her own. This she did, and as he grew up she fell more and more in love with him. She passed on to him the secrets of her magical powers and finally told him of his abduction by her husband. Pradyumna thereupon decided to destroy Śambara. Seven times he attacked the demon, only to be foiled by his enchantments. Then Pradyumna altered his tactics, and turning the eighth spell back against Śambara, killed him and all his followers. Nārada then announced that Pradyumna was really an incarnation of Anaṅga, the mental form of Kāma,[3] the god of love, and Māyādevī an incarnation of his wife, the goddess Rati, whose marriage to Śambara was merely an illusion created to ensure the restoration and return of her husband Anaṅga in the form of Pradyumna.

[1]This rite is prescribed when a girl has been seized by force, and after her kinsmen and friends have been slain or wounded in battle.

[2]Cf. the story of Jonah.

[3]An allusion to the story that Śiva's fiery glance had reduced Kāma to ashes for having inflamed Śiva with passion for Umā. Later, moved by Rati's grief, Śiva restored Kāma to a bodiless existence as Anaṅga, whose place is to be in the heart.

v. Vivāha.

Māyāvatī v. Māyādevī.

Mayūra 'Peacock', said to have been produced from Garuḍa's fallen wing. Like the fabulous bird Garuḍa it eats snakes. Garuḍa presented a peacock to Skanda and Aruṇa gave him a fighting cock.

The peacock is an emblem of love; thus Rāma was roused erotically when he watched some peacocks dancing. This bird is also an emblem of Durgā.[1]

[1]*EM.*, p. 224. Peacock flesh was eaten in the royal household during Mauryan times. They were also kept in the grounds of palaces as pets, and were sometimes trained to fight (Brodrick, *Animals in Archaeology*, p. 123).

Mayūradhvaja The peacock banner or standard of Bāṇa. The breaking of the standard was an omen of impending war.

Mayūrī The pea-hen, said to protect against poison (*RV.*, I.191.14; *AV.*, VIII.56.7).

Medhā 'Intelligence', 'wisdom', personified as the wife of Dharma and the daughter of Dakṣa (*VP.*, I.7). Medhā is a form of Sarasvatī (*SED.*).

v. Śruti.

Medhātithi I. A Vedic *ṛṣi*. Indra is said to have appeared to him in the shape of a ram (*RV.*, VIII.2,40; *ŚBr.*, III.3,4,18).

II. One of the ten sons of King Priyavrata,[1] who divided the earth into seven continents and appointed Medhātithi to rule over Plakṣadvīpa (*VP.*, II.1). Later Medhātithi gave each of his seven sons one seventh of his kingdom.

[1]In *VP.*, IV19, Medhātithi is said to be the son of Kaṇva.
III. Name of a commentator on the *Mānava-dharmaśāstra.*

Medinī A name of the earth-goddess.
v. Kaiṭabha.

Megasthenes An ambassador appointed by Seleucus Nicator to the court of Candragupta. Megasthenes spent eight years (306–298 B.C.) at Pāṭaliputra where he wrote an account of the country; though now lost it has been largely preserved in the narratives of Diodorus Siculus, Strabo, Aelian and Arrian.[1] Megasthenes' frank observations covered many aspects of Indian social, religious, political and economic life. Doubtless the complete freedom to make his observations was due to the friendly relations of the two countries, which had been confirmed by the marriage of Candragupta and Seleucus Nicator's daughter.

Megasthenes mentioned the inferior position held by women and consequently their lack of education. Caste then consisted mainly in distinctions of occupation; seven being noted, including the four mentioned in *RV.*, X.90. The Buddha is referred to and also the existence of philosophical schools, but there is no direct mention of Śaivism or Vaiṣṇavism, only of an Indian counterpart of Herakles, generally assumed to be Kṛṣṇa. Megasthenes refers also to the magnificence of Candragupta's palace, the huge dimensions of Pāṭaliputra, the well-organized economy of the country, and its powerful army.

[1]These were collected and translated by McCrindle, published in the *Indian Antiquary*, and subsequently in book form.
v. Maurya(s).

Meghadūta 'Cloud-messenger.' A Sanskrit poem by Kālidāsa telling of the love of an exiled *yakṣa* for his wife. He sees a huge cloud drifting northwards towards his home in the mountains, and he pours out his longing to it. He describes a bird's-eye view of the country over which the cloud will pass; the magical mountain city of the *yakṣas*; and the beauties of his wife.

Meghanāda 'Cloud-noise', i.e., thunder. Name of a son of Rāvaṇa.
v. Indrajit; Uśanas.

Mekhalā I. A girdle or belt. In the *Tait. Saṁ.*, VI.6.4,2 the girdle is given a special significance, designed to ensure strength, bestow power and other benefits (*ŚBr.*, III.2.1, 10–14).[1] These were achieved by the setting up of a sacrificial post (*yūja*) round which a girdle is wound in a prescribed manner, depending on the particular benefit desired. Thus two girdles must be wound round the post if a man desires two wives; to have a daughter he should intertwine the ends of the girdles; or for a son the girdles should be wound round the top of the *yūpa*. Other methods of winding the girdles are prescribed for other results, such as bringing rain, increase of cattle and so forth.

The wearing of the *mekhalā* had a ritualistic significance for the three superior classes, that of a *brāhmaṇa* should consist of a triple cord of *muñja* grass; of a *kṣatriya* a bowstring made of *mūrvā* fibres; of a *vaiśya* that made of hempen threads (*Manu*, II.42–4).[2]

The *mekhalā* has from ancient times been associated with the supposed protective powers of the circle (*cakra*). According to the *AV.*, VI.133,5,[3] the broad jewelled belt depicted on the terracotta figures of fertility goddesses were regarded as 'a long-life (*āyuṣya*) charm'.

[1]Cf. Aphrodite's girdle, which rendered all who wore it irresistible (James, *Tree of Life*, p. 192).

[2]Girdles were distinguished by the number of threads of which each was composed. Thus a girdle composed of a single strand is called *kāñcī*, of eight, *mekhalā*, of sixteen, *raśanā*, of twenty-five *katāpa* (A. J. Shastri, *India as Seen in the Bṛhat Saṁhitā*, p. 234, n. 1).

[3]In ancient Greece girls before marriage offered their girdles to Artemis (Farnell, *Cults*, II, p. 448). In the Homeric 'Hymn to Demeter', a liturgical chant designed for one of the great seasonal festivals, Demeter is described as 'racked with longing for her deep-girdled daughter' (Gaster, *Thespis*, pp. 453ff.), here also indicating fertility.
v. Parjanya.

II. The cords or lines drawn round an altar (*vedi*) on the four sides of the receptacle in which the sacrificial fire is deposited.

Menā or **Menakā** I. A daughter of King Vṛṣaṇaśva, mentioned in a single passage of the *RV.* (I.51,13). In Paurāṇic mythology she is a mind-born daughter of the *pitṛs* by Svadhā (*VP.*, I.10). According to the *Vāyu P.* she married Himavat (the personified Himālaya), and became the mother of Maināka, Gaṅgā and Pārvatī.

II. Name of the *apsaras* who seduced the *ṛṣi* Viśvāmitra and became the mother of Śakuntalā, whom Kālidāsa enshrined in his famous drama *Śakuntalā*.

Later Menā is said to have abandoned[1] Śakuntalā, and also Pramadvarā whom she bore to the *gandharva* Viśvāvasu.

[1]A practice characteristic of *apsarasas*.
v. Aparṇā; Bharata.

Meru or **Sumeru** I. The name of the mythical golden mountain, the subject of numerous Paurāṇic myths. It represents the central point of the universe, a notion common to many other ancient cosmological theories, and generally associated with a particular mountain or prominent landmark.[1] Such mountains were generally regarded as the meeting place or abode of the gods and as the earth's axis.[2] On its summit the celestial Ganges (*gaṅgā*) falls before dividing into four terrestrial streams flowing to the four points of the compass.

Mountains were generally regarded as protectors, as is indicated by the prayer: 'May the mountains be auspicious to us' (*RV.*, VII.35,8).[3] The notion of a central point, called by various names and described by numerous metaphors in the Purāṇas, is popularly identified with one or another of the Himālayan peaks. According to the *Mārk. P.* (54,15f.) and the *VP.* (II.2), the height of Meru is 84,000 *yojanas*, and its depth below the surface of the earth, 16,000; the diameter of the summit 32,000 *yojanas*, and its base 16,000, and hence the simile 'the seed-cup or lotus of the earth'. Conflicting descriptions occur in other Purāṇas but these divergences are ascribed by the sages to inadequate knowledge. Only Brahmā, it is said, fully comprehends it. Brahmā's square city of gold is situated on its summit. On its outskirts are the eight cities of the eight Lokapālas. The heavens or spheres (*lokas*) of Kṛṣṇa and Viṣṇu are also located on Meru. Beneath the mountain are the seven nether worlds; in the lowest of these resides the giant snake Vāsuki supporting Meru and the worlds on his sevenfold hood. Earth tremors occur when he yawns, and when he finally awakes and uncoils his enormous body at the end of the age, the whole of creation is consumed by his fiery breath. Meru also figures in Buddhist myths.

Among the epithets applied to Meru are: Hemādṛ (Golden mountain); Ratnasānu (Jewel peak); Karṇikācala (Lotus mountain); Devaparvata (Mountain of the gods).

[1]Such as Olympus, Kilimanjaro, Fujiyama, etc.

[2]But Hopkins states that 'the Epic knows nothing ... of Meru as the axis of the world' (*EM.*, p. 11). For the meaning of Meru in tantrism, v. Rawson, *The Art of Tantra*, p. 139.

[3]Cf. Psalm 121,1, 'I will lift up mine eyes unto the mountains, from whence cometh my help'.

v. Amarāvatī; Jambudvīpa.

II. The central or most prominent bead of a necklace (*mālā*).

Meṣānana 'Ram-faced.' A demon injurious to children.

Mīḍhūṣī v. Madirā.

Mīmāṁsā v. Pūrva-Mīmāṁsā; Darśana(s).

Mīnā The name of the mother of fishes, *makaras*, etc.

Mīnākṣī 'Fish-eyed.' The name of an ancient South Indian cult goddess, whose epithet may mean 'having eyes of surpassing beauty',[1] or 'love-filled eyes',[2] the fish being an emblem of Kāma, the god of love. Originally she was regarded as a daughter of Kubera and hence as a *yakṣiṇī*.[3]

A great temple was erected on Mīnākṣī's shrine in the seventeenth century, consisting of a hall of a 'thousand' pillars, but actually of 997 columns all elaborately carved. It also contains a number of courts as well as twin sanctuaries, one dedicated to Mīnākṣī, the other to Śiva.

In front of the Mīnākṣī sanctuary is the rectangular Pool of the Golden Lilies. To bathe in it removes guilt and leads even unbelievers to heaven.[4] It is said that Tamil authors' works were judged here by placing the manuscript on the water, 'If it stank, it sank!'[5]

[1]P. Brown, *Indian Architecture*, p. 113.

[2]Whitehead, *Village Gods of South India*, p. 112, n.2. Mīnākṣī is said to be an incarnation of Pārvatī, as the daughter of a Pāṇḍyan King of Madurai.

[3]Coomaraswamy, *Yakṣas*, pt. i, p. 9.

[4]Diehl, *Instrument and Purpose*, p. 244.

[5]*Fodor's Guide to India*, p. 515.

Miñjika (m.) and **Miñjikā** (fem.) Two spirits begotten by Rudra/Śiva when his semen fell on a mountain. Another myth states that Śiva's semen, when cast upon sunbeams, the earth, trees, etc., produces 'five kinds of demons, especially worshipped as children of Śiva'.[1]

[1]*EM.*, p. 231, n. 1.

Mithuna A 'pair (male and female), or any couple or pair'.

The symbolism of the 'fertile pairs' depicted on temples reflects ancient cosmogonic notions such as heaven and earth, light and darkness, phallus and *yoni*, as well as philosophical concepts like the union of *puruṣa* and *prakṛti*, the unmanifested and the manifested, etc. These ideas were later expressed iconographically by the figures of Śiva and Pārvatī together; or of Viṣṇu and Lakṣmī; or of paired figures of *gandharvas* and *apsarasas*, etc.

The *mithuna* figures carved on the doors of houses and temples are regarded as auspicious, as a symbol of creation. But in some temples, particularly those influenced by Tantrism, the figures became more and more erotic.[1] The two lovers complement each other and when in sexual union become more than either can be alone.[2] Some Upaniṣads also use erotic symbolism, and declare that 'the physical ecstasy of union is an image of the delight of the knowledge of *brahman*'.[3] This is indicated in the *Bṛhad-Ār. Up.* (IV.3,21) which declares that as in the ecstasy of perfect coition between husband and wife, each loses all consciousness of individuality, 'of within and without', so when the mortal self is united with the Universal Self (*ātman*), the illusion of differentiation and duality disappears. From the dismembered body of Prajāpati couples (*mithunāni*) went forth; and from pairs birth originates (*ŚBr.*, IX.4.1,3–5). The *AV.*, VI.141,2, referring to the marking of the ears of cattle, states that they should be marked with a pair (*mithuna*) on both ears with a red (copper?) knife. This is obviously a 'magical' device thought to ensure fertility in the animals.

Sexual 'divinization' can be performed by a man or woman who has reached the necessary spiritual level enabling them to initiate others. Such a 'woman, who has been herself converted into a vessel of the divine energy by sexual intercourse and ritual with one or more divinized Tantrik men, can pass on the initiation by intercourse with male would-be initiates. This ... survives in modern Bengali Tantra. There are plenty of textual references to this particular aspect of the cult. The women were called ... *Dūtīs*, *Yoginīs* or simply *Śaktis*'.[4]

[1] *Mithuna* is equivalent to the sacral coitus carried out by the chief queen and the sacrificial horse at the *aśvamedha* (*ŚBr.*, XIII.5.2,2), and that of the *mahāvrata* festival at the spring solstice when it is necessary to strengthen the sun. The large number of erotic pairs on the Sun temple at Koṇārak may be similarly explained. For the procreative pairs prominent in later art, v. Gangoly, 'The Mithuna in Indian Art', *Rūpam*, 1927, 22–3.

[2] But in Buddhist tantrism this 'pairing' is a subjective inner visualization and not an outward physical act. Gonda considers that the importance of *mithuna* stems 'from the Vedic maxim that a pair (*dvandvam*) means strength and a productive copulation' (*VS.*, p. 56).

[3] Coomaraswamy, *Philosophy of Ancient Asiatic Art*, p. 108, which forms part of M. R. Anand's *Hindu View of Art*. In India the art of love has never 'been regarded as derogatory to the dignity of man' (ibid.).

[4] Rawson, *The Art of Tantra*, p. 80.

Mitra I. A 'friend', 'companion'.[1] In the *RV.* and *AV.*, *mitra* is masculine, in later works generally neuter.[2] Other forms, having the same derivation, occur in these two Vedas, such as *mitrin*, 'united by friendship'; *mitriya*, 'friendly'; and *mithuna*, 'pair'. All these terms imply compatibility, reciprocity, a special mutually dependent relationship, a common aim in the exercise of individual functions in every sphere of life. Thus in a political sense *mitra* refers to the relationship of one ruler and an ally whose territory adjoins that of another regarded as an enemy (*ari*) of both.[3]

In the *RV.* and *AV.* Mitra and his companions Varuṇa and Aryaman are often collectively invoked, or Mitra and Varuṇa jointly. In one hymn (*RV.*, III.59,1) Mitra alone is addressed as 'he who awakens men at daybreak and stirs them to labour'. As sons of Aditi all three deities are referred to by their metronymic Āditya (*RV.*, X.36,3).

Butter that has been churned spontaneously, as by the motion of a cart, is offered to Mitra, and also unbroken rice grains, because he never injures the animate or the inanimate, and hence is the friend of all (*ŚBr.*, V.3.2,6–7).

Mitra and Varuṇa 'by Law uphold the Law', and also encourage self-discipline (*RV.*, I.186,2). In *maṇḍala* VII.66,13–14, law has a moral significance and the two gods are described as 'true to Law, born in the Law, haters of the false'.

Mitra should be worshipped when palaces or houses are erected. Originally Savitar, Sūrya and Mitra were regarded as separate gods, but in later mythology they became one.[4]

To gaze steadfastly at an object with 'the eye of Mitra' is 'a ritual technique to appease that object, that is to annihilate the evil influences adhering to it'.[5]

[1] Cf. the Avestan Mithra—a sun-god and guardian of faithfulness. His Greco-Irānian name was Mithras, and he was widely worshipped in the Roman Empire, especially by legionaries, during the early Christian centuries.

[2] *SED.*, p. 816. The neuter *mitram* means 'a neutral acknowledgement of equality and subsequent exchange of understanding and tolerance' (Heimann, *Facets*, p. 85).

[3] *Manu*, VII.158.

[4] *C. Herit. I.*, vol. I, p. 26.

[5] Gonda, *Eye and Gaze in the Veda*, p. 42.

v. Mitra-Varuṇa.

II. The name of one of the four immediate followers of Lakulīśa, the systematizer of the Pāśupata cult,[1] the others being Kuśika, Gārgya and Kaurasya.

[1] *DHI.*, pp. 450f.; Farquhar, *Outline of the Religious Literature of India*, p. 146.

Mitra-Varuṇa The gods Mitra and Varuṇa conjoined.[1] They are handsome, young, shining, sunlike and terrible; the sacred *soma* plant is pressed for them (*Tait. Saṁ.*, I.4,5). The gods (*devas*) anointed them as kings (*ŚBr.*, V.3.4,3). Sometimes they granted offspring, as can be seen in the account of Manu's sacrifice to them to obtain an eighth son, even more distinguished than the previous seven (*Mārk. P.*, 111, 4ff.).[2]

[1] Pairs of gods, *gandharvas*, etc., are regarded as being particularly auspicious.

[2] Prajāpati also performed a sacrifice in honour of Mitra-Varuṇa and from it Iḍā emerged (*Vāyu P.*,

85, 6–7, *Pl.*).
v. Mithuna; Āditya(s).

Mleccha(s) 'Foreigners.' From the root *mlech*, a foreigner, a non-Indo-Āryan, often regarded as a barbarian.[1] The epithet was also applied to Indo-Āryans accustomed only to speaking a regional dialect and thus assumed to lack a knowledge of brahminic institutions and traditions.[2] They are said to have emerged from the left (i.e., the inauspicious) side of Veṇa's body when it was rubbed by the *ṛṣis*.

The feminine form *mlecchī* sometimes refers to makers of weapons, or to those engaged in agriculture.[3]

[1]The *VP.* (IV.17) mentions lawless *mlecchas* of the North whose princes were the hundred sons of Pracetas.

[2]According to *VP.* (IV.3) *mlecchas* were degraded *kṣatriyas*, but *mleccha* did not always have a derogatory significance, especially when applied to the Greeks.

[3]*SED.*

v. Yavana(s); Niṣāda.

Mohanī I. The 'Beguiler', a demoness who personifies this form of deception. Her brother Nighna eats the foetus, and she causes human offspring to be born as snakes, frogs, etc. Nighna may enter a pregnant woman who has eaten meat; or who sits under a tree at night, or where three or four roads meet, etc. (*Mārk. P.*, 51, 77–80).

II. A magical formula, like that referred to in the *AV.* (III.1,2), employed to confuse an enemy.

Mohinī The beautiful female form assumed by Viṣṇu to bewitch the *asuras* and thus deprive them of their rightful share of the *amṛta* (ambrosia),[1] one of the treasures which had emerged during the Churning of the Ocean (*samudramathana*). In another myth Mohinī is portrayed as the enchantress Lust, whose form Viṣṇu had assumed to test the sages of the Dārukāvana forest who were given to boasting about their chastity.

In a sectarian myth Mohinī is said to have seduced Śiva for the purpose of making him realize the superiority of Viṣṇu's power!

[1]*TT.*, pp. 205 and 225, n.11. Bharati suggests that there may be a link between this myth and the saga-complex of Indo-European origin, in which the giants, after building Valhalla, were cheated of their fee by Thor who had assumed the form of a beautiful woman. v. also Davidson, *Gods and Myths of Northern Europe*, p. 73.

Mokṣa or **Mukti** 'Release'. The *SED.* derives both *mokṣa* and *mukti* from *mokṣ*, 'to free one's self', 'to shake off', but the *PTS.* derives *mokṣa* and its Pāli form *mokkha* from *muc*, 'letting loose', 'releasing', and considers the term to be late Vedic, and to lack the special significance later given it. The *Bṛhad-Ār. Up.* (III.1,5) refers to *mukti* as a fourfold release, ritually effected by the *hotṛ*, *adhvaryu*, *udgatṛ* and *brahman* officiating priests, but which represents only release from the limitations of the psychosomatic relationship. It is further stated (4.4,7) that only 'when all desires that lodge in the heart are liberated (*mukti*) shall a mortal become immortal and attain *brahman*'.[1]

The immortality referred to in the Upaniṣads is unique, being absorption in *brahman*, but some of the references to it reflect the common desire for individual immortality, hence the numerous Vedic *mantras* designed to ensure it. Even in the later Classical Upaniṣads Death (Mṛtyu) is still regarded as the arch-enemy, whose defeat is no longer to be effected by the repetition of *mantras*. According to the *Śvet. Up.* (3,7) men become immortal only when they come to know *brahman* as Lord (*īś*).[2] According to Śaivism deliverance in this very life (*jīvan-mukti*) consists in nothing but the realization that the 'entire universe is my manifestation' (*sarvo mamāyaṁ vibhavaḥ*).[3]

[1]This mystical knowledge occurs with the realization of the 'identification between ritual, cosmic and human entities' (*BIP.*, p. 31, n.4), but this is not the later notion of *mukti*.

The attainment of complete freedom (*mokṣa*) 'lies in the mastery of attitudes of greater and greater concern coupled with less and less attachment or possessiveness' (Karl H. Potter, *Presuppositions of India's philosophies*, p. 10).

[2]Cf. *ŚBr.*, X.4.3,9–10 which declares that those who refuse to surrender their bodies to Death when he so ordains, shall resume their earthly lives and repeatedly become the 'food of Death'.

[3]*EW.*, vol. I, p. 389; v. also Raghavan and Dandekar, *Sources of Indian Tradition*, p. 276.

Mṛgaśiras I. 'Deer's head.' The name of a constellation. Prajāpati (Brahmā) conceived an incestuous passion for his daughter who had assumed the shape of a doe. The gods, seeing what was happening, formed a divine being Bhūtavat (i.e., a Rudra) from their most terrifying forms, who shot an arrow at Prajāpati making him leap into the sky where he became the constellation *mṛga* (*mṛgaśīrṣa*),[1] and his daughter the asterism Rohiṇī (*Āit. Br.*, III.33; and v. *ŚBr.*, I.7.4,1ff.; II.1.2,8–9). This and similar astronomical myths 'acquire significance if we suppose them to have arisen at the time when the precession of the equinoxes finally made it impossible to associate the summer solstice with Spica in Virgo, and the vernal equinox, with Gemini. This occurred about 4000 B.C.'[2]

[1]Another version in the *Śiva P.* relates that when Śiva saw Brahmā (in stag form) pursuing his daughter

across the skies, he cut off his head with an arrow, which remains in the sky as the sixth lunar mansion *ārdrā*, and the stag's head as the fifth mansion.

[2]G. E. Gibson, 'The Vedic Nakṣatras and the Zodiac,' p. 156, *Semitic and Oriental Studies presented to William Popper*.

II. Yajña, the personification of the sacrifice, is also said to have the head of a deer. He was killed by Vīrabhadra at Dakṣa's sacrifice, and made by Brahmā into the constellation *mṛgaśirṣas*.

Mṛtyu 'Death'; 'the personification of death'.[1] References to death in early Vedic literature make it clear that life after death was envisaged as a repetition of life on earth with 'the whole body and all its members' (*sarvatanuḥ sāṅgaḥ*)[2] being restored and capable of enjoying all the pleasures of mortal life (*AV*., V.6,11; *ŚBr*., V.6.1,1).[3] Despite this prospect death continued to be dreaded. This is indicated by the numerous *mantras* in the *AV*. each designed to avert a particular disease or calamity that might result in death, and the equally numerous prayers appealing to the gods to grant longevity (*āyuṣya*), i.e., a hundred years, the Vedic ideal. Dreaded almost as much as death, especially by men, was old age and the loss of physical powers.

Apparently even the gods were originally not immune from death.[4] Prajāpati attained immortality and made his body 'undecaying' by a sacrificial rite (*ŚBr*., X.1.4,1), or by practising austerities (*tapas*) for a thousand years (X.4.4,1). He also instructed the gods by means of a rite how to attain immortality (X.4.3,3ff.). Mṛtyu complained that if mankind came to share this immortality he would have no food and nothing to do. Whereupon the gods decreed that mankind should only become immortal after surrendering their bodies to Death, but those refusing to accept this condition must resume their earthly life, and repeatedly become the 'food of Death' (*ŚBr*., X.4.3,9–10).

A bundle of twigs was tied to the foot of the corpse, thus obliterating its footsteps and so preventing or delaying the return either of Death or the deceased to the land of the living (*RV*., X.18,2). As a further precaution the *adhvaryu* priest erected a mound of earth or stone to prevent Death's return.[5]

Mṛtyu dwells in the sun, hence the world of death is the highest sky (*Kauṣ. Br*., xx.1). The sun's glowing light is immortal; Death does not die for he is within the immortal, and hence it is said, 'within Death is immortality'. Whoever comprehends this passes after death to 'that body and becomes immortal, for Death is his own self' (*ŚBr*., X.5.2,3ff.).

Brāhmaṇas who practise *yoga* and *tapas*, and those initiated into the art of life-giving elixirs, possess the power of warding off Death from the sick (*Suś. Saṁ*., I, p. 266). According to the beliefs of the Siddha Cult death may be postponed indefinitely by 'a psycho-chemical process of *yoga*, known as the *kāya-sādhana* or the culture of the body with a view to making it perfect and immutable and thereby attaining an immortal spiritual life'.[6]

In the Purāṇas Mṛtyu is the theme of numerous myths. The *VP*. (I.7) states that Mṛtyu was generated by Brahmā, or was the son of Bhaya (Fear) and Māyā (Illusion), their children being Vyādhi (Disease), Jarā (Old Age), Śoka (Sorrow), Tṛṣṇā (Greed) and Krodha (Wrath).

[1]Cf. the Babylonian god of death, Mu-u-tu; also the Greek god Thanatos and the Welsh Angau.

[2]The persistence of this belief is indicated in the burial service of the Western Church, which quotes from Job, 19,26, 'Though . . . worms destroy this body, yet in my flesh shall I see God.'

[3]But the post-Vedic view (*MBh*., XII.267,10, Critical Ed.) was that the body became 'five-fold', i.e., it dissolved into the five elements from which it was formed: water, atmosphere, earth, wind and fire, and hence 'to go to fiveness' is synonymous with 'to die'.

[4]Initially only Agni was immortal (*ŚBr*., II.2.2,8). Only Death is fearless for all creatures fear him (*Ait. Br*., V.25).

[5]Diehl, referring to South Indian present-day customs, states that sometimes the traces of the funeral procession are obliterated at cross-roads, or the corpse is removed from the house through a hole in the wall which is afterwards closed, thereby preventing the deceased's return to its old home. Singing and merry-making also take place to deceive the demons who, not realizing that a funeral is taking place, do not attack the corpse (*Instrument and Purpose*, p. 194).

[6]*ORC*., p. 192.

v. Kūdī; Yama; Bhīṣma; Amṛta; Mṛtyupāśa.

Mṛtyupāśa One of Death's many nooses (*pāśa*) which ensnare the living.

v. Mṛtyu; Yama.

Mucukunda A son of Māndhātṛ, a king of the Solar dynasty. As a reward for his assistance to the gods in their struggle against the *asuras*, he was granted the boon of uninterrupted sleep and the assurance that whoever disturbed him would be burnt to ashes by his fiery glance. Kṛṣṇa, being aware of this, lured his enemy, the Yavana king Kālayavana, into the cave of the sleeper who awoke and cast an angry glance at the intruder, reducing him to ashes. Mucukunda then paid honour to Kṛṣṇa who granted him the right to enter any of the celestial realms. When he had enjoyed all their pleasures he would be reborn in a distinguished family, and finally attain liberation (*VP*., V.23,24).

Mudgala A Vedic *ṛṣi* of great generosity who lived a life of poverty but fed thousands of *brahmins* with grain which he gleaned from the fields. This grain never diminished, and even increased when needed.[1]

The ill-tempered *ṛṣi* Durvāsas visited Mudgala and six times devoured all his food, but failed to disturb the *ṛṣi*'s perfect tranquillity. Durvāsas, greatly impressed by this show of self-control, declared that Mudgala would ascend bodily to the heavenly worlds, but in his great wisdom Mudgala, knowing that in heaven even merit is a diminishing asset, preferred to remain on earth, continuing to practise extreme asceticism (*tapas*) until he had attained perfection, when he would be beyond rebirth (*MBh*., Vana pa., 259).

[1]Cf. the feeding of the five thousand, Matthew 14,16–21; and the oil of the widow of Zarephath, I. Kings, 17, 8–16.

Mudrā or **Hasta**[1] A seal or impression; sign or token; its function being to confirm, or to give visible proof of validity, hence it became a manual sign made by particular positionings of the hand, fingers and arm. By means of these *mudrās* a number of meanings may be expressed.[2]

The universal belief in the magical power of hands or fingers probably stems from the fact that the hands are used for so many actions; hence they became a symbol of power. Much of this deep-rooted early magic is associated with the *mudrā*, the practitioner being supposed to transform himself into a conductor of mystic forces actuated by the pronouncing of a particular *mantra*,[3] and hence the objection to pointing in many countries, for in some it is still believed that dangerous magical power flows from practitioner to victim. It is customary for *brahmins* to keep their hands covered when praying, and for Moslems to cover them before a superior, or when visiting. In Christian art St. Peter, when receiving the keys, has his hands covered with the skirt of his cloak, and Cardinals today cover their hands with their capes when paying homage to the Pope.

In Hindu, Jaina and Buddhist sculptures the significance of some of the *mudrās* is similar, three of the commonest being the *dhyāna* or meditative posture, the *abhaya* or the fear-removing, and *varada*, the boon-giving *mudrā*.

According to Hommel the term *mudrā* is derived from the Babylonian *musarū* (seal), which became in Old Persian *muzrā*, the 'z' being changed to 'd' in Sanskrit.[4] Przyluski considers that the literal meaning of *mudrā* is 'seal' and also 'womb'.

Apart from its iconographic significance *mudrā* in Buddhist Tantrism may also be applied to a female adept. In the Hindu Śākta cult it is applied to both parched grain and to kidney beans (considered to be aphrodisiacs). *Mudrā* is the third of the 'five Ms' of the Hindu Tantrists.

[1]*Hasta* usually denotes hand positions in which the arm and hand are shown in a particular ritual or iconographic pose, whereas *mudrā* applies to the respective positions of the palm and fingers.

[2]*Mudrās* are similarly used in the religious practices of Judaism, Christianity and Islam. Indian *mudrās* are used in religious worship, rites, meditation, drama and dances, especially in the Classical Bharata-nāṭya of South India. *Mudrās* have influenced the dance cultures of the Orient, of the South Pacific (especially the Hawaiian *hula*), and of Spain, although in the latter the significance of the symbolism has been lost.

[3]R. H. van Gulik, *Hayagrīva*, pp. 51–2.

[4]*Ehrengabe für Wilhelm Geiger*, pp. 73–84, Leipzig, 1931; and v. S. H. Langdon, 'Gesture in Sumerian and Babylonian Prayer', *JRAS*., 1919, pp. 531–56. For dance *mudrās* v. Poduval, *Kathākil and Diagram of Hand Poses*, Trivandrum, 1930.

v. Hasta I; Nāṭya Veda.

Muhūrta A moment, instant, or any short space of time; the thirtieth part of a day, i.e., forty-eight minutes. v. Muhūrtā.

Muhūrtā The name of one of Dakṣa's daughters, the wife of Dharma (*VP*., I.15), or of Manu. She became the mother of the personified moments of time (*muhūrta*).

Mukhaliṅga A *liṅga* on which is depicted one or more human faces representing various aspects of Śiva. The number of faces depends on the purpose for which the *mukhaliṅga* is required. A *liṅga* with one face should be set up in villages; with two faces, on hills or near the border of enemy country; with three faces, in temples with three doors; with four faces, in four-doored temples; and the five-faced on hills. The last *liṅga* is also used in rites for the destruction of enemies (*abhicāra*), as is also the two-faced *liṅga*.[1]

[1]T. Bhattacharyya, *Canons of Indian Art*, pp. 397f.

Mukhāmbikā 'Mouth-mother.' A shrine in N. Cannanore on the Malabar coast. Only the lower portion of the goddess's head is depicted.[1]

[1]*TT*., p. 98, n.11.

v. Bālāmbikā; Hemāmbikā.

Mukti v. Mokṣa.

Mukundā The wife of the *ṛṣi* Vācaknavī, who was seduced by Indra. To carry out the seduction Indra took the form of King Rukmāṅgada to whom Mukundā was attracted.[1]

[1]*Gaṇeśa P*., 1,36,40; v. *HP*., p. 108.

Mūla The root of a plant or tree. Figuratively, the

lowest part of anything. Since Vedic times (and probably before), roots and plants play an important part in magic and medicine, and some possess real curative properties.

Mūlaliṅga The 'root' (*mūla*) *liṅga* in the central shrine (*garbha-gṛha*) of a temple, which is never moved from the building.

Muṇḍa 'Bald.' Name of a demon slain by Durgā.

Muṇḍaka One of the eighteen principal Upaniṣads.

Muni An inspired person, sage, seer, ascetic, especially one who has taken a vow of silence,[1] who possesses magical powers (*RV.*, 136.2f.), who treads the paths of the *gandharvas* and *apsarasas*, and becomes a friend of the gods.

According to the *Kaṭha Up.* (I.4), a *muni* is one who has transcended all earthly desires, his mind being concentrated on the *ātman*. In Buddhism the term is applied to the Buddha, called Śākyamuni (the Sage of the Śākyas), and to Buddhist *arhats*.

[1]The ancient Egyptians greatly revered the silent man. 'High officials describe themselves "as truly silent" . . . True wisdom is true power; but it means mastery over one's impulses, and silence is a sign not of humility, but of superiority' (Frankfort, *Ancient Egyptian Religion*, p. 66; and v. Wilson in *The Intellectual Adventure of Modern Man*, pp. 114f.). Cf. Psalm 46, 10, 'Be still and know that I am God.'

Muñja A sedge-like grass (Saccharum muñja) which grows to a height of ten feet. Its hollow stem is said to be the home of lightning (*vidyut*). Because of its purifying qualities it was sometimes used as a filter for *soma* (*RV.*, I.161,8). A layer of *muñja* grass was placed in the sacred fire-pan, and was likened to a womb from which the fire (*agni*) was to be born (*ŚBr.*, VI.6.1,23).

Mura or **Muru** A five-headed *daitya* and father of 7,000 sons. He joined the demon Naraka in his fight against Kṛṣṇa, but the latter destroyed them and the sons with flames from the edge of his discus (*cakra*) (*VP.*, IV.29).

Mūradeva(s) A term used derogatively in the *RV.* where Indra and Agni are invoked to kill the Mūradevas (VII.104,24; X.87,2 and 14). Sāyaṇa considers them to be destructive demons (*rākṣasas*); but A.P.B. Shastri suggests that the term may denote an ethnic entity.[1]

[1]'Iconism in India', *IHQ.*, XII, 1936, pp. 335f.

Murugan The Tamil name of Kārttikeya (Skanda) who 'was worshipped with flower offerings and orgiastic dances'.[1] He was the god of Kuriñci, one of the five ancient divisions of the Tamil country.[2]

[1]*HP.*, p. 299.

[2]Diehl, *Instrument and Purpose*, p. 135, n.1 and p. 251, n.1.

Musala A pestle-shaped club (also spelt *muṣala* or *muśala*), carried by Balarāma.

v. Saunanda; Śāmba.

N

Nābha or **Nābhi** 'Navel', 'centre'. In a cosmogonic sense *nābha* signifies a central point, such as the mythical Mount Meru, regarded as the navel of the earth[1] and the seat of the life-force (*ŚBr*., VI.7.1,9). The altar fire is similarly designated (VI.6.3,9). In the Purāṇas Brahmā is said to have sprung from the lotus springing from Viṣṇu's navel, the centre of universal energy.[2] In Śaivism, the *nābha* is the focal point of meditation in the worship of Śiva.

Yakṣas are often depicted with the rhizome of a lotus springing from their navels or from their mouths, perhaps indicating that the life-breath (*prāṇa*) is the vegetative source; or that the saliva represents the waters (*āpaḥ*).[3]

[1]Cf. the Gr. *omphalos* in the Temple of Apollo at Delphi, believed to represent the earth's central point, and to be the meeting place of gods and men. The Babylonians regarded Babylon as the centre of the world ('Mesopotamia' in *Ancient and Medieval Science*, ed. by Taton, p. 77, v. also fig. 10).

[2]An Upper Palaeolithic so-called 'Venus' at Çatal Hüyük (Anatolia) in shrine E. VI.8 has only the navel carefully modelled (Brodrick (ed.), *Animals in Archaeology*, p. 33). For the sexual significance of navel and *vedi* (altar) v. Johannsen, *Ueber die altindische Göttin Dhiṣaṇā*, pp. 51ff.

[3]Coomaraswamy, *Yakṣas*, pt. ii, p. 24 and n.1.

Naciketas A son of Vājaśravas who figures in a story related in the *Kaṭha Up*., intended to illustrate a particular point of view or to point a moral. Vājaśravas is described as a man whose religious zeal impelled him to surrender all his possessions as an offering to the gods. But Naciketas several times reminded him that it is laid down that a man should offer of his best, which the father considered to be a reflection on his zeal. He therefore decided to offer Naciketas—his most precious possession—to Yama, the ruler of the dead.

When Naciketas entered the Hall of Death, Yama was not there to welcome him, an inexcusable breach of hospitality in Vedic India, for which Yama on his return sought to make amends by offering the newcomer three boons. Naciketas gratefully accepted the offer, his first wish being the restoration of his father's affection; the second to know the secret of the mystic fire by which the state beyond the sphere of re-birth is attained; the third to learn the nature of life in the hereafter (1,29).

After the fulfilment of two of the wishes Yama pleaded that the third might be beyond his powers. The refusal of Naciketas to choose another boon is the subject of a dialogue between him and Yama. This is succeeded by a long monologue by Yama on the identity of the individual self with the universal Self. Only towards the end of the discourse does Yama revert to the subject of the afterlife, but beyond declaring that the condition of immortality is a renunciation of all desires and attachments, no attempt is made to define the nature of the hereafter—which Naciketas so urgently desired to know. Instead, the Upaniṣad inconclusively concludes: Then Naciketas, 'having received this knowledge taught by Death and the whole rule of Yoga (meditation) . . . became free from passion and death, and attained *brahman*'.[1]

[1]Müller, *The Upanishads*, Pt. 2, *SBE*., XV, p. 24. Yama also promised Naciketas that the fire which forms a 'bridge' to the celestial world would henceforth be known as the Naciketas fire.

v. Uddālaka Āruṇi.

Nada 'Roarer, bellower, thunderer.' An epithet of a storm-cloud, a bull, horse, etc., as well as of a river when personified as a god.

v. Nadī II.

Nāda 'Sound or tone-vibration.' An important aspect of tantrism, many works (Tantras) being devoted to the study of *mantras* and the science of sound. Reality is believed to consist 'of an immensely complex web of vibrations and "resonances" . . . which all originate, in a logical not a temporal sense, from a single self-originated point of sound, the Nādabiṇḍu, analogous to the creative point in the centre of the Śrī Yantra'.[1] The innumerable vibration patterns are but modifications of the *nādabiṇḍu*.

[1]Rawson, *The Art of Tantra*, p. 195.

Nadī I. Name of a river when personified as a goddess. The differentiated forms of the river-goddesses in northern India are 'directly derived from that of the *yakṣī-dryad*, and this implies that the latter, despite the vegetal and apparently terrestrial habitat, was still primarily a spirit of the waters'.[1]

[1]Coomaraswamy, *Yakṣas*, pt. i, p. 55.

II. In tantrism *nadī* is the channel through 'which energies flow through the human subtle body'.[1]

[1]Rawson, *The Art of Tantra*, p. 207.

Nāga I. 'Snake.' In Indian mythology *nāga* is a general term for both snake and elephant. It is also applied to the mythical serpents Takṣaka, Śeṣa, Vāsuki; and to the serpent offspring of Kadrū. It was believed that man could communicate with the Nāga realm either through caverns or anthills.[1] Serpents are said to be the guardians of the mineral wealth of the earth. Viṣṇu's favourite symbolic animal is the snake Ananta.

Nāgas are sometimes portrayed as handsome men, or as half-man and half-snake, the top half being the torso of a man, the lower half a coiled snake.[2]

[1]Brodrick (ed.), *Animals in Archaeology*, p. 137.

[2]The Mesopotamian serpent-god was similarly depicted (ibid., p. 60).

v. Manasā; Bhogavatī.

II. The name of a people and their country—situated in eastern Assam, and described by L.A. Waddell[1] as part of the Burmese rugged mountain system, and chiefly peopled by tribes collectively called Nāgas. The wilder tribes inhabit the upper valleys, the more civilized tribes being mostly restricted to the tropical central valley fringing the Brahmaputra which connects them with the plains of India. The Nāgas are classified as brachycephalic Negritos from Africa and are among the earliest people to have come to India.[2] The term Nāga is also 'often applied by Tamil writers to a warlike race armed with bows and nooses and famous as freebooters.'[3]

Though traces of the Negrito survive in eastern Assam and in small areas of southern India, they appear to have been mostly killed off or absorbed by subsequent immigrants more advanced than themselves, such as the proto-Australoids, who were in turn partly absorbed by the Dravidians.

[1]'Tribes of the Brahmaputra Valley', *JRASB*., vol. LXIX, pt. iii, p. 8.

[2]*HCIP*., vol. I, p. 142.

[3]*CHI*., vol. I, p. 595.

III. A devotee of an Indian snake-cult,[1] the shrines of which are to be found in many parts of India, particularly in the South and in Bengal and Assam. Serpent-festivals are held at various times of the year according to local custom, one of the most popular being the *nāga-pañcamī*, held on the fifth day of the first half of the lunar month *śrāvaṇa*. These festivals are almost invariably conducted by a low caste villager, such as a potter, shoemaker or fisherman, though occasionally in Hinduized villages a *brahman* may act as priest. On the day of the festival the women of each family bring to the shrine an earthen or clay representation of a serpent, or a pot depicting a serpent, and later they pour offerings of milk and cereals into the snakes' holes. Householders, after giving portions of the daily food to *brahmins*, also throw some to dogs, insects, birds and serpents.[2]

In South India many houses have their own shrine which is often a grove reserved for snakes, consisting of trees, festooned with creepers, situated in a corner of the garden.[3] Often a stone with a snake depicted on it is set up. Similar stones are also erected in villages, often under a tree, and women desiring children visit them. Neglect of the snakes arouses their anger and may result in sickness in the household. Snakes were regarded as part of the property and 'transfer deeds made special mention of the family serpent as one of the articles sold along with the freehold'.[4] In Bengal and Assam the snake-cult rites may vary from village to village, but the devotees are generally united in their worship of the goddess Manasā (also called Viṣaharī 'remover of poison'), the ruler of serpents.

Serpent cults have existed in most countries, originating when early man was most susceptible to the influence of the mysterious and the uncanny. Thus the serpent, because of its curious gliding movement, its hypnotic eyes, its ability to disappear suddenly, the fatal consequences of its bite, and the casting of its skin, made it the subject of many myths and the object both of fear and veneration. This is particularly true of India, which possesses almost every known species of snake, and which has preserved either in its archaeological remains or in its literature an unbroken continuity of evidence of the existence of the snake-cult from the third millennium B.C. Although a serpent-cult is not mentioned in the *RV*.[5] there is ample evidence in the *AV*.[6] of its existence. The attitude of the *RV*. seers to the serpent-cult is referred to by Karmarkar,[7] who considers that the introduction of the Indra-Vṛtra myth was the first step in the Āryanization of the snake-cult of the conquered by the conquerors. The Vedic hymns show that Vṛtra, the enemy of Indra and the *devas*, was represented as an *asura*, *dāsa*, or a *dānava*, and as one of the serpent race of Ahi (*RV*. I.32,11). There are references in the *Bṛhat Saṁ*. (XLV.14; XLVII.25.31,62) to the drawing and worshipping of figures of *nāgas*. Pearls were believed to be in the bodies (or heads) of snakes belonging to the family of Takṣaka and Vāsuki, and to possess the power to cause rain (LXXX.25–6). Those countries in which *nāgas* reside are certain to be drought-free (LIII.111).

The Śaiva Liṅgāyats worship snakes, which are often depicted with Śiva. The serpent-cult also penetrated Buddhism, Jainism, Vaiṣṇavism, etc., where the ambivalent attitude towards them is seen. Viṣṇu's bird vehicle (*vāhana*) Garuḍa is the implacable enemy of snakes; the child Kṛṣṇa subdues the Nāga Kāliya. On the other hand Viṣṇu rests on the snake Śeṣa in the interval between two periods of creation. But here Śeṣa and the cosmic ocean on which he floats are manifestations of Viṣṇu himself.

According to the Purāṇas the Nāgas were born of Kaśyapa and Kadrū, but *Manu* (I.35–7) states they were created by the ten great *ṛṣis*, Marīci, Atri, Aṅgiras, Pulastya, etc.

In Indian art the cobra has always been a dominant motif. It appears on the seals of Mohenjo-daro, which suggests that either the cobra was an emblem of a proto-Śiva, or it was the totem of devotees who worshipped the god of the cobra.[8]

[1]Though serpent cults existed among the Nāga tribes of eastern Assam from remote times, the term *nāga* when used to denote devotees of the cult has no ethnic significance.

[2]J. Auboyer, *Daily Life in Ancient India*, p. 194.

[3]W. Logan, *Manual of Malabar*, Madras (1887), I, p. 183.

[4]C.K. Menon, *Calcutta Review* (July, 1901), cxiii, 21ff.

[5]Vṛtra in the *RV.* may represent the maleficent aspect of snakes, and Ahirbudhnya the beneficent (*HCIP.*, vol. II, p. 472).

[6]*AV.*, V.13; VI.12; VII.56; VIII.7; XI.6, etc.

[7]A.P. Karmarkar, *Religions of India*, vol. I, p. 159, cited by Maity, *Historical Studies in the Cult of the Goddess Manasā*, p. 16.

[8]Maity, op. cit., p. 13.

v. Janamejaya; Nahuṣa; Paidva; Pātāla; Netraviṣa; Nāgadru; Nāgapāśa; Viṣavidyā; Sarpamaṇi; Bhogavatī I, II, IV; Bhūmiya.

Nāgadru A species of Euphorbia[1] sacred to Manasā, the goddess of snakes.

[1]The Euphorbiaceae species of plants, trees, shrubs and herbs has the common property of exciting which varies in degree from a mere stimulant to the most dangerous poison. Balfour states that E. antiquorum (from which is produced the drug euphorium), and E. ligularia are sacred to Manasā (*CI.*, vol. I, p. 1061).

Nāgaloka The underworld realm or sphere of serpents (*nāgas*) which is also called Pātāla.

Nāgāntaka 'Destroyer of serpents.' An epithet of Garuḍa, the enemy of snakes (*nāgas*).

Nāgapañcamī A festival sacred to the *nāgas*, held on the fifth day of the light half of the month *śrāvaṇa*, or in the dark half of the month *āṣāḍha*.

v. Nāga III.

Nāgapāśa Also called Viśvajit, the name of Varuṇa's favourite weapon. A magical noose (*pāśa*) used in battle; originally it may have been a weapon used by the Nāgas and later adopted by Indo-Āryan tribes.

Nāgara One of the three styles of Indian architecture,[1] the Nāgara being distinguished by its quadrangular shape; the Vesara by its round shape, and the Drāviḍa by its octagonal or hexagonal shape.[2] These styles are considered to have originated in particular areas, the boundaries of which are not now clearly traceable.

[1]T. Bhattacharyya, *Canons of Indian Art*, p. 384.

[2]*DHA.*, p. 300.

v. Mānasāra.

Nāgī A female snake (*nāga*) and the name of an aquatic snake-spirit symbolizing 'both the primordial sacrality concentrated in the ocean and the earliest aboriginal cultural forms'.[1]

In South India the snake-goddess is called Durgāmma, and her shrine is built over a snake-stone situated near a *nīm* tree. A silver cobra's head represents her in domestic worship. In Bengal she is the goddess Manasā. Women offer milk to her in the hope that she will protect their children from snake-bite.

[1]Eliade, *Yoga*, p. 351.

Nagnajit A writer on temple architecture mentioned in the *Bṛhat Saṁ.* (LVII.4; 15). Utpala refers to some of his works including the *Prāsādalakṣaṇa* and the *Citralakṣaṇa*, the latter dealing, *inter alia*, with various kinds of weapons.[1]

[1]A.M. Shastri, *India as Seen in the Bṛhat. Saṁ.*, pp. 457f.

Nahuṣa The word occurs in some *RV.* passages as *nāhuṣa*, an adjective meaning 'neighbouring' (V.73, etc.).[1] Other passages refer to the Nāhuṣa tribes (VIII.6,24) and to the noble offspring of Nahuṣa (V.12,6). But there is no clear indication of the identity of Nahuṣa himself or his tribe, nor of his relationship to the five principal Āryan tribes alluded to in (VI.46,7). A single reference to Yayāti as a son of Nahuṣa occurs in a late passage (X.63,1), which may have some historical validity and be the basis of the Nahuṣa and Yayāti legends of the *MBh.* and the Purāṇas.

According to the *VP.* (IV.10) a king called Nahuṣa had six sons,[2] one of whom was Yayāti who succeeded to the throne. Yadu his eldest son was the ancestor of Kṛṣṇa, and Puru, the youngest, the ancestor of the Pauravas and Kauravas. The *MBh.* reverts to the early Vedic Nahuṣa and states that he had by great effort attained the rank of Indra. In keeping with this position Indra's wife Śacī suggested that his litter should in future be born by *ṛṣis*, but they rejected the suggestion and cursed Nahuṣa to fall from his high estate and be reborn as a serpent.[3] Yudhiṣṭhira, the Pāṇḍu prince, is then anachronistically introduced to deliver a series of homilies to Nahuṣa, designed to show that even the great may not insult *brāhmaṇas* with impunity. Finally the humbled Nahuṣa is freed from his serpent form. But the connexion of the Vedic Nahuṣa with Puru, as related in the Epic, is a 'tradition which must be deemed inaccurate'.[4]

[1]VI., vol. I, p. 448.

[2]Hopkins suggests that all Nahuṣa's sons may have been stars (*EM*., p. 53).

[3]Another account states that Agastya and other great *ṛṣis* bore Nahuṣa's chariot across the sky, but Agastya, who was short, stumbled and Nahuṣa touched him with his foot, whereupon the *ṛṣi* cursed him to become a serpent. Yet another version is that by extreme austerities (*tapas*) he acquired the sovereignty of the three worlds and took possession of Indra's throne, but because of his lack of humility was finally ruined (*Manu*, VII.41).

[4]*VI.*, vol. II, p. 187.

v. Netraviṣa.

Naigameṣa A ram-headed demon especially injurious to children. When a child is attacked offerings should be made to Naigameṣa at the foot of a *vaṭa* tree (*Suś. Saṁ.*, III, pp. 159f.). Coomaraswamy[1] calls him antelope-headed and states that he is connected with procreation in both Hindu and Jaina mythology, whilst in the Epic he is a 'goat-faced form of Agni'.

[1]*Yakṣas*, pt. i, p. 12.

Naigameya A form of Skanda, also said to be his son or playfellow.[1] When Skanda is described as goat-headed (*chāgavaktra*), he is then called Naigameya.[2]

[1]*SED.*

[2]*DHI.*, p. 363; cf. p. 562.

Naikaṣeya(s) or **Nikaṣātmaja(s)** The name of the carnivorous demons also called *piśitāśanas* descended from Rāvaṇa's mother Nikaṣā or Naikaṣī.

Nairṛta 'Belonging or consecrated to Nirṛti', goddess of decay, destruction and death.

Nairṛta(s) I. The demon offspring of Nirṛti[1] the goddess of misery, decay and death.

[1]The prefix *ni*, meaning down, back, in, into, within, is prefixed to verbs or nouns; in the latter case it also has the meaning of negation or privation. Cf. Ger. *ni-dar*, *ni-der*, *nieder*; AS. *ni-ther*; E. *nei-ther*.

II. Name of one of the Lokapālas.

Nakṣatra Puruṣa The anthropomorphic form of the *nakṣatras* (asterisms) when represented collectively (*Bṛhat Saṁ.*, CIV.1–6). Each part of the Nakṣatra Puruṣa should be worshipped during the ascendancy of its corresponding *nakṣatra*, which will ensure to the worshipper the fulfilment of all his objects and desires. This stellar deity was also worshipped for the attainment of a fine physique in the next life (*Bṛhat Saṁ.*, CIV.1–13).

The *AGP.* (196,1–7) describes the Nakṣatra Puruṣa as 'an imaginary figure whose body is supposed to be composed of the clusters of asterisms, grouped so as to form its different parts'. It should be invoked and worshipped in a pitcher filled with molasses.

Hari is said to manifest himself as the Nakṣatra Puruṣa.

Nakṣatra(s) A star or a cluster of stars, or a constellation which represents the 27 divisions of the lunar zodiac. In later treatises they numbered 28 independent asterisms, each used in astronomical observation, or as a basis for the casting of horoscopes. The *nakṣatras* represent also the phases of the moon during its monthly orbit of the earth.[1]

The '*nakṣatras* were used to follow the motions of the sun, as well as those of the moon and the planets. The calendars of the Vedic and later periods were . . . luni-solar, for Indian astrologers have always looked upon astronomical phenomena as indivisible'.[2] Only one passage in the *RV.* (X.85,13), occurring in possibly interpolative material, refers to *nakṣatras*, viz., to *maghā* and the *arjunīs* (later called *phalgunīs*). In the *AV.* (XIX.7,1–5; 8,1–7) the *nakṣatras* are implored to grant blessings and wellbeing. In the Brāhmaṇas the lunar zodiac was fully recognized, the stellar groups serving to mark the divisions of the lunar path, and hence the epithet *ma*, 'the measurer', applied to the moon.

To accord with the moon's sidereal revolution (approximately 27⅓ days), it was necessary to have twenty-seven *nakṣatras*, but as the synodal revolution, or interval from one new moon to the next, is about 29½ days, an additional *nakṣatra* called *abhijit* was introduced.[3] Half of them were designated '*deva*', and half '*yama*', the former being regarded as lucky, the other fourteen, because of their association with the waning moon, as unlucky.[4] A particular *nakṣatra* was linked to every occurrence and regarded as an astrological element which must be registered daily for the casting of horoscopes. Thus one *nakṣatra* was propitious for marriage, another at the commencement of a boy's education, others at the beginning of the ploughing season, and so forth. When a natal asterism was menaced by unfavourable planetary conjunctions, propitiatory abstinences were observed. Festivals for the dead were also related to a particular *nakṣatra*.[5]

Abhijit was introduced as the twenty-eighth *nakṣatra*, but was eliminated and the lunar zodiac divided into twenty-seven equal periods, called *bhogas*, or arcs of 800′ each, which Paurāṇic legends personified as the twenty-seven wives of the Moon (Candra). They were the daughters of Dakṣa (representing ritual skill), and hence their association with the correct performance of sacrificial rites.[6]

The nomenclature of the Hindu lunar signs shows considerable variation prior to their final systematization.[7] Thus, though the Indian lunar zodiac originally opened with *kṛttikā* (Pleiades) as the sign of the vernal equinox, it was later relegated to third place and superseded by the *aśvinī*, possibly as the result of Greek influence. But for ritual purposes, the Pleiades, with Agni as the presiding deity, continued to be the first sign.

[1]Often referred to as the moon's light and dark periods, or to its alternate waxing and waning.

[2]Singhal, *India*, vol. I, p. 163; v. also Needham, *Science and Civilization in China*, vol. III, pp. 173ff.

[3]This was eliminated about the twelfth century A.D.

[4]In South Indian ceremonies the performance of *nakṣatra pūjā* is believed to destroy evil omens, drive away foreign armies, pacify the five gross elements, give success, avert untimely death and destroy the malign influence of the nine planets (*navagrahas*) (Diehl, *Instrument and Purpose*, p. 161).

[5]*AGP.*, CXXV.

[6]The highest gods and the *pitṛs* dwell beyond the solar world in the sphere of the stars, and contact with these regions can only be attained by means of sacrificial rites.

[7]The names of the *nakṣatras* are: Aśvinī, Bharaṇī, Kṛttikā, Rohiṇī, Mṛgaśiras, Ārdrā, Punarvasū, Puṣyā, Āśleṣā, Maghā, Pūrva-phalgunī, Uttara-phalgunī, Hastā, Citrā, Svātī, Viśākhā, Anurādhā, Jyeṣṭhā, Mūlā, Pūrvāṣāḍhā, Śravaṇā, Dhaniṣṭhā or Śraviṣṭhā, Śatabhiṣaj, Pūrvabhadrapadā, Uttara-bhadrapadā, Revatī, Abhijit. For further information v. G.E. Gibson, 'The Vedic Nakṣatras and the Zodiac', in *Semitic and Oriental Studies*, University of California, 1951, pp. 149–66; v. also Filliozat in *Ancient and Medieval Science*, pp. 143ff.; and *CHI.*, I, p. 140.

v. Jyotiṣa; Mṛgaśiras; Māsa.

Nakula I. One of the twin Pāṇḍu princes, his brother being Sahadeva, the sons of Mādrī, second wife of King Pāṇḍu. The paternity of the two brothers is mythically ascribed to Nāsatya, one of the twin Aśvins.[1] Nakula was trained in the military arts and the training of horses by Droṇa, and later became the *rāja* of Virāṭa's master of horse.

[1]According to another account, the Aśvins were reborn as Nakula and Sahadeva.

v. Mahābhārata.

II. An ichneumon or mongoose (the enemy of snakes and mice) is said to be able to cut a snake in two and then rejoin the pieces (*AV.*, VI.139,5). It also protects itself against snake-venom by means of the plant called *nākulī* (VIII.7,23).

Nākulī The 'ichneumon plant' (Salmalia malabarica),[1] believed to provide the ichneumon with an antidote to snake venom. Every part of the plant or tree is used by practitioners of Āyurveda.

[1]But it has been shown experimentally that 'neither the flower nor the fruit has any antidotal value against snake or scorpion venom' (Blatter, *et al.*, *Some Beautiful Indian Trees*, p. 125). This is confirmed by Balfour who cites an unpleasant experiment carried out by three British officers in 1863 at Trichinopoly, in which a mongoose was bitten by a cobra, and though deliberately deprived of the *nākulī*, suffered no ill effects, nor did it show any fear of the reptile. After a prolonged fight it killed the cobra (*CI.*, vol. II, p. 977).

Nala I. The King of Niṣada, whose kingdom was situated in the wild forests of the Bhīl country. His bravery, good looks and virtues were matched by the beauty and accomplishments of his bride Damayantī, the daughter of Bhīma, King of Vidarbha. The account of their life appears in the *Mahābhārata* and is basically a simple tale of romantic love, intrigue, adversity and the final triumph of love, interwoven with moralistic propaganda.

II. A chief of a South Indian tribe to whom is ascribed the building of the causeway between India and Laṅkā (Ceylon) over which Rāma and his army were able to cross. His skill earned him the reputation of being able to make stones float on water, and hence his designation, 'son of Viśvakarman' the divine architect (*Rām.*, 1.17.11; 6.22,44).

v. Vānara.

Nalakūbera or **Nalakūvera** A son of Kubera and Ṛddhi, and one of the most overbearing of Rudra's attendants. When drunk he and his brother Maṇigrīva seduced some girls on the banks of the Ganges, for which Nārada cursed them to became trees for a hundred divine years. At the end of this period Kṛṣṇa would release them by uprooting the trees.

Nālāyira-Prabandham v. Ācārya II.

Nāmakīrtana The constant repetition of the name of a god, by which an ecstatic state may be attained. The magical potency of a name is so great that even a 'blasphemous' repetition of Kṛṣṇa's name may secure beatitude. This repetition of a god's names and epithets is a well-known liturgical form of praise and adoration, and also a means of meditatively identifying oneself with the god.

v. Nāman.

Nāman[1] 'Name.' As a means of distinguishing things or persons from one another, and of describing them, name-giving has obviously a remote origin. The numerous customs and conventions relating to it are woven into a mythology which has always underlined its importance. Thus in India it is essential to call a man by his right name, still more so a divinity when invoked, and hence the belief that the mere repetition of the divine name will ensure liberation (*mokṣa*). It may also be said to have creative power,[2] for by means of Name and Form the impersonal *brahman* was able to descend again into the world he had created (*ŚBr.*, XI.2.3,3).

In the *soma* sacrifice a man consecrates himself as Agni; if he hates a man he should mumble his enemy's name, and having become Agni, will burn him up (*Kauṣ. Br.*, VII.3).

The choice of names is limitless, and varies according to regional custom and belief. Thus a boy may be named after a god, or a local or national hero, in the hope that the child may share his respective qualities.[3] Similarly, girls may be named after a goddess, or simply after flowers or gems. Astrology also provides names, the lunar mansion (*nakṣatra*), or the zodiacal sign under which the child is born may be chosen. A change of status may also lead to the assumption of a new name, as when a prince or usurper is consecrated as king, or it may be applied contemptuously by his enemies.[4]

Names may also be augmented or replaced by epithets which reflect an outstanding quality, or be a form of flattery, like 'Piya-dasī' (Beloved of the gods), applied to the Emperor Aśoka. Many names are derived from those of holy places, or have an ethnic or tribal significance, such as Nāga, Rākṣasa, Vānara, etc., or refer to occupation or status, or have originated as caste distinctions.

Manu (II.31–2) declares that 'the first part of a *brahmin*'s name should denote something auspicious; of a *kṣatriya*, power; of a *vaiśya*, industriousness; but that of a *śūdra* should reflect his menial state. The second part of the name of a *brahmin* should imply happiness; of a *kṣatriya*, protection; of a *vaiśya*, prosperity; of a *śūdra*, service.[5] The *VP.* (III.10) states that the name of a *brahman* boy should consist of an even number of syllables, neither too long nor too short, and should not contain too many long vowels. For a girl the name should be easy to pronounce, be pleasing and auspicious, and end in long vowels, such as Radhā, Lakṣmī, etc.

The rules relating to name-giving in some Gṛhya Sūtras, such as the *Gobhila* (II.8,9–16) and *Śāṅkhāyana* (I.24,1–16), state that a boy should have two names, but the *Hiraṇyakeśin* adds a third, which should be secret. This is the most important name, being regarded as 'a ritually generative force',[6] and as the sole part of the individual which does not perish at death.[7] The secret name is thus distinguished from the other names, and is usually known only to its bearer and his preceptor (*guru*) or family priest by whom it (and a secret *mantra*) are whispered into a boy's ear at his initiation ceremony (*upanayana*). The name is also entered in his horoscope, generally in such a way that it is not easily recognizable should the horoscope fall into other hands. This traditional association of personality and name is further indicated by the reluctance of many Hindu women to address the husband by name, and the husband's use of 'mother of so-and-so' when addressing a wife.[8]

In all cultures the name has a mystical and magical importance, being regarded as the 'essence' of the personality, and as such must be guarded from strangers. To know the name of a person or thing is to know the thing itself, and thus be able to control and manoeuvre it to suit one's purpose (*AV.*, VI.83,2).[9] The intimate connexion of the name and its bearer can be seen in the Jewish fear of uttering the name of the god Yahwè, which it was believed would cause a dangerous 'discharge' of divine power.

According to the *ŚBr.* (VI.1.3,9) the giving of a name to a boy frees him from evil, and the greater the number of names the greater the amount of evil thereby removed. The gods have many names and epithets. Viṣṇu has a thousand and Śiva a thousand and eight,[10] the repetition of which bestows great merit; Agni has thirteen, denoting the thirteen months of the lunar year and the thirteen layers and fillings of the fire-altar (IX.3.3,9); in *RV.* (VIII.69,9) Indra is requested to take a fourth, i.e., his sacrificial name.

[1]The etymology is uncertain, but a word cognate with it occurs in almost all IE. languages. Cf. E. *name*; L. *nomen*; Gr. *onoma*, etc.

[2]According to the ancient Egyptian texts of the Heliopolitan priesthood (c. 2480–2137 B.C.) the 'pre-existent ultimate source of all things was created by the utterance of his name and so became Khepri "he who exists by himself"' (S.A.B. Mercer, *Pyramid Texts*, 1466 b-d; 1587 a-d, vols 1–4, 1953). According to the Akkadian Creation Epic the fifty great gods conferred on 'Marduk his fifty names assigning to him the powers of all the gods in the pantheon' (E.O. James, *Tree of Life*, p. 138).

[3]Thus for boys: Devadatta (God-given), Devadāsa (Servant of God), Viṣṇuputra (Son of Viṣṇu); for girls: Lakṣmī, Śrī, Padmā, etc.

[4]Cf. Divodāsa, 'Time-server' (*HCIP.*, II, p. 286n.). Cf. also the taking of religious names by Buddhist monks and Roman Catholic monks and nuns.

[5]The name-giving rite (*nāmadheya* or *nāmakaraṇa*), performed on the tenth or twelfth day after birth, was a solemn religious act, fraught with important consequences.

[6]Auboyer, *Daily Life in Ancient India*, p. 291.

[7]The ancient Egyptians similarly identified the secret or

personal name with the soul; the modern European custom of a family name as well as a given name identifies the individual with the magical power of the family.

[8]Crooke, *Things Indian*, p. 344.

[9]Cf. the Gnostic belief that when each soul knew the names of demons they could then control them (Allegro, *The Sacred Mushroom and the Cross*, p. 161).

[10]Moslems have ninety names for Allah, and Christians about a hundred for God. According to Aristotle Zeus had more than a hundred names.

In India repetition of the names of the god ensures the efficacy of the rite being performed. Farnell points out that the various epithets or designations of an ancient Greek deity in liturgical formulae, may come to form separate deities, 'for in semi-magical ritual the name is all-important and the identity of individuality tends to disappear through variety of names' (*Cults*, vol. II, p. 18, n.a).

Gonda points out that Viṣṇu and Śiva have about eighty epithets and surnames in common, some of which also belonged to ancient deities (*VS.*, p. 16).

Nammāḷvar v. Āḷvār(s).

Namuci The name of a demon and descendant of Kaśyapa and Danu (the mythical progenitors of the non-Āryan Indian tribes called *dānavas*), but he is specifically referred to in the *VP.* (I.21) as the son of Vipracitti and Siṁhikā, the sister of the *daitya* king, Hiraṇyakaśipu.

Indra having defeated all the *dānavas* except Namuci, found himself overpowered by the latter, who agreed to release him on condition that he promised never to slay him by day or night, with staff or bow, with hand or fist, nor with anything dry or wet. Namuci took advantage of this promise to rob Indra of his vital source of strength, the *soma* drink. Indra besought the Aśvins and Sarasvatī to help him regain his power, and as a reward promised to share it with them. Whereupon the Aśvins and Sarasvatī poured out a 'foam[1] of water' to serve as a thunderbolt (*vajra*), which is neither dry nor wet, and with it Indra cut off Namuci's head at dawn. In his head was blood and *soma* juice.[2]

Another version is given in the *MBh.*, where Namuci is said to have been Indra's friend, but Indra killed him and cut off his head. Then, overcome with remorse, Indra went to Brahmā for advice and was directed to perform an appropriate sacrifice and to purify himself by touching the waters at the confluence of the Aruṇā and Sarasvatī rivers, and thus expiate his sins.

[1]Foam is considered identical with lead (v. *Kauśika sūtra* 8.18 for list of substances called 'lead' of which foam is one). Heesterman suggests that Namuci in the *surā* cycle is the restrainer whose death releases the invigorating fluids. Namuci 'plays the same part as Vṛtra in the *soma* cycle. Indra's freeing himself from Namuci may therefore well be compared with his victory over Vṛtra as signifying his birth' (*Ancient Indian Royal Consecration*, p. 110).

[2]For the myth of Namuci in connexion with ritual v. Bloomfield, *JAOS.*, XV, pp. 143f.; in the *MBh.*, v. L. Feer, 'Vṛtra et Namuci dans le MBh.', *Revue de l'histoire des religions*, xiv, 291–307, 1886. In a later myth Indra is replaced by Viṣṇu (Gonda, *VS.*, p. 136).

Nanda I. A cowherd who with his wife Yaśodā became the foster-parents of the infant Kṛṣṇa. To protect him from the attacks of the demons who molest babies, the herdsmen and women threw balls of turmeric at him and sprinkled themselves with butter, curds and milk, which suggests some kind of fertility festival.

For attempting to bathe in the Yamunā river at an unsuitable time, Nanda was seized by an *asura* follower of Varuṇa, but was freed with the assistance of Kṛṣṇa.

II. Name of one of Kubera's nine treasures (*nidhis*).

III. Name of the dynasty which succeeded Ajātaśatru and his line to the throne of Magadha.

v. Pāṭaliputra; Maurya(s).

Nandaka 'Gladdening.' The name of Kṛṣṇa's sword, symbolizing true knowledge and hence wisdom (*VP.*, I.22). It cuts away evil caused by ignorance and false knowledge (*avidyā*), as does the sword of the Mahāyāna Buddhist *bodhisattva* Mañjuśri.

According to the *AGP.* (245,14f.) Nandaka was given by the fire-god Agni to Hari (Viṣṇu) so that he might slay the demon who was obstructing the sacrifice, but the demon gave himself hundreds of extra arms. Finally Hari killed him and cut his body into several pieces which were transformed into iron as they fell to earth. These Hari then blessed, saying, 'Be you converted into weapons on earth'.

Nandaka is one of the eight (or nine) treasures (*nidhis*) of Kubera, and is also one of the eight personified virtues or qualities which may be conferred on the individual (*Mārk. P.*, 68, 4–46).

Nandana The mythical grove of Indra in which grows the divine *pārijāta* tree. Here the good dwell in ethereal form, the reward of their meritorious actions when on earth. The *VP.* (II.2) states that this garden is situated in the region of Ilāvṛta, and from it came the flowers presented by the gods to the goddess Caṇḍikā (Durgā) after her defeat of the demon Mahiṣa (*Mārk. P.*, 84, 27).

v. Mahiṣa II.

Nāndīmukha 'Having a cheerful face.' A class of ancestors (*pitṛs*)[1] for whom a particular *śrāddha* is performed by the father on the birth of a son (*Mārk. P.*,

30, 4–5), or to celebrate an occasion of good fortune, when meat-balls mixed with curds, barley and jujubes are offered to the Nāndīmukhas (*VP.*, III.10 and 13).

[1]These comprise a man's father, grandfather and great grandfather, and his maternal grand, great grand, and great, great grandfather (*AGP.*, 117, 38–43).

Nandin 'The Happy One.'[1] The name of the bull, the vehicle (*vāhana*) of Śiva. It is represented in South Indian temples 'by the recumbent bull placed in front of the chief shrine',[2] or just outside the hall leading to it.

Although the bull as a symbol of fertility and strength[3] is frequently referred to in Vedic literature, and was worshipped in several civilizations of the Middle East, there is no clear evidence of a connexion between Nandin and any early bull-cult.[4] Nonetheless, Coomaraswamy considers that the bull was the theriomorphic form of Śiva, which later became his vehicle when Śiva was represented anthropomorphically.[5] Heimann suggests that the animal form expresses particular qualities more effectively than is possible anthropomorphically.[6]

[1]Also applied to Viṣṇu in the *MBh.* Nandin is also called Bhṛṅgi, etc., and is the embodiment of moral law (*dharma*).

[2]H. K. Shastri, *South Indian Images of Gods and Goddesses*, p. 162; *DHI.*, p. 153.

[3]The Hurrian god Teshub was sometimes depicted standing on a bull representing vital force.

[4]But judging by the Indus Valley seals depicting bulls, it is probable that there was some kind of bull-cult in that area.

[5]*HIIA.*, p. 45.

[6]*Facets*, p. 116. Gonda considers that Nandin represents the fertility aspect of Śiva (*VS.*, p. 76). Up to the present century seed-drills were sometimes ornamented with carved figures of Nandin, Hanumat, the *liṅgam*, etc., all denoting fertility (E. Thurston, *Omens and Superstitions of Southern India*, p. 304).

v. Kāmadhenu.

Nandinī The mythical 'Cow of abundance', often used to denote Northern India as the land of plenty. Nandinī yields all manner of desirable things and her milk rejuvenates mankind for a thousand years.

Nandinī was the offspring (or mother) of Surabhi, (the Cow of Plenty), owned by the *ṛṣi* Vasiṣṭha.

v. Viśvāmitra; Kāmadhenu, n.1.

Nandivaktra v. Pañcānana.

Nara 'Man.' Nara is the general name for 'man' in the *RV.* (I. 178,3; II.34,6, etc.) and the *AV.* (II.9,2; IX.1,3, etc.), but it is seldom used in the later Saṁhitās and Brāhmaṇas. In post-Vedic language Nara sometimes denotes the first man, the progenitor of mankind or secondary creator,[1] and is variously designated according to regional views or those of different priestly schools. But such developments can usually be traced to a legendary or quasi-historical source, and in this instance to Nara and Nārāyaṇa,[2] two eminent *ṛṣis*,[3] the sons of Dharma (Righteousness) and Ahiṁsā (Non-injury), noted for their extreme asceticism and holiness. Their apotheosis as emanations of Viṣṇu (*Bhāg. P.*, 1.2,4, etc.) and the identification of Nārāyaṇa with the Self-existent *brahman* is explained in *Manu* (I.10), which states that 'the waters (i.e., the primeval waters) are called '*nārāḥ*', for they are indeed the offspring of Nara, and his first dwelling place '*ayana*', whence his name Nārāyaṇa,[4] or 'he whose place of motion was the waters'.

[1]Cf. Svayambhū and the role of Manu Svāyambhuva, Prajāpati and Brahmā.

[2]In some Purs. Nārāyaṇa appears as the son of Nara, but the *MBh.* refers to them as brothers. In another existence they are said to have been reborn as Kṛṣṇa and Arjuna (*VP.*, IV.1).

[3]A niche on the outer western face of the Daśāvatāra temple of Deogarh depicts the two *ṛṣis* seated in their peaceful *āśrama*. v. also Banerjea, *RAA.*, p. 40.

[4]This punning explanation of Nārāyaṇa and his identification with *brahman* occurs also in other Purs. (*VP.*, I.4; *AGP.*, 49, 23–4).

Nārada The name of a mythical seer mentioned in the *AV.* (V. 19,9; XII.4,16, etc.). The name occurs in other texts as that of a priest and teacher. But the numerous references to a seer called Nārada appear in various works, composed over several centuries. Śaṅkarācārya explains this apparent coincidence by stating that such perfected beings, though freed from the bonds of ignorance and illusion, continue to be reborn until their divine mission has been accomplished.[1]

Such an explanation gave ample opportunity to the composers of the *MBh.* and Purāṇas to fill in any gaps in the life or lives of Nārada. He is thus said to be one of the Prajāpatis, born from Brahmā's throat or forehead; or a son of Kaśyapa and one of Dakṣa's daughters; or a son of Viśvāmitra, etc.

When Nārada heard of Dakṣa's plan for his five thousand sons to people the earth, he dissuaded them, and so incurred Dakṣa's curse. The sons, realizing their inability to carry out the plan, dispersed aimlessly to other lands and were heard of no more.

Nārada figures in other stories, particularly in that relating to King Kaṁsa whose death at the hands of Kṛṣṇa he foretold (*VP.*, V.1). Some musical works are attributed to him as well as the invention of the *vīṇā* (lute).

[1]S. Radhakrishnan, *Brahma Sūtra*, p. 487.

v. Haryaśvas; Nāradīya Dharmaśāstra.

Nāradīya Dharmaśāstra 'Institutes of Nārada.' A minor law book by an unknown author, but which purports to be by the ancient seer Nārada, doubtless to give it added authority. Internal evidence alone refutes the claim and suggests that it was composed about A.D. 400–500, though it contains laws belonging to a much earlier period.[1] It is specifically a law treatise, unencumbered by disquisitions on the creation of the world, or by theological speculations, purificatory rules, or the question of rebirth and ultimate liberation, which characterize the Institutes of Manu (*Manusmṛti*).

[1]J. Jolly, *Nāradīya Dharmaśāstra*, Intro.

v. Yājñavalkya.

Naraka I. 'Hell', 'place of torment'. One of the hells personified as a son of Nirṛti.

There are said to be many hells; the numbers vary according to different works. The *Mārk. P.* (XII) mentions six; *Manu* (IV.88–90), twenty-one; *Brahmāṇḍa P.* (IV.2.146–50), twenty-seven; and the *AGP.* (352,13f.), twenty-eight, situated under the seventh nether world.[1] These hells lie one above the other, each having one hundred and forty-four sub-divisions. The 'warders' have faces of cats, owls, jackals, vultures, etc.

[1]The Hindu and Buddhist 'hells' are not places of eternal torment, for after the necessary period their inhabitants are reborn either as lower or higher beings, according to their *karman*.

II. Name of a demon, the son of Viṣṇu and Bhūmi (the Earth-goddess), hence his metronymic Bhauma.[1]

Naraka stole Aditi's magic earrings (which were sources of *amṛta* and removers of grief), but at the request of the gods Kṛṣṇa killed him and recovered the jewels which he presented to Sūrya. According to the *VP.* (V.31,36) Naraka also stole Varuṇa's royal umbrella, and demanded Indra's elephant Airāvata, but Indra commanded Kṛṣṇa to cut Naraka in two. Later the spoils of Naraka's city were distributed among Kṛṣṇa's followers, and all the women taken to Kṛṣṇa's harem.

[1]Gonda, *Aspects* (pp. 141f.), suggests that Naraka mainly represents dung, i.e., fertility.

v. Mura; Vajra.

Narasiṁha The man-lion *avatāra* of Viṣṇu, the upper part of the body being a lion, the lower, a man (*AGP.*, 276, 11–12). The ruler Hiraṇyakaśipu was greatly incensed by his son Prahlāda's[1] unswerving adherence to Viṣṇu, and for this reason persecuted him cruelly.[2]

Narasiṁha is the embodiment of valour as a divine attribute, and hence is especially suitable for worship by rulers and warriors (*kṣatriyas*). He is also said to embody the verses of the *Yajurveda* from which spring strength and courage;[3] he is invoked to protect his worshippers from the incantations (*mantras*) of enemies (*AGP.*, 63,3). Two days before the commencement of battle, Narasiṁha should be worshipped, and also on the morning of the second day (236,24).

[1]The Narasiṁha myth has been recast and transformed a number of times. In the *Bhagavadgītā* Prahlāda is a manifestation of Kṛṣṇa's power, which was personified and 'became the principal character of the myth of Viṣṇu's man-lion *avatāra*, to which he originally did not belong' (J. Gonda, *VS.*, p. 104). In the original version he became an *avatāra* to punish the *daitya* king for his dethronement of the gods (ibid., p. 105).

[2]For Hiraṇyakaśipu's reiterated attempts to destroy Prahlāda and his final repentance and reunion with his son, v. *VP.*, I, Chs. 17–20. This work mentions Narasiṁha's slaying of Hiraṇyakaśipu, but gives no details.

[3]*HP.*, p. 169. Narasiṁha is sometimes worshipped exclusively by kings (Banerjea, *RAA.*, p. 38). When frog-fat is consecrated with Narasiṁha's *mantra* and rubbed on the body, it enables one to walk unscathed through fire (*AGP.*, 306,18). v. Maṇḍūka for the supposed cooling properties of frogs.

v. Śarabha.

Nārāyaṇa An archetypal personification of solar or cosmic energy and of creative power identified with the solar Viṣṇu, the symbol of spiritual enlightenment, the interpretation given in the *gāyatrī* hymn (*RV.*, III.62,10). The name is said to be derived from '*narāḥ*', the primeval waters (the source of all life), and '*ayana*', the abode of the creator who moves upon the waters and periodically renews the universe, a belief common to other ancient river-civilizations.[1] Of the several Indian creation theories, held regionally or advanced by independent priestly schools, that relating to the role of Nārāyaṇa, and to the action of the sun upon the waters is possibly a more rational explanation of the appearance of life than some others, and also suggests the natural relationship between the Vedic solar Viṣṇu and the Viṣṇu of the Purāṇas. This is indicated when the world dissolves into its formless (i.e. undifferentiated) state at the end of the age.[2] Viṣṇu then is said to rest on the cosmic serpent Śeṣa, which floats on the primeval waters. When the next age is due to begin, Viṣṇu (Nārāyaṇa) awakes, and re-creates the world. This myth has naturally given rise to many applications, not the least being to the spiritual awakening of the devotee who meditates on Viṣṇu and his many aspects, including that of Nārāyaṇa.

Thus from being just another theory of cosmogonic renewal, Nārāyaṇa became the epitome of them all. Hence it was only a matter of time for Brahmā to be superseded by Nārāyaṇa, and to be acknowledged by both Vaiṣṇavas and Śaivas to be the manifestation of the Universal Essence (*ātman*) which is in all things and is all things.[3] He is invoked in the eight-syllabled *mantra*: 'Om! Namo Nārāyaṇāya'.

According to the *Mārk. P.* (IV. 43–59) Nārāyaṇa lives in quadruple form: The first is inscrutable; the wise see it as bright and covered with garlands of flame; to devotees it is perfection and transcends all attributes; as Vāsudeva it is devoid of egoism. The second is called Śeṣa, who in serpent form supports the world on his head. The third is the active form in which Nārāyaṇa 'descends' to earth in various incarnations (*avatāras*) to re-establish righteousness, etc. The fourth abides in water, reclining on a couch formed by the coils of the serpent Ananta.

[1]Cf. Genesis I.2, 'And darkness was upon the face of the deep; and the spirit of God moved upon the face of the waters'.

[2]'Nārāyaṇa is this primeval universe. He at the time of creation makes the creation; and at the time of world-destruction he devours it again' (*MBh.*, Critical Ed., 12.290, cited by Edgerton, *BIP.*, p. 301). Nārāyaṇa, his serpent-couch, and the waters 'are triune manifestations of the single divine, imperishable, cosmic substance, the energy underlying and inhabiting all the forms of life' (Zimmer, *Myths*, p. 61).

[3]The *Mahā-Nārāyaṇa Up.* (3rd or 4th century B.C.) identifies Nārāyaṇa with the Absolute (cited by Gonda, *VS.*, pp. 29, 97). This Upaniṣad has been translated and annotated by J. Varenne, *La Mahā Nārāyaṇa Upaniṣad*, 2 vols, Paris, 1960. Nārāyaṇa was a god of obscure origin who became identified with Viṣṇu (*WI.*, p. 298).

v. Nara; Puruṣa; Pralaya; Brahmā.

Narmadā The name of one of the great rivers of India (referred to by Ptolemy as the Namadus), and of the goddess[1] personifying it. The river rises in the central highlands and flows from east to west. From the Narmadā valley, the Vindhyas rise abruptly; and from the south appear as a regular mountain range. To the north an undulating plateau is heavily forested, and afforded almost inaccessible retreats for primitive tribes, which retarded the Indo-Āryan penetration of the Deccan.

As a sacred river the Narmadā is considered by many Hindus to rank only second to the Ganges. Its rapid flow has eroded many of its pebbles to the shape of a *liṅga*, a process that has added to its popularity and reputation for holiness. The most meritorious act is to walk from the sea to the source of the Narmadā and then back along the opposite bank, a pilgrimage which takes up to two years to accomplish.

When the 60,000 Mauneyas (sons of Kaśyapa)[2] usurped the subterranean kingdom of the Nāgas (serpent-gods) the latter appealed to Viṣṇu who assumed the form of the ruler Purukutsa[3] (son of Māndhātṛ) whose wife was a Nāgī and the personification of the Narmadā. After the defeat of the *gandharvas* the Nāgas conferred on the goddess Narmadā the gift of annulling the effects of snake-venom in those who invoke her with the *mantra*: 'Salutation in the morning and at night to thee, O Narmadā! Defend me from the serpent's poison' (*VP.*, IV.3).

The water of the Ganges will purify the bather in the course of a single day, but the mere sight of the waters of the Narmadā absolves a man from all sin (*AGP.*, Ch. 113). Śiva is believed to reside 'in every white pebble found in the Narmadā',[4] and he is represented by a white pebble in the *Pañcāyatana pūjā* rite.

[1]She is said to be the daughter of the *ṛṣi* Mekāla.

[2]This legend is probably based on an account of a quarrel between rival tribes.

[3]According to the *VP.* (IV.3) Purukutsa had a son called Trasadasyu by the goddess Narmadā.

[4]Gonda, *VS.*, p. 113.

Nāsatya(s) v. Aśvins.

Naṭarāja 'Lord of the Dance.' A name applied to Śiva (as the Cosmic Dancer) when he performs the Tāṇḍava dance, which represents the continuous creation, maintenance and destruction of the universe, and indicates the perfect balance between life and death. A magnificent (though damaged) figure of Naṭarāja is depicted in cave 14 at Elūrā dating from the eighth century A.D. His wildly moving limbs pervaded by cosmic energy denote the phenomenal world, characterized by the universal illusion of individual existences, whilst the perfect stillness and serenity of the head dominates the whole display—as the Unmoved Mover, the Absolute, beyond time and change. The 'dance is a measured sequence born of . . . space and time, which essentially constitute this world of manifestation. Therefore dance is the prototype of universal creative activity'.[1]

In *RV.*, VIII.81,3, Indra is called the Dancer and the giver of abundant strength. This may refer to a war-dance, as he was the war-god of the Āryans.

The gods, as if dancing, were believed to have formed the earth from the 'thickening cloud of dust' they kicked up (*RV.*, X.72,6).

[1]*CHS.*, p. 168. v. also Coomaraswamy, 'The Dance of Śiva', *Siddhānta Dīpikā*, vol. XIII, July 1912. For the principal temple of the Lord of the Dance, v. Harle, *Temple Gateways in South India*, pp. 27–45.

v. Nāṭya Veda; Apasmāra.

Nāṭyaśāstra An anonymous work on drama, music

and dancing, traditionally attributed to the ancient sage Bharata. Rām Gopāl and other great Indian dancers still abide by the rules laid down in this work.

Abhinavagupta wrote a work called *Abhinava-bhāratī* on the *Nāṭyaśāstra* in which he 'propounded a theory of aesthetics in the context of drama, which has been accepted by almost all the subsequent writers on the subject'.[1]

[1]*EW.*, vol. I, p. 383.

v. Nāṭya Veda; Tāṇḍava.

Nāṭya Veda The art of dancing (*nāṭya*)[1] which in India particularly has been practised from earliest times. It is an intrinsic part of worship, and hence all India's classical dances stem from Hindu temple dances. This art includes the most complicated forms of dancing in the world, in which the mind and body, hands and feet, and the eyes must all be perfectly co-ordinated with the musical accompaniment. *Mudrās* also are of great importance in most Indian dances because they express various meanings according to their particular position. Dancing is thus highly symbolic, every emotion being capable of representation, and the significance of religious truths expressed, like that of the cosmic dance of Śiva.

The four main classical schools of dancing are: 1. Bharata-nāṭya, in which *mudrās* have an important part. 2. Kathakali (in Kerala) which developed from certain forms of mono-acting that stem from ancient folk traditions. 3. Manipuri (in the N.E.) shows local and foreign influences. 4. Kathak (in the N.) reflects Persian influence. It is based on the precepts of Bharata-nāṭya plus Islamic elements, and was much patronized by the Islamic Courts. Expert Kathak dancers can reproduce the exact sounds of drums in their footwork. Furthermore, they wear three rows of anklet bells, and are said to be able to control the sound of any one of them. In Kathak dancing *mudrās* are merely decorative and hence Kathak lacks the sculptural quality of Bharata-nāṭya.

[1]Ahmedabad has an arts academy called Darpana (Mirror) because it mirrors the ancient arts of India. Its principal and founder is Mrinalini Sarabhai, one of the great exponents of the classical Indian dance; v. also A. K. Coomaraswamy, *The Dance of Śiva*, and L. Frédéric, *La Danse sacrée de l'Inde*, Paris, 1957.

v. Naṭarāja; Deva-dāsī(s); Nāṭyaśāstra.

Navadurgā(s) v. Navapatrikā(s).

Navagraha(s) The 'Nine Planets'[1] traditionally designated as the sun (Sūrya), moon (Soma), Mercury (Budha), Venus (Śukra), Mars (Maṅgala or Aṅgāraka), Jupiter (Bṛhaspati), Saturn (Śani), Rāhu and Ketu. These planets are regarded as of the greatest astrological significance and are believed to influence the life of the individual and the course of history. They are especially worshipped in times of danger.

Śani, Rāhu and Ketu are inauspicious, even maleficent, and in South India are believed to be (together with birds and frogs, etc.) responsible for children's diseases.[2] These three planets must therefore be propitiated,[3] their personified representations being placed in every South Indian Śaiva temple, and so arranged that one figure does not face another. During the Gupta period in North India the Navagrahas were generally placed on the lintels of temple doors, to protect the temple and all who enter it.

According to the *Agni Pur.* the wood of certain trees, such as the *palāśa*, *khadira*, *udumbara*, *śamī*, etc., are sacred to the planets.

[1]Some texts give their number as five or seven. In Mithraism the seven degrees of initiation which 'have been left marked in the pattern of the mosaic floors of their meeting-places' were linked with the seven planets (J. M. Allegro, *The Sacred Mushroom and the Cross*, p. 169). The Babylonians personified stars and planets as divinities; and 'the greater gods, even when addressed by name in prayer, were regarded as astral powers' (King, *Babylonian Magic and Sorcery*, p. 109).

[2]Diehl, *Instrument and Purpose*, p. 193. By means of the planets predictions of rain and crops were made (*Bṛhat Saṁ.*, XXIV.6).

[3]The *Suś. Saṁ.* identifies the nine planets with the nine diseases of infants. They have ethereal forms and were created by Agni, Umā, etc., to guard the new-born Guha (Skanda). Until well into the eighteenth century in the United Kingdom, planets were believed by many to cause disease—when paralysis or sudden death occurred the person was said to be 'planet-struck' or 'blasted', and in the late nineteenth century white witches were called 'planet-rulers' (K. Thomas, *Religion and the Decline of Magic*, pp. 633f.).

v. Graha; Grahabali; Grahahoma; Grahakuṇḍalikā; Grahāpasmāra; Navaratna.

Navanīta v. Santāna.

Navapatrikā(s) The 'nine plants'. An autumnal ceremony in Bengal connected with Durgā and indicating her vegetal character. The nine plants comprise the *rambha* (plantain), *kacvī* (Arum colocasia), *haridrā* (turmeric), *jayantī* (barley), *bel* (wood-apple), *dāḍima* (pomegranate), *aśoka* (Saraca indica), *māna* and *dhānya* (rice). Each plant is presided over by one of Durgā's nine forms (Navadurgās), comprising Brahmāṇī, Kālikā, Durgā, Kārttikī, Śivā, Raktadantikā, Śokarahitā, Cāmuṇḍā and Lakṣmī.[1] These nine forms of Durgā are believed to dwell in the nine plants which are invoked to protect their worshippers.[2] In India, the examples of plant theophanies attest 'to the people's consciousness of the divinity and the highly important function of the vegetable kingdom'.[3]

[1]*DHI.*, pp. 490, n.1, and 500, n.1. where variant lists of Navapatrikās are given.

[2]S. C. Mitra, 'On the Cult of the Tree-goddess in Eastern Bengal' (*Man in India*, vol. II, pp. 230–41, 1922). For the relations of the gods with particular plants, v. J. Gonda, *VS.*, pp. 111f.

[3]Gonda, op. cit., p. 113.

v. Navagraha(s); Navaratna.

Navaratna The 'Nine gems'. A much-valued amulet consisting of pearl, ruby, topaz, diamond, emerald, lapis lazuli, coral, sapphire, and an unidentified stone called *gomeda*. Each stone is said to protect the wearer against a particular evil or misfortune.[1] The nine gems are popularly connected with the nine planets (*navagrahas*).

[1]Crooke, *Things Indian*, p. 393.

Nayana-dīkṣā 'Instruction and initiation by the eye.' By looking at his disciple a *guru* destroys the 'fundamental evil conditioning the soul's delusion that it is limited, and in doing so enlightens him'.[1]

[1]Gonda, *Eye and Gaze in the Veda*, p. 54.

Nāyikā(s) I. The eight minor forms of Durgā, which comprise Ugracaṇḍā, Pracaṇḍā, Caṇḍogrā, Caṇḍanāyikā, Ati-caṇḍā, Cāmuṇḍā, Caṇḍā and Caṇḍavatī. II. A class of female personifications of illicit love, comprising Balinī, Kāmeśvarī, Vimalā, Aruṇā, Medinī, Jayinī, Sarveśvarī and Kauleśī.

Neṣṭṛ v. Ṛtvij.

Neti neti 'Not this, not that.'[1] A Vedānta formula expressing non-duality and indicating that the nature of the impersonal *brahman* can be neither represented nor comprehended. It points to that which 'does not fall into the category of "object" and constitutes the inward self of all'.[2] Behind every deity stands the unifying impersonal power of *brahman*, which lends to each only 'a part of its own efficacy'.[3]

[1]Edgerton suggests 'no, no' (*BIP.*, p. 34); others 'not so, not so'.

[2]Radhakrishnan and Moore, *Sourcebook in Indian Philosophy*, p. 538.

[3]Heimann, *Facets*, p. 32.

Netraviṣa The name of the evil existing in the eye of a man or snake. Nahuṣa is said to have possessed the 'poison-look'.

v. Dṛṣṭidoṣa.

Nidāgha The son of Pulastya who practised austerities for two periods of a thousand years each. His *guru* was Ṛbhu by whom he was taught to regard the whole universe as the one undivided nature of the Supreme Spirit called Vāsudeva, and hence to consider himself as one with all that exists in the world (*VP.*, II.15,16).

v. Tapas.

Nidhi(s) A 'treasure'. The word primarily means 'store', or 'container', such as a receptacle for holding juices, etc., (*RV.* I.183,4, etc.), and then 'treasure' generally (II.24,6 etc.). In the plural it refers to the eight (or sometimes nine) personified treasures of Kubera (*Mārk. P.*, LXVIII), viz., Padma, Mahāpadma, Makara, Kaccapa, Mukunda, Nandaka, Nīla and Śaṅkha.[1] They are also connected with Śiva's eight *śaktis* and worshipped by Tantrists. Kubera's *nidhis* suggest a folk origin whose significance is no longer apparent.

In the *Mārk. P.* (LXVIII, 1–46) the *nidhis* are said to be the 'supporters' of a particular kind of knowledge called *padminī* whose presiding deity is Lakṣmī. The *nidhis* 'are demi-gods who preside over and influence the individuals' propensities, pursuits, pleasures, tastes, etc.'[2] throughout life. Thus *padma* reflects the quality of politeness and sincerity; *mahāpadma*, goodness, generosity; *makara*, ignorance, though the ignorant may possess a good disposition; but *kaccapa* represents blind ignorance, the man whose prejudices make him suspicious, mean and incapable of enjoyment; *mukunda* typifies the extrovert, whose interests are chiefly wine, women and song; *nandaka* (or *nanda*) represents wealth, so that the man attracted by it becomes prosperous; the qualities associated with *nīla* are goodness and a passion for collecting all manner of things associated with water, such as pearls and coral, the control of rivers and planting of trees; *śaṅkha* represents self-interest, selfishness being the characteristic of those lacking in affection for family or relatives, and who have no friends.

[1]The list varies in different works and probably reflects different opinions about what constitutes 'treasure' (v. also Coomaraswamy, *Yakṣas*, pt. ii, p. 49).

[2]Pargiter, *Mārk. P.*, p. 415n.

Nidrā The goddess personifying sleep (*nidra*), one of the 'treasures' which emerged from the Churning of the Ocean (*samudramathana*). At the dissolution of the world[1] marking the end of each age, Nidrā enters the body of Viṣṇu who then sleeps on the causal waters until Brahmā instructs Nidrā to depart so that Viṣṇu may awaken and re-create the world (*Mārk. P.*, 81, 53–70).

[1]At the end of each age Mahālakṣmī assumes the form of the secondary goddess Mahākālī, known also as Nidrā or Yoganidrā, Mahāmāyā, Mahāmārī, Kṣudhā, Tṛṣā, Kalarātrī, etc. (*DHI.*, p. 469).

Nigama A term used to distinguish Vedic religious

ideas and practices from those of the Āgama or 'Tantric and Paurāṇic domain of religion and ritual.'[1]

[1]*HCIP.*, I, p. 160.

v. Tantra.

Nighaṇṭu v. Nirukta.

Nikumbha I. A Rākṣasa, son of Kumbha-karṇa. II. An *asura* and king of Ṣaṭpura. He had received a boon from Brahmā that he could not be killed except by the hand of Viṣṇu. Although he possessed great magical powers and could assume many forms, he was finally slain by Kṛṣṇa (Viṣṇu).

Nikumbhilā A tutelary goddess of the Laṅkā Rākṣasas, to whom groves were dedicated, and where dancing, wine (*surā*) drinking, and human sacrifice formed part of her ritual (*Rām.*, V.24,44). By sacrificing to Nikumbhilā before a battle Rāvaṇa's son Meghanāda is said to have been rendered invisible.[1]

[1]*IRA.*, pp. 35f. and 47.

v. Indrajit; Laṅkinī.

Nīla In the *RV.* it denotes a colour, generally dark blue or black. In post-Vedic literature it is the name of one of the eight (or nine) treasures (*nidhis*) of Kubera; of a mythical mountain range situated north of Mount Meru; or of one of the Vānara chiefs who assisted Rāma by building a causeway from India to Ceylon (Laṅkā); or of a Pāṇḍava warrior killed by Aśvatthāman.

Nīlakaṇṭha 'Blue-throated.' The epithet applied to Śiva when at Brahmā's request he swallowed the poison called *halāhala* (or *kalā-kuṭa*) which emerged during the Churning of the Ocean (*samudramathana*).[1]

[1]Another myth states that a second churning took place at the instigation of Śiva who was displeased at the demons being cheated out of their share. Only poison emerged this time (Gonda, *VS.*, pp. 124–5).

Nimba A tree (Azadirachta indica). The stones of the fruit, which are perforated, are used to make 'rosaries' and necklaces. In Northern India salt and mustard burnt on a fire consisting of this wood will exorcize demons. The bitter leaves are chewed by mourners to purify themselves after the performance of funerary rites and before re-entering the house.

Every part of the tree is magical. Bunches of its leaves when tied on the doors of houses[1] indicated a birth or a death, as well as giving protection against spirits, especially the dreaded smallpox goddess Śītalā who must be propitiated with *nimba* garlands and jasmine placed on the beds of smallpox victims.

[1]But its wood was forbidden for building purposes. (*Bṛhat Saṁ.*, LII,118).

Nimi A son of Ikṣvāku, the traditional founder of the Solar Dynasty. Nimi asked the *ṛṣi* Vasiṣṭha to officiate at a sacrifice he wished to perform, but the *ṛṣi* was unable to comply immediately. The impatient Nimi then sought the help of other *ṛṣis*. On hearing of his intention Vasiṣṭha cursed him to become disembodied, and his corpse embalmed. But as the sacrifice arranged by Nimi had not been cancelled, it was performed by the *ṛṣis*. After its completion the gods came to receive their share of the sacrifice, but before acceding to their request, the *ṛṣis* asked them to restore Nimi to life. The gods agreed but Nimi refused the boon, declaring that he no longer wished to suffer again the bondage of the body (*VP.*, IV.5).

v. Animiṣa; Janaka I.

Nimittajñāna 'Knowledge of omens.' One of the sixty-four 'sciences' enumerated by Vātsyāyana, which is particularly associated with astrology. It entails the knowledge of countless inauspicious signs, marks and objects which must be avoided.

v. Jyotiṣa.

Nīrājana 'Lustration of arms.'[1] A politico-religious ceremony conducted by the *purohita* for the king in the month *āśvina* or in *kārttika*, and usually before a military expedition. On an auspicious spot to the north-east of the town a wooden arch was erected, sixteen cubits high and ten wide; also a 'house' made of branches of *udumbara*, *sarja*, etc. Nuts, rice, costus and white mustard seeds were tied together, dipped in saffron paste, and then tied to the necks of the horses, accompanied by *mantras* addressed to the Sun, Varuṇa, Prajāpati, etc. *Śānti* (expiatory rites) were carried out for the horses for a week, during which they were not spoken to harshly or beaten, but lulled by songs and music. On the eighth day a hut was erected to the south of the arch. An altar was placed in front of the hut and various offerings made. Accompanied by a veterinary surgeon and an astrologer the king sat on a tiger-skin facing east in front of the fire. Omens were then drawn from a number of things, including the flames and smoke of the fire, and afterwards from the movements of a horse and elephant which were led under the arch. If the horse stood with its right leg uplifted this portended victory for the king, but if frightened it presaged defeat. The priest then gave the horse a rice-ball duly consecrated with *mantras*. If the horse smelt it, this indicated victory, if not, defeat. The horses, elephants, soldiers, and the king were touched with an *udumbara* twig previously dipped in consecrated water. The ceremony concluded with the worship of the god Revanta, the purification of the army, the chanting of the magical hymns of the *AV.*, and the piercing of the heart of a clay figure of the enemy by the priest.[2] The king then mounted his horse and moved off with his army towards the north-east.[3]

[1]The act of sprinkling horses, elephants and soldiers

with water.

[2]This is an *abhicāra* rite. According to the *Kālikā Pur.*, ch. 80, there was a mock fight consisting in the destruction of earthen representations of enemy troops.

[3]*Bṛhat Saṁ.*, XLIII.3–28. For other *nīrājana* ceremonies v. Gonda, *VS.*, pp. 83, 189, n.278.

Nirguṇa 'Beyond qualities or attributes', an epithet applied to the *brahman*.

Nirṛti[1] A term signifying dissolution, misery, corruption, evil and decay, and its personification as a goddess. Varuṇa and other deities are implored to drive her away (*RV.*, I. 24,9); old age is naturally consigned to her (V.41,17), and with her are identified all who take advantage of the simple and who harm the righteous (VII.104,9).

As part of the *rājasūya* ceremony offerings are made to Nirṛti in a barren hollow, for desolate places belong to her. If she is properly propitiated she will not seize or destroy the king during his inauguration (*ŚBr.*, V.2.3, 2–3).[2]

Nirṛti is black; she seeks out men who do not offer oblations or sacrifices. She is asked to follow the paths of thieves and robbers, and so avoid the paths of good men. She is said to know 'all that is born' (*Tait. Saṁ.*, IV.2,5). Three black bricks dried by a chaff fire are included in the building up of the *gārhapatya* fire-altar and constitute Nirṛti's portion (V.2,4). These bricks are a foot square, and represent evil. Hence when the sacrificer treads on them he symbolically crushes underfoot all evil, corruption, decay, etc. The bricks are unmarked because that which has no signs, marks or characteristics is non-existent.

According to *Manu* (XI.105) a man who has seduced the wife of his *guru* must himself cut off his genitalia and, taking them in his joined hands, walk towards Nirṛti's region (the S. W.) until he dies. A student who has broken his vow should offer a one-eyed ass to Nirṛti at a crossroad (XL.119).[3]

Nirṛti is the daughter (or wife) of Adharma, and Hiṁsā; her offspring are Mṛtyu (Death), Bhaya (Fear) and Mahābhaya (Terror).[4] The owl (*ulūka*) which causes great terror, and the pigeon and hare are sacred to her (*Tait. Saṁ.*, V.5,18). Her dwelling-place is the *aśvattha* tree (Ficus religiosa), the *bodhi* tree of the Buddhists. Though generally feared, Nirṛti protects the crippled or mentally retarded if they are virtuous and kind.[5] Those desiring the acquisition of magical powers should worship her.

[1]v. Nairṛta(s) I, n.1.

[2]*Mārk. P.*, LXXXV,9, calls her the 'goddess of the good fortune of kings'.

[3]In many countries crossroads were much dreaded. Demons, ghosts, murderers, suicides, etc. gathered there, and divination rites were practised. Nirṛti is identified with the dangerous aspects of the earth (J.C. Heesterman, *Ancient Indian Royal Consecration*, p. 17).

[4]Cf. the old Bohemian Tras (Tremor), and Strakh (Terror), who leap on enemies. v. Grimm, *Teutonic Mythology*, p. 208.

In the Purs. Nirṛti is said to be the wife of Virūpākṣa the lord of the Rākṣasas (A. Mitra Shastri, *India as Seen in the Bṛhat Saṁ.*, p. 146).

[5]*HP.*, p. 138.

Nirṛti(s) Destructive powers or potencies. In a *RV.* hymn the priests are said to serve the Nirṛtis, whose origin only they know (X.114,2); but in another hymn (VIII.24,24) Indra is said to know how to avoid these destructive powers. The Nirṛtis should be worshipped by those who wish to destroy their enemies.

v. Nirṛti.

Nirukta 'Explanation or etymological interpretation of a word.'[1] The name of several works, especially of a Commentary on the *Nighaṇṭu* by Yāska. The *Nighaṇṭu* is a list of Vedic words handed down by tradition, which with the *Nirukta* is the oldest surviving Indian treatise on etymology, philology and semantics.[2]

Subsequently, the *Nirukta* led to the systematic development of etymology and was included among the list of *vidyās* or sciences.

[1]*SED.*

[2]Translated into E. by Lakshman Sarup, entitled *The Nighaṇṭu and the Nirukta*.

v. Pāṇini; Sanskrit.

Nirvāṇa Lit. 'extinction'. In Indian mysticism the word, while retaining its original meaning, is applied metaphorically to the extinguishing of all worldly desires (as a flame is extinguished), and the attainment of knowledge free from illusion (*māyā*) and false knowledge (*avidyā*), and hence the nullification of *karman*.

The term *nirvāṇa* was never as generally used in Hinduism[1] as in Buddhism, owing possibly to the special significance given to it by the Buddha, and which, in addition to other specialized terms, remained part of the Buddhist vocabulary. Such terminological distinctions became a prominent feature of each Indian *darśana*. Thus in the Hindu *ātmavāda* schools the term '*mokṣa*' was used to denote 'liberation' and the attainment of brahman, whereas in Buddhism '*nirvāṇa*', whilst denoting 'liberation', particularly denotes '*bodhi*' or the attainment of supreme knowledge.

These subtle distinctions resulted in some confusion among the Hindu and Buddhist leaders, as is indicated by the different interpretations of the several Vedānta schools on the one hand and those of Buddhism on the other, as also by the controversy over the significance of *nirvāṇa* among eminent Indologists like Stcherbatsky and de la Vallée Poussin.[2]

[1]But Heimann (*IWP.*, p. 54) considers that in the widest sense *nirvāṇa* 'is a universal Hindu idea, and by no means confined to a few Buddhistic sects'. Furthermore, it never meant nullity either to Buddhists or Hindus. In ontology it means the dispersion of all definite shape; in logic, the (dis) solution of all definition; in psychology, the (dis) solution of all individual desire.

[2]v. *Nirvāṇa* by L. de la Vallée Poussin, and *The Conception of Buddhist Nirvāṇa*, by Th. Stcherbatsky.

Niṣāda. Name of one of the earliest aboriginal groups in India, a people of Negro origin, probably the survivors of an age prior to the Continental drift which separated Africa and India. From their resemblance to some Australian tribes, they have been called proto-Australoids or Austrics. The Dravidian occupation of India gradually forced them into hills and jungles and the more remote parts of the country, a dispersion subsequently furthered by the Āryan occupation.

The first reference to them by name occurs in the Rudrādhyāya of the *YV*, together with several other tribes, all of whom were held in contempt by the Indo-Āryan superior classes.[1]

Tradition provides a description of the Niṣādas, which the ethnological study of their descendants has generally confirmed. Their origin is described in the legend of Vena, a ruler notorious for the oppression of his people and of the *ṛṣis*. The latter, repeating appropriate *mantras*, slew Vena with the sharp blades of *kuśa* grass. Then, apparently to obtain an heir, Vena being childless, the *ṛṣis*, again using magical *mantras*, pierced (or rubbed) the dead king's right thigh, from which immediately issued a dwarfish figure, black as a charred stick, with flattish nose, blood-red eyes and black hair,[2] from whom the Niṣādas and other barbarians of the Vindhya forests are said to be descended. The fabulous bird Garuḍa is believed to devour them.

[1]R. Chanda, *Indo-Āryan Races*, p. 4.

[2]*MBh.* (XII.59); *VP.* (I.13). Variants of the legend appear in other Purāṇas.

Niṣkala v. Liṅga.

Niśumbha v. Śumbha; Durgā.

Nīti-Śāstra (s) A class of 'ethical and didactic writings of all kinds, including collections of fables and moral precepts'.[1]

[1]*IW.*, p. 157.

Nityā (s) The 'Eternal Ones'. A synonym of *mahāvidyā*.

Ṇya v. Brahmaloka.

Nyagrodha The name of the great Indian fig tree (Ficus indica) which has both ordinary and aerial roots. The latter grow down from the branches until the soil is reached, the new plants repeating the process. The area covered by the roots is sacred to Kālī. The wood of the tree is also sacred and is used to make sacrificial bowls (*Tait. Saṁ.*, VII.4.12,1). The mythical origin of the tree is given in the *Ait. Br.* (VII.30)—when the sacrificial goblets of the gods were tilted over (*nyubjan*) they became *nyagrodha* trees.[1]

The *Chān. Up.* (6.12,2) refers to the imperceptible source of the great *nyagrodha* trees, and likens it to that imperceptible essence (*ātman*) which permeates the immeasurable world.

Gandharvas and *apsarasas* are said to dwell in *nyagrodha*, *udumbara*, *aśvattha* and *plakṣa* trees (*Tait. Saṁ.*, III.4,8). But the *nyagrodha* may also exert a malevolent influence and hence should not be planted near graves (*ŚBr.*, XIII.8.1,16). It is sometimes regarded as a form of Śiva.

Or it emerged from Indra (*ŚBr.*, XII.7.1,1).

v. Vaṭa.

Nyāsa The mental appropriation or assignment of various parts of the body to tutelary deities. This 'ritual projection' is achieved either by mentally assigning them to various organs, or by touching various parts of the body. This was an ancient rite which was revalorized and enriched in Tantrism. Bharati defines *nyāsa* as 'the process of charging a part of the body, or any organ of another living body, with a specified power through touch'.[1]

Among the yogic practices mentioned in the *Ṛgvidhāna* (30. 3–6) is that of 'placing' various organs in the sixteen stanzas of *RV.*, X.90 (the famous Puruṣa-sūkta hymn); the first stanza is 'placed' in the left hand, the second in the right, and so on. As this hymn states that the universe was created by the sacrifice of the Cosmic Puruṣa, the *nyāsa* rite will result in the disciple's 'identification both with the universe and with the gods (who are also believed to have issued from the sacrifice)'.[2]

[1]*TT.*, p. 91. The Pāñcarātrins initiate a candidate with the *nyāsa* rite 'to unite him with spiritual qualities' (Gonda, *VS.*, p. 66). To Śaivas 'the divinities in different parts of the body represent the five aspects or faces of Śiva' (ibid., p. 73; for other kinds of *nyāsa* v. p. 82). For *nyāsa* in Tantrism v. Rawson, *The Art of Tantra*, p. 80.

[2]Eliade, *Yoga*, p. 138. Cf. the practice in ancient Mesopotamia whereby the deceased, to overcome the phantoms encountered after death, assimilated 'his members to those of the various gods, and thus deifying

in a manner his own substance' (F. Lenormant, *Chaldean Magic; Its Origin and Development*, pp.87–8, 1877).

Nyāya 'Logical analysis.' One of the six Hindu 'orthodox' quasi-philosophical schools (*darśanas*), the founding of which is traditionally ascribed to Gautama. It constitutes with the Vaiśeṣika one of the three pairs of *darśanas*, so aligned either because of the similarity of their respective subjects or their methodology. Until recently the founding of the Nyāya was generally regarded as having preceded that of the Vaiśeṣika, but K. Sastri[1] reverses the sequence.

Like the other *darśanas*, the Nyāya and Vaiśeṣika represent a systematization and development of the philosophy of the early *sūtras*, the repository of much earlier ideas. Whilst that may be true of the subject matter, it does not explain the adoption of the Nyāya methodology. Attention has often been drawn to the similarity between the Realism of the Buddhist Sarvāstivāda School and the Nyāya-Vaiśeṣika, and the resemblance of all three to the Greek Peripatetics associated with Aristotle, whose pupil Alexander invaded India at the beginning of the third century B.C. As the Sarvāstivādins were settled in Gāndhāra, close to areas occupied by Alexander's immediate successors, it seems not improbable that the analytic method of the Nyāya and theory of elements of the Sarvāstivādins, and the atomic structural theory propounded by both of them were influenced by, if not entirely derived from, Greek sources. But the ultimate object of the Nyāya-Vaiśeṣika was distinctively Indian: the achievement of individual liberation (*mokṣa*) from *karman*, and escape from the continuous process of life and death (*saṁsāra*). The immediate purpose of the Nyāya was therefore to prove the validity of these notions by logical analysis and philosophical argument, and thus to silence the criticism of Cārvākas, Jains and Buddhists. But the Nyāyikas were limited by both subject and method from completely objective enquiry. Like the Sarvāstivāda, the Nyāya-Vaiśeṣika was empirical, relying too rigidly on perception and inference, and on its inductive premises.

The development of these Realist schools was probably a reaction against the Idealism of aupaniṣadic speculative thought, which was often so abstruse as to be unintelligible, and so unformulated as to afford no solid basis for a coherent philosophy. But the Realist schools, because of their inflexibility, failed to appreciate that the old Idealism had been gradually and quietly maturing. Against its resurgence the influence of the Realist schools waned, until finally they were absorbed, the Sarvāstivāda into the Mahāyāna, and the Nyāya-Vaiśeṣika into the Uttara-Mīmāṁsā (Vedānta).

[1] *HCIP*., II, p. 477.

Nyāya-līlāvatī An important Vaiśeṣika work by Vallabhācārya which anticipated the later Nyāya-Vaiśeṣika philosophy.

O

Odana An oblation usually consisting of grain cooked in milk, or sometimes of curds, meat or ghee, or of rice, beans or sesame mixed with milk.[1] The *odana* rite appears to be of very ancient origin and closely associated with thaumaturgy, as is indicated in some passages of the *AV*. Thus to ensure victory in battle the sorcerer makes an oblation to the altar-fire with the right hand to protect the sacrificer from his foes, and with the left hand an oblation of the *iṅgiḍa* plant to ensure the destruction of an enemy army.[2] Success is further ensured if a goat forms part of the offering (*AV.*, IX.5,22). 'An *odana* whose main motive is escape from death (*ati tarāṇi mṛtyum*) is dealt with in *AV.*, IV.35; another, prepared with succulent sauces and called *viṣṭārin* "spreader", is described in mystic cosmogonic language as conducive to happiness in the other world.'[3]

Like the sacrificial utensils (*āpris*), the vessel used for the *odana* offering was also personified and identified with numerous and quite disparate things. One hymn (XI.3,52) declares that Prajāpati fashioned the thirty-three worlds from one particular *odana*; another hymn likens it to the sun because the *odana* offering was yellow, hot and nourishing.

[1] *VI.*, vol. I, p. 124. *Odana* is also the name of the rice-dish itself (Whitney, *AV.*, II, p. 625; v. also A.M. Shastri, *India as Seen in the Bṛhat Saṁhitā*, pp. 211f.).

[2] Whitney, *AV.*, vol. II, p. 503.

[3] Bloomfield, *The Atharvaveda*, p. 78.

Om, Oṁ or **Aum**[1] A sacred syllable which first appears in the Upaniṣads as a mystic monosyllable, regarded by some as the basis or 'seed' (*bīja*) of all *mantras*.[2] It is the root-syllable of origination and dissolution. Thus *AUM* is the one eternal syllable of which all that exists is but the development. The past, present, and future are all included in this one sound, and all that exists beyond the three forms of time is also implied in it (*Māṇḍūkya Up.*, 1,1).[3]

The *Chān. Up.* (2.23,2–3) and *Tait. Up.* (1,8) assign the origin of language to Prajāpati, from whose meditation on the three worlds arose the threefold knowledge (the three Vedas); from his meditation on them emerged the syllables, *bhur*, *bhuvaḥ* and *svar* (representing earth, atmosphere and sky); and from his meditation on these originated the syllable *Om*, which co-ordinates all speech and represents the totality of the world.[4] The three constituents of *Om* also represent the deities of the Hindu triad (*trimūrti*); Brahmā, Viṣṇu and Śiva respectively.

But Vaiṣṇavism and Śaivism define *Om* according to their respective theological notions. Thus Vaiṣṇavas identify the sound-form of *Om* with Viṣṇu (*AGP.*, 215,1f.), whilst Śaivas claim that Śiva in his form of Nādatanu, i.e., 'consisting of sound', 'is the syllable *Om* from whose five mouths have come forth the notes of the "octave", *sa ri*, *ga*, *ma pa*, *dha*, and *ni*'.[5] Thus by the sound produced from his drum (*ḍamaru*) Śiva successively recreates the world. To the Vedāntins *Om* is the sound-form of the *ātman*, i.e., Absolute Sound (*Maitri Up.*, 6,5; *Māṇḍūkya Up.*, 1.12). The composition, meaning and efficacy of *Om* are expounded by Dattātreya in the *Mārk P.* (Canto XLII) which states that everything—existent and non-existent—can be grasped by uttering the sacred syllable, the 'Supreme *Om*'.

The *Chān. Up.* (I.4,1–5) states that initially only Agni was immortal, and that the other gods, fearing that Death would ultimately destroy them, took refuge in the sound of *Om* which, being immortal and without fear, conferred these qualities on them. Hence the epithet of *Om*, 'Slayer of Death'.

The psycho-therapeutic efficacy of *Om* is regarded as limitless, and its utterance at the beginning and end of a lesson on the Veda ensures that the student will retain the knowledge gained. Its utterance also counteracts errors in the performance of a sacrifice, and protects the devotee against misfortune. Meditation on this sacred syllable satisfies every need and finally leads to liberation (*Kaṭha Up.*, 2,16–17; *Praśna Up.*, 5,7). Its sound is thus more important than all Vedic rites, oblations and sacrifices, for it alone is imperishable (*Manu*, II.84).

The sound of *Om* is said to have emotional effects too subtle to be defined, so that its utterance is regarded as a very personal act. Thus wherever it is uttered, in temple or home, it must be *sotto voce* lest it should be heard by anyone of low caste. But rites once customary among all devout Hindus have tended to become simplified and are often performed perfunctorily. Nonetheless, prayers and the recital of passages from the Veda[6] are still prefixed by the utterance of *Om*.[7]

[1] In Sanskrit 'o' is constitutionally a diphthong, contracted from 'a' and 'u' which when pronounced quickly have the sound of 'o', and which combined with 'm' gives to the whole a resonant, humming sound.

[2]But Bharati (*TT.*, p. 107) states that '*Om* is only a *mantra* by courtesy, and that it becomes a true *mantra* only when it is formally imparted by a *guru* to a disciple in accordance with a particular ritual.' For *Om* in the *Praṇava Up.*, v. Bloomfield, *The Atharvaveda*, pp. 108f.

[3]v. *HP.*, p. 39.

[4]v. Zimmer, *Philosophies of India*, pp. 372–8; Eliade, *Yoga*, pp. 122–4 and 390.

[5]A.A. Bake, 'The Appropriation of Siva's Attributes by Devī', *BSOAS.*, 1955, XVII/3, p. 523; v. also Gonda, *VS.*, p. 67.

[6]Deussen, *Allgemeine Geschichte der Philosophie*, II, pp. 349f.

[7]It was usually referred to as *praṇava*, but occasionally as *akṣara* or *ekākṣara*, and in later times as *oṁkāra*.

v. Yoga.

Omkāra v. Om.

Oṣadhi Probably from *oṣa*, 'shining' or 'luminous'. A plant or herb, especially a medicinal herb. Because of its close association with plant growth the moon is called Oṣadhipati (Lord of herbs), and Oṣadhigarbha (Producer of herbs).

The origin of plants is given in a myth of Prajāpati who, being dissatisfied with an oblation he had prepared, poured it into the fire. From it plants immediately sprang up, hence their name *oṣadhyaḥ* (*ŚBr.*, II.2.4,5). But in the *RV.* (X.97,1) herbs are said to have preceded the gods by three ages (*yugas*). People who partake of these herbs, like the partakers of *soma*, scale the inaccessible heights of heaven (*Suś. Saṁ.*, II. p. 541).

Oṣadhigarbha v. Oṣadhi.

Oṣadhipati 'Lord of herbs.' An epithet of the moon; and the title of a physician, i.e., 'Master of herbs'. v. Oṣadhi.

Oṣṭakarṇaka(s) Members of an aboriginal tribe whose mouths were either unusually large, or whose lips were artificially distended so that they stretched almost from ear to ear.

P

Pāda I. 'Quarter.' Its primary meaning is 'foot'[1] but when applied to quadrupeds it indicates one-fourth, just as *śapha*, the cleft hoof, denotes an 'eighth'.[2]

[1]In the *AV.* it refers to the 'foot or leg or an inanimate object' (Turner, *IAL.*, 8056).

[2]*VI.*, vol. I, p. 516.

II. Oaths were sometimes sworn by a pupil on the feet (*pādas*) of his *guru* (*AGP.*, 255, 49f.).

III. In prosody a measure (foot), a succession of which are arranged in regular order, according to certain types recognized as standards, in verse of a particular length. Such an arrangement of pādas (which may consist of long or short syllables, ranging from a minimum of four to a maximum of twelve) constitutes its respective metre.

v. Chandas.

Padārtha-dharma-saṁgraha (4th century A.D.). A work by Praśastapāda. Though usually regarded as a commentary (*bhaṣya*) on the *Vaiśeṣika sūtra* of Kaṇāda, it is really an independent exposition of Vaiśeṣika philosophy.

Padma I. 'Lotus.' An aquatic plant which has long been an emblem of especial sanctity in many parts of Asia. In Hinduism it is a symbol of the sun and of creation, and also, as in Jainism and Buddhism, of perfection and purity, because its flowers grow on long stalks high above the water, whilst its roots remain in the mud. Its origin is generally assigned to the primeval waters (*Tait. Br.*, I.1.3,5), from which it emerged on the eve of creation or cosmic renewal as a thousand-leafed plant from Viṣṇu's navel (representing the centre of the energy of the universe).[1] Seated on the opened flower was the god Brahmā. Thus in Hinduism the lotus became the 'visible representation of the womb of creation'.[2]

In architecture the lotus is the typical basis or support of a building, as the *padma-pīṭha* is of images and of the so-called 'bell-capitals' of supporting columns. The lotus-petal moulding at the base of columns denotes that the building is supported on an open lotus flower (representing the earth) which rests upon the waters.

The lotus is equated with the Tree of Life—the Cosmic Tree—which originally sprang from the navel of Varuṇa, bearing the deities on its branches. In late Gupta and medieval art it is depicted rising from the navel of Nārāyaṇa (Viṣṇu) and supporting Brahmā.[3] The *padma* is believed to be the direct source of wealth, as can be seen from the *padma-nidhi*, one of Kubera's treasures (*nidhis*).

[1]Cf. the ancient Egyptian belief that 'the lotus issued from the body of the Creators of the Earth and remained "within the pool of the island"' (Reymond, *Mythological Origin of the Egyptian Temple*, p. 70; v. also Gonda, *Aspects*, p. 104). The Egyptian sun-god Re raised himself from the primordial waters concealed in a lotus (James, *Tree of Life*, p. 131), or appeared as a child sitting in a lotus flower (Frankfort, *Ancient Egyptian Religion*, p. 154).

[2]Gonda, *CC.*, p. 326. According to the *AGP.* (XLIX, 24) *padma* represents the material aspect of evolution, the petals its consecutive forms. In medieval symbolism the expanded lotus denotes the manifested universe.

[3]Coomaraswamy, *Yakṣas*, pt. ii, p. 57.

v. Padmanābha; Padmabandhu.

II. Name of one of Kubera's personified treasures (*nidhis*) (*Mārk. P.*, LXV. 2ff.; for a description of them v. LXVIII).

III. Name of one of the four chief yogic positions (*āsana*), the others being called *siddha*, *bhadra* and *siṁha*.

v. Padmāsana.

Padmā I. 'Lotus.' An epithet of the goddesses Lakṣmī, Śrī and Manasā.

v. Padma I.

II. A sixteen-cornered plinth for images, believed to bring good luck.

Padmabandhu 'Friend of the lotus.' An epithet of the Sun whose heat causes the lotus flowers to open. The sun-god Sūrya is depicted holding fully opened lotus flowers.

v. Padma I.

Padmanābha 'Lotus-navel.' An epithet of Viṣṇu,[1] from whose navel emerged the cosmic lotus (*padma*) representing the commencement of a new age.

[1]The *Sātvata Saṁ.* lists Padmanābha as one of the thirty-nine incarnatory forms of Viṣṇu (*DHI.*, p. 391).

Padmapāṇi 'Lotus-handed'; 'holding a lotus in the hand'. An epithet of Brahmā; of Viṣṇu; of the Buddhist *bodhisattva* Avalokiteśvara, and of the Sun (Sūrya).

Padma Purāṇa One of the eighteen principal Purāṇas. It contains an account of ancient times when the world was a golden lotus (*padma*). This Purāṇa is divided into five books and is a treatise on the practice of devotion, but its varied contents suggest that it consists of separate works united under one title.

Padmāsana 'Lotus-posture.' A particular sitting-posture adopted as one of the most suitable positions (*āsana*) for religious meditation, and that in which the Buddha and many Hindu deities are often depicted.

Padminī-vidyā The '*padminī* science', i.e., the knowledge and understanding of the significance of the eight 'treasures' (*nidhis*)[1] of Kubera. The goddess Lakṣmī is the presiding deity of *padminī-vidyā*.

[1]The lists of *nidhis* vary, and Coomaraswamy gives nine treasures which he considers are really water-symbols (cited by Banerjea, *DHI.*, p. 105, n.1).

Pahlava(s) or **Pallava(s)** or **Parthava(s)**[1] An Āryan fair-skinned nomadic people of the Caucasus, who subsequently entered India and moved to Andhra before finally settling on the east coast of Southern India, where they founded a dynasty which flourished from A.D. 250 to 750.

The Pahlavas are frequently mentioned with the Śakas, Kāmbojas, Pāradas, Yavanas and other groups, which entered north-western India during the first millennium B.C. Their extant coins illustrate their eclecticism.[2]

[1]'Pahlava and its Iranian prototype Pahlev are ... corruptions of Parthava, the indigenous name of the Parthians', Bühler, *Laws of Manu*, *SBE.*, XXV, Intro., p. cxv.

[2]*DHI.*, p. 542.

v. Kuṣāṇa(s).

Paidva 'Pertaining to Pedu.' The mythical white horse given to Pedu by the Aśvins (*RV.*, I.116,6; 117,9). The horse had particular significance, being regarded as a symbol of the sun and of knowledge. It is also referred to as a serpent-killer (*RV.*, I.118,9; *AV.*, X.4,5), and as being impervious to arrows. The above *AV.* hymn is a long charm against serpents, and invokes the white horse of Pedu for protection against them, but 'in practice an insect that has come by the name of Paidva is substituted for the unattainable horse (*Kauśika Sūtra*, 32,20ff.)'.[1]

[1]Bloomfield, *The Atharvaveda*, p. 81.

Paiśāca I. 'Relating or belonging to *piśācas*', i.e., infernal, demonic.

II. One of the eight forms of marriage (*Manu*, III.21), the first six being lawful, the remaining two, the *Paiśāca* and *Asura*, being forbidden, not only to the 'twice-born' castes, but also to *śūdras*.

v. Vivāha.

Pākadūrvā Perhaps millet, or an aquatic plant, which was planted where a deceased person had been cremated, the intention being to refresh (or cool) the scorched earth.[1]

[1]*RV.*, X.16,13. Alternatively a frog was placed on the cremation site for the same purpose.

v. Maṇḍūka.

Pālakāpya An ancient *ṛṣi* and the author of several medical treatises. He is said to be an incarnation of Dhanvantari.

Palāla A demon injurious to children.

Palāśa v. Parṇa.

Pañcajana Name of the demon slain by Kṛṣṇa. Pañcajana in the form of a conch-shell (*śaṅkha*) lived under the ocean and from his 'bones' Viṣṇu's sacred conch was made. Its sound terrifies demons, 'animates the gods, and annihilates unrighteousness'.[1]

[1]*BH.*, p. 103, n.2.

v. Pāñcajanya.

Pāñcajanya Kṛṣṇa's conch, formed from the shell of the sea-demon Pañcajana. It is one of Kṛṣṇa's emblems (*VP.*, V.21), and a special *mantra* is associated with its worship (*AGP.*, 25,14).

Pañcākṣara The five-syllabled Śaiva *mantra*—'*Namaḥ Śivāya*', which is said to give spiritual realization, prosperity, and to remove danger and fear.

Pañcāla v. Kuru.

Pañcamukha 'Five-headed.' An epithet of Brahmā who, after having lied by saying that he had seen the pinnacle of Śiva's *liṅga* of light, was deprived of one of his heads by Śiva who had assumed the form of Bhairava.

Pañcānana 'Five-faced.' An epithet of Śiva, representing various aspects of his fivefold nature, such as the five gross elements: earth, water, heat, wind and sky, called Sadyojāta, Vāmadeva, Aghora, Tatpuruṣa and Sadāśiva (or Īśāna) respectively. The Pañcānana also represent the four directions and are called Mahādeva (E), Bhairava (S), Nandivaktra (W), Umāvaktra (N), and the fifth, the zenith, called Sadāśiva, which corresponds to the fifth of the gross elements.

These symbolic 'five faces' of Śiva represent his every aspect, from the easily comprehensible to the highest and most complex (*sadāśiva*). The latter cannot be seen even by the most advanced yogin.[1] The five faces are important subjects for meditation leading to the attainment of true knowledge. Sadyojāta is associated with Śiva's creative function, Vāmadeva with the preservation of the world, Aghora with its continuous process of absorption and renewal, Tatpuruṣa with the power of darkness or obscuration in *saṁsāra*, and Sadāśiva with the process leading to final deliverance (*mokṣa*).

The symbolic significance of Pañcānana is mentioned in the *Mahā-Nārāyaṇa Up.* (i.e., the tenth book of the *Tait. Ār.*). Though the five functions or 'faces' are separately enumerated, they collectively represent 'the Force which rules, absorbs and reproduces the universe, and in performing one of these acts necessarily performs the others'.[2]

[1] *DHI.*, pp. 460 and 573f.; *IT.*, p. 205.

[2] Gonda, *VS.*, p. 48; v. also H. Mitra, 'Sadāśiva in Early Bengal', pp. 42ff. (*Proceedings of the Asiatic Society*, Bengal, XXIX, 1933).

v. Aṣṭamūrti.

Pañcarātra I. Name of the sacred book, or books, of the Pāñcarātra, a Vaiṣṇava cult.

II. A period of five days (nights), specifically that of an *ahīna*, a sacrifice lasting five days.

Pāñcarātra Name of a Vaiṣṇava sect following the doctrine of the sacred texts called Pañcarātra,[1] thought to have originated in Kashmir in the first, or possibly the third century B.C. The significance of the name of the sect, like its early history, is obscure. An early text, the *Ahirbudnya Saṁ.*, states that its name refers to the fivefold nature of Vāsudeva,[2] and does not connect the name with the *ahīna*, a sacrifice lasting five days.

Traditionally the Pāñcarātra doctrines were first systematized about A.D. 100 by Sāṇḍilya who in several sūtras emphasized the duty of devotion (*bhakti*) to Viṣṇu as the supreme deity. But at one stage, the Pāñcarātras whilst emphasizing the unique position of Kṛṣṇa-Vāsudeva, asserted that Saṅkarṣaṇa (another name of Balarāma, Kṛṣṇa's brother), Pradyumna (Kṛṣṇa's son), and Aniruddha (Kṛṣṇa's grandson), are not merely aspects of the divine character, but gods in their own right, as they were with the early Bhāgavatas.[3] A variant of this *vyūha* triad was the worship of Baladeva, Kṛṣṇa and Subhadrā as a single aspect (*ekānaṁśa*) of Viṣṇu. Varāhamihira refers to a combined image of them, and to a devotional inscription from Bhuvaneśvara, addressed to Baladeva, Kṛṣṇa and Subhadrā.[4]

At an early stage of its development the Pāñcarātra appears to have combined with the Bhāgavatas, and later, under the leadership of Yamunācārya to have propounded the doctrine of Viśiṣṭādvaita (qualified non-duality) and to have 'laid the foundation of all the doctrines that go under Rāmānuja's name'.[5]

Other works appeared as the Pāñcarātra influence spread. These dealt with the two classes of 'emanations' of Viṣṇu, *vyūhas* (manifestations), and *avatāras* (incarnations), and finally the recognition of Kṛṣṇa as the supreme (*para*) incarnation of Viṣṇu.[6] But the list of *vyūhas* and *avatāras* varied from sect to sect. The *Ahirbudhnya Saṁ.* includes the Buddha (under the name of Śāntātman).[7]

Many factors influenced the development of the Pāñcarātra and sometimes created inconsistencies, but this sect contributed greatly to the formation of modern Hinduism.

[1] *SED.*, p. 614; v. also p. 577.

[2] Banerjea, *PTR.*, p. 42.

[3] Basham, *WI.*, p. 329.

[4] Thus the Pāñcarātrins relied not solely on textual exposition, but on three-dimensional imagery, and hence their emphasis on having images of Viṣṇu or one or another of his aspects in temples and households.

[5] R.C. Majumdar, 'Religion and Philosophy', in *HCIP.*, vol. v, p. 437.

[6] Cf. the claim of Christ: 'I and my Father are one', Gospel of St. John, X.30.

[7] The *Agni Purāṇa* uses the epithet Śāntātmā in referring to the 'Buddha in its description of his image: Śāntātmā lambakarṇaścha gaurāṅgaśchāmbarāvṛtaḥ, "Śāntātmā, i.e., Buddha (is to be shown with) long (pendulous) ears, (is) white-complexioned and covered with garments (the *trichīvara* of the monks)"' (Banerjea, *PTR.*, p. 47). For Pāñcarātra theories of incarnations v. Parrinder, *Avatar and Incarnation*, pp. 59f.; v. under 'Avatāra' for lists of the various *avatāras*.

Pañcatantra[1] A collection of popular tales and fables comprising five (*pañca*) books (*tantra*), compiled by Viṣṇuśarman. 'The original of this work, now lost, goes back to the early centuries of the Christian era ... In India we have three distinct versions: the north-western, which can be traced in the *Bṛhat-kathā-mañjarī* and *Kathāsarit-sāgara*; two Kāṣmir versions called *Tantrākhyāyikā* and two Jain recensions based on a text akin to it; a southern version from which was derived the Nepalese *Pañcatantra* and the well-known *Hitopadeśa*'.[2] With the exception of the *Tantrākhyāyikā*, which probably belongs to the classical age, the remaining recensions date from the seventh to the twelfth century A.D.

Like most ancient tales (*itihāsas*), those of the *Pañcatantra* probably originated as myths relating to cosmogonic phenomena and their influence on fertility; or to exceptional topographical features, like mountains, rivers and trees; or to particular animals, serpents and birds, all of which were personified and generally endowed with human or superhuman qualities. Such tales are the prototypes of later literary productions, like the Jātakas, Purāṇas, romances, dramas, and the Epics of the post-Vedic period.

Traces of some of these ancient tales are evident in obscure passages in the *RV.* and *AV.*, but their successors reveal a remarkable proficiency in style and in the use of ingenious literary devices, such as enlarging a single fable or story into a succession of them, each subtly related to its predecessor, and all forming a many-faceted but single literary structure like that of the *Hitopadeśa*. Though probably only intended initially for entertainment, some of these tales inculcated moral lessons, and contained wise maxims. The story was usually related in prose, the moral introduced at the end as a short verse, a form intended to fasten it securely in the memory, particularly of the young.

Many of the ancient Indian folk-tales found their way into the literature of the Middle East and thence into that of Europe. They were translated in the sixth century A.D. from Sanskrit into Pahlevi, thence into Arabic and Syriac. The Arabic version or others derived from later recensions, particularly of the *Hitopadeśa*, were translated over the centuries into Persian, Hebrew, Latin, Spanish, Italian and other languages of Europe and Asia.[3]

[1]F. Edgerton has reconstructed the text of the work and given an E. translation under the title Pañcatantra Reconstructed, *AOS.*, 1924; and also by the same translator, *The Pañcatantra*, London, 1965. From translations of translations of this work have come some of the most notable books of medieval Europe such as the *Directorium* of John of Capua (1270), and *Buch der Beispiele* (1483), etc.

[2]*HCIP.*, vol. III, p. 314. Over 200 different versions of the *Pañcatantra* are known to exist in over fifty languages, the majority of which are not Indian (J. Hertel, *Das Pañcatantra, seine Geschichte und seine Verbreitung*, pp. 451f.). For the various translations of the *Pañcatantra* over the centuries, v. Singhal, *India*, vol. I, pp. 204ff.

[3]*HCIP.*, vol. III, p. 629.

Pañcavṛkṣa The five trees of Indra's Paradise (*svarga*), viz., mandāra, pārijāta, saṁtāna, kalpavṛkṣa and hari-candana.

Pāṇḍava(s) Sons of Pāṇḍu,[1] brother of Dhṛtarāṣṭra. Pāṇḍu's sons were Yudhiṣṭhira, Bhīma, Arjuna, by his first wife Pṛthā (Kuntī), and Nakula and Sahadeva by his second wife Mādrī.

The story of the battle between the Pāṇḍavas and their cousins, the Kauravas, is described in the *Mahābhārata*, an epic poem which reveals traces of Vedic mythology.[2]

The Pāṇḍavas are said to have possessed Indra's unfailing javelin (*amoghā śakti*), made by the divine craftsman Tvaṣṭṛ. They worshipped it with perfumes, garlands, food, etc.; it was 'a javelin inspired by *mantras* into an *Indra-astram*.'[3]

[1]The first mention of this name that 'can be dated seems to be in a *vārttika* or supplementary rule to Pāṇini, IV.1,44, attributed to Kātyāyana (c. 180 B.C.). The Pāṇḍus, whatever may have been their antiquity, first come into view with the later Buddhist literature, which recognizes the Pāṇḍavas as a mountain clan' (*CHI.*, vol. I, p. 253).

[2]v. S. Wikander and G. Dumézil, 'La légende des Pāṇḍava et la substructure mythique du Mahābhārata', cited by Eliade, *Yoga*, p. 146.

[3]*EM.*, p. 124.

Pāṇḍu v. Pāṇḍava(s); Mahābhārata.

Pāṇini The author of the *Aṣṭādhyāyī*, the earliest standard Sanskrit grammar, which is regarded as 'one of the most remarkable literary works that the world has even seen ... no other country can produce any grammatical system at all comparable to it, either for originality of plan or for analytical subtlety'.[1]

All that is known of Pāṇini is that he was a descendant of Paṇin, and grandchild of a notable legislator named Devala. He is sometimes known by his metronymic Dākṣeya (his mother's name being Dākṣī), or as Śālāturīya after his birthplace Śalātura in the Gandhāra country.

Pāṇini mentions several grammarians as having preceded him, whose works were ancillary to the study of the Veda rather than to the study of grammar as such, and especially of post-Vedic terminology. Pāṇini's great work consists of eight lectures, each of four chapters, the whole consisting of nearly 4,000 aphorisms or *sūtras*. The work enumerates the technical terms used in grammar, the rules for their interpretation and application. Thus 'Pāṇini's work is a kind of natural history of the Sanskrit language'.[2] The term for grammar (*vyākaraṇa*) means literally 'undoing', and is applied primarily to linguistic analysis and then generally to grammar, but especially to Pāṇini's grammar.[3]

Pāṇini's date is variously estimated between the seventh and fourth centuries B.C., but as he was later than Yāska and earlier than Patañjali and Kātyāyana, the latter century seems more likely. Moreover, the language of the *Aṣṭādhyāyī* is closer to the prose of the Brāhmaṇas than to the Sanskrit of Kātyāyana. So great was Pāṇini's achievement that it was considered of divine origin like the Veda, the direct inspiration of Vāc, the goddess of speech.[4]

[1]*IW.*, p. 172; v. also B. Faddegon, *Studies on Pāṇini's Grammar*, Amsterdam, 1936.

[2]*IW.*, p. 176, citing Goldstücker.

[3]Ibid., p. 171.

[4]Heimann, *Facets*, p. 75; v. also *WI.*, p. 388.

v. Nirukta; Śiva Sūtra.

Paṇi(s) A non-Āryan people often mentioned in the *RV.* with the *dāsas* and *dasyus* as enemies of the Āryans, but their specific identity is uncertain. 'The words

Paṇik or Vaṇik, Paṇya and Vipaṇi, found in Sanskrit, suggest that the Paṇis were merchants *par excellence* in the Ṛgvedic age.'[1] Like the *dasyus* they were despised by the Āryans on religious rather than racial grounds, and especially condemned by the *brāhmaṇas* whose services they rejected and to whom consequently they refused to contribute. They were thus described in the *ŚBr.* (XIII.8.2,3) as niggards and 'scorners of the gods'. It has been suggested that the Phoenicians may have originated from the Indian Paṇis. The latter have been identified 'with the founders of the Indus Valley civilization and by the fact that the people of Carthage were called Pani or Peoni. Thus instead of a Phoenician immigration to India, there was a probable Paṇi exodus from India'.[2] Others have identified them with 'Babylonians ... with Parnians, the Dahae and other Irānian tribes; and with non-Āryan caravan traders'.[3]

[1]*HCIP.*, I, p. 249; V. G. Rahurkar, *Seers*, p. 101. In parts of the Veda they are said to be wealthy, also to be cattle-rustlers (Rahurkar, op. cit., p. 105). The *Tait. Saṁ.* (II.6,11) refers to them as cattle breeders or dealers.

[2]Rahurkar, op. cit., p. 105, n.115.

[3]*HCIP.*, Ibid.

Paṅkti A metre consisting of five *pādas* of eight syllables each. It is called 'five-footed' and accompanies the *gāyatrī* (*ŚBr.*, IV.2.5,21).

Pānśula v. Khaṭvāṅga.

Pāpa I. 'Evil, harmful.' Pāpa is regarded as the personification of the archetypal wrongdoer whom the *AGP.* (40,20) states should be propitiated with offerings of blood, bile and bones.

II. In astrology any celestial phenomenon that portends evil.

Pāpī Lakṣmī The personification of bad luck. With an iron hook bad luck is attached to enemies (*AV.*, VII.115,1). In India it is believed by many that malevolent spirits fear iron in any form.[1]

[1]Iron enters into the folklore of most peoples, either as a charm against sorcery or as a religious taboo.

v. Lakṣmī, n.1.

Paramahaṁsa(s) The highest of the four categories of hermits or ascetics devoted to the attainment of perfection and final liberation (*mokṣa*). Some classes of hermits though 'documented only in comparatively late texts, probably go back to the proto-history of India',[1] as is suggested by the Indus Valley clay figure of a holy man seated cross-legged in the religious position of meditation.

The four classes of ascetics noted for their soteriological aims comprise: Kuṭīcakas, who travel from one monastery to another, where they swallow only eight mouthfuls of food; Bahūdakas, who carry a 'triple-staff', wear red clothing, and beg for their food; Haṁsas (who may not stay more than a night and a day in a village), live on cow urine and dung and practise the *cāndrāyana* fast; Paramahaṁsas who practise a kind of Tantrism. They 'represent an extremely ancient, aboriginal, anti-Brāhmanic ascetic tradition and foreshadow certain "extremist" yogico-tantric schools',[2] whose members, being indifferent to bodily comfort, lived under trees, in graveyards, or in deserted houses, and often went about naked. So absorbed were they in their meditation on the *ātman* and the attainment of liberation that they made no distinction between differing mundane values, nor distinguished opposing moral standards; they also accepted food with the same indifference whether from the lowest or the highest caste.

[1]Eliade, *Yoga*, p. 139.

[2]Ibid., p. 140.

Paramātman The supreme essence, i.e., *brahman*. v. Ātman.

Parañjaya 'Conquest.' The name of Indra's sword.

Parāśara I. Name of a *ṛṣi*, said to be the author of *RV.* hymns I.65–75 and IX.97, and of a law-book.

II. Name of a *ṛṣi* whose father was the son (or grandson) of Vasiṣṭha; his mother was Adṛṣyantī. During her pregnancy her husband was devoured by a *rākṣasa*, but Parāśara remained safely in her womb for twelve years. When he learnt of his father's death he vowed to destroy all *rākṣasas*, and prepared a sacrifice to achieve this end, but Vasiṣṭha dissuaded him[1] Thus he was left with the dangerous magical remains of the unconsumed sacrificial fire which he flung into the northern face of the Himālaya where it is said to blaze forth consuming *rākṣasas* and forests.

Parāśara became enamoured of Satyavatī, whose mother, the *apsaras* Adrikā, though condemned to assume the form of a fish, nonetheless bore Satyavatī, a girl of great beauty, but cursed with a fishy odour. She was left with fisherfolk to rear and subsequently plied a small ferry boat on the river. One of her passengers was Parāśara who lost no time in making his feelings known to her. She repulsed his advances but finally agreed to yield to him provided he rid her of her objectionable smell. The *ṛṣi* readily consented and henceforth she was known as Gandhavatī, the sweet-scented one. The child of their union became the twenty-eighth Veda-vyāsa, called Kṛṣṇa-dvaipāyana, an allusion to his having been born on an island (*dvīpa*) in the Yamunā river (*MBh.*, Ādi pa., 63).

[1]The *VP.*, I.1, states that Parāśara was given a number of boons (as rewards for his forbearance) by Pulastya, a

mind-born son of Brahmā. One boon was that he should become the author of a summary of all the Purāṇas.

III. Name of an ancient Indian astronomer, the author of the *Parāśaratantra*. He is said to have received instruction in astronomy (*jyotiṣa*) from Soma (the Moon), and then imparted it to the Yavanas (Greeks).

Pārāśraya v. Kalkin.

Paraśu 'Battle-axe', made of bronze or iron. This weapon was evolved from the Neolithic cutting tool, examples of which have been found at a number of sites in India.[1] The metal battle-axe was a favourite weapon of the ruling class (*kṣatra*). In some rural communities the axe is regarded as a 'thunderstone'—an uncanny object in which dwells a spirit, and hence it is placed on the pile of stones that form the village shrine.[2]

[1]Many of these are illustrated in *The Birth of Indian Civilization* by B. and F. R. Allchin.

[2]Crooke, *Things Indian*, p. 18.

v. Paraśurāma.

Paraśurāma 'Rāma with the battle-axe' (*paraśu*). Traditional history describes him as a member of the Bhārgavas, a priestly family which claimed descent from Bhṛgu. The family settled in Ānarta (Gujarāt) and became closely associated with the Haihayas after the latter's conquest of Western India.[1] Kṛtavīrya, the Haihaya king, made them his priests and endowed them with great wealth. Kṛtavīrya's family subsequently demanded its return, but meeting with a blunt refusal, forced the Bhārgavas to flee for safety to Kānyakubja. Although *brāhmaṇas*, and thus traditionally forbidden to engage in warfare, the Bhārgavas began to arm themselves and to enter into marital alliances with influential warrior (*kṣatra*) families, one of their leaders Ṛcīka marrying Satyavatī, the daughter of Gādhi, king of Kānyakubja. Their son was Jamadagni, father of the famous warrior Paraśurāma, who was later to avenge both the oppression of his family by the Kārtavīryas and their subsequent murder of his father.

One legend suggests that these tragic events were the motive for his hatred of *kṣatriyas* generally, but the account in the *MBh.* (I.66,48, etc., *EM.*) states that he 'descended' to earth as the sixth *avatāra* of Viṣṇu to re-establish the social order which had been disrupted by arrogant *kṣatriyas* attempting to usurp the spiritual and social leadership traditionally claimed by *brāhmaṇas*. After twenty-one attempts he is reputed to have destroyed all *kṣatriyas* and given their lands to Kaśyapa, but was finally defeated by Rāmacandra (son of Daśaratha), the seventh *avatāra* of Viṣṇu.

Paraśurāma's conquests are the subject of a number of legends all suggesting that he was instrumental in colonizing much of Southern India, where many shrines are dedicated to him.[2] One account states that Kāmadhenu, the Cow of Plenty, which Indra had entrusted to the *ṛṣis*, was the prize for which the *kṣatriyas* fought and which they would have succeeded in gaining had not Viṣṇu's *avatāra* intervened. So littered was the earth after the battle that Paraśurāma had hardly room on which to stand and gaze upon the land that stretched endlessly to the south.

Varuṇa, the god of law and order, apprehensive of Paraśurāma's ambition, told him that he should have only the land within bow-shot, but fearing also his strength and skill, Varuṇa changed Yama, lord of the nether regions, into an ant which gnawed Paraśurāma's bow-string. Thus weakened, its arrow only reached Malabar. Thus the origin of Malabar is traditionally ascribed to Paraśurāma.

Vaiṣṇava legends generally ignore the bloodthirsty aspect[3] of Paraśurāma's character when portraying him as an incarnation (*avatāra*)[4] of Viṣṇu, and refer to him not as Paraśurāma but as Bhārgava Rāma, or call him by his patronymic, Jāmadagni Rāma, names which serve to distinguish him from Rāma (Rāmacandra) son of Daśaratha, and from Balarāma, Kṛṣṇa's brother. Like so many great heroes he is believed to be still living in a cavern in Central India.

[1]History suggests that the Haihaya motive for domination was to control the sea-trade of the West (*HCIP.*, I, pp. 282f.).

[2]The calendar of the Paraśurāma era is still followed in Malabar (*HP.*, p. 172).

[3]The *AGP.*, 276, 22f., refers to the extermination of the *kṣatriyas* as Paraśurāma's mission.

[4]Banerjea considers that Paraśurāma is really an *āveśāvatāra*, i.e., possessed temporarily by Viṣṇu, because he ceased to be an *avatāra* as soon as Rāmacandra (the seventh *avatāra*) appeared (*DHI.*, pp. 419f.).

Paravāṇi 'Peacock.' The vehicle (*vāhana*) of Kārttikeya.

Pārijāta The Indian Coral Tree (Erythrina indica), said to be one of the five trees produced at the Churning of the Ocean (*samudramathana*). It grew in Indra's paradise and its scent perfumed the worlds (*VP.*, I.9). Śacī, Indra's 'wife', loved the tree which provided her with flowery ornaments, but as Kṛṣṇa's wife Satyabhāmā coveted it Kṛṣṇa stole it for her. This led to a fight in which Indra was defeated (*VP.*, V.30), and Kṛṣṇa took the tree to Dvārakā, but after his death it was returned to Indra's Paradise (V.38).

The Coral tree has trifoliate leaves which represent the *trimūrti*, the middle leaflet representing Viṣṇu, the right and left representing Brahmā and Śiva respectively.

Parikṣit A son of Abhimanyu and Uttarā and grandson of Arjuna. After the conclusion of the Bhārata War, Yudhiṣṭhira (the eldest of the Pāṇḍu princes), abdicated the throne of Hastināpura in favour of Parikṣit.

The *Bhāgavata P.* relates that Parikṣit, having offended a hermit, was condemned to die at the end of seven days from snake-bite. The king, in preparation for this event, retired to the banks of the Ganges. He asked what a man should do when about to die, and was told that the *Bhāgavata P.* should be narrated to him, for nothing 'secures final happiness so certainly as to die whilst the mind is wholly concentrated on Viṣṇu'.[1]

[1] *VP.*, Pref., xxxivf.; *Bhāg. P.*, III.74.227,230, *PI.*

Pārikṣita 'Descendant of Parikṣit', the patronymic of a king called Janamejaya, mentioned in the *ŚBr.* (XIII.5.4, 1) as the performer of a horse-sacrifice (*aśvamedha*). This sacrifice and the accompanying lavish gifts to the priestly officiants ended the long-standing feud between them and the Pārikṣitas. The mystery of the latter's disappearance from historical records is referred to in the *Bṛhad-Ār. Up.* (III.3,1) and made the subject of a quasi-philosophical discussion.

Owing to the syncretizing of traditions relating to two kings named Janamejaya, one the grandson of Kuru and ancestor of the Pāṇḍavas, the other a grandson of Arjuna and therefore a descendant of the Pāṇḍavas, little historical value can be attributed to any of the accounts of the Pārikṣitas.

Pāriṣada(s) Mythical beings with various animal or bird heads such as tortoise, cock, crow, owl, dog, fox, boar, elephant, lion, etc.,[1] said to be attendant on Śiva and Skanda.

[1] *DHI.*, p. 356. Cf. the ancient Egyptian divine beings who resembled falcons, lions, snakes and bulls. They formed a protective square round the cult-god (the Falcon) when he was threatened by his great enemy the snake (Reymond, *Mythological Origin of the Egyptian Temple*, p. 195). Cf. also the animal-like demons associated with the European myth of the Wild Hunt (Herzog, *Psyche and Death*, p. 73).

Parjanya The personification of rain or of the rain-cloud as a son of Dyaus.

Parjanya is sometimes represented as a bull and is then equated with Indra (*RV.*, III.55,17, etc.) whom he replaced as a god of rain.[1] He forms the 'germ of life' in cows, mares, plants and women (V.83,1; VI.52,16; VII.102). He gives good health and healing plants, and generates the corn and food offerings of the sacrifice (VI.52,6 and 16). In the same work (V.83,6) he is called an Asura, an ancient epithet 'which originally belonged to Varuṇa and other prehistoric gods'.[2]

In an *AV.* hymn (IV.15,1–16) he is implored to send abundant rain. The *Nir.* (10.10) suggests a number of fanciful etymologies for his name, one of which calls him 'bestower of juices' whom the whole world fears when as the 'rainer' he thunders and strikes down evil-doers (10.11). He moves in a chariot laden with water in skins and mighty vessels which he pours on the earth (*RV.*, V.83, 7–8).[3]

Parjanya should be worshipped during the building of a house. The *AGP.*, 263, 17f., states that the Sun, Moon-gods and Parjanya should be worshipped to prevent any occurrence which might affect the annual rainfall of a country.[4]

[1] Hopkins considers Parjanya to be the 'rain form of Indra, although given a distinct personality' (*EM.*, p. 128).

[2] *BIP.*, p. 56, n.1.

[3] The Canaanite Baal's rain was contained in pails. Cf. Job, 38,37.

[4] For the association of the *mekhalā* (girdle) with Parjanya and the giving or withholding of rain v. *Tait. Saṁ.*, VI.3.4,5.

Parṇa Later called *palāśa*. A magnificent tree (Butea monosperma) which bears masses of brilliant orange flowers, and hence is popularly known as 'flame of the forest'. Its leaf consists of three leaflets, the central (or terminal) being obovate and considerably larger than the lateral ones, which are from four to six inches long, and from three to four and a half broad. The central leaflet, which is shaped like a sacrificial ladle, is used for sacred purposes (*AV.*, XVIII.4,53 and n.), and its wood for making amulets, which ensure victory over rivals, the attainment of wealth, longevity, etc. Of the twenty-one sacrificial stakes (*yūpa*), six consist of *parṇa* wood (*ŚBr.*, XIII.4.4,5).

The sacrificial oblation is offered on the central leaflet of the *palāśa*, because it is truly the *brāhmaṇa* 'the priesthood' (*ŚBr.*, II.6.2,8). The *parṇa* also represents royalty (*Tait. Saṁ.*, III.5,7; *AV.*, III.5,2).

A man who drinks water in which *palāśa* seeds have been washed will be able to beget a male child (*AGP.*, 323,14).

Pārśva The last but one Jaina *tīrthaṅkara*. He lived 250 years before the twenty-fourth and last *tīrthaṅkara*, Mahāvīra.

v. Jaina.

Pārśvadevatā A deity serving as an iconic accessory and placed in a side-niche of the sanctum, but in other shrines the same deity could be the principal cult-object.[1]

[1] *DHI.*, p. 235.

Parvata I. A mountain or mountain-range, especially the snow-clad Himavat (Himālaya), which is personified as Parvata, its presiding deity. The *RV.* (I. 122,3) mentions Parvata and Indra, but only implies their association. The *ŚBr.* (IV.6.9,14) is more explicit, and describes them as warleaders, and the protectors of their devotees.
v. Pārvatī; Parvata(s).
II. A heap of grain, salt, silver, gold, etc., presented to *brāhmaṇas*.
III. A *ṛṣi* and associate of Nārada and the reputed author of *RV.*, VIII.12; IX.104,105.

Parvatāri 'Enemy of mountains.' An epithet of Indra, who 'clipped the wings' of mountains to prevent them moving. Mount Meru alone was excepted.

Parvata(s) Godlings who preside over mountains and clouds. As givers of offspring they are probably connected with an ancient fertility cult (*RV.*, V.41,9).

Pārvatī Daughter of Parvata, the personification of the Himālaya (*Kena Up.*, 3.25). In Paurāṇic mythology she was associated or identified with various goddesses[1] some of whom were probably regional. These were later absorbed into Śaiva mythology, each goddess being regarded as a *śakti*, or aspect of Śiva's energy, which in its entirety was personified as Devī or Mahādevī. Pārvatī was also identified with the *śakti* Jagadmātā, the World Mother,[2] and with *prakṛti*.

Pārvatī's 'consort' was Śiva. One day when she was seated nude on his lap, some *ṛṣis* arrived unannounced, causing her much embarrassment. To placate her Śiva announced that in future any male who intruded would be instantly transformed into a female (*Bhāg. P.*, IX.1,29–32, *PI.*). In another myth she is described as having playfully placed her hands over Śiva's eyes, but immediately another eye appeared in the middle of his forehead, so preventing the whole of creation being enveloped in darkness.[3]

[1]As Umā she was represented on coins as early as the Kuṣāṇa dynasty. Among her other names are Gaurī, Śyāmā, Caṇḍī, Bhairavī, Durgā, and Ambikā. Cf. the ancient Egyptian goddess Isis who was identified with almost every goddess in Egypt (James, *Tree of Life*, p. 169).

The Sumerian mother-goddess, like Pārvatī, was known as the 'Lady of the Mountain' (Levy, *Gate of Horn*, p. 95); she represents the lush vegetation of the mountains (Kramer, *Sumerian Mythology*, pp. 56ff. and v. also Pritchard, *Ancient Near Eastern Texts*, p. 37).

[2]*TT.*, p. 270, n.24.

[3]For further myths, v. *IT.*, ch. 8.

v. Bhṛṅgi I; Gaṇeśa.

Pāśa 'Noose, snare, or fetter.' Many of the post-Vedic references to the noose are apparently intended to be taken literally. Nooses were used in the great Bhārata War; and the *AGP.* (251, 1–6) gives instructions for their manufacture and the way in which they were to be handled. The *pāśa* was picked up by the left hand, passed to the right and cast by whirling it around above the head, and was used by a rider galloping, trotting or cantering. This implies that it was cast like the North American lasso, although this requires the co-operation of a very highly trained horse. On the other hand it may have been thrown like the South American bolas.

In the early literature *pāśa* is used metaphorically.[1] Thus Indra binds Vṛtra the drought-demon and so releases the rain. Rudra, Varuṇa and Agni also carry the *pāśa* (*RV.*, VII. 46,4; X.87,11), but that of Varuṇa is used to bind the evildoer (VI.74,4), and generally has a moral significance in other passages. Illness is also represented in the form of ties or bonds.[2]

[1]From 'Vedic times the "binding" complex, while it remains characteristic and constitutive of the zone of magical sovereignty, yet overflows it both upward (to the cosmological plane: Vṛtra) and downward (to the funerary level; Yama, Nirṛti; the plane of "sorcery")'. (Eliade, *Images and Symbols*, pp. 102f.).

[2]In the Akkadian Tablet IV, Marduk, the god of magic, is invoked to save his worshipper from an evil 'binder', to break the knot of evil and loosen his fetters (Reiner, *Šurpu. A Collection of Sumerian and Akkadian Incantations*, pp. 26f.; v. also King, *Babylonian Magic and Sorcery*, p. 22). The Gr. word *deô*, 'bind' or 'tie' and the L. *ligare* often 'designate the act of enchanting by tying or binding' (Entralgo, *The Therapy of the Word in Classical Antiquity*, p. 21). Tammuz is known as 'Lord of snares'; Yahweh is described as having nets in his hands, ever ready to entangle the guilty (Hosea, VII.12; Ezekiel, XII.13; Job, XIX.6); there are also references to the bonds of Satan in Luke, XIII.16, etc. For Śiva as 'binder of souls' v. *DHI.*, p. 128.

v. Ṭhag(s).

Pāṣaṇḍa 'Heretical', whence *pāṣaṇḍika*, 'a heretic', 'unbeliever'. The epithet was specifically applied to Jains, Buddhists and Cārvākas, but generally it referred to the Śākyas, Vajjians and other peoples of north-eastern India, where Jainism and Buddhism originated. Initially such variant views as those expressed by Mahāvīra, the Jain leader, or by the Buddha were ignored by the *brāhmaṇas*, but the subsequent popularity of these 'heretical' cults, and the royal patronage accorded them were regarded by Vaiṣṇava priests as a cause for apprehension. They therefore appealed to Viṣṇu who emitted from his body an illusory (*māyā*) form, so that the *pāṣaṇḍikas*, having been led astray from the path of the Vedas, may be put to death; for all gods, demons and others shall perish by Viṣṇu's might (*VP.*, III.6).

v. Darśana(s); Pāśupata II.

Paśu I. The collective term for cattle, goats, sheep, etc. It denotes specifically the five sacrificial animals: cows, horses, men, sheep and goats (*AV.*, XI.2,9), but the list varies in different texts. Sometimes camels, dogs, mules and asses are included.

II. A 'soul' which has become associated with impurity (*mala*) or bonds (*pāśa*). By nature all 'souls' are infinite and omniscient, but are called *paśu* when connected with any impurity. Then they experience finiteness and thus limitation.

Paśu-bandha 'Animal sacrifice.' The victims were beheaded or strangled, then cut open and after being roasted were offered to the gods. Jains and Buddhists, like most Hindus, have always opposed animal sacrifice, but goats are still sacrificed to the Tantric goddess Kālī in the Kālīghāt, and at Devīpaṭan, where the right hand of Satī is reputed to have fallen.

v. Yajña.

Pāśupata I. The 'herdsman's staff',[1] also called *brahmaśiras*. It is said to be Śiva's favourite weapon, with which he kills the *daityas* (i.e., unbelievers). Subsequently he presented it to Arjuna, or according to another account it is the weapon he will use to destroy the world at the end of the age.

[1]Cf. the Sumerian divinity Papsukkal called the 'Lord of the Staff' (Reiner, *Šurpu*, p. 28).

II. Generally considered to be the earliest Śaiva sect, the composite name, *paśu* 'animal' and *pati* 'lord', suggesting its prehistoric origin, when such a tutelary divinity was relied upon to protect the cattle and goats upon which the majority depended for their livelihood. This is evident in numerous regional myths which indicate the appeal that the Śaiva cult has had for village folk throughout India. It also helps to explain the diversity of the nature-myths associated with Śiva. The subsequent development of Śaivism as a philosophy was a long process, reflecting various stages of social and religious culture, and a period when there was acute rivalry between Śaivism and Vaiṣṇavism.

Maheśvara (Śiva) is said to have told Brahmā that in the twenty-eighth *mahāyuga* Viṣṇu would be reborn as Vāsudeva and he (Śiva) would become incarnate in the form of a *brahmacārin* known as Nakulin 'after entering a dead body in the burial ground of Kāyārohaṇa, a land of *siddhas*, and that he would have four pupils —Kuśika, Gārgya, Mitraka and Ruṣṭa—who, duly initiated into *Māheśvara-yoga*, would reach Rudraloka whence there is no return ... [a thirteenth-century inscription] records that Śiva became incarnate in the form of Bhaṭṭāraka Śrī Lakulīśa and dwelt in Kārohaṇa [Kāyārohaṇa] in the Lāṭa country, and that he had four pupils, Kauśika, Gārgya, Kauruṣa and Maitreya, who became the founders of four branches of the Pāśupata school'.[1]

Originally the cult consisted of a simple form of asceticism including overcoming greed and anger, the repetition of the sacred syllable *OM*, and deep meditation. Rhythmic songs and dances were performed to induce trance-like states.

The bodies of the initiates were smeared with ashes, and the utterance of particular *mantras* ensured that they would be delivered from the fetters of existence.[2] The cult met with much opposition, some of its practices being of an anti-social nature.

[1]*HCIP.*, vol. II, pp. 453f.; v. also *RAA.*, pp. 53ff.; *DHI.*, pp. 450f.

[2]*DHI.*, p. 451. Sometime between the ninth and twelfth centuries, Gorakhnāth 'accomplished a new synthesis among certain Śivaist traditions (Pāśupata), tantrism, and the doctrines ... of the Siddhas' (Eliade, *Yoga*, p. 303).

v. Liṅgāyat; Liṅga; Rudra.

Pāśupati I. 'Lord of animals', a title of Śiva as the divine Herdsman.[1] In the oldest ritual texts great care was taken to avoid using the name of this terrible god. He is 'referred to as "this god" or "the god whose name contains the word *bhūta* or *paśu* (i.e., Bhūtapati, Pāśupati)"'.[2]

The well-known Indus Valley seal depicting a figure seated in a yogic position and surrounded by animals was thought by Marshall[3] to be a prototype of Śiva, but the evidence is inconclusive.

[1]The Pāśupata cult absorbed many of the local godlings of herdsmen and shepherds. The notion of lordship over animals occurs in the Middle East and elsewhere v. Childe, *New Light on the Most Ancient East*, Pl. 1; Psalm 50, 10, 'For every beast of the forest is mine, and the cattle on a thousand hills'. Cf. the figure of the Master of Animals with a high horned headdress, striding over a bull, depicted on the tympanon of Ida, now in the Heracleion Museum (Charbonneaux, *Greek Bronzes*, illus. p. 43). *Paśu* refers to a domestic or sacrificial animal as opposed to *mṛga*, a wild animal.

[2]*HCIP.*, vol. I, p. 213, n.9. All creatures have either a *liṅga* or a *yoni* and hence all are Śiva's creatures (*EM.*, p. 223).

[3]*Mohenjo-daro and the Indus Civilization*, 3 vols, 1931; v. also two seals illustrated in *HCIP.*, vol. I, Pl. vii, nos. 4 and 6.

II. Name of one of the nine forms of Agni (*ŚBr.*, VI.1.3,12 and 18), and of one of the eight forms of Rudra-Śiva (*VP.*, I.8).

Pāṭā A medicinal climbing plant used in spells to remove a rival wife. 'From out of the earth I dig this plant, a herb of most effectual power wherewith one quells the rival wife and gains the husband for oneself' (*RV.*, X.145,1). With the aid of a talisman of the *pāṭā* plant hostile disputants may also be overcome (*AV.*, II.27).

Pātāla The collective name of the seven nether regions,[1] or the name of one of them, the other six being called Atala, Vitala, Nitala, Gabhistimat, Mahātala and Sutala.[2] Each region is 10,000 leagues in depth and has its own regent. The soil in these regions is of various hues: white, black, purple, yellow, or sand and stone-coloured respectively, but that of Pātāla itself is of gold. All are enclosed in the shell of Brahmā's cosmogonic egg which also contains innumerable mundane eggs,[3] the whole supported on the hoods of the cobra Vāsuki, who is also the ruler of Pātāla whose capital is Bhogavatī. He banned Garuḍa, the great snake-eating bird from Pātāla, but promised him a snake (*nāga*) daily for his sustenance on the shore of the southern sea.

The *ṛṣi* Nārada visited Pātāla and declared that it far exceeded the splendour of Indra's paradise (*svarga*) (*VP.*, II.5).

[1]v. Heimann, *PSPT.*, p. 4. *Tala* means 'lower part'.

[2]Some of the names vary in different works. The *Padma P.* lists them as: Atala, ruled by Mahāmāyā; Vitala, by Hātakeśvara (a form of Śiva); Sutala, by Bali; Talātala, by Māyā; Mahātala, the abode of serpents; Rasātala, the abode of *daityas* and *dānavas*; and Pātāla, ruled by Vāsuki.

[3]*OST.*, vol. I, p. 504.

Pāṭaliputra Name of the capital of Magadha and later, during the reign of Candragupta Maurya (c. 320 B.C.), that of northern India.[1] It derives its name from *pāṭali* 'trumpetflower', Bignonia susveolens. It was situated at the confluence of the Ganges and the Sōn rivers. Pāṭaliputra began as a fortress, built by Ajātaśatru, king of Magadha, as a strategic base from which to defend his domains from attack by his northern enemies the Licchavis. Settlements needed to supply the fortress soon grew up near it, and formed the nucleus of what, by the time of Ajātaśatru's grandson, Udaya, had become a famous city.

At the time of Candragupta Maurya 'the royal palace, although chiefly constructed of timber, was considered to excel in splendour and magnificence the palaces of Sūsa and Ekbatana'.[2] The city was the centre of an efficient administration, which included the systematic registration of births and deaths, thus providing the necessary information for the levying of taxes. To the capital came trade missions from many countries, and the representatives of foreign governments, among whom was Megasthenes, the ambassador of Seleukos, Alexander's successor.

During the reign of Aśoka, Candragupta's grandson, stone superseded timber for building, exemplified by *stūpas* at Sāñcī and elsewhere, as well as the palace at Pāṭaliputra.

At the beginning of the fourth century A.D. the Licchavis of Vaiśālī were its overlords, as is indicated by the marriage of the Licchavi princess Kumāra Devī (c. 308 A.D.) to Candra-gupta[3] the founder of the Gupta dynasty. Her dowry apparently included Pāṭaliputra, which thus became Candra-gupta's capital. To commemorate the event he struck coins in the joint names of himself, his queen, and the Licchavis.

Aśoka's palace, built nearly 700 years before, had been well maintained, for when the Chinese pilgrim Fa-hsien (A.D. 399–414) saw it he marvelled that such magnificence should have been created by human hands. But the conquest of Western India by Samudra-gupta left Pāṭaliputra no longer at the centre of the empire and rendered it unsuitable as the seat of government. It was superseded by Ayodhyā as the premier city, but the former capital remained a magnificent and populous city until it was destroyed during the Hun invasions of the sixth century. Thus when the Chinese pilgrim Hsüan Tsang came to the site in A.D. 640 he found it in ruins. In the ninth century the Pāla kings of Bengal and Bihar attempted to renew its ancient glory, and in 811 held court there.

[1]It stretched for nine miles along the Ganges, part of which must have been the site of settlements contemporary with those of Harappā and Mohenjo-daro on the Indus, as is indicated by numerous terracotta remains since discovered (v. *HCIP.*, I. p. 195).

[2]V.A. Smith, *Early History of India*, 4th ed., 128.

[3]The names of the rulers of the Gupta dynasty are hyphenated to distinguish them from the Maurya.

Patañjali The name of a grammarian and author of Books I–III of the Yoga-sūtras, the earliest systematic treatise on Yoga, who flourished during the second century B.C. But according to Jacobi[1] and Keith[2] the last Book (IV) of the work was added in the fifth century, but attributed to Patañjali by an anonymous *brāhmaṇa* in the hope that it might share the prestige of the earlier portion.

Patañjali admits in the *Yoga-sūtras* (I.1) that he was not the inventor of yogic techniques, his aim being to correct and systematize early doctrinal and technical traditions current among Indian ascetics and mystics. But the controversies concerning the period of the *Yoga-sūtras* are of little relevance, for the yogic techniques given by Patañjali are certainly of considerable antiquity.

[1]'Über das Alter der Yogaśāstra' (*Zeitschrift für Indologie und Iranistie*, VIII, pp. 80–8, 1931).

[2]'Some problems of Indian philosophy', *IHQ.*, VIII, 3, p. 433.

v. Yoga.

Pathyā The 'Auspicious Path',[1] personified as a goddess. She is requested to give prosperity to her worshippers (*RV.*, V.41,14; *ŚBr.*, III.2.3,8), and to protect them at home and when far away (*RV.*, X.63,16). Her role appears to be similar to that of her 'husband' Pūṣan, who was also protector of paths and of travellers. The *Tait. Saṁ.* (VI.1,5) associates her with the eastern quarter of the heavens.

[1]Cf. Zend. *Path* or *pathan*, meaning a path or way; OFries. *pad, path*; E. *path*.

Paṭṭa A slab or tablet for writing or painting upon, especially a copper plate for the inscription of royal grants or orders.[1] *Paṭṭa* is also the name of an early style of painting or engraving associated with a funerary cult. Metal *paṭṭas* on which are depicted figures of Viṣṇu and his ten *avatāras* are worshipped by Vaiṣṇavas.[2]

[1]It may be also a kind of silk.

[2]*IT.*, p. 355.

Paurava (s) 'Belonging to, or descended from, Puru', a king of the Lunar Dynasty. Their quarrel with their cousins the Pāṇḍavas culminated in the Bhārata war.

v. Mahābhārata.

Paurṇamāsī The name of the goddess personifying the full moon (*AV.*, VII.80; *VP.*, II.8). This night is specially sacred.

v. Phālgunīpaurṇamāsī.

Pavana 'Purifier.' The wind, or god of the wind (Vāyu),[1] who as purifying power is called 'lord of life'. It is also a term for vital air or breath (*prāṇa*).

[1]'Parjanya and Pavana are ancient names of "the deities concerned with wind and rain"' (Gonda, *Aspects*, p. 105). Vāyu has many names including Anila, Māruta, Samīraṇa (*Bṛhat Saṁ.*, XXXII.7; XCIX.2; XLV.45).

Payovrata A vow to subsist on nothing but milk. It is also called *sarvayajña* and *sarvavrata*. According to the *Bhāg. P.* (VIII. 16.25–60; 17.1–18, *PI.*), it is an 'offering' consisting of the essence of *tapas* (austerities) practised in honour of Hari (Viṣṇu). On the advice of Kaśyapa, Aditi observed this vow and as a result Hari manifested himself and promised to become her child.

Pedu A royal *ṛṣi* (*rājarṣi*) and protégé of the Aśvins who gave him a white horse known as Paidva (belonging to Pedu), which was renowned for its serpent-killing ability (*RV.*, I.118,9; X.39,10; *AV.*, X.4,5–7).[1]

[1]Cf. *AVB.*, pp. 605f. The horse was closely associated with the solar gods and with kingship in India.

Phālguna I. The eleventh month of the Hindu year (February–March) (*ŚBr.*, VI.2.2.18, n.1). The twelfth day of each month is sacred to Kṛṣṇa, who is worshipped under a different name in each month.[1]

[1]*EM.*, p. 69.

v. Nakṣatra (s).

II. One of several plants used as a substitute for the *soma* plant (*ŚBr.*, IV.5.10,2).

Phalgunī (s) The name of a double lunar mansion (*pūrva* and *uttara*). The *phalgunīs* are jointly Indra's asterism (*nakṣatra*), and correspond to him in name, for Indra is also called Arjuna, this being his mystic name; and they (the *phalgunīs*) are also called *arjunīs* (*ŚBr.*, II.1.2,11).

Phālgunīpaurṇamāsī The day of the full moon in the month *phālguna* on which the great *holī* festival is celebrated.

Phaṭ A syllable (*bīja*) used ritually as an aggressive *mantra* from the earliest times. To the Indian ear its sound 'conveys explosion onomatopoetically ... In Hindi *phaṭ* is a very common colloquial term for "burst, explode".'[1]

[1]*TT.*, p. 116.

Piḍārī One of the *grāmadevatās* (village goddesses) each of whom has a particular function. Piḍārī presides over the spirits of suicides and of those who meet with violent death. If she fails to control them their spirits become malignant demons and a threat to the living.

Pināka A staff or bow, especially that of Rudra-Śiva, which, according to the *Mārk. P.* (63,24ff.), Rudra gave to Svāyambhuva who presented it to Vasiṣṭha, the chief of the *siddhas*.

v. Ajagava II.

Piṇḍa or **Pūraka** A ball of rice or flour offered to the *pitṛs*. In funerary rites five *piṇḍas* are put on the corpse which faces the north. The orifices are filled with ghee and the eldest son or his representative recites the following verse from the *RV*: 'May the guardian deity Pūṣan conduct you on your long journey; may he deliver you to the *pitṛs* ...' (X.17,3). The *piṇḍas* are intended to nourish the deceased (*Manu*, III, 237),[1] and to assist in the formation of a body which his spirit may occupy.

[1]Many ancient peoples made offerings to the dead including the Sumerians, Egyptians and Hebrews. The latter offered 'libations and other means of sustenance at the tombs of the deceased members of the house-

hold . . . the dead were not only active and conscious but also endowed with supernatural power' (E.O. James, *Tree of Life*, pp. 216f.).
v. Ekoddiṣṭa; Śrāddha.

Piṅga A godling invoked to protect a child during the actual process of birth, and implored not to 'make the man a woman', or to let 'the egg-eaters injure the embryo' (*AV*., VIII.6,25).

Piṅgākṣa I. A leader of the Śābaras (a criminal tribe), who once saved some travellers from being robbed and killed. As a reward he was made the regent of one of the four quarters of the heavens.
II. A name of Agni, of Śiva, and of a bird said to be one of Droṇa's four sons who dwell in a cave in the Vindhya mountains (*Mārk. P*.,1,21).

Piṅgala 'Tawny', 'yellow'. An epithet of Śiva; the name of one of Sūrya's doorkeepers, the other being Daṇḍi (*AGP*., I.73,2–3).

Pippala The sacred fig-tree (Ficus religiosa).
v. Aśvattha.

Pipru The name of a drought-demon (or perhaps a leader of hostile aborigines). Pipru was the enemy of Indra's protégé Ṛjiśvan (*RV*., I.101.1,2; IV.16,13), so Indra killed him (VI.20,7).

Piśācā A daughter of Dakṣa and mother of Piśācas.

Piśāca(s) Flesh-eating demonic beings.[1] Their origin is variously given: they were created by Brahmā (*Mārk. P*., 48.37; *VP*., I.5); they emerged from Pulaha; they were born of Krodhā or Piśācā; or produced by Darkness (*Manu*, XII.44), etc.

The *piśācas* are said to 'possess' people but certain *mantras* and herbs (*AV*., IV.37,10) will drive them away.

Piśācas dwell or congregate in cremation grounds together with *bhūtas*, *vetālas*, *yakṣas*, etc. (*Mārk. P*., 8,106–8), and move about at twilight, frequenting deserted houses, royal roads and doorways. One who sees them or other demons will die within nine months (*Mārk. P*., 43,5), therefore it is necessary to propitiate them with offerings to avert their harmful intentions. They are fed on holy days, but their share (*bhaga*) of the offerings are small and mean, such as food that has been sneezed or stepped on, food mixed with hair, insects, tears, or licked by a dog, or unconsecrated food. They are also given offerings of liquor, flesh, sesamum, incense, black cloth, etc.

Piśācas may assume any form at will and also possess the power of invisibility, and hence they can easily enter the mouth of anyone who yawns without covering the mouth or snapping the fingers to ward them off. Once inside the body they penetrate to the intestines and feed on faeces.

[1]Piśāca was also the name of a people whose language or dialect was known as Paiśāci (*PTS*., pt. V, p. 83, col. 2).
It is also the name of a form of marriage (*vivāha*).
v. Prākṛta.

Piśācī A she-devil.
v. Piśāca(s); Tīrthapālikā.

Pīṭha A post-Vedic word,[1] possibly a corruption of *pi-sad*, 'to sit upon', and hence a stool or seat, pedestal (especially of an image), a throne; or a site or centre of particular interest.

In the latter sense *pīṭhas* were places of pilgrimage where the Great Goddess was honoured under her many names: Devī, Śakti, Durgā, etc.

Each of the four *pīṭhas* represents the actual presence of the Great Goddess, as well as being 'aniconic altars, which had acquired their rank as holy places from the fact that ascetics and yogins had meditated and obtained *siddhis* there'.[2] The quaternary symbolism 'expresses the victory of the cult of Śakti in all India (the *pīṭhas* were distributed among the four cardinal points)'.[3] But the number of *pīṭhas* increased rapidly until it reached 108 (all of them associated with Devī).

After Śiva's wife Satī died, Śiva was inconsolable and wandered about the world carrying her corpse. Finally when the gods decided to reduce her body to fragments Brahmā, Viṣṇu and Śani by yogic means entered her body and divided it into small pieces (*Devībhāgavata*, VII.30; *Kālikā Pur*., XVIII, etc.). Other versions state that Viṣṇu divided her body with his arrows, or with his *cakra* (discus). 'The symbolism of dismemberment also occurs, though in different contexts, in lunar mythologies and in Shamanism. In the case of the *pīṭhas*, we have an aboriginal fertility myth incorporated into tantrism.'[4]

[1]Turner suggests that it is of non-Āryan origin, *IAL*, 8222. v. Snellgrove, *Hevajra Tantra*, I, pp. 14f. for names of the Buddhist Tantric *pīṭhas*.

[2]Eliade, *Yoga*, p. 347. Today 'the most important objects of worship in many of these shrines are usually stone blocks covered over with red cloth, which are described as this or that limb of the goddess' (*DHI*., p. 83).

[3]Eliade, op. cit., p. 346. For a list of Tantric *pīṭhas* v. Sircar, 'The Śākta Pīṭhas' (*JRAS*., Bengal, 1948).

[4]Eliade, op. cit., p. 347.

Pitṛ-loka The realm or sphere (*loka*) of the *pitṛs* (ancestors), sometimes identified with heaven (*svarga*) (*AV*., XVIII.4,64), but more often conceived as a nether-world situated in the South beyond the realm of the living. It is sometimes identified with Yamaloka.

Pitṛ(s) The 'Fathers', 'Manes'. It also has the meaning of 'ancestors', the 'begetters' (*janitṛs*), of the family or tribe. As is to be expected in a patriarchal society the father was the protector[1] of his family.

The earliest references to the *pitṛs* occur in the *RV.* (X. 15,1, etc.), and the *AV.* (XVIII.2.48f.) which suggest that they comprised three classes, each class being allotted to one of the three spheres (*lokas*), i.e., the sky, atmosphere, or earth, according to merit. In post-Vedic times seven classes[2] are mentioned, three being incorporeal, but able to assume any form. Numerous myths were invented to account for their origin, such as that they emanated from the sun's rays; or that they were the offspring of the gods whose companionship they shared; or that they were born from Brahmā's side (*VP.*, I.5). As the *pitṛs* are no longer bound by the human time-scale, nothing, past or future, is hidden from them.[3]

The *pitṛs* inevitably became incorporated into brahmanic ritual. The relation of the Devas and Asuras (the joint forces of nature) to the various classes of living creatures thus had to be clearly defined. This was the task assigned by the *brāhmaṇas* to Prajāpati as the secondary creator. To the *devas* he declared: 'The sacrifice shall be your food; immortality your sap; the sun your light'. To the *pitṛs* were assigned swiftness of thought, and Soma (the moon) as their light, and to mankind death (*ŚBr.*, II.4.2,1–2). The reference to the sun and moon is repeated centuries later in the *MBh.* (XII and XIII) which states that: 'Two paths are known, one leading to the gods, the other to the fathers', and that 'the sun is the entrance to the path to the gods, the moon that leading to the fathers'.[4]

In Vedic sacrificial ritual particular objects were held to be sacred to the *pitṛs*, including the unwoven end of the priest's upper garment which was tucked into the waistband; the fringe of threads remaining attached to the loom when the web has been cut off; a red cow with reddish-white eyes; and the lower end of the sacrificial post (*yūpa*) which was sunk into the ground. Such objects subsequently provided the *brāhmaṇas* with a basis for a great extension of the funerary ritual (*śrāddha*), and an augmented list of food offerings considered to be most suitable for the *pitṛs* and for the officiating priests. But the list of foods given in the *Mārk. P.* (32,1–14; *AGP.*, 117, 44–8) should perhaps be regarded as symbolic, as some of them are at variance with Paurāṇic sacrificial tradition. The list includes the flesh of venison, hare, pig, antelope and even rhinoceros. Certain things were banned, such as turmeric, barley, garlic, onions, carrots, sesamum-seed, and anything manifestly salty. But of far more importance than the precise constituents of the offerings was the possession of a son[5] for the performance of the *śrāddha*.[6] The *pitṛs*, though usually associated with death and the underworld, were like Pluto also closely connected with fertility and the continuity of human life.[7] Allegro[8] points out that the 'earth's bowels' were regarded 'as the seat of creation where all life is conceived and after death recreated'.

The spirits of the dead are likened to birds, as in ancient Egypt and elsewhere. In India they are said to be always looking down to earth, and by analogy this led to the custom of feeding birds during the performance of funerary rites.[9]

The disposal of the dead among Indian tribes varied considerably, but consisted of cremation in areas where Indo-Āryan religious practice was predominant. In late post-Vedic funerary rites cremation was an essential condition, without which reunion of the deceased with his ancestors could not be effected. But the Vedic belief that this reunion immediately succeeded death was later superseded by the dogma that a deceased man had first to be a *preta* (an ethereal form) and undergo a kind of purgatorial existence for a year.[10] This was further modified, possibly to conform with the development of funerary beliefs. Instead of first becoming a *preta*, the 'self' of the deceased assumed an *ātivāhika śarīra* form,[11] i.e., one consumed by fire. This form was less 'subtle' than that of the *preta*, and subject to an even more painful existence before reaching the *preta* stage. To effect the transition, the *ekoddiṣṭa* rites were performed at six or twelve monthly intervals for one year, culminating in the *sapiṇḍī karaṇa* rite, at the conclusion of which the *preta* becomes a *pitṛ*, and entitled to share 'in a *pārvaṇa* rite which is the model of all kinds of ancestor-worship popularly known as *śrāddha*'.[12]

The significance of this rite to individual Hindus, whether perfunctorily performed in accordance with convention, or as a reverential act, is generally regarded as obligatory. It ensures that the whole Hindu community shall always remember the relation of the present to the past.

[1] 'Protector' is probably the etymological sense of *pitṛ*.

To the Romans the Manes were the spirits of the dead and the tutelary deities of their families, as were the Fravashis of Zoroastrianism.

[2] But the *Mārk. P.* (96,48) mentions thirty-one classes of *pitṛs*.

[3] In earlier times the gods, men and *pitṛs* could be seen drinking together, but now 'they are invisible to man' (*ŚBr.*, III.6.2.2,26). Cf. Plato, *Philebus* 18: 'And the ancients who were better than ourselves and dwelt nearer to the gods . . .'

[4] But in some Purāṇas the *pitṛs* are regarded not as departed ancestors but as an order of semi-divine beings dwelling in their own celestial world (*pitṛloka*),

who will be joined by all whose funerary rites have been properly performed.

[5]This is illustrated in the myth of the *ṛṣi* Agastya whose ancestors were condemned to remain suspended over a pit, until the childless *ṛṣi*, who was the sole thread holding them to the world of the living, should beget a son.

[6]Failing a son this rite could be performed by the nearest male relative, or as a last resort by a female relative ritually designated male.

[7]In the *Bhāg. P.* (II.3,8, *PI.*) the *pitṛs* are especially invoked to ensure the continuity of the family.

[8]*The Sacred Mushroom and the Cross*, p. 153.

In a rite to overcome infertility in a woman, the Ndembu of N.W. Zambia endeavour to contact the dead. The adepts carry white clay (representing semen) in a phallus-shaped calabash which is placed on the ritual winnowing basket, to the accompaniment of bawdy songs (V.W. Turner, *The Ritual Process*, pp. 53ff.).

[9]*Ancestor Worship*, p. 301. According to Baudhāyana the *pitṛs* assume the form of birds (ibid., p. 311).

[10]Though not identical with the Roman Catholic notion of Purgatory, the belief in the efficacy of prayers for the dead is common to both. Cf. the incantatory formula in the Epistle to the Ephesians, 5,14, 'Awake sleeper! Arise from the dead, and the Christ will give you light'. In its final Greek form this incantation 'is openly related to the necromantic cult from which it is derived' (Allegro, op. cit., p. 159).

[11]*Śarīra*, from *śṛ*, to burn.

[12]*Ancestor Worship*, p. 2.

Pitṛyāna The southern 'Path of the *pitṛs*'. Those householders who have performed the correct rites and sacrifices, during their lives, will after death go to the Moon[1] by the southern path until their *karman* is exhausted. Then they return to earth, firstly as plants, then as a member of one or other of the three castes, but the wicked are reborn as outcastes, dogs or swine. Death (Mṛtyu) follows his own path which is different from the path of the gods (*devayāna*) (*RV.*, X.18,1).

[1]The Irānian dead, if virtuous, went first to the moon and then to the sun; those who were almost perfect entered the eternal light of Ahura Mazda. The Greek Elysian Fields were situated on the moon (F. Cumont, *Recherches sur le symbolisme funéraire des Romains*, p. 184, n.4., Paris, 1942).

Plakṣa One of the trees in which *gandharvas* and *apsarasas* are said to dwell (*Tait. Saṁ.*, III.4,8,3).

Plakṣadvīpa One of the seven continents. It is surrounded by a sea of sugar-cane juice representing abundance. The people of Plakṣadvīpa live to an age of 5,000 years and enjoy good health, wealth, etc. In the midst of the island is the *plakṣa* tree sacred to Śiva (*Bhāg. P.*, V.1,32 etc., *PI.*).

Potṛ 'Purifier', 'cleanser'. Title of one of the priestly officiants of the sacrifice. Agni is identified with the *potṛ* and with other priests (*RV.*, I.94,6) and embodies in himself the functions of the different classes of human priests.

v. Ṛtvij.

Prabhā I. 'Radiance.' Daughter of the *dānava* Svarbhānu (*VP.*, I.21).

The Purāṇas, in an attempt to classify every section of Indian society, have provided a lineage for those of non-Āryan origin, i.e., the *dānavas* (descendants of Danu), the *daityas* (descendants of Diti) and others. Prabhā became the wife of Namuci, and mother of Nahuṣa; or according to the *Matsya Pur.* she was one of Vivasvat's three wives.

II. Name of Sagara's wife, the mother of his 60,000 sons (*Matsya P.*, 12,39,42, *PI.*).

Pracetas I. 'Observant, attentive, wise.' A term applied to the gods, especially Agni and the Ādityas. Like many similar Vedic terms Pracetas was adopted by the composers of the *MBh.*, *Manu* (I.35), etc. to designate one or more of the Prajāpatis (progenitors of mankind).

II. The collective name for the ten sons of King Prācīnabarhis and Savarṇā the daughter of the Ocean-god Samudra. His sons practised extreme asceticism (*tapas*) on the bed of the ocean for 10,000 years. Viṣṇu, being much gratified by their zeal allowed them to emerge from the depths. They found the earth too heavily forested so they burnt it down. They married the beautiful girl Māriṣā, daughter of Kaṇḍu, and from her was born Dakṣa; all mobile and immobile creation; and all two-legged creatures and quadrupeds (*VP.*, *AGP.*, 18, 21–8).

Prācīnabarhis v. Pracetas II.

Prācya(s) A collective name for the 'ungodly' non-Āryan peoples (*asuras*) living east of the Ganges, whose circular burial places are scornfully contrasted with those of the 'godly' which are four-cornered (*ŚBr.*, XIII.8.1,5).

Pradakṣiṇā 'Circumambulation.' 'The prefix "*pra*" indicates a natural pro-cess (urge).'[1] *Dakṣiṇā*, lit. 'south' or 'southern',[2] in this context denotes circumambulatory motion relative to the sun, which at noon is due south, the object circumambulated being always on the right. The *pradakṣiṇā* of sacred trees, animals, shrines, etc., is performed as an act of reverence, respect, submission or sacrifice. Furthermore, it is believed to bestow merit and prosperity; it acts as a protective circle preventing harm coming to the circumambulator; it also delineates a sacred area.[3] Temples[4] are also reverenced in this way for they represent the visible body of an invisible deity. During the horse sacrifice (*aśvamedha*) the King's wives circumambulate the sacrificial horse to make amends to it for its slaughter (*ŚBr*., XIII.2.8,4). But if circumambulation is performed in the opposite direction, it is called '*prasavya*', and has a malign influence resulting in misfortune or death.[5]

Though the *pradakṣiṇā* rite was initially associated with magic, it later became an important part of Vedic ritual and closely linked with the solar Viṣṇu, and with his traditional 'three steps' (which encompassed the world), represented by the triple circuit of a sacred object.[6]

In Tantric literature elaborate instructions are given for the correct performance of the *pradakṣiṇā*; the *Liṅgārcana-candrikā* (a hitherto unpublished text) specifies the number of circumambulations to be made for each deity: for Caṇḍī, one; Sūrya, seven; Gaṇeśa, three; Hari (Viṣṇu), four; Śiva, half of one.[7]

[1] Heimann, *PSPT*., p. 25.

[2] Cf. E. *deasil*, Gaelic *deiseil*, W. *de*, L. *dexter*, 'right', i.e., towards the South, or motion according to the apparent course of the sun (Whitney, *CD*.). v. also *ERE*., III, pp. 657ff.

[3] It was also believed to have a curative function as can be seen by the old Isle of Lewis custom which lasted into the nineteenth century. To prevent disease in cattle a man holding a firebrand circumambulated them thrice in a sunwise direction. This took place at the beginning of winter. A beast with an injured foot could be cured by driving it sunwise round a stone (Radford, *Encyclopedia of Superstitions*, p. 329).

[4] Cf. the present-day circular rides round the holy precincts of chapels in some parts of Germany, such as 'the Leonhardi and Georgi Rides in Tölz, Traunstein and other places' (Herzog, *Psyche and Death*, p. 184).

[5] Cf. the Celtic *cartuasul*; E. *widdershins*; L. *sinister*. In funerary rites, or cases of snake-bite, or of houses subject to snake intrusions, the *prasavya* method is followed by the priest; in the Roman Catholic burial service, the priest similarly circumambulates the bier.

[6] S.W. Nakamura suggests that the rite may have 'developed out of a primitive dance around the fire as a preliminary procedure in sacrificial rites' (*Semitic and Oriental Studies presented to William Popper*, p. 345, Univ. of California, 1951); or it may have had its origin in the Egyptian sun-cult. In the third phase of the building of the Edfu temple a forecourt and enclosure were erected 'which formed an ambulatory around the original structure' (Reymond, *Mythological Origin of the Egyptian Temple*, p. 320).

[7] *TT*., p. 93. Eliade points out that ritual circumambulation of a *stūpa* or temple indicates 'a march towards the center' (*Yoga*, pp. 224–5).

Pradhāna[1] 'Primary or crude matter.' In the Sāṁkhya system *pradhāna* is equated with the Creative Force (*prakṛti*), so-called because it 'produces' ($\sqrt{kṛ}$). It is the fixed material cause of everything except spirit (*puruṣa*). This infinite 'subtle elementary germ, *prakṛti* or *pradhāna*, though one, is supposed to be made up of a triad of co-eternal primordial substances or essences in equipoise (*sāmya*)'.[2] This attempt to explain the nature of things as the product of a bio-psycho-physical combination was used in the *Śvet. Up*. as the basis of a mystical interpretation of *brahman*, which was adopted by Rāmānuja in his exposition of the Vedānta philosophy.[3]

[1] As a synonym of *prakṛti*, the prefix *pra* of *pradhāna* is used in the sense of 'superior' or 'prior' and *dhāna* as belonging to the sphere of logical reasoning and measuring (Heimann, *PSPT*., p. 25).

[2] *BH*, p. 30.

[3] v. Bhandarkar, *VSM*., pp. 106ff.

Pradyumna The son of Kṛṣṇa by his chief wife Rukmiṇī (*VP*., V.26).[1]

Pradyumna appears to have been an historical figure, being one of the five Vṛṣṇi heroes: Saṁkarṣaṇa, Vāsudeva, Sāmba and Aniruddha.[2] The *Vāyu P*. describes them as *manuṣyaprakṛti devas*, i.e., 'deified human beings', four of them, including Pradyumna, being endowed with special sanctity and regarded as primary *vyūhas* (emanations) of the highest god, Para Vāsudeva, in the developed Pāñcarātra (Vaiṣṇava) cult.

[1] He is said to be an incarnation of Kāma, the god of love.

[2] *DHI*., pp. 93f.

v. Māyādevī; Yādava.

Prahlāda v. Hiraṇyakaśipu; Narasiṁha.

Prajāpati 'Lord of creation', from *prajā*, 'procreation or propagation', and *pati* 'lord'. A late Vedic cosmogonic concept, representing not only the personified forces of nature as a single creative force,[1] but also combining and including in the idea the creator theories represented by Puruṣa and Hiraṇyagarbha,[2] until Prajāpati was finally merged in the concept of Brahmā.

The *Tait. Br*. (I.6.2,1) states that Prajāpati formed living creatures[3] out of his sacrificial offerings to the gods, and when these creatures were destroyed by the storm-gods (Maruts), they were re-created. The *AV*. (XI.4,12) identifies Prajāpati's creative energy with Vital Breath (*prāṇa*). Other views associate or identify Prajāpati with the sacrifice, in the belief that only by regular sacrifices were the gods sustained. Hence the saying: 'Prajāpati is sacrifice, for he created it as his own image' (*ŚBr*., XI.1.8,2).[4] Even the remnants (*ucchiṣṭa*) of the sacrifice were held to be sacred to him, for he exists eternally in them.

According to *Manu* (XI.38) the horse is sacred to Prajāpati, and he is said to have assumed this form when he searched for Agni who had hidden in the waters from the gods (*ŚBr.*, VII.3.2,14–15).

Prajāpati's daughter is Uṣas (*Kauṣ. Br.*, VI.1), the goddess of the dawn.[5] The *Tait. Saṁ.* (II.3,5) states that Prajāpati had thirty-three daughters whom he presented to King Soma.

[1]There are thirty-three gods, Prajāpati being regarded as the thirty-fourth (*ŚBr.*, IV.5.7,2) and hence denoting Totality. Thus he is greater than the thirty-three gods and encompasses them and all other beings in himself (*Nir.*, 10,43; *CC.*, pp. 124f.).

[2]Cf. *RV.* (X.121,1): 'In the beginning was Hiraṇya-garbha, the only lord of all created beings'; also X.90, 2 and 8: 'This Puruṣa is all that has been and all that is to be. All creatures are one-fourth of him, three-fourths immortality' (*amṛtam*).

[3]Or he created the world by 'sweating' or 'heating' himself by extreme asceticism (*tapas*) (*Ait. Br.*, V.32,1); according to the *Tait. Br.* (II.2.9,1–10) he is regarded as the product of *tapas*. 'Sweating' is probably connected with Shamanistic practices. Cf. the Nordic giant Ymir who produced the first pair of human beings from his sweat.

[4]Prajāpati is the first sacrificer and at the same time the sacrificial victim (J.C. Heesterman, *Ancient Indian Royal Consecration*, p. 161). Prajāpati engenders Virāj, who in turn gives birth to Prajāpati. This 'reflects the androgynic primal being, whose two aspects give birth to each other' (ibid., p. 161, n.25). Although Prajāpati is the divine counterpart of the earthly sacrificer, he is also Time which leads to 'death, so that the sacrificer himself becomes death, and by that act rises superior to death, and is for ever removed from the world of illusion and trouble to the world of everlasting bliss' (*CHI.*, I. p. 142).

[5]In some myths she is said to be the daughter of Dyaus and Vivasvat. For Prajāpati's creative activity v. *Kauṣ. Br.*, VI.1–9.

v. Prajāpati(s); Kaśyapa; Atri; Bhṛgu I; Śarva; Prāṇa I; Vāc.

Prajāpati(s) The seven, eight, ten or more mythical great sages (*maharṣis*), the mind-born sons of Brahmā; hence they are also called *brahmarṣis* or *brahmaputras*, who are presented as the instruments of secondary creation (*Manu*, I. 1–119) in an attempt to formulate a rational theory of evolution. It begins with the notion of the Self-existent (Svayambhū) 'unknowable and unfathomable' (I.3) who divided his own body and became half male and half female.[1] From the latter, representing cosmic potency, was produced the male Virāj, who called into existence 'ten' great sages, destined to be 'lords of created beings'. These were Marīci, Atri, Aṅgiras, Pulastya, Pulaha, Kratu, Vasiṣṭha, Pracetas [or Dakṣa], Bhṛgu and Nārada (I.32–5),[2] the progenitors of the seven Manus, the gods and godlings, demons, atmospheric phenomena, and all species of animal and vegetal life.

[1]Cf. the ancient Egyptian god Atum who 'mated with himself to produce Shu, the atmosphere and his consort Tefnut, the goddess of moisture' (E.O. James, *Tree of Life*, p. 167).

[2]Considerable variety exists in the lists of Prajāpatis in the *MBh.*, and the Purāṇas, the original list containing seven.

v. Aṅgiras I.

Prākṛta Commonly transliterated 'prakrit'. A 'natural' language as contrasted with the 'artificial' language of Sanskrit. It is also the collective name of provincial or vernacular dialects cognate with Sanskrit.

Prakṛti 'Primal material nature.' 'The prefix "*pra*" indicates a natural pro-cess (urge)',[1] *kṛti* in this context having 'both an active and a passive sense, producing and produced. It is as much action as function'.[2] *Prakṛti* is thus the urge to produce, and 'is called *prasava-dharmin*, in the sense of having the immanent quality of productivity'.[3] All subjects, objects and effects are contained *in potentia* in the 'reservoir of primary Matter before, and after, their actual manifestation. *Prakṛti* is their common efficient and material cause'.[4] It is the only productive force within the empirical world.

Prakṛti is personified as the active female principle through which the inactive male principle of the cosmos is manifested. Together they constitute Nature and its dual function of generation and destruction which are of necessity interdependent. Thus 'all ethical canons fall outside the range of Nature's laws'.[5] *Prakṛti* and *puruṣa*, the interdependent elements of Nature, form the basis of the Sāṁkhya system which has greatly influenced Indian philosophical views.

In mythology *prakṛti* is represented as a goddess, the personification of cosmic will or energy in the evolutionary process, and hence every *deva* is inseparably associated with a *śakti* (energy). Thus *prakṛti* is *nartakī*, 'the (cosmic) dancer . . . [who] dances before the Puruṣa, in a voluntary display of her dynamic capacities'.[6]

[1]Heimann, *PSPT.*, p. 25.

[2]Ibid., p. 24.

[3]Ibid., p. 25.

[4]Heimann, *Facets*, p. 59.

[5]Heimann, *IWP.*, p. 42.

[6]Heimann, *PSPT.*, p. 75. The *Mārk P.* (45, 32) equates *prakṛti* with *pradhāna*.

Pralaya 'Dissolution', lit. a process (*pra*) of melting (*laya*), and hence of dissolution and destruction, i.e., of the world at the end of each age (*kalpa*) or day of Brahmā (*VP.*, I.7). It precedes a new creation or emanation. According to the *VP.* (I.7) there are four kinds of dissolution—occasional, elemental, absolute and perpetual. They are described as follows: 1. when the lord of the world sleeps, this is called the Brahmā dissolution; 2. when the world-egg reverts to its primary element from which it was derived; 3. the absolute 'non-existence' of the world as experienced by the *ṛṣi* who becomes merged in the Supreme Spirit; 4. the constant disappearance, day and night, of all that is born.

At the end of Brahmā's own life (of one hundred divine years) the great dissolution (Mahāpralaya) takes place (*VP.*, VI.1), which is ruled over by the goddess Mahākālī. This disintegration of the world is aptly described by Heimann as a 'de-individualizing melting process'[1] in which all forms disappear into an indiscernible mass.

[1]*Facets*, p. 52.

Pramatha(s) 'Tormentor', 'smiter'. One of the many classes of demons and sprites belonging to ancient Indian folklore, occasionally mentioned in the *AV.* and other early texts. Myths relating to them appear to have been current in rural communities throughout the Vedic and post-Vedic periods and given expression in the Epics and Purāṇas. The *pramathas* (who appear to be the same as the *gaṇas*) are usually associated with Śiva and Gaṇeśa. The former is also lord of *bhūtas* (spirits), and so he is connected 'with the spectre world, where the ghosts roam at his bidding, ghosts with whom he lives in the cremation-ground'.[1]

The *pramathas* are variously described as bearded, terrific, pot-bellied, hunch-backed and dwarfish, who sometimes figure on the lower portion of temple door-jambs, where they are believed to exert auspicious influences (*Bṛhat Saṁ.*, LV.14,5). Nonetheless, because they also possessed malign powers it was necessary to propitiate them, especially at the commencement of religious rites, lest they should obstruct them. At night they plague people who sleep at the foot of a tree, eat 'unholy' food, lie in the wrong direction, pollute water, or do not purify themselves after sexual connexion. Such people have apertures which give admission to these 'Smiters', but those who always carry with them *gorocanā* or orris-root, or keep at home the skin or claws of a hyena, or a hill-tortoise, or a cat, or a black or tawny goat, or keep up the sacrificial fire, are not troubled by them.[2]

[1]*IT.*, p. 133.

[2]*EM.*, p. 44.

Pramlocā A celestial nymph (*apsaras*).
v. Kaṇḍu.

Prāṇa The breath of life[1] or life principle, which distinguishes the animate from the inanimate. Hence the Hindu concept: 'the five life winds, the *prāṇas*, functioning in different directions throughout the human and animal body, are pregnantly formed with appropriate prefixes of motion connected with the verbal root *an*, to breathe. *Pr*(*a*)-*āṇa*, the respiration . . . forwards (*pra*) through nose and mouth; *ap*(*a*)*āna*, the respiration which goes downwards away (*apa*); *sam-āna*, the central circulation (*sam*), which has its seat in the cavity of the navel; *ud-āna*, the breathing out (*ut*), which rises up the throat and enters the head, and *vy-āna*, that which is diffused (*vi*) through the whole body.'[2]

In Indian philosophy breath means 'the vital breath', and is equated with *ātman*, the cosmic essence (*Bṛhad-Ār. Up.*, III.4,1), and with *brahman*. The association of breath with life and its cessation with death[3] is so obvious that it must have been apparent to man at a very early period, though the realization of their metaphysical significance must have been a long process.

The vital air that is immortal is in the upper part of the body and is the inspirer of all thoughts (*ŚBr.*, VI.7.1,11; VII.1.1,24). By the breath from his mouth Prajāpati created the gods; and by the *prāṇa* in the lower part of his body he formed the *asuras* (XI.1.6,7–8).

In the rite of preparing the ground for the fire the sacrificer *inter alia* puts down a naturally perforated brick representing this earth and makes the sacrificial horse sniff it (*Tait. Saṁ.*, V.2.8,1), thereby bestowing 'breath' (*prāṇa*, i.e., vital power) on the object sniffed. Elsewhere (*ŚBr.*, VII.3.2,12) 'the "sniff-kiss" of the horse is explained as a transfer of beneficent power comparable to or identical with the kisses with which the sun puts himself in contact with the creatures'.[4]

[1]Cf. the Gr. psyche which 'must once have meant "breath" but came to denote "spirit"' (Nilsson, *A History of Greek Religion*, p. 102). The ancient Egyptian god Amon, called the 'Hidden One', who manifests himself in the wind, was 'also, as breath, the mysterious source of life in man and beast' (Frankfort, *Ancient Egyptian Religion*. p. 22). The Hebrew term *rūĕh* also means wind, breath, or spirit.

[2]Heimann, *PSPT.*, p. 3. According to the *AGP.* (214, 6–14) there are ten *prāṇas*, each having certain functions; the *Chān. Up.* (III.16) equates the *prāṇas* with the Vasus, Rudras and the Ādityas.

[3]At death the individual *prāṇa* is said to go to the wind (*AV.*, XI.8,31). *Prāṇa* is the moving force of the universe. '"Breath" not only governed respiration but all the other physiological processes as well' (Filliozat, in *Ancient and Medieval Science*, p. 153). Cf. breath (spiritus) which generates the universe by moving about as in a kind of womb (Pliny the Elder, *Historia Naturalis*, II. p. 116). God formed Adam of dust 'and breathed into his nostrils the breath of life' and into animals (Genesis, II. 7, 19).

[4]Gonda, *Eye and Gaze in the Veda*, p. 49. Cf. *ŚBr.* VIII.7.3,10.

v. Prāṇapratiṣṭhā.

Prāṇapratiṣṭhā 'Endowing with breath', i.e., the act of endowing an image with life. Several rites are performed to animate an image. The eyes are opened first, and life is installed inside. The image is now 'god himself',[1] being filled with the vital breath (*prāṇa*) of the deity it represents.

[1]Bhattacharyya, *Canons of Indian Art*, p. 386. Cf. the ancient Egyptian belief as recorded in the Edfu texts 'that the nameless creators were believed to survive in the island in the form of an image ... this theory might have been derived from the belief in the "entering into a body" by a divine power' (Reymond, *Mythological Origin of the Egyptian Temple*, p. 90). Furthermore, the reliefs and statues of the temple 'were thought to be animated and to be filled with latent life' (ibid., p. 294).

Praṇava v. Om.

Prasāda 'Grace, i.e., divine grace or favour', a notion common to several of the Upaniṣads, in which the various interpretations of the term reveal the antinomy that existed between the strict *dharma-karman* doctrine and the as yet unformulated definition of *prasāda*. The former reflects the notion that the apprehension of the *ātman* may be achieved by knowledge, which is the essence of *dharma*, the latter that it is by grace that the individual is freed from illusion and attains immortality (*Śvet. Up.*, 1,6).[1] The *Kaṭha*, 2,23, goes further and presents a Calvinistic view of grace, declaring that the *ātman* is not to be realized by instruction, or by intellectual means, but is only to be attained by the chosen. 'To such a one the *ātman* reveals his own person'.

[1]A similar antinomy is evident at the close of the Old Testament, and also in the New Testament, which refers to the human individual as free and responsible, but whose salvation is nonetheless dependent on the intervention of a Power independent of him.

v. Bhakti.

Prasavya v. Pradakṣiṇā.

Prasena The brother of Satrājit.

v. Jāmbavat; Syamantaka.

Pratardana Son of Divodāsa, King of Kāśī. Pratardana was also called Kuvalayāśva because he possessed a wonderful horse called Kuvalaya (*VP.*, IV.8). Divodāsa's kingdom was conquered and his family killed by Vītahavya, King of the Haihayas, but by means of a sacrifice performed by Bhṛgu, Divodāsa obtained a son, Pratardana, who avenged the family wrongs and regained his father's kingdom.

Prati-nidhi v. Dakṣiṇācāra.

Pratīpa A descendant of Kuru, one of the legendary rulers of South Pañcāla. Owing to frequent wars between the kingdoms of North and South Pañcāla the fortunes of the main Paurava line declined but were ultimately restored by Pratīpa. Traditional history states that he had three sons[1] but legend only one called Śāntanu (*MBh.*, Ādi pa., 97). This legend, or rather legend-sequence, recounts the story of a curse laid on the eight Vasus for an offence of which they were unaware, but which condemned them to be reborn as mortals. To limit the duration of this affliction they successfully appealed to the goddess Gaṅgā to help them. To do so she had to marry a mortal, and as befitted a goddess he had to be a king of great renown.

The legend then recounts that Pratīpa after spending some years as an ascetic at the source of the Ganges, was one day confronted by Gaṅgā who had assumed the form of a beautiful maiden as part of her scheme to aid the Vasus. Soon she was seated on Pratīpa's right thigh, declaring that she wished to become his wife. The king protested, informing her that she had violated the tradition which requires that a woman soliciting a man to marry her should sit on his left thigh, the right being reserved for daughters and daughters-in-law. Thus for him to marry her would be incestuous. Nonetheless, if she should bear him a son and still wished to marry him, he would do so.

Subsequently Pratīpa's son Śāntanu was similarly confronted by Gaṅgā with whom he fell in love and married, but only after he had agreed to conditions which provide the motif for the next episode in the scheme to aid the Vasus.[2]

[1]*HCIP.*, I, pp. 294f.

[2]The other episodes comprising the legend-sequence appear under the entries: Vasus(s), Gaṅgā, Śāntanu and Bhīṣma.

Prātiśākhya(s) Treatises on phonetics written in the *sūtra* style, some anterior, others posterior, to Pāṇini. They form part of the science of proper pronunciation (*śikṣa*), especially that relating to the laws of euphony peculiar to the Veda, such treatises being generally classified as Vedāṅgas.[1]

[1]*IW.*, p. 160; *HIL.*, vol. I, pt. i, p. 146.

Pravargya A ceremony introductory to the *soma* sacrifice, in which a metal cauldron or a large earthenware pot, called *pravarga* or *gharma*, is used. This vessel is identified with Agni, Vāyu, Āditya, and with the solar year, which represents totality (*ŚBr.*, IX.2.1, 21; X.2.5,4). This mystic rite is believed to enable the sacrificer to absorb the sun's strength. It concludes with the sacrificial utensils being so arranged as to represent a man.[1]

[1]*HIL.*, vol. 1, pt.1, pp. 153–4. It appears to constitute a sun-spell (v. *IT.*, p. 229).

v. Mahāvīra II; Dadhyac.

Prayāga 'Place of sacrifice.' A famous place of pilgrimage (*tīrtha*), later called Allāhābād, situated at the confluence of the Gaṅgā and Yamunā rivers and the mythical subterranean Sarasvatī; hence it is called the 'triple braid' (*triveṇī*). The earth of this *tīrtha* is so sacred that even a small portion is said to cleanse from all sin. Women sometimes offer a braid of their hair to Gaṅgā.

Preta(s) Lit. 'deceased'.[1] *Preta* generally denotes the ethereal form assumed by a dead man during the period between death and union with his ancestors (*pitṛs*). But this definition has been qualified by local legend and changing social and religious views, which have resulted in the separation of *pretas* into various groups (v. *Manu*, XII. 69ff.).

Some *pretas*, though not evilly disposed towards the living, may haunt their former homes and may become malicious if not propitiated. They particularly harass children.

The *preta* state appears to be a kind of purgatory which some *pretas* must undergo as a form of retribution for 'sins' committed on earth, such as intercourse by a member of the 'twice-born' castes with a woman of the *śūdra* caste. The correct funerary rites (*śrāddhas*)[2] were essential if the *preta* was to be united with his ancestors; if not performed the *preta* becomes dangerous to the living.[3]

[1]Synonymous with *pra-yāta* and *pra-ita*, which 'denote an intentional forward motion "*pra*" to a further state of development by means of the transition into death', as distinct from the English 'de-ceased' or the German 'ab-scheiden' which merely 'indicate separation from the body or from the world in the moment of death' (Heimann, *PSPT.*, p. 89). Cf. Pā. *peta*, 'dead'; Prakṛt *pea*, 'ghost'; Gujarāti *pariya* (m.pl.), 'forefathers'; Sinhalese *pe*, 'ghost' (*IAL.*, 8998).

[2]In Sumerian demonology the dead who had not had funeral rites performed for them were greatly feared (Hooke, *Babylonian and Assyrian Religion*, p. 78). Cf. the Greek festival of Anthestheria; the Roman Lemuria; the Christian Purgation; i.e., the placation of the spirits of the dead.

[3]The ancient Egyptian dead 'became Akhu [transfigured spirits] through funerary ritual' (Frankfort, *Ancient Egyptian Religion*, p. 100).

v. Bhūta; Pretaloka; Pretacārin; Pretaśilā; Kaṭapūtana; Ekoddiṣṭa.

Pretacārin 'Roaming among the dead.' An epithet of Śiva.

v. Preta(s).

Pretaloka 'Sphere of the *pretas*', where the dead remain for one year or until the *śrāddha* ceremonies are completed.

Pretaśilā 'Stone of the dead.' A stone near Gayā on which *piṇḍas* (balls of rice or flour) are offered.

v. Preta(s).

Priyavrata The name of several teachers, who are distinguished only by their patronymics, as Saumāpi, the son of Priyavrata Somāpi (*Ait. Br.*, VII.34), or Rauhiṇāyana, descendant of Priyavrata Rauhiṇa (*ŚBr.*, X.3.5,14), etc. As '*priyavrata*' signifies 'having desirable ordinances and a regard for obedience', these attributes may be a form of title applied like that of *ācārya* to teachers.

In the *VP.* (I.7) Priyavrata is mentioned as a son of Manu Svāyambhuva and Śatarūpā. Priyavrata's descendants are said to have peopled the whole earth (*Mārk. P.*, 53, 1ff.). Another myth states that Priyavrata attempted to turn night into day by following the sun in a fiery chariot. After he had completed seven journeys, the ruts left by the wheels became the beds of the oceans dividing the seven continents of which his sons became the rulers.

Pṛśni I. 'Variegated', 'speckled', 'spotted', epithets applied especially to cows, frogs, etc. In the Veda it is the name given to the dappled cow (symbolizing abundance), the giver of milk and perhaps of the fertilizing rain.

II. The earth, personified as the goddess Pṛśni, the mother of the Maruts (*RV.*, I.23,10).

Pṛśniparṇī The name of a plant (Hemionitis cordifolia) having a spotted leaf, personified as a goddess of the same name. The leaf is used as a charm to ward off a malevolent being called Kaṇva (*AV.*, II.25) who causes miscarriages, etc.

v. Kaṇva(s) II.

Pṛthā The daughter of Śūra, a Yādava king. In accordance with a promise, Śūra gave his first-born daughter to his childless cousin Kuntibhoja (*VP.*, IV. 14), and hence her secondary name Kuntī. Kuntibhoja frequently entertained *brāhmaṇas* and other visitors to whom Pṛthā acted as hostess. One of them, the irascible ṛṣi Durvāsas, was so 'gratified by her attentions' that he gave her a secret *mantra* by which she could summon any god she chose, and 'by his grace obtain children'. Being curious, Kuntī shortly afterwards invoked the god Sūrya, and subsequently discovered that she was pregnant. Afraid of the scandal the news would cause, she secretly gave birth to the child and left it on the banks of the neighbouring river (the Yamunā), where it was found and adopted by the charioteer Adhiratha and his wife Rādhā, who named him Vasusena (*MBh.*, Ādi pa., LXVII). He was subsequently called Karṇa and became the lifelong rival of his half-brother Arjuna.

Later Pṛthā married Pāṇḍu, the Puru king, by whom—according to traditional history—she had three sons, Yudhiṣṭhira, Bhīma and Arjuna. This is contradicted by legend (*MBh.*, Ādi pa., CXI), which implies that Pāṇḍu was cursed to be impotent as a punishment for having killed a stag whilst it was coupling with its mate. The legend, having thus dealt with the question of Pāṇḍu's relationship, endowed each of the sons with divine paternity, Yudhiṣṭhira's being attributed to Dharma, Bhīma's to Vāyu, and Arjuna's to Indra, each prince being considered also to have inherited the qualities of his divine progenitor.[1]

During the long exile and loss of the Pāṇḍava kingdom owing to Yudhiṣṭhira's gambling with his cousin Duryodhana, Pṛthā kept the secret of Karṇa's birth. Years later, at the close of the war between the two families, when she heard that Karṇa had been killed by Arjuna she admitted that he was her son and hence the half-brother of the Pāṇḍavas. By her silence she had turned the Pāṇḍavas' victory into bitterness.

The story ends with the departure of Pṛthā and the blind King Dhṛtarāṣṭra and his wife Gandhārī (all that remained of the Kauravas) to a hermitage in the forest, subsequently destroyed by a fire in which all three perished.

[1]Nakula and Sahadeva, the twin children of Mādrī, Pāṇḍu's second wife, were also credited with divine origin, viz., that of the Aśvins. But why the birth of Karṇa should have been regarded as shameful and that of the Pāṇḍavas a matter for pride, is a question that the *MBh.* leaves unanswered.

v. Mahābhārata.

Pṛthī v. Pṛthu.

Pṛthivī 'The Wide or Extended One.' The earth and its personification as a goddess. According to *RV.* (VII.99,2–3) the word specifically denotes one of the two parts constituting the physical world: the earth (*pṛthivī*) and the heaven or sky (*div*), which are sometimes jointly personified as Dyāvā-Pṛthivī.

The idea of the earth's motion and its consequent instability is reflected in *RV.*, VII.99, 3, which states that the solar Viṣṇu supported the vault of heaven and firmly fixed the earth in its place. This myth appears in a different form in the *ŚBr.* (II.1.8–10) where the earth is likened to a lotus leaf which tosses to and fro in the wind until the gods securely pegged it down. Another variant occurs in the *Tait. Br.* (I.1.3,5) where the earth is spread out by Prajāpati on a lotus leaf, the roots of the plant being kept in place in the waters by pebbles, but in the *AGP.* (120, 39–41) the earth originated from Viṣṇu's body and assumed the form of a huge lotus traversed by mountain chains and rivers.

Pṛthivī is aptly termed Agni's womb (*ŚBr.*, VII.4.1,8) in which the embryo of existence is formed (*AV.*, V.25,2); hence she is called the Mother (III.23,6). She is thus closely connected with fertility,[1] and associated with the solar Viṣṇu. To the gods Pṛthivī is Aditi, to the agriculturist she is Sītā, and to living beings in general she is the Earth. From Pṛthivī's close connexion with husbandry (the occupation of the great majority of the people), a number of myths and legends grew up. Some of these suggest ecological problems, arising from population explosion that existed even in ancient times. Hence Pṛthivī's declaration: 'I cannot endure all these people',[2] and her appeal to Brahmā to reduce their numbers. His response was to create Death in the form of a beautiful woman, whose tears at having to perform such a task became fatal diseases, often subtle and inexplicable, for Death often comes softly.

The Earth is said to be the final arbiter[3] when innocence or integrity is in doubt, and hence Sītā's appeal to the Earth-goddess when accused of unfaithfulness. The Buddha also appealed to the Earth to bear witness to his integrity and to the truth of his teaching; hence he is often depicted seated and touching the earth with his right hand.

[1]And hence she is sometimes referred to as the divine cow, symbolizing the earth which provides all food. Cf. the Sumerian Earth-goddess called Ki or Nintu, the 'lady who gives birth'. In the ancient Egyptian Memphite theology the primeval hill emerged from the waters of chaos which expresses the 'belief that the earth's power is primary power and hence the source of all existence' (Frankfort, *Ancient Egyptian Religion*, p. 21).

[2]South Indian (Kumbakonan) ed. of the *MBh.* (II.51, 45f.), cited by Hopkins, *EM.*, p. 78.

[3]In ancient Greece the Earth Spirit was most frequently invoked 'for she is always near at hand and could not be escaped from' (Farnell, *Cults*, III, p. 3).

v. Pṛthu.

Pṛthu or **Pṛthī** The son of Vena, a ruler of one of the Vajjian kingdoms whose capital was Vaiśālī (Besārh). It was an important Buddhist centre, as is indicated by the ruins of a large *stūpa* at Kesarīya (thirty miles from Vaiśālī) erected in honour of Vena. Hindu tradition, not unnaturally, describes him as an arrogant and decadent *kṣatriya*, opposed to ritual and priestly authority, and against whom there was a general rebellion in which he was killed.[1] He was succeeded by his son Pṛthu, whose birth is fancifully described as having occurred from the right arm of his father's corpse, the arm having first been rubbed by priests. But traditional history appears to have syncretized the post-Vedic Pṛthu with the Vedic Pṛthī, and to have ignored the existence of the *stūpa* erected by the Buddhists to the post-Vedic Vena. Thus the Vedic Pṛthī or Pṛthu appears in the *RV*. (VI.27,8) as the name of a culture-hero and royal *ṛṣi*, who introduced agriculture (*AV*., VIII.10,24),[2] and the knowledge of medicinal herbs. According to the *Matsya P*. (10.10–35, *PI*.) he levelled the ground from Cape Comorin to the Himālaya, cleared forests and made the country safe.

Pṛthu's wife was Arcis, and they had five ideal sons. In old age Pṛthu entrusted his kingdom to them and retired to the forest to live an ascetic life with his wife. When he died Arcis lighted his funeral pyre and then threw herself upon it and so ascended to heaven (*VP*., IV.23).

[1] *HCIP*., I, p. 271.

[2] Pṛthu is also said to be the first anointed king (*AGP*., 18, 12–15). Once when there was famine he forced the Earth-goddess (Pṛthivī) to become fertile again, and from him she received her name (*VP*., I.13). But according to *Manu* (IX.44) she was his wife.

v. Niṣāda; Rājasūya; Satī.

Pūjā 'Worship', 'homage'. The word, which is not found in any Indo-European language outside India and Ceylon, is probably derived from a root *pūj* which 'appears, like the thing it connotes, to be of Dravidian origin'.[1] Worship in Vedic times involved a household ceremony called the Vaiśvadeva, which was performed for the family by one of its members—unlike the Sandhyā, which was performed by and for a person for himself. The worship of the gods (*devapūjā*) was also performed in public for the 'well-being of the world'. Originally it was 'an invocation, reception and entertainment of God as a royal guest'.[2] It replaced the basic Vedic rite which was sacrifice (*yajña*).

More sophisticated ideas about the nature and purpose of worship, were engendered by aupaniṣadic speculation, the *ahiṁsa* doctrine of Jainism and Buddhism, and by the impact of the *Bhagavadgītā*. Thus in ordinary Hindu practice, there is a great deal of compromise, as for instance in Vedic ritual, in which the worship of an image or a symbol of the divinity is distinguished 'by treating the latter, after it has been consecrated, as a living personality, and bringing before it, as before a living being',[3] simple offerings designed to express gratitude, and not as in Vedic ritual, to propitiate or to act as an inducement to grant favours. Nonetheless, as Gonda points out, there are 'many differences in detail, not only between Śaivas and Vaiṣṇavas' but also among other cults,[4] despite the attempts of liberal-minded *brahmins* to reconcile the differences of Vaiṣṇavas, Śaivas, Śāktas, Sauras and Gaṇipatis, so that their respective deities, Viṣṇu, Śiva, Devī, Sūrya and Gaṇeśa, should be recognized simply as aspects of 'the one absolute god who by himself, was beyond the ken of speech and thought (*avāṅmanasagocaraḥ*)'.[5] The ritual of this fivefold *pūjā*, called the *pañcāyatana pūjā*, is described by Monier-Williams.[6] It includes the placing of five stones in a round open metal dish which perhaps also represents their joint association. The stones are arranged in different positions according to the priority given to the deity represented by it. One is placed in the centre, the remainder being assigned to positions corresponding to the intermediate points of the compass. Thus when Viṣṇu, represented by a black stone, is placed in the centre, a white stone for Śiva[7] is given a position N. E., a red stone for Gaṇeśa in the S. E., a piece of crystal for the Sun in the S. W., and a small piece of metallic ore for Devī, the *śakti* of Śiva, in the N. W. Any of the five deities may occupy the central position and hence the ritual can be shared by all five religious groups.

[1] *HCIP*., I, p. 160; J. Charpentier, 'Meaning and Etymology of Pūjā', *IA*., LVI, 1927, 93–8, 130–5; Eliade, *Yoga*, p. 348.

[2] Gonda, *VS*., p. 77.

[3] *HCIP*., I, p. 160. With the growth of *bhakti* (single-minded devotion) to one's chosen deity, images were absolutely necessary for the various acts of *pūjā* (*DHI*., p. 78).

[4] Gonda, op. cit., p. 76.

[5] *DHI*., p. 541.

[6] *BH*., pp. 411ff.

[7] Śiva is also believed to reside in every white pebble found in the Narmadā river.

Pulaha One of the ten mind-born sons of Brahmā mentioned in *Manu* (I.35), who are frequently referred to as *brahmarṣis* or Prajāpatis.

v. Maharṣis; Kṣamā; Yakṣa(s).

Pulastya One of the ten mind-born sons of Brahmā. In the *Vāyu P*. they number eight, in the *Bhāg*. nine, and in the *Matsya*, ten—the same number as in *Manu* (I.35). Brahmā is said to have communicated the *Viṣṇu P.* to Pulastya who in turn communicated it to Parāśara.

Pulastya's offspring were the Vānaras, Yakṣas, Rākṣasas, and the flesh-eating beings called Piśitāśanas. Among his wives were Iḍāviḍā, Mālinī and Rākā; his eldest son[1] was Viśravas.

According to the *MBh.*, and *Padma P.* Pulastya and the other great *ṛṣis* represent cosmic principles.[2]

[1]Or he was a manifestation of a part of Pulastya himself.
[2]*HP.*, p. 317.

Pulomā A daughter of the *dānava* Puloman and wife of Indra (or of Bhṛgu).

Puloman I. A *dānava* and Indra's father-in-law. Puloman joined Vṛtra in his struggle against Indra.
v. Pulomā.
II. A name of the Lord of the *vidyādharas*.

Puṁsavana A rite to ensure the birth of a male child (*AV.*, VI.11,1–3, etc.), usually performed in the third month of pregnancy (*AGP.*, 75,15). During the rite a hymn is recited when the sacrificial fire is generated between the *śamī* and *aśvattha* wood firesticks (*araṇi*).[1] Heated ghee (prepared from the milk of a cow having a male calf) is then put in the nostrils of the pregnant woman, who is given a drink prepared from honey. Finally wool from a male animal is placed around the fire and subsequently tied to the woman as an amulet (*AVB.*, p. 460).

Diti, desiring a son who would destroy Indra, was advised by Kaśyapa to perform this rite. But Indra, afraid of its result, decided to descend to earth and become her pupil, hoping for an opportunity to destroy the foetus. This occurred when Diti failed to carry out the correct ritual, whereupon Indra with his *vajra* cut the embryo into forty-nine pieces which became the storm-gods (Maruts) and his chief allies.

A *puṁsavana* rite was also performed for Aṅgiras' wife when as a result of an error in the ritual she had given birth to a still-born child. She appealed to Brahmā and was told to invoke Sanat-Kumāra, who would instruct her. As a result of the correct performance of the rite she gave birth to Bṛhaspati, the preceptor of the gods.

[1]*Śamī* wood represents the woman, the *aśvattha* the man, and the flames their child.

Puṇḍarīka I. 'White lotus.' A large erect aquatic plant with leaves and flowers raised high above the water on long stems. It symbolizes purity. It is also a synonym for the manifested world, and in Tantrism is a synonym of *yoni*.
II. A *brahmin* famous for his great filial piety. He was later worshipped as the god Viṭhobā.
III. Name of one of the elephants supporting the south-east quarter of the world.

Puṇḍra I. A son of the *daitya* Bali, ancestor of the Puṇḍras.
II. A sectarian mark worn on the foreheads of ascetics (*sadhu*). Apart from indicating the wearer's religious group, it also expresses or symbolizes 'his living in connection with divine power'.[1]

[1]Gonda, *VS.*, p. 71.
v. Tilaka.

Puṇyajana A good or honest man. This term may be derived from the root *puṇ*, 'auspicious, good, pure, sacred,' etc. In the Paippalāda version of the *AV.* *yakṣas* are called *puṇyajanāḥ* (sacred folk). Later this term and another, *itarajanāḥ* (other folk), became synonyms of *yakṣa*.[1]

[1]*DHI.*, p. 337; v. also *EM.*, p. 148. Cf. the flattering epithets applied to the European fairies: 'good folk', 'good neighbours', 'little people', etc.

Purāṇa A collection of tales of ancient times. In post-Vedic times the Purāṇas became the medium for conveying Vedic teaching to the unlettered, who comprised not only the lower castes, but also the majority of women, to whom education was deliberately denied. These popular versions or proto-purāṇas later became a hieratic type of Purāṇa mainly concerned with Viṣṇu and Śiva. They drew freely on the Vedic gods and demons, who were re-mythologized in new legendary settings, often at the expense of chronistic probability, their chief purpose being to serve the respective interests of the two rival cults.[1]

A Purāṇa should expound five subjects (*pañca-lakṣaṇa*); the creation of the world (*sarga*); its destruction and re-creation (*pratisarga*); the genealogy of the gods and patriarchs (*vaṁśa*); the reigns and periods of the Manus (*manvantaras*); the history of the Solar and Lunar royal dynasties (*vaṁśānucarita*). Though the *pañca-lakṣaṇa* rules may have been observed in the early versions, very few of the extant texts conform to them, which suggests that the later versions include many accretions, including astrology, geography, chronology, anatomy, medicine, as well as on the use of military weapons. Much of the information is in the form of dialogues, in some of which an alleged divinely inspired sage is the principal narrator who answers the questions of a disciple or pupil. Nonetheless, these accretions are valuable and indicate the gradual erosion of Vedic theistic concepts, the development of the *trimūrti*, a diminishing interest in Brahmā, and the rivalry of the Vaiṣṇava and Śaiva cults during the Medieval Period.

Paurāṇic literature comprises two groups, the primary or major (Mahāpurāṇas), and the secondary or minor (Upapurāṇas),[2] each group consisting of eighteen works. The former fall into three categories: those relating to Brahmā are called Rājasa Purāṇas, with the *guṇa rajas* (passion) prevailing; those relating to Viṣṇu, called Sāttvika, with the *guṇa sattva* (purity) prevailing; those relating to Śiva, called Tāmasa, the *guṇa tamas* (darkness) prevailing. The Rājasa Purāṇas comprise: 1. Brahma (also Ādi Purāṇa and Saura P.); 2. Brahmāṇḍa; 3. Brahma-vaivarta; 4. Mārkaṇḍeya; 5. Bhaviṣya; 6. Vāmana. The Sāttvika Purāṇas comprise: 1. Viṣṇu; 2. Bhāgvata; 3. Nārada or Nāradīya; 4. Garuḍa;[3] 5. Padma; 6.Vārāha. The Tāmasa Purāṇas comprise: 1.Śiva;[4] 2. Liṅga; 3. Skanda; 4. Agni; 5. Matsya; 6. Kūrma.

Whilst each division relates in varying degrees to its respective deity, the arrangement is to some extent artificial and does not reflect, as it is supposed to do, a true image of the triple manifestation (*trimūrti*) of *brahman*. Moreover, though some of the Rājasa Purāṇas extol Brahmā, they are mainly concerned in advocating the worship of Viṣṇu or Śiva, and are more appropriate to the second or third division.

The eighteen Upa-Purāṇas comprise: 1. Sanatkumāra; 2. Narasiṁha; 3. Nāradīya or Vṛhannāradīya; 4. Śiva; 5. Durvāsasa; 6. Kāpila; 7. Mānava; 8. Auśanasa; 9. Vāruṇa; 10. Kālikā; 11. Śāmba; 12. Nandi; 13. Saura; 14. Pārāśara; 15. Āditya; 16. Māheśvara; 17. Bhāgavata (thought to be a misreading for Bhārgava); 18. Vāsiṣṭha.[5]

During the destruction of the world at the end of the age, Hayagrīva is said to have saved the Purāṇas. A summary of the original work is now preserved in heaven! (*PI.*).

The extant recension of the Purāṇas can hardly be placed earlier than the Gupta period, the earliest events related by them having occurred more than 2000 years before, an interval during which the original nucleus is likely to have undergone considerable re-editing. 'Besides this distance in time, the traditional account contained in the Purāṇas is vitiated by exaggeration, mythological details, pronounced religious bias, and the divergences in the texts of the different Purāṇas.'[6] Nonetheless, as the sole source of information relating to the early post-Vedic period, they cannot be dismissed as entirely unreliable. This is especially true of the *Viṣṇu Purāṇa*, which more closely conforms to the rules of the 'five subjects' than any other Purāṇa.

[1]It would be possible to collect a large number of instances of the Viṣṇuization or Śivaization of Vedic traditional themes as Gonda has indicated in *VS.*, pp. 134ff.

[2]There are variations in their lists. There are modern Purāṇa-type works also purporting to tell of ancient times.

[3]Several versions are extant but it is doubtful if any of them is the original version.

[4]The *Vāyu P.* may be a part of the *Śiva P.* (*Śiva Purāṇa*, vol. I, Intro., p. xiii).

[5]*IW.*, pp. 489ff.

[6]*HCIP*, I, p. 267. The reading of the titles of the eighteen Purs. and their constant repetition will ensure the same benefits as those derived from a horse-sacrifice (*aśvamedha*) (*Mārk. P.*, VIII.21,2, *PI.*).

v. Purāṇapuruṣa.

Purāṇapuruṣa The Supreme Being, who revealed the Purāṇas to man. He is identified with Nārāyaṇa (Viṣṇu) and Kumāra (*Matsya P.*, 53,2; 61; *Vāyu P.*, 21, 81; 22,13, etc., *PI.*).

Purañjanī Wife of King Purañjana. She symbolizes the intellect (*buddhi*). For a hundred years she lived happily with her husband but disapproved of his passion for hunting (*Bhāg. P.*, IV.25, 20ff., etc., *PI.*).

Pūrṇāvatāra Complete incarnation (*avatāra*) of Viṣṇu. Most Vaiṣṇavas consider Kṛṣṇa to be the only *pūrṇāvatāra* of Viṣṇu, his other *avatāras* being partial manifestations.

v. Aṁśa.

Purohita 'Appointed', 'placed in front', i.e., appointed to an office (*purodhā*) of the Court (*RV.*, VII.83,4). During the early stages of Āryan penetration of India there was no organized government supervised by officials, such as existed under the Mauryas. Instead, the government consisted of the ruler, as commander of the army, and the *purohita* whose function was to counsel and protect him by his magical powers. He also conducted the ceremonies of the *indramaha*, *nirājana* and *puṣyasnāna* for the king. Thus the *purohita* was no ordinary priest, but chosen because of his special capabilities.[1]

The power and prestige of the *purohita* grew, as is indicated in the *Ait. Br.* (VIII.24) where it is laid down that all the offerings of a king to the gods are in vain if he lacks a *purohita*. The establishment of large kingdoms necessitated the appointment of administrative officers, which tended to strengthen rather than weaken the position of the *purohita*. He thus became the chief officiant at the consecration (*rājasūya*) of a new king, and at all important sacrifices, such as the *aśvamedha*, to celebrate a victorious military campaign, and especially that culminating in imperial status for the victor. The *purohita* may have been originally the *hotṛ* priest, the singer *par excellence*, when he took any part at all in the ritual of the great sacrifices with the *Ṛtvij*,[2] (composed of sixteen priestly officiants).

The most notable *purohita* in post-Vedic times was Kauṭilya, the minister of the emperor Candragupta Maurya and of his grandson. Their joint efforts brought almost the whole of Peninsular India under Mauryan rule. The *Arthaśāstra*, or collection of maxims, similar to those of Machiavelli, is attributed to Kauṭilya and became the basis of the very efficient 'Civil Service'[3] instituted by Candragupta's grandson Aśoka.

[1] A.M. Shastri, *India as Seen in the Bṛhat Saṁhitā*, p. 472. Furthermore the *purohita* became the overseer of the whole sacrifice (*HCIP*., I, p. 502), and can be regarded 'as the king's ritual father' (J.C. Heesterman, *Ancient Indian Royal Consecration*, p. 56, n.40). In the *AV*. (VII.5,5–6; X.1,6) the term *purohita* refers to the possessor of powers capable of averting evil influences and counteracting witchcraft. He also enables the king to live a long, full life. According to the *Ait. Br*., VII.25, the king 'dies not again'. v. also Bloomfield, *The Atharvaveda*, pp. 74ff.

[2] *VI*., vol. II, p. 7.

[3] Such as Censors, Provincial Governors, Commissioners, and District Magistrates (V.A. Smith, *Early History of India*, pp. 189f.).

Puru A Vedic Āryan tribe which originally settled on the Paruṣṇī (Rāvī) river (*RV*., VII.18,13; VIII.53,10). One of the Pūru kings was Purukutsa, an ally of Sudās, the Tṛtsu king (*RV*., I.53,7), but later he became his enemy in the war of the ten kings (*Daśarājñya*). His son was known as Trasadasyu, 'He before whom the *dasyus* tremble' (*RV*., IV.42, 8–9), who appears to have restored the fortunes of the Purus after their defeat by Sudās. But this change of fortune appears to have been temporary and ended when the Purus settled on the Sarasvatī river (*RV*., VII.96,2). The gods Varuṇa and Mitra gave a divine stallion to the Purus, which brought them prosperity, longevity, etc. (*RV*., IV.39,2).

In the *MBh*. the post-Vedic Yayāti[1] father of Puru, is syncretized with the Vedic Yayāti (*RV*., I.31,17), apparently to provide a Vedic ancestry for the Pāṇḍavas and Kauravas.

[1] *VP*. (IV.10) states that Puru was the youngest son of Yayāti and Śarmiṣṭhā the daughter of Vṛṣaparvan.

v. Devayānī.

Purukutsa v. Puru.

Purūravas The son of Ilā or Iḍā and Budha and grandson of Candra the founder of the Lunar dynasty.

Purūravas's love for the celestial nymph Urvaśī is described in a cryptic dialogue between the two lovers (*RV*., X.95) which is possibly a fragment of a much earlier and imperfectly understood nature-myth. Nonetheless, its popularity is evident by its appearance in various forms in the Brāhmaṇas, Purāṇas, and *MBh*., and finally as a play by Kālidāsa entitled the Hero and the Nymph (*Vikramorvaśī*).

The *VP*. (IV.6) version recounts that Urvaśī, having incurred the wrath of Mitra and Varuṇa, decided to live on earth as a mortal. As soon as Purūravas saw her he fell in love. She promised to return his affection if he would agree that she should keep her pet rams by her bedside; that Purūravas should never appear naked before her;[1] and that clarified butter should be her only food.[2] Purūravas agreed and they lived happily together for 61,000 years.[3] By this time the *gandharvas* and *apsarasas* desired Urvaśī's return, and Viśvāvasu was appointed to break the conditions laid down by Urvaśī by removing the rams. Immediately Purūravas seized his sword and chased the robbers, hoping that in the darkness his wife would not see his nakedness, but the *gandharvas* sent a flash of lightning, and Urvaśī disappeared. Purūravas wandered forlornly about the world seeking her, until one day he saw her with four other nymphs bathing in a beautiful lake. He ran towards her begging her to return to him, but she told him to come back in a year when she would present him with a son and remain with him for one night. At the end of a year they met again at Kurukṣetra, and she gave him his first-born son Āyus. For five years the meetings took place and five sons were born to them.[4] Then the *gandharvas* offered him a boon and he requested that he should be allowed to live forever with Urvaśī. The *gandharvas* then gave him a vessel of fire, and instructed him to divide it into three[5] in accordance with the precepts of the Vedas. When he had achieved this he was united with his beloved.

[1] Except during sexual intercourse, according to *Bhāg. P*., IX.14, 15–49; *Vāyu P*., 91, 1–52, *PI*. In Greek popular myths a water-nymph (nereid) who marries a mortal disappears as soon as he commits some indiscretion (Nilsson, *A History of Greek Religion*, p. 303).

[2] In the *RV*., X.95,16 account she lives on one drop of butter daily. The conditions vary in the *ŚBr*. (XI.5.1, 1f.).

[3] Or for 'four autumns' (*RV*., X.95,16).

[4] *AGP*., 274,9f, mentions eight sons.

[5] Wilson suggests that Purūravas was probably the innovator of some important ritual practices (*VP*., p. 317, n.6). This is also suggested by his mother who represents sacrificial food. There are two obscure references to him in *Nir*., 10, 46 and 47.

v. Araṇi.

Puruṣa I. 'Man', 'male', or collectively 'mankind' (*RV*., VII.104, 15, etc; *AV*., III.21,1, etc.), but the word is variously applied. In the Puruṣa-sūkta (*RV*., X.90) the

Puruṣa is depicted as a cosmogonic figure,[1] a creative source, the primeval male who envelops the whole earth and who represents totality.[2] This hymn is the earliest account of secondary creation and is of particular interest as the earliest account of the structure of Vedic society, which its alleged composer Nārāyaṇa divides into four occupational or functional categories, each corresponding to a particular part of the sacrificed body of the Puruṣa. This sacrifice became the prototype of all future sacrifices.[3] From the Puruṣa's severed body the *brāhmaṇa* emerged from his mouth, from his arms the *rājanya*; from his thighs the *vaiśya*, and from his feet the *śūdra*. From his mind was produced the moon; from his eye the sun; the wind from his breath; from his navel the atmosphere; from his head the sky, and so forth. Upon this purely symbolic description of the social, political and economic structure of late Vedic society, subsequent Indian 'sociologists' built a caste system, which was ultimately presented in the *Manu-smṛti* as the inviolable expression of divine law. The Puruṣa-sūkta was also prescribed for those desiring a son, for purification, 'and in the ceremonies performed in founding a temple which is constructed in the likeness of the Puruṣa'.[4]

In the *ŚBr.* (XI.1.6,1–2) Puruṣa appears as the secondary creator Prajāpati, who emerged from the golden egg produced by the primeval waters. In the *Ait Up.* (1,1–4) he is also portrayed as a cosmogonic figure, the instrument of secondary creation, from whose bodily parts emerged speech (*vāc*), breath (*prāṇa*), sight (*cakṣus*), hearing (*śrota*), mind (*manas*), etc. But in the Sāṁkhya system the term *puruṣa* denotes the passive complement of the active creative principle (*prakṛti*).

There is nothing higher or beyond the Puruṣa (*Kaṭha Up.*, 3, 11); it represents the material from which the world was made, (i.e., the *causa materialis*) as well as its creator (*causa efficiens*).

[1]Man is limited by his body and sense-impressions, only his inner 'universe' is within his reach; hence the universe, the macrocosm, is depicted as a Cosmic Man. The Unborn was one of the early designations of the World-ground. It was later called Puruṣa, Prajāpati, Brahman or Nārāyaṇa; later Viṣṇu inherited the formula (Coomaraswamy, *Yakṣas*, pt. ii, p. 25).

[2]The hymn contains sixteen verses, this number representing totality.

[3]Puruṣa becomes the oblation = the animal victim of the cosmic sacrifice = creation performed by the gods. 'The self-immolation of the demiurge is conceived in many mythologies to be an essential prerequisite of creation. In Christian mythology the corrupt creation is restored to its pristine glory through Christ's self-sacrifice, which is like a second creation' (*IT.*, p. 335; v. also Eliade, *Patterns*, p. 183). The myth of the sacrifice of the Primordial Giant 'is European, but it has also been found among other ethnic groups, including some of the most archaic' (Eliade, *Yoga*, p. 138, n.112).

[4]Gonda, *VS.*, p. 27.

v. Puruṣamedha; Hiraṇyagarbha.

II. v. Sāṁkhya.

Puruṣamedha 'Human sacrifice' to ensure the renewal of life.[1] The existence of the practice is suggested in the *ŚBr.* (I.2.3,6), and *Tait. Saṁ.* (II.2.2,4), which presents it as the re-enaction of the process of creation and its renewal.[2]

Gonda[3] suggests that the horse sacrifice (*aśvamedha*) may have been the model of the *puruṣamedha*. That the practice existed is evident in the discovery of an ancient altar, and a large quantity of human and animal bones at Kauśāmbī.[4]

[1]This rite ensures the realization of individual identity with the Totality of existence (*idaṃ sarvam*).

[2]The five sacrificial creatures are: puruṣa, horse, bull, ram, and he-goat (*ŚBr.*, VI.2.1,2). But Heesterman does not agree with the theory that man was the primary sacrificial victim and that animals, etc., were later substituted, because it fails to 'take into account the intimate interrelation of man, animal and vegetation, which belongs to the origins of symbolic thinking. The human victim and its substitute will also originally have existed side by side as they do in the Vedic ritual, and in fact till the present day' (*Ancient Indian Royal Consecration*, p. 139, n. 71). The gods slew man as a sacrificial victim (*Ait. Br.*, II.8).

[3]*VS.*, p. 26; *Tait. Saṁ.*, I, p. cxxxviii.

[4]G.R. Sharma, *The Excavations at Kauśāmbī*, 1957–59, pp. 96f. v. also *CHI.*, I, p. 142; and Hillebrandt, *Ritualliteratur*, pp. 149ff. Human sacrifice persisted among some tribes, especially the Khonds, who offered their victims to the Earth-goddess, blood being considered necessary for the cultivation of turmeric which otherwise would not attain its red colour (*ERE.*, VI. 850; *IA.*, VIII (1879) 219); v. also Thurston, *Omens and Superstitions*, ch. vii; S.C. Mitra, 'On a Recent Instance of the Khāsī Custom of Offering Human Sacrifice to the Snake Deity', *JASB.*, XIII, 1924, pp. 192–8. 'Human sacrifices formed part of the cult of Zeus on Mt. Lykaion even in historic times' (Nilsson, *A History of Greek Religion*, p. 58). Most early Āryan tribes practised human sacrifice (Farnell, *Cults*, I, p. 25). Coomaraswamy suggests that possibly both the *puruṣamedha* and the *aśvamedha* are relics of

human sacrifice (as a vegetation ritual) of a temporary king. There is also evidence of human sacrifice to trees or to tree-spirits in India (*Yakṣas*, pt. ii, p. 28).
v. Agnicayana; Śunaḥśepa; Satī; Ṭhag(s).

Puruṣa-sūkta v. Puruṣa.

Pūrva-Mīmāṁsā Generally called Mīmāṁsā. A priestly school whose founder is said to be Jaimini. It is one of the six 'orthodox' Hindu *darśanas*, or media for the expression of quasi-philosophical views. As its name suggests, it presents early (*pūrva*) fundamentalist doctrines as distinct from those of the late (*uttara*) Mīmāṁsā school, subsequently called Vedānta.

The term *mīmāṁsā* is derived from √*man*, 'to think', and means the 'solution of a problem by critical examination', the problem being the achievement of liberation (*mokṣa*) from the sequence of birth, death and re-birth (*saṁsāra*). The solution, expounded by Jaimini, and elaborated by two of his successors, consisted in the performance of 'ritually good' works (*karmānuṣṭhāyin*). Originally faith and ethics played no part in it, its views being expressly based on the Veda, regarded as divine law.

Two schools subsequently emerged from the Pūrva-Mīmāṁsā, whose leaders were Prabhākara and Bhaṭṭa, but apart from slight variations in their theory of the nature of the 'soul', they do not differ from the views of the parent body. The Mīmāṁsā is essentially a systematized code of sacrificial rules which should be interpreted in accordance with the Veda regarded as knowledge divinely 'revealed' or 'heard'.[1] It 'maintained that every word was the reflexion of an eternal prototype, and that its meaning was eternal and inherent in it'.[2]

[1]Cf. the similar claims of Islam regarding the Koran; of Judaism and the Pentateuch, and that of fundamentalist Christian sects concerning the authenticity of the Bible.

[2]Basham, *WI.*, p. 390.

v. Darśana(s); Karman; Śabda.

Pūṣabhāsā v. Amarāvatī.

Pūṣan A deity whose name is derived from the root *puṣ* 'to nourish', and hence his role as the divine giver of fertility, and as protector, guide and tutelary deity. He is associated with Bhaga, the dispenser of tribal property. Though not included in the Vedic list of Ādityas, Pūṣan was subsequently included in the twelve representing the divisions of the solar year (*ŚBr.*, XI.6.3,8), and indicating his association with the sun which, like Pūṣan, directs travellers. Thus Pūṣan is invoked to 'conduct us over our road, to go on before us, to drive away the waylayer, and to lead us to a country of rich pastures' (*RV.*, I.42,1–10); and to 'guard the ways' (*Tait. Saṁ.*, I.2,4).[1] The *Nir.* (7.9) calls him the wise guardian of the universe, whose cattle are never lost, and who guides the dead to the *pitṛs*.

Like the god Thor of Northern mythology, Pūṣan's chariot is drawn by rams or goats (*RV.*, X.26,8), and he carries a golden spear, goad and awl. As a bestower of fertility he is associated with marriage rites (*RV.*, X. 85,26 and 37) and with successful childbirth (*AV.*, I.11). He is bearded and has braided hair. Gruel (*karambha*) was his food after Śiva had broken his teeth because he had attended Dakṣa's sacrifice.[2]

[1]v. also S.D. Atkins, *Pūṣan in the RV.*; E. Sieke, *Pūṣan*. Cf. the Greek Hermes who was also god of the ways.

[2]The *Kauṣ. Br.* (VI.13) states that the gods, after performing a sacrifice, kept the *brāhmaṇas'* share for Pūṣan (among others), but it knocked out his teeth. Cf. *Tait. Saṁ.*, II.6.8,3–4; v. also Lévi, *La Doctrine du sacrifice*, pp. 125f.

Another version states that the gods instructed Rudra to pierce Prajāpati with his dart as a punishment for his incestuous relationship with his daughter. But when their anger had subsided they cured Prajāpati and removed Rudra's dart. To ensure that the part of the sacrifice torn out by the dart would not be lost they offered it to Bhaga, but its brilliance burnt out his eyes; then they offered it to Pūṣan but when he tasted it his teeth fell out (*ŚBr.* I.7.4, 1ff.). Inherent in this 'tale is the conflict of Rudra and the solar gods, whose domination in the Āryan pantheon may have been responsible for the exclusion of the lunar Rudra' (*IT.*, p. 122).

Puṣkara I. The blue lotus flower; an epithet of Śiva and Kṛṣṇa; also the name of one of Varuṇa's sons.
II. A type of cloud (also called *puṣkarāvartakas*), said to cause famine.

Puṣkaradvīpa One of the seven mythical insular continents surrounded by a sea of fresh water (*jala*) (*VP.*, II.2). It is named after the huge lotus which constitutes Brahmā's throne. In the middle of the continent is Mount Mānasottara on the summit of which rotates the wheel of the sun-god's chariot (*Bhāg. P.*, V.I.32, etc.; *Brah. P.*, II.14,14, etc., *PI.*).

Puṣpaka The magical aerial chariot drawn as 'swift as thought' by geese (*haṁsa*), which was given by Brahmā to Kubera, and stolen by Rāvaṇa. Subsequently the latter was killed by Rāma who used the chariot to take Sītā (and others) back to Ayodhyā.

Puṣpaśakaṭikā A mysterious heavenly voice. Divination by means of the sounds of this voice is counted among the sixty-four arts.

Puṣpodakā 'Stream of flowers.' The name of one of the two rivers which flow through Yama's kingdom of the dead. To the good it is sweet-smelling, but to the evil it

appears as a river of pus.
v. Vaitaraṇī.

Puṣṭi 'Thriving.' Name of one of Dakṣa's daughters, the wife of Dharma (*VP.*, I.7). She personifies prosperity and growth (*AGP.*, I, ch. 98).

Puṣya-snāna A ceremonial ablution described in the *Bṛhat Saṁ.* (XLVII, 82 and 85), and held annually by kings, preferably on the full-moon day of *pauṣa* (Dec.-Jan.), that being considered the best time, though it could be observed at other times. The ceremony was conducted by the *purohita* at the *rājasūya* (the consecration of a king), its performance confirming his overlordship and ensuring the birth of an heir. It was also believed to be capable of averting or remedying the consequences of all kinds of unfavourable planetary conjunctions, of eclipses, comets and other evil portents.

Put v. Putra.

Pūtanā A vampire-like demoness who poisons children. She tried to poison the infant Kṛṣṇa by suckling him on her poisoned milk, but was herself sucked to death by him to the amazement of the *gopīs* and *gopas* (*AGP.*, 12, 14–17).

She is sometimes regarded as a *yoginī* and as one of the *mātṛs* attendant on Skanda.
v. Gokarīṣam.

Pūtika Also called *ādāra*. A plant used as a substitute for the *soma* plant. It originated from the vital essence of the personified Sacrifice, i.e., Viṣṇu (*ŚBr.*, XIV.1.2,12).

Pūtkārī v. Bhogavatī.

Putra Son. His chief function, which has magico-religious significance, is 'as an instrument for cleansing his ancestors in the funeral rites which he performs for them'.[1] Hence the necessity for a man to have a son, for without one the deceased members of the family would be condemned to remain in the hell called Put.

[1]Heimann, *Facets*, p. 158; and v. *Mārk. P.*, 75,16–17.
v. Śrāddha; Gotra; Ekoddiṣṭa.

R

Rādhā I. A beautiful cowherdess (*gopī*), wife of Ayanaghoṣa, a cowherd of Vṛndāvana, where lived also the cowherd Nanda in whose care the infant Kṛṣṇa had been placed. As a young man Kṛṣṇa is reputed to have been on intimate terms with the cowherds' wives and daughters, especially with Rādhā. She is immortalized by the twelfth-century Bengali poet Jayadeva in a pastoral drama entitled *Gītāgovinda*, to which much of the popularity of the romantic legend of Kṛṣṇa and Rādhā is owed. This drama has much in common with Hesiod's hymn to the Delian Apollo, which refers to the Ionians who gather with their shy wives, the girls of Delos, to honour Apollo. Ovid also refers to the many wives of Apollo, as do the Purāṇas to those of Kṛṣṇa. In the Bhāgavata-Kṛṣṇa concept 'Rādhā symbolized the second principle necessary for duality . . . and the image became an archetype. Māyā, the wife or feminine principle of Viṣṇu, took the place of Māyā of [the] Vedānta.'[1]

The *Gītāgovinda* has been likened to the Hebrew Song of Songs, and both have been given mystical interpretations. Though Rukmiṇī is traditionally regarded as Kṛṣṇa's favourite wife she never attained the symbolic significance, or had the romantic appeal of her rival Rādhā.

In Tantrism 'Rādhā is conceived as the infinite love that constitutes the very essence of Kṛṣṇa. Woman participates in the nature of Rādhā and man in the nature of Kṛṣṇa; hence the "truth" concerning the loves of Kṛṣṇa and Rādhā can be known only in the body itself, and this knowledge on the plane of "corporeality" has a universal metaphysical validity'.[2]

[1] *IT.*, p. 313.

[2] Eliade, *Yoga*, p. 265. As in all Tantric and mystical schools when man and woman are mentioned they refer to the archetypal man and woman.

II. Wife of Adhiratha and foster-mother of Karṇa.

Rāga A musical note or melody; a particular musical mode or order of sound. The term is derived from the root *rañj*, lit. 'to colour', but figuratively 'to tinge with emotion'. 'The effect of Indian music is cumulative rather than dramatic.'[1] Bharata, traditionally regarded as the author of a manual of dramatic art *Nāṭya-śāstra*, enumerates six *rāgas*, viz., *bhairava*, *kauśika*, *hindola*, *dīpaka*, *śrīrāga* and *megha*, but the names and number of *rāgas* vary with different authors.

Each of the six chief *rāgas* is personified and wedded to one of the five (or six) *rāgiṇīs*,[2] their union resulting in further musical modes. The *rāgas* are classified according to the time of day or night for which they are appropriate. Thus *bhairava* is suitable for a dawn performance, *megha* for morning, *dīpaka* and *śrīrāga*, afternoon, and *kauśika* and *hindola* for night. They are also associated with different emotions, *bhairava* with fear; *kauśika*, joy; *hindola*, *dīpaka* and *śrīrāga* with love; and *megha* with peace and calm.[3]

'The Indian musician was, and still is, an improviser . . . India never devised a true musical notation and the music of her ancient masters has vanished forever. As at the present day, every performance was virtually a new composition.'[4]

[1] Singhal, *India*, I, pp. 219f. The skilled musician leads his audience 'to a depth and intensity of feeling undreamt of in other musical systems' (Daniélou, *Northern Indian Music*, I, p. 115).

[2] A *rāgiṇī* is a modification of the musical mode called *rāga*, and the number of *rāgiṇīs* mentioned are thirty-five or thirty-six (*SED.*). But new *rāgas* are being invented, some of which will join the classical series.

[3] *WI.*, p. 383.

[4] Ibid., pp. 383f.

Raghu An ancient king of the Ikṣvāku or Solar Dynasty, the son of Dilīpa, also known as Khaṭvāṅga, a celebrated *cakravartin*. Both father and son figure in Kālidāsa's poem Raghuvaṁśa. Raghu is regarded as an ideal monarch. He was the great grandfather of Rāma who had the title Raghupati (chief of the race of Raghu), and the patronymic Rāghava (Descendant of Raghu).

Raghuvaṁśa 'Dynasty of Raghu.' The name of a poem by Kālidāsa on the ancestry and life of Rāma.

Rāgiṇī v. Rāga.

Rahasyas Lit. 'the secret portions', i.e., the Upaniṣads and their explanation.[1]

[1] v. *The Laws of Manu*, II.140n. (*SBE.*, vol. XXV).

Rāhu 'Seizer.' The post-Vedic name of the demon responsible for eclipses of the sun or moon, a phenomenon attributed in the *RV.* to Svarbhānu. According to the *MBh.* (Ādi pa., XIX) and some Purāṇas, Rāhu was a *dānava* who appeared in the guise of a god at the Churning of the Ocean (*samudramathana*) and joined the other gods in drinking the sacred *amṛta* (the elixir of immortality), but Sūrya (the sun) and Soma (the moon) recognized him and informed the gods. Viṣṇu immediately struck off his head which rose up to the sky where it uttered loud cries. Thus began the long-standing quarrel between Rāhu's head and the sun and moon and its attempts to seize and swallow the sun,[1] and hence Rāhu's epithet Abhrapiśāca (sky demon).

Malevolence is sometimes attributed to the Sun (Sūrya) who was formerly believed to steal the light of the moon during the day, and thus like Rāhu was known as a Mahāgraha (Great Seizer). In Indian astronomical mythology Rāhu's head is regarded as the ascending and his tail Ketu as the descending node. But in some Purs. Ketu is regarded as the personification of comets and meteors, and in the *Padma* and *Bhāgavata* Purs., he and Rāhu are said to be the demon sons of Siṁhikā, the wife of the *dānava* Vipracitti.

Rāhu's chariot is drawn by eight black horses eternally yoked to it (*VP.*, II.12). He is the regent of the S.W. quarter of the heavens. His sons are the thirty-two comets (*ketus*), who when visible in the sun's disc portend famine, robbery, foreign invasions, the death of the king, etc.

[1]This belief is also common to the myths of the Near East, Greece and China. In Scandinavian mythology the sun is relentlessly pursued by the wolf Skoll; in Lithuanian the demon Tiknis attacks the sun's chariot; in the Jewish, the sun is periodically swallowed by a huge fish (Ginsberg, *Legends of the Jews*, V, pp. 108, 116); and in the Canaanite a dragon or serpent is regarded as the cause of eclipses.

v. Kīrtimukha, n.1; Graha.

Raivata I. Also called Kakudmin. A son of Revata, and ruler of Ānarta whose capital was Kuśasthalī.[1] Raivata, being unable to obtain a suitable husband for his beautiful daughter Revatī, ascended to the paradise of Brahmā to seek his help. But when he arrived the singing of the divine choristers so entranced him that centuries elapsed before he remembered the purpose of his visit.

In reply to Brahmā's enquiry whether he had anyone in mind, Raivata mentioned the names of several eligible princes, and was astonished to learn that these had long since died. After a brief dissertation on the relativity of time and on the immanence of Viṣṇu in every age, Brahmā advised Raivata to seek out Baladeva, who as a partial incarnation (*avatāra*) of Viṣṇu, was living in Kuśasthalī. This was done and Baladeva agreed to marry Revatī.[2]

[1]Subsequent legend shows that it was the same, or built on the same spot, as Dvārakā. Ānarta was therefore part of Cutch or Gujarāt (Wilson, *VP.*, p. 284, n.31).

[2]According to *VP.* (IV.1) Baladeva shortened Revatī with his ploughshare as she was excessively tall.

II. Name of a demon injurious to children.

Rājan King, sovereign, prince or chief. The term occurs frequently in the *RV.*, but except for brief references to a king called Sudās and the 'War of the Ten Kings' (*daśarājñya*) in VII.83,6, etc., it is used only as a title of gods such as Indra, Varuṇa and Agni, regarded as the celestial archetypes of terrestrial sovereigns. With the proliferation of kingdoms, the position of the king was generally regarded as hereditary but by no means secure, as instances of the forced abdication of the ruler occur, as in the *ŚBr.* (XII.9.3,1–2). There are also instances (notably that of the Emperor Aśoka), when the heir-apparent was passed over in favour of another member of the family better qualified to succeed to the throne.[1]

The initial function of the ruler was to lead his warriors (*kṣatriyas*) into battle against the enemies of his people and to defend them (*RV.*, III.43,5). In return for these services the king and his warriors (as also the priests) required that the people (*viś*) contribute to their maintenance. Like his divine counterpart Varuṇa, the king, assisted by his *purohita*, also acted as the administrator of justice.

A king if he so desired could retire to the forest in his later years for meditation, or he could commit ritual suicide by various means, but this decision would only be taken when the succession was assured.[2]

According to the *VP.* (I.13) Pṛthu gained the affection of his people and was the first ruler to whom the title of *rājan* was ascribed. Although a king is said to incorporate in himself many deities such as Dharma, Bṛhaspati, Indra, Prajāpati, etc., he does not attain complete divinity until he dies.[3] A king's touch was believed to possess healing powers both in India, and at one time in Europe.

[1]Crooke, *Things Indian*, p. 398. The *rājan* was the ideal of the *kṣatriyas.* His very presence ensured the prosperity of the country.

[2]Auboyer, *Daily Life in Ancient India*, p. 256. 'In some of the medieval principalities of Malabar the ritual suicide of the king became a regular institution' (Basham, *WI.*, p. 93).

[3]*EM.*, p. 64.

v. Rājanya; Ṛṣi(s); Rājasūya.

Rājanya A Vedic designation of the *Kṣatra* class.

Rājarṣi(s) v. Ṛṣi(s).

Rajas 'The sphere of mist and clouds.' In the Veda it is one of the divisions of the world and distinguished from *div* or *svar*, the 'sphere of light', and *rocanā divaḥ*, the 'ethereal spaces' which are beyond the *rajas*, as space is beyond the atmosphere.

Philosophically *rajas* is the second of the three

guṇas and is the driving power animating the other two *guṇas* (*sattva* and *tamas*). As soon as *prakṛti* (primordial substance) departs from its state of perfect equilibrium and becomes differentiated, it manifests itself in three different ways (called *guṇas*), viz., '*sattva* (modality of luminosity and intelligence); *rajas* (modality of motor energy and mental activity); *tamas* (modality of static inertia and psychic obscurity).'[1] The *guṇas* never appear separately but exist simultaneously, although in unequal proportions, in every physical, biological or psychomental phenomenon. This inequality 'permits the appearance of a "phenomenon", of whatever kind; otherwise, the primordial equilibrium and homogeneity by virtue of which the *guṇas* were in perfect equilibrium would persist forever'.[2]

Brahmā represents *rajas*, the activity from which the myriad forms of the universe arise.

[1]Eliade, *Yoga*, p. 19.

[2]Ibid.

v. Sāṁkhya.

Rājasūya[1] 'Royal consecration.' A Vedic ceremony that seems originally to have been a simple inauguration ceremony, 'which subsequently found admission, with many elaborations, into the *śrauta* ritual'.[2] Thus the ceremony generally associated 'the king with the udumbara tree and with rain-water, and the notion of quickening the royal energy by means of the rite',[3] which suggests a connexion with ancient ritual designed to ensure fertility and cosmogonic continuity, and hence the subsequent adoption of the ceremony as an annual event. Another ceremony, the *vājapeya*, is closely associated with the *rājasūya*, and may represent either an early variant of the royal inauguration, or as Weber suggests, have been 'originally a popular celebration of victory or promotion'.[4]

The *rājasūya* ceremony is outlined in the *ŚBr.* (V.2.3,1, *et seq.*; *Ait. Br.*, VIII. 1–28), and described in the sūtras as 'a succession of sacrificial performances, spread over a period, of one and sometimes two years'.[5] The inaugural ceremony is preceded by a purificatory rite, a *soma* sacrifice comprising four *dīkṣās* or initiation days. This is followed a year later by the *abhiṣecanīya*, the consecration or act of anointing.[6] This is followed at intervals by minor rites and finally by the *kṣatra-dhṛti*, or acknowledgement of the king's sovereignty.[7]

The *rājasūya* is performed by representatives of the three superior classes, *brāhmaṇa*, *rājanya* (including the *kṣatra*), and the *viś* or commonalty. Water-vessels made from the wood of particular trees, and having an appropriate symbolic significance, are used by a member of each social group to sprinkle the king. This joint participation in the ceremony ensured the recognition by the king of the superior status of the *brāhmaṇa*, whilst at the same time the king's sovereignty was recognized and assurance given of the loyalty of the members of his family, the *kṣatriyas* and the people.[8]

[1]Lit. 'pouring upon', an expression not used in either the *RV.* or *SV.*, though it occurs in the *AV.*, but without any definite ceremonial implication. Heesterman suggests that it is best rendered by 'king-engendering' (*Ancient Indian Royal Consecration*, p. 86). The *rājasūya* was also known as *Varuṇasava* indicating 'that the royal sacrificer being anointed impersonates the god Varuṇa' (ibid., p. 85). Varuṇa reproduces the archetypal act with which he himself was consecrated (Eliade, *Patterns*, p. 70), and the king ritually 'realizes his inherent identity with the cosmos and its processes' (Heesterman, op. cit., pp. 225f.).

[2]Weber, *Über den Rājasūya*, pp. 1–6. The *rājasūya* may have been an annual 'rite of cosmic regeneration and rebirth, not unlike the Hindu seasonal festivals the *utsavas*' (Heesterman, op. cit., p. 7). Cf. the annual unction of the *puṣyasnāna*.

[3]*ERE.*, I, p. 23; v. also Basham, *WI.*, p. 81. For a charm to protect the king at the *rājasūya* v. *AV.* IV.8.

[4]*ERE.*, I, p. 24.

[5]Eggeling, *ŚBr.*, III, Intro., p. xxvi.

[6]The anointing of kings and priests is largely imitative in character—the king had to ensure the fertility of the land as the priests ensured that the gods continued to inseminate the land (Allegro, *The Sacred Mushroom and the Cross*, p. 58). Cf. the belief of many African tribes that the chief's own fertility and moral fibre affect the growth and welfare of the whole tribe.

[7]The *rājasūya* also includes *inter alia* the yoking and driving by the king of a quadriga which he stops in the midst of a herd of cows, one of which he touches with his bow, thereby taking the vigour of the herd to himself (*ŚBr.*, V.4.3,1ff.); he then engages in a ritual game with five dice (representing the five regions) which he always wins, so symbolically bringing prosperity to the five regions (V.4.4,6f.), etc. For the ritual dicing v. G. J. Held, *The Mahābhārata: An Ethnological Study*, ch. 5, 1935; K. de Vreese, 'The Game of dice in ancient India', in *Orientalia Neerlandica*, pp. 349–62, Leiden, 1948.

[8]As an ordinary sacrificer was believed to be ritually reborn out of the sacrifice, so the king was believed to be reborn from the *rājasūya*.

v. Nirṛti; Rājan; Rājya; Abhiṣeka; Bṛhaspatisava.

Rāja Yoga v. Yoga.

Rājya 'Sovereign power', 'kingship'. The term occurs in the *AV.* (III.4.2, etc.), and in later texts. Though the *brāhmaṇa* is specifically excluded from exercising regal power, the priestly Bhārgavas took up arms and entered into marital alliances with *kṣatra* families when threatened by the Kārtavīryas.[1]

The *ŚBr.* (V.1.1,13) makes a distinction between the status of a king (*rājan*) and that of an emperor (*samrāj*), and states that the *rājasūya* rite is performed at the consecration of a king, the *vājapeya* being reserved for an emperor. But terms like *rājya*, *samrājya* and others can have been little more than nominal distinctions during Vedic times, because imperial power, like that of the Maurya or Gupta dynasties, was unknown.

[1]v. Paraśurāma.

Rākā The name of a goddess variously described as presiding over the day of the full moon (*VP.*, II.8), or as its consort, or personified as one of the four daughters representing the four phases of the moon,[1] the offspring of Aṅgiras and Smṛti (I.10). Rākā is also associated with childbirth, and invoked to bestow heroic sons and prosperity (*RV.*, II.32, 4–5; *AV.*, VII.48,1–2). Gonda suggests that she was originally a fertility goddess to whom oblations were offered during preparation of the implements for ploughing, sowing, reaping, etc.[2]

[1]Eggeling, *ŚBr.*, IV, p. 264, n.3.

[2]*Aspects*, p. 260, n.131; v. also *Tait. Saṁ.*, III.4,9 and *Nir.*, 11.30. Cf. *Ait. Br.*, III.37.

Rakṣā[1] Any amulet or token used as a charm. Sometimes a piece of thread or silk is bound round the wrist to avert the Evil Eye and protect the wearer against witchcraft. The infant Kṛṣṇa was given such an amulet by Yaśodā to protect him from maleficent forces (*VP.*, V.5).

[1]From the root *rakṣ* 'to guard', 'watch over', 'protect'.

v. Rakṣāmaṇi; Rakṣāmantra.

Rakṣāmaṇi A jewel (*maṇi*) worn as an amulet against evil.

v. Rakṣā.

Rakṣāmantra A collection of Vedic hymns chanted at weddings to protect the bridal pair from maleficent forces.

v. Rākṣasa I; Rakṣā; Rakṣāmaṇi.

Rākṣasa (s) I. 'Demons', including *bhūtas* and other generally malevolent spirits. *Rākṣasas* wander about at night (*Manu*, III.280) and can assume various forms, often those of dogs, eagles, vultures, owls, cuckoos, dwarfs, and of husbands and lovers. In their customary form they have fiery eyes and abnormally long tongues. They are called 'confounders of the sacrifice' who at one time used to lay in wait at fords to kill those who tried to cross (*Kauṣ. Br.*, XII.1).

Rākṣasas are especially dangerous to newly born children, and hence are propitiated with offerings of chaff and husks.[1] Women are also particularly vulnerable; hence at weddings small staves are thrown in the air to blind the *rākṣasas*, who in the form of dogs or apes lie in wait for women. Men also had to beware when eating and drinking lest the *rākṣasas* should enter their mouths and drive them insane.[2] During the day they are generally inactive, but at dusk their strength begins to return and by nightfall reaches its peak. They prefer the dark period of the new moon. They fear both fire and mustard.[3]

[1]Heesterman, *Ancient Indian Royal Consecration*, p. 38 and n.34.

[2]Cf. the Gr. Keres, who were originally sources of evil, if not actually evil spirits, who often entered the mouths of men when eating (Harrison, *Prolegomena to the Study of Greek Religion*, p. 168).

[3]*Rākṣasas* pursued Indra at his birth, but he entered the fire and they were driven off by its sparks.

v. Rakṣā.

II. An epithet applied in the *RV.* to Indian indigenes whose characteristics were likened to those of malevolent *rākṣasas* and other 'demons' of popular folklore. Whereas much of the resistance to Āryan infiltration was made from fortified positions, that offered by less-organized tribes consisted of guerrilla tactics from forest hiding places, which Indra was constantly invoked to burn and destroy (*RV.*, I.76,3, etc.). The Maruts also were implored to search them out and grind them to pieces (*RV.*, VII. 104,18). Because of their skill in evading capture and their successful efforts at interrupting the sacrifices performed by the *brāhmaṇas*, the *rākṣasas* were thought to possess magical powers and to be in league with sorcerers (*yātudhanas*).

To the *rākṣasas* the Āryans were interlopers who sought to introduce strange social customs, religious practices, and an alien language, all of which they initially rejected. Thus the terms *rākṣasa* (demonic) and *vānara* (monkey-man) were applied by Rāma to the indigenes of the Deccan rather than to tribal groups. They were derogatory epithets, applied not only to the ordinary folk, but also to the *rākṣasa* aristocracy like Rāvaṇa and his followers.

The *rākṣasas* (and *yakṣas*) were invested with a mythical origin or parentage, and said to be the offspring of Khasā, one of Dakṣa's daughters (*VP.*, I.21), or of the non-Āryan *ṛṣi* Pulastya,[1] or of Brahmā (*VP.*, I.55), or of Yadu.[2]

[1]Of Pulastya's offspring Kubera only was a *rākṣasa*. Like Rāvaṇa, Kubera became known as Rākṣasendra (Lord of Rākṣasas).

[2]*EM.*, p. 187.

v. Rakṣā, n.1.

III. One of the eight forms of marriage enumerated in *Manu* (III.20 *et seq.*).
v. Vivāha.

Rākṣasī(s) Female *rākṣasas*, whose offspring at the moment of conception are fully adult.
v. Jarā; Pūtanā.

Raktavīja The name of the giant *asura* who fought Caṇḍikā (Cāmuṇḍā). Each drop of blood from his wounds was transformed into a powerful fighter like himself, until Cāmuṇḍā drank the blood as it fell and finally defeated him (*Mārk. P.*, LXXXVIII).

Rāma A number of men bear this name, but the three principal Rāmas are Paraśurāma, sometimes called Jāmadagnya, son of Jamadagni and Reṇukā. He is also called Bhārgava, a descendant of Bhṛgu. Rāmacandra, the son of Daśaratha, also called Rāghava (descendant of Raghu). Balarāma (also called Halāyudha) regarded as the elder brother of Kṛṣṇa.

Rāmacandra Also called Rāma. The suffix probably refers to his moon-like beauty.[1] He was the eldest son of Daśaratha, King of Kosala, who ruled from the capital Ayodhyā. Owing to the intrigues of Kaikeyī (one of the king's four wives), her son Bharata was declared heir-apparent and Rāma and his wife Sītā were exiled to the Daṇḍaka forest. Their subsequent adventures are recounted in the *Rāmāyaṇa* which, 'divested of its miraculous, fabulous, incredible and mythological elements, clearly indicates that he was a great king who spread Āryan ideas and institutions into regions far and wide',[2] especially in Southern India.

After the rescue of Sītā, who had been captured by Rāvaṇa, King of Laṅkā, and the latter's defeat and death, Rāma returned to Ayodhyā and was proclaimed king. Despite Sītā's protestation of loyalty to her husband during her captivity, public opinion rejected her, and Rāma unwillingly accepted the decision.[3]

The original version of the *Rāmāyaṇa*, composed by *Vālmīki*, is comprised in Books II–VI, in which Rāma is described as a prince courageous both in misfortune and in battle, faithful also to the best traditions of his great ancestor Raghu, whence his epithet Rāghava. But in later recensions, and in the Purāṇas, Rāma is raised to divine status as an *avatāra* of Viṣṇu, second only to Kṛṣṇa. His *mantra*, *Rāṁ*, is held by Vaiṣṇavas to represent the universe, and according to the *Padma P.* to be the basic sound from which all languages issued.[4]

[1]Cf. *Nara-candrama* 'a moon among men'.
[2]*HCIP.*, I, p. 291. He represents the ideal of an educated and cultured man of the early Epic period. He was skilled in law, polity, logic, music, military science, and the training of elephants and horses. He was a good and just ruler and the institutor of a 'golden age'. It is probable that he, like Kṛṣṇa and others, were ancient heroes who were deified.
[3]According to *VP.*, IV.4, Sītā underwent the fire-ordeal to purify herself from the contamination of her captivity.
[4]*HP.*, p. 174.
v. Raghu; Rāmasetu; Balarāma; Paraśurāma; Sarasvatī; Tārakā I; Hanumat.

Rāmacarita 'Deeds of Rāma.' A poem by Sandhyākara (12th century). The Rāmacarita 'may be read as applying either to the legendary Rāma of Ayodhyā or to the historical king Rāmapāla of Bengal, who was the poet's contemporary and patron'.[1]
[1]Basham, *WI.*, p. 424.

Rāmānuja The founder of, or principal exponent of Viśiṣṭādvaita, a qualified form of monism. He also wrote long commentaries on the Brahma-sūtras, the *BG.*, and the Upaniṣads. His system, partly founded on that of the Pāñcarātra, stressed that *bhakti-yoga* was the best method to obtain deliverance (*mokṣa*). Thus by concentrated and intense devotion (*bhakti*) to Viṣṇu, the devotee realizes that he is merely a fragment of the deity, and thus wholly dependent on him. Another method was the complete surrender of self to the will of God. He taught that the individual 'soul' stands in a relationship of 'difference-non-difference' (*bhedābheda*) to *brahman*. Rāmānuja's teaching greatly influenced many of the devotional cults of later times.

Rāmānuja is said to have been born about A.D. 1017[1] at Śrī Parambattūr near Madras. Mythologically he is regarded as an incarnation of Śeṣa or Ananta. He taught at Kāñci-puram (Kāñjivaram); travelled twice through India, and finally settled at Śrī-raṅgam, near Trichinopoly, where he died. He is buried in the great temple of Śrīraṅga-nāth.[2]

[1]This date is probably several decades too early.
[2]*BH.*, p. 119. Rāmānuja is also called Yatirāja.
v. Darśana(s); Madhva.

Rāmasetu 'Rāma's bridge.' An outcrop of rocks in the channel between India and Ceylon, described in the *Rām.* as a causeway built of coral by Nala, Rāma's army commander.

Rāmāyaṇa An epic poem consisting of 24,000 *ślokas* in seven books. Of the three recensions, the Northern, the oldest, has suffered least from addition and interpolation; the Bengal has suffered most; and the Bombay occupies a position between the other two. These recensions reflect regional influence, and thus differ on many points; also about one-third of each version is lacking from the others.

The *Rāmāyaṇa* has generally been accepted until modern times as a homogeneous work by a single author,

Vālmīki. Critical examination now suggests not only that it must have passed through many stages of development, but also that it contains numerous interpolations, and the addition of Books I and VII. Moreover, the passages representing Rāma as an *avatāra* of Viṣṇu must also be regarded as additions, hardly consistent with the very human terms in which he is generally portrayed in the original poem. Thus in its present form it is a combination of loosely related elements, comprising romantic and allegorical legends and stories, half-mythical, half-historical, and some scanty descriptions of the aboriginal inhabitants and the country of southern India. Nonetheless, as the first national epic of India, the *Rāmāyaṇa* is unique in the cultural history of the Deccan, relating to a period, if not anterior to Troy and Memphis, as M. N. Dutt[1] suggests, at least to a period subsequent to the Āryanization of the major part of northern India.

The supplementary Books, I and VII, may be regarded as a collection of romantic stories supplementing the adventures of Rāma and his wife Sītā; her abduction by Rāvaṇa, King of Laṅkā; her subsequent estrangement from her husband, despite her protestations of faithfulness[2] to him made before the assembled people; her appeal to the Earth-goddess to attest the truth[3] of her declaration, and to the rending of the earth and the emergence of the Earth-goddess seated on a golden throne, and the dramatic finale of the goddess embracing Sītā and their return to the netherworld.

Weber[4] considers that Sītā 'the furrow' represents Āryan husbandry, which had to be protected by Rāma against the attacks of the predatory aborigines. But such attacks may simply have been the attempts of Rāvaṇa and his so-called demoniacal followers (*rākṣasas*) to protect their lands from those they regarded as predatory intruders.

Attempts to ascertain the date of the composition of the *Rāmāyaṇa* have generally involved its comparison with the date of the *MBh*. The result has been to regard the *Rāmāyaṇa* as the earlier work, though some events to which it refers are later than those of the *MBh*. Thus there is no general agreement about its date, opinions about the nucleus varying from 500 to 300 B.C., and the additions from 300 B.C., to A.D. 200.

[1]Intro. to his translation of the *Rāmāyaṇa*.

[2]v. Rambhā I.

[3]Cf. the Buddhist *bhūmisparśamudrā*, or earth-witness *mudrā*, designed to attest the validity of a declaration.

[4]*History of Indian Literature*, p. 192.

v. Hanumat; Pṛthivī.

Rambhā I. A celestial nymph (*apsaras*) who figures in numerous legends, of differing regional origin, often designed to explain another legend or to serve a particular purpose. She is thus portrayed in numerous guises and also as the wife of several men.[1] She is always described as beautiful, and in the *Rām*. (VII.26) her physical charms are depicted with uninhibited frankness. The story recounts that when on her way to a festival she met Rāvaṇa, King of Laṅkā, who was apparently unaware of her identity. In response to his ardent invitation to rest awhile on the mountainside, she claimed his protection, informing him that she was the wife of his nephew Nalakūbara, and therefore his niece, with the status of a daughter-in-law. Rāvaṇa replied, 'For those who have but one husband your argument is valid, but you are an *apsaras* and as such should never be considered as the wife of any man'. Despite her resistance he ravished her. When she was released from his embrace her jewellery was scattered, her hair and clothes in disarray. Still trembling she at last reached home and told her husband what had happened. Swearing vengeance, Nalakūbara sought to console her. Then he laid a curse on Rāvaṇa that he would never be able to approach another woman unless she loved him. If he should seek to possess a woman who does not love him, his head would split into seven pieces. In later works Rambhā was said to have emerged from the Churning of the Ocean (*samudramathana*), as the embodiment of female beauty. Indra sent her to seduce the *ṛṣi* Viśvāmitra, but she failed and the *ṛṣi* cursed her to become a stone and to remain in that form for a thousand years.

[1]*EM*., p. 143. Banerjea states that Rambhā is one of the six variants of the goddess Gaurī (*DHI*., p. 502).

II. The plantain (Musa paradisaca), to whose smooth and tapering (*rambhorū*) stem the thighs of beautiful women are likened.

Rantideva A king of the Lunar Dynasty and son of Saṁskṛti. He spent his wealth in instituting the daily sacrifice of so many animals that their blood formed a river called Carmaṇvatī.

Rasa Sap, juice, elixir, water, mercury, essence, etc. *Rasa* was said to be mercury (*pārada*), regarded by some as the quintessence of the human body (and of all substances); by others as Śiva's vital essence,[1] i.e., semen. As vegetation-spirits, *yakṣas* are guardians of the vegetative source of life (*rasa* = sap in tree = *soma* = *amṛta*), and thus closely connected with the waters.[2] *Rasa* played an important part in Indian alchemy, which was primarily of interest to Śaivas, and was used in concocting the elixir of life (*rasāyana*), aphrodisiacs and tonics.

[1]Mica (*abhraka*) was also believed to have magical properties and was called the 'seed of Gaurī' Śiva's

spouse.

[2]Coomaraswamy, *Yakṣas*, pt. ii. p. 2.

Rasā Name of a mythical river (*RV.*, V.54,9), personified as a goddess, and said to flow round the world (IX.41,6).

Rāsa The circular dance of Kṛṣṇa and the *gopīs*, during which he multiplied himself many times so that each *gopī* thought that she alone danced with him.

Rāṣṭrakūṭa A dynasty (750–973) of the Western Deccan, claiming descent from the Yādava chief Sātyaki, one of Kṛṣṇa's kinsmen.

Rathaṁtara Name of various chants (*sāmans*), said to be capable of destroying the eyesight of the *udgatar* priest.[1]

[1]Gonda, *Eye and Gaze in the Veda*, p. 30.

Rati 'Desire; passion; love', personified as a celestial nymph (*apsaras*), and name of one of the wives of Kāma, the god of love. As an *apsaras* is not expected to remain constant to any one man, Rati is known by many epithets including Māyāvatī (Deceiver), Rāgalaṭa (Vine of love), Kelikilā (Wanton).

Rātrī 'night', personified as a goddess (*RV.*, I.35,1; 113,1; X.127).

Rātrī is naturally associated with Uṣas, the goddess of the Dawn and invoked as a dual divinity in *RV.*, I.142;188, etc. The two goddesses endlessly follow similar paths, but these never cross, nor is there any rivalry between them, for they are the divine mothers of celestial order (*ṛta*).

Raurava One of the twenty-one hells through which pass all those who disobey the law (*Manu*, IV.88). It is a fearsome fiery hell where the wrongdoer's feet are consumed again and again; later he enters the Niraya and other hells until he is successively reborn as an insect, bird, carnivore, etc. (*Mārk. P.*, X.81ff.).

Raurava is personified as the husband of Vedanā (pain) (*Mārk. P.*, L. 30f.).

Rāvaṇa The King of Laṅkā (Ceylon), and half-brother of Kubera. Rāvaṇa was also leader of the indigenous tribes of the adjoining mainland of South India. He is portrayed in the *Rām.* as cruel, lecherous, and an unscrupulous foe,[1] the arch-enemy of Rāma, who is depicted as the archetype of manly virtue.

Whatever Rāma's real motive for the invasion of the Deccan, the *Rām.* makes no attempt to justify it, but seeks rather to blame Rāvaṇa for resisting it. But it is impossible to regard the war between them as a historical event, or to deduce from its description a valid portrait of Rāvaṇa, largely owing to its mythical character. In addition the purpose of the supplements (Books I and VII), and the interpolations which enhance the romantic story of Sītā and her abduction by Rāvaṇa, serve also to blacken his character. After her rescue Rāvaṇa is slain by Rāma, but in the seventh book he reappears in numerous supplementary legends, all of a derogatory character, especially one recounting the raping of his niece Rambhā.

[1]He had ten heads and twenty arms, denoting his great strength and power. Rāvaṇa is said to be a devotee of Śiva.

v. Janaka; Daśaratha; Kumbhakarṇa; Vibhīṣana; Pulastya; Maṇḍodarī; Śiśupāla; Vānara(s); Rākṣasa(s).

Ravi A particular aspect of the sun, sometimes regarded as one of the twelve Ādityas.

Ravicakra A particular astronomical diagram described in the *Garuḍa P.*, in which the sun is represented by the figure of a man with stars marked on his body.

Ṛbhu(s) 'Skilful workmen.'[1] An epithet applied to Indra, Agni, Tvaṣṭṛ and the twelve Ādityas. A *RV.* hymn (I.20) is addressed to the Ṛbhus, and refers to them as the 'Celestial Race'. They composed the song of praise which brings wealth; formed Indra's horses; wrought by their skill the Aśvins' chariot, and by their pious acts won for themselves a share in the sacrifice of the gods.

They are said to be the three sons of Sudhanvan, a descendant of Aṅgiras, and severally named Ṛbhu, Vibhu (or Vibhvan) and Vāja and styled collectively Ṛbhus from the name of the eldest. Wilson considers that their elevation to divine status suggests the ancient belief that men could become divinities.[2]

The *VP.* (II.15) states that Ṛbhu was a son of Brahmā and also a great teacher.

[1]Cf. German, *elbe*; E. *elf*. The Ṛbhus may have been outstanding craftsmen who introduced new skills.
[2]v. *OST.*, V, p. 227.

Ṛc 'Praise', especially a sacred verse recited in praise of a deity. A collection of *ṛcs* is included in the Ārcika, the first part of the *Sāmaveda Saṁ.*, and consists of 585 stanzas, each with its own melody or chant (*sāman*), and each suited to a particular sacrificial rite.

According to the *ŚBr.* (V.5.5,1–4), the *ṛcs* were within Vṛtra who, becoming afraid when Indra raised his thunderbolt to attack him, gave the formulas to Indra.

v. Ṛgveda.

Ṛcīka One of the Bhārgava priests, all of whom had been forced to seek refuge in Kānyakubja, owing to the persecution by Kārtavīrya, King of the Haihayas. Although traditionally forbidden to take up arms, the Bhārgavas married into influential *kṣatra* families, hoping that their sons might avenge them. In furtherance of this policy, Ṛcīka sought to marry Satyavatī, the daughter of Gādhi, King of Kānyakubja, who being unwilling to give her to a peevish old *brāhmaṇa*, demanded as a nuptial present a thousand white horses, each having one black ear. To obtain them Ṛcīka propitiated Varuṇa, the god of the ocean,[1] who presented him with the horses at a sacred spot called Aśvatīrtha,[2] thus enabling the marriage to take place.

[1]Wilson sees in the procuring of horses a parallel between Varuṇa and Neptune (*VP.*, p. 319, n.11).

[2]Situated in the district of Kanauj, perhaps at the confluence of the Kālanadī and the Ganges.

Rebha A *ṛṣi*, probably a victim of anti-Vedic indigenes, by whom he was fettered and thrown into a stream where he lay for ten days until rescued by the Aśvins (*RV.*, I.116,24).

v. Vandana.

Reṇukā I. A daughter of King Prasenajit, who became the wife of Jamadagni and mother of Paraśurāma.

II. In yogic terminology *reṇukā* (or *reṇu*) refers to semen.[1]

[1]*HP.*, p. 172.

Revā or **Rati** The wife of Kāma, the god of love.

Revanta The son of Sūrya and Saṁjñā in their equine forms (*Mārk. P.*, canto 78; *VP.* III.2).[1] He was born mounted on a horse, clad in armour, bearing a sword and shield, and a quiver of arrows. In canto 108 he is described as the lord of forest sprites (*guhyakas*). Those who call on him for aid shall be safeguarded from forest fires, from the terrors of lonely places and attacks by robbers.

The worship of Revanta appears to have originated in Bengal or a neighbouring area. He is represented by only a few epigraphic and iconographic remains, described by Banerjea;[2] all connect him with hunting and horsemanship (*Bṛhat Saṁ.*, LVII.56). Apart from these there is no general agreement about the precise nature of Revanta's functions.

[1]But the *Matsya P.* states he was the son of Vivasvat and Rājñī.

[2]*DHI.*, p. 442. No iconographic remains relating to him have been found in South India.

v. Chāyā.

Revatī I. A yoginī, sometimes identified with Aditi and Durgā or with the Earth.

II. Name of a daughter of King Raivata and wife of Balarāma.

Ṛgveda Saṁhitā The 'Veda of praise'. A repository of sacred lore, consisting of a collection (*saṁhitā*) of hymns (*sūktas*), composed of verses (*ṛcs*). The collection comprises 1,017 (or 1,028)[1] hymns arranged in ten books (*maṇḍalas*). This is known as the Śākala recension, the text used by the Śākalaka priestly school. It included thirty-six hymns, called *khilasūktas*, not in the original *RV.* nucleus. These were apparently added to provide for additions to or changes of ritual.[2]

In the course of the editing of the *RV.* some passages appear to have lost much of their original significance possibly owing to faulty oral transmission. That the task of editing the successive recensions of the *RV.* must have been formidable is indicated by the compilation of an additional *maṇḍala* (VIII); and the selection of verses from *maṇḍalas* II–VII and their transfer to *maṇḍala* IX. The task also included the compilation of two more *maṇḍalas*, numbers I and X, both obviously supplements, as is indicated by their difference in character and style from the nucleus.

A subsequent arrangement,[3] based on authorship, divides the text into *aṣṭikas* (eighths), each of which was subject to further divisions. Whatever the motive for this arrangement of the hymns, Rahurkar[4] finds it 'difficult to rationalize the particular order of *maṇḍalas* two to seven . . . the order of these *maṇḍalas* indicates neither the chronological sequence of their composition nor the intellectual eminence nor the social position of the different families which are traditionally believed to have composed them'. But Brough[5] 'points out that there is a striking symmetry of arrangement so far as the nucleus of the *RV.* is concerned', which shows that the Gṛtsamadas of *maṇḍala* II are the sole representatives of the Bhṛgus, whilst 'IV, VI, and VIII represent the three well-known subdivisions of the Āṅgirasas, namely the Gautamas, Bhāradvājas, and Kevala Āṅgirasas who are represented by the Kāṇvas. On the other hand Books III, V, and VII belong to the non-Bhṛgu Āṅgiras gotras'.

The *maṇḍalas* differ individually, but they have some characteristics in common. Thus in the hymns of the first eight those addressed to Agni are placed first; those to Indra second; and those to the other gods (Viśvedevas) last.[6] *Maṇḍalas* II–VII are classified as 'Family Books', the composition of each being ascribed to a particular *ṛṣi* or to members of his family. The lists (*anukramaṇīs*) of these names go further and name the composer of each hymn. But such ascriptions represent a traditional device, intended to give greater authority or sanctity to a work, which often contradicts the statements of the hymns themselves.[7] *Maṇḍala* VIII may also be classified as a 'Family Book', but was not included in the original seven 'Family Books' or distributed among them because it was probably compiled later.

Unlike the other *maṇḍalas*, the ninth is confined to a single subject, that of the *soma* ritual, particularly to the *soma pavamāna* rites relating to the extraction and purification of the *soma* juice. The first and tenth *maṇḍalas* include late compositions, some of the tenth being of particular interest because of their speculative, quasi-philosophical character or literary quality. These two *maṇḍalas*, whether by design or coincidence, each contain 191 *sūktas*. Though much of the *RV.* indicates its sacerdotal origin and purpose, it also contains nature poems, and others which, though moralistic, are also secular, like the lament of the gambler (*RV.*, X.34).

The *RV.* represents an attempt to adapt ancient myths, magical incantations and spells of nomadic Āryan tribes, chiefly concerned with ensuring the satisfaction of their immediate material needs. The achievement of these aims under the leadership of Indra is the theme of many early hymns. But with accumulating experience, the reliance on magical formulas was superseded by a systematized mythology which defined the functions of the gods and established a practical relationship between them and their devotees. This is indicated by comparison of the early and late *RV.* hymns, the former depicting the Āryan settlers as communal pastoralists, their agriculture being limited to the cultivation of barley. Though the cow, which they introduced, was highly prized, it was not regarded as sacred. The later hymns reveal the fusion of ethnic groups, the Indian and Āryan, when derogatory terms, denoting colour distinction, cease to be used. The family, rather than the community or tribe, becomes the social unit, and individual occupations, such as medicine, sewing, chariot-building, navigation and hunting are frequently referred to.[8]

In Indian tradition the *RV.* is acknowledged to be the record of direct divine revelation, 'seen' as well as 'heard' by inspired seers (*ṛṣis*), and hence the term *veda*[9] was applied to it. The Pūrva-mīmāṁsā priestly school at one time claimed that even the sound of each syllable in the *RV.* was sacrosanct and the Veda itself eternal, but in response to later criticism of the Uttara-mīmāṁsā school these claims were modified or abandoned.

The *RV.* is the greatest source of information about early Indian social, political, religious and linguistic development. Muir[10] considers that it provides 'far more illustrations of the workings of the human mind, in the period of its infancy, upon matters of religion, than can be found in any other literature whatsoever'.

[1]The number 1,017 excludes, and that of 1,028 includes, the Vālakhilya hymns, usually attached to the eighth *maṇḍala*.

[2]*HCIP.*, vol. I, pp. 225ff.

[3]Another arrangement is based on the number of *sūktas* in each *maṇḍala*, these being successively increased in II–VII.

[4]Rahurkar, *Seers*, p. 1.

[5]'The Early History of the Gotras', *JRAS.*, April 1947, p. 85, cited by Rahurkar, op. cit., p. 1, n.1.

[6]This conforms to the tradition which regards Agni as the deity of the *brāhmaṇa*, Indra as that of the *kṣatra*, and the Viśvedevas as the gods of the commonalty (*viś*).

[7]*HIL.*, vol. I, pt. 1, p. 50.

[8]*RV.*, II. 29–39.

[9]Veda has here the same sense as its L. derivative *videre*, stem *vid*, 'to see'. Mythologically the *RV.* (and other valuable things) are said to have emerged from Brahmā's eastern mouth (*VP.*, I.5).

[10]*OST.*, V, p. 4.

v. Ṛgvidhāna; Veda.

Ṛgvidhāna A late but important work showing the process by which Vedic traditions were Hinduized. It describes some of the *siddhis* (supranormal powers), especially those of being able to fly, to hear from afar, to remember one's former lives, etc., as well as a great deal of other magical, yogic and devotional practices. In it can be seen 'the actual assimilation of practices that are non-brahmanic and very probably non-Āryan; all the technical details of magic, ecstasy, or contemplation are integrated and validated by citations from the Vedic scriptures'.[1] It is also strongly influenced by devotion (*bhakti*).

[1]Eliade, *Yoga*, p. 136. The *Ṛgvidhāna* has been translated into E. by J. Gonda, Utrecht, 1951.

Rikta The name of one of the four varieties of wagtails used for purposes of divination. It has white sides to its face and a dark spot on the neck.

Ṛjrāśva A man who slaughtered a hundred wethers to feed a starving she-wolf. For this deed he was blinded by his father, but as the wolf was one of the Aśvins' asses in wolf-form the Aśvins restored his sight (*RV.*, I.116,16).

Ṛṇam The general term for 'debt' from the *RV.* onwards. Though sometimes used metaphorically as in II. 27,4, the term signifies a gambling debt in X.34,10. The result of non-payment of a debt might be serious, but even more so if the stake was ruinously high, as in the case of the Pāṇḍava Prince Yudhiṣṭhira. In the Brāhmaṇas it has an ethical significance, which covers the whole duty of man. It is the debt due by man to the gods, the *ṛṣis*, the *pitṛs*, to his fellow men, and to all creatures; the abstaining from theft, adultery and murder; the obedience to every aspect of moral law (*dharma*).

Rodasī A Vedic goddess, perhaps the personification of lightning as the wife of Rudra and the mother (or wife) of the Maruts. She is immortal, heroic, and the giver of wealth (*RV.*, I.167.5; VII.34,22).

Roga 'Disease, infirmity, sickness'. From the √*ruj*, 'loss of strength and virility', and thus disease personified as a demon, who acts as Death's charioteer, because illness often leads to Death.

v. Mṛtyu; Yama.

Rohiṇī I. The feminine counterpart of the personified rising sun Rohita.[1] The *AVB.* (I.22,3) states that Rohiṇī is the divinity of cattle. In post-Vedic works she is represented as a daughter of the cow Surabhi and mother of Kāmadhenu, the 'Cow of Plenty'.

[1]*AVB.*, p. 265; v. also *AV.*, XIII.1,22 and n. She is also called Uṣas, Sūryā, Sāvitrī, etc.

II. A stellar divinity, personified as a daughter of Dakṣa and wife of Soma (the moon). Rohiṇī, one of the reddish stars in the constellation of Taurus, is one of Soma's twenty-seven wives, who represent the twenty-seven lunar asterisms (*nakṣatras*).[1] As Soma cared only for Rohiṇī his other wives returned to their father. Soma asked for their return and Dakṣa agreed on condition that he promised to share his affection equally with them. Soma promised, but again he singled out Rohiṇī. Soon after he was stricken down with a wasting disease from which he was cured by the Ādityas.

[1]The *rohiṇī nakṣatra* is equated with offspring and cattle (*ŚBr.*, XI.1.1,7).

v. Jyotiṣa.

III. Name of Balarāma's mother.

v. Devakī.

Rohita[1] I. 'The Red.' A name of the sun-god; his female counterpart is Rohiṇī.

All four hymns of Book XIII of the *AV.* are dedicated to Rohita the Ruddy One, who is extolled as the maker of the sky, of heaven and earth, the measurer of space, by whom the gods achieved immortality. Rohita and Rohiṇī are represented 'allegorically as king and queen ... and the terms in which they are exalted reflect the praise and adulation of terrestrial monarchs'.[2]

[1]The term *rohita* is sometimes applied to a red or chestnut horse, and to the sacrificial horse of the *aśvamedha* (v. *AVB.*, p. 662). Metaphorically it is applied to the horse of the sun, the red horse of the sky. According to the *Jaiminīya Br.* (III.199f.), Indra assumed the form of a chestnut horse.

[2]Bloomfield, *The Atharvaveda*, p. 75.

II. A rainbow which appears as straight instead of curved, when it represents Indra's unbent bow, never visible to mortals.

III. Son of King Hariścandra, and the subject of several legends which recount that his father, having been stripped of all his possessions—and also of his wife—by Viśvāmitra, was then required to sacrifice his son, but finally was permitted to purchase a substitute called Śunaḥśepa.

Ropaṇākā A thrush or, according to Whitney, a species of parrot (*kāṣṭhaśuka*).[1] In a charm against jaundice and similar diseases (*AV.*, I.22,4) the latter are invoked to enter a parrot, thrush, or yellow wagtail (*hāridrava* or *gopītanaka*), and so enable the patient to recover.[2]

[1]*AV.*, vol. I, p. 23n.

[2]The transference of diseases to birds, animals, plants, etc., is common to many countries. Thus by sympathetic magic a yellow disease belongs to yellow objects, etc.

Ṛṣi (s) 'Seer.' There is no general agreement about the etymology of the term, but that suggested by Monier-Williams[1] accords with the significance given it in later compositions. He considers that *ṛṣi* is probably derived from the obsolete root *ṛṣ*, from the root *dṛś* 'to see', whence *ṛṣi-kṛt* 'causing to see' or 'a singer of sacred songs', 'an inspired poet or sage'. This definition appears to be confirmed by Rahurkar[2] who considers 'that the ancient Indian culture-complex is mainly made up of two cultural strands—the *ṛṣi*-culture and the *muni*-culture', the *ṛṣis* representing the Vedic Āryan current of thought, the *munis* its pre-Vedic counterpart. The *ṛṣi* is the ideal or the 'model' by which other men are able to achieve spiritual development. In *AV.* XII.1,39, the *saptarṣis* (Seven Ṛsis) are said to be 'the primal makers of creation'. By means of ritual and *tapas* they brought forth cows.

Various *ṛṣis* or seers and their families are mentioned in the *RV.*, but in post-Vedic mythology they are classified as *maharṣis* or *saptarṣis*, or primary ancestors; *rājarṣis*, those of royal lineage; *brahmarṣis* (priestly seers); and *devarṣis*, i.e., *ṛṣis* possessed of such virtues as to merit the honorific 'divine', bestowed on Nārada, Atri and others. This apotheosis accorded both with the etymological and celestial significance of *deva*, which is associated with *dyaus*, 'the bright sky'.

The *ṛṣis* of the *RV.* may be regarded as an élite group of Vedic priestly families, whose literary gifts and knowledge of sacred lore are chiefly represented in the hymns of the *RV.* These *ṛṣis* not only contributed to Vedic culture during its formative period, but also by example helped to preserve it, and by training their successors, to establish it as an integrated Indo-Āryan culture. It was considered that future knowledge could be acquired by a study of the divinely inspired Veda, and hence the declaration in the *Āpastamba Dharmasūtra* (I.2.5,4–5) that the age of divine revelation, hitherto intuitively apprehended, was now ended.[3] Nonetheless, Āpastamba conceded that some *brāhmaṇas*, by their devotion to the sacred texts, might appear to have achieved a state resembling that of their ancient counterparts.

To ensure the efficacy of the sacrificial rite the sacrificer repeats the names of the ancient *ṛṣis*. Word-magic of this kind became a regular feature of sacrificial ritual, the magically powerful names ensuring an efficacious sacrifice. The *AV.*, a repository of magical formulas, contains some excellent examples of the use of *ṛṣi* names as in hymns II.32,2; VI.137,1; 52,3, etc.[4]

The Purāṇas and the *MBh.* contain many legends of Vedic *ṛṣis*, the title of *ṛṣi* being given to many post-Vedic 'holy men' despite Āpastamba's declaration. Similarly on those not of priestly lineage, the title Bhagavat, Muni, etc. was conferred as an honorific, or as a sign of great respect, as with the Buddha (a *kṣatriya*) who was addressed as Bhagavat (Lord), and known as Śākyamuni (Sage of the Śākyas).

The Buddha and the Buddhist 'Saints' as well as the *ṛṣis* were believed to possess the supernatural power of flight. The Buddhist sages journey to the divine lake Anavaptapta in an instant, and the *ṛṣis* soared through the air to the mysterious land of Śvetadvīpa. These are '"pure lands", located in a mystical space that is at once paradisal and of the nature of an "inner space" accessible only to the initiate'.[5]

[1]*SED.*

[2]*Seers*, Intro., p. xv.

[3]The pretensions of Śvetaketu (*Chān. Up.*, 6.1,1–2) illustrates this point, as does the Judaic parallel that divinely inspired prophecy ceased with Malachi, the last of the prophets.

[4]*EBS.*, pp. 17f.

[5]Eliade, *Yoga*, p. 328.

v. Brāhmaṇa I.

Ṛṣyaśṛṅga 'Deer-horned.' Son of the hermit Vibhāṇḍaka, with whom he lived until he became adult. An obscure legend in the *Rām.* and *MBh.* states that he was born of a doe and had a small protuberance on his forehead, whence his name. He was noted for his magical powers, for when the kingdom of Aṅga was stricken by drought, the priests suggested to King Lomapāda that he should give his adopted daughter Śāntā in marriage to Ṛṣyaśṛṅga on condition that he ended the drought. Agreement was reached and shortly after the rains came.

Ṛṣyaśṛṅga officiated at the successful sacrifice instituted by Daśaratha to ensure the birth of an heir subsequently known as Rāmacandra.

Ṛtam I. 'Fixed or settled order, law, rule (especially in religion), sacred action or custom, divine truth.' It is thus associated with sacrificial rites, which must be performed in the correct manner and also at the fixed or appointed time (*ṛtu*).[1] It was considered dangerous for a person or thing to deviate from its own place. In ontology *ṛta* represents the immanent dynamic order or inner balance of the cosmic manifestations themselves; in theology, divine law; in epistemology, validity, truth.[2]

In the Vedic sense *ṛta* indicates the existence of the fundamental and inherent law of nature by which the true '*ṛta*' is distinguished from the false '*anṛta*' (*RV.*, X.124,5),[3] to determine which is one of the duties of Varuṇa. But the same hymn also declares that 'rule is ever-changing'; thus the interpretation of *ṛta*, like that of *dharma*, is also subject to change. *Ṛta* (truth, creativity, law, etc.) is said to exist in the remains (*ucchiṣṭa*) of the sacrifice, as 'force in force' (*AVB.*, XI.7.17).

Throughout the many changes that occurred during each phase of Indian speculative thought, the notion of truth, law and order, represented by Mitra, Varuṇa and Aryaman, continued to be regarded as the 'abstract hero-gods of the Āryans made visible in the sun, whose path also ran straight on'.[4]

[1]Thus '*ṛtu*' also applies to the various seasonal tasks connected with agriculture.

[2]Heimann, *IWP.*, p. 34. Order in the universe is immanent, *not* 'an externally determined law of preconceived function' (Heimann, *Facets*, p. 37). For this reason the gods are said to be subsequent to the world's emanation (*RV.*, X.129,6). Similarly, to the Greeks of the Classical age 'the gods themselves are subject to the order of the universe' (Entralgo, *The Therapy of the Word in Classical Antiquity*, p. 14).

[3]*Ṛta* also means 'normal' and is equivalent to '*asha* (in the Avesta) or *arta* (in ancient Achaemenid texts). The similarity between these names indicates a common origin in prehistoric times' (Filliozat in *Ancient and Medieval Science*, p. 134).

[4]*IT.*, p. 220. Cf. the ancient Egyptian term *maat* (order, justice). 'It is justice as the divine order of society, but it is also the divine order of nature as established at the time of creation. In the Pyramid Texts Re is said to have come from the primeval hill, the place of creation, "after he had put order (*maat*) in the place of chaos"' (Frankfort, *Ancient Egyptian Religion*, p. 54). 'But we lack words for conceptions which, like Maat, have ethical as well as metaphysical implications. We must sometimes translate "order", sometimes "truth", sometimes "justice"' (ibid.). Cf. the Sumerian *me*, and Gr. *moira*.

II. 'Truth, right, duty or custom', personified as an object of worship and regarded as a child of Dharma.

Ṛtavyā 'Relating to the seasons (*ṛtu*), or to seasonal activities. Two of the bricks used in the building of the fire-altar represented the seasons, the Year, i.e., totality, generative power, the three worlds, etc. (*ŚBr.*,

VIII.7.1,1ff.). Bricks were also the stepping-stones by which the gods ascended from the earth to the heavens, and by which the sacrificer also reached the celestial worlds.

Ṛtu 'Any settled point of time; time appointed for any action, especially for sacrifice and other regular worship.' It is also a division or part of the year, a season. The personified Seasons are worshipped by libations.
v. Ṛtam I; Ṛtvij.

Ṛtuhārikā A demoness who obstructs the menses and causes sterility.

Ṛtvij[1] The collective designation of the priests employed in the performance of the sacrifice. They originally numbered four, subsequently increased to seven, this number coinciding with the *maharṣis*, the instigators of the sacrifice. The seven priests were the Hotar, Potar, Neṣtar, Agnīdh, Praśāstar, Adhvaryu and Brahman. Originally the Purohita was a member of the *ṛtvij*, and was the singer of the most important songs, subsequently the role of the Hotar.

The Purohita also supervised the performance of the sacrifice, but this function was later assigned to the Brahman. The *ŚBr.* (III.6.2,1) refers to 'seven Hotṛs', but this appears to denote the priests of the *ṛtvij* of which the Hotṛ was chief. The Adhvaryu's duties were concerned with the practical side of the sacrifice, his assistant being the Agnīdh. The Praśāstar (also known as the Upavaktar or Maitravaruṇa) was present only at great sacrifices. To him alone particular litanies were entrusted, and his was the sole prerogative of advising the Hotar. The Potar, Neṣtar, and Brahman were concerned solely with the *soma* sacrifice, but at a later period when the *ṛtvij* was enlarged to sixteen,[2] this duty was performed by the Brāhmaṇācchaṁsin, thus distinguishing him from the Brahman, the supervisor of the sacrifice.

Sacrifices performed by the *ṛtvij* on behalf of the king also included his people for whose welfare he was considered to be responsible. The *sattra*, or prolonged sacrificial session, was performed for the sole benefit of the priests.

[1]From '*ṛtu*', the time appointed for any action, and '*ij*' from '*yaj*', the performance of the sacrifice at the proper time (*Nir.*, 3,19).

[2]The number sixteen symbolizes totality or completion. *CC.*, ch. iv, deals with the significance of the number sixteen.

Ruci 'Light', 'splendour'. The name of one of the ten Prajāpatis.
v. Ākūti; Mālinī.

Rudra The Vedic god of the tempest, whose characteristics, thunder and lightning, are represented by their respective epithets, 'Roarer'[1] and 'Red or flashing One', both of which are derived from a common root, '*rud*'.[2] S.K. Chatterji suggests that there may be a connexion between the Vedic Rudra and the Dravidian 'Red god', who was originally identified with an already existing Storm-god.[3] Numerous passages in the *RV.* (I. 43,1, etc.) portray Rudra as the bringer of rain, who thus ensures the fertility of the fields, and the health and well-being of the people. Though his activities might sometimes be overpowering and result in floods, he conforms to the law of Savitar (the Sun), from whom all aerial gods derive their powers.[4]

In some *RV.* hymns Rudra is directly or implicitly identified with Agni and Indra, the latter also being a 'thunder-wielder' (VI.29,1), their activities being frequently associated with the production of rain. This is indicated by the reference to Agni secreting himself in the aerial waters or rain-cloud; by the attacks of Indra on the drought-demon Vṛtra; and by the efforts of Rudra to force the monsoon rains to come to the parched earth. He is aided by his sons the Maruts (Rudras), who come with blasts of wind, clad in robes of rain (V.57,4), and who roar like lions (III.26,5). They are often associated with Indra who also refers to them as his children (I.100,5). Rudra is said to have a hundred weapons; he is called the 'Tufted One' in *AV.* (XI.2,12), and said to be followed by howling dogs (XI.2,30), and by the hosts of the dead, like the Wild Huntsman of European mythology.

Rudra may originally have been a pre-Vedic god, as is suggested by a hymn to him (*AV.*, XI.2,1–17), which identifies or associates him with Bhava and Śarva, the lords of cattle; verse 31 refers to his female attendants, the *ghoṣiṇīs* or 'Noisy Ones', to whom also homage should be paid. The reference to them is significant by its contrast with the general patriarchal emphasis of the *RV.* Rudra was called 'lord of cattle' and other domestic animals. He was also expected to destroy dangerous wild animals, and by inference all maleficent storm-clouds (*ŚBr.*, XII.7.3,20). Rudra's ambivalent character,[5] and his increasing association with fertility and the generative process, remains a recurring theme in the *ŚBr.*, the *MBh.* and the Purs. This is illustrated by a myth in which Brahmā was interrupted whilst meditating on the creative process. His rage at being disturbed burst from his forehead in the form of Rudra who, at Brahmā's command divided himself into male and female forms. These were subdivided and became the eleven Rudras, some mild, others fierce. The female half became manifold, which the *Vāyu P.* declares are the various energies (*śaktis*) of Śiva. Among Rudra's many epithets are Caṇḍa (Wrathful),

Ugra (Fearful), Mīḍhras (Bountiful), Śarva (Archer), Īśāna (Ruler), etc.

The *Śvetāśvatara Up.* (3,2) states that Rudra alone is unaffected by the dissolution of the world (*pralaya*) at the end of the age.

Finally Rudra ceased to have a separate entity and becomes completely identified with Śiva. Although much of the evidence linking them has disappeared, what remains suggests that their ultimate amalgamation is more than a simple coalescence of two cults, but the flow of numerous regional non-Āryan beliefs into the main current of Vedic and post-Vedic Indo-Āryan tradition.

[1]Or perhaps 'Howler', referring to the noise of the thunder-bolt (*hrādinī*).

[2]Cf. E. *ruddy*; Cornish *rud*; Old W. *rudd*, etc.; v. also *HP.*, p. 195.

[3]*HCIP.*, I, p. 162. Cf. *CHI.*, vol. I, p. 145.

[4]Rudra unites in himself both the dangerous and beneficial aspects of the fertility process (Heesterman, *Ancient Indian Royal Consecration*, p. 90, n.44). In the Agnihotra the sacrificer twice holds out the offering ladle to the north to propitiate Rudra. Therefore it is dangerous to stand to the north of the offering when it is made, for this is the vicinity of this dread god (*Kauṣ Br.*, II.2).

[5]No fire oblation was made to Rudra, which indicates that he was more feared than adored, especially as offerings to him were deposited at cross-roads and other ill-omened places.

v. Rudra(s); Rudraja; Rudrakalaśa; Rudrākṣa; Rudrākrīḍa; Rudrānī.

Rudraja 'Quicksilver' (mercury),[1] supposed to have been one of the by-products of atmospheric phenomena, especially of Rudra, the god of lightning and thunder. *Rudraja* is also identified with Śiva's semen.

[1]According to Indian alchemy mercury is 'solar heat', transmitted by atmospheric phenomena and stored in the earth and called *rudravīrya* (*HP.*, p. 196).

Rudrākrīḍa 'Rudra's pleasure-ground', i.e., the burial or cremation place where Rudra is said to dance at twilight.

Rudrākṣa 'Rudra-eyed.' Berries from the tree or shrub (Elaeocarpus ganitrus) used to make Śaiva rosaries. The berries are rough and have five divisions, denoting Śiva's five faces (*pañcānana*). The berries are said to be his tears when on one occasion he wept with rage.[1]

[1]*BH.*, p. 82.

Rudrāṇī Name of Rudra's wife. She is depicted in the Brāhmaṇas as a cruel goddess associated with blood sacrifices, who causes sickness, terror and death to emerge from the depths of the forest. In post-Vedic works she is equated with Durgā.

Rudra(s) 'The Howling or Red Ones.' In the Vedas they are identified with the Maruts, the sons of Rudra. But in the *ŚBr.* (XI.6.3,7) they correspond to the eleven vital life-energies (*rudra-prāṇa*) of the individual, ten of them representing the physical and sensory energies, and the eleventh the self (spirit). When these depart from this mortal body, they cause wailing (*rud*) and hence are called Rudras.[1]

According to the *MBh.* Śiva is surrounded by 1,100 Rudras, who also act as escorts for Yama.

[1]The vital life-energies are referred to in the *Bṛhad-Ār. Up.* (3.9,4; *Chān. Up.*, 3.16,3–4) which at death leave the body and are the 'cause of tears'.

v. Rudraja.

Rudravīrya v. Rudraja.

Rukma 'Bright or radiant.' Probably a golden ornament in the form of a chain or disc worn by the Maruts (*RV.*, I.166, 10, etc.). Rukma is also a Vedic epithet of the sun.

Rukmin The name of the eldest son of Bhīṣmaka King of Vidarbha. His sister Rukmiṇī[1] fell in love with Kṛṣṇa, but Rukmin disliked him and opposed the marriage. Shortly afterwards she was betrothed to Śiśupāla, King of Cedi, but before the wedding could take place, Kṛṣṇa abducted Rukmiṇī. Her brother and his army pursued him but were defeated. During the battle Śiśupāla was killed, and only the intervention of Rukmiṇī saved her brother from a similar fate. Rukmin then founded the city of Bhojakaṭa where he lived until his death.

According to the current rules of warfare Rukmiṇī was now one of the 'spoils of war', whom Kṛṣṇa was free to marry by the Rākṣasa rite, i.e., marriage by capture. Kṛṣṇa exercised his right and from their union was born the illustrious Pradyumna, whom one tradition regards as an incarnation of Kāma, the god of love, and another as one of the *vyūhas* (emanations) of Vāsudeva (Kṛṣṇa).

[1]Like Sītā she is regarded as an incarnation of Lakṣmī who under different names is said to accompany each of Viṣṇu's 'descents' to earth.

v. Vivāha; Māyādevī; Avatāra.

Rukmiṇī v. Rukmin.

Rūpa 'Form, shape or figure.'[1] By means of *rūpa* a body becomes an object of perception. The formless *brahman* is said to have brought forth his own form spontaneously.

The term is applied especially to images or pictures of the gods and thus distinguishes them from objects such as pebbles, rock formations, etc., which are regarded, not as formless, but as natural formations, and designated *a-rūpa* or aniconic. In India any individual shape, even of a god or of a 'world', is considered to be purely accidental and transitory.

[1]B.K. Ghosh considers that it originally meant 'assumed form' as in the *RV*. (*HCIP*., vol. I, p. 423, n.60).

S

Śabala[1] 'Brindled', 'variegated'. Either the name or epithet of one of Yama's two 'four-eyed' dogs,[2] the other being called Śyāma ('black'). But in the *RV.* (X.14,10–12) both are said to be dark-hued, fierce and bloodthirsty. They were the offspring of Indra's bitch Saramā, and guarded the road to Yama's realm of the dead (*AV.*, VIII.1,9). To appease the dogs and thus protect the bodies of those already on their way, the corpses were covered with pieces of flesh from a specially slaughtered cow or goat.

[1]The Greek Kerberos has been identified with the Sanskrit Śabala (*Ancestor Worship*, p. 42). *Karbara*, 'spotted, variegated'; and *śabala*, *śabara*, etc., are from an Austro-Asiatic word-group with various prefixes (*IAL.*, 2882).

[2]Dogs are associated with death and the dead in many mythologies. The *Avestan* Yima had four dogs, and the ancient Egyptian dog or jackal-headed god Anubis was called the 'Opener of the way' (to the realm of the dead).

v. Sārameya (s).

Śabalāśva (s) v. Dakṣa.

Śabara One of the wild Indian tribes living on the borders of the Āryan settlements. 'They can be identified with the Suari of Pliny and the Sabarae of Ptolemy and are probably ancestors of the Savaralu or Sauras of the Vizagapatam hills, the Savaris of the Gwalior territory and the savages on the frontiers of Orissa.'[1] Later the term was applied to any savage or barbarian tribe.

[1]*HCIP.*, I, p. 260.

v. Piṅgākṣa I.

Śabara Mantra (s) Obscure formulas whose meaning has been lost but which are regarded as having great efficacy. They are still used in some Indian magical rites.[1]

[1]*HP.*, p. 337.

Sabardughā The 'nectar-yielding cow' which pours out all treasures (*RV.*, I.134,4; VIII.1,1); or it may be the general term for cows whose milk was used at the sacrifice.

Śabda 'Sound.' In India 'sound' has been from ancient times the subject of intense study,[1] especially by the Udgātar priest, the chanter of the *sāmans*. A pure tone was considered not only to free the sacrifice from evil influences, but also to purify the sacrificer (*Kauṣ. Br.*, XI.1).

Sound is distinguished as: 1. *Sphoṭa*, a self-existent, eternal element, beyond perception. 2. *Nāda*, perceptible only to the divinely inspired poet or seer. 3. *Anāhata*, potentially existent, like thought, but not expressed. 4. *Āhata*, sound of any kind, whether or not within the range of human or animal perception.

The significance of *sphoṭa* and *nāda* is peculiar to the Mīmāṁsā priestly school and was developed as a doctrine of *a priori*, eternal, self-existent essence, revealed in speech (*vac*) whose divine origin rendered its sound (*nāda*) also divine. The doctrine was essentially one of religio-transcendentalism or super-empiricism, to which in some mystical manner the empirical canons of truth were shown to conform. The purpose, Heimann[2] suggests, was to 'empiricize, as it were, unempirical objects to make them more convincing for the *laukika*, the ordinary mind'. This is indicated by the creative power existent in the sound of Śiva's drum (*ḍamaru*). The notion of Śiva as the essence of sound or '*Nādatanu*—consisting of sound—has remained a living concept up to our days'.[3] Thus some *mantras* rely for their efficacy not on a connexion between sound and meaning, but on sound alone.

[1]Speech patterns are crucial in an oral culture, everything having to be 'called up' or 'recalled'. 'For this reason, even in the most laconic early cultures, utterance is attended to and valued in ways it will seldom be once writing takes hold' (Entralgo, *The Therapy of the Word in Classical Antiquity*, Pref., p. xii).

[2]*PSPT.*, p. 20.

[3]A. A. Bake, 'The Appropriation of Śiva's Attributes to Devī', *BSOAS.*, 1958, XVII/3, p. 523.

Śabda-brahman The equation of *sphoṭa*, the primary element of sound (*śabda*), with the essence of existence (*brahman*), expressed by the sound of the mystical syllable *OM*. *Śabda-brahman* thus represents the ultimate significance of sound, i.e., non-sound or abstract sound—sound devoid of all attributes. It is the complete union (*sāyujyatva*) of the individual self (*ātman*) with *brahman* and the attainment of ultimate peace (*nirvṛtatva*) (*Maitri Up.*, 6.22).

Śacī 'Divine power or the source of that power', conceived not as an inherent quality of the gods, but as a quality derived from a divine source. This power is impartially bestowed on various gods and especially on Indra. The notion of divine power was personified

as the goddess Śacī (also called Indrāṇī and Aindrī), the consort of Indra.
v. Śakra; Śākta.

Sadampuṣpā 'Ever-flowering.' An unidentified herb from which amulets are made to enable the wearer to detect and to avoid sorcerers (*AV.*, IV.20, 1–9).

Sadānvā(s) A class of demonesses, believed to inhabit the foundations of houses from which Rudra and Indra are implored to drive them forth. The origin and activities of these maleficent beings belong to a dimly remembered tradition, and because of the mystery surrounding them they are the more greatly feared (*AVB.*, II.14,5). Many amulets are made from the wood of trees noted for particular magical qualities, but none of them gives any protection against the Sadānvās, the only effective amulet against them being one made of pearl shell (*AVB.*, IV.10,3).

Sadāśiva v. Pañcānana.

Sādhanā 'The means of effecting or achieving a particular end.' In Tantrism it denotes 'the exercise of sexual contact under tantric "laboratory" conditions. It is irrelevant, in the final analysis, whether these *sādhanās* were or are literally performed, or whether they are hypostasized entirely into mental configurations'.[1]

[1] *TT.*, p. 228.

Sādhya(s) A class of semi-divine celestial beings, whom Banerjea calls 'intermediate gods' (*vyantara-devatās*). They are referred to in the *RV.* (X.90,16) as the 'gods of old', and in the *Tait. Saṁ.* (VI.3,5) are regarded as having existed prior to the creation of human life. They may be the rites of the Vedas personified. Later they became associated with the *puṣyasnāna* or ablution ceremony which preceded the annual consecration of a king (*Bṛhat Saṁ.*, XLVII, 55), and with the *aśvamedha* or horse-sacrifice (*Tait. Saṁ.*, V.6,17). They also shared the guardianship of the sacrificial horse during its year-long wanderings (*ŚBr.*, XIII.4,2,16).

Sadyojāta v. Pañcānana.

Sagara A king of Ayodhyā and son of King Bāhu.[1] The latter was driven from his kingdom by the Haihayas and forced to seek refuge at the hermitage of Aurva Bhārgava. Whilst there Bāhu's queen gave birth, after her husband's death, to Sagara whom Aurva subsequently trained in the military arts and prophesied that he would become a universal ruler (*cakravartin*). Sagara's marriage to Keśinī, the daughter of the Yādava King Vidarbha enabled him to defeat his father's enemies the Haihayas, and their allies the Śakas, Kāmbojas, Pāradas, Pahlavas, etc. He would have completely destroyed them but for the intercession of his *purohita* Vasiṣṭha. Instead, as a sign of their defeat, he made the Śakas shave half of the hair of their heads; the Kāmbojas the whole of it; the Pāradas were forbidden to shave or trim their hair; the Pahlavas were compelled to cut off their beards,[2] thus rendering them all unfit to perform Vedic rites.

Like his father, Sagara also had two wives; by his first, Keśinī, he had Asamañjas, who became famous and continued the royal line. His second wife Sumatī was delivered of a gourd containing 60,000 seeds which were transformed into sons, all of whom, having offended the *ṛṣi* Kapila, were destroyed by him.

The Sagara legend appears to have been very popular and to have provided a basis for numerous regional variants.[3] Thus it is used to explain the origin of both the celestial and terrestrial Ganges, and the reason for the purifying qualities of the latter; the relation of the Ganges to Sagara's 60,000 sons, and finally to show that from the water of the Ganges the ocean (*sāgara*) was formed.

[1] *HCIP.*, vol. I, pp. 284, 286–7.

[2] The *VP.* (IV.3) states that they were ordered to wear beards.

[3] One of which occurs in the *VP.*, IV.4.

v. Aṁśumat; Bhagīratha; Gaṅgā; Sāgara.

Sāgara The personified ocean.
v. Sagara.

Sahadeva v. Pāṇḍavas.

Sahasrākṣa 'Thousand-eyed', and thus 'all-perceiving'. An epithet of Indra and Vāyu (*RV.*, I.23,3), of Agni (I.79, 12; *Tait. Saṁ.*, V.4.7,2), and of Viśvakarman (*RV.*, X.81,3). The epithet is also applied to an amulet derived from the *varaṇa* tree, which sees all and wards off every malevolent influence (*AV.*, X.3).

Sahasrāra cakra v. Kuṇḍalinī.

Saibyā I. Hariścandra's queen.
II. Wife of Śatadhanu.

Śaiva 'Relating to Śiva'; the 'cult of Śiva' (Śaivism); 'a devotee of Śiva'.

The origin of Śaivism belongs to pre-history, to a period in which primitive beliefs were the product of a diversity of ethnic groups, traces of which are reflected in the *AV.* and Purāṇas.

The term *śiva*, meaning 'auspicious', occurs in the *RV.* where it is used especially of Rudra the storm-god who, though generally regarded as fierce and destructive, was also the bringer of rain. Gradually the association of the epithet with Rudra ceased and the epithet itself was personified as the 'Auspicious One'. After a long process of absorption of local cults Śiva was given what may be termed post-Vedic theistic status in the *Śvetāśvatara Up.*, and subsequently in the Śaiva texts called Āgamas. This was confirmed during the following centuries, during which Śaivism had to contend with another Hindu sectary, the Vaiṣṇava; as well as the popular Buddhist and Jain Orders. But Śaiva and Vaiṣṇava rivalry tended to be the more active, as many passages in the *VP.* indicate. Later, when many of the early differences of the two sects appeared to have been reconciled, various interpretations of the monistic doctrine of the Vedānta still persisted.

Following the absorption of ancient local cults and the formation of a Śaiva system, a number of Śaiva sects were established over the years. Among these were: Pāśupata, whose tenets were based on the two works of Kauṇḍinya—the *Pāśupatasūtra* and *Pañcārthabhāṣya*, the former written about 100–200 A.D., the latter c. A.D. 400–600; the Pratyabhijñā, a Kashmir sect whose doctrine was formulated by Vasugupta (800 A.D.) in the *Śiva sūtra* and *Spandakārikā*, and expanded in successive commentaries by Somānanda, Utpaladeva, Abhinavagupta and his pupil Kṣemarāja, whose *Pratyabhijñāhṛdaya* summarizes the teachings of the sect; and the Vīra or Liṅgāyata (the latter name being derived from the phallic symbol worn by adherents of the cult). It remained relatively obscure until the thirteenth century when it was developed by Basava, a *brahmin* of Kannada in South India; the Śaiva Siddhānta, a South Indian sect[1] which developed during the eleventh to the thirteenth centuries, using Sanskrit texts. These were subsequently superseded by those in Tamil, which greatly increased its popularity.

Śaiva philosophy may be said to typify the entire range of Hindu thought, from idealistic monism to pluralistic realism; from a belief in a personal divinity to that of an abstract principle.

[1] *BH.*, p. 89.

v. Liṅga; Lakulīśa; Śākta; Śakti.

Śaiva Siddhānta The name of the 'early literature of the Pāśupatas and other Śaiva sects ... written in Sanskrit, [which] was supplemented and then virtually superseded by texts in Tamil'.[1] The latter, while recognizing the authority of the Veda and drawing on its teaching, added texts of a devotional character.

The primary sources of Śaiva Siddhānta are the twenty-eight Śivāgamas, the chief being the Kāmikā.[2]

[1] *WI.*, pp. 333f.

[2] *EW.*, vol. I, pp. 370, 374. v. also H. Mitra, 'Sadāśiva Worship in Bengal', *JRASB.*, n.s., vol. xxix, 1933, pp. 171–254.

v. Śiva-jñāna-bodham; Śiva; Śaiva.

Śaivī One of the names of Manasā, the goddess of snakes.

Śaka The name of a nomadic pastoralist people who may have originated 'beyond either the Aral or the Caspian.'[1] The Chinese knew them as Se, the Persians as Śakas, the Romans as Sacae, but they have also been called Scythians, the vaguely specified area of Scythia being to ancient geographers a convenient repository for nomadic tribes of known ethnic but uncertain regional occupation. It is generally assumed that the Śakas were fair-skinned Caucasians,[2] but it is not unlikely that during their nomadic existence they became closely associated with tribes like the Piśāca, Ābhīra and Kekaya and also with their Parthian neighbours. It is probable also that there was some infusion of Turanian blood through intermarriage with women captured during tribal wars.

During the latter half of the first millennium B.C. the Persian kings appointed both Śakas and Parthians as governors or satraps of their provinces in north-western India. It is to them, rather than to Alexander's satraps, that Candragupta Maurya, and especially Aśoka—for some years Viceroy at Ujjain—owed their political and administrative abilities. Thus when the successive conquests of Alexander, and subsequently of the Kuṣāṇas, had been concluded, the Śakas and Parthians continued to act as governors under Kaniṣka. By the end of the second century A.D. they had acquired complete control of Satrapies as widely separated as Kapiśa in Afghanistan, Taxila in Western Punjāb, Ujjain in Mālwā and Nāsik in the Upper Deccan, over which they ruled for three hundred years.[3]

[1] E. H. Minns, *Scythians and Greeks*, pt. i, p. 112.

[2] Like the five tribes of the Hiung-nu, who are described by the Chinese as fair (op. cit., p. 45).

[3] Among the towns they established were Śākala, the modern Siālkot. It was a Śaka ruler, Candravarman, who in A.D. 325 erected the famous Iron Pillar, regarded as a masterpiece of engineering, since re-erected at Mehrauli, Delhi.

v. Śākya(s).

Śāka The teak tree, after which one of the seven mythical islands (*dvīpas*) is named. A *śāka* tree was believed to grow in the centre of the island. The latter is surrounded by a sea of milk (representing abundance) (*VP.*, II.4).

Śākala The final recension of the *RV.*, regarded as the definitive text of the Śākalaka priestly school.

v. Ṛgveda; Śākha.

Śakambhara Perhaps the personification of diarrhoea, regarded as the symptom of various diseases (*AVB.*, V.22,4 and pp. 445f.).

v. Apvā.

Śākambharī 'Herb-bearing'; 'herb-nourishing'. A vegetal goddess, probably of pre-Vedic origin,[1] subsequently identified with Durgā, who in this form produces from her body life-sustaining vegetables (*Mārk. P.*, 91, 43f.).

[1]An oblong Harappā sealing depicts a nude female figure, upside down, from whose womb issues a plant. A similar Gupta terracotta figure has a lotus issuing from her neck (*DHI.*, p. 490; v. also *EM.*, p. 11).

v. Navapatrikā(s).

Śākhā Lit. and fig. 'a branch', and thus 'a branch or school of the Veda (each school adhering to its own traditional text and interpretation)'.[1] The *Caraṇa-vyūha*, a work by Śaunaka, refers to five *RV.* schools: the Śākala, Baṣkala, Āśvalāyana, Śāṅkhāyana and Māṇḍukāyana, the texts of which were subsequently reduced to the extant Śākala recension. But internal evidence, especially of the *RV.*, suggests that the earliest nuclei of the Vedas must have been subjected to excisions, amendments and additions before their final recension. 'It is impossible to imagine, however, any stage in the development of the *Ṛik-Saṁhitā* at which a demand for the new *mantras* was not present, for the ritual in which they were intended to be used was all the time growing in complexity and expanding in range'.[2] Thus a final recension of the *RV.* was probably not attempted until its particular form of ritual began to wither away, and the Veda was re-interpreted by the composers of the Āraṇyakas and Upaniṣads. This event heralded the gradual emancipation of Indian thought from the confines of Vedic dogma and faith in the efficacy of sacrificial rites.

Freed from ancient commentarial and linguistic restrictions, philosophical and 'literary' works were produced in an ever-increasing volume, until today they present what is perhaps the world's most complete record of religious and philosophical thought.

[1]*SED.*, p. 1062, col. 3.

[2]*HCIP.*, I, p. 227.

Śākinī(s) Demonesses attendant on Śiva and Durgā. They are similar to the Mahāyāna Buddhist Ḍākinīs.

Śakra 'Strong, powerful.' The epithet of many gods, especially of Indra, regarded as the personification of power, strength and fearlessness.

v. Śacī.

Śakra-kumarī(s) The five (or seven) small flagstaffs erected near the main flagstaff during the *Indramaha* festival (*Bṛhat Saṁ.*, XLII.39f.). Omens were drawn from the breaking or falling of the flagstaffs, or from birds alighting on them, etc. The breaking of one of the staffs presaged death to prostitutes; the breaking of ropes trouble for children, etc.[1]

[1]A. M. Shastri, *India as Seen in the Bṛhatsaṁhitā* p. 123, n.1. The *śakra-kumaris* are also described as 'decorative wooden dolls attached to the banner of Indra' (ibid., p. 443).

Śakrasṛṣṭa 'Indra-created.' The yellow myrobalan plant, said to have sprung from the ground where Indra had spilt a drop of *amṛta*.

Śākta A Hindu cult based on the concept of divine energy (*śakti*) as the activating principle of existence. The latter is not only grammatically feminine[1] but is also notionally female. Nascent forms of such a belief are apparent in the *RV.* and in subsequent works, but the Śākta as a recognizable cult cannot be traced before the first half of the present era. The recognition of supranormal power, manifested in all phenomena, must have been one of the first things of which early man became aware. The gradual awareness of its significance greatly influenced religious ideas, as is indicated in the Devī-sūkta (*RV.*, X.125) which gives 'one of the greatest and at the same time simplest expositions of the concept of divine Energy or *Śakti* inherent in everything—in gods, men and animals . . . in the universe itself'.[2]

It was perhaps inevitable that the attempts to express religious aspirations and the methods of achieving them should have assumed a variety of forms. On the one hand there was the practice of extreme asceticism, and on the other erotic Tantric practices. Thus these interpretations divided the Śāktas into the so-called 'Right-hand' or *dakṣiṇācāra* the ascetic group; and the 'Left-hand' or *vāmācāra*. The latter, whilst professing to share the aims of the ascetics, combined their yogic techniques with wine-drinking, 'licentious ritual songs, erotic mimicry and probably orgies'.[3] Some Śāktas included magic and alchemy in their techniques.

The Śākta cult flourished in areas like Bengal and Assam, and regions least influenced by the main streams of Indo-Āryan culture. Nonetheless, no region was lacking in the recognition of the importance of the female aspect of nature, whether conceived as Aditi (the mother of the universe) or as a fertility divinity, or as a tutelary mother-goddess, or as Devī, the Supreme Goddess. But its influence on other Indian cults has yet to be fully explained.

Although the Śākta cult is closely associated with that of Śiva, it is clearly distinguished from the latter, as is indicated by the Śākta dictum: 'Śiva is a corpse without Śakti'.[4] This is confirmed by the Śākta elevation of Pārvatī, and the relegation of Śiva to a secondary position.[5]

[1]Cf. the Lat. '*anima*' (vital breath); Hebrew '*rūăḥ*' (the spirit of God), which 'moved upon the face of the waters' (Genesis, I.2). The early Syriac Trinity was Father, Son and 'Mother', with whom the Holy Spirit was identified.

In Mesopotamia, Syria, Anatolia and elsewhere the fertile earth symbolized the female generative principle, personified as the goddess Ninhursaga or Innanna-Ishtar; in Egypt the consort of a god was recognized as the generative principle, the source of life, and its First Cause (E.O. James, *Tree of Life*, p. 166).

[2]*DHI.*, pp. 490f.; v. also *HP.*, p. 35.

[3]Eliade, *Yoga*, p. 342. Allegro (*Sacred Mushroom and the Cross*, p. 81) points out that the sexual power of women was vital also to the Near Eastern mystery cults.

[4]In Buddhist Tantrism the dictum is reversed: 'Without the bridegroom the bride is dead'.

[5]van Gulik, *Sexual Life in Ancient China*, p. 343.

v. Kuṇḍalinī; Ardhanārī; Ājīvikas; Yoga; Śacī.

Śakti I. 'Divine power or energy', personified as female and dynamic as distinct from its male or passive aspect,[1] a concept generally lacking in the *RV.*, where the notion of divine power is contrasted with the limited power of man, and hence his constant appeals to the gods for help. Nonetheless, the power of the gods was not regarded as inherent, but as derived from a separate source called *śacī*. But brief references to the gnās[2] in the *AV.* (VII.51,2, etc.) suggest that 'nature power' had already begun to be associated with female energies long before the advent of Tantric doctrine.

The lack of speculation on the subject in the Vedas and Brāhmaṇas is perhaps because of their preoccupation with ritual.[3] Even the classical Upaniṣads are mainly concerned with secret and esoteric doctrines.

Numerous local cults became assimilated with the main current of Śaiva mythology. Thus many goddesses, like Pārvatī, Umā and others, whose origin lacks any apparent connexion with the energy principle, finally became important aspects of it.

Among these are Ambikā, whose epithet Śākambharī (herb-bearing or herb-nourishing) indicates both her vegetal origin and her association with Śiva, the lord of plants. Another is Durgā, a goddess of ancient Indian origin, who assumes various forms from which other forms emerge. She is sometimes called Ambikā, from whose forehead (regarded as the emotional centre, especially of wrath) sprang Kālī, and from her Cāmuṇḍā, the Destroyer. Though in the *MBh.* and the Purāṇas the Śāktis are variously named, such distinctions never lose sight of the concept that they are all merely aspects of the indivisible Mahādevī. In addition to local goddesses, a particular virtue may be personified, such as Satī, representing the faithfulness of a wife, and given the status of a *śakti*.

The notion of *śakti* as the personification of energy, does not figure prominently in Vaiṣṇavism, though it is said to have eight *śaktis*: Śrī, Bhū, Sarasvatī, Prīti, Kīrti, Śānti, Tuṣṭi and Puṣṭi, regarded as 'the eight channels through which the protective energies of the god can display their beneficent activity'.[4] One reason why the Vaiṣṇava has little need of *śaktis* is that the beneficent activities of Viṣṇu are performed by his *avatāras*; another is that the Viṣṇu tradition was initially brahmanic and patriarchal, whilst that of Śiva owed its origin and development largely to indigenous and matriarchal traditions.

[1]But in a few passages of Hindu Tantric works, particularly the Periyapurāṇam, a canonical text of Tamil Śaivism, the active function is assigned to Śiva, the inactive function to Śakti, as it is also assigned 'in at least two passages of the *Mārkaṇḍeya Purāṇa*, Caṇḍipātha' (*TT.*, p. 213).

[2]Lit. 'women'.

[3]But at an early date the term *śakti* conveyed the idea of an energy by which man might ritually come into contact with the divine (Gonda, *VS.*, pp. 55, 61).

[4]Gonda, *Aspects*, p. 231.

v. Prāṇa.

II. A 'spear' or 'javelin'. Weapons which greatly increased the fighting power of the warrior. The *MBh.* (3,270,3) mentions a *mahāśakti*, a large and powerful weapon adorned with a hundred bells, which was probably displayed only on ceremonial occasions.

A special javelin or spear made of metal was reserved for leading chariot-borne *kṣatriyas*, and hence such weapons were called *ratha-śaktis* (chariot spears), and were probably better finished than those called *ṛṣṭi*, carried by the ordinary soldier.[1]

The *MBh.* (9.17,44. *EM.*) refers to the *vajra* made by Tvaṣṭṛ for Indra as his *amoghā śakti* or 'unfailing javelin',[2] which became the possession of the Pāṇḍu princes, who paid homage to it with perfumes and garlands. The *śakti* is also the emblem of the war-god Skanda.

[1]S. D. Singh, *Ancient Indian Warfare*, pp. 107f.

[2]Cf., the sacred spear called *Ḥtr-ḥr* of the Egyptian Horus (Reymond, *Mythological Origin of the Egyptian Temple*, p. 94).

v. Krauñca II.

Śākuna I. A bird, especially a large one, from which good or bad omens may be drawn. The *Bṛhat Saṁ.* devotes eleven sections (85–95) to the subject.

v. Śakunādhiṣṭhātrī; Śakunajñāna.

II. Charms directed against pigeons, owls and other black birds whose appearance, or contact with, is thought to defile, or to forebode evil (Bloomfield, *The Atharvaveda*, p. 85).

Śakunādhiṣṭhātrī The goddess who presides over omens, usually good.

Śakunajñāna Divination by the movements of birds

(*śakuna*) and animals.

Śakuni Son of King Subala of Gāndhāra and uncle of the Kaurava princes. He was an expert at dicing and advised Duryodhana during his game with Yudhiṣṭhira, when the latter lost the whole of his possessions. v. Pāṇḍava(s).

Śakunī A demoness, the cause of particular diseases in children. She is sometimes associated with Durgā.

Śakuntalā The daughter of the *apsaras* Menakā and the *ṛṣi* Viśvāmitra, or according to the solitary reference in the *ŚBr*. (XIII.5.4,13), she was an unnamed *apsaras* who 'at Nāḍapit,[1] conceived Bharata', the founder of the first empire in Northern India. The birth of Bharata appears in the *MBh*. (Ādi pa., LXXI, *et seq.*) as the excuse for a legend, apparently designed as a genealogical link with his descendants the Kauravas and Pāṇḍavas. Its romantic element is enhanced by selecting a popular genre as its medium, that an *apsaras* or nymph who, subject to certain conditions imposed by her, agrees to become the lover or wife of some notable *ṛṣi* or famous prince.[2]

The condition imposed by Śakuntalā on King Duṣyanta before yielding to his desire was that if she bore him a son, he should be the royal heir.[3] The king agreed and in due course she bore a son who became the illustrious Bharata, Śakuntalā herself incidentally providing Kālidāsa with the title for his most famous drama. This became renowned not only throughout India but also in Europe after its discovery by Sir William Jones, its first translator. The Deva-Nāgarī recension by Monier-Williams, and his translation, completed only after the rejection of numerous Bengali versions, many of which contain spurious additions, is considered to approximate closely to the original of Kālidāsa.

[1]The hermitage of the *ṛṣi* Kaṇva, by whom she was brought up.

[2]Cf. the legend of Satyavatī (also the daughter of an *apsaras*), who became the mother of Kṛṣṇa-Dvaipāyana, whom she bore to the *ṛṣi* Parāśara. Cf. also the legend of the *apsaras* Urvaśī and Purūravas.

[3]Such a union, in those circumstances, was considered valid and was known as the *gandharva* rite, the equivalent of the European 'without benefit of the clergy'.

Śākya(s) 'Derived or descended from the Śakas', from whom the historical Buddha was descended, whence his honorific Śākyamuni, 'Sage of the Śākyas'. As the major migration of the Śakas and Parthians to India does not appear to have taken place before the fourth century B.C., the establishment of a tribe of the Śakas in north-eastern India would seem to have been one of the minor infiltrations from the Caucasus in the later part of the second millennium B.C. v. Pahlava(s).

Śālagrāma I. A village and place of pilgrimage on the Gaṇḍakī river, named after the *śāl* trees growing there, or after a particular type of pebble found in the river. II. The name of fossilized shells of an extinct species of molluscs found in the Gaṇḍakī river and also at Dvārakā, believed by many Vaiṣṇavas to possess magical properties and to be pervaded by Viṣṇu's presence, thereby showing his power to assume any shape, and hence they may be worshipped if no image of Viṣṇu is available.

The *śālagrāmas* are of various colours, nine of which represent the principal *avatāras* of Viṣṇu.[1] An ancient myth is reflected in the belief that a violet-coloured *śālagrāma*, a symbol of the god's anger, should never be kept in the house,[2] whilst those of other colours are regarded as auspicious.[3] These should be wrapped in clean material, and frequently bathed and perfumed, the water used being believed to have acquired 'sin'-dispelling qualities. It is drunk after the performance of the rite.

[1]Gonda, *Aspects*, p. 95; and v. also *VS*., p. 66.

[2]Crooke, *Things Indian*, p. 455.

[3]In addition to the *śālagrāmas*, other stones and rocks, especially meteorites, or those of volcanic origin were regarded as 'sacred because they bear the mark of some spiritual force' (Eliade, *Patterns*, p. 220 and also pp. 228f.).

Śālakaṭaṅkaṭa v. Vināyaka I.

Sālāvṛka(s) Hyenas and jackals and other scavenging animals which prey on corpses left on the battlefield. They are symbolically represented in a Vedic rite based on the myth in which Indra is said to have thrown the demons called *yatis* to the *sālāvṛkas* who ate them on the right side of the altar. Thus any water left over from sprinkling the altar, must be poured away to the right, so that whatever is cruel or evil might thereby be appeased.[1]

[1]In Epic mythology the *sālāvṛkas* appear as demonic forms during battles.

Śālivāhana v. Sātavāhana.

Śālmali I. The silk-cotton tree (Salmalia malabarica), a tall deciduous tree covered with thorns which gradually disappear with age. Practically every part of the tree has a medicinal value and is used in the practice of medicine (Āyurveda), but in *RV*., VII. 50.3, it is regarded as poisonous. Subsequently its wood was used in the making of bridal carriages (X.85,20).

II. Name of one of the mythical hells to which are consigned those who fail to observe the ordinances of sacred law (*Manu*, IV. 87 and 90). There they will be tortured by the thorns of the *śālmali* tree.

III. One of the seven continents (*dvīpas*), named after the tree (*śālmali*) growing at its centre.

Śalya The brother of Mādrī, the second wife of King Pāṇḍu. When the quarrel between the Kauravas and Pāṇḍavas culminated in war, he joined the Kauravas and became Karṇa's charioteer, and finally commanded the remnants of the Kaurava army on the last day of the battle, when he was slain by Yudhiṣṭhira.

v. Mahābhārata.

Śama 'Calm'; 'tranquil'. A state of mind personified as a son of Dharma.

v. Dakṣa.

Samādhi Concentrated thought, profound or abstract meditation, intense contemplation of any particular object, so as to identify the contemplator with the object meditated upon.

Sāman(s) Songs of praise or metrical compositions. They were chanted as part of the sacrificial ritual, most of them being drawn from verses of the *RV.*, their metre being regarded as the 'womb' from which the melody emerged. According to the *ŚBr.* (V.5.5,1–5; XII.8.3,23), after Indra's defeat of Vṛtra the power of the latter passed to the *sāmans*, enabling them to repel the indigenous dissidents who sought to prevent the performance of the sacrifice.

Not all *sāmans* were derived from *RV.* hymns. Some were of ancient non-Āryan origin, and 'were presumably popular melodies, to which in very early times semi-religious songs were sung at solstice celebrations and other national festivals ... others may date back as far as that noisy music with which pre-brahmanical wizard-priests—not unlike the magicians, shamans and medicine-men of primitive peoples—accompanied their wild songs and rites'.[1]

[1] *HIL.*, vol. I, pt. i, p. 146. Allegro considers that in ancient Judaism 'singing was primarily a sexual activity whose function was to stimulate new life' (*The Sacred Mushroom and the Cross*, p. 142). But Combarieu concludes that magical formulas were first sung, then recited, and finally written down, and the latter were sometimes worn as amulets (v. *La Musique et la magie*, Paris, 1909).

v. Chandas; Sāmaveda.

Sāmaveda The Veda of sacred songs (*sāmans*). It consists chiefly of hymns, or portions of hymns, mostly taken from the *RV.*, transposed and re-arranged to suit liturgical requirements. These *sāmans* were chanted by the *udgātṛ* priest or his assistants at the *soma* sacrifices.

Of the 1810, or 1549 verses—if repetitions are excluded—contained in the two parts of the *SV.*, all but seventy-five are to be found in the *RV.*, mostly in *maṇḍalas* VIII and IX. Most of these verses are composed in the *gāyatrī* metre or in a combination of *gāyatrī* and *jagatī*, and were from the beginning meant to be sung. This is indicated by the verb '*gā*' to sing. Thus the text is only a means to an end, the essential element being always the melody, which the *udgātṛ* had first to master before he could assume that office.[1]

The three recensions of the *SV.*, are the Kauthuma Śākhā, current in Gujarāt; the Jaiminīya in the Carnatic; and the Rāṇāyanīya in the Mahratta country.[2]

[1] *HIL.*, vol. I, pt. i, p. 143.

[2] Griffith, *SV.*, Intro., p. iv. The instructions for intoning the *SV.* hymns 'show that the style of liturgical singing in Vedic times was rather like that of medieval plain chant' (Basham, *WI.*, p. 382). The *SV.* chants consisted of 'three to four musical intervals, the earliest example of the Indian tetrachord, which eventually developed into a full musical scale' (Singhal, *India*, vol. I, p. 221).

Śamba A synonym of *vajra*, the thunderbolt of Indra. The *Nir.* (5.24) derives it from the root *śam* (to kill), or from the causal of *śad* (to knock off).

Sāmba (Also written Śāmba.) Son of Kṛṣṇa, the Yādava prince, and Jāmbavatī. According to the *VP.* (V.35), when the daughter of Duryodhana (the Kaurava prince) was holding her *svayaṁbara* for the purpose of choosing a husband, Sāmba succeeded in abducting her.

The story of Sāmba indicates the rivalry that existed among the kingdoms of northern India following the collapse of the Bhārata empire. Quarrels between tribes related by blood were frequent, and into which neighbouring tribes were drawn by intrigues or by motives of self-interest. Sāmba's abduction of Duryodhana's daughter was a case of 'like father, like son', his father Kṛṣṇa having abducted Rukmiṇī in similar circumstances.

v. Kaṁsa.

Śāmbāditya The name of a sun-image at Mathurā, said to have been installed by Śāmba (Kṛṣṇa's son) as an expression of his gratitude to the Sun-god by whom he was cured of leprosy. The sun-cult appears to have developed in North India in the early centuries of the present era, and generally followed the pattern of the eastern Iranian mode of sun-worship.[1]

[1] *DHI.*, pp. 430f. Śāmba may have instituted some new form of sun-cult (A.M. Shastri, *India as Seen in the Bṛhatsaṁhitā*, p. 148).

v. Saura(s); Āditya(s); Sūrya; Savitṛ.

Śambara The name of a 'demon', probably leader of an Indian tribe which resisted the advance of the Āryans in north-western India by diverting and blocking streams, thus flooding whole areas, and then retreating to fortified positions. They are generally referred to in the *RV.* (I.59,6, etc.) as drought-demons whose forts Indra was constantly besought to destroy.

Paurāṇic legend also portrays Śambara as a demon, and elaborates these brief *RV.* references in an account of his abduction of the infant Pradyumna (son of Kṛṣṇa and Rukmiṇī). Śambara threw the child into the sea, where it was swallowed by a fish which was caught and sold to Śambara's wife Māyādevī, who found that it contained the infant abducted by her husband.

Śambhu 'Causing or granting happiness.'[1] A form of Śiva indicating his beneficent aspect when presiding over the re-integration of new life. Śambhu is also worshipped in Buddhist and Jaina Tantric disciplines.[2]

[1]It is applied as an epithet to Agni; to one of the eleven Rudras, and to Brahmā, etc.

[2]*TT.*, p. 135.

Saṁhārāmūrti(s) The destructive forms of Śiva.

v. Anugrahamūrti(s).

Saṁhitā A collection of methodically arranged compositions of a similar character, like those of the *RV.*, *SV.*, and *AV.*, etc.

Śamī A hard-wood tree (Prosopis spicigera or perhaps Acacia suma), believed to contain fire, and hence used to kindle the altar fire. In the ritual of laying it a stick of *śamī* is added 'for atonement' (*Tait Saṁ.*, V.1,9), and for its soothing qualities (V.4,7). But in the *AV.* (VI.30) it is said to intoxicate and to cause baldness (or it may have been used as a remedy for baldness).

Agni is closely associated with the *śamī*,[1] which was personified as the goddess Śamīdevī. The *śamī* was believed to bring peace to the dead, and like the bamboo was also planted to define a particular boundary (*Manu*, VIII.247).

[1]Agni is said to have hidden in the *śamī* wood after Bhṛgu had cursed him (*ŚBr.*, IX.2.3,37).

v. Araṇī.

Śamīdevī v. Śamī.

Saṁjīvīnī-vidyā 'The science of re-vivification.' A power attributed to Śukra, the Bhārgava priest (*MBh.*, Ādi pa., LXXVI).

v. Kaca.

Saṁjñā Also called Tvaṣṭrī. Daughter of Viśvakarman (Tvaṣṭṛ) (the divine master-craftsman), and wife of the sun-god, Sūrya, to whom she bore three children, Manu (Vaivasvata), Yama, and a daughter, Yamī. Being unable to endure Sūrya's dazzling light, Saṁjñā decided to leave him and seek the shade of the forest, but before doing so she left him a substitute called Chāyā 'Shade', who was in every respect an image of herself. Sūrya begot by Chāyā three other children, Śanaiścara, another Manu (Sāvarṇi) and a daughter Tapatī (deified as the goddess of the river Taptī). All continued to go smoothly until Chāyā had occasion to rebuke Yama, and in the ensuing quarrel Sūrya learned the truth about Saṁjñā. Being 'all-seeing', Sūrya easily found her forest abode, where she had assumed the form of a mare.[1] Changing himself into a stallion, Sūrya rejoined her. She bore him three more children, the twin Aśvins and Revanta. He then returned with Saṁjña to the celestial sphere.

To ensure that Saṁjñā should never again have cause to leave her husband, Viśvakarman placed the sun on his lathe and reduced it by seven-eighths.[2] During the process the particles (the rays of the sun) that were being ground off fell blazing to earth and were used by Viśvakarman to make the discus of Viṣṇu, the trident of Śiva, the lance of Kārttikeya and enough weapons to arm all the other gods.[3] Other trimmings from the sun are said to have been used to build the great sun-temple at Konarak, built in the form of the horse-drawn chariot of the sun. Covered with erotic friezes, this temple illustrates the popular association of sexual fire and the virility of the horses of the sun. Śiva, like the sun, is also said 'to have difficulty in finding a wife capable of bearing his *tejas*' (fiery power).[4]

[1]v. O'Flaherty, 'The Submarine Mare', *JRAS.*, 1971, no. 1, p. 16.

[2]The *Matsya P.* says he trimmed the whole of the sun except his feet which were not visible; consequently Sūrya's feet should never be depicted; to delineate them renders the artist liable to leprosy and other diseases.

[3]The above is the version in *VP.* (III.2), variants of which appear in the *Matsya*, *Mārkaṇḍeya* and other Purs.

[4]O'Flaherty, op. cit., p. 17.

v. Saraṇyū.

Saṁkarṣaṇa One of the names of Balarāma which originated when his embryo was transferred from Devakī's womb to that of Rohiṇī (*VP.*, IV.5). But Gonda considers that he was so-called because he draws together and unites (*saṁkarṣayati*) repeatedly in every period of the world.[1] Saṁkarṣaṇa is associated with agriculture, the plough (*hala*),[2] being his emblem.

The *Vāyu P.* refers to Saṁkarṣaṇa as one of the five Vṛṣṇi heroes (*vīras*), whose names appear in an inscription of the first century A.D. at Mora near Mathurā.[3] But his independent worship had spread over a wide area prior to the Mora inscription. In an inscription at Ghosundi he is called Bhagavat and Sarveśvara jointly with Vāsudeva and, according to the *MBh.*, was worshipped by the Kaurava prince Duryodhana.

[1]*VS.*, p. 167, n. 263.

[2]Other emblems are the *muṣala* (pestle to pound corn) and drinking vessel (*pānapātra*) (*DHI.*, p. 306, and v. pp. 386ff.).

[3]*HCIP.*, II, p. 447.

v. Kṛṣṇa I.

Sāṁkhya or **Sāṅkhya** One of the six Hindu 'orthodox' philosophies (*darśanas*). It is a philosophy of dualistic realism and is attributed to the sage Kapila.

The Sāṁkhya was originally atheistic and known as Nirīśvara-sāṁkhya, but was subsequently merged with the theistic Yoga system. It has been variously defined as 'enumeration', 'investigation', or 'analysis', viz., 'of the categories of the phenomenal world'. But as one of the principal aims of the Sāṁkhya is to distinguish the two fundamental constituents of existence—spirit (*puruṣa*) and matter or substance (*prakṛti*)—Eliade suggests the definition, 'discrimination or discernment',[1] whilst Edgerton proposes 'reasoning' or 'ratiocination'.[2] Monier-Williams[3] considers that the Sāṁkhya, instead of being 'an analytical inquiry into the universe as actually existing, arranged under topics and categories', is a synthetical system, based on the notion of an eternally existing essence (*prakṛti*) from which everything else (except 'soul') originated.

The two ultimate realities recognized by the Sāṁkhya are the *puruṣa* (the intelligent principle, whose essence is consciousness) and *prakṛti*, the ultimate cause of the world. *Prakṛti* is an eternal unconscious principle (*jaḍa*) which is always changing. It is composed of three constituents, *sattva*, *rajas* and *tamas* (collectively called *guṇas*). When in a state of equilibrium there can be no manifestation of any kind. The evolution of the world starts when *puruṣa* and *prakṛti* are associated (*saṁyoga*). This disturbs *prakṛti*'s original equilibrium which is a state a non-manifestation.

The *guṇas* are inseparable—one alone cannot produce anything, but the predominance of one of the three determines the dominant characteristic or quality of each individual or thing. The *guṇa sattva* is the subtle principle which determines the qualities of light, knowledge, intellect and the emotions. *Rajas* is the principle of activity, without which *sattva* and *tamas* cannot function effectively. *Rajas* lacks the subtlety of *sattva*, its activities being likened to a fierce forest fire or to a tempestuous wind. When *rajas* predominates emotional unbalance, pain, etc. occurs. *Tamas* is the principle of passivity or negativity.

The Sāṁkhya contends that every 'effect' or 'efficient cause' is inherent in a primary cause, just as every aspect of the phenomenal world is inherent in its causal matrix *prakṛti*, a view that confirms the tradition that the Sāṁkhya was initially, at least, a non-theistic system. The individual real self (later equated with *ātman*) was considered to be completely separated from the body, the ego, the mind, and the senses. Although the real self is immortal and free, it fails to realise its freedom because of the influence of ignorance (*avidyā*), which causes the self to regard the body, senses and mind (*manas*) as the real self. This lack of discrimination (*aviveka*) between the self and the non-self is the cause of all sorrow and suffering. But once discrimination occurs freedom is attained. The events of the world and the individual's changing fortunes, etc. are seen but the real self remains unaffected and unimplicated in them. This supreme state may be attained during life (*jīvanmukti*) or in another life (*videhamukti*). But this freedom cannot be reached by mere intellectual understanding, unless accompanied by a long course of spiritual training[4] and constant meditation on the true self which is pure eternal consciousness, beyond the mind-body complex and the pressures of the world.

Kapila's doctrine was successively transmitted by his followers until it reached Pañcaśikha, and by him was imparted to Īśvarakṛṣṇa, the compiler of the *Sāṁkhya-kārikā* (c. 200–450),[5] the text-book of the Sāṁkhya *darśana*.

[1]*Yoga*, p. 8.

[2]*BIP.*, p. 36, n.1.

[3]*IW.*, p. 90.

[4]This training is elaborated in the Yoga philosophy.

[5]The extant version cannot be dated before A.D. 1400.

Sāṁkhya Yoga v. Sāṁkhya; Yoga; Darśana(s).

Saṁsāra The 'bondage of life, death and rebirth'. A reference to *saṁsāra* appears first in the *Bṛhad-Ār. Up.* (6.2,16), but is more clearly stated in the *Kaṭha Up.* (3,7). It is the cycle of birth and rebirth or metempsychosis,[1] which is dictated by the inexorable law of *karman*, to which every individual is subject. It declared that 'as a man sows, so shall he continue to reap', until by the attainment of true knowledge he shall be released from the bondage of *saṁsāra*. Uncontrolled enjoyment of desires leads to rebirth on earth. Hence only by the control of thoughts and desires can rebirth be avoided (*Maitri Up.*, 1.4; 6, 34). But the Indian doctrine of transmigration 'implies the integration of animals into the same "cycle" as man ... [This] gives them a relatively privileged position, the degree of privilege depending on the place assigned to them, on the basis of their specific characteristics, in the animal hierarchy'.[2]

The rigid doctrine of *karman* and *saṁsāra*, though basically ethical, nonetheless embodies an inflexible notion of reward and punishment[3] from which there was no escape except by the practice of an austere discipline beyond the capacity of most. A reaction to this situation is indicated by the appearance of several schools of speculative thought, led by Kapila (founder of the Sāṁkhya), Parśva and Mahāvīra (Jainism) and

Śākyamuni (Buddhism). This reaction also included the introduction of the doctrine of *śraddhā* (faith) and *bhakti* (devotion), notions that appealed to ordinary folk.

[1]Belief in the transmigration of 'souls' appears in the Orphic texts inscribed on 'gold leaves which in the third century B.C. were laid in the graves of the dead in Southern Italy as a passport for their journey to the other world' (Nilsson, *A History of Greek Religion*, p. 221). The round of rebirths ended when the righteous, having been tested sufficiently, passed into eternal bliss. Zimmer (*Philosophies of India*, p. 184n.) considers that *saṁsāra* was derived from the Indus Valley or non-Āryan strata of religious thought. If transmigration is possible it implies that all life is akin. Pythagoras taught that the apparent distinctions between human and non-human beings are not ultimate.

[2]Auboyer in *Animals in Archaeology* (ed. by Brodrick), p. 116.

[3]Thus for the transmigrating 'individual', 'the hereafter is only another here', and such reincarnation is either progressive or retrogressive according to inherent tendencies (v. Heimann, *IWP*., pp. 60f.). The prefix *sam* indicates 'the wide range of possibilities which lie side by side in this series of rebirths' (Heimann, *PSPT*., p. 14).

Saṁskṛta v. Sanskrit.

Samudramathana or **Samudramanthana** 'Churning of the Ocean.' This is a 'secondary' creation myth which regarded all things as existing *in potentia* in the primordial ocean. Only by superhuman efforts could the ocean be churned and made to give up its treasures and benefits to man. The myth appears in the *MBh*. (Ādi pa., XVII–XIX), and in some Purs.; is briefly alluded to in others, and ignored in the remainder. The *VP*. (I.9) records that only by the aid of Viṣṇu, the 'lord of all' could the enterprise successfully be concluded and the defeat of the gods (*devas*) by the demonic *dānavas* be turned to victory. To achieve it the gods appealed to Viṣṇu who advised them to make peace with the *dānavas* and to enlist their co-operation in the Churning of the Ocean. In return for their help they were to receive a share of the sacred ambrosia (*amṛta*) which would emerge from the ocean and make them also immortal. But Viṣṇu informed the gods that he would not allow the *amṛta* to fall into the hands of the *dānavas*, and that they should only share the labour!

The gods chose Mount Mandara as a churning rod, around which they coiled the serpent Vāsuki[1] to enable them to turn it.[2] The gods held the tail, the *dānavas* the head, each group alternately pulling in opposite directions, whilst Viṣṇu, in the form of a tortoise, served as a base for the churning rod. From the churned ocean various objects began to emerge,[3] the first being Surabhi, the cow of abundance, followed by Vāruṇī, the goddess of wine, then the celestial *pārijāta* tree, a group of heavenly nymphs (*apsarasas*), and the cool-rayed moon. At this juncture poison began to appear, but this was swallowed by the snake-gods (Nāgas).[4] Then Dhanvantari, the physician of the gods, appeared holding a vessel of *amṛta*, the longed-for treasure. Then followed the goddess Śrī, seated on a lotus and holding a lotus flower. The *dānavas* apparently doubted the probity of the gods and seized the *amṛta*, but before they could drink it Viṣṇu, assuming the form of a beautiful girl called Mohiṇī, held them spellbound. Before they could recover, Viṣṇu seized the *amṛta* and gave it to the gods. Immediately they were infused with new vigour and fell upon the incensed *dānavas* and utterly defeated them.

[1]Vāsuki represents the non-evolved form of nature (*prakṛti*).

[2]Rotation implies expansion from a stable centre in all directions. It 'conveys a dynamic image of Cosmic Life, which is concentrated as potentiality in the immovable centre of the Supreme Being, and from there goes forth as manifested existence' (*CHS*., p. 172; v. also Heesterman, *Ancient Indian Royal Consecration*, p. 151, n. 51. According to the Homeric theory 'the Ocean was the origin of all things' (Farnell, *Cults*, vol. I, p. 265, n. b.).

[3]Their number and order of appearance vary. The popular enumeration is fourteen, but the *Rām*., *MBh*. and the *Padma Pur*. specify nine, others ten or twelve. Other objects, not mentioned in the *VP*. account, are the elephant Airāvata, and the white horse (which is said to be water-born (*Tait. Saṁ*., II.3.12,2), and which in at least one account is identified with Uccaiḥśravas. Another variant (*VP*., I. 9, n.8) attributes the seizure of the *amṛta* to Rāhu, the eclipse demon, and omits the references to the *dānavas* and *daityas*.

[4]The *MBh*. version states that Śiva swallowed the poison to prevent it from spreading amongst mankind, thus accounting for the discoloration of his throat by its scorching effect. But the *Hariv*. version (referred to in the *VP*. (I.9, n.8)) states that the discoloration of Śiva's throat was the result of his having been almost strangled by Viṣṇu when he (Śiva) tried to disrupt Dakṣa's sacrifice.

Śanaiścara An epithet of the deified planet Saturn, son of Sūrya and Chāyā (*VP*., III.2).

v. Saṁjñā; Śani.

Sanātana 'Eternal; primeval.' One of the mind-born sons of Brahmā.

Sanat-kumāra 'Eternal youth.' One of the mind-born

sons of Brahmā who chose to remain celibate and thus retain forever the unsullied innocence of youth.[1] He is said to have instructed the *ṛṣi* Nārada in the 'science' of *brahmavidyā*.

[1]Sanat-kumāra is an epithet often applied to any great ascetic. The *Chān. Up.* (VII.26,2) calls him Skanda, which may explain why Skanda, the god of war, became the 'instructor god' in southern India. v. also *EM.*, p. 191.

Śaṇḍa v. Marka I.

Sandhyā 'Juncture', i.e., twilight or the interval between sunset and darkness, or that between night and sunrise, personified as a daughter of Brahmā and wife of Śiva.[1] The term occurs frequently in astrological interpretations of omens and portents. Thus the effects of twilight, good and bad, were ascertained from the movements of wild animals and birds; of the wind, or of a halo round the sun and the moon, or of tree-shaped clouds, etc. (*Bṛhat Saṁ.*, XXX, 1–2). Thus the prolonged howling of a wild animal was considered to indicate the destruction of a village; wild beasts facing the sun or wind on the left of an army was a portent of war; various atmospheric changes meant the death of a monarch or one of his ministers (XXX,19).

[1]The *VP.* (I.5) states that she is an 'abandoned body' (or form) of Brahmā.

v. Mṛgaśiras.

Śani The name of the inauspicious planet Saturn and of its Regent, whose vehicle (*vāhana*) is a crow, an especially inauspicious bird.

v. Navagraha(s); Śanicakra; Śanaiścara.

Śanicakra 'Saturn's diagram', consisting of a circle (*cakra*),[1] used for fortune-telling. It comprises twenty-seven lunar divisions, representing the twenty-seven *nakṣatras*, through which the planet Saturn (Śani) passes in its orbit round the sun.

[1]This circle or ring has no connexion with the so-called ring of miniature moons which rotate round the planet, which were not known until 1659 when Huygens, by means of a new telescope, discovered them.

Śaṅkara or **Śaṁkara** 'Auspicious.' An epithet of Śiva.

Śaṅkarācārya A Tamil Śaiva and one of the most notable of Indian religious teachers (*ācārya*), whose commentary (*bhaṣya*) on Bādarāyaṇa's *Brahma-sūtra* is one of the principal expositions of Vedānta doctrine. This commentary, entitled *Naiṣkarmya-siddhi* was written under the pseudonym Sureśvara, the name Śaṅkara assumed on his conversion in A.D. 800 to the doctrine of monism (Advaita Vedānta).

The views expressed in his commentary and in his lectures and debates are proof of his independent character and intellectual qualities, as his decision to remain a *naiṣṭhika-brahmacārin* (vowed to celibacy), points to his single-mindedness and strength of will. But these virtues sometimes detracted from his ability to understand fully the views of the several Buddhist schools,[1] and to appreciate the significance of the technical terms used by them. These terms, though superficially identical with those used by the Vedāntins, often had an application peculiar to Buddhist philosophy. Some Indian philosophers, whether Hindu, Buddhist or Jaina, often allowed mystical speculation to prejudice philosophical judgment.[2] Śaṅkara was no exception, though paradoxically, so close were some of his conclusions to those of his opponents, the Buddhist Mādhyamikas, that he was sometimes accused of being 'a Buddhist in disguise'.

Despite his fame,[3] little is known of his personal life, except that it was brief, lasting only from A.D. 788 to 820, and that his teacher was Govinda, the disciple of Gauḍapāḍa, author of the *Māṇḍūkya-kārikā*, a commentary on the Upaniṣad of that name. But he found time to establish four colleges (*maṭhas*) for students at Dvārakā in the West, Pūri in the East, Badri in the North, and Śṛṅgeri in the South.[4]

[1]Rāmānuja, and subsequently Madhva, called Śaṅkara a 'crypto-Buddhist' because they saw no difference between his interpretation of *brahman* and the *śūnya* doctrine of the Buddhists.

[2]This is illustrated by Śaṅkara's derivation of the word *upaniṣad* from the root '*sad*', which he insisted was 'so-called because it destroys inborn ignorance and leads to salvation by revealing the right knowledge' (Dasgupta, *History of Indian Philosophy*, I, p. 38). This is contrary to the meaning given in the Upaniṣads themselves and accepted by scholars generally.

[3]Which was such as to link his name with Śiva's synonym 'Śaṅkara', meaning 'auspicious', and thus to his being regarded as an incarnation of Śiva.

[4]Radhakrishnan, *The Brahma Sūtra*, p. 28.

v. Ātman; Buddhism.

Śaṅkha I. The general name for sea-shells, particularly of the conch-shell variety, which were from earliest times used as ornaments or amulets (*AV.*, IV.10,1ff.), and later as libation vessels at the sacrifice. When the point of the conch-shell was cut off, the main body of the shell was used as a horn or trumpet in war, and in Tibet was blown to avert hail-storms. Its very sound was considered auspicious, and capable of averting the Evil Eye and destroying demons.[1] In the *Vārāha P.* it is even said to destroy ignorance (*avidyā*).[2] Because conch-shells resemble the vulva they are also associated with fertility.[3]

In the *Pañcāyatana* ceremony the conch-shell is

invoked in a special formula. It is an emblem of Viṣṇu and sometimes of Śiva.[4] When sounded it awakes the divinity in the temple and drives away demons from the offerings.[5] Although the most usual belief is that the *śaṅkha* emerged from the ocean, its origin is also attributed to Vṛtra in whom all things were initially contained (*ŚBr.*, V.5.5,1); or it was derived from Soma; or from the lightning; or from the bones of the gods (*AV.*, IV.10,7).

[1]v. 'The Indian chank in Folklore and Religion' (*Folklore*, 53, 1942, pp. 113ff.). For the adoration of the *śaṅkha*, v. Gonda, *VS.*, pp. 82f.

[2]*EHI.*, vol. I, pt. i, p. 295.

[3]Their size and colour, etc. varied. Viṣṇu's conch (*pāñcajanya*) is small, slender, black and melodious; Arjuna's, medium-sized, slender, white, high-pitched and called Devadatta; Bhīma's, large, brown, low-pitched and called *pauṇḍra*.

[4]*BH.*, pp. 414 and 93.

[5]Similarly in ancient Crete the triton-shell was sounded to summon the divinity to her shrine. The shells are frequently found in the Megalithic sepulchres of Italy and Sicily and are of great importance in Pacific island ritual. Their use in ritual 'is one more link with the religious customs of the Stone Age' (Levy, *Gate of Horn*, p. 233).

v. Śaṅkhapuruṣa; Āyudhapuruṣa; Śrīphala; Pāñcajana.

II. The name of the demon who stole the Vedas and hid them at the bottom of the sea, whence they were recovered by Viṣṇu in his fish form (*matsya avatāra*).

III. The name of one of Kubera's treasures (*nidhi*), or of its guardian (*Mārk. P.*, 68,42f.).

Śaṅkhapuruṣa The conch-shell (*śaṅkha*) personified.
v. Āyudhapuruṣa.

Sāṅkhya v. Sāṁkhya.

Ṣaṇmukha 'Six-faced.' An epithet of Skanda.
v. Kṛttikā(s).

Sannyāsin One who has relinquished all worldly attachments and values and has chosen a life of religious contemplation or asceticism. It was customary, when economically practicable, for the head of a family 'when he had seen his eldest son's son' to spend his closing years as a recluse. The term was later applied generally to religious mendicants, and particularly to Śaiva itinerant devotees.

A *sannyāsin* is assumed to have attained a state of holiness and thus become immortal, his death being regarded simply as a trance-state (*samādhi*). He is not cremated but buried in a seated, cross-legged posture, as though engaged in meditation. Salt is spread round the body to preserve it, and an earthen pot placed over the skull. The latter is sometimes cracked to provide an exit for the spirit. Flour and pulse, the dead man's gourd and staff, etc., are also buried with him.
v. Brahmarandhra.

Sanskrit (Saṁskṛta). The classical language of India. The name signifies 'perfectly constructed, cultivated, literary speech', in contrast to the common dialects or *prākrits*, such as that of the Aśoka Inscriptions or the *ardha-māgadhi* of the Jains. Sanskrit is the elaborated form of the language of the *RV.*, the earliest Indian 'literary' composition. This Vedic prototype was in the main the language of the Āryans, who are generally believed to have migrated from the Caucasus to Iran, India and Europe about 2000–1700 B.C. From a prototype evolved the principal languages of northern India[1] and those comprising the Āryo-European group.

As its name indicates, Sanskrit is a highly sophisticated language, consisting of 180,000 words or compounds, some of them drawn from Dravidian and other indigenous languages, and others from the languages of the Middle East and the Mediterranean.[2] But Sanskrit, either as a spoken or written language, did not immediately supersede the oral transmission of sacred compositions, possibly because the earliest written form of Sanskrit may have failed to ensure the correct accentuation of a particular syllable or the value of a particular vowel, though this possibility was subsequently remedied.[3] Nonetheless, it became apparent that any fundamental changes in Vedic grammatical constructions would have been impracticable without the aid of writing. The main reason for this perhaps was that Sanskrit is richly endowed with vowels which are often dependent on accent for their meaning, as in the word *kṣáya*, meaning 'abode', whereas *kṣayá*, with the stress on the final syllable, means 'destruction'.[4] Hence the Mīmāṁsā insistence on the correct utterance of the sacred sounds of the Veda and the clinging to the oral tradition, long after the introduction of writing.[5]

It is not certain when an 'alphabetic' arrangement was adopted in India, but **Brāhmī**,[6] the traditional prototype of all Indo-Āryan scripts, may have been introduced in the eighth or seventh century B.C.[7] Some of its signs resemble those of proto-Semitic scripts, particularly the Phoenician which, if not the source of the Brāhmī, appears to have influenced it. Like its Semitic prototype, a script known as Kharoṣṭhī was introduced into north-western India in the fifth or fourth century B.C. It was written in boustrophedon style, i.e., alternately from right to left, and left to right, a characteristic of some rock Inscriptions of Aśoka on the north-western frontier of India.[8]

The Brāhmī script of the Aśoka Edicts, though imperfect, was an improvement on that of the previous century, a few examples of which have recently been found. The signs are crudely formed and grammatically inferior, lacking both long vowels and consonantal combinations. It is evident that before the Brāhmī script could match the refined language (Sanskrit) and express all its grammatical nuances, further improvements would have to be made. Gradually these were introduced, and from the Gupta period a new script was developed called Nāgarī.[9] The earliest documents written entirely in Nāgarī belong to the middle of the eighth century. Though still artistically imperfect, Nāgarī was gradually developed and by the eleventh century became the principal script of northern India, and with variants, was used exclusively for Sanskrit in western and eastern India.[10] In its final form it consisted of forty-eight signs, including fourteen vowels and diphthongs, and thirty-four basic consonants.

But the position of Sanskrit suffered, and its use by learned Hindus and Buddhists was constantly interrupted from the seventh century by persecution, forcible conversion to Islam, and the destruction of centres of learning by successive Islamic invasions. A brief renascence of Indian culture ensued under several rulers of the Mughal dynasty before it fell into decline. As a result of the subsequent Civil Wars, learning suffered a further setback, so that by the early nineteenth century when the Aśoka rock and pillar Inscriptions—long since covered by jungle—were discovered, no Indian scholar was capable of deciphering them. This was accomplished only by the painstaking work of the late James Prinsep, the Secretary of the Asiatic Society of Bengal.

Today the position of Sanskrit is reversed, and though not widely used, is by no means a dead language, but is studied and taught in India and other universities throughout the world.

[1]Including Hindī, Marathī, Gujarātī, Bengalī, Oriya, etc.

[2]Cretan (Linear B) Greek, possibly the oldest Indo-European language of Europe, like the language of the Veda, had its origin elsewhere. Both developed an elaborate syntax and grammar, and as the result of fusion with local ethnic groups—the Āryas with the Dravidians, etc., the Greeks with the Minoans—both languages acquired a large non-Indo-European vocabulary. 'In both cases the language of the conqueror prevailed' (Hall, *Bronze Age Greece*, p. 288). For non-Āryan influence on Sanskrit, v. T. Burrow, *The Sanskrit Language*, Ch. VIII.

[3]According to Pāṇini, this is indicated by adding a final letter to affixes and suffixes, such as the letter 'c', as in *ghura(c)* to show that its derivative *bhaṅgura* should be accented on the last syllable, i.e., *bhaṅgurá*.

[4]Cf. English 'deserts' (expanses of barren land), and 'desérts' (that which is deserved).

[5]There is no exact equivalent in Sanskrit to the Western word for 'literature'. Written works or classes of works are collectively called *vidyā* (from *vid* 'to know'), or *śruti* (from *śru* 'to hear'), *śāstra* (from *śās* 'to teach'), and *smṛti* (from *smṛ* 'to remember'), *tantra*, 'work', etc. Thus the Epics and Purāṇas, which comprise much that the West would regard as literary productions, are classed in India as ancient tales retold, and therefore as *smṛti*, 'remembered' or 'handed down'.

[6]So-called because its creation was attributed to Brahmā.

[7]v. David Diringer, *The Alphabet*, 2 vols, 1968, vol. I, p. 263.

[8]Ibid, p. 266.

[9]Or *Deva-nāgarī*, 'the writing of the gods'.

[10]The South Indian form is generally called *Nandi-nāgarī*.

Śānta 'Calm', 'tranquil'. An auspicious omen, the opposite of an ill-omen (*dīpta*). Inauspicious portents may sometimes be averted by propitiation and become temporarily *śānta*.

Santāna One of the six aspects of Gaṇeśa worshipped by the Gāṇapatyas. These aspects, Mahā, Haridrā, Svarṇa, Navanīta and Unmatta-Ucchiṣṭa, as well as Santāna, gave rise to six Gaṇeśa cults.

Śāntanu The third and youngest son of Pratīpa, a famous ruler of the Kuru-Pañcāla kingdom which he re-established after its decline during the reigns of the successors of Kuru, its founder. Traditional history relates that Pratīpa was succeeded by Śāntanu whose eldest son Bhīṣma (originally called Devavrata) renounced his right to the throne to enable his father to marry the fisher-girl Satyavatī,[1] who had demanded as a condition of her marriage to Śāntanu that her son, and not Bhīṣma, should be heir to the throne. But the story of Śāntanu in the *MBh.* (Ādi pa., 98–101) has little in common with the historical account. The former states that Śāntanu married the river goddess Gaṅgā, who had assumed human form. Like Satyavatī she also stipulated certain conditions before consenting to the marriage. Their eighth child, the only one to survive, was called Gaṅgādatta and subsequently Bhīṣma.

[1]A similar story is told of Parāśara and the fisher-girl of the same name.

v. Pāṇḍava(s); Kaurava(s).

Śānti I. 'Tranquillity'; 'absence of passion', personified as a daughter of Śraddhā (faith).

II. An expiatory or propitiatory rite for preventing disease, averting the effect of curses, adverse stellar influences, or the karmic results of bad actions in a previous existence. *Śānti* rites are also performed at the *Nīrājana*, *Puṣyasnāna* and *Indramaha* ceremonies to counteract procedural errors (*Bṛhat Saṁ.*, XLII.61). The magical rites used by a priest if he wishes to injure the sacrificer are given in the *Ait. Br.* (III.3).

Saptajihva 'Seven-tongued.' An epithet of Agni, whose seven tongues of fire are called Kālī, Karālī, Mano-javā, Su-lohitā, Su-dhūmra-varṇā, Ugrā or Sphuliṅginī, and Pradīptā. These names vary according to the particular rite in which fire is used.

Saptamātṛkā(s) The 'Seven Mothers.' A mother-goddess cult which existed in pre-Vedic India, as is indicated by an Indus Valley seal depicting a nude goddess standing between the parted branches of an *aśvattha* tree (Ficus religiosa), below which stand seven female attendants.[1] Though celestial 'dames' are occasionally alluded to in the *RV.*, and the Seven Mothers specifically in (I,34,8), they are unnamed, and remained so until post-Vedic times. 'The usually accepted list supported by iconographic data consists of Brahmāṇī, Maheśvarī, Kaumārī, Vaiṣṇavī, Vārāhī, Indrāṇī and Cāmuṇḍī [or Cāmuṇḍā], though there are some variants'.[2] They are often depicted in that order together with Vīrabhadra and Gaṇeśa, who act as guardians, a role occasionally assigned to Skanda. The arrangement of the 'Mothers' varies according to the end desired. If for the destruction of enemies, Brahmāṇī must be in the centre; but to increase the population of a village Cāmuṇḍā must occupy the central position. Demons were said to guard the entrances to the shrines of the 'Mothers'.

[1]J. Campbell, *Masks of God*, II, p. 167. The number seven has long been sacred in India and is used to express indefinite plurality; hence the seven divisions of the world; seven cities; seven rivers, etc.

[2]*DHI.*, p. 505. Nārasiṁhī is sometimes substituted for Cāmuṇḍī.

v. Mātṛ(s).

Saptarṣi(s) The 'Seven Seers' (*RV.*, X. 130, 7), whom post-Vedic commentators identify as the seven great *ṛṣis* individually mentioned in various passages of the *RV.* According to the northern tradition, they comprise: Atri, Vasiṣṭha, Kaśyapa, Viśvāmitra, Gotama, Jamadagni and Bharadvāja.[1] In some traditions the list varies only slightly, in others considerably.

Subsequently other names were added as stellar mythology expanded, and astrology and cosmogonic theory developed. The *saptarṣi* tradition also became associated with the notion of descent (*jāti*), not from a single ancestor, but from the tribal group or clan (*gotra*), each represented by one of the original 'Seven seers'. This notion, though only faintly discernible in the Veda, is clearly enunciated in post-Vedic theory, in which the *brahmarṣis*, or mind-born sons of Brahmā, are declared to be the progenitors of the human race.

[1]*EM.*, p. 177.

v. Varṇa; Pravara; Ṛṣi(s).

Saptavadhri An ancient *ṛṣi* mentioned several times in the *RV.* In one passage he is said to have trapped his hand in a tree but was finally released by the Aśvins (V.78,5–6).

Śara 'Arrow.' From *śri* 'to rend or destroy'. *Śara* denotes both an arrow and the particular reed used to make it.

v. Bāṇa I.

Śarabha or **Śarabheṣamūrti** A form (part man, beast and bird), assumed by Śiva to punish Narasiṁha (the man-lion *avatāra* of Viṣṇu), for having killed the Śaiva Hiraṇyakaśipu. The legend reflects the sectarian animosity between the cults of Viṣṇu and Śiva, revealed in the 'concoction of mythological stories and construction of interesting images'.[1] This was a characteristic mode of giving vent to sectarian ill-feeling.

Śarabha is sometimes described as eight-legged,[2] two-handed, with one, two or three horns, long claws, a lion's face, two wings, arrow-like spikes for hair, and a body glowing like fire.

[1]*DHI.*, p. 5; v. also Gonda, *VS.*, pp. 106f.

[2]Cf. Odin's eight-legged horse Sleipnir; also the eight-legged headless horses of Germanic and Japanese mythology, all of which, like Śarabha, are connected with ecstasy and death (Eliade, *Shamanism*, p. 469; Ellis Davidson, *Gods and Myths of Northern Europe*, pp. 142f.).

v. Prahlāda.

Śāradā v. Sarasvatī.

Śaradvat v. Gautama I.

Saramā 'Swift one',[1] the name of the bitch, who acted as Indra's messenger (*AV.*, IV.20,7) or watch-dog. She was the mother of Yama's two 'four-eyed'[2] dogs who guard the road followed by the dead (*AV.*, XVIII.2, 11). She is regarded as the mother of all canines.

When the Paṇis hid some stolen cattle in an almost inaccessible mountain spot, Saramā tracked them to it. The Paṇis begged her to remain with them but she refused (*RV.*, X.108; I.72,8; III.31,6).

[1]The *Nir.* (11,24) derives the name from the root *sṛ* 'to move'.

[2]The four eyes may indicate that the dogs can look in all directions, and are ever alert and vigilant, or it may 'express the idea of an abnormality which, as such, is a source of evil' (Gonda, *Eye and Gaze*, p. 71, n. 15).

v. Sārameya(s); Aśvamedha.

Sārameya(s) The metronymic of the two offspring of

Saramā, probably sired by the mythical dog Sīsara.[1] They are described as 'four-eyed', brindled (or copper-coloured), and broad-nosed, who wait on the road which the dead must take to reach Yama's realm (*AV.*, XVIII.2, 11–13). To pass them safely, it was necessary to place the two kidneys of the sacrificed funerary animal in the hands of the deceased.[2]

[1]Cf. Sīsarama, a dog-demon.

[2]Cf. the Greek Kerberos.

v. Śabala, n.1.

Saraṇyū A daughter of Tvaṣṭṛ. Her twin brother was Triśiras. Her father gave her in marriage to Vivasvat after which she disappeared from the sight of mortal man (*RV.*, X.17, 1–2). According to the *Bṛhadd.* (VI. 162–3; VII.1–6) she bore the twins Yama and Yamī to Vivasvat. Then she created a female similar to herself and left the twins in her care. By her Vivasvat, unaware of the substitution, begot Manu. On learning that Saraṇyū had assumed the form of a mare, he assumed the form of a stallion, but in his excitement on finding her his semen was spilt on the ground. Though the mare merely sniffed it, her action was enough to engender the twin Aśvins called Nāsatya and Dasra.[1]

[1]v. also *Nir.*, 12. 10, 11.

Sarasvat A divinity of the upper region, born of water and plants, regarded as the guardian of the waters and the bestower of fertility (*RV.*, VII.96,4–6), who is associated with the river-goddess Sarasvatī.[1]

[1]Sarasvat and Sarasvatī represent 'divine pairing', and hence those who make offerings to them are assured of offspring (J. C. Heesterman, *Ancient Indian Royal Consecration*, p. 23).

Sārasvata A *ṛṣi*, the son of the personified river Sarasvatī. During a drought the *brāhmaṇas* became so vitiated by hunger that they could no longer recite or even remember the Vedas. But Sārasvata, sustained by a fish given him by his mother, was able to remember them.

Sarasvatī An ancient river of north-western India, personified as the goddess Sarasvatī. It is often erroneously identified with the modern Sarasvatī which loses itself in the sands of Patiala at Vinaśena. Owing to the extreme aridity of the region, combined with the sand-drifting action of the south-west monsoon winds,[1] only its almost dried-up river-bed remains. Of the twenty-five rivers mentioned in the *RV.* the Sarasvatī appears to have been the most renowned, and is described as the 'Best mother, best of rivers, best of goddesses' (*RV.*, II.41,16). The Sarasvatī was probably as large as the Sutlej in Vedic times and actually reached the sea, as is indicated in the *RV.* (VII.95,2). She is also called Sāradā,[2] Vagīśvara,[3] Brahmī, etc.,[4] and is associated in one of the Āprī hymns (*RV.*, VII.2,8) with Bhāratī and Iḷā. As a river-goddess she is connected with fertility and procreation, and particularly with purification. Thus all who bathe in her waters and sacrifice on her banks are cleansed of all impurity (*RV.*, I.3,10).

The land between the Sarasvatī and the Dṛṣadvarī, because of its religious importance, was called Brahmavarta, and it became also the focal point of political development in the subsequent kingdom of the Kuru-Pañcālas (*Manu*, II. 17–19).

Sarasvatī is the tutelary deity of writers and poets, and in libraries she is worshipped with offerings of flowers, fruit and incense.

[1]*HCIP.*, I, p. 86. The name Sarasvatī is derived from *saras* ($\sqrt{sṛ}$ 'to flow', *Nir.*, 9.26), a synonym of water.

[2]In parts of Mysore, she is regarded as the goddess who presides over the sixty-four arts.

[3]The name by which she is called by Hindu and Buddhist Tantrists.

[4]Among her many epithets are Mahāvidyā, Kāmadhenu, Vījagarbha, Dhaneśvarī and Sāradā. She is variously regarded as Dakṣa's daughter; wife (or daughter) of Brahmā; or wife of Viṣṇu, Manu, or Dharma, etc.

v. Sarasvat; Sārasvata; Vāc.

Śārdūla A term which may denote a lion, tiger, panther, leopard or similar beast of prey. It sometimes refers to the mythical animal Śarabha; and also appears in some temple carvings as a kind of leogryph.

v. Śārdūlī.

Śārdūlī The mythical mother of tigers and other beasts of prey.

Śarmiṣṭhā Mother of Puru and daughter of Vṛṣaparvan.

v. Devayānī.

Śārṅga I. The name of the bow made by Viśvakarman for Viṣṇu. It corresponds to the divine power of illusion (*māyā*).[1]

[1]*HP.*, p. 156.

II. A poison extracted from the *śṛṅga* plant.

Sarpa 'Creeping', 'sliding along'; a 'serpent'. Sarpa became a derogatory epithet applied by the Āryan settlers to the Indian indigenes who moved through the forests silently like serpents.

v. Nāga; Sarpamaṇi; Sarpaśānti; Viṣavidyā.

Sarpamaṇi 'Snake-gem.' A jewel believed to be secreted in the heads of serpents (*sarpa*), and having the power to expel poison.

Sarpaśānti A rite for obtaining offspring. Barrenness was regarded as the result of a woman having killed a snake (*sarpa* or *nāga*) in a former life. Diehl states that in South India snakes are conceived as 'soul-animals', and hence are connected with ancestor worship.[1]

[1] *Instrument and Purpose*, p. 254.

Sarpāvidyā v. Viṣavidyā.

Śarva 'Archer.' The name of one of the eight elemental forms of Rudra, the dark-haired archer (*AV.*, VI.93,1).

Both Śarva and Bhava are called 'lords of cattle and of men' (*AV.*, IV.28,1; XI.2,1), a description that applies to Śiva, who in the *MBh.* (III.167,47f.; 173,42ff., *EM.*), is called by his ancient name Śarva.[1]

[1] *EM.*, p. 231.

Sarvam 'Whole,' 'totality'. The Year is ritually regarded as *sarvam*, i.e., a 'cosmological entity', a full time-cycle, and hence by 'winning the Year' one masters the whole of Time.[1]

[1] Gonda, *Loka*, p. 101.

Sarvamedha 'Universal sacrifice'; a 'sacrifice for the attainment of power or supremacy', consisting of a ten-day performance, twice that required for the *puruṣamedha*. The rite is described in the *ŚBr.*, XIII.7,1ff.

The creator Svayambhū offered himself as the oblation at the *sarvamedha*. It was the supreme offering of One who exists in all beings and in whom all beings exist.[1]

This idea resembles that of the Norse god Odin who sacrificed himself so that he might obtain 'magical' knowledge, and thus destroy Chaos (represented by the Wolf) which threatened to destroy the universe.[2]

[1] Cf. the purpose of the Christian doctrine of the Crucifixion of Jesus, the son of God. 'For God so loved the world, that he gave his only begotten Son, that whosoever believeth on him should not perish, but have eternal life. God sent his Son that the world should be saved through him' (Gospel of St. John, III.16–17).

[2] v. H.R. Ellis Davidson, *Gods and Myths of Northern Europe*, p. 205. Viśvakarman performed a *sarvamedha* and finally sacrificed himself (*Nir.*, 10,26).

v. Yajña; Aśvamedha.

Śaśāṅka 'The hare in the moon.' The marks on the moon (*śaśin*) are said to resemble a hare (*śaśa*).

v. Candra.

Ṣaṣṭhī A folk-goddess,[1] regarded as a form of Durgā, who personifies the sixth day[2] after the birth of a child, and is regarded as a protector of children. She is also called Skandamātā, and is worshipped by Bengalī women desiring offspring.[3] The cat is sacred to her and regarded as her vehicle (*vāhana*).[4] Ṣaṣṭhī appears to have merged with the goddess Śrī, perhaps because the former may also represent an aspect of prosperity.[5]

[1] For the worship of this type of goddess, v. Banerjea, 'Some Folk Goddesses of Ancient and Mediaeval India', *IHQ.*, XIV, pp. 101–9, 1938.

[2] When danger to the life of mother and child is considered to be over, and the child's destiny is fixed. The occasion is celebrated by a ceremony called *Ṣaṣṭhījāgara*.

[3] *DHI.*, p. 384, n.1.

[4] *BH.*, p. 328; Crooke, *Things Indian*, p. 59.

[5] Gonda, *Aspects*, p. 219.

Ṣaṣṭhījāgara v. Ṣaṣṭhī, n.2.

Śāstra (s) A 'rule', 'treatise' or 'law-book'. A class of Hindu compilations belonging to the post-Vedic period, and which superseded priestly *sūtra* manuals. The *śāstra* is the formal exposition of particular subjects, which may resemble that of sūtras like the *Gṛhya* and *Dharma*, or include grammatical treatises, or works like the *Arthaśāstra* of Kauṭilya, and the *Kāmaśāstra* of Vātsyāyana. These were prose works, but the Dharmaśāstras followed an older metrical form.

The *Nyāya sāstra*, a manual of logic, is a later production as are the minor scientific and art treatises which though long studied, lacked the systematic form characteristic of the *śāstra*.

v. Vedāṅga (s); Upa-veda (s); Sanskrit.

Śastradevatā A deified weapon, from *śastra*, 'knife, sword, or any cutting instrument', and *devatā*, 'goddess'.

v. Āyudhapuruṣa (s).

Sat Lit. 'Being.'[1] In ontology it means 'existing', 'being'; in ethics 'good'; in epistemology 'true'.[2]

[1] *Sat* is the present participle of the root *as*; Gr. *asti*; Lat. *est*.

[2] Cf. the f. form *satī*, denoting a 'good' wife, and *satya*, the compound form of *sat*, 'true' or 'real'.

Śatadhanu A mythical king whose wife Śaibyā was noted for her womanly virtues, and for her ardent devotion to religious duties. On one occasion, after ritually bathing in the neighbouring sacred river, she and her husband were approached by a Jain, a friend of the king's military preceptor. Out of respect for the latter Śatadhanu entered into conversation with him, despite the interdiction of associating with 'infidels' like Jainas, Buddhists and Cārvākas. But Śaibyā remained silent and turned her gaze towards the sun.[1]

Shortly afterwards the king died, and his wife, faithful to the end, ascended his funeral pyre. Owing to his having conversed with an 'infidel', her husband was successively reborn as a dog, jackal, wolf, vulture, crow and peacock, whilst the undefiled Śaibyā was reborn as the daughter of the King of Kāśī. Wishing to see her happily married, her father requested her to choose a husband,[2] but she deferred her decision, hoping that her former husband's rebirths would finally result in the expiation of his sin, and that he would be reborn as a person of distinction whom she might marry. Her hopes were fulfilled, and when her father died Śatadhanu succeeded to his throne (*VP.*, III.18).

[1]The virtuous must stop to gaze upon the sun after looking at any person who has failed to observe the religious duties required of him.

[2]Either by means of a *svayaṁbara* or similar gathering, when eligible young men presented themselves as prospective bride-grooms.

Śatapatha Brāhmaṇa 'The Brāhmaṇa of a hundred paths', so-called because it consists of that number of lectures (*adhyāyas*). As the largest and most comprehensive of the Brāhmaṇas it is attached to the White Yajus or *Vājasaneyi Saṁ.*, the principal exposition of Vedic ritual which, with the Black Yajus (*Tait. Saṁ.*), constitutes the *Yajurveda*.

The *Vāj. Saṁ.* claims to contain knowledge hitherto not known which was later reflected in the *ŚBr.*, a claim that has some validity, though like the other Brāhmaṇas the *Śatapatha* is characterized by 'wearisome prolixity of exposition ... dogmatic assertion and a flimsy symbolism rather than by serious reasoning'.[1] Nonetheless, it is the only Brāhmaṇa to describe fully the five great sacrificial ceremonies, the *vājapeya*, *rājasūya*, *aśvamedha*, *puruṣamedha*, and the *sarvamedha*. Moreover, it gives the clearest and most comprehensive view of the increasing complexity of social and political conditions in north-western and northern India in late Vedic times, and also of the struggle for ascendancy between the priestly schools and the ruling class (*rājanya*). It reveals also the influence of the *purohita*,[2] (the ruler's priestly adviser) which enabled him to achieve a great degree of political as well as priestly power.

The *ŚBr.* appears to have reached an advanced stage also in literary and linguistic forms. It discarded traditional Vedic versification in favour of prose, and the use of compact forms and expressive Sanskrit particles. Although the schools of the *Vājasaneyi Saṁhitā* are said to have numbered either fifteen or seventeen, only two texts of the *ŚBr.* are known, the Mādhyandina and the Kāṇva.

The Mādhyandina text consists of two parts, the first comprising nine books containing sixty *adhyāyas*, the second five books, containing forty *adhyāyas*. Internal evidence, such as difference of style, geographical references, variations of doctrine, suggests that it originated in two different regions. Thus the first five books refer almost exclusively to places along the Ganges and Jumna, the remaining four to north-western districts. The first five also are confined to doctrines of a general nature, the latter four being chiefly concerned with the *agnicayana*, or construction of the sacred fire-altar 'which had come to be recognized as an important preliminary to the *soma* sacrifice'.[3] The two parts reveal yet another difference; while the first five books frequently quote Yājñavalkya's opinion as authoritative, in the succeeding four books another teacher, Śāṇḍilya, alone is called upon in support of a particular doctrinal interpretation. Nonetheless, these nine books appear to be an early redaction of the Mādhyandina text. But, as Eggeling points out, the tenth book, the Agnirahasya, deals with the same subject as the preceding four books; it also quotes Śāṇḍilya—not Yājñavalkya—as its authority. The list of teachers of the fire-ritual appended to it, and the ascription of its origin to Prajāpati, suggests that the tenth book represents another tradition, contemporary with that of the first nine books. But the last four (XI–XIV) are apparently of later date, and regarded as a separate portion of the work. The last six chapters of the final book (XIV) are a still later addition, and consists of a forest-treatise, the so-called *Bṛhad-Āraṇyaka*, subsequently classified as the first of the early Upaniṣads.

The arrangement of the Kāṇva text differs from that of the Mādhyandina; its grammatical forms also differ, the Kāṇva more closely resembling those of the *RV.* Apart from these differences the two recensions present the same account of the brahmanical ritual procedures in the late Vedic period.

[1]Eggeling, *ŚBr.*, according to the text of the Mādhyandina school, vol. I, Intro., p. ix.

[2]His influence is clearly emphasized in the statement: 'Verily the gods do not eat the food offered by the king who is without a *purohita*; wherefore let the king who wishes to sacrifice place a *brahman* at the head' (*Ait. Br.*, VIII.24–5).

[3]Eggeling, op. cit., vol. V, p. xiii.

v. Brāhmaṇa II.

Śatarūpā 'Having a hundred forms.' Name of the daughter of Brahmā and mother (in some accounts the wife) of Svāyambhuva. Śatarūpā is also called Sāvitrī.

Sātavāhana A kingdom situated in the Kanarese area of the Deccan and ruled by a dynasty of the same name established during the first century B.C. It lasted until the third century A.D., when it was conquered by tribes from north-western India. 'The memory of the dynasty lingers in the story of the King Śālivāhana ... [who] seems to have appropriated to himself the glorious deeds of several distinguished ... emperors of the Deccan.'[1]

[1]*AHI.*, p. 115.

v. Amarāvatī.

Satī I. (Anglicized as 'suttee'.) A feminine noun formed from the verbal root '*sat*', meaning 'real, true, good, virtuous'. Such epithets were applied especially to a widow who on the death of her husband proved her devotion by being burned with him on his funeral pyre.

But early Christian missionaries erroneously applied the term *satī* to the act itself. Though self-immolation may sometimes have been voluntary and a genuine expression of devotion,[1] it was more often an obligation imposed by custom, to show that the duty of a woman to her husband was a bond which even death could not break.

But the practice of *satī* in India, whatever its origin, bears no resemblance to the entombment of the wife, slaves and possessions of a Pharaoh in ancient Egypt or of rulers in Mesopotamia, where neither wives nor slaves had any choice in the matter. But the practice of some Indo-Germanic tribes of immolating a widow of a chieftain so that she might accompany her husband to Valhalla,[2] is not unlike the *satī* rite in India.

In Vedic times *satī* was only a mimetic ceremony, in which the widow climbed on to the funeral pyre and lay beside her husband's body, and was then led away either by a relative or friend, after which the pyre was set alight (*RV*., X.18,8; *AV*., XVIII.3,1). But according to Strabo (XV. ch. 700, 30), writing about the end of the first century B.C., the practice of *satī* was customary for the widows of *kṣatriyas*. Whether the actual, or only a mimetic, ceremony continued to be practised is not certain, but it probably—like the *aśvamedha* (horse-sacrifice)—fell into abeyance. But for a reason that has yet to be explained[3] widow-burning was resumed about the sixth century along the Ganges, and in Bengal and Rājputāna, and was continued among some aboriginal tribes[4] until it was declared illegal in 1829.[5]

[1]Arjuna performed the funeral rites for Kṛṣṇa whose eight wives led by Rukmiṇī embraced their husband's corpse on the funeral pyre and were burned with him (*VP*., V.38).

[2]Davidson, *Gods and Myths of Northern Europe*, p. 150.

[3]Fraser suggests that it was revived under the influence of priests anxious to obtain control of the property of the widow. To 'give the custom a religious sanction, a passage in the *RV*. (X.18,7) which directed the widow to rise from her husband's funeral pyre and go forth in front (*agre*) was altered into to go into the fire (*agneḥ*)' (*ERE*., XI, p. 207). The practice also increased in Bengal during the British expansion (Singhal, *India*, II, p. 282), despite the efforts of Ram Mohan Roy (1772–1833) to prohibit it.

[4]*Ancestor Worship*, p. 51.

[5]This rite was witnessed and described by R. Hartley Kennedy in a booklet entitled *The Sutti*, London, 1855. It took place at Baroda on 25 November 1825. For further information v. E. Thompson, *Suttee*. According to the fifteenth-century Italian traveller Nicolo dei Conti 'as many as three thousand of the wives and concubines of the kings of Vijayanagara were pledged to be burnt with their lord on his death' (Basham, *WI*., p. 188); v. also *CHI*., I, p. 415.

II. Name of one of the daughters of Dakṣa and a *śakti* of Śiva.

v. Vīrabhadra I; Pīṭha.

Ṣaṭkarman Six acts or tantric 'spells' designed to injure enemies, and called *śānti, vaśya, stambhana, vidveṣa, uccāṭana* and *māraṇa*.

v. Mantra.

Satrājita A Yādava prince, son of Nighna and father of Satyabhāmā one of the eight principal wives of Kṛṣṇa. A legend in the *VP*. (IV.13), was possibly designed to refute calumnious rumours about Kṛṣṇa, who was alleged to have killed Satrājita's brother Prasena and robbed him of the magical jewel *syamantaka*,[1] given to Satrājita by the sun-god Āditya. Subsequently it was learned that Prasena had been killed by a lion which in turn was slain by Jāmbavat an aboriginal chieftain. The latter recovered the jewel and gave it to his child Sukumāra as a plaything. Kṛṣṇa finally tracked Jāmbavat to his hiding-place, and after a battle of twenty-one days the chieftain surrendered, convinced that only an '*avatāra* of the sovereign lord Nārāyaṇa' could have defeated him. Jāmbavat returned the jewel to Kṛṣṇa and presented him with his daughter Jāmbavatī. Although the acceptance of a gift from a person of such low degree was a social impropriety, Kṛṣṇa accepted it to clear his own reputation. In the meantime the Yādavas who had accompanied him, after waiting seven or eight days for him, returned to Dvārakā and reported that Kṛṣṇa had been killed. But when Kṛṣṇa and his bride Jāmbavatī arrived at Dvārakā, the jewel was given back to Satrājita and Kṛṣṇa completely exonerated.

Satrājita, realizing that his suspicions had been unfounded, sought to make amends by giving his daughter Satyabhāmā to Kṛṣṇa. As she had been courted by other distinguished Yādavas, their resentment resulted in a plot to kill Satrājita, steal the jewel, and if Kṛṣṇa attempted to intervene, to fight him. Satrājita was killed and the jewel stolen. It finally passed into the possession of Akrūra, one of Satyabhāmā's suitors, who agreed to hold it on behalf of the entire Yādava people.

The story of the *syamantaka* occurs in several Purāṇas and in the *Hariv*. Independently of the part played by Kṛṣṇa, it presents a curious and no doubt faithful picture of ancient manners, particularly of the loose self-government of kindred clans, and their acts of personal violence, of ensuing feuds, and the parts played by the elders and women in the affairs of the community.[2]

[1]Considered to be an inexhaustible source of benefits to a virtuous person, but if worn by an evil-doer it became

a source of disaster.
[2]v. Wilson, *VP*. (IV.14, n.16).

Śatrughna 'Destroyer of foes'. The twin brother of Lakṣmaṇa, and son of Daśaratha and his queen Sumitrā, and half-brother of Rāma.
v. Rāmāyaṇa.

Sattva One of the three *guṇas* or constituents of *prakṛti*.
v. Sāṁkhya.

Sātvata I. Belonging or sacred to Sātvata (Kṛṣṇa); also the name of Baladeva, etc.
II. Name of a Yādava people, who were worshippers of Kṛṣṇa.
III. Name of an early Pāñcarātra Saṁhitā.

Satya I. 'True', 'real'. An epithet of Viṣṇu who exemplifies truth.
II. Name of one of the *Viśvas* (Universal Principles), personified as the son of Dharma and Viśvā, a daughter of Dakṣa (*VP*., I. 15).
III. Name of the first four *yugas* or ages, also called *kṛta*.

Satyabhāmā 'Having true lustre.' Daughter of the Yādava prince Satrājita, and one of Kṛṣṇa's wives. She accompanied Kṛṣṇa to heaven and induced him to steal the divine *pārijāta* tree belonging to Śacī, Indra's wife (*VP*., V.30).
v. Rukmiṇī; Jāmbavatī.

Satyaloka v. Brahmaloka.

Satyavāha v. Aṅgir.

Satyavāhana 'Conveying truth', popularly said of dreams.

Satyavatī I. Daughter of the *apsaras* Adrikā and mother of Kṛṣṇa-Dvaipāyana, the legendary compiler (*vyāsa*) of the *MBh*., born as the result of a liaison with the *ṛṣi* Parāśara. She became the wife of King Śāntanu.
II. Daughter of Gādhi, King of Kānyakubja, and wife of the aged Ṛcīka, a Bhārgava priest.
v. Jamadagni; Paraśurāma.

Satyavrata I. Name of the seventh Manu, also called Vaivasvata.
v. Manu I; Matsya avatāra; Manvantara (s).
II. One of the three kings of Ayodhyā, known also as Satyavrata Triśaṅku who, after the decline of the kingdom, succeeded in restoring it to its former greatness. After being 'expelled by his father at the instance of his family priest [Vasiṣṭha] on account of some excesses, the prince is said to have led the life of a *caṇḍāla* [outcaste] wandering in the woods ... for twelve years'.[1] During his exile there was a great famine, in which Satyavrata, by now well-versed in the art of self-sustenance, supported the family of Viśvāmitra during the latter's absence.

On his return Viśvāmitra, to express his gratitude and his disapproval of Vasiṣṭha, had Satyavrata installed on the throne of Ayodhyā, thus maintaining the royal line from which Rāma was descended.
[1]*HCIP*., I, p. 286.

Saubhari v. Māndhātṛ.

Saumya I. 'Relating to *soma*', i.e., to the juice of the *soma* plant, or to its sacrificial use, or to the moon-god (Soma). It is also the patronymic of the planet Mercury (Budha).
II. A class of ancestors (*pitṛs*), referred to in *Manu* (III, 199).

Śaunaka Name of the author of the *Bṛhaddevatā*, the *Ṛgvidhāna*, and other works.

Saunanda The name of Balarāma's club.
v. Gadā.

Saura 'Relating to Sūrya the sun-god.' The name of one of the Hindu cults whose metaphysical beliefs are represented by the sun (Savitṛ), the source of light and metaphorically of true knowledge and spiritual enlightenment, which is expressed in the short prayer called *gāyatrī* (*RV*., III.62,10). But it is probable that a form of sun-worship was common in India from a very remote age, and which has persisted until modern times, as is indicated by the sacrifice of white cocks, dedicated to the sun, by some aboriginal tribes. Hopkins[1] considers that some of the followers of the Pāṇḍavas were Sauras, one of whom, Arvāvasu, was taught the 'Secret Veda of the Sun'.

The sun as a symbol of enlightenment is recognized also by Śaivas and Vaiṣṇavas, but not as a distinct object of worship. Thus few Saura temples have survived, the best-known being that at Konārak in Orissa.

'From the early centuries of the Christian era the sun-cult appears to have developed in northern India along a certain well-marked line. That its north Indian form was much reorientated by the east Iranian mode of sun-worship is fully proved by many literary and archaeological data.'[2] By the eighth century there were several distinct cults of sun-worshippers, who wore a caste mark of red sandal paste, and garlands of red flowers, and repeated the *gāyatrī*.
[1]*EM*., p. 88.
[2]*DHI*., p. 430.
v. Sāmba; Āditya; Pūṣan; Viṣṇu; Sūryavaṁśa.

Sautrāmaṇī A particular sacrifice in honour of Indra. If a castrated bull or a draught-mare forms the *dakṣiṇā*, the sacrifice will ensure the destruction of the donor's enemies, the fulfilment of all his desires and his ultimate attainment of the celestial world (*ŚBr*., V.5.4,35). The rite is also performed to expiate the sin of immoderate consumption of *soma* by a priest (*ŚBr*., I.6.3,7, n.1), and that by Indra (*AVB*., pp. 328f.), a reference to the myth of the *soma* juice reserved for Tvaṣṭṛ which Indra stole and drank. As a result of this his limbs flew asunder and were not reunited until the Aśvins and Sarasvatī had performed the *sautrāmaṇī* rite for him. According to the *Kauṣ. Br.* (XVI.10), the rite also ensures prosperity, and offspring, etc.

v. Surā.

Sāvarṇa v. Sāvarṇi.

Sāvarṇi or **Sāvarṇa** Son of Sūrya and Chāyā, who became the eighth Manu. 'He was called Sāvarṇi from being of the same caste (*sāvarṇa*) as his elder brother the Manu Vaivasvata' (*VP.*, III.2). The name Savarṇa is used either alone or in combination for all succeeding Manus.

v. Manvantara(s).

Śavasī 'Mighty' Epithet of Indra's mother (*RV.*, VIII. 45,5), v. Indra, n. 4.

Savitṛ (post-Vedic), or **Savitar** (Vedic)[1] The 'Vivifier or Animator'. An epithet of Sūrya, the sun, regarded as the source of life and of light and the antithesis of darkness, and thus metaphorically the source of the light of knowledge and dispeller of ignorance. This is expressed in the celebrated *gāyatrī*, the prayer 'used by every *brahmin* throughout India in his daily devotions'.[2] With his rays Savitṛi measures out the worlds; he leads the sacrificial horse on easy paths to the gods; and returns the bones of the dead to the earth (*ŚBr.*, XIII.2.7,12; 8.3,3).

[1]From the root *sū* 'to bring forth', i.e., the sun as the source of creation.

[2]*IW.*, p. 19. The *Śvet. Up.*, 2,1–3 invokes Savitṛ for inspiration and self-control.

Sāvitrī v. Gāyatrī; Sūrya.

Sāya 'Evening', personified as a son of Dhātṛ and Kuhū.

Sāyaṇa A notable fourteenth-century commentator on the *RV.* and author of numerous works, some of which were probably written in collaboration with his brother Mādhava Vidyāraṇya. The two brothers were prominent during the founding of the Vijayanagara Empire in southern India.[1] Its significance in the history of India is that for almost three centuries it stood as a bulwark of Vedic religion and culture against the pressure of neighbouring Moslem states. The tolerance of the early rulers of Vijayanagara allowed both Śaivas and Vaiṣṇavas their respective temples. The use of Sanskrit and the principal South Indian languages were also impartially encouraged.

Nonetheless, such an environment did not entirely eliminate Mīmāṁsā fundamentalism. Because the Veda was generally regarded as eternal, it was inconceivable to scholiasts like Sāyaṇa that there could be any break in the continuity of the ritual of 1000 B.C. and that of its counterpart in the fourteenth century A.D. He therefore uncompromisingly stated in his commentarial introduction to the first hymn of the *RV.* that not only was it essential for anyone repeating a Vedic hymn to know the name of the *ṛṣi* to whom it was revealed, and that of the god to whom it was addressed, but also to know its metre, and the correct accents and interpretation of the *mantras*. Anyone not knowing these things, he declared, was a 'mantra-thorn' (*mantra-kaṇṭaka*) whose carelessness would assuredly destroy or obstruct the efficacy of its recital.

The authority ascribed to Sāyaṇa and other Indian medieval commentators by early nineteenth-century Western scholiasts has since been questioned by Muir, Max Müller and others, and later by twentieth-century scholars such as Heimann, Gonda, Banerjea and others. Max Müller offers one explanation of the difficulties of the medieval scholiasts: 'As the authors of the Brāhmaṇas were blinded by theology, the authors of the still later Niruktas [etymological treatises] were deceived by etymological fictions, and both conspired to mislead by their authority later and more sensible commentators, such as Sāyaṇa.'[2] But despite many errors, when giving his own unbiased judgment Sāyaṇa's etymological conclusions have often proved to be sound.[3]

[1]But the legend that one or other of the brothers became Prime Minister has not been generally accepted (*AHI.*, p. 366).

[2]Griffith, *RV.*, vol. I, Intro., p. xi.

[3]'Sāyaṇa often gives several inconsistent explanations of a word in interpreting the same passage or in commenting on the same word in different passages ... It is clear from a careful examination of their comments that neither Yāska nor Sāyaṇa possessed any certain knowledge about a large number of words in the *RV.*' (Macdonell, *A Vedic Reader for Students*, Intro., p. xxx).

Śekhara A diadem or ornament representing the crescent of the fifth-day moon which Śiva bears on his brow near his fiery third eye. It represents 'the power of procreation co-existent with that of destruction'.[1]

[1]Karapātṛ, 'Śrī Śiva tattva', *Siddhānta*, II, 1941–2, 116, cited in *HP.*, p. 215.

Senā I. A dart, spear, or similar missile, and subsequently the term denoting an army (*RV.*, I.33,6). It is also the name of Indra's wife.

v. Senānī I and II.

II. An army or battle-array pesonified as the wife of the war-god Skanda.

Senānī I. 'Leader of army', 'Commander'. An epithet

of the war-god Skanda.

II. A term used in the game of dice to denote the highest numbered die (*RV*., X.34,12).

Śeṣa I. 'Remainder.'[1] The thousand-headed cosmic serpent (*nāga*), also called Ananta, the 'Endless or Infinite One'. The head of Śeṣa sustains the earth; the latter supports the spheres and their inhabitants (*VP*., II.5). As a theriomorphic[2] form of Viṣṇu, Śeṣa is a kind of demiurge whose fiery breath at the end of every age destroys the world, whose ashes sink into the primordial waters (representing the undifferentiated state of the cosmos), leaving only Viṣṇu and Śeṣa to continue the work of creation. Viṣṇu reclines on the coiled form of Śeṣa, the coils symbolizing the endless revolutions of Time.

According to the *Hariv*. (12076) Śeṣa hung from a tree for a thousand years in ascetic fervour (*tapas*), distilling the *kalākula* poison from his mouth, and thus burning up the world.

Snakes were thought to incorporate the 'soul'. Thus Śeṣa emerged from the dying Balarāma and entered the earth, where he was welcomed by the other serpents.

[1]Śeṣa represents the residue after the world 'had been shaped out of the cosmic waters of the abyss' (Zimmer, *Myths*, p. 62); or the remains of the universe after its destruction at the end of an age (*HP*., p. 33).

[2]v. Zimmer, op. cit., p. 62, and Gonda, *Aspects*, p. 152.

v. Ananta I; Nārāyaṇa.

II. The name of an architect to whom is attributed the Nāgara style of architecture.

Siddhānta-kaumudī Name of a simplified form of Pāṇini's grammar, by Bhaṭṭojī Dīkṣita.

Siddhānta (s) The general name for scientific treatises, especially those connected with the solution of astronomical and mathematical problems.

v. Vedāṅgas; Jyotiṣa; Sūrya Siddhānta; Śāstra (s).

Siddharasa 'Mercury', popularly called quicksilver because of its silver-white colour, brilliant metallic lustre, and unique fluidity. To the alchemists it was a magical tool by means of which the Siddhas were believed to acquire supranormal powers (*siddhis*).

Siddha (s) A term applied to certain yogins who have acquired the 'eight *siddhis*' or supranormal faculties and have thus reached a state of spiritual perfection. Historically, they are the successors of the ancient *munis* and *ṛṣis* who sought to overcome disease and death and to become immortal. The adept *siddha*[1] attains liberation whilst living (*jīvan-mukti*), his ordinary body being transformed into a perfect one which death cannot touch. When in this state the *siddha* continues to render 'spiritual guidance to innumerable religious aspirants—and this state is the fittest state for becoming a *guru* or spiritual preceptor. It is for this reason that the *siddhas* are the true preceptors in the world'.[2] The great *ṛṣi* Agastya is said to have worked for hundreds of years in full vigour. Now he abides in a shrine from which he watches over the spiritual activities of less advanced *siddhas*. Other great yogins such as the historical Buddha were believed to be able to postpone their deaths indefinitely.[3] Hence a yogin has always been considered by many to be a *mahāsiddha*, a possessor of occult powers, a 'magician'.[4]

The *siddhas* were also great alchemists, and 'if we set aside the folklore that proliferated around the alchemists (as around all "magicians"), we shall understand the correspondence between the alchemist working on "vulgar" metals to transmute them into "gold" and the yogin working on himself to the end of "extracting" from his dark, enslaved psychomental life the free and autonomous spirit, which shares in the same essence as gold',[5] for 'gold is immortality' (*amṛtam āyur hiraṇyam*) (*Maitrāyaṇī Saṁ*., II.2,2).

To Śaivas, Śiva is the Supreme Siddha (Ādi-nātha), the divine source of perfection, of whom all other *siddhas* are incarnations.

[1]But not all *siddhas* were adepts. The first Tantric teachers, such as the eighty-four *siddhas*, were mostly rustic folk with little learning, and thus limited to the vocabulary of the Hindu village (v. *TT*., p. 28).

[2]Dasgupta, *ORC*., p. 219.

[3]v. P.S. Jaini, 'Buddha's prolongation of life', *BOAS*., xxi, pt. 3, 1958, pp. 546f.

[4]Eliade, *Yoga*, p. 88.

[5]Eliade, op. cit., p. 281.

v. Siddhi I; Siddharasa; Siddhīśvara; Gorakhnāth; Matsyendranāth.

Siddhasthālī A magical cauldron from which a Siddha can produce any kind of food.[1]

[1]Cf. the Celtic magical cauldron of Cerridwen.

Siddhi I. 'Successful achievement'; 'fulfilment'; supranormal faculties attained by *siddhas* by means of *haṭha-yoga* and other means. Patañjali states that *siddhi* can even be attained by the application of herbs or medicine (*auṣadhi*).[1] Particular *mantras* also yield *siddhi* in the present (*kali*) age,[2] as do certain rites of the so-called *vāmācāra* tantrists.[3]

[1]*ORC*., p. 193.

[2]*TT*., p. 127.

[3]Ibid., p. 230, and v. p. 120; v. also R.H. van Gulik, *Sexual Life in Ancient China*, p. 349. For some similarities between Shamanism and the *siddhis* v. Eliade, *Shamanism*, p. 409.

v. Siddha (s); Tantra.

II. A goddess personifying perfection or successful

achievement, and popularly regarded as a fitting wife for Gaṇeśa, the overcomer of obstacles.
v. Siddha(s).

Siddhīśvara 'Lord of magical power.' Epithet of Śiva, and name of a district sacred to him.

Śikṣā One of the six vedāṅgas or sets of rules governing the performance of the sacrifice. *Śikṣā* was a sophisticated system of phonetics which included the correct value of each letter, its accent and quantity, and the proper method of articulation, so as to ensure correct pronunciation (*prātiśākhya*) especially in the recital of sacred passages of the Vedas.
v. Chandas.

Śilpa-śāstra The science of mechanics, including architecture. Any book or treatise on this science.

Sīmantonnayana A ceremony performed during a woman's first pregnancy to ensure a successful birth, in which 'Soma is invoked as the *retodhās*—the impregnator of seed, or ... [as] the life-giving power manifesting itself in the cyclical processes of fertility; Soma is the fluid principle of continuity of life'.[1]

[1]Heesterman, *Ancient Indian Royal Consecration*, p. 75.

Siṁha 'Lion.' The lion and its strength were identified with sovereignty and given the title of lord, chief, hero, etc.[1] Thus a king's throne is called *siṁhāsana*, as are those of the Buddha and Viṣṇu. The lion is the emblem of Mahāvīra, the twenty-fourth Jaina *tīrthaṅkara*, and the *vāhana* of Devī when she fought the *asura* Raktavīja.

The lion is regarded as the mythical ancestor of the Sinhalese.[2]

[1]Cf. the title of the Emperor of Ethiopia, 'Lion of Judah'. The Egyptian goddess Sekmet was lion-headed; the great goddess of Phrygia and the Babylonian Ishtar were accompanied by lions.

[2]A.K. Coomaraswamy, *Mediaeval Sinhalese Art*, p. 86.
v. Narasiṁha; Siṁhī.

Siṁhī 'Lioness.' A designation of the northern fire-altar (*uttaravedī*). It is regarded as a lioness overcoming all rivals and giving wealth, etc.

Sinīvālī Name of a lunar goddess who personifies the new moon.[1] The other three lunar phases are personified as the goddesses Kuhū, Anumati and Rākā. All four goddesses preside over procreation.

Sinīvālī helps to fashion the embryo of the child (*AV*., VI.11,3), and is also associated with cattle and conducts them to their byres; Anumati keeps them in place on arrival (*AV*., II,26,2). At the horse-sacrifice (*aśvamedha*) three heifers are offered to Sinīvālī (*Tait. Saṁ*., V.6,18). She appears in the shape of a crescent moon on the headdress of Śiva (also called Kapardin), and hence she is called Kapardin's daughter.

[1]The *Nir*., 11,31, states that she represents the day when the new moon rises but is invisible. It becomes visible the following day, and is then called Kuhū.
v. Sinīvālīkuhūśānti.

Sinīvālīkuhūśānti A ceremony designed to avert the maleficent effects of being born on Sinīvālī or Kuhū days.

Śipiviṣṭa An obscure term[1] whose origin and precise significance remain uncertain, despite the efforts of lexicographers and commentators, both Western and Indian. In the *RV*. (VII.99,7; 105,7) it appears as an epithet of the solar Viṣṇu, and is variously interpreted as 'invested with rays of light', 'luminous', etc. (*Nir*., 5,8). But in another passage it is used as a term of contempt (*Nir*., 5,7), as also in the *Tait. Saṁ*. (II.2.12,5), where it refers to 'a diseased man whose private parts are exposed', i.e., devoid of a prepuce.[2] In the *Nir*. (p. 78, n.2) the term *viṣṇave śipiviṣṭāya* means a 'bald man',[3] but in another passage (5,9) the term denotes the 'master of hymns' who knows the sacred customs, praises the name of Śipiviṣṭa, and glorifies him because of his might. The *Tait. Saṁ*. (III.4,1) states that the redundant portion of the sacrifice is offered to Viṣṇu Śipiviṣṭa, for 'verily in the redundant he deposits the redundant, to appease the redundant'.[4]

[1]v. K. Geldner, *Vedische Studien*, p. 81n., Stuttgart, 1901, and Eggeling, *SBE*., XLIV, p. 293, n.2.

[2]Some authorities consider that *śipi* cannot be dissociated from *śepa* (penis), which according to the *IAL*. (12606) also means 'tail'. Cf. the Sumerian *sipa*, lit., 'stretched horn' or 'penis', which 'sometimes signifies "shepherd"' (J.M. Allegro, *The Sacred Mushroom and the Cross*, p. 24). Gonda does not see any unmistakable reference to a phallic character of the deity (*Aspects*, p. 106). In *RV*. (VII.100,6) Viṣṇu is begged not to hide his *śipiviṣṭa* form from his worshippers.

[3]'Bald-head' was a term of contempt among the Israelites (II. Kings 2,23), as also among the Greeks and Romans. Offerings are made to Viṣṇu, the Bald (*ŚBr*., XIII.1.8,8). Cf. the 'bald' Zeus at Argos which may indicate the decaying year (Farnell, *Cults*, vol. I, p. 37, n.a).

[4]The Commentator Mahīdhara states that *śipi* means one who is present in all creatures.

Sīsara A dog-demon, the father of Kūrkura by the bitch Saramā. If a child falls ill with the 'dog-disease', i.e., epilepsy, the father covers the child with a net and mutters a stanza from the *Pāraskara Gṛhya Sūtra* (I.16,24), imploring Sīsara and Kūrkura to leave his son alone and go away.
v. Sārameya(s).

Śiśnadeva The phallus (*śiśna*), personified as a divinity (*deva*). The *Nir*. (4,18) derives *śiśna* from the root *śnath*, 'to pierce', the significance given to its various synonyms in Indo-European languages.

The ancient remains of the Indus Valley civilization, which include representations of male and female generative organs, suggest the existence of a phallic cult. That some form of it existed in Vedic times is confirmed by *RV.* passages condemning it, and by the explicit ban upon its devotees from sharing in brahmanic sacrificial rites, or from entering sacred areas (VIII.21,5). In another passage (X.99,3) the *śiśna* devotees are called lustful demons, whose hundred-gated fort was captured by Indra. Later, 'when phallicism came to be inseparably connected with the worship of Rudra-Śiva, the orthodox Indo-Āryans who upheld the original Vedic tradition were at first tardy in its recognition'.[1]

[1] *DHI.*, pp. 63f. 'Early Tamil literature refers to the setting up of ritual posts, which seem to have been phallic emblems' (Basham, *WI.*, p. 308).

v. Śiva; Liṅga; Liṅgāyat(s).

Śiśumāra I. 'Child-killer.' The Gangetic porpoise or dolphin, or possibly an alligator.

II. A stellar galaxy, thought to resemble a porpoise, and regarded as a form of Hari (Viṣṇu). Dhruva, the Pole Star, is situated in its tail, to which the other stars in the galaxy are believed to be attached by aerial cords. Thus when Dhruva revolves the other stars revolve with it (*VP.*, II.9). The sight of Śiśumāra at night is believed to expiate 'sins' committed during the day, and to gaze upon it regularly is said to ensure longevity (II.12).

Śiśupāla[1] A Cedi king, one of the rulers invited to the *rājasūya* of Yudhiṣṭhira. Among those present was Kṛṣṇa, who was chosen as the first officiant, but Śiśupāla objected, and in the quarrel that followed, was killed by Kṛṣṇa. Śiśupāla's objection suggests sectarian jealousy, as a legend in the *VP.* (IV.14–15) relates that in a former existence Śiśupāla was King Hiraṇyakaśipu, a devoted Śaiva, who was killed by Nara-siṁha, an *avatāra* of Viṣṇu, for his refusal to recognize Viṣṇu as the Supreme Being.

[1] Lassen considers that Śiśupāla was probably an early name of Śiva (*Indian Antiquities*, vol. I. p. 823, 2nd edn.).

Sītā I. The furrow[1] personified as a goddess and worshipped as the deity presiding over agriculture. She is mentioned in a hymn (*RV.*, IV.57) addressed to the lord of the fields (Kṣetrapati) and to other divinities associated with agriculture. Hence, at the beginning of each sowing season, twelve furrows (representing the months of the year) were ritually ploughed by the king or chieftain in the first field (*Tait. Saṁ.*, V.2,5).[2] As the repository of the seed, furrows were regarded as the earth's female generative organs.[3]

[1] Cf. the Etruscan god Tages who appeared in the furrow ploughed by Tarchon.

[2] The importance of ritual ploughing by the ruler in person occurs in other countries, including Ceylon and China. Hopkins suggests that Sītā is a kind of Corn Mother, and hence is represented by a ploughshare (*EM.*, p. 12). v. also Gonda, *Aspects*, p. 116.

[3] Cf. the French synonyms for 'furrow', especially 'tranche', which is also a slang term for vulva. In one of the marriage hymns of the *AV.* (XIV.2,14) the bride is likened to a field. For woman as the 'everlasting field' v. *MBh.* (Bombay edn.) I. 74,40ff. cited by Basham, *WI.*, p. 182. Cf. Koran (II,22) 'Your women are your plough-land'.

II. The daughter of Janaka, one of the kings of Videha. Probably because of her birth during the Spring, she is poetically described in the *Rāmāyaṇa* as having sprung from a furrow (*sītā*) during the ritual ploughing by her father at the beginning of the Spring sowing, and hence her epithet Ayonijā 'not womb-born'.

Before her marriage to Rāma, heir to the throne of Ayodhyā, her suitors, as was the custom of those seeking to marry princesses, were invited to a *svayaṁbara* to test their valour and skill. Rāma won the contest by bending the great bow which Śiva had given to her father. Owing to a palace intrigue, she and her husband were subsequently exiled. By a subterfuge she was abducted by Rāvaṇa, the ruler of Laṅkā, and held prisoner until her rescue several years later. Owing to her having dwelt in another man's house, objections were raised about her fitness to become queen. Reluctantly Rāma was forced by public opinion to discard her.[1]

This event confirms Sītā's association with the earth by her appeal to the Earth-goddess to rebut the charge of unfaithfulness made against her. This the Earth-goddess did by emerging from the earth, seated on a golden throne, and by embracing Sītā and disappearing with her into the earth from which she had miraculously sprung. Henceforth Sītā is considered to represent chastity and conjugal fidelity and is regarded as an incarnation of Lakṣmī, the wife of Viṣṇu.

[1] But the *AGP.* (X,27–28) states that Sītā underwent the fire-ordeal which proved her guiltless, after which she rejoined her husband.

III. Name of the eastern branch of the four mythical streams of the celestial Gaṅgā which divide after falling on Mount Meru.

Śītalā The goddess of small-pox, who may inflict the disease as well as avert it.[1] Her name means 'cold' or 'shivering',[2] a condition which precedes the high fever of smallpox. When death occurs the victims are seldom cremated, for this would injure the goddess herself who is thought to have entered the body of the patient. Śītalā is still worshipped in Bengal during smallpox epidemics.[3] To the Tamils she is Māriyammai (Mother Death).

Her shrines are generally situated outside villages, under trees or in groves, where she is represented by a stone, a clay image or piece of a pine tree (Pandanus odoratissimus), her own dwelling being the *kikar* tree (Acacia arabuca), which women water, and thus by this act of sympathetic magic cool the victims of the disease. She is frequently depicted as a naked woman, painted red, mounted on an ass, carrying a bundle of sticks, winnowing fan and an earthen pot. It is probable that Śītalā is another name for the inauspicious goddess Jyeṣṭhā.

Śītalā is one of seven sisters, all of whom are associated with disease, against which amulets depicting Śītalā are worn as a protection. In Bengal the priest attending a household afflicted with smallpox is never a *brāhmaṇa*, but a member of the gardener caste. Meat or food containing spices are forbidden to the sufferer, to whose wrist the priest ties a lock of hair, a cowrie shell, and other articles. The patient must continue to lie on a plantin leaf, and drink only water used to bathe Śītalā's image.

[1]The Greek Apollo sent the pestilence and also removed it (Farnell, *Cults*, IV, p. 233). Śītalā also presides over cholera and other fatal diseases.

[2]In the festival in her honour called *Śītalā-saptami*, held on the seventh day of the light half of the month *māgha*, only cold food is eaten.

[3]*IT.*, p. 85.

Śītalāsaptami v. Śītalā.

Śiva 'Auspicious.' The word occurs frequently in the *RV.* (II.33,1–7, etc.) as a propitiatory epithet applied to the storm-god Rudra, who is implored to look upon his suppliants with compassion, and neither to hide the sunlight from them nor be angered should they inadequately extol him. Rudra was evidently regarded as a fierce divinity[1] who ravaged the countryside without discrimination, but who also brought rain, without which the the crops failed and the people starved. It was therefore natural that Rudra should be addressed with placatory epithets, such as '*śiva*', meaning auspicious, propitious, gracious, benign, etc., in the hope of averting his violent activities.[2]

From being an epithet '*śiva*' is attached to Rudra in the Gṛhya rites as a joint name (Rudra-Śiva), a form in common use among country folk, long after Vedic personification of natural forces had been superseded by rational explanation among the literate classes. But by the second century B.C., the epithet '*śiva*' had acquired a separate identity and was represented by an image or likeness (*pratikṛti*) of Śiva as an object of worship.[3] The dis-association of Śiva and Rudra is suggested by the synonym *śaṅkara* (auspicious) often used in the *MBh.* and Purs. when referring to Śiva. Coomaraswamy refers to the close association of the *yakṣas* with a form of Śiva called Śaṅkara, and states that some temples, such as the Virūpākṣa at Paṭṭadkadal, are dedicated to him under names identical with those of *yakṣas*.[4]

In the early Kuṣāṇa period anthropomorphic representations of Śiva, holding a trident (*triśūla*) appear on coins. He is depicted either with two or four arms, and accompanied by his bull-mount Nandin.[5] But in the late Kuṣāṇa and early Gupta periods the phallus (*liṅga*) as well as the trident and bull, are sculpturally represented. That a *liṅga* cult existed in India in pre-Vedic times may be indicated by an ithyphallic figure[6] found in the Indus Valley. Though the cult was subsequently condemned by the Āryans (*RV.*, VII.21,5), the worship of the generative principle, represented by the *liṅga*, *yoni* and the bull, persisted among many aboriginal tribes, even after these cults had become assimilated with that of Śiva. Such traditional beliefs, as well as diverse folk divinities (*laulika devatās*), are reflected in Śiva's numerous titles, names, forms and epithets. It is thus probable that the ithyphallic figurines of the Indus Valley, while indicating the existence of a phallic cult, are not a prototype of Śiva, as has sometimes been suggested, but are merely coincidental and lacking any connexion with the Śaiva representations of the second century B.C. Furthermore, the 'proto-Śiva' of Harappā has buffalo horns, whereas Śiva is associated specifically with the domestic bull.

Whatever the popular Śaiva views may have been some were gradually modified by Sāṁkhya doctrines which, though basically dualistic, regarded existence as a continuous process of generation, destruction and regeneration. Such a concept suited the priestly schools and facilitated the transition from Vedic explanations of natural law to those of the two main sectaries, the cults of Śiva and Viṣṇu. The composite nature of Śiva, reflected in his 1008 epithets and names, and those of his *śaktis* was gradually accepted, because it was recognized as being essentially no different from the Vedic notion of the multiple forms of a single divine power.[7] Śiva represents 'supra-ethical and supra-personal dynamic evolution',[8] and as Mahādeva, is equated with the impersonal *brahman*.

[1]To Vedic man Rudra represented the uncultivated, unconquered and greatly feared Nature 'experienced as a divinity' (Gonda, *VS.*, p. 5). Rudra unites within

himself the dangerous and the beneficent aspects of the fertility process (Heesterman, *Ancient Indian Royal Consecration*, p. 90, n.44). Śiva may be called *śivaṇ*, *śivā* or *śivam*—all his names may be rendered thus in the three genders for he is male, female and neuter (*EW*., I, p. 371).

[2]The personal name of the Hebrew divinity Yahweh, like Rudra, signified 'storm-god' or denoted 'rain-giver' (Hastings, *Dictionary of the Bible*, vol. II, p. 199). Jane Harrison (*Prolegomena to the Study of Greek Religion*, p. 553) states that it was not considered safe to address the gods by a name denoting their fierceness lest by sympathetic magic the anger which the suppliant seeks to avert remains unaffected. The second part of the name of the Greek Zeus Melichios is said to mean 'kindly' and is used euphemistically (Farnell, *Cults*, I, p. 64).

[3]Similarly, such names as Iacchos, Bacchus, etc., which were originally ritual cries, subsequently became the names of Dionysos. v. also Gaster, *Thespis*, pp. 32f.

[4]*Yakṣas*, pt. 1, p. 12, n.2.

[5]Some Indo-Greek rulers in Gandhāra and the Panjāb depicted a bull on their coins, which represented 'in most cases, Śiva in his theriomorphic form' (*RAA*., p. 45). Campbell (*Oriental Mythology*, II. pp. 90f.) cites a number of analogies of Śiva with the ancient Egyptian Ptah.

[6]A similar figure of the ancient Egyptian god Min symbolized the generative force of nature (H. Frankfort, *Ancient Egyptian Religion*, p. 26).

[7]This is confirmed in *Manu* (XII.123); 'Some call him Agni, others Manu, the Lord of creatures, others Indra, others the vital air, and again others eternal *brahman*.'

[8]Heimann, *Facets*, pp. 66f.

v. Śākta; Sāṁkhya; Bhairava; Dakṣiṇāmūrti; Naṭarāja; Pāśupata I and II; Pañcānana; Pāriṣada(s); Pārvatī.

Śivā 'Auspicious.' Though Śivā is a personification of Śiva's energy (*śakti*), her name is merely a grammatical construction, the feminine form of a masculine proper name. In all his different forms he has a *śakti* of the same name, as do some other divinities.

Śiva-jñāna-bodham A thirteenth-century work, thought by some to be by Meykaṇḍa. It consists of twelve *sūtras* with a commentary (*vārttika*) by the author, and is a basic Śaiva-siddhānta.

Śiva jyotis 'Auspicious light.' In ritual, the fire, as the Destroyer (an aspect of Śiva) is called a *liṅga*, an 'auspicious light'.[1]

[1]*HP*., p. 229.

Śivālaya I. The name of 'Śiva's abode' on Mount Kailāsa.

II. Any temple or shrine dedicated to Śiva; also a name of the cremation ground.

Śiva Purāṇa[1] A Śaiva Purāṇa. In its extant form it is an abridgement of the original recension (comprising twelve *saṁhitās*, containing 100,000 stanzas, to one of seven *saṁhitās*, containing 24,000 stanzas), the redaction being ascribed to the sage Kṛṣṇa Dvaipāyana Vyāsa. While most of the Mahāpurāṇa lists include the *Śiva P*., others replace it with the *Vāyu*.

[1]An E. translation has been published in the *Ancient Indian Tradition and Mythology* Series, 4 vols, India, 1970.

v. Purāṇa(s).

Śivarātri 'Śiva's night.' A festival in honour of Śiva, held on the fourteenth night of the dark half of the moon in the month of *māgha* (January–February). During the festival a *liṅga* image is garlanded with flowers, a custom based on the story of a hunter who had killed so many birds that he was unable to collect them all before nightfall. He therefore decided to spend the night in a tree, but was unable to sleep owing to the cold. In his attempts to keep warm the leaves and flowers fell on to a *liṅga* situated at the foot of the tree. His inadvertent act brought him continued good fortune and hence the custom of holding this festival.

Śiva Sūtra I. Name of the aphorisms of the Śaiva philosophy attributed to the god Śiva.

II. Name of the fourteen sūtras with which Pāṇini opens his famous treatise on Sanskrit grammar, containing a peculiar method of arranging the alphabet or alphabetical sounds, said to have been communicated to him by Śiva.

Śivāvidyā 'Jackal-science' (*śiva* or *śivālu* being a euphemism for jackal). A form of divination based on the howls and movements of jackals, generally regarded as animals of ill-omen.

Śivi or **Śibi** One of the five sons of Uśīnara, the king of the country also called Uśīnara, near Gandhāra. According to the genealogies given in the *Hariv*. (1674–9) various tribes of the Panjāb claimed descent from Uśīnara, a claim rejected by the descendants of Śivi (*MBh*., Vana pa., 131). Numerous sub-Himālayan Indo-Āryan and aboriginal tribes also claimed descent from Uśīnara (*Mārk. P*., LVIII).[1]

A Vaiṣṇava legend relates that Viṣṇu, wishing to test Śivi's faith, appeared before him in the form of a *brāhmaṇa* and demanded his son Vṛhadgarbha as a sacrificial victim. Śivi thereupon killed his son, and was then told he should partake of the offering. He was about to do so when he was stopped by Viṣṇu, who praised him for his faith and devotion and restored his son to life.

[1]But according to traditional history, Uśīnara was an Ānava, i.e., a descendant of Anu, eldest son of Yayāti and Śarmiṣṭhā, and therefore not originally of Āryan stock.

Skambha (Vedic) or **Stambha** (post-Vedic) 'Prop, support, pillar', often used in a cosmic sense, as in *RV.* (VIII.41,10) which refers to the pillar connecting the heavens and the earth.[1] The hymns of the *AV.* (X.7 and 8) mystically personify the *skambha*, regarded as a frame (or scaffolding) supporting creation. One passage (8,2) describes the *skambha* as the essence (*ātman*) of all that aspires to the life of the spirit, i.e., 'of all that breathes'. Another passage (7,17) states that whoever apprehends the *skambha* apprehends the centre or essence of all being, the *axis mundi*.[2]

The *stambha* may have developed from the large standing stones or menhirs which were erected in India by prehistoric peoples. Similar stones are still erected by the Khasis of Assam as an abode for the spirit of the dead or as memorials to them.

Numerous metaphors are employed to express the developing significance of the *skambha*, without losing sight of its primary meaning. In the *rājasūya* ceremony the king, when about to receive the unction, stands upright on the throne with his hands raised, thus representing 'the cosmic pillar resting on the navel of the earth (the throne) and reaching to the sky'.[3]

The classic Indian work on architecture, the *Mānāsara* (ch. 15), lists the various types of *stambhas* and distinguishes them according to the shape of the column itself, or the style of the base and capital. A quadrangular pillar is called Brahma-kānta; an octangular, Viṣṇu-kānta; a sixteen-sided or circular, Rudra-kānta; a pentagonal, Śiva-kānta; a hexagonal, Skanda-kānta.[4] These are further distinguished according to their dimensions and ornamental mouldings. The eight component parts of the column are also listed, and though their origin is uncertain their number is identical with that of their Graeco-Roman counterparts.

Stambhas were erected for a variety of reasons, as votive columns to Viṣṇu, Śiva, Rāma, Lakṣmī,[5] Garuḍa, etc., or as memorial and boundary pillars; or to commemorate a victory, or to obtain merit. Some pillars are marked with the *liṅga*; those erected by the Jains are generally *dīpa-stambhas* or lamp-standards; whilst those of the Buddhists bear inscriptions on their shafts, their capitals being decorated with emblems or animal figures. Vaiṣṇava pillars are generally ornamented with representations of Garuḍa or Hanumat, those of Śaivas often being in the form of flag-staffs (*dhvaja-stambhas*).

For originality and variety of design, the pillars of the historical period are without equal. They range from the simple to the great monoliths set up by Aśoka about 250 B.C., and from those to the many others successively erected up to the seventeenth century.

[1]The word *sthūṇa*, used in the *RV.* (I.59,1, etc.), is synonymous with *skambha*; but in the *RV.* (IV.5,1) and *AV.* (IX.3,1) the word *upa-mit* represents 'pillar'.

[2]Cf. the 'giant column' Irminsul, often referred to in Saxon Teutonic literature as being associated with temples as a lofty pillar, i.e., the trunk of a sacred tree symbolizing the world-pillar supporting the sky (E.O. James, *Tree of Life*, p. 160); also cf. the pillar of the Cretan Bronze Age which 'came to be regarded dynamically, as raising itself from earth to sky, as an architectural member, for the support of no visible roof, like Jachin and Boaz before the temple of Solomon' (Levy, *Gate of Horn*, p. 217). The consecrated tree of a *vodun loa* is an 'avenue of divine approach' for the god to make contact with man (Deren, *Divine Horsemen*, p. 36).

[3]Heesterman, *Ancient Indian Royal Consecration*, p. 101.

[4]Acharya, *DHA.*, p. 645.

[5]In villages of eastern Bengal it is the custom for each family to call one of the pillars of their house the Lakṣmī pillar and to worship it (ibid., p. 668).

Skanda 'Attacker.' The god of war. He is known by various names, many of them regional, such as Mahāsena,[1] Sanat-kumāra, Guhu, etc., or as Brahmaṇya or Subrahmaṇya, etc., in South India. But as Banerjea observes, 'if a careful analysis is made of the myths associated with many of these names'[2] it is apparent that from them was derived the unified idea of the god Skanda-Kārttikeya, whose worship was current in northern India in the fifth century A.D. The ancient Tamil deity Murugan was also identified with Skanda. The former was originally a mountain deity, part of whose worship consisted in orgiastic dances.

Skanda is sometimes called 'lord of *grahas*', the 'Seizers' who bring or cause diseases (*Suś. Saṁ.*, III, pp. 144f.). He is the leader of the dog-like demons who cause children's ailments (v. Sīsara). As the stealer of health Skanda is the deity of thieves, euphemistically called Skandaputras 'sons of Skanda'.

This mythological complex appears to have influenced the diverse accounts of Skanda's own origin. Thus one legend states that when Agni's seed fell into the Ganges, he was conceived by the river-goddess Gaṅgā, who subsequently hid him among the rushes on the river bank. Here he was found by the six *kṛttikās* (the personified Pleiades) and reared by them, whence his metronymic Kārttikeya. Subsequently he was assimilated with Śaiva mythology as the son of Śiva[3] and Pārvatī. Many of Skanda's attendants are similar to those of Śiva, such as animal-headed sprites, fiends of various sorts, the seven Mothers, etc.[4] His vehicle (*vāhana*) is a cock, a bird which was also sacrificed to him, accompanied by the ringing of bells.

[1]Under this name he was the tutelary divinity of the early Kadambas and Cālukyas (*IA.*, VI, p. 74; VII, p. 162, etc.).

[2]*DHI.*, pp. 362f.

[3]In Yoga Skanda represents the power of chastity, for he was born when the great yogin Śiva who, having attained complete mastery of his instincts, applied his sexual energy to spiritual and intellectual ends.

[4]*EM.*, p. 228.

v. Viśakha II; Paravāṇi.

Skanda Purāṇa One of the eighteen classical Purāṇas, which Wilson[1] considers to be a fourteenth-century redaction of a ninth-century Tamil work, the *Periapuram*. But a copy of the Purāṇa, written in the later Gupta characters of the sixth or seventh century A.D. has since been found.[2]

[1]*VP.*, Pref., xliv.

[2]Pargiter, *Mārk. Pur.*, Intro., p. xiv.

v. Skanda.

Śloka The chief Epic metre, which was developed out of the Vedic *anuṣṭubh*. It consists of four *pādas* or quarter verses, each of eight syllables, or two lines of sixteen syllables each. The *Rāmāyaṇa* fancifully derives the word from *śoka* (sorrow), an allusion to the tradition that the first *śloka* was composed by Vālmīki when grief-stricken at seeing a bird killed.

Smārta Sūtra Name of any Sūtra work based on Smṛti (traditional law). Such Sūtras are principally concerned with family and domestic rites (*gṛhya*).

Śmaśāna Cremation ground; tumulus or burial mound. But *śmaśānas* are often described as being covered with putrefying corpses among which wandered dogs and vultures. This indicates that many Vedic Indians 'did not cremate their dead, but, like the Zoroastrians of Persia, merely abandoned their bodies to the wild beasts.'[1]

The mounds discovered at Laurīya Nandangarh in Bīhar were identified by Bloch with the *śmaśāna* described in Vedic ritual. Two of them consisted of layers of clay alternating with straw and leaves, with a post (*sthūṇā*) of *sāl* wood standing erect in the centre. There was also a deposit of human bones and charcoal, and a small gold leaf impressed with the crude outline of a female figure 'interpreted as the Earth Goddess, referred to in the Vedic burial hymn'.[2]

The Āryan tradition apparently favoured four-cornered graves, which were customary for those who followed Vedic customs, whilst those of the aborigines and foreigners were limited to circular mounds (*ŚBr.*, XIII.8.1,5).

[1]Basham, *WI.*, p. 177.

[2]*CHI.*, I, p. 616.

v. Śmaśāna sādhana; Śmaśānavāsin.

Śmaśāna sādhana Magical rites performed at cremation grounds (*śmaśānas*) to gain control over malevolent spirits.

Śmaśānavāsin An epithet of Śiva as a dweller in cremation grounds.

v. Śmaśāna.

Smṛti 'Remembered', 'recalled'. A technical term applied to the whole corpus of sacred lore remembered and handed down by tradition. It is thus distinguished from the truths of the Veda which were 'heard' (*śruti*) by the ancient *ṛṣis*. But the term also denoted secondary works. In its widest acceptation *smṛti* includes six principal subjects, viz., the six Vedāṅgas; the Smārta Sūtra; the Dharmaśāstras or Law books; Itihāsas or legendary poems and the Kāvyas, etc.; the eighteen Purāṇas and the eighteen minor Purāṇas (Upapurāṇas); and the Nīti-śāstras.[1]

[1]*IW.*, pp. 155ff.

Ṣoḍaśī Lit. the 'maiden of sixteen'. Sixteen signifies totality and thus perfection. Ṣoḍaśī is third in the list of the ten *mahāvidyās*, and is identified in the *Ṣoḍaśī Tantra* with the goddess Tripurasundarī, who represents 'the light radiating from the three eyes of Śiva.'[1]

[1]*HP.*, p. 278.

Soma I. The name of a particular plant and of its juice which, after being ritually filtered,[1] was sometimes mixed with water, milk, butter or barley. The sap[2] apparently had strong intoxicating or more probably hallucinogenic properties. The *soma* ceremony is generally regarded as identical with the Avestan *haoma*,[3] which constituted the central rite of Zoroastrian worship.

In the *RV.* (III.48,2) the *soma* is said to be 'Mountain-born', or brought from the sky by an eagle (IX.86,24), and thus considered to be of divine origin. In other *RV.* passages its shoots '*aṁśu*' (I.168,3) are described as ruddy '*aruṇa*' (VII.98,1), or tawny '*hari*' (IX.92,1) and its juice called '*andhas*' (III.48,1), though in some passages this may refer to the husk after pressing. But none of these descriptions make it clear if the *soma* was a shrub or species of succulent, or what was the natural flavour of its juice, as it appears after filtering to have varied from sweet to distasteful, and if drunk to excess to produce nausea, as when Indra drank undiluted *soma* (*ŚBr.*, IX.4.4,8; XII.7.1,14).[4]

Soma juice was the essential libation of all early Vedic sacrifices, ostensibly as an offering to the gods, incidentally as a desirable drink for the priestly officiants and those participating in the sacrifice. Like other powerful drugs in many parts of the world, *soma* became an object of worship, the focus of an extensive mystical ritual, and the subject of a vast literature based on the 'Family Books' of the *RV.* In some passages grandiloquent epithets are applied both to plant and juice, enhanced by extravagant metaphor, or veiled in mystical fantasies, so that it is often difficult to distinguish product from process, and the botanical plant from its mythical counterpart in Indra's Paradise. In other passages *soma* is called celestial dew, or rain—the milk of the heavenly cows (clouds). The inspiration of the sacred hymns are also ascribed to its qualities (*RV.*, X.76,4). Its exhilarating effects made 'it possible to share—though fleetingly and imperfectly—in the divine mode of being; it achieves ... the paradox of at once possessing the fulness of existence, and becoming; of being at once dynamic and static'.[5] This is borne out by *Suś. Saṁ.* (II, p. 535) where by means of *soma* man develops the eight godly powers, thus enabling him to emulate the divine Īśāna.

In the *RV.* Indra's power is sometimes derived from *śacī* (energy), but in (III.40,2) it is from the strength-conferring *soma* juice. Later portions of the *RV.* extend the benefits to be derived from it. To these the *YV.* pays little attention, and the *AV.* still less, most references being to its medicinal properties. Such changes are even more marked in the *ŚBr.*, which refers to the difficulty of obtaining the *soma* plant, and recommends the substitution of the brown *phālguna* or the *śyenahṛta*, etc. (IV.5,10,1–6).[6] Other passages interpret *soma* in a metaphorical sense, which appears to lack any connexion with its *RV.* prototype. Another passage (III.9.4,22f.) attempts to explain the deification of *soma* by a clumsy pun, coupled with the use of esoteric terms having no etymological validity.

During the Gupta period the name *soma* was applied to twenty-four species individually classified according to 'the difference of their habitats, structure, epithets and potencies' (*Suś. Saṁ.*, II, p. 530). Though retaining an element of religious significance, the so-called *soma* was mainly applied medicinally 'for the prevention of death and decay of the body'. But the extraction of the juice was still ritually performed, the bulb of the *soma* plant being pricked with a golden needle and the milky exudation collected in a golden vessel. Then a draught was given to the patient who had already undergone the necessary purificatory and other rites (*Suś. Saṁ.*, II, p. 531).

Attempts have been made by botanists and others to identify the Vedic *soma* plant, but only one seems to offer a valid solution. This appeared in a work by von Bibra, entitled *Die narkotischen Genussmittel und der Mensch*, published in 1855. It was the first book of its kind and provided the basis over the next hundred years for the study of the plant-lore of ancient cultures. The study of hallucinogens in the past thirty or forty years owe their success to the data gleaned from many seemingly unrelated fields of investigation, such as anthropology, ethnobotany, medicine, linguistics, etc.[7] During the past century and a half numerous plant species, including the Ephedra, Periploca and Sarcostemma, have been suggested as being the Vedic *soma*, but all for various reasons have been rejected. But the independent researches of J.M. Allegro[8] and R.G. Wasson[9] into the fly agaric mushroom (Amanita muscaria), show that its psychical and physical effects seem to conform very closely to those produced by the Vedic *soma*.[10]

[1]This follows the pressing or 'crushing' of the *soma* plant between stones (*adrī* or *grāvan*). The process is completed when the juice 'flows freely' (*pavamāna*), a result regarded as a divine act rather than the result of physical effort (v. *OST.*, II, p. 469; V, p. 258). After pressing and filtering both *soma* (and *haoma*) are said to be of a yellowish colour.

[2]The sap 'is the manifestation *par excellence* of the life-giving principle' (Heesterman, *Ancient Indian Royal Consecration*, p. 193).

[3]The present Pārsīs of Kermān and Yezd claim that the juice they obtain from the *hūm* shrub is identical with the *haoma* of the *Avesta* (Eggeling, *ŚBr.*, II, Intro., xxivf.). After a lapse of 3000 years, during which many substitutes for the original *soma* plant have appeared, such a claim obviously cannot be substantiated.

According to the *Avesta* the *haoma* became incarnate in the ancient hero called Duraosha and Frashmi (the discoverer of *haoma*) who immolated himself. From his body his divine essence streamed giving wisdom, courage, inspiration, exhilaration, as well as immortality (*Yasna* IX.1; *Yasht.* X.90, cited by James, *Tree of Life*, p. 80; v. also Heesterman, *Ancient Indian Royal Consecration*, p. 109). The *ŚBr.* (III.9.4,17; IV.9.4,14) states that whilst pressing (i.e., killing) the *soma* plant the utmost sympathy must be shown to it.

[4]The *Suś. Saṁ.* (II, pp. 532f.) states that vomiting is a result of the action of *soma* on worm-infested parts of the body.

[5]Eliade, *Patterns*, p. 162. Cf. the Dionysiac drugged frenzies and their accompanying oracular powers.

[6]Changes were also taking place in Iranian sacrificial rites, as is indicated by Zarathustra's attempts to ban animal sacrifice and the excesses of the *haoma* rites

(*HCIP.*, I, p. 221).

[7]R.E. Schulter, *Bulletin on Narcotics*, vol. xxi, no. 3, pp. 1 and 5, July–September 1969, United Nations, New York.

[8]Allegro considers that 'many of the most secret names of the mushroom go back to ancient Sumerian, the oldest written language known to us, witnessed by cuneiform texts dating from the fourth millennium B.C. and which provide a bridge between the Indo-European and the Semitic groups' (*Sacred Mushroom and the Cross*, Intro., p. xvf.).

[9]*Soma, Divine Mushroom of Immortality* (Ethno-Mycological Studies, I, 1968).

[10] Bharati considers that the states of mind described after taking *soma* are 'much closer to alkaloid drug experiences than to alcoholic intoxication' (*TT.*, p. 287). For the use of hallucinogens in Shamanism v. Michael J. Harner (ed.), *Hallucinogens and Shamanism*, Oxford, 1973.

v. Amṛta; Soma II; Indu.

II. From being a divine sacrificial libation of Vedic origin, *soma* is portrayed in the *MBh.* and Purāṇas as the lord of stars and planets, of priests and plants, of sacrifices and devotions (*VP.*, I.22). He is identified with the moon[1] and is said to have married the twenty-seven *nakṣatras* (representing the lunar asterisms), the daughters of Dakṣa.[2] Owing to his failure to share his affection equally among them he became afflicted with a wasting disease for half of each month, an allusion to the waning of the moon.

[1]v. R.G. Wasson, *Soma, Divine Mushroom of Immortality*, pp. 69f.

[2]Cf. the myth in the *Tait. Saṁ.* (II.3,5) which states that King Soma married thirty-three of the daughters of Prajāpati.

v. Soma I; Candra; Oṣadhi; Budha; Bṛhaspati; Rohiṇī.

Somadeva The moon-god and lord of plants.

v. Soma II; Oṣadhi.

Somadeva Bhaṭṭa The writer or compiler of the *Kathāsaritsāgara* (Ocean of the Streams of Story),[1] an eleventh-century collection of more than 350 stories, fables, anecdotes, etc. Somadeva broke with the conventional traditions of story-telling and invested them with realistic imagery.

[1]A complete translation into English was made by C.H. Tawney, originally published by the Asiatic Society of Bengal and later edited with notes by N.M. Penzer.

Somānanda A younger contemporary of Vasugupta. He approached the problems of Ultimate Reality rationally; criticized Śāktyadvayavāda (Śākta monism), as well as the teaching of various Hindu, Buddhist and Jaina schools.

Sphoṭa v. Śabda.

Śrāddha[1] A supplementary rite to the funerary ceremony,[2] performed in honour of a deceased relative and as a reminder that death does not break the link between past and present, or between the living and the dead.

This rite includes the daily offering of water, and on particular occasions an offering of funerary cakes (*piṇḍas*)[3] to the three immediate generations of the deceased's paternal and maternal forbears. This ensures that their ethereal bodies shall not lack nourishment and so be unable to accumulate merit, which would impede their progress through future births and delay their final union with *brahman*. The *śrāddha* may also be a means of accumulating merit for those who perform it sincerely and reverently. On the other hand, unsuitable offerings invalidate the rite. Thus unconsecrated grain or lentils, gourds, garlic, onions, or red vegetable extracts should not be offered. Salt is similarly banned, as is also impure water, or that drawn by night, or the milk of animals having uncloven hoofs, etc.[4] Moreover, the *śrāddha* should be performed in private, or in a secluded place, lest it should be witnessed by a eunuch, an outcaste, a heretic, or a pregnant woman, etc., and result in the rejection by the deceased of the offerings as unclean (*VP.*, III.16).[5]

[1]Faith (*śraddhā*), whence the rite (*śrāddha*) derives its name.

[2]But it may also be connected with occasions of rejoicing.

[3]A custom common in many countries to which it probably spread from Sumeria, where adequate provision was made for the dead and 'sometimes renewed by monthly offerings' (James, *Tree of Life*, p. 213).

[4]According to the *Rām.* (49,9) only the meat of wethers was offered at *śrāddhas* (*IRA.*, p. 204).

[5]v. also *Ancestor Worship*, pp. 157f.

v. Ekoddiṣṭa; Preta; Pitṛ.

Śraddhā 'Faith', and its personification as a goddess. In the *RV.* (X.151), Śraddhā is implored to endow her worshippers with firm belief and confidence, for only by faith is Agni kindled, and without faith offerings to the gods are vain. A single reference occurs in the *AV.* (V.7,5), attributing faith to the drinking of *soma*. But the *Kauṣ Br.* (VII.4) declares that the sacrifice of one whose offerings are accompanied by faith endures forever.

v. Śrāddha; Dakṣiṇā.

Śrauṣat A ritual exclamation used in making an offering with fire to a god or departed spirit. Exclamations like *śrauṣat*, *vaṣat*, *svāhā*, etc. were regarded as possessing protective powers. There are six modes of uttering *śrauṣat*, each being magically potent (*ŚBr.*, XI.4.2,5–12).[1]

A myth, probably intended to indicate that sound is eternal, appears in the *ŚBr.* (XII.3.3,1–3) which relates that when the gods began a sacrificial ceremony requiring a thousand years for its completion, they discovered at the end of five hundred years that the *sāmans*, metres, etc., had become worn out. All that remained of the sacrifice were the ritual exclamations, the *śrāvaya*, *śrauṣat*, *yaja*, *yajāmahe* and *vaṣat*.

[1]Cf. the ritual cries of the ancient Greeks: 'Iacchos', 'Bacchus', etc., which later were personified as gods (Harrison, *Prolegomena to the Study of Greek Religion*, p. 543; Gaster, *Thespis*, p. 32).

v. Śabda.

Śrauta-sūtra(s) Name of particular *sūtras* or *sūtra* collections based on sacred traditions or on texts of the Veda. They were composed to elucidate the sacrificial instructions contained in the Brāhmaṇas, which had become obscure over the years.

There are Śrauta-sūtras for each of the five *saṁhitās* of the Veda. For the *RV.*, the Āśvalāyana, Śāṅkhāyana and Śaunaka; for the *SV.*, the Maśaka, Lāṭyāyana and Drāhyāyaṇa; for the Taittirīya or Black *YV.*, the Āpastamba, Baudhāyana, Satyāṣādha-hiraṇya-keśin, Mānava, Bhāradvāja, Vādhūna, Vaikhānasa, Laugākṣi, Maitra, Kaṭha and Vārāha; for the White *YV.*, the Kātyāyana; for the *AV.*, the Kuśika.[1]

[1]*IW.*, p. 157. But Bloomfield (*The Atharvaveda*, p. 16) also mentions the anonymous Vaitāna.

Śreṇi A guild—a group of men practising the same occupation. Some kind of elementary guild system may have existed in Vedic times, but by the fifth century B.C. guilds existed in all important towns and covered almost all trades and industries, including even a guild of thieves![1] Some guilds became wealthy and acted as merchant bankers and trustees of religious endowments.

The guilds 'created very solid bonds that extended over ... the whole of India ... [and] also constituted a powerful economic lever',[2] often giving a social status to a particular guild that would generally have been denied it, and distinguishing particular occupations from those of aboriginal and other tribes engaged in hunting, trapping, fishing. Such occupations, being tainted by the destruction of life, excluded those practising them from the guild system.

'As a sign of its power, every guild possessed a special seal (*nāmamudrā*) made of bronze, copper, ivory, stone or terracotta, imitating in this the king, his ministers and his dignitaries.'[3] The Buddhist Jātakas enumerate eighteen[4] traditional handicrafts, including those of wood-workers, smiths, painters; workers in stone, ivory, precious metals, copper and iron; weavers, potters, makers of agricultural implements, weapons, etc. With the economic growth of the country, the guilds rapidly increased in number and influence.

[1]Basham, *WI.*, p. 217.

[2]Auboyer, *Daily Life in Ancient India*, p. 102.

[3]Ibid., v. also Shastri, *India as Seen in the Bṛhatsaṁhitā*, pp. 317f.

[4]But Auboyer, op. cit., p. 102, states that about thirty can be compiled from available sources.

Śrī I. 'Prosperity', 'good fortune'; the term occurs once in the *RV.* (VIII.2,19), but frequently in the *AV.* (VI.54,1; 73,1; etc.) and later.

II. Prosperity or Luck[1] (*śrī*) personified as a goddess. The *ŚBr.* (IX.4.3,1–5) describes her as a goddess, resplendent and shining, who emerged from Prajāpati after his creation of all other beings.[2] She is the embodiment of all good things desired by gods and men, the former being even prepared to kill her for them. But Prajāpati rebuked them, reminding them that men do not kill women, and that Śrī would not withhold her gifts. Some of the gods, lacking faith in Prajāpati's assurance, decided to help themselves to Śrī's possessions. Agni chose her 'store of good', Soma her royal attributes, Varuṇa her universal sovereignty, Mitra her royal rank, Indra her power, Bṛhaspati her holy lustre, Savitṛ her dominion, Pūṣan her wealth, Sarasvatī her prosperity, and Tvaṣṭṛ all the manifold aspects of her beauty. Śrī complained to Prajāpati, who told her that the gods had only borrowed her possessions, which they wished to use at the sacrifice they were performing, and that after its completion they would be restored to her.

This brief account of Śrī became the basis for numerous myths, linking her with the goddess Lakṣmī, the post-Vedic goddess of good fortune, who emerged from the Churning of the Ocean (*samudramathana*). The association of Śrī and Lakṣmī and the varied nature of the myths connected with them, suggests the assimilation of numerous folk traditions.

Śrī is said to dwell in garlands (*mālās*), and hence the wearing of them brings good luck, prosperity and victory. When Indra allowed a garland presented to him to fall to the ground he is said to have lost *śrī*.[3] Śrī is also associated with rice cultivation, and after her death a rice plant grew from her navel.[4] Among her other fertility aspects is her association with dung (hence her epithet Karīṣin, 'abounding in dung'), and her connexion with food and soil.[5]

[1]As Demokritos well said: 'Men have feigned an image of Luck, a mask of their own folly' (cited by Farnell, *Cults*, vol. V, p. 447).

[2]Cf. the birth of Pallas-Athene from the aching head of

Zeus. Śrī was adopted by the Buddhists and is often depicted seated on a lotus between two elephants who pour water over her from their uplifted trunks, as in the Hindu Gaja-Lakṣmī images. Śrī is also associated with the metres (v. Gonda, *Aspects*, p. 187).

[3]Gonda, Ibid., p. 224.

[4]Ibid., p. 220, and v. n. 43. Cf. the 'nine plants' (*navapatrikās*) associated with Durgā, one of which is rice.

[5]Gonda, *VS.*, p. 71.

v. Gaurī, n.4; Śrīvatsa.

III. In the primary sense of 'lustre', *śrī* is often used as an honorific prefixed to the name of particular divinities. Thus Rāma is frequently referred to as Śrī-Rāma, Durgā as Śrī-Durgā, etc. The prefix is sometimes repeated two or more times to express great veneration and is often applied to the names of eminent persons.

Śrī-cakra v. Yantra.

Śrīpañcamī The fifth day of the light half of the moon in the month of *māgha* (January–February), when a festival is held in honour of Sarasvatī, goddess of learning, at which books and writing materials are worshipped.

Śrīphala 'Fruit of fortune', i.e., the fruit of the *bilva* tree (Aegle marmelos). On the death of a holy man the *śrīphala* or a conch-shell (*śaṅkha*) is used to crack the skull to allow his spirit to escape.

v. Brahmarandhra.

Śrīvatsa 'Favourite of Śrī', goddess of good fortune. A particular mark or sign (*lakṣaṇa*) denoting a great man or signifying divine quality or status, which is depicted by a triangle, cruciform flower, or simply by a whorl of hair on the chest as on the images of Viṣṇu and Kṛṣṇa.[1]

The *śrīvatsa* is also depicted on certain Buddhist and Jaina images. Its origin is uncertain, as is indicated by the myths invented to explain it, such as the one which explains Viṣṇu's *śrīvatsa* as the result of water having been thrown at his chest by Bharadvāja.[2]

[1]Banerjea mentions two figures in the Madras Museum which combine that of the goddess Śrī and the *śrīvatsa* (*DHI.*, p. 376 and P1. XIX, figs. 1 and 3).

[2]*EM.*, p. 184.

v. Lakṣmī; Śrī.

Sruc A long-handled ladle with a spout made of *palāśa* or *khadira* wood and used for pouring ghee (*ghṛta*) on the sacrificial fire.

v. Juhū; Upabhṛt; Dhruva; Sruva.

Śrutavatī A daughter of Bharadvāja, begotten when he saw the nymph (*apsaras*) Ghṛtācī. She practised extreme austerities (*tapas*) so that she could become Indra's wife.

Śruti 'Hearing.' Sacred knowledge of the Veda 'heard' by the ancient *ṛṣis* and orally transmitted by *brāhmaṇas* from generation to generation. This term originally applied to the Mantra and Brāhmaṇa portion of the Vedas, but was later extended to the Upaniṣads and other works.

Sruva A small wooden spoon used for pouring ghee into the *sruc* (ladle). This spoon, if made of *palāśa* or *vikaṅkata* wood, will prevent *rākṣasas* from interfering with the sacrifice (*ŚBr.*, V.2.4,18).

v. Juhū.

Stambha v. Skambha.

Sthaladevatā A tutelary divinity presiding over a particular region.

Sthānu 'Immovable'; 'standing firmly'. A certain posture taken up by certain holy men (*sādhus*) who vow to remain for months or even years perfectly motionless.[1]

Sthānu is also an epithet of Śiva, and refers to his great ascetic practices (*tapas*) when he stands like a trunk or post until the dissolution of the universe. There are references to the presence of Śiva on columnar altars in the earlier sections of the *MBh.*

[1]v. Gonda, *VS.*, pp. 14; 148, n. 114.

Sthūṇa Wooden memorial columns erected in Vedic burial grounds (*RV.*, X.18,13). Similar columns, called *yūpastambhas*, were erected by kings and nobles to commemorate their performance of various Vedic sacrifices and were probably the prototype of the votive columns (*dhvajas*) erected before temples in honour of Vāsudeva-Kṛṣṇa, Kubera, etc.

v. Indramaha.

Subala A ruler of Gandhāra and father of Gāndhārī, wife of Dhṛtarāṣṭra, the Kaurava king.

v. Mahābhārata; Pāṇḍu.

Subhadrā The sister of Kṛṣṇa, wife of Arjuna and mother of Abhimanyu.

v. Jagannātha.

Subrahmaṇya An ancient Dravidian folk-divinity who became identified with Skanda, the god of war. Subrahmaṇya's Tamil name is Murugan 'the divine child'. He has many names including Kumāra, Mahāsena, Guha, etc., which suggest that there are a number of allied god-concepts 'at the root of the later unified idea of a deity by the name of Skanda-Kārttikeya'.[1]

[1]*DHI.*, p. 362. In South India he is still believed to possess the power to drive away illnesses (Diehl, *Instrument and Purpose*, p. 228).

Śucī One of the six daughters of Tamrā and Kaśyapa. Śucī and her sisters are part of the Kaśyapa creation myth, each of them becoming the mother of particular groups of birds (*VP.*, I, 21).

v. Bhāsī; Śyenī.

Sudarśana 'Fair to see.' The name of Viṣṇu's wheel or discus (*cakra*) symbolizing the limitless power of his mind, and the speed of his thought. During its ceaseless revolutions the worlds are created, sustained and destroyed (*VP.*, I.22).[1] Its symbolism is probably derived from the three-naved wheel on which the three worlds rest, referred to in the *RV.* (I.164,2). Later the wheel became identified with the sharp-edged *cakras* used as missiles in warfare, by which Sudarśana is said to kill all enemies. It is also invoked to 'cut through' malevolent incantations (*AGP.*, 307, 17–19).

Like most emblems of the gods, the Sudarśana was personified and portrayed as a small figure (*cakrapuruṣa*) with round eyes and drooping belly, on whose head the left hand of Viṣṇu rests (*Viṣṇudharmottara*, III.85, 13–14).[2] The *cakra* was adopted by Jainas and Buddhists to represent the teaching of their respective leaders.[3]

[1]v. also *EHI.*, I, Pl. i. and p. 291n.

[2]The fragment of a large sculpture, now in the Ashmolean Museum, Oxford, depicts the *cakrapuruṣa* as a small male figure standing in front of a wheel.

[3]P.D. Mehta, *Early Indian Religious Thought*, p. 105.

v. Āyudhapuruṣa.

Sudās v. Daśarājña; Tṛtsu(s); Bharata.

Sudāsa[1] A king of Ayodhyā and descendant of Sagara of the Solar Dynasty. As the result of Sudāsa's extensive conquests, the North Pañcāla power increased rapidly, but after his death its power declined and the kingdom was finally conquered and divided, North Pañcāla passing to Droṇa, South Pañcāla to Drupada, whose daughter Draupadī became the wife of Yudhiṣṭhira.

[1]'Sudāsa has been identified with the Vedic Sudās of the *daśarājña* . . . but beyond mere similarity of names, there is nothing in support of this identification' (*HCIP.*, I, p. 289).

Śuddha-Śaiva or **Āgamānta Śaiva** A Śaiva cult based on the twenty-eight Śaiva Āgamas, regarded as having been directly revealed by Śiva, and therefore believed to be *śuddha*, i.e., 'pure', 'free from error'.

The three principals of the cult are the Lord Pati, i.e., Śiva; the individual 'soul' (*paśu*); and the fetters (*pāśa*) binding the 'soul' to worldly existence. The four stages of religious life are: practical piety and the correct performance of duties and rites; initiation; the practice of Yoga; and the highest knowledge, which enables the individual 'soul' to attain union with the deity.[1]

[1]S. Shivapadasundaram, *Shaiva School of Hinduism*, pp. 177f.; v. also *EHI.*, II, pp. 361–70.

v. Śūdra.

Śūdra The fourth social class. The origin of the word is obscure and cannot with any certainty be identified with Ptolemy's Sudroi, considered by him to be the name of Indian aboriginal tribes opposed to the Āryans. The word *śūdra* occurs in the *Puruṣa sūkta* (*RV.*, X.90,12). The latter, being a hieratical composition, naturally gave pride of place to the *brāhmaṇa*, next to the *rājanya* or ruling class, then to the *vaiśya* or agriculturalists and craftsmen, and lastly to the *śūdras*, generally assumed to refer to the menial classes, irrespective of their ethnic origin, but particularly to aboriginals or prisoners of war. Nonetheless, the *śūdras*, unlike the wild tribes of mountain and jungle, constituted a part of Vedic society, although not 'twice-born', and hence not eligible for initiation into the Indo-Āryan community. The position of the *śūdra* (mythologically represented as emerging from the feet of the cosmogonic Puruṣa) clearly indicates the *śūdra's* position in relation to the other classes which emerged from what were regarded as the more important parts of the Puruṣa. Nonetheless, two kinds of *śūdras* were recognized: 'not-excluded' and the 'excluded', the latter being almost indistinguishable from those who later became known as Untouchables.

Occupational class distinction appears to have existed in India before the arrival of the Āryans, as is indicated by the use of separate buildings for priests, merchants and craftsmen at Mohenjo-daro. Similarly in other early communities functional differentiation, often implying social distinction, was common. But to the Āryans the initial distinction between themselves and the Indian indigenes was the difference in colour (*varṇa*) of their skins, and hence the contrasting terms, *ārya-varṇa* (white) and *dasyu-varṇa* (dark) or *kṛṣṇa-varṇa* (black).

The conquest of the *dasyus* resulted in the virtual enslavement of the survivors, and the gradual readjustment of the relationship of the three superior classes to each other, as well as their collective relationship to the *dasyus*. But economic expansion, political changes, and the resurgence of brahmanical power and influence during the Gupta period were accompanied by the creation of numerous new occupations and crafts no longer regarded as strictly menial. This is indicated by the gradual and selective fusion of the Āryans with individuals of Dravidian origin, which deprived colour distinction of much of its relevance, so that the term *ārya* came to signify Indo-Āryan. It was contrasted not with *dasyu* but with *śūdra*, and the establishment of two social divisions, like that of master and serf.[1] Nonetheless, there is evidence of flexibility in their relationship, unlike the rigidity of the later caste system. The *Maitri Up.* (7,8) refers to *śūdras* who know the

Śāstras; and the *Chān. Up.* (4.4,1–5) to Satyakāma Jābāla who, despite being the natural son of a *śūdrī*, became a pupil of the *guru*, Hāridrumata Gautama.

Kauṭilya's *Arthaśāstra* (III.13), a civil rather than a hieratical code of laws, records not only contemporary views concerning *śūdras* but also reflects those of an earlier age. It states that a *śūdra* who has been freed might, according to circumstances, be classed as an Ārya; that the selling of a *śūdra* child of an Āryan father, brought up as an Āryan, shall be punishable by a fine; that anyone robbing a slave of his money, or depriving him of his privileges shall also be fined. Furthermore, an Ārya who has sold himself into slavery shall regain his Āryahood (*āryatvam*) on repayment of the purchase price.[2]

Doubtless the status and treatment of *śūdras* varied regionally, but during the late Vedic age they were generally given the protection of the law.[3] Other factors were instrumental in the modification of caste rules, such as the acceptance by the Buddhists of all converts, irrespective of caste. Tantrists and Śuddha-Śaivas also allowed *śūdras* to participate in their rites.

Changed conditions also resulted in the partial break-down of the barriers between *vaiśya* and *śūdra*, and led to the enhanced status of some *śūdras*, who became well-to-do and even succeeded in marrying their daughters into royal families.[4]

As occupational variations both of the skilled[5] and unskilled had always existed, constantly affecting the social status of all sections of the community, a new definition of caste was required to maintain differentiation of the classes. To establish such a system it became necessary to introduce other factors, such as primary lineage (*gotra*), and family lineage (*kula*), so that occupation was no longer the chief criterion of social status.

[1]According to Pāṇini, *ārya* means 'master' (*svāmī*), the term denoting all three superior classes, not because of their Āryan blood, but because they were 'masters', i.e., freemen. The term *śūdra* may have also denoted a conquered people, 'as Karian became synonymous with slave at Athens' (*CHI.*, I, p. 234), but the *śūdras* were not pariahs, and they took part in some domestic rites (ibid.).

[2]*Manu* (II.31f.) states that the first part of a *śūdra*'s name should denote the contemptible nature of his status, the second the particular occupation assigned to him. A dead *śūdra* should be carried out of the southern gate of a town, but a corpse of the 'twice-born' through any of the other gates (V.92; X.41).

[3]Cf. *Ait. Br.*, VII.29.

[4]Sumitrā, one of the four wives of Daśaratha, was a *śūdrī*. There were also *śūdra* kings (Basham, *WI.*, p. 144).

[5]Among the later skills was the making of images, traditionally regarded as a craft of the *śūdras* (Eliade, *Yoga*, p. 403).

v. Brāhmaṇa I; Śreṇi.

Sudyumna v. Iḷā.

Sugrīva I. The so-called monkey or ape-king, a son of Sūrya.[1] After being dethroned by his brother Bālin, he was later reinstated by Rāma at Kiṣkindhyā.

[1]All the great legendary apes, Nīla, Dvivida, Maindra, etc., are said to have had divine fathers. From the description of their exploits they were probably proto-Australoid tribesmen of huge stature and ape-like appearance.

II. The emissary sent by Śumbha to solicit the hand of Ambikā in marriage.

Sugrīvī A daughter of Kaśyapa and Tamrā, who appears in the plan of 'secondary' creation as the mother of camels, horses and asses (*VP.*, I.21).

v. Dakṣa.

Śuka A parrot. The name is probably derived from *śuc*, 'the bright one'. Śuka is invoked to remove jaundice from the worshippers of Sūrya the sun-god, and to transfer it to parrots and starlings, or to *haritāla* trees (*RV.*, I.50,12).

Sukanyā v. Cyavana.

Śūkara The name of one of the hells (*narakas*) to which various types of evil-doers are consigned. To Śūkara, the 'swine hell', go those guilty of the murder of a *brāhmaṇa*, or those who have stolen gold or drunk wine, or any who associate with such persons.

Śukra I. Also called Uśanas. According to one tradition (*MBh.*, Ādi pa., 65), he was the son of a *ṛṣi* who became a priest of the *asuras*,[1] i.e., non-Āryan Indian tribes, or that he acted for them in their disputes with over-zealous *brāhmaṇas*. When at one point indigenous customs conflicted with those of the Āryans, the *brāhmaṇas* appealed to the gods who appointed Bṛhaspati to act for them. In the ensuing struggles both sides suffered casualties, but those of the *asuras* were quickly restored to life by Śukra, of whose skill in the science of re-vivification (*saṁjīvinīvidyā*), Bṛhaspati was ignorant. To obtain the secret, the gods decided that Bṛhaspati's son Kaca should become Śukra's pupil and by stratagem obtain it. This he succeeded in doing after several hazardous experiences.[2]

Śukra is said to be a son of Bhṛgu and hence his patronymic Bhārgava. He is also called Kavi or Kāvya, the poet. Like many other mythical *ṛṣis*, Śukra became a star-god and was made Regent of the planet Venus, whence the *Nir.* (8,11) derives his name, the 'Bright

One', from the root *śuc*, 'to shine'. In other contexts *śukra* means semen, sperm, seed.

[1]According to the *Maitri Up.* (7,9), Bṛhaspati, the preceptor of the gods, became Śukra, the teacher of the *asuras*.

[2]The account of which is given under the entry 'Kaca'.

v. Navagraha; Devayānī.

II. An alternate name of the month *jyaiṣṭha* (May–June), personified as the guardian of Kubera's treasure.

Sūkta A Vedic hymn as distinct from a *ṛc* or single verse. The term later denoted a wise saying, a song of praise, etc.

Sūktānukramaṇī The index of Vedic hymns, generally attributed to Śaunaka.

Śūla v. Triśūla.

Śulva-sūtra(s) The name of 'those portions or supplements of the Kalpa-sūtras, which treat of the measurement and construction of the different *vedis* or altars, the word "*sūtra*" referring to the cords which were employed for those measurements'.[1] The two most important treatises dealing with the subject are the *Śulva-sūtras* of Baudhāyana and Āpastamba.

[1]*DHA.*, p. 800. These sūtras may 'be regarded as the oldest books on Indian geometry' (*HCIP.*, I, p. 475).

Sumati v. Sagara; Gaṅgā.

Śumbha Name of an *asura*. He and his brother Niśumbha are among the chief characters of a dramatic poem, interpolated in the *Mārk. P.* (cantos 85–90). They are referred to as wealthy *asuras*, the possessors of 'gems, precious stones, elephants, horses and of all the most desirable things that exist', the one exception being Ambikā (a form of Pārvatī the goddess of Mount Himavat) whom Śumbha's servants Caṇḍa and Muṇḍa unexpectedly came upon as she was bathing in the Ganges.

The two servants reported their discovery to Śumbha and urged him to acquire 'this gem of womankind'. Śumbha immediately dispatched Sugrīva as his emissary to seek her hand in marriage. Ambikā (here called Durgā) replied: 'Only he who vanquishes me in battle, who can break my pride, or match my strength in the world, shall be my husband. Let Śumbha or Niśumbha come and try!'

In the sanguinary battles that ensued, Durgā assumed various shapes, and successively destroyed the *asura* armies and their generals. When Niśumbha was slain, Śumbha continued the fight, but so sorely pressed was Durgā that only with the aid of the respective energies of Brahmā, Viṣṇu, Śiva and Indra was she able to continue the fight. Only after a succession of horrific battles was Śumbha slain.

v. Śakti(s).

Sumeru v. Meru.

Sumitrā The *śūdra* wife of Daśaratha and mother of Lakṣmaṇa and Śatrughna.

Śunaḥśepa The second of the three sons of Ajīgarta, a poor *ṛṣi*, who figures in the story of Hariścandra, a king of the Solar dynasty who, despite his numerous wives, was childless. Finally he appealed to Varuṇa to grant him an heir, vowing that if his prayer was granted he would offer the child as a sacrifice (*Ait. Br.*, VII,13–18). When the boy Rohita was born Varuṇa reminded the king of his vow, but agreed to postpone the sacrifice. When the boy was old enough to bear arms his father told him of the vow, whereupon Rohita fled to the forest where he lived for three (or six) years. During this time his father, stricken with dropsy, lived miserably with his barren wives.

One day Rohita met the recluse Ajīgarta and offered him a hundred cows if his eldest son would replace him as the sacrifice to Varuṇa. At first the *ṛṣi* refused, but finally agreed to the sale of his second son, Śunaḥśepa, who was then bound to the sacrificial stake (*yūpa*). But his father refused to act as executioner unless he received an additional herd of cows. Śunaḥśepa invoked Viśvāmitra who directed him to pray to Varuṇa, the Aśvins and Agni to save him. He did so and immediately his bonds fell away. Simultaneously his father's dropsy was cured and the vow to Varuṇa was regarded as having been fulfilled.

The reference to a *ṛṣi* of the same name in the *RV.* (I. 24,12f.; and v. V.2,7) who prayed to Varuṇa to release him from the bonds binding him to three pillars, suggests the existence of human sacrifice (*puruṣamedha*) among some tribes in early Vedic times, a practice which the legend finally condemns.

The legend of Śunaḥśepa is recited at the *rājasūya* ceremony probably because of its reputed efficacy in ensuring the birth of sons (*Ait. Br.*, VII.18), the lack of which was considered to retard the course of the universe (*ŚBr.*, IX.4.1,5).

Śunā-sīra 'Ploughshare and plough',[1] personified as agricultural divinities (*RV.*, IV.57,5). A ceremony (*śunāsīrya*) performed at the close of the three four-monthly seasonal offerings for the gaining of *śrī* (prosperity) (*ŚBr.*, II.6.3,2; V.2.4,4). In the *Tait. Saṁ.* (I.8,7) *śunā-sīra* is an epithet of Indra, an allusion to his association with vigour and fertility.

[1]The *Nir.* (9.40) identifies them with Vāyu and the Āditya.

Sūnṛtā 'Gladness', personified as a goddess (*RV.*, I.40,3), and giver of wealth (X.141,2; *AV.*, III.20,3).

Śūnya I. The Indian mathematical sign for 'nought' or zero. Its equation with *ākāśa* 'space' has a literal parallel in the practice of the ancient Egyptian scribes of leaving a blank space to denote zero. The Indian method of numeration, far more comprehensive than that of ancient Egypt or Greece, began with the invention of the nine numerical figures, and the nought (*śūnya*), and of assigning a decuple value to each according to its position in the series, each regarded as of divine origin. Thus the unit (*eka*), with the addition of *śūnya* denoted ten (*daśa*), which with the successive addition of a nought, denoted a hundred (*śata*), a thousand (*sahasra*), ten thousand (*ayuta*), a hundred thousand (*lakṣa*), a million (*prayuta*), ten millions (*koṭi*), a hundred millions (*arbuda*), a thousand millions (*abja* or *padma*), ten thousand millions (*kharva*), a hundred thousand millions (*nikharva*), a billion (*mahā-padma*), ten billions (*śaṅku*), a hundred billions (*jaladhi* or *samudra*), a thousand billions (*antya*), ten thousand billions (*madhya*), a hundred thousand billions (*parārdha*).[1]

[1] *IW.*, p. 193.

II. 'Void', 'nothingness'.[1] As a Hindu philosophical term *śūnya* (zero) 'was originally conceived as a symbol of *brahman* and *nirvāṇam* ... the unifying point of indifference and the matrix of the All and the None'.[2]

Mahāyāna Buddhism, especially the Mādhyamika school, whilst not denying the existence of empirical reality, declared that it was 'void' of ultimate reality when stripped of its empirically conceived attributes.

[1] Dr Guenther in a letter to Bharati (*TT.*, p. 35, n.5) describes *śūnya* 'as neither capable of being made fuller nor capable of decrease ... It is thus a plenum—in the philological Latin sense, not in the philosophical sense'.

[2] Heimann, *Facets*, p. 24.

Suparṇa An eagle or vulture (*RV.*, II.42,2; *Kauṣ. Br.*, XVIII,4), noted for its strength and swiftness. Like the Vedic Garutman, Suparṇa may possibly have been a prototype of Garuḍa[1] who was regarded as the King of Suparṇas. A myth in the *MBh.* (Ādi pa., 33) relates that when Garuḍa flew away with the *amṛta* from Paradise Indra hurled his *vajra* and hit the great bird, but only a single feather fell to earth. So beautiful was it that all who saw it were made happy, and henceforth Garuḍa was called Suparṇa (having fine feathers or wings).

[1] Dange (*Legends*, Pref., x) considers Garuḍa and Suparṇa to be separate deities, but Garuḍa is called Suparṇa in *VP.* (I, 21).

Suparṇī 'Wide-winged', i.e., the heavens (*Tait. Saṁ.*, VI.1,6). In an obscure myth (*ŚBr.*, III.2,4,1–7; 6,2,2–8) Suparṇī and Kadrū are said to be two illusions created by the gods when they wished to bring *soma* down from the sky so that they might sacrifice together. Suparṇī is regarded as the mother of metres, especially of the *gāyatrī*.

Surā 'Intoxicating liquor';[1] 'wine,' and name of the goddess personifying it.[2] The properties of *surā* are likened to those of *soma* juice (*RV.*, VIII.2,12), and if improperly used tend to lead men astray (*RV.*, VII.86,6). But in variant *ŚBr.* passages *surā*, like *soma*, was regarded as a source of strength, and provided Namuci with the means of sharing Indra's *soma*-derived power (XII.7.3,1). *Surā* was therefore sometimes mixed with *soma*, i.e., 'the strong with the strong', thereby endowing with energy the sacrificer partaking of it (XII.7.3,5). The *Ait. Br.* (VIII,8) refers to *surā* as a lordly power and the essence of food.

The *Suś. Saṁ.* (Intro., p. xxxii) refers to *surā* as an anaesthetic, but to some Śāktas it was employed as a stimulant, the goddess (Surādevī) being the presiding deity of the wine used in the ritual of the 'Five M's'. The meat-eating *yakṣas* and *rākṣasas* invariably drank *surā* or some other spirituous liquor at their feasts. The drinking of *surā* plays an important part in the *vājapeya* ceremony. Heesterman considers that it also played an important part in a now lost version of the *rājasūya*.[3]

[1] Perhaps a spirit, as it was 'distilled or matured' (*ŚBr.*, XII.7.3,6). Eggeling (*ŚBr.*, pt. v, pp. 223f.) refers to the ingredients as being malted rice and barley, fried rice, spices, ferments, nutmeg, areca-nut, cloves, ginger, etc. But *Manu* (XI.95) states that there are three kinds of *surā*: that distilled from molasses, ground rice, and madhūka flowers respectively. Hopkins considers *surā* to have been a rice-brandy (*ERE.*, XI, p. 686).

[2] The goddess Surā is equated with Vāruṇī, the consort of Varuṇa. Wine was the most potent 'vehicle of Bacchic possession or divine communion, being the quintessence of that god-life that moved in the "juices and sap of the earth"' (Farnell, *Cults*, V, p. 122).

[3] *Ancient Indian Royal Consecration*, p. 110; and v. Dange, *Legends*, pp. 194 and 234. But *Manu* (XI.94) condemns the practice, declaring that as '*surā*' is the refuse (*mala*) of grain, the drinking of liquor produced from it by *brāhmaṇas*, *kṣatriyas* and *vaiśyas* is strictly forbidden.

v. Madyam; Madirā.

Śūra Name of a Yādava king, the father of Vasudeva and Pṛthā (later known as Kuntī), and grandfather of Kṛṣṇa.

Surabhi or **Surabhī**[1] The 'Cow of Plenty', also called Kāmadhenu, the first of the 'treasures' to emerge from the Churning of the Ocean (*samudramathana*) by the gods and asuras (*VP.*, I.9). She is the subject of numerous myths where she represents the endless proliferation of Nature, and hence her identification with the rich lands of Āryavārta and the Madhyadeśa, whose possession was the cause of constant wars in ancient times, and of the feud between successive Viśvāmitras and Vasiṣṭhas.

[1]Perhaps derived from *su* + root *rabh*, 'affecting pleasantly'.

v. Dilīpa; Jamadagni.

Surādevī v. Surā.

Śūrpa or **Sūrpa** A kind of wicker sieve or winnowing basket[1] used for ritual as well as for domestic purposes. It is sometimes personified as a *gandharva*.[2] Gonda[3] suggests that Lakṣmī may have been originally a corn goddess, as she was believed to manifest herself in seedlings grown in a winnowing basket.

When the *śūrpa* is carried by the goddess Śītalā, it is regarded as a divine attribute.[4]

[1]*Nir.*, 6,9, states that the *syam* is a winnowing basket and *śūrpam* a sieve for winnowing grain, the latter being derived from *śṛ* 'to fall off'.

[2]*SED.*

[3]*Aspects*, p. 218. The Greek Ergane was 'worshipped with winnowing fans set upright' (Farnell, *Cults*, I, p. 315, n. b.). Jane Harrison suggests these fans were a 'memento of the primitive agricultural Athens' (*Classical Review*, p. 270, 1894).

[4]v. Auboyer and de Mallman, 'Śītalā la Froide', *Artibus Asiae*, XIII. (1950), pp. 207ff.

Śūrpaṇakhā 'Having fingernails like winnowing fans.' The name of Rāvaṇa's sister who fell in love with Rāma. When he rejected her she turned to his brother Lakṣmaṇa by whom she was similarly treated. Enraged by her rejection she attacked Rāma and his wife Sītā, but Lakṣmaṇa intervened and cut off her nose and ears.[1] To avenge herself she urged Rāvaṇa to abduct Sītā, an action which led to the death of Rāvaṇa and the destruction of his kingdom.[2]

[1]She was only disfigured, it being regarded as sinful to slay a woman.

[2]Another version is given in the *AGP*. (ch. 7).

Sūrya[1] or **Savitar** The two names most frequently used in the *RV.* to denote the sun and the Sun-god. Sūrya is probably derived from the Vedic *sur* or *svar* 'to shine',[2] the latter being etymologically identical with the Iranian *hvare*, and having the same meaning. The sun may be represented anthropomorphically or by symbols such as the wheel or disc (*cakra*),[3] or by the opened lotus flower (*padma*) to denote its creative function, but in some hymns it is described as a celestial bird called Garutman, or as a beautiful white horse accompanying Ūṣas, the goddess of the dawn (*RV.*, VII.77,3). Sūrya's one-wheeled chariot, representing the annual cycle, is drawn by bay or red mares (I.115,3–4, etc.);[4] or by one horse called Etaśa (VII.63,2).

Sūrya is the Āditya *par excellence*, the other Ādityas, referred to individually by name or collectively as seven (IX.114,3), or eight (X.72,8), though all associated with light[5] are generally only epithets or aspects of the sun.

In the *AV.* Sūrya has a cosmogonic significance; he surveys the whole world, sees beyond the sky, the earth and the primordial waters (XIII.1,45);[6] from him man derives his visionary faculties (VIII.2,3).[7] He possesses curative powers and thus is the preserver of life; as light he represents immortal life, which man may attain after his ascent from the dark valley of death (VII.53,7). But in the *ŚBr.* (II.3.3,7–8) Sūrya is said to represent death[8] as well as life, and to be the intermediary between darkness and light.[9] Thus all creatures in the terrestrial sphere must inevitably die, because they are subject to time; but those who ascend to the celestial sphere attain immortality. Hence Savitṛ (the Sanskrit form of Savitar) is the celestial door to immortality (*Chān. Up.*, 8.6,5), for the sun is the centre of creation, the point where the manifested and unmanifested worlds unite (3,19,1). As the sun consists of fire which forever consumes itself[10] it is identified with the Cosmic Sacrifice, and is the Cosmic Being who rises as life and fire (*Praśna Up.*, 1.6,8).

In the Upaniṣads the notion of the sun is generally expressed in metaphorical terms as is indicated in the *Maitri Up.*, 6,34, which states that 'the splendour of Savitṛ should be constantly meditated upon, because he is the mediator abiding in the intellect.'

Subsequently, Sūrya, like the other Vedic gods, became little more than a Paurāṇic mythical figure, to be superseded by the former minor solar deity, Viṣṇu, who became the second 'person' of the Hindu triad (*trimūrti*), and regarded by Vaiṣṇavas as the supreme manifestation of the Self-Existent (*brahman*).

[1]Cf. the Hittite word for sun '*šurias*' (Hertfeld, *Iran in the Ancient East*, p. 182). A number of Vedic solar deities were merged in Hinduism into the sun-god Sūrya (Basham, *WI.*, p. 312).

[2]*Nir.* (12,14; and v. 16) derives *sūrya* from *sṛ* 'to move'; or from *sū* 'to stimulate', or from *svīr* 'to promote well'.

[3]The Mitanni kings similarly employed these as emblems of the sun (James, *Tree of Life*, p. 115); v. also H. Frankfort, *Cylinder Seals*, Pl. XLII. a,b,e, and o).

[4]A metaphor preserved in North European mythology. Cf. the myth of the sun's stallion (Eliade, *Patterns*, p. 148); and the sun-chariot of Trundholm.

[5]Hence a white animal without blemish should be

offered to the Sun (*Ait. Br.*, IV.19).

[6]Demeter requested the sun-god Helios to find Persephone for her: 'while in the cognate Hittite myth of Telipinu, it is that deity who is first summoned to discover the whereabouts of the missing god' (Gaster, *Thespis*, p. 215 n.). Similarly the sun-goddess retrieves the Canaanite Baal from the netherworld (ibid., p. 215).

[7]According to the Egyptian Hermopolitan tradition the gods emerged from the Sun-god's mouth; men from his eyes (Reymond, *Mythological Origin of the Egyptian Temple*, p. 83). Socrates regarded the eye as having affinity with the sun (Plato, *Republic*, VI.18).

[8]As Death dwells within the immortal sun, he (Death) cannot die (*ŚBr.*, X.5.2,3; v. also verse 4 and n.2).

[9]It was popularly believed that the sun's disc after each journey across the heavens turned over, so that its light side alternately lit up the earth and the stars. The sacrificial fire is identified with the sun's fire (*BIP.*, p. 122, n.4; v. also *Praśna Up.*, I.6,8).

[10]Actually the sun is in a state of equilibrium. Thus as the result of the conversion of hydrogen to helium by nuclear reaction in its interior, the sun's mean molecular weight tends to increase, so that the quantity of energy radiated remains equal to the energy produced. Although our sun is insignificant in the galaxy as a whole, it is the source of life for us (*Atlas of the Universe*, ed. by H. E. Butler).

v. Saura(s); Rohita; Sūryā; Etaśa; Gāyatrī; Tārkṣya; Sūryakānta; Sūryavaṁśa.

Sūryā Daughter of the sun-god Sūrya. In a composite and very late *RV.* hymn (X.6–17) Sūryā is referred to by name, and her impending marriage described in a succession of extravagant metaphors and obscure allusions. The remainder of the hymn, verses 18–47, are devoted to the subject of marriage in general. In a charm to obtain a wife the Aśvins are said to have carried Sūryā away as a bride (*AVB.*, VI,82; cf. *RV.*, I.34,5).

Sūryabhānu The name of Kubera's gatekeeper, slain by Rāvaṇa.

Sūryakānta 'Beloved of the Sun.' The epithet of the sun-stone, believed to be formed from the rays of the sun, as is the moon stone (*candrakānta*) from the rays of the moon.

Sūrya Siddhānta Explanation or 'Solution of the Sun', an Indian astronomical treatise, believed to have been composed in the sixth century B.C. 'The original version was subsequently re-edited, for there are references which coincide with events in the fifth century [A.D.] and possibly even later.'[1] Its mythical ascription to the sun (Sūrya) is explained by the custom of regarding the sun as the source of all knowledge. It has been suggested that the treatise owed much to Alexandrian influence, but this is not apparent in extant recensions.

[1]Filliozat in *Ancient and Medieval Science*, p. 141.

v. Jyotiṣa; Siddhānta.

Sūryavaṁśa The Solar dynasty or line of kings, whose founder Ikṣvāku claimed descent from the sun-god Sūrya. There were two branches of the line, one represented by Ikṣvāku's eldest son Vikukṣı, who ruled at Ayodhyā, the other, represented by a younger son Nimi, at Mithīlā. Both the Buddha and the Jaina *tīrthaṅkara* Mahāvīra, as well as many notable kings, including Rāmacandra, claimed descent from the Solar dynasty.

v. Candravaṁśa.

Sūṣaṇā[1] A goddess invoked to ensure easy parturition by 'loosening' the womb.

[1]The derivation of her name is unknown. Whitney suggests that *sūṣaṇā* may be the name of a female organ. (v. also *AVB.*, p. 244.)

Suṣena I. Son of Kṛṣṇa and Rukmiṇī.

II. A physician attached to Rāma's army. He was believed to be able to restore the dead to life.

Śuṣṇa 'Parcher.'[1] Name of a Vedic demon causing drought, who was overthrown by Indra (*RV.*, I. 11,7).[2] Śuṣṇa was one-horned, probably an indication of his great strength,[3] and was the possessor of 'magical devices' (*RV.*, VI.20,4).

He is sometimes referred to as a *dānava*, who stole the divine elixir (*amṛta*) which he held in his mouth, but Indra transformed himself into a lump of honey, and then into an eagle (*śyena*), and finally snatched it from Śuṣṇa's mouth.

[1]Cf. *śuṣ*, 'drying or withering'.

[2]According to the *ŚBr.* (III.1.3,11) the gods slew Śuṣṇa.

[3]Cf. the power attributed to the mythical unicorn.

Suśruta Saṁhitā[1] 'Compendium of Suśruta.' A medical work compiled by Suśruta,[2] which represents the views of the school of medicine founded by Ātreya, and later developed by Caraka in his *saṁhitā*. These two works are regarded as the basis of the Āyurveda, the science of Indian medicine. Traditionally Suśruta's work is said to represent the doctrines of Divodāsa, an incarnation of the divine physician Dhanvantari, the possessor of *amṛta* or elixir of immortality.

Though Suśruta's work reflects some ancient notions about the demonic cause of disease and about the efficacy of magic as a remedy, it also attempts to present a rational classification of diseases and methods of treating them. Particular attention was paid to breathing, not merely as a respiratory act, but one to which the mind should contribute, because breath is *prāṇa*, the 'vital essence'.

As the study of medicine developed, traditional interpretations and analogies were submitted to critical examination,[3] and logic became an essential element in testing the validity of theory.

[1]An E. translation by K. L. Bhishagratna was published at Calcutta, 1907–18, and reprinted in three volumes in 1963.

[2]The date of its compilation is uncertain, attributions varying from the fourth to second centuries B.C.

[3]Filliozat, 'Ancient Indian Science' included in *Ancient and Medieval Science*, p. 157.

Sūta Originally the general term for a charioteer, whose role was also to relieve the boredom of the king or warrior during long journeys.[1] Later the *sūta* became a court official, usually a royal herald or bard, or possibly 'Master of the Horse'. The *sūta* ranked with the Commander-in-Chief of the Army, and other high officers of the Court.[2]

[1]*HCIP.*, I, p. 431.

[2]*CHI.*, vol. I, p. 297.

Sutāla One of the seven nether-worlds, which extend below the earth for 70,000 *yojanas*. It contains magnificent palaces inhabited by *dānavas*, *daityas*, *yakṣas*, etc. (*VP.*, II.5).

Sūtra(s) Lit. 'Thread'.[1] Later the term was applied to compositions written in an aphoristic style. *Sūtra* may possibly be derived from *siv*, 'to sew', applied to the stitching together of the leaves of manuscripts. The earliest *sūtras* were local law-manuals, called Gṛhya and Dharma Sūtras, the former dealing with the sacrificial rites of the householder and his family, the latter with their relationship to the community and its leaders. These *sūtras* were compiled by individual priestly schools during a period dating from the sixth or seventh centuries B.C. to the second century A.D.,[2] the Gṛhya being naturally influenced by local traditions, the Dharma, because of their more general nature, being less subject to local variation.

The Gṛhya and Dharma *sūtras*, though their source was the Veda, were regarded as *smārta*, whereas the rules relating to the great sacrifices, were regarded as divinely revealed (*śrauta*). But with the growth of population, the founding of larger kingdoms, and the development of the economy, the Gṛhya and Dharma *sūtras* proved to be inadequate and had to be supplemented. They were gradually superseded by successive and more comprehensive Dharma-śāstras, which culminated in the *Manu-smṛti*,[3] written in an expanded metrical, easily memorized form, and not in the terse obscure style of the *sūtra*.

The *sūtra* style was adopted in all Indian quasi-philosophical systems, but necessitated commentaries, such as those on Pāṇini's grammatical treatise called the *Brahma-sūtra*, etc.

[1]Cf. L. *sutor*, a cobbler; E. *suture*, to sew together.

[2]*CHI.*, vol. I, p. 227.

[3]The *sūtras* may be regarded as the first step in the evolution of legal literature: for the metrical *śāstras* or law-books are only the extension and completion of the rules of the Dharma *sūtras* (*CHI.*, vol. I, p. 228).

v. Vedāṅga.

Sūtrātman The spiritual essence (*ātman*) that passes like a thread (*sūtra*) through the whole universe.

Svadhā 'Offering.' The term is applied to the offering due to each god, or to any oblation or libation, especially that offered to the *pitṛs*,[1] who to sustain themselves are said to feed upon the essence of the offering. *Svadhā* is personified as a daughter of Dakṣa and Prasūti, or of Agni. She is regarded as the wife of one class of *pitṛs* and as the mother of others.

[1]In honouring the *pitṛs* 'the word *svadhā* is the highest benison' (*Manu*, III.252). Both *svadhā* and the reverence paid to the *pitṛs* are 'ritual entities' which create a 'place' (*loka*) for them to exist in (Gonda, *Loka*, p. 65).

v. Svāhā.

Svāhā A ritual exclamation or call[1] uttered when making oblations to the gods (*RV.*, I.13,12, etc.). It is the 'terminal constant in all Hindu and much Buddhist ritual, and in *mantras* which accompany oblations and libations, actual or metaphorical.'[2] *Svāhā* also possesses magical powers (*ŚBr.*, VI.6.3,17).

Svāhā is personified as a goddess and identified with Umā, to whom women pray when desirous of offspring.[3]

[1]Cf. the Gr. goddess Ioulô, whom the *iouloi*, or 'howls' of Demeter's devotees were supposed to invoke; the Sumerian god Alala, created from the *alala* or ritual wail; the Basque hero Lelo, lamented in traditional folk songs, is merely 'a projection of the *lelo*, or dirge' (Gaster, *Thespis*, p. 32). In most languages of the ancient world the words for 'howl of pain' and 'cry for joy' are undifferentiated or akin, both going back to a single onomatopoeic root meaning simply 'yell' (ibid., p. 34).

[2]*TT.*, p. 271, n.34; v. also *ŚBr.*, I.5.3,14; 5.4,5.

[3]*EM.*, p. 230.

v. Śrauṣat.

Śvan 'Dog.' It is probable that dogs were not unfavourably regarded in pre-Vedic India, as is indicated by numerous post-Vedic myths reflecting ancient beliefs concerning them. Thus Indra, when he disguised himself as a beggar is accompanied by a dog;[1] Rudra is called lord of dogs (*śvapati*);[2] and Śiva in his form of

Bhairava is usually accompanied by a dog. Yama's realm is guarded by two brindled hounds.

The Macedonian leader Alexander greatly admired the huge hunting dogs of the Indian kings. These animals were probably similar to the modern Tibetan mastiff.[3] Nonetheless, there was prejudice (perhaps regional) against dogs in early Vedic times, and they were regarded as unsuitable as sacrificial offerings. Moreover, if a dog,[4] boar, or ram came near the sacrificial fire when the *agnihotra* offering was placed on it, expiatory rites had to be performed (*ŚBr.*, XI.4.1,4). When the horse sacrifice (*aśvamedha*) was performed, a dog was clubbed to death and its body floated away beneath the belly of the horse, the dog representing the malevolent forces threatening the sacrificer (XIII.1,2,9).

Whooping cough was likened to the barking of a dog, and children so afflicted were said to be possessed by Bhairava.[5] A *MBh.* legend relates that when Yudhiṣṭhira was invited to enter the celestial realm, he was denied entry on refusing to part with his dog, but was recalled by Indra who commended his fidelity to the animal.[6]

Dog-demons were believed to cause epilepsy in children, and hence the necessity of propitiating them. The *Āpastamba Gṛhya Sūtra* (VII. 18,1) gives details of the rite.

[1] *EM.*, p. 137.

[2] Small effigies of dogs made of sugar are offered to Śiva (Herzog, *Psyche and Death*, p. 52). The *Tait. Saṁ.* (IV.5,4) refers *inter alia* to the homage to be paid to 'hunters, dog-leaders, dogs and lords of dogs'.

[3] The Persian Emperor Artaxerxes I (465–424 B.C.) 'exempted the inhabitants of four Babylonian villages from taxation in return for their breeding Indian dogs for war and hunting. These dogs were also known in the Egypt of the Ptolemies' (*WI.*, p. 196). Herodotus (VII.187) records that an immense number of Indian dogs followed the army of Xerxes in his invasion of Greece.

[4] A Persian MS. giving instructions for the magical invoking of spirits, states that if dogs come near the invoker 'his power (*barakat*) will be completely destroyed' (S. Indries Shah, *Oriental Magic*, p. 105).

[5] *Madras Christian College Magazine*, January 1907, VI. no. 7, cited by Thurston, *Omens*, p. 196.

[6] This legend supports the claim that the Pāṇḍavas were probably of non-Āryan origin.

v. Sīsara; Saramā; Sārameya(s); Śvāśva.

Śvaphalka v. Gāndinī.

Svapna 'Sleep'; 'the unconscious state of consciousness'. Śiva as lord of sleep, represents the final dissolution of the personality, the cessation of self-manifestation.[1] According to the *Bṛhad-Ār. Up.* (4.3,9), man is subject to being in this world or in the other world, or in an intermediate third condition, i.e., that of being asleep, when one sees both worlds.

[1] Sleep is one of the 'five sins' which a yogin must 'cut off' (Eliade, *Yoga*, p. 151, n.21).

Svar v. Svarga; Vyāhṛti(s).

Svarbhānu Name of a demon (*asura*) who causes darkness, probably an allusion to a solar eclipse (*RV.*, V.40,5), from which the Atris are said to have rescued the sun (*Kauṣ. Br.*, xxiv. 3 and 4). Indra fought the demon (*ŚBr.*, V.3.2,1), and Soma (the moon-god) and Rudra effectively dispelled the darkness caused by him; in the *AVB.* (II.10,8) the gods are said to have released Sūrya and Ṛta from his clutches. In later mythology Svarbhānu is identified with Rāhu, the eclipse demon.

Svarga[1] The heaven or paradise of Indra. The word is perhaps related to '*svar*',[2] meaning the 'light of heaven', i.e., the sun, or it may refer to the region between the sun and the Pole Star (*dhruva*).

The *ŚBr.* (VI.6.2,4) states that the portal of heaven is in the north-east. In post-Vedic mythology Indra, Kuvera and other gods each have their own heaven, situated on one or other of the mythical mountains of the Himālaya. The notion that the 'good' attain *svarga* occurs in the *VP.* (II.2), and that before entering it they are said to acquire divine forms and to be free of all 'sin'. By the proper performance of a sacrifice, the sacrificer was enabled to attain *svarga*, 'or the quality of a god (*devātman*) after death'.[3]

In the *Chān. Up.* (8.3,4–5) heaven is represented by the notion of the Real (*satyam*) which is presented as *sat-ti-yam*. '*Sat*' represents being, the immortal, '*ti*' the mortal, and '*yam*' that which holds the two together. He who knows this goes to the heavenly world.[4]

[1] The etymology of the word is not known, but some scholars consider that '*ga*' belongs to '*gam*', to go, i.e., going or leading to the light, to heaven, etc. (Gonda, *Loka*, p. 73). Cf. *Svarog*, the Slavonic word for 'heaven' (Sykes, *Dictionary of Non-Classical Mythology*).

[2] When Prajāpati emerged from the golden egg (*hiraṇyagarbha*) he uttered the words *bhūḥ* (or *bhūr*), *bhuvaḥ* (or *bhuvar*), and *svaṇ* (or *svar*), which became the earth, air and sky respectively (*ŚBr.*, XI.1.6,1–5). In the *Chān. Up.* (4.17,3) Prajāpati extracted *svar* from the *sāman* chants.

[3] Eliade, *Yoga*, p. 110.

[4] Hume, *TPU.*, p. 265.

v. Gotra; Preta(s); Pitṛ(s); Brahmaloka; Indraloka.

Svarṇa v. Santāna.

Svasti-devī Goddess of the home who protects, and

confers prosperity (*RV.*, IV.55,3), not only on the household, but also on any of its absent members (*RV.*, X.63,16). Hence she may be identical with the goddess Pathyā-svasti, the personification of the 'prosperous way or path'[1] (*Tait. Saṁ.*, VI.1,5; *AVB.*, III.4,7), and the embodiment of success and well-being.

[1]Cf. Pūṣan, the guardian of roads and travellers, etc. who may be Svasti-devī's male counterpart.

v. Svastika.

Svastika I. 'Swastika.' Lit. 'Of good fortune', from *su* 'well' and *asti* 'being'.[1] An auspicious mark or emblem placed upon persons or things. It is shaped like a Greek cross, the arms bent at right angles 卐 . This is the right-handed *svastika* associated with the sun, and hence an emblem of the Vedic solar Viṣṇu and symbol of the world-wheel, indicating cosmic procession and evolution round a fixed centre.

In astronomy the auspicious form of the *svastika*, represents the solstitial change of the sun to the Tropic of Capricorn, and is regarded as male. The left-handed *svastika*, indicating an anti-clockwise movement, represents the sun during Autumn and Winter, and is regarded as female and inauspicious.

The *Bṛhat Saṁ.* (LV.15) states that the *svastika* and other auspicious marks should be depicted on temple doors.[2] It was often painted on houses[3] and cattle-sheds, etc., to protect families and animals from the Evil Eye. Its origin is uncertain, but examples have been found in the Indus Valley, Mesopotamia and Palestine,[4] South America and on Easter Island, etc.

[1]Whitney, *CD.*, p. 6102.

[2]v. also Acharya, *DHA.*, p. 733; Bhattacharyya, *Canons of Indian Art*, p. 39.

[3]Cf. Hindī *sathiyā* 'mystical mark of good luck'; Gujarātī, *sāthiyo*, an 'auspicious mark painted on the front of a house' (*IAL.*, 13916).

[4]Hrozný, *Ancient History of Western Asia*, pp. 19, 166, 187, fig. 112. Arabs maintain 'that a special virtue resides in its form alone' (S. Idries Shah, *Oriental Magic*, p. 81).

II. Name of a Nāga, and of one of Skanda's attendants. The warriors of some Nāga tribes, particularly those of Magadha, wore *svastikas* when at war.[1]

[1]*EM.*, p. 28.

Śvāśva 'Having a dog for a mount.' An epithet of Bhairava (a form of Śiva) who rides (or is accompanied by) a dog (*śvan*).

Svayaṁbara From *svayam*, 'one's own', and *bara* or *vara*, 'choice', the right exercised in ancient times by girls of noble birth to choose a husband. The *svayaṁbara* was a pre-marriage ceremony, usually a kind of tournament to which were invited eligible young men whose skill in archery, spear-throwing and similar activities was put to the test.[1] The competition was preceded by a recital of the names, lineage,[2] and accomplishments of those taking part. At the end of the tournament, the girl in whose honour the *svayaṁbara* was held, placed a garland of white flowers round the neck of the man of her choice, generally the most skilled competitor, as was Arjuna at Draupadī's *svayaṁbara*. This freedom to choose a husband follows an ancient tradition[3] which was subsequently lost when women became subservient to men (*Manu*, V. 147f.).[4] But the marriage of Draupadī (to the five Pāṇḍu brothers) was a practice common among many Himālayan tribes. Subsequent legends deny that she contracted a polyandrous marriage, which indicates the strong views held by brahmanic traditionalists.

[1]For other forms of *svayaṁbara*, v. *WI.*, p. 169. The Cālukya King Vikramāditya VI (11th cent.) obtained his brides by this method.

[2]The importance of lineage is indicated by Karṇa's rejection at Draupadī's *svayaṁbara*.

[3]Charles Autran, *L'Épopée Indoue*, p. 18, considers that the custom was general in parts of Western Asia, and not unknown in ancient Greece, where a chariot race arranged by the father of Hippodamia was won by Pelops, the man of her choice, whose bride she became, despite her father's objections.

[4]Cf. the freedom accorded to women in the legend of Devayānī and Śarmiṣṭhā and the high status of Buddhist women indicated in I.B. Horner's *Women under Primitive Buddhism*.

v. Mahābhārata; **Arjuna**.

Svayambhū Lit. 'Self-existent', or 'unoriginated'.[1] It is doubtful if such a profound philosophical notion was intended to represent anything more than a Supreme Creator or a personified creative principle, like Puruṣa, Prajāpati or Brahmā. Nonetheless, such a notion confirms the existence of a Vedic tendency to co-ordinate natural forces into a monotheistic concept. Thus Svayambhū in the Purāṇas is made the basis of an elaborate cosmogonic theory, which postulated a succession of worlds, and immense periods of time, each introduced by a 'secondary creator' or Manu, the first being Svāyambhuva the son of Svayambhū. But in the *Bṛhad-Ār. Up.* (2.6,3) *svayambhū* is used as an epithet, signifying the 'self-existent' nature of *brahman*, the essence (*ātman*) of 'being', a notion fully expressed in the *advaita* doctrine of the Vedānta and in the closing passage of the *Manu-smṛti* (XII. 123 and 125).

[1]In the Mahāyāna Ādibuddha system, the Ādibuddha is called the 'self-existent'; the ancient Egyptian god Ptah was also styled the 'self-begotten' (Gaster, *Thespis*,

p. 401); and in an Egyptian morning hymn the sun is addressed as: the 'divine youth who came into being out of thyself' (H. Frankfort, *Ancient Egyptian Religion*, p. 17).

Svāyambhuva Name of the first Manu, and first of the fourteen mythical Creators or Progenitors, who successively rule the fourteen periods called *manvantaras*.

In the *VP*. (I.7) Brahmā is said to have converted himself into two persons, one male, the Manu Svāyambhuva, the other female, called Śatarūpā. Svāyambhuva is thus said to be both born of, and identical with, Brahmā.

v. Svayambhū; Manu I.

Svedaja 'Born of sweat', i.e., engendered by moist and humid conditions, an archaic biological notion of particular pre-Vedic cultures of India, and which, as Eliade observes, 'is very well illustrated by the theory and practice of *tapas*',[1] (lit. 'heat', 'ardour'), a term used generally to denote ascetic effort. Thus by *tapas* ascetics might obtain a degree of power rivalling that of the gods, and hence the reason for sending nymphs (*apsarasas*) to seduce the *ṛṣis* and ascetics.

The sweat generated by the priest during the performance of certain rites was regarded as proof of his devotional fervour (*tapas*). In a rite against enemies sweat is smeared on the points of arrows (symbolizing the potency of the magic being directed against an enemy) (*Kauśika Sūtra*, 47,44).

When Prajāpati wished to create the world, he could do so only by 'heating' himself, i.e., by the practice of extreme asceticism (*Ait. Br.*, V. 32,1). This 'magical sweating' is also a feature of Shamanism.[2]

[1]Eliade, *Yoga*, p. 106; v. also Blair, *Heat in the Ṛig Veda and Atharva Veda*, pp. 108f.

[2]Eliade, op. cit., p. 106.

Śvetāmbara 'White-clad.' One of the two principal Jaina schools, whose ascetic practices are less extreme than those of the Digambaras.

Śvetāśvatara Upaniṣad One of the thirteen principal Upaniṣads. Nallaswami Pillai[1] considers it to be a 'genuine Upaniṣad of the Black *Yajur Veda*, and is one of the oldest of its kind . . . It expounds both a theoretic philosophy and a practical religion, all-comprehensive and all-embracing, a system at once Sāṁkhya and Yoga, dualistic and monistic, and appealing to all classes of society.'

[1]Cited by Hume, *TPU*., p. 469.

Śyāmā 'Black'; 'dark-coloured'. A form of Durgā worshipped by Tantrists.

Syamantaka v. Satrājita.

Śyena An eagle, hawk, falcon or other bird of prey. A mythical eagle is said to have brought the celestial *soma* down to earth.

v. Śyenī.

Śyenī The mythical mother of eagles, hawks, etc, described as the daughter of Tamrā and Kaśyapa (*VP*., I.21).

T

Tāḍakā A female vegetal godling (*yakṣiṇī*) who was changed into a malevolent spirit (*rākṣasī*) for having disturbed the *ṛṣi* Agastya's devotions. She was subsequently killed by Rāma.

Taittirīya Saṁhitā v. Yajurveda.

Takman A kind of fever mentioned in the *AV.*, which occurs usually in the autumn (IX.8,6). Its symptoms consist of extremes of temperature and a severe cough, called the 'missiles of *takman*'. They may also be accompanied by a spotted, reddish or yellow skin condition.[1] Four entire hymns of the *AV.* (I.25; V.22; VI.20; VII.116) are devoted to the disease and its cure. Most of the remedies consist of incantations, or of invocations to Agni to transfer the disease to other tribes, or to 'wanton female menials' (*śūdrī*). A popular remedy was to place a frog against the skin of the sufferer in the belief that its cold and clammy surface would have a cooling effect and also absorb the fever.

[1] In India jaundice often accompanies malaria, which may be one of the forms of *takman*. The *SED.* states that *takman* refers to a number of diseases, especially those of a consumptive nature.

v. Maṇḍūka; Kuṣṭha.

Takṣaka A Nāga chief, a descendant of Viśāla (*AV.*, VIII.10,29); the *VP.* (I.21) states that he is a son of Kadrū.

Bright, blue-hued pearls, believed to be rain-producing, were said to be obtained from the hoods of serpents descended from Takṣaka and Vāsuki (*Bṛhat Saṁ.*, LXXX, 25–6). These two, as well as Śeṣa and the goddess Manasā are still worshipped in Bengal during the rainy season.[1]

[1] *DHI.*, p. 346.

Tāla I. The 'fan-palm', from which a spirituous liquor is produced. The demon Dhenuka is said to have dwelt in a palm-grove.

v. Tālaketu.

II. A hell to which were condemned those guilty of murdering a *kṣatriya*, *vaiśya* or *brāhmaṇa*, or one who violates a preceptor's bed, or engages in other 'sinful' practices (*Manu*, IX.235).

v. Naraka I; Pātāla.

Tālaketu 'Palm-bannered.' A term denoting the palm-tree emblem depicted on Baladeva's banner.

Tamas 'Darkness, disintegration, dispersion, inertia.' One of the three *guṇas* or constituents of *prakṛti* in the Sāṁkhya system. It is the centrifugal force leading to disintegration and dispersion, and is the opposite of *sattva*, the centripetal force of cohesion. As the characteristic of darkness, *tamas* is stated in the *Maitri Up.* (5,2) to have existed alone at the beginning of the world. Only when activated did the process of differentiation commence, giving rise to a multiplicity of forms.

Tamas is also identified with Śiva, as the lord of sleep, who represents the utter silence and darkness into which all activity dissolves at the dissolution of the world.

Tāmisra One of the twenty-one (or twenty-eight) hells to which are condemned those who have accepted bribes from an avaricious king or who act contrary to the institutes of the sacred law (*Manu*, IV.87f.), such as stealing property, or enticing women from their families (*Bhāg. P.*, III.30,28, etc., *PI.*). The specific crimes enumerated include not only injuring a *brāhmaṇa* by a man of the three superior classes, but also threatening to do so, the penalty being a hundred years in the *tāmisra* hell (*Manu*, IV.165).

Tāmra The father of five daughters, the wives of Garuḍa, whose offspring comprised all species of birds (*Brahmāṇḍa P.*, II.19,11–12, etc., *PI.*). This is one of several myths purporting to explain the origin of various forms of terrestrial life.

v. Tāmrā.

Tāmrā One of Daksa's daughters married to Kaśyapa. She produced five daughters: Kakī, Śyenī, Bhāsī, Dhṛtarāṣṭrī and Śukī, who became the mothers of crows, hawks, vultures, ducks, parrots, respectively.

Tāṇḍava[1] The name of Śiva's cosmic dance of creation and destruction.[2] It represents the turning of the Cosmic Wheel, with 'the two different phases of the movement, the active upward drive on one side and the passive downward trend on the other ... [which reveal] the two alternate phases of the cosmic cycle: its emanation and evolution in Space and Time, and its dissolution and reabsorption into one unchanging Essence in all things. With respect to Śiva, they represent the two aspects of his divine Līlā, the forthgoing activity by which he veils himself in the *māyā* of creation, and the withdrawing activity, by which he releases all created forms from ... *Saṁsāra* and reintegrates them into his own Being.'[3] Thus the orbit of his dance is the whole universe; 'its purpose is release'.[4]

The *tāṇḍava* possibly originated as a fertility dance, its symbolism becoming more complex over the years. The connexion between dancing, fertility and creation is indicated in the *RV.* (X.72,6) which relates that the gods, like dancers, stirred up the dust from which the earth was formed.[5]

[1]The name is said to be derived from that of the *ṛṣi* Taṇḍi [or Taṇḍu], the first human being to receive the Śaiva doctrine from the Rudras (*IT.*, p. 143; v. also Singhal, *India*, I, pp. 218f.).

[2]Cf. Dionysos who 'unites the dark side of Death with the most radiant aspects of life' (Herzog, *Psyche and Death*, pp. 115f.).

[3]*CHS.*, pp. 182f.

[4]Kramrisch, *Indian Sculpture*, p. 106.

[5]Cf. the Judaic David who danced mightily before the Lord (II. Samuel, 6,14). This was obviously some kind of fertility dance. Clebert (*The Gypsies*, p. 116) suggests that originally the gypsy dances were ritualistic, and were a 'commonplace rendering of the sacred dances of Vedic India'.

v. Naṭarāja; Maheśvara Sūtra.

Taṇḍi v. Tāṇḍava.

Taṇḍu The name of a skilled musician and the originator of the art of dancing. He is said to be an attendant of Śiva.[1]

[1]*BH.*, p. 79, n.1.

v. Tāṇḍava.

Tantra I. 'Warp and woof'; 'threads woven on a loom', the term applied to works, both religious and secular, composed according to particular patterns. The term *tantra* is specifically applied to the texts of the Tantric cults (Hindu, Buddhist and Jaina), the earliest of which appear to have been written during the Gupta period.

II. The general term for the Tantric cults of India—Hindu, Buddhist and Jaina, whose doctrines are enumerated in texts called Tantras.

The Tantric adepts sought to gain the 'power' resulting from 'the worship of the *śakti* or female energy . . . in conjunction with male energy'.[1] This notion resembles that implicit in Sāṁkhya doctrine which regarded 'power' as the polarization of opposites: *puruṣa* and *prakṛti.* This notion, whether or not expressed by erotic symbolism or abstract theory, is that generally accepted by Tantrists, especially those of the Śaiva and Buddhist Vajrayāna cults. Tantrism, like all Indian mystico-psychical speculation, is invariably associated with yoga, and has only tenuous links with fertility symbolism or with the magico-eroticism of the *AV.*

Though historically regarded as a product of the Gupta period, Tantrism is really an extension of ancient yogic tradition (implicit in the *RV.* notion of *śacī*), and represents a psycho-experimental interpretation of non-Tantric lore. If viewed without the prejudice of some Indian religious leaders, from Śaṅkarācārya onwards, and especially the 'reformists' of the past two centuries, Tantrism may be seen to have profoundly influenced Indian religious development, as other forms of yogic discipline have influenced Indian traditional music and the dance. But Tantrism, owing to its erotic symbolism,[2] and some of its practices, has led to a misunderstanding of its ideology, which P.C. Bagchi[3] considers is due to the failure of some scholars to interpret correctly the technical terms used in the Tantric texts. Their use of esoteric terminology and symbolism, like that of the Upaniṣads, is to reveal truths, in language that would be understood only by the initiated. Hence in Tantrism the use of the so-called 'intentional language' (*sandhyā-bhāṣā*), 'a secret, dark, ambiguous language in which a state of consciousness is expressed by an erotic term and the vocabulary of mythology or cosmology is charged with Haṭha-yogic or sexual meanings,'[4] its aim being the projection of the yogin into the 'paradoxical situation' indispensable to his training.

Whether Tantrism originated in Buddhism or in Hinduism has yet to be determined, but the rejection of caste distinction, and the high status generally accorded to women by Buddhists, which antedates the similar attitude of Hindus, suggest that Tantrism was perhaps first systematized by particular Buddhist schools. This view is supported by S.B. Dasgupta's observation that the extant Buddhist Tantras are also richer and more varied than those of Hindu origin.[5] But perhaps the clearest evidence for the Buddhist systematization of Tantrism lies in the condition of Buddhism during the Gupta period, a condition of scholastic conflict that had been growing in intensity since the Council of Vaiśālī, and which had finally resulted in dividing Buddhism into several distinct schools and numerous splinter groups, all of which provided a fertile ground for variant radical ideas, of which Tantrism was one. On the other hand, there is little doubt that Mahāyāna Buddhism was influenced by the worship of the female (*śakti*) principle.

Hitherto in the early post-Vedic period liberation (*mokṣa*) was to be achieved by meditation, but in Tantrism the emphasis was placed on direct experience. It declared that '*cittavṛttis*, the "eddies of consciousness", cannot be controlled and finally done away with unless they are first known "experimentally"'.[6]

Serious 'work on the Tantras has remained so limited and so specialized, that they have not come to form a genre within Oriental studies, though they are as qualified as . . . the Upaniṣads and the Pāli Canon. For this omission, there is positively no excuse, unless prudishness, fear of social and scientific opprobrium . . . were held to be valid excuses. No doubt, Tantrism is a delicate theme because of its intensive and extensive erotic ramifications.'[7] But owing to abuses and aberrations, found in almost all religious systems,[8] Tantrism has been deliberately neglected, despite the fact that a cult should be judged by its rationale and not by its aberrations. Tantrism should therefore be viewed from two levels: the literal (*mukhya*), the other from the metaphorical interpretation of its doctrine (*gauna*). The former is called *vāmācāra*, or 'left-handed', the latter, *dakṣiṇācāra*, or 'right-handed'.

Though the aim of non-Tantric and Tantric cults is the same: the recognition of the identity of the absolute and the phenomenal modes of existence (whatever the terms used to express the notion), there is a great deal of difference between the means employed to achieve that recognition. In non-Tantric systems contemplative exercises are the means of achieving enstatic,[9] supersensory, and extrarational experience, leading to *samādhi* (the final stage of yoga). In Tantrism both physical and psychical means are used to achieve the realization (*sādhanā*) of the identity of the phenomenal (*vyavahāra*) and the absolute (*paramārtha*) world. It was a 'doctrine inherent in esoteric Hinduism and Mahāyāna Buddhism—especially of the Mādhyamika school . . . [and] the nucleus around which all their speculation was to revolve'.[10] Thus the monistic principle was not to be regarded as a philosophical conclusion, or as a dichotomy resolved by reason, but as a realization achieved by all the constituents of the psychosomatic organism. This is expressed in Tantric erotic metaphor as *kuṇḍalinī*, the latent energy stored at the base of the spinal column, which like a coiled serpent uncoils through the several parts (*cakras*) of the spine and finally reaches the nerve centres of the upper brain (*sahasrāra*).[11] Another exercise relates to the retention of the breath and of the semen (even in actual copulation), the latter an exercise peculiar to Tantrism and the cults influenced by it.

Bagchi and other authorities enumerate a number of Tantras, without attributing any date to their composition, though this can sometimes be inferred from the texts themselves, which indicate a period anterior to the first century B.C. Some extant Tantras are written on bark or palm leaves, and are copies of copies, often written in poor Sanskrit or in one of the vernaculars. This may be accounted for by the wide distribution of Tantrism, many centres being on the periphery of Sanskritic India, others in Turkestan, Tibet, China, etc. Naturally, the existence of such widely separated centres suggests that techniques varied regionally, and that reciprocal influences occurred in particular areas. In addition, 'more than one curious parallel can be noted between Tantrism and the great Western mysteriosophic current that, at the beginning of the Christian era, arose from the confluence of Gnosticism, Hermetism, Greco-Egyptian alchemy, and the traditions of the Mysteries'.[12] The various sects and sub-sects adapted Tantric doctrine according to the deities worshipped and the ritual associated with them.

Much research remains to be undertaken before the classification of even the known Indian Tantras is complete, and still more if those of Tibet, Indo-China and China are taken into account.

Although much Tantric iconographical representation has been destroyed or lost, much remains at Sāñcī, Ellora, Ajaṇṭa and elsewhere.[13] It reveals mankind's affinity with nature, which to the early Tantrists gave a clearer notion of cosmic unity than that experienced by later Tantric adepts. As for the masses, their fundamental desires were identical with those of the plant and animal world, all subject to hunger, thirst and the generative impulse. Thus in Tantric iconography imagination inspired a vast natural world where nothing is inaccessible, whose symbolism is uninhibited but never unnatural, and where the same cosmic force flows through all.

During the Tantric period in India, the practice of alchemy reached its highest development.[14]

[1]Bhattacharyya, *Indian Buddhist Iconography*, p. xviii. Cf. the archaic marital myth of Heaven and Earth, a hierogamy, reflected in the *Bṛhad-Ār*. (VI.4,20), where the husband says to the wife, 'I am the heaven, thou art the earth.'

[2]Which, however, constitutes only a minor fraction of the Tantras, as it does that of the Upaniṣads (*Bṛhad-Ār*., 6.4,21; *Chān. Up*., 2.13,1–2).

[3]*Studies in the Tantras*, pt. i. p. 61.

[4]Eliade, *Yoga*, p. 249. To clarify the confusion that has existed over the meaning of '*sandhyā-bhāṣā*' and '*sandhā-bhāṣā*', he defines the latter as 'great doctrine', the former as the language used to express it.

[5]*Introduction to Tantric Buddhism*, Pref., p. ix.

[6]Eliade, op. cit., p. 40.

[7]*TT*., pp. 9f. But this omission has been largely remedied by the author's own efforts and those of Alex Wayman (USA), Mircea Eliade (France), H. Hoffman (Germany), de Jong (Holland), D.L. Snellgrove (England), H.V. Guenther (Canada), and G. Tucci, the doyen of Tibetan research (Italy).

[8]Dasgupta, *ORC.*, p. xxvi.

[9]Enstasy 'is the ultimate target of all meditative disciplines in Asia, and the term applies equally to Christian mysticism and to Sufism, from the comparativist viewpoint ... Enstasy ... is a non-discursive, quasi-permanent condition of the individual agent, and it is highly euphoric ... it is tantamount to supreme insight or wisdom' (*TT.*, p. 286).

[10]*TT.*, p. 18.

[11]The learned, conservative Hindu objected not only to the erotic symbolism, but also to the unsophisticated terminology used by the early Siddhas, 'who were mostly rustic folk without much' learning (*TT.*, p. 28).

[12]Eliade, op. cit., p. 202.

[13]The temple-complex of Khajuraho (Central India) is a Tantric shrine (v. Auboyer, *Khajuraho*).

[14]P. Ray (ed.), *History of Chemistry in Ancient and Medieval India*, pp. 114f. For Jaina Tantrism v. M.B. Jhaveri, *Comparative and Critical Study of Mantraśāstra*; and Williams, *Jaina Yoga*.

Bharati (*TT.*, p. 309 Bibliog.) points out that the British philosopher C.D. Broad, in his *Mind and Its Place in Nature* (1925), 'propounds a mind-matter view strikingly similar to that of Tantrism'.

v. Śakti; Śākta.

Tantraloka An encylopaedic work by the great Śākta Abhinavagupta, on Śaiva-Śākta philosophy.

Tanūnapāt A mystical name of the terrestrial form of Agni which occurs in some of the *āprī* hymns (*RV.*, I.142,2; III.4,2; cf. *Nir.*, 8,5 and *Ait. Br.*, II, 4), to indicate the unique nature of fire which, though generated by the friction of the fire-sticks (*araṇis*), is regarded as a form of spontaneous combustion, fire being considered to be inherent in the wood itself. Tanūnapāt thus signifies 'self-born' or 'self-produced'.

Tapas 'Warmth', 'heat', and hence 'potential power'. In Indian symbolism heat 'has two forms, mutually opposed: *kāma*, the heat of sexual desire, and *tapas*, the heat generated by ascetic practices, particularly by chastity. These two forms often meet and interact in mythology'[1] as in the myth of Kāma's attempt to divert Śiva from his meditation by arousing his desire for Pārvatī.

The *ṛṣis* are said to owe their origin to *tapas*, and by it the gods overcome death (*AV.*, XI.5,19); it set creation in motion (*RV.*, X.129,3), and enabled Agastya to overhear the storm-gods (Maruts) conversing with Indra (*Bṛhadd.*, IV.46,2; v. also IV.58f.; 66). Prajāpati created this world and 'yonder world' by *tapas* (*Kauṣ. Br.*, VI.10; and v. VI.1).

Tapas was thus both the source of power and the means of gaining it, for it provided the stimuli which combined faith (*śraddhā*) and knowledge (*jñāna*) (*Muṇḍ. Up.*, 3,2,4), and the attainment in solitude of the peace of mind that unites the devotee with *brahman* (1.2,11). To 'the archaic mind' heat indicated a manifestation of magico-religious power.[2] Creation through autothermy is attested in primitive cosmologies as well as in Shamanism.[3]

The practice of *tapas* became a rite to be performed by a sacrificer and his wife before sharing in the sacrificial ceremony. Subsequently *tapas* became a yogic technique, which the *Baudhāyana Dharma Sūtra* (IV.1.23f.) states can be attained by breath control.[4]

According to the Indian view, a positive gain is to be derived from asceticism and renunciation—the force derived therefrom far exceeding the mundane pleasures which must of necessity be given up. A number of myths tell of the alarm felt by the gods when certain ascetics became advanced in this technique. To the popular mind *tapas* is an outward sign of advanced spirituality.

[1]W.D. O'Flaherty, 'The Submarine Mare in the Mythology of Śiva', *JRAS.*, no. 1. 1971, p. 9. v. also Chauncey Blair, *Heat in the Rig Veda and Atharva Veda*.

[2]Gonda, *CC.*, p. 294. Cf. *tapa*, 'consuming by heat'.

[3]Eliade, *Yoga*, pp. 332 and 385.

[4]Ibid., p. 108. *Tapas* is 'a physiological technique, compared with which the strictly psychological technique is subsidiary' (ibid., p. 36).

v. Tyāga; Tapoloka.

Tapatī v. Saṁjñā.

Tapoloka or **Taparloka** One of the seven celestial spheres, situated above the Pole Star (Dhruva), where dwell those deities who by ascetic practices (*tapas*) attain immunity from fire (*VP.*, II.7).

Tara The name of a spell used against evil spirits who are believed to 'possess' certain weapons.

Tārā or **Tārakā** I. 'Star.' Name of the wife of Bṛhaspati, the preceptor of the gods. Whatever the original intention of the Tārā myth, it is used in *VP.* (IV.6) to explain the relation of the Lunar dynasty to Soma (the moon-god), and also his descent from Atri the son of the creator Brahmā.

Soma's conquests and the glory he acquired led to his becoming arrogant and licentious, and to his abduction of Tārā. Despite the efforts of her husband to recover her, the remonstration of the *ṛṣis*, and Brahmā's command that she should be returned, Soma refused to relinquish her.

The gods with their allies then declared war on Soma who was joined by Uśanas (not from any liking for Soma, but because of his dislike of Bṛhaspati). The *daityas* and *dānavas*, following the example of their preceptor Uśanas, also joined Soma's army. The contest for the recovery of Tārā is called the Tārakā war. The Earth, shaken to its very centre, cried out for protection. Then Brahmā interposed, the combatants laid down their arms, and Tārā was restored to her husband. Later when he discovered that she was pregnant he declared that the child should be abandoned, but from the moment of its birth, it was endowed with such splendour that Bṛhaspati and Soma both claimed paternity. To settle the dispute Brahmā appealed to Tārā to declare who was the father, but she refused. The child, incensed by her refusal, declared that unless she answered he would sentence her 'to such a fate as should deter every female in future from hesitating to tell the truth'. Tārā then declared that he was Soma's child, whereupon the father embraced him and said, 'Well done, my son, thou art truly wise', whence his name Budha, 'He who knows'.

v. Ugra-tārā.

II. A Tantric goddess (one of the ten *mahāvidyās*), who figures prominently in Hindu, Jaina and Buddhist Tantric tradition, as well as that of Tibetan Buddhist Vajrayāna. Tārā may be regarded as 'the epiphany of the Great Goddess of aboriginal India', who represents the religion of the Mother-Goddess 'that in ancient times reigned over an immense Aegeo-Afrasiatic territory and which was always the chief form of devotion among the authochthonous peoples of India'.[1]

[1]Eliade, *Yoga*, p. 202. The Sumerian symbol for divinity was a star (Levy, *Gate of Horn*, p. 160). Tārā is an epithet common to all the great Hindu goddesses (*TT.*, p. 61).

Tāraka The name of a valiant *daitya*, son of Hiraṇyākṣa and Diti (*VP.*, I.21).

v. Tripura.

Tārakā I. v. Tārā I.

II. Name of the daughter of the demon Sunda or of the *yakṣa* Suketu. Tārakā incurred the wrath of the *ṛṣi* Agastya who, to punish her, changed her into a *rākṣasī*. She avenged herself by mercilessly ravaging the countryside. Then Viśvāmitra requested Rāmacandra to kill her, but he only cut off her arms, and his brother Lakṣmaṇa her nose and ears, but by her great magical powers she continued to hurl great rocks at them until finally Rāma killed her with an arrow.

v. Mārīca.

Tārkṣya The sun conceived as a white horse which draws the solar chariot across the heavens (*RV.*, I.89,6; X.178,1; cf. *Kauṣ. Br.*, xxx, 5). At daybreak the goddess of the dawn appears leading a beautiful white horse (VII.77,3), but in other hymns the sun is either a bird or mounted on a bird and called Garutman, whence Garuḍa, the *vāhana* of Viṣṇu.[1]

The *VP.* (II.10) states that Tārkṣya is one of the seven beings who ride in the sun's chariot during the month of mārgarśīrṣa (November–December).

[1]*DHI.*, p. 429; v. also *Nir.*, 10,27 and 28; *Bṛhadd.*, II.58.

v. Dadhikrā; Sūrya; Savitṛ.

Tarpaṇa A rite in which water is offered as a libation to the gods and ancestors (*Manu*, III.70).

Tārpya A garment or robe made from some kind of vegetable fibre[1] and used in funerary and other rites. Savitar is said to give the *tārpya* to the dead man to wear in Yama's realm (*AV.*, XVIII,4,31) in place of the garments he wore when alive (2.57).[2] But the *tārpya* is also associated with ritual rebirth as well as with death. In the *rājasūya* ceremony the royal sacrificer dons the robe and ritually 'dies' and enters the womb. When the *tārpya* is removed he is said to be reborn out of the sacrifice. In the five-day consecration ceremony (*abhiṣecanīya*), the king puts on a number of garments, one of which is the *tārpya* in which 'are wrought[3] all forms of sacrifice'; it also represents 'the inner caul of knighthood (*kṣatra*) from which the king is ritually reborn' (*ŚBr.*, V.3.5,20).

During the performance of the horse sacrifice (*aśvamedha*), the *tārpya* was spread on the ground where the horse was to be immolated.[4] According to the *Baudhāyana-śrauta-śūtra* (15,28; etc.) the horse was strangled with the *tārpya*. Later in the same ceremony the robe was used to cover the chief queen and the dead horse during their mimetic copulation.

[1]It may have been made from *tṛpā* grass or from *triparṇa* plants (*ŚBr.*, pt. iii, p. 85, n.1).

[2]Cf. the magic power of clothes; the investing of a person with rank, authority, dignity, etc., or with some quality or attribute.

[3]The commentators consider that the robe was decorated with representations of various sacrificial objects.

[4]Dumont, *L'Aśvamedha*, p. 275.

Tatpuruṣa v. Pañcānana.

Tattvacintāmaṇi A work by Gaṅgeśa Upādhyāya (c. A.D. 1225), written as a reply to the Vedāntin Śrīharṣa's criticisms of the Nyāya-Vaiśeṣika in his work *Khaṇḍana-khaṇḍa-khādya*.

Tattva(s) Principles or evolvents of matter (*prakṛti*); primary subtle elements. They are regarded as 'categories in the evolution of the universe, proceeding from subtle essence to the constitution of material or gross form'.[1] *Tattva per se* is the noumenon, transcending the subjective categories of thought, which 'are of empirical validity and can be significantly used within phenomena only'.[2]

[1]*CHS.*, Glossary, p. 258.

[2]T.R.V. Murti, *The Central Philosophy of Buddhism*, p. 294.

Tat tvam asi 'That thou art.' A phrase which occurs in the *Chān. Up.* (6.8,6), etc., and is used as a *mantra* representing 'the fundamental identity of the macrocosm and the microcosm'.[1] *Tat* (that) represents *brahman*, the universal principle; *tvam* (thou) the *ātman*, the individualized and subjective aspect of *brahman*; but widening the idea of the self to include the All precludes the notion of a subject (which implies limitation).[2] Thus the supremely moral man identifies his 'self' with the 'self' of all other beings and thus delights in their welfare (*BG.*, 5.7,25).

[1]*HP.*, p. 295.

[2]Heimann, *Facets*, p. 51.

v. Vedānta.

Tejas Fiery energy, vital power, spiritual or moral or magical power or influence, glory, majesty, authority. The meaning of the term varies according to its context.[1]

With the *tejas* of the gods Caṇḍikā was formed to overcome the demon Mahiṣa (*Mārk. P.*, 82,8f.); with part of his *tejas* Hari sustained the serpent Vāsuki, and with another part he sustained the gods during the Churning of the Ocean (*samudramathana*). With the brilliant (*tejas*) pieces which Viśvakarman filed off the sun, he made Viṣṇu's *cakra* and Śiva's *triśūla* (*V.P.*, III.2).

[1]Sometimes it means *semen virile*.

Ṭhag(s) 'Thug.'[1] In some parts of India the Thugs are styled 'stranglers'; the Tamils call them 'Moslem noosers'.[2] The Thugs were members of a religious fraternity of professional assassins[3] once prevalent in parts of the central and northern provinces of India and in the Deccan, and though the date of their origin is unknown, they were active in the seventh century, according to Hsüan-tsang, the Chinese Buddhist pilgrim.

The Thugs were devotees of the goddess Bhavānī (a form of Kālī) to whom they offered their victims and a third of the proceeds of their robberies. Kālī is said to have taught her devotees the art of garrotting on a clay dummy, but poison (especially that of the thorn-apple), drowning and burning alive were also practised. Women were not supposed to be murdered as they were unacceptable to the goddess.

Some of the Thugs concentrated their activities in the Ganges area between Banāras and Calcutta, plying boats with crews of fifteen, ostensibly to convey pilgrims, whom they flung into the river after robbing them. Others roamed about the country in small bands or joined up with travellers whose confidence they had gained.

Of the various methods adopted by the Thugs to dispatch their victims garrotting was the more usual, but none of the methods involved the shedding of blood. The victims were buried in a hole dug with a sacred pickaxe, an implement greatly venerated and worshipped by Thugs, and upon which oaths were sworn,[4] and by which they practised divination. When the sacred pickaxe was hidden in a well it 'rose in the morning of its own accord and came of itself into its custodian's hand; its sound made in digging a grave could be heard by none but a Thug; it was more sacred than Ganges water or the Qur'an'.[5] Some Moslems joined the Hindu Thugs but usually they formed themselves into separate bands.[6]

With great difficulty the Thugs were finally suppressed in 1861 in the settled areas of India.

[1]The Prakrit form is *ṭhagga*, the Sindhī *ṭhagu*, the Kāṣmirī *ṭhag* and *ṭhagun*, meaning to cheat or rob (*IAL*).

[2]*CI.*, III, p. 868.

[3]There are some parallels with the Assassins, members of the Shī'ite branch of Islam called Fidā'īs 'devoted ones', who spread terror throughout Persia and Syria during the eleventh and twelfth centuries (Allegro, *The Sacred Mushroom and the Cross*, pp. 188f.). The murderous Moslem Hurs of India, so active in the twenties, thirties and forties of this century, appear to be the modern equivalent of the Ṭhags (v. H. T. Lambrick, *The Terrorist*).

[4]A Thug who swore a false oath on the sacred pickaxe was condemned to death (J.H. Hutton, *Caste in India*, p. 127).

[5]Ibid.

[6]The Moslem Thugs generally were devotees of 'the Moslem Saint Nizam-ud-din Auliya, whose tomb is one of the chief architectural gems of old Delhi' (Crooke, *Things Indian*, p. 475).

Tilaka or **Puṇḍra** A sectarial mark made on the forehead with unguents or mineral or vegetal colouring matter. The devotees of Śrī-Kṛṣṇa apply the *tilaka* to twelve parts of their bodies before commencing daily worship. A kind of white clay is used called *gopīcandana*, obtained from Dvārakā.[1] These visible signs are believed by many to have protective powers.

[1]Gonda, *VS.*, pp. 81f. For illustrations of a number of *tilakas* v. Birdwood, *Indian Arts*, I, p. 105.

Tilottamā Name of an *apsaras* often associated with the sun. During its annual journey between the extreme northern and southern points, it is accompanied during each month by a particular group of seven guardians responsible for temperature and rainfall. The *apsaras* Tilottamā, with Tvaṣṭṛ, Jamadagni, Dhṛtarāṣṭra, etc., are the sun's seven guardians during the month of *māgha* (January–February) (*VP.*, II.10).

Siva became so enamoured of the nymph that he became four-faced so that he could constantly view her great beauty.

Tilvaka The name of a tree (Symplocos racemosa) near which it was unwise to dig a grave (*ŚBr.*, XIII.8.1, 16). The wood of this tree was also used to make the sacrificial post (*yūpa*).

Tīrtha I. A shrine or sacred place of pilgrimage, often situated on the banks of a river or stream. *Tīrthas* may also consist of a mound, a large tree, peculiar shaped stones, or a pool, or any place mythologically associated with the activities of the gods or of holy men. To bathe in a sacred river or to drink from it, both purifies and strengthens. Such water when sprinkled by a priest on the pilgrim expels all 'sin'. To die at a *tīrtha* is especially meritorious.

The place-names of many ancient *tīrthas* often conceal the identity of long-forgotten godlings and cults absorbed by the two principal cults, and which subsequent research has revealed. *Tīrthas* are often dedicated to both gods and goddesses and may contain images of them, but those connected only with goddesses are usually termed *pīṭhas*, i.e., 'the holy seats or resorts of the mother-goddess',[1] or the places where the pieces of Satī's dead body fell.

[1] *TT.*, p. 87.

v. Tīrthapālikā.

II. Certain parts (*tīrthas*) of the hand are regarded as sacred. According to *Manu* (II.58–9), the root of the thumb is sacred to the eternal *brahman*; that of the little finger to Ka (Prajāpati); the tips of the fingers to the gods; and the space between the index and the thumb to the *pitṛs*.

Tīrthaṅkara v. Jaina.

Tīrthapālikā The name of the Piśācī who guards the sacred *tīrthas* and prevents the impure or impious from entering them.

Tithi A lunar day or thirtieth part of a whole lunation of slightly more than twenty-seven solar days. Thus the bright half of the month (the waxing period) consists of fifteen *tithis*, and of a similar number during the dark half (or waning period). The former was called *śukla-pakṣa* and the latter *kṛṣṇapakṣa*. 'According to the system followed in Northern India and much of the Deccan the month began and ended with the full moon, while in the Tamil country the month generally began with the new moon.'[1]

[1] Basham, *WI.*, p. 492, App. III.

v. Nakṣatra; Jyotiṣa.

Tomara A long lance used in fighting from the backs of war-elephants.

Totalā v. Gaurī.

Trasadasyu v. Kuru; Daśarājña.

Trayī vidyā I. The 'threefold sacred science' (of the Veda) comprising the reciting of hymns, performing sacrifices, and chanting. According to the *ŚBr.* (VI.1,8), the *trayī vidyā* was the first creative act of Prajāpati, which provided him with a foundation for all other acts of creation. As everything is contained in the eternal threefold Veda, Prajāpati decided to construct for himself a body which would contain all this lore (*ŚBr.*, X.4.2,21–2).

II. One of the names of the female form of the Power of Time when it became androgynous.[1]

[1] *HP.*, p. 259.

v. Kālī II; Kāla I.

Tretā I. One of the four *yugas* or mythical divisions of cosmic time, the others being *kṛta*, *dvāpara* and *kali* ages. During these periods the world evolves and devolves through a series of cycles of creation, destruction and recreation.

v. Kalpa; Manvantara.

II. The name of one[1] of the four sides of a die, the others being called *kṛta*, *dvāpara* and *kali*.

[1] Or it may have been applied to a die marked four, three, two or one (*VI.*, vol. I, p. 3.).

v. Tretā I.

Trijaṭā The name of the *rākṣasī* who befriended Sītā when she was abducted by Rāvaṇa.

Trika or **Trikaśāsana**[1] The name of the Kāṣmir Śaiva system which, as its name indicates, recognized three ultimate principles: Śiva as All-knowing, All-sustaining Being; Śakti as transcendental energy; and Aṇu as the individual Ātman, bound to *saṁsāra* by the fallibilities of human nature. The school was founded by Vasugupta (770–830), and by the tenth century had become a complex mystico-psychological system, developed by successive commentators to the ultimate degree of yogic subtlety.

[1] The subject is fully dealt with by S. K. Das, *Śakti or Divine Power*; v. also S. Dasgupta, *Obscure Religious Cults*.

Trikoṇa 'Triangle.' A vertical triangle represents Śiva; an inverted one his *śakti*.[1] In India geometrical symbols represent the unapproachable Divine; involved triangles (like the *yantras* of the Tantra cults), being used as 'aids' to meditation and concentration.[2]

[1] Cf. the 'sexual triangle' depicted on some representations of Western Asian goddesses as well as on their ancient Egyptian counterparts (James, *Tree of Life*, p. 179). Also the inverted triangular shape of the entrance to the Queen's Chamber in the pyramid of Cheops.

[2]Heimann, *IWP.*, pp. 124f.

Trilocana or **Trinetra** 'Three-eyed.' An epithet of Śiva, referring to his third eye (usually depicted vertically on his forehead). It is mythically explained as having burst from his forehead when Pārvatī playfully covered his eyes with her hands whereupon the world was plunged into darkness.

Trimūrti 'Having three forms.' The Hindu triad, the three manifestations of the Supreme Being,[1] represented by Brahmā, Viṣṇu and Śiva,[2] each being associated with a specific cosmic function. Brahmā is the equilibrium between two opposing principles (the centripetal and centrifugal), represented by Viṣṇu and Śiva respectively,[3] Viṣṇu primarily symbolizing preservation and renewal, Śiva disintegration or destruction.

[1]There are parallels between the *trimūrti* and the Mexican Ho-Huitzilopochtli-Tlaloc triad. P. Kirchhoff suggests that China, India, Java and Mexico share a common system ('The Diffusion of a Great Religious System, India to Mexico', *Sobretiro del xxxv Congress International de Americanistas*, p. 88. v. also p. 73 for the similar calendraic classification of India and Mexico).

[2]Cf. the Vedic association of the three gods Agni, Vāyu and Sūrya.

[3]*HP.*, pp. 23f. The personification of the three *guṇas* as Brahmā, Viṣṇu and Śiva respectively appears to be a late idea (L. Renou and J. Filliozat, *L'Inde classique*, I. p. 518).

v. Om.

Tripura The 'Triple City'. A fabulous city (or cities) of the *asuras* constructed of gold, silver and iron by the architect Maya for the three sons of Tāraka.[1] These cities, so grandiloquently described in the *MBh.*, probably refer to the ancient fortress complexes[2] of the peoples of the Indus Valley and the Panjāb, against which the energies of the nomadic Āryans, under the leadership of Indra were directed. Wherever the Āryans attacked there seemed always to be a fortress, and hence the myth that the forts were capable of moving themselves from place to place at will. Subsequently the Tripura myth was merged with Śaiva mythology to indicate the passing of the 'old order' and its replacement by the new. Thus Tripura, having survived for a thousand years, was destroyed by Śiva[3] in a chariot drawn by a thousand lions. Only Maya was spared.

[1]*MBh.*, 7.202,64f.; 8.33,16f. (*EM.*, p. 50).

[2]In the Brāhmaṇas a 'tripartite stronghold' is regarded as a secure protection, thus 'the gods made three ritual citadels and instituted a tripartite sacrificial rite called "victories" ... to overpower the *asuras* who had made earth, atmosphere and heaven three fortresses' (Gonda, *VS.*, p. 125).

[3]As a punishment for his destruction of Tripura, Uśanas plucked Śiva's hair out. Each hair became a snake (*IT.*, p. 111).

v. Tripurā Bhairavī; Tripurasundarī.

Tripurā Bhairavī The goddess of the triple city (Tripura). She is also called Mahāmāyā.[1] According to the *Kālikā Pur.* (Ch. 76, 88–93),[2] she emerged from the *liṅgam* which then divided into three parts.

Tripurā Bhairavī is the *śakti* of Śiva when he assumes the form of the all-pervading ruler of death, and it is she who silently carries out Death's relentless work.

[1]*DHI.*, p. 509.

[2]Cited by Bhattasali, *Iconography of Buddhist and Brahmanical Sculptures in the Dacca Museum*, p. 193.

v. Tripurasundarī.

Tripurasundarī The goddess of the triple city (Tripura). She is a form of Durgā[1] and is called the 'Fair One' (*Sundarī*), 'the fairest being in the three spheres, heaven, earth and air.' She is worshipped by Tantrists. The *Ṣoḍaśī Tantra* identifies her with Ṣoḍaśī, who represents the universal creative energy of Devī, manifested as the light radiating from Śiva's three eyes, which illumines the three worlds.[2]

[1]A form of Gaurī is also called Tripurā (*DHI.*, p. 502).

[2]*HP.*, p. 278.

Triṣaṁdhi 'Having three joints.' A divine being, perhaps the personification of the three-pointed *vajra* or some other weapon, regarded as a very effective instrument, capable of giving protection against all manner of enemies (*AV.*, XI.10,1ff.).

Triśaṅku v. Satyavrata II.

Triśiras I. 'Three-headed.'[1] A son of Tvaṣṭar (Tvaṣṭṛ). In the *Tait. Saṁ.* (II.5,1–5) he is called Viśvarūpa (multiformed). He is the twin brother of Saraṇyū (*Bṛhadd.*, VI.162). With one mouth he drank *soma*, with the second, *surā*, and with the third he ate the sacrificial offerings. All that he ate and drank he openly vowed to share with the gods, but secretly he made a similar promise to the Asuras,[2] the ancient non-Āryan rivals of the gods.

The sequel to Triśiras' duplicity states that Indra, afraid that such a diversion of the offerings might lead to a weakening of his sovereign power, cut off the heads of Triśiras with his *vajra*, but realized too late that his act made him guilty of brahmanicide. Indra assumed his guilt[3] and bore it for a year, but many creatures constantly reminded him of it, so he appealed to the Earth-goddess to assume a third of his guilt, and in return granted her the boon that any portion of the earth disfigured by cultivation should not be allowed to remain in that condition. Indra next appealed to the trees, promising them that they should not suffer by being pruned. His final appeal was to women, who chose as their boon that they should obtain offspring and also enjoy cohabitation throughout their pregnancies.[4]

The *MBh.*[5] has another version of the beheading of Triśiras by Indra, and states that from the dead body arose Vṛtra, whom Indra had also to kill, thus making him again guilty of brahmanicide. The possible consequences of his second crime so frightened him that he fled and hid in a lotus-stalk.

[1]Agni, like Triśiras, is described as seven-rayed as well as three-headed (*RV.*, I.146,1).

[2]Probably because he was 'the son of a sister of the Asuras' (*Bṛhadd.*, VI. 149).

[3]In India, as in ancient Greece, guilt was regarded as an actual entity.

[4]For a variant account v. *ŚBr.*, V.5.4,2ff.; also v. XII.7.1,1ff. Both the *Tait. Saṁ*. version and that of the *ŚBr.* are apparently of ritual significance.

[5]*EM.*, pp. 130f.

II. Fever personified as a three-headed demon, representing the three stages of fever—heat, cold and sweating.

III. A name of Kubera, god of wealth.

Triṣṭubh[1] One of the chief Vedic metres, consisting of 4 × 11 syllables. It is said to belong to Indra (*Bṛhadd.*, VIII.106), or to be his portion (*RV.*, X.130,5). According to the *VP.* (I.5) it was created *inter alia* from Brahmā's southern mouth.

[1]It is said to be the 'swiftest metre' (*Nir.*, 7.12). The funeral verses of the *AV.* are in this metre (Bloomfield, *The Atharvaveda*, p. 41).

Triśūla 'Trident.'[1] An emblem of Śiva, denoting his functions 'as Creator, Preserver and Destroyer', or those of the three *guṇas* or 'instruments' of the evolutionary process. According to the yoga theory, 'the trident represents the three subtle arteries of the body, *iḍā*, *piṅgalā*, and *suṣumnā*, which ... ascend from the root centre at the base of the spinal cord to reach the "lotus of a thousand petals" at the summit of the head'.[2]

In early numismatic and sculptural representations the *triśūla* is associated with both Viṣṇu and Śiva.[3] It is also placed on the top of Śaiva temples. Benares (Kāśī) itself is said to stand on Śiva's *triśūla*, and hence the whole area is sacred to this deity.[4]

Combaz considers that the *triśūla* has an affinity with the *cakra*,[5] but Coomaraswamy maintains it is the cosmic pillar holding earth and heaven apart.

[1]*Śūla* means any sharp instrument, stake, dart, lance, etc.

[2]*HP.*, p. 216.

[3]*DHI.*, p. 191.

[4]The *triśūla* is also sacred to Śiva's *śakti* Durgā. The divine weapons of the gods have a place in ritual and also 'in ceremonies for protection' (Gonda, *VS.*, p. 178 n.91).

[5]'L'Évolution du stūpa en Asie', *MCB.*, II, pp. 163ff.

v. Āyudhapuruṣa; Cakra; Tejas.

Trita or **Trita Āptya** I. A minor deity mentioned occasionally in the *RV.* The name is derived from *trita* (third) and *āptya* (sprung from the waters), an allusion to an obscure myth (*ŚBr.*, I.2.3,1ff.) relating to Agni who, probably in the form of lightning, disappeared in 'the waters', whence he was forcibly removed by the gods. Agni spat on the waters because they failed to conceal him.

Trita is the Vedic counterpart of the Avestan Thrita who also figured in the *haoma* ritual. Trita is sometimes regarded as a double of Indra[1] or to be closely associated with him in his demon-killing role (*RV.*, I.52,5), and so became a kind of scapegoat for Indra's many murders, as well as for the 'sins' of the gods. The 'sins' of the latter were the guilt and impurity incurred in the preparation of the sacrifice. The gods 'wiped off', i.e., transferred the guilt to Trita who in turn transferred it to human beings (*AV.*, VI.1).

Trita's great enemy was Tvaṣṭṛ's son, the three-headed Triśiras (*RV.*, X.8,8).[2]

[1]Indra and Trita were originally separate deities. Indra is also called Āptya, perhaps because he causes rain.

[2]Cf. the Avestan Thrita who as Thraetaona prepared the sacred *haoma* and killed the triple-headed dragon Azhi Dahaka.

v. Apāmārga.

II. Name of one of the seven *ṛṣis* of Varuṇa, who officiate at the sacrifice.[1]

[1]*EM.*, p. 120; *Bṛhadd.*, III.58.

Trivikrama The three great strides[1] of the Vedic solar god Viṣṇu as he makes his diurnal journey across the sky and thus manifests his 'holy ways' (*RV.*, I.22, 18–19). This reference is probably the source of the Paurāṇic Vāmana *avatāra* myth.

[1]Cf. the Iranian myth of Ameša-spenta's three steps.

Tṛṇāntarābhibhāṣaṇa Name of a custom in which a person holds up a blade of grass[1] as a sign of contempt when compelled by circumstance to talk or listen to another person. Sītā held up a blade of grass whenever her abductor Rāvaṇa spoke to her.

[1]Dried grass or straw (*tṛṇa*) has from ancient times been a symbol of worthlessness and contempt. Cf. Job, VIII.12; Psalm, I.4.

Tṛṇāvarta A whirlwind-demon who seized the infant Kṛṣṇa and whirled him up into the sky, but Kṛṣṇa seized him by the throat and the demon fell to the ground under the prodigous weight of the divine infant (*Bhāg. P.*, X.2,1; 7,30–2, etc., *PI.*).

Tṛtsu(s) Name of a people or tribe mentioned in the Veda. Their kingdom formed part of that of the Bhāratas,[1] who gave their name to the whole of the country later known as Brahmāvarta. Two of the famous rulers of the Tṛtsus were Divodāsa 'surnamed' Atithigva, and his still more famous descendant Sudās who overwhelmed the confederation of the Ten Kings (*daśarājña*) and firmly established the empire of the Bhāratas. The *RV.* (VII.83,8) describes the Tṛtsus as skilled singers, white-robed and with braided hair.

[1]'The exact relation of the Tṛtsus and Bhāratas cannot be determined and there is a sharp difference of opinion among scholars on the subject' (*HCIP.*, I, p. 246).

Tulasī The Basil plant (Ocimum sanctum), commonly called *tulsī*. In some accounts of the Churning of the Ocean (*samudramathana*), the *tulasī* is added to the list of articles which emerged from it, but the addition appears to be a sectarial one because the plant is sacred to Kṛṣṇa.[1] It is also sacred to his consort Lakṣmī; the essence of these deities pervades it and hence it is itself an object of worship.[2]

One myth recounts that when Kṛṣṇa was pursuing a nymph (*apsaras*) she transformed herself into a *tulasī* as Daphne changed herself into a laurel when pursued by Apollo.

The *tulasī* plant also possesses curative properties and is an antidote to snake-venom. It destroys mosquitoes and other pests and purifies the air. It even wards off the messengers of Yama, the ruler of the dead, who will not enter a house containing a sprig of *tulasī*. When death occurs, the funeral pyre should be constructed of *tulasī*, *palāśa*, and sandal-wood.

[1]Wilson, *VP.*, p. 67, n.8.

[2]Those plants that are sacred to particular divinities are regarded as 'manifestations of the power complexes for which these divine names stand' (Gonda, *VS.*, p. 111). In its roots are contained all places of pilgrimage; its centre contains all the deities, and its upper branches all the Vedas (*BH.*, p. 333).

v. Tulasīvivāha.

Tulasīvivāha A festival held on the twelfth day of the first half of the month *kārttika*, during which Viṣṇu's image is 'married' to the *tulasī* plant, or to a *śālagrāma* pebble, the abode of Viṣṇu/Kṛṣṇa.[1]

[1]*BH.*, pp. 334f.

Tumburu Also called Virādha. The name of the leader of the celestial musicians (*gandharvas*), who had a magic lute called *kalāvatī*. Hopkins[1] suggests that Tumburu may be the 'tambour personified'. In the *Rām.* he is invoked with others to make magic gardens for Bharadvāja.

[1]*EM.*, p. 155.

Tūṇava Name of a wooden musical instrument, probably a flute. When Vāc, the goddess of Speech, was unwilling to agree to the gods' demands she entered the trees, and thus the voice of the trees is heard in the sounds of the drum, lute and flute (*Tait. Saṁ.*, VI.1,4), which are made of wood.

Turaga A name of the white horse which emerged from the Churning of the Ocean (*samudramathana*), and was claimed by the Sun-god (*Matsya P.*, 250,3; 251,3,*PI.*).

Turvaśa(s) A Vedic tribe named after its ruler Turvaśa or Turvaśu, one of the five sons of an ancient sacrificer and the composer of some *RV.* hymns. His name, and that of his brothers, Yadu, Druhyu, Anu and Puru occur in the *RV.* as the names of tribes and their rulers respectively, but they have no connexion with their namesakes in the Purāṇas and *MBh.*

The Turvaśas and Yādavas are notable as the allies of Sudās, the king of the Tṛtsus, and later of the Bhāratas, in the war subsequently known as the *daśarājña*. Later the Turvaśas became merged with the Pañcālas.

Turvaśu A son of Yayāti, an imperial ruler, and Devayānī, the daughter of Uśanas-Śukra, a Bhārgava *ṛṣi*.

The Purāṇas differ about the territories assigned by Yayāti to his five sons,[1] but it appears that Turvaśu was given the south-eastern territory (around Rewa). His kingdom was subsequently merged with that of the Yādavas (bequeathed to his elder brother Yadu) and that of the Pauravas (bequeathed to his half-brother Puru).

[1]The names of the Paurāṇic Yayāti and his five sons also occur in the *RV.*, but there is no historical connexion between them. This similarity is probably the result of Paurāṇic syncretism.

v. Turvaśa(s).

Tvaṣṭṛ (Vedic **Tvaṣṭar**) The divine artisan. The name is derived from the root *tvakṣ*, meaning 'to form or fashion',[1] and in this sense his function is similar to that of the Egyptian Ptah, the god of craftsmen; to the Babylonian Mummu, personifying technical skill; the Phoenician Chusor, and the Greek Hephaistos, etc.

Tvaṣṭṛ is the embodiment of craftsmanship, the 'shaper or fashioner', whose power is divine (*AV.*, XII.3,33). He is also called the 'earliest born', who can assume all forms (*RV.*, I.13,10) and thus create all forms, and hence is invoked in the *āprī* hymns by those desiring offspring. It was customary to offer mares to him by those desiring children.[2]

To Tvaṣṭṛ is also ascribed the fashioning of the sacrificial ladle, from which he later made four ladles

(*RV.*, I.20,6). He also fashioned the chalice of the gods from which the Ṛbhus subsequently made four (I.161,2). In addition Tvaṣṭṛ made Indra's great thunderbolt (*vajra*) (I.32,2; 52,7) from the bones of Dadhyac, thus increasing Indra's strength. He formed heaven and earth and is thus the ruler of all beings, and responsible for their increase and well-being (I.95,5; X.184,1; *AV.*, V.25,5; *Bṛhad-Ār. Up.*, 6.4,21). Thus as the fashioner of the embryo he is surrounded by *gnās* who are the recipients of his generative energy, and hence his epithet Garbhapati, Lord of the Womb. Only animals with testicles, i.e., begetters, should be brought to the sacrifices dedicated to Tvaṣṭṛ. Such an animal must not be slain, but set free after the sacrificial fire has been carried round it. To slay it would end the begetting of offspring (*ŚBr.*, III.7.2,8). The *AV.* (VI.78,3) enlarges the sphere of Tvaṣṭṛ's activities and states that he bestows longevity, allays jealousy (*VII.*74, 3), and increases the speed of the horse (VI.92,1–3).

Tvaṣṭṛ's son was Triśiras (also called Viśvarūpa), and his daughter was Saraṇyū, who married the sun-god Vivasvat.

[1] *IT.*, p. 320. Cf. *Nir.*, 8, 13. In the Vedas the carpenters of the heavy bullock-carts were called *tvaṣṭṛ*, and *rathakāra* in the Buddhist *Jātaka* tales (Auboyer, *Daily Life in Ancient India*, p. 313, n.30).

[2] *IT.*, p. 322.

v. Saṁjñā; Chāyā; Sūrya.

Tyāga 'Ignoring.' One of the Hindu basic virtues which implies the calm and tranquil acceptance of renunciation as opposed to the active asceticism of *tapas. Tyāga* implies non-injury (*ahiṁsā*) towards all creatures, and the giving up of all one's goods, property, and money.

U

Ū The *bīja mantra* of the sun (*Chān. Up*., I.13,2), which implies a promise to protect.

Ucathya Name of a mythical Vedic Āṅgirasa *ṛṣi*, the husband of Mamatā whose son Dīrghatamas, though born blind, was the composer of numerous *RV*. hymns. His father is the reputed author of one hymn only (IX.50).

In post-Vedic mythology Ucathya appears to have been syncretized with Utathya. The Vedic Bṛhaspati is metamorphosed as Utathya's younger brother, the paternity of both being attributed to Aṅgiras.[1]

The account of the birth of Dīrghatamas in the *Bṛhadd.* (IV.11–15) represents a transitional stage in the development of the Ucathya-Bṛhaspati-Mamatā-Dīrghatamas myth and that of the Utathya-Bṛhaspati-Mamatā-Bharadvāja myth related in the *VP.* (IV.9). In both accounts Bṛhaspati is said to have had intercourse with Mamatā, which resulted in the premature birth of the embryo engendered by him. In the *Bṛhadd.* account Bṛhaspati accused Dīrghatamas of having caused the abortion and cursed him to be reborn blind. In the *VP.* version the aborted child is called Bharadvāja, and his half-brother Dīrghatamas, as in the *Bṛhadd.* account.[2]

[1]Wilson, *VP*., p. 70, n.3.

[2]This myth is modified in the *Brah. P.* and the *Hariv*. (*VP*., p. 359, n.15).

Uccadevatā Time personified.

v. Kāla I; Ṛtu.

Uccaiḥśravas 'Long-eared'[1] or 'neighing aloud'. Name of the mythical king of horses. The meaning of the name is uncertain as *uccais* (*uccaiḥ* in compounds) means 'high' and *śravas*, both 'ear' and 'neigh'. According to some Paurāṇic myths Uccaiḥśravas, as the prototype of horses, emerged from the Churning of the Ocean (*samudramathana*).[2] The *RV*. (I.163,1) similarly refers to an unnamed prototype as coming from the sea or from the atmospheric waters,[3] but in the following verse it is said to have been fashioned from the sun by the Vasus, and thus was a fit mount for Indra, the first to ride it.

The horse thereafter was almost always associated with solar gods, and particularly with the horse-headed solar Viṣṇu (called Hayaśiras) who is identified with Uccaiḥśravas, (*MBh*., 5.99,5, *EM*., p. 204), the horse which follows swiftly in the path of the sun. Uccaiḥśravas was moon-coloured, i.e., white, with a black tail, this distinction being the result of 'serpent-magic'.[4] One late Paurāṇic myth relates that Viṣṇu condemned Lakṣmī to become a mare because she lusted after Revanta, the son of the sun when she saw him riding Uccaiḥśravas.[5] Another myth states that when Pṛthu was installed as sovereign of the earth he made Uccaiḥśravas king of horses (*VP*., I.22).

[1]Among the characteristics of comparatively uncrossed breeds of horses in the remote provinces of India is a tendency 'to long ears with points much turned inwards' (Ridgeway, *Origin and Influence of the Thoroughbred Horse*, p. 157). But it is possible that Uccaiḥśravas represented a powerful breed of ass, like the wild species of Ethiopia, said to be faster and stronger than horses. Long ears may have been regarded as a sign of their strength and speed; or Uccaiḥśravas could have been an onager, such as those used in ancient Mesopotamia which were harnessed to Queen Pu-Abi's chariot in the royal tombs of Ur. The ears of onagers are longer than those of horses, they have straight manes, and tails which end in a tuft of hair. They are often mistaken for asses.

[2]He was claimed by Indra and by Namuci (v. *Kathāsaritsāgara*, Ch. CXXIII), leader of the *dānavas*. In the fight that ensued over the division of the sacred *amṛta*, the gods killed many *dānavas*, but Uccaiḥśravas immediately restored them to life by sniffing them.

[3]Horses are said to be 'water-born' (*apsu-yoni*) (*Tait. Saṁ*., II.3.12,2). In ancient Greece horses were often connected with water-deities (Farnell, *Cults*, IV, pp. 20f.); v. also *EM*., p. 125.

[4]de Gubernatis, *Zoological Mythology*, vol. I, p. 288.

[5]*Devībhāgavata Pur*. (6.17f.) cited by W.D. O'Flaherty, *JRAS*., no. 1, 1971, p. 17.

Uccaṭana One of the six magical means of forcing an enemy to give up his occupation and thus ruin him; or to cause an enemy to flee in shame and disgrace; or to blow up houses and dwellings.[1]

[1]*TT*., p. 156.

v. Ṣaṭkarman.

Ucchiṣṭa 'Residue', the 'rejected', 'remnant', especially the 'remains' of the sacrificial offerings, which were of great ritualistic importance, as indicated by *AV*. (XI.7) which describes and eulogizes the *ucchiṣṭa*[1] as a cosmogonic act affecting the entire world. In the same hymn, verses 15 and 16, the *ucchiṣṭa* is personified as the masculine Ucchiṣṭas.[2] Verse 17 states that truth and law (*ṛta*) are implicit in the remains of the sacrifice, as force is inherent in force.

The relation of the *ucchiṣṭa* to fertility and creation is indicated by the myth of Aditi who, desirous of having offspring, cooked food for the Sādhya gods. She ate the remains which caused her to become pregnant, and subsequently she gave birth to four of the Ādityas. She then cooked more food and ate it, but only succeeded in producing an egg[3] which miscarried. A subsequent attempt resulted in the birth of the Āditya Vivasvant (*Tait. Saṁ.*, VI.5,6).

[1]Offerings to a deity are of two kinds, that eaten by the priests (*brahma-odana*) and that thrown into the fire (*pravargya*), the remainder (*ucchiṣṭa*) being the immanent cause of all that exists. Hence the whole world is metaphorically a remnant of food (v. *HP.*, p. 71). Heesterman points out that the last of a series bears all the dangerous aspects contained in the series; from it a new productive cycle arises (*Ancient Indian Royal Consecration*, p. 70, n.5).

[2]*AVB*. pp. 631f.

[3]Cf. the Mārtāṇḍa myth, where one of the Ādityas, born as a lifeless egg, was cast away, but finally became the most powerful of Aditi's sons. Cf. also Śeṣa ('Remainder'), the world-serpent who remains after the periodic evolution and devolution of the universe, and from whom a new creation arises.

v. Ucchiṣṭagaṇapati.

Ucchiṣṭagaṇapati[1] One of the six sub-divisions of the Gāṇapatya cult, details of which do not occur until the appearance of texts of the medieval period. The adherents of this cult are called Ucchiṣṭas who, probably as a cultic practice, leave the remains of food in their mouths. The leaders of these six cults claimed Gaṇeśa as the supreme god and recited the Gaṇeśa-gāyatrī as given in the *Tait. Ār.* (Book X). The description of the object of worship of the Ucchiṣṭas given by their leader, Vāmācāri-Herambasuta, reveals its Tantric character. The worshippers neither observed caste-distinctions nor married. They drank wine and did not perform daily rites. But doubts have been raised about the existence of so elaborate a form of Tantrism as early as the eighth century.[2]

Gaṇeśa is presented as four-armed, three-eyed, holding a noose, an elephant-goad, a club and showing the *abhaya mudrā* (fear-removing pose); 'the tip of his trunk [is] applied to a pot of strong wine; seated on a *mahāpīṭha* . . . and engaged in kissing and embracing his *śakti* sitting on his left lap'.[3]

[1]Also known as Heramba.

[2]*PTR.*, pp. 154f.

[3]Ibid., p. 154.

v. Ucchiṣṭa.

Uddālaka Āruṇi Name of a *brāhmaṇa* of the Kurupañcālas (*ŚBr.* XI.4.1,2), who like his father Aruṇa was one of the most prominent teachers of the Veda. Uddālaka is repeatedly referred to by his patronymic in the *ŚBr.* and the *Bṛhad-Ār.* and *Chān. Up.* Uddālaka later became the teacher of Yājñavalkya (*Bṛhad-Ār. Up.*, 6.3,7). His son Śvetaketu Āruṇeya on assuring the local ruler, Pravāhaṇa Jaibali, that he had been fully instructed by his father, was rebuked by the prince for his inability to answer questions about metempsychosis (6.2,1–2). When Śvetaketu demanded to know why his father had failed to instruct him, his father had to admit that such a doctrine was unknown to him. Uddālaka therefore went to the prince and asked to be instructed and was told that his ignorance was excusable, because knowledge of the doctrine had hitherto been unknown to all *brāhmaṇas*. Thus Uddālaka was the first *brāhmaṇa* to be instructed in it (*Bṛhad-Ār. Up.*, 6.2,8).[1]

[1]There is no trace of the doctrine in the *RV.*, though Hopkins (*Religions of India*, p. 175) considers that a preliminary sign of the doctrine of metempsychosis appears in the *AV.*, but according to Hume, *TPU.*, p. 54) the notion first makes its definite appearance in the *Śatapatha Brāhmaṇa*.

Udgātṛ (Skt.), **Udgātar** (Vedic) v. Ṛtvij; Brāhmaṇa I.

Udumbara or **Uḍumbara** A tree (Ficus glomerata), regarded as sacred, and serving numerous purposes. Sacrificial articles are made from its wood, such as the post (*yūpa*) to which the sacrificial animal is tied (*Tait. Saṁ.*, II.1.1,5); the seat or throne of the sacrificer (*ŚBr.*, V.2.1,23; *Ait. Br.*, VIII.17); as well as a variety of amulets. Thus one of the latter worn by a virtuous person will bring him prosperity; while one 'quickened by Indra' will slay enemies (*AV.*, XIX.31, 1–14), or drive away evil spirits (*ŚBr.*, III.2.1,32). The *udumbara* also symbolizes food and strength (*Ait. Br.*, V.24).

The *ŚBr.* (VI.6.3,2–3) account states that the esteem for the *udumbara*[1] originated during the war between the gods and the anti-gods (*asuras*), when every tree, except the *udumbara*, sided with the *asuras*. After the battle the victorious gods took possession of the trees and transferred their pith and sap to the *udumbaras*, which resulted in their producing more and better fruit[2] and wood than all other trees. In its fruit is the essence of all fruits, as in its wood are the properties of every kind of wood. Thus when Agni is kindled by the wood of the *udumbara*, he is kindled by that of every tree.

The marriage between trees to promote a woman's

fertility has a parallel custom in the placing of a stick of *udumbara* between a newly married couple to represent the *gandharvas* who had the *jus primae noctis*. The 'fertilizing power of the *gandharvas*, embodied in the wood, was considered as consummating the marriage with the bride'.[3]

[1]The fire-sticks (*aranis*) with which the gods pierced hundreds of *asuras* were made of *udumbara* wood (*Tait. Saṁ.*, V.7,2–3).

[2]According to the *Ait. Br.* (V.24), its fruit ripens three times a year.

[3]Eliade, *Patterns*, p. 309.

v. Ulūkhala II.

Ugra I. 'Powerful', 'mighty', 'terrible'. Its basic meaning is 'powerful', a neutral force which may have good or bad effects. Deities (*devas*) and demons (*asuras*) are exponents of this ambiguous concept of power.[1] The significance of *ugra*[2] has its counterpart in the word '*tabu*' (the '*tapu*' of the Polynesians), meaning 'set apart, because forbidden or sacred'. Thus in Vedic religious thought the divine is always *ugra*. But in post-Vedic India, the term was applied to the offspring of a *kṣatriya* and daughter of a *śūdra*, who shares their worst characteristics, being 'ferocious in manners and delighting in cruelty' (*Manu*, X.9).

[1]Heimann, *Facets*, p. 101.

[2]Derived from the hypothetical root *vaj*; from which *ojas*, *vāja* and *vajra* are also derived (*IAL.*, 1631 and p. 653 under VAJ).

II. The name of one of Śiva's four terrible (*ghora*) aspects, the others being Rudra, Śarva and Aśani, which are balanced by his four gentle (*saumya*) aspects: Bhava, Paśupati, Mahādeva and Īśāna.[1]

[1]They are also the names of the eight forms of Agni (*ŚBr.*, VI.1.3,10–18) which were given by Prajāpati to the nameless boy (Kumāra).

Ugrasena King of Mathurā, deposed by his unscrupulous son Kaṁsa who usurped the throne, and later formed an alliance with his father-in-law Jarāsandha, King of Magadha, against the Yādavas led by Kṛṣṇa. Kaṁsa was later killed by Kṛṣṇa, and Jarāsandha by Bhīma, and Ugrasena restored to his throne.

v. Kṛṣṇa I; Sāmba.

Ugratārā The terrifying form of the tantric goddess Tārā, one of the ten *mahāvidyās*. As long as offerings are made to the solar fire the sun will shed its heat beneficially, but should they cease to be made, it will assume the all-consuming form of Ugratārā.[1]

[1]*HP.*, p. 276. Ugratārā is also the name of the Mahāyāna Buddhist tantric goddess who was adopted by the Hindus under the name of Tārā (Bhattacharyya, *The Indian Buddhist Iconography*, p. 76).

Ujjayinī One of the seven sacred Hindu cities, and an important centre politically and commercially in ancient India.[1] Many of its kings were probably Haihayas (a branch of the Yādavas), or Avantis, one of the five branches of the Haihayas, who ruled after the Bhārata War. They were succeeded by the Pradyotas whose first king was a contemporary of Bimbisāra of Magadha, according to Pāli accounts. It was to Ujjayinī that Candragupta, after the founding of the Mauryan Empire, appointed his grandson Aśoka as Viceroy.

In Hindu mythology Ujjayinī is one of the places where a portion of Satī's body fell after she had been cut in pieces by Viṣṇu's *cakra*. In Hindu geography longitude is calculated from Ujjayinī.

[1]Also called Avanti, the name of the state of which it was the capital. It is identified with the modern Ujjain.

v. Tīrtha(s); Kāśī; Maurya(s).

Ulkāmukha I. 'Fiery mouth.' A son of Agni.[1]

[1]*EM.*, p. 104.

II. A demonic form assumed by the departed spirit of a *brāhmaṇa* who has failed to fulfil his sacred duties (*Manu*, XII.71).

Ulūka 'Owl.' This bird is referred to in the *RV.* (X.165,4) as a harbinger of misfortune (*nairṛta*).[1] Thus the owl is one of the offerings made to Nirṛti[2] the goddess of misery, decay, etc., to avert harm from the king during the *rājasūya* (*ŚBr.*, V.2.3,2–3), or during the *aśvamedha* (horse sacrifice), held in recognition of his imperial status (*Tait. Saṁ.*, V.5,18).

Owls and owlets were believed to be among the many forms assumed by demonic powers (*RV.*, VII.104,22).

[1]A belief common to the Romans from whom European folklore appears to have derived it. But in Greece the owl was sacred to Athena.

[2]Pigeons and hares were also offered to her.

Ulūka Kaṇāda The legendary founder of the Vaiśeṣika school.

Ulūkhala(s) I. Demons whom it was necessary to propitiate with offerings of mustard seeds mixed with rice-chaff.[1] The *Brahmāṇḍa* and *Vāyu Purāṇas* call them Piśācas, having sunken eyes and protruding tongues, and wearing mortars or bowls as ornaments.

[1]*DHI.*, p. 70, n.1.

II. A wooden mortar or bowl (*RV.*, I.28,6; *AV.*, X.9,26, etc.), often made of *udumbara* wood. According to the *Tait. Saṁ.* (V.2,8,7) a mortar represents the navel or centre of the sacrificial fire, and also provides a base for the *yūpa* or sacrificial post (VII.2.1,3). The *ulūkhala* may also be the name of a mortar-shaped cup used to hold the *soma* libation.

Umā A non-Vedic Indian mother-goddess with whom

many local goddesses have gradually become identified and by whose names she is also known. Thus she is called Pārvatī, Durgā, Aparṇā, Ambikā, Bhadrakālī, Mahākālī, Rudrāṇī, Mahānidrā, Śākambharī, Gaurī, etc. In the *Kena Up.* (25) she is called Umā Haimavatī[1] the daughter of Himavat (the personified Himālaya), and this may be her original name.[2] Umā is said to nourish the world with life-sustaining vegetables which emerged from her body during the rains (*Mārk. P.*, XCI.43); or she may be a corn-goddess.[3]

The Indian mother-goddess concept is distinguished from that of other ancient cultures by its 'philosophical sublimation' and identification with the distinctively Indian cosmogonic notion of energy, in its constructive and destructive forms represented by the Śiva-Śakti union.[4] Thus at the end of the age (*yuga*) Śiva and Umā manifest themselves to mankind.[5]

[1]Umā may have been 'a female mountain ghost haunting the Himālaya' (*Ancestor Worship*, p. 242).

[2]Oppert (*Original Inhabitants of India*, p. 421) suggests that her name may be derived from Ammā, a common name for Dravidian mother-goddesses, her vehicle (*vāhana*) the cow, being symbolically associated with mother-goddesses in many ancient cultures. v. also Gonda, *VS.*, p. 212, n. 263.

[3]*IT.*, p. 161. Umā also means flax or turmeric (*SED.*).

[4]*HCIP.*, vol. I, p. 162.

[5]*EM.*, p. 226.

Upabhṛt One of the three sets of sacrificial ladles, each made of different wood,[1] and each of great ritual significance (*ŚBr.*, XI.4.2,1ff.; *Tait. Saṁ.*, I.1.11; III. 5,7). As the offerings were believed to sustain the gods, so the sacrificial utensils were thought to contribute in some measure to the stability of the world, the function of the *upabhṛt* being to sustain the atmosphere (*AV.*, XVIII.4,5).

[1]v. Caland and Henry, *L'Agniṣṭoma*, pp. 253ff.

v. Juhū I.

Upajihvikā, Upajīkā,[1] or **Upadīkā** Three forms of a word denoting a species of ant which has considerable ritual significance and is the basis of numerous myths. Ritually an ant-hill represents the earth (*ŚBr.*, VI.3.3,5); it thus has life-giving properties.[2] Ants have the power of locating water possessing healing properties; or they use water given them by the gods to destroy poison (*AV.*, VI.100,2); they also produce a remedy for flux (*AV.*, II.3,4). The earth from ant-hills has long been considered to possess medicinal properties and to be connected with fertility. Ants are divine and the first-born of the world (*ŚBr.*, XIV.1.2,10).

Mythology provides other myths relating to ants and ant-hills. According to the belief of the Korkus of Central India, Śiva (Mahadeo) made man and woman from the red earth of an ant-hill. Viṣṇu's bowstring was gnawed through by ants, its sudden release resulting in his decapitation (*ŚBr.*, XIV.1.1,1–9). Ants are an integral part of the community to whom food should be supplied (*Mārk. P.*, XXXIV.1ff.).

[1]Monier-Williams (*SED.*) suggests that *upajīkā* may be the name of a water-deity.

[2]Keith, *Tait. Saṁ.*, vol. I, Intro., p. cxxxix.

Upamanyu A Śaiva ascetic whose hermitage in the Himālaya became a sanctuary for all kinds of animals, snakes, etc., who lived peacefully together.[1] This idyllic state was made possible by the power derived from self-discipline and austerities (*tapas*), achieved by the perfected *ṛṣi*.

[1]Cf. Isaiah, XI.6ff.

Upanayana I. The introduction[1] to esoteric lore (or to any science); the ceremony in which a *guru* initiates a boy into one of the three 'twice-born' castes.

A spiritual relationship exists between *guru* and pupil, a tie no less real than blood relationship. This led to the practice of the pupil taking the name of his teacher. Thus a pupil could not marry the daughter of his teacher, and so Kaca could not marry Devayānī, the daughter of his *guru* Śukra.

The *upanayana* appears to be the continuation of a prehistoric initiatory rite, like that of the Jünglingsweihe or induction of a youth into full membership of the community, a practice common to early tribal units throughout the world,[2] but it had 'little or no trace of overt sexual symbolism ... [like the] initiation ceremonies among more primitive peoples, as a rite fitting the initiate for sexual life'.[3]

The investiture of the three superior castes with the 'sacred thread' is called *yajñopavīta*.[4] It is worn over the right shoulder and hangs down under the left. It was originally only put on during the performance of sacred ceremonies. In modern times it is assumed by other castes such as the Vaidyas (a medical caste) in Bengal.

[1]*CC.*, pp. 232 and 235.

[2]*ERE.*, VII, p. 323. The 'Zoroastrians had a similar ceremony, a form of which is still practised by the modern Parsīs' (*WI.*, p. 161).

[3]*WI.*, p. 162.

[4]A rite resembling in some respects that of baptism and confirmation in the Christian Church, especially in the regenerative notion of the rite and the naming of the initiate who is considered to be born again. v. *AV.*, XI.5,7 whence the epithet 'twice-born' is applied to those of the three superior classes for whom the appropriate rite (*yajñopavīta*) has been performed. Cf. also the Orphic doctrine of Palingenesia—a sort of

spiritual rebirth (Harrison, *Prolegomena to the Study of Greek Religion*, p. 526).
v. Dīkṣā.
II. One of the twelve purificatory rites (*saṁskāras*) prescribed in the Dharma Sūtras.

Upaniṣad (s) From *upa*, 'supplementary', 'additional', and *ni-ṣad* 'to sit down near a teacher', from whom a pupil received esoteric knowledge. But grammarians differ about the meaning of the word, some defining it as '*tattvajñāna*', the knowledge of reality; others as '*rahasya*', secret doctrine. The Upaniṣads themselves indicate that the knowledge contained in them was esoteric and therefore to be imparted only in secret. But most of the two hundred or more so-called Upaniṣads[1] contain neither esoteric doctrine nor teaching imparted in secret. Of all these texts, whether individual or part of a collection, only thirteen—or fourteen, according to some authorities—actually contain esoteric teaching. The remainder are late compositions which mainly represent the views of Vaiṣṇavas, Śaivas and Śāktas. Winternitz[2] divides them into six classes, which deal with the following subjects respectively: 1. Vedānta doctrine; 2. Yoga; 3. the ascetic life (*sannyāsa*); 4. Viṣṇu; 5. Śiva; 6. other cults.

The dating of the thirteen (or fourteen) classical Upaniṣads is conjectural, but internal evidence suggests that they were composed between 700 and 300 B.C., some of them revealing changes of style and views, and of repeated revision. Their composition may be assigned to three periods. Six belong to the earliest; six to the middle, regarded as pre-Buddhist and pre-Pāṇini;[3] the last two to a time shortly after the establishment of the Buddhist Order. The first group consists of the Aitareya, Kauṣitaki, Taittirīya, Bṛhad-Ār., Chān. and Kena; the second, Kāṭhaka, Śvetāśvatara, Mahā-Nārāyaṇa, Īśā, Muṇḍaka, and Praśna; the third, Maitrāyaṇīya and Māṇḍūkya. Those of the first group resemble Brāhmaṇas in language and style, a simple, slightly clumsy prose, but by no means lacking in beauty.[4] Some of the second group are mainly composed in verse, and unlike those of the first group, reflect Sāṁkhya and Yoga views, though their inclusion may be the result of late recensions. Those of the third group are definitely post-Vedic, both in language and views.

The fourteen Upaniṣads, as well as other 'forest compilations' called Āraṇyakas, were subsequently attached to particular Brāhmaṇas,[5] which in turn were attached to a particular Veda. Thus the *Bṛhad-Ār. Up.*, itself probably a collection of earlier compositions, was attached to the *Śatapatha Brāhmaṇa*, which was attached to the White *Yajurveda*.

That the Āraṇyakas and Upaniṣads originated as a reaction against the stereotyped views of professional sacerdotalists can hardly be doubted. This is indicated by *kṣatriyas* being numbered among the composers of the Upaniṣads, and also by the choice of forest retreats for the discussion and teaching of esoteric doctrines. Once begun, the speculative mood became general and resulted in the formation of other groups opposed to brahminic fundamentalism, such as the Cārvākas, Jainas and Buddhists. Even some priestly schools appear to have been influenced and to have contributed to the final recension of the earliest Upaniṣads, which may account for some of their inconsistencies.[6] The Upaniṣads have thus been criticized adversely for some of their views and the use of false analogies. The explanation lies perhaps in the fact that they are not a single co-ordinated collection but separate compositions, the work of minds not always equally well-equipped for the task.

Nonetheless, the fact remains that the Upaniṣads generally present an objective view of the universe and a rational approach to the problem of reality far in advance even of the flashes of intuitive knowledge that illumine occasional passages of the Vedas and Brāhmaṇas. Thus the expression 'as if' or 'as it were' (*iva*) in the *Bṛhad-Ār. Up.* (II.4,14), accords well with the modern scientific view that, despite the manifold appearances of the phenomenal world, the entire universe, both known and as yet unknown, is essentially one.[7]

[1] 'The practice of taking what is actually not an Upaniṣad as an Upaniṣad appears to have been in existence from the time of Pāṇini' (Bhattacharyya, *Āgamaśāstra of Gauḍapāda*, p. xxxvi).
[2] *HIL.*, pt. 1, p. 209.
[3] With the possible exception of the *Śvetāśvatara*, which Jacobi considers to be apocryphal (*ERE.*, III, p. 156).
[4] *HIL.*, p. 205.
[5] For a full list of the Brāhmaṇas and the Upaniṣads attached to them, v. 'Veda'.
[6] Nonetheless, 'it is a well-known fact that all the later schools of Indian philosophy, which [may] radically differ from each other . . . depend on the Upaniṣads for their basic authorities' (*C. Herit. I.*, vol. II, pp. 67f.).
[7] This is emphasized in the *Īśa Up.*: 'The man who understands that every creature exists in God alone, and thus perceives the unity of being, has no grief and no illusion' (*IW.*, p. 39).

Upa-Purāṇa (s) v. Purāṇa (s).

Uparicara v. Adrikā.

Upa-Veda (s)[1] 'Secondary or supplementary knowledge.' Minor or subordinate Vedas, which have no connexion with the 'revealed' Veda. The Upa-vedas are:

Āyur-veda, the science of medicine; Gāndharva-veda, the science of music and dancing; Dhanur-veda, the science of military science and archery; and Sthāpatya-veda, the science of architecture.

[1]*Upa*, a preposition or prefix to verbs and nouns denotes position, i.e., 'near to', as opposed to *apa*, 'away from'. *Upa* is thus relative and denotes contiguity in space, time, number, degree, resemblance, but always in the sense of inferiority or subordination to the idea of the noun or verb to which it is attached (*SED*.).

Upendra 'Younger brother of Indra', i.e., Kṛṣṇa.

When Indra, jealous of Kṛṣṇa's growing influence, sent a great flood which threatened to destroy the Govardhana mountain and the cowherds (*gopas*) and cattle dwelling there, Kṛṣṇa lifted it up and so provided shelter for them. Indra was amazed at the miracle, and realizing that he was confronted by a power greater than his own, conferred on Kṛṣṇa the epithet Upendra (*VP*., V.12).

Uraga I. A snake (*nāga*) usually represented with a human face.

II. The lunar asterism (*nakṣatra*) Āśleṣa presided over by *nāgas*.

Ūrjā v. Ūrjānī.

Ūrjānī A goddess personifying strength, who is associated with the Aśvins (*RV*., I.119,2). She may be identical with the post-Vedic Ūrjā, 'daughter of Dakṣa who bore Vasiṣṭha seven sons' (*Mārk. P*., L.22–3; LII. 26).

Ūrmyā A Vedic goddess who is the personification of Night. A *RV*. hymn (X.127) is addressed to her:

Kind goddess who at thy coming
Straightway thy servants seek repose
Like birds who nightly nestle in the trees.
Drive thou away, O Night, the wolf,
Drive hence the thief, and keep us safely until Dawn,
Who like one that clears away a debt
Shall chase away this black, yet palpable obscurity[1].

[1]Abridged from the tr. of *MMW*., *Indian Wisdom*.

Ūrva v. Aurva.

Urvarā The name of an *apsaras*.

v. Urvarāpati.

Urvarāpati 'Lord of the cultivated soil'. An epithet of Indra (*RV*., VIII.21,3).[1]

[1]Cf. *urvarā*, meaning 'fertile soil'.

Urvaśī[1] Name of an *apsaras* or heavenly nymph, first obscurely referred to in *RV*. (V.41,19). A later hymn (VII.33,11; also *Bṛhadd*., V.149) refers to the birth of Vasiṣṭha as the result of Varuṇa's and Mitra's ardent love for Urvaśī, a myth subsequently elaborated in post-Vedic literature. Similarly the dialogue between Urvaśī and Purūravas (*RV*., X.95) contains the germ of subsequent myths in the *ŚBr*. (XI.5.1, 1–17), the *MBh*. and Purs., and on which Kālidāsa based his drama 'The Hero and the Nymph' (*Vikramorvaśī*).

The Urvaśī-Purūravas myth has some connexion with the fire-generating ritual, the two fire-sticks (*araṇis*) being called Urvaśī and Purūravas, and the fire thus generated is called their child Āyu (*Tait. Saṁ*., I.3,7). In some Purs. (*Brahmāṇḍa*, III. 7,16 and *Bhāg. P*., II.3,6, *PI*.) Urvaśī is invoked to grant success in love affairs.

[1]For various meanings of her name v. *Nir*., 5,13. Urvaśīs (pl.) are mentioned in *AV*., XVIII.3,23.

v. Kṛpa II.

Ūṣā v. Aniruddha I.

Uśanas Kāvya A famous Vedic *ṛṣi*, the son of Kavi. He is frequently mentioned in the *RV*., where he is closely associated with the fire-ritual (VIII.23,17), and regarded as the composer of four hymns. The first (VIII.73) is addressed to Agni, the remainder (IX.87–9) to Soma Pavamāna. He is repeatedly referred to as the friend of Indra, whose *vajra* he endowed with 'the greatness and strength that rends both worlds apart' (I.51,10);[1] but another passage (I.121,12) states that the bolt was actually fashioned by Uśanas and given by him to Indra.[2] He shares with Indra the victory over the drought-demon Śuṣṇa (V.29,9), and accompanies the gods when Indra and Kutsa stemmed the floods that threatened Yadu and Turvaśa (V.31,8). He is praised for his wisdom and for his championship of the people, as well as for having discovered the mysterious hidden nature of cows. The *Tait. Saṁ*. (II.5.8,5) calls him the messenger of the *asuras*.[3]

In the Epics Uśanas Kāvya is syncretized with Uśanas Śukra, a Bhārgava priest, the *purohita* of Yayāti, the paramount ruler of several non-Āryan Indian kingdoms whose people were derogatively designated *daityas*, *asuras*, or *rākṣasas*. He became the *guru* of Kaca, son of Bṛhaspati, whose object in becoming the pupil of Śukra was to obtain—by fair means or foul—the secret of immortality (*saṁjīvinī vidyā*). His attempts to do so and at the same time repulse Śukra's only daughter Devayānī who wished to marry him, form the theme of a highly coloured story in the *MBh*. (Ādi pa., 76–83).

Śukra, like Agastya, is represented in the *Rām*. as being a 'missionary' to tribes (Rākṣasas and others) in the Deccan. As their preceptor he sought to instruct Meghanāda, son of Rāvaṇa, in Vedic sacrificial rites, but his offer was bluntly refused (*Rām*., 7.25, 6f.).

Śukra was given stellar status[4] and appointed Regent of the planet Venus.

[1]But *RV*. (VI.20,11) attributes the power of Uśanas to Indra.

[2]The fashioning of Indra's *vajra* is generally attributed to Tvaṣṭar.

[3]In the *Mārk. P.* (II. 47ff.) Uśanas encourages the *daityas* to continue their fight against the gods.

For the story of Uśanas being swallowed by Śiva and his emergence from his phallus, v. *IT.*, p. 159.

[4]Śukra (which means luminous or bright) along with other *ṛṣis* achieved this stellar distinction.

v. Bhṛgu; Bṛhaspati.

Uṣas Goddess of the dawn. The *RV.* hymn (I.48) addressed to her refers to her as Daughter of the Sky, the Lady of Light.[1] Like a good matron she comes tending everything, rousing all creatures to activity, encouraging them and assuring them of her bounty. She opens the twin doors of heaven and reveals herself in all-subduing splendour.

There are few references to Uṣas in the *AV.* One refers to a charm to restore virility by means of a particular plant and the influence of Sūrya and Uṣas (IV.4, 1 ff.). The rising sun and Uṣas are especially calculated to dispel the evils associated with night, and by extension with misery and disease.[2] Another hymn (VI.6,7) declares that Uṣas will deliver men from the power of curses.

[1]*Nir.*, 12,5f. derives *uṣas* from the root *vaś* 'to shine; and identifies her with Sūryā (12,7); v. also *AVB.*, p. 503.

[2]*AVB.*, p. 318.

Uṣṇīṣa A turban; head-band; or anything wound round the head. A uṣṇīṣa is put on the head of a king during his consecration (*abhiṣeka*), and is regarded as a source of special power. In ritual the donning of various garments including the *uṣṇīṣa* symbolizes 'the vestures of the embryo' and stages of birth, by which the initiant is reborn (*ŚBr.*, V.3.5,23–4; and v. n.3).

The protuberance depicted on the top of the head of the Buddha is also called *uṣṇīṣa* and denotes great wisdom.

v. Rājasūya.

Usrā 'Morning light, daybreak', personified as a red cow, the source of all good things.

Uṣṭrapāda The name of a *yakṣa*. He was 'a being either human or animal, with the feet of a camel'.[1]

[1]*DHI.*, p. 134.

Utathya v. Ucathya; Mamatā; Dīrghatamas.

Utpalācārya A pupil of Somānanda. Utpalācārya wrote the *Īśvara-pratyabhijñā-kārikā* and two commentaries thereon, in which he refuted the Buddhist objections to the basis of monistic Śaivism.[1]

[1]*EW.*, vol. I, p. 383.

Utpāta Any sudden or unexpected event, or the portent of one, particularly a calamity (*AV.*, XIX.9,7). Man's collective wrong-doing is believed to accumulate and to form an actual entity which causes natural disturbances. The latter are indicated by celestial, atmospheric and terrestrial portents. To appease the gods it was necessary to perform certain expiatory 'rites of aversion' (*śāntis*).

Uttānapad Name of a particular creative agency by which existence became manifest (*RV.*, X.72).

v. Aditi.

Uttara 'Upper, higher', and by extension 'northern',[1] because the northern part of India is high. It is opposed to *adhara*, 'low, lower region'; furthermore it also means *vāma* 'left' as opposed to *dakṣiṇa* 'right', because in praying, the face when turned to the east would place the north on the left hand.[2] *Uttara* later signified 'posterior, future', as opposed to *pūrva*, 'former'. It also meant 'remainder', 'result' or 'conclusion', and thus is the name of the last book of the *Rāmāyaṇa*. These prefixes serve also to distinguish the *pūrva* and *uttara mīmāṁsā darśanas*. In some contexts *uttara* signifies superiority, excellence, competence.

[1]The Hindu sacred mountains of Kailāsa and Meru, whose peaks were said to pierce heaven, are situated in the north. Cf. *uttaramārga*, the way to the north, i.e., heaven. v. Job, 37,22; Psalm, 48,2. The ancient Egyptian gods dwelt on the northern mountain; the Kwan-lun of the Chinese, and the Asaheim of the Norsemen were also in this region. 'The numinous quality of the north also inspires the belief that it is the seat of demons. This idea obtained among the Iranians' (Gaster, *Thespis*, p. 182 n.).

[2]*SED.*, p. 178.

Uttarā A daughter of the *rāja* of Virāṭa and wife of Abhimanyu. Her son was Parīkṣit.

Uttara-Mīmāṁsā v. Vedānta.

Uttara-Rāma-Carita 'Later Chronicle of Rāma', the name of a drama by Bhavabhūti (8th century), on the last half of Rāma's life. It is based on the *uttarakāṇḍa* (the last section) of the *Rāmāyaṇa*.

Uttarāṇi v. Araṇi.

Uttaravedi The northern (or upper) altar (*vedi*) represents the sphere of the gods, the southern the sphere of the *pitṛs*. The *uttaravedi* also represents the whole world. It is equated with Vāc, the goddess of speech, the supreme medium of communication (*ŚBr.*, III.5.1,23), and because of its shape the altar is likened to a woman (III.5.1,35).

v. Vedi; Uttara.

V

Vac (In compounds Vak.) Its primary meaning is language or speech, i.e., the sounds (*śabda*) produced vocally as a means of communication.

Lack of a written language in early Vedic times made oral transmission the only means of recording and communicating the sacred truths of the Veda 'heard' by holy men (*ṛṣis*). Thus arose the necessity not only for correct words, but also for correct intonation and accent, without which the *mantras* and the sacrificial ritual would be ineffectual.

Language not only enabled everything to be named, but was considered to define the essence of the thing named, and to know the name of a thing conferred the power to control it, and hence the Atharvanic belief that if the names of demons were known, they would be rendered harmless.

The *Bṛhad-Ār. Up.* (4.1,2) considers *vac* to be an aspect of the Eternal Principle (*brahman*), for only by means of language can sacred knowledge (or any knowledge) be apprehended. Without it the Vedas, legends (*itihāsas*), ancient lore (*purāṇas*), mystic doctrines (*upaniṣads*), and the sciences (*vidyās*) would have remained unknown.

v. Vāc.

Vāc Speech personified as a goddess. She was initially little more than a folk-divinity, but her influence on Vedic theology became increasingly apparent (*ŚBr.*, III.5.1,18–23) and resulted in her being given precedence over Agni at the sacrifice.

Vāc is identified with the river-goddess Sarasvatī, and thus became associated with nature as well as learning.[1] The banks of the Sarasvatī were one of the most important sites of brahmanical culture.

Like the neo-Platonic 'logos' Vāc was the 'Word',[2] the supreme source of creativity.

Vāc is sometimes called the 'Gladdener' who bestows food and vigour, or a milch-cow, the source of all good things (*RV.*, VIII.89,11).

When the *gandharva* Viśvavasu stole the sacred *soma*, the gods, knowing the *gandarvas*' fondness for women, sent the goddess Vāc to beguile them into returning it (*ŚBr.*, III.2.4,1–7).

[1]Cf. the Celtic goddess Ceridwen who was both a patroness of grain and of poetry and letters. Edgerton regards Vāc as the 'personification of Vedic hymnal composition' (*BIP.*, p. 71). Cf. *RV.*, X.81,7, where Viśvakarman is called 'lord of holy utterance' (Vācaspati).

[2]Eliade, *Yoga*, p. 116. The Vedic notion that Vāc gave birth to the *mantras*, gave rise in Tantric circles to the idea of the *mantra*-mother (*mātṛkā śakti*) or Para-Vāc, the Supreme Logos.

v. Gñā.

Vacā An aromatic root which was ground into a powder and mixed with milk. When consecrated it was believed to improve memory and hearing, and if taken for forty-eight consecutive days would improve eyesight, conduce to longevity, and expiate all 'sins' (*Suś. Saṁ.*, II, p. 526).

Vācaspatimiśra The name of the author of the *Tattvakaumudī*, an important work on the Sāṁkhya *darśana*.

Vaḍabā or **Baḍavā** 'Mare.' The name of the *apsaras* Aśvinī who in the form of a mare became the mother of the twin Aśvins by Vivasvat (the sun).[1]

[1]A variant of this myth appears in the *VP.* (III.1).

Vaḍabāgni 'Mare's fire', i.e., the submarine fire, said to emerge from a cavity called the mare's mouth (*vaḍabāmukha*), situated under the sea at the South Pole.[1] It remains beneath the sea until finally it erupts and destroys the world, and hence has become a metaphor for insatiable energy.

After Śiva had cut off Brahmā's fifth head, he was pursued relentlessly by the demon of brahminicide who is likened to the all-consuming mare-fire (*Bhaviṣya P.*, 1. 22, 14 and 16; *Skanda P.*, 3.1.24, 30–67).

The *Harivaṁśa* (I.45,1–19) associates fire with demons, and in the *Padma P.* (5.18,159–98) the gods instructed Sarasvatī to take the fire before it reduced the world to ashes and to throw it into the ocean, where it remained as the submarine fire.[2]

[1]*SED.* Probably based on the experience of volcanic submarine eruptions. The Greek monster Typhoeus also 'seems to have had some connexion with volcanoes and subterranean forces' (Farnell, *Cults*, I, p. 183).

[2]For other myths v. W. D. O'Flaherty, *JRAS.*, no. 1, 1971, 'The Submarine Mare in the Mythology of Śiva', pp. 9ff.

v. Aurva.

Vaḍabāmukha v. Vaḍabāgni.

Vāgbhaṭa v. Āyurveda.

Vāhana 'Vehicle', 'bearer'. The bird or animal[1] on

which a Jaina, Hindu or Mahāyāna Buddhist deity rides or is associated with. The *vāhana* 'is a duplicate representation of the energy and character of the god'.[2] The term does not occur in the *RV.* in the sense of a vehicle for the gods; in the *Ait. Br.* (IV.9,4; *ŚBr.*, I.8.2,9, etc.) it denotes a 'beast of burden' or occasionally a 'cart'.[3]

Many of the ancient Mesopotamian gods are depicted with *vāhanas* c. 1500 B.C. or earlier, and the idea was probably taken to India from Mesopotamia by traders.

In post-Vedic mythology the *vāhana* and the attributes associated with the various divinities, help to distinguish them. Thus Brahmā has a goose (*haṁsa*); Viṣṇu has the fabulous Garuḍa bird; Bhairava, a dog; Śiva, a bull; Durgā, a lion; Agni, a ram; Gaṇeśa, a rat; Varuṇa, a makara; Skanda, a cockerel; Kāma, a parrot; Kārttikeya, a peacock, etc.

[1]Very occasionally a man is a *vāhana*, as in the case of the dread goddess Nirṛti, and of the non-Āryan divinity, Kubera, overlord of *yakṣas* and god of wealth.

[2]Zimmer, *Myths and Symbols in Indian Art and Civilization*, p. 70 and v. p. 146.

[3]*VI.*, vol. II, p. 293.

Vaidhyata Name of Yama's gate-keeper.

Vaijayanta I. 'Victorious.' Name of Indra's banner, said to be dark-blue, which hung from a yellow staff attached to his golden chariot, Jaitraratha. The banner itself was believed to possess magical powers by which Indra overcame the *asuras*, and hence it became 'the object of a separate cult.'[1]

[1]*HP.*, p. 110.

v. Vaijantī-mālā.

II. An epithet of Skanda, the god of war.

Vaijayantī-mālā 'Garland of victory', the garland (*mālā*) worn by Viṣṇu. It is variously described as consisting of five kinds of gems: emeralds, pearls, bluestones (possibly sapphires), rubies and diamonds, which are associated with the five elements; or as consisting of fragrant wild flowers, symbolizing the different worlds and solar systems (*AGP.*, 201, 1–8). Its very presence ensures victory, as does Indra's banner Vaijayanta.

Vaikuṇṭha I. An epithet of Indra. Several hymns in the *RV.* (X.47–50) are associated with him under the joint name Indra-Vaikuṇṭha. In post-Vedic mythology Vaikuṇṭha is a name of Viṣṇu and of his sphere (*loka*) or Paradise, whose location is said to be either in the depths of the ocean, or on the northern or eastern peak of Mount Meru. It is built of gold and precious stones, and is eternal and beyond even the perception of the gods.

II. An image which combines the three (or four) aspects of Viṣṇu (*Viṣṇudharmottara*, III, ch. 85).[1]

[1]*DHI.*, p. 409.

v. Vyūha(s) n. 2.

Vaiśālī The name of the kingdom whose capital,[1] situated in eastern India, was founded by Viśāla, the son of Tṛṇabindu, whose reign traditional history assigned to the third quarter of the *treta* age.[2]

Vaiśālī subsequently became famous as the scene of the Buddha's activities and as the birthplace of the last Jaina *tīrthankara* Vardhamana Mahāvīra.

[1]Identified with Basārh (Muzaffarpur district) *HCIP.*, I, p. 272.

[2]*HCIP.*, I, p. 292.

Vaiśampāyana Name of an ancient sage, whom post-Vedic mythology declares to be the first teacher of the doctrines of the *Tait. Saṁ.*, and to have been a pupil of Vyāsa. He is also said to have narrated the whole of the *Mahābhārata* to Janamejaya during the intervals of the latter's great sacrifice of snakes (*nāgas*). The latter probably refers to the slaying of the Nāga tribesmen who had killed his forbear Parakṣit.

Vaiśeṣika Name of one of the six Hindu 'orthodox' priestly 'philosophical' schools (*darśanas*), whose founder is said to be the sage Kaṇāda,[1] also known as Ulūka. The name Vaiśeṣika is derived from *viśeṣa*, 'a category of knowledge, denoting essential difference, individuality, particularity', one of the characteristics of eternal substance (*dravya*). These categories or *padārthas* are considered to be so essentially different that one can never be the other.[2]

In Kaṇāda's *sūtras* he enumerates six categories of existence, to which a seventh, non-existence (*abhāva*) was subsequently added, because it was considered to have been implied by him. As substance constituted the basis of the other categories, only it could give them significance. In the Vaiśeṣika system substance is therefore described in comprehensive terms. It comprises earth (*pṛthivī*), water (*āpas*), light (*tejas*), air (*vāyu*), ether (*ākāśa*), time (*kāla*), space (*diś*), essence of being (*ātman*), and mind (*manas*).

The seven categories are: 1. substance (*dravya*); 2. apparent quality or property (*guṇa*);[3] 3. act or action (*karman*); 4. generality or universality (*sāmānya*); 5. particularity (*viśeṣa*); 6. co-inherence or perpetual intimate relation (*samavaya*); 7. non-existence or negation of existence (*abhāva*).[4] But while there was general agreement between the Nyāya and Vaiséṣika systems, they differed on points of epistemology. Whereas the Nyāya recognized four independent sources of knowledge, viz., perception, inference, comparison and testimony, the Vaiśeṣika recognized only perception and inference, regarding comparison and testimony merely as aspects of perception. Another important difference was that the Vaiśeṣika recognized only seven categories of reality. To these the Nyāya added nine, making sixteen in all.

The presence of the Greeks on the north-western frontiers of India, and the contact of Buddhist pilgrims with Persia, Syria, Alexandria and China, led to some interchange of ideas, but such ideas, though similar, were far from being identical owing to ancient prejudices and traditions—religious and mythical.[5]

The Vaiśeṣika attempted to harmonize philosophical theory with both a moral and spiritual attitude to life and theistic faith, but failed to carry their theism to the point where the Supreme Being is the essence of reality and not merely the agent of a release from the law of *karman* and the bondage of *saṁsāra*. Such a point was not reached until the Nyāya-Vaiśeṣika philosophy became integrated with that of the Vedānta.

[1]Probably a nickname, meaning 'Feeder on atoms' (Monier-Williams, *Indian Wisdom*, p. 76, n.1).

[2]*SED*., p. 990.

[3]But a *guṇa*, though existing in a substance, has no existence apart from it, and by itself is never a cause of anything. The Vaiśeṣika lists twenty-four kinds of *guṇas*, which may be further divided and sub-divided.

[4]Chatterjee and Datta, *Introduction to Indian Philosophy*, 6th ed., p. 224.

[5]The Vaiśeṣika enumerated four kinds of atoms, whereas Democritus recognized only one kind. The Vaiśeṣika considered the atom to be the smallest particle, a view that persisted in scientific circles until the atom was split by Rutherford early in the twentieth century.

Vaiṣṇava The cult of Viṣṇu, and a term for a follower of the cult. The Vaiṣṇava is one of the three great divisions of modern Hinduism, the other two being the Śaiva and Śākta.

The Vaiṣṇavas became separated into four principal sects and some minor ones. The former are: the Rāmānujas founded by Rāmānuja; the Mādhvas, founded by Madhva; the Vallabhas, founded by Vallabhācārya; and a sect founded by Caitanya who was regarded as an *avatāra* of Kṛṣṇa.

Vaiṣṇavism was initially connected with the Vedic solar deity Viṣṇu (the Pervader), as the source of light and symbol of spiritual enlightenment, and is thus portrayed in the *gāyatrī* hymn (*RV*., III. 62, 10). Viṣṇu was subsequently assimilated with Nārāyaṇa, the personification of cosmic energy. Later, when the apotheosis of the tribal hero Kṛṣṇa-Vāsudeva was generally acknowledged, his name was linked to those of Viṣṇu and Nārāyaṇa, and all three were ultimately 'equalized by a mysterious process of religious syncretism'.[1]

Vaiṣṇava doctrines are derived mainly from the texts of its several schools, partly from the late classical Upaniṣads, the early Purāṇas, the Epics and the *Bhagavadgītā*. Finally Viṣṇu was regarded both as Īśvara, the Lord or Supreme Being, and the abstract *brahman*.

Vaiṣṇavism reflects the influence of Buddhism, of its tolerance, humanitarianism, and self-discipline. It was also influenced by Tantrism.

During its formative period Vaiṣṇava doctrine appealed strongly to the common people, an appeal that was undoubtedly heightened by the notion of a divine being whose 'descents' (*avatāras*) to earth were made to succour and to protect them in times of great need. The chief *avatāras* were Kṛṣṇa-Vāsudeva and Rāmacandra, but especially Kṛṣṇa who is regarded as a complete manifestation of Viṣṇu, unlike the other *avatāras* who are only partial incarnations.

[1]J. Gonda, *Die Religionen Indiens*, vol. I, pp. 236f.

v. Vedānta; Viśiṣṭādvaita; Bhakti; Śeṣa; Pāñcarātra; Hari-Hara.

Vaiśravaṇa 'Son of Viśravas.' One of the several patronymics of Rāvaṇa and Kubera, whose parentage is variously assigned according to the particular mythological tradition[1] adopted in the *MBh.* and *Rāmāyaṇa* during the various periods of their composition.

[1]Details of which are given by Hopkins in *EM*., pp. 142ff. Vaiśravaṇa is often depicted with flames emerging from his shoulders, which 'represent the fiery energy inherent in a king' (Coomaraswamy, *Yakṣas*, pt.i, p. 1.).

Vaiśvadeva A household ceremony of Vedic origin[1] which begins with an offering to all the gods, and ends with a rite called *bali-haraṇa*, a rite 'far more interesting than the *pañcāyatana-pūjā*, or any other modern form of the *deva-pūjā*'.[2] The ceremony is a form of homage to the gods, the givers of food, and especially to Agni,[3] who is the bearer of the offerings to heaven, and without whose aid the food could not be properly prepared. The fire for the ceremony is contained in a small portable receptacle, called a *kuṇḍa* and is fed with consecrated fuel. Offerings of rice, etc., are thrown into the fire, to the accompaniment of Vedic *mantras*. In the *bali-haraṇa* rite which concludes the ceremony, the food-offering is divided into portions, arranged in a circle, each portion being allotted to a particular deity and accompanied by prescribed formulas.

Towards the end of the ceremony the ashes are removed by a deep-bowled spoon called a *darvi*, and applied with a finger to different parts of the body, accompanied by a prayer to Rudra to refrain from harming any member of the family, or their cattle (*RV*., I.114,8).

[1]It is described in its most ancient form in *Manu* (III.84–

93).
[2]*BH.*, p. 417.
[3]Who is thus addressed: 'O all-wise Agni, come to this our sacrifice as a loved friend and household guest' (*BH.*, p. 418).
v. Pūjā; Nyāsa.

Vaiśvāmitra(s) The patronymic of the family of the Vedic *ṛṣi* Viśvāmitra and the designation of his descendants. Numerous *RV.* hymns are ascribed to the family, to whom also are attributed the development of the cult of Indra and Agni, and that of Vedic sacrificial ritual. In common with other Vedic priestly families, they contributed largely to the social and political advancement of Vedic India.

Vaiśvānara A name of Agni, the god of fire. Agni is the welcome guest in every household; the agent without whom no sacrifice could be properly carried out, or the aroma of the offering reach the gods. According to *RV.* (I.59,2) Vaiśvānara was produced by the gods to be a light for the Āryans.[1]

In the *ŚBr.* (VI.2.1,35) Vaiśvānara is the collective name of the three sacrificial fires, the *ahavanīya*, *gārhapatya* and *dakṣiṇāgni*, and is identified *inter alia* with the Year (=Totality) and with the earth (V.2.5,15, etc.).

Vaiśvānara is also the combined appellation of Ekata, Dvita and Trita (also called Śuci, Pāvaka and Pavamāna), the three brothers of Agni.

[1]Edgerton (*BIP.*, p. 94, n.2) suggests that Vaiśvānara refers to the sacrificial fire that burns in every man's home. This agrees with *AV.* (XII.1,6), but in the *Bṛhadd.* (I.67; 97; VII.142) it is the celestial form of the three forms of Agni. (v. also *Nir.*, 7.23; cf. 7,31.)

Vaiśya A member of the *viś*, the third of the four classes of the community alluded to in *RV.* (I.113,6)[1] and subsequently referred to by name in X.90,12. In post-Vedic texts, especially in the Dharma-śāstras, these classes, called *varṇas*, became the basis of the caste system. In the principal Dharma-śāstra, the *Manu-smṛti* (I.87–91), this fourfold classification follows that of the Puruṣa-sūkta (*RV.*X.90), which forms part of an account of creation. Because of man's importance the purpose of his position in the community is metaphorically related to the four principal parts of the body of the Puruṣa, from which the four classes, the *brāhmaṇa*, *rājanya*, *vaiśya* and *śūdra*, are said to have emerged. The order of precedence is implied by the relation of the four classes to the body of the Puruṣa and by the occupations and duties assigned to each,[2] especially the *śūdra*.

The occupation of the *vaiśya* was cattle-raising, land cultivation, trading of every kind, and also the ability to keep accurate accounts. His religious duties were to bestow gifts (on the *brāhmaṇas*), to offer sacrifices, and to study the Veda (*Manu*, I.90). The subsequent growth of population led to a vast increase in the number of occupations, and the fragmentation of many to prevent unemployment. This resulted in skill becoming the criterion of a particular occupation rather than the limitations dictated by caste. Thus the lot of many unskilled *vaiśyas* became little better than that of the *śūdras*, and 'the social order of the human community is seen as a biological law'[3] rather than that arbitrarily fixed by tradition.

[1]'But verses 4,5,6 seem to be separated ... from the rest of the hymn, and may perhaps be a later addition to it' (Griffith, *RV.*, vol. I, p. 150, n.).
[2]Hence, according to *Manu* (X.97), it is better to perform imperfectly the duties of one's own caste than to perform perfectly those of a superior caste. Cf. the English jingle: 'God bless the squire and his relations, and keep us in our proper stations.'
[3]Heimann, *Facets*, p. 38.
v. Varṇa; Śreṇi.

Vaitaraṇī The name of the foetid river which flows between the earth and the nether regions, and over which the dead pass[1] to Yama's realm.

A river, mythically associated with death and the afterlife, is common to other cultures. Vaitaraṇī, also called Mahānadī, is also the name of a sacred river in Kaliṅga, 250 miles south west of Calcutta. Like the Egyptian Nile or the Greek Styx (in ancient geography said to be the river that flowed by the city of Nonacris in Arcadia) it is associated with funerary rites and the passage of the dead to the other world.

[1]Vaitaraṇī is also the name of the cow presented to the priest during the funerary rites, in the belief that it will carry the dead man safely across the dreaded river. In ancient Egypt a cow was said to guide the dead to the next world; and in Lancashire folklore the Milky Way, the traditional way of the dead, was called the 'cow's lane'. Furthermore, one who gave a cow to the poor would after death be guided by the animal to the heavenly world (Radford, *Encyclopaedia of Superstitions*, p. 116).
v. Naraka I; Puṣpodakā; Preta; Ekoddiṣṭa.

Vaivasvata 'Coming from or belonging to the sun (Vivasvat)'; the patronymic of the seventh Manu, the son of Vivasvat. Vaivasvata, unlike his Hebrew counterpart Noah, found himself completely alone after the Deluge. He therefore performed arduous religious rites and finally cast an oblation on the waters. A year later a beautiful female, the personification of the oblation, rose from the waters, and informed him that she was his daughter Iḍā, who had been engendered by the oblation (*iḍā*), and that if he would make use of her services at the sacrifice he would be assured of both offspring and cattle (*ŚBr.*, I.8.1,1ff.). v. Matsya avatāra; Manvantara.

Vāja I. 'Strength', 'potency'. A term possibly derived from the hypothetical root *vaj*, 'to be strong'.[1] *Vāja* generally 'expresses, not a concept in the modern sense of the word, but a group or complex of ideas, beliefs, conceptions, experiences converging in a "Daseinsmacht", a power usually conceived as substantial in character and, hence, very apt to materialize, a power manifesting in animal and vegetative life, strength, potency,' etc.[2] But the primary significance of *vāja* is never absent from its widely applied usage, which is indicated in compounds like *vājajit*, 'winning a race'; *vājada*, 'bestowing or restoring vigour' (*AV.*, VI.101, 1–2), and thus increasing the speed and power of endurance of the horse (*vājin*) in a race; *vājapeya*, 'the drink of strength,' especially in battle, and hence the name of one of the seven *soma* sacrifices, offered by kings and *brāhmaṇas* aspiring to higher position and increased power.

[1]*IAL.*, p. 653, col. 2. *Vajra*, *ugra*, etc., may also be derived from the same root. In a list of old Indo-Āryan words current in the Veda, but obsolete in classical Sanskrit, Burrow includes *vāja* 'prize, booty' (*The Sanskrit Language*, p. 40).

[2]Gonda, *Aspects*, p. 48.

II. A name of one of the three Ṛbhus (*RV.*, I.111,5).

Vājapeya The 'drink of strength' which ensures victory. It is drunk at one of the seven *soma* sacrifices performed by a king or priest[1] aspiring to high position. In the case of the priest, Eggeling suggests it was a preliminary rite performed before his inauguration as a *purohita*; with a king it preceded his consecration. The *vājapeya* rite also preceded the celebration of the *aśvamedha* (horse-sacrifice), performed to confirm the claim to imperial status, and to witness the acknowledgment of the ruler's suzerainty by his vassals. Keith considers that the original rite was intended to honour Indra alone, but the priests gave Bṛhaspati the place of honour. Nonetheless, 'in sacerdotalizing the rite the priests have still retained its popular features, which makes its inclusion as a form of the *soma* sacrifice obviously a secondary one'.[2]

Included among the elaborate rituals given in *ŚBr.* (V.1.1,1ff.) five *vājapeya* cups are drawn, representing the five seasons of the year. Then seventeen cups of *soma* and seventeen of *surā* are drawn by the priests, making thirty-four in all, for there are thirty-three gods, and with Prajāpati, the thirty-fourth, who represents totality.

A race with seventeen chariots is run round a circular track, the sacrificer's chariot being always the winner, signifying that he 'wins' or 'gains' the terrestrial world. Favourable forces or energies were set in motion by this race, which was also believed to restore the reproductive power of the earth as well as that of the competitors. Heesterman considers that rotary motion is essential for attaining generative power (*vāja*). 'Whether the course takes the character of a race . . . or is performed by a single chariot, as in the *rājasūya*, the track begins and ends at the same point.'[3] Thus the chariot course has cosmic symbolism attached to it—it represents the sun encompassing the whole world.[4] Seventeen drums are placed along the edge of the altar, which in the past are said to have 'caused' Bṛhaspati and Indra to win the race. The *adhvaryu* priest addresses the horses and imbues them with vigour. He implores them to be auspicious to their owners, to keep away the wolf, evil spirits and all afflictions. He takes the *bārhaspatya* pap and touches it, so taking to himself all food (*anna*).

The sacrificial post (*yūpa*) is octagonal and represents the eight-syllabled *gāyatrī*. It is wrapped in seventeen cloths, and on the top is placed a piece of wheaten dough.[5] Before leading the sacrificer's wife[6] to the *yūpa* the *neṣṭṛ* priest makes her wrap herself in a cloth made from the purifying *kuśa* grass, for women are impure below the navel. A ladder is placed against the post and the sacrificer addresses his wife: 'Ascend we to the sky.' He then ascends the ladder (for his wife as well), touches the wheaten piece saying, 'We have gone to the light, O ye gods.' Then he raises his head above the post saying, 'We have become immortal,' and looks in all directions, so taking their power, energy, etc., to himself and his wife. Seventeen bags of salt[7] wrapped in *aśvattha* leaves are thrown up to him. Then he looks down on the Earth (i.e., the Earth-goddess) and pays homage to her, so entering into a friendly relationship with the earth. Descending from the post he steps on to a piece of gold representing immortality.

The sacrificer is led by a priest to a throne of *udumbara* wood, on which is placed a goat-skin[8] (the latter said to represent Prajāpati), and so endows him with royal power. Then sixteen kinds of food are brought to him, but if seventeen (representing Totality) were brought he would appropriate all food to himself leaving nothing for others. Hence one particular food must be forsworn *forever* by the sacrificer. Then the *vājaprasavanīya* oblations are offered, which are designed to promote strength, and Iḍā is invoked, etc.

[1]Winternitz, *HIL.*, vol. I. pt.1. p. 150, considers that the *vājapeya* was offered originally probably only by

warriors and kings, at which besides *soma*, brandy (*surā*) also was offered, a drink otherwise proscribed by brahmanical law. According to the *Śāṅkhāyana Śrauta Sūtra* (XV.1) any Āryan could perform it, so it is likely that at one time it was a popular victory celebration.

[2] *Tait. Saṁ.*, vol. I, p. cx.

[3] *Ancient Indian Royal Consecration*, p. 134; v. Gonda, *Loka*, p. 93; also *Aspects*, p. 50.

[4] Heesterman, op. cit., p. 134. For the fertilizing circular motion of the sun, v. *AV.*, XI.5,12.

[5] A wheel-shaped piece of dough symbolizes the sun (*IT.*, p. 228). In some versions an actual chariot wheel is placed on the top of a long pole.

[6] In another version the *hotṛ* priest recited the formula whilst the *adhvaryu* priest carried out coitus with a woman (*Bṛhad-Ār. Up.*, 6.4.3) who had previously been 'transfigured; she becomes the consecrated place where the sacrifice is performed' (Eliade, *Yoga*, p. 255).

[7] Salt represents cattle and the latter food.

[8] The *udumbara* denotes sustenance; the goat-skin, generative power.

v. Bṛhaspatisava; Rājasūya; Vāja I.

Vājasaneyi-Saṁhitā v. Yajurveda.

Vājaśravas v. Naciketas.

Vājīkaraṇa A treatise on aphrodisiacs.

Vājin 'Swift, spirited, strong, potent', epithets often applied to the horse, especially to the chariot-horse and the courser. *Vājin* also represents the best qualities of warrior and king, and hence the epithets applied to them: 'heroic, manly, strong, virile'.

Subsequently in the *RV.* poetic imagery described the sun-gods as horses (or as having horse-heads), to whom the epithet *vājin* is applied, especially Sūrya or Savitar, and the solar Viṣṇu (the Pervader). Two hymns (IV.39 and 40), addressed to the celestial horse Dadhikrā, call him 'the Courser', a 'guide to mortals', the 'ripener of crops,'[1] 'bringer of food', and 'the strengthener'. He extends himself 'over the nations, and in this he resembles Sūrya'.[2]

The *ŚBr.* (V.1.5,22) gives a variant rendering of the invocation in *RV.* (VII.38,7) to the coursers (*vājins*) to destroy the wolf, the serpent and all evil spirits.[3]

[1] Farnell (*Cults*, III, p. 35) states that the Āryans regarded the last sheaf of corn as animated with the corn-spirit in the form of a horse. In Wales this sheaf was called 'the mare'.

[2] Gonda, *Aspects*, p. 147; v. also p. 149.

[3] In the *vājapeya* ceremony the chariot-horses are similarly invoked, and in *ŚBr.* (VI.3.2,7) the horse is urged to tread down evil and avert curses.

v. Vāja; Vājapeya; Indra.

Vajra The magical weapon of Indra[1] the divine war-leader of the Vedic Āryans. The *vajra* is a weapon befitting his position, the weapon of the Vedic ordinary soldier being the bow. Indra's *vajra* was made of metal (*RV.*, I.52,8), and fashioned by Tvaṣṭar the smith of the gods (I.32,2). It needed to be sharpened periodically (I.55,1). It apparently had a shaft, as it was held by one hand, but sometimes by both (I.81,4); or it was a double-ended trident which was grasped at the centre.

The *vajra*, usually rendered by nineteenth-century translators as 'thunderbolt', i.e., lightning, is described in the *RV.* (X.27,21) as 'whirling down from the misty realm of the sun (Sūrya)'. Whilst this is a poetically adequate description of a transient electrical discharge breaking up the rain-clouds or 'misty realm', it conflicts with the general description of the *vajra* as a very hard, sharp weapon.[2] Moreover the Vedic word for thunderbolt, '*vidyut*', is specifically associated with Parjanya, 'Indra being called *vajrahasta*, never *vidyut-hasta*'.[3] The *vajra* is also deified (*Bṛhadd.*, I.84). The *Tait. Saṁ.*, VI.3.3,1 equates it with the axe, used to cut the sacrificial post (*yūpa*).

The exploits of Indra and his *vajra*[4] and the myths describing them are innumerable, and in late Vedic and post-Vedic texts the functions of the *vajra* also include the driving away of evil spirits, etc. It is equated with vigour (*vāja*); and in Tantrism with the creative principle of the *liṅga*.[5] The Mahāyāna Buddhist Vajrayāna cult based its doctrine on the divine indestructible *vajra* which was equated with *śūnya* (the Real).[6]

The notion of a divine weapon conceived as a thunderbolt is common to numerous non-Indian mythologies. Among these are the Babylonian Eleven Mighty Helpers of Tiamat, who were all armed with invincible thunderbolts; the Syrian Reshpu; the Etruscan gods Summanus and Sethlans; the Greek Zeus; the Roman Jupiter; the hammer or thunderbolt called Miölnir of the Scandinavian god Thor, which could both kill and restore to life. The Vedic divine smith Tvaṣṭar has also counterparts in Hephaistos who controlled the Cyclopean forge; and the Canaanite Koshar, etc.[7]

[1] The Avestan counterpart '*vazra*' was the chief weapon of Mithra, lord of battles, rain-giver, god of faith and light, etc. (Gonda, *Aspects*, p. 43). Turner suggests that *vajra* is derived from the hypothetical root *vaj* 'to be strong' (*IAL.*).

[2] Apte considers the *vajra* was a club or hammer ('Vajra in the Ṛgveda', *ABORI.*, vol. xxxvii, pp. 292–5, 1956).

[3] Singh, *Ancient Indian Warfare*, p. 96.

[4] Indra's hundred-jointed *vajra* is efficacious against witchcraft (*AV.*, VIII.5,15).

[5]In the Brāhmaṇas those entities which are favourable to man, to vegetal growth, and which destroy evil are called *vajras* (Gonda, *Aspects*, p. 41; v. also p. 37).
[6]Bhattacharyya, *Indian Buddhist Iconography*, p. xvii.
[7]Gaster, *Thespis*, p. 148.
v. Dadhyac; Āyudhapuruṣa; Triśiras.

Vaka or **Baka** 'Crane', 'heron'. Figuratively a hypocrite or cheat, the crane being regarded as a bird of great cunning and deceit as well as circumspection.

Vakula v. Bakula.

Vala or **Bala** A leader of the Paṇis, one of the non-Āryan Indian tribes, derogatively called *dasyus*, *asuras*, *daityas*, or *dānavas*, who regarded the Āryan settlers as intruders. These tribes expressed their antipathy (*RV.*, II.12,3; 14,3; VI.17,12, etc.) by cattle-raiding, damming waterways and rivers, interfering with Brahmanic sacrifices, and because of their cunning, were frequently referred to as demons.

The Paṇis were notorious cattle-raiders, whose mountain strongholds made the recovery of the stolen cattle both difficult and dangerous. Thus Indra is frequently invoked to destroy Vala and his followers, and is lauded whenever the cattle have been retrieved. Although Indra is generally given the credit for these exploits (*RV.*, X.67,6, etc.), Brahmaṇaspati (the lord of prayer) is also said to have retrieved the cattle and 'cleft Vala through by prayer' (*RV.*, II.24,3); and Bṛhaspati made Vala 'fall apart' (*AV.*, IX.3,2).

Vālakhilya I. The name of a collection of six, eight, but more usually of eleven hymns of the *RV.*, commonly inserted after VIII.48, but numbered separately as a supplement by some editors.

II. A class of 60,000 divine 'thumb-sized'[1] *ṛṣis* produced from Brahmā's body (or from Kratu), who live for a thousand ages. Sometimes they are classed as Siddhas, who have attained their status through asceticism (*tapas*), but remain associated with mortals.

[1]Cf. the smallness of the individual 'soul' described in *Chān. Up.*, 3.14,2.

III. Name of an ascetic order of mendicants mentioned in the *Vaikhānasmārta-sūtra* (c. 4th century), whose clothing consisted of rags or bark, and whose hair was uncut and matted.[1]

[1]Eliade, *Yoga*, p. 139.

Vāli v. Bāli.

Vallabha v. Vedānta.

Vālmīki v. Rāmāyaṇa.

Vāmācāra The designation of so-called 'left-handed' Tantrists, which is applied to distinguish them from the 'right-handed' (*dakṣiṇācāra*) discipline. Sexual symbolism, which has existed in India since Vedic times, has a role in *vāmācāra* practices, and certain excesses, cruelties and aberrations in Tantrism have seemed to some Indians to be a means of putting themselves beyond the human condition and hence outside society, being no longer bound by its laws and ethics.[1] Bharati maintains that the central rule of both Hindu and Buddhist *vāmācāras* 'is the retention of semen during the sexual act'.[2]

[1]Cf. the ecstatic frenzies of the Greek Maenads who transcended the limits of ordinary consciousness and so attained a feeling of communion with the divine nature (v. Farnell, *Cults*, Vol. V, pp. 161f.; v. also the sexual rites associated with European witchcraft, believed to stimulate the powers of universal fertility (D. Valiente, *An A.B.C. of Witchcraft Past and Present*, pp. 132–5, 1973).
[2]*TT.*, p. 179. In the *Chān. Up.* (II.13,1–2) 'sexual union is transposed and valorized as liturgical chant (*sāman*)' (Eliade, *Yoga*, p. 257).
v. Śakti; Śākta.

Vāmadeva I. Name of a *ṛṣi* to whom are ascribed most of the hymns of the fourth *maṇḍala* of the *RV.* He is mentioned by name (IV.16,18) where Indra is invoked to further Vāmadeva's holy thoughts.

II. Name of one of the 'five faces' of Śiva.

Vāmana 'Dwarf.' One of the 'descents' or incarnations (*avatāras*) of Viṣṇu, the fifth of the ten *avatāras* enumerated in the stereotyped list. The Vāmana myth, describing the three steps of the dwarf *avatāra* is the Vaiṣṇava counterpart of the *RV.* myth of the three strides taken by the solar Viṣṇu (*RV.*, I.22, 16–18; 154, 1–6, etc.).[1]

The Paurāṇic Vāmana myth relates that Bali, a non-Āryan Indian ruler, was too powerful to be coerced into ceding any of his kingdom to the *brāhmaṇas*. They therefore appealed to Viṣṇu, who in the form of a dwarf asked Bali to grant him a portion of land no wider than that which he could traverse in three strides. The king readily agreed to such a modest request, whereupon the dwarf stood up and quickly swelled to an immense size. In three strides he traversed the whole earth, the third stride landing on the king's head and forcing him down into the nether regions. As a reward for Bali's magnanimity he was made ruler of the lower region. The Vāmana incarnation of Viṣṇu is worshipped under the name Trivi-krama, 'the god who took three strides', or the Tamil Ulagalanda-Perumā, 'the lord who measured the universe (with three strides)'.[2] The number three indicates Viṣṇu's universal character, for the universe is tripartite: the upper regions, the earth and the waters (*RV.*, I. 139,11). Furthermore, these three strides, when carried out ritually by the sacrificer, annihilate evil (*Tait. Saṁ.*, I.6.5, etc.).[3]

[1]In the Vedic account Viṣṇu represents the principle of

growth (*VF.*, p. 34).

[2]Shastri, *South Indian Images of Gods and Goddesses*, p. 30. Up to the end of the nineteenth century representations of Vāmana were common 'on demarcation stones of fields granted in charity' (ibid., p. 32).

[3]v. also Gonda, *Aspects*, pp. 55ff.

v. Bali II.

Vāmana Purāṇa Ostensibly a Vaiṣṇava Pur., but being a late composition it lacks any sectarial partiality, and divides its homage fairly evenly between Śiva and Viṣṇu.

It contains an account of the dwarf (*vāmana*) *avatāra* of Viṣṇu, which purports to have been related by Pulastya to Nārada, the names of two ancient seers having been borrowed to lend authority to a *paurāṇic* composition.

Vanamālā A long garland (*mālā*) of woodland flowers worn by Viṣṇu.

v. Mālā.

Vānara 'Monkey', 'forest dweller'. Name of a community of South Indian aboriginal forest-dwellers who because of their strange appearance[1] and timidity were derisorily called monkeys. They had a clan-system, each clan having its own chieftain, and all of them subject to the tribal chief. When properly led, they were formidable fighters.[2]

Their leader was Sugrīva, his army commander Hanumat. The Vānaras are said to have helped Rāma find Sītā, as well as helping him in his fight against Rāvaṇa.

[1]They are sometimes described as having tails, but these were probably worn as emblems or as ornaments (*IRA.*, p. 58), which would account for the fact that Hanumat did not feel pain when his tail was set on fire in Laṅkā. S. Ramdas mentions a class of 'tailed' aboriginals among the Śabaras of Vizagapatnam ('Aboriginal Tribes in the Rāmāyaṇa,' *Man in India*, vol. V, pp. 46ff.).

[2]*IRA.*, pp. 48ff.

Vanaspati 'Lord of the forest.' In *RV.* (I.13,11) it refers to a large tree, the 'sovran of the wood'; in 142,11 to the wooden sacrificial post (*yūpa*) said to be a form of Agni, who is called the 'overlord of forest trees' (*AV.*, V.24,2), or 'protector of trees' (*Bṛhadd.*, III. 26–7). Fire (*agni*) is often identified with the wood of trees because it was believed to exist within the kindling sticks (*araṇis*).

Vandana Name of a Vedic *ṛṣi* probably one of those engaged in attempts to convert the aboriginals to the religion of the Āryans. Though some of the *ṛṣis* were successful, others like Vandana and his companion Rebha were attacked and thrown into a pit from which they were rescued by the Aśvins (*RV.*, I.116,11).

Varada I. 'Bestower of boons.' An epithet applied to some ancestors (*pitṛs*), and to Agni and other divinities. II. A particular *mudrā*, indicating the bestowal of boons or gifts on the worshipper. The hand is held out with the palm uppermost.

Varāha 'Boar.' One of the forms (*avatāras*) of Viṣṇu, which appears to have originated from an archaic cosmogonic or fertility myth,[1] like that of the storm-god Rudra, called the 'boar of heaven' (*RV.*, I.114,5). In the *ŚBr.*, XIV.1.2,11 the boar Emūṣa raised the Earth-goddess on his mighty tusks from the primeval waters. The water poured off his brow purifying the great sages; and as the water flowed through his hoof-marks into the lower worlds, the *munis* sheltered amongst his bristles (*VP.*, I.4).

A fine stone image of Varāha is in the Ashmolean Museum, Oxford. The whole body is covered with rows and rows of small figures denoting the cosmic significance of the boar.

[1]Some theriomorphic cults, especially in Eastern Mālwā, worshipped a divinity in the form of a boar. By about the fourth century A.D. the boar cult became assimilated with the *avatāras* of the Viṣṇu cult (Basham, *WI.*, p. 298). The boar has also long been associated with deities of fertility in Europe.

Varāhamihira A famous Indian astronomer of the sixth century A.D., the author of the *Pañcasiddhāntikā*, a summary of five astronomical works long since lost. His greatest work was the *Bṛhatsaṁhitā* or Great Compendium[1] which deals with the astrological significance of the heavenly bodies and their significance in relation to human behaviour, etc. 'In addition he wrote two books on purely horoscopic astrology, the *Bṛhatjātaka* (Great Horoscopy)[2] and the *Laghujātaka* (Short Horoscopy), which reveal some Greek influence.

[1]English translation by H. Kern, *JRAS.*, 1870–5; another by V. Subrahmanya Shastri and M.R. Bhat, 2 vols, Bangalore, 1947.

[2]English translation by V. Subrahmanya Shastri, Mysore, 1929.

Varaṇa The tree (Crataeva Roxburghii), believed to possess both medical and magical properties (*AV.*, VI.85,1). Amulets were made from its wood.

In Vedic burial rites its wood was used for one of the four pegs which marked out the burial mound; the particular positions intended to ward off (*vāraya*) evil or harm from the dead man.

Vārāṇasī v. Kāśī.

Varcin Name of a member of the Indian aboriginal tribes (*dāsa*) who, with another called Śambara, fought the Āryans. Indra is said to have destroyed Varcin and his tribe; demolished Śambara's hundred forts (*RV.*,

II.14,6; IV.30,14–15), and slain 1,100 of Varcin's men (*Tait. Saṁ.*, III. 2,11).

Varṇa The word is generally used to denote colour, but its primary meaning, derived from the root *vṛ*, is 'screen, veil, covering, external appearance', and hence colour is only one of the many aspects of the term. The most frequent colours mentioned are red and yellow, but both black (*kṛṣṇa*), and white (*śukla*), or light-coloured (*śveta*), frequently occur, as also brown (*babhru*) and reddish-brown (*kapila*). *Kalmāṣa* denotes 'spotted', *śilpa* 'dappled', and *aruṇa* 'ruddy'.[1]

From being a general designation of colour, *varṇa* was used to denote groups having different skin coloration. Thus when the Āryans were confronted with the brown-skinned Dravidians or with the black proto-Australoids they designated them *dasyu-varṇa* and themselves *ārya-varṇa* (*RV.*, III.34,9), etc.). In addition to this ethnic distinction, other differences, such as religion and speech initially widened the gap between the two racial groups, which otherwise might have been closed by gradual integration. But it is questionable whether the *puruṣa-sūkta* (*RV.*, X.90) in dividing mankind into four socially separate but interdependent categories, provided the basis for the caste[2] system, sanctified and legalized in the *Manu-dharma-śāstra*. The *puruṣa-sūkta* itself makes no such claim, but merely attempts to explain the origin of all living creatures. It is primarily a creation myth, and intended to establish the essential unity and interdependence of mankind and all living creatures, and to define in a general sense the occupations regarded as the basis of Vedic society. In this context skin-colour has no relevance, as at the time of the composition of the *puruṣa-sūkta* racial integration had long since begun.

Nonetheless, the four occupational categories, despite their mutual dependence, gradually came to be regarded as having varying degrees of social prestige, probably owing to the assumption that one part of the body is of greater importance than another. Thus the *brāhmaṇa*, having emerged from the head of the cosmic *puruṣa* was regarded as the receptacle of the mind, centre of the sensory organs, and held to be superior to the *rājanya*, represented by the arms, and to the *vaiśya*, represented by the legs, all three being regarded as superior to the *śūdra*, the lowest level, the feet of *puruṣa*. These metaphorical distinctions were observed, not only in life, but also in death, the height of the burial mounds being made in accordance with the relative social status implied in the *puruṣa-sūkta*. Thus the mound of a *brāhmaṇa* was built as high as the mouth of a man standing upright, that of a *kṣatriya* to the level of his outstretched arms, that of a woman to hip-level, of a *vaiśya* to the thighs and of a *śūdra* to the knees (*SBr.*, XIII.8.3,11).

Among the many customs which distinguished the four main classes are the following: The ornaments of the *brahmin* were of gold or silver of the highest quality; those of the *kṣatriya* of inferior quality; those of the *vaiśya* consisted of brass; those of the *śūdra* of iron. The times for initiation were spring for the *brahmin*, summer for the *kṣatriya*, and autumn for the *vaiśya*. Different ritual metres were also allotted. The *gāyatrī* for the *brahman*, the *triṣṭubh* for the *kṣatriya*, the *jagatī* for the *vaiśya*. Furthermore, the *brahman* is permitted four wives, the *kṣatriya* three, the *vaiśya* two, but the first wife must always be of the same caste as the husband (*Manu*, III.12–13). The *śūdra* was permitted only one wife, who must be of his own caste. Penalties for crime also varied among the three superior castes, but theoretically they incurred no penalty for the illtreatment of a *śūdra*. But these distinctions of class were not rigidly observed either in Vedic or later times. Such distinctions occurred only when social and economic considerations, and religious and secular interests were involved. The establishment of a caste system thus ensured a certain continuity, which suited the demands of an expanding civilization. Nonetheless, the system contained potentially divisive and anti-social elements, which gradually led to the formation of numerous sub-castes, and subsequently to the establishment of secondary caste-systems, having their own rules and order of precedence. Thus crafts and occupations were graded according to the degree of skill involved, or according to supply and demand, though all such regarded themselves as superior to the unskilled, and especially to the lowliest of the lowly, the 'Untouchables' (*caṇḍālas*). Such a system, like that of the Medieval Guilds of Europe, or the subsequent apprentice system, ensured a high standard of workmanship and the exclusion of shoddy productions so often seen in modern times.

[1] *VI.*, vol. II, p. 247, n.2.

[2] This term, generally used in the West, was first used by the Portuguese traders to denote the system of social, religious and political distinctions peculiar to India. The word is derived from the L. *castus*, 'pure', and hence *incestus*, 'soiled' or 'impure'.

v. Jāti; Gotra; Kula; Śreṇi.

Vārṣṇeya Patronymic of Kṛṣṇa, a descendant of Vṛṣṇi.

Varuṇa One of the earliest Vedic gods, who is similar in character to the Avestan Ahura Mazda. Varuṇa is thus sometimes called a great Asura (= the Avestan Ahura) or cosmogonic power. The earliest concept of Varuṇa appears to have been that of the all encompassing sky, his name being probably derived from the root *vṛ* 'to cover', or 'encompass', a character 'in keeping with his lordship over the twin spheres of light and darkness ... and with his position as supreme ruler (*samrāj*) of the physical and moral world and as the custodian of *ṛta*'.[1] But in the *RV.* his function and activities are often indistinguishable from those of Indra and Agni. As one of the Ādityas he is associated with celestial order, especially the regular movement of the sun, the appearance of the dawn, and with the timely gathering of the clouds necessary for adequate rainfall (VI.48,14; X.99,10).[2] His responsibility for law and order also extended to sacrificial procedure, a duty shared by Mitra, Agni and Indra, and hence their common title 'Lord of *ṛta*', i.e., of holy sacrificial laws, *ṛta* being also concerned with the seasonal tasks connected with agriculture.

Gradually the notion of *ṛta* acquired an ethical significance, which was associated with man's moral behaviour, the responsibility for which became also one of Varuṇa's functions. Nothing escaped his notice. Wherever two were gathered together, Varuṇa was their unseen companion (*AV.*, IV.16,2). In addition his informants (*spaśaḥ*) reported any infringements of law and order, whether on earth or in the heavens, for from the sun, 'the eye of Varuṇa', nothing is hidden. There are many resemblances in the ethical character of Viṣṇu and Varuṇa.

As apparently quarrels over property rights and false claims about them were frequent in Vedic times,[3] Varuṇa strongly condemned and punished the liar, but forgave truly repentant 'sinners', or those who erred through thoughtlessness. Thus both Varuṇa and Mitra are jointly described as 'true to Law, born in the Law, and haters of the false' (*RV.*, VII.66, 13–14).

Another term, *dharma*, appears in the *RV.*, having almost the same significance as *ṛta*, both in relation to sacrificial procedure and to social duty and moral behaviour. Thus law and order began to be seen not as the sole responsibility of particular gods, but as that of the priestly and secular authorities. This view inevitably led to a gradual deterioration of the position of Varuṇa, as it did subsequently to the status of other Vedic divinities. This is evident in the *AV.*, where Varuṇa is presented as little more than a folk-divinity to whom invocations were mainly prompted by personal considerations. Thus Varuṇa (or jointly with Mitra) is implored by an ardent lover to arouse passionate love in a particular woman (III.25,6), or is implored by a woman to arouse similar feelings in a man for her (VI.132,5). Varuṇa is also asked to remove blemishes from a woman's body (I.18,1–2), to give confidence to a king on the eve of battle (VI.97,1–2), and to ensure that rain shall be withheld from the oppressors of the *brāhmaṇas* (V.19,5).

Varuṇa afflicts with dropsy those who anger him (*AV.*, I.10), but when correctly invoked he removes it (VII.83). But some afflictions he cannot cure, for he himself once became impotent, his virility being restored by a particular herb given him by the Gandharva (IV.4,1).

The horse-sacrifice (*aśvamedha*), originally a fertility rite, identifies Varuṇa's generative forces with those of the stallion, his favourite sacrificial animal. Varuṇa is also overlord of the primordial waters (*āpaḥ*), and hence his vehicle (*vāhana*) is the fabulous aquatic animal, the *makara*.[4] Those who are drowned are said to go to Varuṇa. He also wards off the evil effects of bad omens relating to water. Thus *bali* offerings are made to him before the digging of wells (*Bṛhat Saṁ.*, XLV.50; LIII.124).

Varuṇa's wife Vāruṇānī is probably a personification of the waters (or of night) (*AVB.*, p. 485). The *Tait. Saṁ.*, (V.5,4,1) states that the Waters are his wives.

[1] *HCIP.*, vol. I, p. 365. Manu associates Varuṇa with kingship for he is said to have been the first consecrated king. He is thus the embodiment of kingship and as such belongs to a settled order, to a city state (Coomaraswamy, *Yakṣas*, pt. ii, p. 27).

[2] A South Indian rite called *Varuṇa japa* is performed to ensure rain (Diehl, *Instrument and Purpose*, p. 264). The *RV.* (V.85,3) and *Nir.* (10.4), refer to him as the 'rain-giver'. In many cultures, everything to do with fertility was thought to depend on the king's virtue.

[3] A situation that was partly remedied by the use of boundary stones and pillars, but not completely so until writing was introduced and title deeds were inscribed on copper plates.

[4] Tamil fishermen long worshipped a marine deity, called Varuṇan, in the form 'of a "shark's horn". This god, however, is clearly an indigenous Tamil divinity who had acquired an Āryan name' (Basham, *WI.*, p. 313). Coomaraswamy suggests that the *makara* 'may have been the theriomorphic form of the deity in person' (*Yakṣas*, pt. ii, p. 53). For the association of the horse with Varuṇa and with the ocean, v. Kramrisch, *Unknown India*, p. 57.

v. Varuṇapāśa; Varuṇagraha; Varuṇasava. Puruṣamedha.

Varuṇagraha 'Seized by Varuṇa.' Varuṇa inflicts evil-doers with paralysis or dropsy.

Varuṇānī or **Vāruṇī** Name of the wife (or daughter) of Varuṇa. The *VP.* (I.9) calls her the goddess of wine or of intoxication.[1]

[1]The term *varuṇatmajā* 'Varuṇa's daughter' is applied to intoxicating liquor.

Varuṇapāśa Also called *dharmapāśa*. The noose (*pāśa*) with which Varuṇa seizes or ensnares evil-doers and demons.

Varuṇasava The name by which the *rājasūya* ceremony is also known. It refers to the anointing of a king with water, which identifies him with Varuṇa, the god of the waters.

Varūtrī 'Protectress.' Name of a guardian goddess and the spouse of a deity (*RV.*, I.22,10) who possesses great powers to help her worshippers (V.41,15).

v. Devī.

Vaṣaṭ or **Vauṣaṭ**[1] A ritual exclamation uttered by the *hotṛ* priest[2] at the end of the recital of the sacrificial offering-verse, on hearing which the *adhvaryu* casts the oblation into the altar fire.[3] Such offerings are said to be sanctified by *vaṣaṭ* (*RV.*, VII.14,3, etc.), to unite all living creatures (I.31,5), and to support the sacrifice (*Tait Saṁ.*, VII.5,5). The *vaṣaṭ* also summons the gods to the sacrifice (*AV.*, XI.10, 4), and is sacred to them all (*Bṛhadd.*, VIII. 111).

The *vaṣaṭ* possesses great magical power, and is capable of destroying enemies (*Tait. Saṁ.*, II.6.2,5).[4] It is equated with the sun and with death (*ŚBr.*, XI.2.3,5). But in the Śākta cult, when the Vedic *vauṣaṭ* and *vaṣaṭ* are added to incantations they counteract any opposing forces. They may represent 'quasi-morphemes formed out of the phonetic complex "v/s", which conjures up in the Indian ear speed and superhuman acceleration (e.g., *vidyut* ... "lightning" ... and the notion of power, force contained in the morphemes of *vas*-; *vauṣaṭ* might then be an intensification of *vaṣaṭ* through a sort of folk-*guṇation*'.[5]

[1]Probably a lengthened form of *vaṣaṭan*. Eggeling suggests that it is derived from the root *vakṣ* 'to grow, increase', or from *vah* 'to bear' (*ŚBr.*, pt. v, p. 277, n.2, and 6).

[2]As the *hotṛ* represents winter, the *vaṣaṭ* is not uttered by him during that season, for to do so would result in the wasting away of the cattle of the sacrificers (*ŚBr*, XI.2.7,32).

[3]*BIP.*, p. 84, n.1.

[4]Agni's brothers had been shattered by this call (*Bṛhadd.*, VII.61; *Tait. Saṁ.*, II.6,6).

[5]*TT.*, p. 116.

v. Vaṣaṭkāra; Svāhā.

Vaṣaṭkāra The ritual exclamation of *vaṣaṭ*, and also its personification as a divinity.

Vaśīkaraṇa The act of subjugating or bewitching anyone by means of incantations and spells.

Vasiṣṭha The name of one of the most prominent *ṛṣis* of Vedic tradition and of post-Vedic mythology, though in the latter the affairs of his descendants[1] are often confused with their Vedic progenitor. As one of the great Vedic *ṛṣis* he figures prominently in the seventh *maṇḍala* of the *RV.*, and one hymn (VII.18) suggests that he was its composer.

During the War of the Ten Kings (*daśarājña*) Vasiṣṭha was *purohita* to Sudās, king of the Tṛtsus. Viśvāmitra who had previously held the office of *purohita*, was summarily dismissed by Sudās, and joined his enemies as their *purohita*. Vasiṣṭha's appointment may have been responsible for the subsequent rule that only a *purohita* should act as the officiating *brahman* at the sacrifice (*ŚBr.*, XII.6.1,41), and for the tradition that a king attempting to rule without a *purohita* was destined to fail (*Ait. Br.*, VIII.24). Vasiṣṭha's appointment and Viśvāmitra's dismissal gave rise to numerous legends of the feud[2] that developed between the two *ṛṣis* and their descendants, though no reference to the feud occurs in the *RV*. The feud was subsequently reflected in the rivalry of kings as well as that of the descendants of Vasiṣṭha and Viśvāmitra, and is indicated in the Epics by the fanciful accounts of the wars for the possession of the 'Cow of Plenty', i.e., the Madhyadeśa or heartland of Northern India, which continued until the boundaries of kingdoms became generally recognized, and their relative permanence assured by the intermarriage of royal families or by political alliances.

There is little doubt that Vasiṣṭha contributed greatly to establishing the status of the *brāhmaṇa*, and especially of the *purohita*, resulting in the latter's prestige being progressively enhanced by posthumous fame. Thus Vasiṣṭha was numbered among the seven *maharṣis* or patriarchal ancestors from whom *brāhmaṇas*, and subsequently all 'twice-born' Hindus, theoretically claim descent (*gotra*). The high esteem in which Vasiṣṭha was held is also indicated by the recognition of his miraculous birth, referred to in the *RV.* (VII.33,11), which states that he was 'born of the love of the sun-gods Varuṇa and Mitra for Urvaśī, goddess of the dawn'. According to post-Vedic mythology Vasiṣṭha married Ūrjjā, one of Dakṣa's daughters (*VP.*, I.7). He subsequently became one of the seven stellar *devarṣis* who rise and set in the region of Mount Meru.[3]

[1]The *RV.* Vasiṣṭhas form 'a clan rather than a family in the narrower sense' (Brough, *EBS.*, Pref., xiii).

[2]A curious myth in *Suś. Saṁ.* (II, p. 755) relates that when Viśvāmitra aroused Vasiṣṭha's wrath, drops of sweat formed on Vasiṣṭha's brow and trickled down to the bales of hay reserved for the celestial cow. The sweat changed into a number of venomous spiders which to the present day are found to infest the articles

of royal use because of the iniquity of the royal sage (Viśvāmitra).

[3]*EM.*, p. 182.

v. Sagara.

Vāstoṣpati 'Protector of the house.' Name of a deity who presides over the foundation of a house.[1] He is invoked to grant the family happiness and an increase of cattle (*RV.*, VII.54,1), and to remove disease (VII.55,1). The *Tait. Saṁ.* (III.4,10,3) identifies Vāstoṣpati with Rudra; thus if a sacrificer failed to recognize their identity and omitted to make the appropriate offering to Vāstoṣpati, Rudra would assume a fiery form and slay him.

[1]Also an epithet applied to Indra, who may at one time have been a house-guardian (Bhattacharyya, *Canons of Indian Art*, p. 3).

v. Vāstunara.

Vāstunara or **Vāstupuruṣa** The archetype or ideal design of a house personified as a divinity. Vāstunara is said to be an undefined being whose huge body obstructed earth and heaven. He was seized by the gods, each of whom pressed down a limb on to the ground, and thus each god became the deity of the part he had pressed down.

When a house is to be built homage should be paid to Vāstunara, and a sacrifice performed which will constitute his food. The area of a house should be divided into eighty-one squares (that of a temple into sixty-four), each being sub-divided into nine or eight squares (the central square, in which the diagonals meet, being reserved for Brahmā).[1]

[1]v. Kramrisch, *The Hindu Temple*, vol. I, p. 22; Bhattacharyya, *Canons of Indian Art*, p. 30.

v. Vāstoṣpati; Vāstuśamana.

Vāstupuruṣa v. Vāstunara.

Vāstuśamana A rite performed to pacify spirits living on the intended site of a house, the building of which might disturb them and arouse their hostility.

Vāstuvidyā The science of architecture, one of the sixty-four sciences.

Vasudeva[1] Also called Ānakadundubhi.[2] Name of one of the sons of Śūra who married Māriṣā, a Bhoja princess, both she and her husband being descended from Yādava families. Vasudeva became the chief minister of Kaṁsa, king of Mathurā, also a Yādava, who because of a prediction that he would be slain by a son of Devakī (his cousin), had her first six sons destroyed at birth. By a subterfuge, the seventh and eighth sons, Balarāma and Kṛṣṇa escaped. Kṛṣṇa subsequently fulfilled the prediction.

[1]The *AGP.* (II, p. 1013) states that Vasudeva was an incarnation of Kaśyapa, and Devakī an incarnation of Aditi, the 'mother of the gods'.

[2]The gods, knowing that Ānakadundubhi would be Kṛṣṇa's father, joyfully beat the drums (*dundubhi*) of heaven.

v. Vāsudeva.

Vāsudeva The patronymic of Kṛṣṇa, son of Vasudeva, a member of the warrior class. Nonetheless, the oldest tradition does not mention Kṛṣṇa's father, but only his mother, and calls him the son of Devakī;[1] thus the patronymic belongs to a later period. On the other hand, Baladeva, known as Balarāma and Balabhadra, though a reputed son of Vasudeva, is never called by the patronymic Vāsudeva.[2] But 'very early a god named Vāsudeva was widely worshipped, especially in Western India. It was to this god that the Besnagar column . . . was erected. The inscription . . . shows that by the end of the second century B.C. the cult of Vāsudeva was receiving the support of the ruling classes, and even of the Western invaders. Soon after this Vāsudeva was identified with the Vedic god Viṣṇu . . . and further syncretisms were taking place.'[3]

The Kṛṣṇa-Vāsudeva cult, like Jainism and Buddhism, appears to have originated as a desire by literate members of the warrior (*kṣatra*) class to break away from the uncompromising sacrificial system of the *brāhmaṇas*. Such a view is amply supported by the radical views of the Upaniṣads, and by the *Bhagavadgītā* and the canonical writings of the Jains and Buddhists.

Unlike his brother Baladeva, Kṛṣṇa was widely recognized as the complete manifestation of Viṣṇu. But the assimilation of the Kṛṣṇa-Vāsudeva cult with the Vaiṣṇava system, and the order of precedence accorded to the *avatāras*, appears to have been a complex process, which has led to some minor differences among professed Vaiṣṇavas, and hence the rise of the mystical Pāñcarātra or Bhāgavata school,[4] and of the views of Rāmānuja, etc.

[1]*ERE.*, VII. p. 196.

[2]But the term Vāsudeva may have been used in a literal sense, i.e., as *vasu*, meaning 'good', 'beneficent', etc., and *deva* 'divine', and hence Vasudevatā, the wish-granting goddess, or Vasumat, 'giver of wealth', an epithet of Indra. If so, the conception of Vasudeva as Kṛṣṇa's father must have arisen later (Bhandarkar, *VSM.*, p. 11).

[3]*WI.*, p. 298.

[4]Eliade, *Yoga*, p. 395.

v. Kṛṣṇa I; Aṁśa II; Pūrṇāvatāra.

Vasugupta A Kāṣmirī Śaiva philosopher (770–830). His system of 'idealistic monism' was based on the Śaivāgamas, the Siddhāntas, and Advaita Vedānta. He is the author of the *Śiva-sūtra*.[1]

[1]His cult is known as Kāṣmirī Śaivism, or Trīka or Trīkaśāstra. For further details v. S.K. Das, *Śakti, or Divine Power*, ch. 2.

Vāsuki The mythical serpent-son of Kadrū. Like Śeṣa and Takṣaka, he was one of the serpent (*nāga*) kings. The world was thought to be supported on Vāsuki's many heads, and when he moved earthquakes resulted.[1]

[1]Cf. the Scandinavian serpent Miðgarðsormr, called the 'girdle of the earth' who dwells in the ocean depths. At the end of the world he will furiously lash the seas which will rise and cover the earth.

v. Pātāla.

Vasu(s)[1] 'Good', 'bountiful', 'wealthy'. Name of a class of gods regarded as atmospheric powers like the Rudraṣ, the Ādityas, the Aśvins, and the Maruts, and often associated with Agni and Indra. They are frequently mentioned in the *RV.* and constantly implored to grant aid or material benefits, but have no specific function assigned to them. Nonetheless, they were held in great esteem in early Vedic times, as is indicated by the refrain to each verse of a hymn addressed to the Viśvedevas (I.106): 'Even as a chariot from a ravine, rescue us, O bountiful Vasus, from all distress.' This esteem is further exemplified in a hymn to Agni (I.94,13) which extols him as 'the wondrous friend of the gods, the Vasu of Vasus'. Their special relationship with Indra is indicated by their presenting him with a magic steed which they fashioned from the sun (I.163,2), and by their forming the team which drew Indra's car (III.49,4).

They are invoked with other deities to cure convulsions and other maladies (*AV.*, VIII.1,16); to prevent enemies interfering with sacred rites and ceremonies (II.2,4); to crush enemies (III.1,2); to allay discord (VI.73,1); and to bestow treasures (*Nir.*, 12,42) on their worshippers.

The *ŚBr.* (IV.3.5,1) enumerates three classes of deities: eight Vasus, eleven Rudras and twelve Ādityas. Another passage (IV.5.7,3) adds Heaven and Earth, making a total of thirty-three, the number stated in the *RV.* (I.34,11). The names of the eight Vasus are Āpa, Dhruva, Soma, Dhara, Anila, Anala, Prabhāsa, and Pratyūṣa.

The *Bṛhad-Ār.* (I.4,12) distinguishes them from the high-gods and classes them with the Viśvedevas, the gods of the *viś* or commonalty. In another passage (III.9,3) the Vasus are equated with various atmospheric and stellar phenomena[2] and also with their spheres.

In the *MBh.* (Ādi pa., 98 *et seq.*) the Vasus bear little resemblance to their Vedic archetypes and become little more than folk godlings. They are said to have been cursed by the *ṛṣi* Vasiṣṭha to be reborn as mortals for having ventured near him during one of his periods of meditation. To reduce the penalty to the minimum the Vasus pleaded with Gaṅgā, the river-goddess, that they might be born to her and sired by some illustrious prince who would raise no objection to curtailing the mortal life of seven of them, allowing the eighth to survive, though he must never beget offspring.

Assuming the form of a beautiful girl, Gaṅgā arranged that she should be seen by King Śāntanu whom she consented to marry on condition that should he object to any action of hers she would leave him. Thus she was able to drown at birth seven of her sons, allowing only the eighth to live, enabling the Vasus finally to return to the celestial sphere.

[1]Perhaps from the root *vas* (shine). It also means to 'dwell' (*IAL.*, p. 667, col. 1). The Vasus as said to be preceded by fire and they abound in light (*VP.*, I.15).

[2]Viz., Fire Earth, Wind, Atmosphere, Sun, Sky, Moon and Stars (v. *HP.*, p. 85).

Vaṭa The Indian fig-tree (Ficus indica).[1] In Vedic times its juice was the drink of kings as *soma* was that of priests.

[1]Monier-Williams suggests *vaṭa* may be the *prakṛt* form of *vṛta*, meaning 'surrounded', 'covered', a description that applies to its aerial roots which grow down from the branches and root themselves, smothering the undergrowth, a single tree gradually covering a very large area.

v. Nyagrodha; Vṛkṣa.

Vāta[1] A name of Vāyu, god of the wind (from the root *vā* 'blow'). Vāta is associated with fertility,[2] and like other personifications of atmospheric phenomena, is frequently mentioned in *RV.* hymns addressed to the Viśvedevas, whose functions are closely connected with the welfare of the people. Even Vāta's 'docile harnessed horses' give succour (V.31,10). He is implored to blow the clouds together and so enable Parjanya to send rain (VI.49,6). The *AVB.* (XI.4,15) equates the life-breath (*prāṇa*) with Mātariśvan and with Vāta.

[1]*IAL.*, 11491. According to the *Bṛhadd.* (2,32) it means 'wanderer' and also 'pervader'. The Zoroastrian wind-god also had the same name (*DHI.*, p. 527).

[2]Cf. the old Spanish belief that mares could be impregnated by the wind. In the *Suś. Saṁ.* (vol. I, p. 120) *vāta* became a medical term for flatulence and other digestive reactions.

v. Vātula; Anila.

Vātāpi I. A South Indian native king, brother of Ilvala, who plotted together to kill the great *ṛṣi* Agastya (*MBh.*, Vana pa., 99).

II. Name of a *rākṣasa* brother of Namuci, son of Vipracitti and Siṁhikā (wife of Hiraṇyakaśipu). Vātāpi assumed the form of a ram which was eaten by some *brāhmaṇas*. His brother Ilvala then called to him to come out of their stomachs, whereupon he burst out. Vātāpi tried the same ruse on Agastya but the latter had already digested his portion.

Vaṭeśvara 'Lord of the *vaṭa* tree.' The name of a *liṅga* and of Śiva who is worshipped in connexion with the sacred *vaṭa* tree. Śiva is also associated with the jambu and mango trees, and 'at a shrine south of the Vindhya he is worshipped as Drākṣārāmeśvara, "Lord of the vineyard"'.[1]

[1]*BH.*, p. 447.

Vātsyāyana also called Mallanāga. The reputed author of the *Kāmasūtra* (Art of Love), composed in the fourth or fifth century A.D. It was the successor of similar works by various authors, whose names are known but whose works have not survived. The *Kāmasūtra* deals comprehensively with the subject, gives practical advice about marriage and is very informative about the manners and customs of the time.[1]

[1]*HCIP.*, II, p. 324.

Vātula 'Affected by wind-disease', 'crazy'.[1] According to the medical teaching of the *Āyurveda*, mental derangements of all kinds are caused by wind (*vāta*, *vāyu*), as well as various somatic diseases.

[1]*IAL.*, 11504.

Vauṣaṭ v. Vaṣaṭ.

Vāyu The name of the wind and of its personification; from the root *vā*, 'blow', but the word is used in the sense of 'wind' or 'air', in all passages of the *RV.* except X.90,13, where *vāyu* is said to be 'the breath of Puruṣa', a description which became the basis of much mystical speculation about 'vital breath' (*prāṇa*).

Vāyu was regarded as having purifying powers, and was also capable of freeing one from misfortune (*AVB.*, III.31,2), and of destroying the points of the enemies' bows (XI.10, 16). Vāyu particularly enjoys the companionship of cattle (II.26,1), and white flowers are sacred to him (*Bṛhat Saṁ.*, CIII.47).

In the *RV.* Vāyu is closely associated with Indra, whom he conveys in a shining car, drawn by a pair of red or purple horses, or by several teams consisting of a hundred or even a thousand steeds.

In post-Vedic mythology Vāyu is regarded as one of the five elements, and as one of the eight Vasus, and designated regent of the north-west quarter. In Indian medicine (*Āyurveda*) both *vāyu* and *vāta* became terms for flatulence,[1] and are popularly regarded as wind-demons likely to cause madness unless driven out.

[1]*Suś. Saṁ.*, I, p. 120.

v. Anila I; Vātula; Vāyu Purāṇa.

Vāyu Purāṇa A Purāṇa said to have been revealed by the wind-god Vāyu, the 'breath of *puruṣa*'. It is said to have been composed about the fourth or fifth century.[1]

[1]Gonda, *CC.*, p. 107.

Veda Lit. 'knowledge', a term specifically applied to the 'supreme sacred knowledge' contained in the four collections (*saṁhitās*), called Vedas, to the Brāhmaṇas appended to them,[1] and finally to the Āraṇyakas and Upaniṣads[2] which form a kind of epilogue. Originally the Veda consisted of a single collection of sacred songs or hymns of praise, entitled the *Ṛg-veda.* To this was added two *saṁhitās*: the *Sāma-veda* or collection of melodies (*sāmans*) used by the priest who acted as chanter at the sacrifice; and the *Yajur-veda*, which consisted of sacrificial formulas (*yajūṁṣi*), divided into two sections. The first, the Black Yajus, is preserved mainly in the recension of the *Taittirīya* and *Maitrāyanī saṁhitās*; the second, the White Yajus, is preserved in the *Vājasaneyi-saṁhitā.*

For a considerable time the Veda consisted only of these three collections of which the Āryan priestly class (*brāhmaṇa*) was the sole guardian and interpreter. But the gradual ethnic and cultural fusion of the Āryans and the Indian indigenes, led to the introduction of some local traditions into later recensions of the *RV.* During the process of this assimilation archaic magical formulas, myths, and legends were found, from which another collection was selected, entitled the *Atharva-veda*, which was added to the original Vedic corpus. A few passages of the *AV.* are almost identical with those of the *RV.*, which suggests that they were drawn from a common source, but the *AV.* contributes nothing to the ritual or the exegesis of the original Veda, and was probably intended for the common people (*viś*).

Though each of the Vedas may be regarded as a separate work, their composition must have originated contemporaneously. Thus there is no clear division between the notion of the personification of stellar, atmospheric and chthonic phenomena and the henotheistic and henotic notions that finally superseded them. Some members of the *brahmin* and *kṣatra* classes, and even of the *śūdra*, joined secret coteries in the seclusion of the forest and composed radical Āraṇyakas and Upaniṣads, which rejected ritual sacrifice as the sole means of liberation (*mokṣa*),[3] and introduced a monistic doctrine. Such ideas challenged the stereotyped theological dogmas and revitalized religion in India. So great was their impact that the Āraṇyakas and Upaniṣads were finally regarded as the fulfilment of Vedic nascent aspirations, and therefore called the Vedānta, the end or conclusion '*anta*' of the Veda.

[1]To the *RV.* are attached the *Aitareya Br.*, sometimes called the *Āśvalāyana*, and the *Kauṣītaki* or *Śāṅkhā-*

yana; the *Vājasaneyi-Saṁ*. or White *YV*., has the *Śatapatha*; the *Taittirīya* or Black *YV*., the *Taittirīya Br*. The *SV*. has eight Brāhmaṇas, the best known being the *Prauḍha* or *Pañcaviṁśa* and *Ṣaḍviṁśa*; the *AV*. has only the *Gopatha*.

[2]Some Āraṇyakas were appended to or incorporated in Brāhmaṇas; others were appended to Upaniṣads which in turn were assigned directly to a particular Veda Saṁhitā. Thus the *Aitareya* and *Kauṣītaki Ups*. are appended to *RV*. Brāhmaṇas; the *Taittirīya* to the *YV*. Brāhmaṇas; the *Bṛhad-Ār. Up*. to the *ŚBr*. of the *Vājasaneyi-saṁ*., the fortieth chapter of which also consists of the *Īśa Up*., the only instance of an Upaniṣad being directly incorporated in a *saṁhitā* rather than in a Brāhmaṇa. Of the other Upaniṣads, the *Chāndogya* and *Kena* belong to the *SV*.; the *Praśna*, *Muṇḍaka*, *Māṇḍukya* and *Kaṭha* to the *AV*.

[3]Although the Veda is regarded as forming an unalterable scriptural corpus, it has nonetheless been constantly reinterpreted, as well as assimilating many 'autochthonous "popular" divinities' (Eliade, *Yoga*, p. 113). Some rudiments of classical Yoga are to be found in it (ibid., p. 102). Modern Hinduism purports to be derived from the Veda but in substance it is not 'Vedic at all, but Dravidian; stemming in the main from the Bronze Age complex of the Indus' (Campbell, *Oriental Mythology*, II. pp. 183f.). Both Greek and Vedic religion depends on the performance of ritual acts. Apart from these, man had complete freedom in thought (Harrison, *Prolegomena to the Study of Greek Religion*, p. 156).

v. Brāhmaṇa II; Ṛtvij; Vedāṅga(s).

Vedāṅga(s) Lit. 'limbs' (aṅgas) of the Veda, comprising six treatises 'regarded as auxiliary to, and even in some sense, as part of the Veda'.[1] Their original purpose was to ensure that each part of the sacrificial ceremonies was correctly performed.

The process of ritual development must have been gradual, so that the formulation of the Vedāṅgas may be assigned to a period between that of the later Brāhmaṇas and the early Sūtras, the latter being the style used for the Vedāṅgas. The Vedāṅgas deal specifically with the following six subjects; *Śikṣa*, correct pronunciation; *Chandas*, metre; *Nirukta*, etymology; *Vyākaraṇa*, grammar; *Jyotiṣa*, astronomy; and *Kalpa*, ceremonial, i.e., the general rules governing sacrificial ceremonies.

[1]*SED*., p. 1016.

v. Vidyā(s).

Vedānta 'End of the Veda', i.e., the complete knowledge of the Veda. It is not an appendage to any particular portion of the Veda as were the Brāhmaṇas, but a re-interpretation of its basic truths in the light of aupaniṣadic revelation. The Vedānta is thus associated with the Uttara-Mīmāṁsā 'upper or later examination', regarded as one of the six Hindu *darśanas* which represented the 'views' of particular religious groups, and is distinguished from the Pūrva-Mīmāṁsā, the conservative and fundamentalist appraisal of the original parts of the Veda. The Vedānta views, unlike those of the other *darśanas*, were not initiated by a particular teacher, but were derived from the teaching of the Upaniṣads. As these presented both a doctrine of pure monism (*advaita*) and that of a modified dualism (*dvaita*), the expositions differ. It was not until Bādarāyaṇa produced his Brahma-sūtras (between A.D. 200 and 450) that particular Vedānta views were systematically presented. Despite the lack of indisputable evidence, it is probable that the aupaniṣadic notion of the *ātman* was current in the sixth century B.C., as is suggested by the Buddhist *anattā* (Skt. *anātman*) non-*ātman* doctrine, which by the second century A.D. had become the *śūnyavāda* of the Mahāyāna Buddhists.

There can be little doubt that the Buddhist theory of *śūnya* (the Real) greatly influenced the views of Gauḍa, or Gauḍapāda as he is generally known (*pāda* being an honorific like *ācārya*). He was the first great expositor of Advaita Vedānta, and flourished, according to some authorities about A.D. 500, or to others about A.D. 780. It has been suggested that Gauḍapāda's *śāstra* represents the views of a philosophical school of northern India where Buddhism was currently prominent.[1] It has been said that he was a Buddhist, or at least that he considered the source of the teachings of the Upaniṣads to be similar to those of Buddhism. The latter claim is confirmed by his *Āgamaśāstra* (IV.22) and by his quotations 'from the works of some celebrated Buddhist teachers who flourished between 200–400 A.D.',[2] particularly Nāgārjuna, who rejects the traditional theory of origination and the rule of cause and effect on the grounds that as both are without beginning, neither can come into existence; they are existence.

Śaṅkara's *advaita* doctrine was based on the famous passage in the *Chān. Up*. (6.10,3): 'that thou art' (*tat tvam asi*). He declared that 'thou and that' are not to be regarded as object and subject but as identical, without difference (*a-bheda*), like the real self (*ātman*). Thus the body, the mind (*manas*), the intellect (*buddhi*), and the ego (*ahaṅkāra*) 'are all objects of knowledge and variable and are not therefore the *ātman*'.[3] But not all of Śaṅkara's views were accepted by the expositors of the Vedānta. Among his critics was Rāmānuja (10th cent.) who contended that *ātman* and *brahman* are relative terms—like part and whole (*viśiṣṭādvaita*)—but not identical. Another view was presented by Madhva

(12th cent.) who, like Rāmānuja, was also a Vaiṣṇava, and who, while agreeing with his predecessor's dualistic (*dvaita*) view, rejected any qualification of the uniqueness of *brahman*, whereas Vallabha's view was an uncompromising *śuddhādvaita* or 'pure monism'. Other expositors, expressing variant views, claimed that there was a particular form of identity (*abheda*) of *brahman* and *ātman*; others that there was a specific difference (*bheda*) between them; others that there is distinction but not difference (*bhedābheda*). Such polar notions are the natural outcome of Vedāntic dogma. There is first the assumed polarity between the transcendental Constant and the empirical Transient. On the other hand, there is another kind of polarity to be observed within the sphere of phenomena only.[4] Had such notions been all that the expositors of the Vedānta had to contribute, its teaching would have been confined to a limited circle of scholiasts. But Śaṅkara's views were gradually accepted, possibly because he presented *brahman* both as the cosmic principle and as a personal god (*īśvara*),[5] which added emphasis to the teaching of the later Upaniṣads and to that of Patañjali.

Advaita Vedānta thus reinforced the teaching of the *Bhagavadgītā* and the concept of liberation (*mukti*) by grace (*prasāda*), faith (*śraddhā*), and devotion (*bhakti*). It succeeded in reviving the ancient belief in the affinity of mankind with the world of nature. From being merely one of the *darśanas*, the Vedānta became an element that permeated all Hindu cults and dissolved sectarian distinctions. It gave to the Supreme Essence (*paramātman*), Viṣṇu and Śiva the common, all-inclusive designation, 'Īśvara'. But the Vedānta theory of existence as the first-without-a-second-principle, has defied all attempts to define it in universally acceptable terminology, possibly because of the number of dogmas which have become attached to it. That Vedānta is the corner-stone of modern Hinduism can hardly be denied, but the dogma of *advaita*, and the paradox of its notion of absolute indivisibility and its intuitive cognition by the individual constitute an unsolved philosophical problem. Nonetheless, the aim of Vedāntic metaphysics is clear: it is 'to transgress the limits of this transient world of empirical frame and empirical perception'.[6]

[1]V. Bhattacharyya, *Āgamaśāstra of Gauḍapāda*, p. lxx.
[2]Ibid., p. lxxvif.
[3]S. Bhattacharya, 'Philosophy of Śaṅkara', *C. Herit. I.*, vol. I, p. 552.
[4]Heimann, *PSPT.*, p. 11.
[5]Deussen, *Philosophy of the Upaniṣads*, p. 159, 1919.
[6]Heimann, *PSPT.*, p. 12.

Vedavatī The beautiful and learned daughter of Kuśadhvaja, a *rājarṣi* of the Rāmāyaṇa period. 'After her father's death Vedavatī continued a life of religious discipline in an *āśrama* close to the Himālaya in the Mithilā territory, clad in deer skin and wearing matted hair, and employed, in the manner of *ṛṣis*, in study and learning.'[1]

Her choice of vocation indicated that, though marriage was generally regarded as obligatory, some girls were able to enter *āśramas* and continue their studies.

[1]*IRA.*, p. 168.

Vedavyāsa 'Arranger (*vyāsa*) of the Veda.' The title of a mythical compiler of the *saṁhitās* comprising the Veda. A critical examination of them indicates that such a task could only have been accomplished by many hands over a period of centuries.[1]

The title is erroneously applied to Bādarāyaṇa (A.D. 200–450) an early expositor of the Uttara-mīmāṁsā or Vedānta, which was a re-examination of the later portions of the Veda in the light of the speculative philosophy of the Āraṇyakas and Upaniṣads, rather than a re-arrangement of the Veda.

[1]The *VP.* III.3 mentions twenty-eight *vyāsas* who arranged the Vedas in the *dvāpara* age.

v. Pūrva-Mīmāṁsā.

Vedhasa The part of the hand below the root of the thumb—considered to be sacred to Brahmā.

Vedi 'Altar.' An elevated (or according to some an excavated) piece of ground serving for a sacrificial altar, and having receptacles for the sacrificial fire. The shape of the altar varied, but when narrow in the middle,[1] was given a symbolic significance (*ŚBr.*, VII.3.1,11), likening it to a woman's torso,[2] the lower portion containing the womb. Such symbolism is one of the characteristics of the *ŚBr.*, which, with the *YV.* are the chief sources of information about the altar and Vedic sacrificial rites. Thus the area of the altar is measured in paces according to a ritual formula, the number of paces defining the length and breadth of the three sides enclosing it being given the names of the three principal metres, the *gāyatrī*, *triṣṭubh* and *jagatī* of the chants, apparently for no better reason than the correspondence of the number of paces of each side with the number of syllables of the metres.

In Vedic India the gods were believed to descend into the altar, regarded as situated at the 'centre of the world' (*RV.*, II.3,7; X.1,6). Hence Agni is said to be kindled in the earth's navel (*Tait. Saṁ.*, IV.1,10).

Various objects were placed under the altar, including a lotus leaf; a gold disc (representing the sun and immortality); a live tortoise; a golden figure of a man, perhaps a relic of human sacrifice thought to give permanence and a firm foundation, or it may have represented the Cosmic Puruṣa from which the world originated.

Sacred *kuśa* grass was spread over the altar and the area surrounding it, the latter providing a 'seat' for the gods attending the sacrifice. At its conclusion, the grass was not thrown away, but burnt, because being imbued with superhuman power it would endanger those who came in contact with it. Only fire (*agni*), the cathartic agent *par excellence*, was capable of destroying it.

The *ŚBr*. (I.2.5,1–4) states that the size of the altar was the size of the dwarf (*vāmana*) when he lay down to rest.[3] But in a later part of the *ŚBr*. (III.7.2,1) the *vedi* is said to be as large as the earth, and in other passages to be the focal point of communication between the three worlds (*lokas*)—a link between man and his gods.

[1]'Waisted' altars have been found in Crete (Levy, *Gate of Horn*, p. 127).

[2]In the same work (I.9.2,21) the *vedi* is said to be female and the *veda* male.

[3]But the Śulva-sūtra, included in the *Kalpa-sūtra*, states that altars should be constructed so that their size could be increased without altering their basic shape. This involved advanced geometrical skills (v. Filliozat, in *Ancient and Medieval Science*, p. 148; *IWP*., p. 124).

v. Maṇḍūka; Barhis; Chandas; Apāmārga.

Vena I. A chieftain of the Niṣādas, an Indian aboriginal tribe dwelling in the mountains of the Vindhya range.

v. Niṣāda.

II. A ruler of one of the Vajjian kingdoms whose capital was Vaiśālī.

v. Pṛthu.

Veṇi Hair braided or twisted into one unornamented plait hanging down the back, the style adopted by widows or by those 'mourning' for absent husbands.

Vetāla I. A class of demons, ghouls, or vampires who frequent burial grounds, and are said to re-animate the dead. Their eerie singing, like that of *bhūtas*, *piśācas*, *rākṣasas* is often heard in cemeteries (*Mārk. P*., 8, 115). Numerous stone circles were erected in the Deccan, in the centre of which was a large stone where the chief of the demons was believed to live. The circle of stones represented his followers, or may possibly have formed a 'ghost-hedge' to prevent the demons from leaving the area.[1]

[1]Crooke, *Things Indian*, p. 151.

II. Name of one of Śiva's attendants. Mythology describes him as the father, and Kāmadhenu (the wish-fulfilling cow) as the mother of Śiva's bull, Bhṛṅgi.[1]

[1]*Kālikā P*., adhyāya 91; *HP*., p. 316.

III. Certain *tantras* describe a form of black magic called *vetāla*.[1]

[1]*HP*., p. 310.

Vetālapañcaviṁśati Name of a collection of twenty-five (*pañcaviṁśa*) popular fables recounted by the demon Vetāla to Vikramāditya, king of Ujjain.

Vibhāṇḍaka v. Ṛṣyaśṛṅga.

Vibhīṣaṇa 'Terrifying.' Name of Rāvaṇa's brother. After the two brothers had performed austerities (*tapas*) Brahmā offered to grant them boons. Vibhīṣaṇa, according to the *Rāmāyaṇa*, asked that he should never be guilty of any unworthy action. Not only did he achieve this negative aim, but sought in a very positive way to persuade his brother against making war on Rāma. But his efforts were in vain, and only resulted in his own persecution by Rāvaṇa, until finally he joined Rāma. After Rāvaṇa's defeat and death Vibhīṣaṇa was given the throne of Laṅkā, and according to the *MBh*. Brahmā granted him the boon of immortality.[1]

[1]*EM*., p. 194.

Vibhītaka A large forest tree (Terminalia bellerica) whose nuts were used as dice. It is considered to be unlucky,[1] and hence graves should not be placed in its vicinity.

[1]*EM*., p. 7.

Vibhūti I. The manifestation of superhuman power, consisting of eight special faculties, especially attributed to Śiva, but his devotees may also attain them.

II. The ashes with which Śiva smeared his body, a practice followed by many of his devotees.[1] This custom may derive from Vedic times when ashes from the sacrificial fire were applied to different parts of the body.[2]

Among the great powers attributed to ashes was that of resuscitating the dead, as recounted in the story of the young brahmin Candrasvāmin whose dead wife was about to be cremated. But a Kāpālika ascetic threw some ashes on the girl's corpse which then arose uninjured from the fire.[3]

[1]Cf. the Roman Catholic rite on Ash Wednesday, when members of the congregation go to the altar and are marked with the sign of the cross with the ashes of palms used on Palm Sunday (*BH*., p. 400, n.1).

[2]The purifying and sterilizing properties of fire or extreme heat were well known in Vedic times, and hence ashes were considered to share those properties. They were also said to have fecundating properties as well as the power to avert evil (Gonda, *Aspects*, p. 193).

[3]*Kathāsaritsāgara*, vol. II, pp. 611f., 2nd edn. Delhi, 1968.

v. Bhasman; Pūjā.

Vibhvan v. Ṛbhu(s).
Vicārbhū The throne from which Yama judges the dead.
Vicitra Name of a celebrated king of the Lunar dynasty, the son of Śāntanu and Satyavatī, and so half-brother of Bhīṣma. When Vicitra died childless his mother, anxious to maintain the royal line, requested Vyāsa Kṛṣṇa-Dvaipāyana, her natural son by the sage Parāśara, to marry the two widows of Vicitra. This Vyāsa did and by them had two sons, Dhṛtarāṣṭra and Pāṇḍu, the heads of the Kaurava and Pāṇḍava families respectively. When Vyāsa wanted a third son, the elder of the two widows sent him one of her slave-girls, dressed in her own clothes, who became the mother of Vidura, the wise counsellor of his half-brother Dhṛtarāṣṭra and of his nephews the Pāṇḍavas.

The maintenance of the Lunar line, often by dubious genealogical expedients, gave an added interest to the theme of the *MBh.* and its culmination, the tragic end of the Kauravas and Pāṇḍavas.
v. Mahābhārata.
Vidhātṛ (Vedic **Vidhātar**) 'Disposer', 'dispenser', or 'arranger', an epithet of Viśvakarman, and also the name of one of the fertility gods associated in *RV.* (VI.50,12) with Parjanya, the rain-god, and Vāta, the wind-god.

According to the rites of hospitality, a householder should make a *bali* offering to Dhātṛ and Vidhātṛ at the door of the house (*Mārk. P.*, XXIX, 19).
v. Dhātar.
Vidhavā An epithet of Dhūmāvatī, one of the ten Mahāvidyās, who personifies the destruction of the world by fire. When only its ashes remain Dhūmāvatī is called Vidhavā 'the widow of a dead world'.
Vidveṣa A magical act or formula for exciting hatred or enmity.
v. Ṣaṭkarman; Mantra.
Vidyā Though *vidyā*, like *jñāna*, denotes knowledge, it is more specialized, like that of the sciences and arts. It initially comprised four branches of knowledge:— *Trayī-vidyā*, the knowledge of the triple Veda; *Ānvīkṣikī*, logic and metaphysics; *Daṇḍa-nīti*, the science of government; *Vārttā*, agriculture, commerce, medicine, etc. To these *Manu* (VII.43) adds *Ātma-vidyā*, the knowledge of the Supreme Essence (*ātman*), and hence the term Vidyā-guru, an instructor in sacred wisdom.

Another enumeration comprises fourteen *vidyās*, viz., the four Vedas, the six Vedāṅgas, the Purāṇas, the Mīmāṁsā, the Nyāya, and Dharma or law; or with the four Upa-Vedas, eighteen branches of knowledge. Other lists enumerate thirty-three and even sixty-four sciences (*vidyās*), and the arts of astronomy, geometry, architecture, dancing, music, etc.

Magical skill is also called a *vidyā*, as is the knowledge of hallucinogenic drugs, including one which is said to give the power of ascending to the heavens.[1] Knowledge is also personified as a goddess[2] and identified with Durgā, as a composer of prayers and magical formulas.

In Indian philosophy and metaphysics, *vidyā* denotes the complete knowledge that 'lies before and after the incomplete empirical knowledge (*a-vidyā*) which is . . . veiled by the embarrassing multitude of actual experiences'.[3] Literally it is the knowing of 'all things however apparently different and divergent. *Avidyā* [non-knowledge] . . . like *māyā*, is the fiction of separation'.[4]
[1]Drugs were also used by Shamans, by which they 'ascended' to the heavens and had strange visions.
[2]Cf. the Biblical Sophia, the personification of Wisdom.
[3]Heimann, *Facets*, p. 102.
[4]Heimann, *IWP.*, pp. 94f.
v. Vidyādhara(s); Yoga.
Vidyādhara(s) 'Bearers of Wisdom.' Beneficent aerial spirits of great beauty. They often carry flower-garlands (*mālās*) symbolizing victory, and sometimes swords representing the wisdom (*vidyā*) that cuts through ignorance (*a-vidyā*).[1]

In ancient and medieval Indian art the Vidyādharas are often shown flying towards the principal cult deity, or towards his emblem. They are depicted on the early Buddhist monuments of Bhārhut, Sāñcī, Amarāvatī, etc., and in the Jaina caves of Udayagiri and elsewhere. There are usually two main types: one, a hybrid form with the upper half of the body in human form, the lower half bird-like; the other a complete human form. During the medieval period *vidyādhara* couples are not always depicted flying but playing musical instruments above the *makara* motif, and on each side of the central deity. In late Gupta and in most medieval reliefs, the legs are flexed backwards from the knees.
[1]The females (Vidyādharīs) possess a terrible weapon (*mahāstram vaidyādharam*), but usually they are not warlike (*EM.*, p. 176).
Vidyut 'Lightning.' *Vidyut* is associated with fertility, and forms the stem of many names of *apsarasas* associated with trees, rivers and water, and regarded as bestowers of fertility and plenty. Among their names are Vidyutā, Vidyutparṇā, Vidyutprabhā, etc.,[1] all being connected with lightning, thunder and rain.
[1]Gonda, *Aspects*, p. 40.
v. Muñja; Vidyutśakti.
Vidyutśakti A particular form of energy (*śakti*) manifested as lightning and thunder.
v. Vidyut.
Vighnajit 'Conqueror of obstacles.' An epithet of

Gaṇeśa, who can be both the originator and remover of obstacles, and hence the custom of paying homage to him before commencing any undertaking.
v. Vighnarāja; Vighnāsura.

Vighnarāja 'King (or ruler or controller) of obstacles.' One of the many epithets applied to Gaṇeśa, which refers specifically to his victory over the *asura* Vighna ('Obstruction'). Banerjea points out that Gaṇeśa (Gaṇapati-vināyaka) as Vighnarāja and as Vighna-vināśana (Destroyer of Obstacles), and as Siddhidātā (Giver of Success) becomes benevolent after propitiation. This 'can be traced to the traits of the "imps and evil spirits", the like of whom can even be found in the earlier Gṛhyasūtras'.[1]

[1] *DHI.*, p. 355.
v. Vināyaka(s).

Vighnāsura or **Vighna** v. Vighnarāja.

Vija or **Bīja** v. Mantra.

Vijaya I. 'Victory', 'conquest'. Name of Indra's magic bow, i.e., the rainbow.
II. Name of Rudra's personified lance.
III. Name of the seventeenth hour of the day, the hour of Kṛṣṇa's birth.

Vijayā I. A name of Durgā; of Yama's wife; or of a magical spell, etc.
II. Hemp (Cannabis indica), used by some Tantrists to attain a particular state of mind called enstasy.
v. Tantra; Bhaṅgā.

Vikira 'Scattering', especially of rice on the *kuśa* grass, which is spread on the sacrificial area to propitiate any influences likely to interfere with the performance of the sacrifice. Among these hostile influences are the spirits of dead children who were denied the 'sacrament' of cremation, or the spirits of men who had deserted good wives (*Manu*, III.245).

Vikramāditya According to legend the name or title first assumed by a ruler of the kingdom of Mālwā in the first century B.C., and considered to be the founder of the Vikrama era in 58 B.C. But Sircar[1] rejects the legend as having no historical validity, and states that titles ending with '*āditya*' were not used until their introduction by Gupta rulers. This adoption, or a variant of it, began with Samudragupta (335–376 A.D.), who was called Parākramāṅka. Then followed the titles ending either in *āditya* or *aṅka*[2] which became common. Candragupta (376–414) assumed the title of Vikramāditya, his son Kumāragupta I (414–55) that of Mahendrāditya, his son and successor Skandagupta (455–67) that of Kramāditya or Vikramāditya, and the later descendants of the dynasty continued the practice.

[1] *Ancient Mālwā and the Vikramāditya Tradition*, p. 128.
[2] Cf. the addition of '*varman*' (protector) to the names of Āndhra kings during the fourth and fifth centuries A.D.

Vikṛti v. Virūpa II.

Viliptī The name of one of the 'divine' cows which the gods caused to rise from the sacrifice.[1] The *ṛṣi* Nārada is said to have selected 'the fearful Viliptī for himself' (*AV.*, XII.4,41).

[1] The *SED.* suggests that it refers to a cow at a particular stage of calving, but much of the obscure *AV.* hymn referred to above seems designed to terrify those who might be tempted to withhold 'gifts' of cows to the priests.

Vīṇā An ancient Indian musical instrument, said to have been the invention of the *ṛṣi* Nārada. It was originally a bow-shaped harp,[1] but after the sixth or seventh centuries A.D., the term was applied to a different instrument, a kind of bamboo lute, from either end of which a gourd was suspended. This instrument had one or more strings, and a compass of two octaves, but it has gradually been elaborated over the centuries, resulting in variants, according to the number of strings.[2]

At the horse-sacrifice (*aśvamedha*) the *vīṇā* players sang the praises of former righteous kings, so enabling the individual kingly sacrificer to share the world of his great predecessors (*ŚBr.*, XIII.4.3,3).

[1] Its original form is known from examples found at Harappā and Mohenjo-daro.
[2] v. Marcel-Dubois, *Les Instruments de musique dans l'Inde ancienne*, p. vi, Paris, 1941.

Vinatā I. The wife of the mythical Kaśyapa, sister of Kadrū, and mother (according to some legends) of the egg-born Garuḍa, who was hatched after a thousand years.
II. Name of a *rākṣasī* (demoness) who causes diseases.

Vināyaka I. 'Taking away, removing', and hence 'remover of obstacles', a name of Gaṇeśa.

The *Yājñavalkya-smṛti* (I.271) states that Vināyaka was appointed leader of the Gaṇas by Rudra and Brahmā and given the power to remove obstacles confronting human beings. But in another passage (I.285) four Vināyakas are mentioned, viz., Śālaka-ṭaṅkaṭa, Kūṣmāṇḍarājaputra, Sammita, and Devayajana, but states that they refer to the same Vināyaka.

Varāhamihira (*Bṛhat Saṁ.*, LVIII.9), on the other hand, refers to some Vināyakas and Gaṇas, not as 'removers of obstacles' but as troublesome creatures 'whom he associates with such demonic beings as *piśācas*, *rākṣasas*, *nāgas*, and *asuras*'.[1] It was necessary to propitiate these beings with food offerings placed at cross-roads.

[1] Shastri, *India as Seen in the Bṛhat Saṁhitā*, p. 150.

v. Vighnarāja.

II. Name of particular *mantras* recited over weapons to preserve them and ensure their efficacy.

v. Viruca.

Vināyikā Name of Gaṇeśa's wife, also called Gaṇeśānī.

Vindhya The name of a low, mountainous range stretching across India and dividing the Madhyadeśa from the Deccan.

v. Agastya.

Vindhyācalavāsinī 'Dweller on the Vindhya.' Also called Vindhyavāsinī. A form of the goddess Kālī worshipped by the Ṭhags (Thugs), who garrotted their victims. Kālī was probably a tribal goddess associated with the Vindhya hills[1] and worshipped there with human sacrifices and oblations of intoxicants. Human sacrifice continued in this area into the nineteenth century as part of the religious life of the Gonds, Kols and some other tribes. Kālī is usually depicted with a necklace of newly severed heads (usually of white men) which may indicate that she was a deified princess of the dark-skinned inhabitants of the Vindhya hills who fought against their fair enemies, the Āryans. As Kālī's name also means 'black' (i.e., black-skinned), this too suggests a non-Āryan origin.

[1]Gonda (*VS.*, p. 63) states that Vindhya-vāsinī was the most prominent of the goddesses of the Vindhya mountains. She was adopted by Vaiṣṇavas and connected with Viṣṇu by taking her to be an incarnation of his Yoganīdrā or Yogamāyā.

Vipāśā 'Unbound.' The name of the Vipāśā or Beas river in the Panjāb. The origin of the name is explained in a story of the *ṛṣi* Vasiṣṭha who, after his son's death at the hands of Viśvāmitra, threw himself, bound securely, into the river, but it cast him unbound back on to its banks, whence its name.

Vipracitti v. Namuci; Vātāpi; Hiraṇyakaśipu.

Vīra I. 'Hero, chief, leader.' An epithet applied to Vedic gods like Indra and the solar Viṣṇu, and later to the Buddha and the Jaina Mahāvīra; to any eminent *siddha* who has overcome all earthly impediments by *tapas* (austerity), and to any national or legendary hero.

Those who die valiantly in battle were transported by *apsarasas*[1] in brilliant chariots to Indra's heaven, 'the haven of heroes' (*vīragati*). Vīra is also applied to Śiva, the 'chief of heroes' (*vīreśvara*).

Heroes were sometimes regarded as 'part' of a deity born on earth, or as a unified portion of certain divine powers. 'Hero-stones', closely resembling the classical herms of ancient Greece, were erected to commemorate the deaths of heroes and satīs.[2]

[1]Cf. the Teutonic Valkyries who carried dead heroes to heaven.

[2]v. Harle, 'An early Hero-stone', in *Studies in Honour of Sir Mortimer Wheeler*, *JRAS.*, no. 2, 1970, pp. 159ff.

v. Vīrapāṇa.

II. A Tantric adept who has reached the second of the three dispositions, i.e., the heroic (*vīrabhāva*), the lowest being the animal (*paśubhāva*), the third and highest the divine (*divya-bhāva*).

v. Tantra.

Vīrabhadra I. The name of a frightful manifestation (*bhairavam rūpam*) of Śiva, the living embodiment of his wrath. Sometimes he is regarded as Śiva's son, who emerged from the roots of his father's hair.[1]

Vīrabhadra was created for the express purpose of wrecking Dakṣa's sacrifice, to which Śiva had not been invited.

In the medieval reliefs depicting the Seven Mothers (*sapta-mātṛkā*), Gaṇapati (Gaṇeśa) and Vīrabhadra are generally placed one at each end to act as guardians.

[1]*EM.*, p. 223.

v. Dakṣa.

II. The perfect horse, and thus considered fit to be sacrificed at the horse sacrifice (*aśvamedha*).

Virāḍdeha The embodiment of the universe in the form of Virāj.

Virāj I. 'Ruling far and wide'; 'universal sovereignty'; 'supremely pre-eminent'. Virāj is both feminine and masculine and the term is variously applied, particularly in the ontological sense, as in the *RV.* (X.90), where Virāj is equated with the Puruṣa, by whom all things were engendered, celestial and terrestrial, transcendent and transient. Thus from Puruṣa Virāj was born, and from Virāj was Puruṣa born (X.90,5).[1] This notion of Puruṣa or Virāj was succeeded by other generative agents, distinct from, but not inconsistent with, the notion of Virāj. This is indicated in the *RV.* (X.129) which, though it questions whether anyone knows the origin of creation, assumes the existence of a creator, 'whose eye controls the world'.

In two mystical hymns extolling Virāj he is said to be equivalent to cosmic potency (*AV.*, VIII.9 and 10); especially to any 'bright' feminine cosmic power,[2] such as the cosmic cow (VIII.10,24; XI.8,30); and with *prāṇa*, the vital breath or life force (XI.4,12). In some aspects Virāj resembles a 'culture-hero' introducing agriculture (*kṛṣi*) and grain (*sasya*) for the benefit of mankind (VIII.10,24).

In a later work Virāj is regarded as a secondary creator whom Brahmā, after dividing his own substance into male and female, united with the female half and begot the male power Virāj (*Manu*, I. 32f.).

[1]This is similar to the creation of Dakṣa and Aditi from each other. v. Gonda, *Aspects*, p. 67, and Heesterman, *Ancient Indian Royal Consecration*, p. 161, n.25. Bhattacharji (*IT.*, pp. 330 and 334) suggests that Virāj symbolizes the cosmic waters which formed a base for the production of Puruṣa.

[2]*BIP.*, p. 122, n.1. According to *AV.*, VIII.10,1 the feminine Virāj in the beginning was this universe. (Cf. XI.5,16.)

II. The name of a particular metre consisting of four ten-syllabled lines or eight of five syllables.

The *virāj* metre is used with one or more metres in the same hymn, especially when it is addressed to Agni and Indra, who are associated with the notion of universality, the basic significance of '*virāj*'. Similarly Varuṇa, representing cosmic order, and Mitra, universal co-existence and amity, are specially associated with the *virāj* metre (*RV.*, X.130,5), as the *jagatī* is with the Viśvedevas, who are considered to be united by its metrical form. On the other hand, eleven hymns of the third *maṇḍala*, nos. 62–72, addressed to Mitra-Varuṇa, have seven different metres, not one of which is the *virāj*. Gonda suggests that the ten syllables of this metre 'may have been considered an "accomplissement numérique" or *sampad*'.[1]

Virāj is mystically equated with food in the *Chān. Up.* (4,3,8), and hence invocations should be made in this metre when the object is the attainment of sustenance (*Ait. Br.*, I.4).[2]

[1]*Aspects*, p. 187, n.45; v. also *Nir.*, 7,13.

[2]Boner (*CHS.*, Glos., p. 259) considers that *virāṭ* (*virāj*) is the stage of differentiation of the gross elements in the evolutionary process.

v. Chandas.

Vīrapāṇa The name of a stimulating liquor drunk by warriors before or during battle, a custom that has its counterpart in many armies, as well as that of the former 'rum ration' of the British Navy. Some of Indra's victories were attributed to *soma*, as were those of Odin and the Berserkers to intoxicants.

Vīrarātrī A form of Chinnamastā, the sixth *mahāvidyā*.

v. Mahāvidyā(s).

Vīraśaiva(s) v. Liṅgāyat(s).

Virāṭa Name of a ruler, whose capital was Matsya (near the modern Jaipur). The Pāṇḍu princes and their common wife Draupadī spent the thirteenth year of their exile under the protection of Virāṭa, who subsequently joined them in the war against the Kauravas, in which he was killed by Droṇa.

v. Mahābhārata; Pāṇḍava(s).

Vīriṇī or **Vīraṇī** Also called Asiknī, one of Dakṣa's wives, the mother of the 5,000 mighty sons whom Dakṣa hoped would people the world (*VP.*, I.15).

v. Haryaśva(s).

Virocana I. 'Shining upon', 'illuminating'. An epithet of the sun and of its various personified aspects.

v. Sūrya; Viṣṇu; Āditya(s).

II. v. Bali II.

Viruca A magical formula recited over weapons.

v. Vināyaka II.

Virūḍhaka A *yakṣa*, the guardian of the southern quarter of the world, who is depicted and named with other *yakṣas* on the Bhārhut *stūpa*.

Virūpa I. A Vedic *ṛṣi*, brother of Atri and Aṅgiras, the sons of Priyamedha (*RV.*, I.45,3), to whom certain *RV.* hymns are attributed. Virūpa's descendants are referred to in *RV.* (III.53,7, etc.).

II. A malevolent sprite who lives in the tops of trees, in the ramparts of strongholds, and in the sea. If a pregnant woman should walk under their trees, these spirits will change her foetus with that of another woman (*Mārk. P.*, LI.63f.).

Vīrya 'Virility', 'sexual vigour', symbolized by a fabulous creature called *makara*.

Vīryahārin A malignant sprite who deprives men of their virility (*vīrya*) (*Mārk. P.*, LI.97).

Viś The common people, the ruled as distinct from the rulers, but the significance of the term varies according to social and political conditions. Thus it originally distinguished the agriculturalists, herdsmen, and artificers from the *brāhmaṇa* and *rājanya* or *kṣatra* classes. Later the rival social claims of the *brāhmaṇa* and *kṣatra* resulted in the *viś* being regarded as a socially lower section of the community.

Finally, with the establishment of the caste system, and its complex divisions and sub-divisions, the theoretical status of particular occupations ceased to be relevant.

v. Varṇa; Brāhmaṇa I.

Viṣa 'Poison.' According to the *Suś. Saṁ.* (II. p. 701), the heart of a man who has died from poison is not consumed by the funerary fire.

v. Kaiṭabha; Viṣaharī; Viṣavidyā.

Viṣaharī 'Poison (*viṣa*) remover.' An epithet of the goddess Manasā who protects her devotees from snake-venom.

Viśākha I. A name of Nandin, Śiva's bull.[1]

[1]*DHI.*, p. 117.

II. Possibly the name of Skanda the god of war, or of a god closely associated with him. Hopkins[1] considers that Viśākha may be connected with the month of *vaiśākha*, which coincides with the prevalence of fever.

The *Suś. Saṁ.* (III.29) gives details of the treatment of

a sick child (i.e., one who has been attacked by Skanda in the form of illness). Offerings should be made of cooked and raw meat, fresh goat's blood, milk, etc., and a preparation made from some kind of pulse for the ghosts or spirits. Then the child is bathed at a cross-roads and the physician says: 'O thou, the trusted and beloved friend of the god Skanda ... O thou ugly-faced one whom the world knows by the epithet Viśākha, may good befall this child in distress.'

[1] *EM.*, p. 230.

Viṣavidyā Toxicology or the science (*vidyā*) of poisons (*viṣa*), their sources, effects, and antidotes.

Viśiṣṭādvaita The doctrine of qualified non-duality; from *viśiṣṭa* 'distinct', 'particular', 'peculiar to', and *advaita* 'non-dual'. The doctrine was first introduced by the Vaiṣṇava writer Yamunācārya, and subsequently expounded by Rāmānuja.

v. Pāñcarātra; Vedānta.

Viṣṇu 'Pervader.'[1] A minor Vedic personified manifestation of solar energy, who is described as striding through the seven regions of the universe in three steps.

In the Brāhmaṇas Viṣṇu acquires new attributes and a number of legends unknown to the *RV.* Later he became a deity of major importance and a member of the Hindu triad (*trimūrti*). He is the preserver of the universe, and the embodiment of goodness and mercy. To Vaiṣṇavas he is the Supreme Being from whom everything emanates.

Although it is impossible to trace all the reasons why Viṣṇu became a major deity, two of the main ones are the doctrine of his 'descents' (*avatāras*) to earth in various forms to save mankind from suffering and wickedness, and his ritualistic pre-eminence as the personified Sacrifice.[2] The *avatāra* doctrine enabled historical and legendary personages like Kṛṣṇa-Vāsudeva, Rāmacandra, etc., and the historical Buddha to be absorbed into the concept of Viṣṇu as Īśvara, the Lord of all being.

[1] Or it may mean 'taking various forms' (*IAL.*, 11991). J. Przyluski (*Archivum Linguisticum*, IV.263) and L. Renou (*L'Inde classique*, p. 323) and others consider that the name Viṣṇu is non-Āryan.

[2] For Viṣṇu's pre-eminence v. Gonda, *Aspects*, p. 122.

v. Vaiṣṇava; Kṛṣṇa I; Samudramathana; Kalkin; Saura(s); Yūpa; Śipiviṣṭa; Bali; Nārāyaṇa; Śeṣa; Cakra; Gada I; Gadā; Garuḍa; Hari; Lakṣmī; Sudarśana; Śrīvatsa; Viṣṇu Purāṇa; Vaikuṇṭha II.

Viṣṇu Purāṇa[1] One of the earliest of the eighteen Purāṇas, much of its contents having been composed probably in the first century B.C., though it must have been subject to more than one revision,[2] and to additions as well as excisions. Its language is generally correct Sanskrit and its style elegant, and its presentation that of a carefully constructed whole, qualities that reflect the sophisticated editorial capabilities of a period later than the first century B.C.

The *VP.* is considered to be an exceptional Purāṇa, for not only does it deal with the five subjects regarded as essential, but also deals with them and other matters in great detail. Many myths are recorded relating to creation, the personification of natural phenomena, such as planets, stars, mountains, rivers, trees, plants, etc., and refer to the elemental forces to which they owe their existence. It deals also with abstract concepts, like death (*mṛtyu*), illusion or self-deception (*māyā*), tolerance (*kṣama*), self-discipline (*dama*), fortitude (*dhṛti*), etc., all of which are personified, and given genealogies like those of men and gods. But despite the enormous range of subjects dealt with, it never loses sight of its principal aim, the praise of Viṣṇu, on whom, by faith and worship his devotees may rely for their final liberation (*mokṣa*).

[1] First translated from the Sanskrit by H.H. Wilson and printed in 1840. It was reprinted in 1888 with valuable notes by F. Hall, and reprinted in 1961, with the addition of an introduction by R.C. Hazra of the Sanskrit College, Calcutta.

[2] 'These revisions were responsible for the extension of dynastic accounts down to the time of the Guptas; for its spurious parts, including III. 17–18; and for the elimination of some chapters or verses referred to in others' (Hazra, *VP.*, Intro., pp. k–l).

Viṣṇuyaśas An eminent *brāhmaṇa*, one of whose descendants will be born at the close of the *kali* age as Kalkin, the future *avatāra* of Viṣṇu. His coming will re-establish righteousness on earth, and the return of an age of purity and innocence (*VP.*, IV.24).

Viśpalā Name of a female warrior whose 'leg was severed like a wild bird's pinion' in a night attack against the enemies of her relative Khela, a tribal chieftain. But the Aśvins, learning of her plight, are said to have given her an 'iron leg' (*RV.*, I.116,15) or a 'new leg' (I.118,8), which enabled her to take part in the subsequent battles.

Viśravas v. Pulastya.

Viṣṭārin A particular kind of cooked rice-offering, so-called because the addition of certain ingredients causes it to 'expand' (*viṣṭārin*). Ritually it is equated with the *brahman* and the metres, etc. It is said to be a sacrifice born out of ascetic fervour (*tapas*) (*AV.*, IV.34,1).

The next verse states that when those die who have made the *viṣṭārin* offering, Jātavedas (Agni) does not burn their virile member, and they ascend intact to the celestial world (*svarga*). The next hymn, also dedicated to the rice-offering, states that it will enable the Sacrificer to overcome death and also his enemies.

Viśvajit 'All-conquering.' Name of Varuṇa's noose.

Viśvakarman The divine architect of the universe, the personification of creative power which 'welds heaven and earth together' (*RV.*, X.81,2–3; 82,2).

Viśvakarman not only represents supreme creative power but also universal knowledge and wisdom. He is both the establisher (*dhātar*) and the disposer (*vidhātar*).

According to the *ŚBr.* (XIII.7,1f.), Viśvakarman performed a universal sacrifice (*sarvamedha*) in which he offered up all creatures and finally himself. This sacrifice was believed to be particularly efficacious and to give supremacy over all creatures.[1] This 'dismemberment of the lord of creatures, which took place at that archetypal sacrifice, was in itself the creation of the universe, so every sacrifice is also a repetition of that first creative act. Thus the periodical sacrifice is nothing else than a microcosmic representation of the ever-proceeding destruction and renewal of all cosmic life and matter.'[2] But Viśvakarman's importance was superseded by the notion of the eternal Self-Existent Principle (*brahman*). Finally he appears as the mythical founder of the science of architecture (*vāstuvidyā*).[3]

[1]Cf. Odin's sacrifice of himself to himself.

[2]Eggeling, *ŚBr.*, *SBE.*, vol. XLII, pt. iv, intro. p. xv.

[3]This was also the name of an Āryan master-architect (Bhattacharyya, *Canons of Indian Art*, p. 315).

v. Prajāpati; Puruṣa; Brahmā; Vedāṅga(s); Ghṛtācī; Saṁjñā; Jagannātha; Tvaṣṭṛ.

Viṣvaksena I. 'All-conquering.' An epithet of Viṣṇu-Kṛṣṇa or a form of that deity to whom the fragments of a sacrifice are offered.

II. Name of Viṣṇu's gate-keeper who was killed by Śiva when he was refused permission to enter.[1]

[1]*DHI.*, p. 466.

Viśvāmitra Name of one of the most eminent of the Vedic seers, whose influence and that of his descendants extended throughout the Vedic age, and whose exploits are the theme of many later legends. Viśvāmitra is traditionally the composer of the third *maṇḍala* of the *RV.*, which includes the most sacred of *mantras*, the *gāyatrī* (III.62,10). A number of *AV.* hymns are also attributed to him.

Except for the references to Viśvāmitra as the *purohita* of king Sudās, and later as his adversary in the *daśarājña* (War of the Ten Kings), details of his life and antecedents are few and generally obscure. Later attempts to fill the gap, like those in the *Bṛhadd.* (IV.98), and in the Epics and the Purāṇas,[1] tend to confuse rather than to clarify.

Many of the post-Vedic legends of Viśvāmitra refer to the feud between him and Vasiṣṭha, which was supposed to have originated when King Sudās appointed Vasiṣṭha as his *purohita* in place of Viśvāmitra. This feud[2] is stated in the Purāṇas to have become hereditary and continued for centuries between the descendants of the two *ṛṣis*.

[1]Which refer to Kuśika as the grandfather, and Gādhi as the father of Viśvāmitra.

[2]This may represent the initial antagonism of Āryan and indigenous cultures.

v. Vaiśvāmitra(s); Gotra; Saptarṣis; Aṣṭaka; Menā II.

Viśvarūpa I. 'Multiform.' Name of the three-headed demon Triśiras, son of Tvaṣṭṛ.

II. Name of one of the thirty-nine incarnatory forms of Viṣṇu, listed in the *Sātvata Saṁ.*[1]

[1]*DHI.*, p. 391.

v. Avatāra(s).

Viśvāvasu The chief of the *gandharvas* in Indra's paradise. Viśvāvasu was a skilful dancer and musician.

Viśvedeva(s) Lit. 'All-divine'. A class of minor gods worshipped by the commonalty, *viś*.[1] Numerous references to them occur in the *RV.*, and some hymns are addressed to them. It seems probable that some non-Vedic gods are included among them, as *RV.*, I.27,13, refers to earlier and later gods.

[1]In the *VP.* (I.15) they are the sons of Viśvā, a daughter of Dakṣa. They may be invoked collectively or individually (Heimann, *Facets*, p. 82). They are especially worshipped at *śrāddhas* and at the Vaiśvadeva rite. Hopkins suggests they were originally forms of the Manes, because of 'their constant association with the *pitṛs* at the funeral feast' (*EM.*, p. 174). Travellers invoke them for protection against *bhūtas* (ibid., p. 175). Brahmā and the *pitṛs* gave them the boon of having offerings made to them daily as a reward for their great asceticism (*tapas*).

v. Devatā; Asura.

Vītahavya A Haihaya ruler.

v. Pratardana.

Vivāha 'Marriage.' The relative lack of references to marriage in the first nine *maṇḍalas* of the *RV.* suggests that there was 'considerable freedom on the part of young persons concerned in the selection of a wife or husband'.[1] Nor apparently did their choice require the consent of parent or brother. The only restriction mentioned or implied was that of the marriage of Āryans with the dark-skinned aboriginals (*dasyus*). Indra is thus implored to give protection to the Āryan colour (*ārya-varṇa*) (*RV.*, III.34,9); and to prevent incestuous unions. Only in a late hymn (X.85), known as the wedding-hymn, is the simple Vedic marriage-rite described. It began with the bridegroom and his friends going to the bride's house and escorting her to the wedding-feast, one course of which consisted of cow-beef, the cows having been slaughtered for the occasion. After the feast the ceremony began with the bridegroom taking the bride's hand and leading her round the sacred fire (X.18,8). This simple act sealed the marriage. The consummation was signified by the purification of the bride's garment, a rite probably intended to indicate her virginity.

Most references to marriage suggest that the Vedic Āryans were generally monogamous (I.124,7; IV.3,2; X.71,4; 85,43, etc.),[2] but some passages suggest that polygamy was practised (I.62,11; 104,3; 105,8, etc.), chiefly by the *rājanya* or ruling class, and often for political reasons.

Polyandry is nowhere mentioned in the *RV.*, but it was customary in many hill-tribes of the Himālaya, the result of economic pressures, rather than of female concupiscence. It was subject to rules which stated that the husbands should all be brothers, that the eldest should be acknowledged as the principal husband, and that no two brothers should be at home at the same time. This is confirmed by the story of the banishment of Arjuna, one of the five Pāṇḍu princes, who infringed this rule by coming home when his eldest brother Yudhiṣṭhira was with their common wife Draupadī.

The custom of marrying a girl to a tree or to a bunch of flowers ensured that she should never be a widow. Third marriages are believed to be particularly inauspicious, so when a *brahmin* intends marrying for the third time he is married to an *arka* plant, thus making the real marriage the fourth.[3]

The gradual systematization of marriage rites was coincidental with the expansion of ritual and cultural development generally, which necessitated the composition of *sūtras* for the guidance of both priest and householder. The *Āpastamba* (II.5,11, 15–20; 12, 1–3) states that the basic conditions for marriage are that neither bride nor bridegroom shall be descended from the same original ancestor (*gotra*), nor be related within six degrees (*yonisambandha*)[4] on the mother's or father's side (*pravara*). Six types of marriage[5] are recognized as valid: 1. Brāhma, when the bride's father, before endowing his daughter, satisfies himself about the family of the suitor, his character, learning and health. 2. Ārṣa, when the bride's father bestows his daughter (without any dowry) on a suitor in return for the gift of a bull and a cow. 3. Daiva, the bestowal of a daughter by her father on an officiating priest of the *śrauta* sacrifice. 4. Gāndharva, a love-match, often clandestine, and agreed upon by a young couple, with or without their parents' approval. 5. Āsura, when the father requires a bride-price from the suitor. 6. Rākṣasa, the marriage of a girl who has been abducted by a man and his friends, generally by force if her father and relations offer resistance.

The first three rites only are esteemed. Marriage often involved questions of precedence within the family. Thus an elder brother took precedence in the kindling of the sacred household fire, in the offering of the sacrifice, in marriage and in all matters of inheritance. Any refusal to conform to these customs entailed penalties, successively heavier for each offence. The gradual recognition of caste resulted in further marriage regulations. While the *brahmin* was permitted to have four wives, the *kṣatriya* three, the *vaiśya* two, the first wife must always be of the same caste as the husband (*Manu*, III.12–13). The *śūdra* was permitted only one wife, who must be a *śūdrī*.

The primary importance of marriage was to ensure the fertility of the union.[6] In post-Vedic India the position of sons, especially the eldest, acquired a still more important status. Not only was he expected to ensure the continuity of the family, but also by the performance of funerary rites to ensure that his father should after death achieve union with his ancestors (*pitṛs*). To a father without sons, it was important that he should marry off a daughter as soon as possible after her attainment of puberty[7] (*Baudhāyana sūtra*, IV.1,11) in the hope of obtaining a grandson. These rules and many others indicate the extent of priestly indoctrination of the minds of the people, not unlike that by the Church in medieval Europe.

Nonetheless, romantic views of marriage survived and were nurtured by stories, like those of Nala and Damayantī, and of Rāma and Sītā, though there were not lacking stories of strongly sexed women, like Dhūminī in Daṇḍin's 'Tales of Ten princes' (*Daśakumāracarita*), which reflect the deterioration in the status of women compared with that of Vedic times. How far this may be attributed to Islamic influence is uncertain, but it is significant that after the Moslem conquest of northern India, Hindu women there no longer appeared in public unveiled. But however generally unrealistic the priestly views of sex and marriage had become, an attempt to restore to them a sense of reality was made by Vātsyāyana in the *Kāmasūtra*. Its frank analysis of sex, and the practical advice it offers to the newly married has probably contributed greatly to the legislation that has now restored to the women of India much of their ancient status.

[1] *HCIP*., I, p. 389.

[2] The *AV.* (VII.36–7) confirms the monogamous ideal by the utterance of love-charms by a newly-married

couple. 'Place me within thy heart; may we be of one mind', the husband says to his wife, who replies: 'Thou shall be mine alone; thou shalt not even mention other women to me.' In later works the couple were believed to be together in every birth (*IRA.*, p. 88), even as Viṣṇu's consort Lakṣmī, is his wife in each of his incarnations (*avatāras*).

[3]Thurston, *Omens*, p. 51.

[4]What Manu, Yājñavalkya and others call '*sapiṇḍa*' (*SBE.*, II. p. 126, n.16).

[5]Manu (III.27, *et seq.*) lists eight, which include those of the Āpastamba, the additional two being the Prājāpatya, the marriage of a dowerless girl for whom no bride-price is demanded; the Paiśāca, the seduction of a girl when drunk or drugged, or one of unsound mind. Such a girl is nonetheless neither widow nor virgin and thus not eligible for marriage.

[6]'It is with this object that rice or wheat is poured over the heads of the pair, a custom which has passed from India to Europe' (Crooke, *Things Indian*, p. 319).

[7]But some ancient authorities quoted by Monier-Williams (*BH.*, p. 364, n.1.) state that in olden times girls were married long after they had reached the age of puberty.

v. Vṛkṣa.

Vivasvat 'The Brilliant One.' An epithet of the sun. His Avestan counterpart is Vivahvant.

In post-Vedic mythology, he is said to be one of the Ādityas, sons of Aditi. In Epic poetry he is the father of Manu Vaivasvata.

v. Tvaṣṭṛ; Saraṇyū.

Vopadeva A thirteenth-century grammarian, author of the *Mugdhabodha*, which presents a grammatical system independent of that of Pāṇini.[1]

[1]Weber, *Indian Literature*, p. 226.

Vrata The 'Will', from the root *vṛ*, signifying the exercise of the will.[1] *Vrata* applies also to religious observance, to conduct, to pious practices, such as the making of a solemn vow to fast, to practise chastity, to perform meritorious acts, such as the making of pilgrimages to holy places, etc.

[1]Cf. Lat. *velle*; Slav. *voliti*; Ger. *wollan*, *wollen*; AS. *willan*.

Vrātya I. A name of the supreme *brahman* (*AV.*, XV). Vrātya is also called Ekavrātya (the One Vrātya), whom Eliade considers to be 'the divinized archetype of the Vrātyas'.[1]

According to the *Praśna Up.* (2,11), Vrātya appears as a kind of cosmic being, but Śaṅkara interprets the name as 'uninitiated', i.e., the first-born, and hence without anyone to initiate him.

[1]*Yoga*, p. 105.

II. Name of a tribe of nomads of whom little is known, but who are thought to be one of the earliest of the Āryan tribes to reach India.[1] They gradually drifted to the Deccan, but generally remained outside the sphere of brahmanic culture.

The Vrātyas had horse-, mule- or ass-drawn carts which also served as their place of worship and sacrifice. They wore turbans, necklaces made of coins (*niṣka*), ceremonial earrings, and black garments.

According to the *AV.* they practised a form of *yoga* such as standing erect for a year; breath control and trance states.[2] For some unknown reason the status of the Vrātyas declined over the years,[3] and later works refer to them as the offscourings of society, as pimps, poisoners, drunkards, and of mixed castes. *Manu* (II.38–40) is particularly critical of them, asserting that any member of the superior classes who failed to undergo the *sāvitrī* initiation in the appropriate year would end up as Vrātyas (outcastes), and despised by all true Āryans.[4]

[1]M. N. Ray, *Sarasvatī Bhavana Studies*, vol. V, p. 73.

[2]Eliade, *Shamanism*, p. 408n. They are said to have searched for the elixir of life (Karmarkar, *Religions of India*; *The Vrātya or Dravidian Systems*, p. 25, Lonavla, 1950).

[3]Perhaps because of their association with extreme Śaiva practices. D. R. Bhandarkar considers that the Vrātya cult later 'developed into Śaivism' and had originally come to the Indus Valley from outside India (*Some Aspects of Ancient Indian Culture*, p. 48, Madras, 1940).

[4]The performance of the *vrātyastoma* rite purified and restored them to brahminical society, a rite now used for sanctifying Hindus who have failed to observe the customs, etc., of their caste.

Vṛkṣa The name applied to any tree or to its wood.[1] Because of their continuous growth, trees symbolize reproduction, especially the flower and fruit-bearing species. Godlings, *yakṣas*, etc. were said to dwell in them. Hence any large tree in a village is revered as a power which sustains the community.[2] Among the funerary verses of the *AV.*, the tree is invoked not to oppress the dead (XVIII.2,25), and in another hymn (3.70) it is implored to give back the corpse deposited in it so that he may join Yama. This seems to point to the use of hollow trees as coffins. The dead were also sometimes buried near the roots of trees.

The wood of particular trees, such as the *vikaṅkata* and *udumbara*, was used to feed the sacrificial fire, and for the kindling sticks (*araṇis*), *palāśa* wood (*ŚBr.*, VI.6.3,1–2, and 7). Particular trees have special associations, Agni with the *śamī*; Viṣṇu with the *nyagrodha*, *udumbara*,[3] and *aśvattha*;[4] Śiva with the *vakula* and *bilva*. The *pārijāta* is the tree *par excellence* of Indra's paradise; the *kalpa* is the wish-granting tree.[5] The sap of the *kālāmra*, the giant mango that grows on the eastern slope of Mount Meru, confers eternal youth.

Trees were regarded as sentient beings, and among many of the lower castes a form of tree-marriage is recognized.[6] Those who desire children often invoke tree-spirits.[7]

Trees were consecrated by watering them with a solution of certain drugs; by hanging garlands from every bough, which should also be covered with rice-paste, etc. The blessing of the Earth-Goddess should be invoked from out of the 'hearts of trees' by appropriate *mantras*.

[1]Especially when used for a sacred purpose, or as a flag-pole, or as a symbol of fertility, like the Maypole of medieval European folklore.

[2]Cf. the *vard trad*, the 'protecting trees', on which the well-being of a Scandinavian house depended (James, *Tree of Life*, p.160).

[3]During a conflict of the *devas* and *asuras*, the *udumbara* alone sided with the former who declared that henceforth they would transfer to it the essence of all other trees, so that if the latter again supported the *asuras* they would be as spent as a milked-out cow (*ŚBr.*, VI.6.3,2–3).

[4]Particularly sacred also to the Buddhists.

[5]Cf. the Christmas tree loaded with gifts.

[6]Crooke, *Things Indian*, p. 317.

[7]Coomaraswamy (*Yakṣas*, pt.ii. p.33, n.3) suggests that the connexion between trees and human fertility stems from the time when paternity was not understood. The idea of conception through eating the fruit of a tree is still current in Indian folklore. On trees granting offspring, v. Mehta, *Sexual Life in Ancient India*, pp. 156–8.

v. Vivāha; Araṇi; Caitya.

Vṛndāvana Name of the area in the Mathurā district where the boy Kṛṣṇa lived among the herdsmen and their womenfolk.

v. Gopī(s); Gopāla.

Vṛṣa 'Male; masculine'; a 'male animal, especially the bull', and hence an epithet denoting a strong, vigorous man, hero, or chief. The epithet is applied to Indra and Agni who are likened to bulls (*RV.*, I.177,1; VIII.33,10).

The bull also symbolizes sexual power, and hence Śiva, the great yogin, stands by or on a bull to denote that his power is so great that even sexual energy can be sublimated. The bull is also depicted on Śiva's banner.

In some areas purification after contact with a corpse necessitated touching the tail of a bull. Cf. *ukṣan*, the 'sprinkling bull', i.e., the rain-cloud which causes growth (*Nir.*, 12,9); and *vṛṣaṇa*, 'fertilizing', a name of testicles.

Vṛṣakapi 'Man-ape'—a mysterious semi-divine being. In a late *RV.* hymn (X.86) he is described as a tawny or yellow beast, a great friend of Indra. Vṛṣakapi appears to be associated with the sun.[1]

[1]The names of the sacred sun-apes Vṛṣakapi, Kapindra, etc., are all names of Viṣṇu. v. also *IT.*, pp. 276f.

v. Kapi; Hanumat.

Vṛṣṇi(s) Name of the Yādavas whose descent traditional history traces to Vṛṣṇi, the youngest of the four sons of Bhīma Sātvata, ruler of the Yādava kingdom of north-western India. Vṛṣṇi's descendants included Vasudeva, the father of Kṛṣṇa and Balarāma, and of Pṛthā, later known as Kuntī, the mother of three of the five Pāṇḍu princes.

In the war of the Kauravas and Pāṇḍavas some of the Vṛṣṇi and other Yādava tribes joined the Kauravas, but those connected by marriage with the Pāṇḍu princes joined them. Some years after the Bhārata war most of the Vṛṣṇis and Yādavas of Gujarāt perished in fratricidal strife, shortly before the death of Kṛṣṇa. Thenceforth the name Vṛṣṇi or Yādava is only of historical significance, their descendants being known as Kurus after their more immediate ancestor Kuru.

Five of the Vṛṣṇi heroes (*vīras*), Saṁkarṣaṇa, Vāsudeva, Pradyumna, Sāmba and Aniruddha were originally represented by five statues whose installation was recorded in an inscription at the Mora Well near Mathurā.[1] Four of these deified Vṛṣṇi-vīras, 'Vāsudeva, Saṁkarṣaṇa, Pradyumna and Aniruddha, were endowed with special sanctity and regarded as four primary *vyūhas* of the highest god Para Vāsudeva in . . . the developed Pāñcarātra cult'.[2]

[1]*DHI.*, p. 93.

[2]Ibid., p. 94.

Vṛtra The representative of chaos; the 'demonized power of obstruction'; a malignant influence or demon of darkness and drought supposed to take possession of clouds,[1] and thus withhold rain. But Apte[2] suggests that 'Vṛtra was originally a frost and winter demon from whose grasp the waters have to be wrenched free every year', so that the Vṛtra-myth was more likely to have originated not in India but in a country of severe winters.

Apte also points out that thunderstorms or rains are hardly mentioned in the Indra-Vṛtra myth and that clouds play only a minor part in it; and that as the waters released by Indra are described as running like horses in a race, this is more likely to refer to the flow of rivers rather than of rain released from clouds. Thus Indra is said to pierce with his *vajra* the mountains and so release the pent-up waters. Nonetheless, as the original significance of the Indra-Vṛtra myth receded, its reinterpretation to suit the climatic conditions of north-western India led to many modifications of its original form; including the wide-ranging functions of Indra, from that of rainmaker in collaboration with the Maruts to that of war-leader against the indigenes (*asuras*), whose activities included the damming and diversion of rivers by means of 'forts' or earthworks which Indra was implored to destroy with his *vajra* (*RV.*, III.45,2; VI.32,5, etc.). It is known that the Indus Valley people were highly civilized when the Āryans entered the country, and also had massive fortifications and control of the river system of north-western India.[3] When Indra was not battling against the indigenes, he was fighting Ahi[4] the 'serpent of the sky', and other demons.

It is probable that the Indra-Vṛtra myths owe their diversity to the variant regional conditions confronting the Āryans as they extended their occupation of northern India. But the consistency of the *RV.* legendary Indra-Vṛtra cycle was distorted by brahmanic ritual which in the *ŚBr.* (I.1.3,4–5) describes Vṛtra as covering (*vṛ*) the whole space between heaven and earth, so that when Indra slew him his being flowed forth[5] and polluted the waters, which had to be purified before being fit for sacrificial sprinkling, and hence the loathing thereafter of the waters for Vṛtra. But later portions of the *ŚBr.* attribute Vṛtra's death to the gods, or to the performance of a full-moon sacrifice by Indra.[6]

In post-Vedic compositions the Vṛtra myth merged with fanciful stories having a strong sectarian bias. One of the best-known is that of Triśiras, the priest of the gods, whose growing influence threatened the gods and Indra's own position. Triśiras also sided with Hiraṇyakaśipu, the leader of the *asuras*, a staunch follower of Śiva. Having been unable to persuade Triśiras to change his ways, the gods conspired to obtain a special *vajra*, infused with Viṣṇu-energy, with which Indra decapitated Triśiras, but from his mangled remains arose Vṛtra (another form of Triśiras), which Indra also slew. As Triśiras was a *brāhmaṇa*, so also was his Vṛtra-form, and hence Indra was doubly guilty of brahmanicide. Indra evaded the consequences of his 'sin' by performing a horse-sacrifice (*aśvamedha*) in honour of Viṣṇu, and by distributing his guilt among women, fire, trees and cows, after which he was reinstated as chief of the gods.

[1]From the root *vṛ*, 'to hold back', 'restrain' (*SED.*). v. also Gonda, *Loka*, p. 21.

[2]*HCIP.*, vol. I, pp. 371f.

[3]Piggott, *Prehistoric India*, p. 263; Mortimer Wheeler, *Civilizations of the Indus Valley and Beyond*, p. 78.

[4]Ahi has cognate Greek forms—*ophis* or *echis* 'serpent'. Similar myths of gods fighting serpents occur in the Hittite New Year Purulli festival, the cult-myth taking 'the form of a ritual combat as in the Babylonian Creation Epic and in the Osiris-Horus myth' (James, *Tree of Life*, pp. 118f.); in the Sumerian myth of Ninurta's battle against the monster Asag; in the Canaanite story of Baal vanquishing Mot; the Egyptian Sun-god Ra fighting the serpent Apep; Yahweh who battled against the serpent Leviathan or against Tannin, 'the Dragon'; the Scandinavian thunder-god Thor who conquered the cosmic serpent with his magic hammer Miölnir ('Crusher') which is 'generally identified by modern scholars with the thunderbolt' (Gaster, *Thespis*, p. 148).

[5]The *RV.* (III.45,2) version merely states that Indra released the rain from the clouds, or in VI.32,5 frees the pent-up waters of the rivers.

[6]According to the *AV.* (VIII.5,3) Indra slew Vṛtra with an amulet fashioned from a *srāktya* tree. The *MBh.* states that after Vṛtra's death the personification of the crime, wearing a garland of skulls, emerged from the side of the corpse. This personification stuck to Indra 'like a spell' (*kṛtyā*). Cf. the myth of Brahmā's skull which adhered to Śiva's hand.

v. Dadhyac; Arbuda; Narasiṁha; Pāśa.

Vyādhi 'Disease' (especially leprosy); 'plague'; personified as the offspring of Death (Mṛtyu).

Vyāhṛti(s) 'Utterance', 'declaration'. The *vyāhṛtis* represent the mystical names of the seven worlds: *bhur*, *bhuvar*, *svar*, *mahar*, *janar*, *tapar* and *satya*.[1] The first three names (*Manu*, II.76) are called 'great *vyāhṛtis*' and are uttered after '*Om*' by every *brahmin* at the commencement of his daily prayers. The supreme divinity of the great *vyāhṛtis* is Prajāpati, their individual deities being Agni, Vāyu and Sūrya respectively (*Bṛhadd.*, II.123–4). But according to the *Tait. Saṁ.*, I.6.10,4, the *vyāhṛtis* may also serve evil ends.

[1]The *vyāhṛtis* are personified as the daughters of Savitṛ and Pṛśnī (*SED.*).

v. Mantra; Mahāvyāhṛti.

Vyantara devatā(s) 'Intermediate gods', or folk-godlings, worshipped by Indian village folk.

With the rise of the cult deities, the Vyaṇtara devatās became associated with them, especially with Śiva, generally as attendants, but sometimes as adversaries. There is no doubt that these early divinities and their worship 'lay at the root of the evolution of the various cults associated with brahmanical Hinduism, and to a certain extent with the development of Buddhism and Jainism'.[1]

[1] *DHI.*, pp. 335f.

Vyāsa The general name in late post-Vedic times for 'arranger, editor or compiler' of 'literary' compositions, and variously applied to eminent persons whose names would lend authority to particular works. Hence the title Vedavyāsa, applied to a mythical *ṛṣi* as the 'arranger' of the Veda, a task that internal evidence shows could only have been accomplished by many 'Vyāsas' over a period of centuries.

The title Vyāsa is applied to Kṛṣṇa-Dvaipāyana, the traditional compiler of the nucleus of the *MBh.*, but no historical evidence exists to support the claim.

v. Parāśara.

Vyūha (s) Name of the four appearances or manifestations of Viṣṇu, the Supreme Being. These forms are: *vyūha*; *vibhava* or *avatāra*, the incarnatory; *antaryāmin*, the divine presence in all beings; and the *vigrahas*, the visible embodiment and expression of the divine.[1] But this concept has been variously interpreted among Vaiṣṇavas. For instance, in an inscription at the Mora Well near Mathurā, the four deified Vṛṣṇi-Vīras: Vāsudeva (Kṛṣṇa), Saṁkarṣaṇa (Baladeva), Pradyumna (Kṛṣṇa's son), and Aniruddha (Pradyumna's son), are regarded as the four primary *vyūhas* of the Supreme Being, Para-Vāsudeva, and 'endowed with special sanctity in the developed Pāñcarātra cult'.[2] In some late Śrī-Viṣṇu cults, these four primary *vyūhas* are regarded as special creations of Vāsudeva, which represent particular forces or characteristics of the evolutionary process. Thus Saṁkarṣaṇa, combined with *prakṛti* (primal matter), produced *manas* (mind) which, when combined with Pradyumna, produces *ahaṁkāra* (consciousness), and so forth in an endless succession of *vyūhas*. The absence of any *vyūhas* in the early Bhāgavata texts supports the view that they were a late development in Vaiṣṇava theology.[3]

[1] What Christian theology calls 'the outward and visible sign of an inward and spiritual grace.'

[2] *DHI.*, p. 94. The concept of the 'One in four' is described in cult treatises as '*caturvyūha*' or 'Viṣṇu *caturmūrti*' and represented iconographically as a four-faced and usually four-armed figure. The *Viṣṇudharmottara* (Bk. III, ch. 85) describes this type of icon as Vaikuṇṭha.

[3] V. M. Apte, *HCIP.*, vol. II, p. 447.

v. Avatāra(s).

Y

Yādava(s) 'Relating to or descended from Yadu.' The name Yadu occurs in the *RV*. as that of an early Āryan tribe, while that mentioned in the *MBh*. and the Purāṇas refers to the elder of the two sons of Devayānī, wife of King Yayāti, part of whose kingdom was situated in a region unknown to the Vedic Yadus. The *MBh*. and Purāṇa references either to Yayāti or Yadu indicate the syncretism of post-Vedic names and events with their Vedic namesakes, a literary device to give the impression of antiquity to a particular legend.

There is a great divergence in the Purs. regarding the territories assigned to Yadu and Turvaśu, the two sons of Devayānī, the principal wife of Yayāti, and the three sons of Śarmiṣṭhā, his second wife. Pargiter's collated text suggests that Yadu was given territories to the 'south-west, embracing the country watered by the rivers Charmanvatī (Chambal), Vetravatī (Betwā) and Śuktimatī (Ken)'.[1] There Yadu founded the Yādava line, which became the first Lunar Dynasty to achieve prominence. But under Yadu's sons the Yādavas separated into the Yādava and Haihaya branches, the latter occupying a region south of Mālwā.

The Yādava kingdom was later divided by Bhīma Sātvata among his four sons, and from the youngest, Vṛṣṇi, were descended Vasudeva, father of Kṛṣṇa and Balarāma, and a daughter, Pṛthā, later known as Kuntī (so-called because of her adoption by Kunti-bhoja). She married the Yādava prince Pāṇḍu and became the mother of the three elder Pāṇḍavas, Yudhiṣṭhira, Bhīma and Arjuna.

Contemporary with Vasudeva was Kaṁsa, the ruler of Mathurā who had deposed his father Ugrasena and usurped the throne. Kaṁsa's tyranny finally resulted in his death at the hands of Kṛṣṇa who restored Ugrasena to the throne. As Kaṁsa was the son-in-law of Jarāsandha, the ruler of the powerful kingdom of Magadha, the latter immediately led a campaign against the Yādavas. They were forced to withdraw, but succeeded in establishing themselves under Kṛṣṇa at Dvārakā on the west coast. But towards the close of Kṛṣṇa's life a fratricidal war broke out in which practically all of the Yādava men were killed. Thereafter the Yādava, like other small kingdoms, was absorbed by the Bhārata and Pañcāla kingdoms, though some of them succeeded in emerging with their identity intact.

[1]*HCIP*., I, p. 274.

v. Śukra.

Yadu One of the five Āryan tribes mentioned in the *RV*., enumerated as Yadu, Turvaśa, Druhyu, Anu and Puru. The Yadus and Turvaśas appear to have been closely associated and hence are sometimes mentioned together (*RV*., VIII.9,14, etc.). Occasionally they are alluded to simply as the 'Five tribes' (*RV*., VI.46,7, etc.).

v. Yādava(s); Yayāti.

Yajamāna A sacrificer, or institutor of a sacrifice. His offerings made in this world are said to constitute his body in the next, so that he frees himself from mortality and from his 'sins' (*ŚBr*., XI.2.2,5; 2.6,13; XII. 5.2,8). In the *aśvamedha* (horse-sacrifice), the animal is killed with a gold knife, and by the light of the gold (symbolizing immortality) the sacrificer goes to the celestial world (XIII.2.2,16). The divinized sacrificer possesses 'worlds of his own' like the gods, and by ritual acts withdraws himself from the mundane world and is united with divine power.[1] He is also said to be reborn from the victim. 'Being immolated the victim gives birth to the sacrificer, imparting to him a new identity equal to its own. It is thus that the "birth out of sacrifice, out of brahman"' is realized.[2]

[1]Gonda, *Loka*, p. 91.

[2]Heesterman, *Ancient Indian Royal Consecration*, p. 202; v. also *ŚBr*., I.3,2,1f.

v. Yajña; Dakṣiṇā.

Yajña 'Oblation', 'sacrifice', or 'worship'. The sacrifice was magical rather than religious.[1]

The purpose of the sacrifice was to ensure the fertility and well-being of the individual, his family and domestic animals, and ultimately the whole community. Moreover, it helped to identify each group with the divine—or superhuman—powers of nature. The sacrifice was an offering to the gods, to sustain them in their task of maintaining the world and directing its manifold generative activities,[2] and hence they were invoked to be present.[3]

Some sacrifices were purely priestly ceremonies, others were performed on behalf of individuals.[4] The household sacrifice was performed by the head of the family, its ritual being subsequently enumerated in the Gṛhya-sūtras.

Gradually the belief in the efficacy of the Vedic sacrifice, especially of 'burnt offerings', whose aroma rose like incense to heaven, began to be questioned and a more realistic appraisal of religious needs made in later portions of the *RV.*, *AV.* and in some Brāhmaṇas, Āraṇyakas and Upaniṣads.[5]

[1]Brough, *EBS.*, p. 17; v. also Exodus xxix.39; *HCIP.*, I, p. 500. The *RV.* divine sacrifice of the cosmic Puruṣa was the model for all later sacrifices.

[2]*HP.*, p. 122. By ritual observances men may become gods (*Tait. Up.*, 2.18, 1–14).

[3]The Greek gods were similarly invoked and 'seen coming either in visible form, floating down as a bird, as in the Mycenean representation, or in imagination' (Nilsson, *History of Greek Religion*, p. 148). In the Brāhmaṇas and Sūtras the solar Viṣṇu was the 'personal manifestation of the sacrifice'; in the later Viṣṇu cult, all his *avatāras* were connected with particular forms of the sacrifice (v. *Vaikānasa Smārta Sūtra*, 4.12, cited by Gonda, *VS.*, p. 80).

[4]Some magical elements persisted, the instruments used in the sacrifice being considered to share in its magical power.

[5]The *Muṇḍaka Up.*, 1.2,7–8 states that ceremonial performances are called 'unsafe boats', being ineffective against re-birth and re-death.

v. Yajamāna; Mṛgaśiras II; Ghṛta; Āprī(s); Yūpa; Vedi; Puruṣamedha; Dakṣiṇā; Ucchiṣṭa; Aśvamedha; Rājasūya.

Yājñavalkya A famous sage to whom is attributed the *Vājasaneyi-Saṁ.*, known as the White *YV.*, said to have been revealed to him by the sun in the form of a horse (*vājin*). From this episode he was called Vājasaneya. Those who studied these texts were called *vājins* (*VP.*, III.5).

v. Yajurveda.

Yajñopavīta Investiture with the 'sacred thread'. An initiation rite which appears to be an extension of the *upanayana* or introduction of a son by his father to sacred knowledge and to the religious and other duties henceforth to be performed by him.

The *upanayana* was essentially a preliminary rite, the *yajñopavīta* its culmination, entitling the initiate to be invested with the 'sacred thread', the 'outward and visible sign of an inward and spiritual grace'.

Yajurveda The Veda of the Yajus, a manual for the guidance of the Adhvaryu priest in the performance of the sacrifice. It consists of two closely connected but separate collections (*saṁhitās*), known as the *Taittirīya* or Black *YV.* and the *Vājasaneyi* or White *YV.*

Apart from the introduction of particular views in the *Vājasaneyi-saṁ.*, it differs from the *Taittirīya-saṁ.* chiefly in the presentation of its contents, which are composed of verse-mantras, accompanied by explanatory prose-formulas. The *Vājasaneyi-saṁ.* consists only of verse-mantras, the prose-formulas being attached to its accompanying Brāhmaṇa, the *Śatapatha*. This separation of verse and prose is a practice apparently unknown to the compilers of the *Taittirīya-saṁ.*

A legend in the *VP.* (V.1–3) states that originally the *YV.* consisted of twenty-seven parts, compiled by Vaiśampāyana, who imparted them to twenty-seven of his pupils, one of whom was Yājñavalkya. But he and his preceptor quarrelled about whether or not a rite should be interpreted literally and without regard to the circumstances requiring its performance. The circumstance in this instance was that Vaiśampāyana had accidentally killed his own sister's child, an act which technically made him guilty of brahmanicide, which is defined in *Manu* (IV.235) as a 'mortal sin' (*mahāpātaka*). But this law relates to a wilful act and not to accidental killing. Thus Yājñavalkya considered that his preceptor was blameless and refused to join his fellow pupils[1] in an expiatory rite, which Vaiśampāyana himself regarded as necessary.

The quarrel resulted in Yājñavalkya severing his connexion with his preceptor and expressing his contempt for his teaching by a gesture as though about to vomit. The legend states that he did vomit, bringing up the texts of the *Yajus* taught him by his preceptor. The other pupils immediately transformed themselves into partridges (*tittiri*) and picked up the texts and hence Taittirīya, the name of the *Saṁhitā*. This explanation does not appear in the text and is contradicted by that given in the index (*anukramaṇi*) of the Black *Yajus*, which states that Vaiśampāyana taught it to Yāska, who imparted it to the teacher Tittiri, whence the name *Taittirīya* which according to Pāṇini (4.3,102) means: 'those who read or repeat what was repeated by Tittiri'.[2] This example of paranomasia is but one of many Paurāṇic etymological inventions inserted long after the composition of either the original work or of Pāṇini's Sūtras.[3]

The *VP.* account of the origin of the *Vājasaneyi-Saṁ.* is also fancifully explained. It states that Yājñavalkya, after his quarrel with his preceptor, addressed a hymn to the Sun[4] who acknowledged his homage by appearing in the form of a horse (*vājin*) and revealed to him the Yajus verses called *ayātayāmāni*, meaning new, not hackneyed by long use.[5] This reference applies particularly to the last fifteen (or possibly twenty-two) sections of the forty which comprise the *Vājaseneyi-Saṁ.*

The abandoning of stereotyped doctrine is particularly evident in sections XXXI–XXXIV, which are regarded not merely as new, but as 'secret doctrine' (*upaniṣad*).

Some portions of the *Vāj. Saṁ.*, apparently inserted in section IX, 31–2, are a conglomeration of formulas relating to the metres of the *mantras*, rather than to their contents.

The date of the completion of the *Tait. Saṁ.* has been estimated by Keith[6] to be not later than 600 B.C., but its compilation suggests a long period prior to the final recension. The nucleus of the *Vāj. Saṁ.* must have been later than that of the *Tait. Saṁ.*, and the second half later still.

[1]A special relationship was supposed to exist between preceptor and pupil, like that of father and son, and hence the duty of Vaiśampāyana's pupils to obey their preceptor's order to share in the performance of his expiatory sacrifice, irrespective of their own views regarding the necessity for it.

[2]*VP.*, p. 226, n.3.

[3]Ibid., nn. 3–4.

[4]Winternitz, *HIL.*, I, pt. i, 149, n.2, considers that the 'White Yajus owes its name to this connexion with the sun', the latter symbolizing knowledge as opposed to ignorance, and in this context new knowledge. In contrast the earlier *Yajus* was called 'Black'.

[5]*SED.*, p. 85.

[6]*Veda of the Black Yajus School*, vol. I, Intro., p. xlii.

v. Veda; Yajus.

Yajus A manual for the guidance of the Adhvaryu priest in the performance of the sacrifice.

v. Yajurveda.

Yakṣa(s)[1] The collective name of the mysterious godlings or sprites which frequent field, forest and jungle, and whose activities are the theme of much Indian folklore. They may be either beneficent or malignant, and hence it was considered essential to propitiate them with appropriate offerings.

Yakṣas appear to have been the vegetal godlings of rural communities, whose worship goes back to pre-Vedic times. Such cults were likely to have been ignored by the Vedic priests, and hence the absence of specific references to *yakṣas* in the *RV*. But, as might be expected, they are mentioned in the *AV.*, one passage (XI.6,10) forming part of a prayer for deliverance from calamity, is addressed to the sky, the asterisms (*nakṣatras*), mountains, and *yakṣas*, etc.[2] Another passage (X.7,38) occurs in a late creation myth which speaks of a great *yakṣa* lying on the primordial waters, in the midst of creation.[3] In VIII.10,28 they are called *itarajanaḥ*, 'other folk'; in the Kashmir recension of the *AV.* they are referred to as *puṇyajana*, 'sacred folk'.

The popularity of the *yakṣas* is indicated by their inclusion in Jaina mythology and their representation on the great Buddhist *stūpas* of Sāñcī, Amarāvatī and Bhārhut. In Jainism the *yakṣas* were among the attendants of each of the twenty-four Jaina *tīrthaṅkaras*. Many stories of *yakṣas* occur in Buddhist mythology. One recounts that when the child Siddhartha was taken to the temple of Śākyavardhana (a *yakṣa*), the image bowed before the boy who later was to be called the Buddha.[4] Another story related that the Buddha was asked if he was a *deva*, *gandharva* or a *yakṣa*.

The number of *yakṣas* and other godlings must have been immense, as every village or district had its particular divinity or group of divinities. But the absence of records, and the tendency of the *brāhmaṇas* to suppress such cults, or as in post-Vedic times to assimilate them with sectarian deities, especially with Śiva, resulted in the elimination of many of them. But some retained their picturesque identity and are represented in shrines throughout India. A typical example is that of the *yakṣa* Pūrṇabhadra near Campā, described in the *Aupapātika Sūtra*.[5] The shrine was situated in a grove with a central clearing in which was a great *aśoka* tree. Beneath it was a black, polished, octagonal altar festooned with climbing plants carved on the sides, amongst which were figures of men, wolves, bulls, horses, birds and snakes. Temples were sometimes dedicated to Śiva, one of these at Paṭṭadkedal bearing the name of the *yakṣa* Virūpākṣa,[6] and apparently identifying him with Śiva.

The favourite haunt of *yakṣas* was in the sacred tree common to most villages. There they considered themselves safe from all harm as their presence was believed to ensure the prosperity of the village. Garlands were hung from the branches of the tree and at its foot were placed tiny lamps, cakes and other offerings. Sometimes the *yakṣas* acknowledged these gifts by 'oracular responses', in a strange voice like an echo.[7] Trees and their attendant *yakṣas* and *yakṣīs* were naturally associated with fertility, the *yakṣīs* symbolizing the life-sap of the tree, and hence the belief that barren women could be made fertile by them. Legends of treasure concealed at the foot of sacred trees were common. If no treasure was discovered, the digging up of the ground at least led to more abundant blossoms and a better crop.

Paurāṇic stories made the fullest use of *yakṣa* myths, including that of the pot-bellied Kubera, the god of wealth, regarded as their leader, who is shown in a Bhārhut relief standing on a dwarf *yakṣa*, serving as his *vāhana* or carrier. The *Mārk. Pur.* (VIII.106–9) attributes a macabre role to *yakṣas*, classing them with jackals, *piśācas* and *bhūtas*, the frequenters of cremation grounds. As *yakṣas* can assume any form,[8] including that of beautiful women, their activities were often unpredictable and limitless. Coomaraswamy[9] considers that the *yakṣas* provided the model for the cult images of Śiva, and possibly of Gaṇeśa and others. The Seven Mothers;

the sixty-four *yoginīs*, and some forms of Devī, all appear to have originally been *yakṣiṇīs*.

The custom of providing parentage for mythical beings inevitably included *yakṣas*. Thus the *Mārk. P.* (XLVIII,37) states that they were created by Brahmā; or according to another myth that they were the offspring of Hāritī, originally the tutelary goddess of Rājagṛha, referred to by Hsüan Tsang (the Chinese pilgrim), as the mother of *yakṣas*, to whom people prayed for offspring.[10]

Some *yakṣas*, like the *yakṣagrahas*, caused insanity and all manner of maladies. Thus a person suffering from hydrophobia was immediately bathed at a cross-roads, or with water from a river noted for particular properties, to the accompaniment of *mantras* such as; 'O thou *yakṣa*, who art the lord of dogs, free me from the poison of the rabid dog that has bitten me' (*Suś.Saṁ.*, II, p. 736).

The elephant-headed god Gaṇeśa possesses some *yakṣa* characteristics and is regarded as the beneficent remover of obstacles, the assurer of success.

[1]v *IAL.*, 10395. The etymology of *yakṣa* is uncertain, as is indicated by the various roots from which it is allegedly derived, such as *yus*, *yak-ā*, *vaj*, etc. Fanciful explanations of its origin appear in the Purāṇas (*Mārk. P.*, XLVII.20; *VP.*, I.5, etc.), and other works. Daniélou (*HP.*, p. 137) considers it to be derived from a Vedic word meaning 'mysterious' or 'marvellous'. According to Pāli commentators it is derived from *yaj* 'to sacrifice'. The *PTS.* describes *yakkha* as a 'quick ray of light'; or as a 'ghost', from *yakṣ* 'to move quickly'.

[2] *Yakṣas* are often associated with local hills or mountains. Cf. the German Rübezahl, mountain sprite.

[3]Cf. the Viṣṇu creation myth of Nārāyaṇa resting on the serpent floating on the primordial waters.

[4]W.W. Rockhill *Life of the Buddha*, p. 17. The great Mahāyāna Buddhist master Nāgārjuna is said to have spent twelve years adoring the *yakṣiṇī* who protects the *aśvattha* tree (Ray, *History of Chemistry in Ancient and Medieval India*, II, p. 7).

[5]E. Leumann, *Das Aupapātika Sūtra, erstes Upāṅga der Jaina* (VIII.2), 1883, cited by Coomaraswamy, *Yakṣas*, pt. i, p. 19f.; v. also 'Mahāmayūrī', (*JA.*), edited by S. Levi, p. 38, 1915.

[6]Coomaraswamy, op. cit., pt. i, p. 12, n.2.

[7]Auboyer, *Daily Life in Ancient India*, p. 152.

[8]Śivarāmamūrti, *Amarāvatī Sculptures*, p. 75.

[9]Coomaraswamy, op. cit., pt.i, pp. 9 and 29.

[10]Ibid., p. 9.

v. Yātu; Yātudhāna(s).

Yakṣī or **Yakṣiṇī** v. Yakṣa.

Yakṣma The personification of disease and its general name. The *Mārk. P.* (XXXIV.94,101) lays down the rules to be observed by the householder seeking to avoid disease, and lists the offerings that should be made to Yakṣma.

Yama I. The ruler and judge of the dead. He is called the 'Restrainer', from *yam*, 'to curb', etc., and hence *yama*, 'cessation', 'end'.

Yama is the son of Vivasvat[1] (*RV.*, X.14,1). His celestial world is described as 'the home of heroes' (I.35,6). Because he was the first man to die, he is said to conduct the dead to the realm of the ancestors (*pitṛs*). His sister Yamī is mentioned in hymn X.10, in which she states that their union[2] is essential if the human race is to be perpetuated, but he rejects her proposal. This curious myth is not mentioned elsewhere in the *RV.*

Yama's mount (*vāhana*) is a black buffalo, a form which he himself sometimes assumes. His weapons are the mace (*gadā*) representing punishment, and the noose (*pāśa*) with which he seizes his victims.

[1]Cf. the Indo-Iranian myth of Yima, son of Vivahvant; the Canaanite god Yam (son of El), who judged the dead on the banks of the river before permitting any to cross it to the nether world (Driver, *Canaanite Myths*, p. 12); the Babylonian god of death Mu-u-tu; the Hebrew personification of death, Mawet, 'who has climbed in at our windows and made its way into our palaces, cut off the children from without, and the young men from the streets' (Jeremiah ix, 21). v. also Gaster, *Thespis*, p. 13, and *OST.*, V, p. 288.

[2]Cf. the Lettic song, the theme of which is the incestuous desire of a brother for his sister.

v. Citragupta; Śrāddha; Manu I; Sārameya(s); Vaitaraṇī; Mṛtyu; Naciketas.

II. The 'act of curbing or restraining'; 'self-control'; 'moral obligation or duty'. In yoga *yama* is one of the eight *aṅgas* or means of attaining mental concentration.

Yāmala v. Mantra, n.1.

Yamalārjuna The two magic trees called *yamala* and *arjuna* respectively. They are personified as the enemies of Kṛṣṇa who as a child uprooted them when they blocked his path (*Rām.*, 7.6,35). Later they were identified with Nalakūbara and Maṇibhadra (two sons of Kubera) and called Guhyakas.[1]

[1]*EM.*, p. 144; *VP.*, V.6.

Yamaloka 'Yama's realm.' The realm of the dead, ruled by Yama, originally conceived as the heaven of heroes (*RV.*, I.35,6) and later that of the *pitṛs* (*ŚBr.*, XII.8.1,19).

v. Yama I.

Yamāri 'Yama's enemy', an epithet of Viṣṇu.

Yamī v. Yama I.

Yamunā Name of a river mentioned in the *RV.*

(V.57,17; VIII. 18,19, etc.), commonly called the Jumnā and mythically identified with Yamī. It descends from the Himālaya and is one of the tributaries of the Ganges which it joins at Allahabad. From it is derived a salve possessing great healing properties (*AVB.*, IV.9,10).
v. Balarāma; Gopī(s); Nanda.

Yamunācārya One of the principal expositors or teachers of the doctrines of the Vaiṣṇava Pāñcarātra cult, particularly of the doctrine of Viśiṣṭādvaita (qualified non-duality), subsequently elaborated by Rāmānuja.

The Pañcarātra doctrine was clearly distinguished from that of Śaṅkarācārya, the Śaiva advocate of Advaita (non-dual) Vedānta.

Yantra A mystical diagram believed to possess magical or occult powers. The term is derived from *yam*, meaning 'to hold, curb or restrain', the suffix *tra* denoting the effective instrument, and hence by extension 'fetter, tie, thong, rein', etc. It also signifies any instrument or mechanical device. One such was the *yantra-garuḍa*, an image of Garuḍa mechanically contrived to move apparently by itself.

In Indian medieval medicine surgical instruments were also called *yantras*, but in astronomy the *yantra* was an early form of sextant.[1]

Yantras are intended as a 'chart' or 'machine' to stimulate 'inner visualization' or meditation. The spiritual ascent of the worshipper is from the circumference inwards, the highest states being those closest to the centre.[2] A typical *yantra* is the *Śrī yantra*, consisting of an outer frame composed of straight lines indented on the four sides to form a regular pattern. The frame encloses an arrangement of concentric circles and stylized lotus petals surrounding a series of nine intersecting triangles, the apexes of four pointing upwards, symbolizing the male principle, the remaining five pointing downwards, symbolizing the female principle, the whole culminating in a central point (*bindu*), which is the eternal, undifferentiated principle, *brahman*, or the polar axis seen from above. In Tantrism *bindu* represents the point of concentration of all creative forces, while the nine triangles 'signify the primitive revelation of the Absolute as it differentiates into graduated polarities, the creative activity of the cosmic male and female energies on successive stages of evolution.'[3]

Each deity worshipped has its own *yantra*, which ensures the presence of the deity in it, as in the West the 'magician' remains 'safe' within the magical circle drawn on the floor.

Among the various *yantras* is the Gaṇapati, said to confer wealth and prosperity on the worshipper; the Bhadrakālī, drawn on the floor with rice, turmeric, etc. and worshipped at night. It is said to confer knowledge, strength, health and riches. The same rite performed by an adept facing south for twelve days ensures the death of an enemy; the Sudarśana, engraved on metal and enclosed in a cylinder, when worn as an amulet will relieve the sick or those possessed by evil spirits; the Śarabha cures epilepsy and intermittent fever; the Subrahmaṅya expels evil spirits from houses and from their occupants; the Hanumat gives strength and wisdom and protects the traveller during the hours of darkness; the Cāmuṇḍī, if engraved on lead, and its *pūjā*, performed with offerings of toddy and mutton, will ensure the death of enemies.[4]

[1] The famous fifteenth-century observatory at Samarkand had a masonry sextant, and in India, early in the eighteenth century, Jai Singh constructed several observatories containing similar sextants which he called *ṣaṣṭāṁśa yantras*.

[2] Zimmer, *Myths and Symbols in Indian Art and Civilization*, p. 142; *CHS.*, p. 25.

[3] Zimmer, op. cit., p. 147.

[4] Thurston, *Omens*, pp. 185f. Occasionally the case containing the *yantra* is also worshipped (*EHI.*, vol. I, pp. 330ff.).

v. Trikoṇa; Yoga; Yoni.

Yāska The patronymic of the author of the *Nirukta*, or commentary on the difficult Vedic words in the lists called Nighaṇṭus.[1]

Yāska's date is uncertain, and varies from 500 to 700 B.C., the former being the more likely.[2]

[1] *SED.*, p. 167.

[2] *WI*, p. 387.

v. Pāṇini; Sāyaṇa.

Yaśodā[1] Name of a *gopī*, the wife of the cowherd Nanda, who lived on the banks of the Yamunā (Jumna) river. Yaśodā became the foster-mother of the infant Kṛṣṇa, who was placed in her care to avoid his assassination by Kaṁsa, the tyrannical ruler of Mathurā. One of the many Kṛṣṇa legends reflects an ancient local custom designed to protect infants from evil and to guard them against childhood ailments. According to this legend Yaśodā waved a cow-tail over the infant Kṛṣṇa to protect him from the night-fiend Pūtanā, and anointed the twelve parts of his body, finally cleansing him with cow-urine (*Bhāg. P.*, X.6); or according to *VP.* (V.5) her husband Nanda sprinkled dried cow-dung on his head and gave him an amulet.

[1] *Yaśo* in compounds for *yaśas*, meaning beauty, worth, etc.

v. Yamalārjuna; Kṛṣṇa I.

Yaśodharā Name of the mother of Triśiras and Viśvarūpa by Tvaṣṭṛ.

Yātanā The personification of vengeance and the torments of the hells. The daughter of Bhaya (fear) and Mṛtyu (death).

Yati(s) A mythical community of ascetics associated with the Bhṛgus in praising Indra (*RV.*, VIII.6,18); but in the *Tait. Saṁ.* (III.3,7) Indra is said to have destroyed the *yatis*. A late passage of the *RV.* (X.72,6–7) ignores the earlier description and refers to them as a class of secondary creators or assistants to the creator-deities who produced the world from the dust.[1] Each *deva* has a *yati* to complete his creative work. Śiva is said to be the great *yati* or yogin, the regulating principle of the cosmos.

The Upaniṣads describe *yatis* as ascetics whose natures have been purified by renunciation '*saṁnyāsa-yoga*' (*Muṇḍ. Up.*, 3.1,5; 2,6). The Lord (Īśa), having created his *yatis*, exercises universal overlordship (*Śvet. Up.*, 5,3).

[1]Cf. the Canaanite myth of Talish and Damgiya who were bidden by El to go into the wilderness (representing chaos) and cover themselves with dust and to create particular animals; cf. also the Buddhist Ādi-Buddha system which ascribes the work of creation to the dhyānī-bodhisattvas whilst the dhyānī-buddhas remain eternally in deep meditation. Reymond (*The Mythological Origin of the Egyptian Temple*, p. 63) cites the Edfu texts, which refer to 'a group of nameless deities who existed before the origin of the world, and who were believed to act as a single creating power'.

Yātu or **Yātudhāna** I. An evil spirit; a fiend or demon; the demonic power of evil spirits or sorcerers. Like the medieval Christian Devil the *yātus* had animal hoofs[1] of some kind (*RV.*, X.44,9; 87,12).

The god of fire Agni is the chief expeller and slayer of demons and is specially invoked to burn up female fiends '*yātudhānī*' (*RV.*, X.118,8); and in the *AV.* (I.28,4) he is invoked to compel sorceresses to eat their own children, and then to destroy one another. In another *RV.* hymn (VII.104,15–16) the term *yātudhāna* is applied to a man who has borne false-witness against a neighbour. *Yātudhāna* is equivalent to *yātumant* 'having a familiar demon (*yātu*)'—which the sorcerer 'holds' and can call up.

The *yātudhānas* sometimes used plants to increase the potency of their spells (*AVB.*, IV.28,6), but a particular salve made from Himālayan plants protected the victim both from the 'evil eye' and the spells of the *yātudhānīs* (*AV.*, IV.9.3,6,9). Another plant such as the *apāmārga* annuls their curses. Amulets also protect against their power, one made of *jaṅgiḍa* wood being capable of destroying the power of fifty-three kinds of sorcery (*AVB.*, XIX.34,1–4).

Yātudhānas are sometimes identified with *yakṣas*, the mere sight of which results in pestilence unless averted by expiatory rites (*Bṛhat Saṁ.*, XLV.79), and the *Mārk. P.* (LI.55) insists that such beings should always be pacified by propitiatory rites. In the *MBh.* the primitive folklore of spirits and demons is revived and all manner of calamities relating to the family, especially the ailments of women and children, are attributed to *yātudhānas* and other demons. Thus calamities beset those who have violated marriage-laws; children may be born idiots or deformed as the result of parents' wrongdoing, and so forth. In battle the *yātudhānas* appear as demons.

As *yātudhānas* may reside in the vicinity of large stones, their permission must be obtained should a stone be required for making an image of Viṣṇu, or alternatively, they may be requested to move elsewhere.[2]

[1]Cf. the Hebrew night-hag Lilith, believed to have the hoofs of a goat, or the feet of a goose (L.J.A. Loewenthal, 'The Palms of Jezebel', *Folklore*, vol. 83, 1972, p. 29); and the 'familiar spirits' of medieval European witches and wizards.

In Sumeria laws were passed against sorcerers as early as the middle of the third millennium B.C. In Assyria the penalty for sorcery was death, as it was in the Hebrew codes (Hooke, *Babylonian and Assyrian Religion*, pp. 78f.).

[2]*DHI.*, p. 218.

v. Yātughna; Yātu II.

II. Sorcery, so-called because everything is held in check (*yata*) by the sorcerer (*ŚBr.*, X.5.2,20).[1]

[1]*AVB.*, Intro., xxii.

Yātughna 'Destroyer of *yātus*.' The name of the bdellium (Balsamodendron) plant, whose fragrant gum is said to drive away *yātus*, to avert curses and to protect from disease (*AVB.*, XIX.38,1–2).

v. Yātu I.

Yaudheyas An ancient Indian military tribe who adopted Kārttikeya as their spiritual as well as temporal ruler.[1]

[1]*DHI.*, p. 362.

Yava The Ṛg-vedic general term for any grain yielding flour or meal,[1] but which in the *AV.* usually refers to barley. Some kind of grain appears to have been cultivated in prehistoric times. Traces of barley have been found in the pre-dynastic remains of Egypt,[2] of the type known as Hordeum hexastichon, the most common species cultivated in antiquity. Barley as a sacrificial offering is frequently referred to in the Hebrew writings (Lev., V.5–11; Numbers, V.11). It was the staple grain of the Indus Valley people in the third millennium B.C.[3] It was offered to Indra (*RV.*, I.53,2; IV.24,7) and was sometimes mixed with *soma* (VIII.81,4). *Yava* mixed with water was regarded as the universal remedy (*AVB.*, VI.91,1f.), and rice and barley were called the two immortal children of heaven (VIII.7,20). Barley was also called 'mighty', because it could deliver one from every calamity (XI.6,15), and hence as a gruel (*yavāgū*) was the drink of the *rājanya*. It was also the symbol of Indra's thunderbolt and the guarantor of success (*Tait. Saṁ.*, VI. 2.5,1–2). An amulet of barley (*yavamaṇi*) protects against the Evil Eye.

Because of its importance *yava* represented all plant life, for the gods gave it the sap of every plant, so that though some may wither, the *yava* thrives (*ŚBr.*, III.6.1,10). The pre-eminence of barley generated many fanciful etymologies intended to support the claims made for it, but they are for the most part clumsy puns, such as that in the *Tait. Saṁ.* (I.31) which declares: 'Thou art barley [*yava*], therefore do thou bar [*yavaya*] all foes, all evil spirits, from us.' Elsewhere in the same work (VI.2.10,2) barley and water are poured into a hole for[4] atonement.

[1]Cf. *yavasa* 'grass' on which animals grazed (*RV.*, I.38,5; 91,13); and *yavasād* (grass or grain-eater), an epithet of Agni, who burns up the forests to provide further land for cultivation.

[2]Barley was also represented 'on ancient Egyptian monuments and also on coins of the sixth century B.C.' (*Encyclopaedia Biblica*, p. 484, col. 2).

[3]Childe, *New Light on the Most Ancient East*, p. 176.

[4]The Greeks ritually offered a kind of porridge made of barley meal (*pelanos*) to the Earth and to the underworld gods, their representative snakes and other 'spirits of aversion' (Harrison, *Prolegomena*, p. 90).

v. Kṛṣi.

Yavana(s) 'Greeks', first applied in north-western India to the Greeks from Asia Minor (*yavana-deśa*), especially to the Ionians, who from the sixth century B.C. spread to the north and east, and established settlements in Bactria, the southern borders of the Black Sea and areas adjoining north-western India. It is possible that astrology was introduced into India by the Greeks and ideas exchanged concerning astronomy and other sciences. Later the term was applied to Moslems, Europeans or to any foreigners.

v. Mleccha(s).

Yayāti A Vedic patriarch and sacrificer (*RV.*, I.31,17), traditionally regarded as the father of Yadu, Turvaśu, Druhyu, Anu and Puru, the mythical progenitors of the 'Five Peoples' (I.100,12; 1.7,3). who joined the confederation of ten tribes led by Viśvāmitra against Sudās, the Bhārata king. He is also referred to as Nahuṣa's son (I.63,1), but apart from this the *RV.* gives no information about him.

Nonetheless, from this genealogical reference an elaborate chronicle of love and intrigue was composed by the compilers of the *Viṣṇu Purāṇa* which syncretizes the post-Vedic Yayāti with his Vedic namesake, and the sons of the former with the supposed leaders of the Vedic 'Five Peoples'.

The two marriages of the post-Vedic Yayāti, and the circumstances associated with them, confirm that he was a powerful monarch, and suggest that the country over which he ruled still retained customs not consonant with brahmanic practice. Yayāti was finally cursed by Śukra (at his daughter's instigation) and reduced to complete decrepitude. Such a curse could not be revoked, but Śukra finally agreed to allow it to be transferred. Of Yayāti's five sons only Puru, the youngest, offered to accept it (*VP.*, IV.10).

v. Yādava(s); Devayānī; Daśarājna.

Yoga The 'act of yoking [to] another.'[1] This term is derived from the root *yuj*, its meaning being implicit in virtually all of its derivatives, especially those denoting psychosomatic relationships, in which the purpose of yoking mind and body is to achieve perfect unity, functioning on the profoundest level of the unconscious, beyond the limits of thought and language, and flowing freely in the currents of the energy that pervades space and time. Hence early *yoga* appears to lack any religious connotation.

The ancient origin of *yoga* is indicated by evidence of its embryonic practice in Harappā and Mohenjo-daro,[2] long before its development in Vedic India. Campbell[3] suggests that it was connected with the 'early Bronze Age mythology of ritual regicide, where the king was identified with the dying and resurrected moon', and later associated with the idea of an ever-recurring cycle of cosmic destruction and renewal, or with the Śiva-Śakti notion of the interdependent functions of energy. Eliade[4] sees some similarities between Shamanistic and yogic techniques of concentration, but whereas the final goal of Shamanism is always ecstasy and the soul's ecstatic journey through the various cosmic regions, that of *yoga* is 'final concentration of the spirit and "escape" from the cosmos'.

During its development, *yoga* adopted various media to achieve its aims, ranging from incantation, magic, etc., to the methods of Patañjali;[5] from the performance of religious duties defined by the priest to the ascetic practices of the zealous, or the equally exacting discipline of the mystic. It is not until the later classical Upaniṣads that *yoga* technical terms appeared, such as *ātmā-yoga* (*Tait. Up.*, II,4), and *adhyātma-yoga* (*Kaṭha Up.*, II.12), or that the aim of *yoga* is clearly stated, i.e., as the 'relinquishment of all conditions of existence'.[6] The *Maitri Up.*, 6,25, states that it is the yoking of the whole psychosomatic organism to a single idea. Though such notions mainly reflect the aspirations of mystics, they gradually spread to other circles and gave a great impetus to critical speculation, especially among the Sāṁkhya, Jaina, Buddhist,[7] and Vedānta schools.

Some yogic methods are: *Haṭha*, whereby the body and vital energies can be brought under control. This technique is also applied by exponents of traditional dances, and results in an extraordinary co-ordination of mind and body. *Mantra*, re-integration by hermetic formulae (i.e., *mantras*) and by mystical diagrams (*yantras*), which still the mental agitation so that supreme Reality can be apprehended. *Laya*, re-integration by mergence, in which the mental faculties are completely merged into the object contemplated, or into 'inner sound'. The latter can be made manifest by the practice of breath-control. *Bhakti*, re-integration through love and unswerving devotion. *Jñāna*, re-integration through knowledge. *Karma*, re-integration through action, the performance of religious duties, and the constant application of the mind to the acts or actions ordained by the religious texts. *Rāja*, the royal (*rāja*) way to re-integration. This is the highest form of *yoga*, all other forms being preparatory. When mental agitation is stilled, supra-mental perceptions appear, and the fundamental unity of all that exists is realized.[8]

No system of *yoga* exists in isolation, each being often combined with the elements of another. Being based on the infinite variations of human nature, its appeal is as universal and as fundamental as the age-old instinct for survival. Its practice is common to all religions,[9] from the simplest to the most sophisticated, and whether consciously recognized or not, its discipline is responsible for the achievements of the great artist and musician, for the soldier, statesman and the scientist.[10]

[1]Savitar is invoked to 'harness' the spirit and holy thoughts of the priest (*RV.*, V.81,1). Edgerton stresses that *yoga* never means union with *brahman* (*BIP.*, p. 37, n. 1.); v. also *IAL.*, 10526, 10528, 10529.

[2]Chanda, *Medieval Sculpture in the British Museum*, p. 9; v. also Eliade, *Yoga*, p. 341. Anand (*Hindu View of Art*, p. 17) considers that the Āryans borrowed yogic techniques from the Dravidians.

[3]*Masks of God*, II, p. 206.

[4]*Shamanism*, pp. 416f.

[5]Woods, *The Yoga-System of Patañjali*, *HOS.*, vol. 17, 1966.

[6]Hume, *TPU.*, p. 439.

[7]The Buddha was instructed in *yoga* by two Sāṁkhya teachers (Murti, *Central Philosophy of Buddhism*, p. 22).

[8]Daniélou, *Yoga*, pp. 12ff.; 17ff.

[9]For the influence of *yoga* in Christian mysticism, v. E. Benz, *Indische Einflüsse auf die frühchristliche Theologie*, Wiesbaden.

[10]For the scientific examination of yogic claims, v. S. Lindquist, *Die Methoden des Yoga*, Uppsala, 1932; L. Roesel, *Die psychologischen Grundlagen der Yogapraxis*, Tübingen, 1928.

v. Dakṣiṇāmūrti; Gorakhnāth; Yoganidrā.

Yoganidrā 'Meditation-sleep', a light form of 'sleep' peculiar to yogins, which allows them to withdraw from the stimuli of the outer world while at the same time retaining the full use of their mental powers.

Yoganidrā is personified as a goddess, and represents the interval between cosmic periods (*yugas*) when Viṣṇu is said to sleep. She is a form of Durgā.

Yoginī I. A demoness; a witch or sorceress, or any woman believed to possess magical powers. The number of Yoginīs is variously stated as eight, sixty, sixty-four or sixty-five, and their origin attributed to Durgā who is also known as Yoginī. She created them to serve her and her consort Śiva.

Yoginīs were believed to assume the forms of village godlings (*grāmadevatās*), or were sometimes regarded as epiphanies of Durgā, all representing minor deities of vegetation and destiny, who bring death or wealth, and incarnate the forces of shamanic magic and of *yoga*.[1] But Coomaraswamy[2] considers that the Seven Mothers, the sixty-four Yoginīs, the Ḍākinīs, and some forms of Devī may all—in both medieval and modern cults—be regarded as Yakṣiṇīs. Tantric Buddhism also has its Yoginīs.

[1]Eliade, *Yoga*, pp. 343f.

[2]*Yakṣas*, pt. i, p. 9.

II. A female protective divinity associated with *śakti* worship, and also with the Bhairavas, their consorts or guardians.[1]

[1]*DHI.*, pp. 465f.

III. A girl who has been instructed in Tantric rites by a *guru*, 'and whose body has been consecrated by *nyāsas*. Sexual union is transformed into a ritual through which the human couple becomes a divine couple',[1] a relic of early 'yogic and śaktic complexes incorporated into the mythologies and rituals of vegetation. Certain fairies, moreover, bear the name *yoginī*, as if to emphasize the origin of their magical power, obtained through *yoga*'.[2]

[1]Eliade, *Yoga*, pp. 259f. The sexo-yogic practices of the Bauls of Bengal are similar.

[2]Ibid., p. 343.

v. Mithuna.

Yoni The female generative organs. When associated with the *liṅga* it is a typical symbol of the divine procreative energy. In India birth was a determining hereditary factor, which figures in numerous laws relating to caste and the position of children of polygamous marriages, those of irregular marriages and of those born outside wedlock.[1]

Much folklore, mythology and symbolism is associated with the generative organs in prehistoric India and Western Asia, and in parts of Europe.[2] Very early examples of symbolic genitalia also appear in the fifth millennium B.C. Mesopotamian temple-compounds, enclosed by two high walls of oval shape suggesting the female genitalia.[3] Similarly shaped altars have also been found in Egyptian temples, as have numerous *yoni* and phallic representations in the Indus Valley, including a number of so-called ring-stones, measuring from half an inch to about four feet in diameter, and made of stone, faience, shell, etc.[4]

When depicted alone the *yoni* is referred to as a chalice (*argha*) or water-vessel (*jalaharī*), sometimes shaped like a conch-shell,[5] or represented by a downward pointing triangle.

In southern Indian villages religious life was generally devoted to the worship of local divinities (*grāmadevatās*), regarded as the manifestation of the great goddess, whose 'icons are everywhere simple stone images of the female organ of generation'.[6] But except in temples where Tantric influence once predominated, the generative icons are so stylized as to be unrecognizable as such.

[1]Cf. the story of the servant woman, seduced by an unidentified *brahmin* guest, whose illegitimate son was therefore classed as a *śūdra* (*Chān. Up.*, 4.4,1–5).

[2]'Phallus amulets are common in Italy, and the female genitalia were, until recently, portrayed in ornamental bronze door-knockers at the north entrance of Toledo Cathedral' (L.J.A. Loewenthal, 'The Palms of Jezebel', *Folklore*, vol. 83, 1972, p. 32).

[3]A. Parrot, *Ziggurate et Tour de Babel*, p. 167. Incised triangles representing the *yoni* occur on female figurines of al 'Ubaid which were 'to characterize the female clay figures of western Asia in the Bronze Age' (Levy, *Gate of Horn*, p. 94).

[4]Similar stones found elsewhere were 'believed to have magical powers of various kinds', the smaller ones being used as amulets (Radford, *Encyclopaedia of Superstitions*, p. 191). In some of the small ring-stones from Taxila the figures of a fertility goddess are beautifully carved on the sides of the central hole. v. Marshall, *Mohenjo-daro and the Indus Civilization*, I. pp. 62f. and n.1.

[5]*HP.*, p. 231.

[6]Eliade, *Yoga*, p. 349.

v. Śakti; Tantra; Yoga; Yantra.

Yudhiṣṭhira The eldest son of King Pāṇḍu and Pṛthā (Kuntī), and leader of the Pāṇḍavas.

v. Mahābhārata.

Yuga The four periods or ages of the world's existence. These *yugas* comprise: 1. *kṛta* or *satya*, 2. *tretā*, 3. *dvāpara*, the three periods which have already elapsed, and 4. *kali*, the present period. The duration of each is enumerated respectively as 1,728,000; 1,296,000; 864,000, and 432,000 years, the descending numbers successively reduced by one quarter, being supposed to represent a similar reduction of the physical and moral standards of each age. The four ages total 4,320,000 years and constitute a 'great *yuga*' (*mahā-yuga*).

v. Kalpa; Kāla I; Mahāyuga; Manvantara; Jyotiṣa.

Yūpa A post, pillar or beam, especially a sacrificial post or stake to which the sacrificial victim was attached. This *yūpa* was addressed as 'Sovereign of the forest' (Vanaspati) and anointed at the sacrifice (*RV.*, III.8,3; *ŚBr.*, III.6.4,13; 7.1,14, etc.). In another hymn (*RV.*, IX.5,10) the *yūpa* is extolled as 'ever green, golden-hued, refulgent, thousand-branched', and represented as the cosmic tree, 'an intermediary between the divine world and earthly life',[1] like the *skambha*.[2] It also symbolized *inter alia* the phallus,[3] represented by a knob (*caṣāla*) on the top of the post to which the sacrificial horse was tied during the horse-sacrifice (*aśvamedha*) (*RV.*, I.162,6), and to which a ring or wheel (*kaṭaka*) was attached. The consecrated *yūpa* is included among the *āprī* deities, i.e., the deified objects used at the sacrifice; the first chip of wood from the *yūpa* during its shaping was also used in the sacrifice (*RV.*, VIII.45,2). Sometimes the *yūpa* consisted of three stakes, either bound together, or tied at one end to form a tripod, as in the intended sacrifice of Śunaḥśepa (*RV.*, I.24,13).

The *yūpa* is usually octagonal[4] and likened to an eight-sided *vajra*, and hence was believed to protect the sacrificer against his enemies from all sides. *Yūpas* varied in size (*Ait. Br.*, X.1) and were made from various kinds of wood according to the purpose intended by the sacrificer. One of *khadira* wood ensured the attainment of paradise; one of *palāśa*, a brilliant and splendid future; one of *bilva*, the assurance of food and prosperity. When erected the post was anointed and addressed as 'the tree of divine sweetness', or as 'Lord of the forest'. The position of the *yūpa* may also determine the amount and extent of the rainfall (*Tait. Saṁ.*, VI.3.4,3f.).

In individual sacrificial ceremonies the *yūpa* should be the same height as the sacrificer, who fixes a ring on the top to represent abundance, and then anoints it with butter to glorify Viṣṇu, the personification of the

Sacrifice, and hence the deity of the *yūpa* (*Tait. Saṁ.*, VI.3,4,1ff.).

A girdle of grass is placed round the post by the sacrificer at navel level to represent the strength thereby bestowed upon him. The various portions of the *yūpa* are symbolically differentiated; the base belongs to the *pitṛs*,[5] above that, as far as the girdle, to men; the girdle itself to plants; above it to the Viśvedevas; the top to Indra; the rest to the Sādhyas (*Tait. Saṁ.*, VI.3.4,5–6).

If the sacrificer desires to cause the death of an enemy he should set up a *yūpa* on a base shaped like a grave, one end sloping to the south, the region of the dead.

Originally the sacrificer's wife took part in the ceremony, and when her husband was about to ascend the ladder placed against the *yūpa*, he addresses his wife: 'Come, let us ascend to the sky.' She replies: 'Let us ascend.' He then climbs the ladder,[6] raises his head above the top of the post, saying: 'We have become immortal' (*ŚBr.*, V.2.1,5–17).

[1]Gonda, *Aspects*, p. 81.

[2]Ibid., p. 82.

[3]Ibid., p. 81.

[4]Octagonal pillars, possibly derived from similarly shaped *yūpas*, are much favoured in Indian architecture. The *dhvajastambha* set up before temples sometimes represents the *yūpa*.

[5]But according to *ŚBr.* (V.2.1,7) the hollow at the top of the *yūpa* is sacred to the *pitṛs*.

[6]'Rites of ascent' effect a rupture of planes enabling sacrificers to attain higher spheres (Eliade, *Yoga*, p. 326). The ladder symbol was common also to the ancient Egyptians, one being offered to Ra when about to ascend to heaven (Eliade, *Patterns*, p. 102). Cf. Jacob's dream (Genesis, xxviii,12).

v. Mekhalā I; Yajamāna; Yajña; Vedi.

Bibliography

Abbreviations

ABORI.	Annals of the Bhāndārkar Oriental Research Institute, Poona
BSOAS.	*Bulletin of the School of Oriental and African Studies*, London
Cal.	Calcutta
Calif.	California
Camb.	Cambridge
ch.	chapter
Com.	Commentary
ed.	Editor, or edited
edn.	Edition
EFEO.	L'École française d'Extrême-Orient, Hanoi
HOS.	Harvard Oriental Series
IA.	*The Indian Antiquary*
IHQ.	*India Historical Quarterly*
JAOS.	*Journal of the American Oriental Society.*
JRAS.	*Journal of the Royal Asiatic Society*, London
L.	London
Mass.	Massachusetts
n.d.	no date
n.s.	new series
N.Y.	New York
Or.	Oriental, or Orientalist
ORT.	Orientalia Rheno-Traiectina
Oxf.	Oxford
RAS.	Royal Asiatic Society, London
rev.	revised
repr.	reprint
S.	Series
SBE.	*Sacred Books of the East*
SBH.	*Sacred Books of the Hindus*
SOAS.	School of Oriental and African Studies, London
tr.	translator, or translated
Univ.	University

ACHARYA, PRASANNA K., *Indian Architecture according to the Mānasāra Śilpaśāstra*, Oxf., 1921. Repr. Allahabad, 1927; rev. 1949.

—— *A Dictionary of Hindu Architecture*, Oxf., 1927.

AGARWAL, URMILA, 'The Mithunas', *Or.Art*, Winter 1968, pp. 259f.

—— 'Worship of Viṣṇu' (His incarnations in the Medieval Period), *Or. Art*, Autumn 1970, pp. 252ff.

AGRAWALA, R.C., 'Notes iconographiques', *Arts Asiatiques*, vol. XXIII, 1971, pp. 135ff.

AGRAWALA, VASUDEVA S., *India as Known to Pāṇini*, Lucknow, 1953.

—— *Matsya Purāṇa—A Study*, Varanasi, 1963.

—— *Vāmana Purāṇa—A Study*, Varanasi, 1964.

—— *Śiva Mahādeva*, Varanasi, 1966.

—— *Sparks from the Vedic Fire*, Varanasi, 1962.

AIYANGAR, K.V.R., *Rāja Dharma*, Adyar, 1941.

AIYANGAR, T.R.S. (tr.), *Śaiva Upaniṣads*, Madras, 1953.

AIYYAR, C.V.N., *Origin and Early History of Śaivism*, Madras, 1936.

ALEKSEEV, G.V., *et al.*, *Characteristics of the Proto-Indian Script*, tr. by H.C. Pande and entitled *Soviet Studies on Harappan Script*, Florida, 1969.

ALLAN, J., *Catalogue of the Coins of Ancient India in the British Museum*, L., 1936.

—— *Catalogue of the Coins of the Gupta Dynasties*, L., 1914.

ALLCHIN, BRIDGET, 'The Indian Middle Stone Age', *Bull. of the Institute of Archaeology*, Univ. of London, no. 11, 1959.

——, and ALLCHIN, F.R., *The Birth of Indian Civilization*, L., 1968.

ALLCHIN, F.R., *Neolithic Cattle-Keepers of South India*, Camb., 1963.

—— 'The Stone Alignments of Southern Hyderabad', *Man*, 56, 1956.

——, and JOSHI, J.P., 'Mālvan—Further Light on the Southern Extension of the Indus Civilization', *JRAS.*, no.1, 1970, pp. 20ff.

ALLEGRO, J.M., *The Sacred Mushroom and the Cross*, L., 1970.

ALTEKAR, A.S., *Indian Archaeology—A Review*, New Delhi, 1957–9.

—— *Education in Ancient India*, 3rd edn., Benaras, 1948.

ANAND, MULIK RAJ, *Kāma-kalā—Some Notes on the Philosophical Basis of Hindu Erotic Sculpture*, N.Y., 1958.

—— *The Hindu View of Art*, L., 1957.

——, and KRAMRISCH, S. *Homage to Khajuraho*, Marg monograph, Bombay, 1960.

ANDERSEN, DINES, *A Critical Pāli Dictionary*, commenced by V. Trenckner; rev., continued and ed. by Andersen and Helmer Smith, Copenhagen, 1924–

ANDERSON, J.K., *Ancient Greek Horsemanship*, Calif., 1961.

APTE, V., *Social and Religious Life in the Gṛhya-Sūtras*, Ahmedabad., 1939.

—— 'Vajra in the Ṛgveda', *ABORI.*, vol. XXXVII, 1956, pp. 292ff.

ARBMAN, ERNST, *Rudra*, Uppsala, 1922.

ARNOLD, E., *Vedic Metre in its Historical Development*, Camb., 1905. Repr. Delhi, 1967.

—— *Indian Poetry*, L., 1881.

ARNOLD, W.R., 'Solomon's Horse-Trade', *JAOS.*, 26, 1905.

ATKINS, S.D., *Pūṣan in the Ṛgveda*, Princeton, 1941.

ATREYA, BHIKAN LAL, *The Philosophy of the Yoga-Vāsiṣṭha*, Adyar, 1936.

AUBOYER, JEANNINE, 'Moudrā et hasta ou le langage par signes', *Or. Art*, III, 1951, pp. 153ff.

—— *Le Trône et son symbolisme dans l'Inde ancienne*, Annales du Musée Guimet, LV, Paris, 1949.
—— *Khajuraho*, The Hague, 1960.
—— *Daily Life in Ancient India from 200 B.C. to 700 A.D.*, tr. by S.M. Taylor, L., 1965.
—— *The Art of Afghanistan.*, L., 1968.
AUTRAN, CHARLES, *L'Épopée Indoue*, Paris, 1946.
AYYAR, P.V., *South Indian Shrines*, Madras, 1920.
BAGCHI, PRABODH CHANDRA, *Pre-Āryan and Pre-Dravidian in India* (Essays by S. Lévi, J. Przyluski and J. Bloch), Cal., 1929.
—— *Studies in the Tantras*, Cal., 1939.
BAJPAI, K.D. (chief ed.), *The Geographical Encyclopedia of Ancient and Medieval India based on Vedic, Puranic, Tantric, Jain, Buddhist Literature*, pt. 1, A–D, Benaras, 1967– .
BALFOUR, EDWARD (ed.), *The Cyclopaedia of India*, 3 vols, L., 1885. Repr. 1967–8.
BALL, K.M., *Decorative Motifs of Oriental Art*, L., 1927.
BALLANTYNE, J.R., *The Sāṁkhya Aphorisms of Kapila*. Repr. Varanasi, 1963.
BANERJEA, A.K., *Philosophy of Gorakhnāth*, Gorakhpur, 1965.
BANERJEA, JITENDRA NATH, 'Some Folk Goddesses of Ancient and Mediaeval India', *IHQ.*, XIV, 1938, pp. 101ff.
—— *The Development of Hindu Iconography*, 2nd edn., rev. and enlarged, Cal., 1956.
—— 'Hindu Iconography—Vyūhas and Vibhavas of Viṣṇu', *Journal of the Indian Society of Oriental Art*, XIV, 1946, pp. 1ff.
——*Paurāṇic and Tantric Religion*, Cal., 1966.
—— *Religion in Art and Archaeology*, Lucknow, 1968.
——'Lakulīśa—the Founder or the Systematiser of the Pāśupata Order', *Indian History Congress, Proceedings of the 14th Session*, Jaipur, 1951, pp. 32ff.
BANERJEE, MANINDRA NATH, 'Iron and Steel in the Ṛgvedic Age', *IHQ.*, vol. 3, 1929, pp. 432ff.
BANERJEE, N.R., *Iron Age in India*, Delhi, 1965.
BANERJEE, SARAT CHANDRA, *The Sāṅkhya Philosophy: Sāṅkhyakārikā with Gauḍapāda's Scholia and Nārāyaṇa's Gloss*, Cal., 1909.
BANERJI, P.K., 'Sandhyābhāṣā', *Viśvabhārati Quarterly*, Santiniketan, 1924.
BANERJI, S.C., *A Companion to Sanskrit Literature*, 1971.
—— *A Glossary to Smṛti Literature*, Cal., 1963.
BANTON, M., *Anthropological Approaches to the Study of Religion*, L., 1966.
BARRET, LEROY C., *The Kashmirian Atharvaveda*, American Oriental Society, vol. 18, Baltimore, 1940.
BARRETT, DOUGLAS and GRAY, B., *Painting of India* (Treasures of Asia S.), L., 1963.
BARROW, H.B., 'On Aghoris and Aghorapanthis', in *Proceedings of the Anthropological Society of Bombay*, 1893, pp. 197ff.
BARUA, BENINADHAB, 'The Ājīvikas: A Short History of their Religion and Philosophy', *Journal of the Dept. of Letters, University of Cal.*, II, 1920, pp. 1ff.
—— *A History of Pre-Buddhistic Indian Philosophy*, Cal., 1921. Repr. 1970.
BARY, W. T. DE, *et al.*, *Sources of Indian Tradition*, N.Y., 1958.
BASHAM, A.L., *History and Doctrines of the Ājīvikas*, L., 1951.
—— *The Wonder that was India*, L., 1954.
—— (ed.), *Papers on the Date of Kaniṣka. Submitted to the Conference on the Date of Kaniṣka, L. 1966*, Australian National Univ. Centre of Oriental Studies, monograph iv, 1968.
—— *Studies in Indian History and Culture*, Cal., 1964.
BASU, A., 'Dīkshā', in *Initiation*, ed. by C.J. Bleeker (q.v.).
—— 'Hindu doctrine of Divine Kingship', in *The Sacral Kingship/La Regalità Sacra*, International Congress for the History of Religions, Rome (April 1955), 1959.
BEAL, SAMUEL (tr.), *Chinese Accounts of India*, 4 vols, new edn., India, 1957–8.
BEASLEY, H.G., 'The Scripts of Mohenjo-daro, Harappā and Easter Island', *Man*, 36, no. 199.
BEHANAN, K.T., *Yoga, a Scientific Evaluation*, L., 1937.
BERGAIGNE, A., *La Religion védique d'après les hymnes du Rig-Veda*, France, 4 vols, 1878–97. Repr. 1964.
BHADURI, SADANANDA, *Studies in Nyāya-Vaiśeṣika Metaphysics*, Poona, 1947.
BHANDARKAR, D.R., *Carmichael Lectures on Ancient Indian Numismatics*, Cal., 1921.
BHANDARKAR, R. GOPAL, *Vaiṣṇavism, Śaivism and Minor Religious Systems*, Strassburg, 1913. Repr. 1965.
BHARATI, AGEHANANDA, 'Metaphysics of Tantrism', *Quest*, no. 25, Bombay, 1960.
—— *The Tantric Tradition*, L., 1965.
BHARDWAJ, S.M., *Hindu Places of Pilgrimage in India*, 1973.
BHATT, G.H., *et al.*, *The Rāmāyaṇa of Vālmīki*, critically ed., 6 vols, Baroda, 1960–9.
BHATTACHARJI, S., *The Indian Theogony*, Camb., 1970.
BHATTACHARYA, ASUTOSH SASTRI, *Studies in Post-Śaṅkara Dialectics*, Cal., 1936.
BHATTACHARYA, BRINDAVAN C., *Indian Images*, pt. 1. *The Brahmanic Iconography*, Cal., 1921.
BHATTACHARYYA, A.K., *Indian Coins in the Musée Guimet*, 1971.
BHATTACHARYYA, BENOYTOSH, 'Some Notes on the Mithuna in Indian Art', *Rūpam*, no. 1, Cal., 1926.
—— *The Indian Buddhist Iconography*, Oxf., 1924.
BHATTACHARYYA, T., *A Study of Vāstuvidyā*, Patna, 1948.
—— *The Cult of Brahmā*, Patna, 1957.
—— *The Canons of Indian Art*, 2nd edn., Cal., 1963.
BHATTACHARYYA, VIDHUSHEKHARA, *The Āgamaśāstra of Gauḍapāda* (ed., tr. and annotated), Cal., 1943.
BHATTASALI, N.K., *Iconography of Buddhist and Brahmanical Sculptures in the Dacca Museum*, 1929.
BHISHAGRATNA, K.L., *Sushruta Saṁhitā* (tr. and ed.), 3 vols, Benaras, 1963.
BHOLA NATH, 'The role of animal remains in the early prehistoric cultures of India', *Indian Museum Bull.*, vol. IV, no. 2, 1969, pp. 102ff.
BILLARD, R., *L'Astronomie indienne*, EFEO, 1971.
BIRNBAUM, HENRIK, and PUHVEL, J., *Ancient Indo-European Dialects*, Cal., 1965.
BLACK, J.S. and CHEYNE, T.K., (ed.) *Encyclopaedia Biblica*,

4 vols in 1, L., 1914.
BLAIR, CHAUNCEY J., *Heat in the Ṛig Veda and Atharva Veda*, American Oriental S., vol. 45, New Haven.
BLATTER, E., and MILLARD, W.S., *Some Beautiful Indian Trees*, 2nd edn., rev. by W.T. Stearn, Bombay Natural History Society, 1954.
BLEEKER, C.J. (ed.), *Initiation* (Contributions to the theme of the Study-Conference of the International Assoc. for the History of Religions at Strassburg, 1964), 1965.
BLINKENBERG, C., *Thunder Weapon in Religion and Folklore*, Camb., 1911.
BLOCH, JULES, *L'Indo-Aryen du Veda aux temps modernes*, Paris, 1934. English edn., rev. by author and tr. by A. Master, Paris, 1965.
—— *Les Tsiganes*, Paris, 1953.
—— *Les Inscriptions d'Aśoka*, Paris, 1950.
BLOOMFIELD, MAURICE, *The Atharvaveda* (tr. in part), *SBE.*, vol. XLII, Oxf., 1897.
—— *Ṛig Vedic Repetitions*, *HOS.*, vols XX, XXIV, Cambridge (Mass.), 1916.
—— *Cerberus the Dog of Hades*, Chicago, 1905.
—— *Vedic Concordance*, *HOS.*, vol. X, 1906. Repr. 1964.
—— *The Atharvaveda and the Gopatha Brāhmaṇa*, Strassburg, 1899.
BODDING, P.O., *Santal Riddles and Witchcraft among the Santals*, Oslo, 1940.
—— (ed.), *Santal Folk Tales*, 3 vols, 1925–9.
BODEWITZ, H.W., *Jaiminīya Brāhmaṇa*, I. 1–65, tr. and com., *ORT.*, XVII, 1973.
BOELES, J.J., 'The Migration of the Magic Syllable Om', in *India Antiqua (A volume of Oriental Studies presented to J. Ph. Vogel)*, Leiden, 1947.
BÖHTLINGK, O. VON, and ROTH, R., *Sanskrit Wörterbuch nebst allen Nachträgen*, St. Petersburg, 1855ff. Tr. into E. by M. Mishra; ed. by J.L. Shastri, 7 vols, 1973–
BÖKÖNYI, SÁNDOR, *The Przevalsky Horse*, tr. from the Hungarian by Lili Halápy, L., 1974.
BONER, ALICE, *Principles of Composition in Hindu Sculpture*, Leiden, 1962
BONER, ALICE, and ŚARMĀ, S.R., *Śilpa Prakāśa. A Medieval Orissan Sanskrit Text on Temple Architecture by Rāmacandra Kaulācāra*, Leiden, 1966.
BOSCH, F.D.K., *The Golden Germ*, 's-Gravenhage, 1960.
BOSE, MANINDRA MOHAN, *The Post-Caitanya Sahajiya Cult of Bengal*, Cal., 1930.
BOSE, P.N., *Principles of Indian Śilpaśāstra*, Lahore, 1926.
BOSE, R. (tr. and annotated), *Vedānta-parijāta and Vedānta-kaustubha of Srīnivāsa. Commentaries on the Brahma-Sūtras*, RAS., Bengal, 3 vols, 1940–3.
BOUGLE, C., *Essays on the Caste System*, tr. and ed. by D.F. Pocock, Camb., 1971.
BOUSQUET, JACQUES (tr.), *Praśna Upaniṣad*, Paris, 1948.
BRAHMA, N.K., *The Philosophy of Hindu Sādhanā*, L., 1932.
BRANDON, S.G.F., *Legends of the Ancient Near East*, L., 1963.
—— *The Judgement of the Dead*, L., 1967.
—— (gen. ed.), *A Dictionary of Comparative Religion*, L., 1970.
BRIGGS, GEORGE W., *Gorakhnāth and the Kānphaṭā Yogis*, Cal., 1938.
BRODRICK, A. HOUGHTON (ed.), *Animals in Archaeology*, L., 1972.
BROME, V., *Freud and His Early Circle*, L., 1967.
BROSSE, THÉRÈSE, *Études instrumentales des techniques du Yoga*, Paris, 1963.
BROUGH, JOHN, *Selections from Classical Sanskrit Literature*, Luzac, 1951.
—— *The Early Brahmanical System of Gotra and Pravara*, Camb., 1953.
BROWN, W. NORMAN, *Some Cultural Continuities in India*, Calif., 1966.
BRUCE, G., *The Stranglers: The Thug Cult of Murder and its Overthrow in British India*, L., 1967.
BURGESS, E. (tr.), *Sūryasiddhāntha*, New Haven, 1860. Repr. with introduction, 1935.
BURNOUF, E. (ed. and tr.), *Bhāgavata Purāṇa*, 5 vols, Paris, 1840ff.
BURROW, T., *The Sanskrit Language*, 2nd edn., rev. L., 1965; 3rd rev. edn. 1973.
—— 'Dravidian and the decipherment of the Indus script', *Antiquity*, vol. XLIII, no. 172, 1969, pp. 274ff.
—— and EMENEAU, M.B., *A Dravidian Etymological Dictionary*, Oxf., 1961. Supplement to the above, 1968.
BURTON, SIR RICHARD, *The Kāma Sūtra of Vātsyāyana*, tr. by Burton and F.F. Arbuthnot, 1963.
BUTLER, H.E. (ed.), *Atlas of the Universe*, tr. by D.R. Welsh.
CALAND, WILLEM, *Altindischer Ahnencult; das Crāddha nach den verschiedenen Schulen mit Benutzung handschriftlicher Quellen dargestellt*, Leiden, 1893.
—— *Altindischer Zauberritual*, Amsterdam, 1900. Repr. 1970.
CAMPBELL, JOSEPH (v. also under Zimmer, Heinrich), *The Masks of God: vol. I, Primitive Mythology*, L., 1960; Vol. II, *Oriental Mythology*, L., 1962; Vol. III, *Occidental Mythology*, L., 1965.
—— *The Hero with a Thousand Faces*, N.Y., 1949.
CARMAN, J.B., *The Theology of Rāmānuja. An Essay in Interreligious Understanding*, New Haven, 1974.
CASTIGLIONI, ARTURO, *A History of Medicine*, N.Y., 1958.
CHAKRAVARTI, C., *Tantras. Studies in Their Religion and Literature*, Cal., 1963.
CHAKRAVATI, P.C. *The Art of War in Ancient India*, Dacca, 1941.
CHAKRAVATI, S.C., *The Philosophy of the Upaniṣads*, Cal., 1935.
CHANDRA, MOTI, 'Cosmetics and Coiffure in Ancient India', *Journal of the Indian Society of Oriental Art*, VIII, Cal., 1940, pp. 62ff.
CHARI, S.M. SRINIVASA, *Advaita and Viśiṣṭādvaita*, L., 1961.
CHARPENTIER, JARL, 'The Meaning and Etymology of Pūjā', *IA.*, LVI, 1927, pp. 93ff.; 130ff.
—— *The Uttaradhyayana Sūtra*, 2 vols, Uppsala, 1921–2.
CHATTERJEE, A.D., 'Characteristics of Skanda-Kārttikeya', *Indian Museum Bull.*, vol. IV, 1, 1969, pp. 60ff.
CHATTERJEE, SATIS CHANDRA, *The Nyāya Theory of Knowledge*, 2nd edn., Cal., 1950.

—— and DATTA, D., *An Introduction to Indian Philosophy*, Cal., 1939. 6th edn. 1960.

CHATTOPADHYAYA, D., *Lokāyata. A Study in Ancient Indian Materialism*, New Delhi, 1959. Repr. 1974.

CHAUBEY, B.B., *Treatment of Nature in the Ṛgveda*, Hoshiarpur, 1970.

CHAUDHURI, ANIL KUMAR RAY, *The Doctrine of Māyā*, Cal., 1950.

—— *Self and Falsity in Advaita Vedānta*, Cal., 1955.

CHAUDHURI, J.B., *The Position of Women in Vedic Ritual*, 2nd edn., Cal., 1956.

CHAUDHURI, NANIMADHAB, 'A Pre-historic Tree Cult', *IHQ.*, XIX, 4, 1943, pp. 318ff.

—— 'Rudra-Śiva, as an agricultural deity' *IHQ.*, XV,2, 1939, pp. 183ff.

CHAUDHURI, S.B., *Ethnic Settlements in Ancient India*, Cal., 1954.

CHILDE, V.G., *The Āryans*, L., 1926.

—— *New Light on the Most Ancient East*, L., 1959.

CHOUDHARY, R., *The Vrātyas in Ancient India*, India, 1964.

CLARK, T.W., 'Evolution of Hinduism in Medieval Bengali Literature', *BSOAS.*, XVII/3.

CLARK, W.E., *The Āryabhaṭīya of Āryabhaṭa*, Chicago, 1930.

CLEBERT, JEAN PAUL, *The Gypsies*, tr. by Charles Duff, L., 1963.

COHN, WILLIAM, *Indische Plastik*, Berlin, 1922.

COLEBROOKE, HENRY THOMAS (tr.), *Sāṅkhya Kārikā of Īśvara-Kṛṣṇa*, Oxf., 1837.

COLINET, P., 'Étude sur le mot Aditi', *Museon*, XII, 1893, pp. 81ff.

COMBAZ, GISBERT, 'L'Évolution du stūpa en Asie', *Mélanges chinois et bouddhiques*, Brussels: II (1932–3), pp. 163ff.; III (1934–5), pp. 93ff.; IV (1935–6), pp. 1ff.

CONTENAU, GEORGES, *La Civilisation d'Assur et de Babylone*, Paris, 1937.

—— *Manuel d'archéologie orientale*, 4 vols, Paris, 1927–47.

COOK, A.B., *Zeus. A Study of Ancient Religion*, 3 vols, 1914–40, Camb., Repr. vols I and II, N.Y., 1964.

COOMARASWAMY, ANANDA K., *Hinduism and Buddhism*, N.Y., 1943.

—— 'Sir Gawain and the Green Knight; Indra and Namuci', *Speculum*, Camb. (Mass.), XIX, 1944, pp. 104ff.

—— 'The Tantric Doctrine of Divine Biunity', *ABORI.*, XIX, pp. 1938, 173ff.

—— *The Dance of Shiva*, repr. N.Y. 1957. Rev. edn., Delhi, 1968.

—— 'Satī, A Vindication of Hindu women', Sociological Society, L., 1912.

—— 'Mudrā-Muddā', *JAOS.*, XLVIII, 1928, pp. 279f.

—— *Yakṣas*, 2 vols, Washington, 1928, 1931. Repr. 1971.

—— 'Archaic Indian Terracottas', in *Ipek*, 1928.

—— 'Tree of Jesse and Indian Parallels or Sources', *Art Bull.*, XI, 1929.

—— *History of Indian and Indonesian Art*, L., 1927. Repr. N.Y., 1965.

—— 'Ganesha', *Bull. of the Boston Museum of Fine Arts*, vol. XXVI, April 1928.

—— 'Horse-riding in the Ṛgveda and the Atharvaveda', *JAOS.*, 62, 1942, pp. 139f.

—— 'Philosophy of Ancient Asiatic Art', included in Anand's *The Hindu View of Art* (q.v.).

—— *The Indian Craftsman*, L., 1909.

COWELL, E.B. (ed.), *The Jātaka, or Stories of the Buddha's Former Births*, 7 vols, Camb., 1895–1913.

CROOKE, WILLIAM, *Religion and Folklore of Northern India*, prepared for the press by R.E. Enthoven, Oxf., 1926.

—— *Things Indian*, L., 1906.

DAHLMAN, JOSEPH, *Sāṁkhya-Philosophie*, Berlin, 1902.

DAHLQUIST, ALLAN, *Megasthenes and Indian Religion*, Stockholm, 1962.

d'ALVIELLA, G., *La Migration des Symboles*, Paris, 1891.

DANDEKAR, R.N., 'Pūṣan, the Pastoral God of the Veda', *New Indian Antiquary*, V, Poona.

—— 'The Mahābhārata: Origin and Growth', *Univ. of Ceylon Review*, XII, 1954.

DANGE, S.A., *Legends in the Mahābhārata*, Delhi, 1969.

DANI, AHMAD HASAN, *Indian Palaeography*, Oxf., 1963.

—— *Prehistory and Protohistory of Eastern India*, Cal., 1960.

DANIÉLOU, ALAIN, *Yoga: the Method of Re-Integration*, L., 1949.

—— *The Rāgas of Northern Indian Music*, 2 vols, 1949. Later rev. in 1 vol.

—— *Tableau comparatif des intervalles musicaux*, Pondicherry.

—— *Hindu Polytheism*, L., 1963.

DAREMBERG, C.H., and SAGLIO, E. (ed.), *Dictionnaire des antiquités grecques et romaines*, Paris, 1877–1919.

DAS, BHAGAVAN, *Kṛshṇa. A Study in the Theory of Avatāras*, Madras, 1929.

DAS, D.K., *The Yajña: the Sacrifice in Hinduism*, 1911.

DAS, S.K., *The Educational System of the Ancient Hindus*, Cal., 1930.

—— *Śakti or Divine Power*, Cal., 1934.

DASGUPTA, SHASHIBHUSAN, *An Introduction to Tantric Buddhism*, Cal., 1950. Repr. 1958.

—— *Obscure Religious Cults as Background of Bengali Literature*, Cal., Repr. 1962, 1969.

DASGUPTA, S.N., *A History of Indian Philosophy*, Camb., 5 vols, 1922. Repr. 1952.

—— *Indian Idealism*, Camb., 1933.

—— *A Study of Patañjali*, Cal., 1920.

—— *Yoga as Philosophy and Religion*, L., 1924.

DATTA, B., and SINGH, A.N., *History of Hindu Mathematics*, pts 1 and 2, 1935–8. Repr. 2 vols in 1, Bombay, 1962.

DAVIDS, T.W. RHYS, and STEDE, W., *The Pāli-English Dictionary*, Pāli Text Society, L., 1925.

DAVIDSON, H.R. ELLIS, *Pagan Scandinavia*, L., 1967.

—— *Gods and Myths of Northern Europe*, Harmondsworth, 1964.

DAVIES, C.C., *An Historical Atlas of the Indian Peninsula*, Oxf., 1949.

DE, D.L., 'Pāñcarātra and the Upaniṣads', *IHQ.*, IX, 3, 1933, pp. 645ff.

DELLA VALLE, PIETRO, *The Travels of Pietro della Valle to India*, tr. by G. Havers, 1604. Ed. with a life of the author by

E. Grey, 2 vols, 1891, Hakluyt Society, 1965.

DEONNA, W., *Le Symbolisme de l'oeil*, 1965.

DERRETT, J.D.M., *The Hoysalas*, Oxf., 1957.

DESHMUKH, G. HARI, 'On Hindu Sacrifice', *Journal of the Anthropological Society*, Bombay, 1887, pp. 106ff.

DESHMUKH, P.R., *Indus Civilization in the Ṛgveda*, Yeotmal, 1954.

DEUSSEN, PAUL, *The System of the Vedānta*, tr. by Charles Johnson, Chicago, 1912.

DEUTSCH, E., and BUITENEN, J.A.B. VAN, *A Source Book of Advaita Vedānta*, 1971.

DEVAHUTI, D., *Harsha, a Political Study*, Oxf., 1970.

DEVASTHALI, G.V., *Religion and Mythology of the Brāhmaṇas*, Poona, 1960.

de VREESE, K., 'The game of dice in ancient India', in *Orientalia Neerlandica*, Leiden, 1948, pp. 349ff.

DHARMA, P.C., *The Rāmāyaṇa Polity*, Madras, 1941.

DHAVAMONY, M., *Love of God according to the Śaiva Siddhānta*, L., 1971.

DIEHL, C. GUSTAV., *Instrument and Purpose. Studies on Rites and Rituals in South India*, Lund, 1956.

DIETERICH, A., *Mutter Erde, ein Versuch über Volks-religion*, Leipzig-Berlin, 1905. 3rd edn. 1925, augmented and completed by E. Fehrle.

DIKSHITAR, V.R.R., *War in Ancient India*, L., 1944.

—— *The Purāṇa Index*, 3 vols, Madras, 1951–5.

DIMOCK, E.C. (ed. and tr.), *In Praise of Krishna: Songs from the Bengali*, UNESCO, N.Y., 1967.

DIRINGER, DAVID, *The Alphabet*, 2 vols, 3rd edn. rev. with the collaboration of R. Regensburger, L., 1968.

DOUGLAS, N., *Tantra Yoga*, 1971.

DOWNS, J.F., 'The Origin and Spread of Riding in the Near East and Central Asia', *American Anthropologist*, vol. 63, no. 6, 1961, pp. 1193ff.

DOWSON, JOHN, *A Classical Dictionary of Hindu Mythology and Religion*, L., 1928. Repr. 1968.

DREKMEIER, C., *Kingship and Community in Early India*, Stanford, 1962.

DRENIKOFF-ANDHI, Y., *Le Yoga. Science de l'homme*, Paris, 1967.

DRIVER, G.R., *Canaanite Myths and Legends*, Edinburgh, 1956.

DROWER, E.S., *Water into Wine. A Study of Ritual Idiom in the Middle East*, L., 1956.

DUMÉZIL, GEORGES, *Les Dieux des Indo-Européens*, Paris, 1952.

—— *Ouranos-Varuṇa*, Paris, 1934.

—— *Mitra-Varuṇa*, Leiden, 1943.

DUMONT, PAUL ÉMILE, *L'Aśvamedha. Description du sacrifice solennel du cheval dans le culte védique*, Louvain, 1927.

DUTT, MANMATHA NATH (tr.), *A Prose English Translation of the Mahābhārata*, Cal., 1895–1905.

—— (tr.), *The Rāmāyaṇa*, Cal., 1892–4.

—— (tr.), *Garuḍa-Purāṇam*, *Chowkhamba Sanskrit Studies*, LXVII, 1968.

DUTT, ROMESH C., *The Early Hindu Civilization, B.C. 2000–320*, L., 1888; 4th edn., Cal., 1963.

DVIVEDI, MANILAL N. (tr.), *The Māṇḍūkyopanishad with Gauḍapāda's Kārikās and the Bhāshya of Śaṅkara*, Bombay, 1909.

EDGERTON, FRANKLIN (tr.), (v. also under Mahābhārata), *The Bhagavad Gītā*, Camb. (Mass.), 2 vols, *HOS*. 1944.

—— 'The Meaning of Sāṅkhya and Yoga', *American Journal of Philology*, XLV, Baltimore, 1924, pp. 1ff.

—— (ed.), *The Pañchatantra Reconstructed*, 2 vols, American Oriental S. Monograph 2,3, New Haven, 1924. Repr. 1966.

—— (tr.), *The Mīmāṁsā Nyāya Prakāśa of Āpadevi: A Treatise on the Mīmāṁsā System*, New Haven, 1929.

—— *The Beginnings of Indian Philosophy*, L., 1965.

—— (tr.), *The Pañcatantra*, L., 1965.

—— 'Dominant Ideas in the formation of Indian Culture', *Journal American Oriental Society*, LXII, 1942.

—— *Buddhist Hybrid Sanskrit Grammar and Dictionary*, New Haven, 1953.

EGERTON, SYKES, *Everyman's Dictionary of Non-Classical Mythology*, L., 1952. Rev. 1961 and 1962.

EGGELING, J., v. under *Sacred Books of the East*.

EHRENFELS, O.R., *Mother Right in India*, Hyderabad, 1941.

ELIADE, MIRCEA, 'Cosmical Homology and Yoga', *Journal of the Indian Society of Oriental Art*, Cal., V, 1937, pp. 188ff.

—— *Metallurgy, Magic and Alchemy*, Paris and Bucharest, 1938.

—— *The History of Religions*, Chicago, 1959.

—— *Myth and Reality*, L., 1964.

—— *The Two and the One*, L., 1965.

—— *Birth and Rebirth*, N.Y., 1960.

—— *Techniques du Yoga*, Paris, 1948.

—— *Shamanism: Archaic Techniques of Ecstasy*, tr. by Willard R. Trask, L., 1964.

—— *The Forge and the Crucible*, tr. by Stephen Corrin, N.Y., 1962.

—— *Myths, Dreams and Mysteries*, tr. by Philip Mairet, L., 1960.

—— *Images and Symbols*, tr. by Philip Mairet, L., 1952.

—— *Yoga: Immortality and Freedom*, tr. by Willard R. Trask, L., 1958.

—— *Patterns in Comparative Religion*, tr. by Rosemary Sheed, L., 1958.

—— *From Primitives to Zen*, L., 1967.

ELWIN, VERRIER, *Nāgaland*, Shillong, 1961.

—— *Myths of Middle India*, Oxf., 1941.

EMENEAU, M.B., *The Strangling Figs in Sanskrit Literature*, Calif., 1949.

—— *Dravidian Linguistics, Ethnology and Folktales*, Annamalai, 1967.

—— and BURROW, T., *Dravidian Borrowings from Indo-Āryan*, Calif., 1962.

ENGNELL, IVAN, *Studies in Divine Kingship in the Ancient Near East*, Oxf., 1967.

ENTRALGO, PEDRO LAÍN, *The Therapy of the Word in Classical Antiquity*, ed. and tr. by L.J. Rather and J.M. Sharp, New Haven, 1970.

EPSTEIN, I. (ed. and tr.), *The Babylonian Talmud*, 5 vols, L., 1935–52.

ESNOUL, ANNE MARIE (tr.), *Maitri Upaniṣad*, Paris, 1952.

EVANS-PRITCHARD, E.E., *The Divine Kingship of the Shilluk of*

the Nilotic Sudan, Camb., 1948.
Fables of Pilpay, 'Chandos Classics', rev. edn., n.d.
FABRI, C.F., 'Un élément mésopotamien dans l'art de l'Inde', *JA.*, CCXVII, pp. 298ff.
—— *History of Indian Dress*, Cal., 1960.
FADDEGON, BAREND, *The Vaiçesika-System described with the help of the Oldest Texts*, Amsterdam, 1918. Repr. 1968, 1970.
FAIRSERVIS, WALTER A. JR., *The Harappan Civilization*, N.Y., 1961.
—— *The Roots of Ancient India*, L., 1971.
FARNELL, LEWIS RICHARD, *The Cults of the Greek States*, 5 vols, Oxf., 1896–1909.
FAUSBOLL, V., *Indian Mythology in Outline according to the Mahābhārata*, L., 1903.
FERREIRA, JOHN V., *Totemism in India*. Oxf., 1965.
FILLIOZAT, JEAN, *La Doctrine classique de la médecine indienne, ses origines et ses parallèles grecs*, Paris, 1949. Tr. by M. Ledeserts, and entitled *The Classical Doctrine of Indian Medicine*, L., 1964.
—— *Magie et médecine*, Paris, 1943.
—— 'Ancient Indian Science', in *Ancient and Medieval Science*, (ed.), A.J. Pomerans, L., 1963; and 'Science in Medieval India', ibid.
—— 'Prognostiques médicaux akkadiens, grecs et indiens', *JA.*, 1952.
FINNEGAN, JACK, *The Archaeology of World Religions*, Princeton, 1952.
FINOT, LOUIS, *Les Lapidaires indiens*, Paris, 1896.
FISCHEL, WALTER J. (ed.), *Semitic and Oriental Studies. A volume presented to William Popper on his 75th birthday, 29.10.49*, Calif., 1951.
Fodor's Guide to India, L., n.d.
FORBES, R.J., *Metallurgy in Antiquity: a Notebook for Archaeologists and Technologists*, Leiden, 1950.
FOUCHER, MAX-PÔL, *The Erotic Sculpture of India*, L., 1959.
FRANKFORT, H., *Cylinder Seals*, L., 1939.
—— *Ancient Egyptian Religion*, N.Y., 1948. Repr. paperback, N.Y. 1961.
—— *Kingship and the Gods*, Chicago, 1948.
FRAUWALLNER, E., *Geschichte der indischen Philosophie*, 2 vols, Salzburg, 1953–4, tr. (as *History of Indian Philosophy*) by V.M. Bedekar, 2 vols, L., 1973.
FRAXI, PISANUS, *Bibliography of Prohibited Books*, 3 vols. Repr., N.Y., 1962.
FRAZER, JAMES GEORGE, *The Golden Bough*, 12 vols, L., 1911–27; abridged edn., L., 1923.
GADD, C.F., 'Seals of Ancient Indian Style found at Ur', *Proceedings of the British Academy*, XVIII, 1932, pp. 1ff.
GAIROLA, C. KRISHNA, 'Évolution du pūrṇa ghaṭa (vase d'abondance) dans l'Inde et l'Inde extérieure', *Arts Asiatiques*, Paris, I, 1954, pp. 209ff.
GAIT, EDWARD ALBERT, *A History of Assam*, 2nd edn., Cal., 1926.
GANGOLY, ORDHENDRA COOMAR, *Rāgas and Rāgiṇīs. A Pictorial and Iconographic Study of Indian Musical Modes based on Original Sources*, vol. I, repr. 1947.
—— 'The Mithuna in Indian Art', *Rūpam*, 1925, pp. 22f.
—— *South Indian Bronzes*, Indian Society of Oriental Art, Cal., 1915.
—— 'A Note on Kīrtimukha being the Life-history of an Indian Architectural Ornament', *Rūpam*, I, 1920, pp. 11ff.
—— *Indian Architecture*, Cal., 1928.
—— 'The Cult of Agastya: and the Origin of Indian Colonial Art', *Rūpam*, 25, 1926.
GANGULY, K.K., *Some Aspects of Sun Worship in Ancient India*, Cal., 1965.
—— 'Early Indian Jewellery', *IHQ.*, XVIII, 1, March 1942, and XVIII, 2, June 1942.
GANGULY, M., *Orissa and her Remains, Ancient and Medieval*, Cal., 1912.
GARBE, R. (ed.), *Vaitāna Sūtra: The Ritual of the Atharva Veda*, 1898.
GASKELL, G.A., *Dictionary of All Scriptures and Myths*, N.Y., 1960.
GASTER, TH. H., *Thespis. Ritual, Myth and Drama in the Ancient Near East*, N.Y., 1966.
—— 'Myth and Story', *Numen*, I, 1954, pp. 184ff.
—— *The Oldest Stories in the World*, Boston, 1958.
GAUSDAL, JOHANNES, *The Santal Khūṭs. A Contribution to Animistic Research*, Oslo, 1960.
GELDNER, KARL FRIEDERICH, *Vedische Studien*. Vols 1–3, Stuttgart, 1897.
—— *Der Rig-Veda aus dem Sanskrit ins Deutsche Übersetzt*, 3 vols, *HOS.*, XXXIII–XXXV, 1951, and Index 1957. Repr. 1971.
GERSHEVITCH, I., *The Avestan Hymn to Mithra*, Camb., 1959.
GETTY, ALICE, *Gaṇeśa*, Oxf., 1936.
GHOSE, E.N., 'The Twin Gods of the Ṛgveda', *IHQ.*, 193.
GHOSH, JAJNESWAR, *A Study of Yoga*, Cal., 1933.
GHOSH, MANOMOHAN (ed. and tr.), *Nandikeśvara's Abhinayadarpaṇam; a Manual of Gesture and Posture used in Hindu Dance and Drama*, 2nd edn., Cal., 1957.
—— *The Nāṭyaśāstra*, RAS. (Bengal), 1951.
GHOSHAL, U.N., *The Agrarian System in Ancient India*, Cal., 1930.
—— 'Kingship and Kingly Administration in the Atharva Veda', *IHQ.*, 20, pp. 105ff.
—— *Contributions to the History of the Hindu Revenue System*, Cal., 1929.
GHURYE, G.S., *Bhāratanāṭya and its Costume*, Bombay, n.d.
—— *Caste and Race in India*, L., 1932. 5th edn. Bombay, 1969.
GIBSON, G.E., 'The Vedic Nakṣatras and the Zodiac', pp. 149ff., in *Semitic and Oriental Studies* (v. Fischel, Walter J.).
GILES, H.A. (tr.), *The Travels of Fa-hsien (399–414 A.D.)*, Camb., 1923; L., 1956.
GLADSTONE, M.S., *Viṣṇu in the Ṛgveda*, Camb., 1928.
GLANVILLE, 'Egyptian Theriomorphic Vases in the British Museum', *Journal of Egyptian Archaeology*, vol, XII, pts i and ii, April 1926, pp. 52ff.
GLASENAPP, HELMUTH VON, *Die Philosophie der Inder*, Stuttgart, 1949. Fr. tr. *La Philosophie indienne*, Paris, 1951.
—— 'Tantrismus und Śaktismus', *Ostasiatische Zeitschrift* (Berlin), n.s. XII, 1936, pp. 120ff.

—— *Die Religionen Indiens*, Stuttgart, 1943.
—— *Der Jainismus*, Berlin, 1925. Repr. 1964.
—— *Immortality and Salvation in Indian Religion*, tr. by E.F.J. Payne, Cal., 1963.
GNOLI, G., 'The Tyche and the Dioscuri in Ancient Sculptures from the Valley of Swat', *East and West*, vol. 14, nos. 1 and 2, 1963.
GODE, P.K., *Studies in Indian Literary History*, vols I, II, Bombay, 1953; vol. III, Poona, 1956.
—— 'The Indian Bullock-Cart: Its Prehistoric and Vedic Ancestors', *Poona Orientalist*, V, 1940, pp. 144ff.
GOETZ, ALBRECHT, *Old Babylonian Texts*, New Haven, 1966.
GOETZ, HERMANN, 'The Historical Background of the Great Temples of Khajuraho', *Arts Asiatiques*, vol. V, 1958.
—— *India: Five Thousand Years of Indian Art*, L., 1960.
GONDA, JAN, *Notes on Brahman*, Utrecht, 1950.
—— (ed. and tr.), *The Ṛgvidhāna*, Utrecht, 1951.
—— *Viṣṇuism and Śivaism. A Comparison*, L., 1970.
—— *Eye and Gaze in the Veda*, Amsterdam, 1969.
—— 'Ancient Indian Kingship', *Numen*, 3, 1956, pp. 41ff.
—— *Ancient Indian Kingship from the Religious Point of View*, Leiden, 1966. Repr. 1969.
—— *Aspects of Early Viṣṇuism*, Utrecht, 1954; 2nd edn. Delhi, 1969.
—— *Change and Continuity in Indian Religion*, The Hague, 1965.
—— *Die Religionen Indiens*, I. *Veda und älterer Hinduismus*; II. *Der jüngere Hinduismus*; III. *Buddhismus—Jainismus—Primitivvölker*, Stuttgart, 1961–4.
—— *Notes on Names and the Name of God in Ancient India*, Amsterdam, 1970.
GOPAL, M.H., *Mauryan Public Finance*, L., 1935.
GOPAL, R., *India of the Kalpasūtras*, Delhi, 1959.
GORDON, BENJAMIN LEE, *Medicine Throughout Antiquity*, Philadelphia, 1949.
GORDON, D.H., *The Prehistoric Background of Indian Culture*, Bombay, 1958.
GOUGH, ARCHIBALD EDWARD (tr.), *The Vaiśeṣika Sūtras of Kaṇāda with Comments from the Upaskāra of Śaṅkaramiśra and the Vivṛitti of Jayanārāyaṇa-tarkaparichānana*, Benaras, 1873.
GOWEN, N.H., *A History of Indian Literature*, N.Y., 1931.
GRASSMANN, H., *Wörterbuch zum Rig-Veda*, Leipzig, 1873. Repr. 1964.
GRAVELY, F.H., and RAMACHANDRAM, T.N., *Catalogue of South Indian Hindu Metal Images in the Madras Museum*, 1932.
GRAVES, ROBERT, *The Greek Myths*, 2 vols, Harmondsworth, 1962.
GREENE, W.C., *Moira, Fate, Good and Evil in Greek Thought*, Camb. (Mass.), 1948.
GREGORY, LADY, *Visions and Beliefs in the West of Ireland*, The Coole edn., Gerrards Cross, 1970.
GRIERSON, G.A., and KONOW, STEN, *Linguistic Survey of India*, Cal., 1903–27.
GRIFFITH, R.T.H. (tr.), *The Hymns of the Ṛgveda*, 2 vols, Varanasi, 1963.
—— *The Texts of the White Yajurveda*, Benaras, 1927.
—— (tr.), *The Hymns of the Sāmaveda*, Varanasi, 1963.
GUBERNATIS, ANGELO DE, *Letture sopra la Mitologia Vedica*, Florence, 1874.
—— *Zoological Mythology*, 2 vols, L., 1872.
GUÉNON, RENÉ, *Man and His Becoming, according to the Vedānta*, Luzac, 1945.
GULIK, ROBERT H. VAN, *Hayagrīva, the Mantrayānic Aspect of Horse-Cult in China and Japan*, Leiden, 1935.
—— *Ụrvaśī. A Drama of Kālidāsa*, tr. with intro., text and critical notes, The Hague, 1932.
GUPTA, PARMESHWARI LAL (ed.), *Patna Museum Catalogue of Antiquities*, Patna, 1965.
GUPTA, S.B., *An Introduction to Tantric Buddhism*, Cal., 1958.
GUPTA, SHAKTI M., *Plant Myths and Traditions in India*, Leiden, 1971.
GUPTE, B.A., 'Harvest Festivals of Gaurī and Gaṇesh', *IA.*, vol. XXXV, November 1906.
GURNER, C.W., 'The Fortress Policy in Kauṭilya's Arthaśāstra', *Indian Culture*, VIII, 1941–2, pp. 251ff.
GUSDORF, GEORGES, *Mythe et mètaphysique*, Paris, 1953.
GUTERBROCK, A., 'The Composition of Hittite Prayers to the Sun', *JAOS.*, vol. 78, no. 4, 1958.
HACKER, PAUL, *Untersuchungen über Texte des frühen Advaitavāda*, 2 vols, Mainz-Wiesbaden, 1951 and 1953.
HACKIN, JOSEPH *et al.*, *Asiatic Mythology*, L., 1932. Repr. 1963.
HALL, F. (ed.), *The Sūrya Siddhānta or An Ancient System of Hindu Astronomy*, 2 vols, Cal., 1859–61. Repr. 1974.
HALLADE, MADELEINE, *Arts de l'Asie ancienne. Thèmes et Motifs*, I. *L'Inde*, Musée Guimet, 1954.
HALLIDAY, W.R., *Indo-European Folk-Tales and Greek Legend*, Camb., 1933.
HAMDANI, M. al, and WENZEL, M., 'The Worm in the Tooth', *Folklore*, vol. 77, Spring 1966, pp. 60ff.
HARLE, J.C., 'An Early Hero-stone and a Possible Western Source', in *Studies in Honour of Sir Mortimer Wheeler*, *JRAS.*, no. 2, 1970, pp. 159ff.
—— *Temple Gateways in South India*, Oxf., 1963.
—— 'Three Types of Walls in Early Western Cāḷukya Temples', *Or. Art*, n.s. vol. XVII, n. 1, 1971, pp. 45ff.
—— 'South Indian Temple Bases', *Or. Art*, III, 4, 1957, pp. 138ff.
HARRIS, J. RENDELL, *Cult of the Heavenly Twins*, Camb., 1906.
—— *Picus who is also Zeus*, Camb., 1916.
HARRISON, JANE E., *Themis*, Camb., 1912.
—— *Prolegomena to the Study of Greek Religion*, Camb., 1922.
—— *Ancient Art and Ritual*, L., 1913.
HASTINGS, JAMES (ed.), *Encyclopaedia of Religion and Ethics*, 13 vols, Edinburgh, 1908–21. Repr. in the 1960s.
—— (ed.), *A Dictionary of the Bible*, 5 vols, 8th impression, Edinburgh, 1906.
HATT, GUDMUND, *Asiatic Influences in American Folklore*, Copenhagen, 1949.
HAUER, JACOB WILHELM, *Die Anfänge der Yogapraxis*, Stuttgart, 1922.

—— *Der Vrātya*, Stuttgart, 1927.
—— *Der Yoga*, Stuttgart, 1958.
HAUG, MARTIN, *The Aitareya Brāhmaṇam of the Ṛigveda*, *SBH.*, 1922.
HAYES, W., *The Book of the Cow*, privately printed, 1930.
HAZLITT, W. CAREW, *Faiths and Folklore—A Dictionary*, 2 vols in 1, L., 1905.
HAZRA, R.C., *Studies in the Upapurāṇas*, Cal., 1958.
—— *Studies in the Purāṇic Records on Hindu Rites and Customs*, Dacca, 1940.
—— 'The Kālikā Purāṇa', *ABORI.*, XXII (1941), pp. 1 ff.
HEESTERMAN, J.C., *The Ancient Indian Royal Consecration* (Disputationes Rheno-Trajectinae), 1957.
—— 'Vrātya and sacrifice', *Indo-Iranian Journal*, VI (1962–3), pp. 1ff.
HEILER, FRIEDRICH, *Die Mystik in den Upanishaden*, Munich, 1925.
HEIMANN, BETTY, *Facets of Indian Thought*, L., 1964.
—— *The Significance of Prefixes in Sanskrit Philosophical Terminology*, RAS., Monographs, vol. XXV, 1951.
—— *Indian and Western Philosophy: A Study in Contrasts*, L., 1937.
—— *Studien zur Eigenart indischen Denkens*, Tübingen, 1930.
HEINE-GELDERN, R., 'The Coming of the Āryans at the end of the Harappā Civilisation', *Man*, October 1956.
HELD, G.J., *The Mahābhārata: An Ethnological Study*, L., 1935.
Hemp Drug Commission, Report, 1893–4, 7 vols, and supplement vol. Repr. 1970.
HENDLEY, T.H., 'Indian Jewellery', *Journal of Indian Art*, Vol. XII, 1909.
HENRY, V., *La Magie dans l'Inde antique*, Paris, 1904.
HERTZ, ROBERT, *Mélanges de sociologie religieuse et folklore*, Paris, 1928.
—— *Death and the Right Hand*, tr. by R. and C. Needham, L., 1960.
HERZOG, EDGAR, *Psyche and Death*, tr. by D. Cox and E. Rolfe, L., 1966.
HILL, W.D.P. (tr. and commentary), *The Bhagavadgītā*, Oxf., 1928. Repr. 1953 and 1967.
—— (tr.), *Rāmacaritamanasa. The Holy Lake of the Acts of Rāma*, 1952. Repr. 1971.
HILLEBRANDT, A., *Vedische Mythologie*, 2nd edn., Breslau, 1927–9, 2 vols. Repr. 1965.
—— *Ritualliteratur*, Strassburg, 1897. Repr. 1974.
—— *Alt-indische Politik*, Jena, 1923.
—— *Varuṇa und Mitra*, Breslau, 1877.
—— *Ueber die Göttin Aditi*, Breslau, 1876.
HILLIS, R.K., 'Visual Aspects of Prāṇa', *Or. Art*, Autumn 1969, pp. 190ff.
HIRIYANNA, M. (ed. and tr.), *Vedānta-sāra*, Poona, 1929.
HOCART, A.M. *Caste*, L., 1950.
HOENS, DIRK JAN, *Śānti: A Contribution to Ancient Indian Religious Terminology*, The Hague, 1951.
HOERNLE, A.F., *Studies in the Medicine of Ancient India*, Oxf., 1907.
HOLTZMANN, A., *Das Mahābhārata*, 4 vols, Kiel, 1892–5. Repr. in 1 vol. 1971.
HOOKE, S.H. (ed.), *Myth, Ritual and Kingship*, Oxf., 1958.
—— *Babylonian and Assyrian Religion*, Oxf., 1962.
HOPKINS, EDWARD WASHBURN, *The Great Epic of India*, N.Y., 1901: Repr. Cal., 1969.
—— 'Yoga-Technique in the Great Epic', *JAOS.*, XXII, 1901, pp. 333ff.
—— *Epic Mythology*, repr. Varanasi, 1968.
HORNELL, J., *The Sacred Chank of India*, Madras, 1914.
HOURANI, G.F., *Arab Seafaring in the Indian Ocean in Ancient and Early Medieval Times*, Princeton, 1951.
HROZNÝ, BEDŘICH, *Ancient History of Western Asia, India and Crete*, N.Y., 1953.
HULTZSCH, E., *Corpus Inscriptionum Indicarum*, vol. III., Cal., 1888.
—— *Epigraphia Indica*, vol. IV, Cal., 1896–7.
HUME, ROBERT ERNEST (tr.), *The Thirteen Principal Upanishads*, Oxf., 1921.
HUNASHAL, S., *The Liṅgāyat Movement*, Dharwar, 1927.
HUTTON, J.H., *Caste in India*, Camb., 1946. Repr. Oxf., 1963.
INGALLS, DANIEL H.H., *Materials for the Study of Navya-Nyāya Logic*, *HOS.*, XL, 1951.
IYENGAR, P.T.S., *Pre-Āryan Tamil Culture*, Madras, 1930.
IYER, C.V.N., *The Origin and Early History of Śaivism in South India*, Madras, 1936.
IYER, K.B., *Kathakali. The Sacred Dance-Drama of Malabar*, Luzac, 1955.
JACOB, G.A., *A Manual of Hindu Pantheism: The Vedāntasāra*, tr. and annotated, 1881. Repr. 1972.
JACOBI, HERMANN (tr.), *Gaina Sūtras*, *SBE.*, XXII.
JAINI, JAGMANDERLAL, *Outlines of Jainism*, Camb., 1916.
JAIRAZBHOY, R.A., *Foreign Influences in Ancient India*, Bombay, 1963.
—— *Oriental Influences in Western Art*, L., 1965.
JAMES, E.O., *Cult of the Mother-Goddess*, L., 1959.
—— *Prehistoric Religion*, L., 1957.
—— *The Worship of the Sky-God*, L., 1963.
—— *Sacrifice and Sacrament*, L., 1962.
—— *The Tree of Life. An Archaeological Study*, Leiden, 1966.
JASTROW, MORRIS, *Babylonian-Assyrian Birth Omens*, Giessen, 1914.
JAYASWAL, K.P., *Manu and Yājñavalkya; A Comparison and a Contrast*, Cal., 1930.
JHA, G.M. (tr.), *The Tattva-Kamudī; Vācaspati Miśra's Commentary on the Sāṁkhya-kārikā*, Poona Oriental S., no. 10, 1965.
—— *The Nyāya Philosophy of Gautama*, Allahabad, n.d.
—— (ed. and tr.), *Manu-Smṛti: The Laws of Manu with the Bhāṣya of Medhātithi*, Cal., 9 vols, 1920–6.
JOHNSON, FRANCIS, *Hitopadeśa. The Sanskrit Text with a Grammatical Analysis alphabetically arranged*, new edn., 1884. Rev. by L. Barnett, L., 1928.
JOHNSON, J. (tr.). *The Vedāntatattvasāra Ascribed to Rāmānujāchārya*, Benaras, 1898.
JOHNSTON, EDWARD HAMILTON, 'Some Sāṁkhya and Yoga Conceptions of the Śvetāśvatara Upaniṣad', *JRAS.*, 1930, pp. 855ff.

JOLLY, JULIUS (tr.), *Nāradīya Dharmaśāstra, or The Institutes of Nārada*, L., 1878.

JOSHI, J.P., *Origin and Development of Dattātreya Worship in India*, Baroda, 1965.

JOSHI, R.V., *Le Ritual de la dévotion Kṛṣṇaite*, Pondicherry, 1959.

JOUVEAU-DUBREUIL, G., *Iconography of Southern India*, tr. by A.C. Martin, Paris, 1937.

—— *Dravidian Architecture*, Madras, 1917.

JUNG, C.G., 'On Maṇḍala Symbolism', in *Archetypes and the Collective Unconscious*, tr. by R.F.C. Hull, L. and N.Y., 1955.

KAEGI, A., *Der Rigveda*, 2nd edn., Leipzig, 1881. E. tr. by R. Arrowsmith, Boston, 1886.

KAKATI, BANI KANTA, *The Mother Goddess Kāmākhyā*, Assam, 1948.

KALGHATGI, T.G., *Some Problems in Jaina Psychology*, Dharwar, 1961.

KANE, P.V., *History of Dharmaśāstra*, 5 vols, 1930—, Bhandarkar Oriental Research Institute.

—— *A Brief Sketch of the Pūrva-Mīmāṁsā System*, Poona, 1924.

KANGLE, R.P. (tr.), *Kauṭilya, Arthaśāstra*, Bombay, 1963.

KANIṢKA CONFERENCE, *Papers on the date of Kaniṣka. Submitted to the Conference in L. 20–22nd April, 1966*, ed. by A.L. Basham, 1968 (Australian National Univ. Oriental Monographs, IV).

KARAMBELKAR, V.W., *The Atharva-Veda and the Āyur-Veda*, India, 1961.

KARVE, IRAWATI, *Kinship Organization in India*, Deccan College Monograph S., 11, 1953.

—— *Kinship Terminology and Kinship Usages in Ṛgveda and Atharvaveda*, Annals of the Bhandarkar Oriental Research Institute, 1940.

KAUFMANN, WALTER, *Musical Notations of the Orient*, Vol. I., Indiana, 1967.

—— *The Rāgas of North India*, Indiana, 1968.

KAVIRATNA, A. (tr.), *The Caraka Saṁhitā*, Cal., 1899. Repr. 1912.

KAYE, G.R., *Hindu Astronomy*, Cal., 1924.

KEITH, ARTHUR BERRIEDALE, *A History of Sanskrit Literature*, Oxf., 1928.

—— *Indian Logic and Atomism, an Exposition of the Nyāya and Vaiçeṣika Systems*, Oxf., 1921.

—— *The Religion and Philosophy of the Veda and Upanishads*, Camb. (Mass.), 1925, 2 vols, *HOS.*, XXXI, XXXII. Repr. 1970.

—— (tr.), *Ṛigveda Brāhmaṇas: Aitareya and Kauṣitaki Brāhmaṇas of the Ṛigveda*, *HOS.*, XXV. 1920. Repr. 1971.

—— *The Sāṁkhya System*, L., 1918; 2nd edn., Cal., 1924.

—— (ed. and tr.), *Aitareya Āraṇyaka*, Oxf., 1909. Repr., 1969.

—— 'The Vrātyas', *JRAS.*, 1913, pp. 155ff.

—— and CARNOY, J., *The Mythology of All Races*, 13 vols, *Indian and Iranian*, vol. VI, N.Y., 1917. Repr. 1945.

—— *The Veda of the Black Yajus School entitled Taittirīya Saṁhitā*, *HOS.*, 2 vols, 1914. Repr. 1967.

KENNEDY, MELVILLE T., *The Chaitanya Movement*, Cal., 1925.

KENNEDY, R. HARTLEY, *The Sutti as Witnessed at Baroda, Nov. 29th, 1825*, L., 1855.

KERN, H. (tr.), *Bṛhatsaṁhitā*, *JRAS.*, 1870ff.

KING, L.W., *Babylonian Magic and Sorcery, being The Prayers of the Lifting of the Hand*, Luzac, 1896.

KINGSBURY, F., and PHILLIPS, G.E., *Hymns of the Tamil Śaivite Saints*, Cal., 1921.

KINNIER-WILSON, J.V., *Indo-Sumerian. A New Approach to the Problems of the Indian Script*, Oxf., 1974.

KIRFEL, W., *Die Kosmographie der Inder*, Bonn, 1940. Repr. 1967.

—— *Symbolik des Hinduismus und des Jainismus*, Stuttgart, 1959.

—— *Der Hinduismus*, Leipzig, 1934.

KLUCKHOHN, CLYDE, 'Myths and Rituals: A General Theory', *Harvard Theological Review*, XXXV, 1942, pp. 45ff.

KONOW, STEN, *The Āryan Gods of the Mitanni People*, Kristiania, 1921.

—— *Corpus Inscriptionum Indicarum*, vol. II, pt. 1, Cal., 1929.

—— and TUXEN, P., *Religions of India*, Copenhagen, 1949.

—— *Das indische Drama*, Berlin, 1920.

KOOIJ, K.R. VAN, *Worship of the Goddess according to the Kālikāpurāṇa*, Pt. I. A tr. with intro. and notes on Chs. 54–69. *ORT.*, 1972.

KOSAMBI, D.D., *Myth and Reality*, Bombay, 1962.

—— *The Culture and Civilization of Ancient India in Historical Outline*, L., 1965. Repr. 1969.

KRAMER, S.N., *Sumerian Mythology*, Philadelphia, 1944.

—— *The Sacred Marriage Rite. Aspects of Faith, Myth and Ritual in Ancient Sumer*, Indiana, 1969.

KRAMRISCH, STELLA, *The Hindu Temple*, 2 vols, Cal., 1946.

—— *Unknown India: Ritual Art in Tribe and Village*, Philadelphia, 1968.

—— (tr.), *Viṣṇudharmottara*, Cal., 1928.

—— 'Pūṣan', *JAOS.*, vol. 81, no. 2, 1961.

LACOMBE, O., *La Doctrine morale et métaphysique de Rāmānuja*, Paris, 1938.

LAHIRI, A.N., *Corpus of Indo-Greek Coins*, Cal., 1965.

LAL, B.B., 'The Direction of Writing in the Harappan Script', *Antiquity*, 40, 1965.

LALOU, MARCELLE (tr.), *Kālidāsa Oeuvres Complètes*, Paris, 1921

LAMBERT, W.G., *Babylonian Wisdom Literature*, Oxf., 1960.

LAMBRICK, H.T., *Sind. A General Introduction*, Hyderabad, 1964.

—— *The Terrorist*, L., 1972.

LA MERI, R.M.H., *The Gesture Language of the Hindu Dance*, N.Y., 1941. Repr. 1964.

LAMOTTE, ÉTIENNE, *Notes sur la Bhagavadgītā*, Paris, 1929.

LANCEREAU, E. (tr. and annotated), *Pañchatantra*, Intro. by L. Renou, UNESCO, 1965.

LANGDON, S.H., 'Gesture in Sumerian and Babylonian Prayer', *JRAS.*, 1919, pp. 531ff.

LARSON, G.J., *Classical Sāṁkhya*, Delhi, 1969.

LA VALLÉE POUSSIN, L. de, *Nirvāṇa*, Paris, 1925.

LAW, BIMALA CHURN, *Tribes in Ancient India*, Poona, 1943.

LAW, N.N., *Inter-State Relations in Ancient India*, Cal., 1920.

—— *Studies in Indian History and Culture*, L., 1925.

LEEMANS, W.F., *Foreign Trade in the Old Babylonian Period as revealed by Texts from Southern Mesopotamia*, Leiden, 1960.

LE GRAIN, L.L., 'Horseback riding in Mesopotamia in the IIIrd millennium B.C.', *Bull. of the Univ. Museum*, II (4), pp. 27ff., Philadelphia, 1948.

LENORMANT, FRANÇOIS, *Chaldean Magic*, L., 1877.

LEONARD, G.S., 'Notes on the Kānphaṭa Yogīs', *IA.*, VII, 1878, pp. 298ff.

LEONARDI, G.G., *Bhattikāvyam*, tr. with notes, *ORT.*, XVI, 1972.

LESSING, F.D., 'Calling the Soul: A Lamaist Ritual', in *Semitic and Oriental Studies*, pp. 263ff. (v. Fischel, Walter J.)

LÉVI, SYLVAIN, *La Doctrine du sacrifice dans les Brāhmaṇas*, Paris, 1898, 2nd edn. 1966.

— *et al.*, 'Pré-āryen et pré-dravidien dans l'Inde', *JA.*, CCIII, 1923, pp. 1ff. E. tr. by P.C. Bagchi, Cal., 1929.

LEVY, GERTRUDE RACHEL, *The Gate of Horn*, L., 1953.

LEWIN, LOUIS, *Phantastica: narcotic and stimulating drugs—their use and abuse*, 1931. Repr. L., 1964 (being the E. tr. of *Phantastika—die betaubenden und erregenden Genussmittel*).

LEWIS, BERNARD, *The Assassins: A Radical Sect in Islam*, L., 1967.

LINDQUIST, SIGURD, *Die Methoden des Yoga*, Lund, 1932.

LINGAT, R., *The Classical Law of India*, tr. by J.D.M. Derrett, Calif., 1973.

LOMMEL, A., *Masks: Their Meaning and Function*, L., 1972.

LOOMIS, R., 'Morgain la Fée and the Celtic Goddesses', *Speculum*, 20, 1945, p. 201.

LORENZEN, D.N., *The Kāpālikas and the Kālāmukhas*, Australian National Univ. Centre of Oriental Studies. Oriental monograph S., vol. XII.

LOSCH, H., *Die Yājñavalkyasmṛiti*, Leipzig, 1927.

LÜDERS, HEINRICH L., *Varuṇa*, Gottingen: I. 1951; II. 1959.

—— *Das Wurfelspiel im alten Indien*, Berlin, 1907.

MCCRINDLE, J.W. (tr.), *Ancient India as described by Megasthenes and Arrian*, 6 vols, Cal., 1877–1901.

—— *Ancient India as Described in Classical Literature*, L., 1901.

MACDONELL, A.A., *Vedic Mythology*, Strassburg, 1897. Repr. 1963.

—— 'The god Trita', *JRAS.*, 1893, pp. 419ff.

—— and KEITH, A.B., *Vedic Index of Names and Subjects*, 2 vols, repr. Delhi, 1958 and 1967.

—— *The Bṛhaddevatā of Śaunaka*, *HOS.*, vols V and VI, 1904. 2nd issue Delhi, 1965.

—— *A Vedic Reader for Students*, Oxf., 1917. Repr. 1970.

—— *A History of Sanskrit Literature*, 1889. Repr. 1970.

MCEWAN, C.W., *The Oriental Origin of Hellenistic Kingship*, Chicago, 1939.

Mahābhārata, Critical Edition, ed. by V.S. Sukthankar, F. Edgerton, S.K. De, *et al.* Vols I–XX and XXII. pt.1. Bhandarkar Oriental Research Institute. *The Mahābhārata* by P. Chandra Roy, 12 vols, Cal., n.d., (v. also under Holtzmann, A.; Rice, E.P.; van Buitenen, J.A.B.)

MAHADEVAN, T.M.P., *Gauḍapāda: A Study in Early Vedānta*, Madras, 1952.

MAITRA, SUSIL KUMAR, *Madhva Logic*, Cal., 1936.

MAITY, PRADYOT KUMAR, *Historical Studies in the Cult of the Goddess Manasā*, Cal., 1966.

MAJUMDAR, G.P., *Vanaspati. Plants and Plant-Life as in Indian Treatises and Traditions*, Cal., 1927.

MAJUMDAR, R.C., *Corporate Life in Ancient India*, monograph, Poona, 1922.

—— *Hindu Colonies in the Far East*, Cal., 1944.

—— *et al.*, *An Advanced History of India*, 1946. Repr. with corrections, L., 1953, 1956.

MALALASEKERA, G.P., *Dictionary of Pāli Proper Names*, 2 vols, L., 1937–8.

—— (ed.), *Encyclopaedia of Buddhism*, Ceylon, 1961– .

MALIK, S.C., *Indian Civilization*, Simla, 1968.

MANN, FELIX, *Acupuncture. Cure of Many Diseases*, L. Rev. repr. 1972.

MARCEL-DUBOIS, C., *Les Instruments de musique dans l'Inde ancienne*, Paris, 1941.

MARSHALL, JOHN, *et al.*, *Mohenjo-daro and the Indus Civilization*, 3 vols, L., 1931.

MASCARÓ, JUAN, *The Bhagavad Gītā*, Harmondsworth. Repr. 1970.

MASSON-OURSEL, PAUL, *et al.*, *Ancient India and Indian Civilization*, L., 1934. Repr. 1967.

MASTER, ALFRED, 'The Mysterious Paiśācī', *JRAS.*, pts 3 and 4, 1943, pp. 217ff.

MASUI, JACQUES (ed.), *Yoga, science de l'homme intégral*, Paris, 1953.

MATTHEWS, GORDON (tr.), *Śiva-Ñāna-Bōdham. A Manual of Śaiva Religious Doctrine*, Oxf., 1948.

MAURY, CURT, *Folk Origins of Indian Art*, N.Y., 1969.

MEHTA, J., *Sexual Life in Ancient India*, 1953.

MEYER, JOHN JACOB, *Trilogie altindischer Mächte und Feste der Vegetation*, Zürich and Leipzig, 1937, 3 vols in 1.

—— 'The Monotheistic Religion of Ancient India', *Asiatic Quarterly Review*, no. 28, 1909.

MINNS, ELLIS, M., *Scythians and Greeks*, 2 vols, repr. 1965, N.Y.

MISHRA, K.C., *The Cult of Jagannātha*, Cal., 1971.

MISHRA, R.S., *The Textbook of Yoga Psychology*, L., 1972.

MITRA, RAJENDRALALA (tr.), *The Yoga Aphorisms of Patañjali*, Cal., 1883.

MITRA, SARAT CHANDRA, 'Worship of the Pipal Tree in North Bihar', *Journal of the Bihar and Orissa Society*, VI, 1920.

—— 'On a Recent Instance of the Khāsī Custom of Offering Human Sacrifice to the Snake Deity', *Journal of the Anthropological Society*, Bombay, XIII, 1924–8, pp. 192ff.

MITRA, UMESHA, 'Physical Theory of Sound and its Origin in Indian Thought', *Allahabad Univ. Studies*, II, 1926.

MODE, H., *Indische Frühkulturen*, Basel, 1944.

—— *The Harappā Culture and the West*, Cal., 1961.

MONIER-WILLIAMS, MONIER, *Brahmanism and Hinduism*, L., 1891.

—— *Indian Wisdom*, L., 1875. Repr. 1963.

—— *A Sanskrit-English Dictionary*, rev. edn., Oxf., 1899.

MOOKERJI, N.B., *A History of Indian Shipping and Maritime Activity*, L., 1932.

MOOKERJI, R. KAVIRAJ, *Rasa-jala-nidhi: or Ocean of Indian Chemistry and Alchemy*, 5 vols, 1926–38.
—— *Ancient Indian Education*, L., 1947.
MOOR, EDWARD, *The Hindu Pantheon*, L., 1810.
MORGENSTIERNE, G., *Indo-Iranian Frontier Languages*, Oslo, 1929–56.
MOTWANI, KEWAL, *Manu Dharma Śāstra: A Sociological and Historical Study*, Madras, 1958.
MUIR, JOHN, *Original Sanskrit Texts on the Origin and History of the People of India; Their Religion and Institutions*, 5 vols, 1858–72. Repr. of 3rd enlarged edn., 1967.
MUKERJEE, RADHAKAMAL, *The Culture and Art of India*, L., 1959.
MUKHARJI, N.S., *A Study of Śaṅkara*, Cal., 1942.
MUKHOPADHYAYA, G.N., *History of Indian Medicine*, 3 vols, Cal., 1936.
MÜLLER, R.F.G., *Grundsätze altindischer Medizin*, Copenhagen, 1951.
MURRAY, H.A. (ed.), *Myth and Mythmaking*, N.Y., 1960.
MURRAY, H.J.R., *A History of Chess*, Oxf., 1913.
MURTI, T.R.V., *The Central Philosophy of Buddhism. A Study of the Mādhyamika System*, L., 1955. Repr. 1960.
MUS, PAUL, *Barabudur*, 2 vols, Hanoi, 1935ff.
MUTHU, D.C., *The Antiquity of Hindu Medicine*, N.Y., 1931.
MYLONAS, GEORGE E., *Eleusis and the Eleusinian Mysteries*, Princeton, 1961.
MYSORE, Mahārāja of, *Dattātreya. The Way and the Goal*, L., 1957.
NAKAMURA, SUSUMU W., 'Pradakshiṇa, a Buddhist form of obeisance', pp. 345ff., in *Semitic and Oriental Studies*. (v. Fischel, Walter J.)
NANDIMATH, S.C., *Handbook of Vīraśaivism*, Dharwar, 1942.
——*et al.*, *Śūnyasampādane*, 3 vols, ed. with intro., text, tr., notes, etc. Karnatak Univ., Dharwar: vol. I, 1965; II, 1968; III, 1969.
NARAHARI, H.G., *Ātman in Pre-Upaniṣadic Vedic Literature*, Adyar, 1944.
NATARAJA GURU, *The Bhagavad Gītā*, Bombay, 1961.
NEEDHAM, JOSEPH, *Science and Civilization in China*, 4 vols, Camb., 1954–62.
NEOGI, P., *Iron in Ancient India*, Cal., 1914.
NEUGEBAUER, O., *The Exact Sciences in Antiquity*, Rhode Island, 1957.
NEUMANN, E., *The Great Mother*, N.Y., 1955.
NEWLAND, C.C., *Myself and I*, N.Y., 1963.
NILSSON, M.P., *Primitive Time-Reckoning*, Lund, 1920.
—— *A History of Greek Religion*, Oxf., 1925, tr. from Swedish by F.J. Fielden.
OBERMAN, J., *Ugaritic Mythology*, Yale, 1948.
O'FLAHERTY, W.D., 'The Submarine Mare in the Mythology of Śiva', *JRAS.*, no. 1, 1971.
—— *Asceticism and Eroticism in the Mythology of Śiva*, L., 1973.
OLIVER, R.T., *Communication and Culture in Ancient India and China*, N.Y., 1972.
OPPENHEIM, A.L., 'The Sea-faring Merchants of Ur', *JAOS.*, 74, 1954, pp. 6ff.
OPPERT, GUSTAV, *On the Original Inhabitants of Bhārata-varṣa or India*, L., 1893.
PAL, RADHABINOD, *The History of Hindu Law in the Vedic Age and in Post-Vedic Times down to the Institutes of Manu*, Cal., 1958.
PALMER, R.B., *Dionysus, Myth and Cult*, Indiana, 1965.
PANDEY, K.C., *Indian Aesthetics*, Benaras, 1955.
PANDEY, L. PRASAD, 'The Worship of Revanta in Ancient India', *Vishveshvaranand Indological Journal*, vol. VII, pts. i-ii, 1969, pp. 134ff.
PANDEY, RAJ BALI, *Vikramāditya of Ujjayinī*, Benaras, 1951.
PANDIT, M.P., *Aditi and Other Deities in the Veda*, Madras, 1958.
PANIKKAR, K.M., *Origin and Evolution of Kingship in India*, Baroda, 1938.
PANT, G.N., *Studies in Indian Weapons and Warfare*, New Delhi, 1970.
PARGITER, F. EDEN, *Ancient Indian Historical Traditions*, Oxf., 1922.
—— (tr.), *Mārkaṇḍeya Purāṇa*, Asiatic Society of Bengal, 1904. Repr. Delhi, 1969.
PARRINDER, GEOFFREY, *Avatar and Incarnation* (Wilde Lectures, Oxford), L., 1970.
PATAI, R., *Man and Temple*, L., 1947.
PATHAK, V.S., *History of Śaiva Cults in Northern India*, Varanasi, 1960.
PAYNE, E.A., *The Śāktas: An Introductory Comparative Study*, Cal., 1933.
PENZER, NORMAN MOSLEY (ed.), *Soma-deva's Kathā-sarit-sāgara, or Ocean of Streams of Story*, tr. by C.H. Tawney, 10 vols, L., 1924–8. Repr. 1968, 10 vols in 2, Delhi.
PETTAZZONI, R., *The All-Knowing God*, tr. by H.J. Rose, L., 1956.
PIGGOTT, STUART, *Prehistoric India*, Harmondsworth, 1950. Repr. L., 1962.
—— *Some Ancient Cities of India*, Cal., 1945.
—— (ed.), *The Dawn of Civilization*, L., 1961.
PILLAI, G.S., *Tree Worship and Ophiolatry*, Trichinopoly, 1948.
PISCHEL, RICHARD, and GELDNER, K.F., *Vedische Studien*, 3 vols, 1889–1901.
PODUVAL, R. VASUDEVA, *Kathākala and Diagram of Hand Poses*, Trivandrum, 1930.
POKORNY, JULIUS, *Indogermanisches etymologisches Wörterbuch*, Bern, 1959.
PONNIAH, V., *The Śaiva Siddhānta Theory of Knowledge*, Annamalai Univ., 1952.
POTDAR, K.R., *Sacrifice in the Ṛgveda*, Bombay, 1953.
POTT, P.H., 'Four demonic Gaṇeśas from East Java', in *The Wonder of Man's Ingenuity*, Leiden, 1962, pp. 123ff.
POTTER, KARL H., *Bibliography of Indian Philosophies*, American Institute of Indian Studies, vol. I, N.Y., 1970.
—— *Presuppositions of India's Philosophies*, Englewood Cliffs N.Y., 1963. Repr. 1972.
PRASAD, JVALA, 'The date of the Yoga-Sūtras', *JRAS.*, 1930, pp. 365ff.
PRITCHARD, JAMES B. (ed.), *Ancient Near Eastern Texts, Relating to the Old Testament*, 2nd edn., rev. and enlarged,

Princeton, 1955.
—— *The Ancient Near East in Pictures Relating to the Old Testament*, Princeton, 1954.

PRZYLUSKI, JEAN, 'The Great Goddess in India and Iran', *IHQ.*, 1934.

PURCE, JILL, *The Mystic Spiral*, L., 1974.

PUSALKER, A.D., 'Śiśnadevaḥ in Ṛgveda and Phallus Worship in Indus Valley', *Sarupa-Bharati*, Hoshiarpur, 1954.

RADFORD, E. and M.A., *Encyclopaedia of Superstitions*, ed. and rev. by Christina Hole, 1961. Repr., 1969.

RADHAKRISHNAN, SARVEPALLI, *Indian Philosophy*, L., 1923; rev., 1929; rev., 1931, 2 vols.
—— (ed. with Charles A. Moore), *A Sourcebook in Indian Philosophy*, Princeton, 1957.
—— (tr.), *The Bhagavadgītā*, N.Y., 1948.
—— (ed.), *History of Philosophy: Eastern and Western*, 2 vols, L., 1952–3.
—— *The Principal Upaniṣads*, L., 1953.
—— (tr. with notes), *The Brahma Sūtra*, L., 1960.

RAGHAVAN, V., *Yantras, or Mechanical Contrivances in Ancient India*, Bangalore, 1952.

RAGHAVENDRACHAR, H.N., *Dvaita Philosophy and Its Place in the Vedānta*, Mysore Univ., 1941.

RAHURKAR, V.G., *The Seers of the Ṛgveda*, Univ. of Poona, 1964.

RAIKES, R.L., and DYSON, R.H., Jr., 'The prehistoric climate of Baluchistan and the Indus Valley', *American Anthropologist*, vol. 63, no. 2, pt. 1, April 1961, pp. 265ff.

RAJU, P.T., *Idealistic Thought of India*, L., 1953.

Rāmāyaṇa This work exists in three recensions: Tr. by R.T.H. Griffith, Benaras, 1895; M.N. Dutt, 1892–3; A. Roussel, Paris, 1903–9. (v. next entry.)

Rāmāyaṇa of Vālmīki, tr. by Hari Prasad Shastri, 3 vols, L., 1962; 2nd edn. rev. There is also a critical edn. of the *Rāmāyaṇa*, ed. by G.H. Bhatt, *et al.*, 6 vols, Baroda, 1960ff.

RANADE, R.D., *Constructive Survey of the Upanishadic Philosophy*, Poona, 1926.
—— *Mysticism in Mahārāshtra*, Poona, 1933.

RANDLE, HERBERT NIEL, *Indian Logic in the Early Schools*, Oxf., 1930.

RANGACARYA, M.R.B. (tr.), *The Sarva-siddhānta-saṅgraha of Śaṅkarācārya*, Madras Gov. Press, 1909.

RAO, T.A. GOPINATHA, *Elements of Hindu Iconography*, 4 vols, Madras, 1914–16. Repr. 1968.

RAPSON, E.J., *et al.*, *Ancient India*, The Cambridge History of India, 6 vols, 1914. Repr. 1957–64.

RAWSON, JOSEPH NADIN, *The Kaṭha Upaniṣad*, Oxf., 1934.

RAY, P., *History of Chemistry in Ancient and Medieval India*, Indian Chemical Society, Cal. 1956.

RAY, S., *Music of Eastern India*, Cal., 1973.

RAYCHAUDHURI, H.C., *Materials for the Study of the Early History of the Vaishnava Sect*. Cal., 1920.
—— *Political History of Ancient India*, Cal., 1923. Repr. 1973.

REINER, ERICA, *Šurpu. A Collection of Sumerian and Akkadian Incantations*, Osnabrück, 1970.

RELE, V.G., *The Mysterious Kuṇḍalinī*, Bombay, 1927.

RENOU, LOUIS, *Vocabulaire du ritual védique*, Paris, 1954.
—— and FILLIOZAT, J., *L'Inde classique*, 2 vols, Paris, 1947, 1953.
—— *Religions of Ancient India*, L., 1953. Repr. India, 1972.
—— and BENVENISTE, E., *Vṛtra et Verethragna*, Paris, 1935.
—— *Vedic India*, Cal., 1957.
—— *Études védiques et Pāṇinéennes* (1 to 16 vols published at the time of the author's death), 1955–67.
—— *The Destiny of the Veda in India*, Delhi, 1965.
—— *The Civilization of Ancient India*, tr. by Philip Spratt, 2nd edn., Cal., 1959.

REYMOND, E.A.E., *The Mythological Origin of the Egyptian Temple*, Manchester, 1969.

RIDGEWAY, WILLIAM, *The Origin and Influence of the Thoroughbred Horse*, Camb., 1905.

RIEPE, D., *The Naturalistic Tradition in Indian Thought*, Seattle, 1961.

RISCH, HUBERT, *Le Haṭha-Yoga*, Faculté de Médecine, Paris, 1951.

RISLEY, HERBERT H., *The People of India*, 2nd edn., ed. by W. Crooke, Delhi, 1969.

RODHE, S., *Deliver us from Evil: Studies on the Vedic Ideas of Salvation*, Lund, 1946.

RÓHEIM, GÉZA, *Animism, Magic and the Divine King*, L., 1930.

ROMAIOS, C.A., *Cultes populaires de la Thrace*, Athens, 1945.

ROWLAND, BENJAMIN, *The Art and Architecture of India*, Harmondsworth, 1953.

SACHAU, EDWARD C. (ed.), *Alberuni's India*, 2 vols, L., 1910. Repr. 2 vols in 1, 1964.

Sacred Books of the East Series, first published by the Clarendon Press, Oxf. Repr. Motilal Banarsidass, Delhi.
vols 1, 15: F. Max Müller, *The Upaniṣads*, 2 vols.
vols 2, 14: G. Bühler, *The Sacred Laws of the Āryas*, 2 vols.
vols 4, 23, 31: James Darmesteter and L.H. Mills, *The Zend-Avesta*, 3 vols.
vol. 7: Julius Jolly, *The Institutes of Viṣṇu*.
vol. 8: K.T. Telang, *The Bhagavadgītā*.
vols 12, 26, 41, 43, 44: Julius Eggeling, *The Śatapatha Brāhmaṇa*, 5 vols.
vols 22, 45: Hermann Jacobi, *Jaina Sūtras*, 2 vols.
vol. 25: G. Bühler, *The Laws of Manu*.
vols 29, 30: H. Oldenberg and F. Max Müller, *The Grihya-Sūtras*, 2 vols.
vols 32, 46: F. Max Müller and H. Oldenberg, *Vedic Hymns*, 2 vols.
vol. 33: Julius Jolly, *The Minor Law-Books*.
vols 34, 38: G. Thibaut, *The Vedānta-Sūtras*, 2 vols.
vol. 42: M. Bloomfield, *Hymns of the Atharvaveda*.
vol. 48: G. Thibaut, *The Vedānta-Sūtras* with *Rāmānuja's Śrībhāṣya*.
vol. 50: Index compiled by M. Winternitz.

Sacred Books of the Hindus, tr. into English by various scholars vols 1–31, and extra vols, Allahabad, 1909–26. Repr. in 46 vols, 1974.

SAMADDAR, J.N., *Economic Condition of Ancient India*, Cal., 1922.

SAMBAMOORTHY, P., *History of Indian Music*, Madras, 1960.

SANDAL, PANDIT MOHAN LAL (tr.), *The Mīmāṁsā Sūtras of Jaimini*, *SBH*., XXVII, 1923–5 and XXVIII, 1925.

SANKALIA, H.D., 'New light on the Indo-Iranian or Western Asiatic Relations between 1700 B.C.–1200 B.C.', *Artibus Asiae*, 26, 1963, pp. 312ff.

SARKAR, A., 'Gaṇeśa—the god of the people', *Indian Museum Bull.*, vol. IV, 1, 1969, pp. 84–7.

SARKAR, BENOY KUMAR, *Creative India*, Lahore, 1937.

—— *The Sukranīti*, *SBH*., XIII, 1914.

SARKAR, KISARILALA, *The Mīmāṁsā Rules of Interpretation: as Applied to Hindu Law*, Cal., 1909.

SARMA, K., *A History of the Kerala School of Hindu Astronomy*, India, 1972.

SARMA, M.R.K., *Temples of Telingana*, Hyderabad, 1972.

SARMA, NAGARAJA, *The Reign of Realism in Indian Philosophy. Exposition of Ten Works by Madhva*, Madras, 1937.

SARUP, LAKSHMAN (tr.), *The Nighaṇṭu and the Nirukta*, repr. Delhi, 1967.

SASTRI, H.K., *South Indian Images of Gods and Goddesses*, Madras, 1916.

SASTRI, MADHUSUDANA KAUL (gen. ed.), *The Tantraloka*. 12 vols, Government of Kashmir, 1921ff.

SASTRI, NATESA, *Folklore of Southern India*, 3 pts, Bombay, 1884–8.

SAUNDERS, E. DALE, *Mudrā. A Study of Symbolic Gestures in Japanese Buddhist Sculpture*, L., 1960.

SCHARFE, H., *Pāṇini's Metalanguage*, American Philosophical Society, vol. 89, Philadelphia, 1971.

SCHARPÉ, A., *Kālidāsa-Lexicon*, vol. I. *Basic Text of the Works*; pt. 1. *Abhijñānaśakuntala*, 1954. 2. *Mālavikāgnimitra and Vikramorvaśī*, 1956. 3. *Kumārasambhava, Meghadūta, Ritusamhara and Incerta*, 1958. 4. *Raghuvaṁśa*, 1964.

SCHAYER, S., *Contributions to the Problem of Time in Indian Philosophy*, Cracow, 1938.

SCHOFF, W.H. (tr.), *The Periplus of the Erythraean Sea*, L., 1912.

—— '*The Eastern Iron Trade of the Roman Empire*', *JAOS*., 35, pp. 224ff.

SCHOMERUS, H.W., *Der Çaiva Siddhānta, eine Mystik Indiens nach den tamulischen Quellen bearbeitet und dargestellt*, Leipzig, 1912.

SCHRADER, F. OTTO, *Introduction to the Pañcharātra and the Ahirbudhnya Saṁhitā*, Adyar, 1916, 2 vols.

—— *The Kashmir Recension of the Bhagavadgītā*, Stuttgart, 1930.

SCHROEDER, L. VON, *Mysterium und Mimus im Rigveda*, Leipzig, 1908. Repr. 1972.

—— *Arische Religion*, 2 vols, 1914–16. Repr. 1971.

SCHULTES, RICHARD EVANS, 'The plant kingdom and hallucinogens', pt. 1, *Bulletin on Narcotics*, vol. XXI, no. 3, July–September 1969; vol. XXII, no. 1, October 1969 and January 1970 respectively, United Nations, N.Y.

SEAL, B.N., *The Positive Sciences of the Ancient Hindus*, Delhi, 1958.

SEBEOK, T.A. (ed.), *Myth. A Symposium*, Philadelphia, 1955.

SEN, D.C., *Vaishnava Literature of Mediaeval Bengal*, Cal., 1913.

SEN, M.L. (tr.), *Rāmāyaṇa of Vālmiki*, 3 vols. 3rd edn., L., 1964. (v. also under *Rāmāyaṇa*.)

SENART, E., *Caste in India*, L., 1930.

SHAFER, R., *Ethnography of Ancient India*, Wiesbaden, 1954.

SHAH, SAYED IDRIES, *Oriental Magic*, L., 1968.

SHARMA, B., *Harsa and His Times*, Varanasi, 1970.

SHARMA, CHANDRADHAR, *A Critical Survey of Indian Philosophy*, L., 1960.

SHARMA, D.S., *Dialectic in Buddhism and Vedānta*, Benaras, 1952.

SHARMA, G.R., *The Excavations at Kauśāmbī (1957–59)*, Allahabad, 1960.

SHARMA, H.D., *The Sāṁkhya-Kārikā*, Poona, 1933. (Skt. text and E. tr., with the Commentary of Gauḍapādācārya).

SHARMA, J.P., *Republics in Ancient India, c. 1500 B.C.–500 B.C.*, Leiden, 1968.

SHARMA, P.V., *Indian Medicine in the Classical Age*, India, 1972.

SHASTRI, AJAYA MITRA, *India as Seen in the Bṛhatsaṁhitā*, Delhi, 1969.

SHASTRI, A.P.B., 'Iconism in India', *IHQ*., XII, 1936.

SHASTRI, DAKSHINARANJAN, *A Short History of Indian Materialism, Sensationalism and Hedonism*, Cal., 1970.

—— (tr.), *Chārvāka-shasti*, Cal., n.d.

—— *Origin and Development of the Rituals of Ancestor Worship in India*, Cal., 1963.

SHASTRI, HARI PRASAD (tr.), *The Rāmāyaṇa of Vālmīki*, 3 vols, 1953. Rev. edn. L., 1962. (v. also under *Rāmāyaṇa*.)

SHASTRI, M.N. DUTT (tr.), *Agni Purāṇam*, 2 vols, 2nd edn., India, 1967.

SHASTRI, PRABHU DUTT, *The Doctrine of Māyā in the Philosophy of the Vedānta*, Luzac, 1911.

SHEKHAR, I., *Sanskrit Drama: Its Origin and Decline*, *ORT*., 1960.

SHENDE, N.J., *The Religion and Philosophy of the Atharvaveda*, Poona, 1952.

—— 'Aṅgiras in the Vedic Literature', *ABORI*., XXXI.

SHIVAPADASUNDARAM, S., *The Shaiva School of Hinduism*, Madras, 1934.

SHRIVASTAVA, S.N.L., *Śaṁkara and Bradley. A Comparative and Critical Study*, Delhı, 1968.

SHUKLA, D.N., *Ancient Hindu Canons. Vāstuśāstra*, vol. I. *Hindu Science of Architecture*, 1960; vol. II. *Hindu Canons of Iconography and Painting*, 1960 (Bhāratiya Vāstu-Śāstra Series, VIII).

SIAVE, SUZANNE, *Les Noms Védiques de Viṣṇu dans l'Anuvyākhyāna de Madhva*, Pondicherrv, 1959.

SIEKE, E., *Pūṣan*, Leipzig, 1914.

SIGERIST, H.E., *A History of Medicine*, 2 vols, N.Y., 1951, 1961. The second vol. was never completed, but was published in skeletal form. It includes some complete chs. on the Indus Valley civilization, Vedic medicine, and early medical schools.

SINGER, MILTON (ed.), *Kṛishṇa, Myths, Rites and Attitudes*, Honolulu, 1966.

SINGH, MOHAN, *Gorakhnāth and Medieval Hindu Mysticism*, Lahore, 1937.

SINGH, M.R., *Geographical Date in the Early Purāṇas—A Critical Study*, Cal., 1972.

SINGH, P., *Burial Practices in Ancient India*, Indian Civilization S., XVII, 1970.

SINGH, SARVA DAMAN, *Ancient Indian Warfare with Special References to the Vedic Period*, Leiden, 1965.

—— 'The Elephant and the Āryans', *JRAS.*, 1963, pts. 1 and 2, pp. 1ff.

SINGHAL, D.P., *India and World Civilization*, 2 vols, L., 1972.

SINHA, JADUNATH, *Indian Realism*, L., 1938.

—— *Introduction to Indian Philosophy*, Agra, 1949.

SIRCAR, D.C., *Cosmography and Geography in Early Indian Literature*, Cal., 1967.

—— *Ancient Malwa and the Vikramāditya Tradition*, Delhi, 1969.

—— *The Śakti Cult and Tārā*, Cal., 1967.

—— *Indian Epigraphical Glossary*, Delhi, 1966.

—— (ed.), *Select Inscriptions bearing on Indian History and Civilization*, vol I, from 6th cent. B.C. to 6th cent. A.D., 2nd edn., enlarged Cal., 1965.

SIVARAMAMURTI, C., *Royal Conquests and Cultural Migrations in South India and the Deccan*, Cal., 1955.

—— *A Guide to the Archaeological Gallery of the Indian Museum*, Cal., 1954.

SMITH, V.A., *History of Fine Art in India and Ceylon*, Oxf., 1911. 3rd edn. rev. and enlarged by Karl Khandalava, Bombay, n.d.

—— *The Oxford History of India*, 3rd edn., ed. by Percival Spear. Pt. 1. rev. by Sir Mortimer Wheeler and A.L. Basham. Pt. 2 rev. by J.B. Harrison. Pt. 3 rewritten by P. Spear. Oxf., 1958.

SNELLGROVE, D.L., 'The Notion of Divine Kingship in Tantric Buddhism', in *The Sacral Kingship* (Contributions to the central theme of the VIIIth International Congress, Rome (1955)), 1959.

SÖRENSON, S., *An Index to the Names in the Mahābhārata*, L., 1904. Repr. 1963.

SPELLMAN, J.W., *Political Theory of Ancient India. A Study of Kingship from earliest Times to c.A.D. 300*, Oxf., 1964.

SPINK, W.M., *Krishṇamaṇḍala: A Devotional Theme in Indian Art*, Univ. of Michigan, 1971.

SPITZER, MORITZ, *Begriffsuntersuchungen zum Nyāya-bhāṣya*, Kiel, 1926.

SRINIVAS, M.N., *Religion and Society among the Coorgs of South India*, L., 1952. Repr. 1965.

SRINIVASACHARI, P.N., *The Philosophy of Viśiṣṭādvaita*, Adyar, 1943.

—— *The Philosophy of Bhedābheda*, 2nd edn., rev. and enlarged, Adyar, 1950.

STARR, RICHARD F.S., *Indus Valley Painted Pottery*, Princeton, 1941.

STCHERBATSKY, TH., *Buddhist Logic*, Leningrad 1932. Repr., 2 vols, The Hague, 1958.

—— *The Central Conception of Buddhism and Meaning of the Word Dharma*, 2nd edn., Cal., 1956.

STEIN, M.A., 'On Some River Names in the Rigveda', *JRAS.*, 1917, pp. 91ff.

—— *On Alexander's Track to the Indus*, L., 1929.

STERNBACH, L., 'Juridical Studies in Ancient Indian Law', *Poona Or.*, IX, 1944; X, 1945. Published under same title, 2 vols, Delhi, 1965, 1967.

STEVENSON, W.B., 'Analysis of the Gaṇeśa-Purāṇa', *JRAS.*, vol. VIII, 1845.

STONE, GEORGE CAMERON, *A Glossary of the Construction, Decoration and Use of Arms and Armor in all Countries and in all Times*, N.Y., 1961.

STRAUSS, O., *Bṛhaspati im Veda*, Leipzig, 1905.

—— *Indische Philosophie*, Munich, 1925.

STRZYGOWSKI, J., *et al.*, *The Influence of Indian Art*, L., 1925.

SUBRAMANIAN, K.R., *Origin of Śaivism and Its History in the Tamil Land*, Madras, 1929.

SZASZ, THOMAS S., *The Myth of Mental Illness*, N.Y., 1961.

TARR, GARY, 'The Śiva Cave-Temple of Dhokeśvara', *Or. Art*, Winter 1969, pp. 269ff.

TATIA, NATHMAL, *Studies in Jaina Philosophy*, Benaras, 1951.

TATTON, RENÉ (ed.), *Ancient and Medieval Science. From Pre-History to A.D. 1450*, tr. by A.J. Pomerans, L., 1963.

TAWNEY, C.H. (tr.), *The Kathā Sarit Sāgara or Ocean of the Streams of Story*, 10 vols, 1924–6. Repr. 10 vols in 2, Delhi, 1968.

THADANI, NANIKRAM VASANMAL, *The Mīmāṁsā: The Sect of the Sacred Doctrines of the Hindus*, Delhi, 1952.

THIBAUT, G., v. under *Sacred Books of the East.*

THIÈME, PAUL, 'The "Āryan" Gods of the Mitanni Treaties', *JAOS.*, 80, 1960, pp. 301ff.

—— *Mitra and Aryaman*, Yale, 1957.

THOMAS, KEITH, *Religion and the Decline of Magic. Studies in popular beliefs in 16th and 17th century England*, L., 1971.

THOMAS, P., *Epics, Myths and Legends of India*, Bombay, 1961.

THOMPSON, D'ARCY W., *Glossary of Greek Birds*, Oxf., 1895.

THOMPSON, EDWARD, *Suttee: A Historical and Philosophical Enquiry into the Hindu Rite of Widow-Burning*, L., 1928.

THORNDIKE, LYNN, *A History of Magic and Experimental Science*, 6 vols, N.Y., 1929–41.

THURSTON, E., *Castes and Tribes of Southern India*, 7 vols, Madras, 1909. Repr. 1965.

——*Omens and Superstitions of Southern India*, L., 1912.

TRAUTMANN, THOMAS R., *Kauṭilya and the Arthaśāstra*, Leiden, 1971.

TRENCH, C.C., *A History of Horsemanship*, L., 1970.

TREVELYAN, ERNEST J., *Hindu Family Law*, L., 1908.

TUCCI, GUISEPPE, *Tibetan Painted Scrolls*, Rome, 1949.

—— *Indo-Tibetica*, 4 vols, Rome, 1932–41.

—— *Theory and Practice of Maṇḍala* L., 1961. Repr. 1969.

TURNER, D.R., LADY, *A Comparative Dictionary of the Indo-Āryan Languages: Indexes*, Index vol., SOAS., 1969.

TURNER, SIR RALPH, *A Comparative Dictionary of the Indo-Āryan Languages*, SOAS., 1966.

—— *Studies in Honour of Sir Ralph Turner, including contributions by H.W. Bailey, A.L. Basham, T. Burrow, J. Gonda, L. Renou, et al.*, SOAS., 1957.

—— *The Position of Romani in Indo-Āryan*, Gypsy Lore Society, Monograph no. 4, Edinburgh, 1927.

—— and TURNER, D.R., *Comparative Dictionary of the Indo-Āryan Languages: Phonetic Analysis*, SOAS., 1971.
TURNER, V.W., *The Ritual Process. Structure and Anti-Structure*, L., 1969.
VADER, V.H., 'Twin Gods Aśvinau', *IHQ*., 1932.
VAIDYA, C.V., *History of Sanskrit Literature*, vol. I, *Vedic Period*, Poona, 1930.
—— *History of Medieval India*, 3 vols, L., 1921–6.
VAN BUITENEN, J.A.B., *The Maitrāyaniya Upaniṣad*, Critical essay with text, tr. (Disputationes Rheno-Trajectinae, 1962), Leiden.
—— *The Mahābhārata. Book I*, Univ. of Chicago, 1973.
—— 'Studies in Sāṁkhya', *JAOS*., LXXVI (1956), pp. 153ff., LXXVII (1957), pp. 15ff.; 88ff.
VAN GENNEP, ARNOLD, *The Rites of Passage*, tr. by M.B. Vizedom and G.L. Caffee, L., 1960.
VAN KOOIJ, K.R., *Worship of the Goddess according to the Kālikāpurāṇa*, pt. 1, tr. with intro. and notes of chs. 54–69, *ORT*., XIV, 1972.
VAN LOHUIZEN DE LEEUW, J.E., *The Scythian Period*, Leiden, 1949.
VARMA, SIDDHESHWAR, *Etymologies of Yāska*, Hoshiarpur, 1953.
VASU, R.B.S.C. (tr.), *Shiva Saṁhitā. The Yoga Śāstra*, Allahabad, 1913, *SBH*., no. 54.
VATS, MADHO SARUP, *et al.*, *Excavations at Harappā*, 2 vols, Delhi, 1940
VENKATARAMANAYYA, N., *Rudra-Śiva*, Madras, 1941.
VIDHYARAVASA, S.C. (tr.), *Śiva Saṁhitā*, Allahabad, 1923.
VIDYĀBHŪṢAṆA, SATIS C., *History of Indian Logic*, Cal., 1921.
VIEILLARD, C., *L'Urologie et les médecins urologistes dans la médecine ancienne*, Paris, 1903.
VIENNOT, ODETTE, *Le Culte de l'arbre dans l'Inde ancienne*, (Annales du Musée Guimet, LIX), Paris, 1954.
VOGEL, JEAN PHILIPPE, *Indian Serpent-Lore, or The Nāgas in Hindu Legend and Art*, L., 1926.
—— 'The Woman and Tree or Śālabhañjikā in Indian Literature and Art', *Acta Orientalia* (Leiden), VII, 1929, pp. 201ff.
—— *Catalogue of the Archaeological Museum at Mathura*, Allahabad, 1910.
—— 'Gaṅgā et Yamunā dans l'iconographie brahmanique', *Études Asiatiques*, 1925, pp. 87f.
—— *Indica Antiqua. A collection of Oriental studies presented to J.P. Vogel* (published under the auspices of the Kern Institute), Leiden, 1947.
—— *The Goose in Indian Religion and Art*, Brill, 1962.
VOLWAHSEN, ANDREAS, *Living Architecture: Indian*, L., 1969.
VYAS, S.N., *India in the Rāmāyaṇa Age*, Delhi, 1967.
WALDSCHMIDT, E., *Geschichte der indischen Alterthums*, (Bruckmans Weltgeschichte), 1950.
WALES, H.G. QUARICH, *Siamese State Ceremonies*, L., 1931.
WALKER, B., *Hindu World*, 2 vols, L., 1968.
WALL, O.A., *Sex and Sex Worship*, L., 1919.
WALLIS, H.F., *Cosmology of the Rigveda*, L., 1887.
WARD, DONALD, *The Divine Twins*, Los Angeles, 1968.
WARDER, A.K., *Indian Kavya Literature*, vol. 1, 1972.
WARRIER, A.G.K. (tr.), *Śākta Upanishads*, Adyar, 1967.
WASSON, R. GORDON, *Soma. Divine Mushroom of Immortality* (Ethno-Mycological Studies, I, 1968, limited edn.). Repr. L., 1971.
WATTERS, THOMAS, *On Yüan Chwang's Travels in India A.D. 629–645*, ed. by T.W. Rhys Davids and S.W. Bushell, 1904–5, 2 vols. Repr. 1962.
WATTS, ALAN W. (gen. ed.), *Patterns of Myth*, 3 vols, N.Y., 1963.
WAYMAN, ALEX, 'Notes on the Sanskrit Term Jñāna', *JAOS*., LXXV, 1955, pp. 253ff.
WEBER, ALBRECHT, *The History of Indian Literature*, tr. by J. Mann and Th. Zachariae, L., 1892.
WEBSTER, H., *Magic*, Stanford, 1948.
WEIR, SHELAGH (ed.), *The Gonds of Central India*, L., 1973.
WELLESZ, E., (ed.), *Ancient and Oriental Music*, L., 1957.
WERNER, E.T.C., *A Dictionary of Chinese Mythology*, N.Y., 1961.
WHEELER, SIR MORTIMER, *Early India and Pakistan to Ashoka*, L., 1959.
—— *The Indus Civilization*, 2nd edn., Camb., 1960.
—— 'Harappā, 1946: The Defences and Cemetery', *Ancient India*, no. 3, Delhi 1947, pp. 58ff.
—— *Civilizations of the Indus Valley and Beyond*, L., 1966.
WHITEHEAD, H., *Village Deities of South India*, Cal., 1921.
—— *Catalogue of the Coins in the Panjāb Museum, Lahore*, Oxf., 1914.
WHITNEY, WILLIAM DWIGHT (tr.), *The Atharvaveda*, Camb. (Mass.), 1905. Repr. Delhi, 1962.
—— and BURGESS E., (tr.), *Sūryasiddhānta*, *JAOS*., 1860. Repr., Cal., 1935.
—— *Sanskrit Grammar*, Camb. (Mass.), 1896; 9th issue, 1960.
—— *The Century Dictionary*, 8 vols, N.Y., 1891. Repr. L. and N.Y., 1899.
WICHMANN, HANS AND SIEGFRIED, *Chess: The Story of Chess-pieces from Antiquity to Modern Times*, L., 1964.
WIKANDER, STIG, 'Nakula and Sahadeva', *Orientatla Suecana*, 1957.
WILKINS, CHARLES (tr.), *Fables and Proverbs from the Sanskrit being the Hitopadeśa*, L., 1885.
WILKINS, W.J., *Hindu Mythology*, Cal., 1882; 2nd edn., 1900.
WILLIAMS, R., *Jaina Yoga*, Oxf., 1963.
WILSON, H.H. *Essays and Lectures on the Religions of the Hindus*, ed. by R. Rost, 2 vols, 1861–2.
—— (tr.), *Vishnu Purāṇa* (with notes), L., 1840. Repr. with introduction by R.C. Hazra, Cal., 1961–72.
WINTERNITZ, M., *Some Problems of Indian Literature*, Cal., 1925.
—— *A History of Indian Literature*, 1927, tr. by S. Ketkar, vol. I, pt. i, Cal., 1962. 2nd edn., vol. I, pt. ii, Cal., 1963. vol. III, pt. i, tr. by H. Kohn, Cal., 1959. vol. III, pt. ii, tr. S. Jha, Cal., 1967.
WIRZ, P., *Exorcism and the Art of Healing in Ceylon* (also includes a survey of the healing art in ancient India), 1954.
WOOD, ERNEST, *Great Systems of Yoga*, N.Y., 1954.
WOODROFFE, SIR JOHN (nom-de-plume ARTHUR AVALON) *The*

Principles of Tantra, 2 vols, 1914–16. Repr. Madras, 1952.
—— *The Serpent Power*, 3rd edn., Madras, 1931.
—— *Shakti and Shākta*, 1929. Repr. Madras, 1956, 1969.
—— *Tantrarāja-tantra—A Short Analysis*, Madras, 1952. Repr. 1964.
—— *Garland of Letters (Varṇamālā)*, Madras, 1955. Repr. 1969.
—— *Hymns to the Goddess*, 2nd edn., Madras, 1953.
—— *Introduction to Tantrashāstra—a Key to Tantric Literature*, 3rd edn., Madras, 1956.
—— *Tantra of the Great Liberation*, L., 1913.
—— *The Greatness of Śiva*, Madras, 1953.
—— *Mahā Māyā*, Madras, 1929. Repr. 1954.
—— (tr.), *Kāmakalā-vilāsa. Tantrik Texts*, X, L., 1922.
—— (ed. and tr.), *Mahānirvāṇa Tantra*, Madras, 1927.
WOODS, JAMES H. (tr.), *The Yoga-System of Patañjali. HOS.*, XVII, 1914; 3rd edn., Delhi, 1966.
WOONER, A.C., *Aśoka Text and Glossary*, Lahore, 1924.
WOSIEN, MARIA-GABRIELE, *Sacred Dance*, L., 1974.
WRIGHTMAN, *No Friend of Travellers, the Origin of the Thugs*, 1959.
YAMAUCHI, EDWIN M., *Mandaic Incantation Texts*, American Oriental Society, New Haven, 1967.
YAZDANI, G., *et al.*, *Ajaṇṭā*, 6 vols, Oxf., 1930–46.
—— *Excavations at Kondapur*, Hyderabad, 1942.
YOROI, K., *Gaṇeśagītā, A Study* (Disputationes Rheno-Trajectinae), 1968.
ZAEHNER, R.C., *Zurvan*, Oxf., 1955.
—— 'Utopia and Beyond: Some Indian Views', *Papers from the Eranos Yearbooks*, XXXII, L., 1963.
—— *Hinduism* (Oxf. Paperbacks, opus 12), 1966.
—— *The Bhagavad-Gītā*, Oxf., 1969; new edn., 1973.
ZANNAS, ELIKY, *Khajuraho*, Holland, 1960.
ZEUNER, F.E., *History of the Domestication of Animals*, L., 1963.
ZIDE, A.K. and ZVELEBIL, K., *The Soviet Decipherment of the Indus Valley Script*, tr. and critique (Janua Linguarum, Series Practica, 156), The Hague, 1972.
ZIMMER, HEINRICH, *Kunstform und Yoga im indischen Kultbild*, Berlin, 1926.
—— *Myths and Symbols in Indian Art and Civilization*, ed. by J. Campbell, N.Y., 1946. Repr. 1972.
—— *Philosophies of India*, ed. by J. Campbell, N.Y., 1951.
—— *The Art of Indian Asia*, completed and ed. by J. Campbell, 2 vols, N.Y., 1955.
—— *Maya der Indische Mythos*, Stuttgart, 1936.
—— 'On the Significance of the Indian Tantric Yoga', *Papers from the Eranos Yearbooks*, I, L., 1933.

English Subjects and their Sanskrit Equivalents

To assist the general reader a selected list of subjects in English and the Sanskrit terms relating to them is given below. Deities, demons, plants, mountains, etc. may be found in the main body of the work under their individual Sanskrit names.

Aboriginals	Asura (s); Dasyu (s), etc.
Action and consequences of	Karman
Altar	Vedi
Ambrosia	Amṛta
Amulet	Rakṣā; Maṇi
Ancestors, fore-fathers	Pitṛ(s)
Animals	
Antelope	Īhāmṛga
Boar	Varāha
Bull	Vṛṣa
of Śiva	Nandin
Cow	Go
mythical	Dhenu; Kāmadhenu; Surabhi
Crocodile, mythical	Makara I
Deer, golden	Hemamṛga
Dog	Śvan
bitch, of Indra	Saramā
Elephant	Gaja
mythical	Jalebha
Frog	Maṇḍūka
Gazelle	Hariṇa
Goat	Aja; Chāga
Hare	Śaśāṅka
Horse	Aśva; Haya
mythical	Paidva; Uccaiḥśravas; Kalkin
Lion	Siṁha
Mare	Vaḍabā
Monkey	Kapi; Dvivida I; Hanumat
Serpent	Sarpa; Nāga
mythical	Śeṣa; Vāsuki
Sheep	Avis
Tortoise	Kūrma I
Archery	Dhanurveda
Architecture	Mānasāra; Nāgara
Army	Senā I
tactics	Māyābala
Asceticism; religious fervour	Tapas
Ashes, sacred	Bhasman; Vibhūti II
Asterisms, Lunar	Nakṣatra (s)
Astronomical Diagram	Ravicakra
Astronomy	Jyotiṣa
Auspicious objects, the Eight	Aṣṭamangala
Being, self-existent	Brahman (neuter)
Bell	Ghaṇṭā
Belt, girdle	Mekhalā I
Birds	
Blue Jay	Cāṣa
Cock	Kukkuṭa I
Crane	Bagalā
Dove or pigeon	Kapota
Eagle or hawk	Śyena; Suparṇa
Goose	Haṁsa
Heron	Vaka
Owl	Ulūka
Parrot	Śuka
Partridge	Kapiñjala
Peacock	Mayūra
Yellow Wagtail	Hāridrava
Birds, divinatory	Rikta; Śakunajñāna; Gopīta
Birds, mythical	Garuḍa; Garutmat
Butter, clarified	Ghṛta
Caste and Social class	Varṇa; Gotra; Jati
Cattle and other domesticated animals	Paśu I
Cauldron	Gharma
Chants	Sāman (s)
Chariot, magical	Puṣpaka
of victory	Jaitraratha
Charioteer	Sūta
Circumambulation	Pradakṣiṇā
Conch-shell	Śaṅkha I
Consecration	Abhiṣeka
Cowherd	Gopa (m.); Gopī (f.)
Craftsmen, Agriculturists, etc.	Vaiśya
Creation Theories	Hiraṇyagarbha; Prajāpati
Cremation Ground	Śmaśāna
Dance, Art of	Nāṭya Veda
cosmic	Tāṇḍava
Darkness; inertia	Tamas
Dawn	Uṣas
Day, lunar	Tithi
Death	Mṛtyu; Māra
Demon Mask	Kīrtimukha
Demonology	Bhūtavidyā
Demons	Bhūta (s); Daitya (s); Dānava (s)
Destructive Powers	Nirṛti (s)
Devotion, to a deity	Bhakti; Iṣṭadevatā
Dice	Akṣa; Kali I
Disease	Yakṣma; Āyurveda; Śuśruta Saṁhitā

English and Sanskrit Equivalents

Drugs, potions, etc.	Vidyā
sacrificial and hallucinogenic	Soma
Drum, of Śiva	Ḍamaru
curative	Dundubhi II
Duty, civil, religious, etc.	Dharma
Earth, the	Bhūmi; Pṛthivī
Energy, divine or cosmic	Śacī (Vedic)
	Śakti (Skt)
Epistemology	Darśana (s)
Evil	Manas-pāpman
Existence, individuated essence of	Ātman
Eye	Cakṣu
evil	Netraviṣa
initiation by	Nayana-dīkṣā
Faith	Śraddhā
Family	Kula; Varṇa
Fear	Bhaya
Female pudenda	Yoni
Festivals, Ceremonies, Sacrifices, etc.	Aśvamedha; Dīpāvalī; Holākā; Puruṣamedha; Rājasūya; Sarvamedha; Sautrāmaṇī; Vājapeya
Fever	Jvara
Fire, and god of	Agni
Fire-drill	Araṇi
Firmament	Antarīkṣa
Flesh	Māṁsa
Food	Anna
Form, shape	Rūpa; Mūrti
Fuel, sacred	Edhas
Funerary Rites	Ekoddiṣṭa
Furrow, personified	Sītā
Garland	Mālā
of victory	Vaijantī-mālā
Gems, the nine	Navaratna
Gesture, ritual	Mudrā.
Ghosts, spirits of the dead	Preta; Vetāla
Gifts to priests	Dakṣiṇā
Goddesses	Devī
Gods	Deva
Grace, divine	Prasāda
Grass	Kuśa I
Greeks	Yavana (s)
Hair	Jaṭā
Hand	Hasta I
Herald, etc.	Sūta
Hero	Vīra
Honey	Madhu
Honorific	Śrī III
Horse-sacrifice	Aśvamedha
House goddess	Gṛhadevī
Hysteria	Grahāpasmāra
Ignorance	Avidyā
Illusion	Māyā
Incantation	Mantra
Initiation	Dīkṣā; Upanayana
Insects	
Ant	Upajihvikā
Bee	Bhṛṅga
Cochineal insect	Indragopa
Intoxication	Mada
Island	Dvīpa
King	Rājan
Knowledge	Jñāna; Vidyā
Ladle, sacrificial	Dhruvā; Juhū I; Upabhṛt
Law	Dharma
Law-books	Dharmaśāstra (s)
Leogryph	Śārdulā
Life, breath of	Prāṇa
endowing with	Prāṇapratiṣṭhā
Light	Arcis
Lightning	Vidyut
Lord, 'God'	Īśana; Īśvara
Luck	Lakṣmī
bad	Pāpī lakṣmī
Lucky signs	Kambu
Lunar Dynasty	Candravaṁśa
Lustration of arms	Nīrājana
Madness	Bhūtonmāda
Magic, sorcery, spells	Vidyā; Hiṁsākarman; Ṣaṭkarman; Śānti II; Astramantra; Om; Mantra
Man	Manu; Nara
Marks or signs	Lakṣaṇa; Śrīvatsa; Tilaka; Liṅga
Marriage	Vivāha; Kambala
Matter, primary	v. Sāṁkhya
Medical science	Āyurveda
Meditation	Samādhi; Yoga; Dhāraṇā
Mendicant, religious	Sannyāsin
Menial class	Śūdra
Metre	Chandas
Milk	Dadhi
Milky Way, the	Māndakinī
Mind	Manas
Minstrel	Cāraṇa
Monarch, Universal	Cakravartin
Monism	Vedānta; Brahman (neuter)
Month	Māsa; Jyotiṣa
Moon	Candra; Soma II
Mortar or Bowl	Ulūkhala II
Mountains, mythical	Lokāloka; Mandara I; Cakravāla; Meru I

Mothers	Mātṛ (s)
Mud	Kardama
Music	Rāga.
Musical instruments	
Drum	Anaka; Ḍamaru
Flute	Tūṇava
Lute	Vīṇā
Mystical diagram	Yantra
Name	Nāman
Natural forces personified	Deva (s); Asura (s)
Navel	Nābha
Netherworld	Pātāla I
Night	Rātrī
Noose	Pāśa
Nymphs, celestial	Apsarasas
Oath (sworn promise)	Pāda II
Oblation, sacrificial	Odana; Havis
Ocean, churning of	Samudramathana
Offerings	Bali I; Viṣṭarin; Piṇḍa
Omens, interpretation of	Nimittajñāna; Śivāvidyā
Outcaste	Caṇḍāla
Pair, couple	Mithuna
Parasol, ceremonial	Chattra
Path of the gods	Devayāna
Phallus	Liṅga
Philosophy, schools of	Darśana (s)
Pilgrimage, places of	Tīrtha I
Pillars, memorial, sacrificial	Sthūna; Yūpa; Skambha
Plants, Shrubs, Trees, selection of	Apāmārga; Aśoka I; Aśvattha; Avakā; Bhaṅgā; Bilva; Durva, Guggulu; Haridrā; Khadira; Nimba; Nyagrodha; Padma I; Śāl; Śamī; Soma I; Tulasī; Udumbara
mythical	Kalpadruma; Pañcavṛkṣa; Pārijāta
Ploughing	Kṛṣi
Poison	Viṣa; Viṣavidyā
Pole Star	Dhruva
Power, gained by austerity	Tapas
Prayer	Japa
Pressing-stones	Adri or gravan; Soma
Pride	Darpa
Priestly class	Brāhmaṇa I
Prosperity	Śrī I and II
Rainbow	Indrāyudha
Rain-spell	Kārīrīṣṭi
Release, liberation	Mokṣa
Remnant or residue of the sacrifice	Ucchiṣṭa

Revivification	Saṁjīvinīvidyā
Riddle	Brahmodya
Rites	
for averting evil	Mahāśānti
expiatory	Śānti II
to ensure birth of a male child	Puṁsavana
for offspring	Sarpaśānti
for rain	Kārīrīṣṭi
Funerary	Śrāddha
Ritual exclamations	Śrauṣat; Svāhā; Vaṣaṭ
Rivers	Gaṅgā; Indus, v. under Sindhu; Nadī I; Narmadā; Sarasvatī; Yamunā
mythical	Vaitaraṇī
Royal consecration	Rājasūya
Ruling class	Rājanya; Kṣatra
Sacrifice	Yajña
Sacrificer	Yajamāna
Sage or seer	Ṛṣi
Sap	Rasa
Seasons, relating to	Ṛtavyā; Ṛtu; Jyotiṣa
Shrine	Caitya; Tīrtha I
Sieve	Śūrpa
Sky	Dyaus
Sleep	Nidrā; Svapna
Snake Cult	Nāga III
Solar Dynasty	Sūryavaṁśa
Son	Putra
Sound	Nada; Śabda
Space	Ākāśa
Speech	Vac
Spirits or Ghosts	Bhūta (s)
Sprites, vegetal spirits	Yakṣa (s); Gandharva (s)
Staff	Daṇḍa I and II
Strength, potency	Vāja I
Student, religious	Brahmacārin
Sun	Savitṛ; Sūrya
Supranormal faculties	Siddhi I and II
Teacher	Ācārya; Guru
Temple women	Deva-dāsī (s)
Threefold sacred science	Trayī vidyā
Thugs	Ṭhag (s)
Thunderbolt; meteorite	Aśani I; Vajra
Time	Kāla I; Kalpa I
Toxicology	Viṣavidyā
Treasure	Nidhi
Treatises, learned; scientific, etc.	Śāstra; Siddhānta; Vedāṅga; Vidyā
Tree	Vṛkṣa
Triad, divine	Trimūrti
Triangle	Trikoṇa
Turban	Uṣṇīṣa
Twilight	Sandhyā

English and Sanskrit Equivalents

Unicorn	Ekaśṛṅgin
Vehicle or mount of gods	Vāhana
Victory	Vijaya I
Village goddesses	Grāmadevatā (s)
Virility	Vīrya
Vow	Vrata
Warrior	Kṣatriya
Warrior class	Kṣatra
Water-pot; Ewer	Kalaśa; Kumbha
Waters, primordial	Āpaḥ
Way; Path	Mārga
Weapons	Āyudha
Arrow	Bāṇa I
Axe	Paraśu
Club or Mace	Gadā
Discus	Cakra
Spear; javelin	Śakti II
Sword	Khaḍga
Trident	Triśūla
Weapons, magical	Gaṇḍivā; Kaumodakī
Weapons, personified	Āyudhapuruṣa; Śastradevatā
Wheel	Cakṛa I and II
for fortune-telling	Śanicakra
of Viṣṇu	Sudarśana
Wine	Surā
Witchcraft; Enchantment	Kṛtyā
World	Loka
ages of	Yuga
of the dead	Yamaloka
dissolution of	Pralaya
guardians of	Lokapāla (s)
Worlds, mystical	
names of	Vyāhṛti (s)
Worm	Kṛmi
Worship	Pūjā; Iṣṭadevatā